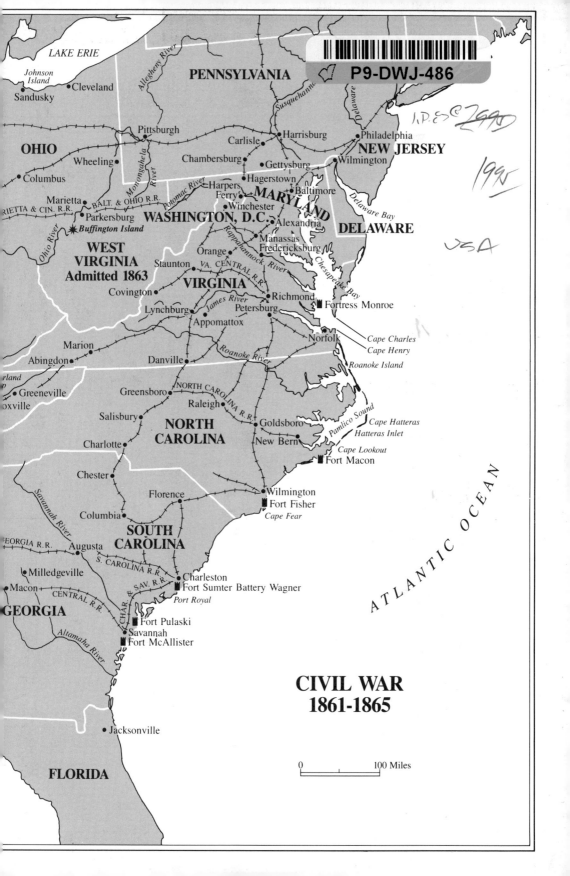

LAKE ERIE

Johnson Island
Sandusky • Cleveland

PENNSYLVANIA

Allegheny River

Susquehanna River

Delaware River

Pittsburgh

Carlisle • Harrisburg • Philadelphia

OHIO

Wheeling

Chambersburg • Gettysburg

NEW JERSEY

Wilmington

Columbus

Monongahela River

Hagerstown

Marietta • BALT. & OHIO R.R.

Harpers Ferry

MARYLAND

Baltimore

MARIETTA & CIN. R.R.

Parkersburg

Winchester

Delaware Bay

Potomac River

WASHINGTON, D.C.

Alexandria

DELAWARE

Buffington Island

Rappahannock River

Manassas

WEST VIRGINIA
Admitted 1863

Ohio River

Orange

Fredericksburg

Chesapeake Bay

Staunton

VA. CENTRAL R.R.

Covington

VIRGINIA

Richmond

Fortress Monroe

Lynchburg

James River

Petersburg

Appomattox

Norfolk

Cape Charles
Cape Henry

Marion

Roanoke River

Roanoke Island

Abingdon

Danville

Greeneville

Knoxville

Greensboro

NORTH CAROLINA R.R.

Raleigh

Pamlico Sound

Cape Hatteras
Hatteras Inlet

Salisbury

NORTH CAROLINA

Goldsboro

Charlotte

New Bern

Cape Lookout

Chester

Fort Macon

Florence

Wilmington

ATLANTIC OCEAN

Columbia

Fort Fisher

Cape Fear

Savannah River

SOUTH CAROLINA

GEORGIA R.R.

Augusta

S. CAROLINA R.R.

Milledgeville

CENTRAL R.R.

CHAR. & SAV. R.R.

Charleston

Fort Sumter Battery Wagner

Macon

Port Royal

GEORGIA

Fort Pulaski

Altamaha River

Savannah

Fort McAllister

**CIVIL WAR
1861-1865**

Jacksonville

FLORIDA

0   100 Miles

TRIAL
BY
FIRE

A
PEOPLE'S HISTORY
OF THE CIVIL WAR
AND
RECONSTRUCTION

TRIAL
BY
FIRE

Page Smith

VOLUME FIVE

McGRAW-HILL BOOK COMPANY

New York / St. Louis / San Francisco / Toronto

Mexico / Hamburg

ISBN 0-07-058571-7

Library of Congress Cataloging in Publication Data

Smith, Page.
Trial by fire.
Includes index.
1. United States—History—Civil War, 1861–1865.
2. Reconstruction.   I. Title.
E468.S64   973.7   81–18573
ISBN 0–07–058571–7   AACR2

*In grateful memory of Josephine Bates and Lewis Scott
and for Beulah Scott, Louise Scott, Dora Johnson,
Genevieve Randolph, Herman Blake, Noah Purifoy, and Bill Moore.*

ALSO BY PAGE SMITH:

James Wilson: Founding Father
John Adams (Two Volumes)
The Historian and History
As a City upon a Hill:
    The Town in American History
Daughters of the Promised Land:
    Women in American History
A New Age Now Begins:
    A People's History of the American
    Revolution (Two Volumes)
The Chicken Book
The Constitution: A Documentary
    and Narrative History
The Shaping of America: A People's History of
    the Young Republic
The Nation Comes of Age: A People's History of
    the Ante-Bellum Years

Contents

Introduction

The British historian, Herbert Butterfield, has written: "Sometimes when the human race has gone through one of its colossal chapters of experience, men in the aftermath have been so appalled by the catastrophe, so obsessed by the memory of it, that they have gone back to the story again and again, finding new angles of research, new aspects of the matter to reflect upon, as one generation succeeds another—a process of thinking and re-thinking, which in special cases is capable of continuing for a thousand years and more." Butterfield is referring specifically to the fall of Rome, but the passage is equally applicable to the American Civil War, called, at least initially in the North, the War of Rebellion and, in the South, the War between the States.

No historian dare approach this episode in our history without a profound degree of awe and even apprehension. It is an event so tragic and so terrible that it was and remains on one level—the level of human suffering and anguish—quite incomprehensible. At the end of the preceding volume I spoke of the onset of the war, with the firing on Fort Sumter as a nightmare become a reality. Americans of all classes and sections had had a nightmare since the earliest days of the Republic, indeed, before. The nightmare had two forms, often intertwined. In one the black slaves of the South rose and slaughtered their masters and mistresses. Despite the occasional uprisings, such as Gabriel's planned insurrection in Virginia in 1800, that of Denmark Vesey in South Carolina twenty-one years later, and the bloody outbreak led by Nat Turner, the feared rebellion never came. In the other related nightmare, the North and South split asunder over the issue of slavery.

We have had occasion more than once to recall George Mason's prophetic words in the Federal Debates: "Every master of slaves is born a petty tyrant. They bring the judgment of heaven on a Country. As nations cannot be rewarded or punished in the next world they must be in this. By an inevitable chain of causes & effects providence punishes national sins by national calamities." Mason was a slaveholder and author of the preamble to the Virginia Constitution from which Jefferson derived the Declaration of Independence. Gouverneur Morris drafted what became, with certain changes, the final version of the Constitution. He declared toward the end of the debates that "he would never concur in upholding domestic slavery. It was a nefarious institution. It was the curse of heaven in the States where it prevailed . . . He would sooner submit himself to a tax for paying for all the negroes in the United States, than saddle posterity with such a Constitution."

The new government had hardly begun its labors before Northerners and Southerners alike were predicting its dissolution. Pierce Butler, who had been a delegate to the Federal Convention, returned as Senator from South Carolina to, in William Maclay's words, threaten "a dissolution of the Union with regard to his State, *as sure as God was in the firmament!*" John Dickinson, famous as the author of the *Letters from a Pennsylvania Farmer*, one of the most influential tracts of the pre-Revolutionary years, apparently resigned himself before his death to the breaking apart of the Union over the issue of slavery. Jefferson himself was moved to reflect frequently on the frightening proposition that "the ten thousand recollections, by the blacks, of the injuries they have sustained at the hands of their masters" would, in time, produce "convulsions, which will probably never end but in the extermination of one or the other race."

The passage of the Missouri Compromise aroused Jefferson's deepest anxieties. It came to this: "Are our slaves to be presented with freedom and a dagger?" It was a "firebell in the night" signaling the end of the Union and the fairest dreams of Republican government.

He was glad, he wrote John Adams, that he could expect to die before that cataclysmic event. Adams replied that he had seen the slavery issue "hanging over [this country] like a black cloud for half a century." He seemed to see "Armies of Negroes marching and counter marching in the air, shining in Armour. I have been so terrified with this Phenomenon that I constantly said in former times to the Southern Gentlemen, I cannot comprehend this object. I must leave it to you."

James Madison left a letter to his fellow citizens to be opened after his death. In it he wrote: "The advice nearest to my heart and deepest in my convictions is that the Union of the States be cherished and perpetuated. Let the open enemy to it be regarded as a Pandora with her box opened; and the disguised one, as the Serpent creeping with his deadly wiles into Paradise."

That such anxieties were both profound and widespread should by now be abundantly clear to the reader. They appear in the pages of our diarists, in the newspapers and journals of the time. They were echoed by perceptive foreign visitors who grew increasingly dubious, with each passing decade, that the Union could be preserved. Count Segur, a French diplomat traveling in the United States in the early years of the century, agreed with the Chevalier de Chastellux that there could be no other outcome to the conflict over slavery but a "separation which could enfeeble and perhaps break this unhappy confederation, which can preserve its power only in being firmly locked and united together."

In 1860 George Templeton Strong remembered "this black bugaboo of 'disunion' since I was old enough to understand the words 'United States.' But till within the last ten years, it was, to me, a mere possibility of disaster, a question for college debating societies. I fear that ugly spectre has risen—too soon—and that we have got to deal with the awful question of dissolution of the Union *now and here*."

The coming of an event so long and so fearfully anticipated has about it a special kind of horror. There was, among many other things—the fratricidal nature of the conflict; the dislocation of individual lives; death in battle and by disease—the fact that the United States was deeply conscious of its mission to redeem the peoples of the world from age-old tyrannies, from poverty, suffering, and exploitation. It had been said at the beginning of the Revolution and reiterated with what was for many observers an infuriating arrogance ever since: American independence foreshadowed "the emancipation of a world." Suddenly that premise was questioned. What was involved was not simply the fate of the United States itself but the hopes of humanity for a more just and equitable human order. If the United States, with its democratic idealism, with its three-quarters of a century of self-government, with its relatively brief but fiercely held tradition of individual freedom, with its unparalleled natural resources, could not hold together, could not "make it," what hopes were there for less abundantly blessed regions and peoples?

Despite all the negative aspects of American life—slavery itself, the appropriation of the Indians' lands, the exploitation of the immigrant population, the crudeness and violence, the materialism, the corrosive anxieties about "getting ahead" or "hanging on"—it was indisputably true that the Revolution and the events that followed it had inaugurated a "new age." An ancient equilibrium had been disturbed; new human possibilities and potentialities had been disclosed; men and women in many lands had been encouraged to think that the future might be better than the past, perhaps, Christianity aside (it was out of Christianity that it had come), the most revolutionary idea ever let loose in the world. Now all that was in doubt. Reaction took heart. The enemies of the people revived old arguments about the shortcomings of democracy and the inability of people to govern themselves. The "Great Experiment" was crashing down in ruins, in the bitterest of internecine conflicts, brother against brother.

Against the coming darkness, it is not too much to say that in some profound, essential way, one man stood. Lincoln was by no means the only man of courage and intelligence, of determination and vision who was resolved to preserve the Union at any hazard, but Lincoln was the essential man. On the Fourth of July, 1861, Lincoln sent a message to the special session of Congress recently assembled. After reviewing the actions of the Southern States, now denominating themselves "the Confederate States," an "illegal organization," Lincoln declared that the issue was far larger than the fate of these United States. "It presents to the whole family of man, the question, whether a constitutional republic or a democracy—a government of the people, by the same people—can, or cannot, maintain its territorial integrity, against its own domestic foes." The question was whether "discontented individuals" can break up their government and thus practically put an end to free government upon the earth. "It forces us to ask 'Is there, in all republics, this inherent, and fatal weakness?' 'Must a government, of necessity, be too *strong* for the liberties of its own people, or too *weak* to maintain its own existence?' "

Lincoln had called for volunteers to preserve the Union and 75,000 militia had responded. A call was made for volunteers to enlist for a period of three years and for "large additions to the regular Army and Navy." All this had been done in anticipation of the approval of Congress. Now Lincoln requested Congress to authorize the recruitment of "four hundred thousand men and four hundred millions of dollars." The South had framed a Constitution and preamble based on the Declaration of Independence, but drafters had omitted the phrase "all men are created equal" and the phrase "We, the People." The omissions were significant, Lincoln insisted. "This is essentially a People's contest. On the side of the Union, it is a struggle for maintaining in the world, that form and substance of government, whose leading object is, to elevate the condition of men—to lift artificial weights from all shoulders—to clear the paths of laudable pursuit for all, to afford all an unfettered start, and a fair chance, in the race of life. I am most happy," Lincoln added, "to believe that the plain people understand and appreciate this." While many officers in the army and the navy had cast their lot with the South "not one common soldier, or common sailor is known to have deserted his flag . . . This is the patriotic instinct of the plain people. They understand, without an argument, that destroying the government, which was made by Washington, means no good to them."

William Wilkins Glenn, the Maryland planter, wrote in 1866: "Living as we do in the midst of great events, knowing many of the leading actors intimately and having every access to information, it is still almost impossible to form an impartial judgment on what is to become history. . . . Still some bold and ignorant men will write books from hearsay and newspapers and call it history. And a hundred years hence some clever fellow in his closet, will say 'now that the smoke of prejudice has passed away and time has allowed us to criticise impartially, we will give to the world a philosophical account of the events of the last century.' What folly! I laugh to think how many great knaves and weak fools will then be historical, and how many men will have credit for great actions who never had brains enough for an original thought or independence enough for manly action."

If history were a conclusion to be reached or a proposition to be proved, a problem to be solved or the sum of academic historians' monographs, we could presumably be done with the Civil War one day. But it is, of course, a part of our lives, of our collective memories, of, indeed, our nervous systems, part of our future. So we will never be done with telling it, wondering over it, immersing ourselves in that tragic and limitless drama.

I feel obliged to make clear to the reader that this is not primarily a military history. Military historians have written volumes on every major battle. It would be presumptuous and futile to try to give a complete tactical account of every engagement. On the other hand, no history of the Civil War can ignore the classic battles. So far as possible, I have dealt with them primarily in terms of the feelings and reactions of the men involved rather than following a more traditional strategic approach.

What cannot be sufficiently emphasized is that since people do not exist for the convenience *or* the scrutiny of historians, a certain violence, or at least disservice, is inevitably done to the full and breathtaking complexity of the truth whenever someone, assuming the role of a historian, attempts to deal with life in the mode called "history." This is most notably true in writing about black people in America. The tragic nature of their collective experience is so profound and the strategies they have devised for living in white America so subtle and so intricate that it is only perhaps in music and in the arts generally that one begins to fathom the excruciating reality. Walter Karp, reviewing Norman Mailer's book *The Executioner's Song*, wrote: "What Mailer has demonstrated . . . is the moral power of an art little esteemed in the higher intellectual circles; the traditional art of narration and its unique capacity to give each person his due." I, too—I trust quite clearly by now—believe in the moral power of the "art of narration," but I am continually and painfully aware of my deficiencies as an uncertain practitioner of the art and nowhere so acutely as in trying, as a white man, to comprehend the nature of what we call today, somewhat glibly, "the black experience."

1

The South on the Eve of War

The Civil War took place because the Southern states felt that they could no longer tolerate their status as members of the Union. Many Southerners had demonstrated a deep and abiding affection for the Union and were strongly opposed to the idea of secession. A substantial number were opposed to slavery itself. That a majority of Southerners were determined to secede should not surprise us, especially when we recall that many Northern abolitionists wished the North to secede from a Union tainted by slavery. Since the Civil War some historians have been disposed to argue that there were other, more essential or more central causes for the secession of the Southern states and, correspondingly, for the war: most commonly economic causes. The North, by this reading, was a great commercial and industrial region with economic interests very different from those of the South. Through such measures as high protective tariffs, the North exploited the South economically and eventually pushed it into seceding to protect its legitimate economic interests. Needless to say, that is not the perspective of this work, which is based unqualifiedly on the assumption that the institution of slavery and, more specifically, the determination of the North to limit it and the South to extend it were the exact and specific cause of the war.

We have had a good deal to say in previous volumes about the nature of Southern society, about the Southern disposition, character, temperament, psyche, or consciousness. Historians of the Civil War have spent more than a hundred years exploring that consciousness without reaching a clear consensus as to its nature. That fact in itself should incline us to proceed with caution and circumspection. But proceed we must in order to set properly the stage for the extraordinary drama of the war and the "reconstruction" that followed it.

In our discussion of Southern life and culture we are fortunate in being able to draw upon a number of remarkably vivid diaries written by Southern women during the war years.

Mary Chesnut belonged by birth and marriage to one of the great families of South Carolina. Her husband, James Chesnut, a United States Senator at the outbreak of the war, had been a leader of the secessionists in his state. The Chesnuts were close to the Jefferson Davises, and James Chesnut was soon serving on the Confederate President's staff. Mary Chesnut was the perfect diarist. Close to the heart of the Confederacy through her friendship with Davis and her husband's role as a politician and aide, she wrote with wit and discernment of everything that went on around her. She described herself, accurately enough, as a "tolerably close observer, a faithful watcher . . . from my youth upward of men and manners." Society had been for her "only an enlarged field for character study." A friend asked, "Why do you write in your diary at all, if, as you say, you have to contradict every day what you wrote yesterday?" Mrs. Chesnut replied, "Because, I tell the tale as it is told to me. I write current rumor. I do not vouch for anything." Mary Chesnut's sister was married to Horace Binney, one of the leading lawyers, philanthropists, and Republicans of Philadelphia.

Emma Holmes was a tall, strong-featured young woman, a schoolteacher and governess, who looked more like the New England schoolmarm of legend than a member of the Charleston elite. An intimate of the Ravenals, the Rhetts, Ruffins, Pinckneys, et al., she loved the classics, reveled in the social life of the city, believed passionately in the justice of the Southern cause, hated Yankees unrelentingly, and kept a detailed diary of her life in South Carolina during the war years. Her first entry, on February 13, 1861, expressed her consternation at the "revolution" which had swept the country in the preceding months, a revolution which had broken the country "into fragments through the malignity and fanaticism of the Black

Republicans. . . . Doubly proud am I of my native state," she wrote, "that she should be the first to arise and shake off the hated chain which linked us with the Black Republicans and the Abolitionists. 'Secession,' said a gentleman, 'was born in the hearts of Carolina women.' " As the finest blood of the city formed into regiments to march off to fight the Yankees, Emma Holmes experienced some fears and misgivings. But she comforted herself with the thought that the Confederate troops, when they met the "fanatics of the North face to face," must quickly rout them, "for we have truth, justice and religion on our side & our homes to battle for."

Kate Stone, another of our female diarists, was twenty years old when the war broke out. She described herself as "tall, not quite five feet six, and thin, have an irregular face, a quantity of brown hair, a shy, quiet manner, and talk but little." She lived with her family on a plantation named Brokenburn, in northeast Louisiana. Her life lacked the glamour and exalted social position of Emma Holmes and Mary Chesnut. Correspondingly it was much closer to that of the great majority of "middling" planters throughout the lower South. Brokenburn itself was a relatively new plantation built on land recently cleared. Of the 11,156 people in Madison Parish almost 10,000 of them were slaves, a ratio of nine to one. Kate Stone's mother, a widow with eight children, owned 1,260 acres of rich cotton land and 150 slaves. The plantation was not far from the Mississippi River, and the sound of Confederate cannon and Union artillery at Vicksburg would often be audible at Brokenburn. Like Emma Holmes and Mary Chesnut, Kate Stone was an indefatigable reader. She read Poe, Hawthorne, Thackeray, Victor Hugo, and Charles Lamb, reminding us again that the literary and intellectual life of the South was largely in the hands (or minds) of the ladies.

Like Mary Chesnut, Elizabeth Avery Meriwether, born and bred in Memphis, Tennessee, hated the institution of slavery. Elizabeth, moreover, was fortunate to marry a young Kentucky engineer, Minor Meriwether, who shared her feelings. Minor's father, Garrett Meriwether, was a prosperous planter with abolitionist leanings, who, as his daughter-in-law wrote, "believed that an All-Ruling Providence designed that the negroes of the South should return to Africa and there Christianize and civilize their savage cousins." He was resolutely opposed to setting his slaves free in America on the ground that "they could never be equal to the Whites, either socially or intellectually, and that consequently friction, if not disaster, would result. . . ." Not only had the elder Meriwether educated his slaves "to fit them to live and do missionary work in Liberia," but he had educated his sons to live by their own labor, not by the labor of slaves. Minor's father had died before his plans to send his slaves to Africa had been achieved, but the son sold sufficient land to pay for the ex-slaves' passage and took them to New Orleans and there put them on a boat for Liberia. Despite the young Meriwethers' opposition to slavery, they were unreservedly Southern in their sentiments, and Minor was among the first men in Memphis to volunteer for the Confederate army, accepting a commission as a colonel in the engineers.

Another of the remarkable diaries of Southern women during wartime was that of Sarah Morgan, daughter of a wealthy Baton Rouge judge, Thomas Morgan, who was a bitter enemy of secession. The seventh child of a seventh child, Sarah had five brothers, one of whom, Harry, was killed in a shotgun duel. Another, Philip, whose sympathies were with the North, took the Union oath of allegiance but refused to bear arms against the South. A brother-in-law was a Union officer in California and helped keep that state from allying itself with the Confederacy. Sarah's three other brothers were all enlisted in the Confederate forces. Shortly before Baton Rouge was seized by Union forces in May, 1862, Sarah Morgan began her diary with the words "Here I am, at your service, Madame Idleness, waiting for any suggestion it may please you to put into my weary brain. . . ." Only a year before, she had been a "happy, careless child who danced through life, loving God's whole world too much to love any particular one. . . ." Now that child was dead; the terrible realities of the war had smashed that idyllic existence. Perhaps the most engaging feature of Sarah Morgan's diary is her determination to be as fair to Yankees as to Southerners and to resist the common Southern disposition to see all Northerners as devils incarnate. She had almost as many Union relatives as secessionists.

The economic foundations of Southern life rested primarily on cotton, tobacco, sugar, and rice, the latter two crops confined largely to the Deep South—Alabama, Mississippi, and Louisiana. But everywhere that soil and climate permitted cotton was "king."

It was a particular and excruciating paradox that Virginia, the state that produced a George Mason and a Jefferson, should have become the premier breeder of slaves. "Slaves were the great staple of the State," Gideon Welles, Lincoln's secretary of the navy, wrote; "their sale brought annually a greater return of money to the State than tobacco or any other product, perhaps than all others; their bondsmen found a market in the States of the South, and nowhere else in Christendom."

A typical cotton plantation had two gangs, each under a black driver. The plow gang had fifteen plows, each drawn by two mules with corn-husk collars. The plow gangs plowed from January until April. (Visiting one plantation, the journalist Whitelaw Reid saw two or three women plowing who were said to be among the most skilled hands on the plantation.) Ahead of the plows moved a colorful band of women and children, chopping out and burning weeds and brush and singing and chattering. When the cotton had been planted and begun to sprout, this band became the hoe gang, following behind the plows and pulling weeds missed by the plowman. A bale of cotton to an acre was a good yield. Half a bale was far from uncommon. In Georgia the great planters were far outnumbered by small farmers cultivating three or four hundred acres of cotton.

Slaves were summoned to the fields at daybreak. They carried their breakfast with them in tin buckets—cornbread, boiled pork, and greens. At eight they stopped work to eat, and at noon they trooped back to their quarters for an hour and a half lunch; the workday ended at dusk. By the middle of August each year the lower bolls on the cotton plants would begin to open; the pickers would move into the fields, and for the months following, as the cotton "bolled out," it would be picked and carried to the gin, which could handle as many as fifty bales a week.

The Reverend David Macrae, the observant Scottish minister who visited the South, remarked, as many others had, on the haphazard utilization of the land by Southern planters and farmers. Even in the cotton states only 39 percent of the arable land was cultivated, and of the "improved" or cleared land 17,000,000 acres were not in actual production. Rather than cultivate 100 properly, many farmers "scratched" 200 or so and kept several times that amount in wilderness. Even the cultivated fields were often dotted with the stumps of trees fifty years old or more. Macrae saw fields that yielded no more than five bushels of corn to an acre; they would have returned a Scottish farmer six times as much. It was a practice—one could hardly call it a system—"lop-sided, wasteful, and superficial," in Macrae's words.

Of all the illusions that sustained the South the most fateful was its conviction that "cotton is king." The most important corollary to this most central proposition was that Great Britain must inevitably and of necessity come to the support of the Southern cause. The South devoutly believed it held the trump card or, better, the whip hand. The superior material and human resources of the North could not prevail against the power of cotton. Even the North must bow before that absolute monarch; starving Northern textile workers must join their British counterparts in demanding that the South be allowed to depart from the Union in peace. The doctrine was given its classic formulation by James Hammond, Senator from South Carolina. On March 4, 1858, three years before Lincoln's inauguration, Hammond declared in the Senate that there could be no war between the North and the South for "no other reason" than that no "sane nation" would "make war on cotton. Without firing a gun, without drawing a sword, should they make war on us we would bring the whole world to our feet. The South is perfectly competent to go on one, two, or three years without planting a seed of cotton. . . . What would happen if no cotton was furnished for three years? I will not stop to depict what everyone can imagine, but this is certain: England would topple headlong and carry the whole civilized world with her, save the South. No, you dare not make war on cotton. No power on earth dares to make war upon it, Cotton *is* King. . . . Who can doubt, that has looked at recent events, that cotton is supreme?"

When William Howard Russell, correspondent for the *London Times,* arrived in the Confederate States to report the war for the readers of England's most famous paper, he was astonished at the depth and tenacity of the Southern conviction that Great Britain had no choice but to come to the support of the Confederacy. "The Yankees are cowardly rascals," a Southern friend insisted. "We have proved it by kicking and cuffing them until we are tired of it; besides we know John Bull very well. He will make a great fuss about non-interference at first, but when he begins to want cotton he'll come off his perch." Russell commented: "I found this was the fixed idea everywhere. The doctrine of 'cotton is king'—to us who have not much considered the question is a grievous delusion or an unmeaning babble—to them is a lively all-powerful faith without distracting heresies or schisms." Russell was told on more than one occasion: "Why, sir, we have only to shut off your supply of cotton for a few weeks, and we can create a revolution in Great Britain."

What, Russell asked, would the Confederacy do if Yankee ships blockaded the Southern ports and prevented Southern cotton from reaching England? All the better: "Why . . . if those miserable Yankees try to blockade us, and keep you from our cotton, you'll just send their ships to the bottom and acknowledge us." When Russell dissented, his companion waved his arm in the direction of some cotton bales piled on a nearby wharf. "Look out there . . . there's the key will open all our ports, and put us in John Bull's strong box as well."

Louisiana and Mississippi were distinguished by the great river that they shared as far north as Vicksburg. On the Mississippi side Natchez was considered the most desirable place to live. Wealthy planters who had plantations for thirty or forty miles up and down the river resided there much of the year, some for as many as six or seven months. Each plantation was usually a thousand acres or more in extent with sugarcane, cotton, and, in the wetter areas nearest the backcountry, rice. Louisiana planters were notorious for their extravagant style of living. A Creole overseer on a plantation told a Yankee visitor that "le proprieter of zis place . . . lived as you would nevare believe. He had over seexty slaves for house servants. Seex carriages stood tere in ze carriage house, for ze use of ze family, besides buggies, saddle horses, et tout cela! . . . And ze dinnares, and ze trips to New Orleans." The garden alone had cost more than $60,000. There were orange trees, a mockingbird in the China tree, and a cork tree which provided cork for bottling the planter's own wines.

Sugar plantations required expensive machinery to crush the cane and boil the syrup to sugar and molasses. Plowers and planters would be followed by hoers in the cane fields to keep down the weeds, and early in October, after the cane had reached maturity, cutters would sever each stalk close to the ground, cutting off the top, which contained "injurious juices." Behind the cutters came broad-tread carts, on which the cane was piled and carried to the mill. There, for three months, fires burned night and day while the cane was processed. Every man was expected to work sixteen to eighteen hours during this period and encouraged by "abundant rations of whisky, presents of tobacco, free draughts of the sweet syrup. . . ." In the last year before the war, the sugar crop was over 440,000 hogsheads produced on 1,291 plantations.

Most of the Louisiana blacks spoke a patois made up of French and English words with some of their own creation mixed in. Each plantation was protected by a levee in front against the inundations of the Mississippi and in the rear against water rising from the swamps that ran back from the drained and cultivated land along the river. The drainage ditches had to be constantly deepened and repaired. The production of sugar involved a heavy capital outlay since sugar mills cost from $20,000 to $150,000.

While the Tennessee plantations along the banks of the Mississippi from Memphis to the Kentucky line conformed to the classic pattern of Southern plantation life, the eastern part of the state, generally, was distinguished by smaller and more diversified farms. The soil was a rich, dark limestone, good for growing corn, oats, hay, wheat, and potatoes and for grazing. Mules, horses, sheep, cattle, and hogs were raised in large numbers. Iron and coal, zinc, copper, and lead, as well as marble, were to be found in most counties. William Blackford, a Virginia cavalry officer, found eastern Tennessee a most unfamiliar terrain. "There are no gentlemen or gentlemen's houses," he wrote; "the people all live in cabins with little cultivated patches of ground around them."

The domestic economy of the Southern plantation was a complex one, demanding constant supervision and attention. Slaves could be maddeningly sly and devious, adept at avoiding work, prone to steal whatever they could and lie with convincing innocence. Such responses were their only defense in a cruelly exploitative system. Powerless, they employed the classic stratagems of those without power.

The slaves' "slavishness" was reinforced by an intricate set of taboos. Certain "white" words must not be used by blacks to describe relationships. Thus, a slave girl who told her mistress that her "mother" had sent her on an errand was whipped for using the word "mother," a "white" word, instead of "mammy," a "black" word. The consequence was a world exotic beyond imagining, where each day was a kind of continuing warfare—the white master or mistress bent on extracting the full measure of labor; the slave on withholding it just short of punishment. Sometimes the "system" broke down. Emma Holmes's sister Carrie and Carrie's husband, Isaac White, had a slave named Margaret who, according to Carrie, had become "so excessively negligent & indifferent to her duties & withal so impertinent" that Carrie had asked her husband to punish her. Since Margaret had been a pet of the family, Isaac considerately took her to the end of the garden after dark, reprimanded her, "& with a light strap gave her two or three cuts across her shoulders." At this, the young black woman tore off her clothes and threw herself into the nearby creek, where she drowned before anyone could reach her. The shocked family recalled that several days earlier she had said that if she were ever touched again, she would kill herself. Emma, as shocked as the rest of the family, comforted herself with the thought that it was an act of "demoniac temper." Isaac was overcome by feelings of contrition, and his sister-in-law wrote in her diary: "Poor fellow, to have his peace of mind destroyed by the blind rage of such a creature is too dreadful." She had never given a hint of such a temper and taken all her other beatings "with utmost indifference."

In addition to this perpetual psychological cold war, there were innumerable things to be *done* to provide for the platoon or army of reluctant workers—food, clothing, medicine for the ailing, care for the aged.

The distribution of labor on small plantations was often haphazard in the extreme. The temptation for the mistress of the house to accumulate servants far beyond necessity simply as a kind of status symbol was a heavy burden on many plantations. One master noted that out of thirty slaves, thirteen were assigned to the house and its dependencies, and eight were too old, too young, or too ailing to work, leaving nine field hands. The house servants were a colony in themselves. Kate Stone's maid Frank, or Francesca Carrarra, was notoriously lazy. Her mistress described her as "a bright yellow mullato, just the color of a pumpkin, with straight black hair and intensive black eyes . . . odd to look at and so unreliable at any kind of work that she was a trial to everybody." Frank and Kate had been playmates as young children, and Kate could not bear to see her whipped, "so she dawdled along, doing as little as possible." At Brokenburn, the youngest house servant was ten-year-old Sarah, whose assignment was to stand or sit just behind her mistress to run errands all day long and to pick up thread and lint off the carpet. "She never spoke unless spoken to and stood like a bronze statue," Kate wrote.

The swollen company of household servants meant increased supervisory duties for the mistress of the house. Kate Stone described the yearly manufacture of slave garments. At Brokenburn each spring and fall a room would be cleared out, and "great bolts of white woolen jeans, Osnabergs, and linseys with bolt after bolt of red flannel for the little ones, would be rolled in and the women with great shears would commence their work." Little attention was paid to fit, and all the clothes were cut to a few simple patterns. "After a day of this work," Kate Stone wrote, "Mama would go to bed quite broken down and Aunt Lucy, the colored housekeeper, would finish the superintending.

... The Negroes often dyed the white suits tan or grey with willow bark or sweet gum."

The political and domestic economy of the South was designed, above all else, to sustain its famous way of life. The South, which took up so exuberantly the guidon of war, was an anomaly in the busy, striving, competitive, restless nation of which it had been for so long a reluctant part. The life of the planter class, or that relatively small portion of it which constituted the ruling aristocracy, revolved around an intricate social life which, in turn, centered on what we call today the extended family. Family dominated everything. Each element of "family" had its respected and well-defined place and role. In no African tribe, feudal fief, or Scottish clan were the ties of kinship more honored. Aunts were a conspicuous category. There were cousins beyond counting—first cousins twice removed, second cousins three times removed, cousins of the third and cousins of the thirty-first degree—and all had their legitimate claims on the affections of all the other cousins, aunts, uncles, nephews. It was a society, it might be said, of sanctified cousinhood, and all cousins were, of course, "kissin' cousins." Naturally, cousins were not confined to the South; they were in evidence wherever old families dominated the social and political life of a region, in Philadelphia, Boston, or, more recently, St. Louis. But nowhere were they so ubiquitous as in the South. The recently published voluminous correspondence of the Colcock Jones family of Georgia included letters of forty-five members, brothers and sisters, aunts, cousins, and various other relatives, scattered about on fourteen or fifteen plantations.

The society was, perhaps above all, patriarchal in the extreme. The oldest male of an extended family was the ruling elder, whose opinions or whims were usually law. He controlled and disposed the material and human resources of the family with the authority of an Old Testament patriarch, whom, in his relentless piety and implacable will, he often resembled. Numerous slaves and numerous children, legitimate and illegitimate, as well as all the "womenfolk," were under his dominion, but he was typically a benevolent despot who saw himself, above all, as the protector, defender, provider for, worshiper and dutiful servant of the "ladies" of all ages and conditions. With most Southern masters, tyranny was always there; it was simply a matter of degree. Mary Chesnut wrote of her father-in-law: "Now this old man of ninety years was born when it was not the fashion for a gentleman to be a saint, and being lord of all he surveyed for so many years, irresponsible, in the center of this huge domain, it is wonderful he was not a greater tyrant." "Old Colonel" Chesnut was deaf and blind, attended in every step by Scipio, a "black Hercules," six feet two and "as gentle as a dove in all his dealings with his blind old master." Colonel Chesnut, his daughter-in-law wrote, "came of a race that would brook no interference with their own sweet will by man, woman, or devil." At Princeton in the 1790s his classmates had called him "the Young Prince." Now he was the last of "a race of lordly planters who ruled this Southern world." *His* father had been a man so imperious that he refused to let his favorite daughter marry a "handsome, dissipated Kershaw, and she, a spoiled beauty . . . went to her room and therein remained, never once coming out of it for forty years," Mary Chesnut wrote. Her father "provided servants to wait on her and every conceivable luxury that she desired, but neither party would give in."

The family was also a kind of extended correctional institution, the members of which thought it their duty constantly to admonish and instruct the other members, especially the female members. "You ought to do this; you ought to do that. . . . They justified their interference with the axiom, 'Blood's thicker than water' . . . and there," Mary Chesnut added, "is where the longing to spill it comes in. No locks or bolts or bars can keep them out. Are they not your nearest family? . . . For stinging you, for cutting you to the quick, who like one of your own household? . . . Did you ever see a really respectable, responsible, revered and beloved head of a family who ever opened his mouth at home except to find fault? He really thinks it is his business in life and all enjoyment is sinful."

In a society dominated by men, far beyond anything known in the North, peace and harmony depended on masculine needs being promptly met. "All the comfort of my life depends upon his being in good humor," Mary Chesnut wrote of her husband. She was acutely aware of the tyranny Southern men, her husband among them, exercised over their wives and daughters. "James Chesnut has been so nice this winter," she wrote in her diary; "so reasonable and considerate—that is, for a man." When Mary came home late from a ladies' party, "instead of making a row . . . he said he was 'so wide awake and so hungry,'" Mrs. Chesnut put on her dressing gown and "scrambled him some eggs, etc., there on our own fire. And with our feet on the fender and the small supper-table between us, we enjoyed the supper and glorious gossip. Rather a pleasant state of things when one's own husband is in good humor and cleverer than all the men outside."

Mary Chesnut was well aware of the deficiencies of her friends and relatives. They had "pluck enough, but they only work by fits and starts; there is no continuous effort; they can't be counted on for steady work. They will stop to play—or enjoy life in some shape." (The comments sound curiously like those made about blacks.) Indolence was, if not an actual virtue, part of a man's style. James Chesnut was famous for his indolence. His cousin Mary Stevens thought him "the laziest man alive" until she encountered his slave Lawrence. "Lawrence," Mary Chesnut wrote, "will not move an inch or lift a finger for any one but his master." Hours after he had been sent on an errand by a member of the household he was observed sitting on the front yard fence. "Didn't you go?" he was asked. "No, ma'am. I'm waiting for Mars. Jeems."

Some men were famous for laziness; some for handsomeness, some for flirtatiousness, some for their sporting talents. Of Nathan Davis Mary Chesnut wrote: "Nathan, all the world knows, is by profession a handsome man." Edmund Rhett was famous for his "very fine eyes and makes fearful play with them," she noted. "He sits silent and motionless, with his hands on his knees, his head bent forward, and his eyes fixed upon you. I could think of nothing like it but a setter and a covey of partridges." Barnwell Rhett was another famous flirt. "The world, you know, is composed of men, women, and Rhetts," a Rhett lady told Mary Chesnut.

Despite the open, sensual nature of Southern society, masculine stoicism was as prized in that section as in the "cool" North. Mary Chesnut could not reconcile herself to that iron self-control. She wrote in her diary: "My husband, as I told him to-day, could see me and everything that he loved hanged, drawn and quartered without moving a muscle, if a crowd were looking on; he could have the same gentle operation performed on himself and make no sign. To all of which violent insinuation he answered in unmoved tones: 'So would any civilized man. . . . Noisy, fidgety grief never moves me at all; it annoys me. Self-control is what we all need. You are a miracle of sensibility; self-control is what you need.'

"So you are civilized," his wife replied. "Some day I mean to be."

The "ladies"—the pure, chaste, undefiled creatures across whose lovely and unclouded brows no shadows were to be permitted to fall, whose shell-like ears must hear no coarse or vulgar words—were, as we know from the diaries many of them kept, a remarkably tough-grained and competent breed that played their assigned roles with graceful compliance. Southern society was organized around them—they were known collectively as Southern womanhood, a phrase pronounced with a quiet reverence that had a slight edge of challenge to it as though daring the listener to cast the mildest aspersion on that sacred category. The rearing or "gentle nurturing" of the ladies, their "coming out" like butterflies emerging from the cocoons of their slightly awkward but nonetheless charming adolescence, the courting and marrying of them, and the subsequent "protecting" of them were the major preoccupations not simply of the males old and young alike but of the whole social order.

The fact was that these idealized ladies, so endlessly attended to, courted, and complimented, were the vestal virgins of the most sacred rite of Southern life—eating. The diaries and letters of upper-class Southern women are filled with accounts of the consumption of food. In Mary Chesnut's diary there are passages of pure poetry describing an especially sumptuous feast. "Columbia is the place for good living, pleasant people, pleasant dinners, pleasant drives," she wrote. In Montgomery, Alabama, there were fewer dinners, and "the society was not smoothed down or in shape. Such as it was it was given over to balls and suppers," while in Richmond it was the breakfasts which were most notable—"the Virginia breakfasts—there were always pleasant people." But the dinners of Columbia were unexcelled. You were asked to stay on a moment's notice, and then came a "perfect dinner." She noted: "You do not see how it could be improved; and yet they had not had time to alter things or add because of unexpected guests. They had everything of the best—silver, glass, china, table linen, and damask, etc." The cooks were as carefully trained as the finest French chefs. A hostess in Columbia who laid a famous table ran a school for the cooks of friends and relatives.

The planning and preparation of such meals demanded the managerial skills of an Astor and the culinary talent of a Brillat-Savarin. Prepared by a squad of black cooks and served by a platoon of black waiters in splendid livery, they required and displayed a dazzling array of silver, crystal, and fine bone China, of epergnes, chafing dishes, urns, platters, and eating utensils of infinite variety and refinement—fish forks and meat forks and salad forks, sugar spoons and nut spoons and teaspoons and coffee spoons. And then there was the food itself in mind-boggling abundance: lustrous-red gleaming

Smithfield hams from lean peanut-fed hogs; country hams and slabs of bacon; the sweet, delicate white and gray-laced flesh of the spring-run shad with their delectable roe; turkey, fresh and smoked; quail, venison, oysters, perch, bass, veal and lamb, chestnuts, creamy dressings, stuffings, chutneys, and endless desserts, prominent among them brandied peaches, "buried in the groun'" to age and sometimes difficult to relocate. And the breads—hot breads, biscuits, rolls, shortbread, muffins, popovers, cornbreads, Sally Lunns, and a dozen variations. In Virginia and South Carolina there was the supreme, endlessly exclaimed-over, and delighted-in terrapin stew, a cloudy mixture of meat and skin with an occasional claw, the most perfect dish of all. And drinks—claret cup, whiskey punch, juleps, slings, and toddies.

Southerners had the settled and doubtless justified conviction that "Yankees and abolitionists"—the words were often interchangeable; a Yankee *was* an abolitionist—existed in a condition of culinary barbarism little better than that of the savages, living on boiled vegetables, overcooked meat, and Indian pudding.

A society which lives to eat, so to speak, was certainly not a new phenomenon in human history. A preoccupation with the gustatory side of life has indeed been characteristic of most aristocracies; it was simply anomalous in a larger culture notorious for treating food as little more than an essential fuel for money-makers and reformers, to be gobbled up as quickly as possible with a minimum of formality.

Everything revolved around a personal code of honor in the South. Lucius Quintus Cincinnatus Lamar went so far as to assure Mary Chesnut that if Charles Sumner "had stood on his manhood and training and struck back when Preston Brooks assailed him," the honor of the North would have been satisfied and the war need not have occurred. Thus, to Lamar it seemed that the Civil War was primarily about Charles Sumner's injured honor. "What an awful blunder that Preston Brooks business was!" he declared.

The sidewalks of Southern towns and cities were a kind of psychological battleground. It was not just blacks who must respectfully yield the sidewalk to a white gentleman. Poor whites must also give way. Southern white pride was, in a sense, on public display on the sidewalk, in part because the sidewalks were typically narrow and the streets were commonly ankle-deep in dust or mud mixed with horse manure and the excrement of hogs. Thus, the sidewalk was not infrequently an avenue to the dueling ground. The Reverend David Macrae was told by a planter he encountered on an Alabama steamboat, "I am as good a Christian, sir, at times, as any man in God's creation; but, sir, I am also a gentleman. And if any man insults me, I will call that man out, and if he refuses to come out, I will shoot him at sight, sir." The result of all this, in Macrae's view, had been "to produce disregard of human life, and a prevalence, in many quarters, of brutal outrages and murderous assaults. For every man who is shot in a duel," Macrae added, "a hundred are 'shot at sight,' or stabbed in the heat of some unexpected quarrel."

Southern honor centered on, although not exclusively, women— ladies, more specifically. A Southerner told Macrae: "A woman, sir, in the South who would seek pecuniary compensation for loss of honour in a court of law, would be regarded as a saleable harlot. . . . Any man who destroyed the virtue of a member of my family I should kill whenever I found him. Any Southern gentleman would do the same. . . ." A Presbyterian minister, he told Macrae, "had an only sister, a widow, to whom a friend made improper proposals. She informed her brother, who was 500 miles distant. The clergyman rode the distance on horseback, found the offender, and killed him." The clergyman was never persecuted by the law or reprimanded by his church. To fail to tip a hat, perform a bow, pull out a chair, in all instances give preference to the ladies was to invite not only unfavorable comment but a challenge to a duel. As late as 1868, William Wilkins Glenn avoided a duel only by the narrowest of margins when he challenged the assertion that the ladies of Richmond were fairer and more virtuous than the ladies of Baltimore.

It is hard to know quite what to say about a society that ran on food and compliments. Clearly it was seductive in the extreme. The most resolute enemies of the South's "peculiar institution" fell under the spell of its languorous and delightfully self-indulgent life. If it was patriarchal, it was also strikingly "youth-oriented." As members of a family—both males and females—reached marriageable age, attention focused on them with disconcerting intensity. Was something to be understood from Nancy's charming blush and demurely downcast eyes? Or from the distracted look on young Peyton's face? There was a whole range of legitimate flirtation, but a line as strict as the meridian marked the boundary between acceptable social "play" and behavior that compromised a young lady's honor; a phalanx of brothers and cousins stood ready to avenge any such transgression. Mary Chesnut described "flirtation" as "the business of society; that is, playing at love-making. It begins in vanity, it ends in vanity. It is spurred on by idleness and a want of any other excitement. Flattery, battledore and shuttlecock, how in this game flattery is dashed backward and forward. It is so soothing to self-conceit." Every aristocracy features elaborate courtship rituals in order to perpetuate itself. In this respect the South was no different from other aristocracies, but there was a strange emptiness at the heart of that charming and romantic existence. After almost forty years of observing it, Mary Chesnut offered the startling statistic that in all that ferment of courtship she had known of only a half dozen unions of real love; the rest was all illusion— accommodation and formalism. She commented to a friend that she thought that two married people could never live any time together "without finding each other out." The friend agreed: "Yes, unless they are dolts, they know to a tittle; but you see if they have common sense they make believe and get on, so so." That was the South. And not, of course, the South alone. It was the species. But in the South willingly entered-into illusions pervaded every aspect of life. Young men and women—Mary Chesnut called them the *jeunesse doré*, the golden youth—lived in this charmed world of happy indolence, of parties, hunts and balls, picnics, breakfasts, sumptuous dinners, and endless "sports" as though there were no future; but when one looked beneath the romantic aura, there were often signs that things were not what they appeared to be.

As in the North, there were in the ranks of the ruling class, especially among its youth, a disconcerting number of breakdowns, physical and psychological. There were drunkards and opium addicts, reckless gamblers (perhaps the most dreaded of all Southern afflictions), inveterate and notorious womanizers, and a substantial number whose eccentricities or inabilities to cope with the world around them grew so marked that they had to be confined to an ever-increasing number of private asylums. Emma Holmes noted in her diary "the saddest of sights, a young girl of beauty, talents, refinement & wealth, whose mind is so clouded by melancholy as to be oblivious of the realities of the present, like poor Connie Lamb whose mind has been so affected by the fate of her various brothers, all drunkards; Augustus burnt to death from spontaneous combustion, George in the Asylum, while his wife (though her mother was a Middleton and her father D. Heyward Hamilton) a woman of abandoned character, & her eldest brother James was long since turned out of the house by his father, & whether dead or not I do not know. . . ." All these disasters had produced in Connie Lamb "a state of melancholy derangement, the ruin of a character. . . ."

Another very striking aspect of Southern society was that its members were constantly in motion, not vertically but horizontally. Geography dominated the life of the South as it did no other section of the country. Many plantation owners owned more than one plantation, though one was usually the preferred habitation for the family. Since it was an accepted principle that most plantations were unhealthy in the humid summers, families migrated faithfully to the nearest "city" for the hottest months—Savannah or Atlanta (or Newport or even Nahant), Camden, Wilmington, Charleston, Richmond, Lynchburg; they retreated there again in winter, when the climate was severe. This meant, of course, maintaining a "town house," which might be occupied by a retinue of servants and an elderly aunt or needy cousin, in the absence of "the family." All moves were complicated and cumbersome, involving not only a number of white adults and children and wagons full of clothes and linens but a substantial quota of personal servants—the cook and her aides, the children's nurses and personal servants, as well as those of the master and mistress. The department of logistics and transportation was usually, like the household management, under the direction of the mistress of the plantation. Since a move from plantation to town or, not infrequently, from plantation to plantation might involve as many as twenty people with their extensive belongings and be made five or six times a year, traveling from one spot to another consumed a vast amount of time, energy, and money. What all this meant was that in striking contrast with the rest of the country, where the details of daily life had in most instances been simplified to an almost Spartan degree in deference to the need to have as much time as possible available for making money, in the planter aristocracy of the South "living" and living "well" were the constant and obsessive preoccupation of both sexes and virtually all ages.

Above all, the South was a world of <u>violence</u>. With all the surface show of gentility and refinement, violence lay at its heart: violence against the slave in the daily litany of whippings and mutilations; violence against animals in the constant hunting and killing; in cockfighting for lower and upper classes alike; in boxing; in wrestling; in gouging and biting, for the lower classes. Jefferson was the most acute analyst of the effect of slavery on the master class. "The whole commerce between master and slave is a perpetual exercise of the most boisterous passions," he wrote, "the most unremitting despotism on the one part, and degrading submission on the other." Children learned it from their parents. "The parent storms, the child looks on, catches the lineaments of wrath . . . gives a loose to his passions, and thus nursed, educated, and daily exercised in tyranny, cannot but be stamped by it with odious peculiarities." The slaves themselves were not, of course, immune to such "odious peculiarities." They learned from the whites. Laura Towne, the New England missionary at Port Royal, was horrified at the brutality of the newly free blacks toward animals, especially toward horses, and when slaves fought among themselves, they often did so with an alarming ferocity. John Davis, a young Englishman, wrote of a fight between two slaves in which the smaller escaped with his life by biting off the toe of his larger opponent.

Finally, the upper-class white Southerner was supremely confident that his style of life and his culture were superior to any other in the world. He and his fellows were truly "the lords of creation." In Albion Tourgée's novel *Bricks Without Straw*, the narrator describes the Southern attitude as follows: "The South believed, honestly believed, in its innate superiority over all other races and peoples. It did not doubt, that, man for man, it was braver, stronger, better than the North. Its men were 'gentlemen'—grander, nobler beings than the North ever knew. Their women were 'ladies'—gentle, refined, ethereal beings, passion and devotion wrapped in forms of ethereal mould, and surrounded by an impalpable effulgence which distinguished them from all others of the sex throughout the world. Whatever was of the South was superlative. . . ."

Describing her life in the ante-bellum South, Elizabeth Meriwether wrote of the family estate on the outskirts of Memphis: "a comfortable home with stables and out houses, a garden and a big, beautiful lawn. . . . Minor rode to town every morning on his big bay horse; Henry [the groom and manservant] drove my Rockaway; Louise looked after the children—in a word we were all as happy as birds." Not the least of Elizabeth Meriwether's blessings was the fact that there was no great company of slaves to attend to; they had been set free, their passage paid to Liberia.

The long, still, warm nights with the night sounds—owls' lonely calling, the bobwhites, the endless music of the crickets, the frogs in the

pond with their hollow *kerchunk*, the barking of a distant fox or the howling of the kenneled hounds—the fireflies, a myriad of winking lights like fairy lanterns dancing across the lawns; the smells of jasmine, honeysuckle, magnolia, night-blooming cereus—they were all together—food, sounds, scents—a gentle seduction of the senses, a subtle invasion of the drugged and languorous consciousness, moments that lingered in the memory like days in paradise. Life was a series of vignettes seen in a softly muted light, candlelight at night and in the daytime light filtered through trees and protecting shrubs. At the handsome DeSaussure mansion in Columbia in the midst of the war, Mary Chesnut sat "in the piazza at twelve noon of a June day" entirely captivated by the "soft, kind, beautiful, dark-grey eyes" of her elderly hostess. "Such eyes are a poem," she wrote, ". . . we were in a dense shade—magnolias in full bloom, ivy, vines of I know not what, and roses in profusion closed us in. It was a living wall of everything beautiful and sweet." That was it—the marvelously realized moment, the muted light, the music of soft voices, the movement of pale, graceful hands, a manifestation of the desire to do all things "perfectly," to create crystalline moments as enduring as diamonds that firmly excluded the confusion and disorder of ordinary life, and, most of all, the inescapable terror of slavery.

Mary Chesnut was clear in her own mind. "Slavery has to go, of course," she wrote in her diary, and then added, strikingly, "and joy go with it." She perceived the irony of the Southern position as few others of her class or section did. Slavery was an evil and must be banished, but she was too unblinking a realist not to know that the "joy" must go with it, that most of what made Southern life such a dream of delicious self-indulgence was built on black servitude.

As much as she disliked slavery, when Mary Chesnut was away from home, she missed "those old grey-haired darkies and their noiseless, automatic service, the result of finished training," men and women "who think for you; they know your ways and your wants; they save you all responsibility even in matters of your own ease and well doing. The butler at Mulberry would be miserable," she added, "and feel himself a ridiculous failure were I ever forced to ask him for anything." She described the principal family plantation at Mulberry Hill near Columbia as resembling nothing so much as a resort or "watering-place where one does not pay" and where there are no strangers, where "one day is curiously like another" with "people . . . coming and going, carriages driving up or driving off." Christmas was only more of everything: "The glass, china, silver, fine linen reserved for grand occasions come forth . . . more turkey, more mutton, more partridges, more fish, etc., and more solemn stiffness."

It was this leisurely exploration of the simple and not-so-simple pleasures of *living* that gave Southern life much of its undeniable charm. Southerners were experts in what we today would call interpersonal relations. All the members of its charmed upper circle were constantly assured that they were, if female, beautiful or, if clearly not beautiful, charming (and that was, after all, better), that their gowns were ravishing, and that they danced divinely; if male, that they were handsome, unflinchingly brave, and splendidly dashing, or, if any such encomiums were clearly so inapplicable as to be patently absurd (if, for instance, the subject was short, deformed, and ugly), he was complimented effusively on his wit, the color of his hair, cut of coat, or, God spare the mark, the polish on his boots. If all that—the eating, drinking, hunting, dancing, courting, the whole world of romantic illusion—seems absurd, we must remember that it has held an apparently inexhaustible fascination for the American imagination. If that world had not been built on the horror of black servitude, its seductions would doubtless have remained irresistible. Discovering how to live delightfully has never been easy, especially, of course, in the United States. We must also acknowledge that just as the consciousness of white people was shaped by their constant contact with their slaves, the consciousness of black people was shaped, not entirely negatively, by the white world of which they were so essential and intimate a part. Did they not learn from their masters and mistresses, despite their debasing servitude, that life was to be, above all, enjoyed and that it was worth expending considerable ingenuity to achieve, however sporadically, that notable end? The model of the world that appealed to the middle- and lower-class citizen of the North, white or black, was that of endless restless striving for material gain or moral redemption. Strife, conflict, and competition, leading to nervous exhaustion and an early grave, seemed to Southerners to be a Northern prescription for a "useful" existence. Tucked away in some corner of the collective consciousness of Americans is the dream of a life not too remote from that of the Wilkes plantation in *Gone with the Wind*, the ultimate expression of the romantic dream.

The structure of ideas that constituted the mental landscape of most white Southerners was simple, largely unquestioned, and amazingly enduring. "Culture" was highly valued, but it was defined primarily as "manners," good food, and good living. Honor, as we have noted, had the status of a philosophical principle and a moral imperative. Christian doctrine provided the general ideological framework, and the traditional virtues, with the exception of humility, were honored. The Christian duty of the master to the slave was fulfilled by exposing the slaves—cautiously, to be sure—to the civilizing effects of Christianity. Scriptural texts which enjoined servants to be obedient to their masters were much favored, and little was said about all being equal in the eyes of God.

The major emphasis in religious instruction for blacks (which, it must be said, was commonly taken very seriously) was on morality—the wickedness of stealing, lying, and, above all, sexual promiscuity. "As far as I can see," Mary Chesnut wrote, "Southern women do all that missionaries could do to prevent and alleviate evil. . . . There are no negro sexual relations half so shocking as Mormonism."

Mary Chesnut was a middle-aged woman before she saw a slave sold at auction in Montgomery, Alabama. "I was walking," she wrote in her diary, "and felt faint, seasick. The creature looked so like my good little Nancy, a bright mulatto with a pleasant face. She was magnificently gotten up in silk and satins. She seemed delighted with it all, sometimes ogling the bidders, sometimes looking quiet, coy, and modest, but her mouth never relaxed from its expanded grin of excitement. I dare say the poor thing knew who would buy her. I sat down on a stool in a shop and disciplined my wild thoughts . . . poor women! poor slaves!" It might, indeed, be said that Southern women had a vested interest in trying to prevail on slave women to be chaste; they might thereby keep them out of their husbands' beds. In modern sociological lingo, Southern whites clearly tried to use the Christian religion as a means of social control. But equally clearly, the vast majority genuinely believed that in so doing, they were simply carrying out their Christian duty. Moreover, whatever the white intention, the fact was that slaves transformed white Christianity into black Christianity, remade it to serve their own needs.

Many of the more sensitive and perceptive Southern women, especially those who, like Mary Chesnut, abhorred slavery, were thoroughly conscious of the incongruity of slaveholding Christians. Kate Stone wrote: "My first recollection is of pity for the Negroes and desire to help them. Even under the best owners, it was a hard, hard life. . . ." Hardest of all was the fact that nothing could change the lot of the slave. "Obedience, revolt, submission, prayers—all were in vain.

Waking sometimes in the night as I grew older and thinking it all over, I would grow sick with the misery of it all. . . . Always I felt the moral guilt of it, felt how impossible it must be for the owner of slaves to win his way into Heaven. Born and raised as we were, what would be our measure of responsibility."

On the level of political ideas Southerners had, as their first article of faith, the Jeffersonian doctrine that the states were prior and superior to the national government and might, whenever they wished, depart from it without so much as a by-your-leave.

When Francis Lieber, the German political theorist who had accepted a chair on the law faculty of Columbia, had discussed with John Calhoun the implications of the fact that the United States had no name but only a description, arguing that the country needed a name like every other country, Calhoun had become furious, declaring that "we were not a nation, and that this want of a name was conclusive proof of it, that we ought not to be a nation, and that if a name could be devised and generally adopted, comprehending the aggregation of states, it would be a public calamity."

At the same time it must be emphasized that many Southerners felt a profound attachment to the Union. George Henry Thomas, a Virginian, a graduate of West Point and an officer in the United States Army, refused to follow his friend Robert E. Lee into the Confederacy. We have already noted that of Sarah Morgan's four brothers, one was loyal to the Union. So it was in a number of Southern families. Many Southerners were passive Unionists; that is to say, they avoided military service so far and as long as they could but did or said nothing to draw attention to themselves. Others who at the beginning of the war had spoken or voted against disunion, fought for the Confederacy because they could not accept the notion of friends and kinsmen fighting Yankee invaders without coming to their assistance.

More basic even than the doctrine of states' rights was the belief that the slave system was the highest form of social organization known and the indispensable condition of Southern "culture." A corollary was that the North was a debased and degraded society made up of "mudsills"—rough and exploited workingmen and newly rich vulgarians whose only interest was in ostentatious display. Southerners were thoroughly contemptuous of democracy—William Wilkins Glenn wrote to a sympathetic English friend that "democracy is only good when the people are not democratic, and in the South where slavery made the institution of caste and separated the common laborer from the landed proprietor, democracy worked very well." Glenn was convinced that the Union would in time split into "half a dozen governments" or be governed by a "military despot." This, he told his friend, was "the inevitable fate attendent upon unlimited Republicanism. . . . It really does seem as if Republicanism were a poison which had no cure when once inoculated in the system and which was inevitably bound to run its fatal course."

Work, especially manual work, was, in the Southern view, demeaning. A gentleman was by definition someone who did not work. David Macrae visited a Virginia family after the war and heard a black maid say to her mistress that a gentleman was at the door to see her. When the lady of the house discovered that the "gentleman" was black, she rebuked the maid in front of her visitor. "How dared you say that 'a gentleman' wished to see me? This is a negro—a man who works. A gentleman is one who doesn't work. A negro may be a very decent man, but he can never be a gentleman."

The white Southern attitude toward manual work was well expressed by a South Carolinian of the old order who ridiculed his North Carolina neighbors for having "no more sense than to work in the field, just like a nigger. If you work with a nigger, he despises you for equalizin' yourself with him. Any man is a dog-goned fool to work, when he can make a nigger work for him."

Work was a necessity, not a matter of choice, for the poor whites or, as they were called in South Carolina, the sandhill tackeys, who were found everywhere in the South. Impoverished, illiterate, indolent, and often plagued with pellagra and other debilitating diseases, they lived a marginal existence, solaced by various forms of evangelical Christianity, which offered an outlet for their bitter passions. Their hatred of blacks was doubtless based in large part on their inability to hate that class of white aristocrats who ruled the South.

The category is, in any event, too inclusive. In the absence of any clearly defined middle class, many small-scale white farmers, industrious and self-respecting, were indiscriminately grouped in the poor white class. It was particularly inappropriate to many of the mountain people of the Appalachian range who had their own life-style, their own customs and traditions, a fierce independence, and a code of honor as demanding as that of any gentleman.

In the hilly backcountry of western Mississippi, Elizabeth Meriwether, fleeing before the invading Yankees, found a temporary refuge with just such a family, the Peppercorns, a mother and three large, angular "darters." All four women were "tall, big boned and exactly alike—the same complexion, the same tawny hair. . . ." Elizabeth Meriwether wrote: "For a moment all four sat perfectly still, then one of the four drew from a pocket of her skirt a twist of tobacco, bit off a piece and set to work chewing it vigorously. . . ." The others followed suit. "After chewing a while all four began to spit across the floor into the fire. It was a full ten feet, but never once did they miss their shot—the sight was to me as astonishing as it was disgusting." The daughters were named Suky, Sally, and Melverina Elverina. Melverina Elverina's twin brother, absent in the Confederate army, was named Alexander the Great or Lexy for short. Melverina was determined to join the army, too. "I can shoot jes as well as he ever did," she declared. "I'm going to jine the fust chance I git."

The next day Elizabeth Meriwether saw approaching the house a tall young man who, from his resemblance to the Peppercorn sisters, she assumed was their brother, Alexander the Great, on furlough. It turned out instead to be Melverina Elverina, her hair cut short and dressed as a man, on her way to enlist in the Confederate army.

Whitelaw Reid described the small planters of the Mississippi upcountry who owned from six to thirty slaves and produced from fifty to several hundred bales of cotton a year as "rough, hairy, wild-looking men, wearing home-spun . . . tobacco-chewing, muddy-footed men from the hills. . . ."

The vast majority of Southerners, it must be said, were neither planters nor "poor whites." Out of a population of some 12,000,000, of whom 4,000,000 were slaves and 250,000 free blacks, only 342,000 owned slaves. The rest were small farmers shading off at the lower end of the economic scale to poor whites. Business and professional men were in the towns and cities (a disproportionate number were doctors, and many were ministers).

The South was, and remains, infinitely mysterious. New England was transparent by comparison—all character and intellect, admirable but not likable, full of stiffness, reserve, punctilio, severe and repressed, not much given to joy or laughter except perhaps in abolitionist circles. But the South was all charm and seduction. Alone in diffuse and chaotic America, the South had formed a coherent "culture." The West had attitudes and attributes, even an identifiable "style," but only the South had "a way of life" that permeated every aspect of society. Even the most determined opponents of slavery could not resist its seductions. From the time the plantation system had taken its characteristic form, say, by the early decades of the eighteenth century until the Civil War, a span of some 150 years, the Old South had changed hardly a whit, and the Deep South had taken its clues from the originals—the Old Dominion, the state of Washington and Jefferson and Madison and a host of others, and South Carolina, the Palmetto State, the citadel of good living and self-indulgence. There were, of course, very considerable differences among the Southern states, but the similarities—or more properly, the similarity, slavery—overrode all the differences. So part of the fascination of the South was its at least relative immutability. Far from lusting after change, priding itself on the "go-ahead" spirit, the South prided itself on remaining the same—yesterday, today, and tomorrow, true and honorable and *right* beyond all peradventure of a doubt. It was thus a bizarre and endlessly intriguing anomaly, a lush island of unchangingness in the midst of restless change. There was the endlessly re-enacted drama of the two races, the perpetual hint of terror behind the charming façades; magnolias and whips; languorous evenings on wisteria-laden porches and terrible mutilations.

Geography was an essential part of the magic. Samuel Shepard, returning to his Virginia home on the eve of the American Revolution, had written: "This place is beautiful. The fields. The mountain. My own trees. The foxes barking in the ravine. The moon a great pearl." It was only one of an infinite number of evocations of Southern landscapes that ranged from the Mississippi River levees, lined with plantations where Spanish moss festooned the ancient oaks, through the rich bottomlands of Alabama to the tidelands of the Carolinas and Virginia. Not all Southern terrain was luxuriant—there were the clay hills of interior Georgia and endless miles of spindly pines getting what nourishment they could from thin, sandy soil. But where the quality folk lived the land was generally abundant, and even if haphazardly tended, it brought forth a profusion of vegetables, flowers, flowering trees, and bushes—the jacaranda, the dogwood, laurel, chinaberry, magnolia, and vines, night-blooming cereus, honeysuckle, bougainvillaea—and cash crops, cotton, rice, and tobacco.

Apart from the hedonistic and self-indulgent life encouraged, indeed, one could almost say, demanded, by the planter culture of the South, there was in the mere physical presence of black people, of a race extraordinarily exotic by white standards, a profoundly compelling drama. Some of the most sympathetic and intelligent observers of slaves, women like Mary Chesnut and Elizabeth Meriwether, confessed themselves totally unable to penetrate to the inner recesses of their slaves' psychic life; they remained, for the most part, a mystery to their masters and mistresses. Slaves and slavery were not new to history, but nowhere else, in no other time, had a culture, or subculture taken the form of the South's "peculiar institution," with such contrasting racial types woven into so intricate and intimate a unity, one so full of unresolvable tensions and tragic paradoxes. A comparative study of slave societies is not within the scope of this work. But such a study would simply cast into sharper relief the uniqueness of slavery as it existed in the Southern portions of the United States. Historians have pointed out that the defeated South, in capturing the imagination of subsequent generations of Americans, might be said to have triumphed psychologically over its conquerors. *Gone with the Wind* and *Roots* bracket uncounted thousands of romances of the South, Old and New. And small wonder, for the dramatic representation of reality is irresistible. However, what is perhaps not yet fully realized, although *Roots* has taken us a long step toward realizing it, is that as appealingly romantic as the story of the ante-bellum white South is, the story of the black South, before and after the war, is, in fact, a richer and more heroic drama.

2

The Response

The election of Lincoln in November, 1860, set in motion a process that, with each passing month, seemed more irresistible. The reactions varied almost as widely as the astonishingly variegated collection of individuals who called themselves Americans. Certainly there were patterns of response. In the South the more militant champions of secession, in places like Charleston, South Carolina, and Memphis, Tennessee, took Lincoln's victory as the signal to begin the dismemberment of the Union. Many other Southerners, like most Northerners, persevered in the hope of some kind of reconciliation— or in the hope that the North would let the South depart in peace. In Charleston, Mary Chesnut noted Lincoln's election in her diary, adding: "The excitement was very great. Everybody was talking at the same time. One, a little more moved than the others, stood up and said despondently: 'The die is cast; no more vain regrets; sad forebodings are useless; the stake is life or death.' 'Did you ever!' was the prevailing exclamation and some one cried out: 'Now that the black radical Republicans have the power I suppose they will Brown us all.' No doubt of it."

Weeks before Lincoln's inauguration the unraveling of the Union began. South Carolina seceded on December 20. On January 6 Florida troops seized the United States arsenal at Apalachicola, and the following day took possession of the Federal Forts Marion and St. Augustine. Each day brought news of some new act of defiance and each week of another state's vote for secession. On January 9 a convention in Mississippi adopted an ordinance of secession by a vote of 84 to 15, while in New York City the Democratic mayor, Fernando Wood, recommended to the City Council that the city secede from the Union along with its Southern friends. In North Carolina, where Union sentiment was strong, armed citizens seized Fort Johnston near Smithville on January 9 and Fort Caswell the following day. Florida passed an ordinance of secession 62 to 7 on the tenth, and in Louisiana Federal forts were occupied by state militia.

In Alabama the vote for secession was 61 to 39. A week later, on January 19, a Georgia convention voted to secede by 208 to 89; soon afterward the Federal arsenal at Augusta was captured. Louisiana voted for secession on January 26. Texas seceded on February 1 by a vote of 166 to 7, and two weeks later the U.S. military posts in Texas were surrendered by General David Twiggs, a Georgian, with a long and distinguished record in the service of the Union.

South Carolina, after passing the ordinance of secession, had called for a convention of slaveholding states to meet at Montgomery, Alabama, in early February. Delegates from South Carolina, Georgia, Alabama, Mississippi, Louisiana, and Florida met on February 4, 1861. One of the leaders of the South Carolina delegation was Mary Chesnut's husband, James. The two most conspicuous delegates were Robert Toombs and Alexander Stephens of Georgia. On February 9, the forty-two delegates approved a hastily drawn-up "provisional" constitution and elected Jefferson Davis president and Alexander Stephens vice-president of the Confederacy. Davis was a Kentuckian, and Kentucky had at this point not yet cast its lot with the Confederacy. He had a distinguished record as an army officer dating back to the Black Hawk War, as well as eight years in the United States Senate and four years as Franklin Pierce's secretary of war.

George Templeton Strong reacted to the atmosphere of anxiety and indecision in New York City by writing in his journal: "The political entity known as the United States of America is found out at last, after imposing on the community of nations for three-quarters of a century. The bird of our country is a debilitated chicken, disguised in eagle feathers. We have never been a nation; we are only an aggregate of communities, ready to fall apart at the first serious shock and without a centre of vigorous national life to keep us together. . . . We are a weak, divided, disgraced people, unable to maintain our national existence. We are impotent even to *assert* our national life. The country of George Washington and Andrew Jackson (!!!) is decomposing, and its elements re-forming into new and strange combinations. . . . I'm tempted to emigrate, to become a naturalized British subject and spend the rest of my days in some pleasant sea-side village in the southern counties of old Mother England. It's a pity we ever renounced our allegiance to the British Crown."

Not long after Texas joined the Confederacy, settlers in that portion of New Mexico Territory called Arizona held a convention and declared themselves out of the Union. They elected a representative to the Confederate Congress and took steps to drive Federal troops out of the area. The officer in the command of the U.S. detachment in the territory surrendered his 500 regulars without a fight, leaving New Mexico and Arizona under the military government of the Confederacy. Encouraged by this easy conquest, the provisional government decided to dispatch a force of 3,500 men (called the Army of New Mexico) under Major Henry Sibley; their mission was to secure the entire frontier along the Mexican border and enter into negotiations with the Mexican states of Sonora, Chihuahua, and Lower California, which would either come into the Confederacy or, if they were reluctant to take such a step, be seized and the authority of the Confederacy established therein. Mexico was once more in a state of turmoil. Benito Juárez headed a liberal government with its capital at Veracruz and was opposed by the conservatives, whose stronghold was Mexico City. With the triumph of Juárez, Napoleon III undertook to try to re-establish a Catholic empire under French rule. In this complicated struggle the future of Mexico seemed uncertain enough to tempt Jefferson Davis and his Cabinet to meddle. Once matters had been concluded with Mexico, they believed, Utah and California would fall into the lap of the Confederate government.

Viewing the confusion and uncertainty all about him, George Templeton Strong wrote: "We are discordant, corrupt, and deeply diseased, unable to govern ourselves, and in a most unfit condition for a war on others." Two days later he added: "Depression today deeper than ever. Most people give up all hope of saving the government and anticipate general bankruptcy, revolution, mob-law, chaos, and ruin."

Particularly demoralizing to Strong was the talk that "disruption" —the splitting up of the Union—was "likely to make the North richer and more prosperous. Capital will desert these combustible, extra-hazardous, seceding communities, they say; and the trade of New Orleans and Mobile will transfer itself to Northern ports. . . . But money cannot pay for our national disgrace," Strong added.

As more and more states joined the ranks of the seceders, Sidney George Fisher, the Philadelphia lawyer and diarist, wrote, "Are these states to be allowed to stay out? I suppose so, for they cannot be brought back by force & coercion, which everyone agrees will not be attempted. Why not say so, legally and officially at once? . . . The present policy of the government . . . seems the only one that can be pursued." To Fisher the "threatening state of affairs . . . shows how completely the whole structure of our government has been under-mined when it thus falls to pieces at a touch. What prospect is there of filling up these rents & gaps, of subduing these animosities, of restoring peace? I can see none. And yet," Fisher added, "the dispute is really about nothing of practical importance, and two sensible men ought to be able to settle it in an hour." The son of George Bancroft, the historian, wrote: "What will become of Father? His occupation certainly will be gone. Nobody will want to read a history of the formation of a government by our forefathers which we have let fall to pieces."

Strong reported that Senator Louis Wigfall of Texas declared that he was disgusted with his Southern friends. "They had sworn that Lincoln should be killed, and now he was peaceably inaugurated after all. He was tempted to say he would have nothing to do with such a d____ set of humbugs."

Emma Holmes wrote: "Old Abe Lincoln was inaugurated today. . . . His speech was just what was expected from him, stupid, ambiguous, vulgar and insolent, and is everywhere considered a virtual declaration of war."

George Templeton Strong's cousin and law partner, Charles Strong, met Lincoln and judged him "a smart country politician and Mrs. Lincoln a very vulgar old woman. . . ." Richard Henry Dana complained to Charles Francis Adams that although Lincoln "has a kind of shrewdness and common sense, mother wit, and slip-shod low-leveled honesty, that made him a good western jury lawyer . . . he is an unutterable calamity to us where he is."

Fisher, who had been favorably impressed with the dignity and simple eloquence of Lincoln's inaugural, was distressed to hear from a friend who had met Lincoln that he was "familiar in his manners, eternally joking and jesting and fond of telling bawdy stories in gross language. If all this be true, it is very bad, considering how much is at stake just now on the wise administration of government." Fisher was concerned that the "high praise" he had bestowed on Lincoln in his book *The Trial of the Constitution* might "turn out to be exaggerated and may appear to some ridiculous. . . . He is uneducated, his manners are uncouth, he wants dignity & reserve befitting his station, & has a vile habit of telling dirty stories. . . ."

Charles Francis Adams, plainly reveling in his new status as a Congressman from Massachusetts (thereby re-enacting John Quincy's congressional career), was reassured by Lincoln's inaugural address, of which he wrote: "As a whole the composition was well aimed, and raised my opinion of him." Adams added: "Thus ends this most trying period of our history. . . . Yet I never in my life felt more serene and clear and confident. It seemed as if I was inspired by a power above me, and supported without effort of my own." Lincoln was "ignorant and must have help," he added. Adams was distressed to learn that the President was considering using force to bring the Southern states back into the Union, but he trusted Secretary of State William H. Seward to make him steer a wise course.

By the end of March, 1861, the uncertainty about the fate of the Republic had permeated the North. "A painful sense of disaster, of a stern and irresistible course of evil impending over the country and over all private interests, oppresses men's minds," Sidney George Fisher wrote. "Disaffection seems to spread everywhere, respect for law and love of country, and confidence in the government, and loyalty are so weakened that we can scarcely be said to have a government at all and seem to be approaching the rule of no rule. There is no King in Israel."

The spirit of doubt and uncertainty pervaded Lincoln's own Cabinet. Salmon Chase, secretary of the treasury, was reported to have told a Philadelphia newspaper editor that in his opinion the only thing left to do was to "call a convention of the people & let them decide how the Union was to be divided, and that they would have to adopt the plan of recognizing secession as a right & provide a legal mode by which a state might secede at pleasure."

"The atmosphere was thick with treason," Gideon Welles wrote. "Party spirit and old party differences prevailed, however, amid these accumulating dangers. Secession was considered by most persons as a political party question, not a rebellion. Democrats to a large extent sympathized with the Rebels more than with the Administration . . . they hoped that President Lincoln and the Republicans would, over-whelmed by obstacles and embarrassments, prove failures." The Republicans, in Welles's opinion, were as violent in their partisan feelings. They wished to see all Democrats turned out. "Patriotism was with them no test, no shield from party malevolence. They demanded the proscription and exclusion of such Democrats as opposed the Rebel movements and clung to the Union, with the same vehemence that they demanded the removal of the worst Rebels who advocated a dissolution of the Union." In the Cabinet Seward was, in Welles's view, the epitome of this unrelenting party spirit.

The firing on Fort Sumter, its surrender to the Confederates on April 13, and Lincoln's call for 75,000 volunteers two days later ended all speculation about the President's intentions. This time the reactions of the various sections were more uniform—an immediate acceptance by the vast majority of Americans, North and South, that a state of war existed. It was as though a spell that had held the entire North immobilized had been broken. Carl Schurz described it as "one of those sublime moments of patriotic exaltation when everyone seems willing to do everything and sacrifice everything for a common cause—one of those ideal sun-bursts in the history of nations." Under all the disorder of American life, the bitter class divisions, the political rancor, the sectional feelings, there was revealed, astonishingly, an essential substratum of devotion to the *idea* of a Union. In Lincoln's marvelous phrase, there were "mystic chords of memory"—common memories, a history that constituted the soul of a people, that was held in the mind, that made the almost incomprehensibly diverse land the strange entity called a nation for which men were ready to lay down their lives. Human motives are never entirely pure. There were other elements involved, of course, many of them much less admirable— deep-seated hostility toward the South; the common human need to transcend the often morally and intellectually debilitating routines of daily life; the need to touch the heroic, to be lifted up into a larger and more dramatic realm of existence, to serve some grand ideal. It was for all that a profoundly revelatory moment, a moment that ranked with the first spontaneous reaction of American colonists to the passage of the Stamp Act by the British Parliament more than ninety years earlier. Then, too, a new and astonishing reality had been disclosed. Now that reality was confirmed and extended.

The ninety-year span arrests our attention. There were men still living when Sumter surrendered who had been born in the tumultuous year of the Stamp Act riots. A modern writer has coined the term "future shock" to describe the accelerating rate of change with which modern man has had to live, has still to live; but the rate and nature of change in the last hundred years in no way equal that of our first, nor will, it seems safe to say, that of the next hundred years. We are today fertile in imaginings, indeed, overimaginings, of intergalactic travel, space colonies, star wars. But even the most prescient eighteenth-century Americans had hardly a glimmering of the strange reality that would unfold in the coming century. Now that reality would be given its severest test.

Even in New York City wild enthusiasm was the order of the day. William Howard Russell, the correspondent to the *London Times*, on his way to Richmond found, "instead of peaceful citizens, men in military uniforms" thronging the streets "and such multitudes of United States' flags floated from the windows and roofs of the houses as to convey the impression that this was a great holiday festival. . . . Fully a third of the people carried arms, and dressed in some kind of martial garb." Walls were covered with recruiting posters, Russell noted, adding: "An outburst of military tailors has taken place in the streets; shops are devoted to militia equipments; rifles, pistols, swords, plumes, long boots, saddles, bridles, camp beds, canteens, tents, knapsacks, have usurped the place of ordinary articles of traffic. . . . Innumerable 'General Scotts' glower at you from every turn, making the General look wiser than he or any man ever was." Children were dressed in miniature uniforms, the most popular version of which was that favored by many of the more prosperous and socially disposed, the so-called Zouave uniform of the French Algerian light infantry, a dizzy sartorial concoction featuring brightly colored baggy trousers, gaiters, a short, braided jacket, and a fez. Many of the soldiers shaved their heads in the fashion of the Algerian originals. It is safe to say that few soldiers in history have fared forth to battle more bizarrely attired. "Mars would die with laughter if he saw some of the abdominous, bespectacled light infantry men who are hobbling along the pavement . . ." Russell wrote.

George Templeton Strong wrote in his journal: "GOD SAVE THE UNION, AND CONFOUND ITS ENEMIES. AMEN." Strong was thrilled by the wave of enthusiasm that swept the North. "My habit is to despond and find fault," he wrote, "but the attitude of New York and the whole North at this time is magnificent. Perfect unanimity, earnestness, and readiness to make every sacrifice for the support of law and national life. Especially impressive after our long forbearance and vain efforts to conciliate, our readiness to humble ourselves for the sake of peace. Still, I expect to hear only of disaster for a long while yet." Strong even prevailed on the "old fogies" on the Trinity Church vestry to fly the United States flag on the church's steeple.

War meant the disruption of everything—families, careers, personal finances. Strong wrote: "I clearly see that this is a most severe personal calamity to me, but I welcome it cordially, for it has shown that I belong to a community that is brave and generous, and that the city of New York is not sordid and selfish. . . . New York is lavishly tendering life and money to sustain a righteous cause, and this without one dissenting voice from Forty-ninth Street to the Battery!" That was overstating the case a bit, but it was a kind of minor miracle that the dissension and divisiveness that had for so long marked the political life of the city seemed to have suddenly disappeared. Strong, who soon became involved in the great voluntary civilian humanitarian enterprise that came to be known as the Sanitary Commission, no longer complained of feelings of futility and unreality in his life. He performed vast labors for the cause, traveling constantly on business of the commission and meeting for long hours with conspicuous benefits to his physical and psychic health. Although, at a rather sedentary forty-one with three children and a wife to care for, he was beyond the age of soldiering, he helped organize the New York Rifles, a kind of citizens' defense company made up primarily of his friends who met for military training several nights a week. There were soon almost two hundred prominent New Yorkers drilling assiduously. "I've found out what 'Eyes Right!' means," Strong noted. "I've long wanted to know the purport of that familiar but mystic phrase. . . . Everybody awkward, but earnest and diligent." Strong was elected "president" until a "military commander" could be found.

In Philadelphia, as in New York, word of the firing on Fort Sumter swept away all doubts and hesitations and "roused the war passions . . . to a fearful pitch." The city itself was, in Sidney George Fisher's words, "in a state of dangerous excitement. Several well-known persons, who had openly expressed secession opinions, had been assaulted in the streets." Some of Fisher's relatives were in imminent danger from mob action. The streets were "all of a flutter with flags, streaming from windows, hotels, stories, etc. The passenger cars were all decorated with them. Indeed, they are needed to protect the houses of persons suspected of 'secession' opinions. . . . Fortunately," Fisher added, "the sentiments of the people are so generally loyal to the government, that tho we are to have the curse of civil war, we are not likely to suffer from the greater evil of partizan war among ourselves." The Democrats were, at least for the moment, thoroughly subdued, but Fisher wrote, prophetically, that "tho the Democrats are quiet now & most of them are zealous in support of the government, the party nevertheless chafes at defeat and will take advantage of any turn in affairs to create trouble. They hate Lincoln and the Republicans cordially and they know how to rouse & direct the brute force of society to serve their purposes."

Despite his gout, Fisher made an effort to enlist in a home guard that was being formed in Germantown. When Fisher met a friend, William Gilpin, the newly appointed territorial governor of Colorado, on the street, Gilpin told him that he considered the South "very formidable." The war would be "a long & expensive struggle requiring an army of half a million of troops. He talks rather wildly," Fisher added, "for I cannot imagine that the South has resources for a long war or even a short one."

In Lima, Indiana, Ted Upson and his father, Jonathan, were husking corn when a neighbor who had just gotten the mail came hurrying across the field. "The Rebels have fired upon and taken Fort Sumter," he called out. "Father got white and couldn't say a word," Ted recalled. "I dont see what has got into those people," he noted later in his diary, "I dont believe any one here wants thier Niggers. And I am sure I dont want to fight for them." Jonathan Upson turned and headed for the house, leaving his son to unload the wagon and put out the horses. When Ted came in for supper, there was no sign of his father. When his mother asked his whereabouts, Ted told her the news. She went upstairs to their bedroom, and after a time they both came down, the senior Upson looking ten years older in his son's view. Ted's grandmother, noticing the strained atmosphere, asked the matter, and when she was told the dismal news, she began to cry, saying, "oh my poor children in the South! Now they will suffer! God knows how they will suffer! I knew it would come! Jonathan I told you it would come! . . . Oh to think that I should have lived to see the day when Brother should rise against Brother." Ted Upson had the sobering thought that his cousins would soon be in the Confederate army. "I wonder," he wrote, "if I were in our army and they should meet me would they shoot me. I suppose they would."

Three days after the surrender of Fort Sumter, Joseph Griner, a young sawmill worker on the Maryland Eastern Shore, wrote to his father: "We have elected Mr. Lincoln but I am afraid it is a-going to call your son from home for a long period and perhaps forever, for I am not the one to stay at home when danger threatens my beloved country, to be called a coward in after years when peace is again declared and prosperity again reigns o'er our land." A week later Griner enlisted in the Philadelphia Light Guards, 1st Division Pennsylvania Volunteers, and was soon on his way to Baltimore, a hotbed of secessionist sentiment. From camp outside Washington he wrote: "How often in boyhood's young days when reading the account of soldiers' lives have I longed to be a man and now the opportunity has offered; but I wish it was with some other foe than our own countrymen. But at present they are the worst foe we ever had. They are all nearly as bad as the Indians and as desperate and savage."

Ulysses S. Grant, who had had a disappointing army career and resigned his commission after the Mexican War, was living in Galena, Illinois, running a leather store, when word came of the fall of Sumter and Lincoln's call for volunteers. "Business ceased entirely," he recalled; "all was excitement; for a time there were no party distinctions; all were Union men, determined to avenge the insult to the national flag. In the evening the court-house was packed." Grant was asked to preside. A company was recruited on the spot, and Grant was asked to be its captain. He declined but gave assurances that he would help in any way he could. The women of Galena got from Grant a description of a United States infantry uniform, bought material, and, with the aid of professional tailors, made up the required number of uniforms. Grant divided the men into squads and supervised their drill, then accompanied them to Springfield, where they were integrated into the 11th Illinois Volunteer Infantry.

The same scene was repeated in thousands of towns and cities in the North and West. There was, indeed, an embarrassment of riches. Far more men wished to enroll than had been called for or than could be equipped, paid, or transported to one of the military sectors. The governor of Illinois appealed to the state legislature to authorize ten more regiments to serve for one month, to be paid by the state but pledged to respond to any Federal call. The governor of Ohio wrote to Secretary of War Simon Cameron begging him to accept a larger number of volunteers from that state. Instead of the thirteen regiments that the state had been called on to provide, he was faced with twenty, adding, "I need not impress upon you the demoralizing results of disbanding the surplus regiments. . . ."

Carl Schurz, starting back east from Wisconsin, found "every railroad station filled with an excited crowd hurrahing for the Union and Lincoln. The Stars and Stripes fluttering from numberless staffs. The drum and fife resounding everywhere. The cars thronged with young men hurrying to the nearest enlistment place, and anxious only lest there be no room left for them in the regiments hastily forming. . . . Social distinctions . . . seemed to have vanished. The millionaires' sons rushed to the colors by the side of the laborers."

While many young Southerners welcomed the beginning of the conflict as an opportunity for heroic deeds and, above all, for the occasion it afforded to humble the arrogant North and prove once for all Southern superiority, others made a more realistic assessment of Southern prospects. Not long after the fall of Sumter, while Charleston was still buzzing with excitement, Mary Chesnut encountered Alexander Stephens of Georgia at a crowded reception and found the Confederate vice-president "not cheerful in his views." When Mrs. Chesnut chided him for being fainthearted, he gave her "some new ideas as to our dangerous situation. Fears for the future and not exultation at our successes pervade his discourse," she added.

Sarah Morgan, the belle of Baton Rouge, assumed the worst. "No more cotton, sugar-cane, or rice!" she wrote. "No more old black aunties or uncles! No more rides in mule teams, no more songs in the cane-field, no more steaming kettles, no more black faces and shining teeth around the furnace fires!"

"The war is making us all tenderly sentimental," Mary Chesnut noted. "No casualties yet, no real mourning, nobody hurt. So it is all parade, fife, and fine feathers. There is no imagination here to forestall woe, and only the excitement and wild awakening from every-day stagnant life are felt. That is, when one gets away from the two or three sensible men who are still left in the world," she added, allowing herself to wonder if the *jeunesse dorée,* with all their dash and glamour, would have the perseverance and stamina to endure a long period of hardship and suffering. The British correspondent William Howard Russell had suggested that white men could not bear the hard labor of campaigning in such a demanding climate, but Mrs. Chesnut noted that "we live in the open air, and work like Trojans at all manly sports, riding hard, hunting, playing at being soldiers."

At Brokenburn in the spring of 1861 the Stone household was

"overflowing with happiness and hope." A record crop was expected, and Mrs. Stone planned "a Northern tour" and a trip to Europe with the older children in the fall. Into this idyllic world came the news of Sumter and Lincoln's call for troops. Kate Stone's brother William was "wild to be off to Virginia," she noted in her diary. "He so fears that the fighting will be over before he can get there." If he signed up fifty men to constitute a company, the state would then commission him to command them, but he could not wait. Kate retired to her room with a new novel and a plate of candy and read until Frank came to summon her to dinner, saying that "the house shorely do look sweet and cool." After dinner, alone in her room, Kate heard her brothers and her uncle Bo, only a few years older than she, playing trios in Bo's room, "the soft sound of violin, flute and guitar." A few days later they all were gone, and Kate wrote in her diary: "Bravely, cheerily they go, willing to meet death in defense of the South, the land we love so well, the fairest land and the most gallant men the sun shines on. May God prosper us. Never again can we join hands with the North, the people who hate us so."

William Stone was soon back temporarily. He had enlisted in the Jeff Davis Guards at Vicksburg and been elected a third lieutenant. He described to Kate the New Orleans Zouaves, the Tiger Rifles, recruited from the very dregs of the city "and commanded by an ex-convict, and the Perrit Guards made up of gamblers who had to demonstrate their ability to 'cut, shuffle and deal.' "

Young Charles Jones, a Georgian, wrote to his father on April 17, 1861: "Can you imagine a more suicidal, outrageous, and exasperating policy than that inaugurated by the fanatical administration at Washington? The Black Republicans may rave among the cold hills of their native states, and grow mad with entertainment of infidelity, heresies, and false conceptions of a 'higher law'; but Heaven forbid that they ever attempt to set foot upon this land of sunshine, of high-souled honor, and of liberty. . . . The conduct of the government of the old United States towards the Confederate States is an outrage upon Christianity and the civilization of the age, and upon the great and just principles of popular sovereignty which we have contended for and embraced for near a hundred years. . . ."

Jones was convinced that anarchy and revolution must follow the defeat of the Union. "Should they be defeated in this fearful contest," he wrote his father, "how fearful the retribution! Who can appreciate the terrors of this lifted wave of fanaticism when, broken and dismayed, it recoils in confusion and madness upon itself?" Charles Jones was determined to play a proper role in the coming conflict, to endure the "dangers and carnage" of battle, he wrote his father, and uphold the good name of his family. "A freeman's heart can beat in no nobler behalf, and no more sacred obligation can rest upon a people than those now devolved upon us to protect our homes, our loves, our lives, our property, our religion, and our liberties, from the inhuman infidel hordes who threaten us with invasion, dishonor, and subjugation." To Jones it was of great significance that the Confederate Constitution "acknowledges in the most emphatic manner the existence and super-intending powers of the living God" while "the old Federal Constitution was a godless instrument." Perhaps, he reflected, the war was God's punishment of the United States for not explicitly acknowledging "His supremacy" in its original "organic law."

In the words of an acquaintance of Mary Chesnut, the South "separated North from South because of incompatibility of temper. We are divorced because we have hated each other so. If we could only separate, a 'separation à l'agréable,' as the French say it, and not have a horrid fight for divorce."

Among those determined to fight for the preservation of the Union was Carl Schurz. Back in Washington to request that he be relieved of his commission as ambassador to Spain so that he might enlist in the Union army, he was received by Secretary of State Seward, who urged him to go to Spain. The war, he assured Schurz, could hardly last more than two or three months, and Schurz could hardly expect to receive such an important post again. Lincoln, though not expressing Seward's optimism, also urged Schurz to retain his commission. As a kind of compromise Schurz prevailed on Lincoln to authorize him to raise a cavalry force of German immigrants who had served in German cavalry regiments before their emigration and "who had only to be armed and put upon horses to make cavalry-men fit for active service." Lincoln sent Schurz to Simon Cameron, who expressed his support and passed him on to General Winfield Scott. Scott did his best to put the damper on the whole idea. "If we were to have a war at all," he declared, "it would be a short one. It would be over long before any volunteer cavalry troops could be made fit for active service in the field." Moreover, Scott anticipated little use for cavalry in any event. The war would be decided primarily in Virginia, and that state was so "cut up with fences and other obstructions as to make operations with large bodies of cavalry impracticable."

Ignoring Scott's objections, Schurz, armed with a letter from Lincoln, hurried on to New York, where he found that a number of his countrymen were already busy forming German companies and regiments. Colonel Max Weber, who had been an officer in the army of the grand duchy of Baden and gone over to the revolutionists in the uprising of 1840, had already recruited several infantry regiments. Colonel Louis Blenker, who had led a revolutionary force in the Palatinate, and Colonel von Gilsa, a former Prussian officer, were similarly engaged. Colonel von Schimmelpfennig and Colonel Mahler, who had been active in the uprisings of 1847, were organizing regiments in Pittsburgh and Philadelphia, while Franz Sigel "and other German revolutionists," as Schurz put it, were recruiting German immigrants in Wisconsin and Illinois. Of all the former German officers, Colonel Blenker was the most colorful. He was already famous as the spectacular leader of the South German insurrection in 1849. He did everything in a lavish and dramatic style. When Schurz met him in New York at his hotel, Blenker rang for a bellboy and ordered a case of Burgundy and a box of the hotel's best Havanas. Later, in the field, his campaign tent was as handsome as a prince's pavilion. Blenker's staff included a number of titled Germans so that he was often heard to give such orders as "Prince A., you instruct Count B. to inspect the pickets tonight, and to take Baron S. with him."

When Blenker's regiment was properly equipped and drilled and it was time to entrain for Washington to join the Army of the Potomac, the colonel led his men in a magnificent parade down Broadway. Thousands of spectators, among them virtually the entire German population of the city, cheered wildly. The regimental band was brilliant, and Blenker marched at the head of his regiment "with a swinging stride that astonished the natives. Nothing," Schurz added, "could have surpassed the lofty grace with which he acknowledged the boisterous acclamations of the admiring throng on the sidewalks and the waving of handkerchiefs that greeted him from the windows."

In New York a number of other immigrant—or, as we would say today, ethnic—groups formed their own regiments. The 69th was an Irish regiment formed a week after the surrender of Sumter. A reporter for the *New York Tribune* saw them at Prince Street in the Irish section, drawing muskets, blankets, and eating utensils from a large truck, while hundreds of women and children watched and cheered and "several Irish civic societies, comprising about 2,000 persons, with waving banners—the harp of Erin kissing the stars and stripes—"

waited to accompany the new recruits in a parade down Broadway. It was an important symbolic moment. The Irish were, almost without exception, Democrats. The South had been a Democratic stronghold, and the alliance between Northern workers, particularly the New York Irish, and the slaveholders of the South had been the keystone of the Democratic Party. Many Southerners assumed that the New York Irish would rise en masse rather than fight alongside those "native" Americans whom they considered their enemies and exploiters. Not a few of their fellow citizens shared the same concern. So when the 69th departed by boat from New York on April 24, the patriotic enthusiasm which accompanied the embarkation of the regiment had in it a substantial element of relief.

A miscellaneous group of foreigners formed the Garibaldi Guards. There were, in addition, the Italian Legion and the Polish Legion, as well as the Cuban Volunteers. Elmer Ellsworth formed the New York Fire Zouaves, who were famous for their splendid drill formations and their riotous behavior. Having been shipped off to Washington, they dazzled the city by the skill and verve with which they extinguished a fire in Willard's Hotel. The Germans also organized the Steuben Volunteers and the DeKalb Rifles. It seemed as though all classes, factions, and sections were pressing forward to demonstrate devotion to the Union.

Every month that passed saw George Templeton Strong and indeed most of his compatriots in the Northern states grow more ferociously patriotic. In May, 1861, Strong wrote in his journal: "This war will soon be universally recognized as waged by an effete corrupt aristocracy of slave breeders against the cause of Progress, Democracy, Free Thought, and Equality (for which, by the way, I have no great respect, though I certainly prefer them to the semi-barbarous system of Mississippi and South Carolina). . . ."

On the other hand, by June many Southerners were confident that the independence of the Confederate States was an accomplished fact. It was generally assumed that North Carolina must soon follow Arkansas, Tennessee, and Virginia. Surely the North, after its initial efforts to coerce the South into reunion, would accept the inevitable. Emma Holmes deplored the "vile deeds of the still viler hirelings and cutthroats of the despotic tyrant, Abe Lincoln, who, in the three months which have passed since his inauguration, has broken every article of the Constitution which he swore to abide by & defend." There was comfort in the news that New York, deprived of Southern

cotton, was "paralyzed, trade totally destroyed & grass literally growing in the streets. . . ." Sobered by the realization that economic ruin
awaited them if they persisted, many Northerners did indeed wish for
nothing so much as the recognition of the Confederacy and the
averting of a civil war.

The abolitionists saw the war as a genuine "revolution," one that
reawakened the echoes of the Revolution of 1776. A prominent
abolitionist, William Goodell, wrote: "The Second American
Revolution . . . has begun. It is in progress. . . . The Revolution must
go on to its completion—*a National Abolition of Slavery*. . . . What but
the insanity of moral blindness can long delay the proclamation,
inviting [the slaves] to share in *the glorious second American Revolution*."
And Moncure Conway, an abolitionist editor and journalist, insisted
that the South not be allowed to appropriate the glorious term
"revolution." It was the North that was fighting "a revolution of
freedom." "WE ARE THE REVOLUTIONISTS."

With Sumter, Wendell Phillips had to reconsider his own well-
known "disunionism." He had declared, from a hundred platforms,
that the South should be severed from the Union because of the
fearful stain of slavery. Now he had to think over that position. He
revealed his doubts to his friend George Smalley, who urged him to
support the war as the best hope of emancipating the slave. "I will tell
you what I once heard a negro say," Smalley told him; " 'When my
massa and somebody else quarrel I'm on the somebody else's side.'
Don't you think the negro knows? Do you really doubt that a war
between the Slave Power and the North, be the result what it may, must
end in Freedom?"

Phillips announced his conversion in a dramatic speech on April
21 at the Boston Music Hall. As word spread throughout the city
excitement grew, and when Phillips rose to speak, four thousand
people had crowded into the hall. He began by acknowledging that he
had often in this very spot "urged . . . the expediency of acknowledging a Southern Confederacy, and the peaceful separation of these
thirty-four States." The beginning of the war had changed all that. "I
rejoice . . . that now, for the first time in my antislavery life, I speak
under the stars and stripes, and welcome the tread of Massachusetts
men marshalled for war." At this the audience was on its feet, cheering
and shouting. "No matter what the past has been or said; to-day the
slave asks God for a sight of his banner, and counts it the pledge of his
redemption. (Applause) Hitherto it may have meant what you thought,

or what I did; to-day it represents sovereignty and justice. (Renewed applause) The only mistake that I have made, was in supposing Massachusetts wholly choked with cotton-dust and cankered with gold. (Loud cheering) . . . When the South cannonaded Fort Sumter the bones of Adams stirred in his coffin. (Cheers) And you might have heard him, from the granite grave at Quincy, proclaim to the nation: 'The hour has struck! Seize the thunderbolt God has forged for you, and annihilate the system which has troubled your peace for seventy years.' (Cheers) . . . I believe in the possibility of justice, in the certainty of union. Years hence, when the smoke of this conflict clears away, the world will see under our banner all tongues, all creeds, all races,—one brotherhood,—and on the banks of the Potomac, the Genius of Liberty, robed in light, four and thirty stars for her diadem, broken chains under her feet, and the olive branch in her right hand. (Great applause)."

The speech was a sensation. It was published by the *Liberator*, and 16,000 copies were sold on the streets. The *Anglo-African* and the *Anti-Slavery Standard* both published the speech, and it was estimated that in New York and other Northern cities well over 200,000 copies were sold.

For some of those gripped by the Protestant Passion, the Civil War marked the prospective beginning of the millennium. For those Americans oriented toward secular redemption, it was to usher in a new age of chastened capitalism.

Many Northerners felt as did the Reverend Herman Humphrey, who asked, in a sermon delivered at Pittsfield, Massachusetts, in January, 1861: "Would He have brought us hither and given us so much work in prospect for bringing in the millennium, if He had intended to pluck us up, just as we are entered upon the work?"

George Templeton Strong's conviction that slavery was a national sin that must be expiated by national suffering led him to lay "much of the moral guilt of this terrible, murderous convulsion at the door of the North. South Carolina," he wrote, "would never have dared to secede but for our toadyism, our disposition to uphold and justify the wickedness of Southern institutions. The logic of history requires that we suffer for our sins far more than we have yet suffered. 'Without the shedding of blood there is no remission of sins.' It is impossible that this great struggle can pass without our feeling it more than we have yet felt it. It is inevitable, but in what particular way we shall be visited I cannot foresee."

The Reverend Daniel C. Eddy of the Harvard Street Church in Boston emphasized the theme of the worldwide significance of the war. The flag of the United States, he declared, "belongs to the world; it is the ensign of the oppressed of all lands. The soil we tread! It is not yours or mine. It does not belong to the cotton lords of the South, nor to the merchant princes of the North. It belongs to constitutional government and human happiness."

To Humphrey and those Christians who lived in anticipation of the millennium, the notion of an impending conflict was thoroughly compatible with the prophecies in the Book of Revelation— Armageddon, the battle of the forces of good against the armies of Satan, to be followed by the return of Christ and His reign for a thousand years on earth.

Slavery was, of course, not the only sin Americans had to answer for to the Almighty. Racial prejudice was everywhere apparent in the North, and even more sobering, the almost universal pursuit of profit was, in the words of George Prentiss, a professor at Union Seminary in New York, a "wild and brutal license which has brought us well nigh to the brink of anarchy." The war must thus be seen as a purgation, a revived revolution. Prentiss announced a "new cycle of events. . . . A fresh chapter . . . in history. Humanity takes a step never taken before toward the fulfillment of its grand destiny." Another prominent Southern apologist wrote: "When individuals or communities have become so sunk in degeneracy, or so wedded and sold to enormous vices, as to be insensible to every motive derived from His goodness, . . . then it is that He makes bare His arm for judgment. . . ." That was the condition of the United States. The war was to be its purification.

Both North and South were now in what we might call Phase I—a period of unrivaled military ardor, self-delusion, and euphoria. Each side trumpeted its own virtues, emphasized its own rectitude, proclaimed the enemy traitors and cowards, and predicted a speedy victory for its heroic soldiers. So it is at the beginning of most wars. Suddenly the mundane business of daily life is miraculously transformed into high drama; parades, bonfires, patriotic rallies, songs, the noise of drums and fifes and military bands preempt the stage. The fragile and imperfect self is caught up in one great exhilarating wave of patriotic fervor. Orators orate; handsome young women contribute agreeable sexual overtones; every man is a prospective hero, and every woman his ardent admirer.

The advantages of the North, at the beginning of the conflict, were simply stated: a sizable navy, a much larger population to draw upon for soldiers, greater wealth, and far greater industrial capacity. Both Henry Adams and his brother Charles Francis, Jr., were convinced that the economic superiority of the North must eventually carry the day: "The long purse, the big guns, and the men . . ." as Henry Adams put it.

The advantages of the South were less readily perceived, but they were nonetheless considerable. Of inestimable importance was the fact that the South had to be invaded by the North. Southerners were fighting for their homes, for their country, as they put it. While they had vastly extended boundaries, they had interior lines of transportation and communication. They could deploy their armies to meet invasions directed against particular points around their perimeter. Moreover, Southerners had a long martial tradition. There were far more Southerners in the regular army officer corps than Northerners, and quite apart from that, the South fed on ideals of chivalric valor and, as we have noted, thirsted for a fight. The Confederate officers, drawn almost exclusively from the planter class at the beginning of the war, had the habit of command, and their soldiers the habit of obedience (although it must be said that discipline was as serious a problem in Confederate units as in Federal ones, especially among soldiers from the border states). This habit of command was particularly important in field grade officers up to the rank of brigadier general, the ranks in which prompt obedience to an officer's orders was most critical and officers were in direct command of units; it was less so in the upper echelons, in which general officers functioned with and through their staffs.

In addition, the South counted heavily on what we would call today a fifth column in the North, the so-called Peace Democrats, who called with increasing stridency for peace at any price. The South did not have to defeat or conquer the North; it had only to persevere until the North grew weary of the cost in money and in blood of trying to restore the Union and recognized the independence of the South. Far from being inconceivable or even farfetched, such an eventuality was not only eminently possible but very nearly realized. The other important factor in Southern calculations related directly to the strategy of exhausting the North's collective will to continue the conflict; it was the anticipation of France and England's recognizing the Confederacy as a belligerent, supplying it with arms and munitions, and, above all, allowing naval ships and raiders to be outfitted in British and French ports.

George Templeton Strong was remarkably prescient in weighing the relative strengths and weaknesses of the two adversaries. The odds seemed to him to be all on the side of the North, but the South had the advantage of interior lines. "Should Providence send them a great general," he wrote, "woe to the North! But I do not expect that Providence will. We have four advantages, viz., money, numbers, the navy, the sympathy of Christendom. They have one vital disadvantage, viz., niggers; and another, the utter want of mechanical skill and educated labor."

John Beatty, Ohio banker turned soldier, had no illusions about the difficulties ahead. Operating with George McClellan's army in the mountainous country of western Virginia, he noted that nature had fortified the country for the rebels. "He is foolishly sanguine," he wrote in his diary, "who predicts an easy victory over such a people, entrenched amidst mountains and hills. I believe the war will run into a war of emancipation, and when it ends, African slavery will have ended also. It would not, perhaps, be politic to say so, but if I had the army in my own hands, I would take a short cut to what I am sure will be the end—commence the work of emancipation at once, and leave every foot of soil behind me free."

The outbreak of the war and the accompanying agitation for emancipation sparked a renewed debate over the nature of black Americans. As we have seen, the abolitionists based their arguments for racial equality not primarily on the question of whether or not the two races were "equal" in physical and mental capacities, but on the Christian doctrine that all peoples were equal in the sight of God and on Christ's message of the brotherhood of man. The thorny issue of whether the races were "equal" in capacities seemed to them, if not an irrelevance, a matter of subsidiary importance. They pointed out that civil rights—the equal protection of the laws, the right to vote, etc.—were parceled out to whites not on the basis of demonstrated intelligence (although it was clear that many Americans would have been pleased to do so, especially in regard to, let us say, Irish immigrants), but on the simple rights of citizens in a democratic republic.

If the abolitionists took the position that the question of the relative capacity of the races was a secondary or tertiary issue in all discussions of enfranchising the blacks, they were nonetheless inevitably drawn into it. In the main they put forward three major propositions. The first, and perhaps least aggressively pressed, was that there were no "racial" differences, simply "cultural" ones. The inescapable differences in white and black manner, style, and temperament were attributed to the circumstances in which members of the respective races had been reared. When blacks were reared in middle-class white families or indeed in middle-class black families, they displayed the same general character traits, ambitions, and capacities as their white counterparts. We might call this the no-difference or culturally determined difference school. Its adherents believed that the education of the freed slaves would transform them into middle-class Americans with black skins.

Those abolitionists who had more acquaintance with lower-class Northern blacks and with Southern blacks were apt to be much more cautious in their formulations. They were disposed to acknowledge basic inherent "racial" differences, but they argued that these had nothing to do with "inferiority" or "superiority." They were simply differences like the obvious physical differences of the thicker lips and kinky hair of blacks or the dark skin, black hair, and brown eyes of certain Caucasians which contrasted sharply with the blond hair and blue eyes of other Caucasians. "It is a mistake to speak of the African as an inferior race to the Caucasian," James Freeman Clarke wrote. "It is doubtless *different* from this, just as this is also different from the Malay, the Indian, the Mongolian. There are many varieties in the human family." To Clarke and, indeed, to the great majority of abolitionists, it was evident that, for example, "the colored man has not so much invention as the white, but more imitation. He has not so much of the reflective, but more of the perceptive powers. The black child will learn to read and write as fast [as] or faster than the white child," but the blacks had not "the indomitable perseverence and will, which make the Caucasian, at least the Saxon portion of it, *masters* wherever they go—but they have a native courtesy, a civility. . . . More than all, they have almost universally a strong religious tendency, and that strength of attachment which is capable of any kind of self-denial, and self-sacrifice. Is this an inferior race—so inferior as to be only fit for chains?" Moncure Conway told an English audience that blacks "seem to me to be weaker in the direction of understanding, strictly speaking, but to have strength and elegance of imagination and expression. Negro sermons, fables, and descriptions are in the highest degree

pictorial, abounding in mystic interpretations which would delight a
German transcendentalist. My belief is, that there is a vast deal of high
art yet to come out of that people in America. Their songs and hymns
are the only original melodies we have."

The third and most radical abolitionist view was one that credited
blacks with essentially superior qualities or, at least, with qualities that,
the abolitionists argued, were conspicuously missing in the dominant
white population and that were desperately needed for the moral
health of the nation. Although "difference" was plainly a two-edged
sword—some using it to argue the basic inferiority of the black—it was
irresistible to many abolitionists because of the possibility that the
difference might be a *redemptive* difference. In *Uncle Tom's Cabin*
Harriet Beecher Stowe had speculated that God, having tried the other
races and peoples of the world, must come at last "in the great drama
of human improvement" to Africa, and life would then "awake there
with a gorgeousness and splendor of which our cold western tribes
have faintly conceived." That continent and its people would "show
forth some of the latest and most magnificent revelations of human
life." Africa and the African would be revealed as "the highest and
noblest in that kingdom which He [God] will set up, when every other
kingdom has been tried, and failed; for the first shall be last, and the
last first."

The principal problem faced by the abolitionists was that of the
most effective tactics. Having been pictured for a generation or more
as wild-eyed fanatics without a shred of political common sense, they
now found themselves directly involved in the political process. They
had the heady experience of helping swing elections, calculating votes
needed, and lobbying hesitant politicos. Under the tutelage of "old
pro" antislavery Republicans like Charles Sumner and Benjamin
Wade, they proved ready learners, quite ready to remain in the
background and pull wires. Lydia Maria Child wrote to John Greenleaf Whittier that "the warmest of the Republicans and the most
unprejudiced of the Abolitionists are laying their heads together, with
no more *publicity* than is necessary, to influence popular opinion,
through the press, and help on the turning tide in the right direction."
Their best writers were recruited to write anonymous articles ("so that
the truths they present may have their due weight, without prejudice")
to be sent out to small-town papers throughout the North—antislavery
boilerplate, so to speak.

The abolitionists also proved adept at forming "front" organizations like the rather innocuously named Boston Emancipation League, made up primarily of old-line abolitionists. Special attention was given to well-known Democrats or conservative Republicans who were known to have liberal chinks in their armor. John Jay worked on "the Butler people" in New York, and Sumner and Phillips brought George Bancroft around. In the year following its founding, the Boston Emancipation League put on nine lectures in Boston and distributed some 100,000 pamphlets in addition to articles and editorials for newspapers. A weekly newspaper, the *Boston Commonwealth*, was started in the fall of 1862. The Boston Emancipation League had its counterparts in other Northern cities, and soon the National Emancipation League in New York City was busy coordinating their activities. In Washington the Smithsonian Institution was rented by emancipationists, né abolitionists, who put on a series of lectures on matters having to do with emancipation and its consequences which were attended by Congressmen and Senators and even, on one occasion, by the President and Mrs. Lincoln. Susan B. Anthony went on the "emancipation circuit."

There were, in the ranks of abolitionists, the so-called amalgamators, the advocates of racial intermarriage. It could hardly have been otherwise. If black people had in their genetic makeup those superior qualities of gentleness, compassion, loyalty, gratitude, and artistic sensibility, qualities desperately needed in order to elevate the American character, what better way for them to be disseminated among the general population than by intermarriage? William Hepworth Dixon, the English journalist, noted sardonically that "amalgamation" was a program favored by Northern abolitionists primarily for the benefit of white Southerners and that such marriages were not conspicuous in the ranks of the abolitionists themselves. "Looked at through the centuries," Theodore Tilton wrote, "the question of races sinks into insignificance. The only generalization that will stand is, not that there are five races of men, or seven, or twelve, but only one—the universal human race in which all men are brothers, and God is father over all."

David Goodman Croly was one of the few abolitionist writers who approached the issue from the point of view of "science" and argued in consequence for "amalgamation" or, in the word he preferred, "miscegenation." In a book of that name, published in 1864, Croly took the line, in the words of one of his chapter headings, that "The Blending of Diverse Bloods [was] essential to American Progress." All history, according to Croly, revealed that progress was the result of the mixing of blood. "The word is spoken at last," his introduction began. "It is Miscegenation—the blending of the various races of men—the practical recognition of the brotherhood of all the children of a common father. While the sublime inspirations of Christianity have taught this doctrine, Christians so-called have ignored it in denying social equality to the colored man; while democracy is founded upon the idea that all men are equal, democrats have shrunk from the logic of their own creed. . . . But Christianity, democracy, and science, are stronger than the timidity, prejudice, and pride of short-sighted men; and they teach that a people to become great, must become composite." Croly was convinced: "If we would be raised to full stature of manhood and womanhood; if we would be as gods, knowing good from evil; if we would fill our proper place in nature, we must mingle our blood with all the children of the common father of humanity. . . . This is a lesson that America, strong with the pride of color and country, should lay well to heart." Croly is interesting as a kind of transitional figure who wishes to combine the Christian notion of brotherhood (obviously paramount in his thinking) with the new credentials of science. He was so aware that his book would enrage most of his fellow citizens that he published it anonymously.

The public discussion of black "nature" was one that blacks entered into with considerable eloquence. William Wells Brown had been born a slave in Kentucky and escaped to the North. Having taught himself to read and write, he was signed on as an abolitionist lecturer and made a name for himself as one of the most effective orators in the movement. In 1863 he wrote a book entitled *The Black Man: His Antecedents, His Genius, and His Achievements.* In biographies of fifty-seven black men and women Brown undertook to demonstrate that even against great odds many blacks had substantial achievements to their credit. The book at once became a best seller, going through ten editions in three years. *The Black Man* was an impressive achievement. The facts were skillfully marshaled, and a tone of irony was evident throughout the work. "In education, in morals, and in the development of mechanical genius, the free blacks of the Northern States will compare favorably with any laboring class in the world," he wrote. "And considering the fact we have been shut out by a cruel prejudice, from nearly all the mechanical branches, and all the professions, it is marvellous that we have attained the position we now occupy."

Frederick Douglass addressed himself to the same issue—the

lumping of all black people together. In his words, "They [blacks] are all bound in one bundle, the ignorant, lazy, thriftless, and unworthy, with the intelligent, industrious, thriving and worthy, and condemned to a common level of degradation."

The *Anglo-African* charged that white Americans "brutalized" black people. "The enormity of your guilt," the paper declared, "the immensity of the wrong does not appear in contemplating what you have made us, but in the consideration of what you have prevented us from being."

John Rock, a black lawyer, placed his finger very clearly on this point when he denounced "the very unjust method of comparing the highest grades of Anglo-American intellect with the lowest forms of negro sensuality . . . to prove our inferiority." It seemed to him mad to argue "that the blessings of citizenship have been especially reserved by our Heavenly Parent for those men who have white skins and straight hair. . . . I tell you gentlemen, we have both physical and moral courage. I believe in the equality of my race. . . . This is our country by birth. . . . This is our native country; we have as strong attachment naturally to our native hills, valleys, plains, luxuriant forests, flowing streams, mighty rivers, and lofty mountains, as any other people. . . . This is the country of our choice, being our fathers' country. We love this land, and have contributed our share to its prosperity and wealth. . . . I will not admit, for a moment," Rock continued, "that we are inferior to you." He compared American blacks with the degraded peasants of Europe, the Russian serfs, the Gypsies, and the Sicilians. Those people had done little or nothing to change their condition. "Not so with the negro; his godlike intellect surmounts the difficulties which surround him, and he stands forth a man." H. Ford Douglass, one of Frederick Douglass's sons, argued that "man's ability depends upon surrounding circumstances. You may take all of those races that have risen from the lowest stage of degradation to the highest eminence of intellectual and moral splendor, and you will discover that no race has ever yet been able, by any internal power and will of its own, to lift itself into respectability, without contact with other civilized tribes. . . ." Douglass also declared himself proud of his race. The black man was, above all, a man, "like other men," and in the United States by his struggle against overwhelming prejudice he had demonstrated "the *highest* element of manhood."

The *Pacific Appeal*, a black newspaper published in San Francisco, defended blacks against the charge that they were by nature lazy and idle, with thievish propensities. "Can they be expected to be scrupu-lously honest," the editor of the *Appeal* asked, "when they are continu-ally, and have been forever, robbed of everything—time, labor, parents, children, the necessaries of life, nay, even life itself? Can they be truthful to those whose every look, every word, every action is a lie, as false as hell?"

To all such arguments the vast majority of white Americans, even in the midst of a civil war fought over the issue of slavery, continued to turn a deaf ear.

3

The Soldiers

Something must be said here about the tens and then hundreds of thousands of young men who poured into Washington or flocked to other newly established military camps in the West to constitute the Union army.

As in the case of the vivid diaries of Southern women written during the war, innumerable soldiers of both armies and of all ranks wrote letters and diaries giving day-to-day accounts in detail of the arduous soldier's life and campaigns of the war. Some of them will be our companions and guides in the pages that follow.

In Lima, Indiana, Ted Upson, barely turned sixteen, nagged his father to allow him to enlist. Many of the young men of the town had already departed. "It is pretty quiet here now," he noted in his diary, "only when some one gets a letter from a soldier at the front they read it in some store and talk it over." Finally Jonathan Upson weakened. "Wont you tell me why you want to go?" he asked his son, "soft and low like." Young Upson replied: "Father, we must have more soldiers. This Union your ancestors and mine helped to make must be saved from destruction. I can better go than some others. I dont feel right to stay at home any longer."

"If that is the way you feel about it," his father replied, "you may go and God bless and keep you my boy." Equipped with a "Six Shooter Colts Revolver" and a hand-me-down uniform, Upson began to drill under the direction of an old veteran of the Indian wars and to enjoy the attention of the girls of the town, who sang "I Am Bound to Be a Soldier's Wife or Die an Old Maid." There were picnics, socials, and buggy rides to pass the days until Upson's unit was filled and mustered into service, and before he left home, he had an "understanding" with "E.S.," presumably one of the girls who was determined to marry a soldier.

When Fort Sumter was fired upon, Alfred Bellard was one of those who wished to volunteer. "My military spirit," he wrote, ". . . rose to a boiling pitch," but he was a carpenter's apprentice and was unable to enlist. When his master departed for Canada, he went to the nearest recruiting office, signed up with the 5th New Jersey Volunteers, and was soon being "initiated in the misteries of keeping our heels on a line. Toes out at an angle of 45 degrees. Belly in. Chest out and such other positions as tend to make a full-fledged veteran out of a raw recruit." One of Bellard's fellow recruits "had his ardor suddenly dampened by the appearance of his wife, who told the captain that her husband was nothing but a drunkard, did not support his family as he ought, and she wanted the captain to send him home, and in order to enforce her argument she pitched into him right and left to the great amusement of the boys. . . ."

Among the New Jersey Volunteers was a young Quaker, Edward Acton, an engineer, ten years married and with three young children. Acton and the New Jersey Volunteers were assigned to Joseph Hooker's division. Like tens of thousands of other soldiers, Acton wrote dutifully to his wife, Mary, giving a picture of the routines of camp life and the highlights of engagements. Having enrolled originally as a staff sergeant, when his three-month enlistment period was over, he re-enlisted, this time as a lieutenant, in Company F, 5th Regiment.

John Beatty, the small-town Ohio banker who had been an early Free-Soil man, a supporter of Frémont in 1856, and a presidential elector, was one of those antislavery, pro-Union sympathizers who responded to Lincoln's first call for volunteers. He helped organize the 3rd Ohio Volunteer Infantry, made up essentially of local militia companies. A week after the fall of Sumter the 3rd Ohio Infantry assembled at Camp Jackson, and ten days after Lincoln's call it was mustered into the United States service with Beatty as lieutenant colonel. Refreshingly lacking in self-importance and with a shrewd eye for the absurd, Beatty kept a lively record of his military experiences. After the war he returned to his bank in Cardington, Ohio, which had been run by his brother during Beatty's term of service in the army, was twice elected to Congress, wrote three novels, and turned out a number of popular paperback books on economic issues.

Walt Whitman's brothers were named Andrew Jackson, Thomas Jefferson, George Washington, Jesse, and Edward. In a close family George Washington Whitman and Walt, ten years his senior, were especially close. George enlisted when Lincoln called for three-month volunteers, re-enlisted in the 51st Regiment of the New York Volunteers, and fought in many of the bloodiest battles of the war. His brother Walt first worked as a nurse in a Brooklyn hospital for Union wounded, then, in part to be nearer his brother, moved to Washington, where he followed George's military ventures anxiously. George, for his part, was a faithful correspondent, writing to his mother—Mammy, as he called her—to his brothers, and to his sister Han, or Hannah. In addition, he kept a rather scant diary which Walt called "a perfect poem of the war," written by one of "a newer larger race of human giants."

Oliver Wendell Holmes, Jr., was twenty years old, still a senior at Harvard, when he enrolled as a private in the New England Guard, a militia unit. When the school year was over and he had been graduated, Holmes was commissioned a first lieutenant in Company A of the 20th Regiment of the Massachusetts Volunteers, which was mustered into the Federal service a few weeks later. It was a unit the officer corps of which was a roster of Boston bluebloods—Hallowells, Lowells, Putnams, Crowninshields, Everetts, Pomeroys, Abbotts, and Cabots.

Among the young men who responded to Lincoln's call for volunteers was a fellow Illinoisan named Lester Ward. Ward was the tenth child of a millwright who had emigrated from western New York to help build the locks of the Illinois and Michigan Canal, not far from Joliet. From Illinois the family moved on to Iowa to claim land due the elder Ward for service in the War of 1812. There young Lester, sixteen years old, spent the hours when he was not working on his parents' farm "roaming over those boundless prairies, always with a gun, killing the game both for sport and for the table, and admiring nature." Unable to find employment in Iowa, he and his brother Erastus made their way to Towanda, Pennsylvania, to work in their brother Cyrenus's wagon hubmaking business.

Charles Francis Adams, Jr., had graduated from Harvard and apprenticed himself to Richard Henry Dana as a lawyer. With the surrender of Sumter, young Adams joined a Boston militia unit and, after several months of tedious drilling, obtained a commission in the 1st Massachusetts Cavalry. His brother Henry accompanied the senior Adams to England to act as his private secretary, and soon the father and his two sons were exchanging frequent letters. Those of young Charles Francis constituted a kind of running narrative of his war experiences.

A soldier's time may be said to be spent 60 percent in camp, 35 percent campaigning (marching and bivouacking), and far less than 5 percent fighting. The proportion of time spent in camp or in the field could, of course, vary greatly, but the amount of time in actual combat was only a tiny fraction of a soldier's life. Many soldiers assigned to forts and strong defensive installations never heard a shot fired in anger. At Drewry's Bluff in Virginia, for instance, William Blackford noted that the men of the garrison had built themselves miniature houses and planted small gardens which kept them supplied with fresh vegetables.

To get a notion of the nature of a soldier's life, we must encounter him in camp. "Camps" were areas, usually well in the rear of the lines of contact between opposing armies, where units rested and drilled between campaigns. They had about them a settled, semipermanent air. Units were established in tents or more weatherproof structures improvised by their occupants, in carefully laid-out company streets, by regiments, brigades, divisions, corps, and armies.

The basic tactical infantry unit was the company, consisting, in the Union army, of between 83 and 102 men and officers. A typical company was commanded by a captain, with one first lieutenant (his assistant and executive officer), one second lieutenant, a first sergeant, four platoon sergeants, and eight corporals. In volunteer units the men commonly elected their company officers, seldom making for the best discipline. An infantry regiment was in turn made up of ten companies (cavalry regiments had twelve) and was commanded by a colonel, who had under him a lieutenant colonel, a major, an adjutant, a quartermaster, a surgeon, two assistant surgeons, and a chaplain. A regiment at full strength (few ever were) ranged from 830 to 1,020 men. Most regiments that had seen any service were at half strength or less. During the course of the war the Union raised, by voluntary enlistment or draft, 2,046 regiments, while the South mustered slightly more than 1,000. In the Union army 1,696 were infantry, 272 cavalry, and 78 artillery.

Brigades, a very commonly employed tactical unit, were made up of two or more regiments; two or more brigades constituted a division. A Federal division usually averaged some 6,000 men and officers to 8,500 for the Confederate division. A corps, correspondingly, was made up of some forty to forty-five infantry regiments organized into two or more divisions.

Armies, which were usually named after the department in which they operated—i.e., the Army of the Ohio or the Army of the Tennessee—numbered some sixteen on the Union side and twenty-three on the Confederate. They varied greatly in size, depending on their mission, and constituted a single unified and independent command under a major general.

In any event, whatever the unit, it typically spent much of its time in camp.

The initial experience of the soldier was that of enlistment (usually accompanied by rudimentary drill and the issuance of clothing and equipment) and transportation to a post or training camp, most commonly by train.

Alfred Bellard, for example, boarded a train with his fellow volunteers at the Pennsylvania Railroad Depot in Trenton, New Jersey. "This," Bellard wrote, "was soon taken possession of and surrounded with friends some of the women crying and wringing their hands, while the boys who were off for a soldier, were laughing and cracking jokes and doing their best to make everyone else feel as happy as themselves."

At Trenton they went through the most perfunctory medical exam by a doctor who asked such questions as "Were you ever sick in your life, have you got the rheumatism, have you got varicose veins, and other questions of like matter," Bellard noted, "instead of finding out for himself by actual examination whether you had or not. If the questions were answered in the affirmative and he had no reason to doubt it, he would give us a thump on the chest, and if we were not floored nor showed any other signs of inconvenience, we were pronounced in good condition. . . ." They were then sworn in "as full-fledged soldiers in the pay of Uncle Sam" and marched off to the state arsenal to be issued a blanket, tin cup, plate, knife, fork, and spoon. Having received their eating utensils, the recruits set about the principal occupation of the soldier—far more important, indeed, than fighting—foraging for food to supplement the monotonous army rations. "There being plenty of farm houses around our camp," Bellard wrote, "we never went short of fruit or corn, for soon after dark when the fog had fairly risen, we would sally out of camp in squads, visit the farms, and return to camp loaded with watermelons or corn." The more adventurous "would sail for the city" and return drunk to find their way past the guard as best they could, or, being apprehended, to spend the night in the guardhouse.

When the train carrying Bellard and his fellows passed through Philadelphia, a large crowd was gathered at the station to cheer them on their journey. "Cigars, tobacco, handkerchiefs and boquets were given away by the young ladies," Bellard wrote. He received a "bunch of cigars," and as the train pulled out of the station, "amid the crack of firearms and the cheers from a thousand throats," the 5th New Jersey Volunteers had their first casualty. In the exuberant firing of guns and pistols a recruit received a pistol bullet in his arm and was discharged on the spot. Passing through Maryland—"rebel climate"—some soldiers amused themselves "by slinging leaden pills [Bellard's name for bullets] at the cows and sheep who were quietly gazing at the passing train."

Ted Upson, who enlisted late in 1861, was sent initially to Camp Allen, Indiana, where the ladies of the vicinity had prepared a "grand dinner . . . in a grove." There the men ate until they could eat no more and then elected their officers. The next day drill began. Upson noted that "some of the boys are aufuly profane and some drink a good deal more than is good for them," but he was determined to hew to the straight and narrow and found a model in forty-two-year-old "Uncle" Aaron Wolford, who had enlisted despite the fact that he had eight children. Uniforms were issued to the new recruits, and Upson wrote: "Evry one was givin a suit, hat, coat, pants and shoes—also shirts and drawers. If they fit, all right; if not, we had to trade around till we could get a fit. . . ." The very short and very tall recruits suffered in the process. A few weeks later, in the wake of the first rains, the men were issued "rubber blankets or 'ponchos.'" Six and a half feet long and three and a half feet wide, they had eyelets by which two could be tied together to make a small tent.

From Camp Allen, Upson and his band of Indiana volunteers were carried down the Mississippi to Fort Pickering on the outskirts of Memphis. From there they began a long march to Holly Springs,

Mississippi, to join the recently formed (March, 1862) Army of the Mississippi. Now all the military and nonmilitary paraphernalia that they had acquired in their weeks of training began to be discarded, and soon the line of march was littered with abandoned "blankets books overcoats and underwear." Some men even discarded their knapsacks. Rain began, cold, soaking rain, a worse enemy to soldiers, especially those not yet adept at mitigating its most chilling effects, than enemy gunfire. Camped by the Tallahatchie River, they endured the interminable downpour as best they could—"an auful wet rain too."

A soldier's day began with reveille, which was sounded, most of the year, at five; breakfast call was at six, sick call at seven, drill at eight, recall at eleven, lunch at twelve, fatigue duty and cleanup thereafter, drill again at four, recall at five, mounting of the guard at five-thirty, parade at six-thirty, tattoo at nine, and taps at nine-thirty.

Drill took two forms—parade ground drill by platoons, companies, and regiments, with the manual of arms and marching and countermarching, by the right flank and the left, forward and to the rear, filing and re-forming; and the complex and demanding movements into battle formations from the march, into closed and extended skirmish lines, and into bayonet charges. The officers were rehearsed in "sending out advanced guard, posting picket, grand guards, outposts, and sentinels. During these exercises," John Beatty wrote, "we rode fifteen or twenty miles and listened to at least twenty speeches." There were further classes on "detachments, reconnaissances, partisans, and flankers." The officers learned their lessons one day and instructed their troops the next.

Formal parades were highly unpopular with the soldiers. John Beatty described "a grand corps drill" conducted under General George Thomas's direction before the Battle of Tullahoma. "The corps," Beatty wrote, "was like a clumsy giant, and hours were required to execute the simplest movement. . . . The waving of banners, the flashing of sabers and bayonets, the clattering to and fro of muddle-headed aides-de-camp on impatient steeds, the heavy rumbling of artillery wagons, the blue coats of the soldiers, the golden trappings of the field and staff, made a grand scene for the disinterested spectator . . ." but with the temperature in the nineties it was hard on the soldiers and produced "an unusual amount of perspiration, and not a little profanity."

The soldiers of both armies had a genius for creating areas of comfort in the midst of discomfort. The pickets of the 3rd Ohio

Volunteers, John Beatty noted, "often make little houses of logs, which they cover with cedar boughs or branches of laurel, and denominate forts, the forts being generally named after the non-commissioned officer in charge." Thus Beatty, making his rounds of the outposts, came on "Fort Stiner," where the men off duty "were sitting around a fire, heating coffee and roasting slices of fat pork. . . ."

In camp near Potomac Run, Virginia, in the bone-chilling cold of Virginia, the Union Army of the Potomac made itself as comfortable as it could, displaying considerable ingenuity in the process. Charles Francis Adams, Jr., wrote that his men had "logged in their tents and built fireplaces, and, as a rule, are well clad and well shod; but, after," he added, "it comes hard on them, this being wet and always sleeping on damp ground. . . ."

When an army was encamped for any period of time, the sutlers descended on it like voracious flies, selling junk food at excessive prices. John Beatty observed that the soldiers "oftenest on the sick list are those who are constantly running to the sutler's for gingerbread, sweetmeats, raisins, and nuts. They eat enormous quantities of this unwholesome stuff and lose appetite for more substantial food. Finding that all desire for hard bread and bacon has disappeared, they conclude that they must be ill, and instead of taking exercise lie in their tents until they finally become really sick."

Along with the sutlers came prostitutes, who swarmed around despite the efforts of the officers to drive them off. Peripatetic strumpets set up tents or established themselves in abandoned houses. Generally their "cover" was that they were laundresses or seamstresses (some of the older and less comely were undoubtedly genuine laundresses); sometimes they were "wives" or "girl friends." This female corps performed a number of functions not strictly sexual. Besides actually laundering and sewing, they frequently acted as impromptu nurses for wounded soldiers; Alfred Bellard, wounded at Chancellorsville, saw a *vivandière*, a kind of female sutler, holding a dying soldier in her lap. Mary Chesnut described the first *vivandière* she saw in Richmond: "She was dressed in the uniform of her regiment, but wore Turkish pantaloons. She frisked about in her hat and feathers . . . played the piano; and sang war songs. . . . She was followed at every step by a mob of admiring soldiers and boys."

John Beatty wrote: "Camp life to a young man who has nothing special to tie him to home has many attractions—abundance of company, continual excitement, and all the fun and frolic that a thousand lighthearted boys can devise. Tonight, in one tent a dozen or more are singing 'Dixie' at the top of their voices. In another 'The Star-Spangled Banner' is being executed so horribly that even a secessionist ought to pity the poor tune. Stories, cards, wrestling, boxing, racing, all these and a thousand other things enter into a day in camp." The uncertain life of the soldier, Beatty reflected, had "a tendency to harden and demoralize most men. . . . The fact that a few hours may put them in battle, where their lives will not be worth a fig, is forgotten. . . . They encourage and strengthen each other to such an extent that, when exposed to danger, imminent though it may be, they do not seem to realize it."

Beatty caught the tedium of war quite exactly when he wrote in his diary on December 29, 1863: "Nothing of interest has transpired today. Bugles, drums, drills, parades—the old story over and over again, the usual number of corncakes eaten, of pipes smoked, of papers respectfully forwarded, of how-do-ye-do's to colonels, captains, lieutenants and soldiers. You put on your hat and take a short walk. It does you no good. Returning you lie down on the cot and undertake to sleep; but you have already slept too much, and you get up and smoke again, look at an old paper, yawn, throw the paper down, and conclude it is confoundedly dull."

One of the conspicuous features of camp life was frequent revival meetings. The less pious organized "impromptu variety theatricles (or free and easys)," in Alfred Bellard's words.

If boredom was the dominant quality of camp life, it was closely followed by irritation at the multitude of petty rules and regulations that limited a soldier's freedom. Camp food was dull and unappetizing, and the opportunities to supplement it, aside from the sutlers' junk food, were severely limited. Military police patrolled the camps, and soldiers absent without leave were subject to severe discipline. Often a soldier returning to camp after a drinking spree and absent without leave would, when challenged by a guard to halt and give the countersign, come forward and place a pint of whiskey in the hand of the guard. Having given the "countersign," he was allowed to pass.

The tents originally issued to the troops were little changed from those used in the Revolution and the War of 1812—the military are not generally notable for innovation. They were heavy canvas structures designed to hold four to six men. They were carried in the regimental baggage train, and since supply wagons tended to get stuck in the mud or other ways delayed, they were often unavailable when most needed. In winter quarters or where a long stay was anticipated, the tents were improved in various ingenious ways. In winter quarters near Alexandria, Virginia, Alfred Bellard and his companions followed the common practice of driving split pine saplings into the ground to create a wall some two feet in height and mounting the tent on top. They would then build a mud and log chimney and fireplace at the rear of the tent, construct rough bunks, and be as snug "as an oyster at high water." But such tents, which had to be carried in a unit's baggage, were impractical for campaigning. Campaigning soldiers had a rubber blanket to keep out the dampness of the wet ground. A ration of whiskey and quinine was dispensed to the troops periodically as a health and morale measure. In the spring of 1863 small two-man shelter tents were issued to the Union soldiers in place of the larger six-man tents. The change was not a popular one. "The boys are very bitter in condemnation of them," John Beatty wrote, "and called them dog tents and dog pens." They wrote on their sides PUPS FOR SALE, RAT TERRIERS, BULL PUPS HERE, DOGHOLE NO. 1, SONS OF BITCHES WITHIN, DOGS, PURPS, and when General William Rosecrans rode by, the soldiers were "on their hands and knees, stretching their heads out of the ends of the tents, barking furiously. . . ."

Most soldiers much preferred the informal life of campaigning, where bivouac areas were occupied at the end of each day's march. A bivouac intended for a night or two might lengthen into weeks. Then the pleasures of military life became more evident. Soldiers had opportunities to forage for themselves. A camping atmosphere of camaraderie and informality prevailed. Charles Francis Adams, Jr., wrote to his mother praising the delights of the field bivouac: "It is strange what a sense of home and home comfort one attaches to the bivouac fire. You come in cold, hungry and tired and I assure you all the luxuries of home scarcely seem desirable beside its bright blaze, as you polish off a hot supper. And such suppers! You've no idea of how well we live, now we've added experience to hunger—hot coffee, delicate young roastpig, beefsteak and an arrangement of cabbage, from the tenement of a neighboring mud-sill. This, with a pipe of tobacco, a bunk of fir branches well-lined with blankets and crackling fire before it left little to be desired. There is a wild luxury about it, very fascinating to me." The dim shapes of the horses and the muffled sounds of their movements on the picket line, the shadows of the trees, and the precious sense of comradeship all were elements of the scene. "My enjoyment," Adams added, "springs from the open air sense of freedom and strength. It's a lawless sort of feeling, making me feel as if I depended only on nature and myself for enjoyment."

Army rations, when they were available, were based on the hardtack biscuit and salt beef and pork. Pork was known to the soldiers as salt junk, and beef as salt horse. Dried peas, beans, and what Alfred Bellard called "desecated vegetables" all were part of the soldiers' fare, along with potatoes and rice. The "desecated vegetables" were dried vegetables that came in a block. Chunks were cut off to put into a pot, "where it would swell out and make a very nice soup." Breakfast and supper were bread and coffee; lunch (dinner) was the main meal of the day. The bean soup was good, Bellard added, but sometimes so thin that the recipe was said by the soldiers to be one bean to a quart of water. Coffee was the one indispensable fuel for the soldier. It was the first thing brewed, the consolation for every hardship—for chilling rain and freezing cold. A cup of coffee pressed to the lips of a wounded man might be his final benediction. Sometimes it was so strong that it was recommended for "cuts and bruises."

Mess pans were used for cooking, for the soldier's ablutions, such as they were, and for washing his clothes. Beef on the hoof were driven along with the army. When a unit needed and qualified for fresh beef, several of the best shots were detailed to go to the drove, select an ox, shoot him, and cut his throat, after which the butcher would cut up the carcass and "issue" it to the company.

The hardtack (biscuit) was so hard in its pristine condition that it was generally too much for the often uncertain teeth of the soldiers. In consequence they commonly fried the hardtack in pork fat after soaking it for an hour or so to make it soft or, if time did not allow for such luxuries, dipped it in their coffee and munched on it as best they could. Fresh bread, available only in camp, was a luxury. One of the soldiers' favorite dishes was made up of any meat they could get their hands on. "Pork or beef, salt or fresh," Alfred Bellard wrote, "was cut up with potatoes, tomatoes, crackers, and garlic, seasoned with pepper and salt [gunpowder was often used when salt was unavailable], and stewed. This we called Hish and Hash or Hell fired stew." Crackers pounded into crumbs and mixed with sugar, raisins, and water made a pudding.

Prior to the start of a campaign, soldiers were typically issued four days' rations of hardtack, coffee, and salt meat, with sixty rounds of "lead pills." Besides coffee the average soldier's greatest consolation was tobacco. Sutlers charged ten cents for a paper of chewing tobacco, $1.50 for "a plug of navy tobacco," and ten cents for smoking tobacco. Chewing was by far the most popular. "A soldier would almost as soon do without his dinner as his chew," Alfred Bellard wrote.

Scrounging for food to supplement the monotonous camp rations was perhaps the soldiers' most absorbing pastime. Technically forbidden (unless official foraging parties were dispatched), it was usually winked at. John Beatty's orderly turned up with a chicken he had "bought," but that, Beatty noted skeptically, was commonly his explanation of how he supplemented the headquarters' rations. Sometimes unauthorized foraging produced no more than wild blackberries or hazelnuts. More often the result was a stray chicken or an unguarded pig. When the Battle of Tullahoma had already begun and John Beatty's brigade was preparing to meet the enemy attack, "at this moment when life and death seemed to hang in the balance, when we supposed we were in the presence of a very considerable, if not overwhelming, force of the enemy," Beatty wrote, "a half-grown hog emerged from the woods and ran across the road. Fifty men sprang from the ranks and gave it chase. . . ."

George Washington Whitman, camped near Cedar Mountain, Virginia, wrote to his mother: "We find plenty of forage in the shape of Beef, Chickens, eggs, potatoes, and the way the cattle and sheep have suffered since we have been here is a caution to secesh farmers. some of the boys go to a house where there is a sheep dog, take the dog and make him catch as many sheep as they want, bring them in and cook them, and you may be sure the yankees get some tall cussing from the farmers."

John Beatty noted in his diary that he "had a blackberry pie and pudding for dinner. Rather too much happiness for one day; but then the crust of the pudding was tolerably tough." The grass had grown high in his tent, and, he noted in his diary, "the gentle grasshopper makes music all the day, and likewise all the night." It was a sweet, incongruous sound amid the strident noises of the camp.

Rivers like the James and Rappahannock abounded in oysters. Fruit trees—peach, pear, cherry, and apple—were a constant temptation and solace to soldiers "fed up" with army rations. The country around most field bivouacs swarmed with game of various kinds. Turkey buzzards (and more occasionally, turkeys), crows, eagles, ducks, and wild geese were plentiful. There were fish in the numerous rivers, creeks, and ponds—yellow perch, catfish, eel, roach, bass—and in the ocean estuaries and rivers that ran to the sea, shad and salmon. Small game—rabbits, squirrels, and opossums principally—were rolled in mud an inch or so thick and placed in the coals of a campfire. After the animal had baked sufficiently, the hardened clay was broken off, the fur with it, and it was cleaned and eaten.

Food was not always so abundant, of course. In the winter, and when Federal supply lines were cut by rebel guerrillas, railroad lines broken up, or tunnels blocked, men often went hungry. John Beatty saw ravenous soldiers following forage wagons and picking up grains of corn that fell from them. The animals suffered most acutely. Hundreds of horses and mules died of starvation before fodder could be secured for them outside Chattanooga.

Swimming was a favorite pastime for soldiers bivouacked near a stream or river. Before the Battle of Malvern Hill, Alfred Bellard and his comrades showered in the water that spilled over a nearby milldam. Someone found a long board, which they anchored on the bank of the millpond, creating a diving board, "and on any fine day the boys could be seen running along the plank and plunging into the water, like so many frogs," Bellard wrote.

As the Union army began to penetrate the Confederacy, the magic Southern landscape seduced the stiffest Yankee soul in spring and summer. At a town with the improbable name of Scrougeville in Tennessee, the night air was filled with the sounds of doves and whippoorwills. Sutlers appeared with pies, "and such pies," John Beatty wrote. Blacks were singing somewhere nearby, and the sounds "floated out on the genial air . . . as we stretched on the greensward . . . smoked our pipes and drank our beer. . . ." It was like a fairyland. Thomas Wentworth Higginson wrote: "There was something luscious, voluptuous, almost oppressively fragrant" about South Carolina, and George Washington Whitman wrote his "Mammy" that he would like to settle in Virginia after the war.

"A brass band is now playing, away over on the Lebanon pike," Beatty wrote in April, 1863, outside Nashville, where the Army of the Cumberland awaited the next engagement. "The pontooniers are singing a psalm, with a view, doubtless, to making the oaths with which they intend to close the night [as they go through their exercises in laying pontoons] appear more forcible. The signals lights are waving to and fro from the dome of the courthouse. The hungry mules of the Pioneer Corps are making the night hideous with howls. So, and amid such scenes, the tedious hours pass. . . . The katydids are piping away on the old, old story. The trees look like great shadows, and unlike the substantial oaks they really are. The camps are dark and quiet. This is all I can say of the night without."

A cavalry encampment was the most romantic scene offered by war. For Walt Whitman it was "a ceaseless field of observation. . . . This forenoon," he wrote, "there stand the horses, tether'd together, dripping, steaming, chewing their hay. . . . Some of the men are cleaning their sabres . . . some brushing boots, some laying off, reading, writing—some cooking, some sleeping. On long temporary crosssticks back of the tents are cavalry accoutrements—blankets and overcoats hung out to air— . . . the squads of horses . . . continually stamping and whisking their tails to keep off flies."

Charles Francis Adams wrote his father: "So here I am, attending daily to the needs of my men and horses, duly seeing that hair is short and clothes are clean, paying great attention to belts and sabres, inspecting pistols and policing quarters and so, not very intellectually and indeed with some sense of fatigue, playing my part in the struggle. . . ."

Many soldiers brought musical instruments with them, and singing was a major form of entertainment—lively songs; sentimental songs; songs of home, of girls left behind, of happier days; comic songs and sad songs. Beatty wrote: "I catch the faintest possible sound of a violin. Some indomitable spirit is enlivening the night, and trenching upon the Sabbath, by giving loose rein to his genius."

A favorite soldier song was "Home, Sweet Home":

> An exile from home, splendor dazzles in vain;
> Oh, give me my lowly thatched cottage again!
> The birds singing gayly, that came at my call,—
> Give me them,—with the peace of mind dearer than all!
> Home, Home, sweet, sweet home. There's no place like
> Home! there's no place like Home!

Beatty wrote in one diary entry: "The night is grand. The moon, a crescent, now rests for a moment on the highest peak of the Cheat and by its light suggests, rather than reveals, the outline of hill, valley, cove, and mountain. The boys are awake and merry. The fair weather has put new spirit in them all. A clear tenor voice sang:

Her golden hair in ringlets fair;
Her eyes like diamonds shining:
Her slender waist, her carriage chaste,
Left me, poor soul a pining.
But let the night be e'er so dark,
Or 'e'er so wet and rainy,
I will return safe back again
To the girl I left behind me."

If war was terrible and sublime, it was clearly a proper subject for poetry, and a vast number of officers and men tried to capture in verse the nature of their experience as soldiers. John Beatty, who loved Keats and Shelley and Burns, tried his hand at it in one of the interminable intervals between battles. He worked away until his head ached, and "this," he wrote, "is the best I could do:

O Lord, when will this war end?
These days of marching, nights of lonely guard?
This terrible expenditure of health and life,
Where is the glory? Where is the reward,
For sacrifice of comfort, quiet, peace?
For sacrifice of children, wife, and friends?
For sacrifice of firesides—genial homes?
What hour, what gift, will ever make amends
For broken health, for bruised flesh and bones,
For lives cut short by bullet, blade, disease? . . .

Hold, murmurer, hold! Is country naught to thee?
Is freedom nothing? Naught an honored name?"

Beatty went on to find solace in the thought which "shall crown the living and the dead, / 'He lived, he died, to God and duty true.' "

A few weeks of campaigning left the best-equipped soldier looking like a ragamuffin. After the Peninsula campaign of 1862 Alfred Bellard wrote: "Our uniforms . . . would have disgraced a beggar. Our pants had worn away so much that they hardly reached the knee, and the bottoms were in tatters. Our overcoats were not much better being burnt here and there in the skirts, by laying too near the fire. The whole uniform being pretty well stained up with mud and ashes." Charles Francis Adams described himself to his father: "My blue trousers are ragged from contact with the saddle and so covered with grease and dust that they would fry well. From frequent washing my flannel shirts are so shrunk about the throat that they utterly refuse to button and so, perforce, 'I follow Freedom with my bosom bare.' " His boots were "long innocent of blacking," and his hair "cropped close to my head, a beard white with dust and such a dirty face, constitute my usual apparel."

Southern soldiers were even more exotically garbed. Near Oxford, Mississippi, in the fall of 1862 Elizabeth Meriwether encountered General Martin Green commanding the 3rd Brigade of Sterling ("Pap") Price's Missourians. "In spite of all retreats their confidence in Price and in the success of the South seemed unbounded," Elizabeth Meriwether wrote. She was struck by "costumes" of the soldiers. "The shirts of some were made of women's shawls, some of window curtains. I saw trousers that were made out of old carpets." When Mary Chesnut watched John Bell Hood's Kentuckians marching through Richmond on their way to join Lee, she was astonished at their ragged appearance and rough ways. "Most garments and arms," she wrote, "were such as had been taken from the enemy. Such shoes as they had on. . . . Such tin pans and pots as were tied to their waists, with bread or bacon stuck on the ends of their bayonets. Anything that could be spiked was bayoneted and held aloft. They did not seem to mind their shabby condition: laughed, shouted, and cheered as they marched by."

Many soldiers found the rough and open life of campaigning, at least when the weather was fine, an exhilarating experience. For sheltered young Harvard men like Charles Francis Adams, Jr., and the younger Oliver Wendell Holmes, their bodies exposed to the elements, hardened and tempered by open air and constant exercise, army life gave a wholly new sense of the physical world and their relation to it. For some it amounted to a revelation of a heretofore-unexplored dimension. Charles Francis Adams's letters to his brother Henry and his father were almost ecstatic. "As for me," he wrote his father in the spring of 1862, "I never was better in my life. The exposure has been pretty severe and the change of life great; but I am always well in the open air and jolly among a crowd of fellows. . . . I like it and like it better than I expected. I fall into the life very easily. . . ."

And to his brother Henry, he wrote: "I am nearer other men than I ever was before, and the contact makes me more human; I am on better terms with my brother men and they with me. You say my mind is lying fallow all this time. Perhaps, but after all the body has other functions than to carry around the head, and few years' quiet will hardly injure a mind warped, as I sometimes suspect mine was, in time past by the too constant and close inspection of print. . . . After being a regular, quiet, respectable stay-at-home body in my youth, lo! at twenty-seven, I have discovered that I never knew myself and that nature meant me for a Bohemian—a vagabond. I am growing and developing here daily, but in such strange directions." Law and business, Adams wrote, seemed "to sit like some terrible incubus on my past . . . the truth is that going back to Boston and its old tread-mill is one of the aspects of the future from which my mind fairly revolts."

If American soldiers were more than ordinarily ingenious in devising ways to increase the minor comforts of army life and relieve the tedium, they were also remarkable for the wry good humor with which they endured its rigors and hazards. At the beginning of the Battle of Chattanooga, John Beatty observed two infantrymen standing by the open fly of their pup tent when a Confederate cannonball struck in front of the tent and rolled into it. "One of the soldiers turned very coolly to the other and said: 'There, you damn fool, you see what you get by leaving your door open!'"

All the general officers had nicknames. Sherman was Uncle Billy; Grant, Old Iron Jaw; Lorenzo Thomas, Pap; Oliver Howard, Old Prayer Book. The men of Ted Upson's regiment composed a song incorporating the nicknames of the regiment's officers and enlisted men:

> Old Leather Britches rips no stitches
> But fights the whole war through
>
> Old Moccasin Sam, with an eighteen shoe,
> And Gunboat Hall the shoe box drew,
>
> The tracks they made may still be seen
> From Richmond back to Bowling Green.

Far more important than what soldiers wore or ate or the nature of their life in camp or bivouac was what we might call their qualities as soldiers—their character—for it was this more than anything else that might be taken as a measure of the success or failure of American democracy. First of all, it must be said that the Union army was an army of nations—Irish and German most conspicuously but French, Hungarian, Scottish, and a dozen others as well. Southerners persisted in describing the Union army as a mercenary force made up primarily of immigrants. However, native-born Americans by far predominated, and the sectional differences were striking.

The New Englanders were conspicuous by virtue of their piety, good order, tidiness, and enterprise. Better educated than their comrades-in-arms from other areas, they more readily accepted military discipline. The New Englanders, Sidney George Fisher believed, were the best troops, "as there the Saxon blood is most pure and civilization, as a consequence, highest. . . . New England is far superior to the rest of this country in its moral and intellectual standards, in its industry & wealth, in morals & literary culture." Walt Whitman, as much as he admired the expansive style of the Westerners, singled out a Massachusetts soldier, Sergeant Calvin Harlowe, Company C, 29th Massachusetts Infantry, 1st Division, as a kind of symbol of the heroism of the Union soldier. Surprised by a rebel raid in the closing weeks of the war, Harlowe, although surrounded by the enemy, refused to surrender and was shot down. Only twenty-two years old, "a tall, slim, dark-hair'd, blue-eyed young man, he would not say, 'I surrender'—and so he died." Whitman added: "When I think of such things, knowing them well, all the vast and complicated events of the war, on which history dwells and makes its volumes, fall aside, and for the moment at any rate I see nothing but young Calvin Harlowe's figure in the night, disdaining to surrender."

New York City produced, as we have seen, the most racially or ethnically variegated units, including "the dregs of the city," a unit called the Lost Children. The Pennsylvanians were "a source of endless delight" to Charles Francis Adams: "[T]hey were so ragged, so independent, and so very peculiar. No officers troubled their repose. . . . They were grave and elderly men and very, very old campaigners. They were curiously clad in defiance of all rule whether military or civil, and we pondered long as to where they could have got their clothes." Apparently, starting in civilian attire, "they had been picking up old soldiers clothes ever since. . . . They had a strange way of leaving camp whenever they saw fit and returning laden with well filled knapsacks; whereat the faces of their comrades would light up with grim satisfaction. Water they had not now and soap they had evidently never known; but they were old soldiers, for they cooked strange messes and when boots and saddles sounded, undisturbed by the cannonade, they would saddle their horses carefully, slowly and meditatively, evidently with respect for the beast if not in the fear of God."

Alfred Bellard's 5th New Jersey Volunteers was made up of a revealing mix of ages and nationalities. Out of the ninety-nine men originally in his company, twelve, including himself, had been born in England. Sixty-two in all were immigrants, most of them Irish and German. The average age was almost thirty, and nineteen members of the company had been over forty when they enlisted. Their occupations were as various as their national origins. Bellard's closest friend, Alfred Austin, had been born in London and worked as an upholsterer. Austin rose through the ranks to become a second lieutenant by the end of the war. John Bell, a native of Liverpool, had been a coppersmith; he was thirty-six when he enrolled. Dennis Buck, twenty-nine, had been a carpenter; Calistro Castro was a Mexican-born cabinetmaker; Charles Conkling, a wheelwright. And so it went—a papermaker, a teamster, a butcher; Joseph Flick, a thirty-four-year-old German shoemaker; Gustavus Goetz, a jeweler, born in Germany, forty years old when he enlisted. William Hill was a laborer from Paterson, New Jersey, who became a second lieutenant. George Lawer was a clerk who was promoted during the war from first sergeant to first lieutenant. George Mitchell, a carriagemaker, likewise advanced through the ranks until he was commissioned first lieutenant. Samuel Starr rose from private to captain. John Switzer, Jr., served with his father, a Swiss immigrant, in the 5th New Jersey Volunteers. Both father and son were privates.

The Westerners were on the whole highly unmilitary. John Beatty found the Indiana regiments often "utterly beyond discipline. . . . The men are good, stout, hearty, intelligent fellows and will make excellent soldiers; but they have now no regard for their officers and, as a rule, do as they please." Observing them in Washington in the summer of 1862, Walt Whitman wrote: "These Western soldiers are more slow in their movements, and in their intellectual quality also; have no extreme alertness. They are larger in size, have a more serious physiognomy, are continually looking at you as they pass in the street. They are largely animal, and handsomely so."

Outside Louisville, the Army of the Ohio grew increasingly restless and insubordinate, a spirit that manifested itself, John Beatty noted, in "an unwillingness to drill, in stealing from camp and remaining away for days. . . . Many non-commissioned officers have been reduced to the ranks by court-martial for being absent without leave, and many privates have been punished in various ways for the same reason. . . . Very many of these soldiers think they should be allowed to work when they please, play when they please, and in short do as they please. Until this idea is expelled from their minds the regiment will be but little if any better than a mob." Beatty himself had to strap on his pistols and threaten to shoot any soldier who tried to interfere with his orders.

In addition to their disregard of army conventions—of saluting and using proper salutations—the Westerners were far more aggressive in "liberating" Confederate possessions. The soldiers from the West, "the Western armies," as George Washington Whitman put it, "burn and destroy every thing they come across and the same number of men, marching through the country will do three times the damage of the army of the Potomac. Sometimes on the march, I have known them to break and destroy, the most costly furniture such as Pianos and Sofas, and I have seen the roads strewn with the most splendidly bound books, that would be taken from the libraries, carried a little distance, and thrown away."

Confederate soldiers, far more racially homogeneous, were as impatient of discipline as the Westerners. Many, indeed, were from Kentucky, Tennessee, Missouri, Arkansas, and even southern Illinois. General Winfield Scott described the typical Southern soldiers as filled with "*élan*, courage, woodcraft, consummate horsemanship, endurance of pain equal to the Indians" but noted that they would not submit to discipline or "take care of things."

There were, of course, numerous cliques and social divisions between the soldiers. Soldiers from a particular town or city, from a county or a state hung together and engaged in raillery and exchanges of insults with "outsiders." Starting good-naturedly enough, such encounters sometimes turned into full-scale riots. Tension between country boys—rubes—and city boys—slickers—was perhaps the most basic division. City units varied far more in their composition and often had, as we have noted in the case of Alfred Bellard's 5th New Jersey Volunteers, a large number of immigrants in their ranks. Country (or county) units were made up almost exclusively of farm boys, more pious and more mannerly than, and lacking the sophistication of, their urban counterparts.

The pious parents of young soldiers worried perhaps as much about the notoriously corrupting influences of army life as they did about their sons escaping death from disease in camp or from an enemy bullet. Ted Upson tried to reassure his mother that he had remained relatively uncorrupted. "When this war is ended and what are left of this Army return to civil life," he wrote, "you will see that they will be accepted as among the best and highest of ideal American citizens. All the roughness will fall away and they will be shining lights in their chosen walks of life." With all the tragedy and suffering, he reminded his parents, the war had brought good as well. The chaplain of the Irish 90th Illinois, for example, although a Catholic, was "greatly loved and respected by all of the men of his and other Regiments. So you see," Upson added, "this war is breaking down the barriers between beliefs and creeds as well as doing many other things you may think more or less desirable. . . . I think we shall move soon and no doubt will again take up the auful task which must be finished before we can have peace. Do not worry about me; I shall try to do my duty as faithfully and well as I am able to do it. . . ."

The soldiers ranged in age from fifteen (in the Confederate army often younger) to the mid-forties, officers, of course, especially the general officers, being substantially older. In many units fathers and sons fought together. Wade Hampton was the son of a Wade Hampton who had been an aide to Jackson at the Battle of New Orleans and the grandson of Wade Hampton who had fought under Washington in the Revolution. An enemy of secession, he enlisted as a private when the war began and subsequently raised regiments of infantry, cavalry, and artillery which became famous as Hampton's Legion. In the Petersburg campaign, Hampton, in command of a cavalry corps, saw his son Preston ride into the thickest of the fighting, unnecessarily exposing himself to enemy fire. Hampton sent his other son, also named Wade, after Preston. Young Wade saw a bullet strike his brother as he rode toward him. He reached him as he fell from his horse, and as he held him in his arms, he himself was hit. The father rode up in time to see Preston die without uttering a word. He took his dead son in his arms, kissed him, handed him to an aide, and, leaving the wounded Wade to be cared for by a surgeon, rode back to his command post to direct the battle.

In one regiment an officer visiting a company commander remarked that the sentry guarding his headquarters looked remarkably like him. "He ought," the captain replied, "he is my father." The other officer said, "I wish I had my father under me, I would pay him off for the whippings he used to give me when I was a boy."

In Washington Walt Whitman saw a fifteen-year-old soldier thinly clad and carrying a musket as large as he was, who looked like a lost child. He had been a soldier for twelve months, he told Whitman proudly, and had borne his part in several historic battles. They talked of the boy's home in East Tennessee, of his parents, his father dead, his mother moved and her whereabouts unknown. The next day Whitman saw a Tennessee regiment marching down Pennsylvania Avenue. "My boy," he wrote, "was . . . stepping along with the rest. There were many boys no older. There did not appear to be a man over thirty years of age, and a large proportion were from 15 to 22 or 23. They all had the look of veterans, stain'd, impassive, and a certain unbent, lounging gait, carrying in addition to their regular arms and knapsacks, frequently a frying-pan, broom, etc."

Sometimes brothers or cousins or even, occasionally, fathers and sons fought in the same battle but on different sides. At the Battle of Kennesaw Mountain in Georgia in 1864, the 15th Corps captured some 3,000 men of General Leonidas Polk, an Episcopal bishop who was killed in the fighting, and Ted Upson found among them his cousin Dayon Hale, "sick" and "in a bad way." He borrowed twenty dollars from a friend and gave fifteen of it to Hale and five to the officer in charge of the prisoners.

Whitman told of staying at the bedside of a young Maryland soldier who had had his right leg amputated, "evidently very intelligent and well bred—very affectionate." The boy held onto Whitman's hand and placed it on his cheek. "As I was lingering," Whitman wrote, "he says to me suddenly, 'I hardly think you know who I am—I don't wish to impose on you—I am a rebel soldier.'" Whitman assured him it made no difference. "Visiting him daily for about two weeks after that while he lived (death had marked him and he was quite alone), I loved him much, always kiss'd him, and he did me." In an adjoining ward, Whitman found the boy's brother, a Union officer. They had both been wounded at the siege of Petersburg. They had not seen each other for four years. Now both were to die in the same hospital.

At Gettysburg Lieutenant Colonel Jonathan Lockwood, commanding the 7th West Virginia Infantry, attacked the 7th Virginia Infantry, commanded by his nephew, who was wounded and captured.

The cases of relatives fighting on opposite sides occurred most frequently in the border states. John Crittenden, a United States Senator from Kentucky, was the father of Major General Thomas Crittenden and Colonel Eugene Crittenden, of the Union army, and Major General George Crittenden of the Confederacy.

The Breckenridge family was similarly divided. John C. Breckenridge, Vice-President of the United States in Buchanan's administration and presidential candidate in 1860, cast his lot with the South, as did his three sons, but one of his cousins had two sons in the Confederate army and two in the Union. In the Battle of Atlanta the Union son captured his Confederate brother.

McKean Buchanan, an officer on the *Congress*, died when that vessel was sunk by the *Merrimac*, commanded by his brother Franklin.

At Perryville on October 8, 1862, William Terrill was killed leading a Union brigade. A year and a half later in May, 1864, his brother James died at Bethesda Church, fighting for the Confederacy.

Mrs. Lincoln's brother and three half brothers were in the Confederate army, giving rise to the rumor that she served as a Southern spy by passing information to her brothers. Philip St. George Cooke, Virginia-born, was loyal to the Union, but his son was a Confederate officer, and his son-in-law was J. E. B. Stuart.

Although many families had five or six members enlisted in the Union or the Confederate armies, the palm for the most family members in either army undoubtedly belonged to the formidable McCook family of Ohio. Although Daniel McCook, a graduate of Jefferson College, was sixty-three at the beginning of the Civil War, he obtained a commission as major and was killed in a cavalry engagement with the Southern raider John Morgan. McCook's brother, John, eight years younger, was a volunteer surgeon in the Union army. Daniel's ten sons all served in the Union army, as did John's five, making a total, fathers and sons, of seventeen McCooks in all.

Daniel was a lawyer in Leavenworth, Kansas, where he was a partner of William Tecumseh Sherman. Starting as captain of Kansas volunteers, he ascended the military ladder with his friend Sherman. At the Battle of Kennesaw Mountain, Sherman chose McCook's brigade to lead the assault on the Confederate lines. Before the attack McCook recited Stanza XXVII of Macaulay's poem "Horatius": "And how can man die better / Than facing fearful odds . . .?" He led his brigade into the Confederate lines and was fatally wounded in the charge.

Robert Latimer McCook organized the 9th Ohio Volunteer Regiment and commanded it under McClellan in western Virginia. Fighting in the Army of the Ohio at the Battle of Mill Springs, in Kentucky in January, 1862, he was severely wounded leading a bayonet charge against the Confederate positions. Promoted to brigadier general, he set out in an ambulance to join his troops before his wounds were fully healed. The ambulance and its escorting soldiers were cut off by guerrillas, and McCook was killed.

Alexander McDowell McCook was one of only two of the younger generation of fighting McCooks to have attended West Point (class of '52); Robert Sheldon McCook had graduated from Annapolis '59, and served on one of the *Monitors*. Alexander, having fought the Apache in New Mexico, was made colonel of the 2nd Ohio Volunteers and commanded that regiment at the First Battle of Bull Run. One of the few officers to distinguish himself in that engagement, he proceeded rapidly through the grades of brigadier and major general until, by July, 1862, he was commanding a corps which he led in the battles of Shiloh, Perryville, Stones River, Tullahoma, and Chickamauga.

There were other McCooks equally combative—Edwin Stanton, three times severely wounded; Charles Morris, a private in the 2nd Ohio Volunteers, killed at the Battle of Bull Run, in the sight of his father; John, a surgeon, serving as a volunteer nurse; John James, a Kenyon student at the beginning of the war, cited for bravery and dangerously wounded at Shady Grove, Virginia; Edward Moody, pioneer settler in Colorado Territory, secret agent, and, with his brother, right-hand man to Sherman on the famous march to the sea; Anson George, traveler to California, volunteer captain in the 2nd Ohio Volunteers at the Battle of Bull Run, where his brother was killed, also with Sherman on the Atlanta campaign in command of a brigade. That does not exhaust the McCooks, but it is enough for now.

A constant problem in both Northern and Southern armies was the disposition of the soldiers and officers to fraternize with the enemy. Before the Battle of Chickamauga, the Union and rebel pickets along the river bathed together and called out pleasantries to each other. After the battle the rebel and Union pickets were, if anything, more friendly than ever, Ted Upson reported, "sitting about on logs together, talking over the great battle, and exchanging views as to the results of a future engagement."

After the Battle of Resaca, Georgia, Ted Upson fraternized with the Confederates at whom he had been shooting only a few hours earlier. Going forward to sketch the Confederate defenses, Upson was hailed by a Johnny, who called out, "Say, Yank, got any thing to trade?" Upson replied that his things were in his knapsack in the Union lines. The Johnny said he would wait while he went for them. The rebel soldier wanted coffee. Upson traded for tobacco, more to be sociable than because he liked chewing, and an Atlanta paper. When they parted, they shook hands and the Johnny said, "Good luck, Yank! Come again some time. I hope you wont git hurt in any of our fights."

Since it was the assignment of pickets—both Confederate and Union—to keep the enemy in sight and guard against surprise attack, the picket lines were commonly within sight of each other, and a cautious socializing often took place between them. It was no different with Captain Charles Francis Adams and his men on the picket lines near Sulphur Springs in early August, 1863. "They're not unlike us," he wrote to his mother, of the Southerners opposite them, "and really pleasant, sociable men—their cavalry, now that we have whipped them out of their conceit. There's much better feeling between Yankee and Southerners now than there ever was before, and now we meet on very pleasant terms."

On New Year's Day, 1864, Ted Upson and his fellows were patrolling the banks of the Tennessee River when they saw rebel scouts on the other side of the river. Upson called to them to come over and get some coffee and a batch of Union proclamations. One got into a canoe and paddled over to enjoy Yankee hospitality, and that night Upson and some friends crossed the river and went to a dance on the rebel side. "We were warmly welcomed and had a fine time," Upson noted. But an excited slave came running to warn them that the "Provo Guards," a kind of home guard, were coming down the road. There was a frantic exit by soldiers and civilians alike, the former making a dash for their boats at the river.

In a break in the fighting at Fredericksburg, several Union and rebel officers met in the intervals between the two armies "and had a friendly chat," as Alfred Bellard put it. "The boys amused themselves by playing cards, while one of the recruits who was a good singer gave us some songs." Meanwhile, the rebels brought up and emplaced "an ugly looking brass battery . . . all ready to lay us out on the morrow." During the night Bellard and his comrades could hear the nearby rebels "singing and laughing, while chopping was going on in the woods. . . ."

Considering the nature of the two citizen armies, it is not surprising that discipline was their most persistent problem. It ranged from classic, if minor, infractions of army rules and regulations, such as failing to salute an officer, drunkenness, being absent without leave, or failing to keep one's arms and equipment clean, to much more serious offenses, such as refusing to obey orders and straggling and desertion, for which latter offense the army code of justice specified execution by firing squad.

One of the common company punishments for some infraction of military regulations was for the culprit to be required to march back and forth all day with a heavy stick of wood instead of a gun on his shoulder. While the abolition of whipping was one of the more notable military reforms, it was still practiced from time to time on civilians, thieves, or other petty offenders.

In a democratic army legitimate discipline must be carefully distinguished from arbitrary actions or brutal punishment. When a Captain Gould of the 5th New Jersey Volunteers ordered two delinquent soldiers tied up by their thumbs, the men untied them and defied the captain. "It was such officers as that," Alfred Bellard observed, noting the incident, "who received a stray ball occasionally on the field of battle."

John Beatty and his 3rd Ohioans were with Robert Anderson's army when it occupied Louisville. The men were held in camp, but the attractions of Louisville were so alluring that they were soon on the verge of mutiny. "Had much difficulty in keeping the men in camp," Beatty wrote, "and this evening, to prevent a general stampede, ordered the guards to load their guns and shoot the first man who attempted to break over." The same order was extended to the officers, and a friend of Beatty's who defied the order was arrested.

In the case of a soldier who had committed an offense serious enough for him to be ousted from the army, his unit would be formed in a square, and the culprit, with his head shaved and the buttons cut from his coat, would be paraded past the brigade to the beat of the "Rogue's March," accompanied by two guards with their arms reversed. One such malefactor, drummed out of Alfred Bellard's brigade, "was as brazen as you please and held his head up as if he enjoyed it."

A not infrequent disciplinary problem involved fighting between soldiers in different units in camp or bivouac. In the Union armies to the friction between Easterners and Westerners was added the animosity of native-born Americans for Irish and German units. Such frictions were especially evident in the case of German soldiers, in which general prejudice against immigrants was reinforced by the language barrier; it was necessary to form the Germans into separate units commanded by English-speaking German officers. In camp bloody fights often broke out among soldiers of different nationalities as well as among soldiers of different sections of the country. John Beatty's Ohio soldiers delighted in singing mock German songs, a typical one of which ran:

> So libft up your ghlass, mine modter,
>> Undt libft up yours, Gretchen, my dear,
> Undt libft up your lauger, mine fadter,
>> Undt drink du long life and good cheer.

The charge of desertion was often difficult to establish. An ill or exhausted soldier dropping by the roadside might intend to return to his unit when rested or might simply slip away, head for home, or, more commonly, attach himself to some guerrilla band, preying on civilians or hanging on the flanks of an army, friendly or hostile. George Templeton Strong estimated that one soldier out of three had "shirked and straggled," adding, "and not one man has been shot down by his commanding officer." Strong blamed the lack of discipline on "the weakness of the President himself." But the fact was that in democratic armies shooting the fainthearted was apt to be, as we say today, counterproductive. Clearly it was against Lincoln's deepest instincts to issue such orders, but had he been somehow prevailed upon to do so, the popular reaction would have been immediate and negative in the extreme. Perhaps in the professional army the occasional shooting of a "coward" can be tolerated or even be exemplary in its effect on his comrades-in-arms. But in a volunteer army, made up of clerks and farm boys, artisans, mechanics, teamsters, miners, common laborers, servants, immigrants, boatmen, lumbermen, and shopkeepers, it is quite another matter. One would have had to begin, in all fairness, with the officers, as Strong himself intimated, and the officers were, for the most part, young lawyers, college students, the scions of prominent and influential families. It would not have worked at all. Moreover, anyone who had ever been in even a modest battle understood very well the impulse to run, the readiness, even of seasoned troops, to panic in the frightening and, perhaps worst of all, *confusing* atmosphere of the battlefield.

As the rolls of deserters mounted, the pressure on Lincoln to approve the execution of captured deserters as a deterrent mounted. When the women members of various "relief societies" from all over the country, meeting in Washington, had an audience with the President, he spoke ruefully of the problems caused by the lack of discipline in the Union armies. "Order the army to march any place!" he said. "Why it's jes' like shovellin' fleas. Hee-yah, ya-hah!" When one of the women asked, "Why don't you order stragglers to be shot, sir?" Lincoln fell silent. The question was repeated, and Frederick Law Olmsted, who was present with the women's delegation, reported that "the President collapsed and wilted down into an embodiment of everything weak, irresolute, perplexed, and annoyed, and he said, 'Oh, I can-an't do *that*, you know.'" It was a revealing moment. Lincoln suffered excruciatingly over the Union casualty figures and only slightly less so, it may be assumed, over those of the Confederate army. His compassion was too deep to add an iota to those terrible columns of the dead. Nonetheless, by the end of the war more than two hundred Union soldiers had been shot for desertion.

The geography of the battlefield was described by Charles Francis Adams, Jr., in a letter to his father. Rifle pits were the mark of the new battlefield. Formerly soldiers had advanced shoulder to shoulder or stood in ranks firing at the enemy. Now fighting became individual. In a nation of individualists, the individual soldier assumed a new relationship to his fellow soldiers. Enormous efforts were, of course, expended in creating elaborate fortified works designed to resist long-term siege. But in the field, where squads, companies, regiments, corps, and divisions maneuvered against each other, the individual rifle ("musket" would have been more accurate a term) pit was, typically, the dominating man-made feature of the terrain. The individual soldier dug a pit even in the briefest interval of fighting to protect his legs and body against enemy fire. The longer he remained on the spot, the deeper the rifle pit became until it was at last a kind of burrow, a semiunderground refuge, like the lair of a large burrowing animal—the hole of a fox, for example. "These scar the whole country," Charles Francis Adams, Jr., wrote, "all along the road of these two armies. You see them confronting each other in long lines on every defensible position, and you never seem to get through them. A rifle pit, in fact, is in the perfection to which they are now carried in these armies, nothing more or less than the most formidable fortifications, alive with infantry and bristling with guns." There were also more elaborate field fortifications. "The instant our infantry, for instance, get into position," Adams wrote, "they go to work with axes and spades and in a very short time there springs up in front of them a wooden barricade made out of fence rails, felled trees, or any material in the reach of men who know what danger is and feel it near them;

and in the rear and front of this a trench is dug, the dirt from the rear being thrown over to the front, so as to bank it up and make it impenetrable to musketry and, except at the top, to artillery. This cover is anywhere from four to six feet high, is often very neatly made, and is regularly bastioned out, as it were, for artillery. As fast as a position is won it is fortified in this way. For defense the same thing is done. The other day I rode down to the front and passed four lines of these intrenchments, all deserted and useless before I came to the fifth, where the line of battle then was, which they were already confronting by a new one."

The tactics were essentially those of the Napoleonic Wars, with the important exception being the greatly increased emphasis on artillery, which was in large part a consequence of the experience of the Mexican War. The result was a marked shift in the balance between attack and defense to the latter. Fortifications were carefully laid out by army engineers. They directed the erection of a timber "framing," and soldiers, armed with the spades and pickaxes which were as familiar to them as their guns, filled in the frameworks with earth. Soil dug from the front of the earthworks formed a ditch which was often soon filled with water. Before the Battle of Malvern Hill, Alfred Bellard noted that his regiment erected earthworks eight feet thick at the base and four at the top. "The brush wood," he wrote, "was cleared away from our front for about 200 yards making a very effective abatis. In front of our brigade we built a battery or redoubt to hold seven guns. . . ."

The emphasis on artillery that was so conspicuous (and indeed decisive) an aspect of the major engagements of the Mexican War continued with the Civil War. Artillery was brought forward into the front lines; batteries of light artillery were usually placed in redoubts in advance of the main infantry lines, from which points they could lay enfilade fire along lines of advancing enemy skirmish lines. Frequently the main assignment of the infantry was to defend the artillery against enemy infantry attacks. At the same time prevailing military tactics laid great stress on the bayonet infantry charge (the same thing was true as recently as World War II), which had so often been the decisive factor in traditional engagements. Tactical doctrine in general had not yet accommodated itself to the fact that artillery was now the dominant element in any large-scale engagement. Conventional infantry tactics, emphasizing massive attacks in waves of skirmishers were still standard. In addition, the soldier in a defensive position had a far better opportunity to load and fire than the soldier in assault, who had to hold his fire until he was within close range of the enemy's works or stop his advance to load his musket. The greater accuracy of the rifled piece as opposed to the smoothbore musket also gave the defender an advantage over the attacker with the rifle since he could begin to fire accurately at a much greater range than he could have with the musket and thus to fire substantially more bullets in the interval between the time the attacker left the protection of his own lines—"point of departure"—and the time he reached the breastworks of the defender. In addition, the percussion cap, replacing the far less efficient firing pan of the Revolutionary era musket, permitted a much higher rate of fire. As late as the War of 1812 a soldier in a defensive position had to hold his fire until, classically, he could "see the whites" of his enemies' eyes. If the attacking forces could weather that single withering blast, they could usually reach the defensive lines, often with their weapons still loaded and their bayonets at the ready before the defenders could reload. Put simply, by the time of the outbreak of the Civil War the defense had far outstripped attack, but military doctrine had yet to take full account of this crucial fact. The results were that in virtually all battles of the Civil War involving conventional assaults, the casualties were appalling. By a rough estimate it might be that the improvement of military technology since the War of 1812 allowed defenders of a well-fortified position to deliver a volume of fire against an attacking force five to ten times greater than that which had been available to their predecessors.

To Whitman the soldiers of the Union army expressed the essence of all that was purest and best in America. "Soldiers, soldiers, soldiers, you meet everywhere about the city," he wrote, "often superb-looking men though invalids dress'd in worn uniforms and carrying canes or crutches. I find it refreshing, these hardy, bright, intuitive, American young men (experience'd soldiers with all their youth). The vocal play and significance moves one more than books. Then there hangs something majestic about a man who has borne his part in battles. . . ."

At Culpeper, Virginia, in the winter of 1864, Whitman stood watching as units slogged by in the rain and mud. "The men had their usual burdens, overcoats, knapsacks, guns and blankets," he wrote. "Long and along they filed by me, with often a laugh, a song, a cheerful word, but never once a murmur. It may have been odd, but I never before so realized the majesty and reality of the American people *en masse*. It fell upon me like a great awe."

Occasionally Whitman met soldiers who seemed to him to have a special, difficult-to-define quality—"specimens of unworldliness, disinterestedness and animal purity and heroism," he put it, ". . . and whose gradual growing up, whatever the circumstances of work-life or change, or hardship, or small or no education that attended it, the power of a spiritual sweetness, fibre and inward health, have also attended. . . . I have met them . . . not seldom in the army in camp, and in the hospitals." Many were from the Western regiments.

Carl Schurz made a systematic analysis of American soldiers. He divided them into three basic types. There were those who, on first going into battle, were filled with dread and responded to that emotion by running away at the first opportunity. There were others who felt the "joy of the conflict" and were impatient to rush forward and cover themselves with glory. A third group, by far the greatest portion, suppressed their fear "in obedience to a sense of patriotic duty or an impulse of honor or of pride," stood their ground, and obeyed the orders of their officers as best they could. Those seasoned in battle simply closed off the emotions of fear and anxiety and focused their attention on the immediate things that needed to be done.

Schurz had a high regard for the Union soldier's courage and intelligence but, above all, for "his moral sense of duty," which induced him to suffer great hardships and dangers. "In what he considered non-essentials his habits were exceedingly loose," Schurz wrote. "The relations between privates and company or regimental, or even higher officers, never were free from that instinctive feeling of equality characteristic of the American. There was no chasm of caste or fixed class distinction between the different ranks, and the consciousness of this led to a forgetfulness of military formalities, and sometimes to a decidedly unmilitary familiarity of tone between subordinate and superior." Saluting, for example, was more honored in the breach than the observance. When a general from another division visited Schurz's headquarters, the sentry did not salute him, and when Schurz later upbraided him and asked why he had failed to salute, the sentry, a Westerner, coolly replied, "Why, sir, that General was never introduced to me."

In another instance, when Schurz was inspecting the picket lines of a Connecticut regiment, one of the pickets turned around and saluted him, removed his cap, and bowed. When Schurz explained that such formalities were inappropriate in the field, the soldier replied that he had heard him speak in the presidential campaign of 1860 and wished to express his respect. "In the volunteer army," Schurz added, "the relations between officers and men were amicable—not to say fraternal—in a degree which in any European army would have been considered subversive of all discipline. . . . There were plenty of men in the ranks who were the equals, if not the superiors, of their lieutenants or captains, or even their colonels in point of intelligence or culture."

When Schurz, years later, visited Prince Otto von Bismarck, the great Prussian prime minister and unifier of Germany, he found the prince to be a close student of the Civil War campaigns. Bismarck asked Schurz about the character of the American soldier, and Schurz described the informal relationship between officers and men. The prime minister and the army officers present smiled condescendingly when Schurz declared that "no country had human material superior to ours as regards physical development, intelligence, and martial spirit; that in the long run our volunteers could outmarch any European troops, surpass them in the endurance of any sort of fatigue; that our volunteers, with incredible skill and rapidity, would build roads, and extemporize serviceable railway bridges and viaducts, with nothing but nails and tools. . . ."

4

The Generals

The officers who commanded the citizen soldiers of the Union and Confederate armies were a mixed lot. The principal categories were West Pointers and political generals, most of whom had been militia officers in their home states. In the urgency of the war's beginning, men who had never experienced a day's military drill were made officers and placed in command of companies and regiments and even brigades and divisions. One brigadier, who wanted to order his men to wheel right in formation for a charge and could not remember the command, shouted, "Come round like a gate, boys," and was thereafter known as General Gates. Another, when he wanted his men to fall in, cried, "Make two rows, boys; make two rows!" In the last year of the war young boys from a military academy were assigned to drill recruits. They were the only ones who knew the formations of close-order and extended-order drill.

A classic political general was a brigadier named Schleich, a former Ohio state senator whose prescription for financing the war was to propose that captured slaves should be sent to Cuba and sold. "He is what might be called a tremendous little man," John Beatty wrote, "swears terribly, and imagines that he thereby shows his snap. Snap, in his opinion, is indispensable to a military man. If snap is the only thing a soldier needs," Beatty noted wryly, "and profanity is snap, Schleich is a second Napoleon." Often in his cups, he upbraided General George McClellan for being too careful of his men. "What are a th-thousand men when [hic] principle is at stake? Men's lives [hic] shouldn't be thought of at such a time [hic]. Amount to nothing [hic]."

The military career of another politician-general was relatively short-lived. Henry Wilson, Senator from Massachusetts, coadjutor of Charles Sumner, and a brigadier general of militia, raised a regiment of volunteers, brought them to Washington, and then applied for a position on McClellan's staff. Wilson, who was forty-nine, found that the sedentary life of a politician had left him ill-prepared for campaigning. McClellan, who, as an enemy of abolitionists, may have been anxious to get rid of him, ordered Wilson to ride out on a thirty-mile tour of inspection of the defenses of Washington; Wilson took to his bed for a week thereafter and promptly resigned from the general's staff.

Of one Indiana officer who was promoted for purely political reasons, John Beatty wrote: "He cannot manage a regiment, and not even his best friends have any confidence in his military capacity." Another Indianan, promoted to brigadier general despite obvious incompetence, was notorious for shouting out, during battalion drill, "Battalion, face right or left, as the case may be, march!"

When Beatty met General James Garfield, a political general par excellence, the general "checked up, shook hands, and said: 'How d'ye do,'" giving a grip "that suggested, 'vote right, vote early.'"

Beatty also encountered his old friend Rutherford Hayes, a major in the 23rd Ohio, "an accomplished gentleman," a graduate of Harvard Law School, and an up-and-coming Ohio politician.

The colonel commanding John Beatty's 3rd Ohio Volunteers was an Ohio politician. Campaigning in western Virginia under McClellan (of whom, incidentally, Beatty had a poor opinion), the 3rd Ohio was ordered to make a dawn attack. The colonel aroused his sleeping men and ordered them to fall out at "the hour when graveyards are supposed to yawn and the sheeted death to walk abroad," Beatty noted, and then "the gallant colonel, with a voice in perfect accord with the solemnity of the hour and the funereal character of the scene," exhorted his sleepy men thus: "Soldiers of the Third. The assault on the enemy's works will be made in the early morning. The Third will lead the column. The secessionists have ten thousand men and forty rifled cannon. They are strongly fortified. They have more men and cannon than we have. They will cut us to pieces. Marching to attack such an enemy, so entrenched and so armed, is marching to a butcher shop rather than to a battle. There is bloody work ahead. Many of you, boys, will go out who will never come back again."

The startled Beatty observed that from the looks on the faces of his men he could tell that they, like him, were reflecting that "it was hard to die so young and so far from home. . . . We thought of mothers, wives, and sweethearts," he added, "of opportunities lost, and good advice disregarded. Some soldiers kicked together the expiring fragments of a camp-fire, and the little blaze that sprang up revealed scores of pallid faces. In short, we all wanted to go home."

Benjamin Butler was one of the most prominent political generals. Butler had been born in New Hampshire in 1818 and been admitted to the Massachusetts bar in 1840. A highly successful corporation lawyer with a reputation for not being overly scrupulous, he wangled himself a commission as a general officer at the beginning of the war and soon became one of the crosses Lincoln had to bear. John Hay, who met him in 1864, noted in his diary: "Gen'l Butler came clattering into the room . . . : he told me how he was administering the oath [of allegiance to the Union] at Norfolk; how popular it was growing; children cried for it; how he hated Jews; how heavily he laid his hand on them; 'a nation that the Lord had been trying to make something of for three thousand years, and had so far utterly failed.' 'King John knew how to deal with them—fried them in swine's fat.' . . . He says he can take an army within thirty miles of Richmond without any trouble; from that point the enemy can be either forced to fight in the open field south of the city, or submit to be starved into surrender. . . ." Butler was better at talking than fighting, and after the failure of his expedition against Charleston, Hay noted in his diary: "Butler is turning out much as I thought he would—perfectly useless and incapable for campaigning." Hay remarked to Lincoln that in his opinion Butler was the only really dangerous general in the Union armies. "McClellan was too timid and vacillating to usurp; Grant too sound and cool-headed and unselfish. . . . Frémont would be danger-ous if he had more ability and energy." "Yes," Lincoln replied, "he is like Jim Jett's brother. Jim used to say that his brother was the d——dest scoundrel that ever lived, but in the infinite mercy of Providence he was also the d——dest fool."

Another notorious general was Daniel Sickles, the New York Democratic Senator. Sickles's reputation as a coarse and brutal man spilled over to his brigade, called the Excelsior. After a battle at Bristoe, Virginia, in the fall of 1863, Alfred Bellard and his regiment passed Sickles's brigade "so drunk that nothing could be done with them. . . . While they were marching past," Bellard noted, "our boys struck up 'Johnny stole a Ham, and Sickles killed a Man,' " a reference to the fact that Sickles had killed his wife's lover.

John Alexander McClernand was an Illinois lawyer, an officer in the state militia, a friend of Lincoln's, and a United States Congressman. Appointed a brigadier general in command of the First Military District at Cairo, Illinois, he became a cross to Ulysses Grant, failing to carry out orders, seizing credit for Grant's achievements, and poisoning Lincoln's mind against his superior.

Many of the political generals were accompanied by friendly journalists who tirelessly inflated their military skills and thereby promoted their careers. "Officers are more selfish, dishonest, and grasping in their struggle for notoriety than the miser for gold," John Beatty wrote. Many reports from units engaged in battle were, in Beatty's view, "simply elaborate essays, which seek to show that the author was a little braver, a little more skillful in the management of his men, and a little worthier than anybody else." The newspaper reporters, John Beatty wrote, were "more vigilant than the rebels and terribly intent on finding somebody to talk about, to laud to the skies, or abuse in the most fearful manner, for they seldom do things by halves, unless it be telling the truth."

Of course, not all political generals were poor leaders. Many compiled enviable records. Among them was Robert Huston Milroy, an Indiana lawyer and politician, who became a major general. Milroy was gaunt and "strikingly Western in character and manners," recklessly exposing himself in battle and exhorting his men to "Pitch in, boys; pitch in!" More than most general officers he felt strong commitment to the antislavery cause, and General Irvin McDowell in his report on the Battle of Antietam described Milroy as "riding up in an absolute state of frenzy, with his sword drawn, and gesticulating at some distance off, shouting to send forward reinforcements to save the day, to save the country." He conferred democratically with his subordinates in deciding on proper tactics and granted them wide latitude for their own judgment and initiative in carrying out his orders.

In the words of Carl Schurz, "the vast majority of the officers' positions, from lieutenancies up to generalships, had to be filled with persons taken from civil life who had no schooling in military service at all, but were selected on account of their general intelligence and their position among their fellow-citizens, which seemed to fit them for leadership on a smaller or larger scale." They had to learn "on the job," and those who proved apt students advanced rapidly, while many of the others fell by the wayside. The system, if it could be called that, worked best in the lower ranks, although it must be said that many junior officers died in battle before they mastered their duties. Among the general officers, most of whom were politicians and/or successful businessmen, the results were more uncertain. The deficiencies of a general officer were inevitably far more obvious and more dangerous than those of a company grade officer, and the weak or inept generals were far harder to dispose of simply because they had numerous influential friends and supporters, some of whom had been instrumental in securing them their initial appointments and subsequently advancing their careers. Schurz himself was such a political general. Although as a young man he had been trained as a soldier during his revolutionary activities in Germany (in one instance by an officer who came to serve under his command), he had never had responsibility for training, caring for, and leading in battle any more than a few dozen men. Thus, his appointment as brigadier general was rather like putting a second lieutenant, whose experience was limited to the command of a platoon of some twenty men, in charge of a division of several thousand.

With a few exceptions—Benjamin Butler was one—the most important Union commands went to West Pointers, many of whom, like Grant, had left the service before the war. Lincoln's most important initial task may well have been that of choosing the general officers—brigadier and major generals—to command the principal armies. General Winfield Scott, "Old Fuss and Feathers," the hero of Chapultepec in the Mexican War, was the army chief of staff, and Lincoln relied heavily on him for recommendations on the appointment of officers and, of course, on strategy as well.

At the fall of Sumter, the regular army consisted of 1,098 officers and 15,304 enlisted men. More than one-third of the officers, most of them in the higher ranks, resigned their commissions to join the Confederate army, and 9 percent of the enlisted men defected.

The officers of the regular army constituted a closely knit family of which Scott was the father. Those who remained in the service (and many, it must be said, who didn't) had been shaped and tempered by their common experiences—the Point, the Seminole War, the Mexican

War, and the expedition to Utah against the Latter-Day Saints. Scott knew them all, and his first choice to command the Union forces was Colonel Robert E. Lee. Lee was fifty-three years old at the outbreak of the war. The grandson of Henry ("Light-Horse Harry") Lee, the brilliant cavalry leader of the Revolutionary War and the author of the classic *Memoirs of the War in the Southern Department of the United States*, Lee had graduated second in his class (1829) from West Point in the era that produced so many gifted officers. After a period of three years, 1852–55, as superintendent of West Point, Lee had been given command of a cavalry unit in Washington and from there had been sent to recapture Harpers Ferry after John Brown's abortive raid.

Scott, who knew of Lee's military capacities at first hand since Lee had fought under him in Scott's campaign against Mexico City, recommended him to Lincoln for the active command of the Federal forces, and Lincoln had offered him that post in April, a few weeks after his inauguration. Lee declined and two days later resigned his commission to take a far more modest role as a commander of troops in his native state of Virginia.

Pierre Gustave Toutant Beauregard was another disappointment. Beauregard, a native of Louisiana and scion of an old and aristocratic French family, was graduated from West Point in 1838, like Lee second in his class. Like so many of his fellow officers, he had distinguished himself in the campaign with Scott and was wounded twice in the final battles at Mexico City. Brevetted major for his courage and enterprise, Beauregard reverted after the war to the rank of lieutenant and served for six more years in that rank before being promoted to captain of engineers. Assigned to duty in New Orleans, he strengthened the fortifications of that city, supervised harbor improvements, and constructed a new Federal customshouse. In January, 1861, after Lincoln's election but before his inauguration, he was appointed superintendent of West Point. He had occupied that position only a few days when a report that he had declared that in event of secession he would cast his lot with the South caused Buchanan to relieve him. Beauregard at once departed for Charleston, South Carolina, where he was given command of the troops besieging Fort Sumter. After the surrender of Sumter, Jefferson Davis ordered him to Virginia, where, in the confused military situation, he took command of a body of soldiers stationed near Bull Run in anticipation of an invasion by Northern troops. Small, intense, sporting a mustache and goatee, Beauregard was the model of a New Orleans aristocrat.

Joseph Eggleston Johnston had been a classmate of Lee's and had served in the Black Hawk War and in the Seminole War, where he had been twice wounded. In the Mexican War Johnston had been in the battle at Chapultepec. Wounded five times in the campaign with Scott, he had been cited for heroism and after the war served as lieutenant colonel of the 1st United States Cavalry in Kansas during the turmoil that followed the passage of the Kansas-Nebraska Act. There the Free-Soil men had accused him of partiality toward the proslavery party. From Kansas, Johnston had gone with Albert Sidney Johnston to Utah to force Brigham Young and his followers to accept the authority of the United States. Casting his lot with the South, he became a major general in the armed forces of the state of Virginia and was placed in command at Harpers Ferry.

The simple recitation of the facts concerning Lincoln's efforts to find officers loyal to the Union to command Federal troops tells nothing of the human drama involved. West Point had been under heavy attack in the period prior to the Mexican War as an elitist institution, a haven for sons of the upper class, an anomaly in a democratic nation committed to the ideal of peace.

The criticisms of the academy, although blunted by the brilliant performance of its graduates in the campaigns of the Mexican War, undoubtedly helped create a special sense of comradeship and mutual affection among the graduates of that institution. The nature of military training, with its emphasis on discipline and authority and the cheerful endurance of hardship, creates a strong bond between young men. If we add to this classic bond the powerful experience of fighting in a common cause—the Mexican War (however bad in fact that cause may be)—and of sharing the terror and euphoria of the battlefield, the result is the creation of the strongest tie that can bind men together. Beyond this, the types of men who serve in the armed forces of a country as professional soldiers are, in general, men with a strong sense of loyalty and obedience. Thus, for the officers of Southern birth to surrender their commissions and disavow their allegiance to the Union was a profoundly traumatic experience.

In addition, there was the question of allegiance to a man. Winfield Scott, if he was pompous, vain, and often fussy, was an excellent soldier and benign "father" to the young officers on his staff, which he called his "little cabinet." He had that most important attribute of a commander—the capacity for generous praise of excellence in his subordinates. In all that "little cabinet," which included many of Lee's classmates and intimate friends, Lee was closest to Scott. The commanding general had come to depend on Lee's skill as an engineer, artillery officer, and collector of intelligence. It was Lee who had been given the task of reconnoitering the terrain in front of Santa Anna before the critically important Battle of Cerro Gordo and subsequently of commanding a division that placed itself on the flank of the Mexican forces covering the vital Jalapa road. A few weeks later, in the attack on Contreras, Lee had played the principal role in developing a general strategy for the march to Mexico City that proved highly successful. As part of the force dispatched to attack Santa Anna's rear, he had established contact with the main body of the army under appallingly difficult circumstances, an achievement that Scott called "the greatest feat of physical and moral courage performed by any individual in my knowledge" during the campaign. "The brilliant victory of Contreras on the following morning," he wrote, "was made possible by Captain Lee's services that night."

Included in Scott's "little cabinet" were such men as George Brinton McClellan, thought to be marked for a brilliant career. The youngest in his class, McClellan had excelled in mathematics and, like Lee, had graduated second in his class (second, for some inscrutable reason, seems to have been much better than first), which included Thomas Jonathan Jackson. Rushing from West Point to Mexico, he arrived in time to fight at Cerro Gordo, Contreras, and Churubusco and be cited "for gallant and meritorious conduct."

Gustavus Woodson Smith, a Kentuckian, who had graduated from the Point in 1842 and had taught engineering there before the war, was another member of Scott's staff destined for distinction as a Confederate major general and, finally, as secretary of war for the Confederacy. John Bankhead Magruder, one of the older officers in the group at fifty-one, was known as Prince John because of his courtly airs and taste for high living. He resigned his United States commission as a captain a few days after his friend and fellow Virginian Robert Lee.

Jesse Reno, a classmate of McClellan's, was another Virginian who had won laurels for bravery in the fighting around Mexico City, but Reno cast his lot with the Union. Braxton Bragg, class of '37, had fought in the Seminole War, and he, too, had won three promotions fighting under Scott. Bragg resigned and accepted a Confederate commission. John Sedgwick, a classmate of Bragg's who had served with him in the Seminole War, with J. E. Johnston on the Kansas frontier, and with Joe and Albert Sidney Johnston in the Utah expedition (in which, incidentally, Jesse Reno served as chief ordnance officer), remained with the Union. Joseph Hooker, a native of Massachusetts, and a member of the class of '37, had resigned his commission and settled in California after the Mexican War. With the outbreak of the Civil War, he offered his services to the Union, but he was in Scott's bad graces and was at first rebuffed.

Fitz-John Porter, a New Hampshire man, was a member of the class of '45. He, too, had been a member of the Utah expedition under Johnston, and he, too, had been wounded in the drive from Veracruz to Mexico City and twice promoted for bravery. Ambrose Powell (A. P.) Hill and George G. Meade, classes of '47 and '35 respectively, were also members of Scott's staff. Hill resigned his regular army commission to become an officer of the Confederacy. Meade, born in Spain of American parents, had resigned his commission after graduation from the Point to become a civil engineer. He had re-enlisted in 1842 but had not had a field command during Scott's campaign in Mexico.

Several points emerge from this review of Scott's officer corps during his Mexican campaign. Of those officers with the most outstanding records in combat, a disproportionate number were Southerners, from which it seems safe to draw certain conclusions. The martial tradition was far stronger in the South than in the North. The existence of a clearly defined Southern aristocracy with a chivalric tradition meant a class with the habit of command. This should not surprise us. In the American Revolution, Southern officers had been more numerous and, in the main, more successful as leaders than their Northern counterparts.

The consequence of all this was that the South, once it became clear that a majority of the regular army officers from that section would resign their commissions in the United States Army and cast their fortunes with the Confederacy, had a conspicuous advantage in the numbers, experience, and capacity of its officer corps. The other fact that is striking is that so many Southerners in the United States Army felt a closer tie to their section and their culture than to the Federal Union. A substantial number had little involvement in the institution of slavery, and some, like Thomas Jonathan Jackson, were actively opposed to it. Their loyalty was clearly to their region and to their "kin," that powerful Southern clan instinct which survives to the present day. The motive of self-interest was certainly not entirely missing. Those Southerners who remained loyal to the Union could be sure that their plantations would be confiscated and they themselves branded as traitors. Lee, for example, had extensive landholdings in Virginia that had come to him by virtue of his marriage to Mary Custis, the great-granddaughter of Martha Washington by her first marriage. Had he accepted Lincoln's offer to command the Northern armies, Lee's name would have become a byword in the South for betrayal of his homeland. The same was, of course, true in varying degrees of the other Southern members of the officer corps.

George Templeton Strong made a shrewd assessment of a Southern weakness that became more evident as the conflict continued to take a terrible toll of Southern officers and men. As the aristocratic planter class, from the ranks of which virtually all the officers of the Confederate armies were drawn, fell in battle from wounds or was cut down by disease, there were no new cohorts to replace its members. What had been a notable advantage to the South at the beginning of hostilities—an officer corps made up of men accustomed to exercise unquestioned domination over those below them in the social order —became, when that original officer cadre had been worn down by ceaseless conflict, a major deficiency in the Confederate forces. In Strong's words, when "the original fire-eating, revolver-flourishing aristocratic 'chivalry' of 1861" was "used up and worn out," the "material to replace it" was "scanty," in large part as a consequence of "the utter debasement of its poor whites."

Irvin McDowell was the officer finally settled on by Lincoln and Scott to command the Union forces in the field. The same age as Beauregard and a member of the same West Point class (1838), McDowell had served during the Mexican War as aide-de-camp to General John Ellis Wool. Assigned thereafter to the general staff in Washington, McDowell became a protégé of Scott's. When Lee and then J. E. Johnston refused the command of the Union armies, Lincoln, on Scott's recommendation, offered the command to McDowell, who had displayed conspicuous abilities in organizing and directing the training of the raw recruits who flooded Washington in response to Lincoln's call for 75,000 three-month volunteers.

In fairness to McDowell it must be said that he was faced with an almost impossible task. If there is one thing that is sure, it is that an army cannot be created overnight. The thousands of young men who poured into the hastily established and ill-equipped camps around Washington did not appear initially to be ideal material from which to create an army. Full of enthusiasm, they considered that they were embarked on a lark. A few months of active campaigning must bring the rebels to their knees. They overflowed with confidence and patriotism and in their euphoria put up cheerfully with the dirt, confusion, and disorder that characterized the initial efforts of Lincoln's administration to create an army. They were an independent lot as well, not much used to taking orders. The officers were as inexperienced as the men. Many had been elected by the men they purported to lead and were acutely conscious that they exercised their authority on sufferance, so to speak. Commissioned and noncommissioned officers were diffident about ordering neighbors about. Cleanliness and sanitation were lacking in the camps. The food was unfamiliar and often unpalatable. In crowded conditions many recruits fell ill and began to think longingly of home.

Not surprisingly there was much hostility and bad feeling between the political generals and the West Pointers, with their inevitable emphasis on "spit and polish" and military punctilio. When William Starke ("Rosey") Rosecrans performed well as head of the Army of the Cumberland, John Beatty, lawyer turned general, attributed it to the fact that "he has been long enough away from West Point, mixing with the people, to get a little common sense rubbed into him."

Interservice rivalry was another serious problem in all combined Union operations. Admiral D. D. Porter expressed a common attitude among naval officers when he wrote to Gideon Welles that he would much prefer to work with a "citizen" general in the Department of the Mississippi than a West Pointer, since the latter was notorious for being "egotistical and assuming and never willing to consider and treat naval officers as equals."

There were also strong sectional differences and animosities. Easterners were suspicious of and hostile to Westerners, who reciprocated enthusiastically. Westerners were firmly convinced that the best commands and most rapid promotions went to Easterners, as was not, in fact, the case since the President's strong Western predilections made him sensitive to that issue.

As we have noted, the ethnic differences, especially those between the "native" Americans on the one hand and the Irish and Germans on the other, were another source of friction. Franz Sigel and Carl Schurz commanding German troops encountered considerable prejudice on the part of the West Point "Eastern" military establishment. They were looked upon as intruders and "obliged to encounter very watchful and sometimes even rancorous criticism."

Finally, it should be noted that some observers were convinced, as the war progressed, that West Pointers in the Union forces stood somewhat in awe of their Southern counterparts, an awe that was rooted in their West Point experience in which Southerners had often excelled in the arts of war. By this theory the poor performance of some Yankee generals could be best accounted for on the basis of a kind of military inferiority complex. John Hay reported a conversation between two Union officers, one of whom declared that "there are a good many officers of the regular army who have not yet entirely lost the West Point idea of southern superiority. That sometimes accounts for an otherwise unaccountable slowness of attack. . . ." The trouble with this theory is that it was not based on the facts. Only in the Virginia campaigns did Southern commanders—most strikingly and almost exclusively Lee and Jackson—have a clear and indisputable edge over their Northern counterparts. Elsewhere Northern generals, in numerous encounters, usually proved themselves the equals or superiors of their rivals.

Carl Schurz was well aware of this fact. In his view, "the most potent influence inspiring troops with more than ordinary courage and daring consists in their confidence and pride in their leaders." Napoleon had said that he would rather have an army of sheep commanded by a lion than an army of lions commanded by a sheep. This leadership principle accounted for the great difference between the Confederate armies of the West and Lee's Army of Northern Virginia. The rebel leaders in the West were, for the most part, ordinary enough generals. There Grant and Sherman dominated. In Virginia it was all Lee.

A striking feature of the war was the number of field and general officers killed or wounded in battle. Company-grade officers, first and second lieutenants and captains, have always been expendable—that is to say, their function is to be in the midst of the action "leading" their men (the motto of the Infantry School in Fort Benning, Georgia, is, for the prospective officer, the rather daunting admonition "Follow Me"). But in modern warfare, lieutenant colonels and "full" or "chicken" colonels—that is to say, most commonly, regimental commanders— are usually reasonably, safely ensconced in their command posts or headquarters to direct the companies—typically three or four—that make up their regiments, and "general" officers—brigadier generals and major generals—are to be found at brigade or division headquarters, well behind the front lines. The high rate of casualties among field grade and general officers in the Civil War was due in part to the nature of the fighting. It surged back and forth—attack and counterattack. Even the most seasoned troops on occasion fled for their lives, sometimes because they had sustained more devastating losses than flesh could be expected to endure, sometimes because that strange infection of panic simply seized them. A misunderstood order might trigger it, or the sight of a nearby unit withdrawing to a stronger position, or a wounded straggler with word that the troops up ahead had broken. In such instances colonels, and not infrequently generals, had to rush forward to rally fleeing men, to restore the lines, to shore up morale by their own examples. Finally, field grade and general officers were mounted on horses, which made them excellent targets. There was, in fact, nothing that they could do on horses that they could not do better on foot except perhaps ride forward with their swords drawn to urge their troops on or to check soldiers fleeing for their lives. Besides offering irresistible targets, horses were a positive hindrance. Alfred Bellard's regimental commander had an Indian pony that always turned tail in the direction of enemy fire, forcing its rider to twist about awkwardly in his saddle to see what was going on. The tremendous increase in the firepower of infantry and artillery had rendered the life of the mounted rider more precarious than ever, but since horses have always been associated with elevated social class, authority, and the right to command, since aristocrats have always ridden and plebeians walked, there was no getting the officers off their horses. Even at the risk of their lives they clung to their dangerously obsolete steeds.

Soldiers and officers are the basic ingredients of all armies. Their strategic dispositions, how they are deployed, what grand strategy directs their movements largely determine the outcome of wars. It is not easy to reconstitute the general air of confusion and uncertainty in which the initial Union strategy took shape. There was a sharp division in the Cabinet and in the army as well over the appropriate strategy to pursue in attempting to subdue the South. At least three grand strategies were proposed. The first, the one favored by William Seward, the secretary of state and the most influential man in the Cabinet, was what Welles called "the border strategy." The notion here was to establish "borders" around the periphery of the Confederacy, assure the Southerners of the goodwill of the North toward them, and wait for pro-Union sentiment in the South to manifest itself and lead to a negotiated peace. This strategy virtually conceded the slavery issue in favor of restoring the Union.

The strategy proposed by Welles likewise rested on the assumption that there were large numbers of Unionists in the South, simply waiting for indications of Northern support to declare themselves. "Instead of halting on the borders, building entrenchments, and repelling indiscriminately and treating as Rebels—enemies—all, Union as well as disunion, men . . . we should," Welles wrote, ". . . penetrate their territory, nourish and protect the Union sentiment, and create and strengthen a national feeling counter to Secession. . . . Instead of holding back, we should be aggressive and enter their territory," Welles added. Both strategies were based on an overestimation of the strength of Union sentiment. Moreover, Welles's strategy ignored the fact that invasion of an enemy's territory invariably arouses the most intense hostility on the part of those invaded.

A third "strategy," one almost indistinguishable in its practical effect from that of Welles, was based on the assumption that only an overwhelming display of superior force demonstrated by an invasion of the South at every vulnerable point could force the Confederacy back into the Union. It was this latter policy that was, on the whole, followed, but the emotional predisposition to the first strategy on the part of many Northerners in and out of the army frequently blunted the effect of the invasion strategy and in the most important theater of the war—Virginia—rendered it a nullity. General Scott himself was for what Welles termed "a defensive policy." As one general put it to Welles: "We must erect our batteries on the eminences in the vicinity of Washington and establish our military lines; frontiers between the belligerents, as between the countries of Continental Europe, are requisite."

As the third strategy became clearly the strategy that Lincoln was determined to pursue—aggressive penetration of the South—the inevitable next question was how was that strategy to be best effected. One needs, first of all, to have reference to the map of the South which constitutes the endpapers of this volume. There it is seen that the South had two major lines of vulnerability: several thousand miles of virtually undefended seacoast running from Norfolk, Virginia, around the tip of Florida and along the Gulf of Mexico to New Orleans and, in the West, almost a thousand miles of the Mississippi River, stretching from St. Louis to New Orleans, which constituted a line of access into the Deep South and, for the Southerners, an obstacle separating them from their trans-Mississippi allies—Texas, Arkansas, and Missouri. Moreover, the Ohio River entered the Mississippi at Cairo, Illinois, and fifty miles to the east of that conjunction, the Cumberland and Tennessee rivers emptied into the Ohio, coming from a southeasterly direction parallel to each other and roughly parallel to the Mississippi. The South had to defend that river network at all costs. In the hands of the North it would leave the South vulnerable to invasion from a hundred points.

New Orleans was the hinge of the lower South—the point where the coastline joined the great arterial waterway of the Mississippi. The Northern strategy was thus, like all proper strategies, dictated in large part by the terrain. Plans were made immediately for three amphibious operations, two combined land-sea operations, directed at vulnerable points on the North and South Carolina coast—one at Roanoke Island, the other at Port Royal, just south of Charleston; the other expedition was directed at New Orleans itself.

Meanwhile, the Army of the Potomac, with McClellan in command, was organized with the mission of capturing Richmond. As the months passed, a series of additional armies were formed along the line of the Ohio and upper Mississippi—the armies of the Ohio, the Cumberland, the Frontier, Kansas, the Mississippi, the Mountain, the Southwest, the Tennessee, the West Tennessee, and, near the end of the war, the Shenandoah, finally fifteen in all (the Confederacy formed twenty-four "armies"). The real story of the war—the battles and campaigns that finally brought it to its bloody conclusion—took place far away from Washington and Richmond, at Shiloh, Tennessee, Vicksburg, Mississippi, Chickamauga, Georgia, and in a dozen other such engagements. But the facts that the capitals of the North and South were so close together, little more than a hundred miles apart, and that the Confederate capital was, moreover, in the extreme northeastern corner of the geographical area covered by the Confederacy produced a strange distortion, first in the war itself and then in our comprehension of it. The grand strategy developed by Lincoln, his Cabinet, and General Winfield Scott and the actual deployment of Union armies certainly took account of the points of Southern vulnerability, but the focus of public attention remained fixed on the two armies that confronted each other in Virginia—the Army of the Potomac and the Army of Northern Virginia.

5

Washington in Peril

We should take note here of two young men whom Lincoln brought with him to Washington at the beginning of his administration. John George Nicolay was born in Bavaria in 1832 and came to the United States with his parents at the age of six. His father settled in Cincinnati, with its large German colony, and Nicolay attended public school there. When he was sixteen, his family moved to Pittsfield, Illinois, where Nicolay went to work for the *Pike County Free Press*—a county and a paper already famous beyond the boundaries of the state. Before he was twenty-one, Nicolay was editor of the paper, which he soon made into one of the most powerful political journals in the state. By 1857, when he went to Springfield to serve as assistant to the secretary of the state of Illinois, he was already a political ally of Lincoln's. Soon the bright and humorous young man, scarcely twenty-five years old, was one of Lincoln's closest friends and confidants.

John Hay's family seems to have had Scottish origins. His forebears had come to America in the eighteenth century by way of the German Palatinate. A son of the original Hay, one Adam, settled in Virginia, and one of *his* sons, John, migrated at an early age to Lexington, Kentucky (after having been, as a child, patted on the head by Washington). A Henry Clay Whig, he married a local belle and reared fourteen children. His antislavery views impelled him to move on to the free territory of Illinois, and he arrived in Sangamon County, the same year (1830) that a twenty-one-year-old Lincoln emigrated to Illinois. John Hay was fifty-five, but he and Lincoln were natural political allies, and the older man was patron and supporter of his ambitious young friend. One Hay son, Charles, two years older than Lincoln, became a doctor in Salem, Indiana, across the Ohio, not far from Springfield. There he married Helen Leonard from Middleboro, Massachusetts, and produced six children. The third was John Hay, born in 1838. As the editor of Hay's letters puts it, the Hays "set their children a standard rather higher than they might have found in the East, where the young generation clung less closely to the ideals of the past." John Hay was sent east to Brown University, and when he was graduated, he established himself in Springfield as a partner in the law firm of an uncle, Milton Hay, whose offices were adjacent to those of Abraham Lincoln. Soon the two Johns, Hay and Nicolay, were devoted friends, both young men disciples of Lincoln, "the cheeriest of talkers, the riskiest of story tellers." Lincoln was obviously charmed by the vivacity and wit of the two young men. Their high spirits and good humor were like a tonic to him, an essential antidote to his tendency to melancholia. Nicolay (Nico to his friend) and Hay studied French together, flirted with the belles of Springfield, and made extravagant plans for their futures.

After Lincoln's election he asked Nicolay to become his private secretary, and it was decided that his friend Hay, six years his junior, should serve as an aide and general handyman around the White House. It was clear that Lincoln cherished the gaiety and exuberance of his young friends. He could discuss the most important questions of state with them or reveal his most intimate feelings without fear of betrayal or misunderstanding.

From the point of view of the historian, it was a most happy decision on Lincoln's part. The intermittent diaries and letters of the two men give a fascinating close-up of the Lincoln White House. Hay referred to the President irreverently as the "Ancient," the "Old Man," and the "Tycoon," but his admiration and affection for the "Boss" were always evident.

When Lincoln called for volunteers to put down the rebellion, the defenses of Washington consisted primarily of a few companies of cavalry stationed near the War Department and some dragoons quartered in stables near Willard's Hotel, plus a few companies of infantry, a battalion of marines, and seventeen militia companies. Cassius Clay, the Kentucky abolitionist who was in Washington, organized the guests at the National and Willard's hotels into a company which he termed the Strangers' Guard. When five companies of Pennsylvania troops, who had made their perilous way through Baltimore, arrived, they were put up in the Capitol. The domeless Capitol building was converted to an improvised fort, and the tread of soldiers' feet reverberated in the halls.

John Hay wrote in his diary on April 18, 1861: "The White House is turned into barracks." A company of Kansas soldiers, "western jayhawkers," was quartered in the East Room. A handsome young lady sought an audience with the President to tell him of a scheme to assassinate him. Hay heard her story and carried the message "to the bedside of the Chief *couché*. I told him the yarn; he quietly grinned."

Amid the deafening clamor of conflicting aims and goals, Lincoln was determined, above all else, to restore the Union of the states. Beside this slavery was a secondary issue. First the Union must be re-established. The border states were all slave states. Any direct threat to their slaves was certain to push them into the ranks of the seceders. Dealing with them was like walking on eggs. Adhering to the Union, however hesitantly, they were an invaluable asset. Kentucky, Tennessee, Kansas, and Missouri held the key to the upper Mississippi Valley. If they were simply neutralized, the North would be saved the vast expenditure of men and money required to subdue them. The psychological effect was hardly less important than the military. To those states that had seceded it was of enormous importance that the slave states form a united front against the Northern enemy. Every defection was a bleeding wound, testimony that some states at least found slavery compatible with union. So Lincoln had, in effect, two wars to fight, one a "hot war" against the states that had seceded; the other what we would call today a "cold war" against the border states. Every military measure directed against the South had to be weighed for its effect on the border slave states. Those states had to be treated with a delicate combination of coercion and blandishment. It is probably not too much to say that if they all had cast their lots promptly and wholeheartedly with the South, the Confederacy would have been sufficiently strengthened to have battled the North to a virtual standstill, in which case England and France would doubtless have recognized the South as an independent nation and the Union would have been permanently severed. George Templeton Strong in effect described Lincoln's policy when he wrote: "Let us keep the comparatively humane and civilized Border States true to their allegiance, if we can, by any compromise or concession."

During the general confusion Lincoln declared a blockade of the ports of the seceding states. It was a bold gesture. The Federal navy was ill-prepared to establish an effective blockade. The South, without a navy, took the course of commissioning privateers to prey on Northern shipping and immediately began a campaign to commission the building of warships in British and French shipyards. Agents from both the North and the South were dispatched to scour Europe for arms and munitions. The problem with the blockade was that since the principal export of the South was cotton to England, the effects of a blockade would be as severely felt by the workers in English cotton mills as by the cotton-producing states of the South. Moreover, the nonbelligerent powers, in this case principally England and France, felt themselves not obliged to obey a "paper blockade"—that is to say, a blockade which could not be backed up by warships capable of closing major ports to the greater part of foreign trade, assuming always that some "runners" would slip through.

Meanwhile, although troops had arrived in Washington by circuitous routes, principally, as we have seen, by way of Annapolis, it became inescapably clear that Baltimore had to be established as a railway terminal for Northern troops moving to Washington in anticipation of invading Virginia. The most delicate problem that faced Secretary of the Navy Gideon Welles in the first months of Lincoln's presidency was that of strengthening the defenses of the U.S. Navy Yard at Norfolk, Virginia, an important base with large quantities of naval stores and armament. Welles's efforts to reinforce it were blocked primarily by William Seward, who argued that any action taken there by the navy might be interpreted as hostile by Virginia, which did not secede until late in May. Welles had no faith in the argument, but Seward and those of like mind prevailed. Confederate forces seized Norfolk, and the blame was placed on Welles's shoulders both in the Senate and by that ferocious partisan Horace Greeley, who, describing the surrender of the Union installation, wrote: "Thus ended the most shameful, cowardly, disastrous performance that stains the annals of the American Navy." Repeating Greeley's sentence with his own account of the procrastinating policy that led to Norfolk's fall, Welles added: "Such is contemporary history."

In each of the border states the pro- and anti-Union factions were large and active, and the conflict between them was exceedingly bitter. The Confederacy spared no efforts to win these states over to its cause; they became highly valuable pawns in a game the stakes of which were union or separation. Maryland was vital to both the Union and the Confederacy. If Maryland entered the Confederate ranks, either Washington would have to be abandoned as the capital of the Union, with a profoundly depressing effect on Northern morale, or the city would be little better than a besieged citadel, hampered in all its civil and military functions. So it was here that the first and in many ways the most crucial drama of the border states was played out. Secessionist sympathies in Maryland were so strong that it had been thought necessary to disguise the train that carried Lincoln through the state to Washington for his inauguration.

On April 18 the report that the Northern Central Railroad would bring thirty-five carloads of troops through Baltimore destined for Washington threw the city into a turmoil. As one chronicler put it, "Large crowds assembled and curses and imprecations were uttered." The soil of Maryland was threatened with invasion, many declared; the state's integrity must be defended. Baltimore was a railroad junction. Soldiers, or regular passengers, arriving from the North had to disembark at the North Station and make their way by cab or on foot to the station at the south end of the city and there take a train for Washington and points south. When six companies of volunteers from Pennsylvania arrived at the Bolton Street depot, several hundred angry citizens were there to meet them, singing "Dixie's Land" and giving Confederate cheers. The unhappy young soldiers, whose first taste of war was to be jeered and hooted at, were formed up by their officers and began the march to the Mount Clare Station through ranks of hostile Southerners (Maryland was, after all, south of the Mason-Dixon Line, the ancient division between North and South. It was a slave state, although slaves were not nearly as important in its economy as in the states to the south of it, and it was thoroughly Southern in its culture and psychology). By the time the soldiers arrived at the Mount Clare Station the crowd had grown bolder. Some soldiers were spit upon; others had their coattails pulled or their hats knocked off amid cries of "Let the police go and we'll lick you" and

"You'll never get back to Pennsylvania." Only the intervention of the police prevented a full-scale battle.

The honor, if it was that, of being the first Northern casualty of the war was claimed by a black attendant of the Pennsylvania troops, Nick Biddle, who was hit on the head by a secessionist rock. Arrived at last in Washington and quartered in the chambers of the House of Representatives, Biddle removed the handkerchief that he had placed over his wound to stanch the flow of blood, and the laceration bled again on the marble tiles of the House floor.

The next day 1,200 Massachusetts militiamen from Lowell and Boston arrived in Baltimore with 1,000 volunteers from Philadelphia. Now the hostile crowd numbered several thousand. The troops were to be conveyed through the city to Camden Station in horse-drawn cars, and when one of them was halted by an impediment, rocks and bricks were thrown through the windows, accompanied by hoots at Lincoln and cheers for Jefferson Davis. The driver of the lead car retreated, and the crowd began to tear up the street and block the track to prevent the passage of other cars carrying Northern soldiers. The soldiers formed up to march to the Camden Station were thereafter ordered to dismount. Again a large crowd intervened, this time brandishing a pole with a Confederate flag attached to it. The soldiers were jostled, abused, pushed, and struck at and their way blocked. When they turned off to detour around the mob, they were again intercepted. As the troops forced their way slowly forward, the attention of the crowd was directed toward the Confederate flag. It was carried to the front so that the Massachusetts soldiers appeared to be marching behind it to the laughter and jeers of their tormentors. When some bold Union sympathizers in the crowd tried to seize the flag, the conflict was escalated by the throwing of rocks, stones, and pieces of lumber at the soldiers. A Massachusetts soldier named William Patch was knocked down by a large paving stone which struck him in the back. As he fell, his musket was seized, and he was badly beaten before the police could come to his aid. Two more soldiers were knocked down and beaten, and their guns taken from them. Their officers directed the soldiers toward a side street on the double, but again their way was barred by groups of men armed with bricks and paving stones. Amid a shower of missiles the officer in command ordered his men to stand and "Fire!" Several shots and then a ragged volley rang out, killing half a dozen members of the crowd and wounding a number of others. One man wrenched a musket away from a soldier and stabbed him with its bayonet, but the crowd gave way, and once more on the double, the troops reached the sanctuary of the Camden Station, where a train waited to take them to Washington. As the troop train moved out of the station, the cars were pelted with rocks and stones.

When the Massachusetts troops arrived in Washington, they were quartered in the Capitol, where John Hay found them, a "throng of bright-looking Yankee boys, the most of them bearing the signs of New England rusticity in voice and manner, scattered over desks, chairs and galleries, some loafing, many writing letters with plough-hardened hands, or with rapidly-glancing clerkly fingers. . . ."

In Baltimore, meanwhile, the city was in a ferment. The crowds grew by the hundreds until it was estimated that eight thousand people were pouring through the streets, looking for trouble. Another train arrived, carrying the 7th Philadelphia Regiment, and it was soon under heavy attack, the windows smashed by rocks and the soldiers inside wounded by flying glass and missiles. Twenty cars of troops now turned back toward Philadelphia. Twelve citizens of the city had been killed in the fray, and four wounded. Four soldiers had been killed— two "young mechanics" from Lowell, a "decorative painter of Boston, and Sumner H. Needham, a plasterer by trade"—and more wounded.

The mayor called out the militia to help restore order and sent a telegram to Lincoln which read in part: "Sir:—A collision between the citizens and the Northern troops has taken place in Baltimore, and the excitement is fearful. Send no troops here." A freight carload of arms and ammunition was seized by city authorities, and the order was given to destroy all bridges on railroad lines to Philadelphia to prevent the passage of more troops. The 7th Philadelphia was sent back to that city, where it was joined by the 8th Massachusetts.

For the moment attention was focused on keeping open the line from Annapolis to Washington. Simon Cameron, secretary of war, ordered that steamboats be collected to carry troops from Philadelphia to Annapolis, and a party of railroad men, among them a young Scotsman named Andrew Carnegie, was sent to Annapolis to facilitate the movement of troops through that port town.

News of the Baltimore riots stirred up a tempest of angry protest in the North, and many newspapers joined in a call for condign punishment of the city. In the words of a Southern historian, "The Northern papers . . . were filled with the most savage denunciations and brutal threats." Rumors circulated that thousands more soldiers were on their way with the intention of subduing the city and assuring the safe passage of troops through it. The response of the Marylanders was to organize companies of armed volunteers and place them under the command of the police board. The mayor of Baltimore and the governor of the state, while joining in affirming that they wished to avoid "a collision with the General Government," were adamant in their insistence that no Northern troops be transported through the city. The *Baltimore County American*, a "Union" paper, put out an extra declaring: "Civil war is in our midst. A riot has occurred between soldiers from the North and citizens of Baltimore, and unarmed men have fallen beneath the musket-shots of soldiers from another State. We have stood long by the Union flag . . . but now we must coincide with Governor Hicks and Mayor Brown . . . and . . . say to our people . . . defend your State."

Lincoln's reply was characteristically conciliatory, if somewhat evasive. Mayor Brown was assured that "no troops shall be brought through Baltimore, if, in a military point of view, and without interruption from opposition, they can be marched around Baltimore." In composing their response, Lincoln and Winfield Scott were very well aware that one way or another Northern troops had to pass through Baltimore, not only to defend Washington but to mount any kind of attack on the northern tier of Confederate states. There was, we are told by a citizen of Baltimore, "considerable dissatisfaction expressed on the streets at the unsatisfactory tone of the President's reply, many being of the opinion that 'these Northern troops should not be allowed to pollute the soil of Maryland by their march to the rendezvous.'" Preparations went ahead to defend the city "in any emergency." An appeal was made for contributions of firearms, money was offered by the bankers of the city to be used in its defense, and "citizens of every class and age" hastened to enroll in volunteer units. Militia units from Frederick, Towson, and Easton arrived to augment the ranks of the defenders of the city. A mob went off to the offices of a German abolitionist newspaper, the *Wecker*, and forced its editor "under threats of death" to hang out a Confederate flag. A German meeting hall was demolished because it was said a group of Germans had departed for Washington to enlist in the Union army. The houses of Germans known to be sympathetic to the Union were attacked, and their occupants forced to flee for their lives.

The next day was Sunday, and the traditional calm of that sacred day was rudely interrupted by the rumor that five thousand Union troops had arrived in Cockeysville and were marching on Baltimore. Drums rolled; "men rushed from the churches as if crazy, to the armories; the females ran shrieking through the streets, supposing the enemy were already in our midst. . . . Hundreds of persons made their appearance at the Marshal's office armed with small bird and heavy duck guns, bowie knives, pistols and every description of weapon." Meanwhile, Mayor Brown was in Washington, conferring with Lincoln, the Cabinet, and General Scott. With the city rapidly taking on the appearance of a besieged garrison, Brown wired the president of the Baltimore & Ohio Railroad, on whose cars the troops had been carried: "Be calm, and do nothing until you hear from me again. I return to see the President at once. . . ." John Hay wrote unsympathetically in his diary: "The whining traitors from Baltimore were here again this morning." Several hours later the mayor sent word that *the troops are ordered to return forthwith to Harrisburg.*

Lincoln's concern for the safety of the capital grew hourly more acute. The telegraph lines were down beyond Baltimore, and Lincoln was unaware of the tremendous burst of enthusiasm in the North, which had sent thousands of troops, on every railroad car available, pouring south toward the Baltimore bottleneck. Fortunately the Confederate forces in Virginia were almost as disorganized as their Northern counterparts and in no condition to launch an attack on Washington. But Lincoln, who had no way of knowing that fact, was acutely aware of the isolation and vulnerability of the city. An aide heard him saying with an edge of desperation in his voice, "Why don't they come? Why don't they come?" Visited by some of the wounded soldiers of the 6th Massachusetts Infantry, he was reported to have said, "I begin to believe there is no North. The Seventh Regiment is a myth. Rhode Island is another. You are the only real thing."

The 7th, as we have seen, was at Annapolis, but sections of the track from Annapolis to Washington had been torn up and the locomotive damaged. When General Benjamin Butler, in command of the troops, asked for a volunteer "who knew how to make an engine," six machinists came forward. One of them was the man who had made the engine, and he was given the job of repairing it.

When Carl Schurz, ambassador designate to Spain, reached Annapolis on his way to the beleaguered city of Washington, he was ushered into Butler's presence. He found the general "clothed in a gorgeous militia uniform adorned with rich gold embroidery. His rotund form, his squinting eye, and the peculiar puff of his cheeks," Schurz wrote, "made him look a little grotesque." It was plain that the new general was delighted with his power and that he "keenly appreciated its theatrical possibilities." He issued orders with a pompous and self-important air and "looked around with a sort of triumphant gaze, as if to assure himself that the bystanders were duly impressed."

At Annapolis Carl Schurz also encountered Colonel Ambrose Burnside with his Rhode Island Regiment "encamped in a grove of tall trees. The camp-fires were still burning brightly, the soldiers, wrapped in red blankets, lying around them in picturesque groups," while Burnside, "the very image of soldierly beauty," proudly greeted all visitors and introduced a select few to the young governor of Rhode Island, William Sprague, heir to a great textile fortune, who had accompanied his state's regiment to Washington. Sprague was dressed in a splendid uniform with a yellow plume in his hat. The Rhode Island troops were already famous for the number of millionaires serving in the ranks as common soldiers.

The engine repaired, Butler's troops then relaid the tracks as they went and rebuilt a partially burned bridge. The next day they were in Washington, where they paraded down Pennsylvania Avenue before citizens who hailed them as deliverers. They were quartered in the House of Representatives, not then in session. With the arrival of the New York 7th Lincoln became far more cheerful. "I intend, at present, always leaving an opportunity for change of mind," he told Nicolay and Hay, "to fill Fortress Monroe with men and stores; blockade the ports effectually; provide for the entire safety of the Capital; keep them quietly employed in this way, and then go down to Charleston and pay her the little debt we are owing her." Day after day more troops, finding their way around Baltimore by various routes, reached the city. By the end of the month there were ten thousand soldiers packed into every corner of the capital in every public and in many private buildings. It was a modest enough number, but at least the city would be able to give a good account of itself if attacked from Virginia.

The problem of recalcitrant Maryland still had to be solved before the District of Columbia could become a staging area for an invasion of Virginia and the march on Richmond that most Northerners felt would end the war.

On April 28, when the Maryland legislature met, Governor

Thomas Holliday Hicks had urged it to adopt a position of neutrality. That body passed a resolution expressing sympathy with the South, declaring that the Federal government's actions to restore the Union were unconstitutional, and calling on Lincoln to stop the war. The legislature defended its failure to pass an ordinance of secession on the ground that this, too, would be unconstitutional. In the period following the riots of April 19 Marylanders had had an opportunity to reflect on the probable consequences of outright resistance to Federal authority. Baltimore had a reputation as a violent city. The actions of the nineteenth were those of an unruly mob. More sober Baltimoreans feared the mob, with its large admixture of Irish and other ethnic groups, perhaps more than they feared Federal troops. Union sentiment was strong in the western part of the state and discernible on the Eastern Shore. The disposition thus grew stronger in a substantial portion of the population to avoid a showdown. The irreconcilables, described rather loosely as "Baltimore roughs" and said to be made up largely of Knights of the Golden Circle, a secret order pledged to fight for slavery, remained determined to oppose any Union forces sent to secure the city.

Meanwhile, Butler had been directed by cautious General Scott to occupy Relay House, a rail junction some nine miles from Baltimore, and to guard the rail lines that converged there. Using the rumors of an attack on his camp by the "Baltimore roughs," Butler marched into the city and took possession of it the next day, arresting a number of city officials and seizing a city arsenal of weapons. For this insubordinate act, Scott relieved Butler of his command, but the occupation having gone with surprising smoothness, the city stayed occupied, and troops were soon moving through the city to Washington unopposed. John Hay described General Scott as "fierce and jubilant" over the capitulation of Baltimore. "No frenzied poet ever predicted the ruin of a hostile house with more energy and fervor," Hay wrote, "than he issued the rescript of destiny against Baltimore. 'We've got 'em,' he said." Delaware's talk of "armed neutrality" infuriated the old man. "The only good use for traitors is to hang them. They are worth more dead than alive."

Union sentiment was strong in Virginia, and while that state had already assumed a military posture with Generals Lee, Johnston, and Beauregard commanding troops there, the state itself had not formally voted to secede. Part of the difficulty was that Union sentiment was especially strong in the western part of the state, where small farmers held few slaves, where antislavery feeling was evident, and where the domination of the state by the seacoast plantation aristocracy had long been resented.

In Virginia the convention called to consider secession had voted 88 to 55 to secede, and several weeks later secession was approved by a popular vote. It was the closest vote of any Southern state, and its most immediate result was the splitting off of the western portion of the state, which set up a government loyal to the Union in a convention held at Wheeling and elected its own Senators and Congressmen. It represented itself as the legitimate government of the state and, when that proved clearly impractical, declared itself the state of West Virginia and applied for admission to the Union as a new state. The governor of Missouri, following the lead of North Carolina, refused to furnish that state's quota of four regiments of infantry, as did Arkansas. More threateningly, U.S. stores of ordnance at Kansas City were seized by state authorities.

Early in May George Strong wrote in his diary: "There has been an election in the savage commonwealth of Arkansas; result uncertain." Perhaps "the treason-eruption has run its course and passed in maximum virulence for Arkansas is constitutionally predisposed to whatever things are unlovely, lawless, and of ill-report." On May 6 Arkansas voted 69 to 1 to secede.

As Washington filled to the bursting point with troops, their tents crowding up to the government buildings and filling every field and open space as far as the eye could see, the pressure mounted for some military action against the Confederate forces in Virginia. At the end of May, Colonel Elmer Ellsworth and his New York Fire Zouaves were ordered to cross the Potomac into Virginia and capture Arlington Heights, which overlooked the southern part of the capital, and Alexandria a few miles to the south. At Alexandria, as Ellsworth dashed up the stairs of the Marshall House Tavern to remove a Confederate flag from the roof, the tavern owner shot him, wounding him fatally, and was shot in turn by one of Ellsworth's Zouaves. A correspondent of the *New York Tribune* gave a graphic account of the episode, and his account was reprinted in newspapers all over the North and in the West, where Ellsworth had achieved considerable fame before the war for the performances of his drill teams.

Having formed his German-born cavalry regiment, Carl Schurz went to pay his respects to the President before his departure for

Spain. He found Lincoln in a reflective mood bearing upon the barrage of criticism leveled at the government. He told Schurz that if his administration had so far more or less "stumbled along," it had on the whole "stumbled along in the right direction." He felt his own inadequacies most keenly in the area of foreign affairs and intended, he told his visitor, to "study up" on the subject. He enjoined Schurz to take the whole subject of European sentiment toward the war as his concern and added, "Remember now . . . whenever anything occurs to you that you want to tell me personally, or that you think I ought to know, you shall write to me directly."

Visitors poured in and out of the White House, intensely curious about its tall, homely occupant. Those who sought the President saw, in Schurz's words, "a man of unconventional manners, who, without the slightest effort to put on dignity, treated all men alike, much like old neighbors; whose speech had not seldom a rustic flavor about it; who always seemed to have time for a homely talk and never to be in a hurry to press business and who occasionally spoke about important affairs of State with the same nonchalance—I might almost say, irreverence—with which he might have discussed an every-day law case in his office at Springfield, Illinois. People were puzzled. Some interesting stories circulated about Lincoln's wit, his quaint sayings, and also about his kindness of heart and the sympathetic loveliness of his character; but," Schurz added, "as to his qualities as a statesman, serious people who did not intimately know him were inclined to reserve judgment."

Charles Francis Adams, Jr., shared the general view that "the Western barbarians had invaded the White House." All of fashionable Washington was atwitter over the faux pas of the President's wife. She intended to economize and announced she would dismiss some of the corps of White House servants, whom she called "help" to the amusement of the sophisticated.

Schurz pointed to an essential element in Lincoln's character. He had, Schurz observed, "great respect for the superior knowledge and culture of other persons. But he did not stand in awe of them. In fact he did not stand in awe of anybody or anything in the sense of a recognition of an apparent superiority that might have made him in the slightest degree surrender the independence of his own judgment or the freedom of his will. He would have approached the greatest man in the world—the greatest in point of mental capacity, or the greatest in point of station or power—with absolute unconcern, as if he had been dealing with such persons all his life." In choosing his Cabinet members, Schurz noted, he chose the foremost political figures of the day, men far more eminent than Lincoln, and did so "without the slightest apprehension that their prestige or their ability might overshadow him." Schurz saw him as the exemplary democratic statesman "risen from the lowest social layer, the class of the Southern poor whites, and lifted from the roughest plebeian surroundings by high moral instinct and intellectual ability to a marvelous level of nobility and statesmanlike leadership, the ideal growth of the American soil, to whom the democratic principle was a simple law of nature. . . ." Lincoln "met great statesmen and titled persons with the absolute natural, instinctive, unaffected self-respect of an equal; he regarded great affairs as simple business he had to deal with in the way of public duty, and he loved to discuss them with his friends in simple and unceremonious language."

Schurz took his cousin, recently arrived from Germany, to visit Lincoln. Before the young man could make a ceremonious and respectful bow, the President had come forward, shaken his hand, greeted him cordially and informally, and invited him to lunch, although "Mary," Mrs. Lincoln, was away. At lunch the President told amusing stories, laughed delightedly, and asked numerous questions about his visitor's homeland. Afterward, Schurz wrote, his cousin "could hardly find words to express his puzzled admiration for a man who, having risen from the bottom of the social ladder to one of the most exalted stations in the world, had remained so perfectly natural and so absolutely unconscious of how he appeared to others—a man to whom it did not occur for a single moment that a person in his position might put on a certain dignity . . . and who bore himself with such genial sincerity and kindliness that the dignity was not missed, and that one would have regretted to see him different."

Lincoln's stories and jokes circulated through the inner circles of government and then, like ripples in a pond, beyond the White House and Washington in ever-widening circles. They became a kind of leitmotiv for the war years; they were, in fact, of very considerable importance in creating the public image of "Uncle Abe," the gentle, compassionate, patiently enduring man in whose large, strong hands rested the destinies of the nation and, as many believed, the wider hopes of humanity. When he had an attack of a mild form of smallpox known as varioloid, he "told some consoling friend that the disease was rather a subject of congratulation. For the first time since he became

President, he felt he had something to give to every man who called on him." Soon the country was chuckling over the President's latest witticisms. Many had to do with his inclination to tease the pompous. One concerned a Prussian nobleman who had been engaged in revolutionary activity in his own country and had come to the United States seeking a commission as an officer in the Union army. Through Carl Schurz, he secured an audience with the President. As Schurz told it, the count "in his ingenuous way . . . explained to Mr. Lincoln how high the nobility of his family was, and that they had been counts so-and-so many centuries. 'Well,' said Mr. Lincoln, interrupting him, 'that need not trouble you. That will not be in your way, if you behave yourself as a soldier.' The poor count looked puzzled. . . ." On another occasion an aristocratic young Englishman who had toured America obtained an interview with the President. Speaking of the social conditions in the United States, the Englishman said that to his astonishment he had learned that many gentlemen in America were in the habit of blacking their own boots. "That is true, but would gentlemen in your country not do that?" Lincoln replied. "No, certainly not," the Englishman answered. "Well!" said Lincoln, "whose boots do they black?"

Lincoln's homely sayings and salty stories circulated even in the South. "We are always picking up some good thing of the rough Illinoisan's saying," Mary Chesnut wrote. The President had said of a certain man, "Oh, he is too *interruptious*." Mary Chesnut commented: "That is a horrid style of man or woman, the interruptious. I know the thing, but had no name for it before." Mrs. Chesnut was not among those Southerners who imagined Lincoln to be a monster. She was told by a friend who had visited him that he was "an utter American specimen, coarse, rough, and strong; a good-natured kind creature; as pleasant-tempered as he is clever, and if this country can be joked and laughed out of its rights he is the kind-hearted fellow to do it."

6

Cabinet and Congress

At the heart of the operation of Lincoln's administration was, of course, his Cabinet. Charles Francis Adams, disappointed at not being included, described it as "a motley mixture, containing one statesman [William H. Seward], one politician, two jobbers, one intriguer, and two respectable old gentlemen." In most administrations throughout our history, Cabinet ministers have been a largely anonymous lot. With the exception of certain secretaries of state who held their office in a period of international tension, they have largely faded from historical memory. This was not the case with Lincoln's Cabinet. For one thing, the Cabinet, despite Charles Francis Adams's disparaging comments, contained far above the average of political figures powerful in their own right. Secondly, the nature of the crisis gave them, as we would say today, increased visibility. The secretaries of war and the navy had enormous responsibilities. Under the pressures of the war, individual failings and frailties that would have passed unnoticed or uncommented on in ordinary times were subject to constant scrutiny and merciless criticism.

Three of the members of Lincoln's original Cabinet—Seward, Salmon Chase, and Simon Cameron—had had presidential ambitions. Seward had been the Republican front-runner in the prenominating convention period prior to the election of 1860. Lincoln was the dark horse that had snatched the prize from him. Seward began his Cabinet service with the conviction that he was Lincoln's superior in knowledge, experience, training, and general intelligence. Lincoln was, in Seward's view, an "accidental" president thrust into a job far too demanding for him to master, a political novice who must look to Seward for the effective direction of the government. Adams described Seward as a "small, thin, sallow man, with . . . [a] pale, wrinkled, strongly marked face—plain and imperturbable—the thick, guttural voice and . . . everlasting cigar." The great beak of nose stuck out over the receding chin; the clothes hung loosely on his body, giving him rather the appearance of a predatory bird in ill-fitting feathers. As Gideon Welles, the secretary of the navy, put it, "Mr. Seward . . . as a matter of course, assumed that he was to be the master mind of the Government . . . he delighted in oblique and indirect movements; he also prided himself on his skill and management, had a craving desire that the world should consider him the great and controlling mind of his party, of the Administration, and of the country. But the President, in a gentle manner gradually let it be understood that Abraham Lincoln was chief."

It was apparently true that Seward had been carrying on friendly discussions with Southerners. "He had done it," Adams noted, "under an entire misapprehension of the real facts of the situation and with an absolutely impossible result in view. . . . He believed in the existence of a strong underlying Union sentiment in the South; he looked forward with confidence to a sharp reaction of sentiment there, as soon as the people of those States realized that no harm was intended them; and he nourished the delusive belief that a recourse to force could be avoided; that, if it was avoided or postponed, the secession movement would languish, and gradually die out." It was the height of irony that the author of the memorable phrase that had so inflamed the South— "the irrepressible conflict"—could not bring himself to face the darkening reality. Seward told George Templeton Strong's friend Charles King in May, 1861, that he "thought there would be no serious fighting after all; the South would collapse and everything be serenely adjusted." Strong added: "Seward pushes consistency to fanaticism."

According to Nicolay and Hay, Seward had the notion of taking such a hard line with France, Spain, and Russia that those countries would be provoked into declaring war on the United States, which in turn would cause such a rush of patriotic feeling all over the country,

North and South, that secession would be abandoned, and the country united against its external foes. Such political methods have not been uncommon on the part of rulers anxious to suppress domestic unrest, but in the circumstances facing the federal government the notion, besides being devious, undemocratic, and thoroughly impractical, was such an egregious misreading of the true situation vis-à-vis the seceding states as to have about it a touch of madness. Lincoln, in any event, squelched the whole project and, remarkably, continued to make use of Seward's undoubted intelligence and experience. It is hard to doubt the justice of Carl Schurz's judgment that Seward's policy, if adopted, "would inevitably have resulted in the ruin of the Republic" and his observation that the behavior of the secretary of state was "one of the psychological puzzles of history."

To soft-pedal the slavery issue in order not to frighten the critical slaveholding border states out of the Union might be expediently necessary, but to state in unmistakable terms that slavery was *not* the issue was a far different matter. And this Seward, in effect, did by instructing Union diplomats not to imply that "any opposing moral principles"—i.e., slavery—lay "at the foundation of the controversy" between the North and the South, adding that "the Territories will remain in all respects the same, whether the revolution shall succeed or fail; the condition of slavery in the several States will remain the same, whether it succeed or fail." The various Union consuls and ambassadors to whom this astonishing message was sent read it, in most instances, with incredulity. As Schurz put it, Seward "thus positively stripped our cause of its peculiar moral force, and he did this by going so far as to say a thing which not only a cautious politician would have found it unnecessary to say, but which, as his own philosophical sense must have told him, could not be true."

Schurz's analysis of Seward is a persuasive one. "Having been," Schurz wrote, "regarded as one of the most radical anti-slavery men before Lincoln's election, he became, after that event, apparently, at least, one of the most timid. As appears from his private correspondence . . . he regarded himself as appointed by Providence as well as by the tacit consent of both political parties to 'compose' the trouble created by the secession movement. He seemed to believe that this composition might be effected by mutual concessions, by compromise with regard to slavery." Perhaps the key to unlock Seward's mysterious tergiversation lies in his long and, for the most part, highly successful career as a politician. "Accommodation" is the breath of life to the politician. To every political problem there *must* be a solution. Otherwise, the system cannot work. The solution may be unsatisfactory in varying degrees to both parties, but *it is a solution*. It usually prevents murder and mayhem. It allows life to go on. Fine and good, but certain problems present themselves in the course of history as not susceptible to such "composition." They are so profoundly moral in their nature that in the last analysis they cannot be compromised. Slavery was such an issue, and on one level of political discourse Seward knew this well enough; hence his "irrepressible conflict." But on another level, that of political action, he simply could not face that terrible reality. High-minded and intelligent as he undoubtedly was, he had been spoiled by a lifetime of small accommodations for the uncompromising commitment to the abolition of slavery that the time required.

Perhaps the most appealing figure in the Cabinet was Gideon Welles, secretary of the navy. Certainly he had the best beard (three Cabinet members were bearded—Edwin Stanton, Welles, and Edward Bates), a splendidly flowing hirsute adornment that gave him the appearance of an Old Testament prophet. Welles, born in 1802 and a native of Connecticut, had been for many years the editor of a staunchly Jacksonian newspaper, the *Hartford Times*. He held several government posts during the period of Democratic hegemony, but left the party in 1856 over the slavery issue and helped organize the Republican Party in his home state. Defeated for governor of Connecticut, he wrote ably and extensively on the issue of slavery. Although, as his opponents were quick to point out, he had never commanded so much as a skiff, Lincoln appointed him secretary of the navy. It was perhaps the best Cabinet appointment. Welles, the only New Englander in the Cabinet, was a man full of the moral rectitude for which that region was famous. He was determined not to be drawn into the Borgian plottings within the Cabinet and equally determined to fend off Seward's efforts to run the Navy Department as well as the government generally. Moreover, he kept a diary, an acidulous and detailed account of the maneuverings of his fellow Cabinet members. It is perhaps as good a general historical rule as any other that diary writers, provided they are vigorous and vivid annalists, always win. Welles's diary is such a valuable source of information about the inner workings of Lincoln's Cabinet that historians have, to a substantial degree, come to see that body through Welles's eyes. Welles gives us a clue to his temperament when he describes the critics of his appointment as "a set of factious fools who think it is wise to be censorious."

Salmon Chase, the secretary of the treasury, was the beau ideal of politicians; "tall, broad-shouldered, and proudly erect, his features strong and regular and his forehead broad, high and clear," as his admiring friend Carl Schurz described him, "he was a picture of intelligence, strength, courage, and dignity . . . one of the stateliest figures in the Senate." Despite an ego somewhat larger than was common even among politicians and a strong disposition to pomposity, Chase was a man of considerable gifts and, as Schurz noted, courage. He had long been a leader of the antislavery forces of Ohio and governor of that state, and indeed, it was his long association with the antislavery movement that, as with Seward, had been the greatest obstacle in his path to the presidency. Schurz observed that Chase's every thought and act were consciously directed toward his goal of becoming, finally, president of the United States. "Chase," Schurz added, "was one of the noblest victims of that disease, and he suffered terribly from it. . . . His repeated disappointments pierced him and rankled in him like poisoned arrows; and he was incessantly tortured by the feeling that his country did not do justice to him, and that his public life was a failure." Lincoln, for his part, became convinced that Chase was sinuous and relentlessly ambitious and that he worked assiduously against him, questioning his decisions, encouraging his enemies. "I am entirely indifferent as to his success or failure in these schemes," Lincoln told Hay, "so long as he does his duty as head of the Treasury Department."

Montgomery Blair, the postmaster general, was a member of the remarkable Blair clan of Kentucky. Francis Preston Blair, the first, had been born in Virginia in 1791. An early supporter of Jackson's and an enemy of the Bank of the United States, he edited the pro-Jackson *Washington Globe* and was a member of the general's Kitchen Cabinet. Blair's strong antislavery feelings drew him into the Republican Party, and he became one of Lincoln's strongest supporters in the Mississippi West. His son Francis Preston Blair, Jr., born in 1821 and a graduate of Princeton, migrated to St. Louis, Missouri, where he soon became a leading figure in the bar and one of the organizers of the Free-Soil Party in Missouri. He was a Free-Soil Congressman, 1856–58, a Republican with the formation of that party, and, like his father, an ardent Lincoln man. Blair's older brother, Montgomery, born in 1813, had attended West Point (class of '35) and then resigned his commission to become a lawyer, a politician, and a protégé of Thomas Hart Benton's. This brought him, with his brother, Francis, into the Benton-Frémont network and cemented the most powerful political alliance in the state. He achieved a measure of national fame as one of Dred Scott's lawyers. Montgomery Blair was a tall, ruggedly handsome man whose most notable features were his dark, deep-set eyes and beetling brows.

The Blairs vastly complicated Lincoln's task. They had their own interests in Missouri and pushed aggressively, within the government and without, policies designed to advance those interests. Lincoln, as we have seen, favored the "radicals" of the state. The Blairs were leaders of the "conservatives." Montgomery Blair declared to John Hay in the fall of 1864, "There is no such thing as an honest and patriotic American radical. Some of the transcendental, red-Republican Germans were honest enough in their moon-struck theorizing; but the Americans imprudently and dishonestly arrogate to themselves the title of unconditional loyalty, when the whole spirit of the faction is contempt of, and opposition to, law. . . ." The fact was the Blairs were very close to being Democrats at heart. Lincoln described them as being like members of a "clan." He told Hay, "Their family is a close corporation." Welles judged Blair to be "as potent with the President" as either Chase or Seward. "With some egotism, Blair has great good sense," Welles wrote, "a better knowledge and estimate of military men than either or both the others, and, I think, is possessed of . . . solid, reliable administrative ability."

Caleb Blood Smith, secretary of the new and relatively unimportant Department of the Interior, had been appointed to the Cabinet as a reward for his efforts in behalf of Lincoln in Indiana. One of Lincoln's earliest and strongest supporters in the upper Mississippi Valley, Smith had seconded Lincoln's nomination at Chicago. Amid the contending giants in Lincoln's Cabinet, Smith steered a cautious course and, finding a year of such servitude all he had taste for, resigned in 1862.

Edward Bates, the attorney general, was the oldest member of Lincoln's Cabinet. He was born in 1793, and his political career in Missouri had been marked by his opposition to the Kansas-Nebraska Act and his early adherence to the nascent Republican Party. The candidate of the border state Republicans for president at the Chicago convention in 1860, Bates had been appointed to the Cabinet as a gesture to that critically important region. Bates, with a fine mane of white hair and short white beard, looked splendidly patriarchal. Like Smith, he did his best to avoid being drawn into the fierce struggle for power in the Lincoln Cabinet.

Simon Cameron, the first secretary of war, was a machine politician in a state—Pennsylvania—notorious for producing an abundance of that breed. But fortunately he was lazy and more interested in the spoils of office than its power. It was evident from the first that he was incapable of managing the vast and complex business of the War Department. "Cameron," Gideon Welles wrote, "does not attempt to deny that he used money, party influence, legislative abuses, and legislative grants to secure an election. In carrying his points he is unscrupulous and cunningly audacious. His party tools he never forgets, so long as they are faithful to his cause and interests, and he freely gives his time, labor, and money to assist them."

Edwin Stanton, Cameron's successor in January, 1862, was a very different type. Born in 1814 in Ohio, he had become one of the most successful corporation lawyers in the country. He had then gone on to serve as special U.S. counsel in the complicated matter of the California land frauds. Buchanan had appointed him attorney general in the last year of his administration, and Stanton had identified himself with the Breckinridge or Union Democrats in the presidential election. Out of office, Stanton had been an outspoken critic of Lincoln's infant administration. Welles heard reports that Stanton, as a member of Buchanan's Cabinet, had kept Seward informed of everything that went on in the government's inner circle, in return for which Seward had engineered Stanton's appointment to Lincoln's Cabinet.

In the words of Gideon Welles, Stanton's "remarks on the personal appearance of the President were coarse, and his freely expressed judgment on public affairs unjust." His loyalty to Lincoln was far from steady. He wrote a letter highly critical of the administration that found its way into the newspapers, and when he came to apologize, Lincoln told him he was "too busy to quarrel with him." Seward, for his part, was confident that having brought Stanton into the Cabinet, he could count him an ally. Stanton was as choleric as he was able; George Templeton Strong described him accurately as "a born tyrant. He likes to use official power to crush and destroy rebels and sympathizers with rebellion and anybody else who may happen to stand inconveniently in his way. . . . He is wholly 'incorruptible' in the ordinary sense, but most corruptible by prejudice and passion." Certainly Stanton's manner was often highly abrasive. He was given to violent tempers and was somewhat of a bully, but he had drive and energy and was, whatever his faults, a vast improvement over Cameron.

Seward clearly intended to run the government, and Welles became the chronicler of that ingenious and determined campaign. The Cabinet meetings themselves were odd encounters. Unplanned, unstructured, unscheduled for a time, they happened whenever a particular crisis arose (and there were, heaven knows, enough of those) or when one of the Cabinet members—usually Seward—pressed for a meeting. Lincoln, rather than give the sessions any overt leadership or direction, allowed them to take their own form, yielding the floor readily to anyone disposed to claim it. This was most often Seward, who, to an uninformed observer, would have appeared to be the leader and dominant personality in the group. Lincoln for the most part listened to his talented and contentious advisers with unfailing courtesy, respect, and, above all, patience. It seemed to most of the Cabinet members that their sessions were often muddled and directionless, yet surprisingly decisions were made, and, indeed, momentous things accomplished. The shrewder members, like Welles, soon came to realize that despite his style, which seemed more that of an interested and intelligent auditor than a leader, Lincoln had increasingly firm control both over the Cabinet and the government. Initially, according to Welles, "the Cabinet-meetings were a sort of privy council or gathering of equals, much like a Senatorial caucus, where there was no recognized leader and the Secretary of State put himself in advance of the President. No seats were assigned or regularly taken," and Seward was "not slow in taking upon himself to prescribe action and doing most of the talking, but often to the disgust of his associates. . . . Discussions were desultory and without order or system, but in the summing-up and conclusions the President, who was a patient listener and learner, concentrated results, and often determined questions adverse to the Secretary of State, regarding him and his opinions . . . for what they were worth and generally no more." Bates eventually expressed his dissatisfaction with such informal proceedings and urged that certain days be set for Cabinet meetings with regular agendas, and Lincoln readily agreed.

A kind of litany of disapproval for the carelessness of Cabinet members in attending meetings runs through Gideon Welles's diary. The consequences of such indifferent attendance, plus Lincoln's disposition to let his Cabinet members run their own departments, led increasingly to what Welles called "departmental administration," the result of which, in Welles's opinion, was that the President was often less well informed than he should be on critical issues. Stanton and Seward, Welles felt, did all in their power to restrict the access of the other Cabinet members to Lincoln. "Both," Welles wrote, "mouse about the President, who, in his intense interest and inquisitiveness, spends much of his time at the War Department, watching the telegraph."

The Congress voted into office with Lincoln was, after the withdrawal of the Southern members, overwhelmingly Republican. Not only did the Republican Party completely control both houses, but the radical, antislavery Republicans controlled the party. Men like Charles Sumner and Thaddeus Stevens, Henry Wilson, William Pitt Fessenden, Zachariah Chandler, and Benjamin Wade, who had labored for years in what so often seemed a lost cause, now had the intoxicating experience of running the congressional show. Men, in the main, of passionate idealism, they were the antithesis of regular machine politicians. Dogmatic and impatient, they were after Lincoln from the first to declare all the slaves within Union lines free and to emancipate the slaves in the District of Columbia, the border states, and wherever the authority of the Federal government reached. They tried to dictate military strategy and threatened constantly to intrude into the domain of the executive. Most of them had little confidence in Lincoln. They considered him no more than the nominal head of the government and looked initially to their longtime friend and ally Seward for direction and leadership. Because they perceived Lincoln as inexperienced, if not incompetent, it seemed to them that they had to run the country and direct the war in alliance with the secretary of state. As in his relationship with the Cabinet members, Lincoln showed infinite patience and tact in his dealings with the radical leaders. His sympathies were with them even when his actions or inaction angered them. He never forgot, in the midst of their persistent harassment, how much the country and the Republican Party owed to their single-minded devotion to the antislavery cause.

If Lincoln's own acute sense of political timing made him often appear reluctant or dilatory, he was, in fact, usually glad to be hurried along, most specifically down the road to emancipation by his congressional critics. He told Hay that "these radical men have in them the stuff which must save the State, and on which we must mainly rely.

They are absolutely uncorroded by the virus of secession. It cannot touch or taint them." In any crisis over the antislavery issue the administration had to side with the radicals. The instrument by which the congressional radicals meant to run the country was the Joint Committee on the Conduct of the War. In the jaundiced opinion of Welles, the committee was made up of "narrow and prejudiced partisans, mischievous busybodies, . . . a discredit to Congress. Mean and contemptible partisanship colors all their acts. . . ."

Charles Sumner had, of course, been *the* abolitionist firebrand in the Senate since his election in 1851, and Preston Brooks's attack on him had made him a hero to antislavery Northerners. But he had had little influence with his fellow Senators because of the extremeness of his views and the intemperance of his language. For Sumner, the war brought a notable accession of influence and power. As one of the leaders of the antislavery Republicans, he had Lincoln's ear and was looked to by Republican Congressmen and Senators alike for guidance and leadership. Over six feet tall, handsome—"godlike" his admirers liked to say—brilliant, eloquent, aristocratic, champion of Radical Republican politics, Sumner dominated the Senate by the power of his intellect rather than by tact or skill in dealing with his colleagues. The caustic Welles considered the Massachusetts Senator deficient as a party leader: "Though he has talents, acquirements, sincerity, and patriotism, with much true and false philanthropy, he is theoretical rather than practical. Is egotistical, credulous to weakness with those who are his friends. . . . He is not a Constitutionalist, has no organizing and constructive powers, and treats the great fundamental principles of the organic law much as he would the resolutions of the last national party convention." Toward the South, Sumner was unrelentingly hostile, "ready to go to extremes to break up not only the system of bondage, but the political, industrial, and social system of all the rebellious States. . . . He would not only free the slaves," Welles wrote, somewhat unfairly, "but elevate them above their former masters. Yet, with all his studied philanthropy and love for the negroes in the abstract, is unwilling to have fellowship with them, though he thinks he is. . . . His knowledge of men is imperfect and unreliable, and hence, while he will always have position with his party and influence its movements he will never be the trusted leader."

Schurz, often his ally in political contests, called Sumner "a born Puritan character, an aristocrat by birth, a democrat by study and reflection, a revolutionary power by the dogmatic intensity of his determination to impose his principles upon the world at any cost," while his friend Ralph Waldo Emerson said of him that he was a "clean, self-poised, great-hearted man, noble in purpose, incorruptible in life, the friend of the poor, the champion of the oppressed. . . . It characterizes a man for me that he hates Charles Sumner for it shows that he cannot discriminate between a foible and a vice." To George Templeton Strong Charles Sumner was "that pedantic twaddler."

Carl Schurz on more than one occasion heard the Massachusetts Senator puzzle over the character of the President. "Lincoln," Schurz wrote, "was utterly unlike Sumner's ideal of a statesman. The refined New Englander, who, after having enjoyed a thorough classical education, had seen much of the great world at home and abroad, and conceived an exalted idea of the dignity of an American Senator and of a President of the great American Republic, could hardly understand this Western product of American democracy." Sumner was intelligent enough to perceive in Lincoln "flashes of thought and bursts of illuminating expression which struck him as extraordinary, although," Schurz wrote, "being absolutely without any sense of humor, . . . he often lost Lincoln's keenest points." The President was "fond of elucidating his arguments with stories, as with a flashlight," Schurz wrote, and Sumner would often come to Schurz "with an air of innocent bewilderment" for an explanation of "such Lincolnisms." To Sumner the war was only about the abolition of slavery, and he grew more and more impatient with the President for not taking a strong line on the subject. Schurz recalled seeing him, on more than one occasion, pacing up and down, declaring, "I pray that the President may be right in delaying. But I am afraid, I am almost sure, he is not. I trust his fidelity, but I cannot understand him." There was simply no referent in Sumner's world of Harvard and Boston for a Lincoln, and, again in Schurz's words, "he could not get rid of his misgivings as to how this seemingly untutored child of nature would master the tremendous task before him." Such misgivings were not, of course, confined to Charles Francis Adams and Charles Sumner. As Schurz suggested, they were shared by every "serious" person, every student of statecraft, and every practical politician.

"For his part," Schurz noted, "Lincoln regarded and esteemed Sumner as the outspoken conscience of the advanced anti-slavery element, the confidence and hearty co-operation of which was to him of the highest moment in the common struggle. While it required all his fortitude to bear Mr. Sumner's intractable insistence, Lincoln did not at all deprecate Sumner's public agitation for an immediate emancipation policy, even though it did reflect on the course of the administration. On the contrary, he rather welcomed everything that would prepare the public mind for the approaching development."

Sumner's political alter ego was his fellow Massachusetts Senator, Henry Wilson. Wilson had been born Jeremiah Colbath of impoverished parents in Farmington, New Hampshire, in 1812 and indentured to a farmer. He moved to Massachusetts and started a shoe factory which prospered, and discovering a bent for politics, he ran for and was elected to the Massachusetts Great and General Court as a Whig. An early Free-Soiler and antislavery man, he had a brief flirtation with the Know-Nothings before finding his home in the newly formed Republican Party and being chosen as a United States Senator. Politics and causes produce strange bedfellows, but surely American politics has produced no stranger matching than Charles Sumner, the Boston aristocrat, tall, handsome, Harvard-educated, and Henry Wilson, rough-spoken, self-taught ex-shoemaker. Wilson had a remarkable ability to understand and respond to the aspirations of the ordinary voter. He could establish an immediate rapport with a working-class audience or, alternately, one made up primarily of young clerks or farmers. In the words of George Hoar, "Wilson supplied almost everything that Sumner lacked. . . . He was a skilful, adroit, practised and constant political manager. He knew the value of party organization, and did not disdain the arts and diplomacies of a partisan. He carried them sometimes farther, in my judgment, than a scrupulous sense of honor would warrant . . . but he never bore malice or seemed to keep angry over night." Most striking of all, in Hoar's view, "was his rare and unparalleled gift of gathering and uttering the sentiment of the people." Hoar told the story of Wilson's reply to a fellow Massachusetts politico who complained that his rural rivals "seemed to have carried their trading and swapping of oxen into politics, and into the higher offices of the state." Wilson responded "that so long as the people were satisfied with the trade, it did not become the oxen to complain."

Thaddeus Stevens was Sumner's counterpart in the House. As different from Sumner as night from day, Stevens had made his way up from the most modest origins to a commanding position in the Republican Party. Starting his political career as an Anti-Mason, he had devoted his life to the antislavery cause. More than any political figure of the day, he identified himself with the enslaved blacks of the

South and the free blacks in the North as well. It was a notorious fact that his housekeeper and common-law wife was a handsome and intelligent mulatto woman.

Stevens, sixty-nine years old at the beginning of the war, was beset by various physical ailments. Born with a clubfoot, he had a merciless and mordant wit. Carl Schurz described the impression that Stevens made on him as "not sympathetic," perhaps an understatement. His face was, in Schurz's words, "long and pallid, topped with an ample dark brown wig" which abandoned all pretense of deception and "beetling brows overhanging keen eyes of uncertain color. . . ." A colleague wrote of him: "In times of emergency he would call on every Republican in the House to sustain the party measures, and boldly defy any conservative to oppose them on pain of being 'read out' of the Republican organization. At such times his manner would be expressive of the bitterest sarcasm, and his voice, cold and trenchant as steel, would strike terror to the hearts of his weaker followers." As he began a speech, another observer noted he would proceed with a "grandfatherly grumbling . . . monotonous, and sometimes incoherent" manner, hunting "mislaid notes or a dropped handkerchief," and then, gathering strength and force as he went, ending with "the iron bolt of his argument." Georges Clemenceau, the French journalist, wrote of Stevens: "When a man of this kind is irascible, vindictive, and vigorous, and when, moreover, he pursues with quite unusual intellectual powers . . . one sole end, with all his strength, and all his force, and all his passions, and prejudices, it is dangerous to stand in his way." Stevens was the conscience and scourge of the House. Ben: Perley Poore, the attentive observer of Washington politicians, described him as "rising by degrees, as a telescope is pulled out, until he stood in a most ungraceful attitude, his heavy black hair falling down over his cavernous brows, and his cold little eyes twinkling in anger." Reaching his full height, he would denounce some errant colleague, "sweeping at him with his large, bony hand, in uncouth gestures, as if he would clutch and shake him."

Stevens made no bones of his hatred of the South. The war and its aftermath, he believed, must be instruments for the chastisement of that proud and arrogant breed. He declared on July 5, 1862, "I would seize every foot of land, and every dollar of their property as our armies go along, and put it to the uses of war and to the pay of our debts. I would plant the South with a military colony if I could not make them submit otherwise."

When the special session of Congress met on July 4, 1861, Lincoln informed that body of the steps he had taken to restore the Union and asked for the support of its members. He gave special attention to the claim of certain border states to remain neutral. "This," he declared, "would be disunion completed. Figuratively speaking, it would be the building of an impassable wall along the line of separation, and yet not quite an impassable one, for under the guise of neutrality, it would tie the hands of the Union men and freely pass supplies from among them to the insurrectionists, which it could not do as an open enemy." There thus could be no neutrality. "It may be affirmed without extravagance," Lincoln concluded, "that the free institutions we enjoy have developed the powers and improved the condition of our whole people beyond any example in the world. Of this we now have a striking and an impressive illustration. So large an army as the Government has now on foot was never before known without a soldier in it but who had taken his place there of his own free choice. But more than this, there are many single regiments whose members, one and another, possess full practical knowledge of all the arts, sciences, professions, and whatever else, whether useful or elegant, is known in the world; and there is scarcely one from which there could not be selected a President, a Cabinet, Congress, and perhaps a court, abundantly competent to administer the Government itself. . . . This is essentially a people's contest. On the side of the Union it is a struggle for maintaining in the world that form or substance of government whose leading object is to elevate the condition of men; to lift artificial weights from all shoulders; to clear the paths of laudable pursuit for all; to afford an unfettered start and a fair chance in the race of life."

Sidney George Fisher read Lincoln's message to Congress and was as impressed as he had been by his inaugural. "It is simple, clear, positive & it is marked throughout by evident sincerity and truth," he noted. "It is wholly free from egotism or desire to produce an effect, but is earnest & candid. It shows, moreover, remarkable power of thought & argument. . . . In this hour of its trial, the country seems to have found in Mr. Lincoln a great man." If Seward had been chosen, or Simon Cameron, the country would have been ruined, in Fisher's view.

7

Bull Run

While McDowell struggled to whip his three-month volunteers into the semblance of an army, pressures mounted on Lincoln to order a drive into Virginia, scatter the small rebel forces there, seize Richmond, and bring the rebellion to a speedy end.

On June 10, 1861, a battle took place at Big Bethel in Virginia. Benjamin Butler, recently relieved of his command for occupying Baltimore without orders, was dispatched by boat with a division to reinforce the U.S. garrison at Fortress Monroe in Virginia. Landing at the fort at the end of the peninsula formed by the York and James rivers, Butler learned that there was a Confederate outpost at Big Bethel some eight miles away. He ordered the 7th New York Volunteers (Duryea's Zouaves) to initiate an attack. The regiment started out to cover the New Market Road. An hour later six other regiments moved out in two columns to join the 7th in an advance on Big Bethel. The columns, as is not uncommonly the case in such circumstances, especially with inexperienced troops, took each other for the enemy and exchanged fire, killing 2 men and wounding 22. After this unpromising beginning the Union troops were intercepted by the 1st North Carolina Volunteers and driven back in disorder, with 2 officers killed (one, Theodore Winthrop, was shot while standing on a fence post exhorting his men) and 74 soldiers out of a force of 4,400 men. The Confederates, with only 1,408 men engaged, lost 11 killed. The plan of attack was faulty, and its execution inept. Butler's mission was to reinforce Fortress Monroe and not to go lollygagging off toward Yorktown, trying to earn points for himself. The encounter was the first land battle of the war, and the Southern "victory" was made much of in the Confederate press. The fact that a handful of Carolinians had defeated a force three times its size was taken as conclusive evidence that the Yankees were both cowardly and incompetent.

An important by-product of Butler's reinforcement of Fortress Monroe was the beginning of the formation of a policy of dealing with slaves who came into Federal lines or who were abandoned by their masters and mistresses in the face of Union advances. Within the extensive Union fortifications extending from Alexandria to Newport News, several thousand slaves were included. The question was: What was to be done with them?

At Fortress Monroe General Benjamin Butler had put three slaves to work with a detail of soldiers to strengthen the fortifications. When a Confederate officer under a flag of truce appeared to claim the slaves, Butler was presented with a dilemma. He was well aware that returning them would stir up a hornets' nest among the enemies of slavery, just as keeping them would inflame the still-loyal border states. He thus hit upon an ingenious solution. Since the Confederate officer claimed the slaves as the property of Southern owners, Butler would declare them to be confiscated property, "contraband of war." The word, with its sly joke, was one of those irresistible terms that, once uttered, enter immediately into the language. Virtually overnight "contraband" became the word for all those slaves of indeterminate status who could not yet be declared free but were, equally unmistakably, not slaves.

Gradually, in response to the exigencies of military life, a rough system for dealing with the contrabands began to emerge. Army commanders were authorized to appoint a superintendent of freedmen's affairs to organize and run the so-called contraband camps. It was a vast work. The ill and aged had to be provided for; food and shelter, found. Those who were able to work were assigned a variety of tasks—working on fortifications, serving as teamsters or as cooks, picking cotton on abandoned plantations, and a dozen other such jobs. Organized into squads of ten, the contrabands went off under the direction of one of their number chosen as leader to work captured plantations in return for wood and rations of meal, bread, bacon, and coffee. Each group of ten belonged to a larger group of one hundred, also headed by a black man, and these reported to a white supervisor.

At the influx of contrabands from Virginia, Elizabeth Keckley, a freed slave, wrote that "many good friends reached forth kind hands, but the North is not warm and impulsive. For one kind word spoken, two harsh ones were uttered; there was something repelling in the atmosphere, and the bright and joyous dreams of freedom to the slave faded—were sadly altered, in the presence of the stern, practical mother, reality. . . ." Mrs. Keckley decided to organize "the well-to-do colored people to go to work to do something for the benefit of the suffering blacks." Mrs. Lincoln gave her full support to the notion and a contribution of $200. Mrs. Keckley's church congregation was enlisted, and soon there were chapters in New York and Boston. At the Metropolitan Hotel in New York the black waiters made a substantial contribution. Mrs. Frederick Douglass chipped in $200, besides lecturing for the cause. Large quantities of clothes and food came from England for distribution to contrabands.

Perhaps the most notable achievement of Northern blacks came in the establishment of schools for the children of freed slaves. The first such school was started by Mary Chase, an ex-slave, in Alexandria, Virginia, a few months after the outbreak of the war. When Virginia contrabands streamed into Fortress Monroe, another black woman, Mrs. Mary Peake, organized a school there the same month that Mary Chase's school started. The New York African Colonization Society, with the coming of the war, turned its attention to starting schools for young contrabands in Washington. A black Catholic parish organized five schools in Washington, and twenty-two other private schools were founded by blacks in that city during and immediately after the war.

Among those who ventured into the South to work in contraband camps, in black hospitals, and in homes for the aged were the veterans of the abolition movement like Frances Dana Gage. A native of Ohio and an early recruit to the women's rights movement, Frances Gage had twice had her house set afire because of her antislavery views. At the age of fifty-four she traveled into the South, following the Union armies, worked as a nurse in field hospitals, taught freedmen to read and write, and worked as an agent of the Sanitary Commission to establish army hospitals in Memphis, Vicksburg, and Natchez, all without pay. Four of her sons fought in the Union army.

Josephine Griffing was another member of the older generation of abolitionists who ministered to the manifold needs of the ex-slaves who crowded Washington. Until her death in 1872 she devoted her energies to the never-ending task.

Abigail Hopper Gibbons belonged to one of those remarkable nineteenth-century families that in successive generations furnished dozens of public-spirited citizens. Her father-in-law, William, a Philadelphia Quaker, had founded a society to prevent the kidnapping of free blacks in Pennsylvania. She, after her marriage, had moved to New York and formed an organization to help women prisoners make their way back into society, founded a home for unwed mothers, and served as president of the German Industrial School for Street Children. In 1862 at the age of sixty she took charge of an army hospital at Point Lookout, Maryland, and when a contraband camp was established nearby, she took that under her wing as well, collecting and distributing supplies for the men, women, and children there and organizing a school. For her pains she received numerous abusive letters, one of which read: "Old Lady you are not needed at this place . . . you old nigger lover yea worse an old hypocrit the devil has his house full of better people than you ever were you old Hell hound. . . ." When the draft riots struck New York City, the Gibbonses' house was one of the first sacked by the mob because of its mistress's well-known antislavery sentiments.

"They come [to Craney Island]," off the Virginia coast, wrote Lucy Chase, a Massachusetts Quaker, of the contrabands, "almost wholly destitute of clothing, covered with vermin, and extremely ignorant, and incompetent for noble, self-originating action of mind or body, uneducated in principle too as they are they ought to enter freedom through the path of moral restraint." That was the heart of the matter. Middle- and upper-class white America was constructed on "restraint," on control, on the faithful observances of innumerable rules of behavior, beginning with cleanliness and ascending through various levels to "pure" and "noble" thoughts and "moral restraints." "The negro marriage-question" was another puzzler for the missionaries and teachers. On Craney Island, Sarah Chase, Lucy's sister, reported that when some black man wished to marry a particular woman, another woman often appeared to claim him as her *de facto* husband and the mother of her children.

When Sarah and Lucy Chase got over the initial shock of contraband ways, they surrendered themselves to the flow of spontaneous black affection that surrounded them, so different from the stiff and awkward manners of their native New England. "They warm my heart, these warm-hearted people," Lucy Chase wrote her "Dear Ones at Home," "one almost worships the wealth of love with which God has blessed them, and willing forgives the barbarous assaults they make on one's patience and forbearance, remembering that slavery alone is responsible for the scars which so disfigure them."

Lincoln had called, after the fall of Sumter, for three-month volunteers to put down the rebellion. The notion that the South could be subdued in three months was probably the most serious error of Lincoln's administration. Three months were hardly enough time to recruit and equip an army, let alone train it to fight.

McDowell, pressed by Lincoln, agreed to attack the Confederate force under Beauregard that was guarding the important road and rail junction at Manassas Junction near Bull Run, a small tributary of the Potomac. (It was an indication of the Southern frame of mind that when rumors spread in Richmond that the Yankees might attack at Bull Run, regrets were expressed that the name of the battle might be so "unrefined.")

McDowell protested that his green troops were not ready for such an ambitious move, but as the end of the volunteers' three-month enlistment period approached, the pressure to make use of his large and expensive army grew irresistible. George Templeton Strong was not alone in his anxiety at the advance of McDowell's column on Manassas Junction. "I fear this move is premature, forced on General Scott by the newspapers. A serious check on this line would be a great disaster," he wrote in his diary.

The plan for the advance provided that General Robert Patterson, who was near Harpers Ferry with 18,000 men, was to move against Joseph Johnston's smaller force at Winchester, thus preventing Johnston from reinforcing Beauregard. One of the oldest officers in either army at the age of sixty-eight, Patterson had been placed in command of the Pennsylvania three-month volunteers by the governor of the state.

McDowell meanwhile crossed the Potomac below Washington with some 30,000 men and reached Centreville on July 18. A basic principle of warfare is prompt attack; but McDowell's inexperienced army was still straggling into its bivouac areas at dusk, and McDowell decided they were not sufficiently rested from their long march under a hot July sun to attack the Confederate force the next morning. Instead, he dispatched the 1st Division under Daniel Tyler to make a reconnaissance force. Tyler, sixty-two years old and a graduate of West Point, class of 1819, had resigned from the army in 1834, never having heard a shot fired in battle, and became, successively, a civil engineer and a railroad president. With the secession of the South he had been commissioned a colonel in the 1st Connecticut Volunteers and had become a brigadier general three weeks later. Now he was charged with making a reconnaissance where an all-out assault was called for. Tyler advanced to the narrow but deep stream of Bull Run, where his men were driven back after a sharp engagement, with losses of 83 soldiers opposed to 68 for the Confederates.

The action of Tyler's division served no better purpose than to indicate to Beauregard the direction of McDowell's anticipated attack. Johnston was ordered to reinforce Beauregard at once. Theophilus Hunter Holmes, West Point '29 (he had been a classmate of Jefferson Davis's) and a veteran of the Seminole and Mexican wars, who was stationed with a Confederate division at Aquia Landing in the Potomac, was also ordered to reinforce Beauregard. Patterson, in disregard of his orders, withdrew from Johnston's front toward Harpers Ferry, thus permitting Johnston to hasten to Beauregard's support. Johnston marched his men to the railroad head at Leesburg, loaded them on trains, and arrived at Manassas Junction twenty-four hours later. McDowell had still not attacked.

On Sunday, July 21, the Union commander began his movements. The attack had, of course, lost any element of surprise. The soldiers, who had started out in high spirits from Washington four days earlier—many of them, it was said, carrying ropes with which to tie up captured rebels—were beginning to experience the strains and stresses, the discomforts and confusions that accompany campaigning: heat, mosquitoes, dust, uncertain and unappetizing rations, breakdowns in supply lines, conflicting orders, and sleepless nights.

Yet a carnival spirit still prevailed. Parties of fashionable Washingtonians rode out to witness the routing of the rebel forces. The carriages of politicians in a picnicking mood were interspersed with the army vehicles and troops that crowded the Centreville road.

McDowell, unaware that Johnston had evacuated his positions at Winchester, planned a classic envelopment of P. T. Beauregard's positions. The fourteen-mile-long march of the two Union divisions— led by David Hunter and Samuel P. Heintzelman—to the Confederate left was observed by Beauregard from high ground, and dispositions were made to meet it. Nonetheless, the initial Union attack at the so-called Stone Bridge, made with gallant spirit, drove back the Confederate defenders in disorder as far as the Henry House Hill, where Thomas Jackson, a furious and commanding figure, rallied the demoralized Confederates and stood, as someone called out, like a stone wall in the path of the oncoming Yankees. Now the tide of battle began to turn. L. Kirby Smith arrived with his rebel brigade from the valley. The Union right, overextended, was vulnerable to counterattack. Two Union batteries that had inflicted heavy casualties on the Confederate left were driven from their positions by J. E. B. Stuart's cavalry. McDowell ordered a retreat, the most demanding of military maneuvers. It began in good order, but suddenly panic swept the green troops. Whole units disintegrated in headlong flight, often led by their officers. Soon the Centreville road was a turbulent stream of fleeing soldiers mixed with civilian spectators, an indescribable scene of disorder.

For the Confederates, as for the Yankees, the battle was their baptism of fire and the scene of innumerable small but poignant dramas. The Virginia officer William Blackford, advancing with his cavalry regiment, saw a friend sitting by the road. When he asked him what the matter was, the man replied that he was wounded and dying. "He said it very cheerfully and did not look as if anything was the matter," Blackford noted, but when they returned an hour later, his friend was dead. Riding over the field after the battle, Blackford noticed among the dead Yankees "an old baby-doll with only one leg . . . just as it dropped from his pocket when he fell. . . ." He dismounted, picked the doll up, and stuffed it into the dead man's shirt.

Among those who had gone out to watch the anticipated victory was Frederick Law Olmsted, the famous landscape architect, who reported to George Templeton Strong that of the soldiers straggling back to Washington "some appeared ferocious, others only sick and dejected, all excessively weak, hungry, and selfish. There was no apparent organization. . . ." The main road was littered not just with abandoned muskets and knapsacks but with picnic baskets of delicacies and ladies' shawls and bonnets abandoned in the wild flight.

William Tecumseh Sherman recalled vividly years later the fearful confusion of the battle, "when for the first time in my life I saw cannon balls strike men and crash through the trees and saplings above and around us, and realized the always sickening confusion as one approaches a fight from the rear; then the night-march from Centreville . . . standing for hours wondering what was meant . . . the terrible scare of a poor negro who was caught between our lines; the crossing of Bull Run, and the fear lest we should be fired on by our own men. . . ."

The Confederate units were too exhausted and undisciplined to make an effective pursuit. They stopped to collect the articles thrown away by the fleeing Yankees.

Until panic descended upon them, the Union soldiers had more than matched their opponents. On the Union side 28,452 men were engaged, of whom 2,645 were casualties—418 killed, 1,011 wounded, 1,216 missing. On the rebel side 32,232 soldiers were engaged (almost 4,000 more than on the Union side). Rebel losses were estimated at 387 killed, 1,582 wounded, 12 missing. Russell, the supercilious correspondent of the *London Times,* noted that the Union army "ran away just as its victory had been assured by the superior cowardice of the South." Russell, George Templeton Strong noted wryly, had "headed the race."

But these, for the Union, somewhat reassuring statistics were not, of course, immediately available. All that was evident was that the Union army, believed to be greatly superior in numbers to the enemy, had suffered a shocking defeat. For more than twenty-four hours weary soldiers filed into Washington, giving that city the appearance of a refugee camp. Walt Whitman watched them pour over the Long Bridge in a drizzling rain and noted "the dust, the grime and smoke, in layers, follow'd by other layers again sweated in, absorbed by those excited souls—their clothes all saturated with the clay-powder filling the air—stirr'd up everywhere on the dry roads and trodden fields . . . all the men with this coating of murk and sweat and rain, now recoiling back . . . a horrible march of twenty miles, returning to Washington baffled, humiliated, panic-struck. . . . They come in disorderly mobs, some in squads, stragglers, companies. Occasionally, a rare regiment in perfect order, with its officers (some gaps, dead, the true braves,) marching in silence, with lowering faces, stern, weary to sinking, all black and dirty, but every man with his musket, and stepping alive. . . . The side-walks of Pennsylvania avenue, Fourteenth street, etc., crowded, jamm'd with citizens, darkies, clerks, everybody, lookers-on. . . . During the forenoon Washington gets all over motley with these defeated soldiers—queer-looking objects, strange eyes and faces, drench'd . . . and fearfully worn, hungry, haggard, blister'd in the feet." Some citizens, conspicuous among them two elderly sisters, with tears streaming down their faces, set up little stands and dispensed hot food to the weary men as long as it lasted. Exhausted soldiers slept on the steps of houses, on sidewalks, in vacant lots. "Some clutch their muskets firmly even in sleep. Some in squads; comrades, brothers, close together—and on them, as they lie, sulkily drips the rain. Meantime in Washington, among the great persons and their entourage, a mixture of awful consternation, uncertainty, rage, shame, helplessness, and stupefying disappointment. The worst is not only imminent, but already here. . . . The dreams of humanity, the vaunted Union we thought so strong, so impregnable—lo! it seems already smash'd like a china plate. One bitter, bitter hour—perhaps proud America will never again know such an hour. . . . But the hour, the day, the night pass'd, and whatever returns, an hour, a day, a night like that can never again return." Whitman saw mobs of officers in Willard's Hotel and wrote indignantly: "There you are, shoulder-straps!—but where are your companies? where are your men? Incompetents! never tell me of chances of battle, of getting stray'd and the like. I think this is your work, this retreat, after all. Sneak, blow, put on airs there in Willard's sumptuous parlors and bar-rooms, or anywhere—no explanation shall save you. Bull Run is your work; had you been half or one-tenth worthy your men, this would never have happen'd."

Lincoln, after the first shock, began to gather up the reins of government once again. "If there were nothing else of Abraham Lincoln for history to stamp him with," Whitman wrote later, "it is enough to send him with his wreath to the memory of all future time, that he endured that hour, that day, bitterer than gall—indeed a crucifixion day—that it did not conquer him—that he unflinchingly stemm'd it, and resolv'd to lift himself and the Union out of it."

All over the North the news of Bull Run was received with shock and dismay. In Boston there was initially a hushed and uneasy air about the city. "A few crowds lingered about the telegraph offices and the newspaper buildings, long closed, and those composing them stood in small knots, talking in subdued tones, and circulating the most awful rumors as to the dead and missing. Nervous excitement was the feature of the night. . . ." George Templeton Strong reacted to the news of Bull Run by calling the day "BLACK MONDAY." "We are utterly and disgracefully routed, beaten, whipped by secessionists. . . . Only one great fact stands out unmistakably: total defeat and national disaster on the largest scale." But a few days later Strong was taking comfort in the fact that the setback at Bull Run would introduce a new note of reality into Northern thinking about the nature and duration of the conflict.

Strong visited McDowell after Bull Run and reported that he could talk of nothing else. He blamed Benjamin Butler and Robert Patterson for not bringing up reinforcements at the critical point in the battle. Strong returned from Washington "depressed and despondent." He had lost faith in the volunteer system, "with its elected colonels and its political major-generals. We are fighting at a sore disadvantage. The men have lost faith in their officers, and no wonder, when so many officers set the example of running away. Of the first three hundred fugitives that crossed the Long Bridge, two hundred had commissions. Two colonels were seen fleeing on the same horse. Several regiments were left without field officers and without a company officer that knew anything beyond company drill." Strong was convinced that the North had to be as remorseless as the South was reputed to be. "We have got to tune ourselves up to the same pitch," he wrote, "hang rebels, arm their niggers, burn their towns, expel all sympathizers with treason that infest our borders. . . ." Many soldiers were mutinous. "We have not yet sounded all the depths of disaster and disgrace," Strong added. "The government seems limp and nerveless and unequal to the crisis."

The usual stories of atrocities circulated, and as is generally the case, a number of them proved to be true. It was reported that when an army surgeon left thirty wounded officers and men for a few minutes to go for medical supplies, he returned to find that they all had been bayoneted by Confederate soldiers in his absence. Two wounded soldiers from a Michigan regiment told Strong, who talked to them in a Georgetown hospital, that they had seen rebel soldiers cut the throats of wounded Yankees.

After the battle Charles Francis Adams, Jr., wrote his father that he was convinced that the "ultimate independence" of the South was "assured." The defeat had had the effect of throwing "the war into the hands of the radicals, and if it lasts a year, it will be a war of abolition," he added, somewhat contradictorily. When Henry Adams received his brother's account of Bull Run, he became impatient to return to the United States to enlist in the army. "Unpursued, untouched, without once having even crossed bayonets with the enemy, we have run and saved our precious carcasses from a danger which did not exist. Our flag, what has become of it? Who will respect it? What can we ever say after this? . . . If we must be beaten, and it looks now as though that must ultimately be the case, I want to do all I can not to be included among those who ran away."

The senior Adams's reaction was a more temperate one. "We have now gone through three stages of this great political disease," he wrote his son Charles. "The first was the cold fit, when it seemed as if nothing would start the country. The second was the hot one, when it seemed almost in the highest continual delirium. The third is the process of waking to the awful reality before it."

When word of the Battle of Bull Run reached Madrid, "like a bolt of lightning from a clear sky," Carl Schurz and the members of the American Legation were plunged into gloom. Most humiliating of all, the fighting qualities of the Union soldiers became the subject of jests in newspapers and cafés. One of the favorite quips was that the battle should be called the Battle of "Patassas" (of the feet) rather than Manassas (of the hands). Whenever Schurz saw a Spaniard smile, he had the paranoid feeling that he was smiling over the cowardice of Union soldiers at Bull Run.

To Southerners the outcome of the Battle of Bull Run was simply a confirmation of their belief that the Yankees were inherent cowards. There were innumerable stories of Yankee panic or dim-wittedness. A weary Union straggler who asked at a plantation house for a glass of brandy rejected it on second thought on the ground that it might be poisoned. His indignant hostess replied, "Sir, I am a Virginia woman. Do you think I would be as base as that? Here Bill, Tom [to two slaves] disarm this man. He is our prisoner." Another soldier was drinking at the well, and a slave girl came up to him and said, "You go in and see Missis." The girl followed him and announced, "Look here, Missis, I got a prisoner, too!" Southerners were especially cheered to hear that the Virginia cavalry found Winfield Scott's "carriage & six horses, with his sword and epaulettes, his table set with silver, champagne, wines and all sorts of delicacies, to celebrate their *intended* victory." Best news of all was the fact that William Tecumseh Sherman's battery of artillery had been captured by a bayonet charge, a charge which General Beauregard, Charleston's special hero, had reportedly declared to be "the greatest the world had ever seen."

The outcome of the battle, far more precarious than was generally realized in the euphoria of victory (Emma Holmes's triumphant entry in her diary that "Every Southerner was a hero on that battlefield" was, in fact, far from the truth), strengthened the South in its conviction that it would win its independence.

Hailed in the South as a great Confederate triumph, the battle brought with it a long and doleful roster of the maimed and killed. Colonel Barlow, a close friend of the Chesnuts', was among the dead, and a military funeral was held for him in Richmond. "The empty saddle and the led war-horse" were grim reminders of the real nature of war. "We saw and heard it all," Mary Chesnut wrote, "and now it seems we are never out of the sound of the Dead March in Saul. It comes and it comes, until I feel inclined to close my ears and scream."

A few Southerners made a more realistic appraisal of the battle's significance. William Trescot, who had been assistant secretary of state in Buchanan's administration, told Mary Chesnut "the victory will be our ruin. It lulls us into a fool's paradise of conceit at our superior valor, and the shameful farce of their flight will wake every inch of their manhood. It was the very fillip they needed."

Certainly the effects of the battle were almost incalculable. Bull Run, while no model of strategy or tactics, belongs in any inventory of the world's most important military engagements. First and most important, it brought the North closer to facing the difficulties that lay ahead in subduing the South. Lincoln and his Cabinet abandoned all notions of three-month enlistments and began to enlist volunteers for three years. The whole scale of the war effort was vastly expanded, and a host of measures adopted in anticipation of a struggle that might extend for a year, or even more, before victory would rest on Union arms.

By the same token, Bull Run encouraged the antiwar Democrats to renewed activity. It was one thing publicly to oppose a war destined to last no more than a few months; it was something very different to oppose a conflict the end of which could not be anticipated.

More dangerous to the Northern cause, Bull Run, by making it clear that the war would be protracted and by placing its eventual outcome in doubt, encouraged the major European powers, particularly England and France, to give covert, and to contemplate seriously giving overt, aid to the South with which the sympathies of their ruling classes plainly rested.

Another important subsidiary effect of Bull Run was to focus the attention of the government, of Lincoln and his Cabinet, of Congress, and of the people of the North in general on the theater of operations in northern Virginia, if not to the exclusion of all other theaters of the war, at least to their decided detriment. This distortion, by placing extraordinarily high stakes on the one Confederate army with clearly superior generalship, made the Union armies appear, in the view of the world, at a conspicuous disadvantage. By opting to test the issue most dramatically in northern Virginia, almost in sight of the Capitol, the North gave a kind of symbolic importance to everything of a military nature that happened there. Every failure was greatly magnified, and the successes elsewhere were minimized or obscured. The notion that the defeat of Lee's army and the capture of Richmond must bring the war to a speedy end possessed the nation and obsessed Lincoln and the general staff. The fact was, as we shall see, that the obsession with defeating Lee prolonged the war, while Lee's victories encouraged the South to believe that it must eventually triumph. The concentration of Union troops and resources on this single objective gave every advantage to Lee and his generals. They fought again and again over terrain as familiar as the palms of their hands. They fought in an essentially defensive mood in which the superiority of the defense over attack was strikingly accentuated, and Lee's brilliance in directing the construction of hasty field fortifications had its maximum effect. One Union general after another appeared to contest the field with Lee, with the result that the Army of the Potomac failed to develop the experienced command staff accustomed to working with each other that is so essential to successful military operations.

The end was thus anticipated in the beginning. The inordinate attention given to defeating Lee under conditions invariably favorable to the Army of Northern Virginia put everything at hazard. Like a gambler who sticks with a "lucky" number while his stake dwindles away, the North kept betting on a series of doomed generals.

George Templeton Strong was appointed to the National Hymn Commission with the task of choosing an appropriate song. The commission had failed to discover a "national hymn" in the piles of "rubbish" submitted for that honor, but in the fall of 1861, with the shock of Bull Run somewhat dissipated, Julia Ward and Samuel Gridley Howe rode out with friends to watch a review of the Union army at Munson's Hill, Virginia. The carriage carrying the Howes and friends of theirs back to Washington was slowed in its progress by soldiers on leave or units whose term of service had expired, marching back to the capital. The Howes and their friends began singing hymns and songs, including "John Brown's Body lies a-moldering in the grave." The soldiers joined in the familiar words. James Freeman Clarke urged Julia to write "some good words for that stirring tune." She woke at daybreak the next morning, and, as she recalled the moment, "as I lay waiting for the dawn, the long lines of the desired poem began to twine themselves in my mind." She got out of bed "and found in the dimness an old stump of pen. . . . I scrawled the verses almost without looking at the paper. . . . Having completed my writing I returned to the bed and fell asleep, saying to myself, 'I like this better than most things I have written.' " What she had written began with the lines:

> Mine eyes have seen the glory of the coming of the Lord;
> He is trampling out the vintage where the grapes of wrath are stored. . . .

The Union had its "national hymn" at last. Julia Howe submitted the verses to the *Atlantic Monthly*'s editor, James Fields, with a peremptory note: "Fields! Do you want this, and do you like it. . . . ? I am sad and spleeny, and begin to have fears that I may not be after all, the greatest woman alive." The magazine paid her five dollars for it. She had given perfect expression to the mixture of piety and patriotic fervor so characteristic of those fighting to preserve the Union.

8

Wilson's Creek

The most prominent casualty of Bull Run was Irvin McDowell, who was superseded by George McClellan and relegated to the role of division commander. McClellan was given command of the Army of the Potomac with the charge of rebuilding that shattered and demoralized organization into an effective fighting force and completing the task that McDowell had undertaken.

McClellan was thirty-six. He had been a boy wonder. His shortcomings were those of an extremely egotistical young man who compensated for his below-average height by natty dressing and an aggressive, if not flamboyant, style. "People came from afar to see him at the head of a brilliant staff," Carl Schurz wrote, "to which princes and counts from abroad were attached, galloping from camp to camp, and holding reviews and inspections. He was the 'young Napoleon,' the pet of the nation. The soldiers adored him, and the commanding officers were attached to him with warm personal devotion." Included in McClellan's staff were the comte de Paris, "tall and handsome," and his brother, the duc de Chartres, "taller, thinner, less handsome," but "remarkably cordial and affable," in the words of Ben: Perley Poore.

Joseph Griner of the Philadelphia Light Guards was one of the soldiers in McClellan's command ready to worship "Little Mac." When the general's birthday was celebrated by his army, Griner wrote ecstatically to his mother: "Patriotic songs was sung by officers as well as privates and all seemed to enjoy the sport . . . the fireworks in the city looked splendid. It was a sight once seen not soon to be forgotten. To see all those grim visaged soldiers standing around a great fire, their breasts swelling with patriotism, cheering for their gallant leader till the very hills seemed to echo back the sound of rejoicing."

Charles Francis Adams wrote to his father that "McClellan has the complete confidence of the people, government securities are rising, money is plenty, and finally the indications are strong that the confederates are being ground to atoms by the very weight of their defensive preparations." It was quite another matter in England, where Charles Francis Adams, Sr., found himself in troubled waters. Earl Russell indicated that the British government intended to take no stand in the contest between the Union and the Confederacy. This, of course, was tantamount to recognizing the legitimacy of Jefferson Davis's government and simply treating the two sections of the country as warring nations rather than accepting the Union position that the South was in rebellion against the legitimate government of the United States. Adams turned his very considerable powers of argumentation on Russell and then, to emphasize his point, broke off further negotiations. The Southern "victory" at Bull Run, or rather the Northern failure to achieve a victory, had caused the current of British opinion, at least in government circles, to run strongly in the direction of the South. Indeed, every month that passed without the Union's asserting decisive military superiority over the South, thereby promising a speedy termination to the war, increased the chances of British meddling in ways dangerous and potentially disastrous to the North. Adams's confrontation with Russell perhaps came at the last moment that Seward and Lincoln still had some leverage left. Adams's hand was fortuitously strengthened by the capture of dispatches from the British consul at Charleston to Russell which "very gravely compromised the British Government" by suggesting active support for the Confederacy.

While McClellan began the task of rebuilding the Army of the Potomac with obvious relish, important military events took place offstage, so to speak, in Missouri. That border state was bitterly divided between pro- and anti-Unionists, and the Confederates were determined to try to secure the state, thereby threatening the whole upper Mississippi Valley.

By the end of July a Confederate force made up of some 10,000 militiamen and volunteers from Missouri, Arkansas, and Louisiana had assembled at the southwest corner of the state with the intention of routing the scattered Federal forces and joining with the secessionist governor, Claiborne Jackson.

Missouri was part of the Union army's Western Department under the command of John Charles Frémont, explorer and ex-presidential candidate. That was Montgomery Blair's doing. Blair was Frémont's principal advocate in the Cabinet. He had insisted that Frémont "must at once be given large and important military command . . . predicting that the genius and energy of this remarkable man would soon astonish the country."

Carl Schurz described Frémont as "a man of middle stature, elegant build, muscular and elastic, dark hair and beard lightly streaked with grey, a broad forehead, a keen eye, fine regular features. . . . His manners seemed perfectly natural, easy, and unaffected, without any attempt at posing. His conversation, carried on in a low, gentle tone of voice, had a suggestion of reticence and reserve in it but not enough to cause a suspicion of insincerity. The whole personality appeared quite attractive—and yet, one did not feel quite sure." Schurz's doubts were well founded. Frémont soon proved a notably inept administrator. Responsibility for checking the Confederate forces devolved on Nathaniel Lyon, a graduate of West Point, class of '41, an ardent Republican, and an ally of the powerful Blair clan. It was Lyon, who, with Frank Blair's encouragement and a small contingent of Union volunteers, had taken charge of the Federal arsenal at St. Louis and prevented it from falling into the hands of the secessionists. As hotheaded as his red hair proclaimed him, Lyon showed a remarkable talent for recruiting and leading volunteer soldiers. It was well known that he hated slavery or any kind of brutality. The story was told of his dismounting and kicking a private he saw beating a dog and then making the man kneel down and apologize to the canine.

Lyon's small force was augmented by Iowans and by a regiment of Missouri Germans recruited and led by Franz Sigel, a veteran of the German Revolution of 1848. A battalion of regulars commanded by Colonel Thomas William Sweeney, a one-armed veteran of the Mexican War, completed the force available to Lyon.

Lyon had seized Camp Jackson at St. Louis a few weeks after Sumter while William Tecumseh Sherman and Ulysses S. Grant watched. In the march through the city an angry crowd had pelted the Union force with stones and sticks, and in the fighting that followed twenty-eight people, one an infant, were killed, and many more wounded. Sherman joined the rush to escape the fire of the soldiers. When word that Lyon had seized the arsenal reached Jefferson City, where the legislature, dominated by Southern sympathizers, was in session, the members, armed to the teeth with pistols and bowie knives, authorized the governor to borrow $1 million to equip a state army. Lyon and the governor thereupon conferred. Governor Jackson promised that if the Federal forces were withdrawn, the state would remain neutral. After several hours of negotiation Lyon declared belligerently: "Rather than concede to the State of Missouri for one single instant the right to dictate to my Government in any manner however unimportant, I will see you and you and you"—indicating each man in the room—"and every man, woman and child in the State, dead and buried. . . . This means war."

Jackson returned to Jefferson City and issued a proclamation calling for 50,000 volunteers, and Lyon made plans to seize the state capital, moving his men up the Missouri River by steamboat. To carry out his plan, it was necessary to round up some experienced pilots. Sam Clemens, who had come to St. Louis to renew his pilot's license, was apprehended and told he would have to pilot one of the boats. He protested that he was a Mississippi, not a Missouri, River pilot, and when his protests were ignored, he slipped away, returned to Hannibal, and joined a "regiment" of guerrilla fighters armed with squirrel rifles and pledged to repel any "Dutch"—i.e., German—invaders from St. Louis. After a few weeks of playing soldier, Clemens and his brother, who had been appointed secretary of Nevada Territory, started off by stage for Carson City, glad to leave the bitterly divided state behind them.

When Lyon and his steamboat flotilla reached Jefferson City, he found it abandoned. Lyon pushed on to Boonville, where Governor Jackson, his nephew John Sappington Marmaduke, and a small militia force barred their way. After a brief skirmish the Missouri militia decamped.

Major Samuel Sturgis was at Fort Leavenworth with a battalion of cavalry and two regiments of Kansas volunteers. Soon they were joined by a regiment of Iowans. Lyon's polyglot force, consisting of 2,350 men, 250 of whom were regulars, followed on Jackson's heels as he moved southeast to make contact with a Confederate force. Sigel's force was sent on ahead.

Franz Sigel was called Professor and ridiculed as "the little fellow in spectacles" who "kept looking around like a weasel," but he was an excellent officer, experienced and tough, who had the complete loyalty of his German soldiers. When he came up with Jackson, the governor was in at least nominal charge of a body of some 4,000 men, including legislators, state officers, militia volunteers, and a United States Senator, along with the official records of the state. Outnumbered three or four to one, Sigel and the Germans attacked. When Sigel's baggage was threatened by Jackson's cavalry, the German officer withdrew, covering his movement with artillery fire, extricating his entire command with the loss of 13 killed and 31 wounded.

When word reached Lyon that Sigel and his Germans had engaged Jackson and needed help, Lyon gave the job to the Iowans, tough young farm boys, and they, discarding their tents, mess kits, and, some said, even their Bibles, set out to reinforce Sigel. Watching them, Lyon exclaimed: "What marching legs! Lord God, see them go. [Watch] the damned Iowa greyhounds and their Happy Land of Canaan." The "Iowa greyhounds" marched forty-eight miles in twenty-four hours, a record not even Stonewall Jackson's "foot cavalry" could match. Private Bill Heustis cheered them up by exclaiming, "I wish I'd stayed at home and sent my big brother," and they sang:

> The time of retribution am a-coming,
> > For with bayonet and shell
> We will give the rebels hell;
> > And they'll never see the Happy Land of Canaan.

Sigel and Lyon joined forces in Springfield and prepared to do battle with Jackson. At Carthage, Claiborne Jackson's contingent was augmented by the Pelican Rifles, a Louisiana regiment in handsome uniforms; by a regiment of Texans commanded by the dashing Ben McCulloch, attired in velvet and carrying an elaborately engraved rifle; and by a brigade of Arkansas volunteers, nicknamed the Butternut Boys. Many of the men were experienced Indian fighters. To this force Jackson added 6,000 of Gideon Pillow's force detached from the defense of the Cumberland River. M. Jeff Thompson, ex-mayor of St. Joseph, commanded his "muskrats," exhorting them: "I understand you want to fight. By God! You shall have it. I am a ripsquealer and my name is fight." William Quantrill of Kansas infamy was with the rebel army, along with Frank James and Coleman Younger.

At Springfield Lyon had some 7,000 men, many of them three-month volunteers whose terms were about to expire, to oppose almost twice that number. Unaware that Jackson had received substantial reinforcements, Lyon decided to attack before his small army evaporated and left the state exposed to Jackson's force. Lyon left Springfield and headed for the rebel force, now under the command of McCulloch, encamped near Wilson's Creek. Having made contact and discovering the enemy far too strong to attack, Lyon began to move back, searching for a place to make a stand against the superior rebel forces. During Lyon's withdrawal an understrength company of Union cavalry—regulars—charged into a column of Senator James E. Rains's Missourians, 1,500 strong, and scattered them in headlong flight. In the delay occasioned by the attack Lyon regained Springfield.

The rebels camped for a distance of three miles along Wilson's Creek, confident that their superior numbers made them immune to attack. At Springfield Lyon learned of the Union defeat at Bull Run. There was no sign of the supplies or reinforcements he had requested from Frémont. It seemed to Lyon that further withdrawal would only expose his little force to piecemeal destruction, not to mention attrition by the expiration of enlistments. Springfield, his officers agreed, was indefensible. The only alternative seemed to be to attack, a notion that dismayed most of the officers but not the irrepressible Sweeney, who flipped his empty sleeve defiantly and declared, "Let us eat the last bit of mule flesh and fire the last cartridge before we think of retreating." The plan was to dispatch Sigel under the cover of darkness with 1,500 men and six guns to strike at McCulloch's left at dawn, while Lyon led the remainder of his force—some 3,500—against McCulloch's front lines along Wilson's Creek. Meanwhile, unbeknownst to Lyon, McCulloch was making plans for a march against Springfield. Lyon went from unit to unit, addressing the uneasy soldiers: "Men, we are going to have a fight. We will march out in a short time. Don't shoot until you get orders. Fire low—don't aim higher than their knees; wait until they get close; don't get scared; it's no part of a soldier's duty to get scared." In the company of Union soldiers moving quietly through the warm summer night dampened by intermittent rain was Wild Bill Hickok in high-heeled boots. A few weeks earlier he had killed the three-man McCanles gang.

At dawn on August 10 Lyon's little army surprised the rebels in their tents. In the bitter fighting that followed, Sigel was initially successful in driving in McCulloch's left, but one of his German companies stopped to loot. Seeing a column approaching, Sigel took it to be Iowans, and before he realized his mistake, the men with him were killed or captured and he barely escaped alive.

McCulloch, counterattacking, was twice driven back. A third Confederate attack gained the high ground from which the Union soldiers had poured a galling fire into the rebel camp. Lyon, seriously wounded, called for his reserve, the 1st Iowans, to restore the line and the men came forward resolutely under heavy fire. But they refused the order to make a bayonet charge, and Major John McAllister Schofield, Lyon's aide, found the general dead on the battlefield, a bullet through his heart. With Colonel Sweeney wounded and Sigel routed, the command devolved on Major Sturgis. For an hour the two lines poured fire into each other's ranks, too weakened by their losses and by exhaustion to press the battle to a conclusion. Finally, the rebels withdrew, but Schofield, riding up to the crest of the hill, saw them being formed up for what was apparently to be a fourth attack. Once more the rebels came on, and once more they were driven back with fearful casualties on both sides. Sturgis, considering his exhausted men, without food since the night before, with their ammunition almost gone, and still greatly outnumbered, ordered a retreat. Schofield was convinced that if the weary men had simply held their ground, the victory would have been theirs. William Tecumseh Sherman was convinced that if Lyon had lived, the Union forces would have carried the day and Missouri would have been secured beyond question for the Union.

The toll of dead and wounded on both sides made Wilson's Creek one of the bloodiest battles of a bloody war. Out of a Union force of scarcely 5,000, 1,317 were killed, wounded, or missing. The rebel losses were 1,230. Regiments that bore the brunt of the fighting lost a third or more of their number. Of 64 men in F Company of the 2nd Kansas, only 24 escaped death or injury. Of those engaged 23 percent were casualties, contrasted with Bull Run, where fewer than 10 percent were lost. Of the Union officers involved 7 would win major general's stars and 23 become brigadier generals, an astonishing statistic.

What was left of Lyon's army retreated to Rolla and thence to Jefferson City. McCulloch occupied Springfield, but his badly battered force was in no condition to carry out the campaign intended to sweep

Missouri into the Confederate fold. If Lyon's death robbed his little army of the fruits of its extraordinary fight against a force outnumbering it two to one, there can be no question that his energy and courage prevented the state from going by default to the rebels, and his brief but spectacular career established him as one of the most brilliant officers of the war.

Equally striking was the fact that Wilson's Creek received little attention in the East. For many Americans Missouri and what happened in Missouri were as irrelevant to the real fortunes of war as if they had transpired on the continent of Asia.

If Frémont was unable to exercise effective command over the Military District of Missouri, he showed an unusual capacity for insubordination. On August 30 he declared martial law in the state and proclaimed that the slaves of all those citizens engaged in rebellion were freed. The proclamation made Frémont an instant hero to the abolitionists and Radical Republicans, and when Lincoln requested him to recall or modify his edict, Frémont refused. The President then rescinded Frémont's proclamation and dispatched Montgomery Blair and General David Hunter, a friend of Frémont's well known for his antislavery sentiments, to try to prevail on him to mind his military p's and q's. Jessie Frémont, meanwhile, hurried to Washington for an angry and tearful interview with the President. To have fired Frémont would have made him a martyr for the Radical Republicans, a destiny Frémont plainly courted.

When Simon Cameron, acting on Lincoln's orders, instructed a still-recalcitrant Frémont to turn over his command to Hunter, Frémont pleaded for a reprieve and then instructed his personal guard not to allow any presidential courier to deliver an order to him to yield his command. A courier, disguised as a farmer, finally served the "summons" on Frémont. Reluctantly he yielded his command to Henry Halleck.

9

Grant Appears

While McClellan was playing with his marvelous toy, the Army of the Potomac, parading, playing host to visiting dignitaries, and, some cynics suggested, indulging his own strategic notions, another engagement that attracted no more attention than Wilson's Creek took place along the Mississippi near Corinth. The Union officer involved was a short, rumpled, reddish-haired man with a passion for horses, Hiram Ulysses Grant. Grant's father, Jesse, had been a farmer and a tanner in Point Pleasant, Ohio, a noisy, blustering man. Named after his maternal grandfather (the Ulysses, in his father's words, after "the great Grecian general who defeated the Trojans by the strategy of the wooden horse"), Lyss Grant, as little more than an infant, showed a fascination for horses that grew into a lifelong obsession. Young Grant was an active, vigorous boy who loved skating, sledding, hunting, and all the outdoor sports and showed some promise as a student, reading a life of Washington at the age of six, according to his father's recollection. Shy and quiet, he had a kind of sober dignity, unusual in a child his age, and it was only as a breaker of intractable horses that he caught the attention of the townspeople as he grew to manhood. When it came time for Grant to consider what his career might be, he made it plain to his father that he had no interest in being a tanner. The notion of being a farmer or a trader on the Mississippi appealed to him, but his pious, teetotaling father urged him to try to get an appointment to West Point. To graduate from the Point did not necessarily mean a military career. Out of more than 1,000 graduates of the academy, only some 400 had remained in the army. Grant consented with no particular enthusiasm and got an appointment when an Ohio friend who held the appointment from that state was forced to leave for disciplinary reasons and Grant was given the vacant place. On his arrival at West Point he found that he was listed as Ulysses S. Grant on the admission rolls, and rather than contend with the admitting officer, he accepted the alteration in his name and let the S stand for Simpson, the name of his maternal grandparents.

At the Point, Grant was plainly a misfit. Awkward off a horse, below average height, with noticeably small hands and feet, he had little in common with the dashing young Southern cadets or the predominately upper-class scions of prominent Northern families. When his name appeared on rosters as U. S. Grant, his classmates entertained themselves by calling him United States Grant and Uncle Sam. One of his fellow cadets, with an odd name of his own, William Tecumseh Sherman—who always signed himself discreetly W. T. Sherman, though he was called Cump—declared years later: "A more unpromising boy never entered the Military Academy."

At drill Grant had a shuffling, behind-the-plow country boy's walk, tilted slightly forward, which made him the despair of his drill sergeants; he was "a clumsy, slow gaited, heavy footed lad," a classmate recalled. The fact that Grant, small as he was, was ready to stand up to any of his larger classmates won grudging respect for him and gave rise to the apparently apocryphal story that he had whipped a much larger classmate and then offered to take on the whole company one at a time, which action, it was said, gave him the new nickname of Company Grant.

Bill Sherman was an upperclassman, tall, slender, slightly simian, always ready for some adventure, famous for his wit and sharp tongue. George Thomas, at twenty-four one of the oldest cadets in the class of 1840, was called Old Tom by Sherman and George Washington by Rosey Rosecrans because of Thomas's dignified, formal, old-fashioned Southern manners. Old Tom, an antislavery Southerner, had defied the law by teaching his father's slaves to read and write.

Grant himself was an adequate, if undistinguished, cadet, demerited primarily for perpetual untidiness. When he was a junior, the entering freshman class had two conspicuous members: fifteen-year-old George B. McClellan, whose family was prominent in Philadelphia society, and nineteen-year-old Thomas Jackson from the hill country of western Virginia. McClellan, strikingly handsome and academically brilliant, had to have the rules bent to admit him to the academy because of his youth. Jackson, wearing homespun clothes and a hillman's rough wool hat, carried most of his possessions in sweat-stained saddlebags. An inquisitive cadet discovered that Old Jack, as he was soon called, "had been to a common school, knew a little grammar, could add up a column of figures, but as to vulgar or decimal fractions, it is doubtful if he had ever heard of them." Clearly not the kind of material out of which to fashion an officer and a gentleman. The odd, reserved Jackson, for his part, noted in his copybook: "It is not desirable to have a large number of intimate friends." He need not have concerned himself.

When Grant was graduated in 1843, he ranked twenty-first in a class of thirty-nine fledgling officers, but at least he had survived. Seventy-three cadets had entered with him. His ambition was to return to the Point as an instructor in mathematics, but that was not to be. Instead, he found himself in the Mexican War, a conflict he despised. "I do not think," he wrote later, "that there was ever a more wicked war than that waged by the United States on Mexico. I thought so at the time . . . only I had not the moral courage to resign: I had taken an oath to serve eight years unless sooner discharged and I considered my supreme duty was to the flag. I had a horror of the Mexican War, and I have always believed that on our part it was most unjust." To the United States Mexico was simply an empire "of incalculable value," coveted by its more powerful neighbor. "The Southern rebellion," Grant wrote, "was largely the outgrowth of the Mexican War. We got our punishment in the most sanguinary and expensive war of modern times."

Nonetheless, Grant was in every major battle of the war with the exception of Buena Vista and ended up a captain. In August, 1848, he married Julia Dent, daughter of a prominent citizen of St. Louis. A series of assignments to remote army posts followed; Grant was often separated from his wife and soon from a small child, Jesse. Although he belonged to the Sons of Temperance, Grant was lonely and unhappy with army life, and he began to drink heavily, a common disposition in army officers similarly placed. Eventually, his command-ing officer insisted that he resign or stand court-martial. Grant resigned and found himself a few weeks later broke and hung-over in a cheap San Francisco hotel—the What Cheer House—without enough money to get back to his family. A fellow officer lent him his fare to New York, and there, once more penniless, he borrowed money from a friend of his West Point days, Captain Simon Bolivar Buckner, to pay for his hotel room. Finally, with money wired by his father, he returned to St. Louis. On land given him by his father-in-law, Grant began hewing out a farm—Hardscrabble he called it wryly—and building a log cabin. To carry him over until the farm began to produce, Grant hauled wood. He was engaged in that occupation when he met Bill Sherman on the street in 1853. Sherman, like Grant out of the army, had recently folded up his banking operation in San Francisco and was now in partnership with his brother-in-law, Thomas Ewing, and engaged in various enterprises with the extensive McCook family.

Caught, like hundreds of thousands of other Americans in the Panic of 1857, Grant could not get enough for his crops to buy seed. Burdened with debt, he sold his team, wagon, and farm equipment and moved into St. Louis to go into the real estate business with a cousin of his wife's. Once again things went badly. By now the Grants had four children and seldom enough food to fill their stomachs. Finally, beaten but not whipped, Grant moved his family to Galena, Illinois, in April, 1860, and took a job as a clerk in his father's leather and hardware store. Grant was working in his father's store when Sumter fell. The next day he wrote his father-in-law, a Southern sympathizer: "The times are indeed startling; but now is the time, particularly in the border slave states, for men to prove their love of country . . . now all party distinctions should be lost sight of, and every true patriot be for maintaining the integrity of the glorious old Stars and Stripes, the Constitution and the Union. . . . I tell you there is no mistaking the feelings of the people. The Government can call into the field 75,000 troops and ten or twenty times 75,000 if it should be necessary. . . . It is all a mistake about the Northern pocket being so sensitive. In times like the present no people are more ready to give their own time or of their abundant means. No impartial man can conceal from himself the fact that in all these troubles the Southerners have been the aggressors. . . . In all this I cannot but see the doom of slavery," Grant added. "The Northerners do not want, nor will they want, to interfere with the institution." On the other hand, they would no longer "give it protection unless the South shall return soon to their allegiance. . . ." Cotton, Grant predicted, would be tied up by the war, thus stimulating its production in other parts of the world. "This will reduce the value of the negroes so much they will never be worth fighting over again."

Although Grant drilled the Galena volunteers, he was anxious to have a command of his own commensurate with his military training and experience. He went to Cincinnati and spent two days trying without success to get to see General McClellan, then in command of the Department of the Ohio. He made another effort with Nathaniel Lyon, a friend from West Point days, after Lyon took over Camp Jackson at St. Louis. Finally, when Grant was about to return to Galena, once more defeated, Governor Richard Yates summoned him and asked him to accept a commission as colonel of the 7th District Regiment, a group of volunteers so unruly that they had been nicknamed Governor Yates's Hellions. Uniformless, wearing an old felt hat, and carrying a tarnished sword, Grant took command on June 16, 1861, and marched his men to Quincy, Illinois, on the Mississippi, where he was assigned to guard the Hannibal & St. Joseph Railroad against Missouri guerrillas.

It was not much of a command for a West Pointer, many of whose contemporaries were, like McClellan, already generals, but it was certainly a step up from clerk in a Galena hardware store. At that point fate intervened. Lincoln, desperately in need of experienced officers for his burgeoning army, asked for names of Illinois candidates. Elihu Washburne, Congressman from the Galena district, sent in Grant's name, and a few days later a telegram arrived appointing him brigadier general of volunteers. Frémont assigned Grant to Cairo, where his responsibilities extended to southern Illinois and southeastern Missouri. A city of 30,000 at the critical juncture of the Ohio and Mississippi, Cairo was a point of departure for all Union efforts to open the upper Mississippi or to penetrate into the interior South by way of the Cumberland and Tennessee rivers. The city was also crucial in its relationship to Kentucky and Tennessee. The governor of Kentucky, like the governor of Missouri, was a secessionist, but the Kentucky legislature was Federal. Jefferson Davis dispatched General (formerly Bishop) Leonidas Polk to hold the state for the Confederacy, and Grant, hearing of the move, dispatched part of his command to Paducah, east of Cairo.

When the inefficient and insubordinate Frémont was relieved by Lincoln, Henry Halleck, a West Pointer and the outstanding military scholar of the army, took his place and soon demonstrated the differences between scholarship and action. Although Grant was definitely not Halleck's kind of textbook soldier, Halleck halfheartedly supported his aggressive probes of the area around Paducah, designed to keep Polk off-balance. Ordered to undertake operations designed to divert Polk while Confederate forces under M. Jeff Thompson were forced out of southwest Missouri, Grant began a movement of his forces down both banks of the Mississippi toward New Madrid on the west bank and Columbus on the east. Grant himself led a small force of 3,114 soldiers protected by gunboats toward the village of Belmont, Missouri, some nine miles south of Cairo. There, hearing that rebel soldiers were moving from Columbus toward the Missouri pocket, Grant decided to attack Belmont. He landed some three miles above the town and advanced with four and a half infantry regiments, two companies of cavalry, and a battery of six guns against six Confederate regiments in Belmont. The attack on November 7, 1861, against a superior force was successful after bitter fighting. The rebels were driven from their camp. "The moment the camp was reached our men laid down their arms and commenced rummaging to pick up trophies," Grant wrote. "Some of the higher officers were little better than the privates. They galloped about from one cluster of men to another and at every halt delivered a short eulogy upon the Union cause and the achievements of the command."

Polk, informed of the attack, ferried a detachment of 10,000 men across the river below Belmont, hoping to cut Grant off from his transports, but Grant extricated his force and even succeeded in carrying off six artillery pieces and a handful of prisoners. Grant himself narrowly escaped capture. Riding back alone to check on his rear guard, he was disconcerted to find it gone, decamped without orders. He realized his own danger as he saw Confederate soldiers advancing through a nearby cornfield. Dressed in a private's greatcoat, Grant managed to escape. When he got back to the landing, Andrew Foote's transports had finished loading the Union troops, and the last one was just pushing off as Grant appeared. Its captain ordered the engines reversed and a plank run out; Grant's horse slid down the bank and made its way across the narrow plank.

Union casualties were 607 out of 3,114 engaged, a heavy rate. The Confederates lost 642 out of some 4,000. At Belmont, Grant displayed those qualities that were to distinguish him as a commander—speed of movement, careful reconnaissance, close contact with all echelons of the troops under his command, the capacity for quick (and generally correct) decisions, an instinct for the particular vulnerability of his opponent, but, above all, aggressiveness, without which all other military talents are nugatory.

In the East the only episode to break the calm that hung over the Army of the Potomac and the Army of Northern Virginia was an abortive foray at Balls Bluff, Virginia, where on October 21 Edward Baker, orator, ex-Congressman, and friend of Lincoln's, a political general pure and simple, was authorized to make "a demonstration" against rebel units at the Poolesville Ford on the Potomac. In this unhappy fiasco, Baker's division was ambushed. Baker and 48 other Union soldiers were killed; 158 men, among them Captain Oliver Wendell Holmes, were wounded; and 714 were listed as captured or missing. Holmes was sure his end had come. "I felt and acted very cool and did my duty I am sure," he wrote his mother from his hospital bed. "I was out in front of our men encouraging 'em on when a spent shot knocked the wind out of me & I fell." Ordered to the rear, he was determined that such a minor blow should not render him *hors de combat* and rushed back to his company. He was waving his sword and calling on his men to follow him when his lungs were pierced by a bullet. His first thought was that the wound was fatal and that he must bleed to death, and he fumbled for a bottle of laudanum which he had carried with him to take if he was mortally wounded and the pain proved too much to bear. But a passing surgeon told him he had a good chance to survive, and he put the laudanum back for possible future use. Evacuated to a crude field hospital, he was visited by his dearest friend, Penrose Hallowell, who told him that half the company had been wounded, killed, or captured, "kissed me and went away again. . . ."

The debacle at Balls Bluff was a blow to Lincoln, already under fire for McClellan's inactivity. "This has been a heavy day," John Hay wrote in his diary at the news of the battle. McClellan's perpetual optimism was as hard to bear as his inaction. John Hay noted that during the course of a conversation with the general "it became painfully evident that he had no plan. . . ." Lincoln did his best to excuse McClellan's immobility. The "Jacobins," as Lincoln called them, were clamoring for action. While Lincoln "depreciated this . . . manifestation of public impatience," he pointed out that it was a political reality that must be taken into account. "At the same time, General," he told McClellan, "you must not fight until you are ready."

"I have everything at stake," McClellan replied; "if I fail, I will not see you again or anybody." It was not a reassuring response. "I have a notion to go out with you, and stand or fall with the battle," Lincoln said.

One of the problems that Lincoln had to deal with was the constant friction between Scott and McClellan. Finally, a week after Balls Bluff, Lincoln decided to accept Scott's resignation and appointed McClellan to Scott's post as commander-in-chief. "I should be perfectly satisfied," Lincoln told his dilatory general, "if I thought that this vast responsibility would not embarrass you." "It is a great relief, Sir! I feel as if several tons were taken from my shoulders, today. I am now in contact with you and the Secretary."

"Well," said Lincoln, "draw on me for all the sense I have, and all the information. In addition to your present command, the supreme command of the army will entail a vast labor upon you."

"I can do it all," McClellan replied.

In his first annual message to Congress Lincoln gave an unmistakable warning to nations "tempted to interfere" and "not . . . able to resist the counsels of seeming expediency and ungenerous ambition. . . . Besides blockading our extensive coasts," Lincoln told Congress, "squadrons larger than ever before assembled under our flag have been put afloat and performed deeds which have increased our naval renown." Lincoln also called for the establishment of a department of agriculture and one of statistics and informed the Congressmen that the territories of Colorado, Dakota, and Nevada had been organized and civil administrations established. Lincoln also brought up what was to become a mild obsession with him—the idea of colonizing those ex-slaves who escaped to Union lines "at some place or places in a climate congenial to them. It might be well to consider, too, whether the free colored people already in the United States could not, so far as individuals may desire, be included in such colonization." Lincoln reminded his listeners of the fruits of his conciliatory policies toward the border states of Maryland, Kentucky, and Missouri, which had provided 40,000 soldiers to the Union army. The President then went on to indict the slave system as an effort to put "*capital* on an equal footing with, if not above, *labor* in the structure of government. . . . Labor is prior to and independent of capital." He declared: "Capital is only the fruit of labor, and could never have existed if labor had not first existed. Labor is the superior of capital, and deserves much the higher consideration. Capital has its rights, which are as worthy of protection as any other rights. Nor is it denied that there is, and probably always will be, a relation between labor and capital producing mutual benefits. . . . No men living," Lincoln continued, "are more worthy to be trusted than those who toil up from poverty; none less inclined to take or touch aught which they have not honestly earned. Let them beware of surrendering a political power which they already possess, and which if surrendered will surely be used to close the door of advancement against such as they and to fix new disabilities and burdens upon them till liberty shall be lost." It seemed to Lincoln that the disposition of the insurrectionists was to try to bring about the progressive limitation of free government. The United States had increased eightfold from the first taking of the census in 1790. There were those living "who if the Union be preserved will live to see it contain 250,000,000. The struggle *of* to-day," he concluded, "is not altogether *for* to-day; it is for a vast future also. With a reliance on Providence all the more firm and earnest, let us proceed in the great task which events have devolved upon us." It was an arresting digression. Lincoln clearly felt it behooved him to constantly remind the nation of the essential basis of a free society.

The Radical Republicans and antislavery forces in general were highly critical of the message. They had hoped for a strong statement on emancipation. Gerrit Smith denounced the speech as "twattle and trash." William Lloyd Garrison called it "feeble and rambling" and Lincoln "a man of very small calibre," who "had better be at his old business of splitting rails than at the head of a government like ours, especially in such a crisis." Lydia Maria Child wrote to Whittier, her most frequent correspondent: "The *people* head in the right direction; but we are unfortunate in the men we have placed in power. Lincoln is narrow-minded, short-sighted, and obstinate. . . . Gerrit Smith writes me that his friends Thaddeus Stevens and Gen. Frémont almost despair of the ship of state."

As the year drew to a close, the Army of the Potomac was marvelous on parade, but its reluctant commander still showed no disposition to advance on Lee, and the criticism of Lincoln and his administration grew increasingly strident. Sidney George Fisher made a shrewd analysis of the situation. "The war is popular," he noted, "the passions of the masses are enlisted in it, and the Democratic party leaders, finding that they could not resist the current, immediately determined to swim with it, if possible into power. . . . The object . . . is, whilst affecting enthusiasm for the war, to denounce the administration for the way in which it is carried on, to magnify all mistakes & reverses, to impeach motives, to deny merit, to disparage & vilify Mr. Lincoln & his advisers in every possible way, so that the operations of the government may be thwarted and embarrassed."

To George Templeton Strong and to many of his fellow Unionists, the war was a kind of penance, a punishment not only for the sin of slavery but for the selfish and self-seeking spirit of acquisitiveness that for so many years had dominated American life. Strong wrote in his diary: "Poor old 1861 just going. It has been a gloomy year of trouble and disaster. I should be glad of its departure, were it not that 1862 is likely to be no better. But we must take what is coming. Only through much tribulation can a young people attain a healthy, vigorous national life. The results of many years spent in selfish devotion to prosperous, easy money-making must be purged out of our system before we are well. . . ." Finishing a volume of his journal "in days that are chilly and grey," Strong saw some faint intimations of "the return of sunshine. So let us hope, and in that hope let us work. If we work faithfully, and do our duty in freely putting forth all our resources, we can hardly fail, with God's blessing, to crush the rebellion and vindicate our existence as a nation. God enable us so to do our duty. Amen."

10

Forts Henry
and Donelson

In January, 1862, McClellan, through Halleck, sent word to Grant to conduct a diversionary movement to assist Don Carlos Buell, commander of the Department of the Ohio. Buell was opposed by a larger force under Grant's old West Point friend Simon Bolivar Buckner, at Bowling Green, Kentucky. Grant's "reconnaissance" was designed to prevent Buckner from being reinforced from Forts Henry or Donelson on the Tennessee and Cumberland rivers.

Buckner, a native of Kentucky, had left the army not long after Grant and gone into the real estate business. With the onset of the war he had done his best to keep Kentucky neutral, and although he was offered a commission by both the Union and the Confederacy, he refused both until Polk moved into Kentucky and Union forces advanced from Cairo to intercept him. Buckner at once reported to Albert Sidney Johnston, was made a Confederate brigadier general, and went with a brigade to reinforce Forts Henry and Donelson. Don Carlos Buell was a native of Ohio who had graduated from West Point two years ahead of Grant, fought in the Mexican War and been severely wounded, and then made his way slowly up the ladder of rank in the small peacetime army. At the outbreak of the war he had been a valuable assistant to McDowell in organizing the first flood of volunteers into trained and reasonably disciplined units and had then been sent to supersede Sherman in the Department of the Ohio after Sherman had infuriated Cameron by stating that 300,000 men would be needed to defeat the Confederates in the West. Now Buell was advancing on Bowling Green. Grant ordered Charles Ferguson Smith to move up the west bank of the Tennessee to threaten Henry and Donelson. Doubtless he felt a little diffident in doing so. Smith, West Point '25, had been an instructor and commandant of cadets when Grant was a plebe. He had remained in the regular army, fought in the Mexican War, and gone on the Utah expedition under Albert Sidney Johnston. Now the fortunes of politics, rather than war—Grant having been essentially a political appointment—had made Grant Smith's superior. If Smith was too generous a man to resent it, Halleck was not. He was outraged at what seemed to him a gross injustice.

John A. McClernand, with 6,000 men, was sent to hold the Confederates at Columbus. McClernand was an arrogant and tactless man, notoriously hostile to West Pointers and always ready with a press release exaggerating his own military accomplishments. The dislike between him and Grant was mutual. Grant accompanied McClernand on the "reconnaissance" through deplorable weather conditions —snow, rain, sleet: in miserable, soaking bivouacs over muddy, rutted roads. It was a numbing but exemplary experience for the relatively inexperienced soldiers, and Grant had a valuable opportunity to test the mettle of his men and officers.

With Buckner held at Fort Donelson, George Thomas, more courtly and dignified than ever, defeated the Confederates at Mill Springs on January 19. Grant, convinced as a consequence of the diversionary movement that Forts Henry and Donelson could be captured, urged Halleck to let him make the attempt, but Halleck rebuffed Grant's proposal and indeed treated that rumpled and unsoldierly figure with a rudeness plainly intended to convey his hostility and contempt. Not to be put off, Grant renewed his solicitations, this time with strong support from Andrew Hull Foote, commander of the Union fleet on the Mississippi. Finally, on February 1, 1862, Grant received Halleck's plainly reluctant consent. *The next day* the expedition was under way. The forts were located at a point where two rivers came within eleven miles of each other, and their defensive positions were extended two miles west and east respectively. They guarded the routes into Kentucky, Tennessee, and as far up the headwaters as Muscle Shoals, Alabama. Their capture would make

Nashville untenable and force the Confederates back far to the east. Because there were not enough boats under Foote's command to convey Grant's force of 17,000 men to the point on the Tennessee where he planned to launch his attack, Grant set up a kind of shuttle service to get his men up the river. Accompanied by seven of Foote's gunboats, Grant led the first contingent of his troops to the point of debarkation. Even before the last of his units arrived, Grant had issued orders for a coordinated attack of gunboats and infantry against Fort Henry and the garrison of some 28,000; Smith was to lead an accompanying movement against Fort Heiman, across the river. Heiman was evacuated before Smith's arrival, and after a brief defense the Confederate commander surrendered Fort Henry with its large supply of ammunition and a number of heavy guns. All but 90 defenders had made their escape from the fort by way of the road to Fort Donelson.

Donelson was Grant's next objective. His principal asset in the attack on that impregnable-looking work was the character of the officers in charge of its defense. John Buchanan Floyd, a former governor of Virginia, was a classic Southern political general (the South suffered from that breed, too). As secretary of war under James Buchanan, he had, in anticipation of secession, devoted much of his energy to dispersing the regular army forces throughout the Southern states in such a fashion as to make them vulnerable to seizure and had also moved large amounts of arms and ammunition from Northern to Southern arsenals. At the beginning of the war he raised a brigade of volunteers and, as was the custom, was given command of it. Grant thought him a traitor and a fool. Floyd's second-in-command was no better. Gideon Pillow, a native of Tennessee and a law partner of James Polk, had got a commission in the army during the Mexican War as a result of the President's influence. Grant had fought under him in several battles and knew him to be a careless and inept leader. Grant thus rode over from Fort Henry to within rifle shot of Donelson, confident that no pickets would be out and no proper military precautions taken. In Grant's own terse statement: "I had known General Pillow in Mexico, and judged that with any force, no matter how small, I could march up to within gunshot of any entrenchments he was given to hold."

Grant's plan for the investment of the fort was a simple one, as most good military plans are. The divisions under his command— Smith's on the left, Lew Wallace's in the middle, and McClernand's on the right—would take their positions on elevated ground in an arc. Foote's gunboats would deliver a preliminary bombardment, and then Grant's infantry would attack. Grant's 15,000 men were badly over-matched by an estimated 21,000 defenders behind strong fortifica-tions, and it was clear he had to have reinforcements. But he was determined to make good use of the time available to him. A prolonged siege would certainly bring Confederate reinforcements from Nashville. "I felt," he wrote later, "that 15,000 men on the 8th [of February] would be more effective than 50,000 a month later." Foote's gunboats had to return to Cairo and then start up the Cumberland. As Grant was moving his army from Fort Henry to Donelson, he was joined by Colonel John Milton Thayer, an experienced Indian fighter, with six regiments of Nebraska volunteers. The units were deployed, and the men settled down to wait for Foote's bombardment. "The greatest suffering was from want of shelter," Grant worte. ". . . During the siege we had rain and snow, thawing and freezing alternately." Campfires could not be built except well in the rear of the lines, and the soldiers suffered intensely from the cold. Many of the inexperi-enced and poorly disciplined men had thrown away their blankets and overcoats on the march from Fort Henry.

On February 14 the bombardment by Foote's fleet began. The damage inflicted on the fort by the small flotilla was difficult to judge, but two of the ships were badly damaged by Confederate fire. That night Grant received word that Foote wished to confer with him.

While Grant was making his laborious way around the Union lines to a skiff that was to take him out to Foote's flagship, Floyd ordered a night attack on the Union right—McClernand's division. Taken by surprise, McClernand's raw troops fired until their ammunition was expended and then took off. On his way back to his command post, Grant was met by a white-faced and frightened staff officer who informed him of the break in the Union lines. Had the Confederates broken through? Grant asked. No, they had fallen back, was the reply. "Some of our men are pretty badly demoralized," Grant said to his aide, "but the enemy must be more so, for he has attempted to force his way out, but he has fallen back: the one who attacks first now will be victorious and the enemy will have to be in a hurry if he gets ahead of me." Grant was convinced that the entire rebel force must have been drawn out of its defensive positions for the attempted breakthrough. Having restored the broken lines and seen that a fresh distribution of ammunition was made, Grant hurried to Smith on the left, explained the situation, and directed him to attack with his whole division. Smith's men were off, Grant noted, "in an incredibly short time," Smith himself leading the charge to be sure that his men did not fire until they were virtually on top of the rebel lines. Everything went as Grant had anticipated, and Smith's division had the reward of spending the balance of the night in the enemy's quarters.

What Grant could not discern was that Floyd and Pillow, turning the command of the portion of the defenses still in Confederate hands over to Buckner, had slipped away by boat with several thousand men, Floyd doubtless anxious to escape capture and possible trial for his treasonable activities as secretary of war. The command thus devolved on Buckner, and the next morning he sent a message to Grant asking for a parley to set terms for the surrender of the fort. When Grant replied that no terms except unconditional surrender would be accepted, Buckner responded that conditions "compel me . . . to accept the ungenerous and unchivalrous terms which you propose." The two men met at the little town of Dover, their first meeting since Buckner, years before, had paid Grant's New York hotel bill. The meeting was friendly, despite Buckner's acerbic note. They reminisced a bit about the Point, and Buckner told Grant he never would have taken the fort as easily as he had if he, Buckner, had been in command, to which Grant replied that had he been, he would never have used the tactics that he had. "I . . . relied very much on their commander to allow me to come safely up to the outside of their works," he told Buckner.

There is wide disagreement on the figures for casualties and captures at Donelson, but the best estimates of losses in killed, wounded, and missing are 2,832 for Grant's army and 16,623 for the Confederates, of whom the great majority were "missing." Grant insisted that rations had been drawn for more than 14,000 prisoners. While account must be taken of Floyd and Pillow's ineptness, great credit goes to Grant. The mark of a true commander is that he exploits the weaknesses of the enemy. The weaknesses of the Confederates were Floyd and Pillow, and Grant exploited them brilliantly. The victory was of vast strategic importance. The doorway to the mid-South was, in a manner of speaking, broken open and the way prepared for the ultimate bisection of the region. Perhaps most important was the fact that the capture of the forts began the close association of Sherman with Grant. Sherman, Grant's senior in point of years of service and in date of commission, had suffered a severe trauma at Bull Run, where his battery had been captured. After he had been sent to command the Department of the Cumberland, his behavior was so eccentric and bizarre that his friends feared he was losing his mind. In the operation against Forts Henry and Donelson he was charged with expediting the flood of men and supplies to Grant, and this he did with exceptional skill and energy, at the same time letting Grant, still very much on trial, feel his own confidence in him and respect for his fighting qualities.

Theodore Lyman, aide-de-camp to George Meade, described Sherman as "the concentrated quintessence of Yankeedom . . . tall, spare, and sinewy, with a very long neck, and a big head . . . a very homely man, with a regular nest of wrinkles in his face, which play and twist as he eagerly talks on each subject . . . his expression is pleasant and kindly."

The fall of Forts Donelson and Henry sent a wave of dismay throughout the lower South. Kate Stone carried her distress to her diary. Her brother, Coley, was busy raising a company. He goes, his sister wrote, "as a bridegroom to his wedding with high hope and gay anticipations." Robert Morris from nearby Salem Plantation went "with a sad foreboding to perform a dreaded duty. . . . He sees danger but presses on. Brother Coley does not even think of it—just a glorious fight for fame and honor."

As for Halleck, he did his best to deprive Grant of the credit due him. Communiqués from Halleck to Grant had failed to reach him and thus remained unanswered. Halleck thereupon wired McClellan, charging Grant with insubordination and disobedience to orders and recommending that he be relieved of his command and placed under arrest pending an investigation. When the brilliant outcome of the campaign became known, Halleck backtracked, but he nonetheless did everything he could to give the credit for the victory to Smith, whom, it was evident, he wished to have replace Grant.

Again, like Wilson's Creek and, to a lesser degree, Belmont, the capture of Forts Henry and Donelson, although it caused widespread rejoicing in the victory-starved North, received less credit than it merited, primarily because it took place so far from the Washington–Richmond center stage.

The consequence was that the opportunities presented to the Union by Grant's successful campaign failed to be properly exploited. In Grant's view the reason was that the Confederate armies in the region were under the overall command of one man, Albert Sidney

Johnston, who could deploy them rapidly as he saw fit. The Union forces opposing him, on the other hand, were divided into four separate departments or commands, which could be coordinated only from Washington by a general staff headed by McClellan and almost wholly preoccupied with events in northeastern Virginia. "If one general who would have taken the responsibility of all the troops west of the Alleghenies had been in command," Grant wrote in his *Personal Memoirs,* "he could have marched to Chattanooga, Corinth, Memphis and Vicksburg. . . ." Such a move would have seriously hampered the already badly pinched Confederate efforts at recruitment in the Tennessee-Kentucky area and, in Grant's opinion, would have substantially shortened the war.

11

The Peninsula Campaign

At the President's New Year's reception on January 1, 1862, Ben: Perley Poore noted that Lincoln appeared in "excellent spirits." Mrs. Lincoln wore a purple silk dress trimmed with black velvet and lace, "her head-dress . . . ornamented with a white plume." Seward was "sphinx-like and impassible"; Chase, bemused; Welles, benign. At midnight the doors of the White House were thrown open to the populace, "and in poured the people in a continuous stream," passing "steadily along, a living tide, which swept in, eddied around the President and his wife, and then surged into the East Room, which was a maelstrom of humanity, uniforms, black coats, gay, feminine attire, and citizens generally."

It was a brief interlude of gaiety in the midst of an otherwise gloomy scene. Lincoln had gone the last mile with McClellan. He had encouraged Scott's resignation when the two men clashed and given the supreme command to McClellan. He had borne with a litany of complaints and demands and done his best to respond to them. By February McClellan had been in command of the immobile Army of the Potomac for six months, and there was every indication that it would be six months more before he undertook a movement into Virginia. Even McClellan's devoted soldiers grew restive at their long inaction. Joseph Griner wrote his mother, lamenting the "mud, mud, mud" and declaring his doubts about "our great commander's judgment in letting us lay idle so long. . . . By my side," Griner added, "lies my three favorites—namely Rifle, Sabre, and Revolver, as bright and clean as labor can make them. My other pet stands quietly eating her hay . . . while I am getting as fat and lazy I can be very well."

Clearly McClellan's powers had gone to his head. When Lincoln and Seward went to his headquarters to confer with him in early January, McClellan passed the door of the room where the President and the secretary of state were waiting, ignored the word that they wished to see him, and, after half an hour, sent a word that he had gone to bed. "I merely record this unparalleled insolence of epaulettes without comment," the indignant Hay added. On the way home Hay protested the general's bad manners, and Lincoln replied that "it was better, at this time, not to be making points of etiquette and personal dignity." But the President began to take a more direct hand in the planning of military strategy. It was clearly too important to be left in the hands of the generals. He indicated in his General War Order of January 27, 1862, that he was determined that the Union armies fight, but "the Army of the Potomac was still sluggish," as John Hay put it. Lincoln assembled its generals at a staff meeting in which, as Seward told Hay the next morning, "we saw ten generals afraid to fight." Lincoln relieved these fainthearted commanders and replaced them by generals, McDowell among them, who showed a disposition to fight. "So," Hay wrote, "things began to look vigorous."

McClellan agreed, reluctantly, to undertake a campaign against Richmond, but he could not, it turned out, be deflected from his ill-conceived notion of transporting his vast army by ships to the peninsula formed by the York and the James rivers and advancing from Fortress Monroe to Richmond. The strategy appears to have been based on the hope that Lee, anticipating an attack across the Potomac, would not turn around. His excuse for going by way of the peninsula was that the roads were better, "but his complaints," Welles noted, "were unceasing, after he got there, of bad roads, water, and swamps."

In March McClellan began a cautious advance from Fortress Monroe up the peninsula toward Richmond. He wrote later in his memoirs that his secondary intention was to lure Joe Johnston into a battle. The advance was also designed "to break up the camps, give the troops a little experience in marching and bivouac before finally leaving the old base of supplies, to test the transportation arrangements and get rid of impedimenta, and thus prepare things for the movement to the Peninsula." The sentence is pure McClellan. With almost twice as many men as the Army of Northern Virginia, and the press of the country clamoring for some decisive military action, McClellan set out for what would be called today maneuvers, a kind of training exercise for his large and by now well-equipped army. He ran at once into a thinly held Confederate defensive position extending from Yorktown along the Warwick River. General J. Bankhead Magruder, known as Prince John for his lordly manners, used one of the oldest military ruses to discourage McClellan's advances. He had his far inferior force file again and again past a point where they were clearly visible to the Union army, giving the impression of many more soldiers than he actually had. McClellan, always eager to find an excuse for delaying an attack, halted, giving Lee precious days to strengthen the defenses of Richmond and deploy his army. McClellan's "theory of an invasion," George Templeton Strong wrote, "is to entrench himself, advance five miles, and then spend three weeks in setting up another line of fieldworks. Perhaps no one whose *spécialité* is military engineering can be a great captain and handle men in the field with decision and promptitude."

McClellan, taken in by Magruder's bluff, began constructing defensive positions in front of the Confederate lines and importuned Lincoln for more troops, declaring that he was opposed by "probably not less than one hundred thousand men, and possibly more." McClellan insisted that he had no more than 85,000 men under his command, to which Lincoln replied: "Your dispatches, complaining that you are not properly sustained, while they do not offend me, do pain me very much. . . . There is a curious mystery about the number of troops now with you. When I telegraphed you on the 6th, saying that you had a hundred thousand with you, I had just obtained from the Secretary of War a statement, taken, as he said, from your own returns." The President exhorted, if he did not order, McClellan to move aggressively and at once. "By delay," he wrote, "the enemy will relatively gain upon you; that is, he will gain faster by fortifications and re-enforcements than you can by re-enforcements alone. And once more let me tell you, it is indispensable to *you* that you strike a blow. *I* am powerless to help this. . . . The country will not fail to note—is now noting—that the present hesitation to move upon an entrenched enemy is but the story of Manassas repeated." He, Lincoln, would do all in his power to support him, "but," he concluded, "you must act."

McClellan thereupon spent a month preparing for an assault on Yorktown, a month which the Confederate forces used to excellent effect to strengthen their defenses around Richmond. One of the most unfortunate results of the delay was that the soldiers of the Union army, compelled to work during the day on extensive fortifications and sleep at night on the damp ground, frequently deluged by cold spring rains, suffered from colds and fevers, the latter often resulting in death. So while McClellan procrastinated, his forces diminished. Finally, on May 6, when McClellan was at last ready to open fire upon the enemy positions at Yorktown, the Confederates, now under the command of Johnston, simply abandoned the town and fell back to Richmond. When McClellan discovered that the fortress was abandoned, he wired Scott: "No time shall be lost. I shall push the enemy to the wall." McClellan did indeed press hard on the heels of the withdrawing Confederates, but they had constructed thirteen lines of fortifications across the path of the Union forces in the time that McClellan had lingered in front of Yorktown, and now these positions, and trees felled across the roads, impeded the progress of the corps of Edwin Sumner and Samuel Heintzelman, and Joseph Hooker's division.

Hooker, pursuing ahead aggressively, was the first to come up with Johnston's rear guard. In sharp fighting the Confederate guns were silenced and the infantry was driven back. Now James Longstreet was assigned by Johnston to check Hooker. Both generals were forced to commit their reserves as the battle developed into a desperate struggle with the now-outnumbered Hooker fighting to keep from being forced back into the Chickahominy. He called on McClellan repeatedly for reinforcements, but none came, in part because of the rain that had made many of the roads virtually impassable and swollen the Chickahominy. For nine hours Hooker's corps maintained the unequal fight, losing almost 2,000 men in the course of the day. Finally, after four o'clock, Philip Kearny's division arrived and afforded some respite for Hooker's exhausted soldiers, many of whom had expended all their ammunition. Harassed by fire from Confederate rifle pits, Kearny ordered Colonel Hobart Howard and his 38th New York Volunteers to drive out the Confederates, and they did in a gallant charge that cost 9 of the regiment's 19 officers.

Meanwhile, on the extreme right of the Union lines, near the York River, Winfield Scott Hancock had taken a position that threatened Johnston's left and with it Williamsburg. Although Sumner refused him reinforcements and ordered him to fall back across Queen's Creek, Hancock delayed, and when he was attacked by a Confederate force, he ordered a bayonet counterattack that drove the enemy back with a loss of some 500 men. Hooker, convinced that prompt reinforcement would have enabled him to win a decisive victory, wrote in his report of the battle: "History will not be believed when it is told that my division were permitted to carry on this unequal struggle from morning until night unaided, in the presence of more than 30,000 of their comrades with arms in their hands."

The opportunity for a decisive Union victory at this point was lost in part at least because of McClellan's failure to assume direction of the advance. He remained at Yorktown, and when members of his staff urged him to go to the front, he is reputed to have replied, "I suppose those in front can attend to that little matter." At the very moment when Longstreet was evacuating Williamsburg, leaving nearly 800 wounded Confederates behind him, McClellan was telegraphing the War Department that the enemy was strongly entrenched in front of him. Again he missed an opportunity to bring on a battle by his dilatory tactics. While he lingered at Williamsburg, waiting for the remainder of his army to come up, the Confederates crossed the Chickahominy and took up defensive positions around Richmond.

Meanwhile, General Wool, acting on the orders of the President, captured Norfolk in a skillfully executed amphibious operation, and the retreating Confederates blew up the *Merrimac* to prevent the vessel from falling into Union hands.

Nathaniel Banks, operating independently in the Shenandoah Valley, evaded Jackson's superior force, reached Winchester ahead of the Confederate general, and there was attacked by Richard Ewell's corps. The outnumbered Union soldiers gave an excellent account of themselves until Jackson arrived in support of Ewell. At this point Banks realized that withdrawal was the only alternative to defeat, and he began a retreat, his men under heavy fire from the residents of Winchester, male and female, who, according to Banks, "vied with each other . . . by firing from the houses, throwing hand-grenades, hot water and missiles of every description." In the entire course of his retreat Banks lost 38 men killed, 155 wounded, and 711 missing as well as 55 wagons out of a train of 500. In a period of forty-eight hours his men had marched fifty-three miles, fighting a number of skirmishes and one full-fledged battle.

The President and Stanton, hearing that Jackson and Ewell were at Winchester, dispatched McDowell to try to cut off their line of retreat to the south and ordered Frémont to join McDowell's corps at Strasburg. The combined force pushed Jackson and Ewell so hard that the Confederate army was forced to turn and fight at Cross Keys on the Shenandoah River. The following day the tide swung in favor of the Confederates as Ewell evaded Frémont and joined forces with Jackson for the Battle of Port Republic, after which Jackson crossed the river on June 9 and Frémont and McDowell's troops were ordered to take positions in defense of Washington while Jackson now was free to join the Confederate army at Richmond.

During the roughly three weeks from the time Banks escaped from Jackson and Ewell at Winchester to Jackson's escape from Frémont at the southern end of the Shenandoah Valley, McClellan's army was deployed along the south bank of the Chickahominy, the main natural barrier barring his advance to Richmond. Meanwhile, gloom pervaded the Confederate forces and the government itself. A niece of Jefferson Davis's wrote to her mother: "Uncle Jeff. thinks we had better go to a safer place than Richmond. . . . He is miserable. He tries to be cheerful and bear up against such a continuation of troubles: but oh, I fear he cannot live long, if he does not get some rest and quiet!" The beleaguered residents of Richmond were not cheered to hear that the president of the Confederacy had been baptized and confirmed by the Episcopal bishop of Virginia. The fact was that Union gunboats commanded both the York and the James rivers and McClellan's large and splendidly equipped army threatened the city with destruction. The government archives were sent to Columbia, South Carolina, and to Lynchburg, and George Wythe Randolph, Thomas Jefferson's grandson and secretary of war for the Confederacy, told a relative, "You must go with my wife to the country, for to-morrow the enemy will be here."

On May 23 and 24 skirmishes took place between the advance guards of the two armies. The Confederates were forced back across the river at two points, and McClellan issued a pompous order to his troops, enjoining them "to bear in mind that the Army of the Potomac" had *"never yet been checked"* and exhorting them to "preserve in battle perfect coolness and confidence, the sure forerunners of success." Aware that Jackson had his hands full contending with Frémont and part of McDowell's corps, McClellan had an additional incentive to make an all-out assault on Richmond before Jackson could reach the city. But "all-out," so essential to military success, was not in Little

Mac's temperament. Despite a flurry of messages from the President urging him on and his own opinion that the defenses of Richmond were "not formidable," he notified Lincoln that he was busy securing his flanks against "the greatly superior forces" of the enemy. While he secured his flanks, whatever that phrase meant in such a context, torrents of rain fell, swelling the Chickahominy and greatly complicating the crossing of it. Nonetheless, on the twenty-seventh, a portion of Fitz-John Porter's V Corps was able to make its way to Hanover Courthouse, northeast of Richmond, cut the railroad line of the Virginia Central, capture 730 prisoners, and inflict 200 casualties. McClellan sent a triumphant telegram to the War Department, claiming "a truly glorious victory" and calling for more soldiers. The following day the Richmond & Fredericksburg Railroad was also cut, further isolating Richmond. More telegrams, one of which proclaimed: "I will do all that quick movements can accomplish, but you must send me all the troops you can, and leave me full latitude as to the choice of commanders."

It was almost as though Joseph Johnston, in command of the Confederate forces around Richmond, were reading McClellan's dispatches. Realizing that a substantial portion of the Union army was north of the swollen Chickahominy while McClellan's main force was still south (and west) of the river, Johnston decided to attack Erasmus Keyes's corps at Seven Pines, some five miles from Richmond. Edward Acton, with the 5th New Jersey Volunteers, wrote to his wife describing the initial phase of what would come to be known as the Battle of Fair Oaks: "Long lines of Waggon trains carrying forward supplies for the immense army in advance. Camps stretching over many acres of ground, with their occupants lying idly in tents, sheltered from the hot noon-day sun or else cleaning their arms. The contraband women and children in their camp flitting from tent to tent and their clear ringing laugh falling musically upon my ear. The many Rail Road cars loading with army stores and passengers; and on the open cars that were loaded with corn and oats . . . all this made up a scene of varied and exciting interest—a scene such as is rarely beheld in a life time. . . . I wish I could describe it to thee just as I saw it—but I cannot."

Alfred Bellard, also in the 5th New Jersey Volunteers, was part of Samuel Heintzelman's III Corps which crossed the Chickahominy to Fair Oaks. After Heintzelman's corps, including Joseph Hooker's 2nd Division, and Erasmus Keyes's IV Corps had crossed the river, heavy rains swelled its banks so that it was impossible to reinforce the two corps, and Johnston hit Keyes at Fair Oaks. The Union soldiers fell back under the force of Johnston's assault. Bellard took a slightly malicious note of the fleeing Zou-Zous or Red Legs, as the Zouave regiments were called by those Yankees less colorfully garbed. In some places the deserters and stragglers were so thick that Bellard's regiment, moving up to try to check the rebels, had to force its way with bayonets. "Any soldier who was wounded in that fight," Bellard noted, "did not lack for help to get out, as everyone seemed ready to give them a lift in order to get as far away from danger as possible themselves." For the first time Bellard experienced fear so intense that he was sick at the stomach, but the sensation passed as soon as he heard rebel bullets passing overhead.

A bridge across the Chickahominy that had been constructed several days before, the so-called Grape-vine Bridge, now became the only means by which McClellan was able to reinforce the hard-pressed units north of the river and prevent their destruction. Three divisions made their way across the bridge just in time to prevent the annihilation of Heintzelman's III Corps at Fair Oaks. The Confederates came on in the face of murderous artillery fire, and at sunset Johnston, directing the attack, was seriously wounded. Soon the rebels themselves were in panicky flight. Riding up to the front after the battle, McClellan passed the 5th New Jersey and called out, "Boys, we've licked them, right, left, and centre, and we're going to Richmond." Bellard wrote in his diary: "This sounded well and put the boys in a good humor." But once again McClellan procrastinated. The army stopped to bury its dead and resupply the divisions.

The dead, Union and rebel, covered the battlefields. Long trenches were dug, and the bodies dragged or pushed into them and covered with a few inches of dirt. Boards or sticks bearing the names of the fallen soldiers, if they were known, were placed over the common graves. The hot weather immediately affected the bodies of the dead rebels. Bellard wrote in his diary: "They had swelled to double their natural size, and as a consequence their clothing had burst exposing their bodies to the sun, and turning them as black as ink. . . ." The Union burial detail found the bodies so badly decomposed that they hit on the expedient of digging a hole eighteen inches deep near each body and then using several fence railings to roll the body into its shallow grave. The dead horses were disposed of by piling brush and fence rails around them and setting them on fire, "our stomachs being so strong by this time," Bellard added, "that we cooked our coffee over their ribs."

Captain Oliver Wendell Holmes, fired at by sharpshooters, noted that "a bullet has a more villainous greasy slide through the air." After the first day's fighting, Holmes and his men "sat under arms waiting sleepless cold wet and hungry for the renewal of the fight." It began at seven in the morning in the woods along the railroad track. When the long day of bitter fighting ended, Holmes was ordered to move his company under the cover of darkness, and as he did, he and his men stumbled over the dead of Confederate soliders, treading "on the swollen bodies already fly blown and decaying." Holmes's regiment suffered terribly. "Our proportionate loss," he wrote his father, "was greater *than any Regts in this whole army during the whole war.* . . . The men behaved like bricks through it all—I think my men like me," he added. "I have heard so, . . . my men cheered me after the fight."

Edward Acton, in charge of the picket lines in advance of Hooker's division, wrote his wife of "the constant roar and din of battle—the hasty and rapid marches—the quick massing of troops and all the phariphinalia of a mighty army—the splendid sight of 60,000 armed men moveing and maneuvering 'neath the early morning sun, all on one field—the horrid sight of mangled bodies, dead and dieing—the shrieks & groans of wounded men on the field of Battle filling the night with sounds of anguish." His company and regiment had been much diminished by casualties and illness. "New officers have taken the places of old ones," Acton wrote, "and the hearty, cheerful courage of the men seems to have been worn down by hard work and sickness to the sort of mechanical courage and performance of duty, in painful contrast to their former high spirits and cheerful alacrity. Our own company number only 43 men for duty—all the others are either dead, wounded or sick." Of the officers one had died in battle and six had been seriously wounded. Acton was the only one returned to duty.

Promoted to captain and assigned to another unit, Acton left his little remnant of a company reluctantly. "Many a brave heart throbs within their manly bosoms," he wrote his wife. "Who could help regreting to leave them after learning to know them as I have—after haveing toiled with them through summer's heats and winter's snows —the Parade ground and the Battle field? . . . This war is terrible. I see around me the sickening evidences of this last battle [Fair Oaks].

Heart-rending discriptions are given that revolts the mind with loathing. Bitter—bitter indeed is the fruit of this war. What punishment can be meted out that is severe enough for the Monsters who inaugurated it? Families bereft—Widows mourning—Orphans helpless—Strong men maimed and shattered—Hundreds of thousands of lives sacrificed—all this for what? Simply to gratify the ambitions of some of the most graceless scoundrels that ever lived; deep—deep will be their punishment."

After the Battle of Fair Oaks, or Seven Pines, rain deluged the armies. "The rain also washed the dirt from the shallow graves, and every morning a detail was sent out to cover up arms, legs and heads that had protruded from the ground during the night," Bellard noted.

Frederick Law Olmsted, at army headquarters with the Sanitary Commission, wrote of "carloads of wounded men dumped on swamply river shores without food, medicine, or attendance; of men with fractured thighs lying neglected and forgotten forty-eight hours in two inches of water, struggling to raise themselves so as to pick the maggots from their rotting wounds and fainting from the effort, and yet keeping a good heart through it." And a few days later Strong noted that "hospitals are in a horrible state, malarious fever and diarrhea prevalent. Scurvy has appeared unmistakably."

The number of Union and Confederate soldiers involved was extraordinarily evenly balanced—41,797 Union soldiers versus 41,816 Confederates; the casualties were 6,134 rebels and 5,031 Yankees. On both sides there were numerous incidents of heroism, of brilliant sallies and stubborn defense. McClellan was saved from the worst consequences of his poor troop disposition by the fighting qualities of his soldiers. Coming almost a year after the Battle of Bull Run, Fair Oaks, or Seven Pines, demonstrated that Yankee and rebel armies had matured into fighting forces of fearful potency. No one who had experienced that bitter and uncertain contest talked again about the superior fighting qualities of one side or the other.

Once again there was procrastination and delay. The Army of the Potomac recoiled from the fighting and attended to its wounds; the defenders of Richmond plucked up courage. A Union hospital was established at Fair Oaks, and it can have done little for the morale of the troops to have scenes of illness and suffering in their midst. Once again fever carried off men faster than enemy bullets. Now it was the weather, McClellan informed an anxious Lincoln, that prevented an all-out attack on Richmond. "The Chickahominy is in a dreadful state," he informed the President;"we have a rain-storm on our hands."

Jackson, having crossed the Shenandoah on June 6, seemed more like a ghost than a corporeal being, eluding all efforts to intercept him and appearing on June 25 at Ashland with 35,000 men, ready to attack the right wing of McClellan's army near Mechanicsville. Not knowing that Jackson had reached Ashland, McClellan had ordered Heintzelman's corps with Sumner's and a part of Keyes's to advance in order "to ascertain the nature of the ground." The result was the Battle of Oak Grove, in which the Union forces lost some 516 killed and wounded to very little purpose. McClellan now received intelligence of Jackson's arrival and wired the President: "I will do all that a General can do with the splendid army I have the honor to command and if it is destroyed by overwhelming numbers, can at least die with it and share its fate. But if the result of the action . . . is a disaster, the responsibility cannot be thrown on my shoulders; it must rest where it belongs." In actual fact, McClellan had under his command 156,838 men, of whom 29,511 were sick, on furlough, under arrest, or absent without leave. Lee, who had succeeded to the command of the Army of Northern Virginia when Johnston was wounded, had some 75,000. The arrival of Jackson brought the armies to roughly equal strength. More important, it made it possible for Lee to assume the initiative. On the twenty-sixth, the day after Jackson's arrival, Lee began his attack on McClellan, with Jackson in advance and the rest of his army directed toward Mechanicsville, leaving only two divisions between McClellan's main force at Fair Oaks and Richmond itself. If McClellan had not been paralyzed by the incorrect assumption that he was vastly outnumbered, he could have driven directly into Richmond. The Union forces were dispersed in well-prepared defensive positions, and the onslaught of D. H. Hill and Longstreet was repulsed with heavy casualties. McClellan's choices were to continue to oppose Lee's attack on his right wing and, when it had spent its force, to counterattack from the Ashland-Hanover Courthouse line; or to hold there and attack Richmond with his main force from his base at Fair Oaks on the left of the Union lines. Instead, McClellan began a retreat to the James.

Pressed hard by Jackson, McClellan ordered Fitz-John Porter to occupy the high ground at Gaines's Mill and be prepared to cover the withdrawal of the Union troops. Porter did as ordered, hastily preparing the defensive positions and emplacing his artillery. At two o'clock on the afternoon of the twenty-seventh, after waiting for hours for Jackson, A. P. Hill hit Porter's pickets and came under heavy fire from the

Union lines. Edward Acton described the battle as commencing with a rebel cannonading by *"Shell, Grape & Cannister"* at two-twenty, showering him and his men with metal fragments and announcing the advance of Stonewall Jackson. Porter's expanded corps of some 35,000 was opposed by twice that number of Confederates, but Porter appealed in vain to McClellan for support. The latter, convinced that the main threat was from Richmond, sent him no help. Finally, at Porter's increasing urgent appeal, McClellan dispatched two brigades. They arrived at the very moment when Porter's men were breaking under the relentless pressure exerted on them. Cheer on cheer rose from the Union lines. "I have never heard anything like it," Acton wrote. "Slowly the fireing . . . ceased as the enemy was driven from their position, the extreme right—here musketry become absolutely terrible. I can give no similey that will give thee the least idea of its terribleness. Almost every moment I looked for our first line to give way. . . . They would not give way. Now the enemys *Battery* is taken, 6 guns—such cheering! It seems as though the very heavens would be rent. The fireing is, if possible, redoubled in fury but slowley, very slowley, at dark the enemy leave. The field is ours."

The Union casualties were 6,837 out of 34,274 men engaged, with 893 killed and 2,836 missing. Of 57,018 Confederate, 8,751 were killed or wounded.

The Union soldiers slept on the field of battle, but their rest was brief and uneasy. After an hour Acton was awakened by picket firing. "It was then," he wrote, "that I heard those terrible groans and shrieks. Some calling for *water*—'for God's sake bring me some water!' others calling frantically for the Doctor—'Doctor! Doctor! Oh my God where is the Doctor?' . . . Again I would hear weeping voices bewaling their fate and begging for some relief from their sufferings and alas! what was more terrible than all, many were blasphemeing and cursing most horridly. . . . [The cries of the wounded] are ringing in my ears now with an awful distinctness and will ring there for many a day to come. . . ."

At the end of the fierce fighting of the twenty-eighth, McClellan sent a dispatch to the secretary of war which read in part: "Had I 20,000 or even 10,000 fresh troops to use to maneuver, I could take Richmond; but I have not a man in reserve. . . . If we have lost the day, we have yet preserved our honor, and no one need blush for the Army of the Potomac. I have lost the battle because my force was too small. I again repeat, that I am not responsible for this. . . ." He must have "very large re-enforcements . . . at once. . . . If you do not do so now the game is lost. If I save this army now I tell you plainly that I owe no thanks to you or any other persons in Washington. You have done your best to sacrifice this army."

Lee assumed that McClellan would either cross the Chickahominy to reinforce Porter and protect his lines of communication or withdraw down the peninsula via Williamsburg, the way he had come. Instead, McClellan decided to pull all his units back to the James in a wheeling movement to the left, ordering Keyes meanwhile to begin the construction of fortifications on Malvern Hill overlooking the James. McClellan directed that the sick and wounded be left behind, with surgeons and medical supplies. What material could not be carried off was to be burned. In the words of a young lieutenant, "Such quantities of elegant new tents; of nice beds for the sick; of fine liquors and cordials and medicines, oranges, lemons, beef, corn, whiskey; immense quantities of hay; boxes on boxes of clothing, and everything conceivable for use and comfort were committed to the flames." McClellan had a twenty-four-hour head start, and his army withdrew in excellent order. As soon as it was clear that his opponent was retreating, Lee, confident that the destruction of the Union army would mean an end to the war, began pursuit.

The first engagement between the pursuers and the pursued took place near the recently abandoned Savage's Station, where Magruder made a fierce attack on John Sedgwick. At the point when Sedgwick's division seemed in danger of annihilation, the brigade of William Burns came to its rescue. Burns, an eyewitness reported, "with clothes and hat pierced, and face covered with blood, . . . rallied and cheered his men." When two companies started to retreat from the force of the Confederate attack, Burns, "taking off his torn hat and throwing it down, . . . besought them not to disgrace themselves and their general." At this appeal the men rallied "and fought more desperately to wipe out the cowardice of a moment."

Captain Oliver Wendell Holmes led G Company of the 20th Massachusetts Volunteers, counterattacking to try to restore the Federal lines breached by Longstreet. "Forward Guide Right," Captain Holmes called out, and forward G Company went. Two men were killed by a Confederate shell before they had crossed the line of departure. The company passed an abandoned Confederate battery with the dead lying thick around it, and then the 7th Michigan on the right broke and ran, and orders came to the 20th Massachusetts to retreat before it was surrounded. The army began its retreat to James, "through terrible rain & mud," Holmes noted, adding that "the anxiety has been more terrible than almost any past experience. . . ." Holmes's spirits failed him when he heard a fellow officer declare they must surrender "or be cut to pieces within 37 hours."

Federal casualties were 2,853, while the Confederates lost 3,615 in one of the bitterest days of fighting of the entire "seven days."

The engagements at White Oak Swamp and Nelson's Farm gave McClellan time to consolidate his defensive positions on Malvern Hill. At sunrise on July 1 Captain Acton climbed a small promontory and for the first time saw virtually the whole of McClellan's army spread out below. "I could hardly conceive *any* power that could overwhelm us. It was a great and grand sight, the like of which in all probability I shall never see again. Lines of Battle were formed almost as far as the eye could reach. Troops were in almost every conceivable position—in Square—in Column closed in mass—in Echelon. Some moving rapidly to their designated places, others with arms stacked resting on the ground. Some kindling fires and makeing coffee, others hastily slinging knapsacks and falling into line. Yonder is a squadron of Calvary in line, *there* is another column, and hereaway, galloping like mad for that belt of woods is still another. . . . In looking over the field I see many of these squadrons. But yonder come Rushes Lancers, the tips of their long lances flashing in the sunlight and the red streamers flaunting sauceily from their lance staffs. . . ."

As Lee massed his army at Malvern Hill for a decisive attack intended to destroy the Army of the Potomac as an effective fighting force, a brief reconnaissance convinced him that the Union positions were most vulnerable on their left, held by Porter's corps. Moreover, an attack on that portion of the Union lines must, if successful, have the effect of cutting off retreat to the James. It was late on the afternoon of July 1 before the Confederate units were in position to begin their assault on Malvern Hill.

The roar of Confederate artillery announced the beginning of the battle. Union soldiers moved forward along draws that offered protection from enemy artillery, and the Union artillery in turn began a heavy fire. It was McClellan's intention to try to overwhelm the Confederate batteries. Acton's company was near a New Jersey battery of ten guns which kept up a lively fire for more than three hours. Finally, as the Union guns began to establish their superiority, the Confederates were ordered forward to storm the tormenting batteries.

"They advanced," Acton wrote his wife, "in the midst of a terrible iron hail; our grape & cannister mowed great swaths through and through their ranks but these gaps were closed up quickly and the rebel hordes still pressed steadily on for the coveted prize; again and again and again were great roads opened in their rank & with the same steady, detirmined, closeing, but at last it was too much for flesh and blood to bear, with a cry of almost terror, they broke and fled from the woods."

A lull followed, and then another Confederate attack. Once more Jackson's men were driven back, and again they came on, now at the double. "Our guns played furiously but the charge was too impetuos to be stoped by artillery," Acton wrote. "Now was the time for infantry. The men stood like statues immoveable—not a shot was fired; on come the Rebels with 100 paces—80 paces—60 paces—still not a shot fired except by artillery—within 50 paces—and still no command except the caution of the officers—'Steady men—Steady men'—40 paces—Ah! now comes the word—'Ready—Aim—Fire' 'Charge Bayonet, double quick, March.'" At the crash of Union fire, the enemy line faltered; they "cannot face the solid wall of gleaming bayonets advanceing so rapidly upon them—they turn and fly pursued by our brave lads," Acton wrote, "who follow them through the woods and capture and secure *their* Battery. . . . The enemy is beaten; it is now near dark, he advances no more." The Union soldiers lay down, once again on the battlefield, to get what sleep they could while the artillery continued its incessant cough. "This night cannonading was beautiful beyond discription," Acton wrote. ". . . It surpassed any exhibition of fireworks that I have evern seen or conceived. With this ended the 7th day of fighting. . . ."

At two o'clock the next morning Acton and his men were roused with word to prepare to move to new positions. "In an incredibly short period," Acton wrote, "we were again on the march. . . ." This time it was a retreat across the James River, accompanied by a torrential downpour that soaked the exhausted men to the skin and turned the mud into ankle-deep yellow clay. "Many men dropped from the ranks unable, from sheer exhaustion, to move further without rest. We plodded on as best we could on our weary way, worn and hungry—for two days we had nothing to eat but hard crackers (about 2 apiece per day) and water, some of the men—but few enough—had a little coffee; on this day we had eaten nothing, yet there was no complaining, I mean comparatively speaking," Acton added, with a Quaker's scrupulous regard for the truth. At ten o'clock in the morning the march stopped, and the men lay down on the wet ground to get what rest they could. Some started to put up tents, and others to collect damp wood to heat water, but again word came to move on, and Acton and his men "trudged . . . very wearily more than a mile through mud now nearly knee deep." Finally they reached a clover field and made camp in the rain. It was after midnight before kitchen trains came up and the men were wakened for a ration of seven hard crackers per man and coffee. For most of the men it was their first "meal" in two days—"Crackers and coffee!—Crackers broken in the coffee and eaten with a spoon. . . ." They had hardly swallowed their meager fare when orders came to move once more. Hooker had called for his *brave Jersey Blues.*" A few miles down the road they were called back to the spot they had just abandoned. It was the Fourth of July. The sun came out; the men's spirits rose. They bathed in a nearby brook "arm pit deep." Their baggage was brought up to them. Bully beef and potatoes seemed like luxuries.

The Seven Days' Battle was over, and the men of McClellan's army were told that they had "lost" the battle. If so, it was only because they had been outnumbered two to one and denied reinforcements at a critical moment "for fear of the overshadowing popularity of one of the greatest living generals [McClellan]," as Edward Acton put it. "They fold their arms calmly and wait to see his army destroyed, his men butchered in an unequal contest in order that they may break him down." Such were the reflections of Acton. It was Stanton and his myrmidons in the War Department who were responsible, Acton wrote, "for the loss of life we have just met—for the terrible ordeal through which we have just passed, and through which only the skill and genius of a McClellan could bring us in safety and with honor. *They* are the *Murderers* who by their clamors prevented us from receiveing the reinforcements which would have enabled us before this to have been in Richmond and virtually have ended the war."

When orders came from McClellan for a general retreat, vast supplies of food and ammunition had to be disposed of. "Everything that could not be carried off," Alfred Bellard wrote, "was . . . burnt or destroyed. Knapsacks and tents were slashed and cut to pieces with swords and bayonettes, crackers and provisions of all kinds were thrown down all the wells we could find, filling them to the brim. . . . The last to disappear was the brigade's sutler's tent. As he did not have waggons enough to carry off his produce, he had to stand by and see the boys help themselves to cans of butter, milk, cheese, and in fact everything he had on hand. . . ."

After three months of snail's-pace campaigning, McClellan had "got safe back," in George Templeton Strong's words. Thousands of lives and millions of dollars had been expended in vain, and Strong noted: "Were I a general, even I, poor feeble, myopic, flaccid, effeminate George T. Strong, I think I could do better than this. . . ."

While McClellan tarried at Harrison's Landing, reorganizing the units under his command, he tried to cast the blame for his failure to capture Richmond on anyone he could find. He wired Stanton: "I have lost this battle because my force was too small. . . . You have done your best to sacrifice this army." The Union armies had lost almost 16,000 men in the Seven Days' Battle. Alfred Bellard's 5th New Jersey Volunteers was "sickened, weakened and exhausted." It had begun the Peninsula campaign with a roster of some 800 men. Now only 441 were present for roll call. Other units had suffered similarly. Joseph Griner wrote his mother: "That retreat was surely a masterly one and shows great generalship on the part of McClellan. That week of battles I shall never forget in all its horrors, for I was in it all. May I never see such another."

A few days after arriving at Harrison's Landing, McClellan wrote an extraordinary letter to Lincoln which he handed to him when the President visited the general's headquarters. It read in part: "Mr. President: You have been fully informed that the rebel army is in front, with the purpose of overwhelming us by attacking our positions. . . . I cannot but regard our condition as critical." With this introduction, McClellan went on to give his own views on the conduct of the war. "Our cause must never be abandoned," he wrote; "it is the cause of free institutions and self-government. The Constitution and the Union must be preserved, whatever the cost in time, treasure, and blood. . . . Let neither military disaster, political factions, nor foreign war shake your settled purpose to enforce the equal operation of the laws of the United States. . . ." The time had come to settle on "a civil and military policy" on the basis of which victory could be won. The rebellion had become a war, and "as such it should be conducted upon the highest principles known to Christian civilization. It should not be a war looking to the subjugation of the people of any State in any event. It should not be at all a war upon population. . . . Neither confiscation of property, political executions of persons, territorial organization of States, or forcible abolition of slavery should be contemplated for a moment." The letter continued with a long list of instructions and admonitions—"pillage and waste should be treated as high crimes. . . . Military arrests should not be tolerated. . . . Military power should not be allowed to interfere with the relations of servitude. . . ." Finally, "a declaration of radical views, especially upon slavery, will rapidly disintegrate our present armies." McClellan warned Lincoln that he must have a commander-in-chief of the army to direct the military forces of the nation along the lines indicated by the letter. "I do not ask that place for myself [although Lincoln might assume, apparently, that he was available]. I am willing to serve you in such position as you may assign me." McClellan's self-pity came out in his remark at the end of his letter: "I may be on the brink of eternity; and . . . I hope for forgiveness from my Maker. . . ." Why, Lincoln, may have wondered, more on the brink than anyone else?

Certainly it may be doubted if any chief of state ever received such a communication from a subordinate general unless it was as a prelude to a military coup. That Lincoln did not at once relieve McClellan of his duties is a measure of the degree to which he was able to subordinate his personal feelings or, perhaps, rise above insolent criticism. For Lincoln, the issue was not the punishment of an insubordinate officer but the cause of the Union.

Offensive as the tone of the letter was, it is not difficult to understand the emotions which prompted it. In a campaign of almost four months McClellan had seen his adored and adoring army badly chewed up to no avail. All that was clear was that the fighting qualities of the two armies were astonishingly similar. In one engagement after another, they had fought each other to a standstill. Of the performance of his soldiers under the most demanding conditions conceivable, McClellan had only reason to be proud. Whatever fault there was lay in his own disposition of his troops. But that aside, he had committed fewer outright blunders than the leaders arrayed against him. If he had failed to capture Richmond, he had shown considerable skill in extricating his army from a series of dangerous extremities. But all that was not enough. He had been hopelessly dilatory; he had failed to take advantage of opportunities presented to him by the fighting qualities of his men and officers; he had been unending in his self-pity and ungenerous with the officers under his command. Now he compounded his misadventures by lecturing his commander-in-chief as though he were a backward schoolboy. Lincoln granted him one wish. He ordered Halleck to Washington to act as chief of staff, and McClellan soon had cause to regret he had ever made such a suggestion.

For almost six weeks the Army of the Potomac licked its terrible wounds at Harrison's Landing and luxuriated in relative idleness, performing the housekeeping functions of every encampment—drilling, maneuvering, going on parade for visiting dignitaries, many of them the "they"—the "murderers"—on whom the army blamed all their misfortunes.

The lesson that cried out to be learned from the Peninsula campaign and that, in a sense, was concealed by McClellan's ineptness and, perhaps even more, by his arrogance and perpetual whining, was that the whole notion of capturing Richmond and, indeed, of defeating Lee and Jackson was chimerical. Yet once Lincoln and his Cabinet and, through them, the nation had committed themselves to that objective, they became its prisoners. Everything was measured by that one standard. What was the latest from Virginia? On that word hung the volatile mood of the Union, the hopes of Democrats, the rise and fall in political favor of the Republicans, the very will to pursue the war to a successful conclusion. There was certainly a consciousness of that dilemma in James Russell Lowell's letter to his editor, James Fields. "Who feels," he wrote, "like asking more recruits to go down into McClellan's beautiful trap, from which seventy thousand men can't get away? Hasn't he pinned his army there like a bug in a cabinet?—only you don't have to *feed* your bug! I feel 'blue as the blue forget-me-not,' and I don't see how we are to be saved but by a miracle, and miracles aren't wrought for folks without heads. . . . Give me victory and I will give you a poem; but I am now clear down to the bottom of the well, where I see the Truth too near to make verses of."

The fact is that if the subjugation of the South had rested on the defeat of Lee and the capture of Richmond, it would never have been subdued. Everything had to crumble away—men, supplies, transportation systems, great clumps of Southern territory, cotton and foodstuffs, the institution of slavery, the homes and plantations of tens of thousands of Southerners—before Lee, still not "beaten" in the conventional military sense, could no longer preserve the will to fight in his exhausted legions.

The nation was not willing to learn the lesson that the Peninsula campaign might have taught, but it was nonetheless a devastating setback. Henry Adams, hearing of the impending campaign against Richmond and assuming, like virtually all Unionists, that it would result in the capture of Richmond and the surrender of the South, had written in May that "before this reaches you I suppose you will be in motion, and I hope that the war will be at an end."

In the bleak summer of 1862 George Templeton Strong confided to his diary: "I find it hard to maintain my lively faith in the triumph of the nation and the law." He feared that the new levies that Lincoln had called for to replace units decimated by the Peninsula fighting would be no better than "Bull-Runagates for six months after they are mustered into service." He added: "McClellan's great name is growing very obscure. . . . As we deified him without reason, I suppose we are free to reduce his rank whenever we like. Prevailing color of people's talk is blue. What's very bad, we begin to lose faith in Uncle Abe." Lincoln was judged to be "most honest and true, thoroughly sensible, but without the decision and the energy the country wants."

Welles reported that Chase visited him with a letter signed by Chase and Stanton to the President "against continuing McClellan in command and demanding his immediate dismissal." It was Chase's conviction that "either the Government or McClellan must go down." Welles confessed that he held no brief for the general, but he protested the approach taken by his fellow Cabinet members. It was not up to them to concert action behind the President's back, so to speak, and present him with "demands." For the moment the matter was put to rest.

12

Diplomatic Matters

What happened in the courts of England, France, or Spain was perhaps as important to the outcome of the Civil War as the Battle of Bull Run or the capture of Forts Henry and Donelson and was directly, of course, related to those and similar military engagements. Napoleon III, ex-habitué of seedy New York hotel bars, was, like a greedy harpy, anxious to batten in any way he could on the crisis of the Union. His sympathies were unabashedly with the South. Earl Russell and the English ruling class in general were of a similar disposition. Spain, the politics of which were of the musical-comedy variety, was as much interested as France and England in making trouble. The means available to the European powers for dealing damaging blows to the Union cause were, short of war—for which there was, it might be said, considerable sentiment in the higher circles of all three countries—the recognition of the South as an independent nation, with the full rights of a belligerent.

The American ambassadors to the four principal European powers—Charles Francis Adams to England, William Dayton to France, John Lothrop Motley to Austria, and Carl Schurz to Spain—had the extremely delicate task of prevailing on the respective nations to which they were accredited to refrain from any actions which would constitute aid and comfort to the South. Their line was that the South was a rebellious section of the country engaged in civil war; the Confederates insisted, of course, that they were a separate nation seeking independence from a tyrannical master, much as the American colonies had sought their independence from Great Britain almost a hundred years earlier. The latter was a notion particularly seductive to the British.

There was a large element of class animus in the reactions of the three nations. America was the seedbed, in their view, of the subversive democratic ideologies spreading all over Europe and keeping the masses in a constant ferment. The defeat and demoralization of the original and model of democracy and the triumph of the Southern aristocracy would, it was believed, strengthen aristocracy and monarchy in every European country. There were, of course, also far more practical considerations, especially in England, tied as it was to the cotton-growing economy of the South in the closest fashion. If the war ended with the independence of the South, its commercial alliance with Great Britain would be complete, and it would be, in all but name, an economic dependency of Great Britain.

The British strategy was thus to give all the covert aid it could to the South by looking the other way while Southern agents contracted with British munitions makers and shipbuilders for arms and for raiders and to come forth as the disinterested friend of peace, offering to assist in negotiations, which, it was assumed, would eventuate in Southern independence.

The fluctuating fortunes of war provided the counterpoint to this strategy of negotiated peace. Obviously every Confederate victory made the European powers more aggressive on behalf of the Confederacy and every Northern victory blunted their efforts.

William Dayton, the United States minister to France, was the least able of Seward's diplomatic corps, but he was shrewd enough to recommend that a "gentleman accustomed to the use of the pen" be sent as a consul to produce Union propaganda for the French newspapers which Dayton found most susceptible to *pourboires*. Such a man "might be of great use in giving a right direction to public sentiment." The man Seward chose, John Bigelow, was a partner in the *New York Evening Post*. It was Bigelow's assignment to try to neutralize "large numbers of Southern men and women" living in Paris "who formed a brilliant and influential society" and whose female members "vied with each other in their endeavors to enlist in support of their

cause everyone connected with the Imperial Court. . . . The consequence was that the Emperor was constantly surrounded by those who
sympathized with the South . . ." an observer of the scene recalled.
"The Emperor was, at times, absolutely beset by these people." Cotton
was freely offered as a bribe to influential court officials.

Bigelow had known Napoleon in the United States, not necessarily
an asset, but he soon proved an abler representative of the United
States than his superior, Dayton, and Seward came to rely heavily on
him for information about Napoleon's inclinations.

Jefferson Davis had chosen three commissioners to represent the
Confederacy to the European courts—Ambrose Dudley Mann of
Virginia; William Lowndes Yancey, an Alabama fire-eater; and Pierre
Rost, a Louisianian. Yancey was accurately described by the British
consul at Charleston as "impulsive, erratic and hot-headed; a rabid
Secessionist [favoring] a revival of the Slave Trade. . . ." Mann was
described as "the son of a bankrupt grocer" and "a mere trading
politician possessing no originality of mind and no special merit of any
description."

Lincoln's inexperience in international affairs and Seward's
strange "hallucinations" left American foreign policy in somewhat of a
shambles. Schurz found a clue to Seward's hallucinations in the
secretary's conviction that cotton was, as the South insisted, "king." So
dependent were the European nations on cotton, Seward argued, that
they would "intervene to prevent the abolition of slavery for the sake
of cotton." This, at least, was Stanton's report on Seward, a view, as
Schurz put it, "so egregiously preposterous" that one was disposed to
think Stanton had misquoted his fellow Cabinet member. But there
was confirmation in a memo that Seward had sent to John Lothrop
Motley, the historian of the Dutch Republic, now ensconced as United
States ambassador to Austria, putting forward the same question:
Would not European nations resist the bestowing of "freedom upon
the laborers whose capacity to supply cotton for European fabrics
depends, or is it supposed to depend, upon their continuance in
bondage?" To which Motley replied, "A thousand times NO!"—a plain
enough answer.

The fact was that Seward's policy (perhaps it should be "Seward's
anxiety" or "Seward's paranoia" rather than "Seward's policy") worked
to just the opposite effect. As Adams, Motley, Dayton, Schurz, and
other American diplomats tried to make clear to Seward (and through
him Lincoln), the reactionary elements in Europe were thoroughly

committed to the Confederacy on the basis of their opposition to the "democracy" represented by the Union, but the mass of the people and all the "progressive" elements in all European nations, many of which had been racked by unsuccessful revolutions a little more than a decade earlier, advocated the cause of the North for the same reasons their enemies supported the South—they saw the South as the symbol of reactionary, feudal politics and the North as democratic and progressive.

The issue of slavery was central for English and European political liberals and radicals and for the working class and large portions of the middle class. Thus, the longer the Lincoln administration equivocated on the slavery issue, the more uncertain and disheartened its supporters on the other side of the Atlantic became. Perhaps they misunderstood. The conflict, which they had assumed from the first was concerned with the great moral principle of human freedom, seemed, with each passing month, to be based on nothing more than a complicated and obscure debate over an essentially legal question— whether under the terms of the Federal Constitution a state, or states, could secede from the Union. It was hard for Europeans to identify, as we say, with this issue. Indeed, in the prevailing mood for "breaking away," becoming "independent" of an onerous ruler, the desire of the South for "independence" struck a responsive chord in many lovers of freedom. Under these circumstances, emissaries of the Fedeal government like Carl Schurz felt an alarming shift in popular sentiment. Southern representatives to the various European powers were doing their best to reinforce the notion that the struggle was not over slavery, which, they insisted, most Northerners were quite ready to accept or at least agree was none of their business, but over the right of Southern states to "freedom," thus, in Schurz's words, taking "what little anti-slavery wind there was left, out of our sail." The threat that all this posed to the Union was that since the ruling circles of most nations sympathized with the South, wished to see it established as an independent nation, and desired to assist it by formal recognition and by an infusion of arms and critically needed supplies, the waning of enthusiasm for the Union among the people at large threatened to leave the ruling classes free to follow their natural inclinations. The result of recognition of the South would have been war with the North, and if Seward had, at the beginning of the conflict, toyed with this idea as a way of reuniting the states, he had abandoned that bizarre strategy and fully supported Lincoln's efforts to keep all European nations neutral.

On his way to his diplomatic post in Spain, Carl Schurz stopped off in London to pay his respects to his counterpart at the Court of St. James's, Charles Francis Adams. "The appearance of the little bald-headed gentleman with the clean-cut features and blue eyes . . . reminded me strongly of the portraits I had seen of President John Quincy Adams," Schurz noted. Although the ambassador declared he was glad to see his guest, he said it in a tone so lacking in warmth as to suggest the opposite. But Schurz soon concluded that "this prim frigidity was purely temperamental and normal," and he left with "the highest impression" of Adams's patriotism, of the clearness and exactness of his mind, of the breadth of his knowledge, and his efficiency as a diplomat. Adams plainly lacked "the gifts of personal magnetism or sympathetic charm" essential to democratic politicians, nor had he, Schurz noted, "that vivacity of mind and racy combative-ness" which had made his father so formidable and dramatic a figure, but he exuded a kind of unflinching moral authority which command-ed "so high a respect that every word he uttered had extraordinary weight. . . ." Schurz left Adams strenghtened in his conviction that the abolition of slavery must be a stated aim of the Union in order to forestall foreign intervention on behalf of the Confederacy.

It was evident that decisions at Whitehall might well determine the outcome of the war itself. "People do not quite understand Americans or their politics," Adams wrote. "They think this is a hasty quarrel, the mere result of passion, which will be arranged as soon as the cause of it shall pass off. They do not comprehend the connection which slavery has with it, because we do not at once preach emancipation." The British believed a "prompt settlement" essential. "If it be by a recogni-tion of two governments, that is as good a way as any other." Adams was convinced that "after all that may be said, there is not and cannot be any assimilation of manners and social habits between Americans and English people. All intercourse with the aristocratic class is necessarily formal. . . . Everyone is civil, but each one has his interests in England, so that a stranger is but an outsider at best. . . ."

At Madrid, Schurz found a most congenial friend in Horatio Perry, a native of New Hampshire and a graduate of Harvard. Strikingly handsome, Perry had come to the legation in 1849 and married a charming Spanish woman, Carolina Coronado, a favorite of the queen's and a famous poetess. Doña Carolina, compliant in every other respect, refused to abandon her home for distant America. Schurz was charmed by her and worked in perfect harmony with

Perry, who was a close scholar of Spanish politics and culture. Schurz lived in the Perrys' palatial country house, Quinta, a perfect Spanish dwelling, one of the residences of the former Queen María Cristina, and ineffably romantic.

Among the members of the diplomatic corps at the Spanish court was a Prussian, Count Galen, the representative of a government that only a few years before had persecuted Schurz "as a revolutionary offender" and "state criminal." Galen was intelligent and well informed. From him Schurz learned that the Prussian aristocracy, like their counterparts in England and France, hated democracy "instinctively" and sympathized with the Confederacy. But an "overwhelming majority" of the Prussian people, "the most intelligent, active and progressive elements, were decidedly and vigorously in sympathy with the North and the Union. . . . The attitude of the Prussian Government was therefore not only one of neutrality, but one of distinctly amicable, well-wishing neutrality."

Queen Isabella, gross and sensual, was openly contemptuous of her mousy husband, the king "with the chicken voice," who "hung about the Court . . . like a charity boarder with a title" while his wife openly took on a series of lovers to the general entertainment of the diplomatic court and her subjects.

So far as the Spanish government had a stand or a policy it was generally favorable to the Confederacy, again on the principle that the South approached more closely a traditional European aristocracy and doubtless with the hope that a conclusion of the war favorable to the South would redound to Spain's interest in Cuba, the Caribbean, and Central and South America. In the relatively brief period that Schurz held his office, Spain threw in with France and England in dispatching an expedition to "restore order" in Mexico and collect debts due from that country to the three European powers. Schurz's insistent queries to the Spanish foreign minister on the intentions of that nation in Mexico were met with bland assurances that the expedition had only the most benign intentions and would be recalled promptly once a stable Mexican government had been established.

It was undoubtedly true that, in the words of Carl Schurz, "foreigners doing business in Mexico were subjected to ruthless extortion and pillage" and that "the official representatives of foreign powers had to suffer insulting demonstrations." England had, it must be said, secured from its partners in the venture a clause to the effect that "the high contracting parties engage not to seek for themselves, in the employment of coercive measures . . . any acquisition of territory, or any special advantage, and not to exercise in the internal affairs of Mexico any influence of a nature to prejudice the right of the Mexican nation to choose and to constitute freely the form of its government." To this clause France had acceded, with, as it turned out, very substantial, if unstated, reservations. The three powers desired to "give new strength and a new impulse to the conservative party in Mexico, and enable it to establish a strong government," the Spanish foreign minister told an uneasy Carl Schurz. Matters were complicated by the fact that when the leader of the conservative or clerical party in Mexico, General Miguel Miramón, visited Madrid to solicit the support of the Spanish crown, he argued that a republic was not a viable form of government for Mexico. A convention should be called for the purpose of establishing a constitutional monarchy and electing a king. While Spain hardly had the resources or national energy for such a dangerous venture it appealed enormously to that ambitious trouble-maker Napoleon III. During 1862 Spain sent twenty-six warships and transports to Veracruz and landed 6,000 soldiers. The British had already sent 700 marines, two frigates, and a battleship, while the French were committed to dispatching an equivalent force.

Schurz became so alarmed over what seemed to him the evident consequences of the Lincoln administration's silence on the slavery issue that he sat down and wrote a long letter to the President on the subject. "It is my conviction," Schurz began, ". . . that the sympathies of the liberal masses in Europe are not as unconditionally in our favor as might be desired, and that unless the war ends soon or something be done to give our cause a stronger foothold in the popular heart, they will, in the end, not be decided and powerful enough to control the actions of those governments whose good will or neutrality is to us of the greatest importance."

At the beginning of the war, most Europeans had seen it "as nothing less than a grand uprising of the popular conscience in favor of a great Humanitarian principle." Had this impression been sustained, the support of those Europeans of humanitarian principles would have been assured, but such friends of the Union had expressed "surprise and disappointment" that the Federal government had "cautiously avoided the mentioning of the slavery question as the cause and origin of the conflict. . . . It is my profound conviction," Schurz continued, "that as soon as the war becomes distinctly one for and against slavery, public opinion will be so strongly, so overwhelmingly in our favor, that, in spite of commercial interests or secret spites, no European government will dare to place itself, by declaration or act, upon the side of a universally condemned institution. . . . It is . . . my opinion that every step taken by the government towards the abolition of slavery is, as to our standing in Europe, equal to a victory in the field."

Surrounded by the seriocomic intrigues of the Spanish court in a setting of decaying feudal splendor, Schurz thought constantly of America and the uncertain progress of the war, which, when he had left the United States, it had been thought would be of only a few months' duration. Now it was clear those months might stretch into years, and Schurz wished for a more active role, preferably in the army. He asked Seward for a leave of absence to return to the United States.

Meanwhile, hopes for improved relations with Great Britain were dashed by what came to be known as the Trent Affair. The British mailship the *Trent* left Havana on the morning of November 7, 1861, with two Confederate agents on board. James M. Mason and John Slidell were traveling to England to try to buy arms and munitions for the Confederate forces and to arrange for ships to be built in British shipyards—ships that would be used to prey on Union shipping. The *Trent* was intercepted by the USS *San Jacinto,* and the Confederate agents were taken off on the orders of Captain Charles Wilkes. Slidell's daughter, it was reported, "with flashing eyes and quivering lips," tried unsuccessfully to bar the way to her father's cabin. Having been carried to Boston, the Confederate agents were imprisoned in Fort Warren while a storm blew up between Britain and the United States over the circumstances of their capture. Mason was the grandson of George Mason, who, seventy-four years earlier in the Federal Convention, had predicted that the United States must pay one day for the sin of slavery. He was a classic Virginia eccentric who called himself Jeems, said "chaw" for "chew," and wore a dress coat to breakfast. Mary Chesnut thought him "the unlikeliest diplomat in the world. But then the English were said to like eccentrics." Slidell, a native of New York and a graduate of Columbia Law School, had been a Louisiana Congressman and a fiery champion of secession.

The British demanded the immediate release of Mason and Slidell and an apology from the government for what it considered an unfriendly and warlike act, in defiance of the laws governing neutral vessels in wartime. Northerners, already indignant with England for its obvious Southern partisanship, breathed defiance. Let old England rage; the Union would not be intimidated. Southerners took heart, hoping that Northern intransigence would provoke England into declaring war or, at the very least, recognizing the rights of the Confederacy as a belligerent and offering it military and financial assistance. Charles Colcock Jones, a lieutenant in the Georgia artillery, was exultant. If the Lincolnites refused to turn Mason and Slidell over, he wrote in his diary, the British and French would declare war on the United States and sweep the North's blockading squadrons from the sea. The future of the Lincoln government was "most gloomy; a God- and man-forsaken people left to work out alone their own destruction."

The line taken by Great Britain was, of course, vastly more important than any actions of Spain. Spain took its clue in foreign and domestic policy largely from France. Napoleon III, by the same token, was anxious to act in concert with the British. The barometer of British sentiment was thus the critical one. England's "upper ten thousand," as the senior Charles Francis Adams called them, continued to revel in every Union setback. "These poor infatuated devils" were, in Adams's opinion, playing a losing game. Adams wrote to his son Charles: "The great body of the aristocracy and the wealthy commercial classes are anxious to see the United States go to pieces. On the other hand the middle and lower class sympathize with us, more and more as they better comprehend the true nature of the struggle. . . . All equally see in the convulsion in America an era in the history of the world, out of which must come in the end a general recognition of the right of mankind to the produce of their labor and the pursuit of happiness."

As weeks passed and Secretary of State Seward sounded as belligerent as any street-corner patriot, the English friends of the Union were thrown into the deepest gloom. It seemed that the United States was determined to become involved in war with Great Britain. "I consider that we are dished, and that our position is hopeless. . . . It is our ruin," Henry Adams wrote to his brother Charles. "What part it is reserved for us to play in this very tragical comedy I am utterly unable to tell. The Government has left us in the most awkward and unfair position. . . . This nation means to make war. Do not doubt it. What Seward means is more than I can guess. . . . We have friends still here, but very few." In his view the South was independent in fact. "I believe the thing to be settled," he wrote his brother. "We cannot bring the South back." Adams continued: "You cannot imagine our existence here. Angry and hateful as I am of Great Britain, I still can't help laughing and cursing at the same time in the accounts of the talk of our people. What a bloody set of fools they are! . . . What do you mean by asserting now principles against which every Adams yet has protested and resisted. You're mad, all of you. It's pitiable to see such idiocy in a nation. . . . It makes papa's position here very embarrassing. . . ."

"Papa" wrote to the same effect. "The leading newspapers roll out as much fiery lava as Vesuvius is doing, daily. . . . The clubs and the army and the navy and the people in the streets generally are raving for war. On the other side are the religious people and a large number of stock jobbers and traders, together with the radical following of Messrs. Cobden and Bright. The impression is general that Mr. Seward is resolved to insult England until she makes a war." Seward's humorous comment to the duke of Newcastle that insulting England was "the only sure passport to popular favor in America" was widely quoted as evidence of the secretary's hostility to Great Britain.

Charles Francis, Jr., not yet aware of the storm created in England by the seizure of the Confederate agents, wrote quite cheerfully that "brute force is all with us. . . . I think there will be a Southern collapse within four months, if only we can hold over that time." When he received Henry's missive predicting war with England, Charles Francis's spirits sank correspondingly. Having blundered all summer long, the United States had "capstoned our blunders by blundering into a war with England. So be it. While there's life there's hope; but I go into the army with a bitter feeling against those under whose lead we have come to this pass, and amid all the shattered idols of my whole life I don't feel as if I cared much when my turn came. . . . Against the rebels I could fight with a will and in earnest. They are traitors, they war for a lie, they are the enemies of morals, of government, and of man. In them we fight against a great wrong." But a war with England would be "a wicked and causeless war wantonly brought about by us and one in which I most unwillingly would go to my death."

Ironically, it was the often implacable Sumner who saw at once that the two envoys must be surrendered and who used all his considerable influence and powers of persuasion to effect that end. In the words of Carl Schurz, "Sumner remained cool. As soon as he heard of what had happened he instantly said: 'We shall have to give up the captives.'" He made a masterful speech in the Senate which conclud-ed: "Mr. President, let the rebels go. The two wicked men, ungrateful to their country, are let loose with the brand of Cain upon their foreheads. Prison doors are opened, but principles are established which will help to free other men, and open the gates of the sea." At the beginning of the New Year, Seward wrote Earl Russell a conciliatory letter, and Mason and Slidell were turned loose to make what considerable mischief they could in England and France.

In the aftermath of the Trent Affair Henry Adams felt that the tide of public, or at least parliamentary, opinion was running strongly against the United States. "If there's not a great success, and a success *followed up,* within six weeks," he wrote Charles, "we may better give up the game than blunder any more over it. . . . This war has lasted long enough to my mind." The death of Prince Albert in 1861 had removed from the English scene a strong advocate of neutrality. "I have given up the war and only pray for its end. The South has vindicated its position and we cannot help it. So, as we can find no one to lead us and no one to hold us together, I don't see the use of our shedding more blood. . . . We dawdle ahead here," he added, "going to dinners, races, balls, dropping a mild dew of remonstrances upon the British Government for allowing rebel armaments in their ports; riding in the parks; dining stray Americans and stately English; and in short groaning under the fardel of an easy life." The latest notion was not military but "moral intervention," which Henry Adams described as "some combined representation on the part of the European powers . . . urging our two parties to come to an understanding." The danger to the Northern cause was that any "understanding" must, almost by definition, leave the South out of the Union and slavery intact. The economic hardship caused by the interruption of the flow of Southern cotton to French and English factories fell most heavily on the mills' operatives thrown out of work. "The suffering among the people in Lancashire and in France is already very great," Adams wrote, "and is increasing every day without any prospect of relief for months to come."

One of the most important long-range consequences of British upper-class partisanship for the Confederacy was that it cured upper-class Americans like the Adamses and George Templeton Strong of their infatuation with England. Strong wrote in his diary that he was "thankful to be cured, at last, of the Anglophilism that has oppressed me ever since I was a boy and made me forget or underrate my own people and my father's house." He was especially indignant with the British *Saturday Review,* in which, it seemed to him, cleverness was much preferred to morality or even common sense. One of the magazine's basic premises seemed to be that Southerners were honorable and "gentlemanly" warriors while Yankees were brutes and barbarians. The author of one such article undertook to prove that while the barbarity of Yankees was due in part to the harshness of the Northern climate, the true reason lay in the tide of immigration. More men had come to the United States than women. Many male immigrants had, therefore, been forced to take Indian women as wives. "Hence, a large infusion of 'Red Indian' blood into the population of the North. Which unquestionable fact fully accounts for the fiendish atrocities and ruffianly brutality Northern soldiers love to perpetuate and Northern communities approve. . . ."

Strong told, with obvious relish, the story of "little Johnny Heckscher," a wounded and furloughed officer at a ball in honor of the marquess of Hartington (later duke of Devonshire). The marquess displayed a "showy little *secesh flag*" in his buttonhole. Heckscher jostled and pushed the young marquess saying, "It was intentional, sir, quite intentional." To which the peer replied, "Hee-aw-w-w-what's the matter. It's really vewy extrawadinary." When Heckscher continued his harassments, the marquess demanded an explanation. "If you do not instantly take that thing out of your buttonhole, I'll pull it out." Strong noted: "So Great Britain took it out and put it in his pocket and apologized. . . ."

Conversely the Civil War reconciled upper-class Americans like Motley, Holmes, Strong, Charles Francis Adams, Jr., perhaps even the latter's father to democracy or popular government by virtue of the fact that the Civil War was so clearly a "people's war." That is to say the people of the North had risen up to defend the Union and to acquiesce in the freeing of the slaves, thus vindicating a political system about which, as we have frequently noted, the upper classes had often retained the gravest misgivings. Certainly those misgivings had not been laid entirely to rest, but when they surfaced again in the last decades of the century, in the so-called Gilded Era, they appeared in a quite different form.

Reading William Howard Russell's account of the early days of the war, Charles Francis Adams, Jr., wrote: "What a shameful, ludicrous time he records, and yet beneath all that humbug, cowardice and incompetence, which makes me weep and blush as one reads, how grand and heroic we who were there and of those days knew that it was at bottom. The enthusiasm, loyalty and self-sacrifice of those days, the sudden upheaving against that which was wrong on the part of a whole great people we felt and knew. . . ." Russell, in his attention to the details of day-to-day events, had missed all this, but it was the essence. "I do admire the people of the North more than I ever did before," Adams added, "and I do believe that history will do credit of their great deeds in this war. . . ."

13

Port Royal

In August, 1861, anxious to take advantage of the Union naval superiority, Benjamin Butler received permission to organize an expedition to seize Forts Hatteras and Clark off the North Carolina coast. The combined operation under Admiral Silas Stringham was made up of seven naval vessels mounting 143 guns and 800 men of the 9th and 20th New York Volunteers. Stringham, sixty-three years old, had fought against the Algerian pirates as a young midshipman in the War of 1812, and he had been appointed commander of the northern Atlantic blockading fleet in the Mexican War. He had participated actively in the navy's transition from sail to steam and seen naval armament and tactics change dramatically. With his little fleet, he carried out a brilliant bombardment of the Hatteras shore batteries. The accepted tactic for ships attacking fortifications was to anchor within range and blast away. The tactic, essential in the days of sailing vessels at the mercy of uncertain winds, had been dutifully followed after the advent of steam. Stringham decided to make use of his steam vessels' independence of wind and current to "move and fire." Steaming past the Confederate forts, his ships made elusive targets for the cumbersome defense guns while soon reducing the rebel forts to rubble. A landing party completed the investment with the loss of only one man. Six hundred and seventy prisoners and thirty-five cannon were captured. Minor though the engagement was, it was brilliantly successful and demonstrated the vulnerability of the South to well-conducted amphibious operations. Stringham, in uncertain health, retired four months later, full of years and honors.

The success of the Hatteras expedition encouraged a far more ambitious undertaking. Lincoln, Stanton, and Welles agreed on a joint army-navy force to seize the splendid harbor of Port Royal between Charleston and Savannah on the Carolina coast. There the confluence of the Board and Port Royal rivers and Archer Creek formed a series of lush islands—the Sea Islands—of which Hilton Head, Parris, and Port Royal were the principal ones, all noted for their rich crops of long-fibered cotton.

When the expedition set out from Hampton Roads at the end of October, it was an impressive flotilla made up of fifty naval vessels and transports carrying some 12,000 soldiers, accompanied by twenty-five coaling ships. The commander of the operation was Samuel Francis Du Pont, a member of the remarkable Du Pont clan. Pierre Samuel du Pont de Nemours, the founder of the family in America, had been a radical French nobleman, a publisher, a member of the school of Physiocrats, and a correspondent of Jefferson's. He had come to the United States with his son, Eleuthère Irénée, in 1799 and established a powder works near Wilmington, Delaware. The War of 1812 made the family fortune. One of Pierre's grandsons, Henry, born in 1838, had recently graduated from the Military Academy (Class of '61) and was already engaged on a brilliant military career that would win him the Congressional Medal of Honor. Samuel Francis was another grandson. Born in 1803, he had been appointed a midshipman at the age of thirteen, commanded Robert Stockton's flagship in the Mexican War, and thereafter, as a senior captain, made notable improvements in the theory and practice of naval warfare. Gideon Welles described him as "a skillful and accomplished officer. Has a fine address, is a courtier with perhaps too much finesse and management, resorts too much to extraneous and subordinate influences to accomplish what he might easily attain directly, and, like many naval officers, is given to cliques,— personal, naval clanship."

Off Hilton Head, Du Pont began his bombardment, which, like that of Stringham, was delivered by his battleships under steam. Three times the Union flotilla passed the Confederate forts, delivering a slow and well-directed fire until they were out of commission and their garrisons had fled in a panic, leaving even coats and watches behind.

The Union losses were thirty-one killed and wounded. Forty-eight cannon and a large supply of military stores were captured. The planters and their families fled, abandoning thousands of exuberant slaves—now "contrabands," following Butler's designation. A number of plantation owners had tried to prevail on their slaves to flee with them. A few, mainly household slaves, had gone, but most had refused. Some of those who refused to leave had been shot by their masters, presumably on the ground that if they must lose their property no one else should have the use of it. A plantation owner on one of the islands who failed to make his escape to the mainland was captured by Federal forces and sent as a prisoner to a Union ship in a boat rowed by his slaves who sang as they rowed:

> De Norfmen dey's got massa now,
> De Norfmen dey's got massa now,
> De Norfmen dey's got massa now,
>   Hallelujah.
>
> Oh! massa a rebel; we row him to prison.
>   Hallelujah.
> Massa no whip us any more.
>   Hallelujah.
> We have no massa now, we free.
>   Hallelujah.

With their white masters gone, many of the slaves began to loot the town houses of Beaufort. One householder, slipping back into town after his fellow planters had fled, found "Chloe, Stephen's wife, seated at Phoebe's piano playing away like the very Devil and two damsels upstairs dancing away famously. . . ." A reporter for the *New York Tribune* wrote: "We went through spacious houses where only a week ago families were living in luxury, and saw their costly furniture despoiled, books and papers smashed, pianos on the sidewalk, feather beds ripped open, and even the filth of the Negroes left lying in parlors and bedchambers."

The seizure of the Sea Islands gave the Union a lodgment in the heart of the Confederacy and led to the most significant nonmilitary event of the war: the so-called Port Royal experiment, carried out by Northern abolitionist teachers and missionaries, or, perhaps more properly, missionary teachers, in partnership with the government. Its avowed purpose was to try to determine what might be done to assist the slaves of the South in making the transition to freedom. What was at issue was no less than the question of the capacity of black Americans who had been enslaved to become assimilated in white America.

Southerners had justified slavery for almost two centuries on the grounds that black people were inherently and irredeemably inferior to white people and that slavery was not only their necessary and inevitable condition but in their best interest. Thousands of Northern abolitionists had staked a substantial portion of their lives on a contrary assumption—that all men were equal in the sight of God; all were rational creatures made in His image. From this it followed that any apparent inferiority was the result of the degrading conditions of slavery. Freedom, accompanied by Christian education, would demonstrate that differences between races, black or white, were only skin deep.

What gave a heightened drama to the unfolding events at Port Royal was that literally millions of Northerners, unpersuaded by the abolitionist arguments for equality, were deferring judgment on the matter (or, it might be fairer to say, had the same conviction that the South did—that black people were inferior to whites). Thus, the consequences of the Port Royal experiment were literally incalculable. Not only was the broad general theological-philosophical issue to be settled one way or another, but specific practical modes of dealing with those millions of slaves who, more and more Northerners were assuming, must eventually be free were to be worked out at Port Royal.

With the capture of Port Royal, as many as 10,000 contrabands, slaves whose masters and mistresses had fled, leaving them free *de facto*, if not *de jure* (since there was yet no governmental policy on slavery, their masters could, presumably, if peace was made on any basis that did not specifically free the slaves, reclaim them), became wards of the Federal government. These slaves without masters had to be provided for. They were, with a handful of exceptions, illiterate, and many of them were, at least initially, unable to care for themselves without the direction of white masters or overseers. Moreover, they had no land; the land still belonged legally to the recently departed owners. The Union might expropriate the land by an act of Congress and sell it to new owners or distribute it to the slaves who worked it—not surprisingly, the recommendation, even insistence, of most of the abolitionists. But even if this latter policy was followed by the Lincoln administration, there was no certainty that the ex-slaves would be able to manage the lands (as opposed to merely working them). To make the transition from a state of complete, almost childlike dependence to the rather demanding role of independent, self-motivated farmer was a far from easy task. A few slaves, mostly household slaves and those slaves who had been given considerable responsibility by their former masters, were capable of fending for themselves with a minimum of assistance from Union agencies or agents. But the great majority were thrust, by the "absquision" (flight) of whites, into a traumatically different world from the one that they had known. A plantation black told Susan Walker, a teacher, that he and his fellows had "been so 'confuse'; they did not know what to do; did not know where they belonged or 'anything about we.' "

Harriet Tubman, the heroine of the Underground Railroad, came to the Sea Islands, where she worked as a nurse and a scout for the Union army. One old slave told her: "I'd been yere seventy-three years, workin' for my master widout even a dime wages. I'd worked rain-wet sun dry. I'd worked wid my mouf full of dust, but would not stop to get a drink of water. I'd been whipped, an' starved, an' I was always prayin', 'Oh! Lord, come an' delibber us!' All dat time de birds been flyin, an' de rabens had been cryin', and de fish had been sunnin' in de waters. One day I look up, an' I see a big cloud; it didn't come up like as de clouds come out far yonder, but it 'peared to be right ober head. Der was tunders out of day, an' der was lightin'd. Den I looked on de water, an' I see, 'peared to me a big house in de water, an' out of de big house came great big eggs, and de good eggs went on throu' de air, an fell into de fort; an' de bad eggs burst before de got dar. . . . Den I heard 'twas the Yankee ship [the *Wabash*] firin' out the big eggs, and dey had come to set us free. Den I praise de Lord. He come an' put he little finger in de work, an' dey Sesh Buckra all go; and de birds stop flyin', and de rabens stop cryin', and when I go to catch a fish to eat wid my rice, de's no fish dar. De Lord Almighty'd come and frightened 'em all out of de waters. Oh! Praise de Lord! I'd prayed seventy-three years, an' now he's come an' we's all free."

Abolitionist missionaries and teachers waited like racers for the starter's gun—the approval of the President—that would send them racing to Port Royal to transmute their faith into fact, to prove that of which they had no doubt—that freed slaves, or slaves treated as though they were free (since, as we have noted, their actual legal and constitutional status was unresolved), would, with education and sympathetic guidance, become distinguishable from whites only by the color of their skin.

On December 20, 1861, only a few weeks after the capture of the islands, Lincoln sent a telegram to Edward L. Pierce asking him to make an investigation of the Sea Islands with recommendations on what should be done for the black population of the islands. Pierce, a graduate of Brown and Harvard Law School, had worked in Salmon Chase's law office and been an early recruit to the Republican Party. Thirty-six years old at the fall of Sumter, he had enlisted as a private in the 3rd Massachusetts Volunteers, and after the capture of Hampton, Virginia, he had been given the assignment of organizing the contrabands to work on the defenses of that town.

After two weeks Pierce drew up a report expressing his opinion that "when properly organized and with proper motives set before them," the blacks of the region "will as freemen be as industrious as any race of men likely in this climate." This, of course, was speculation rather than observation; it was the abolitionist faith and hope. "In spite of their condition," Pierce noted, "reputed to be worse here than in many other parts of the rebellious region, there are such features in their life and character that the opportunity is now offered to us to make of them, partially in this generation and fully in the next, a happy, industrious, law-abiding, free, and Christian people." The tone of caution, the hope for the completion of the task in the "next" generation, hinted at the sobering reality that Pierce confronted among the confused and demoralized blacks.

Lincoln talked with Pierce and, impressed with his intelligence and obvious dedication, authorized Chase to devise a plan to give practical effect to Pierce's very general recommendations. Under the plan that Chase and Pierce submitted, a white "labor superintendent," rather similar in his duties to the plantation overseer he replaced, was to be appointed to each plantation. The superintendents would receive supplies, housing, transportation, and rations from the government, but their salaries would have to be paid by private societies. Pierce set to work at once to organize a network of abolitionist chapters and church congregations to provide both the workers in this new vineyard of the Lord and the money to sustain them. The Union soldiers were quite ready to brutalize and exploit the blacks, and if a heroic effort were not made at once by those devoted to the welfare of the Southern black, they would soon be hopelessly corrupted. In Pierce's words, "If this critical moment be not availed of and some means not taken to make them industrious, orderly and sober, they will become hopelessly demoralized." This was a missionary field far more urgent than India or Africa.

The result of Pierce's exhortations was the formation of the Boston Educational Commission, organized for "the industrial, social, intellectual, moral and religious elevation of persons released from Slavery in the course of the War for the Union." The governor of Massachusetts was elected president, and hundreds of prominent Republicans were soon members, while similar organizations were formed in virtually every Northern state. The National Freedmen's Relief Association was started in New York, and Philadelphia set up the Port Royal Relief Committee. Thus was launched a voluntary philanthropic movement of vast dimensions and significance. When abolitionist journals called for volunteers to go to the Sea Islands as teachers, hundreds applied and fifty-three were chosen. Among them, Pierce noted, were "some of the choicest young men of New England, fresh from Harvard, Yale, and Brown, from the divinity schools of Andover and Cambridge,—men of practical talent and experience. There were some of whom the world was scarce worthy. . . ." Among them were twelve women. One of the company, William Channing Gannett, a Boston teacher, described them, more cogently, as "a queer farrago . . . clerks, doctors, divinity-students, professors and teachers, underground railway agents and socialists . . . white hairs and black. . . . Unitarians, free-thinkers, Methodists, strait-laced, and the other Evangelical sects." Everyone seemed "pretty earnest and quite fraternal." Edward Philbrick, a prosperous young businessman and second-generation abolitionist, who had contributed $1,000 to the cost of the experiment and was serving without pay at Port Royal, was more caustic. To him "a good many looked like broken-down schoolmasters or ministers who have excellent dispositions but not much talent." They were soon termed Gideonites or Gideon's Band by the condescending soldiers in whose midst they began their labors. All but one of the New England members of the contingent had college degrees.

Among the Sea Island missionaries were Samuel Phillips, a nephew of Wendell Phillips, and Edward Hooper, a lawyer from Harvard, who, like Philbrick, was serving without pay. William Channing Gannett was another member of Boston's Unitarian elite who joined Gideon's Band. Austa French and her husband, Mansfield, were two of the most assertive of the group. Mrs. French had graduated from Mary Lyon's school, the precursor of Mount Holyoke, taught with her husband at the Xenia Female Seminary in Ohio, edited a religious magazine, and reared seven children. To her the antislavery cause was the "sacred ark" which she and the other members of the band must carry through the Red Sea. Her first contact with the blacks of Hilton Head was clearly traumatic. "There steals over you," she wrote, "the feeling that you are passing under a great cloud of accumulated wrongs, that you yourself have done something awful, somewhere in the dim past. . . . Slavery is written upon the shore, the trees, the sky, the air. . . . The enormous black hawks, with their screams, seem to be its very spirit. No wonder they caw, caw, over this land—mean vultures waiting for blood." Despite a shaky ornithology, which combined hawks, crows, and vultures in an odd-feathered amalgam, Austa French spoke and wrote eloquently for the extreme evangelical wing of Gideon's Band.

A major theme of this multivolume history has been the American attitude toward work. As the reader is now, I hope, aware, the American view of work has been one of profound ambivalence. According to the Scriptures, "work" was Jehovah's punishment of man for his disobedience in the Garden. Moreover, work was, strictly speaking, physical labor, not writing law briefs or selling something. In America man might be said to have outwitted the Almighty by using work to make money; by constantly and ingeniously devising ways to do less work for more money, to "save time" by lightening labor and thus mitigating the punishment meted out by a displeased deity. Yet Americans, at the same time, glorified and exalted work. We declared that the desire to work long hours at low wages in menial and often dangerous jobs, far from being God's punishment for man's intransigence, was, in fact, the path to salvation, evidence of sterling moral worth (or good character), and, above all, profoundly *American.* The most vocal advocates of this view of work were those who, by William Manning's definition, did no work at all or, by more generous interpretation, did very interesting "work" involving little physical strain or stress or very highly remunerative "work" or both, or, sometimes, in fact, none at all. Sidney George Fisher was appalled at the thought of having to work for a living. Richard Henry Dana was weary and depressed at the prospect, as was George Templeton Strong. Benjamin Franklin, the apostle of work, and Philip Hone retired as soon as they could. Every red-blooded upper-middle- or upper-class young American male wished, as we have seen, to live on dividends or become a writer, about as far from honest labor as one could get. But all were fulsome in their praise of work as an essential character builder for others and indignant whenever they discovered a member of the lower classes who shared their repugnance for it.

We have already noted how this exaltation of work affected the relationship of whites and Indians. It played a somewhat similar role in the relationship of whites to black people. Many free blacks became as work-oriented as the most obsessed white. A number of others, like a number of whites, preferred an economically marginal life, in which what we might call creative leisure was a higher value than work. Considering the kinds of jobs they were limited to by white prejudice and the additional obstacles they encountered in any effort to attain the better jobs which whites for the most part reserved for themselves, the fact that many unskilled blacks showed no special enthusiasm for labor was hardly surprising.

In the South among free blacks and ex-slaves the case, though similar, was markedly different. All African slaves had originally a tribal background. As with the tribes of American aborigines, there was no work in the tribe. Just as tribal consciousness did not make that separation between man and nature that marked "the fall" into modern *self*-consciousness, so it had no notion of "work" as an abstraction, as something that might be done without reference to a specific need to secure food or protect the tribe against its enemies. What work was done—that is to say, the more onerous tasks necessary to maintain tribal life—was commonly done by women or by slaves captured from other tribes. "Work," like "guilt" (both of which, it is important to note, were identified with "the fall"), had not been defined as a category of human activity. The consequence was that for a person of tribal consciousness—i.e., a newly imported slave—to be forced to work and, moreover, to work at the most toilsome and demanding tasks for the benefit of others who did not work and whose superior status *was indicated by the fact that they did not* was to confirm, ironically, the biblical notion of work as punishment, with the additional fact that the slave had committed no "sin" for which the penalty was "work." The work the slave was forced to do appeared to him/her absolutely arbitrary and meaningless, the most remorseless and condign chastisement. The very same Southern master, whose power, authority, and social position rested on the fact that he did no work, waxed wrathful and indignant at the slave who was so "lazy" that he would work only under the constant threat of the lash or some other destructive and degrading form of punishment. And the odd thing was that Americans generally, Americans north and south of the Mason-Dixon Line, accepted it as a basic proposition that blacks must work and that if they did not choose to work of their own volition without any other compensation than the meeting of their barest physical needs, that fact somehow suggested a kind of inherent "racial" inferiority. Even the most devoted abolitionist accepted this basic proposition and worried about its implications incessantly.

To the Southern charge that the black was so morally deficient that he/she would work only if forced to do so, the abolitionist replied that the slave only appeared "lazy"—that is to say, unwilling to work voluntarily because he/she saw no purpose in doing so. The slave could not, like other Americans, better himself; "get ahead" in the "go-ahead age" by working. But as soon as the slave was freed and it was clear to him that benefits would accrue to him from his labor, he would rival or outstrip his white compatriot in the enthusiasm with which he *worked*. But suppose that assumption were wrong? Suppose that the African did not readily and cheerfully adopt what came later to be called the work ethic? Suppose he preferred to explore the possibilities of creative leisure? Then there would intrude the terrible thought that the slaveholder and his system were justified after all because, it was commonly said, there was no place in America for those who would not work—that is to say for those who would not take dangerous, debilitating, and poorly paid jobs primarily for the benefit of others. While all this seemed simple enough to the vast majority of white Americans, it was by no means so clear to black Americans, especially to those who had so recently experienced work as a grievous and perpetual punishment rather than as a mark of sanctification. Thus, work or, more accurately, the white man's notion of it came to be the hinge of the continuing tensions between the white man and the black man, whether or not the latter had been born free or born slave and set free.

The problem was made more complex by the fact that the remarkable subculture that the slave had created and that touched every black man and women, slave or free—the "black consciousness," as we say today—had, in a certain sense, been created in contradistinction, or as antidote, to the "punishment-work" that slaves underwent as the inescapable condition of their lives. Out of the pain and weariness of perpetual labor, slaves created songs of sorrow and endurance, songs and rhythms so powerful and haunting that they would survive a thousand transformations. So to say that freed blacks had, for the best of reasons, an indisposition to work is to understate the case and to raise the question of how anyone could ever have thought that it could have been otherwise. In the end, of course, they had to work, not having the means, as a good many more fortunate Americans did, of avoiding it. If there had been a better understanding among white Americans of the origin, nature, and paradoxes inherent in the very notion of "work," especially as it related to recently tribal peoples who had experienced work only as punishment and the badge of servitude, much misunderstanding might have been avoided.

So the most critical issue at Port Royal was whether contrabands would *work!* One of the immediate problems revolved around the unwillingness of the ex-slaves to plant cotton, the symbol of their servitude. They were quite ready to plant potatoes, corn, and other vegetables and to raise chickens, but they had difficulty understanding the difference between planting cotton for their former masters and planting it for their new master, the Federal government, especially when their pay was often long deferred. Yet the supervisors were under heavy pressure to demonstrate that the cotton production of free blacks would substantially exceed that of slaves (this had been one of the principal abolitionist arguments against slavery—that free labor was far more productive than slave labor). Frederick Law Olmsted had been one of the most vocal champions of this contention. Great attention thus focused on the returns from those Sea Island plantations which were being worked by contrabands under the direction of government-appointed superintendents. In the words of Edward Philbrick, "We found them a herd of suspicious savages who regarded their change of condition with fear and trembling, looking at the cotton-field as a life-long scene of unrequited toil, and hailing with delight the prospect of 'no more driver, no more cotton, no more lickin'.'" They had broken up the cotton gins, the symbols of their servitude, and they were understandably disheartened when their liberators made it clear that they expected them to resume once more the cultivation of that hated crop. A baffled Philbrick threatened to report them to "Massa Lincoln as too lazy to be free." He noted, "I am surprised to find how little most of these people appreciate their present prospects. Once in a while you find an intelligent man who does so, but the mass plod along in the beaten track with little thought about the future and no sort of feeling of responsibility. They feel a sense of relief that no one stands to force them to labor, and they fall back with a feeling of indifference as to whether they exert themselves beyond what is necessary to supply the demands of necessity. . . ." The best part, he added, "go into the field grumbling about 'no clothes, no tobacco, no molasses, no salt, no shoes, no medicine, etc.,' which is all very true and unanswerable." It seemed to many of the blacks that "The Yankees preach nothing but cotton, cotton!" Once it was made clear to them by Philbrick that the proceeds of their work would be their own, they turned to diligently planting and fertilizing two hundred acres of cotton. The cotton gins were hunted up and repaired, and the cotton was ginned.

Directly related to the issue of work was the question of how much help to give the contrabands. Not enough would drive them to starvation or to the acceptance of some new form of white exploitation. But too much, it was argued, would simply make them dependent on a new master—the Federal government. It was, of course, the same argument that had been waged over any form of assistance, public or private, to the needy members of society since the early years of the Republic. When did help for the desperately poor become handouts for the chronically indolent? Disturbed by such reflections, Wendell Phillips wrote: "I ask nothing more for the negro than I ask for the Irishman or the German who comes to our shores. I thank the benevolent men who are laboring at Port Royal—all right!—but the blacks at the South do not need them. They are not objects of charity. They only ask this nation—'Take your yoke off our necks.'" There was a considerable degree of the naïve and the disingenuous in Phillips's sentences. To compare the state of Irish and German immigrants with the condition of the slaves of the South was to demonstrate a failure of understanding, surprising in a man who had given his life to the abolitionist cause.

The "political" abolitionists, as Phillips had increasingly become, were determined to minimize the difficulties of the transition from slavery to freedom; the nonpolitical abolitionists, especially those with any firsthand knowledge of conditions in the South, were convinced that without massive assistance in the form of teachers and "helpers" the freed slaves could not establish themselves as the "equals" of Southern whites. Mansfield French was the leader of those members of Gideon's Band who believed that enough could not be done to assist the freedman in adjusting to white society. "God's programme involves *freedom in its largest sense—Free soil, free schools,—free ballot boxes, free representation in state and national" affairs.* The freedmen needed "teachers, helpers, men who can grasp the destiny and mission of this people.

Men who are not ashamed to bear the cross of the black man. Men who can quarry in the mountains, and bring the tall cedars from the forests. . . ." Edward Philbrick, on the other hand, identified himself with Wendell Phillips's laissez-faire doctrines. He agreed with William Channing Gannett that "all the laws of labor, wages, competition, etc." must "come into play,—and the sooner will habits of responsibility, industry, self-dependence, and manliness be developed. . . . Very little, very little, should be given them; now in their first moment of freedom is the time to influence their notion of it." Gannett took the gloomy view that "nothing will rouse and maintain their energy but suffering."

The debate reflected a far wider tension in American society, a tension of which we have observed numerous examples thus far in this narrative. One tradition reached back to the covenanted communities of New England. It was the spirit that spoke in John Winthrop's "A Modell of Christian Charity" of a people knit together as parts of a single body. Winthrop insisted that Christian love was "absolutely necessary to the being of the body of Christ, as the sinews and other ligaments of a natural body . . . we must love brotherly without dissimulation . . . we must bear one another's burthens, we must not look onely on our own things, but allsoe on the things of our brethren. . . ." This was the Ur document of the community that was "knit together," in which each man or woman cared for his or her brother or sister as himself or herself, and this was the spirit in which Mansfield French called for workers "not ashamed to bear the cross of the black man."

Opposed to the constantly revived hope of the true community was the exaltation of the competitive individual as the highest expression of the modern world, as the fruit of ages of "progress." Adam Smith had preached the gospel of economic laws as inescapable as the law of gravity. Scientific, immutable. To tamper with them was to invite disaster. The freedman, always acted upon, seldom acting, had once again to carry the burden of the white man's contradictory notions of the world and the black man's place in it. The fact was that both dogmas contained considerable truth. The ex-slave needed all the white help, all the love and concern, that he or she could get. There was no truly unselfish act that could not bear some fruit or point the way into the future. But America, for better or worse, was not that true community of brotherly love that the Puritans had yearned for. It was the mercilessly competitive society with which we have become familiar. If everything that could have been done for the freed black had been added to the very considerable things that were, in fact, done, they could not altogether have secured the place of the black man and woman in white society. In the last analysis, only they could do that by claiming it in unmistakable tones as their natural right.

If there was one form of work that virtually all the contrabands were eager to undertake, it was schoolwork. The frustrated superintendents were met, when they tried to impose a strict regimen on the blacks on their plantations, with all the guile and evasiveness that the ex-slaves had learned under their Southern masters. The teachers, on the other hand, were welcomed. They were presumed to carry the key to worldly success, to rapid entry into the privileges and benefits of the white man's world. They became the particular champions and advocates of the black people and often found themselves at odds with the superintendents, who varied widely in their administrative abilities and in their commitment to the Negro cause. Moreover, it was often the case that the more problack a superintendent was, the less capable he was as an administrator, and vice versa.

Elizabeth Botume, a Boston abolitionist who came to the Sea Islands to teach freedmen, wrote of her arrival in Beaufort, South Carolina: "Negroes, negroes, negroes. They hovered around like bees in a swarm. Sitting, standing, or lying at full-length, with their faces turned to the sky. Every doorstep, box, or barrel was covered with them, for the arrival of a boat was a time of great excitement. They were dressed—no, not dressed, nor clothed, but partly covered with every conceivable thing which could be put on the back of a biped. Some of the women had on old, cast-off soldiers' coats . . . and bits of sailcloth for head-handkerchiefs. Many of the men had strips of gay carpeting, or old bags, or pieces of blanket, in which they cut arm-holes and wore as Jackets. . . . Words fail to describe their grotesque appearance." Oblivious "to all this incongruity" they were still "only parts of a whole; once 'Massa's niggers,' now refugees and contrabands." Spoken to, they looked up "with a smile, and put their hands to their foreheads in military fashion, with a 'How d'ye, gineral? How d'ye, missis?'"

To Elizabeth Botume this colorful "whole" presented itself as a problem to be solved. Picturesque and captivating as it might be, it had to be dissolved into its component parts, individuals, and they had to be transformed, if possible, into sober citizens, properly attired, industrious, restrained, literate, middle-class Americans with an incidentally black skin. The culture shock experienced by the high-minded young women who hastened to Port Royal to serve as missionary teachers to the contrabands was considerable. Harriet Ware, a teacher from Massachusetts, had great difficulty understanding her charges' dialect, and Laura Towne, a genteel Philadelphian, wrote a friend that "it certainly takes great nerve to walk here among the soldiers and negroes and not be shocked or pained so much as to give it all up."

Botume discovered that her small black charges either had no identifiable names or changed them at whim. Having made up a list of the names of her pupils, she next day called the roll, but no one answered. "I could not distinguish one from another," she wrote (a not-uncommon reaction of whites to blacks). "They looked like so many peas in a pod. The woolly heads of the girls and boys looked just alike. All wore indiscriminately any cast-off garments given them, so it was not easy to tell 'which was which.'" The next morning the routine had to be repeated all over again. Elizabeth Botume wrote down forty new names. "In time," she noted, "I began to get acquainted with some of their faces. I could remember that 'Vornhouse' yesterday was 'Primus' to-day. That 'Quash' was 'Bryan.' He was already denying the old sobriquet, and threatening to 'mash you mouf in,' to any one who called him 'Quash.'"

Botume had a class of adult contrabands as well. "They rolled up their eyes and scratched their heads when puzzled," she wrote, "and every line in their faces was in motion. If any one missed a word, or gave a wrong answer, he looked very grave. But whenever a correct answer was given, especially if it seemed difficult, they laughed aloud and reeled about, hitting each other with their elbows. Such 'guffaws' could not be tolerated in regular school hours. They joked each other like children; but, unlike them, they took all good-naturedly."

Laura Towne found her pupils equally distracting. They talked aloud, "they lay down and went to sleep, they scuffled and struck each other. They got up by the dozen, made their curtsies, and walked off to the neighboring field for blackberries, coming back to their seats with a curtsy when they were ready. They evidently did not understand me, and I could not understand them, and after two hours and a half of effort I was thoroughly exhausted." But things improved, and Laura Towne wrote a Northern friend that the black people on her plantation were "jolly and happy and decently fed and dressed, and so full of affection and gratitude to the people who are relieving them that it is rather too flattering to be enjoyed." Best of all, they were demonstrating that they could work.

Charlotte Forten was a free black woman from the North who came with the first contingent of teachers and missionaries to Port Royal in 1862 to work with the freed slaves of the islands. She was the daughter of James Forten, who had served as a cabin boy in the Continental navy and become a successful Philadelphia businessman, a philanthropist, and a friend of John Greenleaf Whittier's and Theodore Weld's. Charlotte Forten's response to the contraband children she came to teach at Port Royal was complicated by the fact that she herself was black. She wrote in her diary that the blacks she met were "certainly the most dismal specimens I ever saw." She was an upper-middle-class schoolteacher of that class of reformers whose capital was Boston (she had been teaching in a school in Salem, Massachusetts, before she came to Hilton Head). Her small black charges were as remote from her experience as if they had just arrived from the moon. "Little colored children of every hue were playing about the streets," she wrote, "looking as merry and happy as children ought to look,— now that the evil shadow of Slavery no longer hangs over them." Charlotte Forten was rowed over to the island of St. Helena. "As we glided along, the rich tones of the negro boatmen broke upon the evening stillness,—sweet, strange and solemn:

> Jesus make de blind to see,
> Jesus make de cripple walk,
> Jesus make de deaf to hear.
> Walk in, kind Jesus!
> No man can hinder me."

It must have seemed another and deeper kind of strangeness to Charlotte Forten to feel herself bound to these exotic creatures by the color of her skin.

The next morning she awoke to the sounds of "cheerful voices of men, women, children and chickens," and when she ran to the window, she saw "women in bright-colored handkerchiefs, some carrying pails on their heads . . . crossing the yard, busy with their morning work; children were playing and tumbling around them. On every face there was a look of serenity and cheerfulness. My heart gave a great throb of happiness as I looked at them and thought, 'They are free! so long down-trodden, so long crushed to earth, but now in their old homes, forever free!' And I thanked God that I had lived to see the day."

When Charlotte Forten met her pupils on the first day of school, some of the ambiguities of the situation immediately revealed themselves. She confessed she found it "rather trying." A very different atmosphere prevailed from that of the staid Salem schoolroom with which she was familiar. The children seemed to their harassed teacher "to have discovered the secret of perpetual motion, and tried one's patience sadly. . . . But after some days of positive, though not severe treatment, order was brought of chaos. . . . I never before saw children so eager to learn," she added. "Coming to school is a constant delight and recreation to them. They come here as other children go to play. . . . Of course there are some stupid ones, but these are the minority. The majority learn with wonderful rapidity. Many of the grown people are desirous of learning to read." But with the irresistible desire for "learning" there was an often disconcerting tendency on the part of the pupils, young and old, to be readily distracted. "We found it rather hard to keep their attention in school," Charlotte Forten wrote. Since they had been "so entirely unused to intellectual concentration," it was necessary "to interest them every moment to keep their thoughts from wandering. Teaching here is consequently far more fatiguing than at the North. . . . The tiniest children are delighted to get a book in their hands," she added. "Many of them already know their letters. The parents are eager to have them learn. They sometimes say to me,—'Do, Miss, let de chil'en learn eberyting dey can. We nebber hab no chance to learn nuttin', but we wants de chil'en to learn." The book was a magic talisman. It would seal the freedom of the slaves and open to them all the mysteries of the white world. If they could master the book, learn its secrets, they would become prosperous; they could live like their white masters without work. They could hunt and fish and sing and dance all day long and far into the night.

So there was an overwhelming enthusiasm among the contrabands for books and "learning," which the teachers shared as devoutly as their pupils. But the matter was, of course, more complicated than either teachers or pupils realized. The complex web of ingrained—internalized—values, modes of behavior, even, perhaps "neural circuitry" that prepared the Northern white (or black) pupil to sit quietly at his or her desk and dutifully repeat by rote those things the teacher offered was entirely missing in the environment of the ex-slave and, consequently, of their children. We talk today of brain hemispheres—left side, the emotional, intuitive, passional side; right side, rational, reasoning side. Even if the notion of the brain is, as I suspect, only a metaphor, it is a useful one. Only the left hemisphere of the slave—the emotional, expressive side; the side without which we cannot even survive as human beings—was allowed to develop, and it clearly developed with an unusual richness and potency of affective life. But the other half, the only half that nineteenth-century America for the most part took seriously, the half it thought was the whole, the logical, reasoning half, was hardly there at all. Everything most natural to the freedman and woman, most essentially of themselves, in their sensuous apprehension of life, their capacity for joy, their relation to the deeper rhythms of life, was perceived by most of their Northern well-wishers, black as well as white, to be deficiencies, blemishes, qualities to be apologized for, sources of embarrassment, evidences of inferiority that had to be eradicated as quickly as possible.

In the evening the children often came to Charlotte Forten's schoolhouse "to sing and shout." The "shouts" were, to her, "very strange,—in truth almost indescribable. . . . The children form a ring, and move around in a kind of shuffling dance, singing all the time. Four or five stand apart, and sing very energetically, clapping their hands, stamping their feet, and rocking their bodies to and fro. . . . The shouting of the grown people on this plantation," she added, "is rather solemn and impressive. . . . It is probable that they are the barbarous expression of religion, handed down to them from their African ancestors, and destined to pass away under the influence of Christian teachings." The phrase "Christian teachings" is worth attending to. As we have noted time and again, the most profound expression of black consciousness was its mode of ecstatic Christianity. This mode, which was being enacted before her eyes, Charlotte Forten brushed aside as incompatible with "Christian teachings." To her "Christian teachings" obviously meant a form of restrained piety characteristic of white Northern Protestantism—Quaker, Congregational, Unitarian, Episcopalian, Presbyterian, or whatever. In the North religion was clearly identified far more with patterns of acceptable behavior—dress, manner, morals—than with outpourings of emotion. The difficulty that the high-minded and devoted young black woman from Philadelphia and Salem had in coping with her exuberant and restless charges was a kind of parable of the ambivalent feelings of Northern liberal abolitionists, black and white alike, who ventured into the South to turn ex-slaves into middle-class Americans with incidentally black skins.

Plainly Laura Towne and Elizabeth Botume were disconcerted to discover a substantial degree of ambivalence about them and their fellow teachers and missionaries on the part of the Sea Island blacks. The blacks had been told continuously of the wickedness and depravity of Yankees. Although black people usually took what white people said with more than a grain of salt, such a litany had had in time an effect on black attitudes toward Yankees. Perhaps the most damning thing said to or in the presence of their slaves by Southern whites about Yankees was that they were "common." Black society was as intricately structured as the white society of Newport or Philadelphia. As we have noted before, household slaves considered themselves several cuts above field hands. Indeed, their status among their own people depended in large part on how closely they were associated with their master or mistresses—the closer the contact, the higher the status, generally speaking. The mammy, Aunt Tibia, Aunt Sally, or Aunt Somebody who nursed her mistress's infants and attended to her personal toilet usually dominated the women on the plantation and often the men as well. But that was only the beginning. Slaves were acutely aware of the white social hierarchy as well—who were "quality folks" and, of the "quality folks," who were of the highest quality and, conversely, who were new rich and who were "trash." They patronized and condescended to the slaves of lesser "quality" and were often openly contemptuous of the slaves of "common" whites or trash. The young Northern women who arrived at Port Royal soon discovered that some of the blacks to whom they had come as emissaries of a superior Northern culture thought they were "common" whites, not much better than trash. They did not dress or speak or behave like the masters and mistresses of the former slaves, and the differences were perceived as deficiencies, as evidence of commonness. Not only did they not speak like ladies and gentlemen, but they spoke some incomprehensible jargon that could hardly be understood. When Laura Towne called a venerable black woman Mrs. instead of Aunt, the ex-slave was indignant or amused. Wayman Williams, a former slave, recalled, "Dey didn't know what us mean when us say 'titty' for sister, and 'budder' for brother, and 'nanny' for mammy. Jes' for fun us call ourselves big names to de teacher, some be named General Lee and some Stonewall Jackson. We be one name one day and 'nother name next day. Until she git to know us she couldn't tell diff'rence, 'cause us all look alike to her."

Almost all whites, however well intentioned, had in their attitudes toward the contrabands a substantial element of condescension. Elizabeth Botume noted that white visitors talked about her black charges in front of them as though they did not exist. It was their habit, she wrote, to "treat those who are poor and destitute and helpless as if they were bereft of all their five senses. . . . Visitors would talk before the contrabands as if they could neither see nor hear nor feel. If they could have seen those children at recess, when their visit was over, repeating their words, mimicking their tones and gestures, they would have been undeceived."

We have a valuable witness to the Port Royal experiment in the person of Charles Francis Adams, Jr., whose Massachusetts cavalry regiment was assigned to duty on the island. "Here I am," he wrote to his brother Henry, "surrounded by troopers, missionaries, contrabands, cotton fields and serpents, in a summer climate . . . disgusted with all things military and fighting off malaria with whiskey and tobacco." The island itself was "a small paradise," and army life "a winter picnic. Still," Adams added, "sweets cloy, and drilling in a South Carolina cotton field hour after hour daily for weeks in succession is one of those sweets which cloy. . . . Cotton fields, pine barrens, contrabands, missionaries and soldiers are before me and all around me. A sick missionary is in the next room, a dozen soldiers are eating their suppers in the yard under my window and some twenty negroes of every age, lazy, submissive and as the white man has made them, are hanging about the plantation buildings just as though they were not the *teterrima causa* of this consuming *bella*. . . . No man seems to realize that here, in this little island, all around us, has begun the solution of this tremendous 'nigger' question. . . . Some ten thousand *quondam* slaves are thrown upon the hands of an unfortunate Government; they are the forerunners of hundreds of thousands more, if the plans of the Government succeed, and so the Government may as well now decide what it will do in case of the success of its war plans. While the Government has sent agents down here, private philanthropy has sent missionaries, and while the first see that the contrabands earn their bread, the last teach them the alphabet. Between the two I predict divers results, among which are numerous jobs for agents and missionaries, small comfort to the negroes and heavy losses to the Government." The policy of the government seemed to leave it to private philanthropy to educate the slaves "to the standard of self-support, to hold itself a sort of guardian to the slave in his indefinite state of transition, exacting from him that amount of labor which he owes the community and the cotton market." To Adams it seemed an almost unsolvable dilemma. "Something must be done for these poor people and done at once. They are indolent, shiftless, unable to take care of themselves and plundered by every comer—in short, they are slaves. For the present they must be provided for. It is easy to find fault with the present plan. Can any one suggest a better? For me, I must confess that I cannot."

When it came, the solution would, in Adams's view, be dictated by economic considerations and be one "over which the efforts of Government and individuals can exercise no control. This war is killing slavery," he added. "Not by any legal quibble of contrabands or doubtful theory of confiscation, but by stimulating free trade." The clearest evidence, to Adams, was the hopelessly outmoded and inefficient implements used by slave labor. Let the interested inquirer "handle their tools and examine their implements, and if he comes from any wheat-growing country, he will think himself amid the institutions and implements of the middle ages. . . . The whole system of cotton growing—all its machinery from the slave to the hoe in his hand—is awkward, cumbrous, expensive and behind the age. . . . If fair competition in the growth of cotton be once established a new system of economy and agriculture must inevitably be produced here in which the slave and his hoe will make room for the free laborer and the plough, and the change will not be one of election [of choice] but a sole resource against utter ruin. . . . But how is it," Adams continued, "for the African? Slavery may perish and no one regret it, but what is to become of the unfortunate African? When we have got thus far we have just arrived at the real point of interest in the 'nigger' question."

It seemed to Adams that the ex-slaves had "many good qualities." He noted: "They are good tempered, patient, docile, willing to learn and easily directed; but they are slavish and all that the word slavish implies. They will lie and cheat and steal; they are hypocritical and cunning; they are not brave, and they are not fierce—these qualities the white man took out of them generations ago, and in taking them deprived the African of the capacity for freedom." The prospect was not, therefore, encouraging. They would soon be free "by the operation of economic laws over which Government has no control . . . but their freedom will be the freedom of antiquated and unprofitable machines, the freedom of the hoes they use will be swept aside to make way for better implements. The slave, however, cannot be swept away and herein lies the difficulty and the problem." The essence of the problem was the transition from a servile condition to that of free men in a competitive white society where economic laws seemed to have a ruthless logic of their own. To Adams it appeared that at least a generation would be needed to complete that transition and that new social institutions would have to be devised to superintend it. "Were men and governments what they should be instead of what they are," he wrote, "the case would be different and all would combine in the Christian and tedious effort to patiently undo the wrongs they had done, and to restore to the African his attributes. Then the work could be done well and quickly; but at present, seeing what men are, and how remorselessly they throw aside what has ceased to be useful, I cannot but regard as a doubtful benefit to the African anything which by diminishing his value increases his chances of freedom."

The profoundest irony was that the war would thus "produce untold advantages to the South [by forcing it to adopt the profitable new agricultural technology], to America and to the white race. . . ." But the blacks would still be the losers. "Will they be educated and encouraged and cared for," Adams wrote, "or will they be challenged to compete in the race, or go to the wall, and finally be swept away as useless rubbish? Who can answer those queries?" Adams confessed himself unable to. "One thing I daily see," he noted, "and that is that no spirit exists among the contrabands here which would enable them to care for themselves in a race of vigorous competition. The blacks must be cared for or they will perish, and who is to care for them when they cease to be of value?"

The fact was that there were numerous encouraging signs that the contrabands, properly directed, were disposed to work and work well. Wages were the key. When the Reverend Dr. Richard Fuller, a Baltimore minister, who had owned a great plantation near Beaufort, returned to the islands, he declared, "I never saw as much land here under cultivation—never saw the same general evidences of prosperity, and never saw the negroes themselves appearing so well or so contented." Frederick Eustis, son of a Sea Island planter, who came back to try to make a go of it with free black labor, discovered that freedmen worked far better than slaves and that many older men who had been accounted too old to work, now freed, turned to and did as much work as their younger companions.

Not surprisingly Edward Pierce was convinced that the Port Royal "experiment" was a great success. "I was never so impressed as at this hour with the conviction that the lifting of these people from bondage to freedom . . . is a very easy thing," he wrote to Charles Sumner in March, 1862, "involving only common humanity, and reasonable patience and faith. If white men only did as well under such adverse circumstances, they would be regarded as prodigies."

Not all the attention drawn to Port Royal was favorable. The Northern Democratic press was almost uniformly hostile. The *New York Express* denounced the "band of Abolition socialists, free lovers, and disorganizers of society generally" who had established themselves on the islands and predicted that the inevitable failure of their efforts would result in the downfall of the abolition movement. The *New York Journal of Commerce* spoke of "the nonsensical, wild and fanatical plans of irresponsible men and women" rousing the "sorrow and disgust" of "the intelligent world." Indeed, journalists swarmed over the islands, reporting what it pleased them to report. The correspondents of Democratic newspapers described the indolence, the naïveté, the disposition to deceit of the ex-slaves, qualities which, in their view, rendered the project chimerical. The correspondents for Republican papers, while acknowledging the complexity of the problem, emphasized the positive, and Pierce continued to insist that "the success of the movement . . . has exceeded my most sanguine expectations."

To Craney Island off the Virginia coast, where there were a number of contrabands, came two Quaker sisters, Lucy and Sarah Chase, to teach black children their three Rs. Lucy was forty-two, and Sarah twenty-eight. Their father, Samuel Chase, was one of the most prominent businessmen of Worcester, Massachusetts, part owner of the famous *Massachusetts Spy*, a newspaper dating back to the era of the American Revolution. They found some two thousand contrabands without adequate clothing, food, or shelter. The sisters pitched in at once to help the Federal authorities to bring some kind of order out of the chaos caused by the arrival of the new society. In the days that followed, as they began their teaching duties, combined with a hundred other chores, they wrote of their strange experiences to the "Dear Ones at Home."

Along with the letters of Elizabeth Botume, Laura Towne, and half a dozen other similarly devoted ladies, their correspondence gives us a vivid picture of life among the contrabands. "We are all here for a purpose—we have missions," their father had reminded them, "and if we are true to ourselves we shall seek to know what that mission is, and knowing, endeavour to fulfill it. Whatever our suffering, whatever our privation may be, if we come out of it with the consciousness of having been instrumental in saving a brother, a husband, a father, or soothing their pain in the last struggle of human existence, we feel abundantly compensated. We feel that in as much as we have done something, as it were, for the least of God's creatures, we have done it to Christ."

Two of their coadjutors were William Henry Channing, the idealistic and socialistically inclined son of the famous William Ellery Channing, who was agent of the Sanitary Commission, working under the direction of George Templeton Strong and the other directors of the commission, and Colonel Orlando Brown, a surgeon with the 24th United States Colored Infantry and now superintendent of Negro Affairs under Benjamin Butler.

Like virtually all the other Northern missionary teachers, the Chase sisters were dismayed by the personal habits, especially in regard to cleanliness, of the contrabands and the shouting emotionalism of their religious activities. Orlando Brown cautioned them that only through patience and sympathy could they hope to be of service to the black men, women, and children they had come to help. What was needed most of all was abstention from the often sentimental and romantic notions held by many Northern abolitionists. "To talk of them after the manner of ignorant, enthusiastic philanthropists," Brown warned the sisters, "is giving undue praise to the barbarous teachings of slavery." Lucy wrote her father: "We are to give them a *chance*! which they have never had."

Nonetheless, the sisters were upset to discover that black "religious feeling is purely emotional; void of principle, and of no practical utility. . . . They must know what is *right*! in order to worship aright the God of right."

What began at Port Royal was soon extended everywhere in the South that Union soldiers established Federal authority, but Port Royal, in part because of its ready accessibility and because it was the first such undertaking on a considerable scale, remained both the prototype and the focus of attention.

14

The War in the West

While the war in the East was a series of disappointments or disasters for the Union armies, in the West they enjoyed almost uninterrupted success from the Battle of Pea Ridge on March 7, 1862, to Stones River (or Murfreesboro) at the beginning of the next year. Although the Battle of Pea Ridge, which took place in Arkansas, involved relatively modest forces, it had a major influence on the subsequent campaigns in the West.

After the Battle of Wilson's Creek, the badly battered Confederate forces under General Sterling Price (at 290 pounds, the heaviest general of the war) had occupied Springfield, Missouri. General Samuel Ryan Curtis, West Point '31, was placed in command of what was called the Army of the Southwest by Halleck. Curtis had resigned from the regular army soon after his graduation from the Point and become a civil engineer and lawyer. Returning to active duty during the Mexican War, he had fought with Zachary Taylor. After the war he practiced law in Iowa and served three terms in Congress before resigning to become colonel of the 2nd Iowa Infantry. With a force of some 11,000, Curtis advanced on Springfield, which Price and 8,000 Confederates promptly abandoned. Price then joined forces with Ben McCulloch, the velvet-uniformed Texan, and had his army further augmented by some 2,000 Cherokee, Choctaw, and Creek Indians recruited from Indian territory. General Earl Van Dorn was placed in overall command of a Confederate force of some 14,000 men, with orders to drive Curtis out of Arkansas and, it was hoped, Missouri as well. Franz Sigel, with two divisions made up largely of Germans, constituted the main body of Curtis's army, along with Missouri, Indiana, and Iowa volunteers. Wild Bill Hickok, who had performed valuable services as a scout for General Lyon prior to Wilson's Creek, alerted Curtis to the Confederate advance. Curtis at once concentrated his overextended army at Pea Ridge.

Leaving his campfires burning in the hope of deceiving Curtis, Van Dorn began a complicated night march to try to envelop the Union lines. Van Dorn was ill from the effects of a fall and immersion in an icy river, and his men were weary from a long forced march in freezing rain, but the initial Confederate charge led by the Indians, waving tomahawks and giving war whoops, scattered the German soldiers on the Union left. Behind the Indians came the Texans, who, deciding that the whole thing was a lark, stopped to pillage the Union artillery caissons, putting horse collars around their necks, dancing about, and calling, "Me big In'gen, big as horse." An attack on the right flank of the Union line also succeeded initially, and Curtis was faced with the problem of where to commit his reserve.

Unfortunately for Van Dorn and the Confederates, the Indians proved as difficult to manage as the Texans. Some panicked under Union artillery fire. Others had wished to fight for the Union cause and took the first opportunity to desert. Ben McCulloch, conspicuous in his dove gray uniform, was shot and killed leading a charge of the 16th Arkansas Regiment. James McIntosh, a West Pointer popular with the Indians, was also killed. McIntosh's command devolved on towering Albert Pike, Harvard dropout, Western writer, lawyer for the Creek Indians. Meanwhile, Curtis's Missourians had recovered much of the ridge and discovered a number of Union dead who had been scalped. Hickok, acting as a messenger for Curtis, wore out three horses and had one killed under him.

When the Union left seemed hopelessly routed, a fleeing soldier tossed a burning quilt on an artillery caisson just as rebel soldiers reached the emplacement. The caisson blew up, killing a number of Confederates and disrupting the attack. At nightfall the Union forces, badly battered, had been driven off the ridge at certain points, and the

Confederates, presumably waiting to renew the attack, were so close that they could be heard coughing and talking. Some sang defiantly:

> Jeff Davis is a President;
> Abe Lincoln is a fool!
> Jeff Davis rides a big bay horse;
> Abe Lincoln rides a mule.

The advantage seemed to lie with Van Dorn's army, but Curtis knew that it had lost all of its division commanders and that the Indians were badly demoralized. He ordered his forces to consolidate and prepared to meet a renewed attack. The attack came, preceded by a heavy artillery barrage that killed Churchill Clark, grandson of William Clark. Clark's cousin, William Clark Kinnerly, remembered for years after the sight of a field hospital with piles of amputated arms and legs, many of them still in shirt sleeves and boots.

The Union artillery soon proved its superiority, and the out-gunned Confederates began to withdraw. Further, the rifles of the Germans outranged the Confederate muskets and helped push the rebels back. Finally, Curtis ordered a charge to complete the rout of Van Dorn's army. More than 800 Confederates were captured, along with much artillery and military equipment, and Van Dorn's army was destroyed as an effective fighting force, many of the soldiers deserting to form companies of bushwhackers and freebooters. A Union soldier who had found his brother scalped took nine Indian scalps in revenge, and eleven Indians who surrendered were shot "trying to escape." General Curtis wrote his brother: "The vulture and the wolf have now communion, and the dead, friends and foe, sleep in the same lonely grave."

Pea Ridge was reminiscent of Wilson's Creek. Many of the same soldiers and officers participated, and the fighting was characterized by the same bitterness and ferocity. Van Dorn's use of the Indians proved in retrospect to have been a serious error. While the Union victory at Pea Ridge did not end the fighting in Arkansas, it did put a stop to any serious threat against Missouri and greatly strengthened the Union position in the Mississippi Valley.

After the capture of Forts Henry and Donelson, Grant's next objective was the important rail and river junction near Corinth, in northeastern Mississippi. One railroad there connected with Memphis and the Mississippi River, and the other led South to the cotton states. Albert Sidney Johnston was personally in command of the Confederate forces defending the city. Pittsburg Landing, twenty miles from Corinth, was to be the assembly point and staging area for a joint attack on Corinth by Buell's Army of the Ohio and the Army of the Tennessee under Grant's overall command. The most notable addition to the Army of the Tennessee was Sherman, who had been given command of a division.

The relationship between Grant and Sherman was much like that between Lee and Jackson. Totally different in temperament, they had profound respect for each other's qualities as soldiers, and they soon achieved that perfect union of mind and spirit which is the rarest and happiest fruit of military campaigning. Grant knew that whatever might be uncertain or in doubt, he could count on Sherman as the rock on which all else might rest. That knowledge is worth numerous divisions to a commanding general.

Now, scarcely a month after the capture of Forts Henry and Donelson, Grant was on the move again. By March 19 he was at Columbia, Tennessee, eighty-five miles from Pittsburg Landing. Waiting for the arrival of Buell's army, Grant was inspecting his line in a heavy rainstorm when his horse fell and pinned Grant's leg under him, painfully spraining the general's ankle.

Grant was puzzled by the unusually heavy patrol activity of Johnston's cavalry and skirmishers. On April 6 the Confederates launched a fierce attack on Grant's army, driving the demoralized Yankees out of their bivouacs and pressing them back for a mile or more in most sectors. When McClernand's division fell back precipitously, Benjamin Mayberry Prentiss, an Illinois militia officer and recently colonel of the 10th Illinois Volunteers, now commanding the 6th Division, was cut off, and he and his men were captured.

The losses to both the attackers and the defenders were horrendous, and in the face of such devastating casualties, thousands of soldiers in both armies threw their muskets away and ran for their lives. Grant estimated that more than 10,000 Union soldiers, most of them untested in combat, took refuge under the banks of the river near the landing, and no threats could make them budge. Sherman's division counted few defections, and repeated attacks on his section, which anchored the Union right, were repulsed with heavy losses. By nightfall the Union lines were running from the river along a ravine commanded by a battery of heavy-siege guns to hook up with the division under Stephen Augustus Hurlbut, a lawyer, militia officer, and Illinois state legislator who had taken command of the 4th Division in the absence of a seriously injured General C. F. Smith. McClernand's division extended the line westward, wrapped around a log-house known as Shiloh, and made contact there with Sherman's left, which turned at a right angle and had *its* right on the Owl Creek swamp. Lew Wallace, ordered by Grant to bring his division up from Crump's Landing to the north, had taken the wrong road and did not arrive until the battle of the sixth was over. His division of some 5,000 men was placed in line along with Thomas Crittenden's and Alexander McCook's.

During the Confederate attack on the sixth, Albert Sidney Johnston was killed, and the command of the rebel force devolved on Beauregard.

Grant described the outcome of the day's fighting as "a case of Southern dash against Northern pluck and endurance." Three out of the five divisions engaged "were," he noted, "entirely raw, and many of the men had only received their arms on the way from their States to the field. Many of them had arrived but a day or two before and were hardly able to load their muskets according to the manual. Their officers were equally ignorant of their duties. Under these circumstances it is not astonishing that many of the regiments broke at the first fire."

Sherman, despite the fact that most of his men were raw recruits, "inspired a confidence in officers and men that enabled them to render services on that bloody battle-field worthy of the best of veterans," in Grant's words. Sherman was shot twice, once in the hand, once in the shoulder, the ball cutting his coat and making a slight wound. A third ball passed through his hat.

Despite the staggering casualties his army had suffered, Grant, now reinforced by Buell, was determined to attack the following day. It rained a chill, soaking rain all night long, and Grant's ankle pained him so that he could not sleep. Beauregard, unaware that Buell had arrived, hoped to capitalize on the victory of the preceding day, a victory at least in the sense that the Union forces had been driven back on the landing, Prentiss's division shattered, and W. H. L. Wallace killed. In addition, the Federal army had lost half its artillery. Grant told Sherman that in his view, the situation was much as it had been after the first day's fighting at Fort Donelson—both sides so weakened and demoralized that the one which showed the strongest determination to press the attack would carry the day. In addition, of course, Grant had been substantially reinforced by the arrival of Buell and Lew Wallace. Shortly after dawn on the seventh Grant's attack began along the Corinth road. At first the Confederates fell back, and Grant and Buell recovered much of the area that had been given up the day before, but as the Union army outran its artillery support, Beauregard ordered a counterattack which, for a time, forced the Federals back to the Peach Orchard. There Union artillery came once again into play, and after heavy fighting in the tangled and uneven terrain, the Confederate forces once more began to fall back. Beauregard, anticipating the arrival of Van Dorn, made a desperate effort to hold the ground around Shiloh Church, but when he received word that Van Dorn had not been able to get across the river, the Southern commander decided that his only recourse was to fall back to Corinth.

Grant himself narrowly escaped a serious wound or death when a bullet hit his sword just below the hilt. The heavy rain and the exhaustion of his troops made it impossible for Grant to continue the pursuit of Beauregard's shattered army. The soldiers made camp in the soggy fields, ate their first full meal in almost three days, and slept the sweet sleep of victors. The Union strength had been 33,000 men on the opening day of the battle. Johnston had 40,955. The second day Grant's army was augmented by some 30,000 men minus the casualties of the first day. The Union loss in two days of fighting was more than 13,000—1,754 killed, 8,408 wounded, 2,885 missing. The most serious loss on the Confederate side was Johnston. Beauregard estimated the Confederate casualties as 10,782, of whom 1,723 were killed, 8,102 wounded, and 957 missing. Numbers of missing aside, the Union and Confederate losses were astonishingly close, closer than in any other engagement of the war. And bloodier. Survivors spoke of fields so crowded with dead bodies that one could not walk across them without stepping on a body. The name Shiloh became a synonym for courage and endurance.

Melville wrote a "requiem" for the dead:

> Foemen at morn, but friends at eve—
>   Fame or country least their care;
> (What like a bullet can undeceive!)
>   But now they lie low,
> While over them the swallows skim,
>   All, all is hushed at Shiloh.

Surveying the terrible carnage, Grant realized that his hopes for a speedy end to the war were misplaced. If the South would fight with such ferocity, a long and bitter war was ahead. The fall of Donelson and Henry had disposed him to believe that the South had little fight in it. Shiloh changed his mind. Even so, he believed then and years later that the prompt exploitation of the Shiloh victory would have crippled the Southern armies beyond reconstitution and shortened the war by many months. Again Grant was robbed of proper credit for his victory. Northern newspapers reported that the Union army had been taken by surprise on the sixth and men bayoneted in their beds; that Grant was drunk; and that only Buell's arrival had saved his army from annihilation.

In November, 1861, Grant had made his bold foray against Belmont. On April 7, 1862, he swept the enemy from the field at Shiloh. In six months, he had done more for the cause of Northern arms than all the rest of the vast Union military establishment. More important, he had redeemed Bull Run and restored Northern pride and confidence, albeit at a fearful cost. If anyone in Washington had bothered to pay close attention, he would have perceived that a military leader of remarkable talents had emerged from the pack of professionals and amateurs who made up the ranks of Union general officers. But once again, like a canvas stage drop, the Army of the Potomac obscured all else.

A few days after Shiloh, Halleck arrived at Pittsburg Landing to complete his humiliation of Grant by taking charge of the operation against Corinth. Grant, superseded, was given the nominal title of "second-in-command" and no duties. It was an unmistakable rebuke to the man who had conducted the most successful Union campaign of the war, and it sank Grant into an abyss of fury and despair. The period that followed was undoubtedly the darkest time of the war in terms of his military career. Now it was Sherman who gave essential moral support to Grant in *his* dark night of the soul. Sherman, who had recently been called crazy by a hostile journalist and had come to doubt his own sanity, knew what Grant must be feeling, and he gave hours of his time to bucking up the morale of his friend.

It must be said for Halleck that he was at his best in assembling an army of almost 100,000 men for the delayed attack on Corinth. Sherman gave generous credit to Halleck's organizational skills and Halleck's confidence in Sherman, who was second-in-command of the Army of the Tennessee under his friend Old Tom Thomas, won

Sherman's gratitude and loyalty. When Halleck's army moved against Corinth, Beauregard, the ideal Southern hero and star of Bull Run, evacuated the city without a fight—for which action, or nonaction, Jefferson Davis relieved him of his command of the Army of Tennessee (not to be confused with the Federal Army of the Tennessee) and replaced him with Braxton Bragg.

The advance on Corinth had extended through the month of May, "the most beautiful and valuable month of the year for campaigning in this latitude," Sherman wrote. The advance seemed to Sherman "a magnificent drill, as it served for the instruction of our men in guard and picket duty, and in habituating them to outdoor life; and by the time we had reached Corinth I believe the army was the best then on this continent and could have gone where it pleased." Since Sherman was one of the few who knew Halleck well and had much good to say of him, and since the Ohioan was generally an observant, if ofttimes excessively generous, judge of men, we should attend him. "General Halleck," Sherman wrote in his *Memoirs,* "was a man of great capacity, of large acquirements, and at the time possessed the confidence of the country, and of most of the army. I held him in high estimation, and gave him credit for the combinations which had resulted in placing this magnificent army of a hundred thousand men, well equipped and provided with a good base, at Corinth, from which he could move in any direction."

Sherman was confident that this army could have worked its will, virtually unimpeded, throughout the South if it had been kept intact, but since it was soon dispersed into smaller armies and corps, its usefulness was greatly diminished, and its principal function was to stir the states of the Deep South to what Sherman called a "stupendous" effort to meet its threat.

Grant, meantime, having tagged along unhappily on the Corinth campaign, reached the depths of depression, although his taciturn exterior gave little evidence of his emotions. Sherman heard from Halleck, who was evidently pleased at the news, that Grant had asked for and received a thirty-day leave for unspecified purposes. In a sense Halleck's campaign against Corinth had also been a campaign against Grant. Now Grant was preparing to withdraw. Sherman expostulated with him. He, Sherman, understood Grant's feelings only too well. He too had been within an ace of resigning his commission a few months ago, and look at him now, cock of the walk. There would soon be a reversal of Grant's fortune. An officer of Grant's capacities could not be shunted aside permanently. Too many officers were aware of his remarkable achievements. Sherman made Grant promise that he would do nothing rash until he had consulted with him. Grant agreed to reconsider his application for leave. A few days later he wrote Sherman that he had decided to stick, and Sherman replied: "I . . . am rejoiced at your conclusion to remain; for you could not relieve your mind of the gnawing sensation that injustice had been done you." A little more than a month later Halleck was on his way to Washington to replace McClellan as chief of staff, and Grant was once more in command of the Army of the Tennessee.

Grant's account of Halleck's treatment of him, written years after the event, is characteristically understated: "I was ignored as much as if I had been at the most distant point of territory within my jurisdiction; and although I was in command of all the troops engaged at Shiloh I was not permitted to see one of the reports of General Buell or his subordinate in that battle. . . ." Grant was indignant at the snaillike pace of Halleck's advance on Corinth and confident that what had taken the general the better part of a month could have been accomplished in two days, with heavy losses to the demoralized Confederates and the capture of large amounts of military equipment and many prisoners. Perhaps Halleck felt Grant's silent disapproval, and it deepened his dislike for him and increased his pleasure in humiliating him.

When Halleck left for Washington on July 16, McClernand accompanied him, and the two men combined to denigrate Grant to Lincoln.

While the Army of the Tennessee had been involved in the campaign that resulted in the fall of Forts Henry and Donelson, Major General John Pope had carried out an expedition against Leonidas Polk and Gideon Pillow. Pope was one of the lucky children of fortune who, without ability or intelligence, rise swiftly by their own shrewdness and self-promotion to dizzy heights and fall as precipitously. A graduate of West Point, class of '42, a year ahead of Grant, he was handsome, flamboyant, self-assured, and well dressed. He *looked* like a leader, whereas Grant, by contrast, looked like some general's untidy orderly. So Pope, having served with the army's elite section, the topographical engineers, and having, moreover, in contrast with many of his fellow West Pointers, remained in the regular army, advanced from captain to brigadier general in May, 1861, and then, having had three successive commands, each of a few months' duration, was given command of the Army of the Mississippi. Accompanied by the able Foote, now admiral, he laid siege to New Madrid and Island No. 10 across a bend in the Mississippi from the town itself. In a competently conducted operation against a vastly inferior and poorly led defensive force (1,500 out of 3,500 defenders were ill), Pope captured the island and the town on March 14, thus clearing the Mississippi as far as Fort Pillow and making himself a largely undeserved reputation.

Following the surrender of Island No. 10, Commodore Foote anticipated an opportunity to attack Forts Pillow, Wright, and Randolph, guarding the approaches to Memphis, but Pope was summoned to Corinth, and in the absence of infantry Foote's gunboats were unable to silence the guns of the three forts. Moreover, his small fleet of seven ironclads and one wooden gunboat was opposed by nine Confederate vessels at Fort Pillow with another ten reportedly on their way up the river. Foote was miserable from a wound he had received in the attack on Fort Donelson, and early in May he transferred his command to Captain C. H. Davis and departed to seek medical treatment. A few days later the Confederate ironclads attacked the Union fleet and after a sharp engagement were forced to drop back down the river. The capture of Corinth brought the evacuation of Fort Pillow and its sister forts, leaving only the Confederate gunboats to defend Memphis from the river side. Within sight of the city Davis and the vessels under his command inflicted a crushing defeat on the Confederate ships, sinking or capturing seven of them in a contest that lasted scarcely an hour. Only one Confederate ship escaped while Federal casualties were three wounded. The mayor of Memphis, John Park, surrendered the city to spare it from bombardment, and a few days later Sherman occupied the city while Elizabeth Meriwether and her two young sons watched in unhappy silence. "We felt," she wrote, "as if chains were encircling us." As the Union soldiers marched past, little River Meriwether stood up in the family carriage, pointed a broom handle at the marching troops, and shouted, "Watch me shoot the Yankee!! Bang! Bang!" His mother trembled, but the soldiers only laughed, and one called out, "Bully for the little Reb!"

Sherman, at loggerheads with the citizens of Memphis, ordered all the families of Confederate officers to leave the city. When Elizabeth Meriwether appealed to him for an exemption from the order, he told her curtly, "I am not interested in rebel wives and rebel brats. If you don't leave Memphis in three days you will be locked up in the Irving Block [the city's military prison] as long as the war lasts."

In the aftermath of Shiloh, General Don Carlos Buell was given command of a reconstituted Army of the Ohio with the mission of clearing central Tennessee and invading Alabama. Buell pushed on to Nashville, Murfreesboro, Shelbyville, and Fayetteville, in Tennessee, and Huntsville and Decatur in Alabama, without encountering serious opposition; by the end of August his army controlled Kentucky, Tennessee, and much of Alabama. It was John Beatty's opinion that the army was being misused. "Our forces," he wrote, "are holding the great scope of country between Memphis and Bridgeport, guarding bridges, railroads, and towns, frittering away the strength of a great army and wasting our men by permitting them to be picked up in detail. . . . The climate and the insane effort to garrison the whole country, consumes our troops, and we make no progress. May the good Lord be with us and deliver us from idleness and imbecility; and especially, O Lord, grant a little everyday sense—that very common sense which plain people use in the management of their business affairs—to the illustrious generals who have our armies in hand!" In this situation Bragg and Kirby Smith (there were, incidentally, twenty-two officers named Smith with the rank of general in the war) decided that a strong countermove had to be made to drive back the Union forces, and they began a two-pronged drive against the Army of the Ohio. Hearing that Bragg was on the march for his base in Kentucky, Buell evacuated central Tennessee and started out to intercept the Confederates. The auspices were not good. John Beatty called the first day's march "disagreeable beyond precedent. The boys had been full of whisky for three days and fell out of the ranks by scores." The road for sixteen miles was lined with stragglers. But a few days of marching put new life into the army, and when Buell finally caught up with Bragg at Perryville, Kentucky, his men were in fighting trim. Philip Sheridan's corps was the first to make contact on October 8. Soon the respective Union and rebel forces were deployed, and the fighting began with a strong attack on Sheridan's front which was repulsed. Sheridan then counterattacked and drove the Confederates through Perryville. Buell, who never got his entire force into battle, missed the opportunity to inflict heavy damage on Bragg's army.

John Beatty's Ohioans bore the brunt of the battle. At nightfall they bivouacked in a cornfield. "The regiment had grown suddenly small," he wrote. "It was a sorry sight for us indeed. Every company had its long list of killed, wounded, and missing. Over two hundred were gone. . . . Many eyes were in tears and many hearts were bleeding for lost comrades and dear friends. . . . We are without tents. Rain is falling and the men uncomfortable." But the next day the weather cleared; someone in Beatty's headquarters found a cache of food, and he and his staff dined on "pickled salmon, currant jelly, fried ham, butter, coffee, and crackers." Beatty wrote: "It is now long after nightfall, and the forest is aglow with a thousand campfires. The hum of ten thousand voices strikes the ear like the roar of a distant sea. A band away off to the right is mingling its music with the noise, and a mule now and then breaks in with a voice not governed by any rules of melody known to man."

One of the major objectives of the Confederate campaign was the recapture of Corinth, where Rosey Rosecrans commanded some 23,000 Union soldiers in well-prepared defensive positions. Rosecrans was Ohio-born and West Point-trained. He had become a convert to Catholicism as a cadet to the dismay of his pious Protestant parents and most of his fellow cadets. After four years as an instructor in engineering at the Point, he had resigned his commission and gone into business for himself as a highly successful architect-engineer and oil prospector. At the outbreak of the war he volunteered and was appointed a brigadier general. He had done well in the early fighting in Virginia and had been given command of the left wing of Pope's Army of the Mississippi.

Van Dorn, with 22,000 men, believed the Union army to be much smaller in numbers and attacked fiercely on October 4. A series of assaults were hurled back, and by evening it was clear the Confederate effort was doomed to failure.

Grant, when he heard of Van Dorn's attack, had sent reinforcements to Rosecrans with instructions to pursue and destroy the Confederate force, but the rebel army escaped across the Hatchie River. Once again the casualties in the two armies were almost identical. Rosecrans lost 2,520; Van Dorn, 2,470. The consequences of Corinth were, in Sherman's view, "very great . . . a decisive blow to the Confederate cause in our quarter [which] changed the whole aspect of affairs in western Tennessee."

Buell's failure to press his advantage at Perryville resulted in his replacement by Rosecrans, who began the pursuit of Bragg, who was headed for Murfreesboro. On the march to Murfreesboro a festive air descended upon the Army of the Ohio. The sun came out after days of rain, "the band struck up, and at every plantation," John Beatty noted, "negroes came flocking to the roadside to see us. They are the only friends we find. They have heard of the abolition army, the music, the banners, the glittering arms; possibly the hope that their masters will be humbled and their own condition improved gladdens their hearts and leads them to welcome us with extravagant manifestations of joy. They keep time to the music with feet and hands and hurrah 'fur de ole flag and de Union,' sometimes following us for miles."

The chaplain of the 3rd Ohio Volunteers asked an old man standing with a cluster of blacks, "My friend, are you religious?" "No, massa, I is not; seben of my folks is, and dey is all prayen for your side." An ancient black woman climbed a fence along the road, clapped her hands, and shouted for joy. "Blessed de Lord dat dar was de old flag agin," she exclaimed.

The Federal forces under Rosecrans caught up with Bragg at Stones River, Tennessee, on the last day of the year. Each general, unbeknownst to the other, planned to attack his opponent's right. The two armies launched virtually simultaneous assaults on the morning of January 2, 1863.

John Beatty's brigade formed in the first Union line of advance. "The enemy comes up directly," Beatty wrote of the battle, "and the fight begins. The roar of the guns to the right, left, and front of my brigade sounds like the continuous pounding on a thousand anvils." The Union forces were protected by a wood; the rebels had to advance across an open field, and after a sharp fight the Confederate line withdrew. Soon another wave of rebel soldiers emerged from an opposite wood on the double. The regiments to the right and left of the 3rd Ohio gave way. When the 3rd wavered, Beatty rushed forward to rally them, but his horse was shot under him, and the sight of their colonel on the ground completed the demoralization of his men, who took to their heels, leaving Beatty behind them. At this point the Union artillery opened up with devastating effect on the leading Confederate units and, in Beatty's opinion, "saved the army."

Forced back all along their front by the fierceness of the Confederate attack, the Union forces rallied in a four-acre oak grove that was soon called Hell's Half Acre by the beleaguered soldiers. Repeated Confederate assaults failed to dislodge them; the 8th Tennessee (Confederate) Regiment lost 306 out of 425 engaged.

That night the soldiers of both armies slept as best they could on their arms and ate whatever morsel they might have in their pockets, while burial details carried off the dead and surgeons attended to the wounded. By the light of a small fire, Beatty read Psalm 91: "I will say of the Lord, He is my refuge and my fortress . . . in him will I trust."

The battle resumed the next day, announced by the thunder of the guns. The rattle of muskets grew into "a prolonged and unceasing roll," and then a distant yell rose above the din of the guns. "But whose yell?" Beatty asked himself. "Thank God, it is ours! . . . The enemy has been checked, repulsed, and is now in retreat. . . . The hungry soldiers cut steaks from the slain horses, and with the scanty supplies that have come forward gather around the fires to prepare supper and talk over the incidents of the day." Beatty rode over the battlefield. At one stop he saw an artillery caisson and five horses all "killed in harness and fallen together. . . . Nationals and Confederates," he wrote later, "young, middle-aged, and old are scattered over the woods and fields for miles. . . . We find men with their legs shot off; one with his brains scooped out by a cannon ball; another with half a face gone; another with entrails protruding; young Winnegard of the Third has one foot off and both legs pierced by grape at the thigh. . . . Many Confederate sharpshooters lay behind stumps and rails, and logs, shot in the head. A young boy, dressed in the Confederate uniform, lies with his face turned to the sky and looks as if he might be sleeping. Trees peppered with bullet and buckshot, and now and then one cut down by cannon ball; unexploded shell, solid shot, dead horses, broken caissons, haversacks, old shoes, hats, fragments of muskets, and unused cartridges are to be seen everywhere. In any open space in the oak woods is a long strip of fresh earth in which forty-one sticks are standing, with intervals between them of perhaps half a foot. Here forty-one fellows lie under the fresh earth," Beatty wrote, "with nothing but the forty-one little sticks above to mark the spot." The sticks would rot, and then, Beatty reflected, there would be nothing to indicate that:

> Perhaps in this neglected spot is laid
> Some heart once pregnant with celestial fire;
> Hands, that the rod of empire might have sway'd
> Or waked to ecstasy the living lyre.

Bragg withdrew to Murfreesboro and then to Shelbyville. The Union forces under Rosecrans numbered some 41,400 of whom 12,906 were killed or wounded. The Confederates lost 11,738 out of

34,739. Rosecrans occupied Murfreesboro, which John Beatty described as "an aristocratic town. . . . The poor whites are as poor as rot, and the rich are very rich. There is no substantial well-to-do middle class here. The slaves are, in fact, the middle class here. They are not considered so good, of course, as their masters, but a great deal better than the white trash." A slave said to Beatty: "You look like solgers. No wonder dat to wip de white trash ob de Southern army. Dey ced dey could wip two ob you, but I guess one ob you could wip two ob dem. You is jest as big as dey is, and maybe a little bigger."

In the Army of the Cumberland after Stones River, "absenteeism" grew at an alarming rate. In Thomas's corps alone 16,000 men were, in John Beatty's words, "sick, pretending to be sick, or otherwise." In Beatty's brigade there were 1,600 men present for duty and 1,300 absent. "If every northern soldier able to do duty would do it," Beatty wrote, "Rosecrans could sweep to Mobile in ninety days; but with this skeleton of an army, we rest in doubt and idleness. There is a screw loose somewhere."

In December Grant had ordered Sherman to move down the Mississippi, on the Mississippi Central Railroad, and join him in an attack on Vicksburg, the most important strongpoint on the Mississippi still held by the Confederates and generally considered impregnable. A series of relatively small-scale engagements followed, but the effort to capture Vicksburg failed, and Grant determined to lay siege to the city.

The contrast between the fighting in the East and West is not as stark as the simple narrative of battles and engagements suggests. What is perhaps most striking about all the major battles is that in the great majority of them the percentage of the casualties of the two opposing forces was remarkably close. Often the outcome turned on chance, rather than superior tactics or the fighting qualities of one side as against the other. It is hard not to feel, for example, that the deaths of McCulloch and McIntosh and the flight of the Indian auxiliaries at Pea Ridge had a critical influence on the outcome. In a majority of engagements, East and West, defenders won over attackers—Pea Ridge, Shiloh, Stones River, Malvern Hill, Fair Oaks, indeed, most of the Peninsula campaign and the Second Bull Run. The most advantageous situation an army could have was to be attacked in strong defensive positions on the opening day of the battle, maintain the positions with some degree of success, and be able to counterattack the next day. All this would seem to support the preponderance of the defense over attack in the era of the Civil War. Numerous engagements hung on the seizure, or the failure to seize, a crucial artillery battery. Battles in the Virginia theater of operations that would have been considered standoffs in the West were, not inappropriately, claimed as Confederate victories because the effort to capture Richmond was thwarted. It is not taking anything away from Lee's generalship to point out that in Virginia every advantage was his, every "draw" a victory. In the West a draw was a draw, and since no one Confederate strongpoint was defined as *the* goal, there were opportunities for endless maneuvering, thrusts, and counterthrusts. In this kind of war, superior Federal numbers, supplies, and, often, generalship gave the Union armies an edge that in the main they successfully exploited.

Important as they were, the Western victories made little impression in the East. It is probably not too far off the mark to say that the Western campaigns made more of an impression in Europe than in New York or Washington. That, at least, was the opinion of Charles Francis Adams. "Nowhere," he wrote from London, "has the condition of the western campaign been productive of better effects than in this country. The change produced in the tone towards the United States is very striking. There will be no overt acts tending to recognition whilst there is a doubt of the issue. . . . Every manifestation of sympathy with the rebel success springs from British sources. This feeling is not the popular feeling, but it is that of the governing classes. With many honorable exceptions the aristocracy entertain it as well as the commercial interest."

What bemused serious European observers of the war was its colossal scale, a scale beyond the imaginings of European military strategists, a scale appropriate to a country so vast. "The truth is," Henry Adams wrote to his brother Charles Francis, "as our swarm of armies strike deeper and deeper into the South, the contest is beginning to take to Europeans proportions of grandeur and perfection like nothing of which they have heard or read. They call us insane to attempt what, when achieved, they are almost afraid to appreciate." It was perhaps easier from the perspective of Europe to realize how *awesome* the struggle was. On the other side of the Atlantic there was a growing awareness that a new power had entered unpredictably into the calculus of the Old World. There had, to be sure, been a sense of that for a generation or more, but a fuller realization resulted from the war itself. Europeans might not understand or sympathize with "democratic institutions," might not be able to picture, despite the avalanche of travel books, the real physical dimensions of the country and the remarkable currents of humanity that surged through it. But war they could understand. They knew it very well. "Recognition, intervention, is an old song," Henry Adams wrote Charles Francis. "No one whispers it. . . . And the legion of armies that are winning victory after victory on every side . . . are a cause of study to the English such as they've not had since Napoleon entered Milan some seventy years ago. I feel like a King now. . . . No one treads on our coattails any longer, and I do not expect ever to see again the old days of anxiety and humiliation. . . ."

15

The Abolitionists
and the War

With many of their champions in Congress and Wendell Phillips a brilliant spokesman for their cause, the true-blue abolitionists exerted constant pressure on Lincoln to declare the war a war to free the slaves, rather than simply a war to preserve the Union. John Hay took note of the relentless campaign for emancipation which began, in effect, with the fall of Fort Sumter. Early in May, 1861, Hay found the President watching through a telescope, the end of which he balanced "on his toes, sublime," two distant steamers puffing up the Potomac. Hay told the President that much of his correspondence was made up of letters urging that he declare the slaves to be free and enlist them in the Union army. "For my own part," the President replied, "I consider the central idea pervading this struggle is the necessity that is upon us of proving that popular government is not an absurdity. We must settle this question now, whether, in a free government, the minority have the right to break up the government whenever they choose. If we fail, it will go far to prove the incapability of the people to govern themselves. . . . Taking the government as we found it, we will see if the majority can preserve it."

Richard Henry Dana was of the same persuasion. When Charles

Sumner made an eloquent attack on slavery in the Senate, Dana referred to it as "a magnificent exposition . . . of the sin and horrors of slavery and its ill effect on our politics. . . . He seems to assume that if our twenty millions can be made to hate slaveholders and slavery badly enough . . . all the rest will take care of itself." But Dana was convinced, as he wrote to Charles Francis Adams in London in the fall of 1861, that "we cannot justify war *on the domestic institutions of the Southern States* as an end and object. We must not propagate even Christianity by the sword. The war must be to sustain the Constitution, and prevent the establishment of an independent nation in our limits. . . ."

The abolitionists' priority, on the other hand, was emancipation before all else. George Julian, a Congressman from Indiana in the Thirty-seventh Congress, was one of the first Republicans to describe himself as a radical. He denounced the notion that the war was about the right of secession. "Mr. Chairman," he told his colleagues, "when I say that this rebellion has its source and life in slavery, I only repeat a simple truism. No fact is better understood throughout the country, both by loyal and disloyal men. . . . Sir, this rebellion is a bloody and frightful demonstration of the fact that slavery and freedom cannot dwell together in peace." Southerners were openly contemptuous of work and workingmen. They had described "the laboring millions of the free States as the 'mud-sills of society,' as a 'pauper banditti,' as 'greasy mechanics and filthy operatives.' . . . If we meet them at all, we must necessarily meet them on the issue they tender. If we fight at all, we must fight slavery as the grand rebel. . . . Sir, when the history of this rebellion shall be written, its saddest pages will record the careful and studious tenderness of the administration toward American slavery." Strong, having advocated "any compromise or concession" to keep the border states in the Union, now began to fret at Lincoln's cautious handling of these volatile entities. "Fear of affronting the Border States has kept us hesitating far too long already," he wrote. "When every slave state has cast its lot with the woman-flogging Sepoys of the South, the nation will breathe more freely and act more decisively."

The fact was that sentiment for emancipation grew at a surprising rate. In December, 1861, William Goodell wrote: "Never has there been a time when Abolitionists were as much respected, as at present. Never has there been a time in which their strongest and most radical utterances . . . were as readily received by the people as at present. . . . Announce the presence of a competent abolition lecturer and the house is crammed."

The most spectacular speaker in behalf of the abolition cause was a young woman named Anna Dickinson. Born eleven years after Garrison started the *Liberator*, she had written her first contribution to the paper at the age of fourteen. In 1860 she had startled and delighted an antislavery meeting in Philadelphia by a stirring address. In the spring of 1862 she became a full-time speaker for the Massachusetts Anti-Slavery Society. Her first campaign in Rhode Island was a triumph. A writer in the *Providence Press* declared: "We are at a loss to conceive whence sprung this champion in petticoats of an antislavery war but in sending her forth, the coadjutors have made a wise selection—for, with the tongue of *a dozen women*, she combines the boldness of forty men." After her speech in the Music Hall in Boston before four thousand wildly enthusiastic listeners, Wendell Phillips declared that he had never been so "gratified and deeply moved by a speech." She was in demand everywhere as a speaker, especially in those states where the Republicans felt threatened by Democratic candidates in the fall elections. New Hampshire's beleaguered Republicans begged for Anna Dickinson, for example; she came and conquered the state. "A few of our Copperheads heard her at Moultonboro," one New Hampshire man wrote, "and they are completely shelled out." When the Republicans won the state, much of the credit was given to the girl orator. At Hartford, the hall was filled three hours before Anna's speech. One member of the audience declared afterward: "I am excited. I admit it, I am; it seems as if I was on fire, and everyone else that heard her are about as bad off. . . . [I] never heard anything that would begin to equal it."

In New York, when she spoke at Cooper Union, five thousand people turned out to hear her, and a correspondent for a Connecticut newspaper wrote, "Applause came often and in long-continued storms, hats were swung and handkerchiefs waved and at times the whole house was like a moving tumultuous sea, flecked with white caps. Never have I seen in New York any speaker achieve such a triumph."

The abolitionists were increasingly disenchanted with the President. Anna Dickinson wrote her sister in May, 1862, that Lincoln was simply "an Ass . . . for the Slave Power to ride." William Lloyd Garrison attacked the President in the *Liberator* as "stumbling, halting, prevaricating, irresolute, weak, besotted." Fanny Kemble, who knew at first hand the tragic ambiguities of slavery, feared that the policy of the government would be piecemeal and hit or miss. Military considerations would prevail, she predicted, with the blacks suffering from "one tremendous chapter of accidents, instead of a carefully considered and wisely prepared measure of government." When Wendell Phillips visited Washington in the spring of 1862 under the auspices of Charles Sumner to give a series of lectures at the Smithsonian, he was greeted like a visiting dignitary. "To-day," a correspondent for the *New York Tribune* wrote, "he was introduced by Mr. Sumner on the floor of the Senate. The Vice-President left his seat and greeted him with marked respect. The attentions of the Senators to the apostle of Abolition were of the most flattering character." Phillips's lectures were crowded; he was given a dinner by the Speaker of the House and spent an hour with Lincoln. Angelina Grimké Weld published "A Declaration of War on Slavery" and circulated it among her neighbors for their signatures. All these efforts, plus the working of events themselves and the simple passage of time, had their effect. Senator John Sherman of Ohio wrote his brother, the general, in August, 1862: "You can form no conception of the change of opinion here as to the Negro Question. . . . I am prepared for one to meet the broad issue of universal emancipation."

Even Sumner felt the pressure of the abolitionists. Wendell Phillips, indignant over the President's delay in declaring the slaves emancipated, wrote Sumner in the fall of 1862, urging the Massachusetts Senator to force the President to take action by withholding appropriations. "Lincoln," Phillips declared, "is doing twice as much to-day to break this Union as [Jefferson] Davis is. We are paying thousands of lives & millions of dollars as penalty for having a *timid* & *ignorant* President, all the more injurious because *honest*." Phillips, indeed, rather outdid himself, attacking McClellan for his timidity and adding, "I do not say that McClellan is a traitor, but I say this, that if he had been a traitor from the crown of his head to the sole of his foot, he could not have served the South better than he has done since he was commander-in-chief (applause); . . . and almost the same thing might be said of Mr. Lincoln." The speech, widely reported in the newspapers, caused general indignation even in the abolition ranks, and a Massachusetts Republican wrote to Charles Sumner, urging him to have Phillips committed to a madhouse before he was arrested as a traitor. "If he is sane, the prison is too good for him; if crazy, have him treated gently but not suffered to go at large."

Lincoln added fuel to the abolitionists' fire in the summer of 1862. Horace Greeley had written an editorial entitled "The Prayer of Twenty Millions," suggesting that Lincoln's refusal to declare that the war was being waged to end slavery was undermining the Union cause. "On the face of this wide earth, Mr. President," Greeley wrote, "there is not one disinterested, determined, intelligent champion of the Union cause who does not feel that all attempts to put down the rebellion and at the same time uphold its inciting cause, are preposterous and futile. . . ." Lincoln replied in what was to become one of the most important and widely quoted documents in American history: "As to the policy I 'seem to be pursuing,' as you say, I have not meant to leave anyone in doubt.

"I would save the Union. I would save it the shortest way under the Constitution. The sooner the national authority can be restored, the nearer the Union will be 'the Union as it was.' If there be those who would not save the Union unless they could at the same time save slavery, I do not agree with them. If there be those who would not save the Union unless they could at the same time destroy slavery, I do not agree with them. My paramount object in this struggle is to save the Union, and is not either to save or destroy slavery. If I could save it by freeing all the slaves I would do it; and if I could save it by freeing some and leaving others alone I would also do that. What I do about slavery and the colored race I do because I believe it helps to save the Union; and what I forbear, I forbear because I do not believe that it would help to save the Union. . . . I have here stated my purpose according to my view of official duty; and I intend no modification of my oft-expressed personal wish that all men everywhere could be free."

Every Northern black was an abolitionist, but the reaction of the black community in the North to the outbreak of the war was initially one of uncertainty. In order to understand that reaction, it is necessary to recall that for almost a decade there had been a heated debate in that community about emigrating from the United States to the black republic of Haiti or some other foreign refuge, such as Liberia.

The original resistance of free blacks to the plans of emigration proposed by whites had been based in large part on their faith that the status of free blacks had to improve markedly with the passage of time and the wider acceptance of the principles of Christian democracy and equality. Much of this faith was based on a belief in progress. If a progressive movement was evident in history under God's providence, it followed that the black man must benefit with the white. But the reverse had happened. Free blacks in the North had *lost* ground with each passing decade; they had seen their limited rights as citizens further restricted and the tide of prejudice and hostility rising rather than receding.

In Oregon, California, Iowa, and Illinois, blacks could not testify in court against a white man. With the exception of California, these states also forbade the immigration of blacks. Only in Massachusetts could blacks serve on juries, and in more parts of the North there was *de facto*, if not *de jure*, segregation in public transportation, in schools, and in hotels, restaurants, and theaters. While schools were integrated in most Northern communities, in those cities which had large concentrations of blacks, schools were segregated if they existed at all for blacks. Edward Dicey, a British journalist, wrote in 1862: "I never by any chance, in the Free States, saw a coloured man dining at a public table, or mixing socially in any manner with white people, or dressed as a man well to do in the world, or occupying any position, however humble, in which he was placed in authority over white persons." In Ohio, when Dicey complimented a resident on the beauty of the state, the man replied, "There is but one thing, sir, that we want here, and that is to get rid of the niggers." Dicey wrote: "In every Northern city the poorest, most thriftless, and perhaps the most troublesome part of the population, are the free negroes. . . . The free negro has not a fair chance throughout the North."

Illinois had a law forbidding blacks to enter the state on penalty of a heavy fine. A black convicted of disobeying the law could be sold into temporary servitude to work off his fine. In 1863 eight black people were convicted of entering the state, and seven punished. A Chicago black named John Jones who had made a modest fortune as a tailor became the leader of a movement called the Repeal Association to get the obnoxious law repealed. Every race and nationality had prospered in America, Jones reminded the governor of the state, except the black people. "We," he declared to a state legislative committee, "have been treated as strangers in the land of our birth. . . . To-day a colored man cannot buy a *burying-lot* in the city of Chicago for his own use. . . . And more than this, the cruel treatment that we receive daily at the hands of a portion of your foreign population, is based upon these enactments. . . . Then, fellow citizens, in the name of the great Republic, erase these nefarious and unnecessary laws, and give us your protection, and treat us as you treat other citizens of the State. . . . May God in His goodness assist you to do the right." Illinois did repeal the "black laws," leaving only Indiana, among Northern states, with such restrictions. These were overturned by a state court decision in 1865 and abandoned by the legislature a few months later.

Blacks in New York, as in Philadelphia and most other Northern cities, suffered daily harassment and persecution. J. W. C. Pennington, an ex-slave who became a Congregational minister and a teacher, famous for his eloquence, noted that New York blacks had become the "objects of . . . marked abuse and insult. From many of the grocery corners, stones, potatoes, and pieces of coal, would often be hurled, by idle young loafers, standing about. . . ."

The tobacco factory of Lorillard and Watson in Brooklyn, New York, employed twenty-five blacks, most of them women and children. In August, 1862, it was set afire by a mob of Irishmen whose intent was to burn down the building and murder the black workers in it. The police arrived in time to help put out the fire and rescue the workers. Six months later a white mob sacked and burned thirty-five houses in the black section of Detroit, killing several and leaving more than two hundred people homeless. The *Christian Recorder*, a black journal published in Philadelphia, asked: "What have the colored people done that they should be thus treated? Even here, in the city of Philadelphia, in many places, it is almost impossible for a respectable colored person to walk the streets without being insulted by a set of blackguards and cowards."

When Congress debated confiscating the contrabands fighting against the Union, one Northern Congressman declared: "Pass these acts, confiscate under the bills the property of these men, emancipate their negroes, place arms in the hands of these human gorillas to murder their masters and violate their wives and daughters, and you will have a war such as was never witnessed in the worst days of the French Revolution, and horrors never exceeded in San Domingo."

The City of Brotherly Love was one of the most rigidly segregated cities in the country. Visiting there in 1862, Frederick Douglass wrote of the city that "it has its white schools and colored schools, its white churches and colored churches, its white Christianity and its colored Christianity, its white concerts and its colored concerts, its white literary institutions and its colored literary institutions . . . and the line is everywhere tightly drawn between them. Colored persons, no matter how well dressed or well behaved, ladies and gentlemen, rich or poor, are not even permitted to ride on any of the many railways through that Christian city. . . . The whole aspect of city usage at this point is mean, contemptible and barbarous."

Susan B. Anthony put the matter of Northern prejudice with characteristic succinctness: "While the cruel slave-driver lacerates the black man's mortal body, we, of the North, flay the spirit. . . . Let us open to the colored man all our schools, from the common District to the College. Let us admit him into all our mechanic shops, stores, offices and lucrative business avocations, to work side by side with his white brother; let him rent such pew in the church, and occupy such seat in the theatre, and the public lecture room as he pleases; let him be admitted to all our entertainments, both public & private; let him share all the accommodations of our hotels, stages, railroads and steamboats. . . . Let him vote and be voted for. . . . Let the North thus prove to the South, by her acts, that she fully recognizes the humanity of the black man." The inventory of the rights that Susan B. Anthony believed should be extended to the Northern black was an inventory of those denied him.

Under such social pressure some black leaders began to advocate emigration to the black republic of Haiti. An anonymous letter writer in the pages of the *Anglo-African* urged American blacks to emigrate: "Listen— We want our rights. No one is going to *give* them to us, so perforce we must take them. In order to do this, we must have a strong nationality somewhere—respected, feared. . . . We can make of Haiti the nucleus of a power that shall be to the black, what England has been to the white races, the hope of progress and the guarantee of permanent civilization. . . . From that centre, let the fire of freedom radiate until it shall enkindle, in the whole of that vast area, the sacred flame of Liberty upon the altar of every black man's heart, and you effect at once the abolition of slavery and the regeneration of our race."

J. Willis Menard was another advocate of emigration. "Shall we," he wrote, "always say, 'O America, with thy many faults, we love thee still'? No! let us commit to the care of God the graves of our fathers, and of those who died by the cruel tortures of a slow fire, and go at once to our 'promised land!'"

William Wells Brown, a supporter of emigration early in the war, wrote: "Let us look at facts. It must be confessed that we, the colored people of this country, are a race of cooks, waiters, barbers, whitewashers, bootblacks, and chimney sweeps. How much influence has such a class upon a community?" George Lawrence, the editor of the *Pine and Palm*, echoed the same sentiment: "The scanty pittance of social toleration which is here and there grudgingly doled out to us is only exceptional, illustrating the more strikingly the rule which everywhere excludes us."

A black woman in New York, who supported emigration, wrote that "it is my firm conviction that we as a mass never can rise to any degree of eminence in this country. Our condition may be ameliorated, and individuals may, by dint of severe struggling, manage to keep chin above water and that is about all."

Frederick Douglass, at first sympathetic to the movement for Haitian emigration, turned emphatically against the idea with the outbreak of the war. In June, 1861, he wrote that the plan "has become ethnological, philosophical, political and commercial. It has its doctrines of races, of climates, of nationalities and destinies, and offers itself as the grand solution of the destiny of the colored people in America." The fact of the matter, Douglass wrote, was that blacks in the United States were "Americans, speaking the same language, adopting the same customs, holding the same general opinions . . . and shall rise or fall with Americans. . . ." The history of black people had been, on the whole, "one of progress and improvement," Douglass added, "and in all the likelihoods of the case, will become more so. . . ." All movements of emigration work against black people because "they serve to kindle hopes of getting us out of the country. . . . I hope," Douglass continued, "that there is no such thing as a natural and unconquerable repugnance between the varieties of men. All these artificial and arbitrary barriers give way before interest and enlightenment. . . . The hope of the world is in Human Brotherhood; in the union of mankind, not in exclusive nationalities." The controversy over voluntary emigration was a recurrent one in the black community. Whenever the pressures of white society on blacks have grown unbearable, a "black prophet" has risen to preach the message of a "homeland," sometimes in Africa, sometimes in the Caribbean. Some of the most brilliant spokesmen of what has been called in this century black nationalism have preached the doctrine, and some have tried to practice a variation in their own lives by making themselves voluntary exiles from America. But almost all have discovered the truth of Douglass's dictum—that, for better or worse, American blacks are more American than they are black, or at least as much. They have discovered that being American is, for the vast majority of us, an irreversible condition because we have, with all our considerable blemishes and deficiencies, entered a broader realm of human possibilities.

The outbreak of the war and opposition of Douglass and other leaders dampened the enthusiasm for emigration. James McCune Smith, who had received his medical degree from the University of Glasgow and practiced medicine in New York City, decried the Haitian dream. "Our people want to stay," he wrote Henry Garnet, "and will stay, at home; we are in for the fight, and will fight it out here. Shake yourself free from these migrating phantasms, and join us with your might and main." Several thousand blacks responded to the call of James Redpath's Emigration Bureau and departed for Haiti, but the results were, in the main, tragic. Many died in an uncongenial climate. Most experienced prejudice on the part of the native Haitians almost as merciless as that which they experienced at home. One observer wrote: "The majority of the emigrants [are] . . . not doing well, earning but little money, enjoying miserable health, generally dissatisfied with the country, its prospects, its climate, soil, and the 'old fogy' modes in which business of all kinds are carried on," and welcoming back a group of defeated emigrants from Haiti, the Zion Church of New York resolved that "we view with contempt, as our fathers nobly did, the old Hag, the 'American Colonization Society,' its pet daughter, the 'African Civilization Society,' also its deformed child, the Haytian Emigration Movement, and their efforts to remove the colored man from the United States."

From the first moment of the war Frederick Douglass was tireless in proclaiming that it was, and must be said to be, above all, a war to emancipate the slaves. "Sound policy, not less than humanity," he declared, "demands the instant liberation of every slave in the rebel states. . . . Evade and equivocate as we may, slavery is the sole support of the rebel cause. It is, so to speak, the very stomach of this rebellion. We talk of the irrepressible conflict, and practically give the lie to our talk." To Douglass, "The negro is the key of the situation—the pivot upon which the whole rebellion turns. . . . This war, disguise it as they may, is virtually nothing more or less than perpetual slavery against universal freedom, and to this end the free States will have to come. . . ."

The *Anglo-African*, after news of the surrender of Sumter, wrote: "Men of the North, away with your Balaam-like proclivities, your trifling with truth and trafficking in principles. . . . Look upon us not as outcasts, pariahs, slaves, but as men whom the Almighty has endowed with the same faculties as yourselves, but in whom your cruelty has blurred His image and thwarted *His* intent. . . ."

When the summer of 1861 passed without any official statement on the issue of emancipation, many Northern blacks began to lose heart. A minister of the African Methodist Church in Trenton, New Jersey, spoke for many of his fellows when he expressed his conviction that "The President is not now, and never was, either an abolitionist, or an anti-slavery man. . . . He has no quarrel whatever with the south, upon the slavery question."

Harriet Tubman, her days as a conductor on the Underground Railroad long over, was convinced that "God won't let Massa Linkum beat the South till he do de right ting. Massa Linkum he great man, and I'se poor nigger; but dis nigger can tell Massa Linkum how to save de money and de young men. He do it by setting de niggers free." She had a story to go with Lincoln's stories. "S'pose dar was awfu' big snake down dar, on de floor. He bit you. Folks all skeered, cause you die. You send for doctor to cut de bite; but snake he roll up dar, and while the doctor dwine it, he bite you agin. De doctor cut out dat bite; but while he dwine it, de snake he spring up and bite you agin, and so he keep dwine, till you kill him. Dat's what Massa Linkum orter know."

Free blacks had been in the forefront of those Americans coming forward to serve in the Union army after Sumter, but in all states blacks were barred from serving in the militia by Federal law. Ten days after the fall of Sumter a black drill company was formed in Boston, and Robert Morris, a black lawyer, declared at a meeting of that city's blacks: "If the government would only take away the disability [the law forbidding the enrollment of blacks] there was not a man who would not leap for his knapsack and musket, and they would make it intolerably hot for old Virginia." Massachusetts blacks, followed by those in many other Northern states, drew up a petition to the state legislature stating that black people "have never been wanting in patriotism, but have always exhibited the utmost loyalty to the country, and to the commonwealth, notwithstanding the great national injustice to which they are in many ways subjected on account of their complexion." They asked "in this trial-hour of the republic" to be relieved from the "odious proscription which has so long and so unjustly been directed against them . . . by an illegal act of Congress. . . ." But the Massachusetts legislature equivocated, and Simon Cameron, secretary of war, replied to various Negro petitioners that he had no intention of accepting black recruits. New York City blacks who rented a hall to use for drill were told by the police that they were engaged in an illegal activity and that the authorities could not protect them from attacks by mobs of Negro haters. The same thing happened in Cincinnati and other cities where blacks attempted to form military units. In Cincinnati the efforts of blacks to form a volunteer company were met with the statement that the war was a "white man's fight, with which niggers had nothing to do."

Frederick Douglass now made the issue of enlisting black soldiers his special cause. "Once let the black man get upon his person the brass letters, U.S., let him get an eagle on his buttons, and a musket on his shoulder and bullets in his pocket, and there is no power on earth which can deny that he has earned the right to citizenship in the United States," he declared. In August, 1861, after the Battle of Bull Run, Douglass wrote an article entitled "Fighting Rebels with Only One Hand." "What upon earth is the matter with the American Government and people?" he asked. "Do they really covet the world's ridicule as well as their own social and political ruin?" The government leaders "steadily and persistently refuse to receive the very class of men which have a deeper interest in the defeat and humiliation of the rebels, than all others. . . . What a spectacle of blind, unreasoning prejudice and pusillanimity is this. The national edifice is on fire. Every man who can carry a bucket of water, or remove a brick, is wanted. . . ." But white Americans seemed to prefer to see the structure burn than allow blacks to help put out the flame. "Such is the pride, the stupid prejudice and folly that rules the hour," Douglass wrote. ". . . While the Government continues to refuse the aid of colored men, thus alienating them from the national cause, and giving rebels the advantage over them, it will not deserve better fortunes than it has thus far experienced."

John Rock, a black abolitionist and the first black lawyer accredited before the Supreme Court, wrote in 1862: "The masses seem to think we are oppressed only in the South. This is a mistake; we are oppressed everywhere in this slavery-cursed land." Even in Massachusetts black people were constantly discriminated against. Education was available to Massachusetts blacks, but there was "no field" for educated blacks. "Their education aggravates their suffering," Rock noted. ". . . The educated colored man meets, on the one hand, the embittered prejudices of the whites, and on the other the jealousies of his own race. . . . You can hardly imagine the humiliation and contempt a colored lad must feel by graduating the first in his class, and then being rejected everywhere else because of his color. . . ." If the Union did enlist blacks, Rock wrote, he hoped it would grant them their full rights as citizens—"their manhood." It could hardly be "mean enough to force us to fight for your liberty . . . and then leave us when we go home to our respective States to be told that we cannot ride in the cars, that our children cannot go to the public schools, that we cannot vote; and that if we don't like that state of things, there is an appropriation to colonize us. We ask for our rights."

A California black wrote in the fall of 1862, in a more optimistic view: "Our relation to this Government is changing daily. . . . Our position in the history of the country will, in the future, be entirely different to that which we formerly occupied. . . . The only place the American historian could find for the colored man was in the background of a cotton-field, or the foreground of a cane-brake or a rice swamp, to adorn the pages of geography. . . . But old things are passing away, and eventually old prejudices must follow. The revolution has begun, and time alone must decide where it is to end." Ironically, blacks served with the Confederate army from the earliest days of the war, although only as service troops, as cooks, laborers, and teamsters, or as orderlies for their officer masters.

The consequence of the ban on black enlistments was a division within the black community as to the attitude that Northern blacks should take toward the war. One group urged their fellows to consider the war a war for the rights of all black people in America and support it in every way they could. The other declared that as long as the North continued to discriminate against blacks, black people should not support the war effort. An Ohio black wrote: "If the colored people, under all the social and legal disabilities by which they are environed, are ever ready to defend the government that despoils them of their rights, it may be concluded that it is quite safe to oppress them. . . ." Blacks had, after all, served in the armies of the American Revolution, and if that had not secured their rights for them, it was "absurd to suppose that the fact of tendering our services to settle a domestic war when we know that our services will be contemptuously rejected, will procure a practical acknowledgement of our rights."

Some blacks offered to contribute to the war effort by serving as firemen in the place of white men who volunteered for the army or to enlist in a home guard to defend against possible attacks. The *Anglo-African,* a New York paper, wrote: "There are men among our people who look upon this as the 'white man's war,' and such men openly say, let them fight it out among themselves. It is their flag, and their constitution which have been dishonored and set at naught. . . . This is a huge fallacy," the editorial writer declared. While Northern blacks suffered various forms of discrimination, they had, after all, the "right to life, liberty and pursuit of happiness." The writer asked, "Are these rights worth having? If they are then they are worth defending with all our might, and at any cost. It is illogical, unpatriotic, nay mean and unmanly in us to shrink from the defense of these great rights and priviledges. . . . Talk as we may, we *are* concerned in this fight and our fate hangs upon its issues. The South must be subjugated, or we shall be enslaved. . . . We do not affirm that the North is fighting in behalf of the black man's rights, as such—if this was the single issue, we even doubt whether they would fight at all. But circumstances have been so arranged by the decrees of Providence, that in struggling for their own nationality, they are forced to defend our rights."

The *Anglo-African* was answered by a reader who wrote: "Is this country ready and anxious to initiate a new era for downtrodden humanity, that you now so eagerly propose to make the sacrifice of thousands of our ablest men to encourage and facilitate the great work of regeneration? No! no!! Your answer must be: NO!!! No black regiments unless by circumstances over which we have no option, no control." A Negro schoolteacher in Philadelphia joined in the controversy, writing: "I have seen men drilled among our sturdy colored men of the rural districts of Pennsylvania and New Jersey, in the regular African Zouave Drill, that would make the hearts of secession traitors, or prejudiced northern Yankees, quake and tremble for fear. . . . No nation ever has or ever will be emancipated from slavery . . . but by the sword, wielded to by their own strong arms. It is a foolish idea for us to still be nursing our past grievances to our own detriment when we should as one man grasp the sword. . . . We admit all that has or can be said about the meanness of this government towards us—we are fully aware that there is no more soul in the present administration on the great moral issues involved in the slavery question . . . than has characterized previous administrations; but what of that? . . ." It remained a fact that God helped those who helped themselves. "The prejudiced white men North or South never will respect us until they are forced to do it by deeds of our own. . . . Without this we will be left a hundred years behind this gigantic age of human progress and development."

Petitions were drafted by the dozen and sent to the President and to Congress. One petition to Lincoln declared that the signers, "notwithstanding much injustice and oppression which our race has suffered," cherished "a strong attachment for the land of our birth and for our Republican Government." The petitioners declared that Northern blacks were "strong in numbers, in courage, and in patriotism" and ready to "offer to you and to the nation a power and will sufficient to conquer rebellion, and establish peace on a permanent basis." When a Union officer wrote to Stanton in the summer of 1862 requesting permission to form a black regiment, Stanton not only refused but ordered the officer arrested.

Henry Turner, the black minister of the Israel Bethel Church in Washington, wrote: "Those who have been taught by a God-blessed experience to abhor the monster slavery, and have felt its inhuman crushings" will declare, "Give us the opportunity, show us a chance to climb to distinction, and we will show the world by our bravery what the negro can do. . . . Can you ask more than a chance to drive a bayonet or bullet into the slaveholders' hearts?" Turner asked.

Increasingly the refusal of the government to enlist black soldiers came to be for black leaders a symbol of their inferior status. They were not even to be allowed to fight for the freedom of their own people. The abolitionists promptly allied themselves with the cause of black soldiers. Henry Ward Beecher, Wendell Phillips, and dozens of other abolitionist orators and journalists took up the issue. Even Karl Marx gave his endorsement of the idea, writing to Engels: "A single negro regiment would have a remarkable effect. . . . A war of this kind must be conducted on revolutionary lines while the Yankees have thus far been trying to conduct it constitutionally." But when a delegation of Indiana blacks offered Lincoln the service of two black regiments, he replied: "To arm the negroes would turn 50,000 bayonets from the loyal Border States against us that were for us."

When Lincoln on March 6, 1862, sent a message to Congress proposing Federal compensation for any state "which may adopt the gradual abolishment of slavery," it was hailed by many blacks. The *Anglo-African* declared it had "secured for Abraham Lincoln a confidence and admiration on the part of the people, the whole loyal people such as no man has enjoyed in the present era. We could hardly believe the news. . . . It marks the grandest revolution of the ages, a revolution from barbarism to civilization, or darkness to light, of slavery into freedom." Lincoln said to Owen Lovejoy and Isaac Arnold, a Republican Congressman from Illinois, "Oh, how I wish the border states would accept my proposition. Then you, Lovejoy, and you, Arnold, and all of us, would not have lived in vain! The labor of your life, Lovejoy, would be crowned with success. You would live to see the end of slavery." But Congressman William Wadsworth of Kentucky responded: "I utterly spit at it and despise it . . . emancipation in the cotton states is simply an absurdity. . . . There is not enough power in the world to compel it to be done." To Thaddeus Stevens, on the other hand, the resolution was "the most diluted milk-and-water gruel proposition that was ever given to the American nation." The border states emphatically rejected the President's proposal, but important, if modest, steps toward emancipation were taken during the spring of 1862. A law was passed by Congress forbidding army commanders from returning fugitive slaves who entered Union lines, and legislation prohibiting slavery in the territories and abolishing slavery in the District of Columbia was adopted. The last was the most significant. The persistence of slavery in the Union capital had been pointed to as evidence that the Republicans cared more for political considerations than for freedom. Frederick Douglass wrote to Charles Sumner: "I trust I am not dreaming but the events taking place seem like a dream." A free black went to tell a slave friend that she was free. When he entered the house in which she worked, he wrote a friend, "her and another Slave woman who has a slave son were talking relative to the Bill expressing doubts of its passage & when I entered they perceived that something was ahead and immediately asked me 'Whats the news?' The Districts free says I pulling out the 'National Republican' and reading its editorial when I had finished the chambermaid left the room sobbing for joy. The slave woman clapped her hands and shouted, left the house saying 'let me go and tell my husband that Jesus has done all things well. . . . Were I a drinker I would go on a Jolly spree today but as a Christian I can but kneel in prayer and bless God for the privilege I've enjoyed this day. . . .' "

The *Anglo-African* hailed the abolition of the slavery in the District of Columbia: "Henceforth, whatever betide the nation, its physical heart is freed from the presence of slavery. . . . We rejoice and give thanks to the Almighty for this great boon, we rejoice less as black men than as part and parcel of the American people; for it is clearly a greater boon to the nation at large than to the class more immediately concerned. . . . It is an act of emancipation which frees a hundred thousand white men for every individual black. . . . We can point to our capital and say to all nations, 'IT IS FREE!' "

After the law abolishing slavery in the District of Columbia had been signed by the President, even Lydia Maria Child, an unsparing critic of Lincoln, was willing to give him a modicum of credit. "I am inclined to think 'old Abe' *means* about right, only he has a hidebound soul." Samuel May conceded that even though the government "moves very cautiously, very slowly," its steps were "*forward*—none backward." George Templeton Strong sounded almost like the editor of the *Anglo-African*. "Only the damnedest of the 'damned abolitionists' dreamed of such a thing a year ago," he wrote. "Perhaps the name of abolitionist will be less disgraceful a year hence. John Brown's 'soul's a-marching on,' with the people after it." That a profound alteration in the Northern opinion had taken place was "a great historical fact, comparable," in Strong's words, "with the early progress of Christianity. . . . I think this great and blessed revolution is due, in no small degree, to A. Lincoln's sagacious policy."

"Abolitionism established in the District of Columbia," Strong wrote, "and triumphantly rampant under state laws in Maryland and Missouri. . . . God pardon our blindness of three years ago. But for want of eyes to see and of courage to say what we saw, the South would never have ventured on rebellion."

16

From Bull Run
to Antietam

When Carl Schurz arrived in Washington on leave from his ambassadorial post in Spain, he sought a meeting at once with Lincoln, uncertain whether his letter on the issue of slavery had ever actually reached the President. Schurz reiterated his arguments for the necessity of some positive statement by Lincoln on the subject. "I was still speaking," Schurz later wrote, "when the door of the room was opened and the head of Mr. Seward appeared. 'Excuse me, Seward,' said Mr. Lincoln, 'excuse me for a moment. I have something to talk over with this gentleman.'" When Schurz finished, Lincoln sat silently for a time and then said: "You may be right. Probably you are. I have been thinking so myself. I cannot imagine that any European power would dare to recognize and aid the Southern Confederacy if it becomes clear that the Confederacy stands for slavery and the Union for freedom." Lincoln explained to Schurz that while he was conscious of the importance of the slavery issue as regarded European opinion, he also felt that the Union consensus was a most precarious one and that he was anxious to allow time for domestic antislavery sentiment to grow. "Would not the cry of 'abolition war,' such as might be occasioned by a distinct anti-slavery policy, tend to disunite those forces and thus weaken the Union cause? This was the doubt that troubled him, and it troubled him very much." Lincoln urged Schurz to travel about, talk with people, sound out public sentiment, and report back to him.

Carrying out the President's commission to sample opinion, Schurz noted that "outside of the circles of hide-bound Democratic partisanship" there was "quite general" sentiment "that the time had come for an open movement in outspoken advocacy of emancipation." To encourage this tendency, Schurz and his friends organized an Emancipation Society and arranged for a public meeting at Cooper Union in New York on March 6, 1862. When Schurz reported back to Lincoln the plans for the rally, the President was pleased. "And at that meeting you are going to make a speech?" Schurz said yes, he intended to, and Lincoln replied, "Well, now go home and sketch that speech. Do it as quickly as you can. Then come and show me your arguments and we will talk it over." The line of argument that Schurz developed was ingenious. The war, he predicted, would be long and arduous. When it was over, the Union must be restored as quickly as possible, and sectional feelings minimized. In order for this reconciliation to take place, the principal cause of friction between the two great sections of the country must be removed. That was plainly and inescapably the institution of slavery. No genuine reunion could take place until that terrible bone of contention no longer existed. It was a brilliant stroke to tie the theme of restoration of the Union to the abolition of slavery. The Democrats had contended, and indeed continued to contend, that the North must abandon the cause of abolition in order to effect a reconciliation and reunite the country. Schurz now put forward exactly the opposite proposition—in the final analysis there could be no lasting Union unless the slaves were emancipated. Schurz entitled his prospective address "Reconciliation by Emancipation" and then took it to Lincoln. Lincoln asked Schurz to read the speech to him, and when he had done so, the President said, "Now, you go and deliver that speech at your meeting. . . . And maybe you will hear something from me on the same day."

The emancipation meeting at Cooper Union was crowded to overflowing "with an audience representative of all classes," as Schurz put it. Many people felt that it was the penultimate moment of the long, long crusade against slavery which might be said to have started with the modest appearance of Benjamin Lundy's *Genius of Universal Emancipation*. More than forty years had passed since that time—more than a generation. Garrison, who had started the *Liberator* thirty-one years earlier in 1831, was now a man in his fifties. Arthur Tappan, the bankroller of the movement, was a venerable seventy-six and his brother Lewis, seventy-four. In some instances the pioneers of abolition, the young men and women who had founded the "Church of Abolition," had grown old, and died, and their places in the abolitionists' ranks had been filled by their children. "There was something like a religious fervor in the proceeding," Schurz wrote. Before the meeting ended, the audience rose and sang the well-known hymn "Old Hundred." When it was about to adjourn, Horace Greeley appeared with a telegram from Washington. The President had, that very day, sent a special message to Congress asking for the adoption of a joint resolution by both houses to the effect "that the United States ought to cooperate with any State which may adopt gradual abolishment of slavery, giving to each State pecuniary aid, to be used by such State, in its discretion, to compensate for the inconveniences, public and private, produced by such a change of system." This modest first step was "received by the whole assemblage," Schurz wrote, "with transports of joy."

The ripening process went on. The Radical Republicans in Congress exerted constant pressure on the President, and Lincoln wrote: "Stevens, Sumner and Wilson, simply haunt me with their importunities for a Proclamation of Emancipation. Wherever I go and whatever way I turn, they are on my trail, and still in my heart, I have the conviction that the hour has not yet come." He compared them to Shadrach, Meshach, and Abednego and told Senator John Henderson of Missouri a story of a schoolmate of his who, unable to pronounce the names of the occupants of the fiery furnace, was given a sharp cuff by an impatient schoolmaster every time he stumbled. Finally, in despair, when he came to the names again, he quavered out, "Look there, marster, there comes them same damn three fellers again!"

The old-line abolitionists were not the only emancipationists. There was quite another party, men who professed not the slightest interest in or sympathy with the black man, free *or* slave, who emphasized that their support of emancipation was simply as a war measure designed to weaken and demoralize the South and hasten the end of the war and the restoration of the Union. They deplored the abolitionist-emancipators and went to considerable pains to make clear the differences between the two schools. They denounced "all of that old abolition jargon" about freedom and equality. As far as nine-tenths of the North were concerned, "slaves might have hoed away down in

Dixie" forever. The black man should be regarded "not as a man and a brother," James Gilmore, a leader of the "antiabolitionist" emancipators, wrote, "but as 'a miserable nigger,' if you please, and a nuisance. But whatever he be, if the effect of owning such creatures is to make the owner an intolerable fellow, seditious and insolent, it becomes pretty clear that such ownership should be put an end to."

On May 9, 1862, General David Hunter, in command of the Sea Islands, issued a proclamation stating that all the slaves in Georgia, South Carolina, and Florida were "forever free." Lincoln, again concerned about the allegiance of the border states, countermanded the order ten days later. The news of Lincoln's action spread gloom and dismay among Northern blacks. Frederick Douglass denounced the President for seeking to "reconstruct the union on the old and corrupting basis of compromise, by which slavery shall retain all the power that it ever had. . . ." Lincoln, Douglass declared, "is no more fit for the place he holds than was JAMES BUCHANAN, and the latter was no more the miserable tool of traitors and rebels than the former is allowing himself to be."

There had never been any question in Lincoln's mind about the ultimate goal of emancipation. He had staked his political fortunes on the proposition that the Union could not survive half slave and half free. The question was simply one of timing. It was a question never far from his mind. In the summer of 1862 his instincts told him that the time was at hand. By Welles's account, Lincoln, riding in a carriage with Seward and Welles on the way to the funeral of Stanton's infant son, "first mentioned . . . the subject of emancipating the slaves by proclamation in case the Rebels did not cease to persist in their war on the Government and Union. . . . He dwelt earnestly on the gravity, importance, and delicacy of the moment, said he had given it much thought and had about come to the conclusion that it was a military necessity absolutely essential for the salvation of the Union, that we must free the slaves or be ourselves subdued, etc., etc." The President then asked Seward and Welles for their reaction. Seward replied that it would involve consequences so vast that he felt he must reflect upon it for a time before giving an answer. Welles answered in the same vein. It is plain enough that in Lincoln's mind and in the opinions of his Cabinet members, the issue of emancipation was as much a political as a moral question. "The slaves," Welles wrote, "if not armed and disciplined, were in the service of those who were . . . in rebellion. . . ."

Having sounded out Welles and Seward, Lincoln sat down and wrote out a draft proclamation, called the Cabinet together, "made a little talk to them, and read the momentous document." The act and its consequences were his, he told them, but in Welles's words, "he felt it due to us to make us acquainted with the fact and to invite criticism on the paper which he had prepared. . . . In the course of the discussion on this paper, which was long, earnest, and, on the general principle involved, harmonious," Welles added, the President "remarked that he had made a vow, a covenant, that if God gave us the approaching battle, he would consider it an indication of Divine will, and that it was his duty to move forward in the cause of emancipation." It was his view that "God had decided this question in favor of the slaves. He was satisfied it was right, was confirmed and strengthened in his action by the vow and its results. His mind was fixed, his decision made. . . ." It was clear that certain members of the Cabinet had substantial misgivings. Montgomery Blair, the postmaster general, and Edward Bates, the attorney general, demurred. Even Welles was deeply troubled by the possible consequences. "It is a step in the progress of this war," he wrote in his diary, "which will extend into the distant future. A favorable termination of this terrible conflict seems more remote with every movement. . . ." The outcome must be either emancipation to the slaves or continued submission to their masters. Desirable as it might be, or even essential, it was nonetheless "an arbitrary and despotic measure in the cause of freedom." Chase felt that the proclamation went much farther than was necessary or expedient. Stanton noted: "Chase thinks it a measure of great danger, and would lead to universal emancipation." The uneasiness of Seward and the opposition of Chase persuaded Lincoln to delay the public announcement, and Seward took advantage of the opportunity to urge Thurlow Weed to try to prevail on the President not to announce it since it would be interpreted by many as a hollow gesture, premature and unenforceable.

The issue settled in his own mind, Lincoln felt a calm resolution. Still, the time was not propitious. McClellan's Peninsula campaign had ended in frustration and a staggering toll of casualties. A proclamation, to have the best effect, should be issued in the wake of a Northern military victory. Lincoln put the proclamation in his desk to wait for the right moment. It was a dishearteningly long time coming. McClellan, back from Virginia, once more procrastinated. Chase was convinced that he was traitorous. If he had been president, he told Welles, he would have had McClellan shot. Welles, for his part, confessed that he had given up all efforts to cooperate or even communicate with McClellan. "To me," he wrote, "it seemed he had no plan or policy of his own, or any realizing sense of the true condition of affairs—the Rebels in sight of us, almost within cannon-range, Washington beleaguered, only a single railroad track to Baltimore, and the Potomac about to be closed. He was occupied with reviews, and dress-parades, perhaps with drills and discipline, but was regardless of the necessities of the case." Welles did not agree with Chase that the errant general was an "imbecile, a coward, a traitor, but it was notorious that he hesitated, doubted, had no self-reliance, any definite and determined plan, and audacity to act . . . in short, he was not a fighting general."

It was Welles's conclusion, based on talks with McClellan, that Little Mac "wishes to outgeneral the Rebels but not to kill and destroy them." Indeed, McClellan told Welles that he hated Massachusetts and South Carolina and would "rejoice to see both States extinguished. Both were and always had been ultra mischievous, and he could not tell which he hated most," an odd confession, Welles thought, from a man commanding a large contingent of Massachusetts troops.

Prompted perhaps by McClellan's notorious letter, Lincoln, as we have noted, had summoned Henry Halleck from his post as commander of the Department of the Missouri, where his reputation had profited from the fighting ability of his subordinates. Halleck was the soldier-intellectual, the author of books on military science and translator of a French work on Napoleon's military campaigns. He had given the Lowell Lectures in Boston, seen military service in California, and resigned his army commission to head a prominent California law firm. There he had made mining law his specialty and written two volumes on the subject as well as a treatise on international law. He had been commissioned a major general at the beginning of the war and sent to relieve Frémont as commander of the Department of the Missouri. Nicknamed Old Brains, he was cold and aloof in manner with no gift for conciliating politicians or dealing with his subordinates. He and McClellan were soon at odds. His own cautious temper made McClellan seem bold by comparison.

After the Sanitary Commission's first session with Halleck, George Templeton Strong reported: "We walked away from Halleck's quarters in dismal silence and consternation. Van Buren broke it with the words 'God help us!' That aspiration was never more appropriate. Halleck is not the man for his place. He is certainly—clearly—weak, shallow, commonplace, vulgar. . . . His silly talk was conclusive as to his incapacity, unless he was a little flustered with wine. . . . Heaven help our rulers. Never was so great a cause in the keeping of much smaller men. I still have faith in Abe Lincoln," Strong added.

Of much more significance in the long run than Halleck's appointment was the appointment of another Californian as medical director of the Army of the Potomac. Jonathan Letterman, forty-eight at the time of his appointment, had served in the Seminole War and in army posts on the frontier. When he joined McClellan's army at the end of the disastrous Seven Days' Battle, one-fifth of the men were unfit for duty because of sickness. Medical supplies and field hospitals had been abandoned in the retreat, and twenty thousand sick and wounded soldiers were enduring hellish conditions. Working tirelessly, Letterman evacuated the sick and wounded to Washington, organized an ambulance service, and instituted numerous other reforms, many of them earlier advocated by the Sanitary Commission, that eventually became standard throughout the various Union armies.

While McClellan's Peninsula campaign was in progress, Stonewall Jackson had been raiding the Shenandoah Valley. There he had repeatedly outmaneuvered and outfought the combined armies of Frémont, Nathaniel Banks, and McDowell, slipping away, late in June, to join forces with Johnston (and then Lee after Johnston was wounded) for the bitter fighting of the Seven Days' Battle, where it must be said, his tentativeness and his dilatory execution of orders appeared to cost Lee the chance of a decisive victory over McClellan.

Lincoln, meanwhile, determined to try Pope, who had attracted favorable attention to himself by his capture of New Madrid and Island No. 10. Although there was a notable lack of enthusiasm for Pope among those of Lincoln's advisers who knew him (Montgomery Blair wrote: "Old John Pope, his father, was a flatterer, a deceiver, a liar, and a trickster; all the Popes are so"), Lincoln persisted, and Pope was called to Washington from the Army of the Mississippi and given command. He got off to an inauspicious start by issuing a general order to his new command which declared, "I have come to you from the West where we have always seen the backs of our enemies; from an army whose business it has been to seek the adversary, and to beat him back when he was found; whose policy has been attack and not defense." The order guaranteed the hostility of McClellan and those officers and men loyal to him. (I suspect a study of the style of a general's orders and communiqués would indicate that they were a remarkably accurate index to his performance in battle—the windier the communiqués, the poorer the general.)

When the Army of Virginia was formed by uniting the corps of Frémont, McDowell, and Banks and placing them under Pope, Frémont refused to serve under Pope and resigned. Franz Sigel replaced him in command of the I Corps. Lincoln also ordered McClellan to come to Pope's assistance, but that dilatory general delayed obeying orders until Lincoln sent Ambrose E. Burnside with instructions to supersede him if he did not march at once.

The mission assigned to Pope and the newly formed Army of Virginia was to seize the rail junction at Manassas, near Bull Run, where McDowell had come to grief the year before. Pope, with some 50,000 men, began his advance on July 14. To meet this movement, Lee dispatched Jackson with 12,000 men and then sent A. P. Hill's division to reinforce him.

In Pope's advancing army, Banks's II Corps was intercepted at Cedar Mountain by Jackson on August 9. Banks made an all-out attack on the Confederate line, driving Jackson's men back in confusion. At this point the arrival of A. P. Hill, who attacked Banks's flank, checked the Union assault. Carl Schurz was commanding a brigade in Sigel's corps, which hurriedly broke camp at Sperryville and headed for Cedar Mountain to reinforce Banks. As on many occasions the weather had a marked effect on the outcome of the fighting. When the sun rose, it blazed in a cloudless sky. Not a breath of air stirred. "The dust raised up by the marching column hardly rose above the heads of the men," Schurz wrote, "and enveloped them like a dense, dark, immovable fog bank, within which a black, almost indistinguishable mass struggled onward." Soon the troops began to straggle badly. "As the sun rose higher and the heat grew fiercer, discipline gave way. The men, burdened with their knapsacks and blankets, their faces fairly streaming with sweat, their mouths and nostrils filled with an earthy slime, their breasts panting with almost convulsive gasps for breath, their eyes open with a sort of insane stare, dragged themselves along with painful effort. . . . Wherever there was a run of water, or a well, or a pool, hundreds would rush to it and tumble over one another to slake their ferocious thirst." Many threw away their knapsacks and blankets, and scores dropped by the road, victims of heat prostration, retching and vomiting. Schurz rode along the line, trying to buck up the spirits of his exhausted men. Earlier they had sung German songs, but now, when Schurz tried once more to get them to sing, their parched throats failed them. By the time the columns reached Culpeper some of the regiments had shrunk to little more than platoons. There they heard heavy firing and soon encountered fugitives from the battlefield who told them that Banks had been driven back and "cut to pieces."

Schurz and his fellow officers tried to stop the fleeing and demoralized men and rally them for another stand. A few turned about and joined the ranks of the I Corps. Two batteries of artillery were prevailed on to put their guns in position to form a defensive line. The immediate question was why Lee had not pushed reinforcements forward sooner. The Confederate general lost an opportunity to administer a more crushing defeat in part because of the merciless heat. His own men were worn out by the battle, and a convention was arranged between the two armies to permit the wounded to be removed from the field and the dead buried. Schurz, joining the party of general officers, found himself strongly attracted by the famous cavalry leader J. E. B. Stuart, "looking so gay and so brave."

Lee, meanwhile, discovering that McClellan was withdrawing presumably to reinforce Pope, began a forced march north to join Jackson at Cedar Mountain and strike Pope before McClellan's army could reach him. Although Pope's army substantially outnumbered Lee's, his position was an exposed one and he ordered his force back across the Rappahannock. For several days the two armies felt each other out with the river defining the line between them. Schurz sent Colonel Schimmelpfennig's regiment across the river to reconnoiter, and the enterprising colonel captured eleven pack-mules and a handful of Confederate soldiers. Encouraged by the success of his foray, Schimmelpfennig asked Schurz for reinforcements to guard his line of retreat and pushed farther against a Confederate supply train. Schurz moved to his support, and first Isaac R. Trimble's brigade of Jackson's rear guard and then John Bell Hood's Texas brigade of Longstreet's corps attacked. Only a lively bayonet charge by the 79th Pennsylvania and the 61st Ohio regiments prevented Schurz from losing a large portion of his command on the wrong side of the river. Back on the Union side of the Rappahannock after a skillful withdrawal, Schurz was complimented by Sigel, who had watched the raid from the riverbanks. "Where is your hat?" he asked Schurz. "It must be somewhere in the woods yonder," Schurz replied. "Whether it was knocked from my head by a rebel bullet or the branch of a tree I don't know. But let us say a rebel bullet. It sounds better." Schurz's first important fire fight was the engagement at what was called Freeman's Fort, and he acquitted himself well.

What followed was an unfavorable augury for the success of the Army of the Potomac—marching and countermarching. In any significant engagement involving large numbers of troops a substantial amount of apparently aimless marching falls to the lot of most units. Yet in the equation that spells success or failure on the battlefield, the commander who brings his troops freshest to the fray will be most often successful. The tracks of the general who fiddles and procrastinates can be traced in the footsteps of his weary men.

So it was with Pope. Carl Schurz described the men of his division as engaged in ceaseless marches and countermarches. In one period he himself was in the saddle for thirty hours without respite and his men were "hungry and terribly fatigued," beset with rumors about Jackson's movements. One, that Jackson had circled Pope's army, making a march of fifty miles in thirty-six hours, to fall on the Union forces at Manassas Junction, proved correct. Fitzhugh Lee, acting as Jackson's eyes, had even raided Pope's headquarters on August 22 and got off scot-free. The march of Jackson's so-called foot cavalry was one of the most spectacular feats of the war. It was a brilliant demonstration of what troops could accomplish under a leader who, by his care for them, had earned their respect and love. In counterdistinction to the futile marches of Pope's weary men, Jackson's arrived at Manassas Junction on August 22 full of fight. Still, he was vastly outnumbered, and Pope ordered McDowell and Sigel "to march rapidly on Manassas Junction with their whole force." Jackson meanwhile took up a position west of Bull Run along the Gainesville–Centreville turnpike, waiting for Longstreet to arrive with reinforcements. Now the various components of the Army of the Potomac began to move toward a conclusive battle—Sigel's I Corps, moving into line against Jackson while McDowell's and Fitz-John Porter's corps moved forward. Heintzelman's corps was also headed for what it appeared would be the field of battle, along with the divisions of Hooker and Kearny. Pope's two choices were to fall back to Centreville, shortening his lines and strengthening his command by the addition of two seasoned corps, or to attack Jackson with a superior force before Longstreet could arrive to reinforce him. Pope chose to attack. Sigel's corps was on the right of the Union army, and Schurz's division made up the right of Sigel's corps, amounting to some 9,000 men. On the morning of August 29 Schurz received orders to advance and engage the enemy, keeping contact with the division on his left. Schurz's division formed in order of battle, the main line deployed behind the skirmishers with a second element 150 yards behind still in column. Colonel Schimmelpfennig's brigade was on the right; Colonel Kryzanowski's on the left. The woods to the front were too dense to give any view of the enemy. White smoke hung over them, further obscuring the view, and the tangled undergrowth through which the men had to move made control and contact extremely difficult. Nonetheless, the division moved forward, and shortly Schimmelpfennig sent back two Confederate prisoners with alarming news: Jackson with two divisions, totaling more than 15,000 men, was directly ahead of Schurz, whose division contained no more than 3,000 men.

The "weird clatter" of rebel bullets through the leaves indicated the beginning of a general engagement. Schurz sent word to Sigel, explaining the situation and asking for reinforcements. "The rattling fire" of the skirmishers changed into "crashes of musketry, regular volleys, rapidly firing. . . . Now, 'Steady, men! Steady! Aim low; aim low!'" the officers ordered.

As reinforcements arrived, they were moved forward to augment the attackers. Prominent among them was General Kearny, the old-time enemy of Frémont, now, like Schurz, in command of a division. Schurz found him "a striking, fine, soldierly figure, one-armed, thin face, pointed beard, fiery eyes, his cap somewhat jauntily tipped to the left side of his head," looking rather like a French general. Soon after Kearny arrived, Schurz heard a rebel yell at the center of his lines, and a few moments later he saw the figures of his men running pell-mell through the woods with the rebels in noisy pursuit. He at once ordered a battery of artillery to train its guns on the edge of the woods and emplaced his reserve—the New York 29th regiment—to cover a possible retreat. The artillery and the 29th opened up on the rebels, while Schurz and his staff officers did their best to check the fleeing soldiers. Gradually they were rallied. They presented "a curious spectacle; some fierce and indignant at the conduct of their comrades; some ashamed of themselves, their faces distorted by a sort of idiotic grin; some staring at their officers with a look of hopeless bewilder-ment, as if they did not understand what had happened, and the officers hauling them together with bursts of lively language, and incidental slaps with the flat of their blades."

By late afternoon Schurz's division had been heavily engaged for eight hours while the tide of battle ebbed and flowed through the woods. The men and officers were near the point of exhaustion when the word came that they were to fall back and constitute a reserve. The toll of killed and wounded had been heavy. Years later the scene was almost as vivid in Schurz's memory as it had been at the instant: "The stretchers coming in dreadful procession from the bloody field, their blood-stained burdens to be unloaded at the places where the surgeons stand with their medicine chests and bandages, and their knives and uprolled sleeves and blood-smeared aprons, and by their sides ghastly heaps of cut-off legs and arms—and oh! the shrieks and wailings of the wounded men as they are handled by the attendants, and the beseeching eyes of the dying boy, who recognizing me, says with his broken voice: 'Oh, General! can you not do something for me?'"

By the time Porter's men came up and were engaged the arrival of Longstreet's men had made Jackson's positions, if not impregnable, vastly more difficult to storm. Watching the progress of the attack the next day, Schurz saw "disordered swarms of men coming out of the woods, first thin and scattered, then larger disbanded squads, some at a full run, others at a hurried walk"; finally companies and regiments appeared, still preserving some semblance of order, and here staff officers worked to straighten out units and attach stragglers to them. "Among the retreating mass," Schurz wrote, "there was most conspicuous, a regiment of Zouaves, wearing light-blue jackets and red, baggy trousers . . . the whole field seemed to shine for a while with red trousers and light-blue jackets." Among the Zouaves were two men carrying a wounded companion in a blanket. When a rebel shell burst nearby, they dropped the blanket and fled, whereupon the "wounded comrade" jumped up, ran after them, and overtook them, to the delight of those viewing the scene.

As Schurz's division was covering a general withdrawal, he came on McDowell, surrounded by "a confused mass of men, partly in organized, partly in a disbanded state, and among them army wagons, ambulances, and pieces of artillery, streaming to the rear. Nobody seemed to make any effort to stem the current or to restore order," Schurz noted. Although Porter's corps had been roughly handled, Pope still had 20,000 fresh and uncommitted troops of Sumner's and Franklin's corps, but he had clearly lost his appetite for battle. The Army of the Potomac moved back to Centreville. There the Confederates made another circling maneuver to try to get between Pope and Washington.

Sigel's corps was one of those that were rushed from Centreville to

Fairfax Courthouse in a night march that turned into a nightmare. Two army corps were directed to the same road. "The road," Schurz wrote, "was so densely crowded with men and guns and caissons and wagons and ambulances, that those who were marching absolutely lost the freedom of their movements. One was simply pushed from behind or stopped by some obstruction ahead." The fields and woods on their side of the road were "filled with all sorts of vehicles, a great many of them broken down, and by groups of soldiers, who had straggled from the edges of the column, had gathered around fires and were frying their bacon or heating water for their coffee." Those Union troops who reached Fairfax Courthouse were soon engaged in the fierce battle at Chantilly on September 1.

At the end of the previous day's fighting the prospects for a Union victory seemed bright. Jackson was under heavy attack, and Fitz-John Porter's corps was still uncommitted. According to John Hay, the White House staff went to bed, "expecting glad tidings at sunrise," but at eight o'clock the next morning as Hay was dressing, the President came to his room and said, "Well, John, we are whipped again, I am afraid. . . ." Hay felt a wave of compassion for the President. Careworn as he looked, he seemed more resolute than ever. "It is due in great measure to his indomitable will," Hay wrote, "that army movements have been characterized by such energy and celerity for the last few days."

At Centreville, after the battle, the sanitary commissioners came on the debris of war. "What a scene," Strong wrote. "Acres and acres of huts, some of them burned; the ground literally covered with abandoned baggage and arms, which contrabands were diligently collecting and bundling up in abandoned portmanteaus and chests. Most of the swords and knives had been collected in heaps apparently and burned with more combustible articles so as to destroy their temper; but many were still intact, and we brought off a supply of trophies. Letters abandoned. I could have collected a bushel. . . . All indicate severe distress in secessiondom—want of money and of whatever money can buy." Heavy guns were in such short supply in the Confederate lines that ingenious officers had shaped and painted tree trunks to look like cannon.

Like all Union defeats, the battles that together made up the Second Battle of Bull Run were followed, in the words of Carl Schurz, by "a restless buzzing of ugly rumors, of incrimination and recriminations, charges of treachery and cowardice, and what-not—in short, a general drag-net search for a scapegoat." Clouds hung over McDowell and Porter and McClellan—McDowell for a kind of paralysis of the will; Porter for disobeying Pope's order to come to the aid of Sigel in the initial stages of the attack when he might have turned the tide. As for McClellan, Halleck had sent William B. Franklin to support Pope at Manassas, but McClellan had intercepted Franklin's command, in opposition to orders, on the ground that Franklin might be in danger if he advanced farther. For twenty-four hours Franklin was held back, while Pope, desperately in need of him, contended with Lee's army. It is hard to sort out the blame that should accrue to Pope in all this. Pope was unquestionably, to a substantial degree, the victim of the prejudice that existed against him in the Army of the Potomac. Schurz reported that he heard a group of brigadier generals express "their pleasure at Pope's discomforture without the slightest concealment" and speak of the government "with an affectation of supercilious contempt which disgusted me. . . ." This attitude meant that the corps' and divisions' commanders in many cases did less than their best or, at the very least, failed to display the kind of energy and enthusiasm so essential to successful military operations.

After reading Pope's account of the battle, George Templeton Strong wrote: "Pope is an imaginative chieftain and ranks next to Cooper as a writer of fiction." It was the conviction of Walt Whitman's brother George Washington Whitman, who commanded a company of the 51st New York Volunteers, that the soldiers had fought well, but "we was completely out generald."

Gideon Welles wrote in his diary that Halleck, "destitute of orginality, bewildered by the conduct of McClellan and his generals, without military resources, could devise nothing and knew not what to advise or do after Pope's discomforture. He saw that the dissatisfied generals triumphed in Pope's defeat, that Pope and the faction that Stanton controlled against McClellan were unequal to the task they were expected to perform." Halleck, without discussing the matter with Stanton, concurred with Lincoln's proposal to reinstate McClellan, giving him the task of reorganizing Pope's demoralized forces and subsequently again commanding the Army of the Potomac.

Lincoln told John Hay that "it really seemed to him that McClellan wanted Pope defeated. . . . The President seemed to think him a little crazy. Envy, jealousy and spite are probably a better explanation of his present conduct." Hay added: "He is constantly sending despatches to the President and Halleck asking what is his real position and

command. He acts as chief alarmist and grand marplot of the army."
The defeat of Pope, as a consequence, at least in part, of McClellan's
holding back Franklin's force, strengthened the determination of
Stanton and the other Cabinet members opposed to McClellan to see
him ousted. Welles felt strongly that "this method of conspiring to
influence or control the President was repugnant to my feelings and
was not right; it was unusual, would be disrespectful, and would justly
be deemed offensive; that the President had called us around him as
friends and advisers, with whom he might counsel and consult on all
matters affecting the public welfare, not to enter into combinations to
control him." Lincoln admitted to Hay that McClellan had "acted
badly" toward Pope. "He wanted him to fail. That is unpardonable.
But he is too useful just now to sacrifice. . . . If he can't fight himself,
he excels in making others ready to fight."

Lincoln told Welles: "We had the enemy in the hollow of our
hands . . . if our generals, who are vexed with Pope, had done their
duty; all of our present difficulties and reverses have been brought
upon us by these quarrels of the generals." The word was carried to
Lincoln through a New York Democrat that McClellan had said that
"he had no particular desire to close this immediately, but would
pursue a line of policy of his own, regardless of the Administration, its
wishes and objects." McClellan had reported 20,000 stragglers after
Pope's defeat at Manassas, and Lincoln told Welles that he was shocked
to discover that of the 140,000 soldiers on the payroll of Pope's army,
only 60,000 could be found. Moreover, McClellan had brought away
93,000 men from the Peninsula but could account for only 45,000.
Some Yankee soldiers had, it was said, allowed themselves to be
captured by the rebels in the belief that they would be released on
parole and could return home. The unhappy President asked Welles
the perpetual and apparently unanswerable question: "Who can take
command of this army? Who is there among all these generals?"
Welles, taken rather off guard by the question, suggested Hooker.
Lincoln nodded. "I think as much as you or any other man of Hooker,
but—I fear he gets excited." Montgomery Blair, who was present,
added that the word was that Hooker was "too great a friend of John
Barleycorn." Charles Francis Adams, Jr., wrote from Washington to
his brother Henry: "Do you know that Pope is a humbug and known to
be so by those who put him in his present place? . . . Our rulers seem
to me to be crazy. The air of this city seems thick with treachery; our
army seems in danger of utter demoralization and I have not since the

war began felt such a tug on my nerves as today in Washington. Everything is ripe for a terrible panic, the end of which I cannot see or even imagine. . . . Had McDowell done his duty either for McClellan or against Jackson, we should now have Richmond and McClellan would now be the conquering hero. He did neither and is now in disgrace. . . ."

With Pope checked and the Army of the Potomac demoralized, Lee decided to press into Maryland, hoping to draw that state into the Confederacy and to encourage Northern opposition to the war. The fact that his advance came some six weeks before the fall elections of 1862 was not coincidental.

At the news of Lee's invasion the mood of the South was euphoric. Charles Jones wrote to his father, exulting in the fact that Kirby Smith was "thundering at the gates of Cincinnati; Lee, Jackson, and Longstreet surrounding the beleaguered capital of Lincolndom and pressing to the rescue of Maryland." God's favor was everywhere evident. "Never in the annals of the world has a nation in such a short time achieved such history. Not two years old, and we have already performed such prodigies of valor, given such assurance of greatness, afforded such examples of moral heroism, individual action, and national prowess, and exhibited such proofs of high-toned patriotism, devotion to principle, and love of truth, that we search in vain among the pages of the past for a record to parallel it."

If Bull Run II or the series of battles that culminated in Chantilly added fresh laurels to Lee's crown, it brought increasing fame to Lee's "right arm" Thomas ("Stonewall") Jackson and added a fresh quota of tales and anecdotes about that remarkable soldier. Perhaps more than any other figure of the war, Jackson caught the popular imagination of both North and South. William Blackford, assigned to Jackson's staff, saw Lee and Jackson standing together, talking earnestly. "Lee," he wrote, "was elegantly dressed in full uniform, sword and sash, spotless boots, beautiful spurs and by far the most magnificent man I ever saw. The highest type of the Cavalier class to which by blood and rearing he belongs." Jackson was a striking contrast, "poorly dressed . . . his cap . . . very indifferent and pulled down over one eye, much stained by weather and without insignia. . . . His shoulders were stooped and one shoulder was lower than the other. . . . He seems to have no social life. He divides his time between military duties, prayer, sleep and solitary thought. He holds converse with few."

Such images were etched in the minds of a thousand men. Jackson on his horse, Sorrel, "his faded grey uniform, discoloured with the smoke and dust of a hundred battle-fields; his long, stiff, lank figure; his strange walk, and occasionally abstracted look; his habit of sitting on his horse bent forward, with his knees cramped up and his old cadet-cap tilted so far forward that he had to keep his chin up to let him see—his luminous blue eye, clear and searching—his grace, his stern look—the terrible kindling of his countenance when, in the midst of battle, he rode up with what his men called his 'war-look'. . . ." So, at least, he appeared to Blackford.

Although Jackson was famous for his piety, Mary Chesnut believed he preferred to fight on Sunday rather than listen to a sermon; "failing to manage a fight, he loved best a long Presbyterian sermon, Calvinistic to the core." He was a hard man who "classed all who were weak and weary, who fainted by the wayside, as men wanting in patriotism. If a man's face was as white as cotton and his pulse so low you scarce could feel it," Mary Chesnut wrote, "he looked upon him merely as an inefficient soldier and rode off impatiently. . . . Like the successful warriors of the world, he did not value human life where he had an object to accomplish."

Blackford was continually astonished at the general's air of remoteness and self-containment. On a reconnaissance he simply stopped and, without a word, dismounted, unbuckled his sword, lay down beneath a tree, and went immediately to sleep for five or ten minutes while his staff waited for him to complete his nap. Remote and aloof as he was, Jackson's men adored him. Wherever he passed on his old Sorrel, the troops would raise a shout so that it was a common saying if a shout was heard: "There goes Jackson or a rabbit." His highest praise was "Very commendable, very commendable," sometimes used with startling indiscriminateness as when, told that his messenger had been killed, he murmured, "Very commendable." Blackford called him "Puritanism in action." After Chantilly, Blackford was with Jackson when a young mother brought her infant to the general for his blessing. "Then Jackson, the warrior-saint of another era," Blackford wrote, "with the child in his arms, bowed [his head] until his greying beard touched the fresh young hair of the child pressed close to the shabby coat that had been so well acquainted with death."

That Jackson was as much admired by the Yankees as by the Confederates is indicated by Blackford's story of a captured Yankee soldier, standing beside Jackson's horse, who was observed pulling hairs out of the animal's tail. When Jackson asked him why he was doing so, the prisoner took off his hat respectfully and said, "Ah, General, each one of those hairs is worth a dollar in New York." The general blushed.

With Pope, McDowell, and Porter all discredited and Hooker an unknown quantity, Lincoln felt he had no recourse but to put McClellan, who still retained the devoted loyalty of his officers and men, once more in command of the Union armies. Pope was sent off to fight the Indians, and McClellan moved to intercept Lee.

Lee had ordered Jackson with six divisions to seize Harpers Ferry, while Longstreet with three divisions was to advance toward Hagerstown in western Maryland. The orders found their way into McClellan's hands. The movement of Lee's army gave the Union commander the classic opportunity to attack the divided enemy with greatly superior forces and destroy the Army of Northern Virginia piecemeal. It is the tactical situation every general longs for. The opportunity was, in large measure, lost because McClellan's general dilatoriness plus Halleck's innate cautiousness—he believed it might be a trap—gave Lee time to repair his error. McClellan from his headquarters in Frederick sent Franklin's VI Corps to Harpers Ferry to reinforce the Federal garrison there against Jackson's anticipated attack. Franklin had to fight his way through Crampton's Gap, a mountain pass north of Harpers Ferry, driving back the Confederates. But Franklin delayed and lost the opportunity to reinforce the Union post. Meanwhile, the Battle of South Mountain was developing as McClellan's units encountered rebels blocking the way to Sharpsburg. On September 14, after heavy fighting, the I and IX Corps, United States Army, forced their way through with the loss of 1,813 to 2,685 for the enemy.

Lee, now aware that McClellan knew of his general plan of operation, ordered Longstreet to fall back toward the Potomac. Halleck had ordered the Union garrison at Harpers Ferry to hold it at all cost. Under attack on September 15 by Jackson's superior force, the troops defending the fort surrendered, but not before delaying Jackson's force for almost three days. Lee was withdrawing through Sharpsburg when he heard that Jackson had secured Harpers Ferry. Lee then decided to make a stand at Sharpsburg against McClellan's superior numbers, and on September 17 the Battle of Antietam (named for the creek that ran east of the town), sometimes called

Sharpsburg, began. McClellan's strategy, if it could be called that, seemed to be to make a series of probing attacks against Lee's defenses, searching for a weakness against which he could throw the full weight of his reserves. The most striking drawback to these tactics was that Lee was able to shift his outnumbered defenders from one point in his line to another to meet the Union attacks.

At the Corn Field, West Woods, East Woods, the Roulette house, and Bloody Lane fighting of terrible ferocity took place. Finally, by late afternoon Burnside had forced a crossing of the stone bridge over the Antietam that anchored the Confederate right. As the rebel troops began to give way under the pressure of Burnside's corps, A. P. Hill arrived and counterattacked, driving the IX Corps back and ending the day's fighting. Of some 75,000 Union soldiers, 12,410 were casualties—2,108 killed, 9,549 wounded, and 753 missing. With some 52,000 Confederates engaged the casualties were 13,724 (2,700 killed, 9,024 wounded, and 2,000 missing). The combined total of some 27,000 casualties made it the bloodiest single day's fighting of the war (Shiloh, with 25,000 fewer men engaged, had combined casualties of 23,700 in two days of fighting).

George Whitman estimated after the engagement that "counting the sick and teamsters, Straglers, and cowards we have about 275 men left of the regt we brought from New York less than a year ago [approximately 1,000 men]. The loss of our regt . . . was from 120 to 125 killed wounded and missing." Lieutenant Colonel Paul J. Revere was wounded at Antietam, and his brother, Edward H. R. Revere, assistant surgeon of the 20th Massachusetts, was killed.

Captain Holmes, who had come unscathed through the terrible fighting of the Seven Days' Battle, was wounded at the beginning of the Battle of Antietam—this time in the shoulder, where a bullet had entered and passed through, leaving "some sharp burning pain." Penrose Hallowell was also hit, his arm smashed above the elbow. The two friends lay with other wounded men on the floor of a small house in the middle of the battle while fighting raged all around them. At one point a Confederate soldier stuck his head in the window and asked, "Yankee?" Hallowell replied, "Yes." "Wounded?" "Yes." "Would you like some water?" Again the reply was affirmative, and the reb tossed his canteen to Hallowell, who caught it with his uninjured arm. Fifteen minutes later, after the wounded men had refreshed themselves, the Confederate soldier's face appeared again at the window. This time he was retreating, and he called, "Hurry up there! Hand me my canteen. I am on the double-quick myself now!" The canteen was passed to him, and he disappeared.

George Templeton Strong visited the battlefield of Antietam after the engagement and noted: "Long lines of trenches marked the burial places; scores of dead horses, swollen, with their limbs protruding stiffly at strange angles, and the ground at their noses blackened with hemorrage, lay all around." Many of the more seriously wounded men lay on straw in an improvised hospital in a small church. Young Horace Binney, an infantry lieutenant and son of Strong's close friend, had fought bravely and survived the battle. "In the crowd of ambulances, army wagons, beef-cattle, staff officers, recruits, kicking mules, and so on, who should suddenly turn up," Strong wrote, "but Mrs. Arabella, née Griffith [one of the luminaries of New York society] unattended, but serene and self-possessed as if walking down Broadway." She was nursing her wounded husband and "talked like a sensible, practical, earnest, warm-hearted woman" without a phrase of the "hyperflutination" that characterized her usual conversation.

Lee lingered for two days before he withdrew across the Potomac. McClellan, although he had two uncommitted corps, Franklin's and Porter's, and two fresh divisions totaling more than 42,000 men, failed to renew the attack.

Several days after Antietam, Lincoln went to McClellan's head-quarters to try to prevail on him to pursue the defeated Confederates and "came back thinking he would move at once. But when I got home," Lincoln added, "he began to argue why he ought not to move. I peremptorily ordered him to advance. It was nineteen days before he put a man over the river. It was nine days longer before he got his army across, and then he stopped again, delaying on little pretexts of wanting this and that. I began to fear he was playing false,—that he did not want to hurt the enemy. I saw how he could intercept the enemy on the way to Richmond. I determined to make that the test. If he let them get away, I would remove him. He did so, and I relieved him."

The question of whether McClellan's temperament or his political views best account for his failures as a commander is probably impossible to answer in any definitive fashion. General William Farrar ("Baldy") Smith (Baldy because as a West Point cadet he had thinner hair than that of his classmates) told John Hay that Fernando Wood and another New York Democrat had twice visited McClellan while he was on that general's staff in efforts to induce him to become a candidate on the Democratic presidential ticket. After the first visit

McClellan showed Smith a letter that he had written but not yet sent, "giving his idea of the proper way of conducting the war, so as to conciliate and impress the people of the South with the idea that our armies were intended merely to execute the laws and protect their property, etc., and pledging himself to conduct the war in that inefficient, conciliatory style." Smith was astonished at his commander's political naïveté. "General," he said, as he later reported the incident to John Hay, "do you not see that looks like treason? and that it will ruin you and all of us." The chastened McClellan, according to Smith's account, thereupon destroyed the letter. But soon after Antietam, Wood was back. This time McClellan simply informed Smith that he had agreed to the terms that Wood had proposed.

There was also the implication that Halleck himself was not disposed to an aggressive military policy. A key member of Halleck's staff told John Hay that pursuing the capture of Lee's army after the modest Union victory at Antietam was "not the policy." What was the policy then? he was asked. "It was one of exhaustion" was the reply; ". . . it would have been impolitic and injudicious to have destroyed the Rebel army, for that would have been the end of the contest without any compromise, and it was the army policy at the time to compel the opposing forces to adopt a compromise."

Halleck, on succeeding McClellan, had insisted on being appointed "General-in-Chief . . . responsible for results." Lincoln said to Hay: "We appointed him and all went well enough until after Pope's defeat, when he broke down,—nerve and pluck all gone,—and has ever since evaded all possible responsibility,—little more, since that, than a first-rate clerk." It was left to Lincoln to act, with Stanton's aid, on his own. McClellan's unwillingness to commit his treasured army was certainly in considerable part temperamental, or, as we prefer to say today, psychological. He was, in Freudian terms, a classic anal retentive. He could not let go. It may well have followed from this that he grasped eagerly at a notion of the nature of the conflict that would justify in political terms the course to which his psyche had already committed him. A traitor is one who corresponds with the enemy and seeks to betray his own cause. Certainly there is no suggestion of treachery in McClellan's behavior. He undoubtedly thought that the course he came to pursue was the best one for his country, the one that would lead most directly to the reuniting of the Union. This having been said, the fact remains that McClellan was, if not treacherous to his country, disingenuous and disloyal to his commander-in-chief, the

President of the United States. Egotistical to a degree remarkable even in generals, he was contemptuous of Lincoln, quite ready to frustrate his intentions and to substitute his own judgments for those of the President, commanding general, and general staff. "Thus often," Lincoln remarked to Hay, "I, who am not a specially brave man, have had to restore the sinking courage of these professional fighters in critical times."

On October 18, 1862, Gideon Welles wrote in his diary that five weeks had passed without any action since Antietam. "Certainly the confidence of the people must give way under this fatuous inaction. We have sinister rumors of peace intrigues and strange management. . . . The Secretary of War is reticent, vexed, disappointed, and communicates nothing."

In the aftermath of Antietam, even as enthusiastic a supporter of McClellan as Joseph Griner began to be tormented with doubts, but he was determined to do his duty, "first to my God, second my country, third my mother. Oh my country," he wrote, "how my heart bleeds for your welfare. If this poor life of mine could save you, how willingly would I make the sacrifice, but we must all wait our time. I feel that all will yet be well in the end, and our reverses are but to try our faith and patience. Had we but true and loyal men at our head, I think this cruel war would soon be at an end and rebellion soon crushed to its core. . . . The removal of Gen. McClellan was almost a death blow to the Army of the Potomac, but it has somewhat recovered from the shock."

17

War on the Water

The brightest news was on the naval front. There, at least, the Union enjoyed unquestioned superiority. Gideon Welles was an able and uncorruptible administrator and a shrewd, if severe, judge of men. Besieged by requests for commissions, for promotions, for important commands, he proceeded in his methodical manner, making the good of the cause his only standard. While a number of Southern naval officers resigned their commissions to join the Confederacy, they did not succeed in taking their ships with them. Thus, their only recourse was to commandeer merchant vessels, arm them, and take out letters of marque and reprisal from Confederate authorities, authorizing them to prey on Union shipping.

One of the few Southern naval vessels was the side-wheeler the *Calhoun*, commanded by George Hollins, formerly of the United States Navy. The *Calhoun*, operating out of New Orleans, had seized six merchant ships by the fall of 1861. A few dozen other ships of various tonnages, including a former New York Harbor towboat, the *William Webb*, and several ex-slavers made up the Confederate navy. By the end of the year they had rounded up a total of fifty-eight prizes, fifteen of them captured on the Mississippi.

In October, 1861, General Burnside assembled a division to make amphibious assaults along the coast, and on February 7, 1862, with a flotilla of sixty-five vessels, he landed his force on Roanoke Island after a heavy bombardment, defeated a former Virginia governor, Henry Wise, and captured more than 2,500 prisoners. From there he proceeded down the coast to New Bern, North Carolina, and captured it on March 14, 1862, giving Union forces important footholds at Fortress Monroe, Roanoke, New Bern, and Port Royal.

However, trouble was brewing. There had been alarming rumors for months that the Confederates were building a new type of armored vessel impervious to cannonballs. On March 8, 1862, the Confederate ironclad frigate the *Merrimac* had come down the James River to Norfolk and engaged two U.S. frigates, the *Cumberland* and the *Congress*. The frigates' shells bounced off the *Merrimac*'s iron sides, and both Union vessels were sunk. The result was something close to panic in the North, a panic most conspicuous in the inner circles of the government. A basic element in Lincoln's policy from the first had been to maintain a blockade on Southern ports until the Confederacy was starved into submission by a shortage of supplies and armaments. The navy available to the North was far superior in every way to the handful of vessels mustered by the Confederacy. The crushing and conclusive victory of the *Merrimac*, aside from the loss of two valuable U.S. frigates and the tally of dozens of dead and wounded officers and men, threatened to nullify at one blow the whole strategy of the North. A South that could draw on the vast material resources of Europe, paying for food and arms with its cotton, could fight on for years and might never be subdued.

Stanton was beside himself at the news, Lincoln pale and shaken. Stanton appeared to Welles "at times almost frantic. . . . 'The *Merrimac*,' he said, 'would destroy every vessel in the service, lay every city on the coast under contribution, could take Fortress Monroe; McClellan's mistaken purpose to advance by the Peninsula must be abandoned and Burnside would inevitably be captured.'" Undoubtedly the frigate's first move would be up the Potomac to Washington, where she would "disperse Congress, destroy the Capitol and public buildings." During the course of Stanton's harangue, he kept glaring at the imperturbable Welles, who sat "unmoved and unexcited." Seward, never resolute in the face of adversity, looked the picture of gloom as Stanton went on with his lurid prospectus. Welles could afford an air of studied calm. He knew what none of his colleagues did. Naval intelligence had been well aware that the *Merrimac* was abuilding and the department had a vessel under construction designed to meet and fight the Confederate monster.

Horace Bushnell, the famous Hartford theologian and an old friend of Welles's, had brought the newly appointed secretary of the navy a model of an armored fighting ship designed by an immigrant Swedish inventor, John Ericsson. Ericsson, a classic genius inventor, had designed a number of improved steam power plants as well as the first screw-driven man-of-war, the USS *Princeton*. Combative and irascible, he had also made a number of enemies in the navy, especially among senior officers resistant to change. Welles, impressed by Bushnell's sponsorship as well as by Ericsson's record as an inventor, assumed full responsibility for the decision to rush the construction of the first vessel, which Ericsson assured him could be built in a hundred days.

Anyone familiar with the formidable bulk of the *Merrimac*, with its thick slanting armor plates and rows of heavy-caliber guns, would not conceive that the odd-looking *Monitor* could possibly engage it on equal terms. Welles thought differently, and when Stanton had finished his harangue, the secretary of the navy quietly rebutted his fellow secretary's gloomy prognostication. Washington and New York were safe. The *Merrimac* drew too much water to venture up the Potomac and would hardly risk the voyage to New York. The *Monitor* was on its way from New York. How many guns had the *Monitor*? Seward asked, obviously somewhat disconcerted by the rapid deflation of his doomsday scenario. Two, Welles replied. Stanton's "mingled look of incredulity and contempt cannot be described," Welles wrote, adding that "though unsupported and unassisted, I was not appalled or affected by his terror and bluster. I more correctly read and understood in that crisis his character than he mine. It was the first, and, save a repetition on the following day, the only occasion when he attempted to exercise towards me that rude and offensive insolence for which he became notorious in the discharge of his official duties." During Stanton's harangue both he and the President went from time to time to the window and looked out to the Potomac in the distance, as if they expected to see the *Merrimac* steaming up it to bombard Washington.

Welles's confidence proved justified. After a hair-raising voyage from New York the *Monitor* arrived at Hampton Roads just at the moment when the *Merrimac* was renewing its attack on the badly damaged United States frigate *Minnesota*. The insignificant-looking

Monitor opened fire on the *Merrimac*, which promptly returned the fire. For several hours the bombardment continued, with the cannonballs bouncing off the armor plates of both vessels. Five times the *Merrimac* rammed the *Monitor* in an attempt to sink the smaller vessel. In one clash the *Merrimac*'s timbers were sprung, and the ship began to leak. The *Monitor* was also seriously damaged, but the *Merrimac* had to withdraw, and it was evident that the *Monitor* had at least held its own, thereby effectively neutralizing the *Merrimac*.

Edward Acton, who observed the engagement, wrote to his wife that the *Monitor* looked "for all the world like a *'Yankee Cheese Box on a raft.'*" He added: "No person would suppose a so insignificant looking craft would be capable of such terrible execution. I looked on her in wonder and surprise and thought how much credit and gratitude her inventor deserved and thought how opportune was her arrival here; who could fail to see in it the hand of Providence?"

When Carl Schurz saw the President the next day, Lincoln gave such a vivid description of his delight and relief at the arrival of the news of the "victory" of the *Monitor* that Schurz for years afterward had the distinct impression he had been present when the President first heard the joyful news. George Templeton Strong, reading an account of the battle, "executed a war dance around the hall," to the astonishment of the butler.

Nowhere did word of the contest between the ironclads arouse more intense concern than in England. Charles Francis Adams reported that it "has been the main talk of the town even in Parliament, in the clubs, in the city, among the military and naval people. The impression is that it dates the commencement of a new era in warfare, and that Great Britain must consent to begin over again."

The victory of the *Monitor* assured Union naval supremacy on the ocean and, as important in the long run, on the extensive bays, harbors, and inland waterways of the Confederacy.

Benjamin Butler, never content to rest on his often-disputed laurels, had persuaded Stanton, Welles, and the President to authorize him to assemble an amphibious force to seize New Orleans, thus closing the Mississippi to Confederate trade and shutting off an enormously important outlet for cotton to help finance the rebel cause. Butler was fortunate in his naval counterpart, Captain David Glasgow Farragut, to whose energy and enterprise the capture of New Orleans was primarily owing.

David Glasgow Farragut had been born near Knoxville, Tennessee, in 1801, a descendant of a distinguished Spanish family from Minorca. Farragut's father had migrated from that island to Spanish Louisiana and from there, in 1776, to the newly independent United States to fight in the Revolution. After the war George Farragut settled in Pascagoula, Louisiana Territory, and young Farragut was taken under the wing of David Porter of the United States Navy. In the War of 1812, Farragut, at the age of eleven, was appointed a midshipman and a year later given command of a prize vessel captured by Porter. After a career that read like a boy's adventure yarn, Farragut, now a resident of Norfolk, Virginia, found himself confronted by the choice between loyalty to his adopted state and loyalty to the Union. He chose the Union without hesitation and moved his family to Brooklyn, but it was almost a year before he was given a command. Summoned to Washington, he wrote his wife: "Keep your lips closed, and burn my letters [an injunction which obviously was ignored], for perfect silence is to be observed. . . . I am to have a flag in the Gulf and the rest depends upon myself. Keep calm and silent. I shall sail in three weeks." The "flag" was command of the naval vessels in the amphibious assault on New Orleans.

Farragut rendezvoused with Butler's 15,000 troops on transports at Ship Island some thirty miles below the two forts—Jackson and St. Philip—that guarded the river approaches to New Orleans. Beyond the forts were some fifteen Confederate vessels, including an ironclad ram. Below the forts were two iron chains stretched across the river. Farragut had six sloops of war, sixteen gunboats, and twenty-one mortar boats. For six days and nights the mortar boats threw some 6,000 shells weighing 285 pounds apiece into the forts without substantially damaging them. On April 20 an advance party unfastened the chains under the cover of darkness, and three days later Farragut's little fleet passed the forts, taking heavy fire but raking them with exploding shells and grapeshot. The Confederate fleet was next scattered, with a number of ships sunk or disabled. Union losses were 37 men killed and 147 wounded and one vessel sunk. New Orleans itself fell two days later and was occupied by Butler's troops. The entire operation was a model of careful planning and bold action, and the capture of the city was a devastating blow to Southern morale as well as to the war-making potential of the Confederacy.

After the fall of New Orleans and the institution of conscription in the Confederacy, Kate Stone wrote in her diary: "The conscription has caused great commotion and great consternation among the shirking stay-at-homes. . . . We earnestly hope that these coward souls will be made to go. They are not joining volunteer companies as most of the conscripts are. Not a single man has joined for the last two months. . . .

"Though the Yankees have gained the land," Kate Stone wrote defiantly, "the people are determined they shall not have its wealth, and from every plantation rises the smoke of burning cotton. The order from Beauregard advising the destruction of the cotton met with a ready response from the people, most of them agreeing that it is the only thing to do. . . . We have found it is hard to burn bales of cotton. They will smolder for days. . . . We should know, for Mamma has $20,000 worth burning on the gin ridge now. . . ." For almost a week the air was dark with the smoke of burning cotton. Kate's mother held out eight bales to make cloth for the clothes of the slaves.

New Orleans was the largest and most prosperous city in the South, gateway to the critically important Mississippi River and the network of rivers that ran into it—the Red River, the Arkansas, and just east of its juncture with the Ohio, the Tennessee. There is, moreover, evidence that the fall of the city discouraged Napoleon III from his intention of recognizing the Confederate States and giving open support to the rebellion.

When Farragut returned to Washington, he found himself a national hero. "The more I see and know of Farragut," Gideon Welles wrote, "the better I like him." The admiral (recently promoted) had "ardor and sincerity . . . with the unassuming and unpresuming gentleness of a true hero." When George Templeton Strong met him in a mixed social gathering that included Jessie Frémont, George Bancroft, John Van Buren (the Copperhead son of Martin), and William Cullen Bryant, he found Farragut "a most jolly, conversable, genial old boy; clear-headed, well informed, and perhaps a little dogmatic, but not much."

Butler, in command of New Orleans, promptly stirred up a tempest. One of his first and most spectacular acts was to execute William Mumford for cutting down a Union flag. He next ordered that women of the city who expressed hostility or contempt for Union officers or men be treated like common prostitutes. This latter action touched Southerners on their most chivalric nerve, and Jefferson Davis in retaliation declared that any of Butler's commissioned officers who were captured by Southern forces would be hanged.

On hearing that England and France were considering recognition of the South, Butler was reported to have declared: "Let England or France try it, and I'll be damned if I don't arm every negro in the South, and make them cut the throat of every man, woman, and child in it. I'll make them lay the whole countryside waste with fire and sword, and leave it desolate!" Perhaps the best, if not the last word, on Butler was that of a colonel friend of John Beatty's who served under him at New Orleans. "He says," Beatty noted in his diary, "Butler is a great man, but a *d—n* scoundrel. . . ."

In the aftermath of the capture of New Orleans, Henry Adams wrote to his brother Charles Francis that arriving home, he was "considerably astounded at perceiving the Chief [their father] in an excited manner dance across the entry and ejaculate, 'We've got New Orleans.'" The senior Adams wrote his son: "People here are quite struck aback at Sunday's news of the capture of New Orleans. It took them three days to make up their minds to believe it. The division of the United States had become an idea so fixed in their heads that they had shut out all the avenues to the reception of any other. As a consequence they are now all adrift. The American problem completely baffles their comprehension." Henry wrote: "It acted like a violent blow in the face on a drunken man."

The success of the expedition against New Orleans disposed Stanton and Lincoln to plan a similar expedition against Charleston. Gideon Welles was from the beginning and remained a skeptic about the possibilities of capturing that city. "It will be defended," he wrote, "with desperation, pride, courage, Nullification chivalry, which is something Quixotic, with Lady Dulcineas to stimulate the secession heroes. . . ."

The Charleston expedition, beginning in April, 1863, was commanded by Admiral Samuel Du Pont and made up of "the best material of men and ships ever placed under the command of any officer on this continent and, as regards officers, unequalled anywhere or at any time. . . . There are fifty-two steamers for the work and the most formidable ironclad force that ever went into battle. . . . As a general thing," Welles reflected gloomily, "such immense expeditions are failures. Providence delights to humble man and prostrate his strength. . . . The President, who has often a sort of intuitive sagacity, has spoken discouragingly of operations at Charleston during the whole season. Du Pont's dispatches and movements have not inspired him with faith," Welles wrote; "they remind him, he says, of McClellan." It turned out a most apt analogy. After a rather halfhearted initial foray Du Pont seemed content to fire off a succession of appeals for more ships and men, protesting that Charleston was too well defended to take by assault. "We learn," Welles wrote in April, 1863, "that after all our outlay and great preparations, giving him [Du Pont] about all our force and a large portion of the best officers, he intends making no further effort, but will abandon the plan and all attempts to take it."

Welles confided to his diary that he was "mortified and vexed that I did not earlier detect his vanity and weakness. . . . All Du Pont's letters . . . show that he had no heart, no confidence, no zeal in his work; that he went into the fight with a predetermined conviction that it would not be a success. He is prejudiced against the monitor class of vessels, and would attribute his failure to them, but it is evident he has no taste for rough, close fighting." To the need to find a fighting general to command the Army of the Potomac was added the need to find a fighting admiral to take charge of the Southern fleet and press the attack on Charleston.

The most serious threat to ships sailing under the Stars and Stripes came not from the handful of miscellaneous vessels assembled by the Confederate States but from the shipyards of Great Britain and France. With the passive acquiescence of the British government, Confederate agents had arranged for the building of Confederate cruisers in British shipyards. British law was satisfied if the ships were not actually armed. Armaments were bought from manufacturers of munitions and shipped to France or some neutral port, where the vessels were equipped as commercial raiders. The first such cruiser was a ship temporarily called the *Oreto* and then renamed the *Florida*. Having been outfitted in French ports in the summer of 1862, the *Florida* was soon exacting a heavy toll of United States shipping. Charles Francis Adams, kept informed by American spies, protested vigorously to Earl Russell. (A British customs official, J. Mudie Searcher, appealed to to halt construction on the *Oreto*, examined her, and declared he could find no indication that she was intended for use as a naval vessel.)

With the *Florida* at sea, preying on Union commerce, Confederate agents hurried along the work on the 290, another cruiser being built in the Liverpool shipyards. Adams flooded Russell with evidence that the 290 was being built as a Confederate raider, but Russell fiddled and procrastinated. The evidence submitted by Adams was sent to the queen's advocate for an opinion on whether or not British law was being violated by the building of the 290. He had just gone insane, and his frantic wife ignored the documents from the British Foreign Office. At the shipyards, meanwhile, a band of some thirty sailors appeared, playing "Dixie" on "a fife, concertina, and a cornopean [cornet]." Before the British Foreign Office got sufficiently organized to take any action, the 290 slipped away but not before a number of the sailors' ladies had been put ashore with a good portion of the crew's first month's pay. Outfitted in the Azores with guns and munitions, commanded by Raphael Semmes, and renamed the *Alabama*, she joined her sister ship the *Florida* as a menace to United States shipping on the seven seas. (David Macrae described Semmes as "a small, dark-looking man, thin, wiry, weather-beaten . . . with a fierce-looking moustache, twisted outwards at the ends, and a dangerous look about his black restless eyes.")

Benjamin Moran, secretary of the United States Legation, noted on August 2, 1862, a few days after the *Alabama* had put to sea: "Indifference and connivance characterized the entire proceedings of H.M.'s officers in this matter. . . ." The principal culprit was Price Edwards, collector of the Port of Liverpool, a perjurer and a specula- tor in Southern cotton. The most positive result of the escape of the *Alabama* from the Union point of view was that the British ministry did halt all work on ships intended for the Confederate navy.

The depredations of the *Alabama* were like a bleeding vein in the maritime traffic of the North: five whalers captured and sunk off New England waters; vessels carrying arms and supplies sunk in the Caribbean, in the Gulf of Mexico, off the coast of Florida. Welles dispatched the *Vanderbilt*, especially designed to hunt down and destroy the *Alabama*, but Charles Wilkes, who had created such a furor by arresting Mason and Slidell, diverted the ship from her assigned post and used her as his flagship in the West Indies. It was an open defiance of orders, and Welles decided that he must be relieved of his command and reassigned.

The *Florida* and the *Alabama* wreaked fearful damage on Federal commerce. Before Captain John Winslow in the USS *Kearsarge* came up with Semmes off Cherbourg Harbor, the Confederate cruiser had captured and/or sunk fifty-eight vessels of a value of more than $6,500,000. As word spread that the *Kearsarge* was lying in wait for the *Alabama*, crowds of spectators flocked to Cherbourg to witness the impending naval engagement; among them was Édouard Manet, who had come to paint the scene. The two ships were of comparable size and armament, but the *Alabama* was worn down from her months at sea, and her powder, it turned out, was moldy. On June 19, 1864, the ships engaged, the *Alabama* trying to maintain her distance where her long-range guns would be most effective, the *Kearsarge* attempting to close. The guns of the *Alabama* were inaccurate, and her fire was ineffective. She registered only 28 hits on the *Kearsarge* out of more than 370 shots fired. Firing more slowly and accurately, the Union vessel riddled the *Alabama* and forced her, after an hour of fighting, to strike her colors. Before the *Alabama* sank, most of the officers and crew were rescued—many, including Semmes, by a British yacht that carried them off to England.

As for the *Florida*, she was less successful than her sister ship. She captured thirty-eight Union vessels before she was bottled up in the Brazilian port of Bahia by Napoleon Collins, captain of the USS *Wachusett*, who, in defiance of international law, seized her in port and towed her to Hampton Roads. While Seward apologized to Brazil, the *Florida* was rammed by a United States frigate in the harbor and conveniently sank.

With the *Alabama* at the bottom of the ocean and the *Florida* sunk, the rebel cruiser the *Tallahassee*, bought from British owners, appeared to prey on New England whaling ships. Welles dispatched twelve warships to intercept it, but they came back empty-handed. "With scarcely an exception," the indignant Welles wrote, "the commanders have proved themselves feeble and inefficient. Imputations of drunkenness and of disloyalty or of Rebel sympathy are made against some of them."

The duties of the United States Navy were largely confined to intercepting blockade-runners from Southern ports (as well, of course, as ports in the Caribbean), searching out Confederate raiders like the *Alabama* and the *Florida*, and joining with the army in combined operations such as the attacks on Craney Island, Port Royal, New Orleans, Wilmington, North Carolina, Florida, Charleston, and Mobile. A major naval effort went into the combined operations on the western rivers such as Grant's attack, supported by Foote, on Forts Henry and Donelson on the Tennessee and the Cumberland rivers in 1862, the attack on Vicksburg, and Banks's operations against Port Hudson in 1863. The only spectacular naval engagements in the classic style of ship against ship were the battles between the *Merrimac* and the *Monitor* and between the USS *Kearsarge* and the *Alabama*. At the same time it must be said that the war brought with it very important advances in naval armaments and strategy, the most significant of which was the appearance of the armor-clad frigate, the immediate ancestor of the modern dreadnought. When Henry Adams heard of the battle between the *Merrimac* and the *Monitor*, he wrote his brother Charles Francis: "About a week ago, [the British] discovered that their whole wooden navy was useless; rather a weakness than a strength. . . . To me they seem bewildered by all this. . . . People begin to talk vaguely about the end of war and eternal peace, just as though human nature was changed by the fact that Great Britain's sea-power is knocked in the head." Adams continued: "You may think this all nonsense, but I tell you these are great times. Man has mounted science, and is now run away with. I firmly believe that before many centuries more, science will be the master of man. The engines he will have invented will be beyond his strength to control. Some day science may have the existence of mankind in its power, and the human race commit suicide by blowing up the world. Not only shall we be able to cruise in space, but I see no reason why some future generation shouldn't walk off like a beetle with the world on its back, or give it another rotary motion so that every zone should receive in turn its due portion of heat and light."

18

The Proclamation

The Antietam "victory," if it could be called that, provided Lincoln with the occasion to announce the Proclamation of Emancipation. Five days after the battle, on September 22, the President issued his preliminary proclamation, declaring that if the South persisted in its rebellion, all the slaves of the rebels would be free on January 1, 1863. The effect was electrifying. Frederick Douglass wrote: "We shout for joy that we live to recall this righteous moment. . . . 'Free forever' oh! long enslaved millions, whose cries have so vexed the air and sky, suffer on a few days in sorrow, the hour of your deliverance draws nigh! Oh! Ye millions of free and loyal men who have earnestly sought to free your bleeding country from the dreadful ravages of revolution and anarchy, lift up your voices with joy and thanksgiving for with freedom to the slave will come peace and safety to your country."

William Lloyd Garrison, who had been unsparing in his denunciation of Lincoln, had an immediate change of heart and hailed the proclamation as "a great historic event, sublime, in its magnitude, momentous and beneficent in its far-reaching consequences."

In New Orleans a bilingual newspaper, *L'Union*, started by the free blacks of the city in 1862, spread the word of the Emancipation Proclamation. "Brothers!" it announced. "The hour strikes for us; a new sun, similar to that of 1789, should surely appear on our horizon. May the cry which sounded through France at the seizure of the Bastille resonate today in our ears. . . . Let us all be imbued with these noble sentiments which characterize all civilized people. . . . Let us be resolute. Let us rise up in all the majesty and with the charity befitting Christians, let us preach by example to all men, so that they will follow the road which leads to liberty. . . . Compatriots! May this new era fortify us, and be for us a rampart against persecution; and in sweet accord with our brothers, let us fill the air with these joyous cries: 'vive la liberté! vive l'union! viva la justice pour tous les hommes!'. . . . Down with the craven behavior of bondage! Stand up under the noble flag of the Union and declare yourselves hardy champions of the right."

At Salmon Chase's house in Washington, after the Emancipation Proclamation had been issued, there was a festive air. Everyone "seemed to feel a sort of new and exhilarated life," John Hay wrote; "they breathed freer; the President's proclamation had freed them as well as the slaves. They gleefully and merrily called each other and themselves abolitionists, and seemed to enjoy the novel accusation of appropriating that horrible name."

Austa French was being driven about Beaufort, South Carolina, by her black coachman when she heard the news, and she began exclaiming and praising the Lord. Then she turned to the coachman and asked how the news affected him. "Most beautiful, Missus; onspeakable," he replied. "But why don't you say Hallelujah as I do?" she asked. "I am burning inward, madam," he said.

The proclamation was not without its advocates in the South. Mary Chesnut at least was exultant. "If anything can reconcile me to the idea of a horrid failure after all efforts to make good our independence of Yankees, it is Lincoln's proclamation freeing the negroes. . . . Three hundred of Mr. Walter Blakes' negroes have gone to the Yankees." Like Mary Chesnut, Kate Stone welcomed the freeing of the slaves. "The great load of accountability was lifted," she wrote, "and we could save our souls alive. God would not require the souls of the Negroes at our hands."

The reaction of Lieutenant Charles Colcock Jones was undoubtedly more typical. To him Lincoln's proclamation was "the crowning act of the series of black and diabolical transactions which have marked the entire course of his administration . . . a most infamous attempt to incite flight, murder, and rapine on the part of our slave population."

Nor was every Northerner, by any means, enthusiastic. Edward Ingersoll, brother-in-law of Sidney George Fisher, declared at a Democratic rally: "In the history of the world, what governmental atrocity has equalled this? . . . Do I exaggerate, fellow citizens, or mislead you when I say before the atrocities of this governmental decree, St. Bartholomew and King Herod pale and dwindle?" Fisher found it was wiser in the name of family peace to say nothing about the proclamation to his wife's relatives and connections.

John Hay quoted one of his "C—'s," perhaps Chase, as saying in the aftermath of the Emancipation Proclamation and in reference to the secession of the Southern states, "This was the most wonderful history of an insanity of a class that the world had ever seen. If the slaveholder had stayed in the Union, they might have kept the life in their institution for many years to come. That which no party and no public feeling in the North could ever have hoped to touch, they had madly placed in the very path of destruction."

The effect of the proclamation in Europe was all that Charles Francis Adams and Carl Schurz had hoped for. Henry Adams wrote his brother Charles: "The Emancipation Proclamation has done more for us here than all our former victories and all our diplomacy. It is creating an almost convulsive reaction in our favor all over this country. The London Times furious and scolds like a drunken drab. Certain it is that public opinion is deeply stirred here and finds expression in meetings, addresses to President Lincoln, deputations to us, and standing committees to agitate the subject and to affect opinion, and all the other symptoms of a great popular movement" which "rest altogether on the spontaneous action of the laboring classes. . . ." Henry had gone to "a democratic and socialist meeting, most threatening and dangerous to the established state of things; and assuming a tone and proportions that are quite novel and alarming in this capital. . . . They met to notify the Government that 'they would not tolerate' interference against us. . . . I never quite appreciated the 'moral influence' of American democracy, nor the cause that the privileged classes in Europe have to fear us, until I saw how directly it works. At this moment the American question is organizing a vast mass of the lower orders in direct contact with the wealthy. They go our whole platform and are full of the 'rights of man.' The old revolutionary leaven is working steadily in England. You can find millions of people who look up to our institutions as their model and who talk with utter contempt of their own system of government."

A few days later, writing of a great meeting in the industrial city of Manchester, Adams called it "tremendous, unheard of since the days of reform. The cry was 'Emancipation and reunion' and the spirit was dangerously in sympathy with republicanism. . . . Every allusion to the South was followed by groaning, hisses and howls, and the enthusiasm for Lincoln and for everything connected with the North was immense."

While the proclamation did not change the status of slaves in states not technically in rebellion—i.e., Maryland, Missouri, Tennessee—it did change contrabands into free men and women and provided, as Mary Chesnut's comment indicates, a strong incentive for slaves to seek their freedom in Union lines.

Further, it was a proclamation *in anticipation*. Three months were allowed for states in rebellion to have a change of heart. The proclamation would not go into effect until January 1, 1863, and even then only on the President's confirmation of it. So the proclamation was, in a sense, double-barreled. The first barrel was its announcement; the second would be its confirmation. It was to this date, therefore, that blacks and abolitionists looked as one of the great days in all history.

In the tragicomedy of rotating generals, it fell to a reluctant Ambrose Everett Burnside to command the Army of the Potomac. Burnside, in Carl Schurz's words, was a man whose "sincerity, frankness and amiability of manner made everybody like him." But there was no hint of "greatness" about him, and he himself felt that the responsibility placed on him was too heavy for him to carry, hardly the attitude one looks for in a commanding general but a refreshing contrast with the pomposity of his predecessors. Rather unnervingly he told the general officers of his command that he "knew he was not fit for so big a command; but since it was imposed upon him, he would do his best, and he confidently hoped," Carl Schurz reported, "we would all faithfully stand by him. There was something very touching in that confession of unfitness which was evidently quite honest," Schurz added, "and one could not help feeling a certain tenderness for the man."

Since the principal complaint about his predecessor was that he had been excessively dilatory, Burnside decided that the very least he could do was act promptly. His strategy was simple enough. The combined armies of Virginia and the Potomac would cross the Rappahannock at Fredericksburg and march on Richmond. To carry out this straightforward scheme, Burnside had a splendid army of 120,000 men, most of them veterans of earlier campaigns. He divided this force into "three grand divisions": right, left, and center. The Right Grand Division under General Edwin Vose Sumner consisted of the II and IX Corps. Hooker commanded the center division, made up of the III and V Corps, and the left, under General Franklin, was comprised of the I and VI. The XI Corps, Sigel's, in which Carl Schurz served as a divisional commander, constituted the reserve.

On November 17 Sumner's corps arrived at Falmouth across the river from Fredericksburg. For eight days the Right Grand Division waited for pontoons, during which time Lee disposed his troops in strongly fortified positions on the opposite bank. It was December 11 before the pontoons were laid and the troops began to cross. The night before the battle a member of Lee's staff, William Blackford, dreamed that he heard the enemy cannon firing and the voices of his dead children calling him from heaven, "telling I would soon be with them." When he awoke, he could hear the distant sound of artillery. The battle had begun "under a grey wintry sky." Schurz, watching from high ground on the far bank of the Rappahannock, could see no consistent pattern in the Union attack. At eleven o'clock, Burnside, having occupied Fredericksburg without substantial resistance, ordered an attack on Lee's strongpoint, the heavily fortified lines on Marye's Heights. The Union soldiers moved forward resolutely. "Through our glasses," Schurz wrote, "we saw them fall by the hundreds, and their bodies dot the ground. As they approached Lee's entrenched position, sheet after sheet of flame shot forth from the heights, tearing fearful gaps in our lines. There was no running back of our men. They would sometimes stop or recoil only a little distance, but then doggedly resume the advance."

"Our whole Brigade formed in a line and advanced beautifully over the plain and up to the bank of the creek, under a most terrible fire of Rifle balls, Cannister, and Shell," George Whitman wrote his mother. "A column rushing forward with charged bayonets almost seemed to reach the enemy's ramparts, but then to melt away. Here and there large numbers of our men, within easy range of the enemy's musketry, would suddenly drop like tall grass swept with a scythe." They had dropped to the ground to avoid the storm of lead and were crawling forward. But it was all in vain; Lee's lines were impregnable. The men and officers of the XI Corps watched in an agony of frustration. "Hot tears of rage and pitying sympathy ran down many a weather-beaten cheek," Schurz wrote. "No more horrible and torturing spectacle could have been imagined." When night fell, it was clear that there was no hope of taking the positions on Marye's Heights by direct assault. What was remarkable was that Burnside and his staff should ever have conceived that there might be.

On the eve of the battle Burnside had issued an order declaring that the enemy was "weakened" and that "by the help of providence we would be able to strike a death blow to the Rebellion." Alfred Bellard noted wryly: "But providence didn't help worth a cent." Rain fell relentlessly, turning the roads into quagmires, the mud so deep that Bellard's coattails dragged in it. "Horses, waggons, pontoons and guns were spread around in all directions, stuck so fast in the mud that roads had to be built to get them out," Bellard wrote. One artillery piece and caisson had ten horses attached to it, trying to pull it out of the mud. After a day and night of muddy misery Burnside gave the order to withdraw, a maneuver almost as difficult as the attempted advance, "so," Bellard wrote, "ended the stick in the mud march (so called by the men)." Many men took advantage of the "mud march" to desert or simply stopped struggling and devoted their attention to trying to find a dry spot in some convenient woods. Hundreds of horses and mules could not be extricated and died in their struggles.

Joseph Griner described the scene in a letter to his mother: "Imagine a hundred and seventy heavy guns opening their thunders at once, the screams of the dying and wounded, the incessant rattle of small arms, the cheers of the combatants, the shrill screech of the shells hurled through the air, and a hundred other awful things, and you have a small idea of the battle of Fredericksburg. . . . I have seen some hard fighting, but I never saw anything to compare with that yet. . . ."

At Fredericksburg, as the battle began, Oliver Wendell Holmes, Jr., was in the hospital near Falmouth, Virginia, suffering acutely from dysentery and filled with gloom at seeing his regiment going into battle without him. Gradually word filtered to Holmes's hospital cot of the casualties—Lieutenant Alley, Henry Ropes, close friend and classmate Charles Cabot, and others. Then word of the defeat and the retreat. "It *was* an infamous butchery in a ridiculous attempt in wh. I've no doubt our loss doubled or tripled that of the Rebs," Holmes wrote his father, and Charles Francis Adams, Jr., wrote his brother Henry that "the army of the Potomac is thoroughly demoralized. They will fight yet, but they fight for defeat, just as a brave, bad rider will face a fence, but yet rides for a fall. There is a great deal of croaking, no confidence, plenty of sickness, and desertion is the order of the day."

The splendid Union army had lost 12,700 killed and wounded to 5,300 Confederate soldiers. It was the greatest disparity in casualties of any engagement of the war and more eloquent testimony than words of Burnside's deficiencies as a commander-in-chief of a large army—and of the basic futility of disputing the terrain of northern Virginia with Lee and Jackson. As immobilized as Burnside by the weather, Lee let the Union army slip away unmolested. Burnside remained considerate and courteous in defeat. He eschewed scapegoating and took full responsibility for the failure of the army to dislodge Lee. "He not only did not accuse the troops of any shortcomings," Schurz wrote, "but in the highest terms . . . praised their manly courage and extreme gallantry." The public was impressed by his candor, "but the confidence of the army in his ability and judgment was fatally injured." Many regimental officers, dismayed by the series of reversals, resigned their commissions, and soldiers deserted by the thousands until the names of 85,000 men appeared on the rolls as absent from their units without leave.

Burnside made one more abortive attempt to attack Lee. He tried to cross the Rappahannock at a fording place farther up the river, but the chill winter rain soaked his already demoralized men and turned the countryside into a vast bog, so that it was "fairly covered with mired wagons, ambulances, pontoons, and cannons. The scene," Schurz wrote, "was indescribable. 'Burnside stuck in the mud' was the cry ringing all over the land. It was literally true." Roads were obliterated, and both men and conveyances sank into unseen potholes. "One would see large stretches of country fairly covered with guns and army wagons and ambulances stalled in a sea of black or yellow mire, and infantry standing up to their knees in the mud, shivering and swearing very hard, as hard as a thoroughly disgusted soldier can swear."

Despite the disheartening defeats in Virginia and the failure of Lincoln to find a general, the balance of losses and gains was not as unfavorable to the Union cause as it seemed on the surface. As the year 1862 ended, England and France seemed less inclined to meddle in American affairs. Union forces held a number of forts and islands along the Atlantic coast, the most important of which was Port Royal. The border states had remained at least nominally in the Union. The Tennessee and Cumberland rivers were in Union hands, along with

New Orleans and the Mississippi as far north as Fort Pillow. The Western armies had been almost uniformly successful—none had suffered a defeat. Stones River had been, at best, a standoff.

The South was already beginning to feel an extreme economic pinch. Only a trickle of supplies filtered through the Union blockade. The *Merrimac* had been neutralized and then sunk to prevent its falling in Union hands. The minuscule Confederate navy had lost a number of ships, especially on the Mississippi, that it could not replace. The manpower crisis in the South was so severe that "old men and boys" were ordered out as a reserve corps, and "worst of all," Mary Chesnut wrote, "sacred property, that is, negroes, have been seized and sent out to work on the fortifications along the coast line."

The Confederate government was unwieldy and inefficient, and its efforts were seriously handicapped by touchiness over states' rights. There were bitter feuds within Davis's Cabinet and between Davis and army commanders in the field.

But little of this was apparent in the North, where sentiment against the war seemed to grow with each passing month. Gideon Welles spoke for a number of his countrymen when he wrote in the closing hours of the year: "There is discontent in the public mind. The management of our public affairs is not satisfactory. Our army operations have been a series of disappointments. General Halleck has accomplished nothing, and has not the public confidence. General McClellan has intelligence but not decision; operated understandingly but was never prepared. . . . We have had some misfortunes, and a lurking malevolence exists towards us among nations, that could not have been anticipated. Worse than this, the envenomed, relentless, and unpatriotic spirit of party paralyzes and weakens the hand of the Government and country."

In this mood of deepening pessimism, there was, at least for the enemies of slavery, one bright spot—the eagerly awaited final announcement of emancipation. It was known that a powerful campaign had been mounted to persuade Lincoln to rescind or at least to delay giving effect to the proclamation. But word was that he was resolute.

At the Cabinet meeting on December 29, Lincoln read the final draft of the proclamation and invited criticism. A few small changes were made, and the document was prepared for public announcement. The proclamation declared that anyone in revolt against the United States would be subject to fine and imprisonment and his slaves declared free. Those in that category included all officers in the

Confederate army and public officials of the Confederacy. Further, "all the slaves of persons who shall hereafter be engaged in rebellion against the Government of the United States . . . escaping from such persons and taking refuge within the lines of the army, and all slaves captured from such persons or deserted by them . . . shall be deemed captives of war, and shall be forever free of their servitude, and not again held as slaves." Lincoln enjoined "the people so declared to be free to abstain from all violence, unless in necessary self-defense," and recommended "that in all cases when allowed they labor faithfully for reasonable wages. . . . And I further declare and make known that such persons of suitable condition will be received into the armed service of the United States to garrison forts, positions, stations, and other places, and to man vessels of all sorts in said service."

In Boston, the capital of abolitionism, and in many other Northern cities, free blacks began a vigil at dusk on New Year's Eve. Candles were placed in the windows of black homes, and every black church was filled, as midnight approached, with singing and praying congregations. In many churches, blacks were joined by white friends, who held hands and sang old spirituals calling on the Lord to deliver the slaves from their chains. Fanny and William Garrison, daughter and son of William Lloyd, were among the worshipers. It was a strange and moving moment—the blacks, with their expressiveness of voice and gesture, pouring out their hearts; their white friends, far more inhibited in their expressions of triumph, caught up in the exuberance of the moment. One minister declared: "Brethren and sisters, tomorrow will be de day for der oppressed. But we all know dat evil is 'round de President. While we set here dey is trying to make him break his word. But we have come to dis Watch Night ter see dat he does not break his word. Der ole serpant is abroad tonight wid all his emissaries, in great power. His wrat' is great, 'cause he knows the hour is near. *He will be in dis church dis evening!* As midnight comes on we will hear his *rage!* But brethren and sisters, don't be skeered. We'll pray. He'll go ragin' back to hell, and God Almighty's *New Year will make de United States der lan' of freedom!*" As the preacher spoke of the serpent, the congregation moaned and cried out, and then a great, prolonged sibilant hiss, the hiss of the serpent—the devil—rose with the cry "he's here—*he's here!*" The minister's prayer rose higher to drown out the devil. Then, at the moment when the whole body was swept by the ecstatic sound, the stroke of the clock could be heard sounding midnight. There was a moment of silence and then the first notes of a jubilee hymn.

At the Music Hall in Boston a great crowd of abolitionists gathered to celebrate the expected news of the proclamation. Mendelssohn's *Hymn of Praise*, Beethoven's Fifth Symphony, and Handel's *Hallelujah Chorus* were played, and favorite hymns were sung. All day and into the early evening the vigil was kept. At the Tremont Temple, Frederick Douglass, Anna Dickinson, William Wells Brown, Garrison himself, Harriet Beecher Stowe, and scores of other workers in the cause waited for the final word to come over the telegraph. Shortly before midnight the long-awaited telegram arrived. People wept and shouted, cried and embraced, and pounded each other on the back. There was a call for Garrison in the gallery. He stood up and was given three cheers. Then the crowd called for Harriet Beecher Stowe, who rose and smiled through her tears, acknowledging the deafening applause. The Reverend Charles Bennett Ray began to sing: "Sound the loud timbrel of Egypt's dark sea, Jehovah hath triumphed, his people are free!" Everyone joined in.

In Washington the Reverend Henry Turner, a leader in the fight for black rights and minister of the Israel Bethel Church, going to the offices of the *Evening Star*, in which the final proclamation would be printed, saw "such a multitude of people," black and white, waiting for the edition that he could only with difficulty obtain one, once the paper appeared. Seizing the portion containing the proclamation, Turner ran "for life and death" down Pennsylvania Avenue, waving the torn sheet over his head. When the crowd around the church saw their minister coming, "they raised a shouting cheer that was almost deafening," he recalled. "As many as could get around me lifted me to a great platform and I started to read the Proclamation." But Turner was too out of breath, having run the better part of a mile, and he handed it to a companion, who "read it with great force and clearness." While he was reading it, "every kind of demonstration and gesticulation was going on. Men squealed, women fainted, dogs barked, white and colored people shook hands, songs were sung, and by this time cannons began to fire at the navy-yard . . . great processions of colored and white men marched to and fro and passed in front of the White House and congratulated President Lincoln on his proclamation." Lincoln appeared at the window and bowed to ecstatic shouts and cheers. "It was indeed a time of times," Turner wrote; "nothing

like it will ever be seen again in this life. . . . The first day of
January, 1863, is destined to form one of the most memorable epochs
in the history of the world."

Another Washington meeting was held in a contraband camp,
where ex-slaves who had fled from the South were given temporary
quarters by the government. George Payne, a former slave, addressed
his companions: "Friends, don't you see de han' of God in dis? Haven't
we a right to rejoice? You all know you couldn't have such a meetin' as
dis down in Dixie! Dat you all knows. I have a right to rejoice; an' so
have you; for we shall be free in jus' about five minutes. Dat's a fact. I
shall rejoice that God has placed Mr. Lincum in de president's chair,
and dat he wouldn't let de rebels make peace until after dis new
year. . . ." Payne ended with an admonition: "De lazy man can't go to
heaven. You must be honest, an' work, an' show dat you is fit to be free;
and de Lord will bless you and Abrum Lincum. Amem!"

Another ex-slave also "testified," remembering the time that he
cried all night because his daughter was to be sold. "Now, no more dat!
No more dat! no more dat! When I tink what de Lord's done for us, an
brot us thro' de trubbles, I feel dat I ought to go inter His service.
We'se free now, bress de Lord! (Amens were vociferated all over the
building.) Dey can't sell my wife and child any more, bress de Lord!
(Glory, glory! from the audience.) No more dat! no more dat! no more
dat, now! (Glory!) Preserdun Lincum have shot de gate!"

In Harrisburg the blacks of that town drew up a set of resolutions
in which they declared that the "hand of God" was clearly recognizable
in the proclamation, "and . . . we are constrained to say, roll forward
the day when American soil shall no more be polluted with that crime
against God, American slavery; but all will be able to say, 'Glory to God
in the highest, on earth peace and good will to man.' "

On the Sea Islands there were also ecstatic celebrations of emancipation. Charlotte Forten wrote: "New-Year's-Day-Emancipation Day—
was a glorious one to us. The morning was quite cold . . . but we were
determined to go to the celebration at Camp Saxton [the camp of the
1st South Carolina Volunteers, the black regiment of ex-slaves organized and commanded by Thomas Wentworth Higginson] . . . on this,
' the greatest day in the nation's history.' " On board the ferry carrying
the blacks under Forten's tutelage, "there was an eager, wondering
crowd of the freed people in their holiday attire, with the gayest of
head-handkerchiefs, the whitest of aprons, and the happiest of faces.
The band was playing, the flags streaming, everybody talking merrily

and feeling strangely happy. . . . Long before we reached Camp Saxton we could see the beautiful grove. Some companies of the First Regiment were already drawn up in parade formation—a fine soldierly-looking set of men; their brilliant dress against the trees (they were then wearing red pantaloons) invested them with a semi-barbaric splendor."

Colonel Higginson introduced the chaplain, who read the proclamation, which was cheered to the skies. Two "very elegant flags" were presented to the regiment, and then, before Colonel Higginson could reply, some of the blacks "of their own accord, commenced singing, 'My Country, 'tis of thee.' It was a touching beautiful incident," Charlotte Forten added, "and sent a thrill through all our hearts. . . ."

Then there was a dress parade, black soldiers marching and maneuvering. "To us," Forten wrote, "it seemed strange as a miracle,—this black regiment, the first mustered into the service of the United States, doing itself honor in the sight of the officers of other regiments, many of whom, doubtless, 'came to scoff.' The men afterwards had a great feast, ten oxen having been roasted whole for their special benefit." After the feast Charlotte and her friends gathered on the wall of an old fort nearby while the army band played "Home, Sweet Home." "The moonlight on the water, the perfect stillness around, the wildness and solitude of the ruins, all seemed to give new pathos to that ever dear and beautiful old song. It came very near to all of us—strangers in that strange Southern land." When the *Flora* came to carry them back to their plantation, they all "promenaded the deck of the steamer, sang patriotic songs, and agreed that moonlight and water had never looked so beautiful as on that night." At Beaufort the party took the rowboat for St. Helena, "and the boatmen, as they rowed, sang some of their sweetest, wildest hymns. Our hearts were filled with an exceeding great gladness," Charlotte Forten wrote, "for although the Government had left much undone, we knew that Freedom was surely born in our land that day."

Gideon Welles noted: "The Emancipation Proclamation is published in this evening's *Star*. This is a broad step, and will be a landmark in history. The immediate effect will not be all its friends anticipate or its opponents apprehend. . . . The character of the country is in many respects undergoing a transformation. This must be obvious to all and I am content to await the results of passing events, deep as they may plough their furrows in our once happy land. This great upheaval which is shaking our civil fabric was perhaps necessary to overthrow and subdue the mass of wrong and error which no trivial measure could eradicate. The seed which is being sown will germinate and bear fruit, and tares and weeds will also spring up under the new dispensation."

George Templeton Strong wrote in *his* diary: "Be it remembered, with gratitude to the Author of all Good, that on January 1st the Emancipation Proclamation was duly issued. The nation may be sick unto speedy death and past help from this and any other remedy, but if it is, its last great act is one of repentance and restitution. . . ."

Robert Purvis, the Philadelphia lawyer who had suffered so from discrimination, spoke eloquently of the promise of a new day. He had once denounced the United States "as the basest despotism the sun ever shone upon. . . . I hated it with a wrath which words could not express; and I denounced it with all the bitterness of my indignant soul. . . . I was a victim, stricken, degraded, injured, insulted in my person, in my family, in my friends, in my estate; I returned bitterness for bitterness, and scorn for scorn. . . ." Now he was ready to forget the past: "Joy fills my soul at the prospect of the future. . . . In *spirit* and in *purpose*, thanks to *Almighty God*! this is no longer a slaveholding republic."

The Emancipation Proclamation elevated Lincoln in the minds of many black Americans to a semidivine status. He was the instrument of the Lord sent to set them free from bondage. He came to them in dreams and visions. They declared fervently that he had come to their plantations, shaken their hands, and told them that they were free. If more sophisticated blacks failed to mythologize Lincoln in the same way, they also believed him an instrument of the Almighty. A black congregation in Baltimore raised some $580 to buy a Bible the cover of which depicted Lincoln striking the chains off a slave in a cotton field. The Reverend S. M. Chase presented the Bible to the President, declaring, "Since our incorporation into the American family we have been true and loyal, and we are now ready to aid in defending the country, to be armed and trained in military matters, in order to assist in defending the star spangled banner." The Bible was presented "as a token of respect for your active participation in furtherance of the cause of the emancipation of our race. This great event will be a matter of history. Hereafter when our children shall ask what mean these tokens, they will be told of your worthy deeds, and will rise up and call you blessed." They would, moreover, remember him "at the Throne of Divine Grace" and pray that when he passed "from this world to that of eternity," he would be "borne to the bosom of your Saviour and your God." Lincoln replied, "I can only say now, as I have often said before, it has always been a sentiment with me that all mankind should be free. . . . I have always acted as I believed was just and right, and done all I could for the good of mankind. . . . In regard to the great Book, I have only to say, it is the best gift which God has ever given to man. All the good of the Saviour of the world is communicated to us through this Book. . . . All those things desirable to men are contained in it."

In Georgia, Mary Jones believed that the emancipated slaves were destined to suffer most from the war; "with their emancipation," she wrote in her journal, "must come their extermination. All history, from their first existence, proves them incapable of self-government; they perish when brought in conflict with the intellectual superiority of the Caucasian race. Northern philanthropy and cant may rave as much as they please; but facts prove that *only* in a state of slavery such as exists in the Southern states have the Negro race increased and thriven most." Peace would bring changes in the system of slavery, to be sure, but "when once delivered from the interference of Northern abolitionism, we shall be free to make and enforce such rules and reformations as are just and right. In all my life I never heard such expressions of hatred and contempt as the Yankees heap upon our poor servants. One of them told me he did not know what God Almighty made Negroes for; all he wished was the power to blow their brains out."

19

Black Soldiers

In July, 1862, six months before Lincoln's Emancipation Proclamation, Congress had passed two important acts. The Confiscation Act authorized the President "to employ as many persons of African descent as he may deem necessary and proper for the suppression of this rebellion." The second act repealed an act of 1792 barring black men from serving in state militia and permitting the enlistment of freedmen and free blacks as soldiers. Lincoln and Stanton responded by authorizing General Rufus Saxton, military governor of the Sea Islands, to raise five regiments of black soldiers.

Lincoln's order to begin the enlistment of black soldiers prompted the Confederate Congress to enact a law which read: "That every white person, being a commissioned officer or acting as such, who, during the present war shall command negroes or mulattoes in arms against the Confederate States, or who shall voluntarily aid negroes or mulattoes in any military enterprise, attack or conflict in such service, shall be deemed as inciting servile insurrection, and shall, if captured, be put to death or otherwise punished at the discretion of the Court." Captured black soldiers might be shot or hanged or sold into slavery. Lincoln responded to the threat of the Confederate Congress by declaring "that for every soldier of the United States killed in violation of the laws of war, a rebel soldier shall be executed; and for every one enslaved by the enemy, a rebel soldier shall be placed at hard labor on the public works."

Meanwhile, Benjamin Butler, commanding at New Orleans, wrote Stanton that the Louisiana Negro "by long habit and training has acquired a great horror of fire-arms." Butler was convinced "that this war will be ended before any body of negroes [can] be organized, armed, and drilled so as to be efficient." Nevertheless, Butler found in New Orleans, on closer attention, "a free negro corps" organized for the defense of the city by the state of Louisiana. When the officers of the corps came to offer its services to the Union, Butler was startled to find that "in color, nay, also in conduct they had much more the appearance of white gentlemen than some of those . . . claiming to be the 'Chivalry of the South.'" Although he remained opposed to enlisting black troops, his hand was forced by one of his subordinate officers, who was a devout Vermont abolitionist. Brigadier General John Phelps began to recruit five companies of black soldiers to defend Camp Parapet, some twelve miles from New Orleans. "Phelps has gone crazy," Butler wrote his wife. "He is organizing the negroes into regiments and wants me to arm them. . . . I told him he must set the negroes to work and not drill them and he therefore has resigned."

Phelps stood fast. Chase wrote to Butler that public opinion was swinging toward enlisting blacks (probably all that political general needed to know), and Mrs. Butler informed him, "Phelps' policy prevails instead of yours. The abolitionists will have this a war to free the slaves at once, if possible, nothing else is thought of. The Administration will assent to it just as fast and as far as the Country will go."

Seeing which way the wind was blowing, Butler on August 22 issued his General Order No. 63, authorizing the "Native Guard (colored)" to enlist with the Union. He was delighted by the alacrity with which the city's blacks responded. "I shall . . . have within ten days a Regiment 1000 strong of Native Guards (Colored), the darkest of whom will be about the complexion of the late Mr. Webster," he wrote. By the end of November, 1862, three regiments had been mustered into the Union army. To the correspondent of *The New York Times*, the sight of black soldiers marching down the streets of New Orleans was one of those events that "really mark momentous eras in the history of this revolution."

News of the plan to enlist black soldiers brought some white

308 / TRIAL BY FIRE

regiments to the point of outright mutiny. Ted Upson noted that the 90th Illinois, made up largely of Irishmen, hissed when General Lorenzo Thomas, "dressed in the most gorgeous uniform" Upson had ever seen, read the President's order to enlist black soldiers. The hissing brought an immediate reaction from Thomas. The various units were marched back to their respective parade grounds, and the 90th Illinois was placed under arrest. Upson's colonel called up the officers of the 19th Indiana and announced, "Gentlemen, I congratulate you upon your conduct upon this occasion. In the classic language of Shakespear you have most emphatically shown your ass." Upson added: "The truth is, none of our soldiers seem to like the idea of arming the Negroes. Our boys say this [is] a white mans war and the Negro has no business in it, but a good many say they have stood [for] emancipation. . . . But we don't care to fight side by side with them. However, if Old Abe thinks its the best thing to do, all right: we will stand by him. Lincoln is solid with the boys all right."

The recruitment of black soldiers was carried on in two quite different situations. One effort was directed at recruiting contrabands in the South, or, after emancipation, freedmen. The other was directed at recruiting free blacks in the North.

In the South, the New Orleans Native Guards aside, the logical recruiting grounds were in North Carolina, where General Burnside's landing at Roanoke Island in February, 1862, had established a substantial beachhead in that state, and in South Carolina, where Du Pont's capture of Port Royal freed thousands of slaves and provided a base of operations for military forays into Georgia and Florida.

One of the first black regiments organized under the act of Congress was the 1st South Carolina Volunteers commanded by Thomas Wentworth Higginson. In 1847, as a recent graduate of the Harvard Divinity School, Higginson had written his friend Samuel Longfellow, son of the "good grey poet": "oh, Sam, we can do something to help this poor world along, if we can keep true to ourselves—but to do this we must take the right means." There was so much to be put right that Higginson longed for a "larger center of influence." Four years later he had written to another friend: "All I ask of fate is—Give me one occasion worth bursting the door for—an opportunity to get beyond a boy's play." John Brown's plan to start a slave insurrection in the South had seemed to Higginson just such an "occasion worth bursting the door for." He had been an enthusiastic supporter of Brown's, and when Brown was captured at Harpers

Ferry, Higginson was one of the few who stood by him. He was actively involved in several of the plans to rescue Brown—a raid by sea; a plan to kidnap the governor of Virginia and hold him hostage for Brown's life; an overland expedition led by German refugees to free the prisoner and escape by the horses of the cavalry who were guarding him. "Living, he acted bravely," Higginson wrote after Brown's execution; "dying, he will teach us courage. A Samson in his life; he will be a Samson in his death. Let cowards ridicule and denounce him; let snake-like journalists hiss at his holy failure—for one, I do not hesitate to say that I love him, admire him, and defend him. GOD BLESS HIM!"

Now Higginson had another chance "to get beyond a boy's play." The 1st South Carolina Volunteers, in striking contrast with the elegant Corps d'Afrique of New Orleans, was made up primarily of contrabands. Prince Rivers, appointed sergeant, told his men, "Now we sogers are men—men de first time in our lives. Now we can look our old masters in de face. They used to sell and whip us, and we did not dare say one word. Now we ain't afraid, if they meet us to run the bayonet through them."

Higginson insisted that his officers treat the black soldiers as soldiers. The word "nigger" was banned, as was all demeaning punishment or insulting language. The blacks must first be given a sense of self-respect. Higginson had an unfaltering faith in the ability of blacks to make soldiers as brave and resourceful as whites, and he communicated this feeling to his men. After taking the new troops on an amphibious raiding expedition at the Florida-Georgia border, he wrote euphorically: "Nobody knows anything about these men who has not seen them in battle. I find that I myself knew nothing. There is a fiery energy about them beyond anything of which I have ever read, except it be the French Zouaves. It requires the strictest discipline to hold them in hand. . . . No officer in this regiment now doubts that the key to the successful prosecution of this war lies in the unlimited employment of black troops. Their superiority lies simply in the fact that they know the country, while white troops do not, and, moreover, they have peculiarities of temperament, position, and motive which belong to them alone. Instead of leaving their homes and families to fight they are fighting for their homes and families. . . . It would have been madness to attempt, with the bravest white troops, what I have successfully accomplished with the black ones." He wrote of his regiment: "Their fire and fury appear more like the old Berserker madmen of the Northmen than anything more modern; while their local knowledge gives them a sagacity like that of the Indians. The only difficulty is to coerce them into prudence." He called them his Gospel Army.

Higginson's enthusiasm did more credit to his heart than his head. His men had been in one fire fight and lost one man killed and seven wounded. It was hardly sufficient grounds for such an unqualified endorsement. The moment was, nonetheless, a dramatic one. While it was not the first well-publicized occasion in which black soldiers had fought for the Union cause, national attention had focused on Higginson and his 1st South Carolina Volunteers. If black soldiers fought well, they would have answered one of the most persistent charges against their use—that they were not intelligent or brave enough to make good soldiers. In a society which put a premium on physical, as contrasted with moral, courage, the behavior of black soldiers under fire was taken to be a critical test. Frederick Douglass and a hundred other champions of black rights had welcomed such a test, confident of its outcome. It is not too much to say that the entire future of black people in the United States would be directly and profoundly affected by the performance of black units on various battlefields.

The better Higginson came to know his men, the deeper were his misgivings about their capacity to function in the competitive white society that had freed them. "I cannot believe it," he wrote in his journal on the date of January 8, 1863, after the Proclamation of Emancipation, "but sometimes I feel very anxious about the ultimate fate of these poor people. . . . [T]he habit of inhumanity in regard to them seems so deeply impressed upon our people, that it is hard to believe in anything better. I dare not hope that the promise of the President's proclamation will be kept." It was clear, also, that there was a considerable degree of ambivalence in Higginson's own feelings. "I am conscious of but little affection for individuals among them," he wrote, "if a man dies in [a] hospital or is shot down beside me, I feel it scarcely more than if a tree had fallen." On the other hand, "over their *collective* joy & sorrow I have smiles and tears." That, of course, was precisely the Southern charge against the North—that it had a doctrinaire, liberal, or "radical" obsession with blacks, an oppressed race, but couldn't abide blacks as individuals, whereas the Southerner, however contemptuously or patronizingly he might speak about blacks or "niggers" collectively, liked, indeed loved, innumerable black persons.

One of the most remarkable of the company of young idealists who appeared in the Sea Islands of South Carolina was James Montgomery. Montgomery, who had been a Campbellite preacher in Ohio and a dedicated abolitionist, had joined the Free-Soil pioneers who made their way to Kansas. A lieutenant of John Brown's in the bitter fighting in Kansas, he was as famous for his compassion as for his qualities as a leader of the guerrilla force that he organized and led. A colonel in the 10th Kansas Volunteers, he, like Thomas Wentworth Higginson, was determined to lead black soldiers. Given command of the 2nd South Carolina Volunteers, he joined forces with his old ally Harriet Tubman, who acted as his intelligence staff by collecting information about the disposition of Confederate units and the accessibility of supplies and "contraband." In a raid on the plantations along the Combahee River north of Beaufort, this oddly assorted couple, Tubman wearing the turban that was her trademark, with 250 black soldiers brought back 727 slaves—men, women, and children that they had gathered up in the course of their expedition. A Confederate officer paid unwitting tribute to Harriet Tubman's skill as a collector of intelligence by writing: "The enemy seems to have been well posted as to the character and capacity of our troops and their small chance of encountering opposition."

The slaves were thrilled at the presence of black soldiers. One slave recalled years later his astonishment: "De brack sojer so presumptious. Dey come right ashore, hold up their head. Fus' ting I know, dere was a barn, then tousand bushel rough rice, all in a glaze, den mas'r's great house, all cracklin' up de roof." Harriet Tubman, scout for the expedition, reported: "I nebber see such a sight, pigs squealin', chickens screamin', young ones squallin'." Slaves crowded on the Yankee boats eager to leave "de land o' bondage."

Montgomery, who had been seasoned in the bitter guerrilla fighting of "bleeding Kansas," had a far different view of war from the gentlemanly Higginson, who did his best, usually successfully, to prevent his troops from destroying enemy property. To Montgomery, war was war, and his soldiers were encouraged to burn mansions, "known to belong to notorious rebels." Many of these, "with all their rich furniture and rare works of art, were burned to the ground. . . . Sluices were opened, plantations flooded, and broad ponds and lakes were made where, but a few hours before, luxuriant crops of rice and corn were putting forth their leaves."

With the contrabands gathered in a Beaufort church, Montgomery gave a sermon of "thrilling eloquence," followed by a speech from Harriet Tubman, whose oratory "created a real sensation and recalled the days when she led hundreds of slaves North to freedom with a price on her head."

Another young abolitionist determined to command black troops was James Beecher. Beecher understood, even when he was a young seaman on a China clipper, that it was his destiny to become a preacher like his father, Lyman. "That's my fate," he wrote cheerfully. "Father will pray me into it!" He had attended Dartmouth, where the dissenting temper of the Beecher family resulted in repeated clashes with the college over his course of study until he was suspended. When he was asked why by a friend, he replied: "To give my class a chance to catch up with me." After five years at sea, during which he rose to captain of a clipper ship, James went to Andover Theological Seminary, served a stint as a missionary in China, and returned home at the outbreak of the Civil War to enlist as chaplain in the 1st Long Island Regiment. But James wanted action, and he soon got himself transferred to the command of the 141st New York Volunteers, a regiment of which his brother Thomas became chaplain. When Congress authorized the formation of black units, James Beecher was made colonel of the 1st North Carolina Colored Volunteers, which he recruited and trained at New Bern in that state. As colonel of the 1st North Carolina, Beecher gave as much attention to the spiritual as to the military life of his men. "Had service at 6 P.M. before dress parade," he wrote home. "I formed the battalion into close column then, having no chaplain, gave out, 'My Country, 'tis of thee.' " Then Beecher read Psalm 34: "This poor man cried, and the Lord heard him. . . ." Beecher added: "Then I prayed with them. I had given no directions but they knelt down and bowed their heads—near seven hundred men in United States uniform. It affected me beyond measure. . . . When I spoke of their past lives—of their having been bought and sold like brutes, of their wives and children not their own, of their sorrow and degradation, many wept like children. . . ."

Beecher was in the North seeking proper arms for his men when they fought their first battle at Olustee, Florida, on February 20, 1864, and one of his officers wrote him: "Our men were brave beyond description, and as their comrades fell around them, they stood up nobly without once shrinking. When the right arm of our color sergeant was broken, he knelt down and held up the dear old flag with his left until relieved."

While Beecher and his men were at Beaufort, his wife, Frances, joined him and was soon busy teaching the black soldiers under her husband's command to read and write. "Whenever they had a spare moment," Frances Beecher wrote, "out would come a spelling-book or a New Testament, and you would often see a group of heads around one book." The next year, leading his men at the Battle of Honey Hill, Beecher was severely wounded.

Black regiments were recruited in a number of Northern states. In Xenia, Ohio, a meeting of blacks declared, "We stand as ever on the side of the Government, and pledge to it 'our lives, our property, and our sacred honor,' in its efforts to subdue the rebellion of the slave oligarchy of the country. . . ." By October, 1863, fifty-eight black regiments had been formed in eight Northern and seven Confederate states, with a total strength of 37,482. The *Anglo-African* declared in an editorial: *"White Americans* remember! that we know that in going to the field we will neither get bounty, or as much wages even as you will receive for the performance of the same duty;—that we are well aware of the fact that if captured we will be treated like wild beasts by our enemies;—that the avenue to honor and promotion is closed to us; but for these things we care not. We fight for God, liberty and country, not money. We will fight fearless of capture, as we do not expect quarter so we shall give none. It is infinitely more honorable to die upon the battle field than to be murdered by the barbarians of the South."

A black man named Sayles Bowen, addressing a meeting, expressed the feeling of many blacks. "When we show that we are men," he declared, "we can then demand our liberty, as did the revoluntary fathers—peaceably if we can, forcibly if we must. If we do not fight we are traitors to our God, traitors to our country, traitors to our race, and traitors to ourselves." (Applause.)

With the possible exception of Thomas Wentworth Higginson's 1st South Carolina Volunteers, the most famous black regiment was the 54th Massachusetts Volunteers (Colored). When the 54th was recruited, Governor John Albion Andrew assured the men that his "personal honor" was involved with their success or failure. "I know not, sir," he said, addressing their commander, Colonel Robert Shaw, "when in all human history to any given one thousand men in arms there has been permitted a work so proud, so precious, and so full of hope and glory as the work committed to you." Andrew had recruited officers for the 54th from "those circles of educated Anti-Slavery Society, which next to the colored race itself have greatest interest in the success of this experiment . . . gentlemen of the very highest tone and honor." Robert Shaw's mother, an ardent abolitionist, was thrilled when her son accepted a commission as colonel of the newly formed regiment. A Boston Hallowell was a major, and Garth Wilkinson ("Wilky") James, brother of William and Henry, was also in the original cadre of officers, as were an Appleton, a Homans, a Tucker, and an Emerson. Two of Frederick Douglass's sons were in the regiment.

The 54th Massachusetts carried with it a flag to be presented to the 2nd South Carolina Volunteers, and Montgomery accepted it with the words "The ground over which you march, the fields on which you fight are to be your own. . . . You are to be as free as the winds of Heaven that now kiss these ample folds . . . all depends upon your courage, your obedience to orders, and your constancy in the work of crushing this rebellion."

On a raid against the town of Darien in Georgia, this time accompanied by Robert Shaw and units of the 54th, Montgomery, with "a sweet smile," informed the dismayed Shaw that he had ordered the town put to the torch. Such acts, Montgomery told the Massachusetts officers, would remind the rebels that they would "be swept away by the hand of the Lord like the Jews of old." Higginson wrote to Charles Sumner: "I utterly repudiate" Montgomery's "brigand habits." He added: "This indiscriminate burning and pillaging is savage warfare. . . . and demoralizes the soldiers. . . ."

Charles Francis Adams, Jr., who not long before had expressed skepticism over the possibility of turning ex-slaves into fighting men, had second thoughts and began to pull wires in Washington to get authority to organize a black cavalry company. Once in command of his troops, he wrote his brother Henry: "As for the 'nigs' they are angelic—in all respects. I am now convinced the race is superior to the whites. Their whole philosophy of life is sounder in that it is more attainable. You never saw such fellows to eat and sleep! Send a Corporal to take charge of a working party and go down in ten minutes to see how they're coming on, you'll find them all asleep and the Corporal leading the snore. Now whites haven't that degree of philosophy. Then they're built so much better than white men. Their feet—you never saw such feet! Some of them love to walk in the fields around here, as the road fences are too close together. And their heads! All brain. . . . I assure you, in their presence, I am lost in wonder and overwhelmed with humility! Jesting apart, however, my first impression of this poor, humiliated, down-trodden race is both favorable and kindly. They lack the pride, spirit and intellectual energy of the whites, partly from education and yet by organization; but they are sensitive to praise or blame, and yet more to ridicule. They are diffident and eager to learn; they are docile and naturally polite, and in them I think I see immeasurable capacity for improvement." Adams was convinced that "patience, kindness and self-control" were essential in the proper handling of his black charges. These qualities had not been characteristic of him, he admitted, "any more than they have been characteristics of ourselves as a dominant race." Henry had commented on black men's lack of "self-reliance in their own power." The reason for this deficiency, Charles Francis had concluded, was that "African slavery, as it existed in our slave states, was . . . a patriarchal institution, under which the slaves were not, as a whole, unhappy, cruelly treated or over-worked. I am forced to this conclusion. Mind," Adams continued, "I do not because of it like slavery any the better. Its effects in this case are, no less than in the other, ruinous and demoralizing to both races. . . . I base my opposition to slavery on a broader principle, that, happy or unhappy, it is not good for either that one man should be master and another slave; that such an arrangement is diametrically opposed to the spirit of modern progress and civilization. . . . How far is this war and its tremendous external influences going to revolutionize this miserable, and the more miserable because contented race of slaves?" Adams asked his brother.

"What I see leads me to believe that it is their only chance of salvation. The negro makes a good soldier, particularly in those branches of the service where no high order of intelligence is required. Negro infantry, properly officered, would, I believe be as efficient as any in the world." In the matter of cavalry it was less clear. "[I]n this regiment," Adams wrote of his own men, "if you degrade a negro who has once tried to do well, you had better shoot him at once, for he gives right up and never attempts to redeem himself. . . . The blacks strike me as excellent soldiers in the aggregate, but individually unreliable. The Army, however, is the proper school for the race. Here they learn to take care of themselves. They become, from necessity, conversant with every branch of industry." Army life called for the constant exercise of "industry, versatility and ingenuity" and was thus an ideal training ground. "Thus," Adams continued, "I hope to see the Army become for the black race, a school of skilled labor and self-reliance, as well as an engine of war. . . . My hope is that for years to come our

army will be made up mainly of blacks and number many thousands.
. . . Such is my philanthropic plan for the race and I do not know that I
can do better than to devote to it some few of the passing years of my
life."

General Hunter, whose earlier experiment with a regiment of
ex-slaves had ended in failure, wrote to Stanton announcing his
"complete and eminent satisfaction with . . . the negro regiments in
this department. . . . I find the colored regiments hard, generous,
temperate, strictly obedient, possessing remarkable aptitude for military training and deeply imbued with religious sentiment (call it
fanaticism, such as like) which made the soldiers of Oliver Cromwell
invincible. They are imbued with a burning faith that now is the time
appointed by God, in His All-Wise Providence, for the deliverance of
their race; and under the heroic incitement of this faith I believe them
capable of courage and persistence of purpose which must in the end
exhort both victory and admiration. . . ."

Under constant pressure from black ministers and abolitionists
like Garnet, Turner, and Douglass, the recruitment of Northern blacks
went ahead. A second regiment was formed in Massachusetts. Henry
Turner raised a regiment in Washington and enlisted as its chaplain.
Many whites continued to resist the recruitment of black soldiers, and
some black recruits were chased or beaten by mobs. But when the 20th
U.S. Colored Infantry Regiment marched down Broadway, in New
York City, a vast crowd lined the street. In the words of the *Christian
Recorder,* "A new era has been ushered in, colored soldiers gloriously
welcomed in the streets of New York City . . . their columns headed
. . . by some one hundred of the most influential merchants and
business men of the city; also upwards of twelve hundred of the most
prominent colored men of the country. . . . The national ensign hung
out at every window; on they go, cheer after cheer. Ain't that a
victory? . . ." From the windows of the Sanitary Commission's office at
823 Broadway, George Templeton Strong watched the regiment,
"black but comely," march past, the sidewalks and windows crowded
with cheering, clapping spectators. Strong was confident that the scene
would be the subject of many historical paintings, and he compared
the moment to that when the first regiment from New York, the
famous 7th, had marched down the same broad avenue to ecstatic
cheers. The earlier moment had been more awesome, containing, as it
did, "the fearful anticipation of coming woe, and the new thrill of
national life . . . that stirred all the throng that cloudy, windy after-

noon." Even so, to Strong the sight of "Ethiopia marching down Broadway, armed, drilled, truculent, and elate—was the weightier and more memorable of the two."

Alfred Bellard noted that August 15, 1863, "was a great day for the colored people, as the 1st Regt. Va. Col. Volls passed through the city [Washington]. They marched through the principal streets and made a very good appearance. They had a band of four pieces," Bellard reported, "and were officered by white men. . . . The side-walks were lined with 'cullud pussons' who were laughing, chatting and shaking hands with their military friends."

Great momentum was given to the recruitment of black regiments by the gallant performance of the two Louisiana black regiments at Port Hudson in July, 1863. There was special satisfaction for blacks everywhere in the fact that the officers who led the charge were also black. Among them was Captain André Callioux, who distinguished himself in the attack by urging his men on after his arm had been broken by a Confederate bullet and who fell mortally wounded. A white officer who saw the attack wrote that "you have no idea how my prejudices with regard to negro troops have been dispelled by the battle the other day. The brigade of negroes behaved magnificently and fought splendidly; could not have done better. They are far superior in discipline to the white troops and just as brave," and The New York Times observed that "this official testimony settles the question that the negro race can fight. . . . It is no longer possible to doubt the bravery and steadiness of the colored race, when rightly led."

Two weeks later two recently organized regiments of freedmen beat off a Confederate bayonet charge at Milliken's Bend. The white captain of one of the regiments—the 9th Louisiana Volunteers of African Descent—wrote to his aunt: "We were attacked here . . . by a brigade of Texas troops about 2,500 men in number. We had about 600 men to withstand them—500 of them negroes. . . . We had about 50 men killed in the regiment and 80 wounded [out of 300 in the regiment]; so you can judge of what part of the fight my company sustained. . . . I never more wish to hear the expression, 'the niggers won't fight.' . . . I can say for them that I never saw a braver company of men in my life. No one of them offered to leave his place until ordered to fall back. . . . So they fought and died defending the cause that we revere. They met death cooly, bravely. . . ." Charles Dana, the assistant secretary of war, who was on a tour of the Union armies on the Mississippi, visited the scene of the battle a few days later and wrote that "the bravery of the blacks in the Battle of Milliken's Bend completely revolutionized the sentiment of the army with regard to the employment of negro troops. I heard prominent officers who formerly in private sneered at the idea of the negroes fighting express themselves after that as heartily in favor of it."

It was not just in the army that Port Hudson and Milliken's Bend brought about a dramatic change in attitude. All over the North black men and women found themselves treated better by whites. One of them wrote a friend from Philadelphia that "public sentiment has undergone a great change in the past month or two, and more especially since the brilliant exploits of the several colored regiments. It is the subject of conversation of every crowd. . . ."

Six weeks after Milliken's Bend, the 54th Massachusetts Regiment covered itself with glory in an attack at Fort Wagner in Charleston Harbor. The regiment advanced in the face of devastating fire and had gained the Confederate redoubts when the failure of white units to support it forced it to withdraw. Shaw was killed leading his regiment. Of the 22 officers and 650 enlisted men who went into the battle, 14 officers and 255 enlisted men were killed or wounded. The casualty rate was a staggering 40 percent. A few days after the fight Lewis Douglass, who had been involved, wrote his fiancée, Amelia: "I have been in two fights and am unhurt. . . . The last was desperate we charged that terrible battery on Morris Island known as Fort Wagner, and were repulsed with loss of [many] killed and wounded. I escaped unhurt from amidst that perfect hail of shot and shell. It was terrible. . . . Should I fall in the next fight killed or wounded I hope to fall with my face to the foe. . . ."

Shaw's body was stripped and mutilated by the Confederates and thrown into a common grave with his black soldiers. To news of this desecration, Shaw's father replied: "Our darling son, our hero, has received at the hands of the rebels the most fitting burial possible. They buried him with his brave, devoted followers, who fell dead over him and around him. The poor, benighted wretches thought they were heaping indignities upon his dead body, but the act recoils on themselves, and proves them absolutely incapable of appreciating noble qualities. . . . If a wish of ours would do it, we would not have his body taken away from those who loved him so devotedly, with whom and for whom he gave his life."

Later, when Union forces occupied the fort and there was talk of exhuming the body and returning it to Boston, his father, for years a leader in the abolitionist cause, wrote to Edward Pierce: "We can imagine no holier place than that in which he is, among his brave and devoted followers, nor wish for him better company— . . . what a bodyguard he has!" A widely acclaimed poem captured public sentiment:

> "They buried him with his niggers!"
>   A wide grave should it be.
> They buried more in that shallow trench
>   Than the human eye could see.
> Ay, all the shames and sorrows
>   Of more than a hundred years
> Lie under the weight of that Southern soil
>   Despite those cruel sneers.

Emerson and Lowell also wrote poems commemorating Shaw's death, and a former slave, Edmonia Lewis, established as a sculptress in Rome, made a marble bust of Shaw for Harvard College. A life-size statue of him was also placed in Harvard's Memorial Hall.

Angelina Grimké Weld wrote to a friend: "Do you not rejoice & exult in all that praise that is lavished upon our brave colored troops even by Pro-slavery papers? I have no tears to shed over their graves, because I see that their heroism is working a great change in public opinion, forcing all men to see the sin & shame of enslaving such men."

It is safe to say that no other episode of the war had the emotional impact in New England of the charge of the 54th Massachusetts. The monument erected on the Boston Common to honor the attack was made by Augustus Saint-Gaudens and bore an inscription written by Charles Eliot of Harvard which praised the white officers of the 54th Massachusetts Infantry, who "risked death as inciters of a servile insurrection if taken prisoners," and "the black rank and file," who "served without pay for eighteen months till given that of white troops . . . were brave in action, patient under heavy and dangerous labors. . . ." Together, white and black "gave to the nation and the world undying proof that Americans of African descent possess the pride, courage and devotion of the patriot soldier." William Sinclair, the black historian, wrote: "Fort Wagner opened a new epoch in American history. It changed the thought and current of national life. It showed and sanctified the chattel slave."

Looking back from the perspective of the war's end in September, 1865, the *New York Tribune* reflected: "It is not too much to say that if this Massachusetts Fifty-fourth had faltered when its trial came, two hundred thousand colored troops for whom it was a pioneer would never have been put into the field, or would not have been put in for another year, which would have been equivalent to protracting the war into 1866. But it did not falter. It made Fort Wagner such a name for the colored race as Bunker Hill has been for ninety years to the white Yankees."

At the so-called Fort Pillow Massacre, on April 12, 1864, General Nathan Bedford Forrest, the feared rebel raider, attacked a Union post on the Mississippi River garrisoned by 570 men, of whom approximately half were black. A number of black soldiers were massacred after the fort had been surrendered. The Northern press played up the story as a typical rebel "atrocity," claiming that some 300 Union men were killed in cold blood. The figure turned out to be greatly exaggerated, but no doubt remains that a number of black soldiers and some whites were shot. The Fort Pillow Massacre, in any event, became a battle cry for black units, who swore to avenge the "massacre" by taking no white prisoners.

Grant, who, like the great majority of army officers had had reservations about enlisting black soldiers, wrote to Lincoln in 1863: "I have given the subject of arming the negro my hearty support. This, with the emancipation of the negro, is the heaviest blow yet given the Confederacy. . . . By arming the negro we have added a powerful ally. They will make good soldiers and taking them from the enemy weakens him in the same proportion they strengthen us." Lincoln's own view in the fall of 1863 was: "The Emancipation policy and the use of colored troops constitute the heaviest blows yet dealt the rebellion." When Charles Francis Adams, Jr., wrote his father shortly after Gettysburg, enumerating the accomplishments of the Union, he noted that "we have settled the question of a negro soldiery, and at last enforced the draft, thus opening an unlimited supply of recruits." The Union thus had what it had never had before: "plenty of money and plenty of men." To Adams, "the negro regiment question is our greatest victory of the war so far, and I can assure you," he added, "that in the army, these are so much of a success that they will soon be the fashion. . . . Europe looked to see us exhausted and calling for mediation, without money and without recruits, and behold! the whole African race comes forward to fill our ranks at just the moment when by a wise conscription we are for the first time strong enough without them. . . ."

The *New York Tribune* of March 28, 1863, editorialized: "Facts are beginning to dispel prejudices. Enemies of the negro race, who have persistently denied the capacity and doubted the courage of the Blacks, are unanswerably confuted by the good conduct and gallant deeds of the men whom they persecute and slander. . . ." Lincoln wrote to Andrew Johnson, governor of Tennessee, urging him to press the recruitment of black soldiers, and in New Orleans *L'Union* gave wholehearted support to Nathaniel Banks's efforts to raise additional units of the Corps d'Afrique. Troops were recruited among the freedmen of the Mississippi region, and a Bureau of Colored Troops was set up in the War Department in May, 1863, to facilitate the recruitment of black soldiers throughout the country. Robert Cowden, "recruiting" troops in the vicinity of Memphis, simply sent out cavalry units with instructions to round up all the freedmen they could find and bring them in to be "enlisted." Cowden wrote: "The average plantation negro was a hard-looking specimen, with about as little of the soldier to be seen in him as there was of the angel in Michael Angelo's block of marble before he had applied his chisel. . . . His dress, a close-fitting wool shirt, and pantaloons of homespun material, butternut brown, worn without suspenders, hanging slouchily upon him, and generally too short in the legs by several inches. . . . He had a rolling, dragging, moping gait and a cringing manner, with a downcast thievish glance that dared not look you in the eye. . . ." Under army discipline a remarkable metamorphosis took place. His hair was cut; he was instructed to wash himself thoroughly and was attired in "a clean new suit of army blue," the first suit he had ever owned. Not only was his appearance completely altered, but he was markedly changed in "character and relations. Yesterday a filthy, repulsive 'nigger,' to-day a neatly-attired man; yesterday a slave, to-day a freeman; yesterday a civilian, to-day a soldier." It was clear that to a degree at least, clothes made the man. For someone who had lived most of his life in rags or the crudest forms of body covering, the handsome uniform of a Union soldier was an incalculable morale booster. It was also clearly the case that in order for black soldiers to perform well, their officers had to have both affection for them and confidence in them (the same, of course, was true of white soldiers). Once attired in his splendid new regalia, the black soldier had, in Cowden's words, to unlearn "all that he has ever learned. . . . The plantation manners, the awkward bowing and scraping . . . with hat under arm, and with averted look, must be exchanged for the upright form, the open face, the gentlemanly address and soldierly salute. He must be taught to keep his person, clothes, arms, and accoutrements clean. He must be shown how to stand and step. . . ."

Many slaves, hearing that blacks could become Union soldiers, made their way at considerable risk to enlist. Such a one was Thomas Cole, who, escaping from his plantation with the intention of joining the Union army, found it difficult going. "I eats all the nuts and kills a few swamp rabbits and cotches a fish," he wrote later. "I builds the fire and goes off 'bout half a mile and hides in the thicket till it turns down to the coals, then bakes me a fish and rabbit. I's shaking all the time, 'fraid I'd get cotched, but I's nearly starve to death." In this state Cole was discovered by a patrol from Rosecrans's army, taken to camp, and put to "helping with the cannons." "First thing I know—bang! bang! —things has started, and guns am shooting faster than you can think [it was the beginning of the Battle of Chickamauga in August, 1863], and I look around for the way to run. But them guns am shooting down the hill in front of me and shooting at me, and over me and on both sides of me. I tries to dig a hole and git in it . . . and first thing I knows, the man am kicking me and wanting me to holp him keep the cannon loaded. Man, I didn't want no cannon, but I has to help anyway. . . . I just wants to get back to that old plantation and pick more cotton. . . . I just promises the good Lord if He just let me git out of that mess, I wouldn't run off no more, but I didn't know then He wasn't gwine to let me out with just that battle." A few months later Cole found himself in the Missionary Ridge battle, attacking with a detachment of black soldiers. "I never did git to where I wasn't scared when we goes into the battle," he told a newspaper correspondent disarmingly, adding, "I sure wished lots of time I never run off from the plantation. I begs the General not to send me on any more battles, and he says I's the coward and sympathizes with the South. But I tells him I just couldn't stand to see all them men laying there dying and hollering and begging for help and a drink of water and blood everywhere you looks. . . ."

Elijah Marrs, a Kentucky slave, left his master and set out, in September, 1863, to join the Union army. On the Shelbyville pike, he encountered many of his friends and urged them to accompany him. By the time he reached Louisville, Marrs had collected twenty-seven slaves, armed with clubs and one rusty old pistol. Soon their masters were in the city, trying to reclaim them, but they all had enlisted.

At a meeting at Nashville a black speaker called on all able-bodied blacks to enlist: "God will rule over our destinies. He will guide us, for

He is the friend of the oppressed and down-trodden. The God of battles will watch over us and lead us. We have nothing to lose, but everything to gain. . . . Let us make a name for ourselves and our race, bright as the noonday sun. Let us show, as Greece has done, a people bursting their bonds and rallying for freedom. . . ."

A drummer in a black Kentucky regiment composed a song the concluding verse of which declared:

> We'll get our colored regiments strung
> out 'n a line of battle;
> I'll bet my money agin the South
> The rebels will skedaddle.

And a song popular with black soldiers ran:

> Then give us the flag all free without a slave,
> We'll fight and defend it, as the fathers so brave;
> So, forward, boys, forward! 't is the year of Jubilee!
> God bless America, we'll help to make her free.

Henry Turner, whom we last encountered reading the Emancipation Proclamation to his congregation at the Israel Bethel Church in Washington, was chaplain of the black regiment he had helped to recruit. In North Carolina the soldiers of the regiment took some pains to discover from slaves they encountered the "meanest" plantation owners in the areas they passed through. They would give special attention to such plantations. Turner described one lavish house where the black soldiers destroyed the piano, smashed the china, and demolished the fine furnishings while the owner watched. When he spoke "rather saucily," a black soldier knocked him down. "Oh, that I could have been a Hercules," Turner wrote, "that I might have carried off some of the fine mansions with all their gaudy furniture. How rich I would be now. . . . When the rich owners would use insulting language, we let fire do its work of destruction. A few hours only are necessary to turn what costs years of toil into smoke and ashes."

One of the strangest episodes of the war was recounted by Turner. His regiment had to cross a stream. Hot and dusty, "they took off their clothes and draped them on their bayonets while dozens of white women watched with the utmost intensity, thronging the windows, porticos and yards, in the finest attire imaginable." The naked black soldiers making their way through the water seemed, in Turner's view, "to say to the feminine gazers, 'Yes, though naked, we are our masters.'"

Black troops were often subjected to petty forms of harassment by their white comrades-in-arms. Alfred Bellard told of soldiers from the 5th New Jersey stealing the rations issued to black soldiers by cutting a hole in their mess tent during the night and carrying off "quite a lot of food." But Bellard makes no disparaging remarks about blacks other than to refer to them as "darkeys" and "cullud gemmens." In Beaufort the black soldiers banded together to protect themselves from their white comrades-in-arms. "But we whipped down all dat," a black soldier declared, "—not by going into de white camps for whip um; we didn't tote our bayonets for whip um; but we lived it down by our natural manhood; and now de white sojers take us by de hand and say Broder Sojer. Dats what dis regiment did for the Epiopian race. . . ." Things would never be the same, the soldier concluded, "because we have showed our energy and our courage and our natural manhood."

Once black soldiers had proved themselves on the battlefield, the issue of equal pay and benefits with whites, as well as that of the commissioning of black officers, came to the fore. The lack of both were seen as humiliating discriminations against blacks. Moreover, in the army itself black soldiers suffered from innumerable petty inequities. Far more often than whites, they were assigned to the more menial and laborious tasks that every soldier must perform—digging entrenchments, preparing camps, doing fatigue. The more enlightened officers did their best to check the exploitation of black soldiers by white. On the whole, black and white units got along reasonably well, but the handful of black officers found that they were not welcome to the company of white officers as comrades and equals.

General Daniel Ullman, who had been an unsuccessful Know-Nothing candidate for governor of New York in 1854, was in command of the Corps d'Afrique, the Louisiana unit that distinguished itself at Port Hudson. Ullman wrote indignantly to the antislavery chairman of the Senate Military Affairs Committee, Henry Wilson: "The first point to settle is whether it be intended to make these men soldiers or mere laborers. . . . I fear that many high officials outside of Washington have no other intention than that these men shall be used as diggers and drudges. . . . I have been forced to put into their hands arms most entirely unserviceable, and in other respects their equipments have been of the poorest kind. . . . I assure you that these poor fellows . . . are deeply sensible to this gross injustice. It breaks down their 'morale.'" The Massachusetts 54th and 55th, made up of the most self-conscious and militant blacks, refused to accept any pay at all until their pay was made equal to that of white soldiers. When Governor Andrew of Massachusetts called a meeting of the state legislature to urge that body to make up the difference between the government's pay to black soldiers and that paid to whites, the Massachusetts regiments continued to refuse to accept their pay on the ground that the issue was one not of dollars and cents but of principle. If they were to fight like whites, they must be paid like whites. In the words of one black soldier: "We did not come to fight for money . . . we came not only to make men of ourselves, but of our other colored brothers at home. . . ." The efforts of Thaddeus Stevens and other Radical Republicans to get legislation through Congress equalizing the pay of black and white soldiers were blocked by Democrats and conservative Republicans, who argued that such a law would degrade the whites by implying that blacks were their equals. Stevens declared: "I despise the principle that would make a difference between [white soldiers and black] in the hour of battle and of death. . . . The black man knows when he goes there that his dangers are greater than the white man's. He runs not only the risk of being killed in battle, but the certainty, if taken prisoner, of being slaughtered instead of being treated as a prisoner of war." The result of the soldiers' "strike" for equal pay was much suffering by their families, some of whom were reduced to accepting public charity. One soldier wrote: "My wife and three little children at home are, in a manner, freezing and starving to death. She writes me for aid but I have nothing to send her. . . ." The 55th grew openly mutinous as Congress dallied and delayed. A soldier was court-martialed and shot. A noncommissioned officer in the 3rd South Carolina Volunteers directed his men to stack their arms and resign on the ground that the army had broken its contract with them. He also was court-martialed and executed for mutiny.

Lincoln strongly supported the principle of equal treatment. In a speech given in Baltimore in April, 1864, he declared, "Upon a clear conviction of duty, I resolved to turn that element of strength to account; and I am responsible for it to the American people, to the Christian world, to history, and on my final account to God. Having determined to use the negro as a soldier, there is no way but to give him all the protection given to any other soldier."

In June, 1864, Congress finally equalized the pay of black and white soldiers and did so retroactively, to great rejoicing in black units.

An officer in the 54th noted that the eighteen-month-long injustice had been corrected. "A pretty carnival prevails," he wrote. "The fiddle and other music long neglected enlivens the tents day and night. Songs burst out everywhere; dancing is incessant; boisterous shouts are heard, mimicry, burlesque, and carnival; pompous salutations are heard on all sides. Here a crowd and a preacher; there a crowd and two boxers; yonder, feasting and jubilee."

Besides the issue of equal pay, black soldiers were deeply offended at the initial refusal of the army to commission black officers. Under heavy pressure, the War Department reversed its policy in the face of the outstanding performance of black troops.

In the summer of 1863 John Beatty, now a brigadier general commanding two regiments of Ohio volunteers, was chairman of a board of officers appointed to examine black applicants for commissions. The board met eight or nine hours a day, turning out "about the usual proportion of wheat and chaff," Beatty noted, adding: "There was a time when we thought it would be impossible to obtain good officers for colored regiments. Now we feel assured that they will have as good [as] if not better officers than the white regiments. From sergeants applying for commissions we are able to select splendid men—strong, healthy, well informed and of considerable military experience. In fact, we occasionally find a noncommissioned officer who is better qualified to command a regiment than nine-tenths of the colonels." One of the candidates was a sergeant at least fifty years old, "but sprightly and active . . . of more than ordinary intelligence." Beatty noted: "This sergeant we thought too old," but when he was dismissed, he came to Beatty and asked him if he was a relative of John Beatty of Sandusky. "He was my grandfather," Beatty replied. "Yes," said the sergeant. "You resemble your mother. You are the son of John Beatty of Sandusky. I have carried you in my arms many a time. My mother saved your life more than once. Thirty years ago your father and mine were neighbors. I recollect the cabin you were born in as well as if I had seen it but yesterday." Taking his hand, Beatty said, "I am heartily glad to see you, my old friend. You must stay with me tonight and we will talk over the old times together."

When the sergeant, whose name was Daniel Rodabaugh, left the room, one of the examining officers declared that he supposed the board would have to do something for the sergeant. "He had rendered important service to the country by carrying the honored president of our board in his arms. . . . What do you say, gentlemen, to a second lieutenancy for General Beatty's friend?" Beatty proposed a first lieutenancy and the board concurred. Rodabaugh had been in the regular army, Beatty noted, and richly deserved the appointment.

That black soldiers were a shock to Southern sensibilities need hardly be said. In the words of a New Orleans newspaper, "Our citizens, who had been accustomed to meet and treat the negroes only as respectful servants, were mortified, pained, and shocked to encounter them in towns and villages, and on the public roads, by scores and hundreds and thousands wearing Federal uniforms, and bearing bright muskets and gleaming bayonets. . . . All felt the quartering of negro guards among them to be a deliberate, wanton, cruel act of insult and oppression. Their hearts sickened under what they deemed an outrageous exercise of tyranny."

A soldier in the black 14th Regiment of the Rhode Island Heavy Artillery wrote exultantly that he had "for once in his life . . . walked fearlessly and boldly through the streets of [a] southern city! And he did this without being required to take off his cap at every step, or to give all the side-walks to those lordly princes of the sunny south, the planters' sons!"

Not only was the notion of a black soldier abhorrent and threatening in and of itself, but it raised the whole question of black capacities in a form profoundly troubling to the white consciousness. The South was a region with a martial tradition. Heroes of the Revolutionary War were accorded a special veneration in the South. Monuments commemorated the great battles of the Continental Army or, as it was more accurately called, the "Confederation Army," when "Confederation" meant the states united against Great Britain. The proudest name a Southerner could utter was that of "soldier," a word that summoned up historic memories of unparalleled bravery in defense of freedom and independence. Brothers, sons, and husbands fighting for the present-day Confederacy against the modern counterpart of Great Britain—the Union North—proudly bore that sacred title. Thus, simply to *see* a black man in the uniform of a soldier was a profound affront to Southern sensibilities, a challenge to its deepest convictions about black inferiority, and a stimulus to ancient fears.

Elizabeth Meriwether was dismayed at the presence of black soldiers in Memphis, "men but lately released from slavery, men but a degree removed from savagery. . . ." Such men, she wrote, "sometimes do terrible things when suddenly entrusted with power." The "terrible things" that black soldiers did were, for the most part, confined to forcing white women off the sidewalks, to insults to whites, and, human nature being what it is and soldiers being what they are, to occasional acts of violence. In the Southern mind, insulting a white woman ranked in the list of crimes well ahead of murder, incest, rape, and arson. Indeed, it partook of the nature of all four. In a society in which a thoughtless epithet—say, a heedless "damn" uttered in the presence of a pure, noble, undefiled representative of "Southern womanhood" —could, and not infrequently did, result in a challenge to a duel and in the mutilation or death of one or both of the combatants, it is not surprising that a "black insult" produced a white masculine reaction verging on madness, if it did not, in fact, produce that precise state. American males, North and South, carried on over women of the upper classes in a way difficult to comprehend in modern times. As we have more than once had occasion to note, middle- and upper-class Northern men, while not hesitating to seduce maids or enjoy the favors of mistresses and prostitutes, enveloped the females of their own class with a saccharine coating of sentimentality that transformed them, at least in the male imagination, into ."unsullied," saintly creatures too pure for the world.

Many black soldiers sought out their old masters and mistresses when the tides of war carried them to the vicinity of the plantations on which they had so recently been slaves. These were odd encounters, sometimes suggesting the successful heir returning to visit his home-town and to enjoy the approbation or envy of his friends and mentors. A young black soldier quartered in Nashville used his furlough to return to his plantation, where his former mistress greeted him warmly. "You remember when you were sick," she asked, "and I had to bring you to the house and nurse you?" "Yes." "But now you are fighting me!" "No'm, I ain't fighting you, I'm fighting to get free."

By October, 1864, eighteen months after the army had been authorized to raise black regiments, 140 regiments, totaling 101,950 men, were on active service. In the engagement at Chafin's Farm, Virginia, at the end of September, 1864, thirteen black regiments were involved, and out of a total of thirty-seven Congressional Medals of Honor awarded for that engagement, fourteen were given to black soldiers. The story was much the same in the remaining campaigns of the war. The Battle of Yazoo City, Mississippi, was won, in large part, as the consequence of a charge by black cavalry at a critical juncture in the fighting. General Thomas had eight black regiments under his command at the Battle of Nashville, and again they fought with courage and tenacity. General James Steedman, who had been strongly opposed to enlisting blacks in the army, reported that the greater portion of losses among his black regiments reflected the fact that they carried the brunt of the battle on the left wing of Thomas's army.

At the end of the war 178,985 enlisted men and 7,122 officers, almost 10 percent of the Union army, had served in black regiments. They fought in 449 engagements and 39 major battles, and 17 soldiers and 4 sailors received Congressional Medals of Honor. One-third of the black soldiers—68,178—were listed as dead or missing, of whom 2,751 died in combat. The mortality rate of black soldiers from diseases was three times that of their white counterparts. In addition, it has been estimated that as many as 29,000 blacks served in the Union navy, one-quarter of the total navy enrollment.

A group of Confederate officers, impressed by the performance of black soldiers in the Union army and alarmed over the growing rate of desertion in the rebel forces, signed a petition in January, 1864, urging that slaves be enlisted in the Southern armies. The petition read: "We can see three great causes operating to destroy us: first, the inferiority of our armies to those of the enemy in point of numbers; second, the poverty of our single source of supply in comparison with his several sources; third, the fact that slavery, from being one of our chief sources of strength at the commencement of the war, has now become, in a military point of view, one of our chief sources of weakness. . . . All along the lines slavery is comparatively valueless to us for labor, but of great and increasing worth to the enemy for information. It is an omnipresent spy system, pointing out our valuable men to the enemy, revealing our positions, purposes, and resources." The officers proposed that "we immediately commence training a large reserve of the most courageous of our slaves, and further that we guarantee freedom within a reasonable time to every slave in the South who shall remain true to the Confederacy in this war." If such a step were taken, the problem of spies would be taken care of. Moreover, "there would be no recruits awaiting the enemy with open arms, no fear of insurrection in the rear. . . ."

Jefferson Davis not only rejected the petition but ordered that there should be no more talk of enlisting slaves. In the months that followed, the Confederate cause grew increasingly desperate and finally even Judah Benjamin, the Confederate secretary of state, was won over to the necessity of making soldiers out of slaves. Lee himself was strongly in favor of such a course. He wrote to Davis in March, 1865, urging him to enlist "negro troops," adding, "I think no time should be lost in trying to collect all we can. . . . In the beginning it would be well to do everything to make the enlistment entirely voluntary on the part of the negroes. . . . I have received letters from persons offering to select the most suitable among their slaves. . . ."

The fact is that many slaveholders who joined the army could not bear to march off to war without the attentions of their personal servants. A friend of Mary Chesnut's, watching a Georgia regiment march by in Richmond, calculated that they were accompanied by $16,000 worth of "negro property which can go off on its own legs to the Yankees whenever it pleases." William Blackford found his black orderly deep in Napier's *History of the War in the Peninsula,* "very curious literature for a negro servant," Blackford noted.

Slaves served "informally" with Southern regiments. While most of them performed "fatigue" chores or common labor, some had combat duties: Alfred Bellard saw a Union soldier with a "Telescope rifle" pick off a black sharpshooter who had been causing considerable damage from the shelter of a hollow tree.

But Southern opinion remained sharply divided on the subject of black soldiers, and General Howell Cobb spoke for a substantial number of officers (and more wisely than he knew) when he called the proposition "to make soldiers of our slaves" a "most pernicious idea. . . . You cannot make soldiers of slaves, nor slaves of soldiers. . . . The day you make soldiers of them is the beginning of the end of the revolution. If slaves will make soldiers our whole theory of slavery is wrong."

Hearing of the debate in the South over arming slaves, George Templeton Strong reflected on the irony of it. "The first of all Southern axioms," he noted, "has been for thirty years past that freedom was a punishment to the slave, servitude his normal condition, and that he loved and looked up to and depended on his owner as a good dog does on his master, and that he despised and rejected emancipation just as a good dog would dislike being discharged from his duty of guardianship and kicked into the street to get his own living as best he could."

It is impossible, I suspect, to overestimate the importance of the black soldier in the Civil War. William Sinclair, the black journalist and historian, writing at the end of the century, declared that "the glory and the power of the republic to-day—the foremost and most powerful nation in the world—may be traced to the effective use of the negro as a soldier and as a voter in the most stormy and perilous hour of its existence. He was unquestionably the deciding factor." Such a notion may startle a modern reader, but the case is a strong one. While it would be difficult to argue that black soldiers were a decisive factor in the Union military victory, it is unquestionably the case that their military record altered the white perception of blacks in a way that was an essential precondition of all subsequent political efforts on behalf of blacks by Republican Congressmen and Senators in Congress. It is difficult to imagine that the Radical Republicans could have carried the day for Congressional Reconstruction without the record of black troops to point to. Lydia Maria Child told a revealing story of the change in attitude toward blacks occasioned by reports of their valor in battle. In Wayland, Massachusetts, a navy captain named Wade, who had been a "bitter pro-slavery man, violent and vulgar in his talk against abolitionists and 'niggers'," had returned from duty at New Orleans proclaiming himself an abolitionist as a consequence of the performance of the black regiments of Louisiana. Traveling to Boston on the train, Wade saw a black soldier enter the car in which he was riding and start to take a seat, whereupon a white exclaimed, *"I'm not going to ride with niggers."* At this Captain Wade "rose up, in all the gilded glory of his naval uniform, and called out, 'Come here, my good fellow! I've been fighting along side of people of your color, and glad enough I was to have 'em by my side. Come and sit by me.'" Lydia Child added: "So the work goes on, in all directions."

Joseph Wilson, a member of the 54th Massachusetts, who wrote a history of black soldiers, noted that "every camp had a teacher, in fact every company had some one to instruct the soldiers in reading, if nothing more. Since the war I have known of more than one who have taken up the profession of preaching and law making, whose first letter was learned in camp; and not a few who have entered college." James Monroe Trotter, who rose to the rank of lieutenant in a black company, wrote that many blacks scattered over the country "took their first lessons from some manly officer or no less manly fellow soldier." Not only were white officers active in "this noble work of school-teaching in our colored army, not a few of the best workers were colored chaplains, who wisely divided their time [among] preaching, administering to the sick," and teaching, "while many non-commissioned officers and private soldiers cheerfully rendered effective service in the same direction."

It is unquestionably the case that the performance of black soldiers in the war not only raised immeasurably the pride and confidence of all blacks but provided, in the persons of some 200,000 black veterans, cadres of political leadership for freed blacks in all the Southern states.

20

What to Do About the South?

The Emancipation Proclamation, the enlisting of black soldiers, and their subsequent demonstrations of bravery under fire opened a debate on the future of the freed slaves, or freedmen, as they were called (without reference to the freedwomen). Accompanying this debate and closely related to it was the question of what was to be done about the South—about its "reconstruction"—when the war was over. As Sidney George Fisher put it, the North had "caught a Tartar." He wrote: "Before us lies a path towards freedom, prosperity, & civilization sustained by a wise government & an intelligent people." The North wished to take the "southern people" along this path. "But they will not come. Freedom, civilization, & prosperity are things they do not appreciate & cannot desire. Gladly would we go on without them, but they will not let us. Geographical & other necessities bind us to them. We cannot get rid of them any more than England can get rid of Ireland or Scotland. What then are we to do?" Fisher asked.

Charles Francis Adams, Jr., posed the same question in a letter to his father from Hilton Head, South Carolina, on July 16, 1862. "The questions of the future seem to me too great for us to grapple with successfully and I have begun to fear anarchy and disorganization for years to come. If we succeed in our attempt at subjugation, I see only

333

an immense territory and a savage and ignorant populace to be held down by force, the enigma of slavery to be settled by us somehow, right or wrong, and, most dangerous of all, a spirit of blind, revengeful fanaticism in the North, of which Sumner has come in my mind to be typical, which, utterly deficient in practical wisdom, will, if it can, force our country into any position—be it bankrupt, despotic, anarchial, or what not—in its blind efforts to destroy slavery and the South."

The Reverend Samuel Spears, a Presbyterian minister in Brooklyn, New York, in October, 1862, declared: "The question as to what to do *with* the black man, and what we shall do *for* him . . . is one of the great questions of the age. In its solution he is for the most part dependent upon the friendship, the kind regards, and Christian philanthropy of the white race. He has no power to solve it himself. As he emerges into freedom, he must receive his destiny from those at whose hands he receives that freedom. . . . He cannot conquer his own destiny. His intelligence, powers of combination, and resources of action are not equal to the task."

The debate about what was to be done about the South divided roughly, though not entirely, along party lines. The overwhelming majority of Democrats believed that the Southern states should be brought back into the Union as expeditiously as possible on the same terms as existed when they left. Many Democrats had been opposed to the war from the first. They wished to re-establish the alliance of Northern workingmen and immigrants and Southern planters which for years had given them, if not ascendancy, at least a generous share of national power.

Some Republicans held the same view, a number out of a genuine desire to heal the wounds of sectional conflict and some, like Gideon Welles, out of a fervent belief that the Constitution had been dangerously stretched by the exigencies of the war and that it must be promptly restored to its original purity or the very essence of republican government would be lost. These latter we might call Conscience Constitutionalists. Finally, there were those, thoroughly indifferent to fine constitutional points, who thought it would be good for Northern business to have a prompt reconciliation with the South.

On the other side of the fence were the majority of Republicans who had become increasingly radicalized under the influence of the "radical"—i.e., antislavery—Republicans and even more by the course of the war itself. The Radical Republicans and even the conservative or moderate Republicans were convinced that the conquered Southern states must be kept under military rule until they gave evidence of having accepted what was commonly called the new order. In this camp were those who wished to punish the South for the sin of secession, for disrupting the Union and precipitating one of the most terrible conflicts in history, and those whose basic commitment was to the rights of the ex-slaves. They looked to a radical reordering of Southern society as the only hope for a united and prosperous nation.

This category included virtually all the abolitionists and was in turn divided into those who believed that the freedmen, as represented in places under Federal jurisdiction like Fortress Monroe, Port Royal, New Orleans, and a number of other Federal enclaves, in Kentucky and Tennessee, Mississippi, Arkansas, and Alabama, should have legal and constitutional rights short of the franchise, or that the relatively few literate blacks initially should be given the franchise, which should be extended to others in time as they demonstrated their capacity. Many of these Radical Republicans expressed a willingness to accept a literacy test as a requirement for voting if it was applied uniformly to both whites and blacks. A handful of mostly black abolitionists insisted from the beginning of the debate that freed blacks, if they were to be able to protect their rights, must be given the vote without any limitation or restriction.

In brief, the two questions, related but distinct, now began to occupy the attention of the country, of journalists and politicians (often the same individuals), of preachers and their congregations, of liberal journals, of the freedmen's associations, and of abolitionist orators. Common to all but the most cynical Republicans was the conviction that the country was being purified by the travail and suffering of the war. Like George Templeton Strong, they saw the war as a form of penance for national sins in which the North had been almost as much implicated as the South.

The question of what was to be done "for," or "with" or "to" or "about," the freed slaves of the South was, of course, directly and inescapably part of what was to be done "with" a South the defeat of which seemed increasingly inevitable. A classic statement of what might be called the hard-liners or radicals was made by William Tecumseh Sherman, whose vigorously expressed opinions were given added significance by virtue of the fact that his brother, John, was a United States Senator from Ohio.

At the end of August, 1863, Henry Halleck took it upon himself to write to a number of army commanders soliciting their views on what should be done with the states in rebellion as the Federal government re-established its authority over them, as, for example, in the state of Louisiana. In his reply, Sherman divided the inhabitants of the states bordering the Mississippi into four classes: large planters, smaller farmers, Union men of the South, and the "young bloods of the South." As for the large planters, Sherman wrote, "I *know* we can manage this class but only by *action*. Argument is exhausted, and words have lost their usual meaning. Nothing but the logic of events touches their understanding. . . . If our country were like Europe, crowded with people, I would say it would be easier to replace this class than to reconstruct it, subordinate to the policy of the nation. . . ." But since this was not possible, they must be given a chance to adapt themselves to "the new order of things. . . . Slavery is already gone, and, to cultivate the land, negro or other labor must be hired. This, of itself, is a vast revolution, and time must be afforded to allow men to adjust their minds and habits to the new order of things." Purely military rule must prevail, "able to enforce its laws promptly and emphatically." The small farmers, mechanics, merchants, and laborers made up three-quarters of the white population. They had no real interest "in the establishment of a Southern Confederacy, and have been led or driven into war on the false theory that they were to be benefited somehow—they knew not how." These men made up "the real *tiers état* of the South." They would, as they had in the past, follow their leaders. With the Union men of the South, Sherman professed little sympathy. They had permitted themselves to be bullied and browbeaten. They had "allowed," in Sherman's words, "a clamorous set of demagogues to muzzle and drive them as a pack of curs. . . . They give us no assistance or information, and are loudest in their complaints at the smallest excesses of our soldiers. . . . I account them as nothing in this great game of war." The "young bloods" were "sons of planters, lawyers about towns, good billiard players and sportsmen, men who never did work and never will. War suits them and the rascals are brave, fine riders, bold to rashness, and dangerous subjects in every sense. They care not a sou for niggers, land, or any thing. They hate Yankees *per se,* and don't bother their heads about the past, present, or future. So long as they have good horses, plenty of forage, and an open country, they are happy. This is a larger class than most men suppose [and clearly the one that Sherman identified with most closely], and they are the most dangerous set of men that this war has turned loose upon the world. They are splendid riders, first-rate shots, and utterly reckless. . . . These men must all be killed or employed by us before we can hope for peace."

To Sherman "a civil government now, for any part of [this section of the South] would be simply ridiculous." Reason, logic, and experience all dictated military rule "till after *all* the organized armies of the South are dispersed, conquered, and subjugated." The only issue at the moment was: "Can we whip the South?" Until that issue was settled, all other questions must be suspended. The United States must have the will "to penetrate to every part of our national domain" and make clear to the South "that we will do it in our own time and in our own way; that it makes no difference whether it be in one year, or two, or ten, or twenty; that we will remove and destroy every obstacle, if need be, take every life, every acre of land, every particle of property, every thing that to us seems proper; that we will not cease till the end is attained. . . . If the people of the South oppose, they do so at their peril; and if they stand by, mere onlookers in this domestic tragedy, they have no right to immunity, protection, or share in the final results. . . . The only government needed or deserved by the States of Louisiana, Arkansas, and Mississippi, now exists in Grant's army. . . . The South must be ruled by us, or she will rule us. . . . There is no middle course."

Sherman's letter is arresting on two grounds: first, in anticipation of his famous march; secondly, in the fact that it makes no mention of blacks, slave or free.

Gideon Welles is a representative of that group of Republicans (many of them, incidentally, former Democrats like Welles himself) whom I have called Conscience Constitutionalists. As early as the summer of 1863 he and Chase engaged in discussions about the form that the "reconstruction" of the Union should take. Chase's conviction was that there must be "unconditional and immediate emancipation in all the Rebel States, no retrograde from the Proclamation of Emancipation, no recognition of a Rebel State as a part of the Union, or any terms with it except on the extinction, wholly, at once, and forever, of slavery."

This seemed to Welles far too draconian a policy. At the center of the issue was the question of whether the states in rebellion had come to constitute a belligerent power which, when peace finally came, was to be treated as a defeated nation or whether, since the North had insisted the South had no right to secede and had never *constitutionally* been out of the Union, they should, with the achievement of peace, be accepted back as equal in all respects to the other states of the Union, allowing always for the punishment of individual Confederate leaders like Jefferson Davis. Such, at least, was Welles's view. "The reestablishment of the Union, and harmony," he wrote, "will be a slow process, requiring forbearance and nursing rather than force and coercion. The bitter enmities which have been sown, the hate which has been generated, the blood which has been spilled, the treasure, public and private, which has been wasted, and last, and saddest of all, the lives which have been sacrificed, cannot be forgotten and smoothed over in a day; we can hardly expect it in a generation. By forbearance and forgiveness, by wise and judicious management, the States may be restored to their place and the people to their duty, but let us not begin by harsh assumptions, for even with gentle treatment the work of reconciliation and fraternity will be slow. Let us be magnanimous." Whatever punishment was meted out to a defeated foe should be directed at individuals, not at the states per se.

Chase, meanwhile, was busy trying to recruit Cabinet members to his harsher position. Lincoln he thought much too kindly and easy-going. "He compliments [him] for honesty of intentions," Welles noted, "good common sense, more sagacity than he has credit for, but [thinks] he is greatly wanting in will and decision, in comprehensiveness, in self-reliance, and clear, well-defined purpose." Chase's criticisms were probably accurate enough, as far as they went. Chase, far more the conventional politician than Lincoln, was all for "clear, well-defined purpose," decisiveness, and the unfailing exercise of authority, for the appearance of certitude even if no certitude was possible. Lincoln, on the other hand, was acutely aware of a range of issues and problems, of what we might call, I suppose, human modalities, quite outside the vision of Chase. The President also knew Chase's "goals" and "well-defined purposes" could easily harden into rigid and unrealistic policies, too inflexible to respond to the often unpredictable and uncontrollable course of events. What appeared as indecision to many who observed Lincoln casually, or through the blinders of conventional notions about the appearance and manner of "statesmen," was rather a patient waiting for the time to ripen, for events to come to that point where the application of intelligent pressure might have a decisive effect. It may indeed have been this very patience which was Lincoln's greatest gift. Far more than those around him, he perceived and held fast to the ultimate "purpose": the restoration of the Union and the freeing of the slaves. Every other purpose was subordinate to those two. Every decision or suspension of a decision was made in the hope of advancing the day when the states would be once more united and the slaves free.

Another proposed solution to the problem of the postwar South looked to the voluntary emigration of the ex-slaves to Africa, South America, or the Caribbean islands, where they would, it was presumed, more readily find work and, above all, be free of the hostility of white Southerners. Their places would then be taken by Northern whites, who would help bring the South into the industrial age of the nineteenth century. Lincoln himself was strongly inclined to this way of thinking. In the words of Carl Schurz, the President, "having been born in a slave-holding State, and grown up in a negro-hating community, . . . foresaw more distinctly than other anti-slavery men did the race-troubles that would follow emancipation, and he was anxious to prevent, or at least mitigate them."

In the Cabinet meeting of September 26, 1862, the subject of what was to be done with freed slaves after the war was discussed. The general assumption was that improved technology and the competition of white labor in the South would result in a large surplus of unemployed and unemployable blacks, and the question of how they were to be provided for was one that, as we have seen, troubled many Northerners. One proposal was that an area of land in Central America in what was known as the Costa Rica Chiriquí Grant might be used as a refuge for surplus blacks. The region was said to be rich in coal; colonies of blacks might be established there to mine it. Lincoln was a strong supporter of the notion, but Welles was convinced that it was a giant swindle. Montgomery Blair then "made a long argumentative statement in favor of deportation. It would," he declared, "be necessary to rid the country of its black population, and some place must be found for them." Attorney General Bates was also strong for compulsory deportation. The black would not go voluntarily, Bates argued, for he "had great local attachments but no enterprise or persistency." But Lincoln "objected unequivocally to compulsion. Their emigration must be voluntary and without expense to themselves. Great Britain, Denmark, and perhaps other powers would take them."

When a contingent of blacks visited Lincoln, he told them, "Your race are suffering, in my judgment, the greatest wrong inflicted on any people. . . . The aspiration of men is to enjoy equality with the best when free, but on this broad continent, not a single man of your race is made the equal of a single man of ours." His advice was that American blacks should seek out some corner of the globe where they would be decently treated since it seemed to him impossible in America. He suggested Africa and South America, but his visitors made clear that they considered themselves Americans and intended to remain where they were and fight for their rights. "But for your race among us there could not be war," he told them, "although many men engaged on either side do not care for you one way or the other."

Lincoln's plan for colonization aroused the ire of the *Anglo-African*. Had not the blood and sweat of exploited black people contributed greatly to American prosperity? "Why this desire to get rid of us?" the editor asked. "Can it be possible that because the nation has robbed us for nearly two and a half centuries, and finding that she can do it no longer and preserve her character among nations, now, out of hatred, wishes to banish, because she cannot continue to rob us?"

This was a familiar psychology. "This nation has wronged us, and for this reason many hate us." It was a literal fulfillment of the old Spanish proverb "Since I have wronged you, I have never liked you. . . . When a man wrongs another, he not only hates him, but tries to make others dislike him. . . ." Blacks must remain in America, "not because we prefer being oppressed here to being freemen in other countries, but we will remain because we believe our future prospects are better here than elsewhere."

After Lincoln, in August, 1862, stated to a delegation of black leaders that since most white Americans thought it impossible for blacks and whites to live together as equals, "It is better for us both, therefore, to be separated" and urged them to support the principle of colonization, Frederick Douglass took the President to task once more, writing: "The President of the United States seems to possess an ever increasing passion for making himself appear silly and ridiculous, if nothing worse." The President had displayed "all his inconsistencies, his pride of race and blood, his contempt for negroes and his canting hypocrisy. . . . The tone of frankness and benevolence which he assumes in his speech to the colored committee is too thin a mask not to be seen through. The genuine spark of humanity is missing in it, no sincere wish to improve the condition of the oppressed has dictated it."

Another outraged reply came from A. P. Smith of Saddle River, New Jersey, who wrote: "Let me tell you, sir, President though you are, there is but one race of men on the face of the earth:—One lord, one faith, one baptism, one God and Father of all, who is above all, and through all, and in all. Physical differences no doubt there are; no two persons on earth are exactly alike in this respect; but what of that? . . . Pray tell us, is our right to a home in this country less than your own, Mr. Lincoln? . . . Are you an American? So are we. Are you a patriot? So are we. Would you spurn all absurd, meddlesome, impudent propositions for your colonization in a foreign country? So do we. . . ." For the President's notion of digging coal in South America, Smith reserved his particular scorn. "Pardon, Mr. President," he wrote, "if my African risibilities get the better of me, if I do show my ivories whenever I read that sentence! Coal land, sir! If you please, sir, give McClellan some, give Halleck some, and by all means, save a little strip for yourself."

Isaac Wears, a black leader in Philadelphia, described the President's plan as one that called for black people "to pull up stakes in a civilized and Christian nation, simply to gratify a unnatural wicked prejudice emanating from slavery," and the meeting of a black congregation at Newton, Long Island, declared, "We rejoice that we are colored Americans, but deny that we are 'a different race of people' as God has made of one blood all nations that dwell on the face of the earth, and has hence no respect of men in regard to persons." In the face of virtually unanimous black opposition, Lincoln reluctantly abandoned his colonization proposal.

Carl Schurz was among the influential Republicans who were convinced that Northern emigration into the South was an essential element in reconciling the two sections. He wrote to Charles Sumner that "no better way" could be found to knit the sections together "than by immigration in mass. Of the economic benefits which such immigration would confer upon the owners of the soil, it is hardly necessary to speak," he added.

Many Northerners believed that white Southerners, especially the largely illiterate "poor white" population, was as much in need of education and enlightenment as the freed slave. The editor of the *Independent* declared confidently that "individual regeneration" in the South would be effected by the institute which had "raised the American character in the Free States to its present altitude." He wrote: "The common-school system . . . will, if extended to classes hitherto shut out from it, produce the same beneficent results which are visible about us every day." George Templeton Strong wrote in his diary that "if the Negroes go to work to earn their living, they will fall naturally into their proper place, and hold it to the great advantage of all parties. If they decline to do so, they will starve and perish and disappear, and emigration will supply the labor needed to develop the wealth of secession soil."

The classic abolitionist viewpoint was expressed by William Whiting, a graduate of Harvard Law School and an active antislavery man, who addressed the Union League of Philadelphia in the summer of 1863 on "The Return of the Rebellious States to the Union." He declared, "The war" was "the deadliest struggle between civilization and barbarism—freedom and slavery—republicanism and aristocracy—loyalty and treason." After the war the defeated South would not willingly or readily submit to the restructuring of its social system and to equal rights for the freed slaves. "The foot of the conqueror planted upon their proud necks," Whiting stated, "will not sweeten their tempers; and their defiant and treacherous nature will seek to revenge itself in murders, assassinations, and all underhand methods of venting a spite which they dare not manifest by open war, and in driving out of their borders all loyal men." It was folly to believe that what Union sentiment might survive the war could be protected against a people who had "strained every nerve and made every sacrifice to destroy the Union. . . ." The South, Whiting predicted, would demand full and complete restoration to the Union "under the guise of claiming State rights." It would, moreover, send back to Congress "the same traitors and conspirators who have once betrayed the country into civil war, and who will thwart and embarrass all measures tending to restore the Union by harmonizing the interests and the institutions of the people. . . . The insanity of State-rights' doctrines will be nourished and strengthened by admitting back a conquered people as our equals. . . ."

It was Whiting's conviction, like Sherman's, that the United States has to "continue military government over the conquered district, until there shall appear therein a sufficient number of loyal inhabitants to form a Republican Government, which, by guaranteeing freedom to all, shall be in accordance with the true spirit of the Constitution of the United States."

The great majority of Northerners, who had come along on the emancipation issue with surprising alacrity, had the profoundest misgivings about giving the vote to the ex-slaves. It could hardly have been otherwise since free blacks were disenfranchised in most Northern states, the exceptions being Maine, New Hampshire, Vermont, Massachusetts, and Rhode Island, states containing altogether only 7 percent of the Northern free blacks.

Most upper-class Northerners thought the franchise already much too broad. "The American people," Sidney George Fisher wrote, "worship a villainous Mumbo Jumbo, or Boo-Ghoo-Boo, called universal suffrage. . . . [I]n worship of this idol, they have invited the refuse pauper population of Europe to come over & govern them." Although Fisher had come to be solidly for emancipation of all slaves, he was horrified at the thought of giving them the vote. "Already," he wrote, "universal suffrage is acknowledged by all thinking men to be the chief source of danger to our government because of the ignorance & recklessness of the mob which is brought to bear on our politics, yet these fanatics wish to add the mass of the abject & degraded Negro population to make what was already bad enough, a great deal worse." The *Congregationalist,* a church journal of liberal views, expressed much the same opinion when it asked: "Who will claim that every white man in the slums of northern cities, and every negro in the cabins of southern plantations, ought to vote, or could be allowed to vote with safety to the commonwealth?"

Gideon Welles was ready to concede that the free black was as well qualified to vote "as a considerable portion of the foreign element which comes amongst us." But two wrongs did not make a right. "If the negro is to vote and exercise the duties of a citizen," Welles concluded, "let him be educated to it."

Finally, there was what we might call the exterminationist school, larger possibly than anyone wished to acknowledge. It was these whom Emma Holmes had in mind when she wrote that the Yankees "have freed the negroes & now don't know what to do with them, as the negroes think freedom means freedom from labor & equality with whites, but especially the former, neither of which ideas suit the Yankees in practice, however much they may preach about them. The truth is they hate the negroes and are not only willing for their extermination but assist largely in that mode of abolishing slavery." According to the diarist, when a friend complained to the Union officer in command at Charleston about not being allowed to whip an insolent black man, the officer replied, "Why, shoot the damned rascal, shoot him."

What was common to the debates over the future of the South was the conviction that with emancipation, the major dilemma had been

solved. All that remained was minor in comparison with that achievement and must prove susceptible to some just and reasonable solution.

When the members of the Anti-Slavery Society met in Philadelphia in December, 1863, Frederick Douglass addressed them in an
elegiac tone. The meeting had been one "of reminiscences." He had
begun his "existence as a free man in this country with this association," and he had hopes that it would never be necessary to hold
another ten-year meeting. "We live to see a better hope to-night," he
told his audience. "I participate in the profound thanksgiving expressed by all, that we do live to see this better day. I am one of those who
believe that it is the mission of this war to free every slave in the United
States. I am one of those who believe that we should consent to no
peace which shall not be an Abolition peace. . . . This Society," he
reminded his listeners, "was organized . . . for two distinct objects; one
was the emancipation of the slave and the other the elevation of the
colored people." When the slave had been freed, Douglass predicted,
"we shall find a harder resistance to the second purpose of this great
association than we have found even upon slavery itself. . . . Protest,
affirm, hope, glorify as we may, it cannot be denied that Abolitionism is
still unpopular in the United States. It cannot be denied that the war is
at present denounced by its opponents as an Abolition war; and it is
equally clear that it would not be denounced as an Abolition war, if
Abolitionism was not odious." Douglass expressed no hesitation about
the right of the black man to vote. It had been said that "the Colored
man is ignorant, and therefore he shall not vote. In saying this, you lay
down a rule for the black man that you apply to no other class of your
citizens. I will hear nothing of degradation or of ignorance against the
black man. . . . If he knows an honest man from a thief, he knows
much more than some of our white voters. If he knows as much when
sober as an Irishman knows when drunk, he knows enough to vote. If
he knows enough to take up arms in defense of this Government, and
bare his breast to the storm of rebel artillery, he knows enough to vote.
(Great applause.) . . . Men talk about saving the Union, and restoring
the Union as it was. . . . What business . . . have we to fight for the old
Union? We are fighting for something incomparably better than the
old Union. We are fighting for unity . . . in which there shall be no
North, no South, no East, no West, no black, no white, but a solidarity
of the nation, making every slave free, and every free man a voter."
(Great applause.)

Following Douglass to the rostrum, Wendell Phillips assured his audience that he did not subscribe to the system which trusted "the welfare of the dependent class to the good will and moral sense of the upper class." This was aristocracy. "Our philosophy of government, since the 4th day of July, 1776, is that no class is safe, no freedom is real . . . which does not place in the hands of the man himself the power to protect his own rights." Yet Phillips was also an advocate (as was Douglass) of the "root hog or die" school, which held that as little as possible should be done by philanthropic private agencies or by the Federal government for freed blacks lest they become as dependent in freedom as they had been in slavery.

Many abolitionists like Oliver Johnson related the education and improvement of the freed black directly to the issue of enfranchisement. Johnson disputed Phillips's view that all that was due the freed slave were equal justice under the law and, most important, the vote. "In order that there may be Negro Suffrage," Johnson wrote Phillips, "there must be Negroes, and self-supporting and intelligent ones. . . . That there may be Negroes, they must be fed during the transition stage . . . they must be furnished with . . . protection against extortion and oppression; that they be intelligent, they must have school teachers."

In January, 1864, when Congress was debating the readmission of Louisiana into the Union under a constitution banning slavery, leaders of the black community in that state drew up a petition to be presented to Lincoln asking for black suffrage. It was signed by more than 1,000 Louisiana blacks, 27 of whom had fought with Andrew Jackson at the Battle of New Orleans. Two New Orleans leaders, Jean Baptiste Roudanez and Arnold Bertonneau, took the petition to Washington and presented it to Lincoln, and Charles Sumner presented it to the Senate. The petitioners asked for the vote and the right "to participate in the reorganization of civil government in Louisiana."

From Washington Bertonneau and Roudanez traveled to Boston, where the old abolitionist elite of that city gave them a dinner. Called on to speak, Roudanez declared: "In order to make our State blossom and bloom as the rose, the character of the whole people must be changed. As slavery is abolished, with it must vanish every vestige of oppression. The right to vote must be secured; the doors of our public schools must be opened, that our children, side by side, may study from the same books and imbibe the same principles and precepts from the Book of Books—learn the great truth that God 'created of one blood all nations of men to dwell on all the face of the earth'

—so will caste, founded on prejudice against color, disappear. . . ."

Those Louisiana blacks who pressed for black suffrage were denounced as "radicals" by the white press, and *L'Union* replied: "It is really curious to see what pitiable diatribes against radicalism certain publications inflict on their readers each day. . . . These days, the great crime, the grand malediction, the eternal scapegoat, is radicalism. . . . Our revolutionary ancestors were radicals when they undertook to overthrow British despotism. Jefferson and those who aided him were radicals, and they drafted the most radical political document in the history of mankind—the Declaration of Independence. If we really believe that the great principles of this Declaration are the only sane base for republican liberty, we cannot be too radical in defending them. The truth has no need of halfway believers nor of temporizing disciples."

Louisiana had, since the fall of New Orleans in 1862, been a cornerstone in Lincoln's reconstruction policy. Twelve thousand white Louisianians had sworn loyalty to the Union, accepted presidential pardons, and formed a new state constitution which confirmed the emancipation of the slaves and provided for "giving the benefit for public schools equally to black and white" and allowed for the enfranchisement of black voters at the discretion of the legislature.

Lincoln did his best to nudge Louisiana's political leaders in th direction of enfranchising "the very intelligent" blacks and "those who serve our cause as soldiers." Such an example, he was convinced, would have a salutary effect on other Southern states as the war came to an end and, equally important, on Northern opinion. The experiment was ideally suited to Louisiana because of the state's high proportion of literate and well-educated blacks, most of them concentrated in New Orleans. But white Louisianians were deaf to Lincoln's importunings.

Lincoln had made himself clear on the issue of black suffrage to General James Wadsworth in a letter written not long before the general's death at Chancellorsville. Wadsworth had raised the issue of universal amnesty for all the Confederates, and Lincoln replied that he did not see how amnesty could be offered without "exacting in return universal suffrage, or . . . suffrage on the basis of intelligence and military service. How to better the condition of the colored race," Lincoln added, "has long been a study which has attracted my serious and careful attention." He regarded it, he told Wadsworth, as "a religious duty" to act as "guardian of these people, who have so heroically vindicated their manhood on the battle-field where, in assisting to save the life of the Republic, they have demonstrated in blood their right to the ballot. . . . The restoration of the Rebel States to the Union must rest upon the principle of civil and political equality of races; and it must be sealed by general amnesty."

Perhaps the most important by-product of the debate over the rights of the freed slaves was a concerted drive by Northern blacks to win the franchise in those states where they were barred from the polls. In New York the drive for black suffrage was well organized and well financed. The New York City and County Suffrage Committee of Colored Citizens issued a strongly worded address by James McCune Smith, who declared: "What stone has been left unturned to degrade us? What hand has refused to fan the flame of popular prejudice against us? What American artist has not caricatured us? What wit has not laughed at our wretchedness? What songster has not made merry over our depressed spirits? What press has not ridiculed and condemned us?" In October, 1864, 144 delegates from eighteen states gathered in Syracuse, New York, and gave their support to an "Address to the People of the United States," drafted by Frederick Douglass, which declared, "We want the elective franchise in all the States now in the Union, and the same in all such States as may come into the Union hereafter. We believe that the highest welfare of this great country will be found in erasing from its statute-books all enactments discriminating in favor of or against any class of its people alike. . . . In this department of human relations, no notice should be taken of the color of men; but justice, wisdom, and humanity should weigh alone, and be all-controlling. . . . If you still ask us why we want to vote, we answer, Because we don't want to be mobbed from our work, or insulted with impunity at every corner. We are men, and want to be as free in our native country as other men."

John Mercer Langston was president of the National Equal Rights League, founded in 1865 to agitate for equal rights for blacks. A close friend of Theodore and Angelina Weld's, he had graduated from Oberlin, practiced law in that town, and recruited three black regiments. Under his urging, blacks in half a dozen states formed chapters of the National Equal Rights League. The Pennsylvania chapter, meeting at Harrisburg, declared, "Colored people should adopt the motto that self-reliance is the sure road to independence," and called for removing restrictions which excluded blacks from "libraries, colleges, lecture rooms, military academies, jury boxes, churches, theatres, street cars, and from voting. . . . We ask of the people a patient hearing and admission to our common brotherhood, the human race."

The Ohio chapter followed suit, endorsing the principles enunciated by the Pennsylvania branch. When the Louisiana Equal Rights League met in New Orleans, the *Tribune* hailed the "new era" so eagerly anticipated. "There were seated side by side the rich and the poor, the literate and educated men, and the country laborer, hardly released from bondage, distinguished only by the natural gifts of the mind. There, the rich landowner, the opulent tradesman, seconded motions offered by humble mechanics and freedmen. Ministers of the Gospel, officers and privates of the U.S. Army, men who handled the sword or the pen, merchants and clerks, all classes of society were represented. . . ."

Another issue, related to that of suffrage and equal rights, had to do with the economic prospects of freed blacks. Many Northerners, perhaps a majority, assumed that after the war the South would have to become an industrialized capital-intensive region much like the North, where even agriculture would be reformed along the lines of introducing labor-saving machinery. This transformation would in turn produce a large surplus of unskilled black labor in the South. The question of what was to become of this prospective surplus labor force was a subject of much concern to many Northerners disposed to reflect on such matters.

Henry Adams responded to his brother Charles Francis's speculations about the future of blacks by proposing "free colonies . . . the nucleus of which must be military . . . the old soldiers with their grants of land, their families, their schools, churches and Northern energy, forming common cause with the negroes in gradually sapping the strength of the slaveholders, and thus year after year carrying new industry and free institutions until their borders meet from the Atlantic, the Gulf, the Mississippi and the Tennessee in a common center, and the old crime shall be expiated and the social system of the South reconstructed."

Perhaps the most realistic assessment of the problem of "reconstructing" the South was that of William Kelley, a Pennsylvania Congressman who exhorted his colleagues to assure full civil rights, including the right to vote, for the freed slaves of the South. It had been said that the freeing of the slaves was, with reference to classical times, an instance of history's repeating itself, but Kelley would not have it so. "No, Mr. Speaker, history is not repeating itself. We are unfolding a new page in national life. The past is gone for ever. There is no abiding present; it flies while we name it; and, as it flies, it is our duty to provide for the thick-coming future; and with such agencies as I have . . . alluded to, we need not fear that even the existing generation of freedmen will not prove themselves abundantly able to take care of themselves and maintain the power and dignity of the states of which we shall make them citizens. We are to shape the future. We cannot escape the duty. And 'conciliation, compromise, and concession' are not the methods we are to use."

21

The South in the War

At this point it might be well to take a closer look at the South that Northerners were so eager to "reconstruct," if differing widely on exactly how the reconstruction should be accomplished.

We have already noted the range of feelings in the South in regard to both secession and slavery. The war accentuated them. The news of Sumter broke into that idyllic world with its terrible intimations of tragedy. "A world of trouble fell upon our beautiful Southland," Elizabeth Meriwether wrote, "and for many years Life ceased to be the peaceful, uneventful thing it had hitherto meant for me—it came now to mean storm and stress, anxiety and trouble, hope and despair. . . . Tennesseeans did not want to quit the Union. They grieved when they heard of South Carolina's action and, although they strongly opposed Lincoln and the Republican party, they did not think it wise or necessary to secede." Indeed, the citizens of Tennessee, Minor Meriwether among them, opposed secession by a majority of 67,000. When Lincoln issued his call for volunteers, public sentiment swung strongly the other way. Minor told his wife: "If I stayed at home like a woman you wouldn't love me. You couldn't love a coward. I must go." So off Minor went, commissioned as a colonel in the engineers, with the faithful black Henry, freed but devoted to his former master and determined to serve him. William Blackford, the Virginia cavalry officer campaigning in eastern Tennessee, wrote: "As to patriotism there is none. . . . The people down in these states are not as much enlisted on principle in this war as we are in Virginia. They regard it as a war to protect their property in slaves and when they are lost take no further interest in it. In Virginia we are fighting for the right to govern ourselves in our own way and to perpetuate our own customs and institutions . . . without outside interference."

The plight of the loyalists of Tennessee was vividly described by a Union man to a congressional committee after the war: "Surrounded on all sides by rebel population; suffering every conceivable outrage in person and property; hanged on the gallows; shot by an infuriated soldiery; cast into many prisons; mercilessly conscripted, and hunted like wild beasts and murdered in our places of concealment. . . . More than twenty-five thousand of our number, leaving their homes and families to be pillaged and abused, travelling through mountains or swamps by night and hiding in thickets by day to evade a pursuing and murderous enemy, escaped to the federal lines, and, without bounty or other inducement, enrolled themselves as Union soldiers."

A Virginian told David Macrae after the war that he had had no sympathy for slavery. "It was enough for me that Virginia *had* gone out. If she seceded on the question of the tariff, or on the question of postage-stamps, or on the question of lunar eclipses, it would have been the same thing to me. Where Virginia goes, I follow." A friend of Mary Chesnut's who, she wrote, "does not love slavery any more than Sumner does, nor do I," was Lucius Quintus Cincinnatus Lamar, colonel of a Mississippi regiment, whose father-in-law was the famous Georgia humorist and college president (of five colleges in his time) Augustus Baldwin Longstreet. Wade Hampton had fifteen hundred Negroes on one Mississippi plantation. His daughter told Mary Chesnut that neither of her brothers—Preston or Wade—would fight a day for slavery. "They both hate it as we do." "What are they fighting for?" Mary asked. "Southern rights—whatever that is. And they do not want to be understrappers forever to the Yankees. They talk well enough about it, but I forget what they say."

A Southern Unionist told Whitelaw Reid, the newspaper reporter, after the war: "I knew it was madness, but I could not desert them [his friends and fellow Southerners]." At Bull Run, his closest friend was killed by a Union bullet. From that moment he "was a Rebel, heart and soul. My family, friends, neighbors, old political leaders, all went with the State."

William Blackford reported before Fredericksburg that his regimental commander, Colonel Williams Carter Wickham, tormented by the wound he had received at Williamsburg, complained to him that "it's a damned shame I should have to suffer so much for a cause of which I do not approve. Remember, Blackford, if I am killed tomorrow it will be for Virginia, the land of my fathers, and not for the damned secessionist movement." Mary Chesnut noted in her diary in 1863 that her uncle had told her "the men who went into the war to save their negroes are abjectly wretched. Neither side now cares a fig for their beloved negroes, and would send them all to heaven in a hand-basket . . . to win in the fight," and Johnny Chesnut, Mary's brother-in-law, who shared her distaste for slavery, said, "No use to give a reason—a fellow could not stay away from the fight—not well." Mary Chesnut added wryly: "It takes four negroes to wait on Johnny satisfactorily."

The chivalric code did not, of course, require anything as practical and specific as a "reason" for going to war; honor was quite enough. The South was honorable; the North was mercenary and dishonorable. The Marylander William Wilkins Glenn expressed his faith thus: "I believe in Southern Gentlemen & Southern Generals if Jeff Davis will only let them alone." The Charleston Light Dragoons "stood still to be shot down in their tracks, having no orders to retire. They had been forgotten, doubtless," Mary Chesnut wrote, "and they scorned to take care of themselves." To retreat without orders would have been *dishonorable*.

While there were inevitably differences of opinion about secession and slavery, there was no substantial public dissent from secession. Moreover, severe steps were taken to suppress anybody who questioned the wisdom of continuing the struggle. James Dunwoody Brownson De Bow, the editor of the *Southern Quarterly Review* and the founder of the *Commercial Review of the South,* came under attack for criticizing Jefferson Davis's conduct of the war. "The statistical and chivalric De Bow himself," George Templeton Strong wrote, "whilom apostle of slavery and First Gent-in-Waiting to the late King Cotton, has been suppressed and locked up because for the first time in his life he uttered a little common sense." It was De Bow who had argued "statistically" that the North could not survive economically without Southern cotton and must thus acquiesce in restoration of the Union on Southern terms.

At the Brokenburn plantation in Louisiana there was more

debate about the issue of secession and the justice of the war than would have been allowed at Charleston or at Mulberry Hill. One family friend declared the "whole affair . . . a grand humbug." Kate Stone wrote in her diary: "He cannot appreciate the earnestness and grandness of this great national upheaval, the throes of a Nation's birth."

The South was, perhaps above all, a land of illusion. Thus, it was not surprising that its notion of the North had astonishingly little relation to reality. An article of the Southern faith was that the Union army was made up of immigrants who had enlisted to keep from starving to death. Lieutenant Charles Jones wrote his father: "Our best men are in the field, while we meet in the unequal contest hordes of mercenaries, not one in ten of whom belongs to the race entailing the present miseries [the Yankees of New England] and upon which the avenging rod should fall." His father in turn believed "the Lincolnites" were simply waging the war to distract public opinion and prevent "internal dissensions, civil war, and every manner of turmoil, eventuating in absolute destruction." To the younger Jones, the "Age of Gold" had yielded to the "Age of Iron," and the North stood before the world as "an example of refined barbarity, moral degeneracy, religious impiety, soulless honor, and absolute degradation almost beyond belief."

As the war dragged on and God failed to give victory to Confederate arms, Jones began to read the matter somewhat differently. By December, 1862, he was taking a gloomier view of the conflict. "War," he wrote his mother in a philosophical mood, "is a national judgment of the severest character; it comes from God, and is sent for wise purposes and to accomplish given ends. Among those objects perhaps the most important is the alienation of the hearts of the people from sin and worldliness, and a return of them to . . . the fear and love of God." It seemed to Jones that the South had not yet reached the proper degree of contrition and humility.

Above all, the South was what we would call today an authoritarian society. We have noted often that it literally refused to tolerate any dissenting opinion on the issue of slavery. In March, 1861, Alexander Stephens, the Vice-President of the Confederacy, had declared bluntly that while some people professed to believe that all men were created equal, "Our new Government is founded upon exactly the opposite idea; its foundations are laid, its corner stone rests upon the great truth that the negro is not equal to the white man; that slavery, the subordination to the superior race, is his natural and normal condition. This, our new Government, is the first in the history of the world, based upon this great physical, philosophical, and moral truth."

The Confederate States of America had a constitution and a form of government similar to those of the United States of America. For the words "We, the people . . ." the drafters of the Confederate Constitution substituted "We, the deputies of the sovereign and independent States. . . ."

From the first hour of the existence of the new entity it was riven with dissension. Coordinated action among the individual states was at best difficult and at worst impossible. There was abundant historical irony in the fact that the leader of secession should bear the sacred name of the author of the Declaration of Independence. It was, after all, Jefferson who, in the Virginia Resolutions, had first put forward the doctrine of the right of a state to secede from the Union. It was as though that instantaneous built-in schizophrenia, concurrent with the nation's beginning, had been contained in a single hero who spoke for both human equality and the dissolvability of the recently united states. That the United States should have subsequently been dissolved on the grounds of the irredeemable and perpetual inferiority of black people and led in that dissolution by *Jefferson* Davis (Lincoln always referred to him as "that t'other fellow") reminded the attentive observer that history features the irrational and the paradoxical.

Davis was continually at odds with his Cabinet and with the Confederate legislature. "There is a perfect magazine of discord and discontent in that Cabinet," Mary Chesnut wrote in the fall of 1863; "only wants a hand to apply the torch, and up they go." Even before Davis's inauguration, in February, 1862, "a storm of invective," in Emma Holmes's words, had "burst over him, & the faith of many in him [is] entirely gone." He was criticized for not being more aggressive, for promoting his relatives to military commands beyond their competence, and for engaging in vendettas against generals whom he disliked. In May, 1862, the *Richmond Mercury* declared, "Jefferson Davis now treats all men as if they were idiotic insects."

Davis was mercurial, given to moods of profound gloom, testy, impatient, arbitrary. Before the Battle of Bull Run, Mary Chesnut found the President in a somber mood. He was convinced that Southern soldiers would do "all that can be done by pluck, muscle, endurance, and dogged courage, dash, and red-hot patriotism." Yet all this might not, he feared, be enough. There was a "sad refrain" running through his conversation with Mrs. Chesnut. It would certainly be a long war, whatever its outcome, and "before the end came we would have many a bitter experience . . . only fools doubted the courage of the Yankees, or their willingness to fight when they saw fit," and now, their pride aroused, they would "fight like devils." William Wilkins Glenn wrote: "Mr. Davis' strong point is cultivation. He will talk to you about everything from science down to the shape of a dog's tail, and have something to say about everything, showing that he has read or talked about it before."

Those, like Mary Chesnut, who were close to the government, if in truth it could be called that, so awkward and ill-favored was it, were continually troubled by its ineptitude and the bitter quarrels that agitated its counsels. "Our Congress," Mary Chesnut wrote early in 1864, "is so demoralized, so confused, so depressed. They have asked the President, whom they have so hated, so insulted, so crossed and opposed and thwarted in every way, to speak to them, and advise them what to do."

What can hardly be sufficiently stressed was that the Confederacy was, in essence, a loose alliance of highly independent states. It never took the form of the "nation" it so confidently proclaimed itself to be, and from the first months of war its rickety superstructure threatened to fly apart.

The effect of the war on the South was, of course, cumulative. As each month passed, the toll of dead and wounded mounted. In addition, more and more Southerners came to experience at first hand all the demoralizing consequences of an enemy invasion. Because the population bases of the South were much smaller than those of the North, because the South was invaded, because virtually an entire generation of young males of the planter class enlisted in the Confederate army—the great majority as officers—and because, as we have noted, officers suffered unusually high casualties, the Southern death toll was appallingly high. Sarah Morgan's two young brothers, George and Gibbes, hardly more than boys, were both killed in the same week, and she wrote in her diary: "Dead! Dead! Dead! O my brothers! What have we lived for except you? We, who would have so gladly laid down our lives for yours, are left desolate to mourn over all we loved and hoped for. . . . O my God! I could have prayed Thee to take mother, too, when I looked at her. I thought—I almost hoped she was dead, and that pang spared! But I was wild myself. I could have screamed! —and laughed! 'It is false!' Do you hear me mother? God would not take both! . . . I spoke to a body alive only to pain; not a sound of my voice seemed to reach her; only fearful moans showed she was still alive."

When Mrs. Means, a friend of Mary Chesnut's, heard of the death of her husband and the news that her only son was wounded and a prisoner, she threw a shawl over her head and sat so long without moving that someone ventured to remove the shawl and discovered that she was dead. In Charleston the Cheveses received news of the death of their only son, Edward. His sister, according to Mary Chesnut's account, "kept crying, 'Oh, mother, what shall we do; Edward is killed,' but the mother sat dead still, white as a sheet, never uttering a word or shedding a tear. Are our women losing the capacity to weep?" Mary Chesnut asked herself.

In April, 1862, word reached Brokenburn that Kate Stone's brother, Walter, eighteen years old, had died almost two months before at Cotton Gin, Mississippi. He had died of the "fever," and Kate wrote in her diary: "It wrings my heart to think of him suffering and alone. I hope he did not realize that Death was so near and all he loved so far away. Poor little fellow, he was not used to strangers. He has been surrounded by loved and familiar faces all his short life. . . . He was but a boy and could not stand the hardships of a soldier's life. Four months of it killed him. . . . He has left only a memory and a name."

Encountering a trainload of wounded Confederate soldiers on their way home, Elizabeth Meriwether wept bitterly. "These men, poor and half educated though they were," she wrote, "were God's Noblemen. . . . I told them the time would come when the people of the South would record their deeds on tablets of bronze and on monuments of marble; I said that History would honor them and that posterity, whether we won or lost the war, would ever honor the soldiers of the South as patriots and heroes!"

By the spring of 1862 Mary Chesnut was filled with despair. "Battle after battle has occurred," she wrote in her diary, "disaster after disaster. Every morning's paper is enough to kill a well woman and age a strong and hearty one. . . ." Old Colonel Chesnut wrote from Mulberry Hill: "We can't fight all the world: two and two only make four; it can't make a thousand; numbers will not lie." He had already lost half a million in railroad bonds, he wrote his daughter-in-law. Every Sunday in church the Reverend Mr. Minnegerode "cried aloud in anguish his litany, 'from pestilence and famine, battle, murder, and sudden death,' and we wailed on our knees, 'Good Lord deliver us,' and on Monday, and all week long, we go on as before, hearing of nothing but battle, murder, and sudden death, which are daily events. . . . We live in a huge barrack. We are shut in, guarded from light without."

In the summer of 1863 Mary Chesnut made her way to Portland, Alabama, to her parents' plantation to visit her sick mother. There she saw her beloved sister Sally for the first time in almost two years. She was thin and pale, and when she raised her candle to point something out on the wall, Mary Chesnut saw that "her pretty brown hair was white." It took all her self-control not to burst into "violent weeping," Mrs. Chesnut wrote in her diary. "She looked so sweet, and yet so utterly broken-hearted." Somehow her sister's prematurely white hair and sad, quiet face seemed to Mary Chesnut to symbolize all the loss and tragedy of the war.

Stephen Lee's corps of Johnston's army marched through Lincolnton, North Carolina. The men sang sad, stirring songs. "The leading voice," Mary Chesnut wrote, "was powerful, mellow, clear, distinct, pathetic, sweet. So, I sat down, as women have done before when they hung up their harps by strange streams, and I wept the bitterness of such weeping. Music? Away, away! Thou speakest to me of things which in all my life I have not found, and I shall not find. There they go, the gay and gallant few, doomed, the last gathering of the flower of Southern pride, to be killed, or worse, to a prison. They continue to prance by, light and jaunty. They march as airy a tread as if they still believed the world was all on their side, and that there were no Yankee bullets for the unwary."

Flight before the advancing Yankees and making do with substitutes for the simple necessities of life like buttons and needles and sugar and tea became mythlike themes in the endlessly reiterated stories of survival and endurance. At Brokenburn the Stone family tried sassafras tea in the absence of the real thing, and the ladies of the house set about making shoes, fashioning the uppers out of broadcloth or velvet sewed by a black shoemaker to leather soles. Finally the Yankees reached Brokenburn, and when Kate Stone tried to dissuade one of them from stealing her prize horse, Wonka, he cursed her and said, "I had just as soon kill you as a hoppergrass."

Elizabeth Meriwether, rebuffed in her request to buy corn by a hostile planter, stole what she needed to feed herself and her children and then sent him the money. In Florida, John Hay saw the marks of war's devastation everywhere, in "a lady, well-bred and refined, dressed worse than a bound girl, with a dirty and ragged gown that did not hide her trim ankles and fine legs," and in a "white-haired, heavy-eyed, slow-speaking old young man." There were two black regiments, "gay with banners, fragrant with salthorse."

The Middletons, close friends of Sidney George Fisher's, were ruined. Middleton Place was burned, and the ladies, it was said, were selling nuts and cakes on the street corners of Savannah.

There was also the simple fact of the physical devastation of the land—ruined fences, flooded fields, rampant weeds. Levees broke and remained unrepaired in the countryside around the Brokenburn plantation south of Vicksburg. The whole county was a sheet of water, and no skiff could be bought or borrowed. Mrs. Stone finally secured a huge dugout, and it was loaded with the members of the family and "an assorted cargo of corn, bacon, hams, Negroes, their baggage, dogs and cats, two or three men, and our scant baggage." At Delhi there were "crowds of Negroes of all ages and sizes, wagons, mules, horses, dogs, baggage and furniture of every description . . . thrown in promiscuous heaps—pianos, tables, chairs, rosewood sofas, wardrobes, parlor sets, with pots, kettles, stoves, beds and bedding, bowls and pitchers, and everything of the kind just thrown down pell-mell here and there, with soldiers, drunk and sober, combing over it, shouting and laughing." The planters and their families who crowded the levees above and below the town had lost heavily, Kate Stone wrote. "Some with princely estates and hundreds of Negroes, escaping with ten or twenty of their hands and only the clothes they had on. Others brought household effects but no Negroes, and still others sacrificed everything to run their Negroes to a place of safety. . . . All had their own tales to tell of Yankee insolence and oppression and their hairbreadth escapes. All were eager to tell their own stories of hardship and contrivance, and everybody sympathized with everybody else."

The Stones, forced to flee to Texas from their plantation, found life there a far cry from the pleasures of Brokenburn. Kate and her sisters went to a combination funeral-wedding at a village named Liberty. The women were dressed bizarrely in enormous hoopskirts and flowered flounces. "Many of the men were barefooted," Kate Stone wrote, "and nearly all of their slouched wool hats were decorated with ribbons or an artificial flower. There were few coats but many vests and a display of homemade knit galluses."

Near Columbus, Georgia, pregnant Elizabeth Meriwether was taken in by a kindly Mrs. Winston a few days before Christmas, 1862.

There she gave birth to her third child, a son christened Lee Meriwether, after General Robert E. There were no doctors to be found, so Aunt Tabby, "coal black, strong and self possessed," presided, delivering young Lee, placing him beside his mother, and declaring, "Now, Honey, you go ter sleep and rest yo'self. I'm plum wore out myself an' I must go home an' rest myself." To Elizabeth's feeble protests, Aunt Tabby replied, "Don't you worry, Chile. You doan need me no mo'. I've dun fixed everything handy. Here's de kindlin' wood to make de fire burn and here's a kettle ef yo' needs some hot water. I neber stays wid a lady after I'se got her baby born."

After Elizabeth Meriwether had spent five months with the Winstons, the faithful Henry, detached for the duty from his master, came with a carriage to bring her and the three boys to Tuscaloosa to stay with her sister. Food there was in short supply. The Confederate government distributed to each soldier's wife or widow "one bushel of corn on the cob every day; this was shelled and sent to the mill to be ground into corn meal; in addition to this," Elizabeth Meriwether wrote, "we had field peas which we boiled and made into soup." On this fare her milk failed, and she was glad to be able to turn Lee over to her maid, who had just had an infant of her own, to be nursed.

Like Elizabeth Meriwether, Sarah Morgan, her married sister, her mother, younger sister, and servants moved ceaselessly from one temporary refuge to another—to a friend's, to a cousin's, to rented quarters in a dreary village, back to Baton Rouge when the Union troops were driven out, and then fleeing once more as they returned in greater force. "Still floating about!" Sarah wrote in her diary in September, 1862.

Mary Chesnut alternated among her husband's house in Charleston, the Chesnut family plantations at Mulberry Hill and Sand Hill, her own family's plantation near Montgomery, Alabama, as well as her brother-in-law's plantation at Cool Spring, a house in Camden, South Carolina, and Richmond, Virginia, the seat of the Confederate government.

Yet in the midst of death and devastation the old Southern rituals of eating and courting were maintained with an astonishing tenacity. In Richmond the President's wife spread a lavish table for the ladies of Cabinet members and officers of the government: "Gumbo, ducks and olives, chickens in jelly, oysters, lettuce salad, chocolate cream, jelly cake, claret, champagne, etc." Mary Chesnut noted that some grumblers questioned whether it was appropriate, with the war going so badly, to indulge in such repasts, but they missed the point. It was a ritual of survival, a sacred rite, an act of courage, a gesture of defiance in the face of an unkind Providence. As soon ask them to stop living as to stop feasting. Money was useless. "You take your money to the market in the market basket," James Petigru declared, "and bring home what you buy in your pocketbook."

After a feast Mary Chesnut walked home with General John Breckinridge, a former vice-president of the United States and now a Confederate officer, who asked himself if the man who had spent the evening in gay social chatter was the same man who, not long before, "stood gazing down on the faces of the dead on that awful battle-field [Chancellorsville]. The soldiers lying there stare at you with their eyes wide open," he told Mary Chesnut, adding, "Is this the same world? Here and there?"

On Christmas Day, 1863, with the fortunes of the South at their lowest ebb, the Chesnuts in Richmond enjoyed a splendid feast —"oyster soup . . . roast mutton, boned turkey, wild duck, partridge, plum pudding, sauterne, burgundy, sherry, and Madeira." Mary Chesnut added, "There is life in the old land yet. If it were not for this horrid war," she wrote, "how nice it would be here . . . such beautiful grounds, flowers and fruits; indeed, all that the heart could wish; such delightful dinners . . . jolly talks, such charming people; but this horrid war poisons everything."

There were frequent small but troubling signs that a world was crumbling. Lawrence, James Chesnut's faithful, if indolent, servant, appeared drunk at the breakfast table, and when he was told to move a chair, he raised it high over his head, smashing a chandelier to bits. Chesnut was too furious to trust himself to speak; Mary had to tell Lawrence that he had to go in exile to Mulberry Hill. He went away uncontrite, convinced that his master could not do without him and would soon send for him to return.

Kate Stone's diary, like that of Emma Holmes and of Mary Chesnut, is filled with accounts of courtships and romances, even in the darkest days of the war. Her friend Mollie Hunt, an old school-mate, gave Kate "a full and particular account of her various love affairs, about like the play of *Hamlet* with Hamlet left out" since she would name no names. "She must have had scores," Kate Stone noted. "She says she has four on hand now, all waiting in trembling apprehension of yes or no. She thinks she will say no to all."

As the Union forces penetrated into the South, the Northern soldiers gave special attention, as soldiers will, to the possessions of the enemy. Southern mansions were systematically stripped of everything that could be carried away. While most officers tried, with widely varying degrees of success, to limit or control the depredations of their men, others encouraged them; looting was persistent and, in the last analysis, irrepressible. What the soldiers sought most indefatigably were the vast stores of silver that every plantation prided itself on. The result was a strange drama wherein the plantation people (often the slaves were willing accomplices of their masters and mistresses) employed endless ingenuity in hiding their silver while the Yankee invaders were equally cunning in ferreting it out. In every Southern tale of pillaging by Northern soldiers (and there are thousands upon thousands of them), the effort to preserve the family silver is the central theme. It was concealed (and discovered) beneath the excrement of outhouses, in carcasses in smokehouses, in the cribs of sleeping babies, in the beds of pregnant mothers and ailing old ladies, in eagles' nests, in swamps, beneath barn floors, up chimneys. Plated silver was substituted for sterling in the hope that the invaders would carry it off under the impression that it was the real thing.

Mary Mallard gave a classic acccount of Yankee soldiers searching her home in Arcadia, Georgia. Yankees poured through the house. One asked for whiskey; another, under the pretext of searching for arms, interrogated Mary Mallard about every box and closet and then, not satisfied with her answers, demanded keys to everything locked and broke open those trunks and wardrobes for which keys couldn't be found. One man turned to her and demanded her watch, and when she replied that her husband was wearing her watch, he shook his fist at her and shouted, "Don't you lie to me. You have got a watch!" Mary Mallard persuaded him that she did not. Once again whiskey was demanded, and Mary's mother asked the soldier who appeared to be in command "if he would like to see his mother and his wife treated in this way—their house invaded and searched." In this instance and in many others the Union soldiers tried to engage the women of the plantation in a discussion of the causes of the war.

At Arcadia the visit of the Union soldiers was followed a few hours later by a contingent of marines. Several of them were dressed in bits of finery they had taken from other plantations. Told that the house had already been searched, they asked for food and were directed to the kitchen, where the family meal had been prepared. After eating, they repeated the search of the premises, scattering articles about and taking a gold pencil from Mary Mallard's workbox.

There was a day of quiet, and then forty or fifty horsemen descended on the house, invading the pantry in search of food, "flying hither and thither, ripping open the [food] safe with their swords and breaking open the crockery cupboards," Mary Mallard wrote. Some chickens and ducks had been roasted as a kind of reserve food supply for the family; "these the men seized whole, tearing them to pieces with their teeth like ravenous beasts." Once more the cry was for whiskey. Flour and cornmeal in sacks were thrown across the backs of the horses. The soldiers broke open Mary Mallard's mother's worktable with an andiron, and "failing to find treasure, they took the sweet little locks of golden hair that her mother had cut from the heads of her angel children near half a century ago, and scattering them upon the floor trampled them under their feet. A number of them rifled the sideboard, taking away knives, spoons, forks, tin cups, coffeepots, and everything they wished. They broke open Grandfather's old liquor case and carried off two of the large square gallon bottles, and drank up all the blackberry wine . . . which was in the case. It was vain to utter a word, for we were completely paralyzed by the fury of these ruffians. . . . It is impossible," Mary Mallard concluded, "to imagine the horrible uproar and stampede through the house, every room of which was occupied by them, all yelling, cursing, quarreling, and running from one room to another in wild confusion. Such was their blasphemous language, their horrible countenances and appearance, that we realized what must be the association of the lost in the world of eternal woe. . . . We look back upon their conduct in the house as a horrible nightmare, too terrible to be true."

The ordeal was not over. The next day Mary's mother, seeing a Union officer in the yard, went to him to complain about her house being looted and asked for his protection. He told her that it was against army regulations for soldiers to enter private houses and that the penalty was death. None of his men would be allowed in the house. They were on a foraging expedition and would take only food. Under his direction the soldiers "made the Negroes bring up the oxen and carts, and took off all the chickens and turkeys they could find. They carried off all the syrup from the smokehouse," Mary Mallard noted. "We had one small pig, which was all the meat we had left; they took the whole of it." Finally they rolled out the family carriage and filled it with chickens. "So," Mary wrote, "they were all carried off—carriages, wagons, carts, horses, mules and servants, with food and provisions of every kind. . . ." On many plantations the slaves suffered along with their masters and mistresses from the depredations of the Union soldiers. When one of the slaves at Arcadia spoke affectionately of her former master, the Reverend Mr. Quarterman, to a Yankee soldier, he replied, "He was a damned infernal villain, and we only wish he were alive now; we would blow his brains out." Two blankets were stolen from July, one of the household servants, and a soldier tried to steal his hat, but he resisted. Some of the slaves, to avoid being carried off by the Union soldiers and put to work, feigned ailments. On the Mallard plantation at Arcadia one young slave wore a shawl over her head and tottered about like an old crone. One carried his arm in a sling, another "limped dreadfully," and still another took to his bed, claiming to be ill of the dreaded yellow fever. Yet even here the pattern of black behavior varied, almost from day to day. Susan, nurse to Mary Jones's infant, went off with her husband and joined the Yankee soldiers, informing them that her child's father was Colonel Jones.

The mistress of Arcadia wrote bitterly in her journal of what it meant "to see my house broken open, entered with false keys, threatened to be burned to ashes, refused food and ordered to be starved to death, told that I had no right even to food or water, that I should be 'humbled in the very dust I walked upon,' a pistol and a carbine presented to my breast, cursed and reviled as a rebel, a hypocrite, a devil. Every servant, on pain of having their brains blown out . . . forbidden to wait upon us or furnish us food. Every trunk, bureau, box, room, closet . . . opened or broken open and searched, and whatever was wanted of provisions, clothing, jewelry, knives, forks, spoons, cups, kettles, cooking utensils, towels, bags, etc., etc., from this house taken, and the whole house turned topsy-turvy."

Emma Holmes had taken a position as governess on a plantation near Columbia, South Carolina, owned by a nouveau riche family named Mickle. When word came that Yankees were in the vicinity, the Mickles busied themselves burying their valuables. Emma hid her money and watch in the bodice of her dress and filled her mailbag with handkerchiefs, stockings, and a new pair of shoes and hung them under her hoop skirts. She then composed her spirits and sat down to await the arrival of the dreaded "Yahoos." Two soldiers appeared in time, "followed by two stolen mules & little negroes." They were quiet and polite, asked a few questions, and departed. Soon five more appeared and asked for breakfast and, while it was being prepared, "walked about the house and yard, behaving pretty well." They called for the sideboard keys to look for liquor and then for sugar to make a toddy. After breakfast one of the soldiers handed Mrs. Mickle a Confederate $100 bill as payment. Soon there were more soldiers. They passed freely through the house without taking anything, but they burned the plantation ginhouse, 80 bales of cotton, and 200 bushels of corn. They then ransacked the slaves' quarters, where some of the furnishings of the big house had been distributed, and stole the new breeches of slaves as well as other items of clothing. They called for pillowcases and carried off all the wheat flour, almost all the meat, the turkeys, and chickens. What few items of silverware had been left unburied were carried off as well. The family slaves resisted all cajolings and threats to reveal where the hidden treasures might be and did their best to "help their mistress save something from the 'vile wretches,'" in Emma Holmes's words. Her ink had been spilled on the floor, her "new sealing wax . . . empty purse, new tooth brush & toilette comb stolen. . . ." All in all, she felt, they had not faired as badly as they had expected at the hands of the Yankee monsters. Emma's in-laws, the Whites, who lived at Winnsboro, suffered far more "both at the town house & plantation. . . . The Yankees were very rude to the girls, stole a quantity of house linen & other things, including some jewelry & silver not buried, &, after ransacking the house, put their bombazine bonnets & nicest articles of dress under piles of clothing then trampled on them. But," Emma noted proudly, "the girls held their heads so high & talked so boldly that the wretches left the house in wrathful disgust, vowing vengeance on them."

In General David Hunter's Shenandoah Valley raid, the home of Mrs. Lewis, a friend of Emma Holmes's, "had been sacked, & *every thing* carried off—every particle of grain meat or food in every possible shape, inanimate or living. 15 horses, furniture, clothing, bedding, silver—in fact all she owned in the world, save her wedding ring. . . . The house was not only completely stripped, but the walls ripped open & even the ash barrels & *privies* searched for hidden articles." The story went that when she had protested to General Hunter, "he told her he was glad of it, for that the *women & children were* the *very fiends* of *this war,* sending their husbands, fathers & brothers into the army. He meant to humble the pride of the haughty Virginians to the very dust. . . . The negroes recoiled in horror from the atrocities of the Yankees & refused to leave her." The embattled Mrs. Lewis declared herself willing to lose "10,000 times as much for the cause."

Susan Leigh Blackford, the wife of Captain William Blackford, abandoned Richmond for Charlottesville in the spring of 1865 but found that town threatened by Yankee cavalry. "I took my silver sugar-dish, cream pot, bowl, forks and spoons," she wrote her husband, "and put them into the legs of a pair of your drawers I had in my trunk, tying up each leg at the ankle and tucking the band around my waist. They hung under, and were concealed by, my hoops. It did well while I sat still, but as I walked and when I sat down the clanking destroyed all hope of concealment. Of course the ridiculous side of the situation struck me and I could not restrain my laughter. . . ."

It was General George A. Custer, the beau ideal of a gallant officer, who entered Charlottesville and issued orders against casual looting. Susan Blackford and her friends "had planned all kinds of sarcastic speeches to be hurled" at the Union soldiers "and were almost sorry to miss the opportunity," Mrs. Blackford wrote her husband. Despite Custer's orders, some stragglers found their way to the Gildersleeve plantation on the edge of town. They ran all over the house, ransacking it for silver and female finery, then dressed themselves in "the ladies' underclothes and dresses" and danced wildly about in the yard. Mr. Gildersleeve's sister had put all the family silver in the baby's crib, and the infant was asleep under the watchful eye of her black nurse when the stragglers burst in and, not fooled for a moment, "turned the baby out on the floor," took the hidden treasure, and then shook the indignant nurse to find out if she had any more silver concealed on her person.

General Custer was entertaining the ladies of the Maury household when impish Lizzie Maury, finding a spoon on the floor, brought it to the general and asked if it had fallen out of his pocket, to Custer's indignation. It was discovered that old Mrs. Maury, who had been confined to her bed for years, had struggled out of bed and gotten dressed with the help of her maid. She had heard that the Yankees had said that "in every house in which they found some damned old rebel woman sick she was in bed with the silver, and she did not intend to be dragged out of her bed by men looking for silver she did not have."

Sarah Morgan's pleased surprise at the gentlemanly conduct of the Yankee officers in Memphis turned to fury at the Union troops when, after the Union commander, General Thomas Williams, was shot from ambush, the houses of many of the leading citizens, the Morgan house among them, were pillaged by angry soldiers. At the Jones mansion, four officers appeared, "accompanied by a negro woman, at whose disposal all articles were placed. The worthy companion of these 'gentlemen,'" Sarah wrote, "walked around selecting things with the most natural airs and graces. *This*,' she would say, 'we *must* have. And some of those books, you know; and all the preserves and these chairs and tables, and all the clothes, of course; and yes! the rest of these things.'" The Morgan family fled to the home of friends in the country, and when they returned, they found their house devastated and got a lurid account of its looting by a house servant. "Libraries emptied," Sarah Morgan wrote, "china smashed, sideboards split open with axes, three cedar chests cut open, plundered, and set up on end; all parlor ornaments carried off—even the alabaster Apollo and Diana. . . ." When the black girl, Margaret, protested at the officers' cutting Judge Morgan's portrait from its frame, one of them had put his pistol at her head and threatened to blow her brains out. The invaders had entered Sarah's room, broken her handsome mirror, "pulled down the rods from the bed, and with them pulverized my toilet set. . . . My desk was broken open. Over it was spread all my letters, and private papers, a diary I kept when twelve years old, and sundry tokens of dried roses, etc. . . . how I writhe when I think of all they saw. . . ." One officer had clapped Sarah's bonnet on his head and run out into the street, followed by his companions, similarly attired. The orgy of destruction had been stopped only when Charley, an old household slave, found an officer and reported what was going on. At word that a higher officer was on his way, two of the looters had hidden under a bed and were pulled therefrom.

The Northern soldiers occupying Memphis appropriated Elizabeth Meriwether's cow and with it the milk for her two young children. When she protested to a big, bearded, kindly-looking Yankee, he took the tin bucket little Avery was carrying for the milk and patted him on the head. "I've got a little shaver at home, a boy just about this one's age. I guess his mother would feel bad if he couldn't get any milk for his supper. Just wait here, Marm, I'll be back in a minute." Every morning Elizabeth Meriwether and her son repeated the ritual.

On one plantation, when the Yankee soldiers came, a slave recalled that they simply walked into the house and upstairs and into the bedroom of the mistress of the plantation, "whar my sister, Lucy, wuz combin' Mist'ess long pretty hair. They told Lucy she wuz free now and not to do no more work for Mist'ess. Den all of 'em grabbed dey big old rough hands into Mist'ess' hair, and dey made her walk down stairs and out in de yard, and all de time dey wuz a-pullin' and jerkin' at her long hair. . . ."

On another plantation, soldiers made the women of the house cook and serve a meal for them, Mary Ella Grandberry recalled years later. "De Yankees made 'em do for us lak we done for dem. Dey showed the white folks what it was to work for somebody else."

John Beatty believed that General John B. Turchin's brigade, of the Army of the Ohio, had stolen "a hundred thousand dollars' worth of watches, plate, and jewelry in northern Alabama." While Beatty deplored such thefts, he was more indignant at what he felt was Buell's disposition to treat the rebels with excessive concern, almost deference. "It is said," Beatty wrote, "that it is hard to deprive men of their horses, cattle, grain simply because they differ from us in opinion; but is it not harder still to deprive men of their lives for the same reason?"

Interestingly enough, some of the worst depredations came from the Southern soldiers in the Union army after the surrender. Mulberry Hill had survived the Yankees relatively intact but suffered from what Mary Chesnut called "Potter's raid," when North Carolina "Federals" burned their cotton mills and gins and a hundred bales of cotton. When Mary Chesnut's maid, Molly, appeared from Columbia, she routed some cows out of the swamp and sold butter in town on shares, dividing the proceeds with her former owners, now employers. Old Cuffey, the head gardener, and Yellow Abram, his assistant, would work on, "as long," they vowed, "as old master is alive," and there was plenty of "fresh vegetables,—asparagus, lettuce, spinach and potatoes and soon strawberries in abundance."

A friend of Mary Chesnut's heard an old black man say to his master, "When you had all de power you was good to me, and I'll protect you now. No niggers nor Yankees shall tech you. If you want anything call for Sambo. I mean, call for Mr. Samuel; dat my name now."

Charles Francis Adams, Jr., reported that the cavalry often behaved like Cossacks in looting and pillaging the countryside. He was horrified to hear that the infantry had the reputation for being far worse since the depredations of the cavalry "make my hair stand on end and cause me to loathe all war." One seventy-four-year-old woman appealed to Adams for protection. Her house had been broken into by Union soldiers, her closets and drawers ransacked, her food all stolen, and she herself "abused and threatened. . . . The horrors of war," Adams added, "are not all to be found in the battle-field and every army pillages and outrages to a terrible extent. . . . In the Maryland campaign last year McClellan's army left behind 12,000 fighting men—stragglers, plundering the land."

The case of the border slave states was very different from that of the Old or Deep South. In Kentucky and especially in Tennessee and Missouri the most relentless and sanguinary civil wars took place between Unionists and secessionists, beside which *the* Civil War was a model of gentlemanly restraint. Where the secessionists predominated, Unionists were hunted down like animals or murdered in their beds. When the tide turned, the secessionists were fair game.

Tennessee furnished the North with 40,000 men, as many as Napoleon commanded at Waterloo; Maryland provided 30,000 volunteers to the Confederate armies and half as many for the Union.

Maryland, of course, was a special case. It was firmly in Union hands throughout the war, but it was a hotbed of secessionist sympathies. Baltimore (like Washington and Philadelphia) was full, Sidney George Fisher reported, of "ladies & gentlemen in society who communicate intelligence to the enemy and openly sympathize with the South. The ladies send delicacies to the prisoners of war—wine, cake, morning gowns & embroidered slippers."

Some Southern sympathizers went into permanent hiding. A friend of William Wilkins Glenn's moved constantly about the county, never appearing in the daytime, and kept informed of any searches for him by friendly slaves. W. H. Norris, another Southern sympathizer, "was obliged to dodge about for a long time. It was very funny to see him as you approached his retreat," Glenn wrote, "always on the *qui vive* as he was, warily watching every vehicle, horseman or foot passenger who came towards the house."

William Wilkins Glenn himself was a classic example of a border state man of Southern sympathies and antecedents. Glenn was a planter who owned a number of slaves and had been strikingly successful. The role he chose was that of a newspaper editor (he bought a newspaper primarily to argue the case for Maryland's remaining neutral in the war) and Confederate agent. Twice arrested for his seditious utterances, for his refusal to take the oath of allegiance or even to sign a parole pledging not to engage in activities inimical to the Union, and for his rumored role in facilitating the passage of Southern agents and English journalists through the Union lines, he managed each time to secure his release through influential friends and personal ingratiation. Of his role as an editor, he wrote in his diary: "I was determined to force the Government to have recourse to military power if they wished to muzzle free speech in Maryland."

Locked up in Fort McHenry with a number of other intractable Marylanders, Glenn observed that "some were despondent, one or two got drunk; most of them were thinking of the best way to get free. Jim Maxwell had his fiddle & was very jolly." Glenn was contemptuous of those who gave up their parole in order to secure their freedom. His confinement was relatively gentle. He received bedding and books from home, his wife visited him, and he was "allowed provisions of liquors," which he dispensed generously to his jailers.

Southern agents or simply sympathizers, heading south from Maryland with important dispatches, would often place them in sealed and weighted cans hanging over the sides of their boats by strings which could be cut if capture seemed imminent. Glenn noted that "the underground routes varied constantly. When all communication was entirely stopped on the lower Potomac, it would be opened on the upper—and then again from the Eastern shore." Agents who were caught were often roughly handled. Glenn recorded the case of a governess who was intercepted as she tried to cross the Potomac from the Virginia side. On the ground that she had been seen putting something in her bosom, the commander of the gunboat that intercepted her "thrust his hands in her bosom for the papers he said were concealed there and then tried to excuse the act by declaring that he thought she was a man in disguise." When the lady replied that his "indecent act" should have convinced him of her sex, the officer added insult to injury by declaring "that he had known many men with as large breasts as she had" and continued his searches in his cabin. Not long afterward the inquisitive lieutenant was killed for his license, apparently by a Confederate agent.

As the war dragged on, Glenn found himself more and more involved with smuggling English journalists, army officers, and curious visitors across the lines. It was dangerous and exacting work, often complicated by the eccentricities of his clients. An English officer, who had fought a hundred duels in his days at Heidelberg, was determined to go on a cavalry raid with J. E. B. Stuart. He insisted on taking his elaborate hussar's uniform and cumbersome saber with him. When he reached Richmond and appeared one day in his uniform, the attention it attracted was so great that he was forced to abandon his getup.

Finally, there was that most obscure and least recorded segment of the South—the so-called poor whites. There had been tension from the first between the hot-blooded gentlemen, so eager for war, and their less prosperous neighbors, the sandhill tackeys, as Mary Chesnut called them, adding shrewdly that "those fastidious ones" did not seem "very anxious to fight for anything, or in any way," saying "this was a rich man's war," and "the rich men would be the officers and have an easy time and the poor ones would be privates." Camden, South Carolina, was the site of the other Chesnut plantation. There, Mary Chesnut wrote, "The up-country men were Union men generally, and the low-country seceders. The former growl; they never liked these aristocratic boroughs and parishes; they had themselves a good and prosperous country, a good constitution, and were satisfied. But they had to go—to leave all and fight for the others who brought on all the trouble, and who did not show much disposition to fight for themselves." Kate Stone made much the same observation in Louisiana. Few overseers or lower-class whites hurried to enlist. She noted that they were disposed to let the rich men fight their own battles—"they will stay at home."

The poor whites covered, as we have noted earlier, an astonishingly wide spectrum of human types. Captain Charles Francis Adams described the poor whites of Virginia as permeated "with a sense of hopeless decadence, a spiritless decay both of land and people, such as I never experienced before. The very dogs are curs and the women and children, with their long, blowsy, uncombed hair, seem the proper inmates of the dilapidated log cabins which they hold in common with the long-nosed, lank Virginia swine." By contrast it seemed to John Beatty that the mountains of western Virginia bred a strange, hardy, independent type. Like the country itself, the people were "unpolished, rugged and uneven, capable of the noblest heroism or the most infernal villainy—their lives full of lights and shadows, elevations and depressions." Beatty reported a conversation between a Union soldier and a group of mountain folk, standing by the roadside: "Is these uns Yankees?" "Yes, madam, regular blue-bellied Yankees." "We never seed any you uns before." "Well, keep a sharp lookout and you'll see they all have horns on."

At Chattanooga, Schurz saw Southern "hillbillies" for the first time. Near his encampment he came on a farmhouse occupied by a middle-aged man, his wife, and a flock of children. Although not poor, they lived in a cabin through which the wind blew. "The art of reading and writing was unknown. . . . The children were dirty, ragged, and, of course, bare-footed, sharing the freedom of the house with dogs and domestic animals. . . . The farmer," Schurz noted, "seemed to be a good-natured person, but my conversations with him disclosed an almost incredible depth of ignorance. Of the country in which we lived he had only a vague and nebulous conception." When he asked where all the soldiers came from and Schurz replied by naming such states as New York, Pennsylvania, and Illinois, the farmer confessed that he had heard only of New York. At another cabin Schurz found a pleasant woman, mother of thirteen children, who asserted without embarrassment that she was not married and never had been. Schurz found other farmers "quite illiterate, but intellectually far more advanced and more conversant with the moralities of civilized society. . . . What surprised me most," he added, "was that such people were mostly of pure Anglo-Saxon stock . . . very clearly demonstrating that the element of race is by no means the only one determining the progressive capacities or tendencies of a population, but that even the most vigorous races may succumb in their development to the disfavor of surrounding circumstances."

Large numbers of rebel deserters came into the Union lines. Often, when Schurz arose in the morning, the area outside his tent was jammed with a dense crowd. "They were a sorry lot," he wrote, "ragged, dirty, and emaciated." Most were ravenously hungry and insisted on "taking the oath," the oath of allegiance to the Union. That act, they were convinced, would release food to them. "Among those with whom I talked," Schurz wrote, "I found some who were not without a certain kind of rustic mother-wit. But the ignorance of most of them was beyond belief. There we saw the 'Southern poor white' in his typical complexion." The deserters "had but a very dim conception, if any conception at all, of what all this fighting and bloodshed was about. They had been induced, or been forced, to join the army by those whom they had been accustomed to look upon as their superiors. They had only an indistinct feeling that on the part of the South the war had not been undertaken and was not carried on for their benefit." Many expressed the conviction that "It is the rich man's war and the poor man's fight." Despite such sentiments, they made excellent soldiers. As Schurz put it, "They suffered hunger and all sorts of privations with heroic endurance. They executed marches of almost incredible length and difficulty, and bore all kinds of fatigue without much complaint. And they were good, steady fighters, too, and many of them good marksmen, having been 'handy' with the rifle or shotgun from their childhood up."

Beatty, campaigning in western Virginia, noted that "all avowed secessionists have run away," but a member of the Virginia legislature who professed strong Unionist sympathies declared he did "not relish the idea of Ohio troops coming upon Virginia soil to fight Virginians." Several days later Beatty noted: "The people here have been grossly deceived by their political leaders. They have been made to believe that Lincoln was elected for the sole purpose of liberating the negro; that our army is marching into Virginia to free their slaves, destroy their property, and murder their families; that we, not they, have set the Constitution and the laws, at defiance, and that in resisting us they are simply defending their homes and fighting for their constitutional rights."

The same conditions seemed to obtain through most of the South—the mountain or "hill" men, illiterate though they might be, were hardy, tough, and independent; the eastern flatland sandhill poor whites often conveyed an impression of listless improvidence. Yet all of them had a certain air about them. John Hay found the Southern prisoners at Point Lookout a carefree lot, "dirty, ragged, yet jolly." Great traders and gamblers, they traded every object they could get their hands on—an onion for a piece of coal, for instance—and sold their names and their places in the mess line or on the sick list as well as on the prisoner-exchange roster. They were contained in a thirty-acre lot around which they had put up a fence "with great glee, saying, 'they would fence out all the d——d Yankees and keep respectable.'"

Historians have puzzled over why nonslaveholding white farmers consented to fight for a slaveholding aristocracy in which they had no stake. Such a question presumes in the first place that soldiers in any war make a shrewd assessment of their self-interest before taking up their rifles. Beyond that, there was the fact that Northerners, or Yankees, had been denounced as hostile to the South and its ideals for several generations. Most white Southerners of every class had been reared with a hearty dislike for Yankees, who were most commonly depicted as a sordid, moneygrubbing lot, determined to rob Southerners of their property. The Yankees were thought to be abolitionists and "nigger lovers," bent on inciting blacks to murder white men and especially white women in their beds.

Southern whites were connected to each other by an intricate web of personal ties. Pap Armistead, a dirt farmer with one amiable slave, might be the cousin of Worthington Armistead, master of a vast plantation. Every plantation owner was part of a circle of congenial whites who, whatever their economic status, indulged in the same sports—hunted coon together, raced horses, and fought cocks. By the code of personal loyalty adhered to in the South, a man's concerns were his friends' concerns. Beyond that, secession was represented in the South as something forced on Southerners by Northern intransigence. It was no more than an effort to achieve independence from the greedy capitalists of the North, much as the American colonists had sought independence from the exaction of Parliament and the merchants whose interests Parliament represented. It was, after all, the North that was invading the South; the North that was acting aggressively and intruding on Southern territory. We hear a lot today about "territoriality." The defense of one's own territory, we are solemnly assured by sociobiologists, is the basic instinct of living creatures. The great majority of Southern whites, slaveholders and nonslaveholders alike, believed that they were exercising their right to secede from the Union, a right which no less a figure than Thomas Jefferson had assured them was guaranteed by the Constitution, and defending home and hearth against an intruder who wished to reduce the South to a condition of hopeless dependence and subordination. It was the pride of the South that no such bitter class divisions existed there as in the industrial cities of the North. Indeed, if you had asked a poor white Southern farmer, "Why are you fighting to preserve a system that exploits you?" he would hardly have understood the question. To him there was a far greater commonality of economic interest (not to mention horseracing, cockfighting, etc.) among white Southerners than among the capitalists and workers of the North. There was some truth in the proposition. What bound the North together was simply an idea, the idea of "Union," an idea that had become as powerful a motivating force as the Southern desire for "independence" and the preservation of its social institutions. The poor white, who, by and large, hated blacks, certainly had no interest in seeing them set free to compete on the labor market.

In the last analysis, most of the nonplanters of the South fought because they were forced to, and they fought well because that was their nature. Yet they also deserted in great numbers. Southern deserters were of two varieties: those who deserted to the Union armies and "stragglers" who simply slipped away and returned home or went west. John Beatty wrote as early as July, 1863: "Hundreds, perhaps thousands, of Tennesseans have deserted the Southern army and are now wandering about in the mountains, and endeavoring to get to their homes. They are mostly conscripted men . . . the mountains and coves in this vicinity are said to be full of them."

Deserters from the army became a common sight on the streets of Washington, herded along by a few guards. By early 1864 Southern desertions had reached almost 10,000 a month. The stragglers, by contrast, formed themselves into guerrilla bands that preyed on Southern civilians and Union armies and cut down soldiers who strayed from their units. In western Virginia, where Union feeling predominated, the secessionists took to the woods. Near John Beatty's camp a man, evidently a Union sympathizer, was found by a patrol with his head cut off and his entrails ripped out. There was a kind of vicious, impersonal violence in the irregular warfare between the guerrillas and the soldiers who encountered each other. Beatty recalled that a soldier doing guard duty came on two "Secessionists . . . just sitting down to breakfast," killed them, and then ate their breakfast.

Rhetoric about Southern solidarity has tended to obscure the fact that conscription existed in every Southern state from the spring of 1862, that tens of thousands of Southern men had to be forced to take up arms, and that desertion was a constant and critical problem in the Confederate army. Southern deserters came into Grant's lines by the dozens and sometimes by the hundreds. "All tell the same story," George Templeton Strong wrote, "of compulsory service, hardships, failure of pay and clothing and of rations, and of general despondency. The Confederacy has 'gone up,' they say. 'We all know it, and we know it is useless to fight any longer.'" Many reported that there existed in the rebel army secret societies "whose object was the promotion of desertion. Eleven men from one company arrived yesterday," Beatty wrote, and a rebel officer swam the river and gave himself up.

The Confederate army lost more men from desertions than its Union counterpart, in part because a far higher percentage of the rebel forces were drafted and in part because of the soldiers' proximity to home. The civilian population, it may be said, suffered from their depredations only less than from the Union army itself. At the plantation of Mary Chesnut's parents in Alabama, bushwhackers terrorized her sister Kate. They tried to pour brandy down her throat, and when her maids tried to protect her, they knocked one down with a pistol butt and struck the other a brutal blow.

The entire South suffered beyond the telling of it. Out of that suffering, Southerners fashioned the myth of the "Lost Cause," weaving an intricate web of fact and fancy into a legend of remarkable durability.

22

The War and the Slaves

At the center of everything, of course, was the change produced in the relationship between masters and mistresses and slaves by the simple fact of the war itself, by word of the Emancipation Proclamation, and, most dramatically, by the appearance or simply the proximity of Union soldiers.

For slaves and mistresses alike (most masters were off with the Confederate armies) the war imposed new and unimagined stresses. A few weeks after the fall of Sumter, Mary Chesnut "saw for the first time the demoralization produced by hopes of freedom." Her mother's butler, Lawrence, whom Mary had taught to read when she was a child, avoided speaking to the white members of the family. "He was as efficient as ever in his proper place," she wrote, "but he did not come behind the scenes as usual and have a friendly chat. He held himself aloof so grand and stately we had to send him a 'tip' through his wife." Her mother's maid, Hetty, showed no signs of disaffection. Indeed, as though to make amends for Lawrence's aloofness, she took special pains with Mary's breakfast tray, and when Mary complimented her, "she curtesied to the ground. 'I cooked every mouthful on that tray—as if I did not know what you liked to eat since you was a baby,' "—words supplemented by "a good hug." Trying to fathom the thoughts of the legions of slaves who swarmed everywhere, Mary Chesnut wrote, "It all amazes me. I am always studying these creatures. They are to me inscrutable in their way and past finding out."

Later, in a rented house in Columbia, Mary Chesnut was once more aware of the subtle changes in slave attitudes. When Mary and her husband were at home, her maid, Molly, and her husband's servant, young Lawrence, went about the house "quiet as mice." But when the master and mistress were away, Mrs. Chesnut discovered, "they sang, laughed, shouted, and danced." If the Chesnuts' landlady appeared, Lawrence kept his seat and his hat on. "Lawrence sits at our door, sleepy and respectful, and profoundly indifferent," Mary Chesnut noted. "So are they all, but they carry it too far. You could not tell that they even heard the awful roar going on in the bay [the cannonading of Charleston] though it has been dinning in their ears night and day. People talk before them as if they were chairs and tables. They make no sign. Are they stolidly stupid? or wiser than we are; silent and strong, biding their time?"

At a family plantation near Richmond, Mary Chesnut calculated there were "sixty or seventy people kept . . . to wait upon this household, two-thirds of them too old or too young to be of any use, but families remain intact." She added: "Yesterday some of the negro men on the plantation were found with pistols. I have never before seen aught about any negro to show that they knew we had a war on hand in which they have any interest."

The change in slave attitudes was often registered in infinitely subtle ways. Booker T. Washington recalled that singing "was bolder, had more ring, and lasted later into the night. . . . Now [the slaves] gradually threw off the mask and were not afraid to let it be known that the 'freedom' in their songs meant freedom of the body in this world." What disconcerted their mistresses was that however desperate the situation appeared to be—Yankee soldiers or bushwhackers in the vicinity, food supplies low, or cattle run off—the slaves were determined to observe their traditional celebrations. Catherine Broun, horrified by the word that Sherman's army had burned a nearby town, watched while the plantation slaves engaged in their customary Christmas festivities. "I hear now the sounds of fiddle, tambourine and 'bones' mingled with the shuffling and pounding of feet," she wrote in her diary. "They are having a merry time, thoughtless creatures, they think not of the morrow." On the Stones' plantation at Brokenburn pilfering increased, and the overseer found a barrel of pork in the cornfield, its top knocked off and the meat gone. The plantation storehouse was moved to a safer location, and more locks were added.

In the occupied areas of the South, Northern missionaries and Yankee soldiers found the relationships between Southern whites and their household slaves infinitely mysterious. The Chase sisters, Sarah and Lucy, told the story of Ary, a handsome mulatto contraband, who declared, "Young Master was the father of my baby, and he was very fond of it. He made me dress it clean, three times a day, and he was never tired of playing with it and calling it pet names." The father of Ary's baby was a strong Union man and an enemy of slavery, although he was the son of one of the wealthiest planters in Virginia. When the war came, the "young master" was drafted and taken off in chains. He wrote to Ary, and a young white woman who was in love with his brother was commissioned to read her his letters. "Did your master's sisters know how intimate you were with him?" a startled Lucy Chase asked. "Oh, yes, indeed, and they were all as fond of me as he was, and of the baby too. The baby was very white, and looked just like him."

Startling intimacy and vast distance! When Sarah Morgan was short on bedding in her flight from one uneasy resting place to another, she noted in her diary that she had shared her blankets with her slave girl, Tiche, "thus," she wrote, "(tell it not in Yankeeland, for it will never be credited) actually sleeping under the same bedclothes with our black, shiny negro nurse!"

Elizabeth Meriwether's maid, Evelyn, devoted to "trabblin'" and distressed that her mistress did not plan to take her to Memphis with her, tried to set the family mansion on fire. When charged with the deed, she cheerfully confessed, explaining, "Miss Betty, she dun tell me ef she wuz ter go ter town ter bode in a boden house she'd keep me 'caze I kin dribe de kerredge as well as sew. And Marse Minor, hit's powerful lonesome out here so far frum town. I lubs ter see de folks on de streets en I lubs ter walk 'long en see deir fine close. . . ." Minor asked incredulously: "And you were willing to burn me up, and burn Miss Betty up, just to get a chance to live in town?" Evelyn protested that she intended to wake both Minor and his wife long before they would be in danger. "I wouldn't a burnt you an' Miss Betty not fer nuffin' in de world, caze I jes lubs Miss Betty an' I lubs you too, Marse Minor!"

Everywhere the news of the slaves' imminent liberation disturbed the course of plantation life. Wilbur Shields, the manager of several Louisiana plantations, found it increasingly difficult to control the behavior of his slaves. He wrote one slaveowner "that but very very few are faithful—Some of those who remain are worse than those who have gone . . . they will not even gather food for themselves." Shields estimated that of 146 slaves under his direction, only 16 had been "perfectly faithful" and 100 had "behaved *badly;* many of them outrageously." At another Louisiana plantation the slaves who did not flee with the Yankees, the overseer reported, "remained at home to do *much worse.*" They killed much of the livestock on this and adjacent plantations and pillaged the plantation storerooms. "They deserve to be half starved and to be worked nearly to death for the way they have acted. . . . The recent trying scenes through which we have passed have convinced me that *no dependence is to be placed on the negro*—and that they are the greatest hypocrites and liars that God ever made." The differences in the reactions of slaves were often sectional. In Mississippi and Louisiana, for example, large plantations run by overseers or managers were the norm, and on these slaves felt few pulls of loyalty for an absent master or for the overseer, whom they usually feared but scorned.

Despite the tradition in the Colcock Jones family of kindly concern for their slaves, the younger Jones recommended "terrible corporal punishment, accompanied with close and protracted confinement in the county jail, or public punishment followed by banishment from the county and sale in some distant part of the country," for any slaves who attempted to flee to the enemy. "If allowed to desert," he wrote his father, "our entire social system will be upset. . . ." He was convinced that the Lincolnites intended to help pay for the costs of the war by "stealing and reselling" escaped slaves.

One former slave recalled her master's telling his slaves that the Yankees would never free them, "'cause I gwine free you befo' dat. . . ." At the approach of the Yankees he warned, "I gwine line you up on de bank of Bois D'Arc Creek and free you wid my shotgun. Anybody miss jes one lick wid de hoe . . . or one clap of dat bell, or one toot of de horn, and he gwine be free and talking to de debil lon befo' he ever see a pair of blue britches!"

A Southern regiment—Rutledge's Mounted Rifles—on a raid into a Yankee-held region on the coast was delighted to find the blacks "in such a friendly state of mind," but one servant whispered to an officer, "Don't you mind 'em, don't trust 'em." Later the Southern officer dressed himself in a Union uniform and visited the Negro quarter. The first words he heard were: "Ki! massa, you come fuh ketch rebels. We kin show you way you kin ketch thirty to-night." Southern soldiers often tried to identify slaves disposed to disloyalty by posing as Yankee soldiers. Sarah Debro, a slave, recalled, "Dey acs de nigahs if dey want to be free. If dey say yes, den dey shot dem down, but if they say no dey let dem alone. Dey took three of my uncles out in de woods an' shot dey faces off."

The provost marshal of Adams County, Mississippi, wrote the governor in July, 1862: "There is a great disposition among the Negroes to be insubordinate and to run away and go to the federals. Within the last 12 months we have had to hang some 40 for plotting an insurrection, and there has been about that number put in irons."

Often the instinct of household slaves was to protect a master or mistress to whom they were devoted. When Charley Bryant, a Texas planter, rushed for his gun on hearing of the approach of Yankee soldiers, one of his slaves disarmed him and locked him in the smokehouse to keep him from getting himself killed. "Old massa know dat," an ex-slave recalled, "but he beat on de door an yell, but it ain't git open till dem Yankees done gone."

Lorenza Bell, a slave in the Lipscomb family of South Carolina, recalled: "All my four young massas go to de war, all but Elias. He too old. Smith he kilt at Manassas Junction. Nathan he git he finger shot at the first round at Fort Sumter. But when Billy was wounded at Howard Gap . . . and dey brung him home with he jaw split open, I so mad I could have kilt all de Yankees. I say I be happy iffen I could kill me jes' one Yankee. I hated dem 'cause dey hurt my white people."

Some slaves, like Sara Brown, insisted that they had been free all the time. "Who says I'se free?" she asked defiantly. "I warn't neber no slabe. I libed with qual'ty an' was one ob de fambly. Take dis bandanna off? No, 'deedy! dats the las' semblance I'se got of de good ole times." Another old slave declared, "Missis belonged to him, & he belonged to Missis, & he was not going to leave her . . . he was going to die on this place, & he was not going to do any work either except make a dollar a week." When James Chesnut returned to Mulberry Hill, he was delighted with the effusive expressions of loyalty given him by the slaves there, by their "affection and their faithfulness."

Yet a Georgia "mammy," who told a Union officer that she had suckled all her mistress's children, approved when the soldiers talked of burning down the plantation house, declaring it "ought to be burned, cause there has been so much devilment here, whipping niggers most to dath to make 'em work to pay for it." The behavior of freed slaves toward Southern whites varied greatly, usually in terms of the kindness or cruelty of the master toward slaves. When black soldiers landed near Jamestown, Virginia, two slave women bearing the scars of a recently administered whipping came into their encampment. On a foraging party the soldiers turned up the perpetrator, a man named Clayton. Clayton was tied to a tree and given twenty lashes by one of his former slaves, who was glad to "bring the blood from his loins at every stroke and not forgetting to remind the gentleman of days gone by." The women took their turns next, "to remind him that they were no longer his, but safely housed in Abraham's bosom, and under the protection of the Star-Spangled Banner, and guarded by their own patriotic, though once down-trodden race." The black sergeant, George Hatton, who reported the episode added, "The day is clear, the fields of grain are beautiful, and the birds are singing sweet, melodious songs, while poor Mr. C. is crying to his servants for mercy."

When Margaret Hughes, a young South Carolina slave, heard that the Yankees were coming, she fled to her aunt, who startled her by saying, "Child, we are going to have such a good time a settin' at de white folks' table, a eating off de white folks' table, and a rocking in de big rocking chair."

The most significant index to slave attitudes was to be found in those who escaped, some of whom were killed in the attempt. In Louisiana the war was only a few months old when slaves began to run off. The Stones were sitting on the front porch of Brokenburn on a mild June evening when they heard shouts and running feet. It was a runaway slave. Kate Stone's brothers gave chase, but he escaped. "The runaways are numerous and bold," she wrote. Rumors that a general uprising was being planned were everywhere. "We live on a mine," she added. Even the house servants gave trouble. They were conspicuously lazy and disobedient. Their punishment was exile from the house and a sentence of "going to the field."

Kate Stone noted in a diary entry of June 30, 1862: "The Yankees have taken Negroes off all the places below Omega, the Negroes generally going most willingly, being promised their freedom by the vandals. The officers coolly go on the places, take the plantation books, and call off the names of all the men they want, carrying them off from their masters without a word of apology. They laugh at the idea of payment and say of course they will never send them back." Mrs. Stone was determined to send her slaves off to some safe place, but they in turn were reluctant to go. Moreover, there were fears that if the Yankees arrived and found the slaves gone, they would revenge themselves by burning the buildings on the plantations. "Generally when told to run away from the soldiers, they go right to them, and I cannot say I blame them," Kate Stone wrote. A few days later she wrote again: "Still trouble with the house servants. Aunt Lucy, the head of them all, ran away this morning but was back by dinner. Mamma did not have her punished. All of them are demoralized. . . ."

There were great hazards in any attempt to escape. As the war continued and many slaves grew sullen or unruly, their masters in turn often grew more strict in their disciplinary measures, sometimes requiring that all farm implements that could be used as weapons be locked up at night. One slave woman who escaped reported that her master, furious over the escape of some of the slaves, recaptured several "an' hang dem to a tree, an' shoot dem; he t'ink no more 'nto shoot de culled people right down. . . ." Often slaves hid in swamps or dense forests, stealing back to their plantations at night to get food. Some formed colonies, collecting weapons and foraging for food. A scouting party of whites discovered such a camp in a South Carolina swamp, "well provided with meal, cooking utensils, blankets, etc." as well as twelve guns.

A slave woman and her young son, trying to escape across a river, were shot at by the master's son, whom she had nursed as an infant. "My poor baby is shot dead," she said, "by that young massa I nussed with my own boy. . . . Missus made me nuss her baby, an' set her little girl to watch me, for fear I'd give my baby too much, no matter how hard he cried . . . an' now that same boy has killed mine."

Many slaves who made their way to the Yankees subsequently showed them where silver and valuables had been hidden on their home plantations. Maids dressed themselves in their mistresses' gowns and walked off defiantly. One of the Maury maids, who had "absquated" with the Yankees, returned two days later, announcing, "I'se gwine home, I is! I'se seen 'nuff of the yankees I is. Old missus is good enuf fo' me." Such a story would be preserved in a white family for generations as an example of the affectionate relationships between slaves and their owners.

On the rice plantation of Louis Manigault near Savannah, the slaves showed a disposition to decamp despite threats of the consequences if they were recaptured. Jack Savage was described by Manigault as "the worse Negro I have ever known. I have for two years past looked upon him as capable of committing murder or burning down this dwelling, or doing any act." Savage was one of the first to leave, living in a swamp and stealing livestock from neighboring plantations. Manigault was rather relieved at the defection. But Hector, "always spoiled both by my Father and Myself, greatly indulged," was another matter. He was openly rebellious, "only one of the numerous instances of ingratitude evinced in the African character," Manigault wrote. "This war has taught us the perfect impossibility of placing the least confidence in any Negro. In too numerous instances those we esteemed the most have been the first to desert us!"—a marvelously unself-conscious comment!

Fire was the slaves' classic weapon. For those who planned an escape, setting a fire was a way to distract the attention of possible pursuers. For bolder spirits with a grievance it was a form of revenge. Aware of this, whites often attributed to mutinous blacks fires which had different origins. Thus, blacks often got "credit" for fires with which they had nothing to do, and white paranoia was substantially increased. Mary Chesnut wrote in Columbia in March, 1862: "Last night a house was set on fire; last week two houses. 'The red cock crows in the barn!' Our troubles thicken, indeed, when treachery comes from that dark quarter."

The appearance of Yankee soldiers was often an ambiguous event for slaves. A slave who lived on an Arkansas plantation recalled after the war that a band of Yankee soldiers had appeared and made themselves very much at home, "killed hogs and cooked them. Killed cows and cooked them. Took all kinds of sugar and preserves and things like that. Tore all the feathers out of the mattress looking for money. Then they put Old Miss and her daughter in the kitchen to cooking. Ma got scared and went to bed. Directly the lieutenant come on down there and said, 'Auntie, get up from there. We ain't a-going to do you no hurt. We're after helping you. We are freeing you. Aunt Dinah, you can do as you please now. You're free.' She was free! They stayed round there all night cooking and eating and carrying on. They sent some of the meat in there to us colored folks." But the Yankees had hardly departed before the "secesh folks"—the Southerners —were back. "One night there'd be a gang of Secesh, and the next one, there'd come along a gang of Yankees. Pa was 'fraid of both of 'em. Secesh said they'd kill him if he left his white folks. Yankees said they'd kill him if he didn't leave 'em. He would hide out in the cotton patch and keep we children out there with him."

"This country is in a deplorable state," Kate Stone wrote in March, 1863. "The outrages of the Yankees and the Negroes are enough to frighten one to death. The sword of Damocles in a hundred forms is suspended over us, and there is no escape." A number of blacks had brought wagons and soldiers to the plantations from which they fled and carried off "every portable thing—furniture, provisions, etc., etc."

Mary Jones noted in her journal that the condition of the slaves was "one of perfect anarchy and rebellion. They have placed themselves in perfect antagonism to their owners and to all government and control. We dare not predict the end of all this, if the Lord in mercy does not restrain the hearts and wills of this deluded people. . . . What we are to do becomes daily more and more perplexing. . . . Wherever owners have gone away, the Negroes have taken away all furniture, bedding, and household articles."

Before the Stone family left Brokenburn, a party of armed blacks appeared and ranged through the house, "cursing and laughing, and breaking things open." Kate and her sisters and brothers had taken refuge in one of the upstairs rooms, but the men broke in, went through the bureau drawers and wardrobes, taking what they fancied. Then one came over to Kate and stood on the hem of her dress, snapping his pistol as though he intended to shoot her. When the members of the family went downstairs, they found the house filled with strange blacks, who said nothing, "but," recalled Kate Stone, "they looked at us and grinned and that terrified us more and more. It held such a promise of evil." The next day Mrs. Stone decided to move what she could of her family, possessions, and slaves to Texas. The silver was packed in a barrel and buried in the yard when all the slaves were in their cabins. The old and sickly house servants would be left behind. The flight was complicated by the reluctance of many of the blacks to leave. A planter named Scott living near Brokenburn got up one morning to find "every Negro gone, about seventy-five, only three little girls left. The ladies actually had to get up and get breakfast. . . . Keene Richards has lost 160 from Transylvania and fifty of them are reported dead," Kate Stone wrote. There were only twenty blacks left on Mrs. Tibbetts's five plantations. "The ladies are cooking, washing, etc., while Hiram Tibbetts is wood chopper," Kate Stone noted.

While Kate, her mother, and the rest of the family waited at Fortress Monroe, Kate's brother, sixteen-year-old Jimmy, and some white men stole back to Brokenburn to spy out the lay of the land and try to bring off any remaining blacks. The raiders caught the slaves by surprise and rounded up ten, bringing them back to Monroe to complete the last leg of the trip to Texas. Those blacks who escaped the raid made themselves at home in the big house. A friend who later visited the plantation reported that he never saw so many good things to eat, "barrels of milk, jars of delicious pinkish cream, roll after roll of creamy yellow butter, a yard alive with poultry, and hams and fresh meat just killed. . . . He says," Kate Stone noted in her diary, "they would have been foolish Negroes to run off from a place like that. William and his family were occupying Mamma's room, completely furnished as we left it, and all our other possessions had been divided up among the Negroes."

Many slaves were forced by the Union army officers to work on the plantations on which they had been slaves and for wages far lower than those paid whites for comparable labor. In some instances they were not paid at all, and not a few suffered more from hunger as freedmen than they ever had as slaves. Many of the contraband camps were scenes of "misery and wretchedness." When the government began leasing plantations to individuals, typically Northerners, who contract-ed to work them with free black labor, strict rules were written into the contracts to protect the free blacks, but they were often disregarded. A government inspector who visited a number of leased plantations reported: "The poor negroes are everywhere greatly depressed at their condition. They all testify that if they were only paid their little wages as they earn them, so that they could purchase clothing, and were furnished with the provisions promised they could stand it; but to work and get poorly paid, poorly fed, and not doctored when sick, is more than they can endure." They complained that "they are taken and hired out to men who treat them, so far as providing for them is concerned, far worse than their 'secesh' masters did. . . ."

The report of the American Freedmen's Commission noted that most of the lessees were men devoid of "either loyalty or humanity . . . adventurers, camp followers, 'army sharks,' as they are termed, who have turned aside from what they consider their legitimate prey, the poor soldier, to gather the riches of the land which his prowess has laid open to them. . . ." On ninety-five plantations, taking in 45,745 acres and employing 8,588 freedmen, some 4,800 bales of cotton had been produced. Some land had been leased in small plots to ex-slaves. "There are many instances," a government inspector wrote, "in which a family contrives to get a good support from five acres, farmed with the hoe alone. Many of these add to their resources by cutting wood. . . . One old man I found who had himself, with his hoe only, made ten acres of corn, on land newly cleared. . . . He ought to have the land," the inspector continued. "There is no reason why, under supervision, this whole bend . . . may not be successfully tilled by the blacks in such a way as to remove the support of the people entirely from the shoulders of the Government. . . ."

When General Banks succeeded Butler as commander of the Department of the Gulf, which took in much of Louisiana, large numbers of ex-slaves were living in squalid camps on army half rations. It seemed to Banks that the important thing was to get them to work. Planters who took the oath of allegiance to the United States were permitted to continue to operate their plantations, and the ex-slaves were encouraged to work for their old masters for pay. Workers were to be given "just treatment, healthy rations, comfortable clothing, quarters, fuel, medical attendance, and instruction for children." On the other hand, they could not leave their plantations without passes, and provost marshals were assigned to see that the blacks provided "continuous and faithful service" and showed "respectful deportment, correct discipline and perfect subordination." It was small wonder many freedmen and women wondered whether slavery had been reinstituted under the auspices of the United States Army. Frederick Douglass declared that Banks's policy "practically enslaves the negro, and makes the Proclamation of 1863 a mockery and a delusion." The New Orleans Tribune, like L'Union a bilingual newspaper, noted that virtually all the prohibitions that had been imposed on the slave were "also enforced against the freedman." In March, 1865, a black officer in the Union army named J. H. Ingraham told the Louisiana Equal Rights League, "I recently visited the parishes for the express purpose of inquiring about that system of 'free labor.' Hundreds of people assured me that the laborers were [worse] off under that new system, than they were under the old one."

Banks did encourage the establishment of schools. By the fall of 1864 there were seventy-eight schools with 125 teachers and almost 800 pupils. In the words of the New Orleans Tribune, "there are numerous difficulties to surmount, including racial prejudice." In addition to teachers from the North, "white women of noble heart in New Orleans put themselves swiftly to the task" of educating the black children of the city "and have continued courageously in the face of calumnies, mockeries, and social persecution." Of the teachers 100 were Southern women, and 75 were from Louisiana.

Thomas Callahan, a Presbyterian missionary laboring among the freedmen of Louisiana, wrote a Northern friend in 1863: "You have no idea of the state of things here. Go out in any direction and you meet negroes on horses, negroes on mules, negroes with oxen, negroes by the wagon, cart and buggy load, negroes on foot, men, women and children; negroes in uniform, negroes in rags, negroes in frame houses, negroes living in tents, negroes living in rail pens covered with brush, and negroes living under brush piles without any rails; negroes living on the bare ground with the sky for their covering; all hopeful, almost all cheerful, every one pleading to be taught, willing to do anything for learning. They are never out of our rooms, and their cry is for 'Books! Books!' and 'when will school begin?' Negro women come and offer to cook and wash for us, if we will only teach them to read the Bible. . . . Every night hymns of praise to God and prayers for the Government that oppressed them so long, rise around us on every side—prayers for the white teachers that have already come—prayers that God would send them more."

John Beatty was indignant at the treatment by the Union army of slaves who came into the army camps. "The white rebel," he wrote, "who has done his utmost to bring about the rebellion, is lionized, called a plucky fellow, a great man, while the negro, who welcomes us, who is ready to peril his life to aid us, is kicked, cuffed, and driven back to his master, there to be scourged for kindness to us." Beatty's black orderly told him that a slave had been whipped to death by a planter for giving information to Union intelligence officers. In Huntsville, Alabama, the Union camp had "a superabundance of negroes," in John Beatty's words. One of them was a Georgian who had been in the service of a rebel cavalry officer. "Whither they came to whither they are going," Beatty added, "it is impossible to say. They lie around contentedly and are delighted when we give them an opportunity to serve us. All the colored people of Alabama are anxious to go 'wid yer and wait on you folks.' There are not fifty negroes in the South who would not risk their lives for freedom. The man who affirms that they are contented and happy, and do not desire to escape, is either a falsifier or a fool."

Willis, the black servant of John Beatty, was described by him as "a colored gentleman of much experience and varied accomplishments." He had been a barber on a Mississippi River steamboat and a photographer. He was familiar with much of the South and played a fiddle "with wonderful skill." Hearing him play brought back nostalgic memories to Beatty—the early years of his marriage, when he and his wife were "starting in the world together, when her cheeks were ruddier than now, when wealth and fame and happiness seemed lying just before me, ready to be gathered in. . . ."

Charles Francis Adams, Jr., remarked on the hostility displayed by many of the soldiers toward the freedmen, and a newspaper reporter for the *New York Evening Post* stated that Northern soldiers had displayed "some of the vilest and meanest exhibitions of human depravity that it has ever been my lot to witness. Many, very many of the soldiers and not a few of the officers," he added, "have habitually treated the negroes with the coarsest and most brutal insolence and inhumanity; never speaking to them but to curse and revile them, to say all manner of evil against them, and to threaten . . . them." Charlotte Forten, arriving at Hilton Head in 1862, noted that some of the officers "talked flippantly, and sneeringly of the negroes . . . using an epithet more offensive than gentlemanly." The behavior of the enlisted men was often far more offensive. The soldiers killed cattle, pigs, and chickens, abused black men, and raped black women. It was an unhappy introduction to "freedom."

The Union soldiers in Charleston identified more with the defeated white Southerners than with the ex-slaves. Emma Holmes reported that blacks who broke the law were punished by "gagging, bucking, hanging by the thumb, & shooting—military cruelties, to which whipping is play." When she heard of the abuse of blacks by Union soldiers on the Sea Islands, she wrote: "I have not the slightest doubt their dreadful treatment of the negroes . . . will assuredly strengthen our 'peculiar institution' by teaching them who are their true friends." A Yankee said to Mary Chesnut in Camden, "Why do you shrink from us and avoid us so? We did not come here to fight for negroes; we hate them. At Port Royal I saw a beautiful white woman driving in a wagon with a coal-black negro man. If she had been anything to me I would have shot her through the heart." One indignant slave whose bed had been stolen by a Yankee soldier denounced him bitterly: "Why you nasty, stinkin' rascal. You say you come down here to fight for the niggers, and now you're stealin' from 'em." The soldier replied: "You're a God Damn liar. I'm fightin' for $14 a month and the Union." An enterprising Union officer was charged with gathering a cargo of blacks to sell in Cuba.

Another Northern soldier wrote of a black boy who had attached himself to their regiment: "He is filthy and lazy and seems to know as much as a child of four years and once in a while shows gleams of intelligence beyond his years and condition. He never looks at you when talking, but shifts uneasily from one leg to the other and turns his head from side to side, rolling his eyes and grunting queer laughs. We make all kinds of sport of him."

On the Fourth of July, 1862, deep in Alabama, Union soldiers teased the slaves who hung around their camp by declaring that the day was always marked with Northerners by dining on "roast nigger. It is part of their religion. This is what makes colored folk so scarce in the North." Whereupon the soldiers discussed whether Caesar should be served stuffed or with vegetables.

In Memphis, "Negroes and Germans seemed to accept each other on a basis of perfect equality," Elizabeth Meriwether wrote. "No other white soldier, not even the men from New England, accepted the negroes as their social equals. But the Germans did."

The reaction of Northern soldiers to black women was, not surprisingly, very different from their reaction to the men. A New England soldier in Louisiana wrote his brother: "If I marry at all I believe I'll marry one of these nigger wenches down here. One that the grease runs right off of, one that shines and one that stinks so you can smell her a mile, and then you can have time to get out of the way." And a Massachusetts soldier wrote: "Many of the mongrels are very beautiful with their fine hair, straight or wavy, and their blue or dark eyes, always soft and lustrous and half concealed by the long lashes. They look more like voluptuous Italians than negroes."

Elizabeth Meriwether was indignant at the behavior of her maid, Louise, who, it was reported by her husband, allowed the Yankee soldiers to take liberties with her. "Stead of slappin' deir fool faces," the outraged husband protested, "Louise jes' laughs when dey kisses and hugs her." Mary Chesnut told the story of friends who lived in Montgomery, Alabama, under Union occupation. All their slaves departed except four. These he had given their freedom and employed at "high wages." One day his wife saw some cards on the front-hall table bearing the names of Yankee officers, and when she inquired where they had come from, the maid replied, "Oh, Missis, they come to see me, and I have been waiting to tell you. It is too hard! I cannot do it! I cannot dance with those nice gentlemen at night at our Union Balls and then come here and be your servant the next day.]

can't!" So, one by one, "the faithful few" slipped away, and the family was left to its own devices. "Why not?" Mary Chesnut concluded.

The hope had been that the Emancipation Proclamation would inspire the Southern slaves not necessarily to rise in rebellion but to desert their masters and mistresses in large numbers and to refuse to work any longer on their plantations. In this respect the proclamation proved a disappointment. The great majority of slaves remained on the plantations and farms where most of them had grown up and carried on their accustomed tasks. To understand why this was so, one has to recall the "psychological environment" of the slaves. While many yearned for freedom, they were caught in what we might call a field of force from which it was extremely difficult to extricate themselves. First, there was the general state of dependence and subordination in which they were kept. They were illiterate, and their knowledge of the world, and indeed the terrain beyond the limits of their own plantations, was limited or virtually nonexistent; they were accustomed to looking to their masters for the most basic requirements of life: food, clothing, care in illness—everything that constituted the ground of existence. These needs were supplemented by a more complex state of emotional dependency. I have described the relationship between masters and slaves as a classic love-hate relationship. The white master and, perhaps even more commonly, his wife were an "object of love" for many of the blacks on the plantation. Ambiguous as this emotion undoubtedly was, it was nonetheless real. The white masters and mistresses in turn affirmed that they "loved" their black charges, and it is clear that they often behaved as though they did, so that we have no substantial grounds on which to disclaim this "love," hypocritical as it may appear to the modern reader. The instances that might be cited in support of this contention are legion. Furthermore, the "servile mentality" that we have spoken of was distinguished by an assumption on the part of the slave that the white man was his superior in every respect, knew infinitely more, and, most important, could command far more "power" than he. Indeed, the essence of the slave's situation was that he was completely powerless. Only the arts of ingratiation and manipulation could lighten his burden. Most slaves had no skills, no trade or facility other than with a hoe or some crude agricultural implement, to offer on an uncertain labor market. And to whom, in any case, would they offer it? To leave their master's plantation was to face unimaginable difficulties and hazards, to risk severe punishment and perhaps their lives, to leave everything certain and familiar for the uncertain and the unfamiliar, to tear apart the tissue of relationships, slave to slave and slave to white, that made up the complex plantation world. It has been estimated that by the end of the war more than 500,000 slaves had sought refuge behind the Union lines, but the great majority of these were slaves who had already been drafted for tasks in support of Confederate military installations or operations. Thus, the first and most difficult step had already been taken—separation from the home plantation, from master, and from black friends and relatives. The second step was comparatively easy —to flee, at the first opportunity, to new masters, under whom they would be "free." Thus, every Union army that penetrated into the South immediately acquired a host of slaves who attached themselves to the troops with a cheerful and wholly improvident determination that was often the despair of commanding officers already driven to the limit of their resources in providing food and supplies for their own soldiers.

When General Godfrey Weitzel occupied southern Louisiana in October, 1862, he wrote to army headquarters: "You can form no idea of the vicinity of my camp, nor can you form an idea of the appearance of my brigade as it marched down the bayou. My train was larger than an army train for 25,000 men. Every soldier had a negro marching in the flanks, carrying his knapsack. Plantation carts, filled with negro women and children, with their effects; and of course compelled to pillage for subsistence, as I have no rations to issue them. I have a great many more negroes in my camp now than I have whites."

The attitude of Northern soldiers toward the ex-slaves who gathered about their camps varied primarily according to the section of the country from which the soldiers came. Those from New England, especially from Connecticut and Massachusetts, so long strongholds of antislavery sentiment, were generally kindly and solicitous. One New England soldier wrote home of his first sight of Southern blacks: "I never saw a bunch of them together, but I could pick out an Uncle Tom, a Sambo, a Chloe, an Eliza or any other character in Uncle Tom's Cabin."

Soldiers from such cities as New York and Philadelphia with a long record of working-class hostility toward free blacks were commonly rough and contemptuous, as were those from states, such as Illinois and Indiana, where there was resentment against free blacks and substantial proslavery feeling. A missionary to freedmen at Fortress Monroe, Virginia, wrote of the contrabands there that "there is an irrepressible foreboding which seems to have fixed itself upon the countenance of every one; and not without good cause, for there has been and still is, meanness of every conceivable kind practiced upon them. Officers take advantage of their ignorance in every way possible, and torment them like fiends, while the government retains them on highways and public works, and the quartermaster refuses to pay them."

After the end of the war the Reverend John Jones wrote: "The wave of emancipation coming nearer and nearer, a restlessness was perceived almost universally. Insubordination began to crop out. It was reported at Albany [Georgia]; and two Federals, in blue uniforms and armed, came out, visited the said places, and whipped every Negro man reported to them, and in some cases unmercifully. . . . Another party visited Colquitt [Georgia] . . . and punished by suspending by the thumbs. The effect has been a remarkable quietude and order to all this region. The Negroes are astounded at the idea of being whipped by Yankees. (But keep this all a secret," the Reverend Jones added to his correspondent, "lest we be deprived of their [the Yankee soldiers'] services.)"

Kentucky soldiers had little sympathy with the freedmen, but when they were replaced, at Albany, Georgia, by Illinois troops, "there went abroad," the Reverend John Jones wrote his sister, "a rumor that the true Yankee, the deliverer of the Negro, had come. And immediately commenced an exodus of hundreds into Albany—a stream which has scarcely been stopped. . . ." Refuge, the Joneses' plantation, had lost nine blacks, including a sixteen-year-old girl who had been whipped for being out late Saturday night and "somewhat bruised by the strap." In Albany she exhibited to the Union officers there the marks of the whip. "My heart pities them," Jones concluded, "for I know they will miss their home." Runaway blacks laden with the belongings of their former masters and mistresses often sold their loot to poor whites, "crackers" in Georgia, "sandhill tackeys" in South Carolina. Many a poor white shanty came to boast a handsome bed or chair or rug or mirror.

There was further evidence of the desire of Southern slaves to hasten their day of freedom in the numerous incidents in which they brought valuable information on Confederate troop movements or hidden routes of advance to Union generals. An anonymous black, for example, told Grant where he could most safely land his troops below Vicksburg.

Ted Upson, the young soldier who enlisted in the 100th Indiana Regiment, was placed on detached duty as a scout under the command of Henry Hall, a friend from Lima. Hall, Upson noted, got much information from slaves; "they seem to know everything and are pretty shrewd too," he added. "One of them told us where two field guns were hid."

One of the most successful gatherers of intelligence was a freedman named John Scobell. Allan Pinkerton, chief of the United States Secret Service, described him as a man as "full of music as the feathered songsters. . . . In addition to what seemed an almost inexhaustible stock of negro plantation melodies he had also a charming variety of Scotch ballads, which he sang with a voice of remarkable power and sweetness." Scobell became one of Pinkerton's most trusted agents, ranging far behind Southern lines. Northern prisoners who escaped from their guards were often passed from one black family to another until they were able to reach Union lines.

In their relations with their masters and mistresses and in their contacts with their Northern "deliverers," the black people of the South struggled to understand the nature of their destiny in the new order.

23

For the Public Good

As we have had occasion to note from time to time, Americans had demonstrated from the beginning of the Republic an infatuation with "associational activity"—clubs, orders, societies of every conceivable (and many inconceivable) kinds, partly in an effort to counteract what we have spoken of as the disintegrative effects of American life. They were never so happy as when they could combine associational activity with the improvement of the species or the alleviation of some human ill.

The Civil War witnessed two such enterprises. One, the Sanitary Commission, was a philanthropic venture on an unprecedented scale, designed to augment the inadequate medical services of the United States Army and Navy. The other, the freedmen's associations, were started to assist the contrabands at first and then, after the Emancipation Proclamation, the freed slaves.

George Templeton Strong was one of the founders of the Sanitary Commission, the first chapter of which began business in New York City in the fall of 1861. New York was the staging area and transfer point for troops from all over the Northeast, the Near West, and even California. A regiment made up of ex-Californians living in the East was quartered in a lower story of the building which contained George

Templeton Strong's law offices. He was appalled at the filthy conditions in which the men lived. "I never knew before," he wrote, "what rankness of stench can be emitted by unwashed humanity. . . . It poisons the whole building and, of course, prevails in a concentrated form in the story they occupy, where its absolutely stercoraceous and ammoniacal intensity—nauseous and choking. It half strangles me as I go upstairs." The experience helped strengthen his conviction that the most important single contribution to the Northern war effort would be the introduction of proper sanitary conditions among the troops. Strong was not alone in his concern. In a number of cities and towns, organizations of women had already sprung up spontaneously to make clothing and, above all, to provide care for sick and wounded soldiers. At a meeting at Cooper Union some hundred women social leaders of New York formed the Women's Central Association of Relief. Men followed suit, and a group of doctors founded the Medical Association for Furnishing Hospital Supplies. The problem was that such groups had no official standing. Scattered and hastily organized, they lacked sufficient political weight to achieve any significant reforms in the hopelessly archaic and inefficient Medical Department of the army.

Strong and a number of his friends were convinced that only a national organization, working in conjunction with Lincoln's administration, could have any hope of improving the horrendous conditions in the Medical Department. It was a touchy issue. The surgeon general was incompetent and the army and navy were notoriously resistant to civilian interference in their affairs. Yet the issue was of enormous consequence. Strong and others knowledgeable in matters of sanitation were convinced that the abominable sanitary—or, more accurately, unsanitary—conditions in the camps of volunteers would cause far more deaths from epidemic diseases, particularly typhoid fever, malaria, and cholera, than Confederate bullets would. The problem was to circumvent the secretary of war and win the support of Lincoln. The surest way to the President was through Seward. The problem of proper sanitation among the volunteer units was directly related to the general problem of discipline. The most essential aspect of discipline was cleanliness. In many of the volunteer regiments discipline was conspicuously absent. It recalled the conditions of American soldiers in the Revolutionary War. Then discipline had also been extremely lax, and proper sanitary conditions ignored. It had been Benjamin Rush's great contribution to the cause to institute essential reforms against the bitter resistance of the army's medical chief.

Strong undertook to enlist his friend Francis Lieber, who had emigrated from Germany in 1827, served as professor of political philosophy at South Carolina College, and left the uncongenial political atmosphere of the South in 1856 to take a chair at Columbia, largely through Strong's influence. Lieber had considerable influence with Lincoln as a consequence of his famous work *On Civil Liberty and Self-Government*, published in 1853.

"The old Medical Bureau, was, by the universal consent of all . . ." Strong wrote Lieber, "the most narrow, hidebound, fossilized, red-tape-y of all the departments in Washington." Strong then went on to spell out the demonstrable inability of the Medical Department to care for the wounded after any considerable battle, simply on the basis of its existing table of organization and the resources available to it. The War Department and the Medical Department had demonstrated that they were incapable of dealing with problems of proper medical care in camps *before any fighting had taken place*. It was thus evident that only a large-scale voluntary organization could organize the material and human resources in the form of medical supplies and trained surgeons to deal with the problem.

Strong and his friends decided to call their organization the Sanitary Commission. One of Strong's ablest allies on the commission, besides the indefatigable Frederick Law Olmsted, was Wolcott Gibbs, a professor of chemistry at Columbia. The two men drew up a report containing a number of recommendations for the reform of the volunteer units. They ranged from adequate restrooms at the Washington station for arriving soldiers so that they would not be so disposed to relieve themselves in odd corners about the station to the proposal that soldiers be encouraged to send all or part of their pay home to their families. The thought was that with less money to spend, the volunteers would be unable to engage in excessive drinking and whoring. In addition, the report urged the formation of a corps of military police to help keep soldiers out of saloons and bawdy houses. Fresh vegetables should also be supplied, with competent cooks to prepare them.

The members of the Sanitary Commission had a two-hour audience with Lincoln in October, 1861. "He is lank and hard-featured, among the ugliest white men I have ever seen," Strong wrote. "Decidedly plebeian. Superficially vulgar and a snob. But not essentially. He seems to me clear-headed and sound-hearted, though his laugh is that of a yahoo, with a wrinkling of the nose that suggests affinity with a tapir and other pachyderms; and his grammar is weak." Lincoln charged the commission with "wanting to run the machine"—i.e., the Medical Department and, doubtless, the War Department with it. But he listened on the whole sympathetically to the little company of upper-class Easterners with their refined accents and superior manners. They were especially concerned that the surgeon general be replaced by a vigorous and able man committed to reforming the medical procedures and cooperating with the Sanitary Commission. When Henry Bellows, a member of the commission, chided Lincoln on his irregular eating habits, citing his concern with the President's health, Lincoln replied, "Well, I cannot take my vittles regular. I kind o' just browse round."

Chapters or agencies of the commission were started in Boston, Philadelphia, Chicago, Washington, Louisville, and San Francisco. Its principal offices at Washington and Louisville, "our two chief nervous centres," as Strong called them, "employed some hundred agents with various duties and expended over $40,000 a month." By 1864 the employees of the commission numbered more than 400, and its expenditures ran to $250,000 a month, a staggering sum for a private voluntary agency to dispense.

San Francisco, and indeed all northern California, were generously supportive of the Sanitary Commission. George Templeton Strong wrote that the contributions of that region—from San Francisco to Stockton, Yubaville, Volcano, and "other places new to geographical science"—were "a splendid symbol of . . . national feeling." Among the Unionists who made their way to California and made the northern part of the state a Union stronghold was a Boston Unitarian minister, Thomas Starr King, who told his fellows that they made a mistake by "huddling so close around the cosy stove of civilization in this blessed Boston." He was "ready to go out into the cold and see if I am good for anything." It turned out that he was. Of the more than $1,500,000 raised in California for the Sanitary Commission a large part was due to King's zeal.

In addition to "subscriptions"—contributions by individual businesses and organizations—one of the most popular ways of raising money for the work of the Sanitary Commission was benefit performances by outstanding actors, singers, and public performers. In New York the famous Charlotte Cushman played in *Macbeth* with Edwin Booth, the brilliant young Shakespearean actor, to "an immensely crowded house." The tickets had been scalped for $20 each in Wall

Street. George Templeton Strong was entranced with the performance and thought Charlotte Cushman "beyond all comparison" the best Lady Macbeth he had ever seen. "Macbeth died very game." And the commission cleared more than $5,000.

Almost a year of assiduous lobbying by the Sanitary Commission brought forth from Congress in April, 1862, a bill to reform the Medical Department, or, as George Templeton Strong put it, "a bill to increase the efficiency of that rheumatic, lethargic, paralytic, ossified, old institution. . . ." It had passed, Strong added, "under pressure brought to bear on the Congress by the United States and by the public opinion we have been educating."

Dorothea Dix, busy creating a nursing corps, had her own very strong ideas about how the Medical Department should be reformed and how the Sanitary Commission itself should function. "Miss Dix has plagued us a little," George Templeton Strong wrote. "She is energetic, benevolent, unselfish, and a mild case of monomania. Working on her own hook, she does good, but no one can cooperate with her, for she belongs to the class of comets and can be subdued into relations with no system whatever." In another diary entry Strong referred to her as "that philanthropic lunatic" and added: "She is disgusted with us because we do not leave everything else and rush off the instant she tells us of something that needs attention." She dashed into one meeting of the commission "in breathless excitement to say that a cow in the Smithsonian grounds was dying of sunstroke, and she took it very ill that we did not adjourn instantly to look after the case."

The sanitary commissioners visited McClellan and the Army of the Potomac in March, 1862. There the gentlemen commissioners made out as best they could. "We slept in our shawls and overcoats, on the floor," Strong wrote; "[William Holme] Van Buren snored in a steady, severe classical style; Bellows in a vehement, spasmodic, passionate *sturm und drang* Byronic way, characteristic of the Romantic School." Under McClellan, discipline and its handmaid, proper sanitation, were well attended to.

The Union army hospital at Alexandria, Virginia, had "long been a most scandalous unsanitary nuisance and offense," but the "remonstrances" and the funds of the Sanitary Commission succeeded in turning it into "a model of neatness and order." Strong noted proudly: "It looks like a model New England village, with its long rows of comfortable white huts and shanties, its wide streets, well drained and perfectly policed, its pretty enclosures and green groves." It could accommodate 12,000 sick and wounded soldiers, and the convalescents whom Strong and his fellow commissioners saw looked "orderly and cheerful."

Frederick Law Olmsted grew increasingly difficult to deal with. "Perhaps," Strong wrote, "his most unsanitary habits of life make him morally morbid. He works like a dog all day and sits up nearly all night, doesn't go home to his family . . . for five days and nights together, works with steady, feverish intensity till four in the morning, sleeps on a sofa in his clothes, and breakfasts on *strong coffee and pickles*!!!"

To support the work of the Sanitary Commission, it was decided to give a series of splendid "fairs" in the major cities of the North. When it was proposed to sell chances for handsome items donated to the fairs, the Christian moralists were immediately up in arms to protest against anything that could smack of gambling. The promoters of the fairs met this objection quite ingeniously. It was announced that the chances sold would give the winners the right to designate someone, especially deserving, to whom they would give their prizes. As it turned out, the winners uniformly designated themselves. This caused a scandal with some of the pious, but the general view was that it was admirably "smart." New Yorkers were determined that as the largest city of the Union and its financial capital, the New York fair must outdo all others. For the fair to be a success, the energies of the prominent women of the cities had to be enlisted. So there were two parallel committees, one of leading businessmen like William Henry Aspinwall and John Astor and one of women. They met separately, and the women had constantly to cope as best they could with the vanity, obtuseness, and obduracy of the men, who saw fit "to thwart, snub, insult, and override the ladies' committee," Strong wrote, "in the most disgusting, offensive, and low-bred way." Strong's wife, Ellie, who had done so much as a nurse on the commission's hospital ship *Daniel Webster,* was one of the key members of the women's committee. Every type of labor, every profession and trade, all the literary and artistic societies of the city were involved, and branch committees for the fair were established in Rome, Paris, and London to collect items for display and sale in New York. Two buildings were built to house the fair, one at Union Square and another on Fourteenth Street. There were restaurants, libraries, bookstores, and picture galleries, as well as a cattle and livestock market. An original manuscript of James Fenimore Cooper's was offered for sale, along with the original bowie knife carried by James Bowie at the Battle of the Alamo. Oliver Wendell Holmes wrote a hymn for the occasion. There was a children's department with puppet shows and clowns, a "music hall," and a Knickerbocker Kitchen staffed with society ladies dressed in colonial garb and serving traditional New England food. Albert Bierstadt, the painter of vast Western canvases, directed Indian war dances in a mammoth wigwam. George Templeton Strong confined his purchases to a Russian icon, "one of the marvellous pictures of the Madonna and Child that are found in every Russian habitation, from the palace to the peasant's shanty."

The editor of Beecher's *Independent* saw the fairs as "a sort of pentecostal gathering wherein Catholics, Jews, Presbyterians, Methodists, Unitarians, Swedenborgians, Baptists, Congregationalists, Quakers and Moravians forgot all their differences, and poured into one common reservoir their thank offerings, from the rich gifts of the opulent merchants . . . to the widow's mites of the alleys and byways. No lovelier, [more] soul-satisfying spectacle was ever witnessed on this earth."

An equally impressive eleemosynary enterprise was the network of freedmen's associations, which sprang up, as we have seen, to support the work of educating first the contrabands and then, after the emancipation, the ex-slaves or freedmen and women. The various freedmen's aid societies, as well as the old abolitionist groups (in many instances they were virtually the same; frequently one had replaced the other), constituted an extraordinarily potent network. Never amounting to more than a relatively small portion of the electorate in the Northern and Western states, they exercised an influence out of all proportion to their numbers. In addition to supervising the activities of the white and black teachers and missionaries in the South, the freedmen's aid societies constituted a powerful and highly effective lobby both in the states and in Washington. They poured out a stream of letters to their representatives, admonishing and exhorting. They published a number of magazines, journals, and newsletters; they held numerous meetings and conventions; they drafted and circulated petitions. Typical of the latter was one written by the Reverend George Cheever, a native of Maine and, like his brother, Henry, a Congregational minister and a longtime worker in the abolitionist vineyards. Cheever joined with Parker Pillsbury, another veteran of the abolitionist cause, former editor of the early antislavery journal the *Herald of Freedom*, to draft a lengthy petition setting forth in detail the basis of a republican government. The petition ended with a plea to Congress to guarantee "the freedom of the vote for all citizens of the United States without respect to color or race; and to refuse the admission of any State into the Union, until this condition of Republican freedom be secured in the State Constitutions and laws. The common right of suffrage is one of those immemorial paths of common brotherhood in humanity and Christianity, that run across every State line and enclosure in this country."

J. C. McKee, agent of the Western Freedmen's Aid Commission, found, in the vicinity of Nashville, some "four thousand contrabands who need help and instruction. . . . I find over 40 crowded into one small house. Sometimes 5 or 6 families in one room without fireplace or chimney, cooking their morsel on a few bricks, the smoke filling the apartment and steaming out at the door." When McKee offered to take them back to their former masters, asking, "Would you not feel better with him than here?" the invariable answer was to the effect "Ah, no, Massa. Dese is hard times, sure, but de Lordie do somthin' for us." McKee added: "There is something in their very laugh that makes my heart bleed for them."

Fourteen hundred contrabands died in and about Nashville during the winter of 1863, and McKee estimated that half that number had died of "neglect through hunger, cold, filth and vermin." In the face of such misery "several colored schools have sprung up," he noted, "taught by colored people who have got a little learning somehow." When McKee told them that it was his intention to start a free school and teach it, "such expressions as the following came from all sides: 'Bress de Lor!' 'Oh if I can only learn to read de Bible. I don't care for notin' more.' 'I'm too ole and can't see much no how; but I would like to learn. . . . When will de school begin?' "

In Little Rock, Arkansas, the black citizens formed the Freedman's School Society and established and supported free schools for blacks, the first free schools in the state. Numerous groups in the North, both black and white, rallied support for black schools and for missionary efforts among the freed slaves. The *Christian Recorder* of the African Methodist Church called on "all of our people . . . to give to this cause, for we believe it to be a Christian duty. . . . Let us provide clothing and money to help take care of [the contrabands]; let us send them kind teachers both colored and white." Henry Turner of the Israel Bethel Church observed that the proclamation had laid "grave and solemn responsibilities" on Northern blacks to help their newly freed brethren. There was a note of anxiety in Turner's description of "thousands of contrabands . . . in droves every day perambulating the streets of Washington, homeless, shoeless, dressless, and moneyless. . . . Every man of us now, who has a speck of grace or bit of sympathy, for the race that we are inseparably identified with, is called upon by force of surrounding circumstances, to extend a hand of mercy to *bone of our bone and flesh of our flesh*. . . ." To the middle-class blacks of the North who had worked so long and against heavy odds to achieve "respectability," the sight of hordes of "brothers and sisters" reinforcing the stereotype that they had struggled desperately to transcend was troubling and threatening. They already had to expend considerable effort disassociating themselves from the improvident urban blacks of the North, who were constantly pointed to by whites as evidence of the inferiority of black people generally.

That Northern blacks responded as they did out of the pitifully little that they had is striking testimony to their feeling of solidarity. Black churches, like white, were the centers of support for teachers and missionaries in the South. The Reverend James Lynch, a Methodist minister from Baltimore who had gone to the Sea Islands and been appointed "Missionary and Government Superintendent" there, exhorted the black community to send more black teachers to the South. Lynch declared that while "the white people are doing in the South an educational work that shines forth as the greatest achievement of this world's six thousand years," he did not wish to see "the entire work of education of thousands of our black brethren being carried on entirely by the whites without appealing to my colored friends to be up and doing."

Among the groups formed to assist the contrabands were the Contraband Relief Association of Washington, the Union Relief Association of the Israel Bethel Church, the Freedmen's Friend Society in Brooklyn, and the Contraband Aid Association of Cincinnati. The Washington chapter of the Contraband Relief Association was formed by Elizabeth Meckley, an ex-slave who had purchased her freedom by working as a seamstress and laundress in Washington. Her position as Mrs. Lincoln's seamstress, or, perhaps more accurately, "dress designer," gave her great prestige in the black community of Washington.

In June, 1863, the American Freedmen's Commission issued a report on the condition of the freed slaves in those Southern states occupied by Federal troops, and six months later Congressman Thomas Eliot of Massachusetts submitted a bill to establish a Federal bureau to supervise emancipation. Lincoln's own reconstruction policies had come under sharp criticism from the Emancipation League, a kind of consortium of abolitionist groups, and the President responded to these criticisms by appointing Samuel Gridley Howe, a vice-president of the league, along with Robert Dale Owen of New Harmony fame, and Colonel James MacKaye, a prominent New York abolitionist, to form an "Inquiry Commission" under the auspices of the American Freedmen's Commission. The commission's preliminary report stated clearly the commissioners' doubts about the ability or even the intention of Lincoln's appointees to protect the newly freed slaves from abuse and exploitation by their former masters. "Coming into competition with another race—one among the most energetic in the world—for the first time in the history of our country, on something like equal terms, will he," the commissioners asked, "if left himself, be overborne and crushed?" On one issue the commissioners were in complete agreement—"namely that a scheme of guardianship or protection for one race of men against another race inhabiting the same country cannot become a permanent institution." At the same time assistance in a period of transition was necessary.

As for the potentialities of the freed slaves for full and useful citizenship, the commission was cautiously optimistic. "They have found," the report stated, "unmistakable indications that the negro slave of the south, though in some respects resembling a child from the dependence in which he has been trained, and the unreasoning obedience which has been exacted from him . . . is by no means devoid of practical sagacity in the common affairs of life, and usually learns, readily and quickly, to shift for himself." The commissioners warned against the policy of collecting freedmen and women in military "villages," where they at once became charges of the government. They should be utilized as quickly as possible "as military laborers or on plantations, or in other self-supporting situations." By the same token the government should not run plantations to employ them except as a temporary expedient. "As soon as there are found loyal and respectable owners or lessees of the plantations who will hire the freedmen at fair wages, this is to be preferred. . . ."

The commissioners were cautious on the subject of the distribution of land to former slaves. Small plots of land might be temporarily assigned to them or rented for a moderate charge. The commissioners were unequivocal on "the importance of enlightened instruction, educational and religious, to these uneducated people." They found

PASSION FOR EDUCATION:

them "eager to obtain for themselves, but especially for their children, those privileges of education which have hitherto been jealously withheld from them." Perhaps most important of all, the freedmen needed friends and advisers and a system of justice independent of the local courts to protect them from exploitation by whites, including Southern Unionists and Northern military commanders.

The commissioners concluded their preliminary report with a character analysis of the freed blacks. "The African race," the report announced with confidence, "accustomed to shield itself by cunning and evasion, and by shirking work, whenever it can be safely shirked, against the oppression which has been its lot for generations, is yet of a genial nature, alive to gratitude, open to impressions of kindness, and more readily influenced and led by those who treat it well and gain its confidence than our race, or perhaps than any other." It was therefore essential that the men designated as directors and supervisors of black affairs be men not only of administrative ability "but also of comprehensive benevolence and humanitarian views."

Despite the report, which circulated widely, although it had no official character, nothing was done to establish a regular bureau concerned with the affairs of freedmen for almost two years. The issue was intermittently debated, but Congress gave its attention to presumably more pressing matters. It was thus left to the network, the voluntary freedmen's bureaus under the aegis of the American Freedmen's Commission, to carry the main burden of caring for those ex-slaves who found themselves, or made their way, behind Union lines.

By the end of the war the various freedmen's aid societies had some 900 teachers and missionaries in the South, and it was estimated by General Oliver Howard, head of the Federal Freedmen's Bureau, that in excess of 200,000 freedmen had attended classes taught by its teachers.

24

Hospitals and Prisons

The two places where the horror of the war was most overwhelmingly expressed were the hospitals and prisons of the rival armies. Walt Whitman made himself the chronicler of the Union hospitals.

He described Campbell Hospital in Washington, a typical structure, as having "a long building appropriated to each ward." Ward 6 contained "eighty or a hundred patients, half sick, half wounded. The edifice is nothing but boards, well whitewash'd inside, and the usual slender-framed iron bedsteads, narrow and plain. You walk down a central passage, with a row on either side, their feet towards you and their heads to the wall." The plainness of the walls was relieved by ornaments, silver stars, circles, evergreen branches. "Look at the fine large frames, the bright and broad countenances, and the many yet lingering proofs of strong constitution and physique. Look at the patient and mute manner of our American wounded as they lie in such a sad collection; representatives from all New England, and from New York, and New Jersey, and Pennsylvania—indeed from all the States and all the cities—largely from the west."

The best hospitals were clean and efficiently managed; the worst were mere charnel houses. Charles Francis Adams, Jr., in winter quarters at Point Lookout, Maryland, with time on his hands, visited the post hospital there. "I went through ward after ward," he wrote his mother, "passing up and down long rows of little beds on each of which lay a sick prisoner, with the long matted hair and wild look so peculiar to southern men. The wards were long, wooden buildings, one story high, whitewashed inside, warmed by stoves and scrupulously clean—regular military hospitals. The beds were small and of iron, and each bed had its mattress, coarse white sheets and pillow-case, and two blankets. . . . There was more for a liberal American to be proud of in that hospital than in the greatest achievement of our armies. There was to be found, and that too under circumstances of cruel aggravation, the true spirit of Christianity infused into war. . . ."

Some of the wards were fifty yards long, often arranged around a hollow square with "additional tents, extra wards for contagious diseases, guard-houses, sutler's stores, chaplain's; in the middle," Whitman noted, "will probably be an edifice devoted to the office of the surgeon in charge and the ward surgeons, principal attaches, clerks, etc." There were some thirty to forty such hospitals ringing Washington, often containing fifty to seventy thousand men.

The hospital in Washington where Alfred Bellard was stationed was a large building constructed in the form of a square with some fifty wards, each of which held approximately sixty patients. In the center of the building were the doctor's quarters, dispensary, kitchen, and library. A band gave a concert every day for the wounded, "which livened them up considerably," Bellard noted. One of the most novel features of the hospital was a track that ran down the center of each ward. On it was a small car that distributed hot food to the patients.

The scene after the Battle of Fredericksburg was typical of that which followed all major engagements. The camp brigade and division hospitals were filled to overflowing. They were merely tents, "and sometimes very poor ones," Whitman wrote, "the wounded lying on the ground, lucky if their blankets are spread on layers of pine or hemlock twigs, or small leaves. No cots; seldom even a mattress. . . . The ground is frozen hard, and there is occasional snow."

One of the most distressing periods for the wounded soldier was the time when he was unloaded from a hospital train—usually made up of empty freight cars—at a railroad juncture to wait for another train to take him to a base hospital or to his home if he was convalescent. He might wait for hours or days unattended, with no doctors to dress his wounds or give him medicine and no orderlies to feed him and attend to his personal needs. There thus sprang up in

South Carolina, in the summer of 1862, what came to be known as the wayside home, a kind of nursing station manned by women at the rail junctions where wounded soldiers awaited transportation. Mary Chesnut, who was active in a wayside home in the fall of 1864, wrote: "[S]o much suffering, such loathsome wounds, such distortions, with stumps of limbs not half cured. . . . The end has come. No doubt of the fact."

Whitman, who probably knew hospital conditions as well as any American, was deeply impressed by the quality of the surgeons in the Union army. "I never ceas'd to find the best men, and the hardest and most disinterested workers, among the surgeons in the hospitals. They are full of genius, too," he wrote. While there were serious deficiencies in supply, in management, in general order—"a sad want of system," as Whitman put it—the surgeons stood out in their devotion to their calling and their efforts for their patients. When a soldier seemed in critical condition, the total resources of the ward would be mustered to try to save his life. If it became clear that the cause was hopeless, he would be as quickly abandoned, and the efforts concentrated elsewhere.

The principal diseases were "typhoid fever, diarrhoea, catarrhal affections and bronchitis, rheumatism and pneumonia." At any one time there were twice as many soldiers ill from disease as confined for wounds.

Those soldiers who recovered sufficiently from illness or wounds were returned to active duty, when possible with their original units. Those seriously disabled were discharged. Those needing extended periods of convalescence were sent to the Invalid Corps. Alfred Bellard, our diarist with the 5th New Jersey Volunteers, was wounded at Chancellorsville and, after his recovery in a Pennsylvania hospital and a furlough at home, was assigned to the Invalid Corps to do light duty, most commonly guarding prisoners and acting as military police in the capital and in military camps in the vicinity. The more severely wounded were used primarily as nurses and cooks. In December, 1863, the Invalid Corps had its name changed to the Veterans Reserve Corps, in part because its initials—I.C.—were said to stand for "Inspected—Condemned," army code for rejected military supplies.

The encampment of the Veterans Reserve Corps near Alexandria was like a small city, laid out in streets with stores, a post office, library, barbershop, and photograph gallery. "There was also a fine brass band," Alfred Bellard noted, "that gave us excellent music at headquarters every night, which never failed to draw a large and attentive audience." It was from these veterans that a force was mustered to defend the capital in July, 1864, when two Confederate divisions under Jubal Early threatened the city. Augmented by hastily assembled companies of government clerks, the defensive works protecting the city were manned. Lincoln with a retinue of Cabinet members and Congressmen visited the positions several times, and on one occasion it was said that the President exposed himself so carelessly to enemy sniper fire that Captain Oliver Wendell Holmes, not recognizing the President, shouted, "Get down, you fool."

The nursing corps was made up in large part of women volunteers. George Templeton Strong's wife was such a volunteer. "Ellie enjoys her Bohemian life," Strong wrote, "works hard, sleeps profoundly, finds coarse fare appetizing, and has a good time generally. I have brilliant reports of her energy and efficiency in arrangement, of her cordial acquiescence in drudgery."

However dedicated such women might be, they lacked training and experience and it was Whitman's conviction that men generally made better nurses. He discovered that companionship was often more important to wounded or ill soldiers than medical attention. Some men needed "special and sympathetic nourishment. These I sit down and either talk to, or silently cheer them up. They always like it hugely (and so do I). Each case has its peculiarities, and needs some new adaptation. I have learnt to thus conform—learnt a good deal of hospital wisdom." Although Whitman was not an orthodox Christian, considered himself an agnostic in fact, he did not hesitate to read passages from the Bible or pray with the patients. In many instances he helped dress wounds, and in some cases soldiers would let only Whitman change their dressings. He read aloud to small groups of men or gave "recitations." "They were very fond of it," he noted proudly, "and liked declamatory poetical pieces. We would gather in a large group by ourselves, after supper, and spend the time in such readings, or in talking, and occasionally by an amusing game called the game of twenty questions." He wrote: "One hot day toward the middle of June I gave the inmates of Carver hospital a general ice cream treat, purchasing a large quantity, and, under convoy of the doctor or head nurse, going around personally through the wards to see to its distribution. . . . Once in a while," he added, "some youngster holds on to me convulsively, and I do what I can for him; at any rate stop with him and sit near him for hours, if he wishes it."

Soon he began to lay in a small supply of gifts for the wounded with money given him by well-to-do friends and patrons—oranges, apples, sweet crackers, figs, and, most welcome of all, writing paper and pencils. For those too ill or weak to write or, in some cases, illiterate, Whitman wrote to parents, friends, relatives. He distributed "amusing reading matter, tobacco, and to those without money, five- and ten-cent bills, and sometimes a fifty-cent bill to someone especially in need." Charles Miller, "bed 19, company D, 53rd Pennsylvania," was only sixteen years old, "very bright, courageous boy, left leg amputated below the knee," Whitman wrote; "next bed to him, another young lad very sick; gave each appropriate gifts. In the bed above also, amputation of the left leg; gave him a little jar of raspberries . . . (I am more and more surprised at the very proportion of youngsters from fifteen to twenty-one in the army)."

The oddest hospital was in the Patent Office. "It was a strange, solemn, and, with all its features of suffering and death, a sort of fascinating sight. I go sometimes at night," Whitman wrote, "to soothe and relieve particular cases. Two of the immense apartments are fill'd with high and ponderous glass cases, crowded with models in miniature of every kind of utensil, machine or invention it ever enter'd into the mind of man to conceive. . . ." There, like grim exhibits, lay ill and wounded soldiers.

It was a strangely proper mission for that most American of our poets—to sit, night after night, among the wounded and the dying; to bring them, unwearyingly, the benison of his quiet presence, his gentle hands, his cheering smile, his gifts, his small attentions. He noted their names, the roster of the brave, their units, the legions of a modern *Iliad*. There was Thomas Haley, Company M, 4th New York, an Irish boy come over on purpose to fight, "not a single friend or acquaintance here," shot through the lungs, "inevitably dying." It was useless to talk to him "with his sad hurt, and the stimulants they give him, and the utter strangeness of every object, face, furniture, etc., the poor fellow, even when awake, is like some frighten'd animal." Marcus Small, 7th Maine, "sick with dysentery and typhoid fever"; Thomas Lindley, 1st Pennsylvania Cavalry, in terrible pain from a smashed foot and heavily dosed with morphine, "his face ashy and glazed." Whitman placed a "large handsome apple" by his bed. "In my visits to the hospitals I found it was in the simple matter of personal presence, and emanating ordinary cheer and magnetism," he wrote, "that I succeeded and help'd more than by medical nursing, or delicacies, or gifts of money, or anything else." He prepared for his "tours," day or night, "by fortifying myself with previous rest, the bath, clean clothes, a good meal, and as cheerful an appearance as possible."

As Whitman's descriptions of the hospitals in the vicinity of Washington suggest, the war brought with it vast changes in the arrangement and management of hospitals. Strict standards were established, especially in regard to sanitation, to a large degree through the intervention of the Sanitary Commission. One of the most important reforms was the separation of the administrative offices of the hospital from those areas containing the patients. Heating and ventilation were greatly improved; "efficient water-closets, ablution, and bathing accommodations" were provided; and it was stipulated that "furniture of all kinds" and "suitable quality" should be provided. Those ill of disease were separated from the wounded. Space was provided for the exercise of convalescing patients. Nursing procedures were developed, in large part through the offices of Dorothea Dix, the "philanthropic lunatic" (George Templeton Strong's description), who crowned a lifetime of services to her fellow mortals by organizing the nursing corps and establishing it on a professional basis. Close attention was paid to developing a balanced and healthy diet for the patients; the training of doctors and especially surgeons was much improved; and attention was paid to the psychological as well as the physical needs of the ill and wounded, who received "cordials . . . delicacies, and clothing" which assisted in their recovery.

The consequence of all this was that the Union army had a lower sick rate as well as a lower rate of mortality than any other army of the century. On June 30, 1863, out of every 1,000 men in the army there were 91 in army general hospitals and 44 in field hospitals, making a total of 135 out of every 1,000; of those, 110 were cases of sickness and 25 of wounds—more than four times as many sick as wounded, a ratio that held fairly steady during the war, rising sharply on the side of the wounded, of course, after major engagements.

Whitman estimated that during three years he made more than 600 "visits or tours" to various camps and hospitals and ministered to more than 80,000 of the sick and wounded, "as sustainer of spirit and body in some degree. . . . These visits," he wrote, "varied from an hour or two, to all day or night; for with dear or critical cases I generally watch'd all night. Sometimes I took up my quarters in the hospital, and slept or watch'd there several nights in succession. Those three years I consider the greatest privilege and satisfaction (with all their feverish excitements and physical deprivations and lamentable sights), and, of course, the most profound lesson of my life. I can say that in my ministerings I comprehended all, whoever came in my way, northern or southern, and slighted none. It arous'd and brought out and decided undreamt-of depths of emotion. It has given me my most fervent views of the true *ensemble* and extent of the States." Officers, enlisted men, teamsters—it was all the same with Whitman. "Among the black soldiers, wounded or sick, and in the contraband camps, I also took my way whenever in their neighborhood, and did what I could for them."

Clearly Whitman drew some great affirming strength from the soldiers of both armies. He attended to the ill, the wounded, the dying in the hospitals; made the wards as familiar as the hills and fields and city streets he frequented. He looked into the faces of Wisconsin farm boys, young city clerks, Maine artisans and fishermen, searching out the perpetual riddle of America. Here it was at its purest, near to death, all dross burned away, life at its most elemental, America at its noblest.

In "The Wound-Dresser" he wrote: "An old man bending I come among new faces. . . . To sit by the wounded and soothe them, or silently watch the dead; . . . I sit by the restless all the dark night, some are so young, / Some suffer so much, I recall the experience sweet and sad, / (Many a soldier's loving arms about this neck have cross'd and rested, / Many a soldier's kiss dwells on these bearded lips.)"

In "Ashes of Soldiers," he wrote:

Dearest comrades, all is over and long gone,
But love is not over—and what love, O comrades!
Perfume from the battle-fields rising, up from the foetor arising.

Perfume therefore my chant, O love, immortal love,
Give me to bathe the memories of all dead soldiers,
Shroud them, embalm them, cover them all over with tender pride.

If Whitman was convinced that the real meaning of war was to be found in the hospitals among the ill, the wounded and the dying—that all the rest of the conflict were mere "flanges" around that central theme—much the same could be said of the prisons and prisoners, for the prisons were, for the most part, terrible charnel houses, abodes of the living dead. To enter many of them was to have the sentence of death passed on one, a death preceded by nameless sufferings.

The ideal was, of course, to exchange prisoners, but the terms for exchange were not easily decided. Exchanged prisoners were not supposed to take up arms again, officers being the exception. If officers could not be exchanged directly, one officer was taken to equal a certain number of enlisted men. So many prisoners were taken, well in excess apparently of 200,000 on each side, that both Northern and Southern prisons were jammed with captured soldiers. By the end of the war 121,337 Confederate soldiers had been exchanged for some 110,866 Union soldiers. Some 30,000 rebels were still in the hands of the Federal government at the close of the conflict.

A substantial number of prisoners on both sides escaped, and tens of thousands died. In the South tobacco warehouses were commonly converted into prisons, and the prisoners were theoretically given the same rations as Confederate soldiers. The conditions were nonetheless uniformly bad. The most notorious Confederate prisons were those at Andersonville in Georgia and Libby Prison in Virginia. Holding, by the end of the war, some 35,000 Union prisoners, Andersonville was described as an enclosure of less than thirty acres. The great majority of prisoners were without shelter and, a contemporary account declared, "are exposed to the storms and rains, which are almost daily occurrences: the cold dews of the night, and the more terrible effects of the sun striking with almost tropical fierceness upon their unprotected heads. This mass of men jostle and crowd each other up and down the limits of their enclosure, in storm or sun, and others lie down upon the pitiless earth at night, with no other covering than the clothing upon their backs. . . . Thousands are without pants or coats, and hundreds without even a pair of drawers to cover their nakedness." The men were "fast losing hope," the report continued, "and becoming utterly reckless of life. Numbers, crazed by their sufferings, wander about in a state of idiocy; others deliberately cross the 'dead line,' and are remorselessly shot down."

Of Andersonville, James Blaine, the Maine Congressman, declared, "I have read anew the horrors untold and unimaginable of the Spanish Inquisition. And I here before God, measuring my words, knowing their extent and import, declare that neither the deeds of the Duke of Alva in the Low Countries, nor the massacre of St. Bartholomew, nor the thumb-screws and engines of torture of the Spanish Inquisition begin to compare in atrocity with the hideous crime of Andersonville."

Andersonville was only the most notorious of the Southern prisons. In Salisbury, North Carolina, of 11,000 Union prisoners no more than 2,500 came out alive. Of these, 500, Whitman wrote, "were pitiable, helpless wretches. . . . The regular food was a meal of corn, the cob and husk ground together, and sometimes once a week a ration of sorghum molasses." Meat was seldom served more than once a month. There were tents enough for only 2,000 men, and most of the rest lived in holes in the ground. Some froze to death; others suffered frozen hands and feet. "All the horrors that can be named, starvation, lassitude, filth, vermin, despair, swift loss of self-respect, idiocy, insanity and frequent murder, were there." To Whitman the sight of the released Union prisoners was "worse than any sight of battlefields, or any collection of wounded, even the bloodiest." Whitman asked himself, "Can these be *men*—those little livid brown ash-streak'd, monkey-looking dwarfs?—are they not really mummied, dwindled corpses? They lay there, most of them, quite still, but with a horrible look in their eyes and skinny lips (often with not enough flesh on the lips to cover their teeth). Probably no more appalling sight was ever seen on this earth. (There are deeds, crimes, that may be forgiven; but this is not among them. . . . Over 50,000 have been compell'd to die the death of starvation—reader, did you ever try to realize what *starvation* actually is? in those prisons—and in a land of plenty.)" More Union soldiers died in the rear of the enemy lines than in front of them.

The Confederate prisoners in Union camps usually fared far better than their Yankee counterparts. When Whitman talked with Southern prisoners, he noted: "Some are quite bright and stylish, for all their poor clothes—walking with an air, wearing their old head-coverings on one side, quite saucily." Many had been forced to serve in the Southern army, some months past their periods of enlistment. A huge young Georgian was "complacently eating some bread and meat. . . . It was plain he did not take anything to heart," Whitman wrote. Another, a West Tennessee boy both of whose parents were dead, looked at Whitman with large, clear dark brown eyes and confessed that his only desire in life was a chance to bathe and put on clean underclothes. "I had the very great pleasure," Whitman added, "of helping him accomplish all those wholesome designs."

Ted Upson's first military post was a prisoner of war camp for Confederate soldiers. The camp was under the command of Colonel Richard Owen, son of Robert Owen, the founder of New Harmony. Richard Owen had so far absorbed the philanthropic spirit of his famous father that he ran his prisoner compound more in the manner of a utopian society than of a military prison, in return for which his charges collected funds for a bronze bust of their commandant bearing the inscription "Colonel Richard Owen, Tribute by Confederate prisoners of war and their friends for his courtesy and kindness." It was placed in the Indiana Statehouse and must be among the few such tributes in the history of warfare and prison camps.

Thousands of Southern prisoners were confined in a camp at Point Lookout, Maryland—"a low, sandy, malarious, fever-smitten, wind-blown, God-forsaken tongue of land" Charles Francis Adams, Jr., called it. In a letter to his father in the fall of 1864, Adams described the prisoners' "pens." He wrote: "During the daytime the fashionable streets are thronged with a gaunt, unkempt, strangely clad multitude of all ages and all styles of dress. The peculiar type of southern man, long, wiry, dirty, unshorn and dressed in the homespun yellow, stands strongly out, and mixed in altogether in one cut-throat throng, you meet the pure white trash of the slave states and men bearing the marks of refinement, old men who ought to know better and lads with faces as smooth as an egg. . . . Almost every tent is a work-shop and they manufacture all sorts of pretty trinkets and curious toys which they sell to visitors. They're a dirty set, both naturally and here, almost from necessity, and one of the most marked objects one sees is the large average of men who are always sitting *in puris* picking the vermin off their clothes."

Yet it would be a mistake to assume that the life of a Confederate prisoner was in any way an agreeable one. Many died of disease, and all suffered from their confinement. Mary Chesnut was moved to tears at the sight of Southern soldiers returning home at the end of the war from Northern prisons; they were "so forlorn, so dried up, and shrunken, with such a strange look in some of their eyes, others so restless and wild-looking; others again placidly vacant, as if they had been dead to the world for years."

Hospitals and prisons, so different in intent, so similar in the institutional management of large numbers of individuals incapable of functioning "outside," one from physical incapacity, one from psychological, were two of the great reforms on which the nineteenth century prided itself. It could hardly be said that the incarceration of hundreds of thousands of human beings whose only "crime" was being the enemy advanced in any degree the science of penology. Clearly the case was very different with the hospitals, especially those in the North. There substantial advances were indeed made. But it was in the human dimension that both institutions had their profoundest significance. Whether or not one accepts Whitman's view that the deepest meaning of the conflict was to be read in the ill and dying soldiers, there is no question that in the hospitals its horror was inescapable—and, perhaps even more so (for care and kindness were far less evident), in the prisons. The horror and terror of the battlefield are known only to the soldier who fights thereon. But the hospitals and prisons carried that horror and terror into the heart of the world of noncombatants and gave them an inkling of the true nature of the war and its terrible cost in suffering and in lives.

25

The Democrats in the Ascendancy

The failure of the Peninsula campaign, the debacle at the Second Battle of Bull Run, and the failure of McClellan to take advantage of Antietam brought Republican fortunes to their lowest ebb. In his diary under the date of September 13, 1862, George Templeton Strong wrote: "Disgust with our present government is certainly universal. Even Lincoln himself has gone down at last, like all our popular idols of the last eighteen months. This honest old codger was the last to fall, but he has fallen. Nobody believes in him any more. . . . I cannot bear to admit the country has no man to believe in, and that honest Abe Lincoln is not the style of goods we want just now. But it is impossible to resist the conviction that he is unequal to his place. His only special gift is fertility of smutty stories. . . . If McClellan gain no signal, decisive victory within ten days, I shall collapse. . . . O Abraham, *O mon Roi!*"

Union frustration over the repeated military failures came to focus particularly on the irascible Secretary of War Edwin Stanton, who lacked the temperament to endure such attacks with equanimity. Strong spoke for a substantial body of public opinion when he described Stanton as a "meddling, murderous quack." Strong added: "His name is likely to be a hissing till it is forgotten, and Honest Old

Abe must take care lest his own fare no better. A year ago we laughed at the Honest Old Abe's grotesque genial Western jocosities but they nausate us now." Soon, Strong felt, there would be irresistible pressures on Lincoln to resign and turn the reins of government over to Vice-President Hannibal Hamlin, "about whom nobody knows anything and who may therefore be a change for the better, none for the worse being conceivable."

Gideon Welles wrote in his diary: "The President has good sense, intelligence, and an excellent heart, but is sadly perplexed and distressed by events. He, to an extent, distrusts his own administrative ability and experience. Seward, instead of strengthening and fortifying him, encourages his self-distrust, but is not backward in giving his own judgment and experience, which are often defective expedients, to guide the Executive . . . he runs to the President two or three times a day, gets his ear, gives him his tongue, makes himself interesting by anecdotes, and artfully contrives with Stanton's aid to dispose of measures . . . independent of his associates."

As a consequence of all this, the Democrats were in the ascendancy. There were indeed two factions: the Peace Democrats—or Copperheads, as they were more commonly called, at least in Republican circles—and the War Democrats. The Peace Democrats wanted peace and the restoration of the Union at virtually any price. The War Democrats professed to be determined to prosecute the war vigorously while pursuing every avenue to peace. What united both wings of the party was a willingness to accept slavery as the basis for a negotiated peace. Their strength and their potential for mischief fluctuated almost monthly, rising and falling with the latest war news. A series of military reverses brought a flood of recruits to their banner. Union victories caused a corresponding falling away of the faithful and not-so-faithful. Usually a minority, they had a great potential for making trouble by demoralizing the Unionists and weakening the will to persist in the conflict. John Beatty, the Ohio officer, wrote in his diary: "Surely the effort now being put forth by a great party in the North to convince the troops in the field that this is an unjust war, an abolition or nigger war, must have a tendency to injure the army, and, if persisted in, may finally ruin it."

Most unnerving of all was the sense of the Peace Democrats' constant presence in the wings, so to speak, waiting for the tide of war to swing public opinion decisively in their favor, give them political power, and enable them to negotiate a peace. "As yet," George

Templeton Strong wrote, "the people are sound. They see that stopping the war now would be like leaving the dentist's shop with a tooth half-extracted." Still, there were, besides the "traitors," as Strong called them, the out-and-out enemies of the war and friends of the South, "a great mass of selfishness, frivolity, invincible prejudice, personal Southern attachment, indifference to national life, and so on, quite ready to be used . . . to dam the flood [of patriotic feeling] that broke out so gloriously a year and half ago. Have we, the people," Strong asked, "resolution and steadiness enough to fight on through five years of taxation, corruption, and discouragement? All depends on the answer to that question."

In the Philadelphia social circles in which Sidney George Fisher moved, a disproportionate (compared certainly to New York or Boston) number of his friends and acquaintances were Copperheads, who were sympathetic to the South and the institution of slavery. This was the case most conspicuously among Fisher's relatives. But Fisher's brothers were all "friends of the rebellion," and one, Charles Ingersoll, was so virulent in his denunciations of the Republican administration that he was twice arrested for treasonable utterances and once badly beaten by a mob. He remained unrepentant. A number of Fisher's closest friends were Southerners who, like Pierce Butler, had lived in style in Philadelphia on the proceeds of their plantations and who, again like Butler, departed for the South after Sumter, armed to the teeth and breathing vengeance against the North.

Joseph Allen Smith, although a Pennsylvanian born and bred, was married to a Southern woman. So strong were his sympathies with the South that he changed his name to that of his wife's family—Izard—and headed for South Carolina to fight for the Confederacy.

Charles Biddle, serving a term as Democratic Congressman from Philadelphia, gave a typical statement of a Peace Democrat. "When I see how deeply the Providence of God has rooted the institution of slavery in this land," he declared in a speech in Congress, "I see that it can be safely eradicated only by a gradual process, in which neither the civil nor the military power of the Federal government can intervene with profit. General emancipation can be safely reached only through state action, prompted by conviction and the progress of natural causes."

Charles Ingersoll called for "Conciliation and Compromise!" He said at a political rally: "Fellow citizens, the main difficulty is with the North, not the South, with the party who plotted to dissolve the Union long before South Carolina did. . . . I look on Negro property as being as sacred as any other property, and I sympathize with the South in their desire to preserve it." Edward Ingersoll, brother of Charles, expressed similar sentiments: "It is not African slavery that is the root of all evil, it is the *hatred* of African slavery, it is this mad philosophy of Abolitionism."

At a meeting of Democrats in Independence Square on September 17, 1862, Ingersoll declared, "Negro emancipation [is] . . . alike unconstitutional and impolitic. . . . Negro slavery is an incalculable blessing to us. . . . We must rouse ourselves and assert the rights of the slaveholder and add such guarantees to our Constitution as will protect his property from the spoilation of religious bigotry and persecution, or else we must give up our Constitution and Union."

Joshua Fisher, Sidney's cousin, continued to rage against Lincoln and the war. He denounced the President as "an ignorant blackguard" and declared, "Liberty is destroyed, all security for property at an end, refined & gentlemanlike life henceforth impossible, & he wished his children were all dead rather than see them live in such a country & under such a government."

A few months later the Pennsylvania state Democratic convention passed a resolution declaring that "the party fanaticism or crime, whichever it may be called, that seeks to turn the slaves of Southern States loose to overrun the North and enter into competition with the white laboring masses, thus degrading and insulting their manhood by placing them on an equality with Negroes in their occupation, is insulting to our race and merits our most emphatic and unqualified condemnation." The convention further resolved: "That this is a government of white men and was established exclusively for the white race; that the Negro race are not entitled to and ought not to be admitted to political and social equality with the white race." The North was to blame for the war because "Abolitionism is the parent of secessionism." If the Democratic Party acceded to power, it would immediately halt the fighting and say to the insulted South, "Gentlemen, name your terms." Only then would a sound and lasting peace be achieved.

Sidney George Fisher wrote of the Democrats that they "can see in this great war only a party contest. Every victory of the government they lament as a defeat of their party; in every success of the rebels they see a party victory and hail it with triumph. In all possible ways they oppose the administration & thus encourage the enemy to persevere. . . . Division is weakness and weakness is strength for the enemy. We have thus to contend against the South, the Democrats, and England also, whose unconcealed good wishes as well as services induce the Southern people to hope for active aid if they can hold out long enough."

The *Age,* the journal of the Peace Democrats, lamented the "miseries" the people must endure "while the clown and buffoon at the head of the government, with a vulgar jest upon his lips, and the echo of the ribald song he called for at Antietam ringing in his ears, asks the American people to re-elect him to the high position he has so utterly disgraced." Another Democratic orator declared, "I yield to no man in sympathy for the people of the South, a gallant people struggling nobly for their liberty against as sordid and vile a tyranny as ever proposed the degradation of our race—nay, I go further, and with Jefferson, Madison, and Livingston, I fully embrace the doctrine of secession as an American doctrine. . . ."

Fortunately for the Union loyalists, the "Southrons," as George Templeton Strong called them (when he was not calling them "slave-breeding, women-floggers"), were entirely intractable. To the talk of Copperheads or Peace Democrats of reunion on the basis of Northern acceptance of slavery, the South replied with derision. They "would not take 'Yankees' back even as their slaves." Strong wrote: "Were the South only a little less furious, savage, and spiteful, it could in three months so strengthen our 'Peace Democracy' as to paralyse the nation and destroy all hope of ever restoring its territorial integrity."

In New York a number of important business leaders were notorious Copperheads—including August Belmont and the revered old aristocrat Gulian Verplanck. Politics invaded even the sacred precincts of the Century Club, the city's premier gathering place of intellectuals, literary figures, and artists. Verplanck had started the club seventeen years earlier and been its president ever since. Now he was to be ousted for his "Copperheadism." George Bancroft, whom Strong termed "a erudite ass," was put up to oppose him and carried the day. Strong reported that "twenty people said to me tonight, in substance: 'How unpleasant it is to vote for a snob like Bancroft, and against my old friend Verplanck!' But Verplanck's Copperhead talk is intolerable."

In this atmosphere, Carl Schurz could not forbear to write to Lincoln in November, 1862, placing the blame on his administration for not prosecuting the war more vigorously. "You think I could do better," Lincoln wrote back; "therefore you blame me already. I think I could not do better; therefore I blame you for blaming me. . . . I need success more than I need sympathy. . . . I will not perform the ungrateful task of comparing cases of failure." A few days later a note came from Lincoln to Schurz at his divisional headquarters inviting him to come to the White House. There Schurz found the President "seated in an arm chair before the open-grate fire; his feet in giant morocco slippers." When Schurz had taken a seat beside him, Lincoln clapped his hand on Schurz's knee and said, "Now tell me, young man, whether you really think I am as poor a fellow as you have made me out in your letter!" The disconcerted Schurz protested that it had not been his intention to cause the President pain. He explained his own perplexity and his reasons for writing, and when he finished, Lincoln replied, "Well, I know that you are a warm anti-slavery man and a good friend to me. Now let me tell you all about it." The President then proceeded to "unfold in his peculiar way his view of the then existing state of things, his hopes and apprehensions, his troubles and embarrassments." He was beset on all sides, he reminded Schurz, by the most aggressive advocates of every conceivable policy, pressed to make dubious appointments for political purposes, denounced for doing nothing and for doing too much, for being weak and vacillating and for being a tyrant.

Finally he slapped Schurz once more on the knee, gave his loud, guffawing laugh, and exclaimed: "Didn't I give it to you in my letter? Didn't I? But it didn't hurt, did it? I did not mean to, and therefore I wanted you to come so quickly. . . . Well," he added, "I guess we understand one another now, and it's all right."

The capital was pervaded by gloom. George Templeton Strong, having traveled to Washington on the business of the Sanitary Commission, described it unflatteringly: "Crowd, heat, bad quarters, bad fare, bad smells, mosquitoes, and a plague of flies transcending everything within my experience. They blackened the tablecloths and absolutely flew into one's mouth at dinner. Beelzebub surely reigns, here, and Willard's Hotel is his temple." Those who had any pretense to escape from the city and its steamy environs did so gratefully. Abandoned by official Washington, Lincoln and his young aide Hay entertained themselves with Christian Sharps's breech-loading repeating rifle. Invented by the New Jersey machinist—"a quiet little Yankee who sold himself in relentless slavery to his idea for six weary years before it was perfect," Hay wrote—it was to revolutionize modern warfare, bringing with it the brass cartridge and greatly increasing the firepower of modern armies. The military, of course, was dead set against it, preferring the cumbersome, muzzle-loading percussion-cap musket, little changed in two hundred years of warfare. John Hay described the President's pleasure in the "wonderful gun, loading with absolutely contemptible simplicity and ease, with seven balls, and firing the whole, readily and deliberately, in less than half a minute. The President made some pretty good shots," he added.

The old man and the young man looked at the moon through the telescope at the naval observatory and went together to the Soldiers' Home, where the Lincolns stayed to escape the summer heat. The President read to Hay from Shakespeare's *Henry V*. The French king gives the hand of his daughter to Henry as a pledge of the reconciliation of the warring kingdoms:

> Take her, fair son, and from her blood raise up
> Issue to me, that the contending kingdoms
> Of France and England, whose very shores look pale
> With envy of each other's happiness,
> May cease their hatred; and in this dear conjunction
> Plant neighbourhood and Christian-like accord
> In their sweet bosoms, that never war advance
> His bleeding sword 'twixt England and fair France.

And the beginning of *King Richard the Third* with Gloucester's famous lines:

> Now is the winter of our discontent
> Made glorious summer by this sun of York;
> And all the clouds that lour'd upon our house
> In the deep bosom of the ocean buried.
> Now are our brows bound up with victorious wreaths:
> Our bruised arms hung up for monuments;
> Our stern alarums changed to merry meetings,
> Our dreadful marches to delightful measures.

Gloucester goes on to lament that he is little shaped for "sportive tricks," "Cheated of feature by dissembling nature, / Deform'd, unfinish'd, sent before my time / Into this breathing world, scarce half made up, / And that so lame and unfashionable / That dogs bark at me. . . ."

Clearly in the symbolic union of France and England, Lincoln anticipated the reconciliation of the North and South, and possibly he played on Gloucester's words as well, suggesting that with victory in sight he would have no peacetime role and perhaps even making fun of his own homeliness—"deform'd, unfinish'd, sent before my time / Into this breathing world, scarce half made up." Whatever thoughts were in the President's head as he read, he soon noticed his young aide's drooping eyelids and sent him to bed.

The Army of the Potomac was plagued by absenteeism. Officers and men on sick leave delayed returning to their units. Lincoln issued an order directed against unauthorized extended leaves and desertions. Any officer "whose health permits him to visit watering places or places of amusement, or to make social visits or walk about the town, city, or neighborhood in which he may be, will be considered fit for military duty. . . ." If he did not return promptly to his unit, he would be subject to court-martial. The President also took "military possession of all the railroads in the United States" and, a few months later, issued a proclamation directed against "all persons discouraging volunteer enlistments, resisting militia drafts," or "affording aid and comfort to rebels against the authority of the United States" and suspending the writ of habeas corpus in all such cases. There was an immediate outcry at the severity of the edict, which, strictly interpreted, could place a substantial portion of the Democratic Party in jail. Disturbed by stories of Sabbath breaking and profanity in the armed forces, Lincoln published a general order "Respecting the Observance of the Sabbath Day . . ." quoting Washington's first general order after the Declaration of Independence: "The General hopes and trusts that every officer and man will endeavor to live and act as becomes a Christian soldier defending the dearest rights and liberties of his country."

The elections of the fall of 1862 were a grievous blow to loyal Unionists. Almost everywhere the Democrats made substantial gains. Horatio Seymour, a notorious Copperhead, became the Democratic governor of New York by a margin of 11,000 votes, carrying New York City by a large majority. The Democrats captured New Jersey and made inroads on Republican strength in Pennsylvania and Ohio. In Lincoln's home state of Illinois the Republicans also suffered a severe setback.

The vote was widely interpreted as indicating a lack of confidence in Lincoln and his administration. Strong, deeply depressed, called the election "a great, sweeping revolution of public sentiment. . . ." Did it mean that "the loyal, generous spirit of patriotism that broke out so unexpectedly in April, 1861," was "nothing but a temporary, hysteric spasm?" He consoled himself by reflecting that the popular reaction was more like that of "a feverish patient who shifts his position in bed, though he knows he'll be none the easier for it. Neither the blind masses, the swinish multitude, that rule us under our accursed system of universal suffrage . . . can be expected to exercise self-control and remember that tossing and turning weakens and does harm." If, on the other hand, the vote represented a long-term trend, the prospects for "national life" were bleak indeed. Then the vote could be understood only as "a vote of national suicide. All is up. We are a lost people . . . the Historical Society should secure an American flag at once for its museum of antiquities. . . . But I will not *yet* believe that this people is capable of so shameful and despicable an act of self-destruction as to disembowel itself in the face of the civilized world for fear Jefferson Davis should hurt it."

Such were the circumstances in which Lincoln delivered his second annual address to Congress. He began by declaring that "while it had not pleased the Almighty to bless us with a return of peace, we can but press on, guided by the best light He gives us, trusting that in His own good time and wise way all will yet be well." Once more he urged the colonization of "freemen"—"the voluntary emigration of persons of that class to their respective territories [Liberia and Haiti, primarily], upon conditions which shall be equal, just, and humane." While Lincoln admitted that there had been very little response from free blacks to the idea of colonization, he was convinced that "opinion among them in this respect is improving, and that ere long there will be an augmented and considerable migration to both these countries. . . ."

The Western territories were in a turmoil from Indian raids. Many of the tribes had renounced their treaties with the United States and given their support to the insurrectionists. In August the Minnesota Sioux had "attacked settlements in their vicinity with extreme ferocity, killing indiscriminately men, women and children. . . . It is estimated that no less than 800 persons were killed by the Indians. . . . The State of Minnesota has suffered great injury from this Indian war," Lincoln noted. The Department of Agriculture had been organized, and Lincoln looked forward to "highly beneficial results in the development of a correct knowledge of recent improvements in agriculture, in the introduction of new products, and in the collection of the agricultural statistics of the different States." He wished to call the particular attention of Congress to the mineral and agricultural resources of the region between the Mississippi and the Rocky Mountains. In the Great Plains "the production of provisions, grains, grasses, and all which proceed from them" would make this region "naturally one of the most important in the world." It was an almost inconceivable challenge to work and ingenuity. But splendid as that domain was, "Our national strife springs not from our permanent part," Lincoln added, "not from the land we inhabit; not from our national homestead. . . . Our strife pertains to ourselves—to the passing generations of men—and it can without convulsion be hushed with the passing of one generation." In this healing the undeveloped West could play a crucial role.

Lincoln gave special attention to the conflicting views of Unionists "in regard to slavery and the African race amongst us. Some would perpetuate slavery; some would abolish it suddenly and without compensation; some would abolish it gradually and with compensation; some would remove the free people from us, and some would retain them with us; and there are yet other minor diversities. Because of these diversities we waste much strength in struggles among ourselves. By mutual concession we should harmonize and act together." The solution that Lincoln proposed was gradual emancipation between the termination of the war and the end of the century, a policy, he argued, which would save the slaves themselves from the "vagrant destitution" which might be their fate if they were suddenly freed without any means of livelihood assured to them. The plan would leave each slave state to work out its own plan. Compensation for freed slaves would be only a fraction of the cost of the war itself. "*Heretofore* colored people to some extent have fled North from bondage, and *now,* perhaps, from both bondage and destitution. But if gradual emancipation and deportation be adopted, they will have neither to flee from. . . .

"Fellow-citizens," Lincoln concluded, "*we* can not escape history. We of this Congress and this Administration will be remembered in spite of ourselves. . . . We *say* we are for the Union. The world will not forget that we say this. . . . In *giving* freedom to the *slave* we assure freedom to the *free*—honorable alike in what we give and what we preserve. We shall nobly save or meanly lose the last best hope of earth. . . . The way is plain, peaceful, generous, just—a way which if followed the world will forever applaud and God must forever bless."

Robert Purvis fastened on Lincoln's reference to the cost of emancipating the slaves. Was everything in America, he asked, "to be sacrificed to this insane and vulgar hate. . . ? It is in vain to talk to me about 'two races' and their mutual antagonism. In the matter of rights, there is but one race, and that is the *human* race. . . . Sir, this is our country as much as yours, and we will not leave it." Congress, and the country generally, were hardly more receptive.

On December 19, 1862, a "Republican caucus," made up of a group of prominent Republican Senators—Sumner, Fessenden, Lyman Trumbull, and Preston King among them—presented Lincoln with a kind of ultimatum. Seward must resign as secretary of state. Accompanying the letter was one from Seward offering his resignation. The senatorial missive charged the secretary "with indifference, with want of earnestness in the War, with want of sympathy with the country in this great struggle, and with many things objectionable and especially with too great an ascendancy and control of the President and measures of administration."

The action of the Senators was, first of all, a violation of the principle of the separation of powers. Beyond that, they professed to wish to save the President from himself. The implication was that he was not in charge of his own official family. Lincoln was, of course, quick to perceive that fact, and he was understandably indignant, an indignation shared by other Cabinet members. Yet the caucus—Welles preferred to call it a cabal—was made up of powerful Senators whom the President dare not offend. The problem facing Lincoln was to devise a strategy to protect this secretary of state while giving least offense to the officious, if well-intentioned, congressional meddlers. One of the ironies of the situation was that Seward had, in a large measure, brought this chastisement on himself by his efforts to convey to the world at large, especially to the members of Congress, the impression that he, not the President, was running the country. Thus, it was not surprising that when things went badly, there was a strong disposition to blame the man who claimed to be covert manager.

Lincoln's strategy was to stall for time. He invited the Senators to meet with the Cabinet—Seward, of course, being absent—and there Lincoln read them a firm but tactful lesson on the relationship between the legislative and executive branches of the government. "He spoke," Welles noted, "of the unity of his Cabinet, and how, though they could not be expected to think and speak alike on all subjects, all had acquiesced in measures when once decided." The President confessed that there was often less than complete consultation on important

issues, and other Cabinet members concurred. The Senators expressed their opinion that since all Cabinet members "were more or less
responsible," they all should be "consulted on the great questions
which affected the national welfare, and that the ear of the Executive
should be open to all and that he should have the minds of all."
Montgomery Blair protested the notion of what he called a "plural
executive," saying, "The President was accountable for his administration, might ask opinions or not of either and as many as he pleased, of
all or none of his Cabinet." Again in the words of Welles, "the
President managed his own case, speaking freely, and showed great
tact, shrewdness and ability. . . ." He asked each member of his
Cabinet for his view of Seward's resignation, and each in turn opposed
it. The committee then revealed its own internal division, with Sumner
heading those still determined to force Seward's resignation. But Ira
Harris, a New York Senator, declared that the effect of Seward's
resignation in his home state would be "calamitous."

Welles's feelings were typical of those of most members of the
Cabinet. He had no love for Seward, certainly. He believed the
secretary had "brought upon himself a vast amount of distrust and
hostility on the part of the Senators by his endeavors to impress them
and others with the belief that he is the Administration." On the other
hand, Welles was convinced that "a Senatorial combination to dictate to
the President in regard to his political family in the height of a civil war
which threatens the existence of the Republic cannot be permitted to
succeed, even if the person to whom they object is as obnoxious as they
represent; but," Welles added, "Seward's foibles are not serious
failings." When Welles expressed his views to Lincoln, the President
wholeheartedly concurred. The secretary of the navy then pledged his
support to Seward himself, to which the latter replied, Welles noted a
bit wryly in his diary, with a recitation of "his long political experience;
[and] dwelt on his own sagacity and great services. . . ." Seward tried to
"suppress any exhibition of personal grievance or disappointment, but
is painfully wounded, mortified, and chagrined," Welles concluded.
Welles, acting as intermediary for the President, urged Seward to
withhold any action on his resignation, and the embattled secretary
readily acquiesced. At this stage Chase appeared and informed Lincoln that he had drafted his own resignation to be submitted in the
event that Seward's was accepted. " 'Where is it?' the President asked,
his eye lighting up in a moment." Here, he thought, might be a
solution to the difficulty. " 'I brought it with me.' Chase said, taking a

letter from his pocket. 'Let me have it,' Lincoln said, reaching his long arm and fingers towards C., who held on seemingly reluctant to part with the letter. . . ." Before Chase could say a word, the President had the letter and had opened it. " 'This,' he said, turning toward Welles, with a triumphal laugh, 'cuts the Gordian knot. I can dispose of this subject now without difficulty. I see my way clear.' " Welles noted that "an air of satisfaction spread over [the President's] countenance such as I have not seen for some time."

Now it was Stanton's turn. "Mr. President," the secretary of war said in his self-important way, "I informed you day before yesterday that I was ready to tender you my resignation. I wish, sir, you to consider my resignation at this time in your possession."

"You may go to your Department," Lincoln replied. "I don't want yours. This is all I want; this relieves me; my way is clear; the trouble is ended. I will detain neither of you longer."

The President then made a public announcement of the offers of resignation of both the secretary of state and the secretary of the treasury and of his refusal of them. The partisans and the enemies of Chase and Seward respectively were thus played off against each other, the integrity of the Cabinet was preserved, the efforts of the Senators to intervene were rebuffed, and the principals, Sumner and Trumbull, it was hoped, chastened. It was the kind of solution that delighted Lincoln, whose political instincts were usually unerring. As for Welles, a long talk with a thoroughly subdued Preston King strengthened his suspicion that Stanton and Chase were in varying degrees responsible, perhaps unwittingly, for the senatorial interference. They had, Welles suspected, "without concert" spread alarm among their "Senatorial intimates" with stories of Seward's undue influence on the President. As for the President himself, he was clearly dependent on Seward, although by no means under his sway. In Welles's view, both Chase and Seward were important to Lincoln: "The President feels that he is under obligations to each, and that both are serviceable. He is friendly to both. He is fond of Seward, who is affable; he respects Chase, who is clumsy. Seward comforts him; Chase he deems a necessity."

The crisis was over, but clearly the coming year must bring some improvement in the fortunes of the administration if it and the Union were to survive.

26

Chancellorsville

The euphoria produced, at least in antislavery circles, by the Emancipation Proclamation was short-lived. An atmosphere of gloom and, indeed, impending disaster, was evident everywhere. The streets of Philadelphia were virtually deserted, but Chestnut Street in the center of the city was thronged with men, "chiefly of the working classes, many of them vicious & ill-looking, wandering about apparently without a purpose," Sidney George Fisher noted. "Recruiting parties were marching about . . . followed by a few ragged boys—recruiting offices empty, taverns and grog shops full. The people looked careless & indifferent. There was no excitement. The same street," Fisher reflected, "presented a very different scene in April 1861 when the war broke out. Then it was fluttering with flags & filled by a crowd of agitated, earnest men. War was a novelty then; it is an old story now, and the demagogues have spread abroad the opinion that the administration is corrupt & imbecile, that it is impossible to conquer the South & that we ought to have peace now on any terms." Old General Patterson, whose dilatoriness in coming to the aid of McClellan at the First Battle of Bull Run was blamed by that unhappy warrior for the Union defeat, told Fisher that it was his opinion that the Union was "on the verge of anarchy, that the Democrats will be able to stop the war, &

[he] thinks that they will insist on calling a national convention to restore the Union & alter the Constitution." Charles Ingersoll announced triumphantly to Fisher that opponents of the war would soon "resort to mob law & physical force to carry out their views."

However dark the prospects, Fisher never wavered in his admiration for Lincoln. He credited him, in a fine phrase, with "a wisdom that is above learning, and of an honest, sincere & loving nature. He is certainly, in my judgment," Fisher added, "the best *man* we have had for President since Jno. Q. Adams, he is the man for this crisis, worth, in the strength of his mind and character & purity of purpose, all the rest of the cabinet put together, and if he lives to complete his term of office, I believe the nation will think so, too."

George Templeton Strong noted gloomily that "(between me and my journal) things do in fact look darker and more dark every day. We are in a fearful scrape, and I see no way out of it. Recognition of the 'Confederacy' is impossible. So is vigorous prosecution of the war twelve months longer." After a visit to Washington in March, 1863, Richard Henry Dana wrote to the senior Charles Francis Adams: "As to the politics of Washington, the most striking thing is the absence of personal loyalty to the President. It does not exist. He has no admirers, no enthusiastic supporters, none to bet on his head. If a Republican convention were to be held tomorrow, he would not get the vote of a State. He does not act or talk or feel like the ruler of a great empire in a great crisis. This is felt by all, and has got down through all the layers of society. It has a disastrous effect on all departments and classes of officials, as well as on the public. He seems to me to be fonder of details than of principles, of tithing the mint, anise and cumin of patronage, and personal questions, than of the weightier matters of empire. He likes rather to talk and tell stories with all sorts of persons who come to him for all sorts or purposes than to give his mind to the noble and manly duties of his great office." Dana confided that Lincoln had "a kind of shrewdness and common sense, mother wit, and slipshod, low levelled honesty, that made him a good western jury lawyer. But he is an unutterable calamity to us where he is," Dana concluded. "Only the army can save us. . . . Chase looks and acts as if he meant to be the next President."

Certainly Dana's was not the last word on the subject, but even Gideon Welles fell victim to the general malaise. England was once more threatening to intervene on behalf of peace, meaning, literally, a divided Union and the perpetuation of slavery. Welles wrote in his diary: "We are in no condition for a foreign war. Torn by dissensions, an exhausting civil war on our hands, we have a gloomy prospect, but a righteous cause that will ultimately succeed. God alone knows through what trials, darkness, and suffering we are to pass. There is a disinclination to look these troubles which threaten us boldly in the face." Earl Russell had given indication that "the English Government do not intend to interpose to prevent the Rebels from building, buying, and sending out from England cruisers, semi-pirates, to prey upon our commerce. In plain language, English capital is to be employed in destroying our shipping interests. . . . I close my book and this month of March with sad and painful foreboding," Welles added. "The conduct and attitude of Great Britain, if persisted in, foreshadow years of desolation, of dissolution, of suffering and blood. . . . She has no magnanimity, no sense of honor or of right. She is cowardly, treacherous, and mean, and hates and fears our strength. In that alone is our security." A wider war, Welles was convinced, would mean a general upheaval throughout Europe which would result in "the overthrow of governments and dynasties. The sympathy of the mass of mankind would be with us rather than with the decaying dynasties and old effete governments. Not unlikely the conflict thus commenced would kindle the torch of civil war throughout Christendom, and even nations beyond."

The President felt the weight of office more heavily upon him with each passing month. The torrent of criticism that poured out of the press dampened his spirits. Perhaps Lincoln's most onerous task was reviewing the cases of soldiers under sentence of death by courts-martial for desertion. John Hay was "amused at the eagerness with which the President caught at any fact which would justify him in saving the life of a condemned soldier. . . . Cases of cowardice he was especially averse to punishing with death. He said it would frighten the poor devils too terribly to shoot them. On the case of a soldier who had once deserted and reenlisted, he endorsed: 'Let him fight instead of shooting him!' "

On March 30, 1863, Lincoln issued a proclamation calling for a day of prayer and fasting, "insomuch as we know that by His divine law nations, like individuals, are subjected to punishments and chastisements in this world. . . ." The "awful calamity of civil war," which had desolated the land, might well be "but a punishment inflicted upon us for our presumptuous sins, to the needful end of our national reformation as a whole people. . . ." Americans had, after all, been singularly blessed: "Preserved these many years in peace and prosperity; we have grown in numbers, wealth, and power as no other nation has ever grown. But we have forgotten God. We have forgotten the gracious hand which preserved us in peace and multiplied and enriched and strengthened us, and we have vainly imagined, in the deceitfulness of our hearts, that all these blessings were produced by some superior wisdom and virtue of our own. Intoxicated with unbroken success, we have become too self-sufficient to feel the necessity of redeeming and preserving grace, too proud to pray to the God that made us. It behooves us, then to humble ourselves before the offended Power, to confess our national sins, and to pray for clemency and forgiveness."

Hanging over Lincoln like a cloud was the question of the Army of the Potomac. Who could command it? That question had become the nightmare, the incubus of Lincoln's administration, the yardstick by which all else was measured.

There was also the problem of filling up the ranks of the Union armies, depleted by the terrible casualties of the Peninsula campaign, of Shiloh, Bull Run, Antietam, Fredericksburg, Stones River, and a hundred lesser engagements and by the equally devastating toll from illness and disease. The Confederacy had instituted a draft in the spring of 1862, and in August Lincoln had taken a reluctant step in that direction by accompanying a call to the states for 300,000 militiamen to serve for nine months, with instructions to draft from the militia if the quota could not be filled. The result had been riots in Indiana, Wisconsin, and Pennsylvania, which had led Stanton to suspend the drafting provision. Soon after the meeting of the new session of Congress that body passed the Enrollment Act, providing for a draft if state quotas could not be filled by voluntary enlistments.

Meanwhile, Lincoln resumed his search for a general to command the Army of the Potomac. The hostility of Halleck to Grant ruled him out. Lincoln's choice fell finally on Joseph ("Fighting Joe") Hooker, West Point '37. Hooker had served with no special distinction in the Mexican War and had outraged Scott by siding with Gideon Pillow in that political general's quarrel with his commander. He had resigned after the war and become a rancher in California. At the outbreak of the war Hooker had volunteered but been rebuffed primarily because of Scott's hostility. Commissioned a brigadier general in May, 1862, he had commanded the 2nd Division under McClellan in most of the major battles of the summer and fall of 1862, been advanced to commander of the V Corps at Antietam (where he was wounded), and then given command of the Center Grand Division at Fredericksburg; there his men had borne the brunt of the bloody and futile attacks on Marye's Heights. Fighting Joe Hooker was known to be a bitter critic of the administration, and it was rumored that he had been heard to advocate a military dictatorship, but Lincoln decided to appoint him commander of the Army of the Potomac "and sent him, with the commission," Schurz wrote, "a letter full of kindness and wise advice."

Hooker set about at once to reorganize the demoralized Army of the Potomac. He improved the quality and tastiness of the food, instituted a policy of furloughs, and saw to it that the men were paid on time. He had colorful patches designed to be sewn on the shoulders of the men's uniforms to indicate what corps they belonged to and conducted frequent drills and inspections to see that the men and their camps were clean and orderly.

Fighting Joe told John Hay that the Union army was "the finest on the planet. . . . It was far superior to the Southern army in everything but one. It had more valor, more strength, more endurance, more spirit; the Rebels are only superior in vigor of attack," an important deficiency, to be sure, and one that Hooker blamed on McClellan, "a baby, who knew something of drill, little of organization, and nothing of the morale of the army. It was fashioned by the congenial spirit of this man into a mass of languid inertness, destitute of either dash or cohesion." Hay, obviously impressed by Hooker's air of self-confidence, described him as having "a tall and statuesque form —grand fighting head and grizzled russet hair,—red, florid cheeks and bright blue eyes. . . ." Hooker expressed only contempt for Lee. He had never been "much respected in the army," he declared. "In Mexico he was surpassed by all his lieutenants. In the cavalry he was held in no esteem. . . . He was a courtier, and readily recommended himself by his insinuating manner to the General [Scott]. . . ."

By April, Hooker had amassed an army of 130,000 men, well trained and well equipped, and, most important of all, had restored the morale of the Army of the Potomac. Sigel was relieved of command of the XI Corps, in Schurz's view because of Eastern prejudice against Germans and Westerners, and General Oliver O. Howard took his place as corps commander. A West Pointer who had lost an arm in McClellan's Peninsula campaign, Howard was a slender and dark-haired young man "of rather prepossessing appearance," as Carl

Schurz, who now served as general of the 3rd Division under him, wrote.

Schurz's division was made up of three regiments: the 82nd Illinois Regiment, commanded by Colonel Friedrich Hecker, one of the most outstanding figures in the German revolution of 1848; the 26th Wisconsin, also made up of German-born immigrants from Milwaukee; and the 119th New York, commanded by Colonel Elias Peissner, rumored to be the illegitimate son of Ludwig I of Bavaria.

Hooker's plan was to cross the Rappahannock well above Fredericksburg, turn Lee's flank, and force him to come out of his defensive positions and fight in "the field," where the superior numbers of the Union forces could carry the day. On the morning of April 27, the V, XI, and XII corps headed for Kelly's Ford, some twenty-seven miles above Fredericksburg, while General John Sedgwick made a feint as though to attack Lee directly. The army, Carl Schurz wrote, "was in superb condition and animated by the highest spirits . . . there was no end to the singing and merry laughter, relieving the fatigue of the march." The crossing of the river was effected expeditiously, and on April 30 Hooker issued a grandiloquent general order announcing that "the operations of the last three days have determined that the enemy must ingloriously fly, or come out from behind his defenses and give us battle on our own ground, where certain destruction awaits him. . . ." The order was uncomfortably reminiscent of earlier proclamations by McClellan and Pope.

As Hooker's army crossed the Rappahannock, Captain Charles Francis Adams, Jr., and his regiment were dispatched on picket duty along the lines of advance. As Adams and his men moved forward to take up their positions ahead of the Union lines, they heard carbine shots and then encountered "pell-mell, without order, without lead, a mass of panic-stricken men, riderless horses and miserable cowards" from the picket lines, "driving down the road upon us, in hopeless flight. Along they came . . . throwing away arms and blankets, and in the distance we heard a few carbine shots and the unmistakable savage yell of the rebels." It was the first time Adams had seen Union soldiers in headlong flight. He did his best to stop the rush, to rally the men and establish a skirmish line, but to his dismay his own horse, caught up in the flight, took the bit in his teeth and "dashed off after the rest." Adams wrote: "It was disgraceful! Worse than disgraceful, it was ludicrous." Finally, he formed a line of some thirty men, but he had

hardly got them in place before the rebels appeared and the painstak-
ingly formed line began to dissolve. Adams called to the men to fire,
and "an abortive volley was the result. Poor as it was," he wrote, "it did
the work. A few saddles were emptied and the rebs grew at once more
prudent."

Once more his line started to drift away. Perhaps leading would
work better than driving, Adams thought, and shouting, "Come on,
follow me," in the most approved fashion he spurred his horse
forward, but as he looked over his shoulder, he saw his "line" vanishing
from the center and both flanks. "Then wrath seized my soul," Adams
wrote his brother Henry, "and I uttered a yell and chased them. I
caught a hapless cuss and cut him over the head with my sabre. It only
lent a new horror and fresh speed to his flight. I whanged another over
the face and he tarried for a while. Into a third I drove my horse and
gave him pause, and then I swore and cursed them. I called them
'curs,' 'dogs,' and 'cowards,' a 'disgrace to the 16th Pennsylvania, as the
16th was a disgrace to the service,' and so I finally prevailed on about
half my line to stop this time." Adams's men gave a good account of
themselves, and soon the rebels were in retreat.

By May 1 Hooker's vast army was across the Rappahannock, in
itself no mean accomplishment. Sedgwick, who had been assigned the
role of making a diversionary move, was in position, and the outnumbered rebels were falling back along the Richmond road. Having made
an encouraging beginning, Hooker hesitated just at the moment when
he should have been most aggressive. Lee was given precious hours to
redeploy his forces, and when Hooker pressed forward on the first of
May, he soon encountered Lee's skirmishers. Lee knew well that most
basic rule of military tactics—to strike with the maximum force and
decisiveness at the moment of contact when the situation is most
uncertain and the opposing forces are not yet fully deployed. When
that critical contact was made, Lee drove forward, and Hooker
recoiled, ordering his army to take up defensive positions. Hooker's
whole strategy was based on the notion of drawing Lee into a battle of
maneuver, where the great numerical superiority of the Union army
would be felt. By drawing back in a defensive alignment, Hooker at
once abandoned his strategy and allowed Lee to do what he did best:
maneuver his inferior force with skill and imagination. Lee's reputation overawed his Union counterpart. Nerve is the most essential
element in battle. Hooker's failed him. The army sensed the fact
immediately, and uneasiness quickly pervaded it.

Dr. Daniel Garrison Brinton, Yale '58, was a volunteer surgeon with the Army of the Potomac, assigned to the XI Corps under Howard. The corps was located in a pine woods near Hartwood Church. The road to the camp for twenty miles was filled with wagon trains and infantry moving across the Rappahannock. "The day," Brinton wrote, "was very hot for the season, & the road was strewn with overcoats, blankets, & other articles thrown away by the troops in the hurry of march. In other places, where troops were still encamped they were burning and tearing to pieces such articles, expecting to be soon engaged in the fight which we could already hear commencing on the extreme left. Sadder spectacles than this occasionally presented themselves where some poor fellow worn out by the heat or commencing disease lay helpless and uncared for by the roadside." After marching forward some five miles to the accompaniment of sounds of fighting on the left, the corps in military fashion marched back again. The headquarters unit to which Brinton had been assigned dismounted and waited for further orders. "We had now kept our horses saddled for 36 hours, acc'y to orders," Brinton wrote. "A silent anxiety was visible in every one, & their mirth was forced."

In Hooker's defensive alignment, Howard's XI Corps was placed on the extreme right of the Army of the Potomac. There the men dug hasty entrenchments and developed a "line" oriented in the direction from which it was assumed Lee's attack would come. Carl Schurz was soon aware that all was not as it should be. He saw and heard indications that the rebels were moving to turn the army's right flank—that is, they could be seen marching parallel to the hastily established Union lines, searching for their terminus. But when Schurz tried to persuade Howard that new dispositions should be made to check a flanking and turning maneuver, that officer rejected his warning. Lee was retreating toward Gordonsville, he declared. Howard then retired to catch up on lost sleep, leaving Schurz in charge of his headquarters. Schurz soon received from Hooker a dispatch alerting Howard to the flanking movement of the rebels. Schurz awoke Howard and forwarded Hooker's message. Again Howard rejected Schurz's plea to alter the alignment of the XI Corps. Finally, on his own authority, Schurz moved two regiments on new positions; "as for the rest," he wrote, "the absurdly indefensible position of the corps remained unchanged." Shortly after three in the afternoon the Confederate attack that Schurz had anticipated began to form up within sight of the Union lines. Schurz made haste to inform Howard, who still remained strangely unconcerned. Howard had fresh information from Hooker that Lee was retreating, which he apparently considered more reliable than the testimony of his own division commander. Hooker, in fact, had asked for several brigades to reinforce Sickles, who was presumably in pursuit of Jackson's wagon train. "Within little more than rifle-shot of our right flank," Schurz wrote, "there stood Stonewall Jackson with more than 25,000 men, the most dashing general of the Confederacy with its best soldiers, forming his line of battle, which at a given word was to fold its wings around our feeble flank. . . ."

The construction of field fortifications had been going on for hours. Word came at last to Daniel Brinton that his men might unsaddle and feed themselves and their mounts. The saddles had scarcely been removed when heavy musket fire poured in from their right flank. It was Stonewall Jackson attacking. Before Jackson's "terrific rush" several deer and a bear "were driven from thickets at the edge of the 'wilderness' & in an agony of terror rushed upon our men in the van of the rebels." They were followed by the crash of artillery, the rattle of musket fire, and the "savage screech of the 'rebel yell.'" For a time Schurz's division stood fast, but the men were soon overwhelmed; some were captured, others fled. The 75th Ohio in reserve was engulfed, its colonel killed, and its men were scattered in many instances without a chance to fire their muskets—"telescoped" was Schurz's word.

Schurz and his staff rallied the remnants of the shattered regiments and formed a line which checked the rebel advance long enough to allow a relatively orderly retreat to the Chancellor House, where Hooker had earlier established his headquarters. Schurz calculated that the XI Corps, made up of some 9,000 men, had impeded the attack of the vastly superior force under Jackson for an hour and a half. "Not a man nor a gun came to their aid," Schurz wrote, "during their hopeless contest." Schurz was convinced that the delaying tactics of the corps had prevented the destruction of the greater part of Hooker's army. The shattered corps was placed in reserve, and fate intervened to save the Union army from the worst consequences of Hooker's ineptitude. Stonewall Jackson, returning with his staff officers to his own lines from a reconnaissance, was mistaken by rebel pickets for a Union officer and shot and fatally wounded. One of Jackson's most frequent expressions was: "All things work together for good to them that love God." Mortally wounded, he repeated the verse. His wife, who had been sent for after he was wounded, told him that he was dying, and Jackson replied, "Very good; God does what is best. It is all right." Some hours later, he roused himself and said in a loud, clear voice, "A. P. Hill, prepare for action!" and then: "Let us cross over the river and rest in the shade of the trees." The loss was an incalculable one for the Army of Northern Virginia. Jackson was Lee's right arm, his alter ego, the indispensable adjunct of his army. For a long mournful moment the Confederate forces paused, immobilized by grief and horror.

Walt Whitman, searching for his brother, witnessed much of the fighting and described the latter stages of the battle. "The light from cannons, from flares and from portions of the woods set on fire by sparks gave an eerie light to the battle-field, the crashing, tramping of men," Whitman wrote, "—the yelling—close quarters—we hear the secesh yells—our men cheer loudly back . . . hand-to-hand conflicts, each side stands up to it, brave, determin'd as demons . . . a thousand deeds are done worth to write newer, greater poems on—and still the woods on fire—still many are not only skorch'd—too many, unable to move, are burn'd to death . . . amid the woods, that scene of flitting souls—amid the crack and crash and yelling sounds—the impalpable perfume of the woods—and yet the pungent, stifling smoke—the radiance of the moon, looking from heaven at intervals so placid . . . those silent buoyant upper oceans . . . the melancholy, draperied night above, around. . . . What history, I say, can ever give—for who can know—the mad, determined tussle of the armies, in all their separate large and little squads—as this—each steep'd from crown to toe in desperate, mortal purports?"

Alfred Bellard's New Jersey regiment had repulsed a rebel attack, counterattacked, and captured "seven stands of colors, besides a lot of prisoners," but it was one of the few bright spots in a general Union debacle. The New Jersey men soon found themselves in an extremely precarious position with the units on their right and left falling back, and they themselves had to give ground, abandoning most of their prisoners in the process. Had the 5th New Jersey Volunteers been promptly reinforced and their modest success exploited, the tide of battle might have turned. Bellard himself was wounded in the leg. He made his way as best he could to an army field hospital, where, after he had been given some crackers and a bowl of soup by a lady from the Sanitary Commission, the first sight that met his eyes was a team of doctors operating on wounded soldiers, "cutting off arms and legs, a pile of which lay under the table."

Meanwhile, Hooker drew up some 90,000 men in strong entrenchments before the Chancellor House. Sedgwick, with 22,000 men, was bearing down on Lee's rear. Lee was about to be caught in a pincer movement. For a brief time it seemed as if something might, after all, be retrieved from the disaster of May 3, but Lee was equal to the occasion. Jackson's corps, now under the command of Stuart, made a furious attack on Hooker's lines, threatening to penetrate it at several points, while Lee with a force superior to Sedgwick's fell on the IV Corps, driving it back across the Rappahannock.

"One corps . . . Sedgwick's, fights four dashing and bloody battles in thirty-six hours," Whitman wrote, "retreating in great jeopardy, losing largely but maintaining itself, fighting with the sternest desperation under all circumstances, getting over the Rappahannock only by the skin of its teeth, yet getting over."

With Sedgwick's corps shattered, Lee turned back to join Stuart in front of Hooker's defensive position at the Chancellor House. Hooker, in Schurz's words, "seemed to be in a state of nervous collapse." Soon he was in a state of physical collapse as well. Struck on the head by a wooden pillar dislodged by a rebel cannonball, he was unconscious for an hour. In a mood verging on panic, he ordered his vast army to begin a withdrawal to the Rappahannock. As Schurz put it, Hooker had allowed himself "to be literally scooped up in his entrenchments by a greatly inferior force without making any effort to bring into action some 35,000 to 40,000 men of his own who had hardly fired a shot, and stood substantially idle all the time." Dr. Brinton overtook Hooker, "silent & moody." The pontoon bridge over which they passed was covered with boughs to muffle the sound of marching men and the hooves of horses. "The night was dark and a cold rain that chilled the troops helped to cover the withdrawal." The swollen river threatened to sweep away the three pontoon bridges and leave the Army of the Potomac stranded and at the mercy of Lee. Schurz, coming up with his division, was appalled to see at dawn in the cold, soaking rain 70,000 or 80,000 men jammed together, "waiting to file away in thin marching columns, regiment after regiment, over the bridges." A few well-placed artillery pieces pitching their shells "into this dense, inarticulate mass of humanity, substantially helpless in its huddled condition," would have produced a wild panic.

Oliver Wendell Holmes, Jr., recovered from an attack of dysentery and his wound received at Antietam, was once more in command of Company G. First held in reserve as a part of John Gibbon's division of the II Corps, the 20th Massachusetts moved forward on the night of May 2–3, crossing the Rappahannock and advancing through Fredericksburg. Waiting to cross the canal before Marye's Heights, Holmes was hit by a piece of shrapnel—"whang the iron enters through garter & shoe into my heel," he wrote his mother. "I've been chloroformed & had bone extracted probably shant lose foot" was his reassuring postscript.

William Blackford described the hillside below Marye's where Sedgwick's corps had broken through a Mississippi division after four attacks as "extremely ghastly, the grimmest spectacle" he had ever seen. The Union soldiers had "charged across the field in wave after wave, until it might have been crossed at any point on the bodies of the dead and dying. . . ." Blackford's own home was nearby, and it was soon converted into an army hospital. The dining-room table served as an operating table, "and a small table by its side," he noted, "had a pile of arms and legs upon it." There were barrels of old letters scattered about in the yard, among them a letter from Light-Horse Harry Lee, General Lee's grandfather, to Blackford's grandfather. "The whole house was covered with mud and blood," Blackford wrote, "and it was hard to realize it was the dear old house of my childhood."

After their initial engagement Captain Charles Francis Adams and the 1st Massachusetts Cavalry spent the battle in reserve, combing rumors, waiting restlessly and anxiously to be committed to the battle, hearing the distant sounds of cannon and musket fire, moving forward, and ordered back to their bivouac area. Riding up to try to get some notion of how the tide of battle was flowing, Adams struck the main road "with its endless confusion—reinforcements, supply and ammunition trains and messengers going to the front; stragglers, ambulances and stretchers with the loads of wounded and dying men toiling to the rear; cattle, horses and mules; wounded men resting, tired men sleeping, all here looking excited and worn out with fatigue." The XI Corps had fought but not well, and soon more discouraging news filtered back. "I felt sick of the war," Adams wrote his brother Henry, "of the army, almost of life. I thought of you and of this result abroad; it seemed too much and I felt despairing." The next day he was back at the Potomac Bridge after "the four toughest weeks campaigning that I have ever felt—mud and rain and mud, long marches and short forages. . . . It is strange," he added, "how I like the life though, in spite of its hardships and beastly slavery. . . . On the whole things might be much worse; but the army must be kept in motion and the enemy engaged. If Hooker rests, he's lost, and so I look to being in the field again at once. . . ."

In the capital an apprehensive Lincoln waited for news of Hooker's army. By nightfall, May 6, the truth was all too apparent. Charles Sumner rushed into Welles's room and threw his hands into the air, exclaiming, "Lost, lost all is lost!" Sumner had just come from talking with a deeply dejected Lincoln.

There were a thousand unanswered questions about the latest defeat. "Our people, though shocked and very much disappointed," Welles wrote the next day, "are in better tone and temper than I feared they would be. The press had brought the public mind to high expectation by predicting success which all wished to believe." Charles Francis Adams, Jr., noted that the word that reached the troops was that after "Sedgwick's disaster," Hooker "got frightened and . . . seemed utterly to lose the capacity for command—he was panic stricken. Two thirds of his army had not been engaged at all. . . . Had he fought his army as he might have fought it," Adams added, "the rebel army would have been destroyed and Richmond today in our possession." It seemed to him that Hooker was the least able of all the commanders of the Army of the Potomac. "I never saw him to speak to," he wrote his brother Henry, "but I think him a noisy, low-toned intriguer, conceited, intellectually 'smart,' physically brave. Morally I fear, he is weak; his habits are bad and, as a general in high command, I have lost all confidence in him. But," Adams continued, "the army is large, brave and experienced. We have many good generals and good troops, and, in spite of Hooker, I think much can be done if we are left alone. Give us no more changes and no more new generals!"

Chancellorsville casualties were so great that for ten days after the engagement the wounded were still being brought back to field hospitals. At the Potomac Creek Hospital, Alfred Bellard saw a lieutenant from his company who had been accidentally shot through the lungs by one of his own men and had lain on the battlefield for three days before he was attended to by rebel surgeons. The wounded came in by the boatload to Alexandria. It rained violently on the exposed and helpless men. Whitman, who was present, wrote: "The few torches light up the spectacle. All around—on the wharf, on the ground, out on side place—the men are lying on blankets, old quilts, etc. with bloody rags bound round heads, arms and legs. The attendants are few. . . . The men, whatever their condition lie there, and patiently wait until their turn comes to be taken up," put in ambulances, and carried off to a hospital. More than 30,000 men in both armies were killed, wounded, or missing. Of 133,868 in Hooker's forces 17,278 were casualties. For the army of Northern Virginia the statistics were 60,892 engaged and 12,821 casualties.

With the battle over, the now-familiar scapegoating began. Everyone blamed Hooker, and he in turn did his best to pass the buck. The most accessible goat was the unfortunate XI Corps. Since it was made up largely of Germans, against whom very considerable prejudices existed, the temptation to charge it with responsibility for the general disaster proved irresistible. It was, the newspapers claimed and Hooker's dispatches implied, the failure of the XI Corps to protect the army's flank from Jackson's attack that had opened the door to defeat. Schurz, who had done his best to warn Howard and Hooker of Jackson's flanking movement and repeatedly urged changing the realignment of the corps' defensive lines to meet such a movement, whose men had fought with considerable resolution and courage, and who had lost many of his best officers, was infuriated, his officers and men angry and demoralized. Schimmelpfennig wrote Schurz that members of his brigade had come to him, "filled with indignation . . . with newspapers in their hands," to ask "if such be the reward they may expect for the sufferings they have endured and the bravery they have displayed. The most infamous falsehoods have been circulated through the papers in regard to the conduct of the troops of your division. . . . General," Schimmelpfennig concluded. "I am an old soldier. To this hour I have been proud to command the brave men in this brigade; but I am sure that unless these infamous falsehoods be retracted and reparation made, their good-will and soldierly spirit will be broken. . . ."

Schurz, in his detailed and careful report of the events of May 2 and 3, did his best to repair the damage done to the reputation of the division and corps, demanding an investigation of the charges made against them. In the echelons above, there was evasion and procrastination. No board of inquiry was appointed, and Schurz came to the conclusion that the reputation of the XI Corps was to be sacrificed since it could, "on account of the number of its German regiments and officers, easily be misrepresented as a corps of 'foreigners,' and a 'Dutch corps,' which had few friends, and which might be abused and slandered, and kicked with impunity."

From the perspective of the army, it seemed to Charles Francis Adams, Jr., that "the wretched policy in Washington . . . perpetually divides and dissipates our strength. . . ." In spite of "the acknowledged mediocrity of our Generals," he added, "our sheer strength is carrying through this war. In this Army of the Potomac affairs are today truly deplorable, and I lose and the army loses no heart—all underneath is so sound and good. We know, we *feel*, that our misfortunes are accidents and that we must work through them and the real excellence which we daily see and feel must come to the surface. . . . Sickles, Butterfield and Hooker are the disgrace and bane of this army; they are our three humbugs, intriguers and demagogues. . . . We do not need geniuses; we have enough of brilliant generals; give us in the due course of promotion an honest, faithful, common-sensed and hard-fighting soldier, not stupid, and we feel sure of success."

The cause of the debacle of Chancellorsville, as the confused and indecisive fighting of the first week of May, 1863, came to be known to history, was, plainly, Hooker's incapacity. In order to fight a large army properly, its commander must first *imagine* it. In small unit operations up to, let us say, a division in size, where personal physical courage, example, and exhortation can be demonstrated by a commanding officer and the better part of the field of battle *can be actually seen,* the quality of imagination is of relatively small importance; but when corps and armies are the units in question and critical segments of battles rage far out of the sight of the commander, imagination becomes essential. The commander must not only be able to "imagine" his army but be able to see "in his mind's eye" as well as on sometimes misleading maps the entire field of battle, indeed the theater of operations. Certainly the map is essential, but it must rise from its two-dimensional form into three dimensions. The commander's eye must instantly convert the tracings on paper into hills and declivities, fields, ravines, defensible knolls, lines of fire, roads for quick supply, defiladed positions for artillery batteries, observation posts, concealed approaches to the enemy lines, points of debouchment for attack, concealing woods.

Knowledge of the personal idiosyncrasies of one's fellow officers, of one's superiors and subordinates is the most essential knowledge that a soldier can have. Everything that happens on the field of battle is based, in greater or lesser degree, on *trust,* the confidence that the person who receives an order will execute it faithfully or, best of all, the certain knowledge that if the opportunity presents itself to act "beyond" the other, to meet an unexpected contingency with some bold and enterprising maneuver not covered by the order, or even perhaps contrary to the order, the superior of the officer or soldier involved will have sufficient *trust* in his courage and good sense to support his action. When lives and, sometimes even more important, reputations are at stake, that kind of trust is slowly and often painfully earned. Yet it is the essence, the soul of a body of fighting men, from a platoon up to an army. In this quality, certain Southern armies excelled, and none so much as Lee's. Where mutual sympathy and understanding existed, military articulation followed and greatly increased the effectiveness of every operation. With officers long accustomed to that most profound and deadly of human exercises—battle —a few words, gestures, expressions told volumes, affirmed understandings, sealed unspoken covenants. Part of it was a class matter, a code of honor, a pride, a conscious sense of superiority. Lee and his generals, in modern parlance, often "psyched out" their opposite numbers. And it was here, again, that a quality of imagination was most evident. The great commander not only "imagines" his own army —that is to say, encompasses it with his mind—but penetrates into the psyche of his adversary; he invades his *being* before he penetrates his entrenchments. Every Union general who took the field against Lee, once the myth of the Southerner's invincibility was firmly established, did so with a substantial advantage in men and material and at an immense disadvantage psychologically.

A major factor was that the Army of the Potomac was too near Washington. It thereby suffered from the atmosphere that pervaded the War Department and, to a degree, the Cabinet—the feeling that the North was doing all that was necessary if it simply rebuffed Southern efforts. Such influential figures as Seward and Chase never entirely suppressed the notion that the South must soon "come to its senses" and accept a negotiated peace which would bring it back into the Union and perhaps provide for the eventual emancipation of the slaves. That proposition was *reasonable* enough, and plainly a large number of Americans shared it. The consequence was that the South was always "playing for keeps," for survival, for territory, to preserve its cherished way of life, to keep its women from being violated by the brutal soldiery of the North, and for a dozen other such imperatives. The North was, too often, merely "playing for time." It seems evident that this fatal tentativeness on the part of the North manifested itself in everything that affected the Army of the Potomac. General Scott was its victim. Halleck, his successor, added to it personal deficiencies of character that greatly magnified its effect. With some generals it was doubtless merely a subconscious element. With McClellan there is evidence that it was a conscious policy followed in deliberate defiance of the aims of Lincoln's administration—to seek out the enemy, destroy his capacity to wage war, and force him, by merciless military attrition, to capitulate completely. If this argument be true, then it must follow that every aspect of the Northern military effort in the Virginia theater of operations was compromised by this "psychology of restraint," its sinews unhinged, its resolution diminished, the fighting prolonged almost beyond endurance. The question that remains is: Could it have been otherwise? Would other, more resolute generals—a general, let us say, with the terrible persistence and tenacity of a Grant—have destroyed Lee's army, captured Richmond, and brought the war to an end in 1862 or '63?

The question assumes, of course, that the defeat of Lee's army and the capture of Richmond would have brought about the surrender of the South. The proposition is a doubtful one. There were three or four theaters of war, and there was war by sea as well as by land. The war-making capacity of the South had to be totally destroyed and the Southern will to fight completely broken before there could be peace. So perhaps George Templeton Strong, Gideon Welles, and those of their compatriots who came to feel that there was some terrible quota of suffering and sacrifice that had to be filled before there could be peace were, in essence, right.

The Battle of Chancellorsville came to have a special place in the history of the military campaigns of the war in part because it was the penultimate effort to capture Richmond. Until Grant took command of the Army of the Potomac a year later, the entire focus of the war shifted to the West. Equally important, Chancellorsville was the prelude to Gettysburg, the most crucial engagement of the war, and, in the opinion of many historians, its turning point. And, finally, of course, there was the death of Jackson.

Herman Melville wrote:

> Dead is the Man whose cause is dead,
> Vainly he died and set his seal—
>
> > Stonewall!
>
> Earnest in error, as we feel;
> True to the thing he deemed was due,
> True as John Brown or steel.

27

Gettysburg

After Chancellorsville, the badly battered Army of the Potomac luxuriated in three weeks of rest and recreation. Daniel Brinton distracted himself with his library, which consisted of the Bible, a copy of army regulations, Carlyle's *Sartor Resartus,* and Wilhelm von Humboldt's *Letters to a Female Friend.* On the night of June 3 he had hardly fallen asleep when Captain Fred Stowe, son of Harriet Beecher and an aide to Hooker's adjutant general, stuck his head in Brinton's tent and called out, "Hello, Doctor, get up & pack your things, we have just got a telegraph from Gen. Hooker, to prepare for marching at once & have the Division drawn up under arms & in line of battle by daylight." The division fell out, waited for five hours—sleeping in ranks—and then further orders came to send all baggage to the rear and prepare three days' field rations. Soon heavy firing was heard in the direction of Fredericksburg. Colonel Adin Ballon Underwood's 33rd Massachusetts Regiment was formed up and dispatched to join an elite striking force of 2,000 men capable of marching eighteen miles a day. Word had come that Lee was invading Maryland. The Virginian, it turned out, had decided to try to bring the conflict to a conclusion by carrying the war to the North.

The elections of the fall of 1862 had demonstrated strong

Democratic sentiment in the North favorable to a negotiated peace. The South, not unnaturally, made far more of this phenomenon than it in fact deserved, as, to be sure, did most Northern Republicans (including, as we have seen, the President himself). The failure of Hooker swelled the chorus calling for peace. Carrying the war onto Northern soil might well be the act that would break the Northern will to persist in a war already far longer in its duration and more costly in lives and material than even the most pessimistic Northerners had anticipated two years earlier. Finally, there was the continually renewed hope that even if the North fought on, a successful foray into Pennsylvania would give English friends of the Confederacy the occasion to recognize the South as an independent nation and accord it all the privileges of that status. Lee thus persuaded Jefferson Davis and the Confederate government at Richmond to support his strategy.

Lincoln's initial reaction to the news of Lee's invasion was one of exhilaration. "We cannot help beating them," he told Welles, "if we have the man. How much depends in military matters on one master mind! Hooker may commit the same fault as McClellan and lose his chance. We shall soon see, but it appears to me he can't help but win." Others were far less confident. Washington showed signs of panic. Orders were issued and countermanded. Companies of government clerks were turned out to drill, and in Baltimore, William Wilkins Glenn wrote, "the most absurd little forts were erected about in spots, around the city"; often they were made of hogsheads of tobacco and sugar. Lincoln, yielding to congressional pressure, called for 100,000 volunteers from Maryland, Pennsylvania, New York, and Ohio. Meanwhile, Welles wrote, "Halleck sits, and smokes, and sweats, and scratches his arm . . . but exhibits little military capacity or intelligence; is obfuscated, muddy, uncertain, stupid as to what is doing or to be done."

Lincoln's anxieties about Hooker were confirmed by that general's request to be relieved on the ground that he had not been given sufficient support. Perhaps more basic was Hooker's lack of confidence in his own capacities. Lincoln lost no time in appointing George G. Meade to succeed Hooker. "Of Meade," Welles wrote, "I know very little. He is not great. His brother officers speak well of him, but he is considered rather a 'smooth bore' than a rifle. . . . Meade has not so much character as such a command required," Welles added. "He . . . will be well supported, have the best wishes of all, but does not inspire immediate confidence."

As Lee's army crossed the Potomac on its way to Pennsylvania, a crowd of curious onlookers lined the banks of the Maryland side to greet them. William Blackford heard one of his men call out to the spectators, "well, boys, I've been seceding for two years and now I've got back into the union again!" Another called to a woman he took to be a Union sympathizer: "Here, we are, ladies, as rough and ragged as ever but back again to bother you."

Meade now began a kind of race to place an army across Lee's line of advance. In this movement Howard's XI Corps was in the van; by June 14 it was in the vicinity of Hartwood Church. The only rations available were crackers and coffee, and in the course of the day Daniel Brinton's detachment "half captured half purchased a small pig and a couple of chickens." There was a brief rest, and the weary, hungry troops pushed on again toward Manassas and Centreville, marching on into the night under lowering skies until they could no longer see the way ahead and then making an awkward camp for "a brief & broken nights rest, getting up again at 3 A.M." At the Monocacy River, Brinton's unit found quarters in a church where the prayer books and hymnbooks lay on plush seats. "To all the solemn & sacred associations that these called forth," Brinton wrote, "the sight of saddles, bridles, sabres, and horse blankets scattered about the pews, soldiers lying about the seats smoking, joking, and swearing, the churchyard around with its graves & monuments turned into a horse yard & a slaughter pen for killing sheep, these offered a strange & novel contrast."

Brinton described the scene on the Frederick road, as his unit moved north in pursuit of Lee: "Droves of cattle, ammunition & supply trains, squadrons of cavalry, stragglers of all sorts obstructed the way and created an atmosphere of chaos." When the corps reached Emmitsburg, Maryland, officers found quarters in "an enormous farmhouse," where the farmer "brought up from his cellar a pitcher of excellent old rye whiskey for our solace," Brinton wrote. Orders had come down that Brinton's unit was to be ready to march at 4:00 A.M., so without taking off his boots or spurs, he lay down to snatch a few precious hours of sleep. The infantry did not reach camp until midnight, and at daybreak "they were hastened into line without breakfast, to march through a drizzling rain, over a greasy clay road. . . ." All day long the exhausted men struggled on, making camp at four-thirty in the afternoon after having covered thirty-eight miles in twenty-four hours, one of the most exacting marches of the war. It was no wonder that Brinton, who, after all, had ridden the whole way, found the men "in no very good humor."

In Chambersburg, Pennsylvania, sullen Unionists lined the streets to watch Lee's army pass through the town. One bold young woman had a small Union flag pinned across her bosom, at which a Confederate soldier called out, "Look here, Miss, you'd better take that flag off!" She replied, "I won't do it. Why should I?" The soldier answered: "Because, Miss, these old rebels are hell on breastworks."

In the Pennsylvania farmland, especially among the so-called Pennsylvania Dutch, actually Germans with a strong tradition of ethnic separatism, Sidney George Fisher reported that there was little interest in or sympathy with the war. "The country people displayed entire indifference" even in the face of Lee's invading armies, "saying the war was a mere quarrel between abolitionists & secessionists & that they did not care which won. They were only anxious about their farms and would be glad to have peace on any terms."

As the Confederate army moved in a northwesterly direction, Lee settled on Cashtown, Pennsylvania, as a favorable site for the general engagement which both armies sought. But, as is so often the case, fortuitous circumstances, rather than strategic considerations, determined where the battle was to be fought. The Confederate general Henry Heth, who had succeeded A. P. Hill as brigade commander at Chancellorsville, now commanded a division. Heth, so the story goes, decided to probe into the town of Gettysburg to see if he could find shoes for his men, many of whom were barefoot. General O. O. Howard's XI Corps, which included Carl Schurz's 3rd Division and Daniel Brinton's medical unit, was already in the vicinity. As Howard neared the town, word reached him that General John Reynolds's I Corps had made contact with Heth's advance units. Howard instructed Schurz to hurry his men forward to support Reynolds. Schurz did so, encountering in the process a stream of refugees—primarily of women, children, and older men. One woman, who hurried a small child along, tried to intercept Schurz, calling out, "Hard times at Gettysburg! They are shooting and killin'! What will become of us!"

Shortly before noon Schurz joined Howard on a hill east of the town cemetery. Gettysburg lay in a shallow valley. "Beyond and on both sides of it, stretching far away," the two officers could see "open landscape dotted with little villages and farmhouses and orchards and tufts of trees and detached belts of timber. . . ." The town was the hub of a number of converging roads—the Hanover, Huntertown, Carlisle, Harrisburg, Cashtown, Hagerstown, Baltimore, and Taneytown roads and the York and Chambersburg pikes. The promontory on which they stood was Cemetery Hill, the northern end of a ridge which ran due south to two "steep, rocky partly wooden knolls, called Round Tops." To their right a half mile away was Culp's Hill, and to the left a mile or so off and running more or less parallel to Cemetery Ridge was wooded Seminary Ridge, so called from the Lutheran seminary located there.

The tiny figures of soldiers, impossible to distinguish as Unionists or Confederates, were visible on Seminary Ridge. The scene appeared to Schurz like some toy miniature of battle "in the large frame of the surrounding open country," but even as they stood there, the body of General Reynolds, killed by a Southern sharpshooter, was carried by. With Reynolds's death, command of the I Corps passed to the commander of the 3rd Division, General Abner Doubleday, a graduate of West Point, class of 1842. Doubleday, a native of New York State and resident of Cooperstown, enjoyed some modest fame as the inventor, at the age of sixteen, of a game which he called baseball. He had, additionally, been present at the siege of Fort Sumter and fired the first gun in its defense. With Doubleday in command of the I Corps, Schurz took command of the XI, and Howard assumed the overall direction of the two corps. If the engagement was limited to a portion of Lee's army, the task of the two corps was to drive the rebels off. If, on the other hand, Heth's corps was the advance element of Lee's main army, the most essential task was to prepare strong defensive positions on the assumption that the Virginian had to attack. Clearly in the latter eventuality Cemetery Hill and its two Round Tops made an ideal defensive position with a wide field of fire. Howard ordered Schurz to go to the support of Doubleday and the I Corps with two divisions, while he held the 2nd Division with the artillery in reserve. As Schurz's division reached Cemetery Hill, Schurz sent General Schimmelpfennig forward with the 3rd Division, Schurz's own, which had the primary responsibility of preventing the rebels from turning Doubleday's right flank, and committed Barlow's division (1st Division) to cover Schimmelpfennig. At this point the I Corps had pushed the enemy back with relative ease and captured the better part of a brigade in the process, but soon it was clear that Heth was being rapidly reinforced, and the tide of battle began to turn. After climbing to the roof of a house near the developing battle lines, Schurz could see that his men were in danger of being overwhelmed by superior numbers and cut off from the position on Cemetery Hill. He sent off a hasty message asking Howard for support from the reserve. Ewell's corps and that of A. P. Hill, estimated at a combined strength of 30,000, were pressing on fewer than 14,000 men in the portions of the I and XI Corps. Schurz had hardly dispatched his request for support before the Confederates were in the attack. The fighting grew more intense by the moment. "Regiment stood against regiment in the open fields," Schurz wrote, "near enough almost to see the white in one another's eyes, firing literally in one another's faces. The slaughter on both sides was awful." At this juncture Schurz got word from Howard to withdraw his divisions to Cemetery Hill. He also received a brigade of the 2nd Division, which he placed in position to cover the withdrawal of the 1st Division. It proved more difficult to extricate the 3rd. The maneuver was finally accomplished with heavy casualties. The 2nd Brigade of the 3rd Division lost all its regimental commanders, and several regiments had half their number killed or wounded. Colonel Mahler, who had fought with Schurz in the German fortress at Rastatt in 1849, was mortally wounded and waved a farewell to Schurz. The two corps, more or less intermixed, made their way through the streets of the town crowded with military vehicles, and some lost their way and were captured by the rebels. But the main body of survivors reached Cemetery Hill by midafternoon, hot and weary. There they found that Meade had sent Hancock forward to assume command from Howard.

General Winfield Scott Hancock was a seasoned regular army officer. A member of the West Point class of '44, he was, at thirty-nine, one of the youngest corps commanders in the Union army. He had served in the Mexican War with great distinction and repeatedly distinguished himself in the campaigns of the Army of the Potomac until his reputation with both soldiers and officers was as high as that of any general officer. His arrival at Cemetery Ridge gave the Union troops, in Schurz's words, "a new inspiration." Schurz added: "His proud mien, and his superb soldierly bearing, seemed to verify all the things that had been told about him. His mere presence was a reinforcement, and everybody on the field felt stronger for his being there." Acting on Meade's orders, Hancock was, in effect, the commander of the Union forces in the fighting which was to ensue. The XI Corps was placed in position on Cemetery Hill nearest the town itself. The I Corps extended the line toward the Round Tops except for James Wadsworth's division, which occupied Culp's Hill. After the troop dispositions had been made and entrenchments and breastworks constructed, Hancock and Schurz sat down on a stone fence near the crest of the ridge and studied with their binoculars the movements of the Confederate forces. Although the Union positions were strong ones, the two corps, their ranks considerably thinned by the day's fighting, appeared to be far outnumbered by the rapidly growing Confederate army on the opposite hillside. The XII Corps was on its way, and in its absence both officers confessed some uneasiness about their ability to check a strong assault by Lee's divisions. But the rebels showed no immediate disposition to attack, and at dusk the XII Corps arrived to augment the dangerously thin Union lines. A portion of the III Corps came up in the gathering darkness. Military historians, North and South, would debate for years to come the question of whether or not, if the Confederate forces had attacked Cemetery Hill as soon as the XI and I corps withdrew from Gettysburg, the Confederates would not have routed those two battered units, intercepted Meade's main army in its advance, and achieved another brilliant victory. Schurz at least was convinced otherwise. One of his company commanders, who had been trapped in the town when the Union forces withdrew, later told him that he had heard an officer courier say to General Richard Ewell that Lee wished him to attack Cemetery Hill at once, to which Ewell had replied "that if General Lee knew the condition of his . . . troops, after their long march and the fight that had just taken place, he would not think of such an order, and that the attack could not be risked."

It was now clear that a major battle was unfolding. That night in the lower gatehouse of the Gettysburg Cemetery six or seven generals gathered around a table improvised from a barrel, with a candle stuck in a bottle's neck for light. There, sitting on boxes and on the floor, the corps and division commanders discussed the upcoming battle and the suitability of the ground on which they found themselves. They all were agreed that Meade could hardly do better than to contest Lee's advance here, where the terrain so favored the defense. "There was nothing of extraordinary solemnity in the 'good-night' we gave one another when we parted," Schurz wrote, in concluding his account of the impromptu gathering. "It was rather a common-place, business-like 'good-night,' as that of an ordinary occasion." The men and officers of the XI Corps lay down, in the mild summer evening, wrapped in their blankets, and slept among the gravestones.

When the sun rose on the morning of July 2, the Union soldiers could see the Confederate lines with artillery batteries scattered along its length in position to support an attack. While four Union corps were in position, more were on the march. They could be located by the dust they raised as they marched down the Taneytown road and Baltimore pike to take up positions already marked out for them. Around eight o'clock Meade appeared at the cemetery, accompanied by an orderly and a staff officer. Schurz thought he looked "careworn and tired," as if he had not slept. "This simple, cold, serious soldier with his business-like air did inspire confidence," Schurz wrote. Schurz greeted Meade and explained the disposition of the Federal troops. Meade nodded, satisfied, and Schurz asked him how many men he had under his command. "In the course of the day," Meade replied, "I expect to have about 95,000—enough, I guess, for this business." And then, reflectively: "Well, we may as well fight it out here as anywhere else."

Lee and his staff had meanwhile held a council of war. Longstreet, always cautious, was reluctant to attack at all. He favored a policy of "strategic offense—tactical defense." Heretofore Lee had known the terrain over which he was fighting like the proverbial palm of his hand. In addition, he had had his eyes, Jeb Stuart's cavalry, and his alter ego, Jackson. Now he was venturing into unfamiliar country, without his eyes and without the general on whom he had often and successfully relied. The results were quickly apparent. Without adequate reconnaissance, Lee had an incomplete picture of the Union dispositions. He assumed that the southern (or left) flank of the Union line, along the Emmitsburg road, was the strongpoint (and thus the key to the Federal defenses). It was therefore against this sector that he decided to send Longstreet.

Meanwhile, across the valley, just at daybreak, the II, the V, and the balance of the III corps came up, followed by the Artillery Reserve. Sedgwick's VI Corps arrived after a forced march of thirty-four miles. A strange anticipatory quiet hung now over the scene as the two armies "felt" one another, in Schurz's word, broken by the "occasional sputtering of musketry and abrupt discharges of cannon, like the growling barks of chained watchdogs when you approach them too closely." Finally, as the sun passed its meridian and the heat of the day broke, the Confederate attack began. By now the to-become-famous "fishhook" positions of the Union army were well filled out. Henry Slocum's XII Corps with Wadsworth's division of the I Corps held Culp's Hill and the saddle between it and Cemetery Ridge. These formed the hook. The shank was made up of elements of the XI, the I under Doubleday, and the II. The III Corps under Sickles was pushed out to a peach orchard considerably in advance of the main line. The Round Tops on the left of the III Corps were unoccupied.

To every defensive position there is a key, a point of vulnerability, often not immediately apparent, the capture of which endangers the whole line. Now, while the Union soldiers watched, stirring uneasily in their hastily constructed entrenchments and rifle pits, the Confederate lines formed in a great semicircle, Ewell's corps on the left facing Culp's Hill and Cemetery Hill, A. P. Hill in the center, opposite the II and III corps, and Longstreet's corps on the right. The Confederate artillery opened, firing rather too high, and Union artillery answered. Longstreet's corps moved forward in the attack on the Round Tops, and the rattle of musket fire grew increasingly intense, punctuated by the thump and crash of artillery shells. As Longstreet's attack developed toward the Round Tops, General Gouverneur Kemble Warren, West Point '50 and a topographical engineer, now commanding the II Corps, saw the danger and immediately started reserve units up to occupy the tops. It was too late to reach Big Round Top, the larger of the two promontories. That was already in the hands of Colonel William Calvin Oates and the contingent of rebels from the 15th Alabama. The 20th Maine Regiment, portions of O'Rorke's 140th New York, and young Stephen Weed's 3rd Vermont made it to Little Round Top along with Hazlett's D Battery, of the 5th United States Artillery. For a time there was a bloody and bitter struggle for the tops, a struggle in which four of the Union officers in command of the units that Warren had hastily gathered together and rushed into position and were killed before Little Round Top was secured. The Confederate general John Bell Hood, trying to exploit the seizure of the Big Round Top, had his arm smashed by a Union bullet. Sickles's salient position in the peach orchard now became the focus of Confederate attacks. The III Corps was driven back with heavy casualties, and a dangerous break in the Union lines was prevented only by plugging the gap with divisions drawn from four other corps.

Ewell, meanwhile, had delayed his attack on the northern end of the Federal lines, hoping that his artillery would silence the Union batteries. The reverse happened. The Union batteries on Cemetery Hill and Culp's Hill beat down Ewell's artillery, and under the weight of this disheartening setback, Ewell, at six in the evening, ordered the divisions of Robert Rodes, Early, and Edward ("Allegheny") Johnston to advance on the Union lines. Early, in the center, succeeded in penetrating the Union lines on Cemetery Hill, but Adelbert Ames rallied the fleeing Union defenders and, with reinforcements from Samuel Carroll's brigade, drove the rebels back and restored the Union lines. Ames, West Point '61, had been, with twenty-one of his classmates, in the First Battle of Bull Run and there, as an artillery-man, won the Congressional Medal of Honor, one of the few Union officers to distinguish himself on that unhappy day. Now, by his courage and initiative, he added conspicuously to his laurels.

Culp's Hill had been left to General George Sears Greene, West Point '23. Greene had taught mathematics and engineering at the academy and then resigned his commission in 1836 to become a successful railroad engineer, an engineer for the Croton Reservoir, and the designer and builder of the city reservoir in Central Park, New York. His son, Samuel Dana Greene, a graduate of the Naval Acade-my, had manned the gun on the *Monitor* in her memorable engage-ment with the *Merrimac* and commanded the vessel after Lieutenant Worden was wounded. Now Greene's seriously depleted corps was faced with fighting off Johnston's division. Fortunately only three Confederate brigades found their way across Rock Creek in time to attack Culp's Hill. One of these, led by George H. ("Maryland") Steuart, occupied the entrenchments that had been abandoned by those portions of the XII Corps sent to reinforce Sickles. The other two were checked at the base of the hill by the fire of Greene's troops, who stood fast under heavy fire until reinforced by, among others, several regiments from Schurz's XI Corps.

Schurz was with Howard on Cemetery Hill, exchanging in the gathering darkness congratulations on the repulse of the Confederate attack, when heavy firing broke out from the batteries on the right of Cemetery Hill. The rebels were pressing a final desperate attack on the batteries. If they could be seized and their guns turned on Culp's Hill, Johnston could resume his attack there, and the whole section of the Union line running south to the Round Tops could be taken under enfilade fire. It was a perilous moment. Schurz gathered up two nearby regiments, ordered them to fix bayonets, and directed them to the support of the batteries. "Arrived at the batteries," Schurz wrote, "we found an indescribable scene of melée. Some rebel infantry had scaled the breastworks and were taking possession of the guns. But the cannoneers defended themselves desperately. With rammers and fence rails, hand spikes and stones, they knocked down the intruders." A rebel officer, brandishing his sword, shouted, "This battery is ours!" To which a German artilleryman replied, "No, dis battery is *unser*," and knocked him down with a sponge staff. It was a proud moment for Schurz and his fellow Germans, and several years later Howard took account of their achievements in a magazine article on the battle, writing: "The Dutchmen showed that they were in no way inferior to their Yankee comrades, who had been taunting them ever since Chancellorsville."

The end of the fighting on the second day found the Confederates in possession of an important stretch of the Emmitsburg road and occupying the entrenchments on the forward slope of Culp's Hill. The main Federal lines, on the other hand, had held firm and indeed been strengthened by withdrawing what might be called the Sickles salient in the peach orchard and, most important of all, by taking firm possession of Little Round Top. Casualties on both sides had been heavy. The rebels, as the attackers, had lost large numbers of men killed and wounded. The Southern dispositions had been, in many respects, faulty. Lee's plan of attack had been overly ambitious, and there had been numerous instances of confusion and disregarded or misunderstood orders. Meade used effectively the tactic so often employed by Lee of shifting his men about to meet attacks on different sectors of his front. He was able to do this in part because the Confederate attack was poorly coordinated. Ewell's long delay in attacking, for example, allowed Meade to shift part of the XII Corps from Culp's Hill to restore the Union line at the peach orchard. The tentativeness of the attack of A. P. Hill and W. D. Pender against the line of Cemetery Ridge, which was, to be sure, intended for no more than a diversion, again allowed the commitment of Union reserves to capture Big Round Top.

On the Union side, the promptness and energy with which Warren reacted to Hood's seizure of Big Round Top was clearly a decisive point in the battle, as was the action of Ames in plugging the gap at the peach orchard. Finally, there was the resolution of the men of the XI Corps in turning back the late attack on the Cemetery Hill battery after dark.

Charles Francis Adams's cavalry regiment was heavily involved, and Adams was convinced that the Union army had escaped destruction "by the skin of our teeth." He wrote: "At Sunset we were whipped and night saved the army. I never felt such sickening anxiety." The cavalry had been placed in a wood a mile and a half from the front and slightly behind the right wing of Meade's army. By evening the position was in danger of being outflanked, and the infantry began to give way. "Presently," Adams wrote, "they came swarming through our camp in demoralized squads, wounded and well, officers and men—so that we were forced out and obliged to move back." The order came to retreat twenty miles, but before the orders could be carried out, they were countermanded. At nightfall the Union positions were still largely intact.

Longstreet protested vigorously but futilely Lee's decision to renew the battle the next day. Despite its heavy losses, the morale in the Confederate army was high, and George Pickett's fresh and well-disciplined division had arrived during the night to strengthen the Confederates. Meade had decided that the abandoned Union entrenchments on Culp's Hill, which had been occupied by Steuart without resistance and heavily reinforced during the night, must be retaken, and the morning of the third opened with the sounds of fierce fighting at that spot.

Both armies seemed willing to wait upon the outcome of that contest, which continued for almost six hours before the Confederates were driven out. Again one wonders why Lee, having decided to attack, did not take advantage of the Union action to launch his own assault. After the successful Union attack a strange silence fell over the valley. "That the battle should have come to a short stop would have surprised nobody," Schurz wrote, "but when that stop lengthened from minute to minute, from half hour to half hour, and when it settled down into a tranquility like the peaceful and languid repose of a warm midsummer morning in which one might expect to hear the ringing of the village church-bells, there was something ominous, something uncanny, in these strange, unexpected hours of profound silence, so sharply contrasting with the bloody horrors which had preceded, and which were sure to follow them." Some of the soldiers "sat silently on the ground munching their hard-tack." Others slept while the officers collected in small groups to speculate on the meaning of the interlude of calm. Then, at one o'clock, two guns at Longstreet's lines on the far left coughed, and as though in answer, the entire array of Confederate batteries opened up, some 130 guns, aiming their fire at the Round Tops and Cemetery Hill. Those Union pieces that could be brought to bear on the enemy batteries—some 80—replied, and in Schurz's words, "one of the grandest artillery duels in the history of wars followed." At times Schurz could make himself heard only by cupping his hands and shouting. Most of the shells were aimed high and flew harmlessly overhead, but even so "the screaming, whirring" sound as they passed was unnerving.

It was a severe testing of the Union soldiers. Schurz rightly called heavy artillery fire "one of the hardest trials of the courage and steadfastness of the soldier. . . . It bewilders the mind of the bravest with a painful sense of helplessness as against tremendous power. . . ." Schurz found that the sight of him walking calmly about smoking a cigar was steadying to his men. Many relaxed by performing such minor military chores as cleaning their muskets, polishing the buttons on their uniforms, or sewing up holes in their clothes.

One of Schurz's aides, young Captain Fritz Tiedemann, who thirty years later would marry one of his commanding officer's daughters, was narrowly missed by an enemy shell that exploded just as he moved away to search for some biscuits for Schurz. After the bombardment had continued for an hour or more, the artillery commander ordered various Union batteries to cease firing, in part to conserve ammunition and also to give the Confederates the impression that their fire had silenced the Northern guns. As is so often. the case in artillery bombardments, the actual damage to the Union forces was far less than the vast outpouring would have led an observer to believe —Schurz called the results "very trifling" and the number of men and horses killed "astonishingly small considering the awfulness of the turmoil."

The principal consequence of the fire was to give the rebel officers and men the illusion that the Union lines were badly battered, if not wholly shattered, and that a determined assault on them must succeed. Thus sustained, they formed up in a splendid military panoply, line on line of infantry, battle flags waving and bayonets flashing in the sun. The Union defenders watched the successive, extended lines of skirmishers emerging from the concealing woods, until some 15,000 soldiers, their officers mounted on horseback, covered the hillside below Seminary Ridge. They had almost a mile of open field and meadow to cross to gain the Union entrenchments, and before they had traversed more than a few hundred yards, they discovered that the Union artillery had been far from silenced. It opened with overpowering effect. Schurz and his fellow officers, observing through field glasses, could see great gaps torn in the ranks of the advancing companies and regiments; but the gaps were quickly closed up, and the lines came on unwaveringly. Confederate artillery resumed its fire, but the Union guns, charged with shrapnel, continued their destructive fire. The Confederate lines disappeared in a fold in the terrain and emerged, still in good order and now at a faster pace. As they came within range of rifles and muskets, the crackle of that fire was added to the roar of artillery until it seemed that no one could face such a merciless hail of metal without breaking.

The initial attack was centered on the peach orchard, where the Union line had been broken the day before, but it was accompanied by a strong movement against the positions of the XI Corps on Cemetery Hill.

Some thirty pieces of Union artillery were loaded with grape and canister and given the order to fire when the rebels were within five hundred yards. The results were devastating; those Confederates still on their feet fled for their lives, pursued by Union skirmishers. The sound of heavy firing on the left, where the terrain was hidden from sight by a spur projecting from the ridge, indicated that troops were hotly engaged there and the outcome still presumably in question. At last Schurz saw "first little driblets, then larger numbers, and finally huge swarms of men in utter disorder hurrying back the way they had come," pursued by blue-clad skirmishers gathering in prisoners. There could be only one conclusion—the rebel attack had shattered against the Union positions. A great wave of exultant sound rose from the Union lines, and here and there soldiers began to sing "John Brown's Body," until the "song swept weirdly over the bloody field." To many, it was the moment for an all-out assault on the fleeing and demoralized rebels. The V Corps, held in reserve, was fresh for the task, and men who had been only marginally engaged were eager to administer the coup de grace; to avenge at last all the defeats and humiliations that the Army of the Potomac had suffered at the hands of the rebels. That such a blow might end the war flashed into the minds of many on the field of battle. But no such orders were issued. Night came, and the exhausted men slept where they lay, while medical corpsmen and stretcher-bearers carried the wounded to field hospitals behind the lines.

Carl Schurz rode down into Gettysburg the next day, the Fourth of July. The town was filled with Confederate stragglers and Union soldiers rounding them up as prisoners. Wounded men of both armies still lay in the battlefield amid the dead bodies of their companions. Schurz found General Schimmelpfennig, whom he had given up for dead. The general, Schurz's "military instructor in the old German days," had been caught in the town when the XI Corps withdrew and had hidden under some straw in a pigsty through the two days of fighting without food or water. With the departure of the rebels Schimmelpfennig had come out of hiding, found some eggs in the house, and prepared a breakfast of which he invited Schurz to partake.

After breakfast Schurz visited the battlefield. Most of the wounded had been removed, but the bodies of the dead were everywhere. "There can be no more hideous sight than that of the corpses on a battlefield," Schurz wrote, "after they have been exposed a day or more to the sun in warm weather—the bodies swollen to monstrous size, the faces bloated and black, the eyes bulging out with a dead stare, all their features puffed out almost beyond recognition, some lying singly or in rows, others in heaps, having fallen one over another, some in attitudes of peaceful repose, others with arms raised, others in a sitting position, others on their knees, others clawing the earth, many horribly distorted by what must have been a frightful death-struggle. . . . I rode away from this horrible scene," Schurz added, "in a musing state of mind, finally composing myself with the reaffirmed faith that in our struggle against slavery we could not possibly be wrong; that there was an imperative, indisputable necessity of fighting for our cause. . . ."

The thousands of wounded were carried to farmhouses behind the Union lines. "The houses, the barns, the sheds, and the open barnyards were crowded with moaning and wailing human beings," Schurz wrote, "and still an unceasing procession of stretchers and ambulances was coming in from all sides to augment the numbers of the sufferers." A heavy rain began, as it often did after a battle, and many of the wounded lay unprotected. Operating tables had been placed in the open, where the light was best, and when the rain began, tarpaulins were hastily rigged to shelter doctors and their patients. The surgeons stood, their sleeves rolled up, their bare arms and their linen aprons alike splattered with blood, "their knives not seldom held between their teeth, while they were helping a patient on or off the table . . . around them pools of blood and amputated arms or legs in heaps, sometimes more than man-high." Schurz saw surgeons too tired to stand and some with "hysterical tears" streaming down their faces. Some of the wounded men were in such pain that they called out, "Let me die!" Others, delirious, called for their mothers or fathers. "There are people," Schurz wrote, "who speak lightly of war as a mere heroic sport." They could not do so if they had been witnesses of such scenes. Schurz reflected on "the untold miseries connected with them that were spread all over the land." Only an inhuman brute would not admit "that war brought on without the most absolute necessity, is the greatest and most unpardonable of crimes."

From the first of July to the fifth, Daniel Brinton and his fellow surgeons had been at work ceaselessly, taking a few hours of sleep whenever there was a lull in the flow of wounded and dying men —"very hard work it was, too . . . four operating tables were going night and day." On the Fourth of July, when it was believed that victory had at last crowned the Union army, 1,000 men were in the hospital. Shells fell within twenty feet of the room in which Brinton was operating. Captain Stowe was the only corps staff officer to be wounded, and Brinton extracted a fragment of shell from his leg.

In the aftermath of Gettysburg, Lincoln and his Cabinet waited impatiently for word that Meade was in hot pursuit of Lee's retreating army, but no such word came. The word was, rather, that "our army is waiting for supplies to come up before following,—a little of the old lagging infirmity," Welles wrote in his diary. "If they are driven back, Halleck will be satisfied . . . too many of our officers think it sufficient if the Rebels quit and go off, . . . that it is unnecessary to capture, disperse, and annihilate them."

Lincoln was depressed by Meade's dispatches, Hay noted. "They were so cautiously and almost timidly worded,—talking about reconnoitering to find the enemy's weak place, and other such." The President feared, above all else, that Meade would allow Lee's shattered army to escape. Word that his fears were realized soon came. "We had them within our grasp," Lincoln said; "we had only to stretch forth our hands and they were ours. And nothing I could say or do could make the army move." Meade started off on the wrong foot with the President when he issued an orotund general order to his troops, exhorting them "to drive the invader from our soil." Much more was called for than that comparatively modest task. "This is a dreadful reminiscence of McClellan," Lincoln said to Hay. "The same spirit that moved McClellan to claim a great victory because Pennsylvania and Maryland were safe. The hearts of ten million people sank within them when McClellan raised that shout last fall. Will our Generals never get that idea out of their heads? The whole country is our soil."

For Lincoln, Meade's dilatoriness in pursuing Lee was the last straw. At a Cabinet meeting on July 7, Welles noted that the President's face betrayed his "sadness and despondency." The Potomac had been swollen by rains, and Lee was delayed in crossing. Another missed opportunity.

At first George Templeton Strong, taught by painful experience to be skeptical about claims of Northern victories, refused to believe the news of a decisive victory at Gettysburg over the invincible Lee. Finally the news seemed conclusive. "The woman-floggers" had been "badly repulsed." Strong added: "This may have been one of the great decisive battles of history." The next day he had further reflections: "The results of this victory are priceless. Philadelphia, Baltimore and Washington are safe. The rebels are hunted out of the North, their best army is routed, and the charm of Lee's invincibility broken. The Army of the Potomac has at last found a general that can handle it, and it has stood nobly up to its terrible work in spite of its long disheartening list of hard-fought failures, and in spite of McClellan's influence on its officers." Strong was convinced that Lee's defeat saved New York City "from an organized Copperhead rising . . . headed by sneaking Horatio Seymour's underlings—traitors, bolder but not baser than their chief." He was also proud to note that the medical officers of the Sanitary Commission cared for 13,000 Union and 7,000 Confederate soldiers at Gettysburg and distributed $72,000 worth of clothing and provisions, including 10,000 shirts, 11,000 pounds of mutton and poultry, and 12,000 loaves of bread.

It is safe to say that no battle in history has been as closely studied and as much commented on as the Battle of Gettysburg. The noble but futile attack of Pickett's division is as well known as the charge of the Light Brigade and for somewhat the same reasons. Although it was not so vainglorious and error-ridden an act as its English counterpart, it was perhaps as misguided. Longstreet, Lee's most experienced "lieutenant" after Jackson's death, was bitterly opposed to Lee's plan of attack. He had declared to Lee, "General, I have been a soldier all my life. I have been with soldiers engaged in fights by couples, by squads, companies, regiments and armies, and should know, as well as anyone, what soldiers can do. It is my opinion that no 15,000 men ever arrayed for battle can take that position."

Why Lee persisted in his plan for an attack on the center of the Union lines when his military reputation had been built on his skill at maneuvering large bodies of men, at drawing his opponents into battle under conditions most favorable to him, was and remains a mystery. Longstreet was convinced that the Union right was vulnerable to a flanking movement. If Lee had simply moved *around* Gettysburg, Meade would have had to move to intercept him and thus, almost inevitably, would have been forced to fight on less favorable ground. Perhaps Lee, increasingly aware of the precariousness of his situation and the difficulty of maintaining his lines of supply, decided to stake everything on one roll of the dice, however unfavorable the odds. While it appears in retrospect that the second day of fighting, July 2, was the decisive day, it was also the case that the Confederate forces appeared to come close enough to victory to encourage the hope that they might, with one final heroic effort, demolish Meade's army.

In Lee's defense, it must be said that no battles ever go entirely according to plan. Every attack is dogged by error and confusion. The critical moment almost invariably comes when the original plan, however brilliant its conception, has failed and officers and leaders must improvise. There luck and leadership sustain each other. The most inspired leaders *make* the luck—seize the moment. Lee's mistake was not so much in his plan of attack as in his determination to invade Pennsylvania, thereby conceding almost every "edge" he had enjoyed on his own turf. Once he was in the presence of the Union army, Lee's error was to attack at all. On the other hand, having invaded the North, he could not retreat without a battle. The remarkable thing is that Lee's troops came as close to victory as they did. It is, perhaps above all, a tribute to the fighting qualities of his veteran soldiers. To a substantial degree Lee was a victim of his success. That success had encouraged, in as wise and cautious a general as Lee, the illusion of invincibility. Charles Francis Adams, Jr., was convinced that "finer fighting material" than the "rebel army in Virginia" would be hard to find. "I should say," he wrote his father, "that Lee's army at Gettysburg was in every respect superior to the Army of the Potomac, superior in numbers, better officered, a better fighting material, as well armed, better clothed and as well fed. The spirit of his army was much better than ours, and I saw no evidence of their ever having been short of rations or demoralized by want or misfortune. Their tone was of the very best." On the other hand, Adams's estimate of Lee was not high. He believed, as many Union men did, that Jackson had been the real strength of Lee's army, the only real military genius produced by the war. Lee could have crushed Burnside at Fredericksburg, in Adams's opinion, and had let him escape. Hooker had "surprised" and "outgeneraled" Lee, who had been saved only by Jackson's intervention. "And now, finally at Gettysburg, with every chance in his favor, and against a dispirited army and a new General, he has incurred a disaster to the Southern army which belittles our defeat at Fredericksburg or their own at Malvern Hill. Thus I cannot share in the general admiration of Lee."

Northern reaction to the battle—hailing it as a great victory—was an index of how high the reputation of the Army of Northern Virginia and its great general stood. Simply stated, some 75,000 Confederate soldiers had attacked Meade with more than 88,000 men entrenched in ideal defensive positions and, after having come disconcertingly close to rolling back the Union lines, had withdrawn to their own line of departure on Seminary Ridge with heavy losses. The Confederates are estimated to have lost almost 4,000 killed and more than 18,000 wounded, with 5,400 missing. The Union losses were only slightly less—3,155 killed, 14,529 wounded, and 5,365 missing. Combined Confederate losses: 28,063 out of 75,000 engaged; Union: 23,049. The Confederate losses were one-third of their effective strength at the start of the battle; those of Meade's army, one-fourth—both enormous casualty rates.

Schurz wrote very truly that "the political value of the results achieved at Gettysburg [he did not term it a victory] can hardly be overestimated. Had Lee defeated us on that battlefield, and marched with his victorious hosts upon Washington, there would have been complications of uncalculable consequence." Communications between the capital and the rest of the Union would have been disrupted, Maryland might well have seceded from the Union, and "the disloyal partisan elements in the Northern States might have been greatly encouraged to aggressive activity." Perhaps most dangerous of all, England and France might very well have recognized the Confederacy and eventually intervened in its favor.

In the words of Whitman: "Washington feels that she has pass'd the worst; perhaps feels that she is henceforth mistress. So here she sits with her surrounding hills spotted with guns, and is conscious of a character and identity different from what it was five or six short weeks ago, and very considerably pleasanter and prouder."

28

Vicksburg

While Fighting Joe Hooker was preparing for the "final" assault on Richmond that resulted in the Battle of Chancellorsville, Ulysses S. Grant was investing the supposedly impregnable Confederate fort at Vicksburg. In order to appreciate Grant's accomplishment in capturing Vicksburg, it is necessary to review the defensive arrangements of that city. Vicksburg was (and is) situated on the Mississippi River in the Southwest quadrant of the state of Mississippi, approximately halfway between Memphis and New Orleans at a portion of the river that doubles back on itself with unusual sinuosity. It was located on a bluff high above the river while the land on either side dropped off to alluvial floodplains, rivers, and bayous that for all practical purposes limited the land approaches to the high ground running west along the line of the Vicksburg–Jackson Railroad and parallel to the highway. The river below Vicksburg was blocked by Port Hudson, almost four hundred miles to the south, which prevented the passage of Federal gunboats up the river, and by the strongly fortified point at Grand Gulf, some nine miles below Vicksburg. Just north of Grand Gulf, the Big Black River emptied into the Mississippi, curving north roughly parallel to the river, flooding the intervening area in periods of high water. To the north the Yazoo entered the Mississippi at Haines's Bluff, another well-fortified strongpoint occupied by some 5,000 soldiers and several batteries of heavy artillery. From Haines's Bluff to Grand Gulf Confederate batteries were placed wherever the banks were high enough along the river to support them. The only practical points at which to land troops for an attack on Vicksburg were south of the city from the area of Bruinsburg and Port Gibson to Grand Gulf. North of Grand Gulf the land was too deeply flooded to permit the passage of troops. This meant that Federal gunboats, troop transports, and supply barges had to run the gauntlet of rebel fire for a distance of some twenty miles. River batteries, as contrasted with shore batteries, had all the advantage over boats. The narrowness of the river sharply limited the maneuverability of naval vessels. They had literally to sail through a wall of enemy fire. They could not move in and out of range or engage in evasive tactics; they had simply to take their lumps, return fire as best they could, and pray that the greater part of their ships would get through.

To believe, in the face of the manifold natural and man-made obstacles, that Vicksburg could be captured was in itself a daring leap of the imagination that Grant was virtually alone in making. Even Sherman advised Grant to return upriver to Memphis and wait until Banks was able to join him and a larger force could be assembled, but Grant was determined to push on with the campaign whatever the hazards. With little concern for politics, he was nonetheless convinced that the state of morale in the North was so bad and the will to sustain the conflict in the face of the repeated failures of the Army of the Potomac so diminished that it was essential to carry through a vigorous campaign in the Mississippi Valley. To "make a backward movement as long as that from Vicksburg to Memphis," he wrote in his *Memoirs,* "would be interpreted, by many of those yet full of hope for the preservation of the Union, as a defeat, and . . . the draft would be resisted, desertions ensue and the power to capture and punish deserters lost. There was nothing left to be done but to *go forward to a decisive victory.*"

The winter of 1862–63 was a trying one. In the constant rain and flooded bayous and plains it was difficult to find high ground on which the men might pitch their tents, poor shelter though they were. Malaria, smallpox, and measles ravaged the troops, but the field hospitals were so well staffed and efficiently run that the loss of life was kept to a minimum. Grant himself was constantly harassed by a swarm of war correspondents who, believing themselves now experts on all things military, wrote lengthy dispatches to their papers criticizing him for being "idle, incompetent and unfit to command men in an emergency" and clamoring for his removal.

During the winter months, in the face of merciless cold rains, Grant set his troops to probing possible avenues of access north of Vicksburg, less with the hope of finding or cutting through to the approaches to Vicksburg (much of the work consisted of trying to divert the flow of bayous and creeks to create channels deep enough to bear ships) than with the desire to keep his troops actively engaged in physical tasks. By early spring it was evident that all such efforts (Grant lists four major ones) were doomed to failure and that the expedition, to have any hope of success, had to run down past the Confederate batteries. Once again Grant's happy capacity to find an alter ego manifested itself. William David Porter was the foster brother of David Farragut and the son of Commodore David Porter, who had carried out one of the most spectacular voyages of the War of 1812, raiding British shipping in the Pacific until he was captured by the British at Valparaiso. Another son, David Dixon Porter, was in command of the mortar fleet under Farragut in the capture of New Orleans. William, who was fifty-two at the beginning of the war, had been appointed a midshipman in 1823 and was serving in the United States Navy when the war began. He had been second-in-command to Foote in the expedition against Forts Henry and Donelson and had succeeded in the Mississippi command when Foote was promoted to rear admiral and given command of the United States fleet at Charleston. Gideon Welles wrote of William Porter: "Like all the Porters, he is a courageous, daring, troublesome, reckless officer." Now he cooperated with Grant in preparing his vessels to run down the river to Bruinsburg. Bales of cotton, reinforced by tree trunks, were placed along the bulwarks of the boats, and the engines were similarly protected. When some of the naval crews balked at so perilous a venture, Grant called for volunteers from his own army who were experienced in piloting steamships and made up his own crews. It was not the first or the last time he found officers and men competent to perform tasks far beyond the requirements of ordinary infantry soldiers.

The journey past the Confederate batteries was made at night. To illuminate the river, the rebels built great bonfires on the east bank and set fire to houses and barns so that the spectacle was, in Grant's words, "magnificent but terrible." Every gunboat was hit numerous times, but the protective measures were effective, and all got through with minor damage. One transport was sunk, but no soldiers were killed and only a few wounded. Grant's initial move was directed against Grand Gulf, but the fort proved a hard nut to crack, and while Grant was considering his next maneuver to get his army across to the Vicksburg side of the river, an escaped slave appeared in the Union camp with the information that a good road ran from Bruinsburg to Port Gibson behind Grand Gulf. Grant landed his troops at Bruinsburg, started for the Big Black River, and sent word to Sherman, still north of Vicksburg, to make a diversionary attack on Haines's Bluff. It was well he did so.

John Clifford Pemberton, West Point, class of '37, although a Pennsylvanian, was married to a Virginia woman and had therefore accepted a Confederate commission. He and Grant were old friends from Mexican War days. Now he was on his way with a much superior force to attack Grant's disembarking army when he heard of Sherman's move against Haines's Bluff and turned north. This gave Grant the opportunity to bring his full force, soon supplemented by Sherman's brigade, across the Mississippi from Hard Times and to prepare for the final stage of the campaign. His army over the river, Grant wrote, "I felt a degree of relief scarcely ever equalled since. . . . I was now in the enemy's country, with a vast river and the stronghold of Vicksburg between me and my base of supplies. But I was on dry ground on the same side of the river with the enemy. All the campaigns, labors, hardships and exposures from the month of December previous to the present time that had been made and endured, were for the accomplishment of this one object."

Grant had some 40,000 men in his command. Opposing him at Vicksburg, fifty miles east, at Jackson, the state capital, at Grand Gulf and Haines's Bluff was a total of almost 60,000 men, all on familiar terrain with assured lines of supply. Grant's supply depot was at Memphis, a hundred miles upriver. He could count on no reliable supply or reinforcement in view of the fact that Confederate batteries still commanded the river from Haines's Bluff to Grand Gulf. First Grand Gulf had to be captured to secure a suitable crossing from Hard Times and a landing site for whatever supply barges were successful in running past the rebel guns.

Grant's thirteen-year-old son, Frederick, dogged his father's footsteps. Charles Dana, veteran of Brook Farm, ex-editor of the *New York Tribune,* and now undersecretary of war, also turned up, obviously a plant by Halleck and Stanton, deeply troubled by what seemed to them

Grant's reckless undertaking. "My son accompanied me throughout the campaign and siege," Grant wrote, "and caused no anxiety either to me or to his mother, who was at home. He looked out for himself and was in every battle of the campaign."

At Port Gibson, Grant rounded up every vehicle that could move—hansom carriages, ancient wagons, "everything that could be found in the way of transportation . . . either for use or pleasure," drawn by horses, mules, or oxen with every kind of improvised harness. Dana and Fred found ancient dray horses. Grant himself was without his baggage, no bedroll or tent or clothing. He slept, like his men, where he could find a place to lay his head. The Confederates, faced with the danger of being cut off by Grant's force, evacuated Grand Gulf, and there Grant took his first bath in days, had a square meal, and borrowed clean underclothes from a naval officer.

Banks, with 5,000 men, was making slow progress in his attack on Port Hudson. Grant had hoped, once his base at Grand Gulf was secured, to detach a corps to aid in the capture of Port Hudson and then, augmented by Banks's army and with his supply lines from New Orleans open, to proceed with the attack on Vicksburg. But Banks's message that he could not complete the investment of Port Hudson and reach Grand Gulf before May 10 determined Grant to push on without him. Far more risky than Banks's absence was the fact that Grant had no sure line of supply.

When Grant announced to his staff his determination to advance into the heart of enemy territory, badly outnumbered by foes on three sides of him, and without open supply lines, even Sherman expostulated with him, pointing out in private that he was defying the most basic rules of warfare. He should, at the very least, explain his plan to Washington and get Halleck's consent and promise of support. That, Grant replied, would take too long. Moreover, the cautious Halleck would never consent. Grant would use what transport he had to carry coffee, salt, and hardtack. For the rest the men would have to forage and live off the countryside. Sherman was unconvinced. "Beef, mutton, poultry and forage were found in abundance," Grant wrote. "Quite a quantity of bacon and molasses was also secured from the country. . . ." Bread and coffee were in short supply but every plantation had a mill to grind corn, and these mills were kept in constant operation as the army moved forward so that there was a large supply of cornbread, not much to Yankee taste but filling. At one point, when

Grant rode among the marching soldiers, they shouted, "Hard Tack, Hard Tack."

The army, moving along the ridge lines, the only routes not deep in mud or water, headed for the town of Raymond, southwest of Clinton, which, in turn, lay two-thirds of the way to Jackson from Vicksburg. Now, in a series of dazzling moves, Grant drove back an enemy force at Raymond on May 12; sent the main portion of his army under Sherman against the city of Jackson, where Joseph E. Johnston, detached by Lee from the Army of Northern Virginia, was in command of the Army of Mississippi; drove the Confederates from that key city, transportation junction, supply depot, and manufacturing point; and began the destruction of all military matériel there. Union losses were 37 killed and 228 wounded, while Johnston lost 845 killed, wounded, and captured. Having evacuated Jackson, Johnston now tried to effect a union with Pemberton's force, instructing him to move north to join him in an assault on Grant. Pemberton, however, decided a wiser move would be to drive southeast across Grant's supply line, cut that, and then turn back to engage Grant, catching him between two armies—Pemberton's and Johnston's. "I, however, had no base," Grant wrote, "having abandoned it more than a week before." Grant now became Pemberton's pursuer, hoping to intercept him before he could return to Vicksburg. Pemberton chose the high ground of Champion's Hill astride the Vicksburg–Jackson Railroad, destroyed by Union engineers, to check his pursuer. The Battle of Champion's Hill on May 16 lasted some four hours of intensive fighting, at the end of which Pemberton barely got back to Vicksburg; Pemberton's losses, in Grant's calculation, were some 3,000 killed and wounded and 3,000 captured, to Union losses of 2,500, a heavy casualty rate for the 15,000 men engaged.

The way was now clear for an attack on Vicksburg itself. Grant pushed forward with characteristic speed, but when three assaults were beaten off with heavy losses to the Union attackers, he settled down for a siege of the city, building extensive defense works of his own both at his front and at his rear to cover himself against a possible attack by Johnston. Now it was simply a matter of starving the city's defenders into submission.

We might leave it to Grant himself to summarize the lightning campaign which, if it had an extremely protracted beginning—from early December to April 30—had a whirlwind finish. In twenty days "five distinctive battles (besides continuous skirmishing) had been fought and won . . . the capital of the State had fallen and its arsenals, military manufactories and everything useful for military purposes had been destroyed; an average of about 180 miles had been marched by the troops engaged; but five days rations had been issued, and no forage; over six thousand prisoners had been captured, and as many more of the enemy had been killed or wounded; twenty-seven heavy cannon and sixty-nine field pieces had fallen into our hands; and four hundred miles of the river, from Vicksburg to Port Hudson, had become ours." Grant had had, at most, 43,000 men, opposed to 60,000 Confederates. "We were fortunate," to say the least, Grant added, "in meeting them in detail. . . . They were beaten in detail by a force smaller than their own, upon their own ground."

From May 19 to July 4 the Union noose tightened around Pemberton. Naval guns were dismounted from their ships and placed in batteries, and by June 30, 220 guns were ready to fire on the city. While all this was going on, streams of curious visitors arrived behind the Union lines. "Some came to gratify curiosity; some to see sons or brothers who had passed through the terrible ordeal; members of the Christian and Sanitary Associations came to minister to the wants of the sick or wounded." Often the visitors brought poultry only to find that the besiegers were stuffed to repletion with Southern chickens, ducks, and turkeys. And everywhere there were journalists and correspondents, now more respectful in their manner and flattering in their dispatches.

In the lines around Vicksburg, Union and Confederate soldiers fraternized constantly despite their officers' rather half-hearted attempts to prevent it. Men came out of their respective "works" to trade and talk with each other. Much was good-natured banter, the rebels challenging the Yanks to try to take the city, and the Union soldiers replying that they were waiting until the Confederates had eaten up all their supplies. The Yanks threw hardtack into the rebel positions, and the Johnnies would call, "Come to my house Yank when the war is over and I will give you a square meal." Upson wrote: "I hate to have to fight such splendid fellows."

Word reached Grant that Pemberton had tried to prevail on the defenders to build boats and try to escape by water, but the hungry and demoralized men had refused to make the attempt and had indeed become mutinous. It now seemed only a matter of time before Vicksburg had to surrender. The bombardment was increased, and on

July 1, Pemberton asked the opinion of his division commanders, and they advised surrender. On the third two officers appeared at the Union lines with a white flag. They desired a negotiation. Grant replied that he would accept nothing but unconditional surrender. Would he meet with Pemberton? He would. The two greeted each other as old friends. It was not unlikely that Pemberton realized he was an unwilling participant in one of the great campaigns of history. He asked that his men might be allowed to march out with their arms and honors of war. Grant refused. Pemberton replied: "The conference might as well end." Grant, after conferring with his division commanders, offered to let the Confederates march out of Vicksburg after signing their paroles not to take arms again against the Union, the officers to retain their sidearms. "The rank and file will be allowed all their clothing, but no other property" except cooking utensils and supplies. Pemberton accepted the terms, and on the Fourth of July, Vicksburg was surrendered. "Our soldiers were no sooner inside the lines," Grant wrote, "than the two armies began to fraternize. . . . I myself saw our men taking bread from their haversacks and giving it to the enemy they had been so recently engaged in starving out."

Pemberton defended surrendering on the nation's greatest holiday on the grounds that he thought he could obtain better terms by appealing to the vanity of the Union soldiers. Grant wrote dryly: "This does not support my view of his reasons for selecting the day he did for surrendering."

In Vicksburg the Yankees discovered that a large part of the population had burrowed underground. All along the river, caves had been hewn from the cliffs, "some of them carpeted and furnished with considerable elaboration," Grant wrote. The city rested on a thick yellow clay, and this had been honeycombed with chambers for the storage of powder and shelters against Union shells. When, a week after the fall of the city, the paroled rebel prisoners passed out of "the works they had so long and so gallantly defended, between lines of their late antagonists, not a cheer went up, not a remark was made that would give pain." It was one of the war's most poignant moments. A sense of final Southern defeat hung in the heavy midsummer air. In Lincoln's soon-to-be-famous phrase, "The Queen of waters once more flowed unvexed to the sea." So ended what was, by any measure, one of the greatest military campaigns in history, clearly the greatest of the war. Grant had displayed every military virtue, every essential quality of leadership. He had imagined and carried through a brilliant strategy against seemingly insuperable odds. He had given attention to the smallest detail concerning the movement of his troops and their welfare. He had been everywhere, displaying his own offhand courage, pushing on a laggard division commander here, a skirmish line there. He had preceded every action with a careful reconnaissance. He had used each subordinate commander with a remarkable intuition for his strengths and weaknesses. His most brilliant decision had been that of abandoning his base of supplies and living off the countryside. That was a bit of daring hard for a layman to appreciate unless he might know the hold of tradition on the military mind. Grant thereby taught Sherman the lesson that made him great in his own right. Finally and perhaps most important of all, he imbued the men under his command, from generals to privates, with his own fierce will for victory and his unquenchable conviction that it could be achieved.

It is common to discuss the relative stature of the two great military leaders of the Civil War, Lee and Grant, often to the former's advantage. The comparison is misleading and irrelevant. Lee never conceived or brought off an action to compare in brilliance and daring to the Vicksburg campaign. His was a different kind of excellence. Like his fellow Virginian, George Washington, his talent was for endurance, for survival. He fashioned a marvelously articulated fighting force bound together by the deepest bonds of confidence and trust and fought it, on most occasions, with skill and daring that were admirable but, in the last analysis, conventional. There is no indication that he had anything like Grant's strategic imagination. His boldest strategies, the invasion of Maryland in the fall of 1862 after Fredericksburg and the Gettysburg campaign, both ended in sharp setbacks. He fought over ground as familiar as his own backyard—it was, indeed, his own backyard—and for the most part, he fought defensively. There is certainly no wish here to denigrate or diminish Lee's remarkable accomplishments, but only to insist that they never reached the level of Grant's finest campaign.

In all the vast literature on the Vicksburg campaign, the finest work, by all odds, is Grant's *Personal Memoirs*. A close second and most essential is that of Sherman. The two works complement each other much as their authors did in battle. Alfred North Whitehead wrote: "Style is the ultimate morality of mind." Grant's style is a proper measure of the man. Simple, austere, reserved, direct, informed by a severely suppressed passion, by the determination to do justice to everyone concerned, friend and foe alike, the memoirs are given a profound poignancy by the fact that they were written when Grant, impoverished by unfortunate speculations, was dying of cancer; written to free his wife and children from the burden of debt and to provide some competence for them after his death. It belongs with that select company of great military memoirs that we can count on the fingers of both hands—Xenophon's *Anabasis*, Caesar's *Gallic Wars*, the *History of the Crusades*, the *Siege of Malta*, and Light-Horse Harry Lee's *Memoirs of the War in the Southern Department of the United States*.

Sherman's *Memoirs* belong beside his commander's. Where Grant is spare and almost dry, Sherman is vividly anecdotal and discursive, opinioned if not quite opinionated, lively, even garrulous, but unfailingly interesting. He turns aside to note that in the fighting around Raymond he found himself in the yard of a farmhouse, and when he stopped for a drink of well water, he saw on the ground a copy of the Constitution of the United States with the name of Jefferson Davis written on the title page. Inquiring of a slave, he discovered that the plantation was owned by the president of the Confederacy and that the mansion house was nearby. There he found Davis's brother Joe, "an old man attended by a young and affectionate niece."

The news of Vicksburg arrived in Washington immediately after word of Gettysburg. When Gideon Welles returned to his office after a Cabinet meeting, he found a telegram from Admiral Porter announcing the fall of the Confederate stronghold. He hurried back to the White House with the news. The elated President said, "I myself will telegraph the news to General Meade." By Welles's account, "he seized his hat, but suddenly stopped, his countenance beaming with joy; he caught my hand, and, throwing his arms around me exclaimed: 'What can we do for the Secretary of the Navy for this glorious intelligence? He is always giving us good news. I cannot, in words, tell you my joy over this result. It is great, Mr. Welles, it is great!'"

The capture of Vicksburg, following on the heels of the Union victory at Gettysburg, both occurring on the Fourth of July, in the words of Gideon Welles, "excited a degree of enthusiasm not excelled during the war. . . . Admiral Porter's brief dispatch to me was promptly transmitted over the whole country, and led, everywhere, to spontaneous gatherings, firing of guns, ringing of bells and general gratification and gladness." There was a common feeling that the war was, for all practical purposes, over. A few more campaigns, a few more victories for Northern arms, and the South must capitulate.

Grant believed that the fall of Vicksburg marked the virtual end of the Confederacy, and Sherman concurred. Gettysburg and Vicksburg, "occurring at the same moment of time, should have ended the war," he wrote, "but the rebel leaders were mad, and seemed determined that their people should drink of the very lowest dregs of the cup of war, which they themselves had prepared."

When Charles Francis Adams, Jr., heard the news of the capture of Vicksburg, he wrote his father: "This . . . settles in our favor the material issue of the war, and, in a military point of view, I do not see how it can fail, with the recognized energy of our western Generals, to make the destruction of the confederacy as a military power a mere question of time."

The Vicksburg and Gettysburg victories brought an ecstatic response from Henry Adams. "I wanted to hug the army of the Potomac," he wrote. "I wanted to get the whole army of Vicksburg drunk at my own expense. I wanted to fight some small man and lick him." The news from Vicksburg was especially sweet since British military experts had declared flatly that the city was impregnable and could never be captured. "It is utterly impossible," Henry wrote to his brother, "to describe to you the delight that we all felt here and that has not diminished even now. . . . I preserved sobriety in public, but for four days I've been internally singing Hosannahs and running riot in exultation." Among the pro-Southern Englishmen, "the spirit of hatred" had never before "shown itself so universal and spiteful as now," Adams added, and his father wrote in the same vein: "Great has been the disappointment and consternation here. . . . The Salons of this great metropolis are in tears; tears of anger mixed with grief. . . . They madly struggle with the event, denying that it was possible. Fate cannot be so cruel!"

In Sherman's view the capture of Vicksburg also had less fortunate consequences—"a general relaxation of effort, and desire to escape the hard drudgery of camp; officers sought leaves of absence to visit their homes, and soldiers obtained furloughs and discharges on the most slender pretexts; even the General Government seemed to relax in its efforts to replenish our ranks with new men, or to enforce the draft. . . ."

In the aftermath of Gettysburg and Vicksburg, Lincoln issued a proclamation setting August 6 "as a day for national thanksgiving, praise, and prayer" to invoke the influence of the Holy Spirit "to subdue the anger which has produced and so long sustained a needless and cruel rebellion. . . ." And early in October, 1863, he set the last

Thursday in November as an official day of thanksgiving, a day to be accompanied by "humble penitence for our national perverseness and disobedience," for thanksgiving for those blessings vouchsafed and special prayers for "all those who have become widows, orphans, mourners, or sufferers in the lamentable civil strife. . . ."

The Gettysburg "victory" was clouded by Meade's dilatory pursuit of Lee. By July 14, Lee had his army across the Potomac. The President overtook Welles walking back to his office from a brief and abortive Cabinet meeting. "He said," Welles later wrote in his diary, "with a voice and a countenance which I shall never forget, that he had dreaded yet expected this; that there has seemed to him for a full week a determination that Lee, though we had him in hands, should escape with his force and his plunder. And that, by God, is the last of this Army of the Potomac! There is bad faith somewhere, Meade has been pressed and urged, but only one of his generals was for an immediate attack, was ready to pounce on Lee; the rest held back. What does it mean, Mr. Welles? Great God! What does it mean?" When Welles expressed his opinion that Halleck was the culprit in not ordering Meade to attack, Lincoln replied, "Halleck knows better than I what to do. He is a military man, has had a military education. I brought him here to give me military advice. His views and mine are widely different. It is better that I, who am not a military man, should defer to him rather than he to me." Welles expressed a contrary opinion. He was convinced, he told the President, that he "could more correctly, certainly more energetically direct military movements than Halleck, who, it appeared . . . could originate nothing . . . On only one or two occasions," Welles wrote, "have I ever seen the President so troubled, so dejected and discouraged." When Welles saw him next, a few hours later, in Stanton's office at the War Department, Lincoln was stretched out on a sofa, "subdued and sad," but "calm and resolute."

29

Affairs Political and Military

The North had little time to relish the twin victories of Gettysburg and Vicksburg. Scarcely a week later, on July 13, the worst riots in the country's history broke out in New York City, where the city's Irish and other workers violently resisted the draft law. In the opinion of Gideon Welles and many others, the draft law was "crude, and loose, and wrong in many respects." Not the result of Cabinet consultation, it had been conceived hastily by Stanton in conjunction with the military committees of Congress and voted into law in March. Thaddeus Stevens called it "a rich man's bill, made for him only who can raise his $300, (the price of exemption) and against him who cannot raise that sum." It had been under heavy attack by Democrats from the moment it was first proposed. Congressman Chilton White of Ohio declared, "I fear me, sir, that this is part and parcel of a grand scheme for the overthrow of the Union and for the purpose of building up on its ruins a new government based on new ideas—the idea of territorial unity and consolidated power.... Arm the Chief magistrate with this power—and what becomes of the State Legislatures? What becomes of the local judicial tribunals? What becomes of State constitutions and State laws?" *Frank Leslie's Illustrated Newspaper* declared "this law converts the Republic into one grand military dictatorship."

476

In addition to the charges that the draft law rode roughshod over states rights, the working classes had far more practical grievances against the government. Inflation had driven up prices by 43 percent since 1860; wages had risen by only 12 percent. The effects were felt most acutely by artisans and laborers. Governor Seymour, of New York, in a widely quoted speech, declared: "Remember this, that the bloody, and treasonable, and revolutionary, doctrine of public necessity can be proclaimed by a mob as well as by a Government." To many Republicans it seemed as though the governor were coming dangerously close to inciting a riot.

Yet there were no indications that trouble was brewing. Even when the drawing of names to be drafted began in the various wards of the city, there were cries of "Good-bye, Patrick!" "Good-bye, Brady!" But when the names of some members of the volunteer fire fighters known as the Black Joke Engine Company were called out, trouble began. The highly political fire fighters believed that they should be exempt. They expressed that view by vandalizing the draft office and setting it on fire. A mob gathered and began to loot the adjacent houses. Soon policemen and police stations were under heavy attack. Growing by the hour, the mobs brushed aside a detachment of wounded veterans, the so-called Invalid Corps, and began setting more buildings on fire. A Virginia lawyer harangued a crowd besieging the United States marshal's office on Third Avenue. He had told the city officials recently "that Lincoln, this Nero, this Caligula, this despot, meant by this Conscription Bill to let the rich man go on and earn more money by shoddy contracts and have the poor man dragged from his family and sent to the war to fight for the negro and not to restore the Union. . . . Resist the draft. . . . Organize to resist it! Appoint your leader," he shouted.

The crowd responded with a roar of approval and fanned out through the city, wreaking destruction as it went. Ellen Leonard, visiting her brother, saw First Avenue swarming "with thousands of infuriated creatures, yelling, screaming and swearing in the most frantic manner; while crowds of women, equally ferocious, were leaning from every door and window, swinging their aprons and handkerchiefs, and cheering and urging them onward. The rush and roar grew every moment more terrific. Up came fresh hordes faster and more furious; bare-headed men, with red, swollen faces, brandishing sticks and clubs or carrying heavy poles and beams; and boys, women and children hurrying on and joining with them in this mad chase up the avenue like a company of raging fiends." Soon stores were sacked, as were the apartments above them and private dwellings.

The cry was raised: "Down with the bloody nigger!" "Kill all niggers!" A crowd gathered outside the Colored Orphan Asylum at Fifth Avenue and Forty-third Street in the afternoon. The orphans, some 237 of them, were hurried out the back door just ahead of the mob, which pillaged the building and set it on fire. When firemen arrived to try to extinguish the blaze, their hoses were cut, and they were badly beaten. Negro boardinghouses, scattered about the city, were a favorite target of the rioters, and many of them were soon on fire. Several blacks were hanged or burned to death, and many more killed. A Mohawk Indian named Peter Heuston was taken for a Negro and beaten to death.

George Templeton Strong stayed up far into the night of July 14, listening to the distant noises of the rioters, writing in his journal, and dozing off from time to time, to be awakened by shouts and what sounded like reports of artillery or "perhaps only falling walls" from gutted houses. The next day the city remained in a state of siege, and Strong noted: "Rabbledom is not yet enthroned any more than its ally and instigator, Rebeldom." Strong was delighted by the story of young Elbridge Gerry, grandson of the Elbridge Gerry who had been one of the delegates to the Federal Convention that framed the Constitution. Gerry, who lived in a handsome house with extensive grounds on Nineteenth Street and Broadway, had, like many members of his class, prepared himself and his mansion to withstand the assaults of rioters. He armed himself and his family and servants with muskets and pistols and then, as he told Strong's wife, Ellie, did his best to make his very conspicuous house as modest-looking an establishment as possible. When he was proudly describing his defense measures, Ellie Strong protested, "But your house is always conspicuous; the beautiful birds in your courtyard always attract people's attention." Gerry had, indeed, peacocks and rare pheasants. "Ah," said Gerry, "I provided for that. Just as soon as the disturbances commenced, I sent for my coachman and I ordered him to pull out all the tails of all the birds." In consequence, when the tailless peacocks flew up on a fence, they lost their balance and teetered over forward.

For four days mobs roamed the streets. Among other destructive acts, the rioters looted the well-known gentlemen's haberdashery Brooks Brothers, at the corner of Catherine and Cherry streets, and continued their rampage attired in high silk hats, fashionable derbys, tweed jackets, and velvet-collared coats. It was not until 800 Federal troops, drawn from nearby forts and military installations, invested the city that order was restored. Strong was especially incensed by the attacks on the city's blacks, what he called "the unspeakable infamy of the nigger persecution. They are the most peaceable, sober, and inoffensive of our poor, and the outrages they have suffered during this last week are less excusable—are founded on worse pretext and less provocation—than St. Bartholomew's or the Jew-hunting of the Middle Ages." It was estimated that casualties ran as high as 1,000 killed and wounded, while the damage to property from fire and looting was said to be well over $1,500,000.

In the words of William Pennington, a black historian, an "infuriated band of drunken men, women, and children paid special visits to all localities inhabited by the blacks, and murdered all they could lay their hands on, without regard to age or sex. Every place known to employ negroes was searched; steamboats leaving the city, and railroad depots, were watched, lest some should escape their vengeance." Blacks, fleeing for their lives, begged to be admitted to jails and police stations. "Blacks were chased to the docks, thrown into the river and drowned; while some, after being murdered, were hung to lampposts." William Powell, a black physician, barely escaped with his life, and three daughters, one a cripple, were saved from a mob by "a little deformed despised Israelite—who, Samaritan-like, took my poor helpless daughters under his protection to his house." Powell's eldest son was serving as surgeon in the United States Army. He lost his house and all his possessions. "I am now an old man, stripped of everything," Powell wrote, ". . . but I thank God that He has yet spared my life, which I am ready to yield in defense of my country."

Pennington summarized the effects of the riots on the black citizens of New York. "The loss of life and property," he wrote, "makes only a small part of the damage. The breaking up of families; and business relations just beginning to prosper; the blasting of hopes just dawning; the loss of precious harvest time which will never again return; the feeling of insecurity engendered; the confidence destroyed; the reaction; and lastly, the gross insult offered to our character as a people, sum up a weight of injury which can be realized [only] by the most enlightened and sensitive minds among us. . . ."

It seemed to Gideon Welles, in the aftermath of the draft riots, that New York was "leprous and rotten." He asked: "How can such a place be regenerated and purified?" Contemplating the city's corrupt politics, Welles found himself doubting the principle of free suffrage. "It was becoming a problem," he wrote, "whether there should not be an outside movement, or some restriction on voting to correct palpable evil in municipal government." Welles recalled his "old enthusiasm of former years, when in the security of youth I believed the popular voice was right, and that the majority would come to right results in every community; but alas!" he added, "experience has shaken the confidence I once had. In an agricultural district, or a sparse population the old rule holds, . . . but my faith in the rectitude of the strange material that compose a majority of the population of our large cities is not strong. The floating mass who have no permanent abiding-place, who are the tools of men like Wood and Brooks, who are not patriots but party demagogues, who have no fixed purpose or principle, should not, by their votes, control and overpower the virtuous and good. Yet they do. Some permanent element is wanting in our system. We need more stability and character."

There was clearly a substantial amount of class animosity as well as racial hostility in the New York draft riots, enacted on a lesser scale in a number of other cities. The draft was only the occasion for an outpouring of rage and bitterness smoldering just below the surface of daily life. The Irish population of the city suffered various forms of discrimination. Many of them were not even U.S. citizens; now they were threatened with being drafted into a war to free "niggers."

When news of the draft riots reached Washington, Alfred Bellard reported, all the soldiers in the veterans' hospitals who could walk volunteered to form a regiment to go to New York to help suppress the rioters. Word of the draft riots prompted George Whitman to write his mother that the news was "almost enough to make a fellow ashamed of being a Yorker . . . it strikes me that it would have been a good idea to have taken Fernando and Ben Wood Gov Seymour and a few more of the wire pullers and strung them up to one of the trees in the city Hall park. . . . As for myself I would have went into that fight [against the rioters] with just as good a heart, as if they belonged to the rebel army."

The new draft call included George Templeton Strong, although he was forty-three. He set out to find a substitute and came up with "a big 'Dutch' boy of twenty or thereabouts, for the moderate consideration of $1,100. . . . My *alter ego* could make a good soldier if he tried," Strong noted. "Gave him my address, and told him to write to me if he found himself in the hospital or in trouble, and that I would try to do what I properly could to help him."

One of the most troublesome consequences of the draft law was that a disconcerting number of Democratic judges, when appealed to by draftees, issued writs of habeas corpus, effectively preventing their induction. It seemed evident to Lincoln and his Cabinet that the President would have to issue an executive order suspending the right of habeas corpus in all cases involving, as the draft clearly did, military matters. On this point Lincoln was inflexible. Chase was the sole opponent of such an order. If the President acted on executive authority, he predicted that a civil war in the "Free States" would be inevitable.

Despite Gettysburg and Vicksburg, George Templeton Strong was still not certain that the will to persist to the bitter end, to complete Southern subjugation and freeing of the slaves, existed in the populace of the North. "We hardly appreciate, even yet," he wrote, "the magnitude of this war, the issues that depend on its result, the importance of the chapter in the world's history that we are helping to write. . . . God forgive our blindness! It is a struggle of two hostile and irreconcilable systems of society for the rule of this continent. Since Mahometanism and Christendom met in battle this side of the Pyrenees, there has been no struggle so momentous for mankind." The great generals of the war would, in the future, be better known than the commanders of Napoleon's legions, "not as greater generals, but as fighting on a larger field and in a greater cause than any of them. So will our great-great-grandchildren look back on them a century hence, whatever be the result."

In mid-August, John Hay described Washington to the absent Nicolay "as dismal now as a defaced tombstone. Everybody has gone. . . . The Tycoon," he added, "is in fine whack. I have rarely seen him more serene and busy. He is managing this war, the draft, foreign relations, and planning a reconstruction of the Union, all at once. I never knew with what tyrannous authority he rules the Cabinet until now. The most important things he decides, and there is no cavil. I am growing more and more firmly convinced that the good of the country absolutely demands that he should be kept where he is till this thing is over. There is no man in the country so wise, so gentle and so firm. I believe the hand of God placed him where he is." And in his diary a few days later Hay noted the President's "good spirits." He wrote: "He thinks that the rebel power is at last beginning to disintegrate; that they will break to pieces if we only stand firm now."

With Vicksburg and Jackson in Union hands the communications hub of Chattanooga on the Tennessee River was the next objective. Rosecrans and Burnside were ordered to drive the Confederates out of the upper Tennessee Valley. On September 6 Rosecrans, acting on reports that Bragg had abandoned the city, scattered his forces in the hope of cutting the rebel line of retreat and issued one of those communiqués promising the annihilation of the enemy which, Lincoln knew from painful experience, were usually preludes to disaster. Indeed, it often seemed as though one could measure the incompetence of a general by the florid rhetoric of his dispatches and general orders. Bragg chose favorable terrain near the Chickamauga Creek and prepared to attack Rosecrans. On September 18, Thomas, reconnoitering, encountered Confederate units advancing near the creek. A full-scale battle developed, involving three Union corps against the main body of Bragg's troops. At nightfall neither side had any clear advantage, but Rosecrans claimed victory. The next day the fighting resumed in wooded and hilly terrain where contact and control was almost impossible to maintain. By an unhappy chain of misunderstandings, Rosecrans ordered one of his divisions out of the line of battle to reinforce his right flank at the moment when Longstreet attacked that section of the Union lines. Phil Sheridan's division was taken by the flank and ground up by Longstreet. A general air of panic and disorder seized the Union army; Rosecrans fled to Chattanooga under the impression that the day was lost. Only the determined stand of Thomas's corps prevented a general Union rout. The next day Rosecrans ordered Thomas to withdraw to Chattanooga.

Bragg occupied the high ground on Missionary Ridge outside Chattanooga, and Rosecrans found himself besieged with a long and precarious supply line. In the two days of fighting he had lost some 16,000 men out of a force of 58,222, while the Confederates had lost 18,454 out of 66,326 engaged. The percentage of loss of both armies was almost exactly the same—28 percent, one of the highest of the war. Had Rosecrans not panicked and had he supported Thomas, the Federal forces might have turned the tide and routed Bragg.

If Rosecrans had failed, Bragg, it appeared, had also been dilatory. Angry charges by Longstreet brought President Davis to the scene to conduct a kind of informal investigation. Longstreet told Davis uncompromisingly that he had not been a half hour under Bragg's command before "he saw that General Bragg was incompetent to manage an army or put men into a fight; that his intentions were all good, but he knew nothing of the business. . . ." Other officers spoke with similar candor, but Davis ended up by supporting Bragg, who was subject to terrible migraine headaches and more than once seems to have been virtually incapacitated during critical battles, and by urging the dissident officers to reconcile their differences. The common opinion was that Davis was excessively partial to Bragg because of a famous incident during the Mexican War involving Davis's father-in-law, Zachary Taylor, and Bragg, then a young artillery officer. "A little more grape, Captain Bragg," Taylor had ordered, thereby saving the day at Buena Vista.

The dispatches telling of the fighting at Chickamauga reached Lincoln at his refuge at the Soldiers' Home on September 21, 1863, just after he had fallen asleep. He read them and rose and dressed and went to the War Department to await further word. It appeared that a major disaster had been averted only by General Thomas's refusal to panic in the face of a general Union retreat. It seemed clear that the blame must be laid at Halleck's door. Grant had been sent across the Mississippi, too far away to support Rosecrans. Burnside was idle in northeastern Tennessee, while Meade dawdled in front of Lee. Most disheartening of all was the fact that Halleck apparently had no intelligence reports on the movement of Longstreet's corps to the aid of Bragg. When Welles asked Lincoln why Meade had been so inactive, the President replied, "It is the same old story of this Army of the Potomac. Imbecility, inefficiency—don't want to *do*—is defending the Capital. I inquired of Meade what force was in front. Meade replied that he thought there were 40,000 infantry. I replied that he might have said 50,000 and if Lee with 50,000 could defend their Capital against our 90,000,—and if defense is all our armies are to do,—we might, I thought, detach 50,000 from his command, and thus leave him with 40,000 to defend us. Oh, it is terrible, terrible, this weakness, this indifference of our Potomac generals, with such armies of good and brave men."

"Why not rid yourself of Meade," Welles asked, "who may be a good man and a good officer but is not a great general, has not breadth or strength, certainly is not the man for the position he occupies? The escape of Lee with his army across the Potomac has distressed me almost beyond any occurrence of the War. . . . He is faithful and will obey orders; but he can't originate."

The President agreed with Welles, but, he asked, "what can I do with such generals as we have? Who among them is any better than Meade? To sweep away the whole of them from the chief command and substitute a new man would cause a shock, and be likely to lead to combinations and troubles greater than we now have. I see all the difficulties as you do. They oppress me."

When word of Chickamauga reached Grant, he ordered Sherman to head for Chattanooga and, rounding up every division he could find, set out for the city himself. Sherman hurried his army to Vicksburg to board steamers for the run upriver to Memphis and to make a forced march from there to the beleaguered Rosecrans. Sherman's son, Willie, who, dressed in a miniature sergeant's uniform, had become the pet of the 13th United States Regular, caught typhoid fever on the way and died on board the steamer *Atlantic*. It was a devastating blow to Sherman. In reply to a letter of condolence from the captain of the company so attached to Willie, Sherman wrote that he could hardly stop to grieve. "On, on I must go, to meet a soldier's fate, or live to see our country rise superior to all factions, till its flag is adored and respected by ourselves and by all the powers of the earth. . . . God only knows why he should die thus young. He is dead but will not be forgotten till those who knew him in life have followed him to that same mysterious end."

It was the middle of November before Sherman and his army joined Grant in Chattanooga. As Lee had sent units of the Army of Northern Virginia to reinforce Bragg, Halleck had dispatched Hooker's corps of the Army of the Potomac to augment Sherman's Army of the Tennessee. Carl Schurz, who was in Hooker's corps, saw Grant for the first time riding with General Thomas to inspect the Union lines. "There was absolutely nothing of the fuss-and-feathers style, nothing of the stage or picture general about him," Schurz noted. "His head was covered with the regulation black felt hat. He wore a major-general's coat, but it was unbuttoned and unbelted. . . . On his hands he had a pair of shining white cotton gloves and on his feet low shoes which permitted a pair of white socks to be seen, all the more as his trousers had perceptibly slipped up. He smoked a large black cigar with great energy and looked about him in a business-like way with an impassive face."

By the last week of November, 1863, Grant was ready to attack Bragg, who had unwisely detached Longstreet's corps to fall on Burnside at Knoxville. Bragg's forces were entrenched on Missionary Ridge. Sherman was to assault the right of Bragg's army at Tunnel Hill, then turn and drive on the rebels from the flank. Ewing's division of the XV Corps was assigned the difficult task of attacking up the side of Lookout Mountain. This assignment appeared far more hazardous when Sherman discovered that an impassable ravine lay between his corps and the Confederate right. When Schurz, assigned as Sherman's reserve, came up to that officer, he found him giving "vent to his feelings in language of astonishing vivacity." For the time there seemed to be nothing to do but watch the increasingly laborious advance of Ewing's Division. Suddenly, from the direction of Chattanooga, there was a great roar and clouds of white smoke rising into the air. It marked, as it turned out, the unexpectedly easy capture of Missionary Ridge. With Sherman's advance blocked, Grant had ordered a movement against the Ridge with the intention of drawing some of Bragg's force from Sherman's front and thereby allowing him to traverse the ravine.

Ted Upson and the 100th Indiana Volunteers were at the Battle of Missionary Ridge as part of the XV Army Corps. The 90th Illinois Regiment took heavy losses. Upson heard a soldier declare that their colonel, the dashing O'Meara, had been killed. "No," said another, "its not so bad as that; he's badly wounded." "Indade he is kilt; I heard him say so wid his own mouth." And so it turned out. When Captain John Brouse, commanding K Company of the 100th Indiana, was desperately wounded, he was attended by his chaplain father, John Brouse, who won the hearts of the Indiana men by his labors for the wounded, "praying with the dying, doing all that his great loving heart led him to do."

The men of the IV Corps, once launched, could not be restrained. "With irresistible impetuosity, without orders,—it may almost be said against orders,—they rushed forward, hurled the enemy's advanced lines out of their defenses on the slope, scaled the steep acclivity like wild-cats, suddenly appeared on the crest of the ridge, where the rebel host, amazed at this wholly unlooked-for audacity, fled in wild confusion, leaving their entrenched artillery and thousands of prisoners behind them. It was a soldier's triumph," Schurz concluded, "one of the most brilliant in history."

We have spoken before of the fact that there is almost invariably a key to any defensive position. This key may be found by careful reconnaissance, by a probing attack, or, perhaps most often, by luck since it is seldom where it appears to be. The fact that the men of the IV Corps "found" it in their spontaneous attack on Missionary Ridge suggests that they were lucky, but more than that, it raises the suspicion that if authority could, in such cases, be transferred from commanding generals, who seldom have adequate knowledge of the terrain over which their forward echelons are advancing or the actual military situation to the soldiers themselves, the success rate of such attacks might be considerably improved. In other words, it may often be the case that when a given plan of attack is followed most exactly, the consequences are often disastrous, as in the case of Pickett's attack on Cemetery Ridge.

The fleeing rebels were pursued, and some 6,000 prisoners captured, along with a large number of artillery pieces and the Confederate supply train. To John Beatty, the Battle of Chattanooga seemed to have been conducted with a degree of skill and quality of sureness too seldom encountered in the Union army. "I detected in the management," he wrote, "what I had never discovered before on the battlefield—a little common sense. Dash is handsome, genius glorious, but modest, old-fashioned, practical everyday sense is the trump, after all, and the only thing one can securely rely on for permanent success in any line, either civil or military. This element . . . dominated in this battle." Beatty had a special admiration for Thomas: "The field is his home, the tent his house, and war his business."

Alarming reports came, meanwhile, from Burnside, besieged at Knoxville by Longstreet. He was short of food and ammunition, he wired, and must soon surrender. When word was brought to an anxious Lincoln that heavy firing was reported at Knoxville, the President was considerably cheered. Anything that showed that Burnside's army was still functioning was encouraging. "Like Sally Carter," Lincoln said, "when she heard one of her children squall, would say, 'there goes one of my young ones, not dead yet, bless the Lord!' "

Grant ordered Sherman to set out for Knoxville with the XI Corps to relieve Burnside. On the march Schurz stopped off at a farmhouse along the road in search of something to eat and found Sherman there. A few minutes later General Howard entered. Howard was famous for his piety and his horror of bad language, which had won him the nickname of the Christian Soldier. Sherman greeted him: "Glad to see you, Howard! Sit down by the fire! Damned cold this morning!" At this fearful blasphemy Howard stiffened and paled, replying primly, "Yes, General, it is *quite* cold this morning." Sherman caught the rebuke and thereafter let loose a torrent of "damns," meanwhile winking at one of his staff officers, at which point Howard beat a hasty retreat, more discomfited than if the "damns" had been bullets, and Sherman said, "Well, that Christian soldier business is all right in its place. But he needn't put on airs when we are among ourselves."

Before Sherman reached Knoxville, Longstreet, hearing of his approach, departed for Virginia, and the weary men marched back to Chattanooga, many of them shoeless, their feet wrapped in rags, living off the countryside. At Chattanooga the Army of the Cumberland settled down for the winter. Schurz soon found himself embroiled in a controversy with Hooker, and when the XI and XII corps were reorganized as the XX under Hooker's command and Schurz was assigned to a training command at Nashville, he decided to resign his commission and take up his political career once more, campaigning, especially among German immigrants, for the re-election of Lincoln.

Rosecrans, McCook, and Crittenden all were charged with misconduct at Chickamauga, and although they were acquitted, Rosecrans was replaced by Thomas and held no combat command through the remaining months of the war. George Templeton Strong took note of the rumors that "opium-eating, fits of religious melancholy, and gross personal misconduct at Chickamauga" had been cited as reasons why Rosecrans was succeeded by Thomas.

With Longstreet and Hooker detached from the Army of Northern Virginia and the Army of the Potomac respectively to reinforce Bragg and Grant respectively, Lee and Meade engaged in a series of maneuvers, interspersed with cavalry and infantry encounters through the month of October, known collectively as the Bristoe campaign, which ended inconclusively when Lee failed to cut off Meade's line of retreat. The most important battle was at Bristoe's Station, where Lee's losses were three times as great as Meade's.

In November, John Hay was part of the extensive presidential party, consisting of most of the members of the Cabinet, which made its way to Gettysburg for a memorial service at the cemetery where so many Northern and Southern soldiers had been buried in the aftermath of that bitterly fought engagement. Hay and young Edwin Stanton, son of the secretary of war, "foraged around for a while, walked out to the College, got a chafing dish of oysters," drank some whiskey with the Washington journalist John Forney, and sang "John

Brown." Then the party, all slightly tipsy, ventured out to harangue whoever might be found on the streets to listen. When some curious bystanders cheered Forney's bibulous speech, the journalist became suddenly serious and challenged his listeners: "You have no such cheers to your President down the street. Do you know what you owe to that great man? You owe your country—you owe your name as American Citizens."

The next day Hay rode out to the cemetery with the President and his party. "The procession," he wrote, "formed itself in an orphanly sort of way, and moved out with very little help from anybody." There was some confusion and delay. A minister "made a prayer which thought it was an oration," as ministers are apt to do on such occasions, and Edward Everett, the greatest orator of the age, came forward to give the principal speech. He spoke, Hay noted, "as he always does, perfectly; and the President, in a firm, free way, with more grace than is his wont, said his half-dozen lines of consecration,—and the music wailed, and we went home through crowded and cheering streets. And all the particulars are in the daily papers."

Everett had orated for more than an hour. Lincoln's "lines of consecration" were, by comparison, disconcertingly brief. Delivered in the President's high-pitched voice, they were inaudible to many in the audience:

"Four score and seven years ago our fathers brought forth on this continent, a new nation, conceived in Liberty, and dedicated to the proposition that all men are created equal.

"Now we are engaged in a great civil war, testing whether that nation, or any nation so conceived and so dedicated, can long endure. We are met on a great battle-field of that war. We have come to dedicate a portion of that field, as a final resting place for those who here gave their lives that that nation might live. It is altogether fitting and proper that we should do this.

"But, in a larger sense, we can not dedicate—we can not consecrate—we can not hallow—this ground. The brave men, living and dead, who struggled here, have consecrated it, far above our poor power to add or detract. The world will little note, nor long remember what we say here, but it can never forget what they did here. It is for us the living, rather, to be dedicated here to the unfinished work which they who fought here have thus far so nobly advanced. It is rather for us to be here dedicated to the great task remaining before us—that from these honored dead we take increased devotion to that cause for which they gave the last full measure of devotion—that this nation, under God, shall have a new birth of freedom—and that government of the people, by the people, for the people, shall not perish from the earth."

Sidney George Fisher was among those attending. "The orator," he noted, "was Mr. Edward Everett. His speech was long but commonplace, tho well-written & appropriate. Mr. Seward made a good speech, Mr. Lincoln a very short one, but to the point and marked by his pithy sense, quaintness, & good feeling."

While Vicksburg and Gettysburg raised Republican spirits and seemed to presage an end to the war, the Democrats, having scored substantial gains in the midterm elections the previous fall, redoubled their efforts, concentrating their principal fire on the unpopular draft and clearly hoping to win more voters at the coming fall elections. The acknowledged leader of the Copperheads was Clement Laird Vallandigham of Ohio, one of the most powerful political figures in the state. General Burnside, who had been assigned to the command of the Department of the Ohio, used or abused his new office to arrest Vallandigham and lock up the editor of the *Chicago Times*. There was an immediate storm of protest that, while rooted in the Peace Democrats, extended substantially beyond that faction. Gideon Welles wrote: "A state of war exists; violent and forcible measures are resorted to in order to resist and destroy the government, which have begotten violent and forcible measures to vindicate and restore its peaceful operation. Vallandigham and the *Chicago Times* claim all the benefits, guarantees, and protection of the government which they are assisting the Rebels to destroy. . . . While I have no sympathy for those who are, in their hearts, as unprincipled traitors as Jefferson Davis, I lament that our military officers should, without absolute necessity, disregard those great principles on which our government and institutions rest."

Such arrests seemed to Sidney George Fisher "wholly unjustifiable." They had usually been made by "military authority instead of civil, which has given them a more odious character," Fisher noted, adding, "They are also, in my judgment, illegal, and the violation of the Constitution was entirely unnecessary."

William Wilkins Glenn, the Marylander planter with strong secessionist sympathies, encountered Vallandigham in Canada, to which he had fled to escape prosecution for treason. Glenn noted that Vallandigham had told him that he was committed to having the Western states join the Confederacy and that "in the success of the South lay the only hope for the preservation of Republican liberty on this continent." It was Glenn's settled opinion that Vallandigham was a "political prostitute" who would say anything to get elected governor of Ohio. Nonetheless, as the fall elections approached, there appeared to be at least a possibility that the champion Copperhead might become governor of the third largest state in the Union. Vallandigham had declared that if elected, he intended to defy the President, return to Ohio, and undertake to "array [the state] against Lincoln and the war," whatever that meant.

It is not surprising that Republicans in general made little effort to discriminate between those Democrats who, honestly differing in opinion from the main body of the Republicans about the objectives of the war, nonetheless loyally supported the President, enlisted in the army or responded to the draft, and fought and often died for their country, and the comparatively small number who were openly treasonable. The Republicans, partly for political ends, partly out of genuine conviction, did their best to hang the mantle of treason on their political enemies, who had for so long dominated the American political scene.

The Democrats, on the other hand, were inclined to view the Republicans as simply ex-Whigs wrapped in the mantle of self-righteousness, toadies to the interests, allies of the capitalists, aristocrats, and nabobs with little sympathy for or interest in the immigrant, the workingman, the poor farmer, the exploited mill worker, the mason, or mechanic, struggling to form a union, reduce his hours of labor, or educate his children. The bitterness of party feeling during the Civil War can be understood only in terms of the depths of class divisions in the half century prior to the rebellion. Seen in this light, the indifference or outright hostility of working-class Democrats toward blacks, free and slave alike, was simply a measure of the precariousness of their own economic and social situation. Tolerance is, it might be argued, a luxury most readily accessible to individuals who have risen well above the desperate struggle for existence that characterizes the lives of those at the lowest levels of society. Southerners like George Fitzhugh had been most ingenious in pointing out the nature of the "wage-slavery" of working-class whites in the North and comparing it with, in a modern term, "the cradle-to-grave security" enjoyed by Southern slaves. Whatever the defects of this argument may have been, the Northern laborer whose life was often a nightmare of economic insecurity, who had no recourse when he was fired from his job in hard times and no provision for his old age (which he had not much expectation of achieving in any event), could understand it quite well. After the first ecstatic moment of patriotic fervor, he came, as months and years passed, to see the war as having the unhappy residual effect of rendering him politically (and, it followed inevitably, economically) impotent. What had begun as a war to preserve the Union was increasingly declared to be a war to free the slaves and, at least prospectively, to flood the North with cheap and degraded labor, thereby riveting on the Northern workingman the chains of the capitalist, the most onerous weight of which he had managed to evade primarily by virtue of his alliance with the slaveholding aristocrats of the South. The Democrats thus came to understand that they were literally fighting for their lives as a political party and, in a sense, for the hope of economic and social justice for that segment of Northern society which, in large part, they represented.

If the Republicans should enfranchise the former slaves, they could have a reasonable assurance of herding them into the ranks of Republican voters, thereby preventing the Democrats of the North from re-establishing their Southern alliance and regaining power. The return of the Democrats to political power posed, in the opinion of the Republicans, two major threats (besides, of course, the loss of political patronage). First, it was assumed that the Democrats, hostile toward abolition and emancipation, would conspire with the Southerners to keep the freed blacks in a state of peonage only slightly removed from the condition of slavery, a state having, indeed, the disadvantages of freedom without its benefits, such as the elective franchise and civil rights. In addition, the return to power of the Democrats would mean power for the "dangerous classes": Irish and German immigrants, radical labor leaders, unions, and "demagogues"—i.e., politicians who espoused their cause. The apprehensions of both parties were, as events would prove, well justified. It was one of those classic "double binds" in which history abounds. The rights and interests of one large group of Americans—freed blacks *or* economically marginal whites —were bound to suffer whatever the outcome. The historian is tempted to prefer the cause of the Radical Republicans because it contained, despite its substantial weight of self-interest, a long idealistic tradition and a genuine commitment to equality for free blacks. But he must at the same time keep in mind other "costs" and the fact, before mentioned, that idealism comes more easily on a full stomach. Man's most basic impulse is to provide the bare essentials of life for himself and his family. Only when that has been attended to is he inclined, generally speaking, to give rein to his nobler instincts.

Buoyed up by Union military successes and anxious to stem the Democratic tide that had risen so alarmingly in the fall elections of 1862, the Republicans made an all-out effort to carry the elections. Among other things, John Hay got a free ticket from Washington to New York and back for Walt Whitman, "who is going to New York to electioneer and vote for the union ticket," Hay noted.

In spite of, or perhaps because of, the renewed Copperhead activities, Republicans made substantial gains in the elections of 1863. Not only was Vallandigham decisively defeated, but Republicans more than recouped their losses of the preceding year. William Dickson, an Ohioan, recalled election day in Oberlin some years later. "It was," he wrote, "unlike any other I ever witnessed. The day itself was calm and pleasant; business had voluntarily ceased; the streets had a Sabbath like quietness; there was no noise or confusion at the polls; the number in attendance was less than usual; no military whatever. I felt at first that there was to be a small vote, and it caused me some apprehension, but I was soon undeceived. A steady stream of voters poured along; they formed themselves into a line of their own motion. . . . It was indeed a solemn thing. It was a vote for the draft and taxes." And for the Union.

In Pennsylvania, where George Washington Woodward, a Democratic judge with well-known Southern sympathies, appeared to be a shoo-in against an incumbent Republican in the gubernatorial race, George McClellan wrote a letter warmly endorsing Woodward. Woodward lost, and it is probably safe to say that the unfortunate missive did more to put the damper on McClellan's presidential ambitions than his failures at Antietam and Fredericksburg. John McCunn, the Copperhead mayor of New York, "that nasty sewer-rat," Strong called him, retained his office by a narrow margin, but Maryland voted for "unconditional Union and immediate emancipation." The resident vote was 27,000 for abolition and 29,000 against, but the absentee ballots of the Maryland soldiers decided the issue. "The elections," the historian John Lothrop Motley wrote, "I consider of far more consequence than the battles."

Lincoln was elated at the election returns, but his delight was clouded by the fact that "one genuine American . . . could be induced to vote for such a man as Vallandigham." George Templeton Strong exulted over the defeat in Ohio of the "pinchbeck martyr to free speech" and over the decline in McClellan's popularity. The latter might be "a good general," Strong wrote, "but he is a bad citizen, doing all he can—ignorantly, I hope and believe—to weaken and embarrass the government and help the public enemy."

The news from Europe was equally heartening. "Every day," Henry Adams wrote to his brother Charles Francis, "I am bewildered by new instances of the radical change in policy." England found itself with Russia, Denmark, and Germany to contend with. Henry Ward Beecher visited England to try to rebut some of the falsehoods and misconceptions about the war that were especially strong in the upper classes and in the universities and returned to America to try to diminish "the bitter anti-Anglicanism" prevalent in the United States by assuring his countrymen that while it was true that Northerners were "hated by the aristocracy, the establishment . . . the plutocracy, and the large portion of the leading non-conformists, the great mass of the people is with us."

"Good Mr. Peabody," the millionaire cotton manufacturer of Boston, gave the poor of London £150,000 as a gesture of goodwill, and Charles Francis Adams found himself besieged by applicants for the cotton manufacturer's largess.

Two ironclads were being built for the Confederacy in British shipyards, and Charles Francis Adams "and all our other supernumerary diplomats," as Henry Adams put it, worked to try to prevail on the government to prevent their sailing. But in Adams's words, "The law officers of the Crown were funky" and seemed unwilling to intervene. Finally, under intense pressure, the government acted. The ironclads were forbidden to sail. "Undoubtedly to us this is a second Vicksburg," an exultant Henry Adams wrote his brother. But the level of upper-class hostility remained high, and Henry Adams, getting the news of Union success at Chattanooga days before word appeared in the newspapers, took a perverse pleasure in seeing his British acquaintances, "innocently dancing and smiling on the volcano, utterly unconscious of the extent of hatred and greediness for revenge that they've raised."

Northerners were especially pleased at the news that Charleston was under siege by a Union fleet and being constantly shelled. George

Templeton Strong wrote that "she deserves it all. Sowing the wind was an exhilarating chivalric pastime. Shelling Anderson out of Sumter was pleasant; resisting the whirlwind is less agreeable; to be *shelled* back is a bore."

The most encouraging news that Lincoln had to report to Congress in his third annual message in December, 1863, was that Great Britain had finally come to its senses and exercised its "authority to prevent the departure of new hostile expeditions from British ports," and the emperor of France had done likewise. The Indians were still keeping the frontier in a state of alarm, and "the mineral resources of Colorado, Nevada, Idaho, New Mexico, and Arizona" were "proving far richer than has been heretofore understood." Lincoln recommended to Congress the establishment of "a system for the encouragement of immigration" since there was "still a great deficiency of laborers in every field of industry, especially in agriculture and in our mines, as well of iron and coal as of the precious metals." He noted: "It is easy to see that under the sharp discipline of civil war the nation is beginning a new life." Almost 4,000,000 acres of land had been sold or homesteaded on during the year past. There were numerous other hopeful signs: "The policy of emancipation and of employing black soldiers gave to the future a new aspect, about which hope and fear and doubt contended in uncertain conflict. . . . Eleven months having now passed, we are permitted to take another review." Tennessee and Arkansas had been cleared of rebel forces and had "declared for emancipation." Missouri was ready to follow suit. "Of those who were slaves at the beginning of the rebellion full 100,000 are now in the United States military service, about one-half of which number actually bear arms in the ranks. . . . So far as tested, it is difficult to say they are not as good soldiers as any." The recent elections had given indications of growing Union sentiment. "Thus we have the new reckoning. The crisis which threatened to divide the friends of the Union is past. There had been talk of retracting or modifying the proclamation of emancipation in the hope of shortening the war." Indeed, Lincoln, in August, 1863, had declared that he would do or undo anything that was necessary to restore the Union regardless of its consequence for the slaves. Now he took a much stiffer line. "While I remain in my present position," he told Congress, "I shall not attempt to retract or modify the emancipation proclamation, nor shall I return to slavery any person who is free by the terms of that proclamation or by any of the acts of Congress." After reading the President's message, George Templeton Strong wrote: "Uncle Abe is the most popular man in America today. The firmness, honesty, sagacity of the 'gorilla despot' may be recognized by the rebels themselves sooner than we expect, and the weight of his personal character may do a great deal toward restoration of our national unity."

There was, indeed, as Strong's comments suggest, a kind of Lincoln "revival." James Russell Lowell, the editor of the *North American Review,* who had been one of the first members of the American literary establishment to appreciate Lincoln's greatness, in an article in the *Review,* published at the end of 1863, praised Lincoln's administration and, above all, his direction of the war. The President was patently pleased. He recommended the article to Gideon Welles. He thought it "very excellent, except that it gave him over-much credit."

An interlude that cheered the President was the appearance at the White House of James Henry Hackett, the Shakespearean actor-impresario, most famous for his portrayal of Falstaff. The President, John Hay reported, showed "a very intimate knowledge of those plays of Shakespeare where Falstaff figures." Hackett was "an amusing and garrulous talker," and the next night Lincoln, Hay, and Nicolay went to see Hackett play Falstaff in *Henry IV.*

On the last day of 1863 Gideon Welles wrote in his diary: "The heart of the nation is sounder and its hopes brighter. The national faith was always strong, grows firmer. The rebels show discontent, distrust, and feebleness. They evidently begin to despair. . . . The President has well maintained his position, and under trying circumstances acquitted himself in a manner that will be better appreciated in the future than now. . . . The Cabinet, if a little discordant in some of its elements, has been united as regards him."

Congress, however, remained a cross. The assignments and promotions of officers, even "the petty appointments and employment of laborers in the navy yard," Welles wrote resentfully, were dabbled in by legislators. "The public interest is not regarded by the Members, but they crowd partisan favorites for mechanical positions in place of good mechanics and workmen, and when I refuse to entertain their propositions, they take offense. I can't help it if they do," Welles added, a bit self-righteously. "I will not prostitute my trust to their schemes and selfish personal partisanship."

In the last week of the year Lincoln told John Hay of a dream. "He was in a party of plain people, and, as it became known who he was, they began to comment on his appearance. One of them said:—'He is a very common-looking man.' The President replied:—The Lord prefers common-looking people. That is the reason he makes so many of them."

30

Grant Encounters Lee

The year 1864 arrived heavy with portent. It was the year of the presidential election and, it was widely assumed, the last year of the interminable war. Nerves were drawn to the breaking point. The year opened with the Republicans apparently in the ascendancy. The nomination of Lincoln and his re-election by a grateful nation seemed assured. He had never been so popular, or his enemies so discredited. Yet within three months everything was in disarray. Lincoln's popularity had plunged to its lowest level. Many Republicans were bold to say that he must step aside to allow a stronger and more electable Republican to be nominated. Peace talk was in the air, and Horace Greeley had appointed himself special adviser to Lincoln on peace negotiations. The Copperheads were more rancorous than ever; the draft was being resisted wherever men dared.

In January, 1864, the periods of enlistment of many soldiers expired. A concerted effort was made to persuade them, usually with little success, to re-enlist. Let the new conscripts have their turn, most of the veterans reasoned. But one seasoned veteran was worth half a dozen recruits. Charles Francis Adams wrote to his father that "the re-enlistment question has destroyed all discipline and nearly broken our hearts. It has reduced our regiment to a Caucus and finally

497

three-quarters did not re-enlist." Adams added: "My company alone had kept up to the mark." It was plainly because his men trusted him—"They seem to think that I am a devil of a fellow. To be egotistical, I think I see the old family traits cropping out in myself. These men don't care for me personally. They think me cold, reserved and formal. They feel no affection for me, but they do believe in me, they have faith in my power of accomplishing results and in my integrity. . . ."

A major reason for the precipitous decline in Lincoln's popularity and the political prospects of the Republicans was the fact that the war dragged on, month after weary month. Even Strong came close to despair. He felt, he wrote, like performing some desperate act, "like going south in disguise as the modern Charlotte Corday and shooting Jefferson Davis." Various prospective presidential candidates were advanced by newspapers hostile to Lincoln's administration. McClellan was, of course, frequently mentioned, and the *New York Herald* in its "slashing, slangy" editorials pressed Grant as a candidate on the Democratic ticket.

In February, 1864, Sidney George Fisher met George William Curtis, "graduate" of Brook Farm, reformer, and editor of *Harper's Weekly*. Curtis had been to Washington and talked with Lincoln, Seward, and Sumner. Seward, he told Fisher, "despairs of the success of democracy & has lost faith in the intelligence of the people." Sumner thought that "the true way to restore the South to the Union is to extend the suffrage to the Negroes, after they are emancipated, as a counteracting power to that of their former masters, who will, he thinks, never again be loyal to the Union, but a disaffected element, always ready to intrigue with a foreign enemy." Lincoln, too, Curtis reported, "has lost faith in the vitality of the nation and the ability of the people to meet and dispose of all difficult questions as they arise." At the same time, Fisher reported, Curtis spoke "in the highest possible terms of Mr. Lincoln, of his sagacity, firmness of purpose, unostentatious performance of duty, high-minded and pure integrity, and wonderful power to perceive the true wishes of the people." Fisher replied that he "took some credit" for having praised Lincoln in his *Trial of the Constitution*. It had been considered excessive by many when the book was published, but time had confirmed Fisher's judgments. "Yes," Curtis replied, "fully."

Richard Henry Dana was another of Lincoln's visitors. The President complimented him on his pamphlet on the Supreme Court's jurisdiction over maritime cases. "It cleared up his mind on the subject entirely," he told Dana. "I cannot describe the President," Dana wrote to his cousin Thornton Lothrop; "it is impossible. He has sobered in his talk, told no extreme stories, said some good things and some helplessly natural and naive things. You can't help feeling an interest in him, a sympathy and a kind of pity; feeling, too, that he has some qualities of great value, yet fearing that his weak points may wreck him or wreck something. His life seems a series of wise, sound conclusions, slowly reached, oddly worked out, on great questions, with constant failures in administration of details and dealings with individuals."

The stiff, proper Bostonian was touched by Lincoln's kindness. "He put his arms around me," he wrote his son, "as if he had been my father, and seemed to want to keep me." It was a strangely paternal gesture for a man only six years Dana's senior. Perhaps Lincoln sensed in Dana the quality of sadness, of disappointment with life and with himself, of promise unfulfilled that had been so much a part of Lincoln's own experience.

The newspapers, the *New York Tribune* prominent among them, were busier than ever telling the President how to run the country and the war. An "Abolition Cabal," it was said, was actually running the country. The President had surrendered the helm and contented himself with meddling in the military pie, about which he knew nothing. He should leave military matters to the generals, primarily, many editors felt, to McClellan. "The truth is," Hay wrote to Nicolay, "if he did, the pie would be a sorry mess. The old man sits here and wields like a backwoods Jupiter the bolts of war and the machinery of government with a hand equally steady and equally firm." His last message to Congress, in Hay's opinion, despite some "bad rhetoric —some indecorums that are infamous," would take "its solid place in history as a great utterance of a great man. . . . I do not know whether the nation is worthy of him for another term. I know the people want him."

Undoubtedly the most momentous event of the new year was the appointment of Grant as general-in-chief of the Union armies. Grant's long string of military victories made him the inevitable choice once it was clear that Meade was inadequate.

When Grant was called east by Lincoln, Sherman succeeded him in command of the Military Department of the Mississippi. Grant had his headquarters in Nashville with his wife, Julia, and his son Fred, while he transferred his command to his friend. On March 18 Grant appeared at Sherman's headquarters and invited him to come to a ceremony. Grant was to be presented with a sword, sash, and spurs by the corpulent and self-important mayor of Galena, Illinois. Mrs. Grant, her son, and four or five officers of Grant's personal staff were present. The mayor read sonorously the resolutions of the City Council while Grant stood by, "as usual, very awkwardly." When the mayor had finished, Grant began fumbling in his pockets, "and after considerable delay he pulled out a crumpled piece of yellow cartridge-paper and handed it to the mayor," Sherman recalled, saying: "Mr. Mayor, as I knew that this ceremony was about to occur, and as I am not used to speaking, I have written something in reply." The answer, when read, Sherman noted, was "most excellent, short, and concise. . . . I could not help laughing," Sherman added, "at a scene so characteristic of the man who then stood prominent before the country. . . ."

Charles Francis Adams, Jr., was cheered by the news that Grant was to take over the Army of the Potomac. "I find unexampled military confidence prevailing in Washington," he wrote his father, "under an impression that Grant means to be, in fact as well as name, the head of the Army." There was great curiosity to see the hero of Vicksburg, the only Union general who seemed to have the golden touch of victory. Welles, attending a presidential reception, "saw some men in uniform standing at the entrance, and one of them, a short, brown, dark-haired man, was talking with the President." It was Grant, Welles realized. "There was," he noted, "hesitation, a degree of awkwardness in the General, an embarrassment in that part of the room, and a check or suspension of the moving column." Seward took Grant by the hand and led him to Mrs. Lincoln. As the general passed through the East Room, there was scattered clapping and "a cheer or two . . . all of which," Welles wrote, "seemed rowdy and unseemly."

Richard Henry Dana noticed an untidy little man at Willard's Hotel. "There was nothing marked in his appearance," he wrote a friend. "He had no gait, no station, no manner, rough, light-brown whiskers, a blue eye, and rather a scrubby look withal. . . . Who could it be? He had a cigar in his mouth, and rather the look of a man who did, or once did, take a little too much to drink." Dana asked someone standing near who the odd little figure was. "That is General Grant," he was told, and joined the starers. "I saw that the ordinary, scrubby-looking man with a slightly seedy look, as if he was out of office and on half-pay, and nothing to do but to hang around the entry of Willard's, cigar in mouth, had a clear blue eye and a look of resolution, as if he could not be trifled with, and an entire indifference to the crowd about him. . . . His face looks firm and hard, and his eye is clear and resolute, and he is certainly natural and clear of all appearance of self-consciousness. How war, how all great crises bring us to the one-man power," he added.

Joseph Griner, by now a seasoned veteran of Sheridan's cavalry, wrote his mother: "Grant, I think, is the right man in the right place. I also think if him and Meade cannot accomplish the downfall of Richmond, there isn't any use of anybody else trying. The Niggers fight well and that is all the praise I can give them," Griner added.

During the spring Grant slowly and patiently established his authority over the army. The officer corps was made up of a residue of officers loyal, respectively, to McClellan, Burnside, Pope, Hooker, and Meade. We have already seen how divisive and debilitating those loyalties were. While there were few avowed McClellanites left, his successors were well represented. In the words of Charles Francis Adams, Jr., now attached to the headquarters of the Army of the Potomac as part of a cavalry escort, "the feeling about Grant [was] peculiar—a little jealousy, a little dislike, a little envy, a little want of confidence—all in many minds and now latent; but it is ready to crystallize at any moment," Adams added, "and only a brilliant success will dissipate the elements."

At the end of April, 1864, Grant was ready for *his* drive against Richmond. The atmosphere at the White House was electric with tension, with the hope that the moment of victory might be near at hand and the fear of yet another defeat by Lee's armies. At midnight, as Hay was writing his diary entry for April 30, the President appeared in Hay's office in a nightshirt that barely covered his long, bony legs, to read him a passage from Thomas Hood, the English poet and humorist who was a favorite of Lincoln's, and show him a cartoon that especially tickled his fancy. The President, Hay noted, seemed "utterly unconscious that he . . . was infinitely funnier than anything in the book he was laughing at." Hay added: "What a man it is! Occupied all day with matters of vast moment, deeply anxious about the fate of the greatest army of the world with his own fame and future hanging on the events of the passing hour, yet has such a wealth of simple *bonhomie* and good fellowship, that he gets out of bed and perambulates the house in his shirt to find us that we may share with him the fun of poor Hood's queer little conceits. . . ."

Grant began his advance into Virginia on May 4, crossing the Potomac and the James. Lee decided to engage the advancing Union armies in the Wilderness, a dense forest that Charles Francis Adams, Jr., described as "a most fearfully discouraging place—an enemy always in front. . . ."

On the morning of May 5, Grant's army made contact with the Confederate forces along the so-called Plank Road. Two days of bitter fighting followed, a nightmare of bloodshed made more terrible by the fact that the woods caught fire and many of the wounded were suffocated or burned to death. The maneuverings of the two armies were constant and complex, with the advantage shifting constantly. As the attackers the Union regiments suffered unusually heavy casualties. Of 101,895 men engaged, 2,246 were killed and 12,073 wounded, compared with 7,750 Confederate casualties out of 61,025 for the Army of Northern Virginia.

The Union army, Charles Francis Adams, Jr., wrote, "got very much discouraged and took blue views of life. The straggling became terrible and you saw men the whole time and officers sometimes living in the woods or wandering around the country." But slowly Grant's "presence and power" began to be felt. Instead of retreating on the ground that his first responsibility was to defend Washington, he called for every available soldier from the capital and reinforced his exhausted troops—"Every new man who came up from the rear served to revive the spirits of those who had been here before."

Melville wrote in "The Armies of the Wilderness":

> None can narrate that strife in the pines,
> A seal is on it—Sabaean lore!
> Obscure as the wood, the entangled rhyme
> But hints at the maze of war—
>
> Vivid glimpses or livid through peopled gloom,
> And fires which creep and char—
> A riddle of death, of which the slain
> Sole survivors are.

Having withdrawn from the line formed by the Plank Road, Grant attempted to turn Lee's flank by moving south. Both armies began a race for the commanding ground around Spotsylvania Courthouse. The Confederates won and formed their defensive lines on favorable terrain. There Lee put his men to work building what a modern historian has called "the most intricate and complete field fortifications yet seen in warfare." When Winfield Scott Hancock's corps attacked, Lee's army was waiting for it. Allegheny Johnson's division, formerly under the command of Stonewall Jackson, crumpled under the Union advance, but the Confederates, rallied by Lee himself, drove back Hancock's men from what came to be known as the Bloody Angle.

"The army news is interesting," Gideon Welles wrote on Friday, May 13, 1864, "and as well received as the great loss of life will permit. Hancock has made a successful onset and captured Edward Johnson and two other generals, with about fifty other officers and four thousand prisoners, thirty pieces of cannon, etc." The next day Lincoln received word (prematurely, as it turned out), that the Confederate forces had abandoned Spotsylvania, and he appeared in his nightshirt to inform Hay and Nicolay. "I complimented him on the amount of underpinning he still has left, and he said he weighed 180 pounds. Important if true," Hay added. Unfortunately it was not true. The rebel lines held, and Grant turned west to the North Anna River.

After Spotsylvania, William Blackford wrote his wife that he had not seen so many Union dead since Fredericksburg. "Thus far," he wrote on May 19, 1864, "Grant has shown no remarkable generalship —only a bulldog tenacity and determination in a fight, regardless of the consequences or the loss. . . . Ultimately such bloody policy must win, and it makes little difference to them, as the vast majority of the killed and wounded are foreigners, many of whom cannot speak English. . . . We are being conquered by the splendor of our own victories, and Grant accepts defeat with that consolation." Grant had anticipated this kind of fighting, but the bitterness and costliness of it shocked him. He had never seen anything like it in the West, Charles Francis Adams wrote his father. "Today [May 29]," he added, "as near as I can see, results stand as follows: these two great armies have pounded each other nearly to pieces for many days; neither has achieved any real success over the other on the field of battle. Our loss has probably been greater than theirs . . . but we have a decided balance of prisoners and captured artillery in our favor. The enemy, I think, outfight us, but we outnumber them, and, finally, within the last three days one witnesses in this Army, as it moves along, all the results of a victory, when in fact it has done only barren fighting. For it has done the one thing needful before the enemy—it has advanced. The result is wonderful. Hammered and pounded as this Army has been; worked, marched, fought, and reduced as it is, it is in better spirits and better fighting trim today than it was in the first day's fight in the

Wilderness. Strange as it seems to me, it is, I believe, yet the fact, that this Army is now just on its second wind, and is more formidable than it ever was before."

The Army of the Potomac had been so ineptly and uncertainly led through so many long months that the consciousness of a strong hand at its helm, which had quickly communicated itself down through the ranks, had worked miracles. Nothing is more salutary for an army's morale than to go forward instead of back. The individual soldier has very little sense of whether the action he is engaged in is a victory or defeat. He knows only the tiny sector of a vast battlefield where he engages his opposite number, but he does indubitably know the difference between forward and back. The Confederate army, on the other hand, grew correspondingly discouraged. Adams was confident that "Grant will not let his Army be idle, nor will he allow the initiative to be easily taken out of his hands."

A few days later Adams noted: "Things . . . work in the Army charmingly. Grant is certainly a very extraordinary man. He does not look it and might pass well enough for a dumpy and slouchy little subaltern, very fond of smoking. . . . He sits a horse well, but in walking he leans forward and toddles. Such being his appearance, however, I do not think that any intelligent person could watch him, even from such a distance as mine, without concluding that he is a remarkable man. He handles those around him so quietly and well, he so evidently has the faculty of disposing of work and managing men, he is cool and quiet, almost stolid and as if stupid, in danger, and in a crisis he is one against whom all around, whether few in number or a great army as here, would instinctively lean. He is a man of the most exquisite judgment and tact. . . . He has humored us, he has given some promotions, he has made no parade of his authority, he has given no order except through Meade, and Meade he treats with the utmost confidence and deference. The result is that even from the most jealously disposed and most indiscreet of Meade's staff, not a word is heard against Grant."

In a lull in the fighting William Blackford wrote his wife, Nannie: "The world, our world, is making history now. During all our lives the histories which will be written will be partisan and the truth will not be in them. It is hard to get the truth of what happens now and happens just in our front, and of course the difficulty will increase."

On June 2, Grant again found Lee across his line of advance at Cold Harbor. Once more he tried a frontal assault, and what followed was the bloodiest fighting of the entire war, with 7,000 men killed or wounded in the space of fifteen minutes. In a month Grant had lost some 50,000 men.

A few days later Oliver Wendell Holmes, Jr., unnerved by the bitterness of the fighting and the death of his friend Henry Abbott, wrote his parents of his intention to resign his commission. "I started this thing a boy; I am now a man and I have been coming to the conclusion for the last six months that my duty has changed." He could "do a disagreeable thing or face a great danger coolly enough" when he knew it was a duty, "but," he added, "a doubt demoralizes me as it does any nervous man—and now I honestly think the duty of fighting has ceased for me—ceased because I have laboriously and with much suffering of mind and body earned the right . . . to decide for myself how I can best do my duty to myself, to the country, and, if you choose, to God—"

As the weeks passed, it became increasingly clear that the war in Virginia was no longer a matter of a defeat here, a semi- or inconclusive victory there, discrete events on the outcome of which Union hopes ebbed and flowed; a *process* had begun, the patient, relentless erosion of the Southern war-making capacity, a cruel grinding. Lincoln's spirits rose notably. He said to Hay, "How near we have been to this thing before, and failed! I believe if any other General had been at the head of that army, it would not have been on this side of the Rapidan [i.e., retreated]. It is the dogged pertinacity of Grant that wins." When one of Grant's staff remarked that the rebels seemed disposed to make a "Kilkenny cat fight of the affair"—a sporting event in which tomcats are tied together by their tails—Grant answered, "Our cat has the longest tail." Lincoln was delighted with the remark when it was repeated to him. That was his kind of language. It strengthened his conviction that he had at last found his general.

Time and again Lincoln had tried to persuade his generals to utilize their superior numbers by simultaneously applying pressure on all Confederate forces at every possible point of contact. Piecemeal military operations, a thrust here, a probing attack there, simply allowed the Confederates, with their interior lines, to shift their troops from one sector or region to another to meet each Union assault with equal or superior numbers, thereby nullifying the numerical advantage of the Union army. In Grant he had a general of a far different fiber. Quite on his own initiative Grant perceived the problem and its solution, i.e., "to move at once upon the enemy's whole line so as to bring into action our great superiority in numbers." It was the President's "old suggestion so constantly made and as constantly neglected. . . ." Lincoln was especially taken with Grant's statement that he intended to utilize every man—"those not fighting could help the fighting." Lincoln added: "Those not skinning, can hold a leg." In Mary Chesnut's words, Grant "don't care a snap if men fall like the leaves fall; he fights to win, that chap does. He is not distracted by a thousand side issues; he does not see them. He is narrow and sure—sees only in a straight line. . . . Yes, as with Lincoln, they have ceased to carp at him as a rough clown, no gentleman, etc. You never hear now of Lincoln's nasty fun; only of his wisdom. . . . He has the disagreeable habit of not retreating before irresistible veterans."

Charles Francis Adams wrote his mother: "He [Grant] has all the simplicity of a very great man, of one whose head has in no way been turned by a rapid rise. A very approachable man, with easy, unaffected manners, neither stern nor vulgar, he talked to me much as he would have had he been another Captain of Cavalry whom I was visiting on business." Adams's mission was to secure a commission to raise and command a regiment of black cavalry. While Adams waited for his orders to be prepared, Grant "went on discussing the enemy and their tenacity, talking in his calm, open, cheerful, but dignified way. . . . I have long known," Adams added, "that Grant was a man of wonderful courage and composure—self-poise—but he must also be a man of remarkably kind disposition and cheerful temper."

As Grant's remorseless campaign went on, the country was appalled at the interminable casualty lists. The toll of dead and wounded was especially hard to accept since the feeling that the war was in its final stages was prevalent. "Great confidence is felt in Grant," Gideon Welles wrote, "but the immense slaughter of our brave men chills and sickens us all. The hospitals are crowded with the thousands of mutilated and dying heroes who have poured out their blood in the Union cause." Despite the dishearteningly slow progress of the campaign, there was, in Charles Francis Adams's view, one definite and, in the long run, decisive gain. "In it the rebellion will feel the entire strength of the Government exerted to the utmost. If Grant takes Richmond, even without a battle, I think Lee's army will be essentially destroyed; for they will lose their prestige. The defense of Richmond keeps them alive. They will never fight again as they do now when once that is lost. . . . As to endurance and fighting qualities, the two armies are about equal, all things being considered, and the enemy's lack of numbers is compensated for by the fact of their acting on the defensive."

Thwarted in his efforts to break through Lee's defenses or to turn his flanks, Grant crossed the James and prepared to attack Petersburg. As the Union army crossed that legendary river, Charles Francis Adams, now on Meade's staff, wrote that "with green swelling banks, it flowed quietly and majestically along . . . giving to me at least, one heated, dusty and anxious soldier, a sense of freshness, repose and eternity, such a feeling as I should have expected from the sea, but hardly from the James. There it flowed! We had fought the Indian, the Englishman and the Virginian upon its banks . . . and long after we have fought and toiled our way out of this coil and our battles and sufferings have become a part of history, it will flow on as broad and as majestic as when the vanguard of the Army of the Potomac hailed it with almost as much pleasure as Xenophon's Greeks hailed the sight of the sea." There on the banks of the river the army rested. The soldiers bathed and washed their worn and dirty garments. "The fields were heavy with clover, but full of the graves of Northern soldiers and the debris of old camps; the houses around were ruined and the inhabitants gone; the fences were down and a spirit of solitary desolation reigned over all the region."

In a magic interlude, when the bounties of nature, marred though they were by the scars of war, seemed sweet beyond bearing, Adams and his fellows found "a shady camp . . . where we had a very pleasant time, getting many good things to eat and drink, . . . entertaining guests, . . . and, in fact, having a sort of picnic."

The idyll was short-lived. The next day the army was once more pressing toward Petersburg. Adams saw, for the first time, black soldiers, "and they were in high spirits; for the evening before . . . they had greatly distinguished themselves and the most skeptical on that score were forced to admit that on that occasion the darkies had fought and fought fiercely." Indeed, there was evidence that the rebels "now dread the darkies more than the white troops; for they know that if they fight the rebels cannot expect quarter. . . . If [the black troops] murder prisoners, as I hear they did, it is to be lamented and stopped, but they can hardly be blamed." Adams noted: "The weather was hot and dry, and the dust has accordingly been intense. The men have suffered much in marching and the incessant fatigue and anxiety of the campaign, combined with the unhealthy food, must soon begin to tell on the health of the Army. Meanwhile the fighting has been incessant, the question simply being one of severity." The bands of stragglers were no longer in evidence, but the country was, in Adams's words, "terribly devastated. This Army is, I presume, no worse than others, but it certainly leaves no friends behind."

At Fort Pillow, before Petersburg, as Union casualties piled up in horrifying numbers, Charles Francis Adams's faith in Grant faltered for the first time. "We have assaulted the enemy's works repeatedly and lost many lives," he wrote, "but I cannot understand it. Why have these lives been sacrificed? Why is the Army kept continually fighting until its heart has sickened within it? I cannot tell. Doubtless Grant has reasons and we must have faith; but certainly I have never seen the Army so haggard and worn, so worked out and fought out, so dispirited and hopeless, as now when the fall of Richmond is most likely. Grant has pushed his Army to the extreme limit of human endurance. It cannot and it will not bear much more. . . . Grant doubtless has his plan, but the Army cannot see it and it now cries aloud not to be uselessly slaughtered. I hope that tactics will change soon, for we cannot long stand this."

In the siege of Petersburg itself, Burnside's division was closest to the elaborate and apparently impregnable fortifications of the city. Burnside, using a number of Pennsylvania coal miners, decided to begin mining operations with the intention of digging a tunnel under the fortifications, blowing them up, and pouring troops through the breach in the Confederate defenses. The project went as planned, and when, on August 4 or 5, the mine was detonated, it produced "a most beautiful and striking spectacle—an immense column of debris, mixed with smoke and flame, shooting up in the form of a wheat sheaf some hundred and fifty feet, and then instantly followed by the roar of artillery." George Whitman, commanding a company of Burnside's division, wrote: "Taking it altogether, I think it was the most exciting sight I ever saw." The assault troops rushed into the crater created by the explosion, but there things bogged down. Under withering fire from those parts of the fortification not affected by the blast, the men milled about uncertainly and then broke and fled with heavy casualties. In the words of a rebel soldier, "We recaptured all our lines, driving the enemy into the crater like a herd of frantic buffaloes. Then such a scene ensued as I hope never to see again—a crater filled with a seething mass of men—hundreds and thousands of them—some firing back upon us, some struggling wildly to escape. Shattering volleys were fired into the seething abyss, till it became a perfect hell of blood. . . . Hand grenades were tossed in, and as they exploded you could see heads and legs and arms and legs and go up into the air. Our men sickened at the carnage and stopped. The enemy lost that day more than four thousand men. They left the crater choked with dead."

Among the shock troops were a number of black soldiers. Initially the blame for the failure of the attack was placed on them, but Charles Francis Adams was convinced that its failure was due far more to Burnside's eccentric method of selecting the assault party by lot. The black troops, Adams wrote his father, "seem to have behaved just as well and as badly as the rest and to have suffered more severely." Moreover, the division itself was a green one, untested in battle. "Volunteers might have been called for, a picked regiment might have been designated; but, no, Burnside sent in a motley crowd of white and black, heavy artillery and dismounted cavalry, and they wouldn't come up to scratch." Adams felt the keenest sympathy for Grant. "I should think his heart would break," he wrote. "He had out-generaled Lee so, he so thoroughly deserved success, and then to fail because his soldiers wouldn't fight!"

In George Whitman's view the almost fifteen-minute-long delay of the 1st Division in moving forward doomed the attack to failure. Also, no ladders had been provided for the assault troops to use in climbing out of the crater once they were in it, so they became like fish in a barrel, the targets for the rebel defenders looking down on them. The black soldiers, in any event, were exonerated. An officer in the 22nd U.S. Colored Infantry wrote to a Philadelphia newspaper: "The problem is solved. The negro is a man, a *soldier*, a hero. . . . I am now prepared to say that I never, since the beginning of this war, saw troops fight better, more bravely, and with determination and enthusiasm."

The failure at Petersburg, especially Burnside's eccentric choice of the assault troops by lot, alarmed Welles. Admiral Porter had always argued that there was some deficiency in Grant which was supplied by Sherman and that "the two together made a very perfect general officer and they ought never to be separated." Welles was afraid that Grant was too dependent on Meade. If Grant, minus Sherman, should prove a failure, Welles reflected, the terrible loss of life in the Wilderness campaign could "never be atoned for in this world or the next. . . . A blight and sadness comes over me like a dark shadow," Welles wrote, "when I dwell on the subject, a melancholy feeling of the past, a foreboding of the future. A nation's destiny almost has been committed to this man, and if it is an improper committal, where are we?"

But Grant was unrelenting. If his heart was broken, he gave no sign, and a week later Adams wrote admiringly: "Grant is a man of such infinite resource and ceaseless activity—scarcely does one scheme fail before he has another on foot; baffled in one direction he immediately gropes round for a vulnerable point elsewhere. . . . He has deserved success so often that he will surely have it at last."

Grant settled down to lay siege to the city. When the Sanitary Commission visited his camp outside Petersburg, the camp seemed suspended in a cloud of choking dust. "Miles and miles of what were meadow and cornfield," Strong wrote, "are now seas of impalpable dust of unknown depth, and heated to a temperature beyond what the hand can bear. Through this, and over such roads as are still defined and distinct, though equally dusty, or worse, passes all Grant's enormous transportation. . . . A drove of cattle or a mule-train creates a fog so dense that in passing them this afternoon, our leaders were invisible."

Charles Francis Adams, enjoying a respite from fighting, took every opportunity to observe the commanding general and enjoy those modest privileges which came to him as a member of army headquarters. He and a college classmate found "an attractive cherry tree, ascended it and chatting over old times and old friends, [ate] our fill of that delicious fruit, while we watched in the distance the tired and dusty column toiling along."

Adams wrote his father: "I have unbounded confidence in Grant, but he puzzles me as much as he appears to the rebels. He fights when we expect him to march, waits when we look for motion, and moves when we expect him to fight. Grant will take Richmond, if only he is left alone; of that I am more and more sure. His tenacity and strength, combined with his skill, must, on every general principle, prove too much for them in the end." Grant and Meade were constantly together, "surrounded by a swarm of orderlies and in a cloud of dust, pushing through columns and trains. . . . It is very wearying and tiresome," Charles Francis Adams noted, "this always moving in procession. . . . The men look dirty and tired; they toil along in loose, swaying columns and are chiefly remarkable for a most wonderful collection of old felt hats in every stage of dilapidation. Their clothes are torn, dusty and shabby; few carry knapsacks and most confine their luggage to a shelter-tent and blanket which is tied in a coil over one shoulder."

It seemed to refresh Lincoln to visit Grant's headquarters. The two men instinctively liked and trusted each other. After the succession of pompous and posturing generals that Lincoln had had to endure, the directness and simplicity of Grant were a tonic to him. Even the general's notorious sloppiness, somewhat of a military scandal, was reassuring to Lincoln. On June 23, 1864, Hay wrote in his diary: "The President arrived to-day from the front, sunburnt and fagged, but still refreshed and cheered. He found the army in fine health, good position, and good spirits; Grant quietly confident; he says, quoting the Richmond papers, it may be a long summer's day before he does his work, but that he is as sure of doing it as he is of anything in the world."

In England Charles Francis Adams, Sr., so often despairing of the outcome of the war, exuded optimism. More than that, he saw the war as placing the seal on American greatness. "It may take us fifty years to recover from this effort," he wrote Captain Adams. "That is a mere moment in comparison with the blessing it will give to our latest posterity to be free from the recurrence of such a calamity from the same cause. . . ." Adams recalled the words of Jefferson: "Indeed, I tremble for my country when I reflect that God is just." The moral evil "which we consented to tolerate for a season has become a terrific scourge, that brings the life blood at every instant of its application. How long this chastisement is to be continued, it is idle to attempt to predict. Only one thing is clear to me, and that is the paramount duty to future generations of not neglecting again to remove the source of that evil. It is this that completes the great idea for which the struggle was endured. It is this, and this only, that will compensate for the calamities that attend the second. The very ferocity and endurance with which they fight for their bad principle only contribute to prove the necessity of extirpating it in its very root. This is not simply for the good of America but likewise for that of the civilized world. The sympathy directed in Europe with this rotten cause among the aristocratic and privileged classes, is sufficient proof of the support which wrongful power hopes to obtain from its success. . . . The laws of nature are uniform. The question with the South is only of more or less annihilation by delay. . . . If the great trial have the effect of purifying and exalting us in futurity, we as a nation may yet be saved. The labor of extricating us from our perils will devolve upon the young men of the next generation who shall have passed in safety through this fiery furnace."

In the spring of 1864 Napoleon III dispatched Maximilian, a

jobless Austrian archduke, whose brother Francis Joseph had stripped him of his offices, to Mexico. Responding to the request of Mexican royalists, who wished to establish a monarchy, hoping thereby to bring some stability to the chaotic political conditions in their country, Napoleon persuaded Maximilian to accept the Mexican "crown." Maximilian and his beautiful wife, Carlotta, arrived to find themselves opposed by the majority of Mexicans, who were loyal to Benito Juárez. The United States, well aware that Napoleon would not have dared undertake such a venture unless the country had been wholly preoccupied by the war, took it as another instance of the hostility of the emperor to the Union cause. "Revolutions," Charles Francis Adams wrote to his son Charles, "are worked by the steady spread of convictions rather than the sudden impulse of physical force. The existence of the United States as a prosperous republic has been the example against which all reasoning contrary to the popular feeling has been steadily losing strength. It was the outbreak of the war that in an instant gave such revived hopes to all the privileged classes in Europe. . . . Napoleon's Mexican empire, as a bridle upon the movement of American republicanism, is the only practical result of our crisis. What that will amount to, the moment our troubles pass over and we settle down into a nation, it is not very hard to foresee. An Austrian prince, aided by French soldiers three thousand miles from any base without an aristocracy and with a people little used to respect authority of any kind, in a country which has no sympathy with either Germans or French, has not a very brilliant prospect of founding a dynasty."

The North found a new hero to go with Grant. Philip ("Little Phil") Sheridan was an odd, short-legged man. George Templeton Strong described him as "a stumpy, quadrangular little man, with a forehead of no promise and hair so short that it looks like a coat of black paint." Mounted on a horse, he took on an imposingly martial air. He was painfully shy, "the most modest, bashful, and embarrassed little fellow," especially in the company of ladies. At the age of thirty-four, Little Phil, West Point '53, was one of the youngest general officers in the Union army. Involved in a brawl with his cadet sergeant, whom he had threatened with a bayonet and subsequently beaten with his fists, Sheridan had had his graduation at the Point delayed a year, and his advancement in the army had been notably slow. At the beginning of the war he had been assigned to the Quartermaster

Corps and there narrowly avoided a court-martial. Appointed colonel of the 2nd Michigan Cavalry through the good offices of a friend, Gordon Granger, Sheridan at once displayed such brilliance as a cavalryman in a raid on Booneville, Mississippi, that he was appointed brigadier general and given command of the 11th Division in the Army of the Ohio. Perryville, Stones River, Chickamauga, and Chattanooga added to his laurels (his division broke the Confederate line at Missionary Ridge), and Grant brought him east to head the Cavalry Corps of the Army of the Potomac. There, like a medieval knight, he sought out the premier Confederate cavalryman, J. E. B. Stuart, and in the engagement at Yellow Tavern on May 11, 1864, Stuart's famous cavalry was badly beaten and Stuart himself killed.

Corporal Joseph Griner was with Sheridan on the raid around Richmond. He spoke with some justice of Sheridan's expedition as "one of the greatest raids ever known, completely turning Lee's right flank, gaining his rear and burning all his commissary stores, capturing a large number of wagons, recapturing 500 prisoners of ours on their way to Richmond, and burning a great many cars, locomotives, tearing up railroads and injuring the Rebels to a vast extent. . . . We were gone about twenty days and during that time had very little rest, and had not the country been rich we should have fared very hard for food. As it was we had nothing sometimes for two or three days." The Union cavalry had lost some 5,000 in killed and wounded.

In July the Confederates, well aware of the antiadministration feeling, mounted a raid by Jubal Early into Maryland and made a feint against Washington that caused considerable anxiety in the city. Welles was convinced that it offered no real threat, but the fact that the rebels ranged at will within five miles of the capital angered him. "On our part," he wrote, "there is neglect, ignorance, folly, imbecility, in the last degree. The Rebels are making a show of fight, while they are stealing horses, cattle, etc., through Maryland. They might easily have captured Washington. Stanton, Halleck, and Grant are asleep or dumb." Welles rode out to Fort Stevens, one of the strongpoints guarding the approaches to the city, and there found the President, "sitting in the shade, his back against a parapet towards the enemy." The two men watched Union soldiers and artillery driving back the rebels and on the way back to the city passed numerous stragglers. "Some were doubtless sick, some were drunk, some weary and exhausted" by the excessive heat of the day, Welles noted. Some were on horses, some on mules, some rode in wagons, and many walked. "It was exciting and wild," Welles noted in his diary. "Much of life and much of sadness."

The principal result of Early's Washington raid was to bring terrible retribution to the Confederate commander and his army, based in the Shenandoah. In August Grant detached Sheridan to close down the Shenandoah Valley from Frederick, in western Maryland at the north end of the Blue Ridge, down to Monterey at the entrance to the Alleghenies. The region had been Stuart's stamping, or riding, ground and the granary for Lee's army. "Leave nothing," Grant is reported to have told Sheridan before his raid, "to invite the enemy to return. Destroy whatever cannot be consumed. Let that valley be so left that crows flying over it will have to carry their rations along with them." Sheridan would comply in spectacular fashion.

31

Election of 1864

If the news from Grant's army was persistently encouraging, despite the heavy casualty lists, other less savory pots were coming to a boil in the summer of 1864 as the Democrats and associated troublemakers, including the outright treasonous, concerted plans to defeat Lincoln at the polls in November. General Rosecrans, relieved after Chickamauga and given command of the Department of the Missouri, was full of alarms over the Order of American Knights, a pro-Southern underground group with plans which Rosecrans professed to have unearthed, to assassinate the President and take over the government. Lincoln sent Hay to confer with Rosecrans and bring back whatever evidence had been collected of the conspiracy. John Hay described Rosecrans as "a fine, hearty, abrupt sort of talker, heavy-whiskered, blond, keen eyes, with light brows and lashes, head shunted forward a little; legs a little unsteady in walk . . . chatty and sociable. . . ." Rosecrans revealed what he knew of the conspiracy. The intention was to oppose the war in all possible ways, including, in the border states, "to join with returned rebels and guerrilla parties to plunder, murder and persecute Union men and to give to rebel invasion all possible information and timely aid." Rosecrans estimated the number of Knights to be 13,000 in Missouri, with 140,000 in Illinois and almost as many in Ohio, Indiana, and Kentucky. Vallandigham was the key figure. He was to return from Canada to the Democratic convention and try to stampede it into an antiwar, proslavery position. If any move was made by Federal authorities to arrest him for treason, the Knights everywhere were to rise in his defense and begin a kind of civil war in the North.

To make matters worse, the draft went on slowly. In Maryland, for example, the Baltimore City Council allowed $200 for every man who could furnish a substitute, and the state $300 more. With the Federal payments added, the cost of enlisting a soldier came to something in the neighborhood of $1,000. Thus, 30,000 soldiers cost $300,000,000, a staggering sum, especially considering that number was not much more than the Union casualty rate in two or three bloody battles.

John Murray Forbes, a highly successful capitalist who had made a fortune in the China trade and in railroading, completing the Michigan Central and building the Hannibal & St. Joseph, had helped form a black regiment and had built a cruiser which he had presented to the navy. Forbes visited Welles to try to persuade him to support Salmon Chase as an alternative to Lincoln. Lincoln, Forbes insisted, was a weak president; he lacked "energy, decision, promptness, in consequence of which the country suffered." Welles gave him no encouragement. As the secretary of the navy summarized the attacks on Lincoln, "He is blamed for not being more energetic and because he is too despotic in the same breath. He is censured for being too mild and gentle toward the Rebels and for being tyrannical and intolerant."

Gold, a remorseless barometer of the lack of public confidence, rose to $250 an ounce, and George Templeton Strong sensed even among sincere Union men a mood akin to despair. The losses of men and the expenditures of money seemed to be without end. Strong came back constantly to the notion of a price that must be paid in suffering for the sin of slavery before the war could end. The South, being the greater sinner, had plainly to bear the greater burden of suffering, but the North had its heavy, if lesser, share in the sin that had to be expiated. "What further humiliation and disaster, public and private, we must suffer before we reach the end," Strong wrote, "God only knows; but this shabbiest and basest of rebellions cannot be destined to triumph. . . ." And a few days later he took up the same theme: "We have no right to expect speedy victory in this war, or to ask that rebellion be suppressed till we have suffered more than we yet have done by way of atonement for the many years of servility and of anesthetic processes applied to our moral sense, without which the South would have never dared rebel."

Gideon Welles wrote in his diary: "This war is extraordinary in all its aspects and phases, and no man was prepared to meet them. . . . I have often thought that greater severity might well be exercised, and yet it would tend to barbarism." Welles's own ambivalence was clearly demonstrated by his concluding observation in his diary entry for June 1, 1864: "I apprehend there will be very gentle measures in closing up the Rebellion. The authors of the enormous evils that have been inflicted will go unpunished, or will be but slightly punished."

In the Republican presidential nominating convention held in Baltimore on June 7, 1864, the President was renominated with only the Radical Republican delegation from Missouri dissenting. "There was much intrigue and much misconception in this thing," Welles wrote. The principal issue was whether to renominate Hannibal Hamlin as Lincoln's running mate. Hamlin was an undistinguished man who had made no notable contributions to the Union cause, and a movement to replace him by Andrew Johnson, the military governor of Tennessee, swept the convention. John Hay reported: "Everybody came back from the convention tired but sober. Little drinking—little quarreling—an earnest intention to simply register the expressed will of the people, and go home." The delegates had been "intolerant of speeches—remorselessly coughed down the crack orators of the party."

Even after his nomination the Republican pressures on Lincoln to retire continued. When Carl Schurz returned to Washington in the summer of 1864 from his service as commander of the 3rd Division, he was disturbed at the degree of division in Republican ranks. A number of Eastern Republicans expressed displeasure "with Mr. Lincoln's somewhat loose ways of conducting the public business, with his rustic manners, and with the robust character of his humor. . . ." They wished for a more "presidential" president, one with more dignity. "The administration party," Schurz wrote, "could not have been in a more lethargic and spiritless condition. Its atmosphere was thoroughly depressing." Lincoln invited Schurz to spend an evening with him, and when the younger man arrived at Lincoln's cottage at the Soldiers' Home, the President spoke with an unusual degree of feeling about the attempts of men he considered his friends to persuade him to withdraw from the presidential race. He gave voice, Schurz wrote, "to the sorrowful thoughts distressing him. . . . 'They urge me with almost violent language to withdraw from the contest, although I have been unanimously nominated, in order to make room for a better man. I wish I could. Perhaps some other man might do this business better than I. I do not deny it. But I am here, and that better man is not here. And if I should step aside to make room for him, it is not at all sure—perhaps not even probable—that he would get here. It is much more likely that the factions opposed to me would fall to fighting among themselves, and that those who want me to make room for a better man would get a man whom most of them would not want at all. My withdrawal, therefore, might and probably would, bring on a confusion worse confounded. God knows, I have at least tried very hard to do my duty—to do right to everybody and wrong to nobody. And now to have it said by men who have been my friends and ought to know me better, that I have been seduced by what they call the lust of power, and that I have been doing this and that unscrupulous thing hurtful to the common cause, only to keep myself in power.'

"So he went on," Schurz wrote, "as if speaking to himself, now pausing for a second, then uttering a sentence or two with vehement emphasis." The shadows of evening deepened in the room. The voice, touched with sadness, went on, and Schurz thought he saw tears in the President's eyes, his face "working strangely, as if under a very strong and painful emotion." He stopped speaking, and there was a long moment of silence before Schurz responded with assurances that the people of the Union "believed in him and would faithfully stand by him." The conversation went on to other, more practical matters, and Lincoln's gloom lifted. When Schurz at last rose to excuse himself, the President found the spirit for some "humorous remarks," shook Schurz's hand, and said, "Well, things might look better, and they might look worse. Go in, and let us all do the best we can."

A far more dangerous opponent than Vallandigham or Forbes was Horace Greeley. Approached, as it was to turn out, by self-appointed "peace agents" of the Confederacy, Greeley wrote Lincoln: "I venture to remind you that our bleeding, bankrupt, almost dying country . . . longs for peace; shudders at the prospect of fresh conscriptions, of further wholesale devastations, and new rivers of human blood. And a widespread conviction that the Government and its prominent supporters are not anxious for peace, and do not improve proffered opportunities to achieve it, is doing great harm now, and is morally certain, unless removed, to do far greater in the approaching elections." Greeley neglected to mention that he had played a major role in encouraging the notion that Lincoln was "not anxious for peace."

Having admonished the President, he went on to propose the terms that Lincoln should offer to the Southern emissaries, concluding, "Mr. President, I fear you do not realize how intently the people desire any peace consistent with the national integrity and honor, and how joyously they would hail its achievement and bless its authors. With United States stocks worth but forty cents in gold per dollar, and drafting about to commence on the third million of Union soldiers, can this be wondered at?" It was Greeley's argument that a legitimate and generous offer of peace should at least be made by Lincoln; such an offer "may save us," Greeley concluded, "from a Northern insurrection."

The President's response was an ingenious one. "If you can find any person, anywhere," Lincoln wrote on July 9, "professing to have any proposition of Jefferson Davis in writing, for peace, embracing the restoration of the Union, and abandonment of slavery, whatever else it embraces, say to him he may come to me with you. . . ." Lincoln sent his letter to Greeley by Hay. Greeley was disconcerted at having Lincoln give him the task of meeting with the negotiators. Hay noted: "He didn't like it . . . thought . . . that as soon as he arrived there the newspapers would be full of it; that he would be abused and blackguarded. . . ." He would have to have safe-conduct for four persons. Finally the preliminaries were concluded, and Greeley left for his rendezvous, uncomfortably conscious that he had been outmaneuvered by the President. In Niagara Greeley discovered that the negotiators lacked credentials.

Greeley realized he had been bamboozled. Rather than admit it, he forwarded the request of the quartet, known as Davis & Co., to the President. Lincoln gave instructions that no steps were to be taken unless the requirements of reunion and the freeing of the slaves were first accepted as the conditions for further negotiations. Greeley insisted that Lincoln offer to open negotiations without any conditions. Even word that negotiations were going on would boost the value of the dollar and improve the chances of Republican candidates in the fall elections. At the door of the Clifton House, Hay and Greeley were met by George Sanders, "a seedy-looking Rebel, with grizzled whiskers and a flavor of old clo'." After some desultory conversation, the two men were taken to the room of James Philemon Holcombe, former professor of law at the University of Virginia, Confederate Congressman, and now commissioner to Canada. Holcombe was described by

Hay as "a tall, solemn, spare, false-looking man, with false teeth, false eyes, and false hair." Hay delivered the President's peace terms. The three men shook hands all around, and Hay and Greeley departed. Before returning to New York, Greeley, unbeknownst to Hay, had a further confab with the most colorful of the "negotiators," William ("Colorado") Jewett. Jewett and his allies wrote a letter to Greeley, charging that Lincoln had not undertaken the negotiations in good faith, and broadcast it to the press. Thus, the very notion that Greeley had declared he wished to avoid was conveyed to the impressionable —that Lincoln was placing obstacles in the path of peace.

Greeley did his best to shift the responsibility for the whole unsavory episode to the President. Lincoln declined to prolong the controversy. He told Hay he feared that such a public row would be "a disaster equal to the loss of a great battle" if it were known that the editor of the *Tribune* "was ready to sacrifice everything for peace" and was "frantically denouncing the Government for refusing to surrender the contest." When Lincoln invited Greeley to Washington, the latter refused, writing: "The cry has been steadily, No truce! No armistice! No negotiation! No mediation! Nothing but surrender at discretion! I never heard of such fatuity before. There is nothing like it in history. It *must* result in disaster, or all experience is delusive. . . . I beg you, implore you, to inaugurate or invite proposals for peace forthwith. And in case peace cannot now be made, consent to an *armistice for one year*, each party to retain, unmolested, all it now holds, but the Rebel ports to be opened. Meantime, let a national convention be held, and there will surely be no more war at all events."

Certainly Greeley's behavior was both egocentric and eccentric. William Roscoe Thayer, Hay's biographer, wrote caustically of Greeley: "He dipped his pen of infallibility into his ink of omniscience with as little self-distrust as a child plays with matches. A list of Greeley's misjudgments," Thayer, who was himself a sometime journalist, wrote, ". . . would serve as a warning against the deteriorating effects of journalism upon even a ready intellect and a well-developed conscience." To Lincoln, Greeley was "an old shoe." "In early life," he told Welles, "and with but a few mechanics and but little means in the West, we used to make our shoes last a great while with much mending, and sometimes, when far gone, we found the leather so rotten the stitches would not hold. Greeley is so rotten that nothing can be done with him. He is not truthful; the stitches all tear out."

Beset on one side by Greeley, who was hardly to be distinguished at this point from Vallandigham or August Belmont and the Peace Democrats, Lincoln found himself under fire from the Radical Republicans in Congress as well. Far from wanting a negotiated peace, they were determined to set severe terms for reconstruction.

As evidence gradually accumulated that Southern whites were determined to resist anything approaching equal rights for their ex-slaves, pressure mounted in Congress for the passage of statutes that would protect the emancipated slave in the exercise of his newly acquired rights. The movement was given momentum by a growing impatience with the President's own reconstruction policy and a strong feeling in Congress that it was that body's function, rather than the President's, to determine the course of reconstruction. The challenge to presidential leadership was muted by anxiety over the results of the upcoming presidential election. Radical and moderate Republicans had closed ranks to insure the nomination of Lincoln as their party's standard-bearer, but as soon as the nominating convention was over, mutiny broke out in the form of a bill presented by Benjamin Wade, the Ohio abolitionist, and H. Winter Davis, the outspoken Maryland Congressman. As a boy Davis had been an avid sportsman. Hunting with his father's slaves, he developed a deep sympathy for them. "They spoke with freedom before a boy," he later recalled, "what they would have repressed before a man. They were far from indifferent to their condition; they felt wronged, and sighed for freedom. They were attached to my father, and loved me, yet they habitually spoke of the day when God would deliver them." A talented orator with impeccable social ties, Davis was a leader of the antislavery forces in his own state and prominent in the abolitionist councils of the nation. He shared Wade's conviction that Lincoln had extended the executive powers of government far beyond their proper constitutional limits. Where Lincoln had stipulated that a rebel state might be readmitted into the Union when one-tenth of its population had taken an oath of loyalty to the government of the United States and formed a constitution conformable to republican principles, the Wade-Davis bill required "a majority of the persons enrolled in the State" to take the oath. The bill also excluded from political activity any person "who has held or exercised any office, civil or military, State or Confederate, under the rebel usurpation or who has voluntarily borne arms against the United States." The franchise was thereby limited to white Southerners of such strong Union sentiments that they had evaded fighting in the Confederate armies. As we have seen, many Southern whites of strong

Union sentiment had served in the rebel armies, convinced that it was their duty to defend their land against invaders. Others had simply been unwilling or unable to resist the laws which drafted them into the Confederate army. The plain intention of the Wade-Davis bill was to place political control of the Southern states in the grasp of a handful of Southern white Unionists, including a substantial number who had left the South to enlist in the Union army or who, refusing to serve in the rebel forces, had been imprisoned or placed under virtual house detention.

The Wade-Davis bill passed the Senate and House on July 2, 1864. It was the most serious challenge to Lincoln's leadership yet offered by Congress, and from a purely political point of view it came at a most inappropriate time—a few months before the presidential election, the outcome of which was far from certain. Lincoln's response was a pocket veto, failure to sign the bill into law before the end of the session, accompanied by a mildly worded message. He was, he declared, unwilling, by signing the bill, "to be inflexibly committed to any single plan of restoration." He was also, he declared, "unprepared to declare that the free state constitutions and governments already adopted and installed in Arkansas and Louisiana shall be set aside for naught. . . ."

The pocket veto of the Wade-Davis bill brought an angry "manifesto" from its authors. After a detailed attack on the President's message, Wade and Davis declared, "It was the solemn resolve of Congress to protect the loyal men of the nation against three great dangers: (1) the return to power of the guilty leaders of the rebellion; (2) the continuance of slavery; (3) the burden of the rebel debt." The inadequacy of the oath required by former rebels under the President's plan was a special object of the authors' scorn. After a lengthy enumeration of the shortcomings and flaws in Lincoln's plan, the authors added: "Such are the fruits of this rash and fatal act of the President—a blow at the friends of his Administration, at the rights of humanity, and at the principles of Republican Government." The President must understand, they concluded, "that the authority of Congress is paramount and must be respected; that the whole body of the Union men of Congress will not submit to be impeached by him of rash and unconstitutional legislation; and if he wishes our support, he must confine himself to his Executive duties—to obey and execute, not make the laws—to suppress by arms armed rebellion, and leave political organization to Congress."

Meanwhile, Horace Greeley kept up his attack on Lincoln. In the *Tribune* of August 9, 1864, he wrote that nine-tenths of all Americans "are anxious for peace—peace on almost any terms—and utterly sick of human slaughter and devastation." A fortnight later he wrote: "Lincoln is already beaten . . . he cannot be elected . . . we must have another ticket to save us from utter overthrow." The anti-Lincoln faction of the Radical Republicans met in Cleveland (Welles called them "strange odds and ends of parties, and factions, and disappointed and aspiring individuals") and nominated John C. Frémont as their candidate for president and John Cochrane for vice-president. Welles was caustic. He had supported Frémont in 1856, but now he considered him "reckless, improvident, wasteful, pompous, purposeless, vain, and incompetent," while Cochrane had been by turns "a Democrat, a Barnburner, a conservative, an Abolitionist, an Anti-Abolitionist, a Democratic Republican, and now a Radical Republican."

Lincoln himself was close to despair. At a Cabinet meeting in late August he wrote two sentences on a piece of paper: "This morning, as for some days past, it seems exceedingly probable that this administration will not be re-elected. Then it will be my duty to so cooperate with the President-elect as to save the Union between the election and the inauguration, as he will have secured his election on such ground that he cannot possibly save it afterward." He dated the note, August 23, folded the paper, and asked each Cabinet member to write his name on it as a witness of its authenticity.

With talk that the Peace Democrats in the North could only be outmaneuvered and the coming presidential elections won by some modification of the Emancipation Proclamation, Lincoln stated that as long as he was president, he would not "retract or modify" that document, and if popular clamor to abandon it proved irresistible, he would resign as president rather than carry out such a policy.

Chase was an increasingly discordant element in the Cabinet. "Chase, though a man of mark," Welles wrote of his fellow Cabinet member, "has not the sagacity, knowledge, taste, or ability of a financier. His expedients will break down the government. There is no one to check him. The President has surrendered the finances to his management entirely." Lincoln had no taste for financial matters. The controversy between the hard- and soft-money men seemed to be an impenetrable riddle. When Chase offered his resignation, to everyone's surprise, the President, equally surprisingly, accepted it and offered the office to David Tod, governor of Ohio and a hard-money man, in contrast with Chase's soft-money policies (which so distressed Gideon Welles). But when Tod refused the job, Lincoln turned to Senator William Pitt Fessenden, the Maine Republican. Fessenden, often ailing and irascible, had a notable record as chairman of the Senate Finance Committee. A powerful debater, much respected for his intellectual acuity, he had been one of the first political figures to propose an income tax as a just way of raising revenue to support the military forces of the Union. "The President's course is a riddle," Welles wrote. "Tod is a hard-money man; Fessenden has pressed through Congress the paper system of Chase. One day Tod is selected; on his refusal Fessenden is brought forward. This can in no other way be reconciled than in the President's want of knowledge of the subject." Lincoln proved a more accurate judge of Fessenden's monetary inclinations than Welles. Fessenden, without political ambitions, joined the Cabinet in July, 1864, and did his best to put a check to his predecessor's inflationary policies.

Fessenden was described by Schurz as "a man who might easily have been overlooked in a crowd." Prim and austere, he was noted for his fairness. Prior to a meeting of the Cabinet, Lincoln was reading the early comers passages from Petroleum V. Nasby. Fessenden did not hesitate to make it evident that he "thought it hardly a proper subject for the occasion, and the President hastily dropped it," Welles noted.

At the insistence of Sumner, Lincoln appointed Chase to the position of chief justice made vacant by the death of Roger Taney. According to Welles, Lincoln told a friend "that he would rather have swallowed his buckhorn chair than to have nominated Chase" for the post.

Lincoln continued to draw strength from his visits to Grant's headquarters with the Army of the Potomac. Walt Whitman often passed Lincoln on his way from his quarters at the Soldiers' Home, some three miles north of the city. He was always accompanied by a cavalry guard and usually rode "a good-sized, easy-going grey horse, is dress'd in plain black, somewhat rusty and dusty, wears a black hat, and looks about as ordinary in attire, etc., as the commonest man. . . . I see very plainly ABRAHAM LINCOLN's dark brown face, with the deep-cut lines, the eyes, always to me with a deep latent sadness in the expression." The middle-aged poet and the President became so familiar to each other that they exchanged cordial bows as they passed.

They made a remarkable trinity—Lincoln, Grant, and Whitman —the politician, the soldier, and the poet. The democracy had drawn them up in its hour of greatest need. They were cut of common cloth. The casual and indifferent character of their attire—Lincoln's rusty and unpressed old clothes; Grant in a rumpled private's uniform, sprinkled with ashes; Whitman in the simple garments of a working-man poet—suggested a common impatience with the forms of respectability.

The politician and the general discovered their affinity. It was in their supreme naturalness and simplicity and their fierce, implacable will that the Union should be restored. Whitman wrote of Lincoln: "He has a face like a Hoosier Michael Angelo, so awful ugly it becomes beautiful, with its strange mouth, its deep-cut, criss-cross lines, and its doughnut complexion." The poet had made himself the speaker and singer of the democracy, and in his life with the ill, the wounded, the dying, he had searched for the final meaning of the democracy, its sturdy inner spirit, the soul of America, and found it in the terrible suffering, the heroism, the deaths of young men; their burial in unmarked graves. For Whitman the vast numbers of unknown soldiers buried in unmarked graves symbolized the mysteriousness of the conflict and the sacrifices it demanded. He returned again and again to the theme: "No history ever—no poem sings, no music sounds, those bravest men of all those deeds. No formal general's report, nor book in the library, nor column in the paper, embalms the bravest, north or south, east or west. Unnamed, unknown, remain, and still remain, the bravest soldiers. Our manliest—our boys—our hardy darlings; no picture gives them."

The most memorable event of the war years for Sidney George Fisher was his meeting, as a member of the Union League, with Lincoln when the President visited Philadelphia in the summer of 1864. "Nothing," he wrote in his diary, "was said beyond ordinary salutations & shaking hands. I had all that I wanted, an opportunity to see & observe the man. Was much pleased by his countenance, voice & manner. He is tall, slender, not awkward & uncouth as he has been represented, well dressed in black, self-possessed and easy, frank & cordial. The pictures of him do great injustice to his face. His features are irregular & would be coarse but for their expression which is genial, animated & kind. He looked somewhat pale & languid & there is a soft shade of melancholy in his smile and in his eyes. Altogether an honest, intelligent, amiable countenance, calculated to inspire respect, confidence & regard. His voice, too, is clear & manly. Am very glad I have seen him. His whole bearing & aspect confirm the opinion I had formed of him."

While the political fortunes of the Republicans ebbed, the military fortunes of the Union army flowed strongly. Sherman penetrated to the heart of the Confederacy in Georgia, and Sheridan soon made his presence felt in the Shenandoah Valley.

Jubal Early, whose mission it was to protect the valley, augmented by Joseph Kershaw and an understrength cavalry brigade, attacked Sheridan at Cedar Creek on October 19. At first the attack was successful, driving the Union force back past successive defense lines; but Early's men became distracted, looting the Federal baggage train, and Sheridan was able to rally his troops and overwhelm Early, killing or capturing a large portion of his command. Lincoln issued a special general order on the occasion of Sheridan's victory at Cedar Creek, where "his routed army was reorganized, a great national disaster averted, and a brilliant victory achieved over the rebels for the third time in a pitched battle within thirty days. . . ."

The news of Sheridan's defeat of Early threw Northern cities into an orgy of celebration. It took George Templeton Strong an hour to make his way a few blocks through the cheering crowds. "From the Park to Madison Square all New York seemed in the streets, at the windows, or on the housetops." A hastily assembled parade took more than three hours to pass a single point. In the evening Union Square was the scene of an extravagant display of fireworks. Charles Francis Adams, Jr., wrote his brother Henry, mentioning "Sheridan's great victory, a victory, to my mind, likely in its consequences to be second to none in importance." He thought of the delight with which his brother and father would receive the news. These were the moments he longed to share with them "when, after long days of doubt, anxiety and almost despair, among a foreign and unsympathetic people, you at last suddenly see the smoke of the battle lifted and the country you loved and feared for so much lifting itself up again as strong, as firm and as confident as in the first days of the war."

Sheridan's crushing victory over Early brought a revival of Republican hopes. Now everything rested on the continued success of Union military operations. George Templeton Strong wrote exultantly: "General Philip Sheridan has knocked down gold and G. B. McClellan together. The former is below 200, and the latter is nowhere."

After a smaller engagement at Fisher's Hill, Sheridan concluded his Shenandoah campaign and rejoined Grant. "I have destroyed over 2,000 barns filled with wheat, hay, and farming implements," he wrote Grant, "over 70 mills filled with flour and wheat . . . and have killed and issued to the troops not less than 3,000 sheep." In fertile Loudoun County alone his men seized or destroyed "3,772 horses; 545 mules; 10,918 beef cattle; 12,000 sheep; 15,000 swine . . . 435,802 bushels of wheat; 77,176 bushels of corn; 20,397 tons of hay; . . . 500 tons of fodder; . . . eight sawmills; one powder mill; . . . 1,200 barns; . . . one railroad depot, 947 miles of rail. . . ." More than any single battle or campaign Sheridan's devastation of the valley marked the end of the Army of the Northern Potomac.

Sherman, in command of the Military Department of the Mississippi, had some 100,000 men in seven infantry corps and a cavalry corps. His orders from Grant had been "to move against Johnston's army, to break it up, and to get into the interior of the enemy's country as far as you can, inflicting all the damage you can against their war resources. . . ." Sherman decided that Atlanta best fulfilled Grant's requirements, and on May 7, as Grant was starting his campaign against Richmond, Sherman began his advance on Atlanta. Driving southeast, along the Chattanooga–Atlanta railroad line, Sherman forced Johnston back, turning his flanks in a series of brilliant maneuvers. Each time Johnston prepared to make a stand, Sherman threatened to envelop him, and Johnston was forced once more to retreat. Finally, at Kennesaw Mountain on June 27, Johnston established a strong position, which Sherman attacked. In the fierce fighting that followed, the Union forces failed to penetrate Johnston's defenses. Of the 16,225 Federal soldiers engaged (versus 17,733 Confederates) almost 2,000 were killed or wounded, opposed to 270 rebels, a ratio of ten to one.

Once again Sherman threatened Johnston's rear, and the Confederate commander was forced to withdraw. At this point Jefferson Davis, impatient with Johnston's cautious delaying tactics, replaced him with the more aggressive Hood. In the Battle of Peach Tree Creek on the outskirts of Atlanta, Hood lost heavily and withdrew into the city's defenses. On July 22 Hood attempted another foray which was checked with the crushing loss of more than 8,500 killed and wounded.

A month of minor probing attacks followed as Sherman attempted to cut the railroad lines leading into the city. Ted Upson wrote: "Our boys are living on fruit diet mostly now. The blackberries are so thick in the abandoned fields that one can pick a ten quart pail in a few minutes. The boys make puddings, pies and evry thing they can think of."

On September 1 Hood, afraid of having his last line of retreat closed, evacuated the city. Three days later Sherman occupied Atlanta, and much of it was burned. "We have utterly destroyed Atlanta," Ted Upson wrote. "I dont think any people will want to try and live there now. It is pretty tough to rout people out of their homes in this way, but it is war, and General Sherman is credited with saying that 'War is Hell.' I think that it is."

Charles Francis Adams, Jr., busy recruiting and training a troop of black cavalrymen, was moved to tears by the news of the fall of Atlanta. "How superbly Sherman . . . has handled that Army!" he wrote his father; "the boldness, the caution, the skill, the judgment, the profound military experience and knowledge of that movement, all resulting in its brilliant success and condensed in that one immortal line, 'So Atlanta is ours and is fairly won.' Who shall say," the exultant Adams added, "that to the enemy belong all the skill? . . . Unquestionably it is *the* campaign of this war; not more brilliant or so complete as that of Vicksburg, but, viewed as a whole, with its unheard of lines of supply and unceasing opposition, it rolls along like a sonorous epic. . . . Of the results, whether great or small, which will follow this fall of Atlanta, I don't pretend to form any opinion. I only look at the campaign in an artistic point of view, as a poem. So viewed, to my mind, it is perfect."

The President told Hay that he believed that the Democrats, angry and frustrated, would go to the Democratic nominating convention at Chicago with the intention of turning that body to "some violent end" but that they could not carry the mass of the party with them. Hay thought the reverse to be true: that the party managers would "try to do some clever and prudent things, such as nominate Grant without [a] platform; but that the bare-footed democracy from the heads of the hollows, who are now clearly for peace would carry everything in the Convention before them." It turned out much as Hay had predicted. The New York delegates who came to "intrigue for Grant" and a vague platform could get no hearing. "They were as a feather in the wind in the mist of that blast of German fanaticism," Hay wrote. Taking a long-needed vacation in Warsaw, Indiana, he wrote to Nicolay, holding the fort at the White House, that Republicans were "waiting with the greatest interest for the hatching of the big peace-snake at Chicago."

There was in the rural districts throughout the West "a good, healthy Union feeling," but "everywhere in the towns the copperheads are exultant, and our own people either growling and despondent or sneakingly apologetic." Even in his own family Hay found fainthearted individuals. An uncle had expressed a disposition to vote for the Democratic or "peace" candidate if the Chicago nominee was a good man. "I lose my temper sometimes," Hay wrote, "talking with growling Republicans. There is a diseased restlessness about men in these times that unfits them for the steady support of an administration."

The Democrats, to no one's surprise, expressed strong support for Vallandigham and chose McClellan as their standard-bearer. The Democratic convention gathered in, in Welles's words, "extreme partisans of every hue—Whigs, Democrats, Know-Nothings, Conservatives, War men and Peace men, with a crowd of Secessionists and traitors to stimulate action. . . ." Horatio Seymour helped frame a platform which called for an immediate cessation of hostilities and negotiations for peace. "After four years of failure to restore the Union by the experiment of war," the Constitution "disregarded in every part and public liberty and private right alike trodden down," efforts should now be made for a "convention of the states" to restore the Union and, by implication, accept the institution of slavery in those states still in rebellion.

McClellan's acceptance speech was a masterpiece of evasion. To George Templeton Strong it was "made up of platitudes floating in mucilage, without a single plain word against treason and rebellion . . . and no suggestion of magnetic power in word, phrase, or thought."

A Republican journalist drew up a "McClellan Creed," which read: "I believe in one country, one Constitution, one destiny. And in George B. McClellan, formerly general in chief of the armies of the United States; Who was born of respectable parents; Suffered under Edwin M. Stanton; Was refused reinforcements, and descended into the swamps of the Chickahominy; He was driven therefrom by fire and by sword. . . . He returned to the Potomac, fought the battle of Antietam, and was removed from his high command, and entered into oblivion; From this he shall one day be elevated to the Presidential chair. . . .

"I also believe in the unalienable doctrine of State Rights; In the admission of slavery into the territories; In the illegality of the Confiscation Act, of the Conscription, of the Suspension of Habeas

Corpus, of Arbitrary Arrests, and of the Proclamation of Emancipation; And I finally believe in a Peace which is beyond everybody's understanding. . . ."

The Democrats had hardly disbanded before word came of Sherman's capture of Atlanta. The news cast a chill over Democratic aspirations. "While the true Unionists," Welles wrote, "are cheerful and joyous, greeting all whom they meet over the recent news, the Rebel sympathizers shun company and are dolorous. This the demon of party—the days of its worst form,—a terrible spirit, which in its excess leads men to rejoice in the calamities of their country and mourn its triumphs."

Despite the capture of Atlanta, things looked bleak for Lincoln and the Republicans. The Knights of the Golden Circle were doing their best "to spread disaffection among western farmers and tradesmen." There were rumors that they were stockpiling weapons to be used in a general uprising against the administration. Strong was more pessimistic than ever. "The great experiment of democracy may be destined to fail a century sooner than I expected in disastrous explosion and general chaos," he wrote, "and this our grand republic over which we have bragged so offensively may be cast down as a great millstone into the sea and perish utterly—and all this within sixty days. . . . So much for traitors, demagogues, and lunatics! All the South and half the North are absolutely demented. Neither Lincoln nor McClellan is strong enough to manage so large and populous an asylum. Who is?" Satan seemed in charge. Strong quoted a Puritan of the English Civil War of 1660: "Our sins were ripe. God could not longer be just if we were prosperous." Lincoln, although honest and able, seemed to Strong at that point incapable of coping with the rapidly deteriorating state of Union morale. Glumly watching a McClellan parade marching up Broadway, Strong was led to reflect on the irony of the fact that "working men were carrying banners on which Lincoln is held up to ridicule as a 'railsplitter.' . . . Even our comparatively intelligent mechanics (or many of them)," Strong added, "are too brutally stupid to see that Lincoln is their representative and is fighting their battle against 'Little Mac,' the champion of sympathy with and concession to a rebellion that asserts the rightful supremacy of capital over labor."

Sidney George Fisher shared the anxieties of his New York counterpart. "It is impossible to say what disaster the success of

McClellan would bring," he wrote in his diary. "What would the army say, which is almost unanimous against him & for the war, at degrading terms of peace now that victory is assured and almost within their grasp? And would the Northern people consent that the immense sacrifices of the war should be made in vain? Two things are necessary for a permanent & satisfactory peace—the utter destruction of the military power of the rebels & the actual emancipation of the slaves."

Among the severe critics of Lincoln's policies in regard to black people was Frederick Douglass, but after the nomination of Frémont by Republican dissenters, Douglass declared that while he had former- ly withheld his support from the President, "that possibility is no longer conceivable. . . ." With McClellan as the Democratic candidate, Douglass urged every enemy of slavery to "rally with all the warmth and earnestness of his nature to the support of Abraham Lincoln."

When Charles Francis Adams, Jr., on leave in Washington from his cavalry unit, visited Seward in late August, 1864, his impressions of the state of mind of the secretary "were not cheerful," as he wrote his father. "The old Governor didn't seem to feel firm about the future and retired himself largely into his philosophy. His tone was very different from that of last spring, when he seemed to me so buoyant and confident of the future. . . . He . . . gave the impression which all here do of 'going it wild,' and not seeing where this thing is going to come out; but while others have a reckless and excited manner of going it, he, on the contrary, looked like a thoughtful and wise man, troubled at seeing the machine pass beyond control." Adams himself was scarcely more sanguine. "For all I can see, we must go floundering on indefinitely through torrents of blood and unfathomable bankrupt- cy. Yet I never felt more confident than now of our power to crush out this rebellion."

Precipitously (and mysteriously) as Lincoln's stock had declined, it now rose. Certainly the news that Sherman had captured Atlanta helped considerably, as did Sheridan's spectacular campaign in the Shenandoah Valley and the naval victory of Farragut at Mobile Bay, Alabama, in August.

George Templeton Strong, contemplating the significance of the coming election, wrote: "What political issues have arisen for centuries more momentous than those dependent on this election? They are to determine the destinies—the daily life—of the millions and millions who are to live on this continent for many generations to come. They will define the relations of the laboring man toward the capitalist in 1900 A.D., from Maine to Mexico."

By the end of September, Schurz, who made many speeches in Lincoln's behalf in New York, in Pennsylvania, and as far west as Wisconsin, felt the tide of public sentiment was running so strongly in favor of the President that "they were really superfluous." The campaign seemed to run itself; "it became more and more a popular jubilee as the election approached." On the eve of the election, Lincoln reaffirmed the last Thursday of November "as a day of thanksgiving and praise to Almighty God" and of prayer "for a return of the inestimable blessings of peace, union, and harmony throughout the land which it has pleased Him to assign as a dwelling place for ourselves and for our posterity throughout all generations."

The November elections were anticipated by elections in several states a month earlier. These were judged to be straws in the political wind and were watched with anxious attention by both parties. On the evening of October 11, 1864, Lincoln went to the War Department with Hay and Nicolay to see the dispatches as they came in by wireless. Stanton had locked all access doors to the building and retreated to the telegraph room. Finally the President and his aides found their way in by a side door. As the county tallies came in, they were compared with those of two years before. In Noble County, Indiana, the administration had gained 400 votes. It proved a favorable augury. Wires came in from Pennsylvania, indicating even greater gains there; the President relaxed and, fishing out of his voluminous pockets a copy of the "Nasby papers," read several chapters of "the experiences of the saint and martyr, Petroleum V." Petroleum Vesuvius Nasby was the pen name of David Ross Locke, a journalist on the *Findlay* (Ohio) *Jeffersonian*, who made the Reverend Nasby a caricature of a proslavery man, the epitome of irrational prejudices and hostility to the policies of Lincoln's administration. After the little group had scattered, immensely cheered by the good news, Hay wrote in his diary: "I am deeply thankful for the result in Indiana. I believe it saves Illinois in November, I believe it rescues Indiana from sedition and civil war. A copperhead governor would have afforded a grand central rallying point for . . . lurking treason. . . ."

Seward, Welles noted, was "quite exultant . . . feels strong and self-gratified. Says this administration is wise, energetic, faithful, and able beyond any of its predecessors; that it has gone through trials which none of them has ever known, and carried on, under extraordinary circumstances and against combinations such as the world have never known, a war unparalleled in the annals of the world." Among those hastening to scramble on the Union bandwagon was Hamilton Fish, the New York politician. "If you want to know which way the wind blows, throw up Hamilton Fish," Strong wrote caustically.

The outcome, only a few months before so uncertain, no longer seemed in doubt. Charles Francis Adams wrote his father: "I draw a long breath and say, thank God! Is it not wonderful! One after another how miraculously we have tided over the shadows and piloted through the rapids. Now the end of a Presidential election sees our enemy downcast, and only in sweat and agony anywhere holding his own, while we, flushed with success, find ourselves more firmly pledged to war than at any previous time. Thus the very Presidential election which we all dreaded so greatly and deplored as an unmitigated evil, bids fair to turn out the most opportune of occurrences. . . ."

The senior Adams replied to his son from London: "This strife between two conflicting principles is one of the grandest that ever took place on earth. It has enlisted in its support on the two sides a greater physical power than was ever brought to bear on any other question for the same length of time. I do not except even the wars of the reformation. As an example of the popular will acting energetically and unitedly in execution of a specific purpose, it is the most extraordinary event of all time. Thus far the spectacle is sublime."

On the day of the presidential election—November 8—the White House was "still and almost deserted," Lincoln sad and pensive. His election seemed certain, but the rancor and bitterness that surrounded it depressed him. "It is a little singular," he said to Hay, "that I, who am not a vindictive man, should have always been before the people in canvasses marked for their bitterness:—always but once. When I came to Congress it was a quiet time. But always besides that, the contests in which I have been prominent have been marked with great rancor."

Once more Lincoln and his aides headed for the War Department to get the returns. The night was "rainy, stormy and dark," and the President and his aides splashed through mud puddles to the door of the building, "where a soaked and smoking sentinel was standing in his own vapor with his huddled-up frame covered with a rubber cloak." Already the good news was coming in—a big gain in Indianapolis over the October vote for governor; a 15,000-vote majority in Baltimore, 5,000 in the state. Boston by 5,000. Captain Thomas Eckert, in charge of the telegraph office, came in wet and muddy; he had slipped and fallen. The President was reminded, "of course," Hay wrote, of a slip of his own. "For such an awkward fellow, I am pretty sure-footed. It used to take a pretty dexterous man to throw me." When Douglas had beaten him for the Senate in 1858, he had started home on a night much like the present one, slipped on the path, but recovered his balance and said to himself, thinking of the election, "*It's a slip and not a fall.*"

Lincoln was back at the White House by midnight, assured of victory. Called out by the cheers of a happy crowd of celebrators, he told them: "The election, along with its incidental and undesirable strife, has done good. It has demonstrated that a people's government can sustain a national election in the midst of a great civil war; until now, it has not been known to the world that this was a possibility. . . . It shows, also, to the extent yet known, that we have more men now than we had when the war began. . . . Now that the election is over, may not all, having a common interest, reunite in a common effort to save our common community? For my part I have striven, and will strive, to place no obstacle in the way. So long as I have been here, I have not willingly planted a thorn in any man's bosom. While I am deeply sensible of the high compliment of re-election, it adds nothing to my satisfaction that any other man may be pained or disappointed by the result. May I ask those who were with me to join with me in the same spirit toward those who were against me?"

Carl Schurz wrote years later in his *Reminiscences*: "When I read those noble words, which so touchingly revealed the whole tender generosity of Lincoln's great soul, the haggard face I had seen that evening in the cottage at the Soldiers' Home rose up vividly in my memory."

Lincoln felt that the moral authority given him by his re-election would, if used "in a friendly and magnanimous spirit," in a phrase of Carl Schurz's, enable him to prevail on the more intransigent spirits in his own party to accept a policy of reconstruction designed to bring the South as rapidly as possible into full membership in the Union. In the period between the election and his inauguration, however, Lincoln would find himself engaged in a struggle with Charles Sumner, the leader in the Senate of those who wished to chastise the South severely for its sins. Sumner had developed a theory of what he called "state suicide." The states that had seceded had, in effect, committed suicide, given up all claim to be equal members of a restored Union. The

Federal government might do with them as it wished without any constitutional constraints. The contest between the President and the Senator would grow so warm that the story that the two men were no longer on speaking terms would spread around Washington.

The day after the election George Templeton Strong wrote in his diary: "November 9, 1864 *Laus Deo!* The crisis has been passed, and the most momentous popular election ever held since ballots were invented has decided against treason and disunion. My contempt for democracy and extended suffrage is mitigated. The American people can be trusted to take care of the national honor. Lincoln is reelected by an overwhelming vote. . . . This election, peacefully conducted in a time of such bitter excitement, and with a result recognized and acquiesced in by a furious malcontent minority, is the strongest testimonial in favor of popular institutions to be found in history."

There was, of course, the very considerable fact of Sherman's spectacular march to Atlanta and the reckless platform of the Democrats, which in effect declared the war a failure and all the sacrifices in vain. But Carl Schurz perhaps best expressed the real ground of Lincoln's support: "more potent than all else, the tender affection of the popular heart for Abraham Lincoln [which] burst forth with all its warmth. This tender affection," Schurz added, "cherished among the plain people of the land, among the soldiers in the field, and their 'folks at home,' was a sentimental element of strength which Lincoln's critical opponents in the Union party had wholly ignored." Captain Charles Francis Adams expressed similar sentiments. "This last election," he wrote to his father, "has given me a new and almost unbounded faith in the faculty of a free *and intelligent* people to manage their own affairs . . . it has convinced me that our people, to come to correct conclusions, need only full and able discussions, time to think and honest and clear thinkers to guide." When the news of the election reached Henry Adams, he responded in a similar vein: "I never yet have felt so proud as now of the great qualities of our race, or so confident of the capacity of men to develop their faculties in the mass. I believe that a new era of the movement of the world will date from that day, which will drag nations up still another step, and carry us out of a quantity of old fogs."

William Mason Grosvenor, a native of Massachusetts, a graduate of Yale, an ally of Carl Schurz's, and a budding journalist, was a Union veteran who, like James Beecher, Higginson, Charles Francis Adams, Jr., and so many young men of strong abolitionist convictions, had commanded a black regiment made up largely of Louisiana ex-slaves. Grosvenor was rhapsodic about the outcome of the presidential contest, "conducted with the utmost license of speech and of the press even in the face of a great civil war," with the opposition free to employ "all the influences which could pervert the judgment, sap the loyalty, or shake the purpose of the people. . . . Conservative dry rot, hostility to all reform, and especially hatred of the negro and the abolitionist; prices, taxes, and pecuniary burdens already more grievous to sordid souls than any national dishonor or calamity; dread of the phantom of usurpation and of the prospect of another draft; influence of foreign agents, of rebel sympathizers, and of secret organization . . . the magic spell of a party name, and the yet mightier power of a church and a foreign-born clan"—over all these elements the basic intelligence and good sense of the American people had triumphed.

Three days after the election Lincoln made another visit to Grant's headquarters. This time the general was spruced up for his visitors. "His hair," John Hay noted, "was combed, his coat on, and his shirt clean, his long boots blackened till they shone." The general was "deeply impressed with the vast importance and significance" of the election. Like Hay himself, Grant believed it to be "the pivotal centre of our history—the quiet and orderly character of the whole affair. No bloodshed or riot,—few frauds, and those detected and punished in an exemplary manner." It proved that free institutions could survive great stress and strain without "running into anarchy or despotism." Grant expressed his opposition to the idea of the states filling out their draft quotas by signing up ex-slaves for Sherman's army at $300 a head. "Sherman . . . knows he can get all these negroes that are worth having anyhow, and he prefers to get them that way rather than to fill up the quota of a distant State and thus diminish the fruits of the draft." Grant found the blacks "admirable soldiers in many respects; quick and docile in a charge; excellent in fatigue duty." But he had serious doubts that an army of them could have stood "the week's pounding at the Wilderness and Spotsylvania as our men did," but then, in Grant's view, "no other troops in the world could have done it."

Re-elected, Lincoln found himself more besieged than ever by importuning politicians. He told Welles he was amused by "the manners and views of some who . . . tell him that he is now reëlected and can do just as he has a mind to, which means he can do some unworthy thing that the person who addresses him has a mind to." A few weeks after the election attempts were made by Copperheads in Boston, New York, and Philadelphia to set those cities on fire by planting incendiary devices in the leading hotels. From Canada a party of eight men had been dispatched to New York under the leadership of one Martin. The men visited eleven hotels and Barnum's Museum. They rented rooms at the hotels under assumed names, saturated the beds with camphene, and placed sticks of phosphorus on the camphene with the intention of producing a delayed combustion. In every instance these highly inefficient techniques failed to start a major conflagration.

When the lame-duck Congress assembled, the Republicans were in a euphoric mood. Forgotten were the recent attempts to oust Lincoln from the leadership of the party. The President's fourth annual message to Congress dwelt at length on the relations of the United States with various foreign nations. The act which Congress had passed to encourage immigration had been put into effect promptly with desirable results. "I regard our immigrants," Lincoln declared, "as one of the principal replenishing streams which are appointed by Providence to repair the ravages of internal war and its wastes of national strength and health." It was notable that even with the terrible losses on the battlefield the "steady expansion of the population, improvement, and governmental institutions over the new and unoccupied portions of our country have scarcely been checked, much less impeded or destroyed, by our great civil war. . . ." Homesteading had continued at an accelerating pace, and the mines of the Rocky Mountain region and the Sierra Nevada had produced minerals estimated to be worth in excess of $100 million in the past year. The population in the organized territories had tripled in the four years of war. ". . . We have *more* men *now* than we had when the war *began;* . . . we are not exhausted nor in the process of exhaustion; . . . we are *gaining* strength and may if need be maintain the contest indefinitely. This as to men. Material resources are now more complete and abundant than ever."

The story was very different in the exhausted South. The fall was marked by constant rain. Mary Chesnut, "full of miserable anxiety," felt the rains presaged some terrible conclusion to the long struggle. "There is nothing but distraction and confusion," she wrote. "Freeing negroes is the last Confederate Government craze," Mary Chesnut noted in December, 1864. "We are a little too slow about it; that is all."

Back in Columbia, South Carolina, she waited for the end. Her husband's aides filled the house, "and a group of hopelessly wounded haunt the place. . . . The drilling and marching go on outside. It rains a flood." Her friend Mary McCord exchanged $16,000 in Confederate money for $300 in gold. Hood was back after his defeat by Thomas and the disintegration of his army. His artificial leg allowed him to stand without his crutch and move slowly about, but he sat mostly by the fire, staring into its flames and speaking about "my defeat . . . my army destroyed, my losses, etc., etc." It pained Mary Chesnut's tender heart inexpressibly. "He is going over some bitter scene," Hood's aide, Jack Preston, told Mrs. Chesnut. "He sees Willie Preston with his heart shot away. He sees the panic at Nashville and the dead on the battlefield at Franklin. . . . That agony on his face comes again and again. I can't keep him out of those absent fits."

Mary Chesnut fled to Lincolnton, North Carolina, and found dingy, cramped lodgings there. Her landlady offered her religious tracts, but she declared herself already provided with the "Lamentations of Jeremiah . . . the denunciations of Hosea, and, above all, the patient wail of Job. Job is my comforter now," she wrote in her diary. She hoped things would be no worse. Her husband had survived. She kept herself alive by trading off what was left of her wardrobe for food—"we are devouring our clothes," she added wryly. And still the rain came. Mulberry Hill was raided by Yankee soldiers, who carried off all the horses and mules and much of the poultry and pigs, but according to Lawrence, who gave Mary a detailed account of the episode, James Chesnut's sister was proud of having lost from the family's personal possessions "only two bottles of champagne, two of her brother's gold-headed canes . . . and her own carriage." The only slave who deserted to the Yankees was "a fly-brush boy called Battis, whose occupation in life was to stand behind the table with his peacock feathers and brush the flies away." Claiborne, a "black rascal" who had been suspected of treasonable intentions, talked the Yankees out of burning Mulberry Hill by arguing that the only ones hurt by such an act would be blacks themselves since "Mars Jeems hardly ever come here and he takes only a little sompen . . . to eat when he do come."

The end of 1864 was a time of "sad remembering" for Mary Chesnut, recalling "all the true-hearted, the light-hearted, the gay and gallant boys who have come laughing, singing, and dancing in my way in the three years now past; how," she wrote, "I have looked into their brave young eyes and helped them as I could in every way and then saw them no more forever; now they lie stark and cold, dead upon the battle-fields, or moldering away in hospitals or prisons, which is worse—I think if I consider the long array of those bright youths and loyal men who have gone to their death almost before my very eyes, my heart might break, too. Is anything worth it—this fearful sacrifice, this awful penalty we pay for war?"

An air of impending doom hung over the Capitol at Richmond. If Jefferson Davis remained stubbornly unaware of it, it was plain enough to Mary Chesnut. Longstreet was in Lynchburg, his shoulder smashed by a bullet. "He is very feeble and nervous," William Blackford wrote his wife, "and suffers much from his wound. He sheds tears on the slightest provocation and apologizes for it. He says he does not see why a bullet going through a man's shoulder should make a baby of him."

32

The End

On January 1, 1865, Gideon Welles noted in his diary: "The date admonished me of passing time and accumulating years. Our country is still in the great struggle for national unity and national life; but progress has been made during the year that has just terminated, and it seems to me the Rebellion is not far from its close. The years that I have been here have been oppressive, wearisome, and exhaustive, but I have labored willingly, if sometimes sadly, in the cause of my country and mankind."

As indications of an imminent Southern collapse grew stronger, the Copperheads and Peace Democrats hastened to fall in line, vowing their devotion to the Union and their desire for a Northern victory. England too bestirred itself and began to find heretofore unperceived virtues in the Northern cause and in Lincoln's administration. Palmerston and Disraeli vied with each other in praising "the energy and discretion" of the Union government. "Poor, mean, shabby, fallen, old England restores us the tribute of her shop-keeper's civility and compliments the moment she discerns that we may win our unpromising lawsuit, after all . . ." George Templeton Strong wrote.

Meanwhile, a series of hysterical exhortations issued from the Confederate Congress. Its members warned their fellow Southerners that in the event of a Southern defeat the Union would wreak havoc and destruction upon the South. "Our enemies," one such communiqué declared, "with a boastful insolence unparalleled in the history of modern civilization have threatened not only our subjugation, but some of them have announced their determination if successful in this struggle to deport our entire white population, and supplant it with a new population drawn from their own territory and from the European countries. . . . Think of it!" The same address ended on a note that touched the absurd: "Failure will compel us to drink the bitter cup of humiliation even to the dregs of having the history of our struggle written by New-England historians."

The Radical Republicans, led by Henry Winter Davis, Charles Sumner, Thaddeus Stevens, and Lyman Trumbull, concerted their efforts in the winter and early spring of 1865, as the war was clearly approaching an end, to framing measures designed to insure the active political participation of the freed slaves. The interest of the Radical Republicans in the fate of Southern blacks was, as many political matters are, a combination of idealism and self-interest. The Radical Republican leaders had been abolitionists from early on. Having endured obloquy and abuse for years, they now found themselves in power or at least on the verge of it. They had only to displace the more moderate wing of their party to be in full command of Congress. Most of them had only the dimmest notion of the reality of black life in the South and the complications attendant upon giving political power to free blacks. The blacks they knew were, with very few exceptions, those able and sometimes brilliant individuals, of whom Frederick Douglass was the prototype, who were most active in the abolition movement. Another less worthy but nonetheless entirely understandable goal was to secure in perpetuity the dominance of the Republican Party. It was, after all, the Democrats who had worked almost as doggedly as their Southern allies to undermine the Union war effort, to bring about a premature and discreditable peace, a peace that would have left the slaves in bondage and the South independent. In Republican eyes they were disloyal political partisans who put hunger for power and for office ahead of the good of their country, who conspired against their government and gave aid and comfort to the enemy.

Gideon Welles was alarmed by "a wild, radical element in regard to the rebellious States and people. They are to be treated by a radical Congress as no longer States, but Territories without rights, and must have a new birth or creation by permission of Congress. These are the mistaken theories and schemes of Congress." Charles Francis Adams, Jr., also discerned an attitude toward the South "as ugly and vindictive as possible. They [Radical Republicans] don't want peace," he wrote his father, "unless with it comes the hangman. They will insist upon it that this mighty revolution was, after all, only a murderous riot and that the police court and the constable are just about what it needs to quiet it. To this I can't assent." It seemed to Adams that the thirst for vengeance was strongest of all in his homeland of New England, and he regretted that his father could not be at home to help combat it.

Poised for his dramatic march to Savannah and the sea, Sherman left Atlanta on November 16, a week after Lincoln's election. Ted Upson, "Little Mother" as the men of his company called him because of his care for ill and wounded comrades, wrote proudly that "such an army as we have I doubt was ever got together before; all are in the finest condition. We have weeded out all the sick, feeble ones and all the faint hearted ones and all the boys are ready for a meal or a fight and dont seem to care which it is. We have learned to get along with little in the way of baggage too. All a good many carry is a blanket made into a roll with thier rubber 'poncho' which is doubled around and tied at the ends and hung over the left shoulder." Each man had, in addition, his haversack and canteen and forty rounds of ammunition. All the rest the countryside had to yield.

"The next day [November 17, 1864]," Sherman wrote, "we passed through the handsome town of Covington, the soldiers closing up their ranks, the color-bearers unfurling their flags, and the bands striking up patriotic airs. The white people came out of their houses to behold the sight, in spite of their deep hatred of the invaders, and the negroes were simply frantic with joy. Whenever they heard my name, they clustered about my horse, shouted and prayed in their peculiar style, which had a natural eloquence that would have moved a stone. I have witnessed hundreds, if not thousands of such scenes; and can now see a poor girl, in the very ecstasy of the Methodist 'shout,' hugging the banner of one of the regiments, and jumping up to the 'feet of Jesus.'"

One of the ironies of Sherman's march was that the cotton fields of the state had been converted to the growing of corn to feed the Southern armies. It was, in essence, this corn that enabled Sherman's army to "live off the land." One old black woman told David Macrae, "We know'd it [Sherman's army] was a-comin', 'cos we prayed so for it.

Specs we so tormented de Lord, He was obleeged to send Massa Sherman dis yar way."

As Sherman's army progressed, it collected a strange assortment of slaves, in many instances whole families on foot or in rough wagons, with a goat or cow or ancient mule liberated from its masters, plus a motley assortment of poor whites. The soldiers themselves were often arrayed in odds and ends of Confederate finery stolen from plantations along the route. When some black runaways expressed the wish to see General Sherman, they were directed to a soldier wearing an expropriated "red cutaway uniform with a three corner cocked hat with a feather in it." Although everything was done to discourage blacks from leaving their home plantations, their numbers increased with every mile the army covered.

Sherman's men, marching through Georgia, sounded out a kind of wild music of cries and chants. Commenced by one regiment, they would be taken up by brigades and corps until a vast diapason of sound rose from the tide of marching men. "It was one of the characteristic expressions of the western troops," a newspaper correspondent wrote, "and became a habit, serving as a relief and outlet to the men—a vent for their feelings of victory, returning peace, etc. Morning, noon, and afternoon, spontaneous, for occasion or without occasion, these huge, strange cries, differing from any other, echoing through the open air for many a mile, expressing youth, joy, wildness, irrepressible strength, and the ideas of advance and conquest, sounded along the swamps and uplands of the South."

Sherman's foragers carried maps of the country, "with every village and plantation marked, and all the roads and paths through the forest by which any place could be reached," David Macrae wrote. "They seemed to know what men were away in the Confederate army and what men might be found at home, and how much booty was to be expected at each plantation." They were not particular about the nature of their plunder. It included, again in Macrae's words, everything from "turnips, fowling pieces, and ladies underclothing, chickens and communion service, whips, spoons, pictures, and eatables and drinkables of every description." The story was told of one bummer, or marauder, who poured molasses into his saddlebags rather than abandon it. On some plantations that Macrae visited, Sherman's foragers had burned books, slashed paintings, destroyed family records, and smashed clocks and pianos. All this was, of course, in defiance of Sherman. "The army will forage liberally on the country during the march," he had ordered. Each brigade commander was directed to organize a foraging party under the leadership of a "discreet" officer and gather "corn or forage of any kind, meat of any kind, vegetables, cornmeal, or whatever is needed by the command." A ten-day supply should be kept on hand at all times. It was also specifically stated that "Soldiers must not enter the dwellings of the inhabitants, or commit any trespass." Mills and private property were not to be destroyed, Sherman ordered, unless guerrillas or bush-whackers from the vicinity had molested the troops. Since they almost invariably did, individual commanders had in effect carte blanche to destroy what they wished. Commanders were instructed to "discriminate . . . between the rich, who are usually hostile, and the poor or industrious, usually neutral or friendly. . . . In all foraging of whatever kind, the parties engaged will refrain from abusive or threatening language . . . and they will endeavor to leave with each family a reasonable portion for their maintenance."

Bushwhackers hung on the army like leeches. Foragers from Ted Upson's 100th Indiana Regiment were fired on by bushwhackers, and one was captured and shot down as he begged for his life. "While moving out this morning we saw the lifeless bodies of several citizens swinging from trees," Upson wrote, "with a placard upon each which read: 'This is done in retaliation for the unwarranted attack made upon my foragers yesterday. Any repetition of this offense will be similarly punished. . . . W T Sherman, General Commanding.'"

That there was wholesale destruction and "liberation" of Southern property cannot be denied, nor that the provocation was great. But the wildest stories of Sherman's depredations circulated throughout the South and found ready believers everywhere: that Sherman had personally collected two hundred gold watches among his loot, and an infinite number of similar tales. The truth was grim enough; it hardly needed embellishing.

Carl Schurz, who discussed with Sherman the charges against his army of brutal pillaging and misuse of the civilian population along the route, gave a balanced and reasonable defense. There was no question that officers and men alike helped themselves to rebel property pretty much as they wished, a practice of invading armies which, if not commendable, is for the most part habitual. Schurz, joining Sherman at Goldsboro, North Carolina, saw soldiers frying bacon on silver platters, and in a general's tent he was treated to

Madeira wine poured from a silver pitcher into silver goblets. Sherman admitted that the necessity of "living on the country"—that is to say, constantly dispatching foraging parties to round up food for his soldiers—provided more opportunities for looting than would ordinarily have been the case and made it much more difficult to control. That a party of men sent out to round up any hogs they could find would help themselves to less eatable objects was not to be wondered at. That they might be rude and threatening in the bargain was also not surprising. The Southerners, after all, considered them brutes and barbarians. This spirit was especially evident in the march through South Carolina, a state which the soldiers blamed for precipitating the war. "Before we got out of that state," Sherman told Schurz, "the men had so accustomed themselves to destroying everything in the line of march that sometimes, when I had my headquarters in a house, that house began to burn before I was fairly out of it. The truth is," Sherman continued, "human nature is human nature. You take the best lot of young men, all church members, if you please, and put them into an army, and let them invade the enemy's country, and live upon it for any length of time, and they will gradually lose all principle and self-restraint to a degree beyond the control of discipline. It always has been and always will be so. When a fair-minded man who knows something about war, examines the conduct of my troops under the circumstances, he will not be surprised at what they did, but he will be surprised that it was no worse. At any rate, I was very glad when I had my army out of those States." We might very well let the case for Sherman's army rest there.

On November 22 a substantial Confederate force, numbering by Ted Upson's calculations six brigades, attacked the wagon train. A severe fight followed, in which the 100th Indiana Regiment lost 13 killed and 79 wounded. Upson was convinced that it was only the repeating rifles in the hands of the Union soldiers that prevented the rear guard from being overwhelmed. The Confederate losses were severe, more than 300 killed and more than 1,000 wounded. The greatest loss to Upson was "Uncle" Aaron Woolford, whose maturity and unfailing good humor had been so often an inspiration to the younger men in the regiment. Upson had stood picket duty with him the night before and found him depressed by the foreboding that he had not long to live.

Ted Upson wrote Uncle Aaron's wife, telling her "what a good man he was, how much help he had been to all the boys, how brave and faithful to duty he was, all that I could think of to tell her about him. . . . I never saw her," Upson added, "nor any of the 8 children now left without a Father, but I hope she will realize what a grand soul he had. I also sent his watch, Testament, and money by Express prepaid."

In the skirmishes between Sherman's troops and the retreating Confederates, the most disheartening aspect for the rebels was the superior efficiency of the Union repeating rifles. "They say we are not fair," Upson wrote, "that we have guns that we load up on Sunday and shoot all the rest of the week. . . . I should think those fool Johnnys would quit," he added. "They might as well try to stop a tornado as Uncle Billy and his boys."

In the North there was considerable uneasiness at the vagueness and contradictoriness of the reports on Sherman's progress. "No positive intelligence from Sherman," George Templeton Strong wrote. "Rebel newspapers report that he has been defeated. . . . His failure would be a fearful calamity. Even Richmond papers seem not certainly to know what has become of him. Perhaps he will never be heard from again, like King Arthur and Don Sebastian." Widespread anxiety was expressed at Sherman's recklessness in abandoning his supply line, much too extended in any event to withstand the persistent raids of Morgan and Forrest.

Meanwhile, at Fort McAllister, some ten miles south of Savannah, Sherman's soldiers were preparing for the final assault on that city by making breastworks of saplings or poles fastened together with grapevines. Some sixty feet long and four feet in diameter, the breastworks could be rolled forward by riflemen until they were close enough to shoot into the embrasures protecting the Confederate artillery. In this fashion battery after battery was silenced until the Union soldiers broke into the fort. Even then the Johnnies retreated into their "bombproofs" and had to be dug out "in detail." With Fort McAllister captured, and the Federal fleet blocking the harbor, General William Hardee, in command of the Confederate forces in Savannah, had no choice but to extricate his forces across the causeway leading to the city and begin a long retreat toward Charleston.

At last the word came—Savannah had fallen. On December 22 Sherman's army occupied the city—"a fine Christmas present for Uncle Abraham and the folks at home," Ted Upson noted. Fine present it was indeed. Everyone was conscious of the fact that it was an epic achievement.

Much as white Southerners suffered from the war, blacks suffered more. In the wake of every movement of the Union army thousands of slaves abandoned their plantations and set out on the Jubilee Trail to freedom that was so often marked by terrible hardship, suffering, and death. William Gannett, who had traveled to Savannah to help deal with the tide of black refugees crowding into that city after its fall to Sherman, described the arrival of a ship carrying hundreds of ex-slaves too hungry and ill to stand. "Long, bony, and still, they lay along the decks, the flies swarming around them, as if they lit upon the dead. The silence of four *was* that of death. . . ."

Melville wrote a poem, which ended:

> For behind they left a wailing,
> A terror and a ban,
> And blazing cinders sailing,
> And houseless household wan,
> Wide zones of countries paling,
> And towns where maniacs ran.
> Was it Treason's retribution—
> Necessity the plea?
> They will long remember Sherman
> And his streaming columns free—
> They will long remember Sherman
> Marching to the sea.

For almost six weeks Sherman's weary soldiers enjoyed the luxury of staying put. Upson and his sidekick, Possum, built a kind of mansion six-and-a-half feet long, three-and-a-half feet wide, and four feet deep, lining it with boards from an old house, roofing it with their tent, and covering the floor with hanging moss. The two friends explored the defenses of the city, counting more than three hundred guns in one sector of the positions, some of them large enough for Upson to crawl into until just his head stuck out. "This is a beautiful city, and very old," Upson wrote his parents. "In the Cemetery lie such men as Pulaski and many Revolutionary heroes. The famous Shell Road [made of crushed oyster shells] is more than 5 miles long and smooth as a house floor with great magnolia trees on either side."

Now the war, so endlessly and agonizingly protracted, rushed to its conclusion. Grant ordered Sherman to move his army north through the Carolinas, while Meade was to take the offensive in

Virginia; Lee would at last be caught in pincers from which he could not escape.

Sherman, delayed by heavy winter rains, started his army north the first week of February, accompanied by a corps of now-respectful journalists reporting on every word and gesture of the great military hero. The democratic atmosphere of Sherman's army shocked most observers. Arthur Sumner, a journalist, wrote: "The officers and men are on terms of perfect social equality. . . . On duty they drink together, go arm in arm about town, call each other by the first name in a way that startles the Eastern man." At the same time the Westerners were more hostile to blacks than other Union soldiers. Again in Arthur Sumner's words, they were "impatient with darkies, and annoyed to see them so pampered, petted, and spoiled. . . ." Sherman's men were described by Sumner as "trooping through the streets, roaring out songs and jokes, making sharp comments about all the tidy citizens, and overflowing with merriment and good-nature. Their clothes were patched like Scripture-Joseph's. Hats without brims, hats without crowns. . . . One man had a live cock on his knapsack —the bird had been with him twenty-two months—all the way from Wisconsin. It was a treat, I assure you," Sumner wrote, "to see some real soldiers, who had won battles."

From Savannah, Ted Upson's corps was transported by boat to Beaufort, South Carolina. During the voyage Upson and several of his friends got a "porpoise hook" and, positioning themselves at an open skylight above the officers' dining room, fished up chickens and hams as fast as a black waiter brought them from the galley. "We had pretty well cleaned out everything," Upson wrote, "when we spied some boxes of cigars. In fishing them up one box came open and scattered the cigars all over the table. That gave it away. . . ." The thieves had gobbled up the food so hastily that when the ocean grew rough, they all became seasick and had to "give up their stolen dinner after all."

When Sherman arrived in the Beaufort district with his tatterde-malion army, accompanied by thousands of ex-slaves, Secretary of War Stanton traveled there and met with twenty black leaders to listen to their complaints and solicit their advice. It was, for the times, a remarkable gesture. Among the questions Stanton asked them was whether they would prefer to live in mixed communities of blacks and whites or in their own black communities. The feeling was virtually unanimous for their own communities, "for," as one said, "there is a prejudice against us in the South that it will take years to get over. . . ." Then, to Sherman's indignation, Stanton questioned the black leaders privately about Sherman's attitudes toward Negroes. Although reports had circulated in the North that the general had "an almost *criminal* dislike" of blacks, the blacks were strong and unanimous in their praise of him.

The principal consequence of Stanton's visit to Beaufort was Special Field Order No. 15, which designated the region from Charleston south to the St. John's River and thirty miles inland as an area reserved for settlement by freedmen in tracts of not more than forty acres, "until such time as they can protect themselves, or until Congress shall regulate their title." Hundreds and then thousands of freed slaves flocked to General Rufus Saxton's headquarters to lay claim to allotments of land. A thousand acres were distributed in a few days. The Reverend Ulysses Houston, heading a band from Georgia, told a Port Royal missionary: "We shall build our cabins, and organize our own government for the maintenance of order and the settlement of difficulties." A reporter for an antislavery journal noted: "He and his fellow-colonists selected their lots, laid out a village, numbered their lots, put the numbers in a hat, and drew them out. . . . It was Plymouth colony repeating itself. They agreed if any others came to join them, they should have equal privileges. So blooms the Mayflower on the South Atlantic coast."

From Beaufort Sherman's army pushed on toward Columbia, the state capital. "We have been skirmishing, building corderoy roads, fording streams across swamps, marching through mud and rain over the worst roads that can be imagined," Ted Upson wrote his parents. On February 15 the advance units of Sherman's army entered the city. As they passed a large tobacco warehouse, blacks threw plugs of tobacco to the men, and soon the soldiers encountered Negroes with buckets of whiskey. When Sherman and his staff rode into town, they were greeted by a tipsy soldier, dressed in a figured dressing gown and a high hat, who stepped fearlessly up to the general, lifted his hat, and declared, "I have honor (hic), General, to present (hic) you with (hic) the freedom of the (hic) City." Upson reported: "Uncle Billy turned his head around to us and I saw him grin."

Someone had set bales of cotton on fire in Columbia. Sherman said Wade Hampton, the Confederate general, had done so before he evacuated the city; Hampton said the deed was done by the Yankees. In any event, a strong wind came up, fanned the smoldering cotton into flames, and blew burning wads about until half the city was on fire. The Union soldiers tried to help extinguish the flames and aid the terrified inhabitants. "As to the talk among some of the citizens that we deliberately destroyed the City," Upson wrote, "its all bosh. We had no desire to destroy the City, and did all we could to care for the inhabitants in their distress."

With Sherman's army approaching Charleston, Mary Chesnut sat down at her window in the beautiful moonlit summer night "and tried hard for pleasant thoughts." A piano and flute began to play in a nearby house, "Ever of Thee I Am Fondly Dreaming" and, then, "The Long, Long, Weary Day." She thought of her absent husband and friends, of the living and the dead, the dreamlike memories of charming parties and brilliant conversations. "I broke down," she wrote in her diary. "Heavens what a bitter cry came forth, with such a flood of tears the wonder is there was any of me left." A pervasive sadness hung over the city. "When you meet people," Mrs. Chesnut wrote, "sad and sorrowful is the greeting; they press your hand; tears stand in their eyes or roll down their cheeks, as they happen to possess more or less self-control. They have brother, father, or sons as the case may be, in battle. And how this thing seems never to stop. We have no breathing time given us. . . . The proportion of trouble is awfully against us." It was the women especially who suffered, in Chesnut's view. "Does anyone wonder so many women die?" she wrote. "Grief and constant anxiety kill nearly as many women at home as men are killed on the battle-field."

When the Confederate forces evacuated Charleston on February 17, 1865, the first Union troops to march into the city were the soldiers of the 21st Colored Infantry, followed by the Massachusetts 54th and 55th. An officer of the 55th described the welcome "given to a regiment of colored troops by their people redeemed from slavery." As "shouts, prayers, and blessings resounded on every side, all felt that the hardships and dangers of the siege were fully repaid." "John Brown's Body" was sung, followed by "Babylon Is Fallen" and Julia Ward Howe's "Battle Hymn of the Republic." "The glory and the triumph of this hour may be imagined but can never be described," the officer added. "It was one of those occasions which happens but once in a lifetime, to be lived over in memory forever." An old slave woman chanted:

Ye's been long a-comin'
Ye's been long a-comin'
Ye's been long a-comin'
For to take de land.

With Charleston evacuated by the Confederate forces and black soldiers patrolling the streets, Charlestonians had a substantial adjustment to make. "Negroes," Emma Holmes wrote, ". . . are encouraged to insult their former masters by every petty way malignity can suggest, while a saturnalia reigns among 'the colored ladies' who presented several flags & are considered 'prettier than those of other cities, save New Orleans,' Yankee women are invited to hasten to come and enlighten the young ideas of Africa," she noted, "no doubt with a similar result to the Beaufort experiment. O Heavens, the mind and heart sickens over the revolting thoughts—miscegenation in truth & in our city!"

The white soldiers made camp in the city park, while the blacks were assigned to the lower end of the town and there, according to Emma Holmes, "committed some gross outrages—violating a young lady at Mrs. Baxley's & behaving so dreadfully that she shrieked for help. . . ." The black soldiers held a camp meeting. "Tremendous excitement prevailed," Holmes wrote, "as they prayed their cause might prosper & their just freedom be obtained. Great numbers of servants went off from town really crazy from excitement & the parade. . . ."

A few weeks later the city's blacks organized a "jubilee of freedom." After the 21st Regiment came the black ministers of Charleston, "carrying open Bibles." Behind them came a cart on which were fifteen black women dressed in white dresses to represent the fifteen slave states. They were followed by some eighteen hundred children singing "John Brown's body lies a-moldering in the grave, *We* go marching on!"

Then came the various trades of the city: masons, carpenters, fishermen, teamsters, drovers, coopers, bakers, blacksmiths, barbers, wheelwrights, painters, each carrying the tools of his trade. The last float was the most moving of all. It carried an auctioneer's block and a black man who had been sold several times as a slave, now acting out the part of a slave trader, auctioning off two women and a child. As the cart moved along, the mock auctioneer rang his bell and cried out, "How much am I offered for this good cook? She is an excellent cook, gentlemen, she can make four kinds of mock turtle soup—from beef, fish or fowl. Who bids?"

Many of the black spectators burst into tears as the float passed. Inevitably one is reminded of the Grand Procession in Philadelphia in 1788 in celebration of the ratification of the Federal Constitution, when the leading figures of the city paraded, followed by floats representing the Federal Union and the Constitution and by all the professionals and the artisans of the city, the latter also carrying the tools of their trades. Separated by eighty-three years, the two episodes neatly bracket what might be called the era of slavery in the United States. The Charleston jubilee, modest as it was in comparison with its far more elaborate predecessor, had about it a special kind of poignance. It must have been planned with its historical referent—the Grand Procession—in mind. As such it can be taken as a symbol, once again, of the power of common memories. Through all the degradations of slavery, the black men and women of Charleston had clung to a dream of freedom and human dignity that they now enacted. It was now they, not the sullen and indignant whites who watched from curtained windows, who embodied the spirit of the nation's original charters, the Declaration of Independence and the Constitution.

Reading of the Union occupation of Charleston, George Templeton Strong recalled the impudent telegram sent to Lincoln four years earlier by the young gentlemen of the city:

> With mortar, cannon and petard,
> We tender old Abe our Beau-Regard.

"What do you think about that day's job now?" Strong asked. "But I suppose," he added in a more somber note, "a large majority of the young gentlemen who got more or less gloriously tipsy that memorable night are in their graves before this. Heaven forgive them their share in the colossal crime that has cost so many lives. Wiser, cooler, and better men might have been as blind, mad, and criminal had they grown up as members of a slaveholding caste in a woman-flogging and a baby-buying country."

When Gideon Welles visited Charleston a few weeks later, he was moved to similar reflections: "Their young men . . . considered themselves to be knights and barons bold, sons of chivalry and romance. . . . Cotton they knew to be king, and slavery created cotton. . . . The results of their theory and the fruits of their labors are to be seen in this ruined city and this distressed people. Luxury, refinement, happiness have fled from Charleston; poverty is enthroned there. Having sown error, she has reaped sorrow. She has been, and is, punished. I rejoice that it is so."

Lincoln's Second Inaugural Address on March 4 was almost as disconcertingly short as his Gettysburg Address. It seemed as though he had hardly started before he was finished. He recalled his first inaugural, four years earlier. "One eighth of the whole population was colored slaves, not distributed generally over the Union, but localized in the southern part of it," Lincoln declared. "These slaves constituted a peculiar and powerful interest. All knew that this interest was somehow the cause of the war." The South had committed an act of aggression against the North in trying by force to withdraw from the Union. The issue had been committed to the test of war. Both sides called on the Almighty for assistance. " 'Woe unto the world because of offenses; for it must needs be that offenses come, but woe to that man by whom the offense cometh.' If we shall suppose that American slavery is one of those offenses which, in the providence of God, must needs come, but which, having continued through His appointed time, He now wills to remove, and that He gives to both North and South this terrible war as the woe due to those by whom the offense came, shall we discern therein any departure from those divine attributes which the believers in a living God always ascribe to Him? Fondly do we hope, fervently do we pray, that this mighty scourge of war may speedily pass away. Yet, if God wills that it continue until all the wealth piled by the bondsman's two hundred and fifty years of unrequited toil shall be sunk, and until every drop of blood drawn with the lash shall be paid by another drawn with the sword, as was said three thousand years ago, so still it must be said, 'The judgments of the Lord are true and righteous altogether.'

"With malice toward none, with charity for all, with firmness in the right as God gives us to see the right, let us strive on to finish the work we are in, to bind up the nation's wounds, to care for him who shall have borne the battle and for his widow and his orphan, to do all which may achieve and cherish a just and lasting peace among ourselves and with all nations."

The correspondence among the three Adameses—Charles Francis, Sr.; Charles, Jr.; and Henry—is remarkable for the almost total absence of any reference to Lincoln. It was as though for the Adams clan the President of the United States simply did not exist or was of no importance in the progress of the war. Seward's name, of course, appears frequently, as do those of Stanton and Chase, but Lincoln is conspicuous by his absence. After the second inaugural, however, even Charles Francis, Jr., condescended to take notice. "What do you think of the inaugural?" he wrote his father. "That rail-splitting lawyer is one of the wonders of the day. Once at Gettysburg and now again on a greater occasion he has shown a capacity for rising to the demands of the hour which we should not expect from orators or men of the schools. This inaugural strikes me in its grand simplicity and directness as being for all time the historical keynote of this war; in it a people seemed to speak in the sublimely simple utterance of ruder times. What will Europe think of this utterance of the rude ruler, of whom they have nourished so lofty a contempt? Not a prince or minister in all Europe could have risen to such an equality with the occasion. . . ."

Gideon Welles described the inauguration as being marked by "a great want of arrangement and completeness in the ceremonies. All was confusion and without order,—a jumble." Most disconcerting of all were the remarks of the new vice-president, Andrew Johnson. Johnson, tense and nervous and feeling ill, had apparently been sipping brandy in the office of the retiring vice-president, Hannibal Hamlin. When he was called on to take the oath of office, he was plainly inebriated, and he began, in Ben: Perley Poore's words, "a maudlin, drunken speech," addressing the diplomatic corps and the Cabinet "in the most incoherent, and in some instances, offensive manner." Welles conjectured that Johnson may have "taken medicine, or stimulants, or his brain from sickness may have been overactive. . . . Whatever the cause, it was all in bad taste." Welles had said to Stanton, sitting on his right: "The man is certainly deranged. Johnson is either drunk or crazy." Stanton replied: "There is evidently something wrong."

Walt Whitman saw Lincoln returning from his inauguration. "He was," Whitman wrote, "in this plain two-horse barouche, and look'd very much worn and tired; the lines, indeed, of vast responsibilities, intricate questions, and demands of life and death, cut deeper than ever upon his dark brown face; yet all the old goodness, tenderness, sadness and canny shrewdness underneath the furrows. I never see that man," Whitman added, "without a feeling that he is one to become personally attach'd to, for his combination of purest, heartiest tenderness, and native western form of manliness."

The inaugural reception was just such a mad crush as all such occasions had become. Ben: Perley Poore found a rare seat and entertained himself watching the crowd. It was curious "to hear the gay laugh, the busy hum of conversation, and the jingle of plates, spoons, and glasses; to see hands uplifted, bearing aloft huge dishes of salads and creams, loaves of cakes and stores of candies, not infrequently losing plentiful portions on the way. Many an elegant dress," he added, "received its donations of cream, many a tiny slipper bore away crushed sweets and meats. . . ."

Frederick Douglass was there. "For the first time in my life, and I suppose the first time in any colored man's life, I attended the reception of President Lincoln on the evening of the inauguration," he reported. As Douglass approached the door, he was seized by two policemen, who barred his way. Douglass, a large, powerful man, brushed the two officers aside and entered the White House. Inside, two more police intercepted him. "Oh," said Douglass, "this will not do, gentlemen," and to another guest passing by, he called out, "Just say to Mr. Lincoln that Fred. Douglass is at the door." In a few moments Douglass was ushered into the East Room of the White House. "A perfect sea of beauty and elegance, too, it was," he wrote. "The ladies were in very fine attire and Mrs. Lincoln was standing there. I could not have been more than ten feet from him when Mr. Lincoln saw me; his countenance lighted up, and he said in a voice which was heard all around: 'Here comes my friend Douglass.'" As Douglass approached him, the President reached out his hand "and gave me a cordial shake" and said, "Douglass, I saw you in the crowd to-day listening to my inaugural address. There is no man's opinion that I value more than yours: what do you think of it?"

Douglass replied, "Mr. Lincoln, I cannot stop here to talk with you, as there are thousands waiting to shake you by the hand." Lincoln repeated the question, and Douglass replied, "Mr. Lincoln, it was a sacred effort."

"I'm glad you liked it," Lincoln said.

Meade, meanwhile, continued to integrate newly drafted soldiers in the Army of the Potomac. Sheridan carried out a protracted raid, cutting Confederate lines of communication. At Five Forks on April 1 he undertook to break the supply lines to Petersburg. Lee sent Pickett with 19,000 men to block Sheridan's advance, but in a sequence of skillful maneuvers, Sheridan realigned the forces under his command, threatened Pickett's rear, and captured half his force (5,200 out of some 10,000 engaged). It was in this battle that Frederick Winthrop, George Templeton Strong's young friend, now a brigadier general, was killed. Winthrop's cousin, Theodore, had been one of the first Union officers killed; he was one of the last. Also among the last to be killed was Joseph Griner, who had enlisted four years earlier and survived so many bloody battles. There were no personal possessions to send his mother. The rebels stripped his body even to the clothes. A companion wrote his mother that "Joseph was much beloved among his comrades, making friends and companions of all whom he met." Griner's letters to his mother are among the more modest of the vast inventory of letters, diaries, and memoirs that survived the war, but the picture of Griner that emerges—unfailingly cheerful, undauntedly patriotic, and stoically enduring—is thoroughly appealing.

Petersburg, still under siege, was crowded with refugees and soldiers; people slept on bare floors, and every yard was crowded with tents and improvised shelters. The shelling of the city went on intermittently with surprisingly few casualties. But there was a growing air of demoralization. "There have been more desertions of late than ever before," William Blackford wrote his wife, adding, "I hear that even some Virginians have deserted to the enemy. The hard lives they lead and a certain degree of hopelessness which is stealing over the conviction of the best and bravest will have some effect in inducing demoralization hitherto unknown." And a few weeks later he wrote: "Our living now is very poor; nothing but corn-bread and poor beef,—blue and tough,—no vegetables, no coffee, sugar, tea or even molasses. I merely eat to live. . . . You would laugh or cry to see me eating my supper,—a pone of corn-bread and a tin cup of water. We have meat only once a day. It is hard to maintain one's patriotism on ashcake and water."

On March 31, 1865, a constitutional amendment, the Thirteenth, passed the House, prohibiting slavery anywhere in the United States. "Who thought four years ago," George Templeton Strong wrote, in taking note of the momentous vote, "that John Brown would march so fast. And here has the Supreme Court of the United States just been admitting a colored person [John Rock] one of its attorneys and counsellors, on the motion of Charles Sumner!!! I can scarce believe the evening papers. The dust that was Roger B. Taney must have shivered in its tomb. . . ." A great meeting of Negroes and whites was held in the Boston Music Hall to celebrate the passage in Congress of the Thirteenth Amendment. There were songs and speeches, and the Reverend Rue, pastor of the African Methodist Church, led the audience in singing the spiritual that had been sung on the night of the Emancipation Proclamation, two years earlier. William Lloyd Garrison described the moment in a letter to his wife: "It was a scene to be remembered—the earnestness of the singer, pouring out his heartfelt praise, the sympathy of the audience, catching the glow & the deep-toned organ blending the thousand voices in harmony. Nothing during the evening brought to my mind so clearly the magnitude of the act we celebrated, its deeply religious as well as moral significance than 'Sound the . . . timbrel o'er Egypt's dark sea, Jehovah has triumphed, His people are free.'" In the celebrations over the passage of the Thirteenth Amendment, Lincoln was congratulated and replied: "In the midst of your joyous expressions, He 'from whom all blessings flow' must first be remembered."

On April 2 the Confederate lines west of Petersburg were breached by Union raiders. General A. P. Hill, who rose from a sickbed to try to get some grasp of the situation, encountered two Federal soldiers and was shot and killed. It seemed the last straw. Lee advised that Richmond be abandoned, and Davis and his Cabinet fled from the city by the last train south, ordering that the public buildings be burned. Davis paused in his flight to issue another plea for continued resistance: "We have now entered a new phase of the struggle. Relieved from the necessity of guarding particular points, our army will be free to move from point to point to strike the enemy in detail from his base. Let us but will it, and we are free. . . . Let us not despond, my countrymen, but, relying on God, meet the foe with fresh defiance, with unconquered and unconquerable hearts."

With the government departed, the Richmond City Council resolved to destroy the supplies of liquor in the city. Hundreds of cases of wine and brandy and barrels of liquor were smashed in the streets until the whole city reeked of the fumes. Before the work could be completed, straggling soldiers got hold of whiskey, "and the streets began to ring with the yells of infuriated men and the shrieks of terrified women." Soon the floating rams on the river began to blow up, and then the tobacco warehouses, ordered burned by General Ewell, lit up the city with their flames, adding the pungent smell of tobacco to that of alcohol. The Confederate commissary was broken into, and blacks and poor whites alike carried off flour, coffee, cornmeal, and other staples. Shops were pillaged in a night-long frenzy of joyous looting. "Ah ain't nevuh knowed nigguhs—even all of dem nigguhs," an ex-slave present that night recalled, "could mek such ah ruckus. One huge sea uh black faces filt de streets fum wall ruh wall, and dey wan't nothin' but nigguhs in sight."

The prisoners in Lumpkin's jail chanted:

> Slavery chains done broke at last!
> Broke at last! Broke at last!
> Slavery chains done broke at last!
> Gonna praise God till I die!

Major Charles Francis Adams and his black cavalry were in the van of those entering the city on April 3. "Nine o'clock," he wrote his father, "found me in the suburbs of Richmond. . . . I am confounded at the good fortune which brought me there." This was the supreme moment so long hoped for, so long deferred, the last hours of the Confederacy. "To have led my regiment into Richmond at the moment of its capture is the one event," he wrote, "which I should most have desired as the culmination of my life in the Army. That honor has been mine and now I feel as if my record in this war was rounded and completely filled out."

As Adams and his troopers entered the city, slaves and poor whites were "pillaging freely," but Adams's men helped put a stop to the looting. The spirit of the white Virginians seemed at last broken. The next day many stood in line to take the oath of allegiance to the Union. "The war is really over," Adams wrote. "These indications are new to me." Everywhere desolation was evident in ruined houses, bare chimneys where mansions had once been, abandoned earthworks, rifle pits, and abatis scattered across the fields and through the woods, and in front of Petersburg "the whole soil . . . burrowed and furrowed beyond the power of words to describe . . . nature must bring forth new trees and a new race of men must erect other habitations," Adams wrote, before the grim calligraphy of war would be erased.

When Charles Francis Adams, Sr., heard of his son's presence at the occupation of Richmond, he wrote that "it was a singular circumstance that you, in the fourth generation of our family, under the Union and the constitution, should have been the first to put your foot in the capital of the Ancient Dominion, and that, too, at the head of a corps which prefigured the downfall of the policy which had ruled in that capital during the whole period now approaching a century. How full of significance is this history, which all of us are now helping to make! It is literally the third and fourth generation which is paying the bitter penalty for what must now be admitted were the shortcomings of the original founders of the Union." Adams recalled once more Jefferson's words: "Indeed, I tremble for my country when I reflect that God is just" and added: "We have had it all to do at a period when the dangerous evil had reached the plentitude of its power and threatened to expand its sway over all."

On the bulletin board of the *New York Commercial Advertiser* was written: "Petersburg is taken." A clerk was writing laboriously another bulletin on a sheet of brown paper as a crowd gathered around. "Richmond is—" he wrote, while voices cried out, "What's that about Richmond?" He worked doggedly away, "with a capital *C*, and a capital *A*, and so on," until the word "CAPTURED!!!" was completed to loud cheers. As the news spread, the crowds grew until the streets were jammed. "Never before," Strong wrote, "did I hear cheering that came straight from the heart, that was given because people felt relieved by cheering and hallooing. All the cheers I ever listened to were tame in comparison, because seemingly only inspired by a desire to shew enthusiasm. They were spontaneous and involuntary and of vast magnetizing power." The crowds sang "Old Hundred and Doxology," "John Brown's Body," and "The Star-Spangled Banner." "I think I shall never lose the impression made by the rude, many-voiced chorale," Strong added. "It seemed a revelation of profound national feeling, underlying all our vulgarisms and corruptions. . . . Men embraced and hugged each other, *kissed* each other, retreated into doorways to dry their eyes and came out again to flourish their hats and hurrah."

The editor of the *Independent* wrote: "Who can ever forget the day? Pentecost fell upon Wall Street, till the bewildered inhabitants suddenly spake in unknown tongues—singing the doxology to the tune of 'Old Hundred!' Shall we ever see again such a mad, happy, delightful enthusiasm of a great nation, drunken with the wine of glad news. The city of Richmond . . . Babylon the Great, Mother of Harlots and Abominations of the Earth. . . . Rejoice over her, thou Heavens, and ye holy apostles and prophets: for God hath avenged you on her. And a mighty angel took up a great millstone, and cast it into the sea, saying, Thus with violence shall that great city be thrown down, and shall be found no more at all."

Washington was in an uproar all day, Gideon Welles noted. "Most of the clerks and others left the Departments, and there were immense gatherings in the streets. Joy and gladness lightened every countenance. . . . Flags were flying from every house and store that had them. Many of the stores were closed. . . ."

Several days after the evacuation of Richmond, Welles wrote in his diary: "*Memo.* This Rebellion which has convulsed the nation for four years, threatened the Union, and caused such sacrifice of blood and treasure may be traced in a great degree to the diseased imagination of certain South Carolina gentlemen, who some thirty and forty years since studied Scott's novels, and fancied themselves cavaliers, imbued with chivalry, a superior class, not born to labor but to command, brave beyond mankind generally, more intellectual, more generous, more hospitable, more liberal than others. Such of their countrymen as did not own slaves, and who labored with their own hands, who depended on their own exertions for a livelihood, who were mechanics, traders, tillers of the soil, were in their estimate, inferiors who would not fight, were religious and would not gamble, moral and would not countenance duelling, were serious and minded their own business, economical and thrifty, which was denounced as mean and miserly. Hence the chivalrous Carolinian affected to, and actually did finally, hold the Yankee in contempt. The women caught the infection. They were to be patriotic Revolutionary matrons and maidens. They admired the bold, dashing, swaggering, licentious, boasting, chivalrous slave-master who told them he wanted to fight the Yankee but could not kick and insult him into a quarrel. And they distained and despised the pious, peddling, plodding, persevering Yankee who would not drink, and swear and fight duels." And who, Welles might have added, was as self-righteous as the Southerner was arrogant.

Southerners, "impregnated with the romance and poetry of Scott," believed themselves "knights of blood and spirit." Only a war, Welles was convinced, could have wiped out "this arrogance and folly. . . . Face to face in battle and in field with these slandered Yankees, they learned their own weakness and misconception of the Yankee character . . . the Yankee was proved to be as brave, as generous, as humane, as chivalric as the vaunting and superficial Carolinian, to say the least." Thus, the South learned the costly and bitter lesson that their "ideal" type belonged "no more to the Sunny South than to other sections less arrogant and presuming but more industrious and frugal." Whether or not in fact Sir Walter Scott had much to do with the actual formation of the Southern consciousness (a modern historian has written a book to prove he did), his works were certainly congenial to that consciousness and Welles's "*Memo*" gives us a revealing insight into the "Yankee consciousness," with its exaltation of the "Protestant Ethic" of hard work and frugality. Two other aspects of the "*Memo*" might be mentioned—the explicit resentment of the support by Southern women of the chivalric ideal (readers will be aware that many Southern women were thoroughly disenchanted with slavery) and Welles's desire to claim some of that chivalric ideal for "other sections less arrogant and presuming but more industrious and frugal." Chivalry was, according to Welles, a reality found in the "frugal" North and raw West as well as in the aristocratic South.

Welles was ready to admit that the North had underestimated "the energy and enduring qualities of the Southern people. . . . It was believed that they were effeminate idlers, living on the toil and labor of others, who themselves could endure no hardship such as [was] indispensable to soldiers in the field." He added: "It was also believed that a civil war would inevitably lead to servile insurrection, and that the slave-owners would have their hands full to keep the slaves in subjection after hostilities commenced."

Rather quixotically Lincoln suddenly decided to visit the captured capital of the Confederacy. Over the protests of his staff he visited Richmond April 4. A correspondent of the *Atlantic Monthly* reported on Lincoln's entry into the city. The freed slaves "gathered around the President, ran ahead, hovered upon the flanks of the little company, and hung like a dark cloud upon the rear. Men, women, and children, joined the constantly increasing throng. They came from all the by-streets, running in breathless haste, shouting and halooing and dancing with delight. The men threw up their hats, the women waved their bonnets and handkerchiefs, clapped their hands and sang, 'Glory to God! Glory! Glory! Glory!' rendering all the praise to God, who had heard their wailings in the past, their moanings for wives, husbands, children, and friends, sold out of sight; had given them freedom, and after long years of waiting, had permitted them thus unexpectedly to behold the face of their great benefactor." T. Chester Morris, a black correspondent for the *Philadelphia Press*, wrote: "There is no describing the scene along the route. The colored population was wild with enthusiasm. Old men thanked God in a very boisterous manner, and old women shouted upon the pavement as high as they had ever done at a religious revival. . . . One enthusiastic old negro woman exclaimed: 'I know that I am free, for I have seen Father Abraham and felt him.'"

One incident impressed itself upon the minds of all those who witnessed it. In the long walk the President stopped to rest, and an old black man came up to him, removed his hat, bowed, and with tears running down his cheeks, said, "May de good Lord bless you, President Linkum!" Lincoln removed his own hat and bowed silently in turn. It was a moment of perfect expressiveness, spontaneous and beyond contriving, perhaps, when all is said and done, as revealing of Lincoln's own spirit as any act of his which history has preserved.

After evacuating Richmond, Lee planned to head south and try to join up with Joseph Johnston. Together they might defeat Sherman and then turn back to meet Grant. This strategy required that Lee and his armies reach the Richmond & Danville Railroad so that they might make the juncture with Johnston, but Sheridan's cavalry cut the line, and Lee moved westward, with Ewell covering his rear. On April 6 Ewell was cut off and captured at Sayler's Creek, along with Lee's son Custis.

Union cavalry blocked the path of Lee's retreat at Appomattox Station two days later. The Confederate army, its supplies of food exhausted and many of the soldiers barefoot and half-naked, was literally disintegrating. Lee made one final desperate stand the next day. At last the Army of Northern Virginia and its remarkable leader had "gone to earth," in the fox hunter's term. Lee's general order to his troops announcing the surrender of his army declared: "After four years of arduous service, marked by unsurpassed courage and fortitude, the Army of Northern Virginia has been compelled to yield to overwhelming numbers and resources.

"I need not tell the brave survivors of so many hard fought battles, who had remained steadfast to the last, that I have consented to the result from no distrust of them. . . . By the terms of the agreement officers and men can return to their homes and remain until exchanged. You will take with you the satisfaction that proceeds from the consciousness of duty faithfully performed, and I earnestly pray that a Merciful God will extend to you His blessing and protection. With an increasing admiration of your constancy and devotion to your country, and a grateful remembrance of your kind and generous considerations for myself, I bid you all an affectionate farewell."

The tidings of Lee's surrender were "spread over the country . . . and the nation seems delirious with joy," Welles noted the next day.

"Guns are firing, bells ringing, flags flying, men laughing, children cheering; all, all jubilant. This surrender of the great Rebel captain and the most formidable and reliable army of the Secessionists virtually terminates the Rebellion." Crowds eddied around the White House, calling for the President. Lincoln, who had written out some "remarks," came out on the balcony, holding a candle in his hand, and read them in his high-pitched voice, which carried as far as Lafayette Square. As he finished each page, he would let it fall on the floor. His son Tad would retrieve each one, occasionally calling impatiently, "Give me another paper!" When he had finished his brief speech, Lincoln turned to the nearby navy band which had been serenading him and said, "Now I am about to call upon the band for a tune that our adversaries over the way have endeavored to appropriate. But we fairly captured it yesterday, and the Attorney-General gave me his legal opinion that it is now our property. So I ask the band to play 'Dixie!'"

In the entry in his journal for Monday, April 10, George Templeton Strong wrote in capital letters: "LEE AND ARMY HAVE SURRENDERED! Gloria in Excelsis Deo." Strong had been awakened with the news that "the rebel army of the Peninsula, Antietam, Fredericksburg, Chancellorsville, The Wilderness, Spotsylvania Court House, and other battles, has ceased to exist. It can bother and perplex none but historians henceforth forever. It can never open fire again on loyal men or lend its powerful aid to any cause, good or bad. There is no such army any more. God be praised!"

In the aftermath of the news of Lee's surrender Strong revised his estimate of the President once more. It was true that "many loyal men" held Lincoln, "a sensible, commonplace man, without special talent, except for story telling, and it must be admitted," Strong added, "that he tells stories of a class that is 'not convenient' and does not become a gentleman. . . . But his weaknesses are on the surface, and his name will be of high account fifty years hence, and for many generations thereafter."

Even Herman Melville's dark vision lightened, and he expressed an ecstasy common to his countrymen:

> The Generations pouring
> From times of endless date,
> In their going, in their flowing
> Ever form the steadfast State;

And Humanity of growing
    Toward the fullness of her fate.

Thou Lord of hosts victorious,
    Fulfill the end designed;
By a wondrous way and glorious
    A passage Thou dost find—
    A passage Thou dost find:
Hosanna to the Lord of hosts,
    The hosts of human kind.

James Russell Lowell expressed a sentiment common to the young men who had fought in the war when he wrote to Charles Eliot Norton on the word of Lee's surrender: "The news, my dear Charles, is from Heaven. I feel a strange and tender exaltation. I wanted to laugh and I wanted to cry, and ended by holding my peace and feeling devoutly thankful. There is something magnificent in having a country to love. It is almost like what one feels for a woman. Not so tender, perhaps, but to the full as self-forgetful. I worry a little about reconstruction, but I am inclined to think that matters will very much settle themselves."

News of Lee's surrender reached Sherman's army while they were still bivouacked near Goldsboro, North Carolina. Ted Upson had just been posting his guards when General Charles Woods, the division commander, came out of his tent and said to him, "Dismiss the guard, Sergeant, and come into my tent." The startled Upson so far forgot good military orders as to ask why. "Don't you know that Lee has surrendered?" Woods asked him. "No man shall stand guard at my Quarters tonight. Bring all the guard here." When the guard had assembled, Woods told Upson to have them stack their arms and send two of them to his tent. Inside the tent the general had "a great big bowl setting on a camp table. Evry body," Upson noted, "was helping themselfs out of it." Woods handed the sergeant a tin cup and told him to drink up. Upson took a cautious dip, and then, provided with a pail full of punch, he took it out to the rest of the guard. Woods followed and made a brief speech, telling the men that the war had come to an end "and that we should celebrate as we had never done before. . . . After a while a Band came. They played once or twice, drank some, played some more, then drank some more of that never ending supply of punch, then they played again but did not keep very good time. Some of them could not wait till they got through with a tune till they had to pledge Grant and his gallant army, also Lee and his grand fighters. . . . The Band finaly got so they were trying to play two or three tunes at once." In the midst of the festivities, Colonel Johnson, Upson's commanding officer, took him by the arm and conducted him "back to General Woods' tent," where he praised him as one of the finest soldiers in the regiment. Very well, Woods would make him an instant lieutenant. No, Johnson replied, he deserved a higher rank. Captain then? Captain it should be. Upson had the feeling it might soon have been major or colonel if General Woods had not gone out to find out what had happened to the band. The musicians, it turned out, were "very tired," lying about in various stages of inebriation. Whereupon the general took up the drum, assigned his staff officers the other instruments, and started out on a tour through the camp, "evry fellow blowing his horn to suit himself and the jolly old General pounding the brass drum for all it was worth. The men fell in behind and some sang," or tried to sing, "When Johnny Comes Marching Home" and "John Brown's Body" and "Hail, Columbia" and "The Star-Spangled Banner," but somehow they all got mixed together so that the result while not a "grand success from the artistic point . . . let out a lot of pent-up exhuberant feeling that had to have an outlet."

Ted Upson's promotion to captain disappeared with the daylight, but General Woods dispatched him to Washington with papers for the provost marshal of the city. There Upson found himself something of a celebrity, a forerunner of Sherman's almost legendary army. The provost marshal quizzed him about the famous march and then, delighted with Upson's lively account, called in other officers and had him repeat his stories. The engaging young soldier charmed the officer, who gave him a Secret Service pass, a uniform, and a badge and turned him loose to explore the city. First, though, he was ordered to go to a photographer's studio and there dress himself up like a bummer from Sherman's army. Adopting "the Devil may care" look that "our boys have," Upson reported, he had his picture snapped. A captain took him to supper in one of the city's best hotels, and Upson heard one black waiter say to another, "Dere he is! Dats one of Massa Sherman's men."

In his Secret Service uniform Upson was not allowed to pay for anything—food, cigars, fruit, or newspapers. He went to the theater, "the first real theatre I ever was in," he wrote his parents. The play was *As You Like It*, he added, and he felt like saying, "I like it first rate." With an escort of officers, Upson visited the Patent Office and Mount Vernon, where he "got some photos and other relics." At Mount

Vernon he encountered his company, and a few days later he joined them for the parade throughout the city.

For days after the surrender the wildest rumors circulated through the South. Emma Holmes reported that the South could return to the Union "on the footing we had previously been, all our rights, privileges, property & negroes as far as possible, on condition we would fight the French [in Mexico]." After this entry in her diary, she wrote: "To go back into the Union!!! No words can describe all the horrors contained in those few words. Our souls recoiled shuddering at the bare idea. What can ever bridge over that fearful abyss of blood, suffering, affliction, desolation, and unsummed anguish stretching through those past four years . . . ? Peace on such terms, is war for the rising generation. We could not, we would not believe it. Our Southern blood rose in stronger rebellion than ever and we all determined that, if obliged to submit, never could they *subdue* us." At the end of May she wrote: "Anarchy and chaos seemed to rule everywhere as our ship of State foundered, & I felt as if I could not bear to record the disgrace of my country and my state."

Hearing the news of Lee's surrender in Camden, South Carolina, where they had fled in the face of Sherman's advancing army, Mary Darby shrieked to Mary Chesnut, "Now we belong to negroes and Yankees!" Her brother said, "I do not believe it." Only a year before, the South had seemed invulnerable. Mary Chesnut had stood beside the grave of Jefferson Davis's son Joe, deeply moved by the sadness and beauty of the moment. "Now," she wrote, "we have burned towns, deserted plantations, sacked villages." When she spoke of her feelings to her husband, now "General" Chesnut, he chided her: "You seem resolute to look the worst in the face."

"Yes, poverty, with no future and no hope. . . . You see we are exiles and paupers."

"Pile on the agony," her husband replied.

"How does our famous captain, the great Lee, bear the Yankee's galling chain?" Mary Chesnut asked.

"He knows how to possess his soul in patience. If there were no such word as subjugation, no debts, no poverty, no negro mobs backed by Yankees; if all things were well, you would shiver and feel benumbed," James Chesnut declared, pointing at his wife "in an oratorical attitude." He added: "Your sentence is pronounced—'Camden for life.'"

"All things are taken from us, and become portions and parcels of the dreadful past," Sarah Morgan wrote in her diary, hearing the news of Lee's surrender. When those about her spoke of peace, her heart cried, "Never! Let a great earthquake swallow us up first! Let us leave our land and emigrate to any desert spot of the earth, rather than return to the Union. . . ."

33

The Death of Lincoln

When Lincoln and his Cabinet met on the morning of April 14, everyone was anxious to hear news of Sherman. Grant, who was present, expected to receive some word at any moment. Lincoln was sure it would be favorable. That night, he told the Cabinet (and Gideon Welles reported), he had "the usual dream which he had preceding nearly every great and important event of the war. Generally the news had been favorable which preceded this dream, and the dream itself was always the same . . . [he said that] he seemed to be in some singular, indescribable vessel, and that he was moving with great rapidity towards an indefinite shore; that he had this dream preceding Sumter, Bull Run, Antietam, Gettysburg, Stones River, Vicksburg, Wilmington, etc."

At this point Grant broke in, rather oddly, to say, "Stones River was certainly no victory, and he knew of no great results which followed from it." Stones River, better known as Murfreesboro in Tennessee, was generally taken to include Halleck's advance on Corinth as well as Bragg's invasion of Kentucky. Lincoln took Grant's cavil in good spirit. However that might be, he replied, his dream preceded that fight. "I had," the President continued, in a curiously abstracted way, "this strange dream again last night, and we shall, judging from the past, have great news very soon. I think it must be from Sherman." It was the Friday preceding Easter Week.

That night Welles had just dozed off when his wife woke him with word that someone was at the door with a message for him. Sitting up in bed, Welles heard a voice from the street outside calling to his son, John, whose bedroom was on the floor below. Welles opened the window, and the messenger, James Smith, called up to him that Lincoln had been shot and that Seward and his son Frederick, the assistant secretary of state, had also been assassinated. Welles could not believe the story. "Where was the President when shot?" he asked. At Ford's Theater. Alarmed by Smith's urgency, Welles dressed and accompanied him to Seward's house on Fifteenth Street. A crowd had gathered outside, and Welles had to push his way through. The frightened servants confirmed Smith's story and conducted Welles to Seward's bedroom. "The Secretary," Welles wrote later in his diary, "was lying on his back, the upper part of his head covered with a cloth. . . . His mouth was open, the lower jaw dropping down." Stanton came in soon after Welles.

The two Cabinet members decided it was their responsibility to go to the bedside of the desperately wounded President. Lincoln had been carried across the street from the theater to the house of a Mr. Peterson. The two men rode in Stanton's carriage through streets already filled with crowds of quiet, anxious people who had heard the news, most of them hurrying in the direction of the theater. At the Peterson house they climbed a flight of stairs to the room where Lincoln lay surrounded by doctors. One of them, whom Welles knew, told him that the President was in practical fact dead, although he might linger for a few hours. "The giant sufferer," Welles observed, "lay extended diagonally across the bed, which was not large enough for him. He had been stripped of his clothes. His large arms, which were occasionally exposed, were of a size which one would scarce have expected from his spare appearance. . . . His features were calm and striking. I had never seen them appear to better advantage than for the first hours, perhaps, that I was there. After that his right eye began to swell and that part of his face became discolored." Soon Sumner appeared, and then Schuyler Colfax, the Speaker of the House, and other members of the Cabinet filed into the small room until it was crowded to the point of discomfort. Mrs. Lincoln came and went, weeping and distraught, and Robert Lincoln lingered in the hallway.

The night was gloomy and dank. Some of those present drifted away. Others kept the death watch. At six o'clock of a dreary, overcast morning, Welles, feeling faint, took a short walk. Small clusters of people stood about in the somber streets. It began to rain. Here and there a person, recognizing Welles, stopped him to ask the condition of the President. "Intense grief was on every countenance," Welles noted, "when I replied that the President could survive but a short time. The colored people, especially—and there were at this time more of them, perhaps, than of whites—were overwhelmed with grief." Back at the Peterson house, Welles took a seat in the parlor with the other Cabinet members, some of whom were asleep in their chairs. Around seven he returned to the room where Lincoln lay. The death struggle had begun. Robert stood by his father's bed, half supported by Sumner. At twenty-two minutes past seven on the morning of Saturday, April 15, the labored breathing stopped. Stanton pronounced the dead President's most enduring epitaph: "Now he belongs to the ages."

The Cabinet members then assembled in the parlor once more and drafted a letter to the Vice-President informing him that the duties of president had devolved on him. James Speed, the attorney general, took the communication to Johnson. Salmon Chase was summoned and administered the oath of office in front of a handful of Johnson's friends.

After breakfast Welles went to the White House in the "cheerless rain." On Pennsylvania Avenue in front of the Executive Mansion were "several hundred colored people, mostly women and children, weeping and wailing their loss." Through the cold, wet day, they kept the vigil; "they seemed not to know," Welles wrote, "what was to be their fate since their great benefactor was dead, and their hopeless grief affected me more than almost anything else, though strong and brave men wept when I met them."

At twelve o'clock, by Welles's arrangement, the Cabinet met with the new President. Someone raised the question of whether Johnson should give an inaugural address, and he replied that "his acts would best disclose his policy. In all essentials it would . . . be the same as that of the late President."

Sidney George Fisher, hearing of Lincoln's assassination, wrote: "I felt for some time a mere dull & stupified sense of calamity. What disasters, what wide-spread misfortune may not these events produce. A vague feeling of coming ill & real sorrow for Mr. Lincoln, deprived me of the power to think & reason on the subject. I felt as tho I had lost a personal friend, for indeed I have & so has every honest man in the country. . . . Mr. Lincoln's character was so kind, so generous, so noble, that he inspired personal attachment in those who can appreciate such qualities. . . . He was indeed the great man of the period. On his integrity, constancy, capacity, the hopes of the country rested. He possessed the entire confidence of the people. His perfect uprightness & purity of purpose were beyond all doubt. His ability to comprehend all the questions before the country & to deal with them in an efficient, practical manner, his firmness & purpose & strength of will, were equally well known, whilst his frank, easy, animated manners and conversation, his entire freedom from vanity, or pride, or self seeking or apparent consciousness of his position, except as to its duties, won all hearts. His death is a terrible loss to the country, perhaps an even greater loss to the South than to the North, for Mr. Lincoln's humanity & kindness of heart stood between them and the party of the North who urge measures of vengeance & severity."

An Illinois soldier, who had known Lincoln in Springfield, said to Walt Whitman, "The war is over, and many are lost. And now we have lost the best, the fairest, the truest man in America. Take him altogether, he was the best man this country ever produced. It was quite a while I thought very different; but some time before the murder, that's the way I have seen it."

"I have been expecting this," George Templeton Strong wrote in his diary; ". . . I am stunned, as by a fearful personal calamity, though I can see that this thing, occurring just at this time, may be overruled to our great good. . . . We shall appreciate him at last." And so the country felt—as if a beloved relative or a dear friend had been suddenly struck down. "Above all," Strong wrote, "there is a profound, awe-stricken feeling that we are, as it were, in immediate presence of a fearful, gigantic crime, such as has not been committed in our day and can hardly be matched in history."

Whatever feelings of compassion Strong may have felt at the news of Lee's surrender were quickly dissipated by the assassination of Lincoln, which was widely believed to be the consequence of a conspiracy supported and encouraged by the leaders of the Confederacy. "Let us henceforth deal with rebels as they deserve," he wrote. "The rose-water treatment does not meet their case. I have heard it said fifty times today: 'These madmen have murdered the two best friends they had in the world!'" (It was incorrectly thought that Seward could not survive his wounds.) A feeling began to emerge that "Lincoln had done his appointed work; his honesty, sagacity, kindliness, and singleness of purpose had united the North and secured the suppression of the rebellion," Strong wrote, adding, "Perhaps the time has come for something besides kindliness, mercy, and forbearance, even for vengeance and judgment. Perhaps the murdered President's magnanimity would have been circumvented and his generosity and goodness abused by rebel subtlety. . . ." After the first great wave of anguish passed, Strong wrote: "What a place this man, whom his friends have been patronizing for four years as a well-meaning, sagacious kind-hearted ignorant old codger, had won for himself in the hearts of the people! What a place he will fill in history! I foresaw most clearly that he would be ranked high as the Great Emancipator twenty years hence, but I did not suppose his death would instantly reveal—even to Copperhead newspaper editors—the nobleness and glory of his part in this great contest. . . . *Death* has suddenly opened the eyes of the people (and I think the world) to the fact that a hero has been holding high place among them for four years, closely watched and studied, but despised and rejected by a third of this community, and only tolerated by the other two-thirds."

When Strong heard that Lincoln had dreamed the night before his assassination of "a fine ship entering harbor under full sail," he wrote in his diary: "A poet could make something out of that." A poet did. Whitman wrote:

> O Captain! my Captain! our fearful trip is done,
> The ship has weather'd every rack, the prize
>   we sought is won,
> The port is near, the bells I hear, the people all
>   exulting,
> While follow eyes the steady keel, the vessel
>   grim and daring;
> But O heart! heart! heart!
> O the bleeding drops of red,
> Where on the deck my Captain lies,
>   Fallen cold and dead.

It was all too much to take in, too sudden, too traumatic. Charleston had been occupied by Federal troops at the end of February; Lincoln's inauguration followed a week later. On April 3 Richmond was abandoned. Lincoln visited Richmond on the fourth and fifth. Lee surrendered at Appomattox Courthouse on April 9. Five days later, on the anniversary of the surrender of Sumter, Lincoln was assassinated.

That same day the Union flag was raised once more over the ruins of that fort by none other than Captain (now General) Robert Anderson, who had four years earlier been forced to strike those same colors. William Lloyd Garrison was there as one of the official guests of honor, and Henry Ward Beecher gave the principal address. Having been met at the Charleston docks by a crowd of some three thousand blacks and carried on their shoulders to his hotel, Garrison visited Calhoun's grave and pronounced slavery to be buried deeper than its famous champion. A week later, in Boston, one of his sons reported that "father has [not] quite 'come to himself' yet, his trip was so crowded with delightful wonders. It was like dreamland."

The city and indeed the country were meanwhile given over to mourning for their leader's death. Almost every house displayed some piece of black cloth as a mark of the grief of its occupants. Such signs were especially noticeable on the houses of the poor. To Welles "the little black ribbon or strip of black cloth from the hovel of the poor negro or the impoverished white" was most moving. From Sunday through Tuesday of Easter Week, the dead President's body lay in state in the rotunda of the Capitol while thousands of citizens filed by to look for the last time on that strangely beautiful face. The funeral was on Wednesday, the nineteenth, "imposing, sad and sorrowful." As the procession formed in front of the White House to move down Pennsylvania Avenue to the Capitol, all businesses were closed, and the streets were thronged with silent, often weeping people, black and white, sharing a common sorrow. The procession took two hours and ten minutes to pass a given point and was estimated to be more than three miles long. Welles and Stanton rode together, two not very congenial men, wrapped in their own thoughts. The casket, now sealed, was placed once more in the rotunda. Mr. Ralph Gurley gave a brief prayer, and, Welles wrote in his diary, "we left the remains of the good and great man we loved so well."

The Joint Resolution of Congress upon Lincoln's death dated April 17, 1865, contained a paragraph that read: "Whereas Abraham Lincoln's originality of manner, his humor, wit, sarcasm, and wondrous powers of ridicule, were weapons peculiarly his own, which no one else could imitate. Add to these qualities courage, will, and indomitable persistence of purpose, which never flagged or faltered, and he was a power felt and acknowledged by the nation. Take him all in all, it will be long ere we look upon his like again;

"Whereas he is dead; but the days of his pilgrimage, although in troublesome times, were full of honor, love, and troops of friends. The nation mourns. Peace be with him."

Jack Flowers, a Sea Island black, told a Northern teacher, "I 'spect it's no use to be here. I might as well stayed where I was. It 'pears we can't be free, nohow." A community of blacks at Hilton Head held a meeting and resolved: "That we . . . look upon the death of the Chief Magistrate of our country as a national calamity, and an irrepressible loss beyond the power of words to express, covering the land with gloom and sorrow, mourning and desolation." It was "Almighty God" who had chosen Lincoln for the work of liberation and "crowned the career of this great and good man with a blessed immortality, sealed by his blood, and embalmed in the memory of future generations."

Edgar Dinsmore, a black soldier from New York stationed in South Carolina, wrote: "Humanity has lost a firm advocate, our race its Patron Saint, and the good of all the world a fitting object to emulate. . . . The name Abraham Lincoln will ever be cherished in our hearts, and none will more delight to lisp his name in reverence than the future generations of our people."

Charles Sumner wrote his English reformer friend John Bright: "Family and friends may mourn but his death will do more for the cause than any human life, for it will fix the sentiments of the Country—perhaps of mankind. To my mind few have been happier." George Templeton Strong noted in his diary: "No prince, no leader of a people, was ever so lamented as this unpolished Western lawyer has been and is. His name is Faithful and True. He will stand in history books beside Washington, perhaps higher."

There was a curious appropriateness in James Russell Lowell's Harvard commemoration "Ode," delivered three months after Lincoln's death. It was in praise of Lincoln, most un-Harvard-like of men, a new human type, "Not forced to frame excuses for his birth, / Fed from within with all the strength he needs." The nation had "Wept with the passion of an angry grief" at his death. In him Nature had shaped a "hero new," / "Wise, steadfast in the strength of God, and true / How beautiful to see / Once more a shepherd of mankind indeed." It was presumptuous to praise him.

> He knew to bide his time,
> And can his fame abide,
> Still patient in his simple faith sublime,
> Till the wise years decide.

Our children shall behold his fame.
The kindly-earnest, brave, foreseeing man,
Sagacious, patient, dreading praise, not blame,
New birth of our new soil, the first American.

"The first American" had been a phrase reserved for Washington.
At least Washington had been praised as "first in war, first in peace,
and first in the hearts of his countrymen." So different in so many
ways, the two men were perhaps most alike in their patient enduring-
ness; their courage and perseverance in the face of what often seemed
insurmountable adversities. It is difficult to doubt that America would
not have, in time, won its independence from Great Britain if there
had been no Washington or if he had been mortally wounded in his
first major engagement with the British forces—say, at the Battle of
Kip's Bay, where he so recklessly risked his life, trying to rally his
fleeing soldiers. Certainly it is as safe as any historical generalization to
say that the nation which would have emerged from a Washington-less
revolution would have been very different from the one that did;
indeed, it might well not even have been a single nation. By the same
token it is very hard to believe that the North could have won the Civil
War, restored the Union, and ended slavery without Lincoln's leadership. Washington was as essential to the nation's birth as Lincoln to its
rebirth. Seen in another perspective, Lincoln finished the work that
Washington had begun in the sense that, as we have argued, the nation
could not truly "begin" until the cruel paradox of slavery in "the land
of the free" had been eradicated.

How much Lincoln bore! Foremost, the Army of the Potomac.
That was his cross. One thinks of the Peninsula campaign alone, of
McClellan's arrogance and insolence, his numerous dispatches implying that Lincoln had sabotaged his efforts and that the lives of
thousands of men had been sacrificed in vain by a heartless and
indifferent government. The hours of waiting for news, so often bad,
from one battlefield or another were undoubtedly the most wearing
hours of his presidency. In addition to the incompetence of successive
commanding generals of the Army of the Potomac, Lincoln had to
endure the petty rivalries and bickerings in his own Cabinet, disputes
that set Chase against Stanton and Welles against both, and the
intrigues within his own party as congressional leaders attempted to
undermine his authority and usurp his powers; the remorseless venom
of the Democratic press, the subversive activities of the Copperheads,

and the angry clamors of the abolitionists at his dilatoriness in proclaiming emancipation. Horace Greeley set himself up as the publicly proclaimed conscience of the President, and even such staunch supporters as Carl Schurz burdened him with their doubts and criticisms. It is probably not too much to say that at one time or another during the course of the war virtually every American living north of the Mason-Dixon Line questioned either Lincoln's motives or his ability to discharge the vast and complex duties of his office, sometimes both.

In addition to the tribulations that fell upon him in consequence of his formal political responsibilities, Lincoln suffered in his personal life, first and most acutely in the death in 1862 of his adored son Willie and then in the erratic behavior of his wife. Mary Todd, always a difficult and demanding woman, became increasingly eccentric after the death of her son. Her eccentricity took the form, among others, of running up wildly extravagant bills for her personal wardrobe and for furnishings for the White House, bills that exceeded Lincoln's ability to pay. His wife's state of mind was more distressing to the President than the embarrassment of the bills themselves, which were given wide publicity by his political enemies.

Finally, it has been often noted how much Lincoln suffered over the terrible casualty lists that followed every major battle. They perhaps took the most terrible psychic toll of all. Not surprisingly his health was often bad, and he was frequently troubled by nightmares. Indeed, his dreams were a special source of interest to him, and as we have seen, he often reflected on their meaning. Undoubtedly his humor, so often criticized as coarse or inappropriate, preserved his life and sanity. It was an essential antidote to the strain of morbidity in his nature.

There is no end to the telling of Lincoln's greatness (the Library of Congress catalogue lists five thousand books about him); it is woven into the fabric of our history. It is palpable: in the ground beneath our feet; in the air we breathe. He was the Whitmanesque hero, feeling the greatness of the land, the power of common labor, the surge of humanity across the inconceivable landscape. His words are evocations of our dearest dreams and best aspirations. He was Father Abraham, the Lord's anointed, who stirred the profoundest memories of the race, who elicited with an unerring touch those "mystic chords of memory" that he promised would reunite all Americans when we were at last moved "by the better angels of our nature." Patient and enduring, compassionate, suffering, and at the same time as rough and unfinished as the famous rails he split, he promised a deeper and wiser humanity. He was the paschal lamb, the sacrifice, the bearer of the manifold sins of America, the leader of an "almost chosen people." He was, with all that, an unblinking realist. John Hay spoke of his looking through a fraud "to the buttons on the back of his coat," and his law partner, William Herndon, who knew him perhaps better than anyone else, stressed his "cold" intelligence. "To some men," Herndon declared, "the world of matter and of man comes ornamented with beauty, life, and action, and hence more or less false and inexact. No lurking illusion—delusion—error, false in itself, and clad for the moment in robes of splendor, woven by the imagination, ever passed unchallenged or undetected over the threshold of his mind. . . . He saw all things through a perfect mental lens. There was no diffraction or refraction there. . . . He was not impulsive, fanciful, or imaginative, but cold, calm and precise." Herndon's analysis is one of the most remarkable that we have of Lincoln. It has the ring of truth about it; it confirms what we already know. Such men as Herndon describes are typically cynics; Lincoln's greatness was that seeing the world as he did, utterly without illusion, he loved it and its odd inhabitants with a remarkable passion.

The fact was that no simple idealist could have made his way through the quagmires of provincial Illinois politics to the presidency of the United States. The extraordinary strategic sense with which Lincoln mapped the campaign that was to carry him to the highest office in the Republic and the implacable will with which he made poor Douglas carry him there tell volumes about the quality of his mind —about, as we used to say, his character.

Whitman celebrated him in one of the most moving and mysterious of American poems—"When Lilacs Last in the Dooryard Bloom'd":

> For the sweetest, wisest soul of all my days and lands—
> and this for his dear sake,
> Lilac and star and bird twined with the chant
> of my soul,
> There in the fragrant pines and the cedars
> dusk and dim.

And what of the strange company of conspirators who, it appeared, had plotted the deaths of Lincoln, Seward, Stanton, Grant, and Johnson? John Wilkes Booth was the youngest son of the famous tragedian Junius Brutus Booth. His older brother, Edwin, was one of the most admired actors of the day, famous for his Shakespearean roles. John Wilkes Booth was twenty-six when he assassinated Lincoln. He was a Marylander by birth and an ardent secessionist. Lincoln appeared to him (as he did, of course, to hundreds of thousands of Southerners) as the most malevolent of tyrants, and in his sentimental and romantic imaginings, Booth came to see himself as a modern-day Brutus, freeing the country from an evil dictator, becoming, in consequence, the hero of a real-life drama. A charismatic and compelling figure, with hot, luminous eyes, Booth was able to assemble and dominate as odd a bag of conspirators as ever plotted. Their headquarters in Washington was the home of Mary Surratt. Mrs. Surratt was a member of a well-known family and owned, in addition to her Washington house, a tavern at Surrattsville. In addition to Mary Surratt, those most directly involved in the plot were her own son, John, David Herold, George Atzerodt, Lewis Powell (Paine), Samuel Arnold, Michael O'Laughlin, and Edward Spangler. Ben: Perley Poore later described them as follows: "Samuel Arnold was of respectable appearance, about thirty years of age, with dark hair and beard and a good countenance. Spangler, the stage-carpenter, was chunky, light-haired, rather bloated and whisky-soaked looking man. Atzerodt had a decidedly lager beer look, with heavy blue eyes, light hair, and sallow complexion. O'Laughlin might have been mistaken for a native of Cuba, short and slender, with luxuriant black locks, a delicate moustache and whiskers, and vivacious black eyes. Payne [Powell] was the incarnation of a Roman gladiator, tall, muscular, defiant, with a low forehead, large blue eyes, thin lips . . . with much of the animal and little of the intellectual. Davie Herrold was what the ladies call a pretty little man with cherry cheeks, pouting lips, an incipient beard, dark hazel eyes, and dark, long hair." Mrs. Surratt was a stout middle-aged woman with, again the phrase is Poore's, "feline gray eyes."

After shooting Lincoln, Booth, his leg broken, hobbled to the stage door, where a horse chosen for speed and endurance awaited him. Herold, who had been acting as a lookout, joined him, and the two men rode ten miles to Surrattsville with Booth in great pain. At Surrattsville they stayed at the tavern owned by Mrs. Surratt, where they picked up two carbines left for them, and then made their way to the home of Dr. Samuel Mudd, who set Booth's leg. For nearly a week Booth and Herold hid in the vicinity while a dragnet of detectives and U.S. cavalry closed in on them. Booth, dismayed to discovered that far from being hailed as a deliverer, he was almost universally execrated, confined his feelings to a diary. "Until to-day," he wrote, "nothing was ever thought of sacrificing to our country's wrongs. For six months we had worked to capture; but our cause being lost, something decisive and great must be done. But its failure was owing to others, who did not strike for their country with a heart. I struck boldly, and not as the papers say. I walked with a firm step through a thousand of his friends, and was stopped, but pushed on. A colonel was at his side. I shouted, 'Sic semper!' before I fired. In jumping, I broke my leg. I passed all his pickets, rode sixty miles that night with the bone of my leg tearing the flesh at every jump. I can never repent it, though we hated to kill. Our country owed all our troubles to him, and God simply made me the instrument of his punishment. . . . I care not what becomes of me. I have no desire to outlive my country." Booth deplored the fact that despite his brave and noble act, he was "hunted like a dog through swamps, woods . . . wet, cold, starving, with every man's hand turned against me. . . . And why? For doing what Brutus was honored for, what made Tell a hero. And yet I, for striking down a greater tyrant than they ever knew, am looked upon as a common cut-throat. My action was purer than either of theirs. . . . God can not pardon me if I have done wrong. Yet I cannot see my wrong, except in serving a degenerate people. . . . So ends all. For my country I have given up all that makes life sweet and holy; brought misery upon my family, and I am sure there is no pardon in Heaven for me, since man condemns me so. I have only heard of what has been done, except what I did myself, and it fills me with horror. God, try and forgive me, and bless my mother." Abandoned by the world, he "felt the curse of Cain upon—" The sentence was unfinished as though he could not bear to add the "me."

On April 25, Booth and Herold were run to ground in a tobacco barn near Port Royal, Virginia. With the barn surrounded, the two men were called on to surrender. Herold came out, but Booth refused, calling that he only wanted "fair play." The barn was set on fire, and as Booth tried to escape, he was shot by Sergeant Boston Corbett. He was carried out of the flaming barn still conscious. He asked for water, and when it was given to him, he murmured, "Tell mother I died for my country." He fainted, revived, and said, "I thought I did for the best." Then he asked that his hands be raised so that he could see them and said, "Useless! useless!"

As Booth was making his assault on Lincoln, Powell had gone to Seward's house, forced his way in, rushed up the stairs, and, when Seward's son Frederick tried to intercept him, fractured his skull with a blow from his pistol, and, drawing a knife, began stabbing at the already injured Seward. Seward's attendant, a convalescent soldier named Robinson, grappled with Powell, while Seward's daughter threw open a window and screamed, "Murder!" Powell broke away from Robinson and fled, heading for Mary Surratt's house. There he was intercepted by the police, who had already arrested Mrs. Surratt and her daughters.

John Surratt, Mary's son, escaped to Canada and then to Italy and finally to Egypt, where he was arrested and returned to the United States for trial.

Atzerodt's assignment was apparently to kill Johnson. He had taken a room at Kirkwood House, where Johnson was staying, and a loaded pistol and several bowie knives were found in his bedroom, but he evidently lost his nerve and fled to Middlesburg, Maryland, where he was captured several days later. The conspirators were tried by a military commission and sentenced on July 6. Atzerodt, Herold, Powell, and Mrs. Surratt were hanged. Dr. Mudd, O'Laughlin, and Arnold were given life sentences, and Spangler was sent to prison for six years. There remains a question of the degree of the complicity of the defendants. Several of the accused insisted that the assassination had been Booth's own scheme and that they had not even known of his intention until a few hours before the act. Powell had clearly tried to kill Seward, and though he had failed, he was deeply implicated in the plot. Mudd had done little more than set Booth's leg, but the court was not in a frame of mind to make such distinctions. With Booth dead, public sentiment demanded some severe measures of revenge.

34

The Dream of
the New Union

Despite Lee's capitulation, there had been no surrender of the Confederacy as such. This final act, it was presumed, would take place with Johnston's surrender of *his* army to Sherman.

When Sherman met Johnston in North Carolina on April 18, 1865, to receive the surrender of the Southern armies, he went far beyond his authority and granted terms of peace that immediately raised a storm in the North, coming, as they did, immediately on the heels of Lincoln's assassination. The treaty provided that the Confederate soldiers proceed to their home states and deposit their arms in the state arsenals; that the President would "recognize the several State governments on their officers and legislatures taking the oaths prescribed by the Constitution of the United States . . ."; that "the people and inhabitants of all the States be guaranteed, as far as the Executive can, their political rights and privileges, as well as their rights of person and property . . ."; and, finally, that "war was to cease, and general amnesty be granted on condition that the armies be disbanded, the arms distributed, and peaceful pursuits resumed." What was perhaps most remarkable about this unauthorized document was its spirit of humanity and conciliation. That it should have come from a victorious general to a defeated foe was the more remarkable. It was ironic that a soldier showed himself far more tolerant of the enemy than politicians were willing to be. The peace terms stirred up a hornet's nest. People seemed quite ready to forget Sherman's great services to the Union in their fury at his apparent intention of snatching their victims from them.

The treaty was at once repudiated, and Sherman was sternly rebuked by Stanton. When Stanton's telegram reached Sherman, the general was meeting with his officers in the large, bare room of the Governor's Palace in Raleigh, North Carolina. Sherman, Schurz wrote, "paced up and down the room like a caged lion, and, without addressing any body in particular, unbosomed himself with an eloquence of furious invective which for a while made us all stare. . . . He berated the people who blamed him for what he had done as a mass of fools, not worth fighting for, who did not know when a thing was well done. He railed at the press, which had altogether too much freedom; which had become an engine of vilification; which should be bridled by severe laws. . . ." Grant helped to put matters right by hurrying to Raleigh to smooth the ruffled feathers of his comrade in so many campaigns.

With Lincoln dead and the war at last over, one final ritual remained to be observed. The Union armies must pass in review to receive the plaudits of a grateful nation. Their triumphal march took two days and was made up, in the Army of the Potomac alone, of 151 regiments of infantry, 36 regiments of cavalry, and 22 batteries of artillery. The marching troops were only a portion of the army, and yet it was the greatest military display the world had ever seen. The Union forces had been involved in 2,265 major and minor engagements. In 333 of those, 100 or more Union soldiers had been killed or wounded.

On May 23 four armies, with "polished shoes and brass trimmings," twenty-six miles long, marched through Washington for six hours, the blue lines swinging along to the music of the numerous bands scattered throughout their length—more than 100 in all—the men walking with the proud step of veteran soldiers. It was an exultant moment. Ben: Perley Poore, watching with thousands of his ecstatic fellow citizens, thought of "the legions of imperial Rome, returning in triumph along the Appian Way . . . the conquering hosts of Napoleon the Great" returning from the Italian campaign, or the British Guards returning from the Crimea. None could have received a more "heartfelt ovation." There were 200,000 veterans in the apparently endless ranks, bearing in their battle colors such storied names as Chancellors-ville, Antietam, Vicksburg, Shiloh, Gettysburg, Missionary Ridge, Cold Harbor. Invisible thousands marched with them—the dead and the maimed, the absent veterans who had served their time and returned home. They all were now part of history, as Poore noted. The bands played, the crowds cheered—the Army of the Potomac, the Army of the James, the Army of Georgia, the Army of the Tennessee, and the cavalry led by Phil Sheridan. "To behold such a spectacle men came from every portion of the North," Poore wrote; "fathers brought their sons to see this historic pageant, while historians, poets, novelists, and painters thronged to see the unparalleled sight. . . . In that great display [marched] heroes whose names will live while history endures."

Over the reviewing stand in front of the White House was a long pavilion decorated with flags and displaying the names of the principal victories. On the stand sat the diplomatic corps, the department heads, President Johnson, General Grant, and the members of the Cabinet. In everyone's mind was the figure of the dead Lincoln.

Among the spectators was Lester Ward, who succeeded, as he wrote, "in seeing my old regiment and all the heroes which remained to it. Everyone was joyful on account of the end of the terrible war which has so long ravaged the land. O our country, the glory of Rome is abased to nothing near her! Renewed by the war, cemented with blood, may she march through the ages of the future in a majesty unequalled among the nations of the earth, to accomplish the great object of her establishment. May crowns tremble, may kingdoms totter. . . ."

Carl Schurz's experiences had developed in him a "profound abhorrence of war as such," but he confessed that when he saw the battle-tested veterans of the Union armies parading down Massachu-setts Avenue, his heart "leaped in the consciousness of having been one of them." They came swinging along, "bronzed veterans—the men nothing but bone and muscle and skin—their tattered battle-flags fluttering victoriously over their heads in the full pride of achievement . . . a spectacle splendid and imposing beyond description." Even more moving to Schurz was the thought that "every man that had wielded the sword or the musket or served the cannon in terrible conflict" would go "quietly home to his plow, or his anvil, or his loom, or his counting-room as a peaceable citizen. That this transition from the conditions of war to those of peace, this transformation of a million soldiers into a million citizen-workers, could be accomplished so suddenly, without the slightest disturbance, even without a comprehension of its difficulty, was in its way a greater triumph of the American democracy than any victory won on the battlefield."

The second day was given over to Sherman's Army of the Mississippi. Sherman's bummers were to march in their tattered makeshift uniforms—"just as we come from the front," Upson wrote, "without any extra fuss or feathers." When the army formed up on the Virginia side of the river, Upson was back in ranks with his company, his soiled uniform on and his bedroll slung over his shoulder. His regiment led the line; only Sherman and his staff preceded them. As they started down Pennsylvania Avenue, "our boys fell into the long swinging step, evry man in perfect time, our guns at the Right Shoulder Shift, and it seemed to me," Upson wrote, "that the men had never marched so well before. The sidewalks were packed with people, and my! how they cheered! It was a constant roar, our tattered flags bearing the names of the Regiments and of the principal battles in which they had fought." A multitude of ex-slaves had attached themselves to Sherman's army. A colorful and motley company that grew to thousands, they carried, pushed, or hauled with them their earthly possessions and anything they were able to acquire along the route—bedclothes, bits and pieces of furniture, chickens, goats, scrawny mules, reluctant hogs, an occasional cow. Now they were reconstituted for the great procession—"the strangest huddle of animation, equine, canine, bovine, and human, that ever civilian beheld," Poore wrote, "mules, asses, horses, colts, cows, sheep, pigs, goats, raccoons, chickens, and dogs led by negroes blacker than Erebus. Every beast of burden was loaded to its capacity with tents, baggage, knapsacks, hampers, panniers, boxes, valises, kettles, pots, pans, dishes, demijohns, bird-cages, cradles, mirrors, fiddles, clothing, pickaninnies, and an occasional black woman."

As Sherman's army passed the reviewing stand, all the dignitaries rose to their feet "and with bared heads cheered and cheered." Upson "glanced down the line . . . evry man had his eyes front, evry step was perfect; and on the faces of the men was what one might call a *glory look*. . . . My but I was proud of our boys."

The only jarring note was Sherman's refusal to speak to Stanton, who had rebuked him so stingingly for the terms of surrender he had offered to Joe Johnston. Stanton had tried to prevent Sherman from riding at the head of his army, but President Johnson overruled him, and the wildest shouts of enthusiasm greeted his erect and graceful figure as he rode along, his horse bedecked with flowers, his hat in his left hand, his sword at salute. After Sherman passed the reviewing stand, he dismounted, climbed the steps to the stand, and shook hands with Grant and Johnson, pointedly ignoring Stanton's outstretched hand with the remark "I do not care to shake hands with clerks," or so it was said.

A few days later the 100th Indiana was on a freight train headed for home. At the Ohio River they transferred to steamboats. One incident stuck in Ted Upson's memory. The boat stopped near a little hamlet, and the captain told the men they had an hour to explore the town. Upson dallied until he heard the steamboat whistle blow and then set off on the run, afraid of being left behind. As he turned the corner of the town's single street, he ran into a motherly woman, badly out of breath. "Oh," she said, "I was so afraid I could not get there in time. Here is something for you," and she thrust a fresh-baked loaf of bread into the hands of the startled soldier.

At Indianapolis the men of the 100th Indiana were mustered out with speeches, ceremonial meals, and an abundance of acclaim. "We returned to our home," Upson wrote. "But all did not return. Of the thousand officers and men who started out with us four hundred and seventy-four were not with us now. Many had met death on Southern battle fields; some in hospitals far from home and friends. . . . They sleep their long last sleep neath the whispering pines. Others, unable to stand the strains, trials, and exposures of Army life had left us before the end of the war and came home—some to die, others to linger along broken in health. But from those who have lived to return comes no words of regret. They are content their duty is done, and well done. What matters the loss of all these years? What matters the trial, the sickness, the wounds! What we went out to do is done. The war is ended, and the Union is saved!"

George Templeton Strong wrote in his diary: "Never did human events make such news before. Southern newspaper articles of three or four years ago made me feel very old. They seemed medieval relics. When I remember having read them on their first appearance, my sensations were those of the Wandering Jew refreshing his recollections of political literature under Commodus." Four years ago he had started a new volume of his diary headed simply "War." "We have lived a century of common life since then." The sin of slavery had been expiated; the national life restored. The cost had been beyond calculating.

The estimates of the number of men engaged on both sides and the casualties vary widely, not to say wildly. This is especially true of the Confederate army, which was even more casual about keeping accurate statistics than its Union adversary. *Harper's Encyclopedia of United States History* states that "the whole number of men called into the military service of the government in the army and navy . . . was 2,656,553." It lists 60,000 killed in action and 35,000 "mortally wounded," adding that "disease in camps and hospitals slew 184,000." Another equally authoritative text gives figures of 2,128,948 in Union service, of whom 67,058 were killed in battle, 43,012 died of wounds, and 224,586 of disease. Of the Union army 1,933,779 were listed as volunteers, 43,347 as draftees, and 73,000 as paid substitutes. The *Encyclopedia of American History*, R. B. Morris, editor, does not even give an overall figure for the Union forces but simply states that the Union dead numbered 359,528, including 110,070 killed in battle or died from wounds, and that the wounded totaled 275,175. Confederate figures are given as 258,000 (94,000 wounded in battle or died from wounds, "wounded, 100,000 minimum"). Benson Lossing gave a figure of 2,772,408 Union soldiers and sailors and approximately 600,000 Confederates. In the face of such contradictory statistics all that we can say with certainty is that more than 2,000,000 soldiers and sailors served in the Union forces and some 600,000 fought for the Confederacy, with Confederate and Union casualties roughly equal.

It has become such a commonplace to take the line that the vast superiority of the Northern states in matériel and manpower made a Union victory inevitable that it might be well to review briefly the relative advantages enjoyed by the two adversaries.

The North was, after all, fighting for an idea—that of Union. The Southerners believed that they were fighting for their very existence as a people. If any one of a half dozen likely eventualities had come to pass, the South would in all probability have won its freedom. Had Grant failed at Vicksburg; Lee won at Gettysburg; Vallandigham become governor of Ohio in 1863; England recognized the Confederacy; Sherman been beaten in Tennessee or pinned down in front of Atlanta; draft riots broken out again in major cities; or Lincoln failed of re-election (as he might well have done had the fighting continued to go badly), pressure in the North for a negotiated peace would have been enormous.

And then there is, of course, the final imponderable. It is hard, indeed impossible, at least for this historian, to believe that any other president but Abraham Lincoln could have sustained the Northern will to fight and carried the nation successfully through the war. There was nothing in Lincoln's past, nothing in his manner, his pronouncements, even his actions in the early months of the war to suggest that he was to become the greatest wartime leader of a nation in all history. The rock that the South finally broke upon was the rock of Lincoln's will; only that, in the last analysis.

So it appears that mad as the secession of the South from the Union was in one sense, in another the odds were all in favor of its winning independence. That it didn't, far from being in the historical cards, was the result of enough conjunctions of fortunate events to convince the pious of Divine Providence. Be that as it may, the titanic struggle was over. Walt Whitman pronounced its epitaph: "And so good-bye to the war, I know not how it may have been or may be, to others—to me the main interest I found, (and still on recollection, find,) in the rank and file of the armies, both sides, and in those specimens amid the hospitals, and even the dead on the field." All these—the dead, the maimed, those who survived—illustrated "the latent personal character and eligibilities of these States . . . (As so much of a race depends on how it faces death, and how it stands personal anguish and sickness). . . . Future years will never know the seething hell and the black infernal background of countless minor scenes and interiors . . . and it is best they should not—the real war will never get in the books. . . . Its interior history will not only never be written—its practicality, minutiae of deeds and passions will never be even suggested. The actual soldier . . . with all his ways, his incredible dauntlessness, habits, practices, tastes, language, his fierce friendship, his appetite, rankness, his superb strength and animality, lawless gait, and a hundred unnamed lights and shades of camp, I say, will never be written—perhaps must not and should not be. . . . Of that many-threaded drama, with its sudden and strange surprises, its confounding of prophecies, its moments of despair, the dread of foreign interference, the interminable campaigns, the bloody battles, the mighty and cumbersome and green armies, the drafts and bounties—the immense money expenditure like heavy-pouring constant rain—with, over the whole land, the last three years of the struggle an unending, universal mourning-wail of women, parents, orphans—the marrow of the tragedy concentrated in those army hospitals—(it seem'd sometimes as if the whole interest of the land, North and South, was one vast central hospital, and all the rest of the affair but flanges)—those forming the untold and unwritten history of the war—infinitely greater (like life's) than the few scraps and distortions that are ever told or written."

The peace so longed for was a vast, imponderable fact the meaning of which could hardly be penetrated. Only two things were unmistakably clear. The Union was restored and restored free of the fearful incubus of slavery. But that was all that was clear. What the war itself had meant, it was perhaps impossible to say. During the war the conviction that the United States was indeed growing in "moral energies" which it would be "as futile . . . to try to dam up [as] the waters of Niagara" deepened among the faithful. In the last days Whitman wrote: "Over the carnage rose prophetic a voice, Be not dishearten'd, affection shall solve the problems of freedom yet, Those who love each other shall become invincible," and the American Home Missionary Society expressed its faith that the time had come after Appomattox "for this great, loving, self-denying effort. . . . Everything has been unsettled by the war," its journal declared. "The elements of society are now soft and plastic, ready to be moulded and stamped."

Henry Adams believed that the war would work some reformation in the habits of the masses of the people. Adams hoped that the order and discipline of military campaigns would teach them "to give up that blackguard habit of drinking liquor in bar-rooms, to brush their teeth and hands and wear clean clothes, and to believe that they have a duty in life besides that of getting ahead, and a responsibility for other people's acts as well as their own." The war was a call to a new heroic spirit in peacetime. "I doubt," Henry wrote to Charles Francis, "whether any of us will ever be able to live contented again in terms of peace and laziness. Our generation has been stirred up from its lowest layers and there is that in its history which will stamp every member of it until we are all in our graves. We cannot be commonplace. The great burden that has fallen on us must inevitably stamp its character on us. I have hopes for us all, as we go on with the work. . . ."

For those young Americans like Henry and Charles Francis Adams, Jr., and Lester Ward, for Ted Upson and John Beatty, for Oliver Wendell Holmes, Jr., and tens of thousands like them, peace seemed to hold the promise of a new age; a reformed and reconstructed America, free of slavery, of exploitation, of poverty and injustice. For most older Americans—for the abolitionists certainly—the implications were cast in the more specifically theological terms of a redeemed and Christianized America where all men, finally equal in the eyes of the law, as they had been in the eyes of God, would be brothers (and, for the more advanced, where all women would be sisters). Doubts and misgivings could now be banished. In "Rise, O Days, from Your Fathomless Deeps" Whitman spoke of the doubt of America that had earlier assailed him in the midst of his beloved cities and on country roads. "One doubt, nauseous, undulating like a snake . . . Continually preceding my steps. . . ." Now the conclusion of the war had removed that doubt. ". . . I no longer wait—I am fully satisfied—I am glutted; / I have witness'd the true lightning—I have witness'd my cities electric; / I have lived to behold man burst forth, and warlike America rise. . . ." In "Turn O Libertad," he wrote:

> Turn from lands retrospective recording proofs of the past, . . .
> To where the future, greater than all the past,
> Is swiftly, surely preparing for you.

In "Years of the Modern" he asked:

> Are all nations communing? is there going to be
>   but one heart to the globe?
> Is humanity forming en-masse? . . . The earth, restive,
>   confronts a new era . . .
> No one knows what will happen next—such portents
>   fill the days and nights;
> Years prophetical! . . .
> This incredible rush and heat—this strange ecstatic
>   fever of dreams, O years!
> Your dreams, O years, how they penetrate through me!
>   (I know not whether I sleep or wake!)
> The perform'd America and Europe grow dim, retiring
>   in shadow behind me,
> The unperform'd, more gigantic than ever, advance,
>   advance upon me.

Henry Ward Beecher's younger brother Edward declared: "Now that God has smitten slavery unto death, He has opened the way for the redemption and sanctification of our whole social system." Writing to his old correspondent Leslie Stephen after the evacuation of Richmond, Lowell reminded him that he had once declared that "I had no gift of prophecy but that I had an *instinct* that the American people would come out of the war stronger than ever." To Lowell it seemed clear that "the one thing worth striving for in this world is a state founded on pure manhood, where everyone has a chance given him to better himself, and where the less costume and the more reality there is, the better." In his "Ode Recited at the Harvard Commemoration," Lowell spoke for the hopes of reconciliation and renewal:

> O Beautiful! my Country! ours once more!
> Smoothing thy gold of war-dishevelled hair
> O'er such sweet brows as never other wore,
>   And letting thy set lips,
>   Freed from wrath's pale eclipse,
> The rosy edges of their smile lay bare,
> What words divine of lover or of poet
> Could tell our love and make thee know it,
> Among the Nations bright beyond compare?

A Methodist clergyman named Gilbert Haven declared that the triumph of the Union had "insured the essential extension of America over the world. Already the United States of Europe are openly advocated . . . and that more distant and dubious title, the United States of Asia, looms up mistily on the far horizon. Even the United States of Africa will be born in due time into the family of republics; while the United States of America shall encompass the whole continent in her oceanic lines. Thus from the victory over the rebellion will arise a fraternity of nations, few in number, divided by no alienation of language, government, or faith; ultimately to become one with each other, with Christ, with God."

Since the war was a great moral struggle of good against evil, the soldiers who fought in it had to be strengthened in devoutness and Christian fortitude. Returning home after the conflict was over, they would reverse the trend toward degeneracy and effeminacy, the result of "luxury and ease," and insure "a purer and more stable Republicanism." The experience of war had a mystical dimension about it. The physical hardship was part of it: the terror and exultation and comradeship of battle; the bearing of wounds; the sense of having come through, although almost always with some scar or mutilation. The man who had fought and survived knew something about himself that peacetime life could never teach, had reached some limit of endurance and gone on beyond it. He had entered the terrible furnace of war and come out alive. He knew things in themselves incommunicable, things to be shared only with those who had gone through the same fire. It was not just that he had experienced the unspeakable. He had trusted his life to the God of battle in the name of the preservation of his country, the vindication of its government, its ideals, its democratic aspirations, in the name of justice and equality and a new and better human order. It set him apart from his fellows. "Through our great good fortune," Oliver Wendell Holmes, Jr., declared in a Memorial Day Address in 1884, "in our youth our hearts were touched with fire."

Henry Ward Beecher was confident that the United States had, with the end of the war, "entered a new era of liberty. The style of thought is freer and more noble. The young men of our time are regenerated. The great army has been a school, and hundreds of thousands of men have gone home to preach a truer and nobler view of human rights. . . . Everywhere, in churches, in literature, in natural science, in physical industries, in social questions, as well as in politics," the new spirit was manifesting itself.

Perhaps above all, democracy was vindicated by the war. Whitman wrote: "The movements of the late Secession War and its results, to any sense that understands well and comprehends them, show that popular democracy, whatever its faults and dangers, practically justified itself beyond the proudest claims and wildest hopes of its enthusiasts. . . . What have we seen here if not, towering above all talk and argument, the . . . last-needed proof of democracy? . . . That our national democratic experiment, principles, and machinery could triumphantly sustain such a shock, and that the Constitution could weather it, like a ship in a storm, and come out of it as sound and whole as before, is by far the most signal proof yet of the stability of that experiment—Democracy—, and of those principles and that Constitution."

George Loring, a Massachusetts abolitionist, set forth the terms on which, in his view, the rebel states should be readmitted to the Union. "When *all the citizens* of a state reach the point at which they are ready to return, upon the basis of government which the war has made for us all, let them return. But not until the institutions of these states conform to the highest civilization of the land. . . ." The South must learn "the lesson of freedom"; only then would Americans at last become a "high-toned and moral people." If the United States could be thus "regenerated" and "perfected . . . valiant in the field, and wise, religious, Christian in council and aims, I shall feel that I was born in a blessed hour." It was marvelous to him "how the people had been elevated" by the war, "how self-sacrificing and courageous and lofty" they had become "under its trials and responsibility." He had no patience with those who would restrict "the free ballot as an instrument of power which the people shall use, and use well in deciding all the great questions of the day. . . . There is a great, almost unknown, inestimable power, that sends truth into the hearts of the people; and the grander the truth the more quickly their instincts run to it. The history of the war teaches us this lesson. . . . It is on this estimate of popular intelligence and right, that we of the North have established the exercise of free ballot—of universal suffrage. . . . When . . . in the future some wise and profound historian shall look back and record this chapter on his pages, he will at least be compelled to acknowledge that never before has a people risen in its might and stricken down all political heresy, all social wrong, and moral iniquity, and obtained . . . that lofty eminence which an enlightened and faithful and intelligent people ought to possess. Let us thank God that we have lived to see this day. . . ."

The democracy that had been vindicated was not simply American democracy but democracy on the globe; the theme that the war had been a war on behalf of mankind was constantly reiterated. "Not on the Polish plains," the editor of the *Independent* wrote, "or in Grecian glens, or in Parisian faubourgs, or upon English scaffolds, are the shrines of the truest martyrs for Man. For those fought and died chiefly for themselves. . . ." American soldiers, on the other hand, were fighting for themselves "and all the world."

For many Americans, the free blacks of the South were an essential part of the redemptive process. George Ide, a Baptist minister, declared: "A race, acted on by the three mighty levers, Education, the Gospel, and the Ballot, must rise. No force of prejudice, no power of custom, no ban of exclusiveness can keep it down." With the slave truly emancipated, the United States must "tower up in MATCHLESS STRENGTH AND GRANDEUR, THE MARVEL OF THE AGES, AND THE HOPE OF THE WORLD."

Besides the theme of a redeemed and purified America and a vindicated democracy was the complementary theme of a "completed" America. The Founding Fathers, great as their accomplishments had been, had been unwilling or unable to cope with the most crucial reality in America: black servitude. The consequence was that while the United States called itself a nation and displayed many of the attributes of nationhood, it remained, in fact, two very different and basically incompatible cultures—*unfinished*.

In the view of Wendell Phillips, the United States, prior to the war, had been simply "a mercantile partnership, not a nation. . . . You will be surprised to learn that this nation was a Yankee pedler [sic] for forty years. . . . Outside of our financial and mercantile arrangements the Union is all incomplete. Our fathers never finished their work. The Founders left the United States to float like a balloon in the air. . . . I . . . say that now is the time to complete the machine which our fathers left incomplete. . . . What I want is a government so broad, so impartial, so founded on an average of national interests, that no local prejudice, no local malignity, no local wealth, can hold up its hand against the peaceful exercise of the citizenship under its flag. . . . I want a common school system which shall not rest on the charity of the North. If Alabama doesn't set it up, we will, and send her the bill. I will complete their government. . . . God has given us one corner-stone upon which to fortify, and that is the negro."

Richard Henry Dana, far more conservative than his fellow Bostonian, was convinced that "*the one point* to be gained by this war is the settlement forever, at home and abroad, of the fact as well as the theory that our republic is a government,—in the philosophical sense, a state,—created by the people of the republic, acting directly on individuals, to which each citizen owes a direct allegiance from which no power on earth can absolve him, and from which neither state nor individual has any recourse except to the moral right of revolution. . . . To my mind, the preservation of our combined national and state system—our solar planetary system—is the *sine qua non* of everything else. If that fails, the negro question, so far as it concerns *us*, would be of little consequence."

In the words of the young journalist William Grosvenor, the shock of the war "revealed the fact that we have never been one people, and that a true nationality, embracing all the States and sections, had never existed. Heterogeneous populations, hostile systems, and irreconcilable ideas had only been . . . held to bare juxta-position by a constitutional compact. No chemical union had ever taken place; for that the white-hot crucible of civil war was found necessary." The war had brought in its train a host of new problems—questions about a standing army, tariff for revenue or direct taxation, and, above all, "the problem of the future of the negro race. . . . The change to which we are called is radical. It is the new-birth of the nation," Grosvenor concluded.

The United States had at last acquired a "history." This was the theme of an address by Horace Bushnell, the famous transcendental minister, to a gathering of Yale alumni shortly after the end of the war. "No argument transmutes a discord or composes a unity where there was none," Bushnell declared. "The matter wanted here was blood, not logic. . . . These United States, having dissolved the intractable matter of so many infallible theories and bones of contention in the dreadful menstruum of their blood, are to settle into a fixed unity, and finally into a nearly homogeneous life." The war appeared to raise the issue of whether or not liberty could be preserved only by *dying* for it. Was that the lesson of the war? Bushnell asked. "Nations can sufficiently live only as they find how to energetically die. In this view," he added, "some of us have felt, for a long time, the want of a more historic life, to make us a truly great people. This want is now supplied; for now, at last, we may be said to have gotten a history." The nation had begun in an instant, so to speak, without the long period of historical gestation that had characterized the rise of other nations. Created, it might be said, by a single act of remarkable intellectual power, by force of will, by the Word made Constitution, it had existed in a kind of historical limbo, an odd accident of history, a by-product of the historical process (many Americans, of course, saw it as the consequence of divine intervention). In that historical "limbo," like an organism in a culture dish, it had followed its own curious logic of growth, like some brilliantly colored and exotic fungus. But the conflicts, the potential of disease inherent in the culture from the first, could not be suppressed indefinitely or forever ignored. They produced an extreme crisis in the body politic; they introduced the tragedy of History into the Garden of Innocence.

In a shattering and traumatic moment it was demonstrated that the United States was as susceptible to the tragic dilemmas of history as the rest of humanity. Bushnell was one of the few reform-minded Americans of his day to recognize the implications of that fact. Most of his compatriots in the ranks of Christian reformers preferred to see the war as a renewed anticipation of the millennium rather than as an entry into the anguish of historic time. Whatever the war's meaning, Bushnell was certainly right in declaring that the United States "at last . . . may be said to have gotten a history." But Bushnell was too

American not to believe that the outcome of our Armageddon would be progress and the enhancement of the common life. Even the names of the battlefields would become magic and talismanic words —Chancellorsville, Antietam, Shiloh, Missionary Ridge, Gettysburg, Atlanta. "Our very soil" was now "touched with a mighty poetic life." The "huge floodtide" of the war had opened "loftier ranges of thought . . . lifted our nationality," given us "new sentiments and finer possibilities," "to create, and write, and sing . . . to be all poets."

In other countries history lay all about, richly textured, perceptible in the weathered façades of cathedrals and palaces, in the timeworn stones of streets and walls. In countries of the Old World it had accumulated like a patina on bronze, richly colored, an element in the air, palpable, beyond the need of explication or analysis; told in the names of streets and châteaux and rivers. In America it was to be found only in words, the names of people, a few hallowed sites of Revolutionary fame—Yorktown, Saratoga, Trenton—and the names of the Founders—Washington, Jefferson, Adams, Franklin. The Civil War changed that to a substantial degree, gave the nonnation without a history a history of terrible drama and power. The flood of monuments, "sacred graves," "memorial parks and statues" that the writer in the *New Englander* called for was produced in abundance. Especially the statues. They rose like mortuary mushrooms in every town and city across the nation. Most poignantly, out of their desperately meager resources innumerable Southern towns erected memorials to those who had given their lives in the "Lost Cause." Certainly the physical objects did not obviate the need for the words. They poured out in an endless, apparently inexhaustible stream. Every survivor had a memory (and, as we have seen, many who did not survive left behind letters or diaries) and seemed determined to commit it to paper. Generals and colonels and lieutenants and corporals and even privates added to the voluminous official records their own recollections and reflections. Those of the generals were, with a few notable exceptions, exercises in self-justification, accusatory, exculpatory, trying to retrieve tarnished reputations, explain inexplicable lapses, rebut unfair charges.

Since the war changed everything else in American life, it is not surprising that it changed the relationship of Americans to their past. Prior to the Civil War there had been hardly more than a half dozen "historians"—one could almost count them on the fingers of one hand: Palfrey, historian of Puritanism and relatively obscure; Motley, historian of the wars of the Dutch Republic; Prescott, historian of the Spanish conquests in the Americas; Parkman, historian of the French in the New World; George Bancroft, historian of colonial America and the Revolution; Hildreth, the only one bold enough to tackle post-Revolutionary America. Now they rushed forth, a legion, professionals and amateurs alike, to mark the entry of the United States into history.

In the initial euphoria of peace it was widely assumed that the problem of black Americans had been settled by emancipation. Old-line black abolitionists like Frederick Douglass were uncertain what direction their energies should take in the future. "What should I do?" Douglass wrote. "Outside of the question of slavery my thought had not been much directed and I could hardly hope to make myself useful in any other cause than that to which I had given the best twenty-five years of my life." One thing is abundantly clear—*no* Americans, black or white, politicans, reformers, theorists, or seers, had any idea of the difficulties inherent in the notion of "reconstructing" the South.

35

Freedom

Perhaps a half million slaves had ventured into the strange, un-mapped realm of freedom before the war's end. For another four million or so the surrender of the armies of Lee and Johnston and the ratification of the Thirteenth Amendment on December 18, 1865, brought freedom. But for the vast majority of ex-slaves it was far from clear what freedom meant. On an Alabama plantation the slaves heard the news of their freedom from their master in silence. "We didn't hardly know what he means," one of them recalled years afterward. "We jes' sort of huddle together like scared rabbits, but after we knowed what he mean, didn' many of us go, 'cause we didn' know where to of went."

James Lucas, a former slave of Jefferson Davis's, reflected on his reactions and those of his fellow slaves. "Dey all had diffe'nt ways o'thinkin' 'bout it. Mos'ly though dey was jus' lak me, dey didn' know jus' zackly what it meant. It was jus' somp'n dat de white folks an' slaves all de time talk 'bout. Dat's all. Folks dat ain' never been free don' rightly know de *feel* of bein' free. Dey don' know de meanin' of it."

A Virginia slave named Moble Hopson remembered the reaction of the slaves on his plantation to the end of the war. When they went to the fields to work, there was no one to direct them, "An' dey stan 'round an' laugh an' dey get down an' wait, but dey don' leave dat field all de mawning. An' den de word cum dat the Yankee was a comin', an' all dem blacks start tuh hoopin' and holl'rin', an' den dey go on down to deer shacks an' dey don' do no work at all dat day."

At a plantation near Yorktown, Virginia, when a young slave woman heard her white family talking of Lee's surrender, she rushed out of the house and across the fields until she was out of sight and hearing of the house, and then, she recalled, "I jump up an' scream, 'Glory, glory, hallelujah to Jesus! I's free! I's free! Glory to God, you come down an' free us; no big man could do it.' An' I got sort o' scared, afeared somebody might hear me, an' I takes another good look, an' fall on de groun', an' roll over, an' kiss de groun' fo' de Lord's sake, I's so full o' praise to Masser Jesus. He do all dis great work. De soul buyers ca' neber take my two chillun 'ef ' me; no, neber take 'em from me no mo'."

Morris Sheppard, an Oklahoma slave, believed that it was his master, not Lincoln, who had set him free. "Abraham Lincoln and none of his North people didn't look after me and buy my crop right after I was free like old Master did," he recalled, adding, "Dat was de time dat was de hardest and everything was darkness and confusion."

Another slave, hearing of the end of the war and the passage of the Thirteenth Amendment, waited respectfully for his mistress to mention it. "Ye see," he told a puzzled Northern reporter, "I felt it to her honor to talk to me about it, because I was afraid she'd say I was insultin' to her and presumin', so I wouldn't speak first." But he made it clear that his restraint was not without a time limit—Christmas, 1865.

One slave woman recalled that when she heard she was free, she was working the fields. She dropped her hoe and ran to her mistress, "looked at her real hard," and cried, "I'se free! Yes, I's free! Ain't got to work for you no mo'. You can't put me in yo' pocket now!" At which her mistress broke into tears. On another plantation, a former slave recalled, "Missy, she cries and cries, and tells us we is free and she hopes we starve to death and she'd be glad, 'cause it ruin her to lose us."

Emma Holmes told the story of an old black woman, recently "freed," who sat by the side of the road and wailed loudly. When someone asked her the trouble, she burst forth, "I'm too old to learn to read, and me fingers is too stiff to play the pianny."

One of Lucy Chase's adult pupils on Craney Island, when asked how he felt at being free, gave a reply that charmed his teacher: "I'm free to hold myself, to learn, to show my best behavior to everybody, to serve my country, and to be always a gentleman but I'm not free to do anything else. I want to do all I can to show the white people our race is of some account."

A self-educated slave named Henry Adams, twenty-two at the end of the war, recalled in later life how the news of the passage of the Thirteenth Amendment had been communicated to the slaves on the plantation where he worked. The slaves were gathered together and told that they were free and could go where they wished. But their former master urged them to remain with him and work for wages. "The bad white men," he said, "was mad with the Negroes because they were free and they would kill you just for fun." There was, it turned out, more than a little truth in the prediction. All of Adams's fellow ex-slaves signed a contract to work for their master except Adams and a young friend named Jefferson. When Adams set out for Shreveport, he was stopped by four white men, who asked him to whom he belonged. When Adams replied that he belonged to no one, his interceptors began beating him with a stick and declared that they were going to kill him and every other black who told them that he did not belong to anyone. Between his home plantation and Shreveport, Adams saw "over twelve colored men and women, beat, shot and hung. . . ." When he returned to the plantation, he found a number of blacks ready to leave because of their indignation at the brutal whipping of a fifteen-year-old girl. Eleven men and boys headed for Shreveport. On the way a party of whites fired on them, beat some of the blacks, and, in Adams's words, took "all of our clothes and bed-clothing and money. . . . The same crowd of white men broken up five churches (colored). . . . They killed many hundreds of my race when they were running away to get freedom. . . . To my knowledge there was over two thousand colored people killed trying to get away after the white people told us we were free. . . . This was between Shreveport and Logansport."

At Lombardy Grove in Virginia, young Myrta Lockett Avery's father summoned his slaves and addressed them much as follows: "You do not belong to me any more. You are free. You have been like my own children. I have never felt that you were slaves. I have felt that you were charges put into my hands by God and that I had to render account to him of how I raised you, how I treated you. I want you to do well. You will have to work, if not for me, for somebody else.

Heretofore, you have worked for me and I have supported you, fed you, clothed you, given you comfortable homes, paid your doctor's bills, brought you medicines, taken care of your babies before they could take care of themselves; when you were sick your mistress and I have nursed you; we have laid your dead away." He had to know who was willing to stay and who was determined to go, so that he could make plans for the year's planting. One man called out, "Law, Marster! I ain't got nowhar tuh go ef I was gwine!" and other voices chimed in a chorus of loyalty and affection.

A planter in Lowndes County, Alabama, told his former slaves that he was no longer obliged to care for them. "Being free men, you assume the responsibilities of free men. You sell me your labor, I pay you money, and with that money you provide for yourselves. You must look out for your own clothes and food and the wants of your children. If I advance these things for you, I shall charge them to you, for I cannot give them like I once did. . . . Once if you were ugly and lazy, I had you whipped, and that was the end of it. Now if you are ugly and lazy, your wages will be paid to others, and you will be turned off, to go about the country with bundles on your backs, like the miserable low-down niggers you see that nobody will hire. But if you are well-behaved and industrious, you will be prosperous and respected and happy."

Some owners, returning to plantations which had been abandoned to the slaves who had lived on them during the war, were greeted with the old extravagant expressions of joy but soon made to understand that their ex-slaves considered themselves the owners of the plantations. The return of others was met by sullen resentment and manifest hostility. Thomas Pinckney, a descendant of the diplomat who had been Washington's minister to Great Britain, upon returning to El Dorado, his plantation on the Santee River in South Carolina, found that his former slaves first hid at the news of his arrival; when they finally appeared, they addressed him as "you" or "Capt'n" rather than "Master." They told him they had no intention of working "fuh no white man." Where then, Pinckney asked, would they work? "We gwine wuk right here on de lan' whar we wuz bo'n and what belongs tuh us."

When Adele Allston undertook to retrieve her South Carolina plantations from the possession of her ex-slaves, there were hints of an outright revolt. Finally she forced her will on the blacks by securing possession of the symbolic keys to the rice and corn barn. Still it was clear that she and her daughter were faced with serious resistance. Blacks surrounded them, singing:

> I free! I free!
> I free as a frog!
> I free till I fool!
> Glory Alleluia!

"They revolved around us," her daughter wrote, "holding out their skirts and dancing—now with slow, swinging movements, now with rapid jig-motions, but always with weird chants and wild gestures."

Freedom meant a host of problems large and small (often it was hard to distinguish the large from the small). For many slaves it meant learning to eat with "white folks'" eating utensils. It meant that most mysterious acquisition of all—a name, more than Caesar or Pompey or Cuff or Lawrence. There was a special poignance in choosing a name. The men and women on his plantation, an overseer told Whitelaw Reid, had had "the greatest time picking names. . . . No man thought he was perfectly free unless he had changed his name and taken a family name. Precious few of them . . . ever took that of their old masters." One man called himself Squire Johnston Brown, and another chose States Attorney Smith. One black man encountered by Lucy Chase was named Harrison's Landing and another Friday. North Carolina was a seamstress for Orlando Brown's wife. They gave their children splendidly resonant names—Fesus Edwin Leander Gannett was one, and Cornelia Felicia Thursday M'Arthur another.

To be able to buy things was a new and exhilarating experience for former slaves, and it is not surprising that a disproportionate amount of their wages, when they were paid, went for vivid scarves, gaudy pins, and brilliantly colored material. But they bought chairs and dishes and knives and forks as well. The Reverend David Macrae found Southern blacks fond of "gaudy colours," especially a deep crimson called "freed men's envelopes." A black woman fancied such color combinations as a red parasol, a green turban, and a yellow dress, Macrae recorded, while "the black dandy sports a white hat, red necktie, and flowered vest," and he often carried a cane, in part because to have carried a cane in slavery days would have resulted in his being whipped or fined. It was thus a symbol of his freedom. Macrae also found blacks everywhere addicted to big words, often mispronounced, and to extravagant titles such as Worshipful Patriarch and Grand Scribe. Hundreds of thousands of Northerners had read Harriet Beecher Stowe's prediction, in *Uncle Tom's Cabin*, of a day when African life would awake "with a gorgeousness and splendor of which our cold western tribes faintly have conceived," displaying "new forms of art, new styles of splendor." But this new "revelation" was, after all, to take place in *Africa*, not in the United States. It is not surprising that it did not occur to white Americans that they were witnessing, in the "black style," a transmuted form of that "gorgeousness and splendor" that Mrs. Stowe had so boldly anticipated.

Meanwhile, there was no lack of black leaders to denounce the attempts of their brothers and sisters to emulate white fashions. "We wear fine clothing, silks, satins, broadcloth, and trinkets, for the purpose of representing our wealth, while every person possessing a grain of common sense thinks quite to the contrary," William Whipper wrote.

Many household slaves disappeared in the night—and then came back a few days or weeks later, drawn by sentiment, by attachment to "home" and to "their families." Some were impudent, and some were threatening. So they tried, by constant experiment, to understand and define their new relationship, a relationship of which neither white nor black had had any intimation. The fact was there could be none. Congress was busy debating the specific nature of that relationship. Many Northerners wished to disturb it as little as possible; many others wished to "revolutionize" it completely. On some plantations, the freedmen and women moved into the big house, the plantation manor, crowding the ex-master's family into a room or two. Emma Holmes's uncle and aunt were reduced to living in "*one* room in his house with a few old pieces of furniture, drawing rations of a peck of rice or grist apiece a week and bringing it home himself." Uncle James insisted that his ex-slaves vacate the rooms since he had to rent them to try to bring in money enough to feed himself and his wife. The senior Gadsdens, friends of the Holmeses', had been, like many families, burned out and taken in by friends. They had been abandoned by old Agrippa, "who turned against them, the old, favored family servant." They had dispatched him to their plantation to get provisions, but he had dug up the family silver and distributed it to the blacks who remained on the plantation. The rather outspoken and sometimes defiant cook of another of Emma's uncles had brought her little boy to Emma's aunt Lizzie and, knowing her to be in desperate need of money, offered to pay her to teach her son to read. Emma herself earned money or, since Federal money was unavailable and Confederate money worthless, bartered sewing for food and other needed items.

Freedom meant, for field hands, new and unfamiliar notions of personal care and cleanliness. It meant new ideas of the relations of men and women to each other. No slaves, for instance, were married in the eyes of Southern law. Now men and women who had lived as husband and wife for decades and reared children were told they must be "married." Strangest of all was the matter of defining the new relationships between master and mistress and their former slaves.

In the months following the end of the war, a great part of the correspondence of Southerners was taken up with the reactions of their slaves to their new status as free men and women. Mary Jones wrote to her son Charles Colcock Jones complaining of a slave named Cato who had been "most insolent, indolent, and dishonest." She wished to keep those who were "obedient and industrious" and send the rest away. Porter and his wife, Patience, longtime household servants whom Mary Jones considered "members of the family," were a grievous disappointment to her. Another slave, Sue, had shown "a very perverse spirit," Mary Jones added, "I do remember all her former fidelity. . . ." Mary's brother, the Reverend John Jones, replied, "I would not allow them to live with me unless they gave full evidence of repentance; and yet I cannot say any more of my own servants. Not one can I depend on to remain with us another year. . . . I am thoroughly disgusted with the whole race."

Laura Buttolph, cousin of Mary Jones, wrote her on June 20, 1865: "There are to be *no more bondsmen and no more whippings*, the Yankees told the Negroes here. A Yankee officer told the servants at the Creek this week that they were to stay at home and work harder than they had ever done in their lives, and not run about and steal. . . . They (the Nigs) were quite disgusted. . . ."

Eva Jones, writing her mother-in-law, called the freeing of the slaves "a most unprecedented robbery." She noted: "There has been a great rush of freedmen from all families in the city [Augusta, Georgia] and from neighboring plantations. Adeline, Grace, and Polly have all departed in search of freedom, without bidding any of us an affectionate adieu. . . . We have lost many of our servants, but a sufficient number have remained to serve us, and as yet these appear faithful and anxious to please. On our plantation everything is 'at sixes and sevens.' One day they work, and the next they come to town. . . . We here have been most unfortunate for being so near to the city, our Negroes are under all the baleful influences of the vile abolitionists (of which the worst specimens are in our midst); and they (the Negroes) work or not just as it best suits their convenience and pleasure. . . . Besides this the Negroes and Yankees have broken into our smoke-house and swept it of *every piece* of meat."

The Reverend John Jones wrote to Mary Jones at the end of August, 1865, that the quietude of Refuge, the Jones plantation, had dissipated. "The dark, dissolving, disquieting wave of emancipation has broken over this sequestered region," he noted. "I have been marking its approach for months and watching its influence on our people. It has been like the iceberg, withering and deadening the best sensibilities of master and servant, and fast sundering the domestic ties of years." When two field hands at Refuge "openly rebelled" against the overseer, the Reverend Mr. Jones sent for some Maine and Kentucky soldiers at nearby Albany, who "came promptly, and by use of the strap and sometimes a leather trace they restored order generally. The Negroes were mystified, thunderstruck that they should receive such treatment (and in some cases very severe, even cruel) at the hands of their friends."

There were innumerable ironies and minor tragedies or come-dies. The free blacks in Charleston, "the really respectable class of free negroes," Emma Holmes wrote, "whom we used to employ as tailors, bootmakers, mantua makers, etc." refused to associate with the "par-venue free" and made frequent expressions of sympathy "to the Charleston gentlemen they meet, taking their hats off & expressing their pleasure at seeing them, but regret that it is under such circumstances, enquiring about others, etc."

But "negro insolence," as Emma Holmes called it, was far more common. She reported that an ex-slave had pushed his way into the house of a friend and told his daughter that "he had long been in love with her & had now come to marry her. . . ." The daughter had rushed to the window and called for help, whereupon a Yankee appeared and shot her importunate suitor. There was circulated a rumor that a regiment of black troops was planning to murder the white soldiers and proclaim Charleston and the environs "an African instead of a Yankee colony."

Household servants began requesting wages. In many instances the request was met by the answer that there was no money to pay them, as was, in fact, usually true. They might remain and continue to do what they had done before and be fed and cared for. Or they might leave and try to find work and wages elsewhere. Other household servants announced that there were certain menial jobs like washing and ironing and, in some cases, cooking that they would not do anymore; not infrequently they consented to teach their mistresses how to do such simple domestic chores. Emma Holmes recounted how her maid taught her to iron the men's shirts and collars and congratulated her on the speed with which she learned. Chloe, the Whites' cook, taught Edwin, Emma Holmes's brother-in-law, how to make biscuits, and he in turn taught the women of the family. With two of the maids sick, Emma tried making up her own bed and dusting and sweeping as well and found that they were not as difficult as she had imagined. Patty, Carrie's maid, "tried capers" with her mistress—i.e., refused to wash or iron the baby's clothes—but when Carrie without protest washed and ironed them herself and even ironed her husband's shirts, a chastened Patty reappeared, apologized for her bad behavior, and "went to work briskly." "Our servants," Emma Holmes added, "are generally respectful and willing to work as well as teach us what we want to learn from them, praising us for our industry and 'smartness.' We have told them what is coming, & how they will have all their own expenses to pay. . . ."

There seemed no pattern, among the freed slaves, as to those who left and those who stayed. Isaac Holmes lost Marcus, who "he thought would never leave him, so indulgent and bountiful a master had he always been to him," Emma Holmes wrote. One by one, as the weeks passed, the household slaves disappeared. "Mother," Emma Holmes noted, "had a talk with Chloe [the old family cook] & told her, if she wanted to go, not to sneak away at night like the others had done, but to come & say she wanted to go." The Holmeses had not freed their servants, she told Chloe, because their status was not settled yet. "Matters might be arranged on a different footing but negroes were still obliged to remain with their masters— . . . she could not pay her, as she knew, but, if she was willing to remain, she would feed herself & three children as usual." Chloe vowed she would never leave, but in a few weeks she was gone. "In almost every yard," Emma Holmes wrote, "servants are leaving but going to wait on other people for food merely, sometimes with the promise of clothing, passing themselves as free, much to our amusement."

An elderly, ailing black woman named Ann left two months after Appomattox, abandoning the Holmeses to do their own ironing. "Poor deluded fool," Emma Holmes commented, ". . . off she went while we girls went to ironing."

Nina, another one of the Holmeses' household servants, departed to work for a tailor and after a few days came back and had a "long talk" with Emma's mother, "saying she wanted to make some regular arrangement about working for us and to know exactly how matters stood. For she said with tears in her eyes & much feeling, she had lived too long with us for there to be any misunderstanding now. . . ." A tearful reunion followed with mutual apologies and forgivings.

At the Bell plantation near Nashville several months after the end of the war, the owners found only the houses and one or two Negroes remaining there. The furnishings had been disposed of by the ex-slaves, and some were recovered in the city from shops. Albert Walker found "his large elegant establishment occupied by his own servants, whom he had left, & who were as humble, respectful & attentive as of old, everything being kept in the neatest and cleanest style. . . . The Courtney's and Conner's fine houses [were] filled with negroes cooking in the drawing rooms."

On some plantations there were murders. William Allen, an old friend of Emma Holmes's, was chopped to pieces in his barn, an example, Emma wrote, of how the "devilish Yankees" had instilled in "peaceful & happy" blacks "the foulest demoniac passions."

While in many instances household ex-slaves stayed on as paid servants with their former masters and mistresses, field hands generally preferred to work for someone else. The reasons seem clear enough. First of all, a field hand seldom had those strong emotional ties that bound a mistress and her personal maids or a master and his servants together. That being the case, he preferred to work for someone with whom he had never been in a servile relationship and of whom, therefore, he did not stand in awe or fear. A new employer meant a clean break with the slave past and the consciousness of being "his own man."

As remarkable as any aspect of Reconstruction was the general disposition of freedmen and women to forgive their former masters and mistresses for the "accumulated wrongs" they had suffered. If there were numerous instances of what the whites regarded as insolence, there were remarkably few cases of violence, of physical assault by freed blacks against their former masters, or of the murder of white men by ex-slaves. This, after all, was the horror that had obsessed white minds for generations. Now it was proved groundless.

A group of freedmen in Claiborne County, Mississippi, petitioned the governor of the state in 1865: "All we ask is justice and to be treated like human beings. . . . We have good white friends and we depend on them by the help of god to see us righted and we not want our rights by Murdering. We owe to much to many of our white friends that has shown us Mercy in bygon dayes To harm thaim." One North Carolina white woman was kept from complete starvation by a former slave who shared his wages with her and, when he died, left her $600. Elizabeth Botume reported coming on a young black woman drawing water from a well for her former mistresses. "Us going to well fur water fur the lady what bring we up, an' was like a muther to we," she explained, half-apologetically. She couldn't "stan seein' her workin' fur herself, bringin' water, an' sick-like, fur she been very kind to we."

The spirit of forgiveness extended even to Jefferson Davis. In the words of one of his former slaves, "I . . . can say to Mr. Jefferson Davis, 'Peace! you have suffered! Go in peace.' The Scriptures had, after all, taught forgiveness as the highest Christian virtue. Christ had said, 'blessed are ye, when men shall revile you, and persecute you, . . . I say unto you, That ye resist not evil; but whatsoever shall smite thee on thy right cheek, turn to him the other also. . . .'"

John Roy Lynch, a Mississippi black, expressed a characteristic compassion for the defeated whites: "Many of these proud sons, gallant fathers, cultured mothers and wives and refined and polished daughters found themselves in a situation and in a condition that was pitiable in the extreme. It was not only a difficult matter for them to adjust themselves to the new order of things and to the radically changed conditions, but no longer having slaves upon whom they could depend for everything. . . ."

Ironically, the forbearance and, in many cases, compassion of the blacks for their former owners won them little credit with whites. The whites, for the most part, attributed the blacks' attitude to cowardice or to ingrained habits of subordination while continuing to fear that suppressed black hostility might at any moment break out in an orgy of killing and destruction. Indeed, it was necessary for whites to hold to such views if they were to persevere in their attempts to intimidate the freed blacks and re-establish unquestioned domination over them. So the willingness of the great majority of blacks of all classes to let bygones be bygones, to "let the dead bury the dead," as one black politician expressed it, was generally interpreted as fear.

The most poignant journey of freed blacks was in search of

relatives—children, sons and daughters—who had been sold away from them years before. Many former slaves who had escaped to Canada came south to seek friends and relatives from whom they had been long separated.

In addition to searching for relatives, many freedmen simply wished to travel—to move unimpeded through space. They came and went endlessly and often purposelessly for the simple pleasure of coming and going at will, without passes, permission, punishments, without let or hindrance, so that the South was filled by black men and women traveling about, going from their plantations to hire out at a neighboring one, sassing their mistress (and less often their master) for the mere assertion of their new condition. They considered a thousand alluring prospects, most of them quite illusory. Women considered going to Atlanta or Charleston and setting up as seamstresses. Men considered trades or professions, considered going north or west or into the next county. Most of the freedmen and women yearned, above all, for a small plot of land of their own. Politicians appeared with glittering promises of political and economic power. Missionaries urged them to be pious, to learn to read and write, and, above all, to observe the Seventh Commandment. Charles Colcock Jones wrote his mother from Augusta: "Stepney and Pharaoh are very desirous of going to Arcadia. . . . Little Tom has ever since my absence been working on his own account upon adjoining plantations. He says he is going with his father to Liberty, and his father plans to return to White Oak with Martha and the rest of the children. William, Kate, and family expect to go to Liberty. . . . Robert and family, Niger and family, Pharaoh and family, and Hannah expect to do the same thing. Maria is going to hunt for Dick [her husband]. Rose says she is going with Cato. . . . Peggy wishes to go with Sue." And so it went, in total a vast, restless stirring.

Freedmen and women flocked to the cities, and when the Reverend David Macrae inquired the reason, he found that "while some had come to eat the bread of idleness, many had come for safety; others to get their children to school; others to seek work that would be paid for." As for the reputed black aversion to work, Macrae found "more activity and more desire for work amongst the poor negroes than amongst the poor whites." What to whites often appeared an unwillingness on the part of blacks to work was, in fact, a determination not to be taken advantage of by a white employer.

According to a Northern journalist, the freed blacks regarded the white proprietor who was negotiating for their services "as an adventurous swindler, without any money at all, or as a Croesus, made of money." Newly employed blacks were "suspicious and watchful" until they were satisfied that the "boss" was both solvent and fair in his dealings with them. Satisfied of this, they then began to do their best to wring some additional favor or perquisite from him. Many of the old techniques of wheedling and manipulation learned as slaves—"puttin' on ole massa," as it was called—were, not surprisingly, practiced by free blacks. Their fears of being taken advantage of were certainly well founded. A journalist told of an ostentatiously pious South Carolina planter who, when he added up a net profit of $30,000 at the end of a season, gave a bonus of 6¼ cents to every slave. Whitelaw Reid gave an example of the confusion of freed blacks over what constituted a fair wage. When Reid asked a black railroad worker what his wages were, the man replied, "Twenty dollahs a month, sah; but I'se gwine to quit. 'Tain't enuff, is it?" Reid assured him that it was a good deal, as much as the average white laborer received in the North and more than was being paid in Richmond for similar labor. "Well, den, sah, I'll do as you say," the man replied. "I was afeared of dese men cheatin' me, because I knowed dey would if dey could . . . if you say wuck on, I'll do it."

As we have noted, many blacks, not surprisingly, identified freedom with not having to work. Since slavery meant work, it was a by no means illogical conclusion. David Macrae, visiting the home of a black family, found the man of the house still in bed at noon. When he inquired of his wife if he was sick, she replied, "Oh, he's quite well, sah, but he says he's free now, and can lie in bed when he like." White and black officers of Negro regiments often undertook for a fee to recruit their former soldiers to work on a particular plantation, and some, Whitelaw Reid was told, received as much as $2,000 or $3,000 a year for such a service. Since most of them knew nothing about raising cotton, their sole function was to insure that hands turned out to work as specified by their contracts. "I told a nigger officer," a Mississippi planter said to Whitelaw Reid, "that I'd give him thirty dollars a month just to stay on my plantation and wear his uniform. The fellow did it, and I'm havin' no trouble with my niggers." When a black regiment was demobilized, dozens of Mississippi and Louisiana planters visited the camp with alluring offers and various blandishments, including treats of tobacco and whiskey, but most of the discharged soldiers were too suspicious to commit themselves. Some were offered $20 a month plus food and lodging, and corporals and sergeants were offered $30 or $40 on condition that they bring a certain number of men with them.

Many freedmen and women found life distressingly difficult. Laura Buttolph, writing to her cousin, noted that "the starving people who had no work were 'very plenty.' " The reference was to those blacks who were without work and without Federal rations. Belton O'Neall Townsend, a correspondent for the *Atlantic Monthly*, described the food eaten by poor Southern blacks as "coarse and barbarously prepared. . . . Their dwellings," he added, "have usually but one room, in which they sleep, cook, eat, sit, and receive company. . . . Their food rarely includes more than hominy, cornbread, rank fat bacon sides, coffee and cheap molasses. . . . The gardens of the Negroes contain only a few specimens of plants: sweet potatoes, Irish potatoes more rarely, peas, beans, watermelons and collards. . . . A family that can afford it keeps a pig impounded during the year, fattening it to kill at Christmas. . . . Many of them have invested their earnings in a cow, and most of them rear fowls."

More eloquent than abstract arguments were the statistics on the death rate among Southern blacks. In the period prior to the Civil War the death rate among slaves had been less than a percentage point greater than that of whites. In the years after the war the annual death rate per thousand black persons rose from 26.45 to 43.33, while the white death rate fell slightly. Ironically, one substantial element in the precipitous rise in the black death rate was the fact that ailing slaves, as valuable property, got the best medical attention available, far better than that of Southern poor whites. After the war they got what they could afford, which was precious little. In addition, most white doctors were reluctant to take black patients, and black doctors were few in number and poorly trained.

One of the most striking consequences of emancipation was the importance and often dominance of black women in black families. This was a legacy of slave days, when the "mammy" was a figure of central importance in the domestic economy of the plantation; where there was often a question of the father's identity or when, as was the case when the master of the plantation was the father, his identity was to be at least formally obscured, and a child's identification was much more commonly with his mother than his father. The slave tradition was strengthened by the fact that there was little or no established domestic order for freedmen and women. They thus worked out their own relationships, and many black women enjoyed far more equality vis-à-vis black males than did their white sisters, North or South. "The women are the controlling spirits," Charles Colcock Jones wrote his mother.

Whenever ex-slaves were beyond the protection of Union soldiers or agents of the Freedmen's Bureau, they were apt to be objects of white violence. Emma Holmes noted in her diary in July, 1865, that there were "daily altercations between lower class whites & blacks, in which the latter always suffer, & four or five of them [are] murdered every day—while in Columbia & other places, they are suffering greatly for want of food, for no one will hire those who have children to be fed."

The most basic reality of the freed slaves was their "black Christianity." The center of black life was the black church, and the minister exercised an enormous influence over his flock. Whitelaw Reid attended a service in a converted barn in Louisiana. On the walls were pictures of General Grant and General Sherman, and near the pulpit was an enlarged photograph of Lincoln. The only other decoration was a calendar. The minister's sermon was interspersed with cries from his congregation of "Oh, yes, Lord," "Merciful Father" and other pious ejaculations. Prayers alternated with singing. To Reid it seemed "very absurd," but to the members of this and thousands of other similar congregations it was the breath of life. In slavery days the minister had been more than once whipped for preaching the words of Scripture and thereby exposing his fellow slaves to dangerous doctrines. A British traveler, Sir George Campbell, described the black ministers as "a sort of Christian Brahmins" among their congregations, but "still . . . very democratic in their arrangements. The people like to have a large voice in all their religious affairs. These preachers . . . are a rather funny-looking set, with their black faces and white ties, but they seemed hearty and pleasant." Sir George found the one he listened to "a stirring and effective preacher. . . . The colored preacher is a philosopher and a consummate actor. He is thoroughly acquainted with his race. He knows how to excite each slumbering emotion of the soul."

For many ex-slaves, Christianity, central as it was to their lives, was an ambiguous legacy. While they had extracted from it the conviction that all souls, rich and poor, black and white and yellow or red, were equally precious in the eyes of the Lord, that was not the message that their masters and mistresses wished to convey. Freedom meant, for pious blacks, freedom to hear preached (and eventually, they hoped, to read themselves) the word of God uncensored by white intermediaries. In the words of a Mississippi ex-slave, "Ole missus used to read de good book tu us, black 'uns, on Sunday evenin's, but she mostly read dem places whar it says, 'Sarvints obey your masters,' an' didn't stop tu splane it like de teachers; and now we is free, dar's heaps o' tings in dat ole book we is jes' sufferin' tu larn."

Orlando Brown, a freedmen's missionary, catechized his maid, Nancy, a devout black woman. "Do you think the slave-holders will go to heaven with all the rest of the just?" he asked her. "If Massa's good he'll go to heaven with all the rest of the just." "What is your idea of God, Nancy?" "He's all in a smile; he smiles on the just and he frowns on the unjust. . . . It is the pure in heart who see God."

Henry Johns, an observant young Massachusetts soldier stationed in Louisiana, came from a strong abolitionist background and gave close attention to black life. After attending a black church, he reported, "When praying about their enslaved condition, or for the dying, or for the salvation of poor sinners, they unitedly break out into the most plaintive chorus imaginable. I can't describe it, but to my dying hour I shall remember it. It seemed like the *incarnation of sadness*. I could think of nothing but a mother in heaven wailing for her lost son. . . . Almost like a nightmare it clings to me, ever presenting depths of sadness and resignation beyond my conception."

Prayers, like the songs, were usually spontaneous and full of vivid images. One man prayed, "Lord, when we'se done chawin' all de hard bones, and when we'se done swallerin' all de bitter pills, take us home to Thyself." David Macrae himself was often included in the prayers as "de white gemman in de corner" or "de white brudder near de door." An old man in Hampton, Virginia, prayed, "O Lord, will ye please heyst the diamond winders of heaven, roll back yer lubly curtains, and shake yer tablecloth out, and let some of the crumbs fall among us."

Macrae was touched by the passionate attachment of blacks to the Bible. Those who were illiterate often begged him to read favorite passages to them when he visited their homes. The missionary of a school on a Texas plantation where there were only two Bibles said that every day "a little crowd of scholars" appeared "with messages from parents and grand-parents at home, begging for the loan of one of the Bibles for the night, that they might have it read to them by their children." Macrae wrote: "Nowhere in America does one find such simple and childlike faith, such a strong belief in the presence and power of God, such fervor and religious enthusiasm, as among the pious negroes. They seem to see God bending over them like the sky, to feel His presence on them and around them, like the storm and the sunshine."

Singing and praying and preaching were the standard elements in black worship. Songs, hymns, spirituals were often improvised with one singer starting out with a three times reiterated "line" so that the rest of the congregation could "get it" and then adding a chorus, after which other voices would add verses to the same rhythm and chorus:

> Jordan's river I'm bound to cross,
> Bound to cross, bound to cross,
> Jordan's River I'm bound to cross
> Poor sinners, fare ye well.
>
> That long white robe I'm bound to wear,
> Bound to wear, bound to wear . . .
> Them golden slippers I'm bound to wear,
> Bound to wear, bound to wear . . .

And:

> O! Fader Abraham
> Go down into Dixie's land;
> Tell Jeff Davis
> To let my people go.
> Down in the house of bondage
> Dey have watch and waited long,
> De oppressor's heel is heavy,
> De oppressor's arm is strong.

One of the problems that the missionaries had to face was how to react to the religious practices of the blacks. The shout was a classic example of religious ecstasy, a wild outpouring of emotion and celebration of the Lord, accompanied by singing, dancing, handclapping, and shouting. The Unitarians were, for the most part, appalled at such goings-on in the name of religion, while the Baptists, Methodists, and other evangelicals, if initially disconcerted, were much more readily reconciled to these exuberant outpourings, not unlike camp meetings in their extreme emotionalism.

One of the principal reasons that the older, established black churches lost membership was that their ministers often tried to force a more discreet and genteel form of worship upon the members as part of an effort to "civilize" the former slaves. This was resisted by many blacks, who were determined to worship as they wished. The result was a much less inhibited black religion than that which existed before the war, when whites kept a tight rein on excessive emotionalism and services were often conducted by white ministers. Now pent-up black feelings poured out. "With freedom," Myrta Lockett Avary wrote, "the negro, *en masse*, relapsed promptly into the voodooism of Africa. Emotional extravaganzas, which for the sake of his health and sanity, if for nothing else, had been held in check by the owners, were indulged without restraint. It was as if a force long repressed burst forth. 'Moans,' 'shouts' and 'trance meetings' could be heard for miles. It was weird."

In Charleston, shortly after the surrender of the city, the cornerstone was laid for a new African Methodist Episcopal church. The AME church had been driven out of Charleston thirty years before for the supposed complicity of some of its members in Denmark Vesey's plot. Now it was to be rebuilt, and the architect was Robert Vesey, son of Denmark. Three thousand of the city's blacks participated in the ceremonies. A year later there were eleven black churches in the city; the most fashionable was the Episcopal St. Mark's. A black man named Ed Barber who tried to cross the class line to St. Mark's described it as a church "dat all de society folks of my color went to. No black nigger welcome dere, he told me. Thinkin' as how I was bright 'nough to git in, I up and goes dere one Sunday. Ah, how they did carry on, bow and scrape and ape de white folks. . . . I was uncomfortable all de time though, 'cause they was too hifalootin' in de ways, in de singin', and all sorts of carryin' ons."

Henry Turner, steeped in the liberal theology of the day, complained that black Christianity stressed "Hell fire, brimstone, damnation, black smoke, hot lead, etc." as "man's highest incentive to serve God, while the milder and yet more powerful message of Jesus was thoughtlessly passed by." On another occasion he wrote: "Let a person get a little animated, fall down and roll over awhile, kick a few shins, crawl under a dozen benches, spring upon his feet . . . then squeal and kiss (or buss) around for awhile, and the work is all done." Ironically, whites were often more sympathetic to forms of black worship than black ministers, who plainly felt that the uninhibited behavior of black congregations might be interpreted as an indication of black inferiority. The black leader Thomas Cardozo, a graduate of the Edinburgh Theological Seminary, wrote: "I cannot worship intelligently with the colored people, and, consequently, am at a loss every sabbath what to do."

The problems of the Northern missionary were suggested by the complaint of a Kentucky teacher who wrote: "The idea seemed to be inherent with them [the freedmen] that the duty of Christians consists primarily in boisterous prayers and weird singing and shouting . . . rather than in pure and upright living." The Old School Presbyterians expressed similar sentiments in their General Assembly, complaining that "superstition permeates their whole society, and manifests itself as an atmosphere about the world of piety they inhabit. Visions, revelations, and rhapsodies sweep through their confused ideas of worship, until their religion becomes an inebriation."

The most striking fact about black religion after the war was that it provided an avenue of access for Northern black leaders, the great majority of whom were Protestant ministers, to the freedmen and women of the South. The ablest and most intelligent ministers became inevitably the political leaders of the Southern blacks. Henry Turner, James Lynch, Arthur Waddell, Jonathan Gibbs, and Richard Cain were only the most prominent among dozens who came south to teach and preach and stayed to become active politicians. One of the first to go south had been James Lynch, who had gone to the Sea Islands as a missionary. After several years of missionary work Lynch went to Philadelphia to edit the missionary journal the *Christian Recorder.* There he chafed at his remoteness from the scene of action, and in June, 1867, declaring that "convictions of duty to my race" made it impossible for him to continue as editor, he announced his determination to go to a Southern state and "unite my destiny with that of my people, to live with them, suffer, sorrow, rejoice, and die with them." In Mississippi his intelligence and dedication made him one of the principal political figures in the state.

The wedding of black religion and black politics strengthened both. While the upper-class white churches of the North grew less and less relevant to the daily lives and needs of ordinary people, becoming more and more upper-class sanctuaries and centers of such essentially middle-class preoccupations as temperance and municipal reform, the black churches of the South confirmed and strengthened their function as the repository of black hopes and aspirations as well as of specific political accomplishments. The ministers and the black veterans of the Union army provided the indispensable cadres of black leadership during the Reconstruction Era. They were a remarkable band deserving of far more attention than they have received. When we look back at their achievements, it is not too much to say that defeated as they ultimately were, they succeeded brilliantly in drawing out and nurturing the seeds of a black consciousness that while still retaining residues of the "slave mentality" they often and eloquently deplored, provided the essential grounding for the contemporary "consciousness" of black people, consciousness that grew in the "souls of black people" (as W. E. B. Du Bois put it) until Rosa Parks struck the spark that Martin Luther King, Jr., fanned into the flame of the civil rights-black liberation movement of the 1960s. To put it another way, these leaders created common black memories which, if they faded in their specific historical details, greatly strengthened the psyches of Southern blacks by disclosing new possibilities to them. Indeed, we have only to try to imagine the situation of the post–Civil War freedmen and women in the absence of white and black teachers and missionaries, especially the latter, to realize how crucial their role was. So it is not enough formally to recognize their contributions; a proper assessment of them is essential to an understanding of the period of Reconstruction.

Even before the war there had been in Southern and Northern cities free blacks who constituted a black "upper class." In the North these were most often teachers, doctors, lawyers, ministers, and small-business men; in the South, waiters, craftsmen, barbers, and caterers. After the war black society was augmented by government workers, ex-Union soldiers, and the growing corps of black teachers. The relation of these upper-class blacks toward the black masses was often characterized by the same attitudes held by upper-class whites toward *their* inferiors—snobbery and condescension. But more striking was the fact that given strong incentives to "distance" themselves from their poor and often illiterate black brothers and sisters, most upper-class blacks identified themselves with the less fortunate members of their race and worked for the improvement of their status and the extension of their rights. In these efforts of upper-class blacks, there was undoubtedly a measure of self-preservation, a feeling that all "blacks" whatever the hue of their skin, from the faintest hint of brown to the darkest black, were in the same boat and must sink or swim together. But much deeper and more fundamental were the suffering and degradation that all blacks experienced by virtue of being "black" in a white civilization. The feeling of essential brother- and sisterhood engendered by generations of common tribulations proved in most instances far stronger than the common human instinct to rise higher in the social and economic scale, if not at the expense of one's fellows, at least with a measure of indifference.

Many members of the black upper class modeled their style of living, their manners, their speech, their dress, their entertainments, and their social events upon those of the white middle and upper classes. To the black elite, the classical racial characteristics of lower-class blacks—their often happy-go-lucky and improvident ways, their so-called promiscuity, their expressive emotional life, their songs and music—were often an acute embarrassment. Since they had chosen a path designed to prove themselves "equal" to whites and, in doing so, had of necessity accepted white definitions of what they should strive to be equal to, the black elite was dismayed by the persistence with which lower-class blacks clung to their own culture. Indeed, they did more than cling to it; they elaborated and enhanced it, made it strikingly distinct from white culture and from that upper-class black culture which strove to emulate the white world of fashion. In doing so, ordinary black people continually posed for upper-class blacks the question of whether indeed blacks in general were, as so many whites insisted with increasing stridency and confidence, inferior. It was in many ways a losing battle. If you allow the dominant group in a society to establish the standards for approved and desirable social behavior, you can be sure that the standards will be those at which the dominant groups excel.

Thus, the black upper class found itself in an increasingly schizophrenic situation. Determined to suppress all character traits which whites might identify as "black" and therefore as inferior, they invited the contempt and ridicule of those lower-class blacks who had created, or were in the process of creating, their own subculture, one that emphatically rejected most white values. Not only were they denied full acceptance by the white society that they attempted to imitate, but they were often also denied the leadership roles in their own race that they felt they deserved by virtue of their "success" in emulating whites. After all, they had "proved" that blacks could "make it," "get ahead," compete with whites, that they were "equal." However, it was evident that the whites, in the last analysis, had no intention of accepting upper-class blacks as equals in any real meaning of that word, regardless of their accomplishments. So, it turned out, they had given up their "black consciousness" for a stone. They must still toady and bow, be polite, deferential—"good niggers," in the parlance of old plantation days. It was the final and most cruel exaction. Worst of all, it deprived the generality of blacks of their natural leaders, the ablest and most capable among them. White society had said to the blacks, free and freed, "Prove yourselves our equals, and then we will accept you without barriers and constraints as our equals." The most able and ambitious had responded with unquestionable ability, intelligence, skill, and even good humor, only to encounter the same old barriers and obstacles, the same old arguments, the same apparently ineradicable prejudices. Even their social gatherings, their weddings, and their balls were mocked for their pretentiousness.

A fact that must be kept in mind was that while there was a vast gap between the best educated and most accomplished Northern free black and the illiterate black field worker on an Alabama or a Mississippi plantation, there were differences almost as great among the Southern slaves themselves. There was, as we have seen, the distinction between household slaves, who, in their constant contact with their white masters and mistresses, acquired white ways and manners and often a considerable degree of sophistication, and the field hands who were, in most practical respects, another class. There were also, of course, striking differences between slaves performing conventional domestic and agricultural tasks on plantations and farms and those in the towns and cities who practiced trades or were, like Frederick Douglass, rented out as skilled laborers. Many in this latter category had taught themselves to read, and a number to write as well. Finally, the region of the South was an important determinant in the character and capacities of particular slaves. It was notorious that those who worked rice fields of the Deep South were generally least "acculturated," most deprived and degraded. In the border states, where the plantation system was less ubiquitous and where slaves, in consequence, were commonly engaged in small-scale farming, in domestic work, and in trades, the rate of literacy, the knowledge of the white world, and the capacity to function in it were far higher. What was common to virtually all "classes" and subdivisions of "black culture," North and South, was a deep Christian piety. It was this devoutness, formed in the face of such extraordinary diversity, that was the substratum of what we today call black consciousness, this and the persistent and inescapable fact of white prejudice, which forced a

Frederick Douglass or Robert Purvis into the same category as the most primitive field hand on a Georgia plantation.

We have taken note earlier of the activities of the various freedmen's bureaus, funded by Protestant churches and private philanthropy, which had followed the Union armies of occupation during the war, operating most notably at Port Royal.

After the report by the Freedmen's Inquiry Commission (a body which included Samuel Gridley Howe and Robert Dale Owen), no action was taken by Congress until the last months of the war. On March 3, 1865, Congress established the Bureau of Freedmen, Refugees and Abandoned Lands under the aegis of the War Department. Its first head was General Oliver Otis Howard, West Point '54, at thirty-six one of the youngest generals (and undoubtedly the most pious) in the Union army. Howard, an ardent abolitionist, had a brilliant war record. Awarded the Congressional Medal of Honor for bravery at Fair Oaks, where he lost an arm, he fought at Antietam and Chancellorsville and was cited for unusual skill and bravery at Gettysburg. Later, when he was in command of the XI Corps in the Army of the Cumberland, Sherman had teased him for his extreme piety. Through all of Sherman's campaign to Atlanta and then to the sea, Howard's corps, and later the Army of the Tennessee under his command, played a prominent role.

The job facing the Freedmen's Bureau was a staggering one. It was no less than providing for the physical, psychological, and educational needs of the freed slaves and, indeed, all Southerners, white or black, in need of help. One of the most controversial aspects of the bill which created the bureau was its dependence on army officers as its principal agents. On the other hand, a substantial degree of the support for the bureau in Congress was based on the desire to provide jobs for a large surplus of army officers, many of whom had had valuable experience in the occupation forces.

The agents of the Freedmen's Bureau, soon recruited by the hundreds, ranged from simpleminded abolitionists who poured out "gushes of unctuous cant," in Carl Schurz's words, to individuals who showed hostility and contempt for their charges. Most agents of the bureau, Schurz and other observers believed, evidenced to a remarkable degree the "strict integrity, sound sense, discretion and tact" required for the proper exercise of their demanding duties.

Many men trained under the auspices of the American Freedmen's Aid Union simply moved over to the Freedmen's Bureau, providing a critical nucleus of experienced agents. Many Northern blacks, like Martin Delany and James Lynch, were first employed by the bureau and then, after the passage of the Reconstruction Act, took leadership roles in black politics. Frederick Law Olmsted, back from his utopian gold-digging community at Mariposa, California, took a job with the Freedmen's Bureau.

A reporter for the *New York Tribune* gave an account of a typical day in a Freedmen's Bureau in Goldsboro, North Carolina. After breakfast the bureau agent, an army captain, and two clerks began the business of the day. Some five hundred people, "of all colors and classes," waited for a hearing. The blacks came, for the most part, "to get hired out . . . to make complaint against former masters for wages retained, for rations, and the settlement of all disputes." Rations were given only in cases of clear necessity, and no Negro could make a complaint "unless he or she has made some contract for support for the ensuing year. . . . Thus, you see," the reporter wrote, "all the stuff about the Freedmen's Bureau being a refuge for indolent negroes is so much falsehood. All contracts for labor are made through the bureau. . . . Consequently there are always a large number of planters constantly besieging the bureau for laborers." The *Tribune* correspondent told of a case in which two freedmen brought charges against a former master for withholding their wages. The charges were given a hearing, with the master having an opportunity to present his side of the case. When it was proved that the old master clearly owed the wages in question, he produced a long list of items charged to the account of the freedmen. They in turn protested a number of the charges, and when the planter was asked to swear on a Bible to the accuracy of the bills, he faltered and refused to swear. The case was dismissed, and he was ordered to pay the wages in question.

On many plantations the slave relationship was replaced by a contract which called for the freedmen and, in some instances, women to perform certain labor in the rice or cotton fields in return for food, shelter, and a wage. In the absence of a convenient Freedmen's Bureau contracts were drawn up by the plantation owners, and they were seldom generous to the black laborers. There was no standard contract, although in some areas the Freedmen's Bureau suggested contract terms. Once the contract had been agreed to by field hands, doubts and resentments often arose. Word might come of another contract more favorable to the hands, and there would be angry charges or open rebellion. Mary Jones's experience at Montevideo was typical. In the middle of the planting of the cotton she learned that two of the freedmen, Jesse and July, had gone to the Freedmen's Bureau in Savannah with a copy of the contract. They came back and announced to their fellow workers that the contract was unfair, and "the people one and all . . . declared they would not strike another lick with the hoe. . . ." Mary Jones immediately gathered up the dissenters, Jesse and July, and drove to Savannah, where she confronted Mr. Yulee, the agent of the Freedmen's Bureau. According to Mary Jones's account, "he made some shifting remarks about 'public opinion' and its being customary to give 'half the crop,' etc." Mary Jones replied that the terms of the contract had been approved by a Federal officer. Was there a legal standard for contracts? she asked. No, there was none, the agent admitted.

"Is my contract, then, a legal one?"

"Yes, madam."

"Are the people, then, not bound to comply with its terms?"

"Certainly."

"I now, then sir, appeal to you as an agent of the bureau to restore order upon my plantation!"

The agent then summoned the rebellious Jesse and July and told them that if they did not observe the terms of the contract, he would have them put in a chain gang to work on repairing the streets of Savannah. Doubtless wondering anew at the strange ways of white people, they expressed their willingness to comply, and back at the plantation the indignant Mrs. Jones "told the people that in doubting my word they had offered me the greatest insult I ever received in my life; that I had considered them friends and treated them as such, giving them gallons of clabber every day and syrup once a week, with rice and extra dinners; but that now they were only laborers under contract, and only the law would rule between us. . . ." The fact was, of course, that it was virtually impossible to say what a fair contract was under the circumstances. Presumably it was what the field hands, informed of the resources of the plantation and the going rate for labor, could negotiate. But they lacked the information and the experience to carry on such a negotiation. When employers, North or South, believed it not only proper but *moral* to pay not a cent more than the minimum that would buy a man's labor, it would have been utopian to expect the average planter to pay his ex-slaves a fair wage if it had been possible to determine what a fair wage was. The system of "free labor" consisted, in large part, of the right of the employer to exploit his employees to the greatest degree possible. As we have noted in an earlier volume, the efforts of Northern workers to combine in order to raise their wages had been commonly judged by the courts to be illegal conspiracies.

Every plantation had a store where workers could buy a wide variety of goods, usually at exorbitant prices, to be charged against their wages. The tally at one plantation store against a black plowman included mackerel, sardines, candy, cheese, whiskey, tobacco, candles, a hat, a skillet, and eight rings, which were distributed to young black women on the plantation who caught his fancy. Not surprisingly many hands found that they had little money coming to them when the twice-yearly payday came. Ex-slaves who had only the sketchiest notion of the value of articles they desired and no notion of "deferred gratification" had to learn the hard way to refrain from purchasing all the alluring articles that the plantation store displayed. This was especially the case in the months following emancipation. Many freedmen and women were unable to calculate the value of objects they bought as against the wages due to them.

Under the contract system that came to prevail on the great majority of plantations, hands were paid from $10 to $15 a month, and a careful record was kept of the day's work. When payday came, half of all wages owed were held back against the fulfillment of the contract, or, in other words, to discourage hands from decamping in defiance of the terms of their contract. When freedmen did so, the nearest Freedmen's Bureau was usually asked to prevail upon them to return or, in extreme instances, to put them in jail if they refused. Where the lessees were former Northern officers, the Freedmen's Bureau was especially disposed to require strict observance of contracts if they seemed fairly drawn.

On many plantations a system of tickets was used, with one ticket issued for each day's work; at payday the tickets, with store charges deducted, could be cashed in. The more provident waited to make their purchases until they had been paid; they then would buy a cake of soap, some sugar, a paper of needles, or "two bits worth o' candy."

By 1866 in many states the Freedmen's Bureau was distributing more rations to whites than to blacks. In January, 1866, in Arkansas, for example, 59,532 rations were distributed to whites, 11,696 to freedmen, 4,663 to refugees. In Tennessee an agent of the Freedmen's

Bureau testified to a congressional committee that the poor whites of that state received ten times the number of rations issued to the freedmen.

The Department for Tennessee and Kentucky had 113,650 freedmen in its care. "These," the report noted, "are now disposed as follows: in military service, as soldiers, laundresses, cooks, officers' servants, and laborers in the various staff departments, 41,150; in cities, on plantations, and in freedmen's villages and cared for, 72,500." Of these latter, 62,300 were self-supporting—"the same as any industrial class anywhere—as planters, mechanics, barbers, hackmen, draymen, etc., conducting enterprises on their own responsibility, or as hired laborers." Government subsistence payments were made to 10,000 freedmen, and of these 3,000 were cultivating 4,000 acres of cotton and would pay back the government "advances." Some 7,200 were old, ill, or crippled. But even they had 500 acres of corn, 760 of vegetables, and 1,500 acres of cotton under cultivation. The cutting of wood had been an important subsidiary occupation for many freedmen. Like all such reports, the figures were doubtlessly more impressive than the true situation warranted, but they indicate that much had been done in that region to assist ex-slaves in the transition to freedom.

The Freedmen's Bureau was established by Congress initially for a year. Of its beginnings, General Howard declared: "It would have required more than human foresight to have wholly met the difficulties of this dark period of our Governmental history, but the friends of the measure hoped that . . . the experience of one year of active operation under the eye of our most energetic and able Secretary of War would demonstrate the value of the Bureau sufficiently to warrant at least another year's trial." A year later Howard had substantially revised his estimate of the amount of time required to complete the work of Reconstruction. He told a Cooper Union audience in March, 1866, "If we can hold a steady hand now, in five years there will be no need of a Government control over these people [the freedmen]. The military power can make it [work]." More than the initial year would be needed "but the leaven is working. The influx of men who believe in education, and the negroes who so greatly need it, will doubtless secure the desired end."

When Lyman Abbott reported to the international antislavery convention in Paris in the late summer of 1867 on the accomplishments of the Freedmen's Bureau, he pointed out that its work would have been impossible without the support of "nearly every philanthropic, Christian and religious organization." They combined forces with the "non-ecclesiastical" freedmen's aid societies, which united their efforts under the banner of the American Freedmen's Aid Union. Of the thirteen hundred teachers who had been sent into the South, nearly all had been sustained by "voluntary societies," Abbott pointed out. "The books have been furnished, the school apparatus has been provided, the ground has been surveyed.... In the various cities, towns and villages of the North, local societies have been organized, chiefly among the ladies, who, by sewing Societies, fairs, church contributions, and other instrumentalities, obtain the money to carry on this work." In many instances a particular town undertook the support of a teacher and was rewarded by vivid accounts of the teacher's experiences.

From July, 1865, to July, 1867, Abbott stated, the government had expended roughly $5,278,000 on services to the freedmen. In the period from 1862 to 1867 "the amount in money and kind contributed through the various Freedmen's, Missionary and Church Associations, and by private benevolence" was estimated at more than $5,500,000 of which more than $1,000,000 had been contributed from abroad. In Albion Tourgée's words, "the Freedmen's Bureau acted as the black man's guardian and friend, looked after his interests in contracts, prohibited the law's barbarity, and insisted stubbornly that the freedman was a man, and must be treated as such."

That the Freedmen's Bureau was an agency inadequate to the task at hand is certainly not surprising. What is unquestionable is that despite its numerous failures and shortcomings, the situation in the South would have been infinitely more chaotic without it. Its accomplishments were enormous, and its influence pervaded every area of Southern life. When all is said and done, the greatest tribute to the efficacy of the bureau was the hostility of the South toward it.

In the interminable debate during the war on what was "to be done" with the freed slave, many white Americans, including Lincoln, looked toward a large-scale program of voluntary colonization on the ground that the end of the war would be marked by the application of vastly more efficient farming techniques to Southern agriculture, thus resulting in a surplus of unskilled labor. No one seriously contemplated moving black families north to compete for jobs in the depressed labor markets of industrial cities. Charles Francis Adams, Jr., observing the effects of army discipline on black morale and the black "self-image," as we would say today, believed that the freed blacks should be recruited into the army and, upon their discharge, formed into agricultural communes. Others recommended wholesale migration to the unsettled lands of the West—to Nebraska, the Dakotas, New Mexico Territory. This had already been attempted, before the war, with small groups of manumitted slaves, with results that were discouraging. Early in the war the *New York Anglo-African* published an editorial entitled "What Shall Be Done with the Slaves?" Its remedy, which was soon taken up by black leaders and white sympathizers, was to distribute the land confiscated from rebel landlords to the slaves who had worked it for so many generations. "What course can be clearer, what course more politic?" the editor asked. "What course will be so just, so thoroughly conducive to the public weal and national advancement, as that the government should immediately bestow these lands upon these freed men who know best how to cultivate them. . . ."

George Julian, the Indiana abolitionist, in an address to his colleagues in Congress, in January, 1865, made the first serious proposal offered in that body for the redistribution of rebel lands to the veterans of the war. "The people expect," he declared, "that Congress will provide for parceling out the forfeited and confiscated lands of rebels in small homesteads among the soldiers and seamen of the war, as a fit reward for their valor, and as a security against the ruinous monopoly of the soil in the South." According to Julian, "the people" also expected "the complete enfranchisement of the negro."

Wendell Phillips was equally adamant: "Now, while those large estates remain in the hands of the defeated slave oligarchy, its power is not destroyed. But let me confiscate the land of the South, and put it into the hands of the negroes and white men who have fought for it, and you may go to sleep with your parchments. . . . You do not build governments like clap-board houses; you plant them like an oak. Plant a hundred thousand negro farmers and by their side a hundred thousand white soldiers, and I will risk the South, Davis and all."

The black lawyer John Rock sounded the same note. There had been talk of compensating slaveowners for the loss of their slaves. Rock mocked the notion. "It is the slave," he declared, "who ought to be compensated. The property of the South is by right the property of the slave."

Daniel Foster, a dedicated abolitionist who commanded the 3rd North Carolina Colored Volunteers, wrote in 1864: "The slaves, with almost entire unanimity, long for a little land, that they may own a home of their own. I trust the Government will make provision for them to buy land when they wish." The *New Orleans Tribune* took up the issue, proposing that the government divide confiscated plantations into five-acre lots and distribute them to freedmen.

Increasingly the Radical Republicans called for the breaking up of Southern plantations and the redistribution of the land to Union veterans, freed slaves, and poor whites. "The freedmen . . . who are on the spot," the *Independent* declared, "will form the nucleus of the new society. . . . Next the soldiers, sailors and laborers of our national forces, without distinction of color or race, are entitled to homesteads at the disposal of an appreciative country. Lastly, the field should be thrown open to the best stock of our Northern States, who will seek a new Eldorado." The "radical reconstructors" were divided on how much should be done for the freedman. Too little would leave him dependent on his former masters; too much would make him dependent on the Federal government. It was a delicate equation. Francis Wayland, former president of Brown University, wrote to a missionary friend at Port Royal: "To free the negroes and pay them wages for their labor, will be hardly a blessing, unless you teach them the responsibilities of freedom. If they begin by having such wages as they never dreamed of, and besides this, have their *clothes* given to them, they will be ruined. They will expect it, and be idle, loafing beggars, without an atom of self-respect." Needless to say, Wayland was opposed to any distribution of land to the freedmen.

Many Republicans who were opposed to giving land to freedmen believed they should be assisted in buying portions of the plantations on which they had once worked as slaves. The alternatives were selling the land to Northern speculators and investors or holding it until the rights of its former owners had been determined. Many freedmen had been encouraged to cultivate abandoned lands at Port Royal, and Mansfield French estimated that a thousand Sea Island blacks had taken up such land and, in many instances, built their cabins on it.

The policy of the government was marked by excessive vacillation. Salmon Chase on his tour of the South was besieged on the one hand by prospective Northern purchasers of Southern lands and on the other by the missionaries and teachers of Port Royal, who espoused the principle of preemption, which would allow blacks to purchase land at a purely nominal cost on credit with generous provisions for paying off their indebtedness.

Although the legal aspects of the matter were complicated, the administration did take certain tentative steps in the direction of trying to provide land for ex-slaves. In June, 1862, Congress gave the president the power to calculate the taxes due the government and offer for sale at public auction the lands of those who were judged delinquent. On the Sea Islands some 16,749 abandoned acres were sold, of which 2,000 were bought by freedmen, the rest going to Northern speculators. The white teachers and missionaries on the islands were indignant and raised a considerable ruckus, finally prevailing on the government to allow black families to claim up to 40 acres of abandoned land at the cost of $1.25 an acre.

The tax commissioners and the speculators together mustered enough support to defeat the plan, and at a subsequent sale of some 60,000 additional acres, freedmen were able to purchase only 2,750. One of those unable to purchase land, a farmer named Don Carlos Butler, who had been a slave of Theodosia Burr, Aaron Burr's beautiful and talented daughter, wrote Lincoln in May, 1864, asking "whether the land will be sold from under us or no, or whether it will be sold to us at all. I should like to buy the very spot where I live," Butler wrote. "It ain't got but six acres, and I have cotton planted on it, and very fine cotton too; and potatoes and corn coming on very pretty. If we colored people have land we shall do very well—there is no fear of that."

Another Sea Islands black dictated a letter to the white woman who had been a teacher on his island—"My Dear Young Missus." He had, he reminded her, been a leader in the church. Now he was in danger of losing the land he was farming, and he appealed to "one of dese yere little white sisters . . . dat the Lord sends from the Nort for school we chilen, to write oona for me to ax of onna so please an' will be so kind . . . to speak to Linkum and tell him how we po' folks tank him and de Lord. . . . *Do*, my missus, tell Linkum dat we wants land—dis bery land dat is rich wid de seat ob we face. . . . We born her; we parents' graves here . . . dis yer our home. . . . Where Linkum? We cry to him, but he too far for hear we. . . . Do missus speak ter um for we, an' ax Linkum for stretch out he hand an' make dese yer missionaries cut de land so dat we able for buy. Speak softly next time you meets Massa Linkum. Tell him bout me, and de Lord will keep you warm under he feathers, he will gather oona to he breast, for he love dem what help de poor."

As we have seen, Sherman in his march to the sea acquired

thousands of ex-slaves. When he reached Savannah, he was at a loss as to how to provide for them. The men and women who had attached themselves to his army could hardly be sent back to their plantations. Savannah did not have the resources to provide for them. Stanton, appealed to by Sherman, hurried to Savannah. The general and secretary of war met there with a delegation of black ministers, fifteen of them former slaves. The ministers proposed that land be distributed to the freedmen. "The best way we can take care of ourselves," one of them declared, "is to have land, and turn it and till it by labor—that is, by the labor of the women, men, and children, and old men—and we can soon maintain ourselves and have something to spare. . . . We want to be placed on land until we are able to buy it and make it our own." The consequence of the meeting was Order No. 15, issued by Sherman, which set aside the coast and riverbanks thirty miles inland from Charleston to Jacksonville for freed slaves. Each family could take up to forty acres until Congress "shall regulate the title." General Rufus Saxton was put in charge of the distribution of land, and within six months more than 40,000 freedmen and their families were settled on the designated lands.

When planters began to return to the Sea Islands to reclaim their lands, a crisis followed. General Howard, whom the freedmen trusted, was sent to tell them they must vacate the land they had come to think of as their own. When he addressed a group of freedmen, he got a hostile and defiant reception. "No! no!" one voice called out. "Why, General Howard, why do you take away our lands? You take them from us who are true, always true to the Government! You give them to our all-time enemies! That is not right!" Colonel James Beecher, Harriet Beecher Stowe's younger brother, acting as an agent of the Freedmen's Bureau, found himself in the middle of the controversy. As the freedmen grew more and more obdurate, Beecher became increasingly touchy and indignant. He had his orders, unpleasant as they were, and he expected the freedmen to comply. Meanwhile, the administration, increasingly annoyed with Saxton's disposition to side with the freedmen, removed him from his office, and his successor issued an order declaring: "The former owners of the land in the Sea Islands on the coast of South Carolina and the owners of land on the Main embraced in General Sherman's Special Field Orders will be permitted to return and occupy their lands."

By the end of 1866 only 1,565 out of more than 40,000 freedmen still occupied the land allotted to them in South Carolina. The situation was somewhat similar in Virginia, where after Hampton had been burned and abandoned by the rebels, the government had distributed the land in and about the town to some 800 black families. Now they, too, were told they must vacate or return to work as contract labor for their former masters. In a petition to the government, the black farmers of the Hampton area described their efforts to establish churches and schools and then "Resolved, that we will not leave our happy homes unless compelled to do so by legal authority . . . we will oppose, in all legal ways, the opening of the decrees of confiscation."

South Carolina, under the influence of the predominantly black postwar legislature, was the only Southern state to undertake to facilitate the buying of farms by freedmen. An agency was set up to purchase plantations, divide them up, and sell them on easy terms to small farmers. Groups like the Belle Ville Farmers Association operated under severe handicaps because white bankers commonly refused to lend them money. The Atlantic Land Company, having devoted several years and a substantial sum of money to attempt to establish a cooperative plantation, lost everything when the Charleston banks refused a critically needed loan. In Colleton County, another cooperative effort described as "Colored Communism" was actually a combination of individual enterprise and mutual support. A plantation was purchased, and the land distributed equally among the investors, each of whom was free to grow whatever crop he wished and dispose of it as he judged best. The sick, if they could not care for themselves, were cared for by the society.

In Mississippi a more ambitious project was launched on a plantation which had belonged to Jefferson Davis and his brother, Joseph. Benjamin Montgomery, who had been a Davis slave, advertised in the *New Era* in 1866 that he and a group of fellow entrepreneurs had secured leases on the Hurricane and Briarfield plantations formerly belonging to Joseph Davis. He intended to "organize a community composed exclusively of colored people to occupy and cultivate such plantations and invites the co-operation of such as are recommended by honesty, industry, sobriety and intelligence. A tax to be assessed by the council will be collected to provide for the education of the young and the comfortable maintenance of the aged and helpless." By 1870 the undertaking was such a success that the renters were able to buy the plantations, and they were a magnet for visitors from the North who were concerned with plans to establish freed blacks on a sound economic basis. Frances Harper, a black poet who visited Davis Bend, as the plantation was called, wrote ecstatically to a friend that hundreds of black people were farming between five and six thousand acres containing schools and churches in a venture that turned over hundreds of thousands of dollars yearly in goods and produce. Montgomery's wife and children were as actively involved as he, both supervising the work of others and themselves joining in. One daughter was postmistress and assistant bookkeeper. Another kept the community store. Among the founders of the association were individuals clearly familiar with the New England town, for the association's bylaws provided for a "Road Master to see all Public Roads cleared of brush and dirt . . . [the] Hog and Cattle Reeve to keep all hogs, cattle & horses within enclosures" and "the Market Inspector to see that no diseased meats or vegetables are disposed for sale. . . ."

The simple fact was that the dimensions of freedom seemed infinite; they comprehended every aspect of existence, exhilarating, mysterious, terrifying. Relations between black people and white people in the South had always been filled with nuances and subtleties; things unspoken, glances and gestures decipherable only by the initiated. Now this old code had to be rewritten or at least reinterpreted, new signals devised, new social forms adumbrated, new burdens assumed, new forms of pain endured. Whatever might be said of the horrors of slave life, on the simple level of animal needs it offered a substantial degree of certitude and security for the more fortunate. Now nothing was certain or secure. Freedom, it turned out, was rather like emerging from the womb into a largely incomprehensible world where the Christian religion was the only sure reference point. In the long travail of man, loosely denominated "history," there has been no more profound and poignant experience than that which befell those black Americans who, having been slaves, were now free.

36

The Postwar South

Sidney George Fisher spoke for what may well have been a majority of white Americans when he wrote in his diary a few months after the end of the war: "It seems our fate never to get rid of the Negro question. No sooner have we abolished slavery than a party, which seems to be growing [in] power, proposes Negro suffrage, so that the problem—What shall we do with the Negro?—seems as far from being settled as ever. In fact it is *incapable* of any solution that will satisfy both North & South, because of the permanent difference of race. No position for the Negro that would satisfy the South would agree with enlightened opinion in the North. But how can the North enforce its views? Only by such an exertion of the power of the general government as would be inconsistent with its plan & theory. The South, moreover, when restoration is fully complete and accomplished, will again hold the balance of power, will make another bargain with a northern party, as they did before, the condition of which will be as before—support in all the southern plans for governing the Negro race. . . . I see no way out of these difficulties consistent with the preservation of the Union & free government." Yet that was precisely the question—the "Negro question"—to which the new administration had to address itself.

Aside from the spectacle Andrew Johnson had made of himself at Lincoln's second inauguration, the best-known facts about the new President were that he had been an illiterate tailor and that his invalid wife had taught him to read and write. David Macrae described him as a man with "small, quick, restless" eyes, "peering and glittering from between his puffy eyelids like the eyes of an Indian, conveying a look of deepness, vigilance, and subtlety."

Carl Schurz had met Johnson, then governor of Tennessee, at Nashville after the defeat of Bragg. "His appearance was not prepossessing," Schurz wrote. He reminded Schurz of Stephen Douglas, but without Douglas's "force and vivacity." Schurz sensed rather something "sullen, something betokening a strong will inspired by bitter feelings. I could well imagine him," he wrote, "leading with vindictive energy an uprising of a lower order of society against an aristocracy from whose lordly self-assertion he had suffered, and whose pride he was bent on humiliating." When Schurz wrote those words, he had the benefit of hindsight, which may have induced him to alter his original impression, but it was a view shared by others, some of them admirers of the Tennesseean. "He was a demonstratively fierce Union man," Schurz added, "—not upon anti-slavery grounds, but from constitutional reasons and from hatred of the slave-holding aristocracy, the oppressors and misleaders of the common people. . . . When, in the course of our conversations, I suggested, as I sometimes did, that there were in the reconstruction of the Union other objects to be accomplished fully as important as the punishment of the traitors, he would treat such suggestions with polite indulgence. . . ."

Although Johnson did not deliver a formal inaugural address, he issued a brief statement that was not without its own eloquence. "The best energies of my life," he declared, "have been spent in endeavoring to establish and perpetuate the principles of free government, and I believe that the Government in passing through its present perils will settle down upon principles consonant with popular rights more permanent and enduring than heretofore. I must be permitted to say, if I understand the feelings of my own heart, that I have long labored to ameliorate and elevate the condition of the great mass of the American people. Toil and an honest advocacy of the great principles of free government have been my lot. Duties have been mine; consequences are God's."

As vice-president Johnson had called for a punitive policy toward the leaders of the rebellion, declaring: "Treason must be made odious,

and traitors must be punished and impoverished. Their great plantations must be seized, and divided into small farms, and sold to honest
and industrious men. The day for protecting the lands and Negroes of
those authors of rebellion is past." James Blaine reported a similar
conversation between Benjamin Wade and Johnson not long after the
President had taken office. While Johnson, according to Wade, wished
for executions, a "bloody assize," Wade argued that the hanging of a
"baker's dozen," including Davis, Toombs, Slidell, and Mason, would
satisfy Northern opinion. More, indeed, would offend it.

For the abolitionists, of course, the critical issue was the new
President's position on the rights of the freedmen. When Sumner and
Chase visited Johnson to sound him out on the subject, they found him
thoroughly responsive. The only difference, it appeared, between the
President and his visitors was that he was anxious to try to persuade the
Southerners themselves to take the initiative in extending the rights of
citizenship to their ex-slaves rather than impose such rights by congressional fiat. To this end it was decided to send Chase on a tour
through the South to spread the word of the President's wishes and try
the gentle art of persuasion. Although Sumner doubted that *equality
before the law*" could be achieved "without *Federal authority*," he was
willing to experiment. At the end of the discussion Johnson told Chase
and Sumner, "There is no difference between us."

When Congress adjourned in the early summer of 1865, the
abolitionist-Republicans left Washington in high spirits, confident that
the President would do everything in his power to protect the rights of
the newly freed blacks of the South.

It was in this spirit that Chief Justice Salmon Chase undertook his
presidential mission. Accompanying Chase was a young newspaper
reporter for Horace Greeley's *New York Tribune,* Whitelaw Reid. Only
twenty-nine at the time, the son of pious Presbyterian parents who had
a farm near Xenia, Ohio, Reid had attended Miami University and
become editor of the *Xenia News* at the age of twenty-one. A friend of
Sumner's and Henry Winter Davis's, he was also acquainted with John
Hay and John Nicolay. William Dean Howells described him as "a tall,
graceful youth with an enviable black moustache and imperial, wearing his long hair in Southern fashion, and carrying himself with . . .
native grace. . . ."

After completing his official tour with Chase, Reid set out on his
own to see the South without the constraints inevitably imposed by
Chase's office. Perhaps his most significant conclusion was that in the

period immediately after Appomattox, the South, still in a state of shock and feeling thoroughly defeated, was in a mood to comply with whatever dictates or directives came from the Federal government. In Reid's words, "the National Government could at that time have prescribed no conditions for the return of the Rebel States which they would not have promptly accepted. They expected nothing; were prepared for the worst; would have been thankful for anything. . . . They asked no terms, made no conditions. They were defeated and helpless—they submitted. . . . Filled with the hatred to the negroes, nearly always inspired in any ruling class by the loss of accustomed power over inferiors, they nevertheless yielded to the Freedmen's Bureau, and acquiesced in the necessity for securing civil rights to their slaves. . . . They were shocked at the suggestion; but if the Government required it, they were willing to submit. The whole body politic was as wax." A few months later Reid found that Southerners had begun to talk of their rights. A note of resistance and defiance appeared in their conversations and in the public print. The North had insisted the South had no right to secede from the Union. It had proved its point or, if not proved it, at least enforced it. Now the Southern states must be taken back without stipulations or penalties. The Constitution required it.

Port Royal was one of the first stops on Justice Chase's Southern tour. Whitelaw Reid described the scene of the chief justice's meeting in a Beaufort church with a substantial portion of the island's black population. "Some, black and stalwart, were dressed like quiet country farm laborers, and had probably come in from the country, or had been field hands before the war. Others, lighter in color and slighter in build, were dressed in broadcloth, with flashy scarfs and gaudy pins. . . . Others looked like the more intelligent class of city laborers; and there were a few old patriarchs who might recollect the days of Denmark Vesey. On the other side of the church was a motley but brilliant army of bright-colored turbans . . . and hats of all shapes that have prevailed within the memory of this generation. . . . Some of them wore kid gloves, all were gaudily dressed, and, a few . . . had the air and bearing of ladies." When General Saxton introduced the chief justice, the audience cheered long and enthusiastically. Chase yielded to the calls for a speech, his only one of the entire trip, advising his auditors to "industry, economy, and good morals" and expressing his personal support for their right to vote. "A great race, numbering four millions, has been suddenly enfranchised." The whole world was watching to see the consequences. "Your enemies say you will be disorderly, improvident, lazy; that wages will not tempt you to work; that you will starve rather than labor. . . . You need not feel much anxiety about what people say of you. Feel rather that, under God, your salvation must come of yourselves."

The Reverend Dr. Richard Fuller was a South Carolinian of antislavery sentiment who had inherited a large Sea Island plantation and done everything in his power to improve the condition of the slaves on his estate. Although he had responded to a call to a church in Baltimore, his memory remained green in Beaufort, and when he returned on the occasion of Chief Justice Chase's visit, it was a great event for the islanders. Whitelaw Reid wrote that "eyes grew moist and ancient negresses could be heard vehemently whispering, 'Bress de Lord, bress de Lord!' 'Hebenly Marster!' "

An old man rose to lead the company in singing:

> Ma-a-a-assa Fullah a sittin' on de tree ob life;
> Ma-a-a-assa Fullah a sittin' on de tree ob life,
> Roll, Jordan, roll.

When the ceremonies were over, his former slaves crowded around the beleaguered Fuller as though they could hardly believe he was real. "They pushed up against him," Reid wrote, "kissed his hands, passed their fingers over his hair, crowded about, eager to get a word of recognition. 'Sire, yau 'member me, Massa Rich'd; I'm Tom.' 'Laws, Massa Rich'd, I mind ye when ye's a little 'un.'" A Union officer, watching the scene, said to Reid, "I haven't liked him much," but "I'd give all I'm worth, or ever hope to be worth, in the world, to be loved by as many people as love him."

Fuller wrote of his visit: "I never saw as much land there under cultivation—never saw the same general evidences of prosperity, and never saw the negroes themselves appearing so well or so contented." One thing seemed clear: Whenever freedmen had their own land, they worked far more conscientiously than when they were simply under contract to a plantation owner. The islands' blacks had saved $156,000, deposited in their own bank.

A critical symbol of freedom for the ex-slaves was the use of money. Whitelaw Reid, present at a plantation payday, wrote that those who received their money "looked at it with a puzzled air, took the money as if it were fragile glass, and must be handled very carefully or it would be broken, and went off very much with the air one always imagines, the man must have worn who drew the elephant in a raffle."

The uneasiness of whites over the determination of freedmen to buy guns was understandable. As slaves blacks had been prohibited, under penalty of death, to own guns. The gun was a symbol of the white man's power and authority, and it is not surprising that free blacks regarded guns as marks of their freedom. Mary Jones wrote her daughter that the blacks of Montevideo, once the crop was in and they had been paid, went to Savannah and bought guns, although they needed bread. Muskets, double-barreled shotguns, and pistols were much in demand.

As we have noted earlier in the matter of the Port Royal blacks, attention was focused on the issue of whether the freedmen and women would work. The evidence was, not surprisingly, mixed. Even some blacks accepted the stereotype of their race as incurably indolent. A black brakeman of a Georgia railroad said to Whitelaw Reid, "One-half dese niggers ought to be killed, any how. Dey don't do nuffin' but hang around and steal from dem dat work." An overseer named Jim on a Louisiana plantation expressed his disgust at the refusal of the freed blacks to work. "I sposed, now we's all free," Reid reported the overseer as saying, "dey'd jump into de work keen, to make all de money dey could. But it was juss no work at all. I got so 'scouraged sometimes I's ready to gib it all up, and tell 'em to starve if dey wanted to. . . . When I scold and swear at 'em dey say, 'we's free now, and we's not work unless we pleases.' Sah, I got so sick of der wuflessness dat I sometimes almost wished it was old slavery times again."

As Whitelaw Reid noted of the freedmen, "The uncertainty of their tenure of the land, the constant return of old proprietors and the general confusion and uncertainty as to the ownership of real estate, under the confiscation and abandoned property laws, combined to unsettle both them and the Superintendents of Freedmen, who are trying to care for them."

The blacks of Wilmington, North Carolina, showed much more sophistication than their country cousins. They formed a Union League to "stimulate to industry and to secure combined effort for suffrage," Whitelaw Reid wrote, "without which they insist that they will soon be practically enslaved again." A delegation of Wilmington blacks visited Chief Justice Chase and, in Reid's words, "certainly looked as well and talked as lucidly as any of the poor whites would have done. There are very few of the whites," Reid added, "who encourage them; but, in general, the bitterest prejudice against these black Unionists, is still among those who have been the only white Unionists—the often-described poor white trash." The blacks told Chase that for all practical purposes slavery still existed; "the negroes are worked as hard as ever—in some cases a little harder—and they have no more protection from the cruelty of the whites than ever."

One of the ironic twists in the situation was that since slaves were no longer property, whites were more disposed to kill them if infuriated by resistance or impudence than they had been when the slaves were worth $1,000 or more. In Salisbury, North Carolina, Reid was told that two "prominent men" were on trial for killing a black man, and Temple Neeley, one of "the wealthiest, most refined and respectable young ladies" in the county, was under indictment for shooting a young black woman who had tried to intervene to prevent her child from being whipped. In New Orleans, Reid heard of the shooting and killing of an ex-slave who had refused to take off his hat in the presence of his former master. Such cases were certainly exceptional, but there is no question that freedmen and women were constantly subject to violence at the hands of whites. "I tell you, sah," a freedman told Reid, "we ain't noways safe, 'long as dem people makes de laws we's got to be governed by. We's got to hab a voice in de 'pintin' of de law-makers. Den we knows our frens, and whose hans we's safe in."

In Savannah, Chase received numerous delegations of intelligent and articulate blacks, and with several of them he debated the question of Negro suffrage. They were clearly well informed and capable of exercising the franchise responsibly, but what about their illiterate fellows on isolated plantations who were sunk in the most abysmal ignorance? How could it be argued that they should vote, too? To this his black visitors had a ready answer: "Oh, we'll tell them how to vote, sir! we have means of reaching them; and *they'll follow us sooner than they will their old masters or any white man.*" After all, no one knew the white man better than the black. His life had depended on making a careful study of the characters and temperament of white men and women. "Some of our people stand behind these men at the table," a freedman told Chase, "and hear 'em talk; we see 'em in the house and by the wayside; and we *know* 'em from skin to core, better than you do or can do, till you live among 'em as long, and see as much of 'em as we have." It was a remarkable colloquy, summing up, in a few words, the whole history of the patient study of whites by blacks. To blacks, whites were, first of all, figures of power and danger, but then they were figures of absurdity, of endless hilarious mirth, an infinitely strange breed, accounts of whose behavior could reduce blacks to helpless laughter. White evasions and hypocrisies, white formalities, habits, customs, when not threatening to blacks, seemed most often ridiculous or sidesplittingly funny.

A delegation of blacks from "the country" complained to Chase that their old masters were still exploiting them, whipping them and doing their best to "retain them in a state of actual, if not nominal slavery." Those who had tried to set up for themselves cutting and selling wood had been harassed and threatened. "Others," Reid reported, "had tales of atrocities to tell, whippings and cutting off of ears and the like, for crimes of going where they pleased and assuming to act as freemen. . . . No one," he concluded, "who saw or conversed with the leading Savannah negroes, would doubt their entire capacity to support themselves. They were all well-dressed, in clothes bought by their own earnings; many of them were living in large and well-furnished houses; some owned their own residences, and not a few had quite handsome incomes."

Yet Georgia whites displayed the same prejudices as those of Virginia and Carolina. They indicated that they had every intention of keeping blacks in a state of subordination as close as possible to the condition of slavery. Above all, it was clear, to Reid at least, that most of them had no intention of "working" themselves; working was not "a part of their philosophy of life. Work is for 'niggers'—not for white men." One aristocratic Georgian told Reid loftily, "I'm no book-keeper or counter-jumper. I never learned a trade; I have no profession. I own these lands, and, if the niggers can be made to work, they'll support me; but there's nothing else I know anything about, except managing a plantation."

In New Orleans Chase and Reid went to a fair held by Catholic blacks of the city, most of whom spoke French fluently. The fair was held in the former home of an ex-Senator from Louisiana, Pierre Soulé. Soulé, who had been mixed up discreditably in the infamous Ostend Manifesto and was considered by many to have inherited the mantle of John Calhoun as a secessionist leader, had fled to Mexico after the war, and the black elite of the city were holding a bazaar in his abandoned home to support a school for the children of ex-slaves. Whitelaw Reid was completely captivated by the beauty of the "elegantly dressed ladies, beautiful with a beauty beside which that of the North is wax-work," he wrote enthusiastically; "with great, swimming, lustrous eyes, half-veiled behind long pendant lashes, and arched with coal-black eyebrows. . . . Many of them had been educated in Paris, and more than one Parisian wardrobe shimmered that evening under the . . . chandeliers. . . . But they were only niggers. They might be presented to the Empress Eugénie; they might aspire to the loftiest connections in Europe; but they were not fit to appear in a white man's house in New Orleans." Reid puzzled over the bizarre picture of "negroes raffling fans and picture-frames and sets of jewelry . . . ; negroes selling ice-cream in the Soulé dining-room; negroes at his piano; negroes in his library . . . as handsome, as elegantly dressed, and in many respects almost as brilliant a party as [Soulé] himself ever gathered beneath his hospitable roof."

Reid and Chase were frequently asked the critical question by the freedmen they encountered on their journey: What good did it do them to be free in a region where status rested on landownership unless they owned the land which they had made productive? "Gib us our own land," one spokesman said, "and we take care of ourselves; but widout land, de ole massas can hire us or starve us, as dey please."

The Convention of Colored People that met in Charleston in 1865 framed "An Address to the White Inhabitants of South Carolina," in which the delegates emphasized both their conciliatory spirit and their sense of themselves as Americans. "The dust of our fathers mingles with yours in the same graveyards; you have transmitted into our veins much of the rich blood which courses through yours; we talk the same language, and worship the same God; our mothers nursed you, and satisfied your hunger with our pap; our association with you has taught us to revere you. This is your country but it is ours too; you were born here, so were we; your fathers fought for it, but our fathers fed them." From a black convention in Kentucky came a similar manifesto: "We love our country and her institutions. We are proud of her greatness, her glory and her might. We are intensely American."

Tennessee and Kentucky, although slaveholding, were frontier states with strong Union sentiment. There were relatively few great plantations; most of the farms were of moderate size. The "plantation culture" of the old slaveholding states was missing from the border states—the high style of living, the intricate network of old families, the legions of household slaves, the "society." The people of eastern Tennessee, for example, were described by Whitelaw Reid as living "very comfortably" in "a rude way." But Southern sympathies ran deep, nonetheless, and in every border state "civil war" was much more of a reality than in the Old South, where the almost universal determination to resist the Northern "aggression" united the population in a war against the invaders. In the border states it was far more often neighbor against neighbor, towns and counties divided against themselves in the bitterest of internecine warfare. Reid noted that Tennesseeans who had gone off to fight for the Confederacy often returned not only to encounter open hostility but to be told that they must move elsewhere on pain of being shot. Some, indeed, were shot first. But strong Union feelings stopped short of sympathy for freed blacks. Here the poor-white hatred of Negroes was unrelieved by the sentimental ties between master and slave that often softened the harshness of the relationship in the older seaboard states.

As Reid's account makes clear, the most basic fact about the post-Civil War South was the physical devastation of the region. The psychological consequences of this devastation were, not surprisingly, profound. A residue of bitterness and hostility exists more than a hundred years later. The Reverend David Macrae wrote: "When the war closed in 1865, the South presented a spectacle of wreck and prostration probably without parallel in modern times. . . . The people had shared in the general wreck, and looked poverty-stricken, careworn, and dejected." First there were the discharged soldiers and the maimed veterans. "And then each day as they came, homeless, penniless, clothesless, with the past an awful quivering wreck, and the future a blank whose gloom was only made the deeper by memory of former happiness & peace and the anticipation of greater wrongs and suffering, added another pang," Emma Holmes wrote. Her brother was not the only one who talked of fleeing the orbit of Union authority. "All talked of emigration somewhere beyond Yankee rule," she noted. Some defectors invited the opprobrium of their families and neighbors by heading north on the shrewd calculation that the South was ruined and they must seek their fortunes elsewhere. Others lapsed into a "state of utter passiveness without anything to do to support themselves & families." Still others turned to any task at hand. Gentlemen, who had never done anything more strenuous than ride to hounds, cut and hauled firewood to work on the repair of roads or clerked in stores. The possession of a mule or a scrawny horse was a lifesaver since the animal and its owner could contract out to haul crops to market or to plow. An enterprising soul traveled north and came back with a machine to straighten out railroad rails. Soon he had a crew at work rebuilding critical railroad lines. When gentlemen seemed paralyzed by the extremity of their situation, the more intelligent and energetic (and sometimes the less scrupulous) of the poorer class of whites, held down for so long by a rigid class structure, pushed forward to take advantage of opportunities created by the collapse of the old order.

In Charleston old Edmund Ruffin shot himself. Others reacted with rage; still others, with passive despair. Some, in the opinion at least of their former slaves, died of broken hearts. One plantation mistress walked past her slaves, exclaiming, "Damn you, you are free now," and others "jest walked up an' down out in the yard a-carrin'-on, talkin' an' a-ravin'." When Billy Ninnely returned to his plantation and found the slaves departing, he slashed his throat, leaving a note saying that he could not bear to live because the slaves were freed. The reaction of the planters depended, in large part, upon their age. Many of the younger masters and their wives, like Minor and Elizabeth Meriwether, showed a courageous determination to build new lives. The old owners felt that their last years, instead of being spent in peacefulness and prosperity, were to be years of hardship and danger. For all practical purposes their lives were over, ended in want and desolation.

To those determined to reconstruct the old order in a form as close as possible to the original, the suppression of the freedmen and women was, of course, an essential task. The new-old order must be built on the continued dependence and subordination of black people. That there might be another course was never seriously considered by most whites.

There were those, perhaps a minority, who wished to put the war behind them and devote all their energy to creating a new life, and there were those who could not cope with the new reality; they created a world of nostalgia, of glorious memories, often considerably embellished, of the way things were "before the war." Emma Holmes spoke for the latter when she noted in her diary: "Everybody or almost everybody seems to be trying to forget the war & the past four years of agony & bloodshed, but I never can & rather cherish every memory connected with it." The new spirit of unsentimental realism was typified for Emma by her friend Lizzie Burnet. When Emma spoke with veneration of old Edmund Ruffin, who had fired the first shot at Fort Sumter and then shot himself when Lee surrendered, Lizzie

Burnet referred to him contemptuously as an "old fool." Emma was shocked. She had always "loved & honored the heroic old man."

Many Southerners talked of migrating to Brazil or of following Bedford Forrest, Jubal Early, and John Magruder to Mexico to fight for the emperor Maximilian, who found himself opposed by Mexican revolutionaries. A few wanted to get away from "sassy free niggers" by going North. Judah Benjamin slipped off to England, where he sought admission to the "English Bar."

Charles Colcock Jones went to New York to try to make his living as a lawyer. When he got there, Charles wrote to his mother, asking her to try to engage the sometimes errant Adeline to come to New York to cook for the family. Polly had joined Silvia as a nurse for the Joneses' children, and Charles Jones expressed his regret that the death of his ex-servant, George, had prevented him also from joining the New York establishment. A year after the end of the war Charles Colcock Jones and his wife had, as their servants in their house on Eighty-fourth Street, three of their former slaves. There were many similar cases in every large Northern city and, of course, in Southern cities as well.

The plight of the South struck close to home for Sidney George Fisher, so many of whose friends were Southerners. One, Williams Middleton, was the grandson of Henry Middleton, one of the Founders, and the son of Henry Middleton, who had been governor of South Carolina, Congressman, U.S. minister to Russia, and a leader of the Union faction in his state. Fisher heard that Middleton barely escaped with his life from the vengeance of his slaves, who had burned the famous family mansion with its treasury of fine paintings, silver, and imported furniture. Before the house was burned, Middleton had sent his wife and children off to a house in a small village. On the way they had been intercepted and robbed of everything but the clothes on their backs. Williams Middleton went through the harrowing experience of being put on trial for his life by his slaves, who debated in a mock court the arguments pro and con for taking his life, weighing his kindnesses against his severities. Three times the "court" sentenced him to hanging and three times changed its decision. When he was at last free to follow his wife, with such personal belongings as he could carry, he was intercepted and robbed by guerrilla raiders and escaped with his life only by taking refuge in a swamp, where he remained for days without food until a passerby rescued him.

Dr. William Byrd Page, a Philadelphian who went to Mississippi at the beginning of the war to prevent the confiscation by the Confederacy of his wife's plantation near Natchez, returned to Philadelphia for a visit. When Sidney George Fisher saw him, Page told Fisher that the "privation & suffering" around Natchez were "chiefly among people of property, caused by the loss of articles supplied by commerce —luxuries & refinements for the most part—and by the desertion of household servants. . . ." Page kept his former slaves, paid them wages, and planted a crop which paid him well.

The veterans came back, many wounded, all ragged and impoverished, to desolated homesteads. Emma Holmes's brother, Alester, "mere skin and bone from chill & fever," came home, "having walked over 60 miles and lost all save what was on his back." Returning soldiers and especially officers were liable to be waylaid by bushwhackers and robbed of every meager possession they owned—including, sometimes, the very clothes on their backs—or shot. Although Alester was too weak to walk, he talked of going to the Trans-Mississippi to join Jefferson Davis, who, it was said, had with him a cavalry troop of some 3,000 men and the Confederate gold that he had carried off from Richmond.

In the midst of ruin and despair there circulated stories of Confederate officers and public officials who were trying to batten on the common misery. Emma Holmes noted in her diary that corruption seemed to exist everywhere, "and the greater as the rank ascended —everybody seeming to consider the breaking up of our government and army, the opportunity for a 'grab game,' each striving to seize and appropriate what they could of public stores & property, while they in turn were mobbed and robbed by the town & country people—villages sacked in Yankee style by lawless mobs, and every man returning from the army on mule or horse, having to guard his animals & himself with loaded weapons." Alester had a fine horse which had survived the war, but it was such an object of desire that for his own safety, he decided he had to sell it. "My heart sank," Emma added, "at the fearful picture & we could not but acknowledge the bitter, humiliating, truth . . . that we had showed we were incapable of self-government. With all our endurance & heroic courage, our desolations and afflictions, that national lesson has yet to be learned."

Edwin White, one of Emma Holmes's brothers-in-law, not only learned to make biscuits but got a job running a steam-driven sawmill at St. John. Porcher Smith rented mules and hauled lumber, getting up at dawn each day and eating a cold breakfast.

David Macrae told of a Southern woman who at the end of the war had $150,000 in worthless Confederate paper and ex-slaves once worth more than $50,000. "One of the most prominent men of the Confederacy," Macrae wrote, "was trying to earn a living in the pea-nut business." One of Beauregard's staff, an officer with a famous Southern name, was teaching in a small day school. Others were acting as clerks, and some as farm laborers. Macrae met "three cultured Southern gentlemen," one a former general, one an ex-captain, and one an ex-lieutenant, living together in a little hut, two of them working in a railroad office and one looking for any job he could find. Another formerly wealthy planter lived in three rooms of his once-elegant mansion.

One of the signs of the times was that gentlemen began to be seen carrying bundles on the streets. Noting the fact, Kate Stone wrote: "In proportion as we have been a race of haughty, indolent, and waited-on people, so now are we ready to do away with all forms and work and wait on ourselves." Emma Holmes noted that "as all our negroes will be going, we will need white servants. Joe left us last week, and . . . we had to try our hands one day for dinner. . . . I succeeded in washing the rice, but not the grist, & Lila undertook the corn bread. But, when a fowl was to be roasted (Mary Ann having picked it & cleaned the pots, John cutting wood & making the fire) we were compelled to call Patty [the black laundress] for no one knew how to commence. . . ." Uncle Ta Gibbs made $60 by making and selling 800 fishing lines and some additional money by repairing clocks and watches.

William Blackford, after Lee's surrender, stayed for a time with his wife, Nannie, at Charlottesville. "I purchased flour on credit," he recalled; "we had some bacon and with the money [left] we bought some sugar and coffee which we hoarded. Strange as it may appear the time passed pleasantly, for all were trying to make the best of everything. There were a great many charming people there at the time and a great many pretty girls. . . . Vegetables and milk were given us by Mr. Colston and others and we got along very well." Life was suddenly reduced to the simple level of day-to-day survival. Blackford was asked for a legal opinion and received fifty cents in hard money for his services. It seemed like a small fortune. With it he bought the first herring and slice of cheese he and his wife had had for four years. Soon there was more legal business. The Blackfords returned to Lynchburg and began a new life.

William Wilkins Glenn, seeing General Lee at White Sulphur

Springs, found him impenetrably reserved. The general seemed happiest when he could find "a nice little girl, young fresh, or two at a time and forget himself for a moment. With ladies," he added, "he will talk rather soberly but somewhat freely. With men not at all. It was painful to be with him. He reminded me of a man who feels that life has closed over [him] and that there was nothing left for him but death."

Laura Buttolph wrote to her cousin Mary Mallard that New Orleans was in a distracted state: "No meat, no butter, very little meal. Negroes starving with laziness. Military paralyzing all efforts to make them work. Country ruined: South has no future! Things worse and worse. No help as far as I can see. People generally dissatisfied with their homes; too poor to go away. Seasons unfavorable; too poor to live at home! . . . The Nigs get the best, and are in the majority in this country. . . . And things get worse and *worse here*."

Florida seemed in many ways the most backward of the Southern states. Huge profits were to be made by renting and working plantations that were lying fallow. On the other hand, many Florida blacks had only the vaguest intimation that they might be free and hardly understood what that might mean. In the backcountry they remained "on the little cracker plantations," Whitelaw Reid wrote, "and neither masters nor negroes succeed in more than making a rude living."

A month after Lee's surrender Mary Chesnut wrote in her diary: "We are shattered and stunned, the remnant of heart left alive within us filled with brotherly hate. We sit and wait until the drunken tailor who rules the United States of America issues a proclamation, and defines our anomalous position."

Eva Jones wrote to her mother-in-law, Mary Jones, bemoaning "the dark, crowding events of this most disastrous year. We have seen hope after hope fall blighted and withering about us, until our country is no more—merely a heap of ruins and ashes. A joyless future of probable ignominy, poverty, and want is all that spreads before us. . . . The degradation of a whole country and a proud people is indeed a mighty, an all-enveloping sorrow. . . . My poor brother Edgeworth feels his glory departed, and lays aside his captaincy with a sigh as he opens an up-country store. He goes bravely to work, and says he'll gain an honest livelihood; and many of his best friends here are delighted with his independence and energy. But these times try men's souls—and women's too!"

William Colbert, an Alabama slave, watched the disintegration of his master's plantation. "De massa had three boys go to war," he recalled, "but dere wuzn't one to come home. All the chillun he had wuz killed. Massa, he los' all his money an de house soon begin droppin' away to nothin'. Us niggers one by one lef' de ole place and de las' time I seed de home plantation, I wuz standin' on a hill. I looked back on it for de las' time through a patch of scrub pines and it look so lonely. Dere warn't but one person in sight, de massa. He was a-settin' in a wicker chair in de yard lookin' out ober a small field of cotton an cawn. Dere wuz fo' crosses in de graveyard in de side lawn where he wuz a-settin'. De fo'th one wuz his wife." Colbert, whose own wife had died, felt a bond of sympathy with his old master.

"Newspapers report that society in certain regions of Georgia and Alabama has gone to chaos and disintegration," George Templeton Strong wrote, "—asthenic, passive, dry gangrene and death. Most property there, public and private, is destroyed. The bare soil is left. . . . Cuffee will not work because Mass'r has no money to pay him. Cuffee is distrustful and suspicious, and gives no credit. Mass'r belongs to a First Family, was not born to work, and would rather starve than work; and he and his house seem to be starving, partly for the sake of spiteing the Yankees. . . . Parts of Secessia may have to pass through a period of absolute anarchy and barbarism, longer or shorter, before they become Christianized and civilized."

It was November, 1865, before the Stones returned to Broken-burn. "At home again," Kate Stone wrote, "but so many, many changes in two years. It does not seem the same place. The bare, echoing rooms, the neglect and defacement of all. . . ." But the stately oaks were intact, and the grass was green and luxuriant. Her brothers were soon off hunting and fishing. Old Uncle Bob had served as a kind of custodian after all the other blacks had left, and he was "as humble and respectful as ever," bringing up presents of candy, raisins, and nuts to Mrs. Stone. He had discovered the buried silver and moved it to a safer hiding place. Now it was retrieved, a major triumph. Uncle Bob wanted to rent some of the land and plant for himself, and Mrs. Stone let him have several acres rent-free. Slowly other families returned. Some had never left, clinging to their plantations in the face of every hazard. At Major Bryan's plantation everything had been saved, and the same house servants stayed on to work for wages. Soon Kate Stone was being courted by the strikingly handsome Lieutenant Holmes, cotton was planted, and some of the ex-slaves filtered back, looking for work. With them came some former black soldiers, still wearing their uniforms and full of fight. Johnny, Kate's brother, got in a fight with an independent-minded field hand and shot and nearly killed him. In an instant he was surrounded by an angry crowd of blacks, shouting, "Kill him, kill him!" Only the intervention of Uncle Bob and another black kept Johnny Stone from being lynched on the spot. "It came near breaking up the plantation," Kate Stone wrote. The young black recovered, and Johnny was sent off to school. "He never speaks now of killing people as he formerly had a habit of doing," Kate added.

In rural North Carolina the hardship and destitution were far more evident than in Louisiana. The ravages of the war were everywhere. A Union officer wrote that "window-glass has given way to thin boards. . . . Furniture is matted and broken. . . . Dishes are cemented in various styles, and half the pitchers have tin handles. A complete set of crockery is never seen. . . . A set of forks with whole tines is a curiosity. Clocks and watches have nearly all stopped. . . . Hair-brushes and tooth-brushes have all worn out; combs are broken, and are not yet replaced; pins, needles, thread, and a thousand other such articles . . . are very scarce. . . . At the tables of those who were once esteemed generous providers, you will find neither tea, coffee, sugar, nor spices of any kind. Even candles, in some instances, have been replaced by a cup of grease. . . ."

"Southern affairs," George Templeton Strong noted in his diary, "do not improve. There are wide districts there in which society seems dissolving; in which the white race seems not only insolvent but prostrate, despondent, apathetic, and paralyzed, and short of food besides, while the blacks are idle, shiftless, and predatory. . . ." Such at least was the word in the Democratic press, which blamed conditions on the radical Congress. Strong was more inclined to lay the responsibility on the white South, which had always been "improvident and lazy, and lived in dependence on Cuffee, just as the slaveholding ants depend on their hexapod nurses and breadwinners."

Many whites were living on government rations in Richmond, and a Northern journalist found a descendant of one of the Founding Fathers destitute and kept from starving by bacon and hardtack issued by the U.S. Commissary. Some justified taking government rations by declaring, "It is taking from the United States Government a very small portion of what it owes us," and "As long as the Yankees have taken possession of Richmond, of course it's their place to feed us." There was a particular irony in the fact that destitute white citizens of Mobile, Alabama, received 59,000 rations during the months immediately following the end of the war, while only 11,000 had been distributed to needy blacks, and by the end of June the blacks were drawing only one-tenth the number of weekly rations drawn by whites. "A stranger might have concluded," a journalist wrote, "that it was the white race that was going to prove unable to take care of itself, instead of the emancipated slaves. . . ."

Gradually life settled, if not into its old patterns, into new ones, reminiscent in many ways of the old. An agricultural society is quick to mend. You planted seeds—cotton and corn and wheat and rye and vegetables—in the rich soil, and they came up. Hens laid eggs and hatched chickens. Wild turkeys ran in the woods. Mary Jones wrote her granddaughter from Montevideo, evoking the old sights and sounds. Where insolent Yankees had tramped not long ago, carrying off everything not nailed down, the doors and windows "stand wide open," without fear of intruders, "and the bright sunshine peeps in, and the cool breezes filled with perfume from the tea-scented olive and the sweet roses and flowers of the garden come freely through the entry and the halls. The avenue of oaks, the grove, the lawn are all beautiful; the laurels in full bloom." Squirrels ran cheerily through the trees; the birds sang, "thanking God for His kind care of them." The Yankees had left only one old goose out of a flock of seventy, but she had found a gander and now was busy herding a brood of goslings about the lawn, driving off cats and dogs with angry quacks. A pigeon that had pecked at the window for corn and peas had found a mate, "and now," Mary Jones wrote, "they have a fat little squab just fledged." Those freedmen and women who wished or were prevailed upon to stay had settled into the familiar routines of plantation life, and some who left had come back, drawn by homesickness and chastened by the difficulty of making their way in the outside world.

There were, of course, many Southerners who had considered themselves staunch Unionists—men in every slaveholding state who opposed, directly or indirectly, the movement of secession. When Lincoln made clear his determination to use force to preserve the Union, many of these Southern Unionists completely abjured loyalty to the United States and cast their lot wholeheartedly with the South, believing that they were defending their soil and their way of life against a merciless intruder. Others remained passively loyal, knowing that to speak out for the Union cause would be to court disaster. At the end of the war a number of Unionists of both classes came forward to cooperate with the Federal government, some out of a genuine desire to effect a reconciliation between the sections, knit up the Union once more, and assist in creating a vigorous Southern economy utilizing Northern money and "know-how." Others, undoubtedly, were simply opportunists who wished to take advantage of the Yankee presence to advance their own interests. To the "loyal" Southerner there was little or no distinction between the two categories—the unselfish and the self-interested. When a name so ancient and an individual so honorable as to be above reproach came forward to cooperate with the victors, an exception might be made. But generally cooperating Southern whites—"scalawags"—were more bitterly hated than the carpetbaggers from the North. As great a tragedy as any of those that marked the period of Reconstruction was the hatred that fell upon that relative handful of white Southerners who, in good conscience and out of essentially idealistic motives, tried to help heal the breach. Perhaps even more than the blacks they suffered obloquy, constant danger, and final historical oblivion; they were "nigger lovers," one of the South's (and the North's) most opprobrious epithets. One such was Thomas Durant of New Orleans, described by a Northern correspondent as "an intense radical," who "speaks at negro meetings, demands negro suffrage, unites with negroes in educational movements, champions negroes in the courts. The resident Rebels hate him with an intensity of hatred due only to one whom they regard as an apostate. . . ."

In the North many champions of reconciliation clung to the conviction that the Unionists of the South, given encouragement, would take hold of political power and join forces with the moderate Northern Republicans. Close observers of the defeated South had a different opinion. They could see no evidence that those Unionists who were still identifiable as such had any substantial degree of political power or any prospect of achieving it except under the bayonets of Northern soldiers. The Southerners who had been the leaders in secession and who had fought to repel the Yankee invaders were the natural leaders of the postwar South, Reid insisted. "No reorganization [of the Southern state governments] was possible on a white basis," he wrote, "which should not leave these men in full control of civil government by an overwhelming majority. . . . All the concomitants and outgrowths of slavery and State sovereignty, doctrines which lie at the foundation of secession, and beliefs which reject the possibility of free negro labor, or the prudence of conferring legal rights upon free negroes, remained in full strength. . . . They were part and parcel of the accepted faith of the people. They would be given up as was slavery—not otherwise. Every step must be by compulsion."

Whitelaw Reid believed that there were three distinguishable groups in the South: those who were ready to accept defeat in a spirit of resignation; a smaller group of Union men who were willing to abide by Federal enactments, "if the negroes can be kept under, and themselves put foremost"; and a third class of irreconcilables—"violent and malignant Rebels," Reid called them—who would submit to Federal authority only if no other course were open to them.

Toward the Yankee, the despoiler of the South, the destroyer of its sacred institutions and treasured way of life, the South could feel only hatred, a hatred that in time congealed into an aspect of character or temperament. As in some cultures, particular courtesies become ritualized traits, so in the South "hatred" of the Yankees became a fact of life like the weather or birth and death. William Wilkins Glenn's cousin Mary Ficklin wrote him from Charlottesville in October, 1865: "I have lost heavily during our great struggle but I have enough left and better than that an undying hate to the Yankee that will last me as long as life. I saw much of the Cavalry and Artillery from Maryland. While I recollect them, I must & will hate the Yankee."

Southerners—especially those who hadn't fought in the war —were addicted to the view that Southerners had proved themselves far superior to Northerners as soldiers and thereby validated a general claim of Southern superiority. It was only the sheer weight of numbers and the vast wealth of the North that had overcome the finer breeding and higher principles of the South. "You had three things too many for us," a Georgian told Whitelaw Reid, "the Irish, the niggers, and Jesus Christ." A Mississippi rustic described the Yankees as all cowards who "would never have overpowered us if they hadn't called in the Dutch, Irish, niggers, and all the rest of their superiors in creation, to help them."

In April, 1866, John Richard Dennett, writing for Godkin's *Nation*, described a conversation with a Northerner: "I came out with the kindest feelings for these people down here; I wanted to see it made easy; we had whipped them, and I wanted it to rest there. I thought the South wanted it to end there. But I was tremendously mistaken. They hate us and despise us and all belonging to us. They call us cut-throats, liars, thieves, vandals, cowards, and the very scum of the earth. They actually believe it. . . . And I've heard and seen more brag, and lying, and profanity, and cruelty, down here, than I ever saw or heard before in all my life." The only people Dennett found with any friendly disposition toward Yankees and the Federal government were the Negroes. "I'm convinced," he wrote, "they can vote just as intelligently as the poor whites. A Southerner would knock me down if I said that to him; but it's true. I tell you I'm going home to be a radical. Fight the devil with fire. I've learned to hate Southerners as I find them, and they can hate me if they want to. I'm a Sumner man after I get back. . . ."

While many Southern newspapers continued to pour forth hatred of the Yankees and to breathe defiance, others, George Templeton Strong noted, "dwell rather on the advantages of free immigration, the importance of encouraging it, the undeveloped resources of every Southern State, the value of skilled mechanics to the community and the dignity of labor!!!! The world moves indeed!"

Southern women became the custodians and perpetuators of "hating the Yankees." George Templeton Strong took note in his journal of the flood of reports from southward "of bitter hatred of all Northmen, especially among Secesh women." Their hatred of Yankees became legendary, more bitter and enduring than the hatred of those who had fought and who bore the manifold scars of battle. They kept the hatred alive, passed it on to their children through successive generations like a precious family heirloom. When Lucy and Sarah Chase traveled through the South several years after the war, they were told repeatedly that Southerners would teach their children to hate the Yankees as bitterly as they did. One man said, "We know we must take things as they are and make the best of 'em, but our women are unconquerable; like Hannibal's mother, they teach the brats at their knees undying hatred."

A particular source of Southern bitterness was the treatment of captured Jefferson Davis. As critical as many Southerners had become of Davis's direction of the war, he was still the symbol of Southern resistance, and the apparent disposition of the Federal government to punish and humiliate him was bitterly resented. He had first been allowed freedom on his own parole and then, in the face of outraged protests in the North, confined at Fortress Monroe with orders to manacle him if he gave any provocation. Davis supplied the provocation by throwing a plate of food at one of his soldier guards. The commandant of the fort thereupon ordered Davis placed in irons. When a detail in command of a Captain Titlow went to carry out the order, he found Davis beside himself at the prospect of being placed in chains. He asked for an opportunity to appeal the order to Stanton, and when that was denied, he declared that he would die before he would submit and "walked the cell, venting himself in almost incoherent ravings," in Ben: Perley Poore's words. At one point Davis picked up a stool and struck at Titlow. Finally the captain ordered his men forcibly to restrain the prisoner. It took four men to hold the ex-President of the Confederacy while the manacles were placed on his legs. When the task was finished, Davis slumped onto his cot and burst into tears. A physician called in insisted that the prisoner's health was endangered, and the irons were removed, but the damage had been done. In the opinion of Ben: Perley Poore, "The manacling of Mr. Davis delayed the work of reconstruction for years, and did much to restore the feeling of sectional hatred which fair fighting had overcome." Whether this judgment was true or not, the treatment of Davis was certainly more deeply resented in the South than any other act by Union officials.

While David Macrae found many Southerners who were quite prepared to defend the institution of slavery, he found none who was sorry to see its demise. "I like it better than slavery," one Southerner told him. "I would not go back to the slavery system if I could. Labour is cheaper now and more easily managed. . . . In slave times you had to keep the factory going whether you were making money or not. . . . Now you have nothing to do, if a bad season comes, but turn the hands off, lock the door, put the key in your pocket, wait for better times, and let the men look out for themselves. Every one for himself is the rule now. . . . Saves money at any rate."

Macrae wrote that "notwithstanding the loss to which Emancipation has subjected the Southern people, and the agony of the process by which it was accomplished, I scarcely met a single man or woman, who expressed regret that slavery was gone. The South," he added, "feels like a man who has been subjected against his will to a severe operation—an operation which he thought would kill him, which has terribly prostrated him, from which he is still doubtful if he will completely recover, but which being fairly over, has given him prodigious relief."

The war, Macrae pointed out, had swept away the cause of that region's increasing alienation from the rest of the civilized world and thus lifted from its conscience the terrible weight of universal opprobrium.

37

Whites on Blacks

The most critical issue in the postwar South was not the attitude of white Southerners toward "Yankees," important as that issue was. It was, rather, the feelings of whites toward free blacks.

If Whitelaw Reid gave us one of the best factual accounts of the postwar South, another young man, Albion Tourgée, is our most valuable ally in our efforts to penetrate the consciousness of that South. Tourgée's ancestors included French Huguenots, English Pilgrims on the *Mayflower*, and immigrants from the German Palatinate. Born in 1838, he grew up in Ohio, attended the University of Rochester, taught school, and, in the first week of the war, enlisted in the 27th New York Volunteers. He was wounded in the spine in the First Battle of Bull Run on July 1, 1861, only a few weeks after he had enlisted, and was discharged a month later. A year later, although his recovery was slow, he re-entered the army with the lieutenant's commission as a member of the 105th Ohio Volunteers, only to be arrested for insubordination. The Proclamation of Emancipation had not yet been issued or even seriously considered, and slaves who escaped to the Union lines were subject to be claimed by their owners. An escaped slave warned Tourgée of an imminent attack by rebel soldiers and, in Tourgée's view, saved his company from surprise and probable annihilation. When his commander demanded that the runaway be turned over to the provost marshal for possible return to his owner, Tourgée defied the order.

Captured by the Confederates a few months later and exchanged, Tourgée returned to Ohio and married his childhood sweetheart, Emma Lodoiska Kilbourne. Back with his company, Tourgée fought at Tullahoma, Chickamauga, Lookout Mountain, and Missionary Ridge. Unable to throw off the effect of his wounds, he retired from the army and began to study law; he was admitted to the Ohio bar in 1864. Restless and undecided about his future, Tourgée was taken with the notion of going south to participate in what was already being referred to as its reconstruction.

Albion Tourgée believed that the prompt reconciliation of the two sections was essential to the future welfare of the country. It seemed to him that the devastated South was sorely in need of help from sympathetic Northerners. Educated and idealistic Yankees could, Tourgée felt, perform a real service by helping the freedmen make the transition from slavery to freedom. In addition, he, like so many other visitors to the South, had been strongly drawn to the land and the people. Tourgée was convinced that bigoted and mistaken as they might be, Southern whites would in time accept the new state of affairs and indeed come to realize that the destruction of slavery had been as much a deliverance for them as for their slaves. Meanwhile, he felt confident that the disinterested assistance of a Northerner, who, like so many of his Southern counterparts, had fought and suffered painful wounds for a cause in which he believed, would be welcomed by a people famous for their hospitality. Matters turned out very differently from Tourgée's anticipations. Tourgée and his wife suffered acutely from the animosity directed at "carpetbaggers." But he had his revenge. At the end of Reconstruction he wrote a clearly autobiographical book entitled *A Fool's Errand,* which, published in 1879, became a best seller and was followed by an even more penetrating analysis of Reconstruction, *Bricks Without Straw.*

In his effort to do justice to the Southern frame of mind, Tourgée, in the person of the fictional hero of *A Fool's Errand,* Comfort Servosse, describes the condition of the once-wealthy planter: "The home where he had lived in luxury was almost barren of necessities; even the ordinary comforts of life were wanting at his fireside. A piece of cornbread, with a glass of milk, and bit of bacon, was, perhaps, the richest welcome-feast that wifely love could devise for the returning hero. Time and the scath of war had wrought ruin in his home." It was not surprising, Servosse declared, that reduced to such conditions, the white Southerner believing in the "accepted dogma" of the "inherent inferiority" of his former slaves, as well as "a very general belief of its utter incapacity for the civilization which the Caucasian has attained," should look with "distrust and aversion, if not with positive hatred," at the notion of giving political power to the freedman. "That this should arouse a feeling of very intense bitterness when it came as the result of conquest and the freedom enjoyed by the subject-race was inseparably linked with the memory of loss and humiliation in the mind of the master, would seem equally apparent," Servosse concluded. Only three classes of people failed to take account of the power of this feeling on the part of the defeated South: "martyrs, who were willing to endure ostracism and obloquy for the sake of principles; self-seekers, who were willing to do or be anything and everything for the sake of power, place, and gain; and fools, who hoped that in some inscrutable way the laws of human nature would be suspended. . . ." Servosse-Tourgée clearly belonged to the last class.

In Albion Tourgée's words, the Southern whites "considered the freeing of the slave merely a piece of wanton spite, inspired, in great measure, by sheer envy of Southern superiority, in part by angry hate because of the troubles, perils and losses of the war, and, in a very small degree, by honest though absurd fanaticism. . . . Regarding it as inherently fraudulent, malicious and violent, they felt no compunction in defeating its operation by counterfraud and violence."

A Union officer in Danville, North Carolina, wrote on June 21, 1865: "The belief is by no means general here, that slavery is dead, and a hope that, in some undefined way, they will yet control the slaves, is in many minds, amounting with some to a conviction. They look for its restoration through State action—not yet comprehending that the doctrine of State sovereignty has been somewhat shattered by the war. Here, as in Richmond, the people, instead of grappling with the fact that the war has liberated the slaves, are very busy proving the utter worthlessness of the negroes, and treating them with additional cruelty and contempt, neither offering them fair inducements to work, or working themselves." In Alabama, at least, there was a general assumption among the planting class that in the absence of state legislation, the freedmen could not be prevailed upon to work the cotton plantations of the region. There were a number of contingents of black troops in Mobile. "They marched very handsomely," Reid wrote, "and made, perhaps, the best appearance of any regiments in the column; but every citizen seemed to consider their appearance as a personal insult to himself. That the 'miserable runaway niggers' behaved so handsomely only aggravated the offense." One intractable white muttered, "There's my Tom. . . . How I'd like to cut the throat of the dirty, impudent good-for-nothing."

In the words of Colonel Samuel Thomas, assistant commissioner of the Freedmen's Bureau for Mississippi, "The whites esteem the blacks their property by natural right, and, however much they may admit that the relations of masters and slaves have been destroyed by the war . . . they still have an engrained feeling that the blacks at large belong to the whites at large, and whenever opportunity serves, they treat the colored people just as their profit, caprice or passion may dictate." Carl Schurz's experience confirmed the colonel's analysis "at every step; and the worst of it was," Schurz added, "that, as I had to confess to myself, it was under existing circumstances as natural as it was terrible and distressing."

To a young Southern friend, Sam Griffin, Sidney George Fisher remarked that he "hoped to see the Negroes of the South in the position of a peasantry, working for wages and enjoying all civil rights but not the right of suffrage, but that I feared the southern people would never permit this." What, Griffin asked, did Fisher mean by civil rights? The right to acquire property, make contracts, sue and be sued, give testimony in court, work where he pleased, and have the right of self-defense. For example, if a white man struck a Negro and the Negro struck back, what would the white man do? Fisher asked. "Most men," Griffin replied, "would kill him." Fisher asked: "And public opinion would justify the act?" "Certainly," was the reply, "more than justify, almost require it." Fisher commented: "This shows how much must be changed in the South before the Negro can become equal with the white before the law, and there is a long way from that to Negro suffrage."

George Trenholm spoke for most Southern whites when he told the Augusta, Georgia, Chamber of Commerce, in 1866, "Sir, we have educated them [the slaves]. We took them barbarians, we returned them Christianized and civilized to those from whom we received them; we paid for them, we return them without compensation. Our consciences are clear, our hands are clean."

A Southern Unionist told Whitelaw Reid: "With us, the death of slavery is recognized, and made a basis of action by everybody. But we don't believe that because the nigger is free he ought to be saucy; and we don't mean to have any such nonsense as letting him vote. He's helpless, and ignorant, and dependent, and the old master will still control him. . . . It is possible that a few might be willing to let the intelligent negroes vote—after some years, at any rate, if not now." More than one Southerner insisted to Whitelaw Reid that the freedmen must be under the control of the state legislators with the "authority to fix their wages and prevent vagrancy."

Charles Colcock Jones wrote to his mother that his mother-in-law had been sued by three of her house servants for wages, "a most unwarrantable procedure." He added: "We will all have to recognize the fact at once that our former slaves have been set free and that we have no further legal claim on their services, and that if they continue with us we must pay them for services rendered."

A primary article of the Southern faith held that only a Southerner could "understand" blacks. "You know, and every Northern man knows," a Georgian said to Whitelaw Reid, in what had by now become a wearisome refrain, "that we have been the best friends the nigger ever had. Yet this is the way they treat us." White Southerners spoke perpetually of their former slaves' "ingratitude," and Reid noted on more than one occasion that he was solemnly assured that "nothing short of . . . 'being born among negroes' " could qualify a white man to comprehend their nature. The prevailing Southern attitude toward the freedman, Reid wrote, was that "he was saucy and rude; disposed to acts of violence; likely, by his stupid presumptions, to provoke a war of races, which could only end in his extermination. In this the Freedmen's Bureau encouraged him, and thus became solely a fomenter of mischief. The presence of negro troops tended to demoralize the whole negro population. . . . As to negro suffrage, none but the black-hearted Abolitionists who had brought on the war . . . would dream of asking the South to submit to so revolting a humiliation."

Despite individual exceptions, Reid characterized the attitude of most Mississippi whites toward blacks as "one of blind, baffled, revengeful hatred. 'Now that you've got them ruined, take the cursed scoundrels out of the country.' 'Damn their black souls, they're the things that caused the best blood of our sons to flow.' 'The infernal, sassy niggers had better look out, or they'll get their throats cut yet. . . . ' Such were the voices I heard on every hand," Reid wrote, "—in the hotels, on the cars, in steamboat cabins, among the returned soldiers, grave planters, outspoken members of the 'Legislature,' from every party, and from men of all ages and conditions. More or less the same feeling had been apparent in Tennessee, Georgia, Alabama, and Louisiana. . . . However, these men may have regarded the negro slave, they hated the negro freeman."

The *New Orleans Daily South* of November 19, 1865, declared: "The white seems to be forgotten in the recent gabble about the eternal negro. Negroes care nothing for 'rights.' They know intuitively that their place is in the field; their proper instruments of self-preservation, the shovel and the hoe; their *Ultima Thule* of happiness, plenty to eat, a fiddle, and a breakdown. Sambo feels in his heart that he has no right to sit at a white man's table. . . . Unseduced by wicked demagogues, he would never dream of these impossible things. . . . Every real white man is sick of the negro, and the 'rights' of the negro. Teach the negro that if he goes to work, keeps his place, and behaves himself, he will be protected by *our* white laws; if not, this Southern road will be 'a hard one to travel,' for the whites must and shall rule to the end of time, even if the fate of the Ethopian be annihilation."

To a moderate Virginian who took the line that once a black man had demonstrated that he could acquire property, hold down a job, and educate himself, he should be allowed to vote, an Alabaman replied that he could not prove himself a man because "the nigger ain't a man at all."

"Not a man!" the astonished Virginian replied.

The Alabaman then proceeded to enumerate the differences between white and black and then to argue that in the biblical story of Genesis the serpent was really a black man. By this interpretation, Eve was also black, and God's punishment of Adam was for marrying a black woman and producing mulatto offspring. "I love the nigger in his proper place," the Alabaman concluded, "but his place is not as the white man's equal, but as his slave." This proposition left the Virginian speechless, and David Macrae, apparently, as well. Macrae had never encountered so extreme a position on the black-white issue. Much more typical was the argument that Africans "needed protection; they needed tutelage; they had to be dealt with as a race of infants. It was a thing of mercy, a thing of kindness to keep them in slavery. They were happier in slavery; and it will be manifest to you," a Southerner told Macrae, "as it has been manifest to us, that they are not fit for freedom."

"We figured up," another planter told Whitelaw Reid, "I don't know how many millions of coolies there are in China, that you can bring over for a song . . . they'll live on next to nothing and clothe themselves, and you've only got to pay 'em four dollars a month. That's our game now."

Whitelaw Reid was told that blacks were shot every few nights in the back streets of Knoxville, Tennessee. "Nigger life's cheap now," a white Tennesseean informed Reid; "nobody likes 'em enough to have any affair of the sort investigated; and when a white man feels aggrieved at anything a nigger's done, he just shoots him and puts an end to it." The prejudices against blacks were so strong, Reid added, that "if any way of driving them out of the country can be found, it will be very apt to be put in force."

In the Old South—Virginia, the Carolinas, and Georgia—and especially the Deep South—Alabama, Mississippi, Louisiana, and Florida—the need for labor on plantations mitigated the plight of the freedmen and women. A degree of consideration had to be paid them in order to prevail on them to work at all. But in the border states slave labor had been much more peripheral to their economies, and freed black laborers were much more easily replaced by whites. Ironically, there was little support among Tennessee Unionists for Tennessee's native son, Andrew Johnson. One man burst out to Reid, "Why don't he hang Jeff Davis, as he said in the Senate he would?" Tennessee was generally for "more hanging and fewer pardons."

Underneath all the white talk of the laziness and improvidence of blacks was a strong current of fear. Every black gathering was assumed to be devoted to plotting the murder of whites. Newspapers warned of massacres more bloody than those of Santo Domingo. "We have authentic information," one editor wrote, "of the speeches and conversations of the blacks, sufficient to convince us of their purposes. *They make no secret of their movement.*" The failure of some free blacks to perform all the minor observances demanded of slaves in the presence of their master aroused both fear and anger in whites. In the words of Reid, "Negroes neglected to touch their hats to overseers or former masters whom they disliked; and straightway it was announced that they were growing too saucy for human endurance. They held meetings and sung songs about their freedom, whereupon it was conjectured that they were plotting for a rising against the whites. They refused to be beaten; and, behold, the grossest insubordination was existing among the negroes."

Carl Schurz told the story of a plantation owner who appealed to the Union general commanding in his district for help in dealing with the "terrible state of insubordination" that existed among his hands. When the general asked the nature of the insubordination, the planter cited the fact that after their day's work instead of going promptly to their quarters for the night as he directed them to, "they roam about just as they please. . . ." Not only that, they entertained visitors from neighboring plantations and often sang and danced. When the general replied that this all seemed harmless enough, the planter replied that his mother-in-law's maid had refused to be whipped for not performing her duties properly, concluding, "Now, this is an intolerable state of things."

A major anxiety of white Southerners revolved around the theme of miscegenation. Emma Holmes reported that "two of the Brownfield's former negroes have married Yankees—one a light colored mustee had property left to her by some white man whose mistress she had been. She says she passed herself off for a Spaniard, & Mercier Green violated the sanctity of Grace Church by performing the ceremony. The other, a man, went north and married a Jewess—the idea is too revolting."

There were, in fact, a number of interracial marriages in the aftermath of the war, the most famous perhaps being the marriage of Mississippi state senator Albert Morgan, to Carrie Highgate, a black teacher from New York who had come south to open a school for black children.

David Macrae, trying to find an explanation of the Southern rage and anxiety toward blacks, hit on the Southern horror of racial intermarriage. Political equality, the Southern argument ran, must lead to social equality and that in turn to intermarriage. "And if we have intermarriage," a Southern gentleman told Macrae, "we shall degenerate . . . we shall become another Mexico . . . we shall be ruled out from the family of white nations. Sir, it is a matter of life and death with the Southern people to keep their blood pure." Macrae could not help reflecting on the irony of such an attitude when the South was filled with "thousands upon thousands of mulattoes, quadroons, octoroons, and so on, presenting every variety of shade from pure black to pure white, and so forming an unbroken bridge across the gulf that separated the two races at first." Whatever black blood might do to contaminate white had, it was abundantly clear, already been done.

Abolitionists and Radical Republicans generally were already talking about at least a limited franchise for literate free blacks, but the mere suggestion enraged most Southerners. Like many upper-class

Northerners, members of the Southern aristocracy believed the franchise was already extended too far. Whitelaw Reid was told: "The gentlemen of the country should be the ruling class of the country. . . . Too many voted now, instead of too few." Educational and property qualifications should be established to exclude the poor white vote, but blacks, "educated or ignorant, rich or poor . . . must be kept down."

Perhaps the feelings of the white South are best suggested by an editorial from the *Memphis Advocate* of April 22, 1866. The Northern radicals were, the editor declared, "actuated by a devilish hate and a fiendish malice. . . . Since they cannot, in this part of the State, assassinate, kill, and murder rebels, and take possession of their property, they propose to give a greasy, filthy, stinking negro the right to crowd them from the polls." The same editor undoubtedly went home, after writing the editorial, to a house full of black servants with whom he existed on terms of the greatest intimacy, who cooked his food and nursed his children and for whom he expressed warm affection.

Many Southerners agreed with the editor of the *Memphis Appeal*, who wrote that if the "curse and inconceivable calamity" of Negro suffrage were forced on the South, "it would be a solemn duty . . . to annihilate the race."

One of the few prominent Southerners favoring limited black suffrage was the war hero Wade Hampton. Hampton had been opposed to secession, but he had fought heroically in the war. He and his brother were among the Southerners who professed to welcome Negro suffrage. Hampton's brother's principal concern, expressed to Whitelaw Reid, was that the blacks themselves would be "unbalanced" by having their votes solicited by unscrupulous whites. On the other hand, Hampton was confident that "the old owners would cast the votes of their people almost as absolutely and securely as they cast their own. If Northern men expected . . . to build up a Northern party in the South, they were gravely mistaken. They would only be multiplying the power of the old and natural leaders of Southern politics by every vote given to a former slave," in Reid's paraphrase of Hampton's remarks. "If the suffrage of the Negro is properly handled and directed," Hampton declared, "we shall defeat our adversaries with their own weapons. The negro is Southern born. With a little education, and a property qualification, he can be made to . . . fight with the whites."

Whitelaw Reid found Hampton's confident assurance that the

freedmen would follow the lead of their former masters in political questions "preposterously false." He wrote: "Not one negro in a thousand hoped for the success of the rebellion, or was without some pretty distinct notion of his personal interests in the issue. They often served or saved masters to whom they were personally attached, even in the most critical moments of danger, but this not in the slightest degree affects their desire for the triumph of the Yankees." To Reid it was simply another example of the delusive world the Southern white lived in.

There was another profound contradiction in Southern attitudes. While Southerners insisted that blacks were irredeemably lazy and would work only under coercion, they refused, for the most part, to lease or rent land to freed blacks. "In many portions of the Mississippi Valley," Whitelaw Reid wrote, "the feeling against any ownership of the soil by the negroes is so strong, that the man who should sell small tracts to them would be in actual personal danger. Every effort will be made to prevent negroes from acquiring land; and even the renting of small tracts to them is held to be unpatriotic. . . ."

Mary Jones wrote her daughter: "You can have no conception of the condition of things, I understand Dr. Harris and Mr. Varnedoe will rent their lands to Negroes! The conduct of some citizens has been very injurious to the best interest of the community." The implication was plain enough—renting land to Negroes was a betrayal of the white community.

On the question of the black ownership of land, there were two complications. The first was that of establishing a legal basis for the confiscation of land that belonged to former rebels. This proved impossible. When Southerners who had abandoned their plantations in the face of the advancing Union soldiers returned to claim them, the courts, with few exceptions, recognized those claims, and the free blacks working the land were dispossessed even when they had "bought" the land. White Southerners might be said to have "conspired" to prevent blacks from owning land of their own by exerting heavy pressure on prospective sellers of land not to sell to black purchasers and by finding various legal subterfuges to recover land already owned by blacks (such as heavy tax assessments and foreclosures).

In 1870 a black, Henry Adams, formed a group of ex-soldiers into a self-appointed committee to investigate the actions of whites against Southern blacks. "We worked our way from place to place and from

State to State," Adams reported, "and worked amongst our people in the fields to see what sort of living our people lived. . . . At one time there was five hundred of us." Adams's report, which he turned over to a Senate Committee, is a somber story of misery and exploitation. On plantation after plantation where blacks raised cotton on shares, they were cheated out of a major portion of the money due them. Many blacks were afraid to talk to Adams and his fellows for fear they would be observed and punished. One group told Adams that "the whites take all we make and if we say anything about our rights they beat us."

A congressional committee, investigating conditions in the South in 1872, was told virtually the same story in state after state. Southern whites declared that "if you suffer the colored people to own land we cannot get any laborers." In some instances black farmers had had their cattle and hogs killed by whites jealous of their modest prosperity and determined to keep the freedmen economically dependent. Caesar Robinson, eighty years old and an ex-slave, farmed ten acres near Shreveport, Louisiana, with four houses on it. When he attempted to register the land, he was told he would have to pay exorbitant fees. His money was taken. His land was not registered. A white man claimed it and Robinson was forced off without any compensation for his improvements and told that he would be thrown in jail if he protested.

A stratagem to prevent free blacks from undertaking any business venture was that of requiring a large bond. In Vicksburg no one could become a drayman, hack driver, or teamster without posting a $500 bond. Since blacks were not allowed to own property, they could not post bonds and no white man would do so for them.

Finally, there was that vast, strange realm of Southern "honor." For a black man to look a white man in the eye was to impugn his honor or to give evidence of insolence or the crime of "uppityness," which was so vaguely defined as to include anything that gave the least indication of black pride or ambition.

In Jackson County, Florida, a young black man named John Gilbert who was driving a cart loaded with wood was shot and killed by a former Confederate soldier when he didn't move his cart quickly enough to the side of the road. Such incidents could be multiplied without number. There were literally endless stories, as George Templeton Strong noted, of "infamous cruelties and outrages upon freedmen, and so on. . . . Soreness, and wrath ill suppressed, and spite expended in maltreatment of niggers. . . ."

In all discussions of the post-Civil War era it is essential to keep in mind that the white men and women of the devastated and impoverished South never abandoned their conviction that like their Revolutionary forebears, they had been fighting in the cause of freedom and independence. They fought for "their nation" against the forces of despotic materialism. The fact that they lost the cause did not, to them, make it any less right. Indeed, it might be said to have ennobled it, made the "Lost Cause" a symbol of heroic resistance in the face of overwhelming odds, of courage beyond calculation in defense of the homeland against a ruthless invader. Nor was the Southern frame of mind improved by the inescapable fact that while the South, fighting in the cause of freedom, had been mercilessly pillaged and desolated, its conqueror had waxed surpassingly fat on the conflict. The war for the North, the terrible casualties aside (the North lost approximately 6 percent of its young men of an age to serve in the Union armies, while the South lost 23 percent, almost four times as many proportionately), ushered in a period of unparalleled prosperity, a boom time that heralded the era of modern industrial capitalism.

White Southerners, desolate, devastated, their social system destroyed, their livelihood gone in many instances, their houses and cities and plantations often in ruins, their best young men dead or bearing grievous wounds, faced the bleakest of futures. Today we are very conscious of the psychological effects of warfare on the soldiers and civilians involved. Clinics are established to assist them adjust to peacetime existence; psychologists and psychiatrists are recruited to counsel them; aid programs are instituted to rebuild shattered economies. The collective trauma suffered by the defeated white South was certainly painful beyond our comprehension. On top of these "huge miseries"—the phrase which Fanny Kemble used in describing the condition of slaves on her husband's plantation before the war and which now could be well used to describe the condition of the South, white and black alike—the South perceived the North determined to punish it still further by imposing on it "Negro domination," the final insupportable, ultimate humiliation and degradation. And "domination," as it called any effort on behalf of the rights of free blacks, it was determined to resist.

In the attitude of Southern whites toward their former slaves lay the key to Reconstruction. To have admitted that black men and women were capable of functioning in a free society would have been to admit that slavery was wrong, not to say, evil; that all that their bitterest enemies—the abolitionists—had said was true and that the terrible suffering and bloodshed of the war, the ruin and devastation of the South were not a glorious "Lost Cause" fought for truth and honor but a tragic and ghastly mistake. To believe that the South might make such an acknowledgment was, to say, the least, unrealistic.

38

Presidential Reconstruction

THE THREE DOMINANT FIGURES in the Cabinet that Johnson inherited from his predecessor were, of course, Stanton, Welles, and Seward. Welles and Seward were thoroughly unsympathetic to Southern blacks. Welles wrote in his diary: "Whenever the time arrives that he should vote, the Negro will probably be permitted. I am no advocate of social equality, nor do I labor for political or civil equality with the negro. I do not want him at my table, nor do I care to have him in the jury box, or in the legislative hall or on the bench."

The reader will recall that Welles, like Chase, had started his political life as a Jefferson Democrat and had abandoned that party only over the slavery issue. He thus may be assumed to have had strong residual inclinations toward that party. This undoubtedly affected his attitude toward Reconstruction in two ways. He distrusted the motives and the principles of the ex-Whigs who made up such a large portion of the Republican Party. He considered them tainted with elitist notions and a strong probusiness bias. Further, he shared the strong states' rights views of the Democratic Party.

While Welles grew more and more like a stern Old Testament prophet, prophesying that the country would go to ruin if the

Constitution were not at once restored to its prewar purity, Seward, once the darling of the newly founded Republican Party, became at last the gray eminence he had aspired to be, constantly at Johnson's side. Always thin, his body grew ever more spare until he seemed hardly to inhabit his loosely fitting clothes. His sharp features—his large nose, thin and blue—grew sharper; his chin receded. In body and spirit he appeared strangely diminished. Recanting his pro-Negro heresies, he joined forces with Welles to plump for states' rights. E. L. Godkin reported that the secretary of state had said to him not long after the war: "The North has nothing to do with the negroes. I have no more concern for them than I have for the Hottentots. They are God's poor; they always have been and always will be so everywhere. They are not of our race. They will find their place. They must take their level. . . . The North must get over the notion of interference with the affairs of the South."

President Johnson's problems were compounded by the fact that he stood, inevitably, in the shadow of Grant. With Lincoln's death the general was the most revered and admired American. When Grant visited New York, he and his wife dined with Ellen and George Templeton Strong to Strong's intense satisfaction. "Mrs. Grant," he wrote, "is the plainest of country women, but a lady, inasmuch as she shows no traces of affectation or assumption, and frankly admits herself wholly ignorant of the social usages of New York." Thousands gathered near the Fifth Avenue Hotel to catch a glimpse of the hero, who entered, escorted by General Hooker and William Astor, to meet a company of generals—Meade, Burnside, Frémont, and Dix among them—five Senators, including the new Senator from Nevada, W. M. Stewart, and Thurlow Weed, William Cullen Bryant, Horace Greeley, and Samuel Tilden. Grant was nearly crushed in the rush by the other guests to see him and to get a portion of the oysters and champagne being dispensed at the hotel. The *Tribune* next day described the reception as "one of the most imposing ceremonies ever witnessed in this city. . . ."

On Tuesday, May 9, 1865, the Cabinet had a long discussion on the issue of amnesty for the defeated rebels. "No great difference was expressed," Welles noted, "except on the matter of suffrage. Stanton, [Postmaster General William] Dennison, and Speed were for negro suffrage; [Secretary of the Treasury Hugh] McCulloch, [Secretary of the Interior John P.] Usher and myself opposed. It was agreed, on request of Stanton, we should not discuss the question, but each express his opinion without preliminary debate." After opinions had been given, Welles announced, "I am for no further subversion of the laws, institutions, and usages of the States respectively, nor for more Federal intermeddling in local matters, than is absolutely necessary, in order to rid them of the radical error which has caused our national trouble." Later, noting the discussion in his diary, Welles added, "This question of negro suffrage is beset with difficulties growing out of the conflict through which we have passed and the current of sympathy for the colored race. The demagogues will make use of it, regardless of what is best for the country, and without regard for the organic law, the rights of the States, or the troubles of our government. There is a fanaticism on the subject with some, who persuade themselves that the cause of liberty and the Union is with the negro and not the white man. White men, and especially Southern white men, are tyrants. Senator Sumner is riding this one idea at top speed."

Welles was ready to acknowledge that "there may be unjust prejudices against permitting colored persons to enjoy the elective franchise, under any circumstances; but this is not, and should not be, a Federal question. . . . In most of the Free States they are not permitted to vote," he added. "Is it politic, and wise, or right even, when trying to restore peace and reconcile differences, to make so radical a change,—provided we have the authority, which I deny,—to elevate the ignorant negro, who has been enslaved mentally as well as physically, to the discharge of the highest duties of citizenship, especially when our Free States will not permit the few free negroes to vote?" That, it seemed, to Welles, was the crux of the matter. By what right did Northerners, unwilling to grant the franchise to their own free blacks, demand of the South that in defiance of every instinct, it extend the vote to freedmen presumably far less qualified to exercise it than their Northern counterparts?

Put in those terms, the question was unanswerable. The Founding Fathers had drawn up the charter for a democratic republic with the emphasis on "republic." They had supported the principle of public education on the ground that a republic could survive only if it had an informed and intelligent—that is to say, educated—citizenry. That seemed to be the inescapable lesson of history. By that measure, immigrants, illiterate or uninstructed in the principles of free govern-ment, were a threat to republican government and might have their right to vote restricted. To impose a restriction on the franchise not contained in the Constitution proved awkward, or, indeed, impossible. So the upholders of the old faith had to watch in indignation and dismay while hordes of Irish and German immigrants, aided by native demagogues, subverted municipal and state governments and, indeed, the Federal government itself, by electing Democrats to office year after year.

But the Founding Fathers had another principle upon which they placed great emphasis—that all societies were made up of different and, to a large degree, competing interests and that those "interests" who managed, one way or another, to grasp political power would invariably, since man was by nature selfish and "self-aggrandizing," use their power to exploit those with less power and, most cruelly of all, the powerless. Therefore, governments must be so constructed and power so distributed that all legitimate "interests," those of the poor as well as of the rich, could be protected. So, if it were conceded that freed blacks must constitute a very substantial portion of the "body politic" with very particular and unique interests, it thus followed that their most basic and essential and "constitutional" protection against exploitation was their franchise. In this reading it made no difference how ignorant or intelligent or even literate they might or might not be. They must be presumed to know what was best for them and have the right to vote for those individuals who best represented their interests.

The Cabinet discussion and Welles's reflections in his diary are revealing. From the earliest days of his administration the stronger figures in the Cabinet urged Johnson to leave the issue of freedmen's rights to the respective states. The results were soon apparent.

If the Radical Republicans in Congress—Sumner and Stevens and their adherents—left Washington in June confident that the President would pursue a policy designed to insure the rights of free blacks, they were soon disillusioned. Johnson's first step prefigured the rest. He appointed a provisional governor of North Carolina and directed him to hold elections for a constitutional convention to be chosen by white voters loyal to the Union. When word of the President's actions reached Sumner, he could only believe that Johnson was the victim of a "strange hallucination." Johnson's North Carolina proclamation, more than any other utterance or document, revived Southern hopes of establishing control over their own affairs and, as one New Orleans citizen expressed it, "putting an end to the career of nigger agitators in

Louisiana." Thomas Wentworth Higginson wrote: "What most men mean to-day by the 'president's plan of reconstruction,' is the pardon of every rebel for the crime of rebellion, and the utter refusal to pardon a single black loyalist for the crime of being black. . . . The truth is that we are causing quite as much suffering as a conqueror usually does. It is simply that we are forgiving our enemies and torturing only our friends."

In the South, President Johnson, whom Emma Holmes once referred to contemptuously as "a tailor who used to make suits for Mrs. Boykin," got more favorable notice. "Andy," Emma Holmes wrote in her diary, "intended to leave the important matter of negro suffrage to the state legislatures," adding, "& of course there is no longer any doubt on that point. Andy said he intended the negro to be free and, if the Southern people accepted the fact cheerfully and made their arrangements for the new order of things, that every facility would be afforded the country to return to its former prosperity. . . ."

Republicans were disconcerted to find President Johnson besieged by ex-rebels petitioning for everything under the sun. In Whitelaw Reid's view, the supplicants played skillfully on Johnson's Southern antecedents and prejudices. The President was challenged to denounce the abolitionists as fanatics and as enemies of good government and of reconciliation and to cast his lot with his true friends, the ex-rebels, now ready to become once more loyal citizens if only they would be allowed to manage their own affairs. "Such were the voices," Reid wrote, "day by day and week by week, sounding the President's ears. He heard little else and was given time to think little else."

Disturbed by the indications that Johnson was pursuing a policy designed to turn over power to the leaders of the rebellion with no guarantees for black rights, a delegation of blacks led by Frederick Douglass secured an audience with the President. From the start it went badly. Johnson made it clear that he had little interest in securing the franchise for blacks, that it was a matter for the states. The story was told that after the delegation departed, Johnson said to a private secretary, "Those damned sons of bitches thought they had me in a trap! I know that damned Douglass; he's just like any nigger, and he would sooner cut a white man's throat than not."

Despite the increasing alarm and resistance of the Radical Republicans, Johnson pressed stubbornly ahead with his own plan of Reconstruction, a plan based essentially on the readmission of the ex-Confederate states pretty much on their own terms. Ex-generals and colonels of the rebel armies were conspicuous among the newly appointed and elected officials of all the Southern states, to the indignation of the Republicans. Most disconcerting of all, in North Carolina Johnson placed Northern soldiers, officers, and freed blacks in particular jeopardy by restoring the right of the writ of habeas corpus, which had the direct effect of inhibiting the army and the Freedmen's Bureau in their efforts to protect blacks and Union whites. It made army officers liable to civil suits for damage to Southern property, the cases to be tried in state courts, where Yankees had little hope of justice.

In June, 1865, Johnson appointed provisional governors for the former Confederate states, and the state legislatures in turn repealed their ordinances of secession. Stevens, increasingly uneasy over Johnson's policies, wrote him on July 6, 1865: "I am sure you will pardon me for speaking to you with a candor to which men in high places are seldom accustomed. Among all the leading Union men of the North with whom I have had intercourse, I do not find one who approves of your policy. They believe that 'Restoration' as announced by you will destroy our party. . . . Can you not hold your hand and wait the action of Congress . . . ?" Lincoln had often taken what appeared, at least from the congressional point of view, high-handed and arbitrary actions and infringed on territory that Congress considered its own, but he had almost invariably softened the effect of such actions by consultations, small courtesies, and tactful consideration. Not so Johnson. He ignored Stevens's letter.

Sumner, unable to gain the President's attention directly, in a number of conversations with Welles did his best to induce the secretary of the navy to try to prevail upon Johnson to change his course, warning him that Congress was determined to oppose the presidential policy.

Historians have sometimes conveyed the notion that Sumner and Stevens, by their obdurate resistance to Johnson's policies, drove him into increasingly rancorous opposition. It is plain that at least initially, both men did their best to prevail on the President to work with Congress to effect a national policy on Reconstruction. When argument and exhortation failed in the face of Johnson's stubborn determination to pursue his own course, Sumner, in a sense, declared war on the Johnson administration by telling Welles that the President's policy "on the question of organizing the Rebel States [was] the greatest and most criminal act ever committed by any government." Moreover, Sumner declared Welles the principal culprit. He, a New England man, "New England's representative in the Cabinet, [had] misrepresented New England sentiment. McCulloch was imbued with the pernicious folly of Indiana, but Seward and myself were foully, fatally culpable in giving our countenance and support to the President in his policy." Welles promptly reported the conversation to Johnson, and a few days later Sumner sent Welles a newspaper editorial calling for the impeachment of the President.

Johnson, aware of the determination of the Radical Republicans to draw the freedmen into the political process in the South, if only to insure the hegemony of the party, passed the word *sub rosa* to his correspondents in various Southern states, urging them at least to make a show of allowing a handful of cooperative blacks and white Unionists to vote and hold minor offices, thereby assuring the Radical Republicans of their good intentions. But even such token compliance was unacceptable to Southern Democrats, or Conservatives, as they were at first called.

In South Carolina, which was holding a constitutional convention under the terms set down by the President, a number of Charleston blacks drew up a memorial requesting that at least a limited franchise be extended to those blacks qualified to exercise it, but the convention refused to receive it. "It cannot but be the earnest desire of all members that the matter be ignored *in toto* during the session," the *Charleston Daily Courier* noted.

On September 28, 1865, a young French doctor, twenty-four years of age, named Georges Eugène Benjamin Clemenceau arrived in New York. On his way from France, he had stopped off in England to visit John Stuart Mill. An idealist and political activist, Clemenceau was intensely interested in the United States and the progress of democracy since the days of Tocqueville. He found a home in the French Colony of New York City, where French shopkeepers sold French hats and dresses, gloves, and artificial flowers, then very much in style. In later years he recalled that America in that day had "no general ideas and no good coffee," but he found much else to interest him and was soon writing anonymous dispatches on American affairs for the radical French newspaper *Le Temps*. "The vital question just now in American politics," he wrote in one of his first articles, "is that of negro suffrage. Johnson declares that he will allow each state to settle it independently, whereas the radical Republicans would like to have him assert his authority and settle it once and for all."

One of the most telling measures of Johnson's hardening attitude on the issue of Reconstruction was to be found in his reaction to another "fact-finding" expedition, on which he had, at Chase's suggestion, dispatched Carl Schurz. Welles was critical of the President's choice. "Schurz," he wrote, "is a transcendental red republican of a good deal of genius, but national, with erroneous views of our federal system." Schurz, for his part, had been reluctant to undertake such a taxing assignment, but Stanton and Chase both urged him to go on the ground that the President seemed to be increasingly surrounded by pro-Southern advisers and needed firsthand information from a relatively objective observer. In the South Schurz "sought conversation," as he put it, "with everybody I could reach—planters large and small, merchants, lawyers, physicians, clergymen, guests I met at city hotels or country taverns, fellow travelers on railroads or steamboats, men who had served as officers or private soldiers in the war, men who had stayed home—and whatever different opinions or feelings as to other subjects they might cherish, or with whatever degree of heat or moderation they might express them—on one point they were substantially unanimous with very, very few individual exceptions: 'The negro will not work without physical compulsion. He is lazy. He is improvident. He is inconstant. He may sometimes work a little spell to earn some money, and then stop working to spend his money in a frolic.'" Schurz informed the President that the whole South was virtually monolithic in its resistance to any legal protection for the rights of the ex-slaves.

Most striking to the visitor was the general bewilderment of Southerners over the question of dealing with blacks as free labor. It was not so much prejudice, though that was amply evident; it was primarily an incapacity of the white imagination to conceive of a new relationship. Many "honest and well-meaning people," Schurz wrote, "admitted to me with a sort of helpless stupefaction that their imagination was wholly incapable of grasping the fact that their former slaves were now free." Coercion seemed to Southerners the only way to deal with the problem.

Schurz gave particular attention to the unhappy situation of Southerners with strong Union sympathies as well as Northern men in the South. Southern leaders did not hesitate to tell Schurz that once Federal troops were removed, such men would be in danger of their lives.

As Schurz's preliminary reports reached the President, Johnson's displeasure became more and more apparent. It was Schurz's conviction that "Southern society was still in that most confused, perplexing and perilous of conditions—the condition of a defeated insurrection leaving irritated feelings behind it, and of a great social revolution only half accomplished, leaving antagonistic forces face to face." This was not what Johnson wished to hear. In the weeks following Schurz's departure, the President, pressed hard by Welles and other advocates of reconciliation, had moved rapidly in the direction of restoring white Southern Conservative or rebel control in the South and leaving the fate of the freedmen in their hands. This drift was doubtless due in part to Welles's constant reiteration of the theme that the Constitution must be restored and that *any* action that violated its sacred tenets must be abjured.

"Violent efforts were made by white people to drive the straggling negroes back to the plantations by force," Schurz wrote, "and reports of bloody outrages inflicted upon colored people came from all quarters." Schurz himself saw, in various improvised hospitals, "negroes, women as well as men, whose ears had been cut off or whose bodies had been slashed with knives or bruised with whips, or bludgeons, or punctured with shot wounds. Dead negroes were found in considerable number in the country roads or on the fields, shot to death or strung upon the limbs of trees. In many districts the colored people were in a panic of fright, and the whites in a state of almost insane irritation against them."

In his formal report to the President, Schurz warned against the determination of many Southerners to reinstitute "another 'peculiar institution' differing only in name from slavery. . . . I entreat you," he wrote, addressing Johnson directly, "to take no irretraceable step towards relieving the States lately in rebellion from all national control," until it was clear that the South was ready to acquiesce in the new order. The problem of the "status of the negro in Southern society" could be solved only "if he has a voice in the matter. In the right to vote he would find the best permanent protection against oppressive class-legislation, as well as against individual persecution," Schurz wrote. While objections that the mass of black people were not yet far advanced to merit the ballot might be made, it seemed to Schurz "idle to say that it will be time to speak of negro suffrage when the whole colored race will be educated, for the ballot may be necessary to him to secure his education. . . . The only manner in which the Southern people can be induced to grant to the freedmen some measure of self-protecting power, in the form of suffrage, is to make it a condition precedent to readmission," Schurz concluded.

When Schurz returned to Washington, Johnson made his displeasure evident. The indignant emissary wrote to a friend: "The President received me with civility, indeed, but with demonstrative coldness. I was painfully surprised." Johnson, he learned, had been told that Schurz had taken advantage of his mission to spend his time trying to strengthen the Republican Party in the various states he visited. Schurz hotly denied the accusation and wrote to Charles Sumner, giving an account of his treatment: "That the views expressed in my letters to the President were radically at variance with his policy, is quite probable, but I do not see how, as a sensible and fair-minded man, he could make that the occasion for a personal rupture. In one word I am completely in the dark." Sumner replied that the President wished to move too rapidly. "He revives the old Slave Oligarchy, envenomed by war, and gives it a new lease of terrible power. This Republic cannot be lost; but the President has done much to lose it. We must work hard to save it. . . ."

When Congress assembled in December, Johnson tried to use a somewhat less emphatic report from Grant on conditions in the South to negate that of Schurz's (even Grant had stated unequivocally that "in some form the Freedmen's Bureau is an absolute necessity until civil law is established and enforced, securing to the freedmen their rights and full protection . . .") and appended to it a determinedly sanguine preface which was in sharp contrast with the report itself. "As the result of measures instituted by the Executive," Johnson wrote, the people of the Southern states had reorganized their respective state governments and "are yielding obedience to the laws and governments of the United States, with more willingness and greater promptitude than . . . could reasonably have been anticipated." The Thirteenth Amendment had been ratified by all states except Mississippi. Everywhere the defeated Confederacy demonstrated loyalty to the government and "a prompt and cheerful return to peaceful pursuits," confident that the Federal government's "fostering care will soon restore them to a condition of prosperity." While there were some adjustments to be made in the relations between "the two races . . . systems are gradually developing themselves under which the freedman will receive the protection to which he is justly entitled." "Sectional animosity" was "surely and rapidly merging itself into a spirit of nationality. . . ."

Johnson's first annual message to Congress was delivered on December 4, 1865, and written, in large part, by George Bancroft. It began with a gracious tribute to Lincoln and an affirmation of the new President's determination to uphold the Constitution, in which "The hand of Divine Providence was never more plainly visible." Its drafting was "beyond comparison the greatest event in American history." He asked rhetorically: "Is it not of all events in modern times the most pregnant with consequences for every people of the earth?"

He had, Johnson reminded Congress, found the states under military governments. These he felt obliged to replace as quickly as possible by civil governments. Retained, they would soon have "envenomed hatred rather than have restored affection" and have "occasioned an incalculable and exhausting expense." He had acted "gradually and quietly and by imperceptible steps . . . to restore the rightful energy of the General Government and of the States."

As for the "4,000,000 inhabitants whom the war had called into freedom," the Constitution clearly left it to the states to determine their eligibility as voters. "In my judgment," Johnson declared, "the freedmen, if they show patience and manly virtues, will sooner obtain a participation in the elective franchise through the states than through the General Government, even if it had power to intervene." At the same time Johnson exhorted all Americans to make the experiment of having the "two races . . . live side by side in a state of mutual benefit and goodwill."

Johnson ended his message by evoking Washington and the now-familiar litany of America's blessings—"fruitful soil, genial climes, happy institutions. . . . Here the human mind goes forth unshackled in the pursuit of science. . . . Where in past history does a parallel exist to the public happiness which is within reach of the people of the United States?"

The immediate response to the President's message was almost uniformly favorable. Georges Clemenceau praised the speech and called Johnson's policies "eminently wise and patriotic." He added: "No one has any doubt that the blacks will have the right to vote now that slavery is abolished. It should be so and will be so. Mr. Johnson wishes it to be so, as much as any radical. . . . Whatever one may think of the policies of Mr. Johnson, it has to be admitted that he seems to have won out definitely over the leaders of the extreme radicals. He persists in his ideas with a logical strength which does not encounter grave opposition." For the moment it looked as though the President had triumphed. He (or Bancroft) had shrewdly planted himself on the sacred ground of the Constitution. It was the rock, the grail, the holy writ that contained the soul, the essence, of America, and it must be kept inviolate. To question or to tamper with it was blasphemous, or worse; it was to imperil everything that had been fought for, to jeopardize what had been secured with such terrible sacrifice—the Union. Having chosen the high ground, Johnson had only to hold to it with dignity and restraint to prevail over his enemies, but that was not his nature.

The principal problem with the President's message was that it failed notably to engage the facts—the reports of Chase, Reid, Schurz and others did not at all conform with the President's optimistic phrases. Sumner denounced it promptly as "a white-washing message like Pierce on Kansas." As evidence accumulated on every hand of increasing violence toward blacks, a disillusioned Henry Turner declared, "I charge Mr. Johnson with the murder of thousands of our people; for though he does not kill them personally, yet he abets, or gives aid to those murderers, so that it actually amounts to a direct encouragement."

39

Congress Fights Back

Encouraged by President Johnson's evident intention to return to them the management of their own affairs, Southern legislators, elected by white voters, passed what came to be called Black Codes. Their very evident purpose was to reduce free blacks to a new kind of legal servitude distinguished by all the disadvantages of slavery and none of its advantages—a state, many argued, that was worse than slavery itself. That the Black Codes were not the result of a brief lapse in judgment on the part of Southern legislatures or the work of extremists but rose, rather, out of the famous grassroots is indicated by an ordinance passed immediately after the war in the small town of Opelousas, Louisiana; it stated that "no negro or freedmen shall be allowed to come within the limits of the town of Opelousas without special permission from his employers. . . . Whoever shall violate this provision shall suffer imprisonment and two days' work on the public streets, or pay a fine of five dollars." Any Negro found on the streets of the town after ten o'clock in the evening had to work for five days on the public streets or pay a $5 fine. The ordinance further provided: "No negro or freedman shall be permitted to rent or keep a house within the limits of the town under any circumstances. . . . No negro or freedman shall reside within the limits of the town . . . who is not in the regular service of some white person or former owner. . . . No public meetings or congregations of negroes or freedmen shall be allowed within the limits of the town. . . . No negro or freedman shall be permitted to preach, exhort, or otherwise declaim to congregations of colored people without a special permission from the mayor or president of the board of police. . . . No freedman . . . shall be allowed to carry firearms, or any kind of weapons. . . . No freedman shall sell, barter, or exchange any article of merchandise within the limits of Opelousas without permission in writing from his employer. . . ." In the parish of St. Landry it was required "that every negro [is] to be in the service of some white person, or former owner. . . ."

In Alabama the Black Codes stipulated that it was the duty of all "Civil officers" of a county to report "the names of all minors . . . whose parents have not the means, or who refuse to support said minors." They might be treated in the same way, arrested, fined, and then sentenced to work off their fines. In bidding for the services of "said minor . . . the former owner . . . shall have preference." In Mobile unemployed blacks, those who had no "fixed residence or [could not] give a good account of themselves," were required by another section of the code "to give security for their good behavior for a reasonable time and to indemnify the city against any charge for their support. . . ." In the event they could not meet this requirement, they were, again, "to be confined to labor for a limited time, not exceeding six calendar months . . . for the benefit of said city." Also in Alabama, municipalities were authorized to "restrain and prohibit the nightly and other meetings or disorderly assemblies of all persons and to punish for such offences by fixing penalties not exceeding fifty dollars for any one offence. . . ." Again if the accused were not able to pay the fine, he or she might be sentenced to labor for a period of time not exceeding six months.

The laws of Florida resembled those of Alabama but were, if anything, more severe since a vagrant might be hired out for twelve months. No "negro, mulatto, or person of color" was allowed in Florida and most other Southern states to "keep any bowie-knife, dirk, sword, firearms, or ammunition" without a license. A black owning any weapon "of any kind" had to surrender his arm or arms to the informer, "stand in the pillory . . . for one hour, and then [be] whipped with thirty-nine lashes on the bare back." The same penalty might be invoked for "any person of color . . . who shall intrude himself into any religious or other public assembly of white persons or into any railroad-car or other vehicle set apart for the accommodation of white persons." The South Carolina legislature decreed that no black man "shall pursue the practice, art, trade or business of an artisan, mechanic, or shopkeeper, or any other trade or employment besides that of husbandry, or that of a servant under contract for labor, until he shall have obtained a license from the judge of the district court, which license shall be good for one year only." A black shopkeeper or peddler had to pay $100 a year for a license. If a black man under contract for his labor left or was fired before the end of his contract time, he must "forefeit his wages for that year up to the time of quitting." Moreover, any person "giving or selling to any deserting freedman, free negro, or mulatto, any food, raiment, or other things shall be guilty of a misdemeanor" punishable by a fine of up to $200, and be subject to suit by the employer. In virtually every instance the inability to pay a fine would result in a sentence to labor for a period ranging from six months to a year.

A section of the Louisiana code stipulated that "every adult freed man or woman shall furnish themselves with a comfortable home and visible means of support within twenty days after the passage of this act," and anyone failing to do so "shall be immediately arrested by any sheriff or constable . . . and . . . hired out . . . to some citizen, being the highest bidder, for the remainder of the year." Laborers under contract were not allowed to keep livestock, and all time spent away from the job was to be charged against them at the rate of $2 a day, to be worked out at the end of the contract period. An earlier Louisiana law required that all agricultural workers "make contracts for labor during the first ten days of January for the entire year." In the case of sickness the laborer lost his wages for the days absent, "and where the sickness is supposed to be feigned for the purpose of idleness, double the amount shall be deducted. . . ."

In addition, poll taxes were imposed in every state, ranging in amount from Georgia's $1 per head on every man between the ages of twenty-one and sixty to $2 in Alabama on every person between the ages of eighteen and fifty, and to $3 in Florida. A black man could not buy or rent land except in a city. South Carolina required that a black man pay an exorbitant fee to engage in trade or open a store. Nor, in that state, could he serve on juries. Unemployment was treated as a crime, and the unemployed could be sentenced to work without pay.

In order to understand the impulse behind the Black Codes, we must keep in mind that white Southerners were entirely convinced that the freedmen presented a fearful menace to white society both by refusing to work (thereby becoming public charges and, more serious, bankrupting all planters who depended on them as a labor force) and by performing violent acts against their former masters. But plainly the principal motivation for the Black Codes was economic. White Southerners were determined to force freed blacks to work for them on the terms and under the conditions they prescribed. They were determined to dominate their ex-slaves almost as completely as they had dominated them under the institution of slavery itself. There was nothing about the simple fact of emancipation to alter, in the slightest degree, the white image of the black man or woman. Quite the reverse. As we have seen, under slavery many blacks had been protected to a degree at least by the closest personal contacts with their masters and mistresses (as well as by their dollar value). Both races had trusted these ties to mitigate the harshest aspects of the system. Emancipation destroyed many, if not all, of these relationships or substantially altered them. Whites could no longer, for example, assume that loyalty and, indeed, love would be part of a relationship with any black man or woman. Removed from the "civilizing" and "refining" influences of the plantation (at least that was how the former masters and mistresses viewed it), the freed blacks must lapse back into that "savagery" and "barbarism" from which slavery had rescued them. Bizarre as such a notion seems in retrospect, it was the virtually universal paranoia of the South. Only by keeping these facts constantly in mind can we begin to understand the recklessness with which the South defied Northern opinion by enacting the Black Codes. One would think that a few minutes' reflection would have convinced any reasonable white man south of the Mason-Dixon Line that the simplest dictates of self-interest required that they act with caution and forbearance in regard to the rights of their newly freed slaves. Any other course had to play into the hands of the most intractable enemies of the South. Undoubtedly there was some typical fire-eating Southern intransigence in the enactment of the codes. But it must also be conceded, I believe, that the men who passed them believed literally that they had to do so to preserve themselves, their families, and what was left of their fortunes from a rising tide of blacks determined to devour their substance, rape their wives, and exact a bloody vengeance for years of suffering and cruel oppression. That this corrosive fear, this incapacitating anxiety, did not relate to any substantial body of real facts made it not less compelling to white Southerners. They were a people, after all, schooled in violence. A violent response to a threatened danger was the only response they knew. They could not have been wholly indifferent to or unaware of the risks they were running in terms of anticipatable Northern reactions. But the immediate issue—what was to be done with the freedman—was a far more pressing matter than possible congressional reactions. In addition, the South undoubtedly misread the political situation in the North. The words and actions of the President produced a false sense of security in Southern minds.

In any event, we can hardly fail to agree with William Sinclair, the black historian of Reconstruction, who wrote apropos of his discussion of the Black Codes: "The ballot probably would not have been bestowed upon [the black], certainly not at the time nor in the way and manner it was, if the South had been lenient toward him and shown a disposition to respect the Emancipation Proclamation and the Thirteenth Amendment as accomplished results; and protected him in life and property, the right of contract, marriage relations, locomotion, the privilege of schools, and other just and equitable relations, irrespective of the ballot. . . ." All true enough, but to have accomplished this, the white South would have had to forget or reject everything it had believed and maintained for the previous century and more. It would have had, virtually overnight, to confess that it had been wholly mistaken about the nature and character of people of African origin and that slavery, the heart and essence of its famous "culture," had been a horror based on a misconception. Such a course might have gratified the North (which gave no material indication that it was prepared to go so far in regard to its own black citizens), but it was asking more of the South than it was possible for it to concede without losing what we today like to call its identity. Individuals can express repentance, ask for forgiveness from those they have wronged, and thereby experience "redemption." But I am not aware that a nation or a large segment thereof has ever done so. It was evidently the one thing that the South could not do; it could not collectively repent. So the tragedy of slavery could not end; the nightmare had to continue. The South was given a chance to put its own house in order in a form that would not violate the newly achieved rights of black citizens and, even more important, Northern opinion, and it emphatically rejected it. There are deeper levels of irony. If the South had simply been resourceful enough to bide its time, perhaps making a few tentative gestures toward the free blacks, any disposition in the North for "radical" Reconstruction would have been disarmed. "The hands of the nation," in Sinclair's words, "would have been tied hard and fast. The insistence on state rights would have prevented any legislation by Congress which might have interfered with the Black Code. The Fourteenth and Fifteenth Amendments to the Constitution of the United States, would, obviously, have been impossible." Taking off from Sinclair's analysis, we cannot emphasize too strongly the doubleness of the South's dilemma. The fact that the Southern states were unable to follow the course that reason and political expediency dictated is incontrovertible evidence that it was psychologically impossible for them to do so. Viewed another way, *it was even necessary that they should not.* If Sinclair was right; if some surface accommodation on the part of the South would have handcuffed the champions of Radical Reconstruction in the North and aborted the Fourteenth and Fifteenth Amendments, then must we not conclude that just as the actions of the South were *inevitable*, so they were *essential* to the passage of Radical Reconstruction and to the initiation of that process by which black people came eventually to be able to begin to claim their rights as American citizens?

The Black Codes are important for another reason. A substantial class of historians of both Northern and Southern origins (it turned out that Jefferson Davis's anxieties about having New England historians tell the story of the South's "struggle" were largely groundless; it might be argued that, on the whole, Northern historians have done better by the South than by the North) has been disposed, over the years, to argue that Radical, or Congressional, Reconstruction was a terrible error; that the South should have been left alone to work out its problems in its own way and by its own lights. But the prompt passage, under Presidential Reconstruction, of the Black Codes is an insurmountable stumbling block to this thesis. By their passage the Southern states made crystal clear their Rhadamanthine determination to deny freed blacks the most basic political, social, economic, and constitutional rights. When we have said everything that it is possible to say in explanation and exculpation of the codes, there can be no question that they were entirely incompatible with any conceivable theory of democratic government or social justice. For the United States to have acquiesced in them would have been to have made a mockery of thirty years of antislavery agitation and, indeed, to have conceded to the South the most doggedly held article of its faith—the irredeemable inferiority of African Americans and, beyond that, their inability to function as citizens of a democratic society. It would be another two or three decades, when the war, for most Americans, had faded to a romantic dream, before any substantial number of Americans living north of the Mason-Dixon Line would be willing publicly to acquiesce in that dogma. By that time the generous ardor of the abolitionists for black rights had been largely forgotten.

It must also be added that the Black Codes alone did not fully measure the intractability of the South. Southern Unionists on September 3, 1866, met in a convention in Philadelphia and presented a resolution to Congress calling for support and protection by the government. "Every original Unionist in the South," it read, "has been ostracized. . . . More than one thousand devoted Union soldiers have been murdered in cold blood since the surrender of Lee, and in no case have their assassins been brought to judgment." A few months earlier, in July, a convention of Union men meeting in New Orleans was raided by ex-Confederates and more than two hundred Union men were killed or wounded.

While the Black Codes of Virginia and North Carolina were less severe than those of the other Southern states and while in Tennessee the effort to pass such a code was defeated by Unionists, the critical point is that the South did not believe them to be in any way harsh or unfair. Even Welles had to admit that "the tone of sentiment and action of people of the South is injudicious and indiscreet in many respects. I know not if there is any remedy, but if not, other and serious disasters await them,—and us also perhaps, for if we are one people, dissension and wrong affect the whole." When the municipal elections in Richmond were overturned by the military commander there, Welles wrote, "the Rebels have been foolish and insolent, and there was wanting a smart and stern rebuke rightly administered. . . . From various quarters we learn that the Rebels are organizing through the Southern States with a view to regaining political ascendency, and are pressing forward prominent Rebels for candidates in the approaching election."

In addition to framing constitutions little different, in most instances, from those under which they had fought the war and electing wholly white legislatures that proceeded to pass Black Codes, most states elected Senators and Representatives to serve in the Congress of the United States who had been active in the rebel cause.

All this was done with at least the tacit approval of the President, who clearly hoped to present Congress when it assembled in the fall with a *fait accompli*. According to William Wilkins Glenn, Johnson told a group of Radical Republican Congressmen: "The South has done more in fourteen months than I expected to see accomplished in several years. Slavery is abolished. The Confederate debt is repudiated. The people are submissive. What more do you want? Why do you go on demanding exaction after exaction? You are actually trying to cut the heads of the Southern [men] and thus leave the legs to manage political affairs. I must oppose such policy."

Johnson's policy of restoring the rebellious states to the Union at once and virtually without conditions as regards the civil rights of blacks brought him into immediate conflict with the congressional leaders of his own party, most spectacularly Sumner and Stevens.

Over six feet tall and strikingly handsome—"godlike" his admirers liked to say—Sumner had never married, devoting most of his time outside his political duties to attending to his ailing and imperious mother, who never gave him the love and approval he needed but held him in classic thrall. Subject to terrible spells of loneliness and depression, he was the perfect case of a man whose career was his whole life. To some of his New England friends his untiring and uncompromising championing of the rights of free blacks was an indication of serious emotional instability. "If I could hear that he was out of his head from opium or even New England rum," Richard Henry Dana wrote Charles Francis Adams, Sr., in March, 1865, "not indicating a habit, I should be relieved." Sumner's arguments seemed to Dana "boyish or crazy, I don't know which." A month later Dana described Sumner as "a good seer, but a bad guide. He never did care a farthing for the Constitution, is impatient of law, and considers his oath to have been not to the Constitution, but to the Declaration of Independence. If the negro votes he does not care how the result is obtained or what else may follow."

Sumner, like much of humanity, had the vices of his virtues. They were the familiar symptoms of long use of extensive powers and continual exposure to public adulation, the thickening, one might say, of the membranes of the ego—a disposition to mistake one's own will for that of the Almighty, interpreting differences of opinion as personal opposition and reacting with mounting hostility to criticism of the mildest sort. Even his friends and admirers noted the change.

Henry Adams wrote that Sumner's mind "had reached the calm of water which receives and reflects images without absorbing them; that it contains nothing but itself."

If Sumner was the high-minded idealist who put principles before party, Stevens was the archetypal party man. Schurz reported that when a fellow Congressman, a member of a committee to decide a disputed election, declared that both candidates were rascals, Stevens replied, "Well, which is *our* rascal?"

Elizabeth Meriwether, who encountered Stevens in President Johnson's anteroom, described him as "thin, meager, garbed in citizen's dress which seemed to have been worn a long time—the coat and trousers were rusty and dirty and shiny." Stevens's face seemed to her stamped with "both bodily and mental pain." *Harper's Weekly* declared: "Mr. Stevens has no single quality of a statesmen, except strong conviction and fidelity to principle. He is strictly a revolutionary leader: reckless, unsparing, vehement, vindictive, loud for the rights of conquerors, intolerant of opposition, and as absolutely incapable of fine discrimination and generous judgment as a locomotive of singing. Of a pleasant humor and personal kindliness, he is no more fitted for the task of reconstruction which devolves upon Congress than a jovial blacksmith to repair a watch. . . ." William Wilkins Glenn wrote that the Pennsylvania Congressman was "not a bad hearted man. He will curse you or ruin you or pick your pocket or confiscate your property, if he can make anything by it, but he will not cut your throat needlessly. He promised Mrs. [Jefferson] Davis to work for the release of her husband but she did nothing to help her own case by declaring that President Johnson was determined to keep him in jail until he learned to sew."

Stevens's management of the Senate and House caucuses was shrewd, and he directed the House with great skill. Rutherford Hayes, recently elected to Congress, wrote his wife that Stevens was "witty, cool, full and fond of 'sarcasms,' and thoroughly informed and adequate. . . . He is radical throughout, except, I am told, he don't believe in hanging. He is a leader." When a New Jersey Congressman ranted for several hours against black suffrage in the District of Columbia, doing his cause more harm than good, Stevens said: "I move that he be allowed to go on for the rest of the season!"

Certainly there was a strong punitive streak in Stevens. That this should have been so, considering his commitment to the uplifting of black people, is hardly surprising. "Strip a proud nobility of their bloated estates," he told his colleagues; "reduce them to a level with plain republicans; send them forth to labor, and teach children to enter the workshops or handle the plow, and you will thus humble the proud traitors. Teach his posterity to respect labor and eschew treason. Conspiracies are bred among the rich and vain, the ambitious aristocrats."

"He, Stevens," Gideon Welles wrote in his compendious diary, "intends to play the part of tyrant and dictator to the South for years, will not permit them to be represented, intends to exclude them and to confiscate the property of the Rebels. . . . The North," he added, "must retrieve itself from its errors growing out of resentment and evil passions, and in retrieving itself will extricate the country from the slough in which the Radicals have plunged it."

There was, undoubtedly, much truth in Welles's charge that Sumner and Stevens were indifferent to the Constitution. They made no bones about their reservations in regard to that document. If it were to turn out that it stood in the way of doing justice to the freed slaves, they were perfectly willing to warp or, if necessary, discard it. In a conversation with an ex-Confederate general, Richard Taylor, Stevens was said to have referred to the Constitution as "a worthless bit of old parchment." Sumner's approach was to insist that "anything for human rights is constitutional. . . ." adding, "There can be no State rights against human rights." And in a speech urging the passage of the Fourteenth Amendment Stevens freely confessed that "in my youth, in my manhood, in my old age, I had fondly dreamed that when any fortunate change would have broken up for awhile the foundations of our institutions," Americans would take the opportunity so to "remodel all our institutions as to have freed them from every vestige of human oppression, of inequality of rights, of the recognized degradation of the poor, and the superior caste of the rich." But that dream had vanished, and he now realized that "we shall be obliged to be content with patching up the worst portions of the ancient edifice. . . ." For himself he was resigned to the amendment "because I live among men and not among angels; among men as intelligent, as determined, and as independent as myself, who, not agreeing with me, do not choose to yield their opinions to mine."

A number of congressional Republicans under the leadership of Stevens in the House and Sumner in the Senate were convinced that the South must be punished for its transgressions. This conviction was based on two assumptions, one moral and the other practical. The moral assumption was, quite simply, that there was a moral order in the universe in terms of which evil was punished and virtue rewarded. Congress was in this the agent of the Almighty in seeing that justice was done. The most crucial aspect of this justice was insuring the civil rights of the freed slave. The perfect appropriateness of this task was that Congress, by insuring the civil rights of Southern blacks, would, at the same time, punish the rebel South.

George Templeton Strong confessed himself concerned about the intensity of the desire to punish the South. "The punishment already inflicted on the Southern people is fearful to think of. . . . the devastation, the breaking up of their social system, general destitution, the bitterest humiliation of the most arrogant of mankind, the most splendid and confident expectations disappointed, universal ruin, bereavement, and shame—these are among the terms of the sentence God has pronounced and is executing on rebellious slaveholders. Never, in modern times, at least, has so vast a territory been so scourged." Thousands of these proud men and women had seen their "plantation homesteads . . . plundered and burned," their "husbands, brothers, sons, cousins . . . killed," and, bitterest of all, seen "soldiers that once were 'their niggers' mounting guard in the streets of Savannah, Charleston, or Richmond." At the same time "Darky Suffrage" was "a dark and troublesome question, and it must be met," Strong wrote. "That freedmen, who have as a class always helped the national cause to the utmost of their ability, at the risk of their lives, should have political rights at least equal to those of the bitter enemies of the country who are about to resume those rights, sullenly and under protest, only because they are crushed, coerced, and subjugated, is (abstractly considered) in the highest degree just and right. But the average field hand would use political power as intelligently as would the mule he drives. . . . Were I President, I should aim at securing political rights to property-holding Ethiopians and to such as could read and write."

The practical dimension was that, as Sidney George Fisher noted, unless the South was punished by loss of political power, it would simply renew its ante-bellum alliance with the Northern Democrats and take over the reins of government. In that case the loser would become the winner and any hope of protecting the rights of freedmen and women would vanish once and for all. As one Alabaman put it to Whitelaw Reid, "We'll unite with the opposition up North, and between us we'll make a majority. *Then* we'll show you who's going to govern this country." That was the Republican nightmare.

The compromise in the Constitution on the issue of slavery had provided that for purposes of determining representation in Congress, the slave populations of the Southern states would count as three-fifths of a similar number of white voters. This provision had, of course, been one of the principal objects of attack by abolitionists and, indeed, by all Northerners and Westerners who resented the disproportionate weight of the South in a succession of administrations as well as in the halls of Congress. A freed slave was, presumably, no longer equal to three-fifths of a white man; for purposes of representation he was exactly equal to a white man. If, in addition, he were denied the right to vote, in one way or another, the white population of the South would have improved its political position vis-à-vis the North by two fifths—thereby, it might be argued, gaining in defeat a political edge over its victorious opponent. Elizur Wright, a native of Connecticut and Yale graduate who had served as a professor at Western Reserve College and made a name for himself by developing greatly improved actuarial tables for life insurance companies, made much of this paradox in a widely read pamphlet published in March, 1865, and entitled *Suffrage for the Blacks Sound Political Economy*. Wright, recruited for the antislavery cause by Theodore Weld, insisted that it would "take a long period of military subjugation, after the overthrow of the rebel armies, to educate [the South] out of its rebel propensities, so that a majority of it can be relied on for loyal State government." The only way to avoid a substantial loss of political power to the South in the postwar period would be to enfranchise the freedmen. For Wright, indeed, such enfranchisement was the "*sine qua non* of reconstruction. . . . We have then nothing to do but to convert whites enough to make a majority, when added to the enfranchised blacks, to have State governments that can be trusted to stand alone. . . ." There was little more sentiment in Wright's argument than in his actuarial tables. "I am not disputing about tastes," he wrote. "A negro's ballot may be more vulgar than his bullet," but the alternative was to throw away the fruits of the Northern victory so dearly won. As Thomas Wentworth Higginson put it, "Ignorant men are governed by instinct, like children, and know their friends. And when in the present case, their friends are the nation's friends [i.e., the Republicans] and their enemies are the nation's enemies [Southern Democrats], this is quite enough for them to begin with." The worst thing that could happen would be to have "a consolidated body of rebels in Congress, equally malignant, and eleven votes stronger," as a consequence of the fact that the black population of the South could now count two-fifths *more* population for the purpose of congressional representation.

In the face of these developments, the strategy of the Republican leaders was simple and ingenious. Caucusing before the new Congress convened, they determined to bar the Southern Congressmen from their seats until a congressional investigation had been made to determine the true conditions in the South, most specifically whether the rebellious states were giving Unionists, Southern Republicans, freed blacks, and Northern emigrants the full protection of the law. The agency by which this was to be accomplished was the Joint Committee on Reconstruction, formed by concurrent resolution on December 13, 1865, and instructed to inquire into conditions in the Confederacy and report "whether they or any of them are entitled to be represented in either House of Congress." It was Stevens's strategy to prevent the seating of the Representatives and Senators chosen under the terms of Johnson's Reconstruction. The committee was divided into subcommittees to take testimony and collect evidence in each of the "districts" of the South.

Early in the new year the House passed the District suffrage bill giving the vote to blacks in the District of Columbia, and James Mitchell Ashley of Ohio presented a resolution for the impeachment of the President. The President vetoed the District suffrage bill, and the Senate passed it over his veto, as did the House.

Having established the Joint Committee and launched it on its investigation, Congress, early in 1866, passed a bill to extend the life of the Freedmen's Bureau indefinitely, widen its powers, and make it less dependent on the War Department by providing it with its own budget. Johnson promptly vetoed the bill and accompanied his veto with a lesson on constitutional principles. "After giving his sufficient reasons for this veto in statesmanlike style," George Templeton Strong wrote, "Johnson goes out of his way to lecture congress for not letting in Southern Representatives, wherein I think he shews himself impertinent, and what's worse, radically unsound. I am sorry, for I do not want to lose my faith in Andy Johnson."

The South was exultant over Johnson's veto. The *Montgomery* (Alabama)*Ledger* declared, "The old Tennesseean has shown his blood and bearded the lion in his lair, 'The Douglass in his hall'—'glory enough for one day'—glorious old man, and let the earth ring his praises to the heavens. The South and the Government are in the same boat one more time, thank the gods."

Johnson, exhilarated by the acclaim accorded his veto, gave an impromptu address to a crowd of admirers who gathered at the White House on Washington's Birthday evening. Responding to cheers, he launched a bitter attack on Sumner, Stevens, and Wendell Phillips. The trio was denounced as "opposed to the fundamental principles of this government, and as now laboring to destroy them." These men and their followers, Johnson implied, were bent on his assassination. "Have they not honor and courage enough to effect the removal of the 'Presidential obstacle' otherwise than through the hands of the assassin? . . . Does not the blood of Lincoln appease the vengeance and wrath of the opponents of this government? I do not fear assassins, but if my blood must be shed because I vindicate this Union, let it be so."

The President's harangue was so intemperate and paranoid in its references to assassination and his comparison of himself to Lincoln that word once more spread that Johnson had been drunk. But while many Conservative Republicans and even Democrats were appalled, the *Chicago Times,* a Democratic organ, urged Johnson to arrest Stevens, Sumner, and Phillips and "order the army to drive Congress out of their chambers."

Stevens's response to Johnson was to take the line that the President's speech was simply a hoax invented by the press. He also asked the clerk of the House to read a year-old editorial from the Democratic paper the *New York World,* which had enthusiastically acclaimed Johnson's attack on the Radical Republicans. Following Lincoln's inauguration, the same paper had described the then Vice-President as a "drunken and beastly Caligula," adding, "And to think that only one frail life stands between this *insolent, clownish drunkard* and the Presidency! May God bless and spare Abraham Lincoln!"

George Templeton Strong was appalled when he read Johnson's speech. "It is a very long speech," he wrote, "and full of repetitions. Its bouquet seems to me (as to others) to be that of Old Bourbon, largely imbibed by the orator just before taking the rostrum. Anyhow it is bad, egotistical, diffuse, undignified, intemperate, unwise, and sure to do great mischief. . . . This speech is a national calamity," he added. But the general effect was less calamitous than Strong anticipated. A few days later he wrote that "all indications are that Johnson's policy gains ground with the people, and that the extreme Left in Congress is losing heart." Strong feared that any presidential policy that seemed reasonable would be accepted by the people of the North "so anxious are we to have affairs settled, however illusory and temporary such settlement may be, and however dangerous and disastrous."

Lyman Trumbull, the Illinois Republican, followed the Freedmen's Bureau bill with a civil rights act designed to guarantee the civil rights of all Americans. Under its terms "all persons born in the United States" were declared to be citizens and "without regard to any previous condition of servitude . . . shall have the same right in every State and Territory . . . to make and enforce contracts, to sue, be parties, and give evidence, to inherit, purchase, sell, and convey real and personal property, and to full and equal benefit of all laws and proceedings for the security of person and property." Perhaps most important, "the district courts of the United States" were given exclusive "cognizance of all crimes and offences committed against the provisions of this act." The judgments of lower courts might be taken on appeal, in civil rights cases, to the Supreme Court. Federal marshals and Federal troops were directed to "prevent the violation and enforce the due execution" of the act.

When the President quizzed his Cabinet on the civil rights bill, Seward said that he "thought it might be well to pass a law declaring that negroes were citizens. . . . The rest of the bill he considered unconstitutional in many respects. . . ." Welles, for his part, considered it "very centralizing and objectionable." He wrote indignantly in his diary: "No bill of so contradictory and consolidating a character has ever been enacted. The Alien and Sedition Laws were not so objectionable." The President never wavered in his determination to veto the bill.

"Another veto," George Templeton Strong wrote. "A. Johnson has put his foot on the Civil Rights Bill. So the crack spreads and widens. His message is less strong than against the Freedmen's Bureau, but very able, perhaps sound, possibly a little disingenuous. . . . I am losing my faith in him, by no logical process, but by instinctive distrust of anyone who is commended by the *Express* and *Daily News* and *World,* the London *Times,* and the Richmond papers. . . . There should be no 'restoration' till all possible safeguards have been set up. The question 'would you make the South a Poland?' causes me no shudder. I reply, by all means, if it be expedient."

For many Conservative Republicans, among them John Sherman,

the President's veto was the last straw. Sherman wrote his general brother that Johnson, having been made by the "Union party . . . now deserts and betrays it. . . . I almost fear he contemplates civil war." With Sherman's strong support, the bill was promptly passed over Johnson's veto.

With the passage of the Civil Rights Act of 1866, the Federal government, for the first time in the history of the Republic, took the responsibility for extending the protections afforded in the Bill of Rights of the Constitution to all Americans in whatever state or territory they might reside. Such a dramatic broadening of Federal power would have been unthinkable in the period prior to the Civil War, and indeed after, if it had not been for the fact that Andrew Johnson had embarked on a program that seemed to many Americans to give away much of what the war had been fought for, including, at least prospectively, control of the Federal government. The friends of the free blacks hailed the Civil Rights Act joyfully. John Jay, veteran of decades of labor in the abolitionist cause, termed it "the last great victory in the war against slavery." It was the necessary and proper accompaniment to the Thirteenth Amendment, "since it relieves all misapprehensions as to the position which the American Republic is henceforth to occupy before the world, as regards the relationship of our people towards each other."

As the tide turned, and it became increasingly clear that Congress was determined to impose its own Reconstruction policies on the South, Emma Holmes wrote in her diary: "Oh, my God, when will the dark days end which seem enveloping our stricken land in deeper and deeper gloom, day by day. After our national wreck had shrouded it in awful grief & desolation & the gloom of the grave, months of weary despair & waiting for events bade us hope a little. . . ." The people of the South had tried "to conquer evil destiny by rousing, with all of manhood's energy & woman's faith, to the new and onerous duties laid upon us," and for a time it had seemed that the clouds might lift. President Johnson had struggled against "the ferocious Black Republicans for the rights of the South and the white man," while the Republicans were trying to make the government of the South "an almost unlimited military despotism, holding the South as conquered territory—by granting 'universal suffrage' to the negro (who now [are] the curse that clogs us at every step, I pray [it] may be theirs & prove their destruction). . . . Despair is laying its icy hand on all. Day by day it becomes harder to get money here for the necessaries of life; the little cotton saved has given a galvanized life. . . . No man can tell what the day may bring forth. . . . Liberty is precious, &, though crushed & bleeding under the trampling feet of fanatics & fiends, her [the North's] attitude proves that Secession is Right—and though God does not always permit Truth & Justice to triumph at first, for his own wise purpose, yet I do not forget that 'The mill of the Gods grind slowly, but it grinds exceeding small.' "

As the rift between Congress and the President widened, influential Republicans tried to prevail on Johnson to be more conciliatory in his dealings with Congress. Among them was old Peter Cooper, one of the "founding fathers" of the locomotive, sponsor of the transatlantic cable, and founder of Cooper Union. "I have thought it strange and unaccountable," he wrote, "that you should so severely censure the large majority in Congress, for adopting so mild a form of measures as a means for the guaranty of a republican form of government in the States so lately in rebellion. . . ." Cooper then went on to quote a long list of hostile statements by Johnson directed against the leaders of the rebellion, such as "treason must be made odious; . . . traitors must be punished and impoverished." The list was long and damning. "To my mind," Cooper added, "our nation must live in everlasting infamy if we fail to secure a full measure of justice to an unfortunate race of men who were originally hunted down in their own country, and carried off and sold like beasts into an abject slavery. . . . The enemies of our country and government are now trying to persuade the community to believe that a war of race would result from giving the black man the same measure of justice and rights which the white men claim for themselves. This will be found to be a groundless fear. Our national danger will always result from unequal and partial laws."

The issue of enfranchising the freed blacks was, as we have noted, entwined with the issue of states' rights. Once it was clear that the rights of the freedmen in the South could be protected only by the intervention of the Federal government, the critical question became: How can such intervention be justified in constitutional terms?

Richard Henry Dana had developed what he called "the Grasp of War" theory to justify government intervention in the affairs of the Southern states. It held, simply enough, that even after the peace that concluded the four years of bitter fighting, the "Confederate States were still in the 'grasp of war.' " The Constitution had no provision for the course to be followed if a number of states should secede and "wrongfully form a *de facto* nation. . . ." It thus followed that the South must be treated as a defeated "foreign" power. In Dana's words, "We have a right to hold the rebels in the grasp of war until we have obtained whatever the public safety and the public faith require."

The states' rights position was reiterated throughout Gideon Welles's diary. "While I am not inclined to throw impediments in the way of universal, intelligent enfranchisement of all men," Welles wrote, "I cannot lend myself to break down constitutional barriers. . . . When pressed by arguments which they cannot refute, the advocates of black enfranchisement turn and say if the negro is not allowed to vote, the Democrats will get control of the government in each of the seceding or rebellious States, and in conjunction with the Democrats of the Free States they will get the ascendency in our political affairs. . . . People—individuals—have rebelled but the States are sovereignties, not corporations, and they still belong to and are part of the Union. We can imprison, punish, hang the Rebels by law and constitutional warrant, but where is the authority or power to chastise a State, or change its political status, deprive it of political rights and sovereignty which other States possess? . . . The States have not seceded; they cannot secede, nor can they be expelled. . . . The rights of the States are unimpaired; the rights of those who have participated in the Rebellion may have been forfeited." Slavery had been forbidden by the Thirteenth Amendment "but conferring on the black civil rights is another matter. I know not the authority. The President in the exercise of the pardoning power may limit or make conditions, and, while granting life and liberty to traitors, deny them the right of holding office or voting. While, however, he can exclude traitors, can he legitimately confer on the blacks of North Carolina the right to vote? I do not yet see how this can be done by him or by Congress."

Although George Templeton Strong was a lawyer, he considered the "constitutional issue" a distraction from the first. On July 15, 1865, he wrote in his diary: "The *World* and the *News* and their rapidly diminishing train of followers continue wailing over a violated constitution. . . . What fools they are! Of course, subordination of government to the Constitution and to law is good—very good —among the very best things. But it's not the only good thing. To save the country is also good. . . . Emergencies are certainly conceivable that justify a little unconstitutionality. Perhaps our recent experiences are of that kind. The only people I know that maintain their constitution absolutely inviolate no matter what happens are the Chinese.

. . . Respect for written law and constitutions may be excessive and no less deadly than hypertrophy of the heart. A nation (or a church) that has finally crystalized into permanent, definite form and become incapable of developing new organs or agencies to meet new conditions is *dead,* and will begin to decompose whenever time brings the new conditions. *Anno Domini* 1861 brought us a batch of new conditions, and Abraham Lincoln met them wisely and well. He saved the country. If learned counsel prove by word-splitting that he saved it unconstitutionally, I shall honor his memory still more reverently than I do now. In A.D. 1865, the situation is wholly changed once more. The whole South is in a state of subjugation, indignation, emancipation, ruination, and starvation. It's a chaos of hostile elements mitigated and quieted by bayonets, a collection of acids and bases hardly restrained from fizzing into furious, disastrous reaction at any moment. Our constitution makers never dreamed of this state of affairs and made no provision for it. One would think it most desirable to get the South into good order again without delay. But our Chinese conservatives protest against any step that way, unless chapter and verse of the Constitution can be cited for it. They are political Pharisees, who would let the government perish . . . rather than see it saved 'on the Sabbath Day.' "

Theophilus Parsons, speaking in Faneuil Hall in the summer of 1865, attacked the doctrine of states' rights as simply a cover for persecution of free blacks. The South despised "political equality and free labor," Parsons declared, and to support their peculiar system, "they invented and used, as a most effectual weapon, the dogma of State Supremacy, which they disguised under the name of State Rights. It may, therefore, be fairly said that three ideas had complete possession of Southern society,—Slavery, Aristocracy and State Supremacy." When Parsons had finished his speech, those present endorsed a set of resolutions the most important of which read: "The public faith is pledged to every person of color in the rebel States, to secure to them and their posterity forever a complete and veritable freedom. Having promised them this freedom, received their aid on the faith of this promise, and, by a successful war and actual military occupation of the country, having obtained the power to secure the result, we are dishonored if we fail to make it good to them." It might be said that the Faneuil Hall resolutions contained the essence of what the antislavery movement felt must be the consequence of the Union victory. For ten years they would be the guiding principles of Radical Republican policy, and when the Republicans at last admitted defeat, those who remained true to the cause did not try to gloss over the reality of that defeat, caused in large part, by indifference or hostility in the mass of Northerners to the ultimate fate of black Americans as well as to the intractability of the South.

It is essential to keep in mind the fact that the end of the war found very few Northerners, even in the ranks of the abolitionists, who were disposed to argue in favor of the general enfranchisement of Southern blacks. William Lloyd Garrison and the *Liberator* came out against immediate black suffrage, and Thomas Wentworth Higginson canceled his subscription. His view, he wrote in an article in the *Boston Weekly Commonwealth,* was that "It might be very pleasant to have . . . [Southern States] consist entirely of college graduates, or of gentlemen in white kid-gloves or of albinos with pink eyes. But as all these classes seem likely to be small in those regions, for some years to come, it will be necessary to go beyond those precious and privileged classes and take the best we can get."

Richard Henry Dana supported the enfranchisement of all *Northern* blacks. Speaking at Faneuil Hall in June, 1865, he declared, "Ah! there are negro parents whose children have fallen in battle; there are children who lost fathers, and wives who lost husbands, in our cause. Our covenant with the freedman is sealed in blood! It bears the image and superscription of the republic! Their freedom is a tribute which we must pay, not only to Caesar, but to God! (Applause.)" The freedmen must also have the right to hold land, to testify in courts, to bear arms as soldiers in the militia. But Dana drew the line at giving them the vote. "Some persons may say that. . . . every human being has an absolute and unconditional right to vote." But, Dana declared, "There never was any such doctrine! We do not mean, now, to allow about one half of the South to vote. (Applause.) Why not? Why the public safety does not admit of it. (Applause.)" Half the population of Massachusetts—the women of the state—was excluded from the ballot. "The question of who should vote had been hedged about with many restrictions, property, residence, and now, in Massachusetts, literacy. . . . The greatest good of the greatest number must decide it."

Dana went on to argue that giving "free negroes [of the North] the voting franchise is a revolution. *If we do not secure that now, in the time of revolution, it can never be secured, except by a new revolution.* (Loud applause.) Do you want, some years hence, to see a new revolution? —the poor, oppressed, degraded black man, bearing patiently his oppression until he can endure it no longer, rising with arms for his rights—do you want to see that?" Cries of "No! No!" to which Dana replied, "Then 'Now's the day, and now's the hour.' (Loud applause.) They are in a condition of transition; a condition of revolution; seize the opportunity and make it thorough! (Renewed and hearty applause.)"

The freedmen of the South were a different matter. "Slavery," he explained, "has degraded the negroes. It has kept them ignorant and debased. It has not, thank God, destroyed them. The germ of moral and intellectual life has survived; and we mean to see to it that they are built up into a self-governing, voting, intelligent population. (Applause). They are not that today." That would take time. Meanwhile, they could not, in their present benighted condition, be allowed to vote. The hope of the ballot would be "a part of our educating and elevating process. . . . When the free man of color," Dana continued, "educated in the common schools, deposits a vote which he can write himself, gives a deposition which he can read and sign, and pays a tax on the homestead he has bought," then he must be fully enfranchised. That was the stumbling block. No matter how ardent a black man may have been in the cause of freedom and Union he could not vote until he could read and write. Such a restriction would, of course, bar the vast majority of freedmen from the polls.

Frederick Douglass was one of the few public figures favoring "the immediate, unconditional, and universal 'enfranchisement of the black man, in every State in the Union.' " Addressing the Massachusetts Anti-Slavery Society at the end of the war, he declared, "Without this his liberty is a mockery . . . for in fact if he is not the slave of an individual master, he is the slave of society, and holds his liberty as a privilege, not as a right." Douglass believed "that women, as well as men, have the right to vote [applause] and my heart and my voice go with the movement to extend suffrage to women." But for him the most pressing issue remained the vote for the freed blacks. "We want it because it is our *right,* first of all. . . . We want it again as a means for educating our race. Men are so constituted that they derive their conviction of their own possibilities largely from the estimate formed of them by others." More important, the enfranchisement of blacks was essential to the Union if the consequences of the war were to be secured against the already clearly demonstrated determination of the South to undo them. Southerners, Douglass predicted, "will endeavor to circumvent, they will endeavor to destroy, the peaceful operation of this government." Where, he asked, "will you find the strength to counterbalance this spirit, if you do not find it in the Negroes of the South?" The North's heart had never been in the cause of the slave. The South had fought for decades to extend the limits of slavery; the North, to restrict them, "both despising the Negro, both insulting the Negro." Douglass admitted that blacks were "virtually inferior" to whites. "We walk about among you like dwarfs among giants. Our heads are scarcely seen above the great sea of humanity. The Germans are superior to us; the Irish are superior to us; the Yankees are superior to us; they can do what we cannot, that is, what we have not hitherto been allowed to do. But while I make this admission, I utterly deny, that we are originally, or naturally, or practically, or in any way, or in any important sense, inferior to anybody on this globe. (Loud applause.) This charge of inferiority is an old dodge." Looking about the country, Douglass saw innumerable white organizations devoted to "benevolence" to the black. "What I ask for the Negro," he declared, "is not benevolence, not pity, not sympathy, but simply *justice*." He heard constantly from abolitionists the question "What shall we do with the Negro?" To which he had only one answer: "Do nothing with us! Your doing with us has already played the mischief with us! Do nothing with us!" If whites saw a black child on his way to school, "let him alone, don't disturb him! If you see him going to the dinner table at a hotel, let him alone! If you see him going to the ballot box, let him alone, don't disturb him! (Applause.) If you see him going into a workshop, just let him alone,—your interference is doing him a positive injury. . . . Let him fall if he cannot stand alone! If the Negro cannot live by the line of eternal justice . . . the fault be not yours, it will be his who made the Negro, and established that line for his government." There was a profound truth in Douglass's words. The only trouble was that some whites would not let the Negro alone, and thus, other whites must defend him against those who wished to deny him justice. So he was beset on every side by those who were determined to abuse and degrade him and those determined to protect and uplift him.

Frederick Douglass pleaded with the leaders of the American Anti-Slavery Society, among them William Lloyd Garrison, not to disband. Their work would not be done, he insisted, until the word "white" was erased from every law and statute book in the country. The ready passage of the Thirteenth Amendment had given rise to false hopes. The South, "by unfriendly legislation, could make our liberty, under that provision, a delusion, a mockery, and a snare." Even in the Northern states of Illinois, Indiana, and Ohio, "no black man's testimony" could be received in a court of law. Slavery would not be "abolished until the black man has the ballot. . . . Let the civil powers of the [Confederate] States be restored, and the old prejudices and hostility to the Negro will revive," Douglass predicted. "Aye, the very fact that the Negro has been used to defeat this rebellion and strike down the standards of the Confederacy will be a stimulus to all their hatreds, to all their malice, and lead them to legislate with greater stringency towards this class than ever before. The American people are bound—bound by their sense of honor . . . to extend the franchise to the Negro . . ." and the American Anti-Slavery Society must persevere in that essential work.

Even John Stuart Mill was drawn into the debate. In October, 1865, William Dickson of Oberlin, Ohio, published an address on *The Absolute Equality of All Men Before the Law, the True Basis of Reconstruction*. The principal interest of Dickson's pamphlet was that it contained a letter from John Stuart Mill to Dickson, giving the English social philosopher and reformer's views on the subject of Reconstruction. Mill spoke of Reconstruction as an issue of "concern to all mankind, almost as much as of the United States, that the conquests achieved by your great and arduous struggle should not be, in the very hour of victory, carelessly flung away. . . ." It was true that the slaves had been made "nominally free. But this is about the amount of all they will have gained, if the power of legislation over them is handed over once more to their old masters, and to the mean whites by whom they are despised as much [as], and probably hated more, than even by their masters, and who have been fighting these four years to retain them enslaved."

What action would the North take? Mill asked. To do nothing was "to abandon the negroes to the tender mercies of those from whom, at so terrible a cost, you have so lately rescued them? No party or set of men in the free States are so shameless as to propose this combined turpitude and imbecility. . . ." On the other hand, there were those who insisted that "a censorship will have to be exercised over all the acts, both legislative and administrative, of the State governments; the Federal authorities will, by military coercion, prevent all proceedings calculated to interfere with that equality of civil rights which they are bound by every consideration both of duty and of interest, to secure to the freed race." But such a course must be continued for "a very great length of time." In Mill's opinion at least two generations "must elapse before the habits and feelings engendered by slavery give place to new ones. . . ." Meanwhile, it would be necessary to "rule tyrannically over the whole Southern population, in order to avoid depriving the white half of that population of the power of tyrannizing over the black half." The latter course was unthinkable in Mill's view.

Only an alliance of enfranchised blacks and "white immigrants from the North" could be counted on to neutralize a white people "who have been corrupted by vicious institutions." It was thus necessary to enfranchise the freed blacks promptly. "I have no objection," Mill concluded, "to requiring, as a condition of the suffrage, education up to the point of reading and writing; but upon the condition that this shall be required equally from the whites." The problem with that formula was that while it was one thing to deny the franchise to those who had never had it on the ground of illiteracy, it was quite another to take it away, on the same ground from those who already exercised it.

George Templeton Strong expressed the dilemma: "What shall we do with them? . . . We cannot leave our black soldiers, now mustered out, to the mercy of their late masters. We have a Southern wolf or hyena by the ears. Letting go would be ruinous. Holding on awhile is inconvenient. . . . It seems clear that no Northern man, no Yankee, can live at the South in any moderate safety yet. Negroes are oppressed, tortured, and murdered by their *ci-devant* owners. We may have to undertake another civil war. . . . Nothing but physical exhaustion keeps the Southern hyena from instantly flying at our throats. . . . There is a quarrel among his keepers, much to be regretted. This Republican party is cracked, and the crack is spreading and widening. Andrew Johnson seems more and more inclined toward what is called conservatism. . . . The 'Radicals' are firm. I am sure their doctrine is gaining ground with the people. Every change I notice in anyone's political sympathies is that way. Almost every one had changed a little during the last six months, and become a little more Radical or Conservative."

As Georges Clemenceau put it for his French readers, "There is a widespread feeling of pity for the blacks who behaved so admirably during the war . . . and shed their blood for the Union. . . . Now they are being forced to bargain for, perhaps in the end to lose entirely, the rights which they have already purchased so dearly."

The Black Codes which spelled out in unmistakable terms the

intentions of the white South toward the freed slaves, and the intractability of the President worked, as George Templeton Strong's observations indicated, a profound change of opinion in the North. Abolitionists, if they were initially reluctant to accept the notion of enfranchising the freedmen, soon came, in the main, to support the franchise for blacks. Substantial numbers of Republicans followed their lead.

One of the few issues that failed to divide Congress and the President was the acquisition of Alaska. In 1855, during the Crimean War, Russia, in order to forestall the anticipated seizure of Alaska by the British, prepared a fictitious sale of the region by the Russian American Company to a San Francisco concern called the American Russian Company. The Grand Duke Constantine, brother of the czar, was hostile to the Russian American Company, in part because of its inefficiency and in part because of its ruthless exploitation of the Alaska natives. He pressed for the region's sale to the United States, and in 1859 California Senator William McKendree Gwin offered Russia $5,000,000 for Alaska, apparently at the instance of President Buchanan. The Civil War brought a halt to negotiations, but the friendly attitude of Russia, which did its best to keep the European powers neutral, sent its fleet to New York in 1863 as a gesture of support for the Union, and was said to have "loaned" Admiral Farragut 500 men for the attack on Mobile, created an atmosphere favorable to the purchase of Alaska. In December, 1866, the Russian ambassador, Baron Edward de Stoeckl, broached the matter to Seward, who was an unabashed expansionist. Russia was prepared to sell Alaska to the United States for $7,000,000. There was a notable lack of enthusiasm for the purchase in the country generally, and Johnson himself was cool to the notion; but Charles Sumner made the cause his own, and with the combined efforts of Sumner and Seward the deal was consummated just before the adjournment of Congress at the end of March, 1867 and in an air of considerable secrecy and haste. The price was $7,200,000. Sumner wrote to John Bright: "Abstractly I am against any further accessions of territory but this question was so perplexed by considerations of politics and comity and the engagements already entered into by the government, I hesitated to take the responsibility of defeating it." That was not quite candid. He worked with characteristic zeal to bring it about.

The territory thus acquired, almost inadvertently, one might say, was one of the most remarkable regions of the world. Extending northwest from the farthest tip of the state of Washington, a heavily indented, island-strewn coastline abutted on British Columbia and then the vast Yukon Territory of Canada. Turning directly west, past the Kenai Peninsula, the coast bent sharply south along the Shelikof Strait separating the mainland from the fur and fish-rich island of Kodiak, to the Alaska Peninsula, which terminated in the string of islands reaching 1,000 miles farther west to Attu Island. North of the Alaska Peninsula, again with innumerable inlets, harbors, and rivers, the coastline reached the Seward Peninsula, where, across the Bering Strait, hardly 52 miles in width, lay Siberian Russia. Still farther north were the Arctic Ocean and the northernmost projection of land at Point Barrow. At the southern tip of Alaska lay the beginning of the Inland Passage, 1,000 miles of waterway protected by an island chain to the north of Juneau. Covering an area of more than 590,000 square miles—larger than Texas and California combined—35,000 miles of coastline, Alaska added almost a third to the landmass of the United States. It had, in addition, as wide a range of climate as that between Maine and Florida, extending through 20 degrees of latitude and 54 degrees of longitude—2,500 miles from the easternmost point to Attu in the west. Some of the highest peaks in the world marked its mountain ranges—Mount St. Elias (18,000 feet), Mount Fairweather (15,300), Mount Blackburn (16,523), and, tallest on the North American continent, Mount McKinley (20,320). Glaciers, ice fields, icebergs, and active volcanoes were features of the landscape. This extraordinary "world"—"state" or "territory" does not at all suggest its scale or the variety of climates and topographies— abounds in exotic plant, animal, and human life. Its natural bounties are prodigious; the rivers teem with fish, salmon being only the most notable; its mountains and forests, with moose, bear, caribou; its bays and inlets, with seal and walrus. Its aboriginal people—the Eskimo and the various interior tribes of "Indians"—strengthen the conviction of an ancient migration across the Bering Sea from Asia. Demonstrating in spectacular fashion man's capacity to adapt to hostile environments, the Eskimo created one of the most compelling and dramatic aboriginal cultures in the world. Even today, with the smallest population by far of any state in the Union—some 270,000—scattered over its immense reaches, its future seems as uncertain as its past is mysterious.

On this strange world, the final acquisition of the "westerning impulse" so strong in the American psyche, its previous owners, the Russians, had made only modest inroads—a handful of trading posts reinforced by missions and chapels of the Russian Orthodox Church. Too vast to comprehend, it would remain, a gold rush aside, on the periphery of the nation's consciousness for a generation or more.

40

Congressional Reconstruction

After the passage of the Civil Rights Act, Congress had turned to the drafting of a constitutional amendment to incorporate and extend the provisions of that legislation. The debate over the amendment was prolonged and increasingly acrimonious as Sumner and Stevens tried to add to it ironclad provisions to protect black civil rights and bar any form of racial discrimination.

Wendell Phillips attacked what would eventually be the Fourteenth Amendment for its failure to insure black voting rights. It is important, parenthetically, to note the close interaction between the most influential abolitionists in Congress, like Sumner and Stevens, and those outside, most notably Phillips and Douglass. Phillips insisted that no compromise was possible on the question of the rights of the freed slaves. The Reverend George Cheever followed a similar line in a pamphlet, published the same year, which emphasized the importance of world opinion. "European nations are watching the result," he declared. "Convocations of Christian churches, the most illustrious in the world for piety and patriotism, have addressed similar appeals, on religious grounds, to the people and churches of this country. The leading patriots of Great Britain and France . . . have by letter, speech, and public protest, implored in the name of humanity, and for the sake of the possibility of anticipated impartial freedom in the Old World, the just and right decision of the question here. Nothing injures the republican party so much as the assumption and defence of an injustice so palpable, so shameful, so unnecessary. . . . Better to lose a thousand such amendments than accept the curse with them."

Stevens, now seventy-five years old and in bad health, so feeble he could hardly stand, attacked the amendment with all his old fire. In the words of his ally George Julian, "Eloquence, irony, wit, and invective, were charmingly blended in defense of his positions. . . ." To the Democratic argument that "this is a white man's government," Stevens replied with abundant scorn. "What is implied by this?" he asked. "That one race of men are to have the exclusive right forever to rule this nation, and to exercise all acts of sovereignty, while all other races and nations and colors are to be their subjects. . . . If we have not yet been sufficiently scourged for our national sin to teach us to do justice to all God's creatures, without distinction of race or color, we must expect the still more heavy vengeance of an offended Father. . . ."

Stevens told a Republican rally: "We shall hear repeated, ten thousand times, the cry of 'Negro Equality!' The radicals would thrust the negro into your parlors, your bedrooms, and the bosoms of your wives and daughters. They would even make your reluctant daughters marry black men. And then they will send up a chorus from every foul throat, 'nigger,' 'nigger,' 'nigger!' 'Down with the nigger party.' . . . A deep seated prejudice against races has disfigured the human mind for ages. . . . This doctrine [black rights] may be unpopular with besotted ignorance. But popular or unpopular, I shall stand by it until I am relieved of the unprofitable labors of earth. . . .

"What is negro equality, about which so much is said by knaves, and some of which is believed by men who are not fools?" Stevens asked. "It means, as understood by honest Republicans, just this much and no more: every man, no matter what his race or color; every earthly being who has an immortal soul, has an equal right of justice, honesty, and fair play with every other man; and the law should secure him those rights. . . . The same law which gives a verdict in a white man's favor should give a verdict in a black man's favor on the same state of facts. Such is the law of God and such ought to be the law of man."

In the midst of the debate over the Fourteenth Amendment public opinion was greatly enflamed by two race riots—one in Memphis and one in New Orleans. On May 1, 1866, a fight broke out in Memphis between discharged black soldiers, who were celebrating in South Street bars, and the policemen of the city. There was an exchange of shots, and two policemen and six soldiers were killed in the melee. The soldiers withdrew to the nearby fort. The chief of police tried to organize an attack on the fort itself, and when that failed, he and his men went on an orgy of looting and killing through the black district of the city. The chief was reported to have said to his men, "Boys, I want you to go ahead and kill the last damned one of the nigger race, and burn up the cradle." Before the bloody work was done, forty-six blacks had been killed and some eighty more wounded, including a number of patients in the Freedmen's Bureau Hospital. Ninety houses occupied by blacks and twelve schools were burned to the ground. More than $100,000 worth of black property was consumed in fires or stolen by whites in riots extending over a period of three days. At least five black women were raped. Sleeping blacks were torn from their beds, their belongings ransacked, their money stolen. Typically the raiders declared they were searching for illicit guns; under that pretense, they raped black women and stole money and personal belongings, beating or killing any who resisted.

New Orleans had been occupied by Federal troops during much of the war, and with the end of the war and the evacuation of the troops the citizens turned on all those who had been involved with the Union forces. A hundred and ten teachers accused of Union sympathies were fired; all Union men on the police force were replaced by ex-Confederates and the Southern Cross Association was formed to keep freed blacks in line. On the Republican side the Reconstruction governor, J. Madison Wells, convinced that he could expect no support from Johnson, encouraged a group of white and black Republicans to call a constitutional convention to amend the state Constitution of 1864 to give blacks the right to vote. The promoters of the plan gathered together almost half the original delegates under the leadership of Rufus Howell of the Louisiana Supreme Court. The governor undertook to order elections to fill the remaining seats. The Democrats responded by calling a grand jury to indict all members of the convention for misdemeanor and perjury. Having traveled to Washington, Howell got what he was convinced were promises of support from Radical Republican leaders, and plans to convene the convention on the first of May went forward in an atmosphere of growing tension. Democrats appealed to Johnson and were assured that he would not "countenance" the meeting or anything issuing from it.

On the day set for the assembling of the delegates, a "parade" of blacks estimated at from 60 to 130 men was attacked by a mob led by the sheriff, an ex-Confederate general. Shooting began, and many of the marchers took refuge inside the Mechanics' Institute. There they were hunted down like animals and shot in cold blood, in many instances by the police officers of the city. To the cry "We surrender —we make no resistance," the reply was "God damn you, not one of you will escape from here alive." The count was 48 killed, 68 severely wounded and 98 slightly wounded.

In the congressional investigation that followed, one black testified that a policeman shouted, "There goes one damned nigger captain, the son of a bitch. Kill him." Charles Gibbons, a house painter and a former captain in a Louisiana black regiment, told of being fired at by a policeman as he ran for his life; a friend beside Gibbons was shot by other officers. One, L. Capla, who had stood near the Mechanics' Institue, testified to the committee that "he saw policemen shooting poor laboring men, men with their tin buckets in their hands and even old men walking with sticks. They tramped upon them and mashed their heads with their boots after they were down."

General Sheridan was the military commander of the district. He had done his best to protect the rights of Unionists and blacks in Louisiana and before that in Texas, although he had alienated Texas by declaring angrily that if he owned Texas and hell, he would rent Texas and live in hell. Sheridan wrote to Grant: "The more information I obtain of the affair the more revolting it becomes. *It was not a riot. It was an absolute massacre by the police, which was not excelled in murderous cruelty by that of Fort Pillow. It was a MURDER which the Mayor and Police of the city perpetrated without the shadow of a necessity.* Furthermore, *I believe it was premeditated,* and every indication points to this."

When Stanton read to the Cabinet the telegrams from Sheridan describing the events in New Orleans, Welles noted disapprovingly that the secretary of war showed obvious sympathy with black victims (whom Welles called "the rioters"). Welles was convinced that the riots were the initial phase of a Radical Republican conspiracy to trigger "a series of bloody affrays throughout the States lately in rebellion." Johnson by his silence seemed to condone what had been done, and *Harper's Weekly* called the President's apparent indifference "the most alarming incident in this sad affair." When Johnson did speak out, it was to blame the Radical Republicans for trying "to supersede the organized authorities in the State government of

Louisiana." The responsibility for the massacre was theirs. In the classic manner of megalomaniacs, Johnson, having compared himself earlier to Lincoln, now compared himself to Christ, whose enemies had carried him before Pontius Pilate, "and this same persecuting, diabolical, and nefarious clan today would persecute and shed the blood of innocent men to carry out their purposes."

The congressional committee wrote a scathing report on the two riots, describing that in Memphis as "an organized and bloody massacre of the colored people, inspired by the press and led on by officers of the law, actuated by feelings of the most deadly hatred." The same clearly had been true in New Orleans.

The massacres insured the passage of the Fourteenth Amendment, which was making a slow way through Congress. Stevens took the occasion to urge the retention of the third section, which denied the vote to all Southerners "who had voluntarily adhered to the late insurrection," until July 4, 1870. He would not agree to admit the rebels "except as supplicants in sackcloth and ashes." To those who urged conciliation, he replied, "Let not those friends of secession sing to me their siren song of peace and good will until they can stop my ears to the screams and groans of the dying victims at Memphis. . . ." The House then approved the amendment 128 to 37.

The Fourteenth Amendment provided that "All persons born or naturalized in the United States . . . are citizens of the United States and of the State wherein they reside. No State shall make or enforce any law which shall abridge the privileges or immunities of citizens of the United States; nor shall any State deprive any person of life, liberty or property without due process of law; nor deny to any person within its jurisdiction the equal protection of the laws." The amendment left the question of eligibility to vote with the states, providing only that nonvoters could not be counted for purposes of representation.

George Julian, the Indiana Congressman, shared Stevens's dislike of the amendment that finally emerged, and although Wendell Phillips, convinced that a better bill could not be passed, gave it his reluctant support, Julian was outspoken in his criticism. Years after the event he wrote: "It left the ballot in the hand of white Rebels, and did not confer it upon the black loyalists. It sought to conciliate the power it was endeavoring to coerce. . . . This perfectly inexcusable abandonment of negro suffrage was zealously defended by a small body of conservative Republicans . . . of whom Mr. Blaine was the chief. . . ."

On the other hand, many moderate politicians agreed with Carl Schurz that the clause in the Fourteenth Amendment which disbarred most of the natural white leaders in the South from political roles was, "irrespective of justice or generosity, a grave blunder in statesmanship."

Johnson so far turned his back on the freedmen as to urge the Southern states to reject the Fourteenth Amendment. The fact that ten of the eleven states that had been in rebellion did in fact refuse to ratify the amendment put ammunition into the hands of the Republicans that they did not hesitate to use. The vote, they insisted, had unmasked the true intentions of the Southern states, their adamant resistance to anything like justice for Southern blacks. Johnson and Southern leaders could scarcely have devised a strategy more suited to advance the Republican cause. By putting their intractability on the record, the Southern states, in effect, challenged the North to chastise them. "Thank God, the Southern oligarchy are blind," the black editor of the *New Orleans Tribune* wrote. "This stubbornness of the conquered to refuse the mild and generous terms offered by the conqueror, can only bring the latter to exact stronger guarantees. . . . Their folly will save us and our liberties for the future. It is better for us that the work of reconstruction be protracted. Let the rebels do our work."

In Tennessee the Republican governor, William G. Brownlow, convened a special session of the Tennessee legislature to ratify the Fourteenth Amendment, but only fifty-four members showed up, two shy of the necessary quorum. Three-fourths of those present then voted to ratify the amendment. Champions of the Constitution like Welles were horrified at such dubious actions.

Johnson's greatest mistake may have been in condoning a program of legal harassment directed at Union officers by unrepentant Northern Democrats in the form of damage suits for recruitment or security activities that had taken place during the war. In at least eight states sixteen such suits were filed. The same policy was being followed in the reconstructed states, where army officers and agents of the Freedmen's Bureau were haled into state courts and enjoined from carrying out their duties. The harassment of the army officers and Freedmen's Bureau agents brought Stanton, Grant, and O. O. Howard into the picture. As commanding general Grant was determined to protect the officers, and on January 12, 1866, he issued General Order No. 3, instructing all "Military Division and Department Commanders" in "any of the late rebellious States" to "issue and enforce orders protecting from prosecution or suits in the State or Municipal Courts . . . all officers and soldiers of the armies of the United States . . . charged with offenses for acts done in their military capacity. . . ." All "loyal citizens" were to be similarly protected. Johnson could hardly have made a graver strategic error than allowing a situation to develop where Grant would be forced to come forward as the champion of the men and officers of the Union army.

Republicans still loyal to Johnson met in Philadelphia on August 14, 1866, with a large delegation of Southern representatives to dramatize the President's policy of reconciliation. Republican leaders, among them Thurlow Weed and James Doolittle of Wisconsin, entered the hall arm in arm with Southern delegates; hence its popular name of the "arm-in-arm convention." James Russell Lowell, writing to his English friend Leslie Stephen, described Johnson as having "all the obstinacy of a weak mind and a strong constitution. . . . Johnson is really foolish enough to think he can make himself President for a second term by uniting in his favor the loyalty [Southern sympathizers] of both ends of the country."

"I predict," George Templeton Strong wrote in August, on the heels of the "Philadelphia Convention," "that the fall elections will sustain the President. He has a strong case on the merits; the Radical project of Negro suffrage must find little favor with any but theorists, and the great law of reaction will tell in his favor. Perhaps it may prove best that the President's policy prevail. But I find my faith in A. Johnson growing daily weaker."

The Radical Republicans held a convention of their own two weeks later, featuring Southern "loyalists," who told horrendous tales of persecution by ex-rebels, pointing out that more than a thousand Union citizens in the South had been murdered since Lee's surrender. Army veterans held pro- and anti-Johnson conventions of their own.

At this moment the President, increasingly confident of victory in the fall elections, decided to tour the country with his Cabinet, taking his case to the voters and challenging his congressional opponents on their home grounds. Stanton begged off with the excuse that his wife was sick. Alexander Williams Randall, the new postmaster general, was a somewhat reluctant member of the party, which included Welles and his wife, General Grant, Admiral Farragut, and a bevy of generals, the most conspicuous of whom was handsome, golden-haired young George Custer.

In Cleveland, when hecklers called out, "Hang Jeff Davis," Johnson replied, "Why not hang Thad Stevens and Wendell Phillips? I tell you, my countrymen . . . having fought traitors at the South, I am prepared to fight traitors at the North." In a number of the cities visited—Baltimore, Philadelphia, and Pittsburgh among them—the municipal authorities failed to put in an appearance, and the governors of Ohio, Indiana, Illinois, Michigan, Missouri, and Pennsylvania were also conspicuous by their absence when the presidential party arrived at their states. Welles, not surprisingly, blamed Seward for much of the expedition's failure. "He has," he wrote, "throughout the excursion generally seconded the President, assented to all his positions, rather encouraged his frequent speeches, which I opposed, for it was always the same speech, sometimes slightly modified, which was soon burlesqued and published in anticipation of its delivery."

Yet the trip was not all gloom. If prominent Republicans were absent, large crowds turned out in many cities to hear the President and cheered his fulminations against the Radical Republicans and his proposals to hang Wendell Phillips, Stevens, and Sumner. At Chicago and St. Louis the President experienced a "cordiality and sincerity unsurpassed," Welles noted. And at Alton, Illinois, where Elijah Lovejoy had been martyred years before, thirty-six steamers crowded with admirers of the President made their appearance. But the overall effect was decidedly negative. "The President 'progresses' and speechifies," George Templeton Strong noted. "Every speech costs 'my policy' many votes, I think. No orator has used the first personal pronoun in all its cases (I-me-my) so freely since the days of Erskine, the 'Counselor Ego' of the *Anti-Jacobin*. It is an unhappy mistake and may paralyze all his efforts to do the country service." Strong was equally severe with Seward's "auxiliary harangues." Strong added: "If the fall election sustains Congress, the President will have his own unruly tongue to blame for the result. I think he had the inside track three months ago, but he has lost it by his exhibitions of petulance and egotism during his stump pilgrimage." It was said that an unhappy Grant had declared that "he didn't like attending a man who was making speeches at his own funeral."

As the bitterness between the Radical Republicans, a category that each month included more Republican "regulars"—moderates and even conservatives—and the President increased, Johnson began ousting Republican officeholders whose loyalty to him was in doubt and replacing them with Democrats or proadministration Republicans.

He justified the firing by declaring in a speech in St. Louis: "I believe that one set of men have enjoyed the emoluments of office long enough. . . . God willing, I will kick them out as fast as I can." George Templeton Strong wrote: "He is certainly active in displacing Lincoln's appointees and putting very bad Copperheads into office as postmasters, collectors, and the like. . . . If the country is to avoid ruin, it must sternly repudiate A. Johnson and his 'policy.' " By fall, 1866, thirteen hundred postmasters had been replaced, most of them by Democrats. Johnson's new appointees were soon known as the bread-and-butter brigade, the implication being that they had sold out their party for purely material considerations.

In addition, the President in all his public statements began to refer to Congress as "a body called, or which assumes to be, the Congress of the United States, while, in fact, it is a Congress of only a part of the United States." The implication was clearly that the President was questioning the legitimacy of Congress and, by extension, the constitutionality of all its enactments. He could hardly have issued a more inflammatory challenge.

Georges Clemenceau, who had earlier praised Johnson's policies, had written to Le Temps: "We are threatened with seeing the nullification of all measures taken by Congress to do justice in the ex-Confederate states, by having them tainted with unconstitutionality. Thus it is likely that the year will see a struggle between the President, supported by the Supreme Court and the Southern States on one side, against the Congress."

The approaching elections generated such strong partisan feelings and such an atmosphere of strain and anxiety as, in Carl Schurz's view, "to affect men's balance of mind." He was convinced that the suicides of at least two Republican politicians—Preston King of New York and James Lane of Kansas—were directly attributable to the extreme emotional atmosphere surrounding the elections.

The Radical Republicans took the line that nothing less than the outcome of the war was at stake—whether or not Johnson, allied with Northern and Southern Democrats and Conservative Republicans, would undo all that the Union victory had achieved or, perhaps more accurately, still promised to achieve. The Boston Republican, an organ of the Conservative Republicans, put the matter succinctly: "To reject Thaddeus Stevens and Charles Sumner and support Mr. Johnson is one thing, and to go to bed with Copperheads and rebels is another; and many eager for the first will hesitate long before doing the last."

The October elections of 1866 brought a great victory for the antiadministration Republicans. They swept Pennsylvania by 16,000, Ohio by 10,000, and Indiana by 13,000. The results were a taste of what was to come. In November only Maryland, Delaware, and Kentucky failed to end up in the Republican column. The Republicans had a more than two-thirds majority in both houses, and it was clear that the Radical Republicans were firmly in the driver's seat and determined to force party discipline on moderate or fainthearted members. Even the *Chicago Times,* a strong Democratic and proadministration paper, trimmed its sails, announcing that henceforth the Democrats must support the principle of "Impartial Suffrage in the Southern States" or "become extinct." If the Democratic Party went so far, Strong wrote, it would alienate "all the brutal Irishry—all the great multitude of low corner-grocers, of brothel-bullies, of professional gamblers, and their decoy ducks. . . ."

The Reverend George Cheever called the heavily Republican vote an "uprising of the people . . . to sustain their own Congress to compel the rebel States to obey the Constitution and the laws, making all men equal before the law, and giving to all Citizens their rights, without respect to color or race." The South was bent on the "moral assassination of the whole colored race. . . . For if the right to vote can be taken away from them, every other right will be seized whenever prejudice and cruelty and contempt indicate. . . . The right to vote is the back-bone of all . . . other rights. A man crawls upon his belly in the dust the moment that right is taken away. So we propose to make worms of the black race, for the rebel white race to tread upon. The pretence of protecting their civil rights when taking away their political is base and hypocritical. . . ."

The success of the Republicans was, in the view of most of Johnson's dwindling company of supporters, due in large part to the obtuseness of the Democrats, who, instead of realizing that their best hopes lay in rallying to the President's standard, were so blinded by party considerations that they supported men who had opposed Lincoln and the war. In the fall of 1866, when the Democratic disposition to go whole hog in nominating party regulars was evident, Gideon Welles wrote in his diary: "Instead of openly and boldly supporting the President and the policy of the administration, showing moderation and wisdom in the selection of candidates, they are pressing forward men whom good Unionists, remembering and feeling the recent calamities of the War, cannot willingly support. In this way they have put in jeopardy the success of the cause of the Administration, which is really their own in most of the States." Undoubtedly Democratic folly was based primarily on two considerations. The first was the desire for political spoils. Hungry for the rich harvest of state and Federal offices that must fall to them when the Republicans were ousted, they were unwilling to form a coalition with the moderate and conservative Republicans with whom they would have to divide the spoils. Second was the obvious disarray of the Republican Party itself. Public resistance to its more extreme measures encouraged the Democrats to believe that popular reaction to the Radical Republicans would give them the whole pie without the necessity of compromise with the Johnsonites. In fact, just that intractability on the part of the Democrats perhaps more than anything else insured the continuation of the Radical Republicans in power.

As Congress prepared to meet in December, 1866, George Templeton Strong placed himself squarely in the camp of those supporting the notion of impeaching the President. "A. Johnson disgraces high place and deserves to be impeached," Strong wrote, "but the ultraists, as, for example, B. F. Butler, are no less violent in talk and revolutionary in aspiration than A. Johnson himself." Strong hoped the Radical Republicans would use their accession of power with wisdom and moderation, remember "that it is excellent . . . to have a giant's strength, but tyrannous to 'use it like a giant.' . . ."

In his annual message Johnson listed the accomplishments of his administration in healing the wounds of the war. "One thing, however, yet remained to be done before the work of restoration could be completed, and that was the admission of loyal Senators and Representatives from the States whose people had rebelled against the lawful authority of the General Government." This Congress had refused to do. So to deprive the states was to violate the principle of "no taxation without representation." The result must be "in the end absolute despotism."

As he looked back over the events of the past year, it seemed clear to Georges Clemenceau that "nothing will bring the South into the fold. The whole region has become impossible as a dwelling place for those who believe in the Union." Johnson's "strange scruples as to constitutionality, the successive vetoes which he opposes to all protective measures passed by Congress . . . have shaken his conservative supporters and given heart to his enemies." If Congress was overborne by the President and Southerners admitted to that body on equal terms, "there will be no more internal peace for a quarter of a century. The slave party of the South combined with the Democrats of the North will be strong enough to defeat all the efforts of the abolitionists, and the final and complete emancipation of the colored people will be deferred indefinitely." Clemenceau did not find much evidence of Northern hatred of the South. There was, rather, a determination that the war should not have been fought in vain. "The North is not hostile to the South," he wrote. "The reverse is true. The South hates the North, the latter wishes to guard against the effects of this hatred; that is all."

Emboldened by their victory at the polls, the Radical Republicans pushed ahead with their own plan for the reconstruction of the recalcitrant South in the form of a bill based on the findings of the Joint Committee on Reconstruction. A Congressman from Ohio, James Garfield, pointed out that that body had done its best since the end of the war to "restore the states lately in rebellion by co-operation with their people" and that such efforts had "proven a complete and disastrous failure. . . ." Frank Brandegee from Connecticut declared that "fifteen hundred Union men have been massacred in cold blood (more than the entire population of some of the towns in my district), whose only crime has been loyalty to our flag. . . . In all the revolted states, upon the testimony of your ablest generals, there is no safety to the property or lives of loyal men." George Boutwell, Massachusetts Congressman, declared: "Today there are eight millions or more of people, occupying six hundred and thirty thousand square miles of territory . . . who are writhing under cruelties nameless in their character, and injustices such as have not been permitted to exist in any other country of modern times."

The testimony taken by the Joint Committee on Reconstruction was certainly damning. Since witnesses testifying before congressional committees have a tendency to be people whose testimony is designed to provide a rationale for legislation that the committee intends to pass, it often has a monotonous sameness about it. Such, certainly, was the case with the testimony taken by the joint committee. Witness after witness—military commanders, agents for the Freedmen's Bureau, Southern Unionists, freed blacks—told much the same story. The main burden was that the freedmen and women of the South, Republicans, and Union men, as well as Northern teachers and missionaries, would be in peril, not just of their legal and political rights but of their lives, if Federal troops were withdrawn from the South. Another line common to most of the witnesses was that in the initial shock of defeat white Southerners had been ready to accept any conditions imposed by the victorious North for the reorganization of Southern society along lines that would be compatible with Northern principles of individual rights and social justice. The announcement of Johnson's Reconstruction policies, however, by conceding more than they had dared hope for, had encouraged the notion that the South would not have to pay for its disruption of the Union after all and might, indeed, by ingeniously devised legislation, place its ex-slaves in a condition that had for the whites all the advantages of slavery without its drawbacks. The point is a critical one. It became the major thesis of the critics of Presidential Reconstruction that if Johnson had held fast to the policy of Lincoln, as he had intimated to Sumner and Chase in May, a rational plan of Reconstruction could have been devised. Such a program must have had as its most essential point the protection of the rights of the ex-slaves and free blacks as well as a fair treatment of white Southerners. Moreover, it must have been the result of close cooperation between the executive and legislative branches in order to make clear to the South beyond doubt or cavil that the Republican party was determined that justice be done and that the South could not claim full and equal membership in the Union until it made evident that it was prepared to accept blacks as citizens. This argument rests on the assumption that in the first moment the white South would have acquiesced in at least the beginnings of black political equality. Hence the constant reiteration of this theme in the testimony of witnesses before the joint committee. In order for the Radical Republicans in Congress to justify wrenching the direction of Reconstruction from the hands of the President it was essential to establish the disastrous consequences of Johnson's policies.

A succession of witnesses thus appeared to testify to conditions in the states recently in rebellion. A Virginia farmer of Union sentiments was quizzed by a committee member as follows: "What effect has the President's liberal policy toward the rebels and the rebel States had with reference to the increase or diminution of loyal feeling toward the government of the United States?" "Answer: I think it has brought forward a class of men as representative men, who would not other-wise have come forward. I think it has brought forward the original leaders of the rebellion, who would not have sought position if they had not thought they could get it through this policy."

Another witness was led along the same line. "Question: What effect has the liberal policy of President Johnson in granting amnesty and pardons, and restoring property that was confiscated, had upon their [the white Virginians'] minds?" "Answer: The general feeling and sentiment of the people appears to be . . . getting worse, getting more unfriendly to the government. It appears to me that the leniency of the President was very bad for the Union people."

Justice of the Peace Joseph Denny of Warren County, Virginia, told the congressional committee, "It seems to me there is an animosity between rebels and negroes which will never be settled in this world. . . . It is not an uncommon thing to see five or six of these young aristocrats, who never worked a day in their lives, and who are depending on bank stock which is not worth a cent, cursing and damning the negroes for not working. . . ."

The military commander of the southern counties of Virginia, Major General John Turner, testified that there was a bitter anti-Negro feeling among the rural whites of his section of the state—"an impulsive feeling of aggression—a desire to hit the negro out of the way. They do not think about his rights; they do not appear to know what it means; only they feel that the negro has something now that he did not have before; that he is putting on airs." Where they had half a chance the freedmen were quite ready to defend themselves. Turner acknowledged that as among any group of people, there were lazy and idle blacks, but the majority were anxious to work, and he had found no instance of an employer who was fair in his treatment of a black employee and willing "to accord to him all his civil rights as a free man" who had not been able to hire and retain a labor force.

A Federal district judge, John C. Underwood, testified that a "candid rebel gentleman" of Alexandria had told him: "Sooner than see the colored people raised to a legal and political equality, the Southern people would prefer their total annihilation." Underwood was, of course, not an unprejudiced witness (indeed, it might be said that none was available). An ardent Free-Soiler, he had been driven from Virginia for his heretical opinions and would soon be presiding over the state constitutional convention of 1867.

An agent of the Freedmen's Bureau, Colonel W. H. Beadle, who was stationed in North Carolina, testified to the constant whippings, beatings, and harassment of freed blacks. When he was asked if blacks were generally armed, he replied in the affirmative. Whites tried to prevent it. Often the police raided black houses on the ground that it was illegal for blacks to possess firearms. "They go in squads and search houses and seize arms," he declared. "These raids are often made by young men . . . some of them being members of the police and others not. The tour of pretended duty is often turned into a spree. Houses of colored men have been broken open, beds torn apart and thrown about the floor, and even trunks opened and money taken. A great variety of such offences have been committed by the local police or mad young men. . . . Mules and horses given to negroes by the army have been taken away. . . . Such acts greatly interfere with the efforts of the bureau to restore confidence between laborer and employer."

The Reverend William Thornton, an ex-slave, testified that in Surry County, Virginia, far from any Federal troops, black people lived under a reign of terror and were whipped, beaten, and abused almost daily. "There are no colored schools down in Surry County," he declared; "they would kill anyone who would go down there and establish colored schools." Bands of ten or fifteen whites "patrolled" black communities, "searching the houses of colored people, turning them out and beating them." Many blacks in the county were not convinced that they were actually free.

Occasionally the testimony ranged far more widely than the specific consequences of presidential policy. The Reverend Robert McMurdy, an Episcopal clergyman in Alexandria, Virginia, turned out to be somewhat of a theorist on racial matters. A committee member queried him on the respective capacities of blacks and whites, and McMurdy replied with the common wisdom on the subject. Blacks, in his view, "learn to read more rapidly, they learn to write more rapidly, and they make better writers. They learn music by ear more rapidly. In short they acquire everything more rapidly than whites where imitativeness is brought into requisition. But where ratiocination is concerned, where the powers of logic or the powers of induction are concerned, where reasoning is concerned . . . they are very inferior to whites." It was easy, of course, to concede black superiority in "imitativeness" if white superiority in "reasoning" was maintained since clearly reasoning was a much higher quality of mind and character than imitativeness. Depressed and dependent people have always "imitated" their masters and mistresses—the dominant class. And as for black "reasoning," there was already a substantial company of black intellectuals like William Wells Brown, Henry Turner, Henry Garnet, John Mercer Langston, Robert Purvis, and Frederick Douglass, to name only the most prominent, whose reasoning powers, sharpened by the excruciating racial dilemmas they had experienced, rivaled those of any of their white compatriots. McMurdy, clearly a friend and advocate of black people despite his conventional prejudices, went on to endorse black leadership. "The best person to manage the blacks of the South," he declared, "are those blacks who have the capacity to control, for they have so much suavity, so much gentleness with them, and their effort to govern is not so much by force as by expedience and tact; blacks have always succeeded most handsomely when they had that power." McMurdy was convinced that the postwar period would witness "a great struggle, which struggle, on the part of the blacks, will have the effect of giving them more character. God designs that people shall grow strong through suffering. This suffering will make the blacks strong and vigorous; will give them a different position from that which they could possibly have had were they taken care of as mere children. As slaves they would always be children. They have got to grow into men by being allowed, to a great extent, to work out their own destiny. I conceive that the great policy of government should be simply to protect these people in their rights, and let them be perfectly free to work out the results just as white people work out the results."

Tennessee, the joint committee was told, had an additional problem. "It is a melancholy fact," reported General Clinton B. Fisk, head of the Freedmen's Bureau for the district that included Tennessee, "that among the bitterest opponents of the negro in Tennessee are intensely radical loyalists of the mountain district—men who have been in our armies." The great slaveholding areas of the state—Middle and West Tennessee—containing "the largest and wealthiest planters," had cooperated more readily with the bureau's efforts to assist the freedmen and women than the pro-Union East Tennessee. Fisk acknowledged that in the western portions of the state "there are slaveholders and returned rebel soldiers . . . who persecute [Negroes] bitterly, and pursue them with vengeance, and treat them with brutality, and burn down their dwellings and schoolhouses. But that is not the rule. . . ." Moreover, according to Fisk, there was "more brutality to negroes, and more wicked, malicious persecution of loyalists in the State of Kentucky today than in the State of Tennessee." Fisk, disguised as a traveler, had gone about Kentucky and found "the opposition to the freedmen . . . in many localities . . . very great—in fact to freedom itself."

Colonel William Spence, a Tennessee Unionist, reported to the joint congressional committee that the situation of the freedmen in his county was "very good." The freedmen had conducted themselves discreetly and most were working at wages of approximately $15 a month. "The poor classes of white," Spence said, "are not getting along so well. They have no schools, and where they have no land they cannot get employment as readily as the colored man can. The richer men will not employ them, for the truth is, they are not as valuable for laboring as the negroes are. According to my judgment the poorer classes of white people, not only in Tennessee, but all over the South are scarcely able to take care of themselves. They are inclined to be idle and lazy, and think it degrading to work." There was, as we have noted, a serious split in the Union ranks of the state over the rights of freed blacks. An old Union man had told Spence, "If you take away the military from Tennessee, the buzzards can't eat up the niggers as fast as we'll kill 'em."

The attitude of the Southern sympathizers in Tennessee, the Unionists of that state declared, was that "of deep-seated hatred, amounting in many cases to a spirit of revenge toward the white Unionists of the State, and a haughty contempt for the negro, whom they cannot treat as a freeman. The hatred of the white loyalist is intensified by the accusation that he deserted the South in her extremity, and is, therefore, a traitor. . . ." If the protective arm of Federal authority was withdrawn, the Tennessee Unionists warned, "restrictions will be thrown around the freedom of the negro, and his elevation in the scale of being discountenanced, if not actually prohibited. He will be excluded from the courts, from common schools, and probably from all means of education, from business and privileged occupations, and, perhaps, from the acquisition of property. . . . He will be forced to seek an asylum in other lands, or perhaps he will become a declining race, relapse into barbarism and disappear from the face of the earth. . . ."

There was a disposition of some of the committee members to argue that the old planter aristocracy was more tolerant and more favorably disposed toward the freedman than the "lower classes" of whites. One of the committee members pressed General Turner on the point. It was his impression, he declared, that the old planter class was the most adamant in its resistance to black rights. "They are reluctant even to consider and treat the negro as a free man, to let him have his half of the sidewalk or the street crossing."

"Is this feeling of dislike of the negro more intense and bitter with the lower classes of whites than with the upper?" a committee member asked. Turner answered: "I think that, as a rule, even the more intelligent classes cannot look upon the negro in any other light than as a negro." There was less physical abuse of the Negro by upper-class whites, but Turner considered the prejudice against them no less pervasive. Like most of the witnesses before the committee, Turner testified that when he first took over his command, "it was my conviction . . . that the people were disposed to accept the results of the war, but that they were not very clear as to what those results were. . . . If some of their people had stepped forward and told them what they would have to do, they would have yielded a ready acquiescence to almost anything."

A group of Georgia freedmen who called themselves the Civil and Political Association sent a report to Congress describing the treatment of Georgia blacks by their former masters. After recounting a long story of harassment and murder, the authors concluded: "Thus matters went from bad to worse and the first day of January, 1867 found the colored people in a condition similar if not worse than that of slavery."

It seemed to General O. O. Howard, head of the Freedmen's Bureau, that "the whole white population [was] engaged in a war of extermination against the blacks." The white bands operated under various names in the winter of 1866–67—Regulators in North Carolina, the Jayhawkers in Georgia, the Ku Klux Klan in Tennessee. Emerson Etheridge, Democratic nominee for governor in Tennessee, declared, "The negroes are no more free than they were forty years ago, and if anyone goes about the country telling them that they are free, shoot him; and these negro troops, commanded by low and degraded white men, going through the country ought to be shot down."

In the end a vast amount of evidence was accumulated on the attitudes of Southern whites toward the Federal government and, above all, on the determination of many of them to use every device to keep their ex-slaves in a state of complete subordination. If that proved impossible, they would drive them out of the region or, if need be, exterminate them.

The report itself stressed the fact that the Confederacy was "in a state of utter exhaustion. The people of those States were left bankrupt in their public finances, and shorn of the private wealth which had before given them power and influence. They were also necessarily in a state of complete anarchy. . . ." Moreover, it was not for the President "to decide upon the nature or effect of any system of government which the people of these States might see fit to adopt. This power," the report insisted, "is lodged by the Constitution in the Congress of the United States. . . ." In the view of the committee the President had acted without knowledge of the real conditions in the Southern states and without requiring evidence of loyalty to the Union. The elections conducted under the terms set down by the President had resulted, "almost universally, in the defeat of candidates who had been true to the Union, and in the election of notorious and unpardoned rebels, men who . . . made no secret of their hostility to the government and the people of the United States."

Finally, the report took the line that the President's policies had the effect of leaving the free slaves at the mercy of their former masters. "It was impossible to abandon them," the report continued, "without securing them their rights as free men and citizens. The whole civilized world would have cried out against them for such base ingratitude and the bare idea is offensive to all right-thinking men." The report then came to what was, in a real sense, the heart of the matter: "By an original provision of the Constitution, representation is based on the whole number of free persons in each State, and three-fifths of all other persons. When all become free, representation for all necessarily follows. As a consequence the inevitable effect of the rebellion would be to increase the political power of the insurrectionary States, whenever they should be allowed to resume their positions as States of the Union. . . . It did not seem just or proper that all the political advantages derived from their becoming free should be confined to their former masters, who had fought against the Union. . . ."

The conclusion of the committee was that "the so-called Confederate States are not, at present, entitled to representation in the Congress of the United States; that, before allowing such representation, adequate security for future peace and safety should be required; that this can only be found in such changes of the organic law as shall determine the civil rights and privileges of all citizens in all parts of the republic, shall place representation upon an equitable basis . . . and protect the loyal people against future claims for the expenses incurred in support of rebellion. . . ."

On the ostensible basis of the report of the Joint Committee on

Reconstruction, Congress drafted legislation designed to force compliance with Federal legislation designed to protect the rights of the freedmen. The first reconstruction bill divided the "said rebel States" into five military districts under the command of "an officer of the army" supported by "a sufficient military force to enable such officer to perform his duties." Chief among those duties was the protection of "all persons in their rights of person and property, to suppress insurrection, disorder, and violence, and to punish, or cause to be punished, all disturbers of the public peace and criminals." Moreover, if civil courts failed to function in such a way as to uphold the laws, the military commanders might establish military "commissions or tribunals for that purpose."

The bill provided for the election of delegates by voters "of whatever race, color, or previous condition . . . except such as may be disfranchised for participation in the rebellion" to draw up state constitutions. When the constitutions had been ratified, submitted to Congress, and approved by it, and when "said State . . . shall have adopted the amendment to the Constitution of the United States . . . known as article fourteen," the state might be represented in Congress. Any restrictions on the franchise must apply to black and white voters alike.

Sumner was dissatisfied with the Reconstruction Act of March 2, 1867. At the last moment, he rose in the Republican caucus to present an amendment to Sherman's bill requiring that the Southern states allow all qualified citizens to vote. The amendment was adopted and Sumner was convinced that in winning "the direct requirement of universal suffrage, without distinction of race or color," he had achieved "a prodigious triumph." He declared, "Since Runnymede there has been nothing of greater value to Human Rights." But he was disturbed that the states were initially to be placed under military rather than civilian authority. He tried to attach to a supplemental act a section providing for Federally funded schools. "Free schools," he stated, are "an essential condition of Reconstruction. . . . I now move to require a system of free schools, open to all without distinction of caste. For this great safeguard I ask your votes." He failed to get them, and the supplemental act, which passed on March 23, 1867, did little more than specify the conditions under which the state constitutional conventions should meet.

The Reconstruction Acts of 1867 stipulated, among other things, that in each of the seceded states, until a popularly elected convention drew up a state constitution acceptable to Congress, the state would remain under Federal military rule. Furthermore, blacks must be given the right to vote for delegates to the conventions and to be delegates themselves, and no state constitution which failed to provide for black suffrage would be considered acceptable to Congress.

The Reconstruction Acts put new heart into Southern blacks. The *New Orleans Tribune,* a black newspaper, reported in May, 1867: "The people of New Orleans witnessed last night one of the noblest scenes of which an American city can boast—a phalanx of freemen walking the streets with national colors flying and transparencies enunciating the principles of a free government. This marks a new and glorious era in our history." Rampart Street was illuminated with 15,000 Chinese lanterns and torches, the *Tribune* noted. "The banners and flags were flying to the breeze; the drums were beating and the fifes playing." Again the various black organizations of the city were represented —the "Free School Open to All," the Third Ward Club carrying a sign which proclaimed, "Eight Hours—A Legal Day's Work." Another sign read: "No Contract System." Skyrockets and a street dance completed the festivities.

By the same token the acts vastly increased the alarm of white Southerners about the prospects of black domination, accompanied in the minds of some by the wholesale confiscation of property and, indeed, the murder of whites in their beds. While some whites armed themselves in anticipation of a final bloody racial war, others suggested that the proper strategy was to let the black politicians demonstrate their utter inadequacy; a reaction must set in, and whites will be restored to power. "Give them the necessary amount of rope," a Charleston lawyer advised, "let them have their representatives *all black,* in the Convention, let their ignorance, incapacity, and excesses have full scope and accomplish its end; don't attempt to modify it, with white sauce, let it be all black, and it will soon cure itself." Black rule must be "the most galling tyranny and most stupendous system of organized robbery that is to be met with in history." What was unthinkable was that black politicians might govern ably and fairly.

In the words of Elizabeth Meriwether, the Reconstruction Acts "disfranchised all white men who had not actively sided with the North . . . and enfranchised all black men! Thus began the period of 'Reconstruction' which more properly should be called 'Destruction' —for this law destroyed the homes and happiness of the South to an extent not caused even by the Federal armies in a hundred great battles. . . . The white men of the South, men of brains and property, the men with a long line of cultured, civilized ancestry were forbidden either to vote or to hold public office."

The consequence of the Reconstruction Acts was a vast campaign to register black voters and inform them of the political issues, the foremost of which was that they all should vote Republican. In many Northern states where the black population was, on the whole, far better educated and more literate, the voting rights of blacks were restricted or denied. Now Congress had directed that hundreds of thousands of blacks, the great majority of them unable to read or write or even sign their names, were to have their votes counted as equal to those of white Southerners who had graduated from Princeton or the University of North Carolina. Even some of the educated Northern blacks working in the South as missionaries or teachers had substantial misgivings and as we have seen, white abolitionists themselves were initially divided on the issue. But the Radical Republicans believed that the only way to forestall the re-enslavement of the freedmen and women was to give them political power and protect them in the exercise of it by Northern soldiers. The practical effect was to occupy the white South with enfranchised blacks, backed up by Northern force.

What complicated the whole issue of black enfranchisement enormously was that in some sections of the South it was impossible to give the vote to the freedman without at the same time giving him political dominance over his former masters. While in the South overall whites outnumbered blacks three to one and thus seemed to be in no danger of losing political power on a simple numerical basis, blacks outnumbered whites in some counties and in two states. Moreover, the electoral cards were, to some degree, stacked against the whites by virtue of restrictions on the voting rights of those whites most active in the rebellion. Beyond this the white Unionists in the South were constantly on the defensive. Far from being able to emerge, as Northern Republicans had naïvely thought, as the postwar leaders of the South, most of them were branded as traitors. Finally, Southern Democrats, hoping for an alliance with the Northern wing of the party, a prompt return to power, and the cooperation of the Northerners in undoing the most objectionable aspect of Reconstruction, remained aloof from all political activity that involved contact with black politicians or an appeal to black voters. Politically active blacks were thus left to operate in a kind of vacuum. Deprived of interaction with able, principled, and well-disposed white politicians, they sometimes fell under the influence of the most venal and self-serving whites. At the same time it must be said that the carpetbaggers as a group have generally got much worse press from historians than they deserved. Among them were many able and intelligent men, genuinely devoted to the cause of the black people and dedicated to making black political power in the South a reality.

However much the main body of Radical Republicans assured themselves that they had no alternative to infringing states' rights if they were to see justice done to the freed blacks, it was clearly a painful decision for many of them, and the mood of the country in regard to the issue remained volatile in the extreme. One indication was an editorial by E. L. Godkin in the *Nation,* on July 18, 1867, upbraiding those who were "so anxious to be considered 'radical' in their views that they fear to stop even when they have attained all that is really desirable or practicable." In Godkin's view, "universal suffrage is so nearly established, appears so certain, that some who are more anxious to be radical than to be right are already casting about for some new demand for the benefit of those who were lately oppressed." Godkin believed there were more pressing problems closer to home which demanded the attention of the civic-minded citizens—an inequitable system of taxation, "rotten legislatures, municipalities, and judges, with systems of education grossly defective, with extravagance and inefficiency the rule in government rather than the exception." The limits of Godkin's reformist zeal were indicated by his attack on the champions of the eight-hour day. With the passage of such legislation, "who," he asked, "would suffer so much as the workmen, whose wages would be cut and whose employers would largely abandon enterprises undertaken under different expectations?"

The editorial was a bellwether of middle- and upper-class reformist inclinations. Already the problem of the South with the attendant problem of the freedman was beginning to pall on many Northerners who considered themselves reformers. The word "radical" was, after all, a new word in the American political lexicon. Like the much earlier "Puritan," it had been first applied in derision by enemies of the most devout antislavery Republicans and then nailed proudly to the masthead of the Republican flagship. But it was still not a word with which the generality of Americans were comfortable. "Liberal," "conservative," perhaps even "revolutionary" came more easily to the American tongue. "Radical" had a foreign sound; it smelled of the Paris communes and the upheavals of 1848. It suggested an all-out uncompromising dedication to "a new social order"—in the South at least. The "Southern problem" was so vast, so complex, and its political implications so uncertain, that cautious and ambitious politicians were disposed to steer clear of it. The question of municipal reform, the spectacular pillage of a big-city boss like Tweed, or the defalcations of the new captains of industry, alarming as they were, appeared infinitely more manageable than the question of race relations in the South. Most important, these issues affected the daily lives of ordinary citizens and, most significantly, the pecuniary interests of investors and taxpayers, that is to say, the most articulate and aggressive segment of Northern society.

Even George Templeton Strong was afraid that the Radical Republicans were "going a little too fast for the masses." He noted that "many honest, patriotic people who exult over the downfall of slavery are startled at the prospect of negro sovereignty south of the Potomac and Ohio, and are by no means sure they would like to see the Honorable Mr. Quashee Hampton or Sambo Davis claiming a seat in Congress as a representative or a senator from South Carolina or Mississippi. . . . People hesitate about the Negro senator, not because of his dark cuticle, but because he belongs to a race the average intellect whereof is (in 1867 at least) of lower grade than ours; because we are familiar with the notion of a nigger servant, bootblack, barber, or field hand, and not familiar with that of a Negro legislator. . . . To the Northern man of plain, ordinary, common understanding, a colored person helping to regulate our national finances and our foreign relations seems out of place and anomalous."

In the opinion of Henry Adams the resistance to the Reconstruction Acts "rested primarily on their violation of the letter and spirit of the Constitution as regarded the rights of States. . . ." Their advocates, Adams wrote, did not even try to defend them on constitutional grounds but on the ground of "overwhelming necessity. . . . The measures were adopted with reluctance by a majority of Congressmen, they were approved with equal reluctance by a majority of the people. . . ."

Yet it is hard to quarrel with the defense of the Reconstruction Acts by William Sinclair, the black journalist and historian who wrote: "The ex-Confederates had been exercising full control over the government of every Southern state for two years after the war, and had defied the national laws and authority, and persistently thwarted the work of reconstruction."

The South, meanwhile, rose again, or, more accurately, its cities rose while its countryside languished. When Whitelaw Reid returned to Mobile, Alabama, a year after the end of the war, he could hardly believe the transformation in the city. "A fleet of sail and stream vessels lined the repaired wharves," he wrote. "The main thoroughfare resounded with the rush of business. The hotels were overflowing. The 'new blood of the South' was, of a truth, leaping in riotous pulsations through the veins of the last captured city of the coast. Everywhere throngs of cotton buyers around the reeking bars, at the public tables, in the crowded places of amusement, two classes, crowded and commingled—Northern speculators and Rebel soldiers." "New men" were much in evidence—Yankees, and the more aggressive members of the cracker, poor white, or sandhill tackey class.

Yankees, many of them former Union officers or soldiers, were highly conspicuous. Much of the business was monopolized by Northerners, who imported merchandise of all kinds from plows and hoes, needles and thread, to dresses and ribbons—trade the Southerners were, for the most part, glad to surrender into Northern hands since "tradesmen" stood near the bottom of the Southern social hierarchy. The North was, after all, considered a race of "clerks and shopkeepers," who had no notion of true cultivation. In Montgomery a Baptist preacher, who boasted to Whitelaw Reid that he had his money safely invested in the North, declared, "I'm tired of this crowd of Yankees that is pouring down here . . . they are a totally different class of people, and can never assimilate with us Southerners. What a miserable picayune way of doing things by retail they have, to be sure!"

Two factors contributed to make cotton lands available to Northern speculators. First, and the more important, was the fact that the "old planters" clung stubbornly to their conviction that free black labor could not be used to raise cotton. Secondly, there was a shortage of capital to revive plantations which had been neglected. The consequence was that old planters were in many instances content to rent their land to Northerners and let them try the experiment of using free black labor. There was constant talk among planters of that persuasion of importing white laborers from the North. One proposal that Whitelaw Reid heard warmly advocated was to bring Chinese labor to the South to replace blacks. Brazil was constantly spoken of, and an expedition headed for the city of Pará on the Amazon set off, carrying farming equipment and supplies for six months.

Atlanta had more than recovered from Sherman's devastation. By the latter part of 1866 it was doing a third more commercial business than it had before the war. Skilled labor was in great demand to rebuild the city, and floods of Northern capital poured in to expedite the process. Whitelaw Reid estimated that more than four thousand artisans were at work in reconstruction, and so many merchants were opening new stores that space was at a premium. "The streets," he wrote, "were blockaded with drays and wagons. The four railroads were taxed to their utmost capacity, without beginning to supply all the demands upon them." By the same token, crime, especially armed robbery, had reached alarming proportions, and it was not safe to go into the streets at night in certain areas of the city. Murders were commonplace. In all this atmosphere of hurry and bustle, the dominant spirit was, according to Reid, "overwhelmingly secessionist." One Southern Union man complained that he and his likeminded friends suffered virtual ostracization. "We are in no sense upheld or encouraged by the Government . . ." one of them complained to Reid. Johnson was praised by former Rebels "because he is conservative on the nigger." Another Atlantan declared: "Johnson knows niggers. He's not going to let any such cursed radicalism as inspired Lincoln trouble him. If Johnson had been President, we wouldn't have been embarrassed by an infernal Emancipation Proclamation." Still another announced defiantly, "I've got just the same rights now that any of the damned Yankees have, and I mean to demand my rights. I'm pardoned; there's nothing against me. . . ."

Outside Atlanta, with its air of frantic activity, the true face of the war devastation was visible. All along the recently repaired railroad lines were burned houses, often marked by no more than the chimneys. On the train that Reid traveled, "aimless young men in gray, ragged and filthy, seemed, with the downfall of the rebellion they had fought for, to have lost their object in life. . . ." They "stared stupidly at the clothes and comfortable air of officers and strangers from the North." Here and there were brief glimpses of desperate hardship—a gaunt, halfclothed woman with her children about her, crouched over a small fire, cooking some bit of scavenged food; a respectable-looking old man rummaging sheepishly in garbage cans. Yet there was the same intractable spirit everywhere. One Georgian told Reid the North had only three alternatives—re-establish slavery, give the whites the power to compel the blacks to work for them, "or colonize them out of the country. . . . Such waste and destruction all about," Reid exclaimed, "and still these insatiable men—these handsome tigers—want more conciliation."

Selma, Alabama, was the center of the richest cotton-growing region of the state. Whitelaw Reid found there a more obdurate hostility to the North and to Northerners than elsewhere in the South. Nonetheless, the town was filled with Northerners, many of them recently officers in the Union army. Reid calculated that a Northern farmer, working in the fields himself, could, with six hired blacks, make a handsome profit for himself on a year's cotton crop, but Southern landowners were reluctant to lease or sell small portions of their land. Selma had been well on the way to becoming the arsenal of the Confederacy, and when General James Wilson captured the city in the closing months of the war, he had destroyed its gun foundries and machine shops. A hundred or more guns were lying about in the debris, from heavy siege guns to field artillery pieces, and in the ruins of a factory that had been making muskets, gun barrels and bayonets were piled about, fused together by the heat of the fire that had destroyed the factory. It was ironic that it had been only their desperate need for armaments that had induced the Southerners to develop the coal and iron mines near Talladega and create an industrial complex that rivaled those of the North.

The rebuilding of Selma, like the rebuilding of Atlanta, went on apace, largely in the hands of black carpenters and masons. An old black man told Whitelaw Reid that he was paid a dollar a day, adding, 'By de time I pays ten dollars a month rent fo' my house, an' fifteen cents a poun' for beef or fresh po'k, or thirty cents fo' bacon an' den buys my clo'es, I doesn't hab much leff. I's done tried it, an' I knows brack man cant stan' dat."

Reid himself could not resist the fever of speculation. He took his savings and rented several large cotton plantations near Natchez, hoping to make a fortune in the inflated market. He wrote to Anna Dickinson: "I now have about 300 of these beings under my control. They work well; but life among them is a fearful thing for one's rose-colored ideas. The present generation is bad material to develop. We shall do better with the next." Six months later, having lost most of the money he had invested in his cotton venture, he wrote to Miss

Dickinson again: "I am fearful more than ever, since my experience here—of negro suffrage as a sufficient remedy for our troubles. I would rather see the South governed territorially by militia and wait several years yet." Reid's liberal principles had apparently not survived his entrepreneurial disaster.

41

The Reconstructed
Governments

With the executive and legislative branches of the Federal government more bitterly divided than ever before in the country's
history, the fall elections of 1867 approached. The extreme volatility
of public opinion was indicated by the widespread uncertainty about
the outcome. Only a year before, the Republicans had crushed their
opponents, and then, heady with their victory, they had proceeded to
push the Reconstruction Acts through Congress, alarming Conscience
Constitutionalists in both parties. In addition, the prohibition forces in
the Republican Party, especially in New England, had taken advantage
of their dominance of state legislatures to pass laws, directed primarily
at Irish workingmen, that closed saloons on Sundays. In Boston there
were bloody riots between the Irish and the police over the Sunday
closing law, and in New York there were rumors that the "Celts and the
Teutons," as George Templeton Strong called them, were determined
to stage a riot against the temperance ordinances "that close all
grog-shops and lager-bier saloons on Sunday." The laws seemed to
Strong "a severe strain on the endurance of the *hoi polloi*. . . ."

Municipal, state, and Federal corruption was another issue. Each
department of the national government—Interior, the Navy, the Post
Office—had its sensational revelations of corruption and fraud.

Inflation was raging in the fall of 1867, and Strong wrote in his diary: "I am maddened by the cost of living. Things tend from bad to worse. . . ." The need to dip into capital left Strong "nauseated and wretched. . . . I am *living beyond my income*, pauperizing Johnny and his little brothers. That is what is slowly killing me, and killing me by slow torture." His wife was ready to give up her parties and "social enjoyments," but, Strong wrote, "I would rather die than ask her to give them up and subside into a dull, humdrum existence. These things are her life. . . . If I cannot afford her these social enjoyments, the sooner I die the better. . . . My incapacity for work and duty grows worse every day. I confess myself 'played out' and 'used up.' My only hope is in the fact that our Lord raised men from the dead. . . . I am in living death." It was estimated in December, 1867, that more than fifty thousand men and women were out of work in New York City alone.

As the 1867 elections approached, a spirit reminiscent of the feverish temper a year earlier was evident. Once more there was a sense that the fate of the Republic somehow hung in the balance. Francis Lieber, the Columbia University professor and political scientist, wrote to a friend: "Neither you nor I have agreed with everything Congress has done; but when it comes to choosing between Congress and *that* man—a faithless, ruinous and rebellious executive—who can hesitate? Congress is the country."

Particular attention was given to the outcome of the voting in Pennsylvania because, as Georges Clemenceau noted, "there is a proverb running: 'As goes Pennsylvania, so goes the country.'" The news from Pennsylvania was anything but encouraging; the Democrats made large gains in the Keystone State. New York went Democratic by a margin of almost 50,000 votes. In Ohio a Democratic legislature was elected, and in Wisconsin, Minnesota, and Kansas the Republicans won only by narrow margins. Moreover, Negro suffrage amendments to the state constitutions of Kansas, Minnesota, Wisconsin, and New Jersey were defeated. In all, the Democrats increased the number of states under their control from three to eleven. Johnson responded to the news of the Democratic victory in Ohio by sending a wire to the head of the state's Democratic council which read: "Ohio has done its duty and done it in time. God bless Ohio."

The Democratic victories may have been the party's undoing. Everywhere Democrats, anticipating victory in the coming presidential elections, gave way to extravagant joy; in New York City a cannon kept firing at intervals for two days. Yet with all this, Georges Clemenceau wrote: "It is certain from now on that the political equality of the two races is only a question of time. There has been a gradual growth of public opinion towards this end. . . ." Then Clemenceau added a typically Gallic aside: "To anyone who knows how peculiarly difficult it is to dislodge a prejudice which has somehow succeeded in getting hold in one of the out of the way corners of the right Anglo-Saxon brain," a change of "this kind bears some resemblance of a triumph." He hoped that the principal consequence of the Republican defeat would be "curing the radicals of their puritanical intolerance."

Perhaps the most notable aspect of the elections of 1867 was the fact that under the constitutions framed in the terms of Congressional Reconstruction, tens of thousands of blacks of every description and condition turned out in all the extravagant panoply of American elections with flags, bands, and banners to cast their first votes as free citizens of the Republic. Only the celebrations that greeted the Emancipation Proclamation rivaled the exuberance of the moment. In every Southern state white Republicans, Unionists, and blacks came forth to provide leadership for the largely illiterate freedmen. The Southern whites, called scalawags by the Southerners, contained in their ranks radical idealists like Albert Gallatin Mackey of South Carolina and Thomas Durant of Louisiana, and opportunists like Franklin Moses, also a South Carolinian.

The Northern whites had the same mixture—high-minded reformers like John Albion Andrew, Daniel Chamberlain, Rufus Saxton, and Albion Tourgée and such odious adventurers as Christopher Columbus Bowen, a native of Rhode Island, a faro dealer and gambler who had been dismissed from the Confederate army and thereafter indicted for plotting the murder of his commanding officer. Freed by Sherman's army, he soon became a prominent Republican political figure.

" 'Carpet-Bagger,' " Albion Tourgée wrote, "had . . . all the essentials of a denunciatory epithet in a superlative degree. It had a quaint and ludicrous sound, was utterly without defined significance, and was altogether unique." It was, Tourgée added, "in some sense the lineal descendant of 'abolitionist' . . . very proper for a second edition, a considerable improvement on its immediate predecessor." For Southerners, "the word expressed all that collective and accumulated hate which generations of antagonism had engendered, intensified and sublimated by the white-heat of a war of passionate intensity and undoubted righteousness to the hearts of its promoters." In the words of William Sinclair, "Among the so-called 'carpet-baggers' and 'scalawags' were men as pure in purpose, as lofty in patriotism, as bright in intellect, as unselfish in the discharge of public duties, as honest, courageous, and noble in spirit as America has ever produced."

Certainly black political activity had not waited on passage of the Reconstruction Acts. Soon after the end of the war blacks began to hold meetings and rallies to advance their interests and express their determination to become involved in politics if only as a means of protecting those interests. Soon after the South Carolina legislature passed its Black Code, a black convention met in Charleston to make known the political aspirations of black people. Out of six days of deliberations came a set of resolutions addressed to white Americans in Congress and in the state of South Carolina. They began with a preamble which declared: "The laws which have made white men great, have degraded us because we were colored. But now that we are freemen, now that we have been lifted up by the providence of God to manhood, we have resolved to come forward, and like MEN, speak and *act* for ourselves."

The debate over the propriety of giving the vote to illiterate and "primitive" freed blacks found a poignant expression in a meeting on April 10, 1867, at Montgomery, Alabama. "One very intelligent, educated Negro said, 'I don't want the colored people to vote for five years. Here, and for twenty miles away they'll vote right but farther off they will vote for "Mass William" and "Mass John" to get their good will.'

"Whereupon an old Negro called out, 'Every creature has got an instinct—the calf goes to the cow to suck, the bee to the hive. We's a poor humble degraded people but we know our friend. We'd walk fifteen miles in wartime to find out about the battle. We can walk fifteen miles and more to find out how to vote.' "

The black leaders were of four general classifications. First were blacks free before the war, most of them from the larger Southern cities—Richmond, Charleston, Savannah, New Orleans; they had been barbers, waiters, artisans, the few occupations open to free blacks. Many of these men were literate (in South Carolina alone there were more than nine thousand blacks before the war who could read and many of whom could write). Among them were a high percentage of mulattoes; a substantial number were known to be the sons of white planter fathers and slave mothers.

In Louisiana, where the black aristocracy of New Orleans was bilingual and, in many instances, more cultivated than its white counterparts, there was certainly no dearth of able black leadership.

Second category of black leaders was made up of ex-soldiers, veterans of black regiments, many of them formerly noncommissioned officers in the Union army like Prince Rivers and Robert Smalls.

Still another category was composed of blacks from the North, many of whom had gone south during the war to establish and teach in schools in areas like New Orleans, Memphis, and West Tennessee that contained large numbers of contrabands. This group was, for the most part, the best educated, and its members soon found themselves drawn into politics by necessity.

Finally, and perhaps most important, were the ministers of black congregations, many of them eloquent orators, the natural leaders of their people.

All these various groups and subdivisions, with their diverse, if not conflicting, aims and personal ambitions, now found themselves suddenly thrust onto the stage of history. Their task was an enormous and complex one—to introduce the masses of illiterate (but not necessarily, of course, unintelligent) blacks of the South to political activity and, far more awesome, to political power; to do this with the assistance of primarily two agencies of the Federal government—the army (which was to say, Federal troops commanded by Federal generals) and the Freedmen's Bureaus, which functioned as subagencies of the military district in which they were located; and to do this in the face of massive and often violent opposition from the white population.

Henry Turner, minister of the Israel Bethel Church in Washington and Chaplain of a black regiment, was active in organizing the freedmen of Georgia. "We want representative men," he declared, "without regard to color, as long as they carry the brand of negro oppression. We need power and intellectual equality with the whites. It does not matter whether he be a pretty or ugly negro; a black negro or a mulatto. Whether he were a slave or a free negro; the question is, is he a negro at all? . . . We want power; it only comes through organization and organization comes through unity. Our efforts must be one and inseparable, blended, tied, and bound together."

At a meeting in Savannah, Georgia, attended by seven thousand blacks from all sections of the state, the dominant figure was James Sims, an ex-slave and former waiter who had taught himself to read and write and become a minister and teacher at the end of the war. He was the same James Sims who, with his brother Thomas, had first enlisted the sympathies of Richard Henry Dana when they had been captured under the provisions of the Fugitive Slave Law and returned to their master in Georgia. The Southern whites who professed to understand blacks, Sims declared, really knew nothing of their inner life. All blacks had been compelled to use "dissimulation" toward their masters. Now, for the first time, they could tell them the truth. "Colored men are not fools. They knew enough to fight right and they will vote right. . . . Offices should be filled by both whites and colored men who are capable of serving with honor. I would have white and colored aldermen and white and colored policemen and the sooner people know it the better." Sims's speech was "applauded to the echo. . . . His clear musical voice, distinct enunciation and elegant style of delivery impressed everyone and greatly astonished those who had never heard him speak before," the *New Orleans Tribune* noted proudly.

In New Orleans, initially, the free blacks of that city assumed leadership in black politics, but Richard Cain, the black minister from Brooklyn, New York, was impressed by the rapidity with which freedmen came forward to assume leadership, often on the ground that the free blacks were too "white" in their manners and attitudes to lead ex-slaves. "It is remarkable," Cain wrote, "that the former leading men in these parts, those whom we would have recognized as the great minds of the South among the colored people, have relapsed into secondary men; and the class who were hardly known have come forward and assumed a bold front, and are asserting their manhood."

The first task was simply to register ex-slaves as voters. Thousands of meetings were held throughout the South. Often the nucleus was a church congregation led, as we have seen, by a minister. Not infrequently, the meetings took place under the hostile scrutiny of armed whites. That the enterprise succeeded was a testimonial to the energy and dedication of those who carried it out. We know far too little about how it was done, but it is safe to say that no more impressive political operation has ever been conducted in the history of the country. We have an account of a black political rally from the pen of Mary Jones of Montevideo, who wrote her granddaughter: "Yesterday there was a great mass meeting (political) of the freedmen at Newport Church. I am told there was never such a turnout in this country." On a stage flanked by American flags, their minister, the Reverend Mr. Campbell, now owner of the old Belleville plantation, farmed by a colony of blacks, exhorted them to work hard, "hold fast to the Radicals and give the Democrats a wide berth. This," Mary Jones added, "is the onward progress to (I fear) a war of races." Yet there was, perhaps surprisingly, little indication that the mass of black people had any inclination to "war." A few nights later there was another meeting of freedmen with "a Yankee Negro the speaker." Assurances were given that in the coming year land would be taken from the whites and redistributed to the freedmen in forty-acre parcels. The freedmen from Montevideo were present, and Mary Jones added, "A fearful state of things! Where will it end?"

In Charleston, Lucy Chase reported on a "colored meeting" she attended which had been addressed by "a colored preacher of considerable general intelligence, a great talker, a crowd collector, a truly eloquent man . . . [who] does not believe in being ruled by the North, is for the whole country, has a right to think and speak what he pleases. Advises his people to trust no one, to join no party because it says its principles are true, to keep one eye open while they pray. . . ." At night the Charleston blacks gathered again "with lighted torches, lanterns, and transparencies, and went, with bands of music, and with songs of liberty, to the houses of their prominent political men . . . drinking in at every point, words of encouragement and hope."

A Freedmen's Convention in Raleigh, North Carolina was attended by more than four hundred blacks. Behind the speaker's lectern was a bust of Abraham Lincoln. The motto above it read: "With malice toward none, with charity for all, with firmness in the right."

Blacks were organized into Union Leagues the motto of which was "Liberty, Lincoln, Loyal and League." The league had secret signs and passwords. When registration to vote began in South Carolina in August, 1867, 78,982 blacks—some 94 percent—were registered within a month. Those registered were steered to the registrars by members of the Union League. Many had only the vaguest notion of the significance of the action. A reporter for the *New York Herald* noted that "quite a number brought along bags and baskets 'to put it in,' and in nearly every instance there was a great rush for fear we would not have 'enough to go around.' Some thought it was something to eat, others thought it was something to wear; and quite a few thought it was the distribution of confiscated lands under a new name." Such stories made the accomplishment of the black leaders the more remarkable, and if many of the freedmen did not know what registration was initially, they soon found out.

Needless to say, it took considerable courage to be a black politician in the reconstructed South. James Alston, a member of the Alabama legislature, was described by a white Republican as having "a stronger influence over the minds of the colored men in Macon County than I ever saw exerted by any man." He was a shoemaker and a musician, one of the founders of the Union League Club of Tuskegee. A band of whites surrounded Alston's house and fired more than 265 shots through the windows and walls, two of the bullets striking Alston himself. After he had recovered from his wounds, he was told by a vigilante group that he must leave the county and when he refused, his house was again surrounded and another attempt was made to capture and kill him. Alston escaped by taking refuge in a swamp and made his way to Montgomery, but as he told a congressional committee, he had been barred from his own property for sixteen months, one of his horses was killed and his buggy destroyed. Along with five other black men from Macon County he had been a delegate to the Republican convention. The other four had all been killed; he was the only survivor.

George Houston, a crippled tailor and Republican legislator in Alabama, reported to the same committee that he had attended two sessions before he was shot. Black friends guarded his house until he could be carried away to comparative safety in the Sucarnoochee swamp. The incident was apparently the basis of a similar event in Albion Tourgée's *A Fool's Errand.*

By the fall of 1867 more than 700,000 black men in the South had registered to vote. If we calculate the black population of the South at some 4,000,000, of whom substantially more than 2,000,000 must be assumed to be women and children, it seems apparent that more than half the black males of the South had registered to vote. They outnumbered the far more numerous whites in registration by the margin of some 40,000. From this it followed that a substantial number of the delegates to the various state constitutional conventions were blacks, in some states a majority. Southern newspapers were bitter and derisive about the black-dominated conventions. They were called the "Black and Tans," "The Menagerie," and "Ring-Streaked and Striped Negro Conventions," and the black delegates were termed "baboons" and "monkeys."

In South Carolina, when the actual voting took place for delegates to the state constitutional convention, 87 percent of the blacks voted—68,875—as against 22,221, or less than 5 percent of the white voters. An intensive campaign had been launched by white politicians to persuade white voters to abstain from voting as a protest against the enfranchisement of blacks. Many black votes were cast for white delegates, and when the convention met in January, there were 48 white delegates and 76 blacks. Only in South Carolina were whites outnumbered by blacks in the state constitutional convention. The fact that this should have been the case in South Carolina, the leader in secession and the symbol of Southern intransigence, gave the convention of that state particular dramatic focus. The bitterest denunciations of the Southern press were reserved for its black delegates—"African savages," "gibbering, louse-eaten, devil worshipping barbarians," and the like. One newspaper called the convention "the maddest, most unscrupulous and infamous revolution in history." The recently deposed governor of the state predicted "a war of races" which would be "the most terrific war of extermination that ever desolated the face of the earth in any age or country." The honorary chairman of the convention was a prosperous white businessman, Thomas Robertson, a graduate of the University of South Carolina. Robertson told the delegates that they had met to draw up a "just and legal constitution" to guarantee, among other things, equal rights, "regardless of race, color or previous condition. . . . I trust there will be no class legislation here. I hope we will act harmoniously, promptly, judiciously and in such a manner as will reflect credit on ourselves, and secure the confidence of the people of the State whom we represent."

The permanent chairman of the convention was Albert Gallatin Mackey, son of a Charleston newspaper editor and pioneer mathematics teacher. Mackey himself was a classic character. At sixty-six by far the senior member of the convention, he was a graduate of the medical department of the College of South Carolina, an authority on the Talmud and on cabalistic writings, and a tireless writer on Freemasonry. It was soon evident that the convention contained an unusually large number of able black politicians. One of the most mysterious of the black leaders to emerge in that state after the war was Robert Brown Elliott. Although he referred to an English education that culminated at Eton, there was no record that he had ever attended that school or any explanation of how he was carried to England and returned in a day when few blacks had the resources or the freedom to travel. It was clear, however, that Elliott had, indeed, a classical training, spoke several languages, and had mastered at least the rudiments of the law. He was also a gifted speaker. A Southerner named James Morgan recalled many years later that Elliott "was one of the most brilliant orators I ever heard speak." His wife, Nancy, was renowned as the "most beautiful mulatto girl" in Columbia, South Carolina, a city where beautiful mulatto women abounded. He was also a protégé of Richard Henry Cain, a publisher and editor of the *South Carolina Leader,* a black newspaper. Cain had formerly been minister of the African Methodist Episcopal Church in Brooklyn, New York, and Cain and Elliott had been among the organizers of the Colored People's Convention held at the Zion Church in Charleston in November, 1865, to express dissatisfaction with the work of the state constitutional convention assembled under the terms of Johnson's Reconstruction. Elliott's law partner told of an occasion when Elliott addressed a predominantly white and actively hostile audience. He began by placing a copy of the Constitution on the lectern and on either side of it a large Colt revolver. He came, he informed his listeners, to discourse on the Constitution and was prepared, if necessary, to defend it.

Other prominent black leaders were Robert De Large, a mulatto tailor employed by the Freedmen's Bureau, and Alonzo J. Ransier who had been born free and had been a clerk for a Charleston merchant. Joseph Rainey, twenty-eight years old, had been born in the District of Columbia of parents who were both slaves. Having purchased their freedom, the Raineys moved to Charleston, South Carolina, and young Joseph, self-taught, became active in Republican Party politics at the war's end.

Francis Cardozo, a free Charlestonian, had been educated at the University of Glasgow. Son of Isaac Cardozo of Charleston, an economist, newspaper editor, and one of the most prominent literary figures of the South, Francis Cardozo and his brother, Thomas, had been leaders in establishing freedmen's schools. Francis was principal of the Avery Institute, a school supported by the American Missionary Society. The Reverend David Macrae, who had known Francis as a fellow student at theological seminary in St. Andrews, Scotland, described him as "a man of middle size, but of dignified appearance and refined manners . . . well-read" with "a clear head . . . an excellent argumentative speaker, and a first-rate organizer and man of business."

Another prominent black was William Whipper, a lawyer from Pennsylvania who was the son of a leading black abolitionist. Robert Smalls of Beaufort had achieved the status of Union hero by escaping from Charleston with a small Confederate vessel carrying guns and ammunition. When Smalls was a child, his slave mother had taken him to see a slave auction, hoping thereby to instill in him a hatred of slavery.

Prince Rivers had been a Union soldier, and his commanding officer had said of him, "If there should ever be a black monarchy in South Carolina, he will be its king." Benjamin Franklin Randolph was a graduate of Oberlin and a chaplain in a black regiment who worked for the Freedmen's Bureau after the war. He had doubtless been a slave on one of the plantations of the numerous Randolph clan; indeed, the chances that he carried the aristocratic Randolph blood in his veins were great.

Martin Delany, born in West Virginia, reared in Xenia, Ohio, and described, somewhat inadequately, in the *Concise Dictionary of American Biography* as "physician, journalist, Negro leader," was one of the most remarkable Americans of his age. Accepted at the Harvard Medical School under the deanship of Oliver Wendell Holmes, he was forced to leave by the revolt of his fellow students who resolved: "That we deem the admission of blacks to the medical lectures highly detrimental to the interests and welfare of the Institution." The father of eleven children, all named after famous black figures such as Toussaint L'Ouverture and Alexandre Dumas, he was the first black officer commissioned in the United States Army. Delany had been present at the ceremonies when the United States flag was raised over Fort Sumter on the fourth anniversary of its capture and there met Robert Smalls, with whom he had formed an immediate alliance.

Delany, the reader may recall, had been an advocate of Afro-American settlement in Santo Domingo or Africa, a position which alienated him from many other black leaders. As subassistant commissioner of the Freedmen's Bureau, in charge of the district of Hilton Head, Delany labored to establish the freed blacks of the region as farmers. But he found the task wearisome and frustrating. Whites exerted, as we have seen, constant pressure to regain their confiscated lands. The freedmen themselves proved maddeningly mercurial. They were often as evasive with Delany as with white officials. He was in the awkward position of trying to prevail on the freedmen to fulfill the terms of labor contracts that he had helped frame. Attempting to prevent the exploitation of black workers on "share," Delany established his own cotton-marketing operation and encouraged the workers to bring their cotton to him to get a better price. B. F. Perry, governor of South Carolina under Johnson's Reconstruction government, wrote of Martin Delany, "I must say he has exhibited, in his speeches and addresses, more wisdom and prudence, more honor and patriotism than any other Republican in South Carolina, white or black."

Beverly Nash was a tall, handsome man who had been a slave. After he was freed, Nash became a bootblack at a Columbia hotel and subsequently active in Republican politics. A black colleague said proudly of Nash, "The lawyers and the white chivalry, as they call themselves, have learned to let him alone. They know more law and some other things than he does; but he studies them all up, and then comes down on them with a good story or anecdote, and you better believe he carries the audience right along with him. . . . No, sir there is now nobody who cares to attack Beverly Nash."

Among the white delegates were two men destined for important roles in the state's political history. Franklin Moses, a Confederate veteran, twenty-eight years old, was the son of a judge of the State Supreme Court, scion of an old and distinguished family. Daniel Chamberlain, a native of Massachusetts, had graduated from Yale in the class of '62 and served in the army as a lieutenant in the 4th Massachusetts Colored Cavalry. Deciding to try the life of a cotton planter, he had bought a plantation near Columbia. There his experiences as a white officer in a black regiment made him a natural leader of the newly enfranchised freedmen. Chamberlain was thirty-one.

The minutes of the convention disclose an impressive degree of common sense and liberal principles. When the motion was made to ban a reporter of the *Charleston Mercury* from the convention hall because of that paper's scurrilous attacks, black delegates took the lead in opposing the motion. To exclude him, Cardozo declared, "would be only to exhibit a smallness, a pettiness of spite unworthy of our character." Another black delegate termed the proposal "a stab at the liberty of the press." A white delegate objected to having the phrase from the Declaration of Independence "all men are created free and equal" incorporated in the constitution of South Carolina, where in the aftermath of the freeing of the slaves it took on, for the whites, troubling new connotations. Benjamin Franklin Randolph defended the phrase. It was not, of course, intended to refer to men in a physiological sense. Obviously they varied widely in physical and temperamental attributes. "It refers," Randolph declared, "to the rights of men politically speaking and in that I understand and defend it. All men are born with certain inalienable rights which it is their privilege to enjoy." To Randolph's proposal for a clause in the constitution that would forbid discrimination against any man on the basis of class or race, white delegates objected on the ground that amendments to the Federal Constitution already proposed by Congress obviated the need for such a clause. To this Francis Cardozo replied prophetically that he was convinced that the vast majority of white South Carolinians were determined to deprive blacks of their rights as citizens. "I want to fix them in the Constitution," he declared, "in such a way that no lawyer, however cunning, can possibly misinterpret the meaning."

William Whipper reminded the delegates that their "sole object should be to pass laws that will benefit the whole people. And if we see any class suffering, it is our duty to relieve them. . . . Here we should forget all prejudices and not be swerved from our purposes for anything. . . ." No actions should be taken simply for revenge. "When I left the army at the close of the war," Whipper said, "I was zealous to see the leaders of the rebellion hung and every man engaged in it disfranchised and their lands confiscated." The government, however, had decided on a different policy. "For us to suffer anything to be done that savors of vengeance is wrong, cruel and unjust."

Cardozo was chairman of the Committee on Education, which put forward a plan for a system of free public schools, as well as state institutions for the blind, the deaf-mute, and the insane, and for the establishment of a state university. Section 11 specified that "all the public schools, colleges and universities supported by the public funds shall be free and open to all the children of the state without regard to race or color." There was immediate and determined resistance on the part of the white minority in the convention. A black delegate, Jonathan Wright, declared, "This provision leaves it so that white and colored children can attend school together, if they desire to do so, but I do not believe the colored children will want to go to the white schools and vice versa. The colored people do not want to force what is called social equality; that is a matter which will regulate itself. No law we can pass can compel associations that are distasteful." Cardozo was more disposed to urge desegregation as a way of overcoming prejudices between the races. If young children attended school together, "prejudice must eventually die out; but if we postpone it until they become men and women," he declared, "prejudice will be so established that no mortal can obliterate it." It was not that there should not be any separate schools. "In Charleston, I am sure the colored pupils in my school would not like to go to a white school," but in small schools in rural districts the maintenance of separate schools would be absurd.

Another resolution that was warmly debated required compulsory school attendance for all children between six and sixteen. Robert De Large was one who objected on the ground that "It is just as impossible to put such a section in practical operation, as it would be for a man to fly to the moon." But Elliott insisted that it was "republicanism to educate people without discrimination. . . . The question is not white or black united or divided, but whether children shall be sent to school or kept at home." A white delegate argued that the compulsory education clause should be dropped because it would never be accepted by the white people of the state, but Francis Cardozo replied that it was now or never. "We know," he declared, "that when the old aristocracy and ruling power of this State get into power, as they undoubtedly will, because intelligence and wealth will win in the long run, they will never pass such a law as this. . . . They will take precious good care that the colored people shall never be enlightened."

The delegates devoted a good deal of attention to the question of how compulsory education was to be paid for. When a poll tax was suggested, the objection was raised that some parents who might not be able to pay the tax might be denied the right to vote *or* send their children to school. Elliott insisted that "no person shall ever be deprived of the right of suffrage for nonpayment of said tax."

One of the motions put before the convention was to appropriate $1,000,000 for the purchase of land to be distributed to the freedmen. Richard Cain argued for it. "The abolition of slavery," he declared, "has thrown these people upon their own resources. How are they to live? I know the philosopher of the *New York Tribune* says root hog or die. . . . My proposition is simply to give the hog some place to root."

Some Radical Republicans in Congress were pressing for the confiscation of rebel plantations and their distribution to freedmen, but the South Carolina convention disavowed confiscation. In its place the delegates urged that the Federal government purchase lands and give blacks an opportunity to buy them on easy terms. While Cardozo did not support confiscation, he was emphatic in his conviction that "we will never have true freedom until we abolish the system of agriculture which existed in the Southern States." The large plantations which required dozens and often hundreds of hands to work them, perpetuated a mode of labor which worked against independence for blacks by keeping them in economic, if not legal, bondage. On a resolution to distribute land to the freedman the vote was 101 to 5 in favor.

There was by no means unanimity among the black delegates. The question of the franchise was an especially sensitive subject. When Randolph suggested that a literacy test be required for voters after 1875, a number of his fellow black delegates rose to rebut him. Robert Elliott declared: "This Convention has met for the purpose of laying down a basis of universal suffrage. How would you face your constituents? Would you say to them, you sent us to lay the foundations of liberty deep and broad for your children and your children's children but after getting to Charleston we found out you were not fit for it . . . consequently we have taken it away from you."

Beverly Nash told his fellow delegates, "We are not prepared for this suffrage. But we can learn. Give a man tools and let him commence to use them and in time he will learn a trade. So it is with voting."

Alonzo Ransier was equally strong on the issue. "The right to vote," he declared, "belongs alike to the wise and the ignorant, to the virtuous and the vicious, and I cannot consent to any qualification . . . . It is our chief means for self-defense." He was followed by Richard Cain, who said, "I would not deprive any being, rich or poor, of that franchise by which alone he can protect himself as a citizen. Whether learned or ignorant he has an inalienable right to say who shall govern him. He may not understand a great deal of the knowledge that is derived from books but he can judge between right and wrong."

Whipper made the most radical proposal of all. "However frivolous you may think it," he told his fellow delegates, "I know the time will come when every man and woman in the country will have the right to vote. I acknowledge the superiority of women. There are large numbers of the sex who have an intelligence more than equal to our own. Is it right or just to deprive these intelligent beings of the privileges which we enjoy? The time will come when you will have to meet this question. It will continue to be agitated until it must ultimately triumph. However derisively we may treat these noble women who are struggling for their sex, we shall yet see them successful in the assertion of their rights." The motion to strike out the word "male" in the clause on the franchise was "decided in the negative."

Before the convention adjourned, the permanent chairman, Albert Gallatin Mackey, congratulated the delegates on their accomplishment. For the first time in the history of the state, "the great doctrine of universal manhood suffrage was distinctly recognized," he told them. "Here we have stricken every vestige of serfdom from our situation and that too in so emphatic and unambiguous a way that no doubt can ever be entertained of our determination that this relic of barbarism shall never again in any form pollute our soil. . . . Here we have made every needful arrangement for the free education of our people. . . . Here too we have obliterated from our political system that most pernicious heresy of State sovereignty. . . . We do not claim for ourselves a preeminence of wisdom or virtue, but we do claim that we have followed in the progressive advancement of the age; that we have been bold enough and honest enough and wise enough to trample unworthy prejudice underfoot."

It was, in fact, a marvelous moment. The debates of the convention and Mackey's concluding address belong among the classic documents of our past. Here, in the first instant of black and white government, it seemed that all the hopes of the friends of freedom and equality were to be realized. The level of discourse had been notably high, the arguments seriously sustained, rising at times to the heights of genuine eloquence. The black delegates had more than held their own with their white colleagues. A liberal spirit had prevailed, and much had been accomplished—the framing of the state's first divorce law and provisions for the direct election of the governor and various state officials formerly appointed by the legislature, as well as clauses protecting creditors and extending the property rights of women. Mackey's praise was not excessive. The failures, the disappointments, the abuses and corruptions that followed should never have been allowed to obscure the achievements. From having been, in its constitution, laws, and policy, one of the most retrograde of all the states, South Carolina advanced to the forefront as a consequence of the work of the "Black and Tan" assembly and "the Congo Convention," as it was termed by the hostile press, which also indulged in virulent personal attacks on the black delegates—Cain was "black, ugly and shabby"; Cardozo had "neither abilities or accomplishments"; De Large was part of the "scum" thrown up by "the great social revolution."

What the convention proved beyond contravening (although, of course, numerous persons set about at once to contravene it) was that black politicians could, at the very least, hold their own with their white counterparts; that, moreover, they had a keener sense of what constituted justice for all people than white politicians. Perhaps most striking of all, the majority of the black delegates showed a remarkable disposition to abstain from words or actions provocative to the whites. To be sure such measures as compulsory public education alarmed and dismayed the great majority of South Carolina whites. But there was little hint of the retributive or vindictive in the debates of the convention. Black and white delegates alike knew that in the long run reconciliation with the "Confederate" party offered far more for both races than confrontation.

When the constitution was submitted to the voters of the state for ratification, intense pressure was brought to bear on blacks to vote against it. Jordan Jackson told a congressional committee that his white employer declared, "I should not stay on his place, or any man who voted a ratification ticket. On election day," Jackson testified, "Captain Snead got me drunk and took away from me forcibly a ratification ticket and gave me a Democratic ticket and made me vote it. He also said he would give me no meat or bread if I voted the ratification ticket." Pink Campbell related that when he went to vote, white men intercepted him and asked him how he intended to vote. When he replied, "For the radical ticket," one white said, "God, boy, if you vote the radical ticket you will be ruined."

Black politicians fought fire with fire. Robert Smalls urged the women in his audiences to tell their husbands that if they voted Democratic, they would not give them "any of that thing." The single women should not marry any black Democrats, and "those that is married don't service them in bed."

The constitution was approved by a vote of 70,758 (by far the greater part of it black) to 27,288, with some 35,551 registered voters, mostly whites, remaining away from the polls. It is worth noting that when those whites opposed to the constitution protested to Congress, they cited among its most objectionable features the fact that it provided for the establishment of 1,800 schoolhouses in the state, with 1,800 teachers at a total yearly cost to the taxpayers of almost $1,000,000, an enormous sum in that era. When Thaddeus Stevens read the petition of the constitution's opponents, he noted wryly, "What the protest claimed as grievances . . . [we regard] as virtues."

With the South Carolina constitution ratified by the voters, albeit largely by black voters, and accepted by Congress, the next step was the election of a legislature and state officials under the new frame of government. When the new administration took up its duties in July, 1868, the Senate contained twenty whites, six of whom were Democrats, and ten blacks. The House, on the other hand, had seventy-eight blacks and forty-six whites. Robert K. Scott, a Pennsylvanian who had been assistant commissioner of the Freedmen's Bureau for the district, was chosen governor, and Robert Elliott narrowly missed out as lieutenant governor to Franklin Moses. Although historians have sometimes given the impression that the black majority in the South Carolina convention gobbled up a disproportionate number of public offices, the fact was that they showed remarkable restraint. Jonathan Wright, a Pennsylvania lawyer, became an associate justice of the South Carolina Supreme Court. Francis Cardozo became secretary of state. Both the governor and lieutenant governor were white; and the county treasurers were all white, as were the eleven lower court judges and twenty-one of the thirty-one school commissioners.

The inauguration of Scott was accompanied by an outburst of wild enthusiasm by the largely black crowd who witnessed it. Scott replied in his inaugural address by calling for separate schools for white and black children, the withdrawal of Federal troops, the removal of political constraints on former Confederates, and the elimination of the Freedmen's Bureau. The speech was thoroughly conciliatory. The fact that Scott had so little notion of the precariousness of his own tenure serves to remind us that if black Republicans had strong misgivings about the readiness of "the old class" to accommodate themselves to Congressional Reconstruction, white Republicans persisted in that illusion.

Having ratified the Fourteenth Amendment, the South Carolina legislature went on to other pressing matters. Robert Elliott was in the forefront of those proposing legislation aimed at counteracting the effects of racial prejudice. He introduced a bill designed to prevent discrimination in all public facilities from trains and theaters to hotels. A white opponent of the measure asked why South Carolina should seek to be in advance of Massachusetts, South Carolina already had universal suffrage, whereas the home of abolitionism required a literacy test for voters.

Congressional Reconstruction followed much the same pattern in other Southern states, although overall only approximately one-fourth of the delegates to the state constitutional conventions were black. In the Alabama constitutional convention the black leader was James Rapier, a graduate of the University of Glasgow. In the Mississippi convention one of the most conspicuous black leaders was James Lynch, a graduate of Dartmouth and of the Princeton Theological Seminary. Lynch was described by a white man as "a great orator; fluent and graceful. . . . He was the idol of the Negroes who would come for miles, on foot, to hear him speak. . . . He swayed them with as much ease as a man would sway a peacock feather with his right hand. They yelled and howled, and laughed and cried, as he willed."

Another leading Mississippi black was also named Lynch. John Roy Lynch was born in Concordia, Louisiana, in 1847, of a white father and slave mother. As in the case of Archibald and Francis Grimké, his father intended to free him and his mother by the terms of his will, but after his death the executor of his estate declared his mother was part of the estate and hence still a slave, and her son with her. Young Lynch, sixteen years old, was living in Natchez when that town was occupied by Union troops. He began attending night school taught by missionary teachers, learned to read, and thereafter taught himself, mastering the trade of a photographer. The first Republican governor of the state appointed Lynch justice of the peace, and two years later his black constituents elected him to the state legislature. In 1871, at the age of twenty-four, he was elected Speaker of the House. In 1913, having outlived many of his fellow actors in the drama of Reconstruction, he wrote a book entitled *The Facts of Reconstruction*. The title is misleading since it is largely an account of Lynch's own political career as a black Republican from a Southern state. Perhaps as notable for what it does not say as what it does, Lynch's book is one of the most important works by a black political figure. He had endeavored, he wrote in his preface, "to give expression to his ideas, opinions and convictions in language devoid of bitterness, and entirely free from race prejudice, sectional animosity, or partisan bias." To a remarkable degree he succeeded. At a time when white historians were contending that the enfranchisement of freed blacks by the Republican Congress was a tragic error, Lynch's main purpose was to refute such arguments by showing that black politicians and black voters had conducted themselves in an intelligent and responsible manner and that the prospects for the integration of blacks into the political system had been excellent until the unexpected resurgence of the Democrats in the midterm elections of 1874.

James Hill, an ex-slave who became Mississippi's secretary of state, was described by his friend Thomas Cardozo as "in appearance very much like Mr. Sumner, tall and aristocratic in bearing, and with the same fall of hair over his forehead. . . . He is always direct in his remarks, wears an ugly and grim countenance when speaking and contends for that which he thinks is right."

Another Northern Negro, Israel Shadd, had published an abolitionist newspaper in Canada before the war. Arriving in Mississippi, he found employment as a bookkeeper for Davis Bend, the black farm cooperative. Shadd's brother, a graduate of the newly founded Howard University, was a successful lawyer, and his sister, Mary Ann Shadd Cary, was a teacher and writer.

Hiram Revels was a Methodist minister, born in Fayetteville, North Carolina, of mixed Cherokee and African blood, and educated in the North. Coming to Mississippi in 1865 as the ruling elder of the African Methodist Church, he soon found himself involved in politics. Blanche Bruce had grown up a slave on a Mississippi plantation. The son of the master of the plantation, he had been educated with his white brothers and gone to college at Oberlin after the war. Bruce's white blood was clearly evident in his features. He was a notorious dandy.

In the Mississippi state constitutional convention a majority of the delegates were white, and most of them had been born in Mississippi or had lived there for some years before the war. John Lynch pointed out that although Adams County, which contained the city of Natchez, had a large black majority, two of the delegates elected to the convention from that city were white men. The Mississippi Reconstruction Constitution was an excellent one and would, in John Lynch's opinion, have been adopted by a large majority in the state except for the fact that it contained an "unwise and unnecessary clause" which had the practical effect of disenfranchising all Southerners who had held office under the government of the United States and subsequently given their allegiance to the Confederacy. The effect of this clause was to exclude many ex-U.S. army and navy officers who had fought for the Confederacy or held Federal offices prior to the war. These men constituted the natural leadership of the states, and the exclusionary clause was bitterly resented. Moreover, as Lynch pointed out, it was unnecessary since by the policy of "masterful inactivity" most of the white Southern leaders already abstained from politics.

In New Orleans a convention made up of blacks and whites—the

"Black and Tan Convention," one newspaper called it while another termed it the "Bones and Banjo Convention"—met to draw up a new constitution for the state of Louisiana. Pinckney Benton Stewart Pinchback was a leader of the state's Republicans. Pinchback's father was a prosperous white planter who had freed his sons and their black mother and sent the sons to school in Ohio. When his father died, Pinchback's white relatives denied him his inheritance and threatened to have him seized and sold into slavery if he protested. After a career as a Mississippi River boatman, gambler, and brawler, Pinchback at the end of the war entered Louisiana politics and formed an alliance with the Reconstruction governor, Henry Warmoth, which brought him, successively, to the offices of lieutenant governor and of senator. He was a handsome man with a waxed mustache, curly hair, and piercing dark eyes, and he proved himself an adept practitioner in the murky waters of postwar Louisiana politics.

Under the Reconstruction Constitution, Oscar Dunn, a black Union army veteran, became lieutenant governor of the state. The event was recorded in the *New Orleans Picayune,* which twenty-seven years earlier had carried an advertisement which read: "$5 REWARD. RUNAWAY from the subscribers . . . the negro boy, Oscar Dunn, an apprentice to the plastering trade. . . ."

In his address to the Senate, Dunn said: "I hope that progress will continue until everywhere throughout this land intelligence will be respected, whatever the color of the skin. Not that I claim intelligence for myself," Dunn added, "but that I hope by your assistance and kindness toward me and my race to prove worthy of every advantage bestowed upon us. . . . Myself and my people . . . are not seeking social equality; that is a thing no law can govern. . . . We simply ask equal opportunity of supporting our families, of educating our children, and of becoming worthy citizens of this government."

The Reverend David Macrae found the North Carolina convention "of mixed black and white delegates . . . engaged in revising the Constitution." The press had been excluded because of offensively comic reports of the delegates' deliberation under such headlines as "Bones and Banjo Convention" and because the newspapers added "nigger" after the name of each black delegate.

James Hood, one of the leading members of the Raleigh convention, was a black minister from Bridgeport, Connecticut, who was elected chairman of the convention. He exhorted the delegates "that we and the white people have to live here together. . . . We have been living together for a hundred years and more, and we have got to live together still; and the best way is to harmonize our feelings as much as possible, and to treat all men respectfully."

James Harris, another delegate, had been born a slave, been freed in 1850, and then started out on a pilgrimage to try to find a home for free blacks in some part of the world. Addressing the delegates he agreed with Hood that North Carolina was the proper home for Southern blacks. He had covered forty thousand miles in his search for another refuge. As for the North, there was, if possible, more animosity there toward blacks than in the South, Harris declared.

David Macrae also observed the Virginia constitutional convention, which had a substantial number of black delegates, debating a new frame of government. One black member expressed his indignation that in courts of law one Bible was kept for whites to kiss and another for blacks. "This," he declared, "is a mockery of God and an outrage on our races! Black men have played an important part in history, but white men have tried to keep them out of sight, and are trying to do so still." George Teamah, a runaway slave who had become a brickyard worker in the North and returned to Virginia to play a prominent role in the politics of that state, recalling his experience in the Virginia constitutional convention, declared that "many of us could neither read or write, had gone there from the farm yards etc. . . . But in spite of their disqualifications, my people seems to have been possessed of a natural itching to meet, in open debate, every question which came up for discussion."

In Georgia two black senators and twenty-five black representatives were elected to the state legislature under the Reconstruction Acts, among them Henry Turner and Tunis Campbell. After serving as chaplain with black troops, Turner had settled in Georgia, preaching and helping to organize black voters. Delivering a speech, he had been threatened by armed whites. "I was, on one occasion," he wrote in the *Christian Recorder*, "lecturing to young men on the political prospects of the colored people, when it was announced they were preparing outdoors to shoot, and commenced speaking on as I had been. . . ." Members of his audience set up a picket line outside the church.

Turner had already submitted two bills, one calling for an eight-hour day for all laborers and the other forbidding discrimination on "common carriers," when he and the other black delegates were threatened with eviction. He gave an eloquent defense of his right to sit in the Georgia legislature. "The scene presented in this House," he declared, ". . . is one unparalleled in the history of the world. From this day, back to the day when God breathed the breath of life into Adam, no analogy for it can be found. Never, in the history of the world, has a man been arraigned before a body clothed with legislative, judicial or executive functions, charged with the offense of being a darker hue than his fellow men. . . . The Anglo Saxon race, sir, is a most surprising one. . . . I was not aware that there was in the character of that race so much cowardice or so much pusillanimity. The treachery which has been exhibited in it by gentlemen belonging to that race has shaken my confidence in it more than anything that has come under my observation from the day of my birth. . . .

"You may expel us, gentlemen, by your votes, today; but, while you do it, remember that there is a just God in Heaven, whose All-Seeing Eye beholds alike the acts of the oppressor and the oppressed, and who despite the machinations of the wicked, never fails to vindicate the cause of justice, and the sanctity of His own handiwork."

The legislators were unmoved by Turner's appeal. He and his companions were expelled for no better reason than their blackness. Grant sent General Alfred Howe Terry into Georgia with Federal troops, the black legislators were reinstated, and the whites who had replaced them were evicted. It would prove a brief and barren triumph.

With the ratification of most of the Reconstruction constitutions there were, indeed, grounds for optimism. None of the white fantasies of "black domination" had come to pass. Blacks had conducted themselves with disconcerting intelligence and restraint and shown a disarming readiness to cooperate with (and often defer to) whites. There seemed every reason to believe that once the "Conservatives" or Democrats had accepted black suffrage as a political fact of life, the new order might at last assert itself.

"Niggers," George Templeton Strong wrote, "seem helping to reconstruct the chivalric South with a degree of sense and moderation I did not expect." Strong was annoyed by the disposition of the Northern newspapers to treat the state constitutional conventions and their black members as jokes. "The freedmen," he added, "voted for a reconstruction convention in each state. The whites were against it (preferring the continuance of military rule), and the freedmen have prevailed. In Alabama and Louisiana the whites were apathetic and kept away from the polls. . . . It looks as if the two races were to be henceforth hostile and antagonistic." The whites, Strong was convinced, could have prevented such an outcome by "tact and conciliation." Instead, they had, "by all accounts, treated the freedmen as their natural enemies, and studiously displayed hatred and contempt toward them. . . ." Such a reaction promised to "make the black race master in the South. . . . Very bad for the ex-chivalry, and not very good for us at the North, or for the nation. It may keep us unsettled for an indefinite period. . . . Dethroned tyrants are apt to be nervous and scarey-y."

The Reverend David Macrae echoed Strong. "The enfranchised negroes, in general," he wrote, "exercised their new power quietly, considerately, and well—with far more regard for their old masters, and far less prejudice of race than could have been anticipated." In attending a number of the state constitutional conventions, Macrae had been much impressed by the fiscal and political responsibility shown by the black delegates.

The *Nation* of July 18, 1867, stated that "it is now admitted that the negro can fight, will work, and is both capable of receiving education and eager for it." But many Southerners, and Northerners as well, clung to the notion that the freedman was not interested in voting. In refutation of this argument, the writer in the *Nation* pointed to the fact that "a far larger proportion of the resident colored voters have registered than of whites." In Virginia, if all the whites had registered, they would have outnumbered the black voters by a margin of forty thousand. "The freedmen," the *Nation* concluded, "in every place where they have been properly protected from intimidation, manifest an eagerness to be enrolled for which there is no precedent among white people North or South." Like Strong, the *Nation* was favorably impressed by the performance of black constitution writers and legislators.

As for physical types, the black political figures of the Reconstruction Era represented a remarkable spectrum from individuals with the features of their aristocratic white fathers and skin so light that they might well have passed for "white" to those with classic Negroid features and the darkest of skins. The predominance of mulattoes was clearly not, as some racial theorists were disposed to argue, due to their higher percentage of "white" blood but rather to the fact that as the offspring of their white masters they had enjoyed special opportunities for education, a few having been, like the Cardozos, sent to college in England or in the North by white fathers who had taken interest in their training. Even biased white observers like James Pike, the author of the sensational *The Prostrate State,* noted that they could observe no difference in intelligence and ability between the "African" blacks and those who were virtually "white." Robert Elliott was a case in point. His dark skin and Negroid features indicated that he was "pure" black, although genetics being what they are, appearances in that regard were often deceiving. The fact was that since white masters often preferred as their mistresses slave women of light complexion who already had strong admixtures of white blood, many "blacks" with strikingly Caucasian features had far less black blood or, more accurately, genes than white.

Not surprisingly Southerners were furious at the political activity of their former slaves. What was most offensive to them was the fact that blacks were not allowed to vote in a number of Northern states where their numbers were small. Under such circumstances it seemed to them the most brazen hypocrisy for Congress to insist that Southern blacks, assumed to be far less qualified to exercise the franchise, be given the right to vote by congressional intervention. At a North Carolina banquet, a friend wrote Elizabeth Meriwether in 1868, the company included three ex-governors, two former members of Congress, and an ex-justice of the Supreme Court, "but the only persons in The Banquet Hall who could either vote or hold public office were *the negroes who waited on the table!*" David Macrae found the Southern whites immovable in their conviction that enfranchising the freedmen could lead only to chaos and the extirpation of all whites. In Macrae's opinion the fears of the South were "absurdly" exaggerated. "The idea of the negro ruling the South is preposterous," he wrote. Whites outnumbered blacks roughly 12,000,000 to 4,000,000. In the Gulf states the black population was estimated 45 percent, running down to 12 percent in Missouri. In addition, white Southerners controlled virtually all the wealth of the South and, indeed, had every other advantage, psychological and practical. It seemed clear to Macrae that the white population of the South would, in all likelihood, increase faster than the black, so that simply on a numerical basis the possibility of blacks' "ruling" the South had to diminish with each decade. Macrae, in fact, found that most Southerners with whom he talked were convinced that the black population was declining at a rapid rate. General Beauregard stated that there were 500,000 fewer blacks in the Gulf states in 1868 than there had been in 1860. "They are dying fast," he added. "In seventy-five years hence they will have vanished from this continent along with the red man and the buffalo."

In the face of such attitudes, it is hardly surprising that Southern blacks were unable to "prove" their ability to participate in the political process.

42

Black Education

It was in the realm of education that Northern whites (and Northern blacks) and Southern blacks encountered each other most dramatically. We have had occasion in the story of Port Royal to take note of the labors of Gideon's Band. It had innumerable counterparts.

Between 1861 and 1865, 450 schools were started in Southern states occupied by Union soldiers, and more than 250,000 freedmen and women, young and old, enrolled. In South Carolina alone, David Macrae was told, 25,000 emancipated slaves had learned to read the Bible, while in Texas the number was estimated at 50,000, and in Louisiana the number of reasonably literate blacks was as large as the literate white population. One old black man, struggling to learn the alphabet, told Macrae, "I sees de first letter clar enough but after dat, 'pears to me like puttin' out my foot in de dark. I dunno whar to find de next step. But Mose [his son] lor', sah, dat boy can go slick thro' a word a long as dat"—measuring half the length of his arm. "I 'specs they'll make a scholard of him."

An old black woman who despaired of learning to read was shown the letter *O* in a book. "You see this round thing," her teacher said.

"Yes, mahm."

"That's 'O,' let me hear you say 'O'?"

"O."

"Well, that is one of the letters of the alphabet. Whenever you open a book and see that letter, you will know that it is 'O.'"

The old woman was delighted with her accomplishment. She picked the O out of every Scripture text on the schoolroom wall, hurried home to demonstrate to her family her mastery of O, and soon was able to read.

In Mississippi, in the period of Federal control, more than 150 schools had been started for black children, and 265 teachers were employed to give instruction to more than 14,000 children and 5,000 adults. In New Orleans there were 19 schools employing 104 teachers, with a daily average attendance of 5,724 pupils. The superintendent of schools in the city estimated that 50,000 blacks had been taught to read.

In Goldsboro, North Carolina, two ex-slaves, who had only recently learned to read and write, had gathered together 150 pupils. In New Orleans the correspondent of the *New York Tribune* visited a school of 300 students run by "educated colored men" that "would bear comparison with any ordinary school at the north. Not only good reading and spelling was heard, but lessons at the black-board in arithmetic, recitations in geography and English grammar . . . and all the older classes could read or recite as fluently in French as in English."

Black schools were a kind of critical testing ground for the whole issue of black equality. The black regiments of the Civil War had put to the test the question of whether or not blacks were "brave," whether or not they would, by fighting for their freedom, give witness to their desire to have it. Now the attention shifted to the schools. Could black children learn as quickly and as well as white children? The answer seemed to be a cautious yes. Whitelaw Reid was much impressed with the best black schools in New Orleans. "The progress in learning to read is exceptionally rapid," he noted. "I do not believe that in the best schools at the North, they learn the alphabet and First Reader quicker than do the average of these slave children."

A hymn that the Chase sisters heard went:

> Oh happy is the child who learns to read
> When I get over
> To read the blessed book indeed.

Chorus:
When I get over, when I get over
'Twill take some time to study
When I get over.

William Hepworth Dixon, an English journalist visiting Richmond some months after the end of the war, expressed an opinion of the black man similar to that which he had rather mockingly charged the abolitionist with holding. He believed "that the negro is fitted by his humour, by his industry, by his sociability, for a very high form of civil life." He struck up an acquaintance with Eli Brown, the head waiter at his hotel, an ex-slave who had taught himself to read while still in servitude and was now learning to write. Brown pleased Dixon by declaring that he had no interest in voting yet because he felt that he had not yet sufficient knowledge to vote intelligently. Dixon accompanied his black guide "on a series of peeps into the negro schools" of Richmond. "They are mostly up in garrets," he wrote, "or down in vaults; poor rooms, with scant supplies of benches, desks and books. In some, the teacher is a white; in many he is a black or half-caste. Old men, young lads, were equally intent on learning in these humble schools . . . they have begun the work of emancipating themselves from the thraldom of ignorance and vice." There were forty such schools in the city.

At Port Royal Whitelaw Reid paid particular attention to the school. In a "barn-like structure" he found "row after row of cleanly-clad negro boys, from the ages of six and seven up to sixteen and seventeen." Of 374 pupils enrolled, 200 were present. Reid had never seen "such masses of little wooly heads, such rows of shining ivories, and flat noses and blubber lips." The teachers were convalescent soldiers from a nearby army hospital. Reid had the by-now-familiar anxiety about excessive paternalism. The freedmen of all ages needed to be taught their ABCs, but more than that, "that liberty means, not idleness, but merely work for themselves instead of work for others. . . . The way to do this was not to gather them into colonies at military posts and feed them government rations, but to throw them in the water and them learn to swim by finding the necessity of swimming."

When Charles Sumner brought the Marquis de Chambrun to visit Richard Greener's school at Port Royal, Greener called on one of his pupils, who recited Lincoln's Gettysburg Address. It was a moving moment for Sumner, who had been present at Gettysburg. Lincoln himself, he told Greener, had not done it better.

The attitude of free blacks toward education varied, largely in terms of class and locale. Urban blacks were especially eager for "education." Soon after the fall of Savannah the blacks of the city formed an organization called the Savannah Educational Association, made up primarily of ministers and members of black churches. The association set about to recruit teachers from among the most literate members of the black community. The same response had been strikingly evident in New Orleans, Charleston, and Richmond. On the other hand, rural blacks, especially in the Deep South, often echoed their former master's contempt for "book 'larnin'." Whitelaw Reid quoted a plantation hand who spoke contemptuously of his fellows who were trying to learn to read. "Wat's the use?" he asked. "Wat'll dey be but niggers when dey gets through? Niggers good for nothin' but to wukin the fiel' and make cotton. Can't make white folks ob you'selves, if you *is* free." On other plantations blacks asked the proprietors to take money out of their wages to hire a teacher to teach their children.

We have taken note in an earlier volume of the fact that the Grimké sisters discovered that they had black relatives in Charleston when two light-complexioned black boys named Archibald and Francis Grimké presented themselves at the Morris Street School. The principal, Mrs. Francis Pillsbury, the sister-in-law of Parker Pillsbury, editor of the *Anti-Slavery Standard,* suspected that there was more than a casual relationship between them and Sarah and Angelina. Mrs. Pillsbury arranged for them to attend Lincoln University in Pennsylvania. Admitted despite their youth, they made good progress. Two years later Angelina Grimké, having read an article about the school that mentioned the Grimké boys, wrote to Archibald: "As the name is a very uncommon one, it has occurred to me that you have probably been a slave of one of my brothers and I feel a great desire to know all about you." Archibald Grimké's letter was more than Angelina had bargained for. He and his brother, he wrote, were the sons of Henry Grimké, Angelina's brother. After the death of Henry's wife, "he took my mother, who was his slave & his children's nurse," as his mistress, Archibald wrote. Nancy Weston had three children by Henry, who, dying in 1853, left Nancy and her children in the care of his son "to be treated as members of the family." The son ignored his father's instructions, neglected Nancy and her children until the children were old enough to serve him, and then claimed them as his slaves. When

Francis, still a child, had tried to escape and been recaptured, his master had sold him south. Freed at the end of the war, the family had been reunited, and Francis Pillsbury had traced their parentage. "I hope, dear Madam, you will excuse this badly written epistle," Archibald Grimké concluded. "Perhaps you would like to see our pictures. They are enclosed."

The sisters promptly acknowledged their "black" nephews, surely the most dramatic such reconciliation of the postwar era. "I am glad you have taken the name of Grimké," Angelina wrote. "It was once one of the noblest names of Carolina. I charge you most solemnly by your upright conduct and your devotion to the principles of justice and humanity to lift this name out of the dust where it now lies and set it once more among the princes of our land." There was an affecting meeting between the two now-elderly heroines of the abolitionist movement and their young nephews—Sarah was seventy-six and Angelina sixty-three—and though in modest circumstances themselves, they helped to finance the graduate education of Archibald and Francis. Archibald got a law degree at Harvard, wrote biographies of Charles Sumner and William Lloyd Garrison and became president of the American Negro Academy. Francis became a prominent minister.

Linda Slaughter, a Northern schoolteacher, had her black pupils in Virginia write to white schools in the North. One such letter, written by a black boy named George Wells, began: "I am a little black boy. I don't suppose I'll ever be white. . . . I eat with a fork. I used to sit on the floor and eat with my fingers and get grease and molasses all over myself. I didn't have any manners nor anything to eat hardly. Now I have everything nice and I try very hard. I am a temperance boy. . . . I learn Latin, too . . . *Ille, illa, illud.* . . . Perhaps I shall get on the cars some time and come to see you. Would you speak to a black boy? I shall be eight years old next in May."

Perhaps the most eloquent testimony to the work of Northern teachers came from a young Georgia black. "Now," he wrote a Southern friend, "the white people south says that the yankee are no friend to the southern people. That's a mistaken idea. The northerners do not advise us to be at enemity against any race. They teach us to be friends. . . . If you say the yankee is no friend how is it that the ladies from the north have left there homes and came down here? Why are they laboring day and night to elevate the collored people? Why are they shut out of society in the South? The question is plain. Answer it. . . . I'm going to school now to try to learn some things which I hope will enable me to be of some use to my race. These few lines will show that I am a new beginner. The Lord has sent books and teachers. We must not hesitate a moment, but go on and learn all we can."

Especially notable, in David Macrae's eyes, was the love expressed by both children and adults for the white men and women who had come from the North to teach them and try to smooth the transition from slavery to freedom. "Never a day passed at any mission home I visited," Macrae wrote, "but some little presents were brought to school, sometimes from the parents, sometimes from the children themselves—an orange, a flower, or a stick of candy—anything to express their gratitude." The children, when they had learned to write, often wrote letters to their teachers, such as one Macrae quoted: "My dear Teacher, . . . I love you so well, and I always love you, for you are so good. . . . Dear Mrs. B., I try to do right to please you every day, but sometimes I does wrong. But I never means to do wrong, for I love you to the bodum of my heart."

The role of white teachers extended far beyond the classrooms. Often they boarded with black families when whites would not take them in. They participated in community activities, attended the churches, gave tactful instruction in hygiene and the new science of domestic economy. Martha Schofield spent forty years teaching in a black school, Abby Monroe forty-five years, and Laura Towne, who began her labors at Port Royal, persisted for thirty-eight years.

It was inevitable that the exaggerated and unrealistic expectations of the Northern reformers should be defeated by the impenetrable black consciousness. The wariness that characterized the relationship of *all blacks toward all whites* had its roots in the bewildering fluctuations of government policy as well as in what was, from the black point of view, the bewildering "oddness" of white behavior and manners and the uncertainty that characterized all contacts. Would a black man or woman be complimented, featured, praised, addressed as "Mr." or "Mrs.," or would he or she be cursed and abused? Either response was almost equally demoralizing. So gradually the high hopes dimmed. The enthusiasm of the contrabands for schools and books had delighted the bookish New Englanders as their "shouting" Christianity had pleased the evangelically inclined missionaries. But for the ex-slaves books were simply white man's form of magic, guaranteed to transport them into a new and better world. There was frustration and

disappointment when the "magic" proved both slow and laborious
and, finally, largely inefficacious. The suspicion that man, though he
might be created in the image of God, was not essentially a rational
creature grew in the minds of many missionary teachers. Even more
disheartening was the suspicion that the African, perhaps after all,
bore some racial taint, some ineradicable genetic inadequacy. Charles
Ware complained of the "untrustworthiness" of black people and their
disposition to dissemble and to take advantage of their white benefac-
tors. Arthur Sumner, who had been charmed by his "little black-birds,"
began, in Laura Towne's opinion, to take "a planter's view of all
things." The vexations of running a plantation had "fostered a spirit of
disgust toward the negro," he confessed. They were a "very low and
degraded class of beings," he declared, and went happily back to
teaching black children. They were at least more tractable.

For Northern black missionary teachers the problems and difficulties attendant on their labors seemed almost as hard to deal with. In
addition, they were far more vulnerable to attacks by outraged
Southern whites. Francis Cardozo was minister of the Temple Street
Congregational Church in New Haven before he came south to
become principal of a black school in Charleston supported by funds
from the American Missionary Association. In order to make his
school an example of the learning capacities of black children, Cardozo, it was charged, excluded poor black children and admitted only
those from middle-class black families of free men, some of whom
indeed had owned slaves themselves before the war, who came with a
substantial degree of training and sophistication. Although Cardozo
preferred white teachers over black on the ground that they were
usually better prepared, he ran the school with an imperious hand,
dismissing teachers bold enough to criticize his exclusionist policy.
Cardozo, who had attended theological seminary with Macrae at St.
Andrews, Scotland, showed him proudly through his school for black
students with an enrollment of more than eight hundred. "I feel more
interest and more pride in these classes," Cardozo told Macrae, "than I
ever did in New York. The children there had been taught from
infancy, and were being helped at home; but here most of the scholars
depend entirely upon the training they get from us, and we see the
effect of our work upon them. It is a perpetual enjoyment." Cardozo
soon found himself drawn into politics, "being," as he wrote a
Northern friend, "the *only educated* colored man here."

Some black teachers who came south and taught in schools with white teachers found that they were expected to stay with black families rather than in the mission house, where the white teachers lived. This discrimination, one black teacher was told, was necessary to prevent outraging local whites.

Typical of Northern black teachers who ventured south was Edmonia Highgate, who taught school in Binghamton, New York. In January, 1864, she wrote to the American Missionary Association volunteering to teach freedmen: "I know just what self-denial, self-discipline and domestic qualifications are needed for the work and modestly trust that with God's help I could labor advantageously in that field for my newly-freed brethren." After a stint teaching in Virginia, Edmonia was sent to Louisiana, where she taught a "constant-ly growing day school, a night school and a glorious Sabbath School of near one hundred scholars." She had been twice shot at, and several of her adult night school pupils had been wounded by hidden gunmen; among the injured was "an aged freedman" whose arm and leg had been broken. Most distressing to Edmonia was the prevalence of "adultery." Out of three hundred couples only three were legally married.

In the parish adjacent to New Orleans, whites refused to rent buildings to blacks for schools. One black teacher named Le Blanc had been whipped, another stabbed, and another beaten to death. The beaten man, George Rugby, a native New Yorker, was dragged from his house, thrown into a nearby creek, and struck with pistol butts. His attackers declared that they "did not want to have any damned nigger school in that town and were not going to have it."

Virginia Green, a black missionary teacher, opened a school on a plantation at Davis Bend, Mississippi, the former Jefferson and Joseph Davis plantation. "I class myself with the freedmen," she wrote, "though I have never known servitude they are . . . my people . . . I look forward with impatience to the time when my people shall be strong, blest with education, purified and made prosperous by virtue and industry."

Benjamin Franklin Randolph, who started the Lloyd Garrison School for black children in New Orleans, wrote to the *Liberator* asking for "a little assistance from Boston in the shape of apparatus to illustrate astronomy, a gyroscope and microscope, conic sections, cube-root blocks, a magnet and such other instruments as will enable us to fight this battle for our race against ignorance."

The *New National Era* painted a dismal picture of the status of public education for black children in the South. Most Southern states were in the process of establishing "free schools," but these seldom provided for the education of black children. Virginia led the way with a recently enacted free school law, but Georgia was "where she was before the war, utterly against schools," and Texas was equally resistant. It seemed to one black school superintendent in Texas that the only hope was "to get teachers among the educated colored people of the North or Christian white people who are willing to endure privation among the heartless whites of the 'sunny South.' "

With all the missionary labors, it became increasingly evident that the needs of education for white and black children alike could be met in the long run only by the use of public funds. After 1867 most of the reconstructed state governments voted funds to establish public schools, the major issue being whether the schools should be racially segregated. But even when money was allocated by state legislatures to local school boards for public education, the proportion given to black schools was wholly inadequate. The Savannah School Board in 1873 disbursed $64,000 for white schools and less than $3,000 for blacks, despite the fact that black children outnumbered white in the school district.

Those black Congressmen, like Josiah Walls of Florida, who supported a Federally funded school system, argued cogently that the Southern states could never be relied on to appropriate the necessary moneys. "Can we suppose," Walls asked, "that these firm adherents to slavery and States rights are willing to educate the Negro and loyal whites and thereby enable them to wield the controlling power of the South? No, sir, I should think not." In South Carolina, where public education was more advanced than in any other Southern state largely as a result of the efforts of the black-dominated state legislature, only 66,000 out of 206,000 school-age children actually attended school. Much of the opposition to Federally funded education arose from the fear, common to white Congressmen from the North as well as the South, that Federal support for education would mean integrated schools. Only the schools of New Orleans were integrated under the direction of a white Northern superintendent. When the superintendent, Thomas Conway, first declared that all schools must be open to black children as well as white, the white children departed, leaving the "teachers, pale as ghosts, wondering whether their school was ruined and their vocation gone. And the neighbors, black and white, stood half bewildered and half frightened." After a few days the white pupils filtered back, and soon the schools were a balance of black and white children, "with no single indication of ill-feeling," Conway wrote.

Louisiana, Arkansas, Florida, and Mississippi all had black superintendents of public instruction in 1874. In Florida, Jonathan Gibbs, a Presbyterian minister and superintendent of schools, introduced black history and exhorted his charges to take inspiration from it. "The future is to the young man of color who is in earnest *glorious*," he wrote. "Everything is before him, everything to win."

Although hundreds of dedicated white Northerners went South to teach in black schools, impelled by a missionary zeal to prove their pupils as capable of learning as white children, some certainly were time servers, and others, who started with the noblest of intentions, were overwhelmed by the complexities of their task. With little sympathy for or insight into the black temperament they often became impatient when their pupils failed to respond as they felt they should. In addition, they were disconcerted by the hostility of the local whites. However prepared they were in theory to encounter opposition, the depth of white resentment unnerved them (not, of course, to mention the grosser forms of intimidation). Finally, the Northern teachers not infrequently discovered that they were perceived by black ministers as rivals for the loyalty of black families. William Wells Brown, the black abolitionist who traveled through the South in the 1870s to observe the status of black education, was highly critical of the white teachers. "These people," he wrote, "have no heart in the work they are doing and simply go through the mechanical form of teaching our children for the pittance they receive as salary."

Another obstacle to blacks in black education was the appearance of history textbooks in the schools which glorified the "Lost Cause." William Tunstall, superintendent of public instruction in Houston County, Texas, wrote to the *New National Era and Citizen* in June, 1873, pleading for "a uniform set of textbooks from Maine to Texas. I do not ask for books abusive of the South or laudatory of the North," he wrote, "but books patriotic and national in tone." Hearing of a series of primary and secondary history texts to be written by the faculty members of the Washington and Lee University, Tunstall suggested that "Jeff Davis, in the character of Mother Goose, write the nursery tales of the series." Even Northern texts depicted blacks as inferior to whites. Faith Lichen, a contributor to the *New National Era*, wrote eloquently of the feelings of a black schoolboy constantly confronted by images of black inferiority. "Have you ever studied Smith's *Geogra-*

phy," he asked his readers, "with that very worst type of Negro presented in painful contrast to the most perfect Caucasian on the opposite page? Have the words 'superior to all others,' referring to the latter, ever stuck in your throat. . . .?"

Despite the resistance of black culture to the efforts of well-intentioned white teachers and missionaries to transform it speedily into white culture, education continued to be seen as the panacea. If Southern blacks clung to their own "identity" with disconcerting tenacity, the cure *must* be larger and larger doses of education. Charles Sumner was perhaps the most indefatigable champion of this doctrine. He tried, initially, to amend the bill establishing the Freedmen's Bureau to provide for a national system of free public education open to all blacks as well as whites. When this effort was defeated, he proposed a national bureau of education, and finally, he tried to insert such a program into the Fourteenth and Fifteenth Amendments. Unsegregated public schools in the South meant unsegregated public schools in the North. This was clearly going farther than most Northerners were willing to go. In addition, the efforts of Sumner and other Radical Republicans to establish a national system of education ran counter to two of the most deep-rooted and long-lived traditions in America—local control of schools and the ever-present emblem of states' rights.

In the debate over the proposal in the Forty-second Congress to make public education the responsibility of the Federal government and to pay for it through the sale of public lands, Joseph Rainey, the South Carolina Congressman, tackled the issue of "mixed" schools boldly. What harm would result? he asked. "Why this fear of the Negro since he has been a freedman, when in the past he was almost a household god, gamboling and playing with the children of his old master? And occasionally it was plain to be seen that there was a strong family resemblance between them. . . . The Republican party proposes by this measure . . . to educate the masses so that they will be enabled to judge for themselves in all matters appertaining to their interests, and by an intelligent expression of their manhood annihilate the remnant of that oligarchical spirit of exclusiveness which was so prominent in the past."

In George Hoar's opinion, what defeated the proposal for a "liberal National expenditure for education" was ultimately the fear that in the Southern states Federal funds "would not be fairly expended as between the two races, and that it would be made a large corruption fund for political purposes." General O. O. Howard spoke for this point of view when he warned of the dangers of a school system set up by the Federal government. "You do not want to run an immense machine like this from Washington," he told a convention of Western freedmen's associations in 1867. "You do not want your schools in Illinois to be run and controlled by any one at Washington, but you want to run and control your own schools." Yet Albion Tourgée became convinced that only a Federally supported public school system could lift the freed black out of the ruck of slavery.

It was unmistakably clear that the great majority of Southern whites were bitterly opposed to the education of blacks. The Reverend David Macrae commented on the opposition of Southern whites. Most of them professed to believe that the white teachers were "only there to stir up the black people against their old masters. They would not even visit the schools to see what was actually done," Macrae added. One Southerner accompanied Macrae to the door of a black school but refused to enter. "I don't enter nigger schools," he declared. In one school the two young Northern women who taught there were sent notes warning them that they would be killed if they did not leave —whereupon one of them bought a pistol and began very conspicuously practicing with it.

Charles Colcock Jones wrote his mother in December, 1866: "By all means *deny consent* to the establishment of a schoolhouse upon Arcadia land. It would, in the present condition of things, be but an opening to complications, losses, etc., etc."

In Forsyth, Georgia, a freedman wrote to the Freedmen's Bureau that two Northern teachers had been shot by "Rebel Ruffians for no other cause than teaching School." In another black community a schoolhouse which had been built by freedmen was burned, and when an attempt was made to rebuild it, local whites refused to make lumber available. A Vicksburg paper wrote: "If any radical was ever black enough to suppose the people of Mississippi would ever endow negro schools, for their ilk to teach . . . hatred of their former master . . . such chaps had better take to marching with John Brown's soul. . . . The State has not opened them, nor has she the slightest idea of doing anything of the kind."

On the level of higher education the founding of black colleges, again primarily under the aegis of Northern church denominations, went on apace. Howard University, named after General O. O.

Howard, the first commissioner of the Freedmen's Bureau and later founding president of the University, opened its doors to men and women of both races in 1866, and Lizzie Ward, Lester Ward's wife, was one its earliest students.

Howard had a distinguished law faculty and a medical school. Chief of surgery was Dr. Charles Purvis, son of Robert Purvis, the Philadelphia lawyer and abolitionist leader whose children had been tutored by Georgiana Bruce. Purvis wrote to Gerrit Smith that "the professors are not confined to any particular class, *men & women, white & black share the professorial honors.* An institution so democratic deserves the earnest support of all true lovers of human equality." If Howard was not unique, it was certainly exceptional.

Under the Reconstruction government of South Carolina, blacks were admitted in 1873 to the University of South Carolina, a state-supported institution, founded in 1805. When a black medical student was admitted, a number of the faculty and students left the college. T. McCants Stewart, who was among the first blacks admitted, wrote that "the institution is calculated to do much good for South Carolina and the Negro race. If the time ever comes when the descendants of the Rutledges and the Marions shall believe in the unlimited brotherhood of man, the University of South Carolina will have a dwelling-place in the breast of every Afro-American.

"The two races," he wrote, "study together, visit each other's rooms, play ball together, walk to the city together, without the black's feeling honored or the whites disgraced. . . . Every Negro ought to be very much interested in this State," Stewart continued. "There is a bright future before it—bright for the friends of humanity and progress." Under a government that was "democratic in deed and in truth," the efforts of blacks to better themselves must be successful.

The strategy employed by other states to prevent the admission of blacks to white state colleges or universities was, as we have seen, to establish black state colleges. Alcorn University in Mississippi was named, ironically, after the governor of that state, who announced, when he signed the law founding it, "Now let Oxford be for white Southerners and Alcorn for the children of white carpetbaggers and Negroes." Hiram Revels, the first black man to sit in the United States Senate, was appointed president of Alcorn, but after three stormy years he was removed, and the appropriation for the school cut by two thirds.

Two black cadets were admitted to West Point in 1870 under pressure from Radical Republican Congressmen. One of them, James Smith of South Carolina, reported that his drill sergeant said to him, "Stand off from the line, you d[amne]d black [dog]. I want you to remember you are not on an equal footing with the white men and what you learn you will have to pick up, for I won't teach you a d——d thing." His father, a former slave, exhorted him to persevere. "You must not resign on any account," he wrote, "for that is what the Democrats want. They are betting here that they will devil you so much that you can't stay. Stand your ground. . . ." Smith stood it for four years and then, on the eve of his graduation, was dismissed for a "deficiency in Philosophy." He had a few successors. Henry Flipper graduated in 1877, other black officers in 1887 and 1889, and then, fifty years later, Benjamin Davis.

Hampton Institute at Hampton, Virginia, was headed by another Yankee abolitionist, former General Samuel Chapman Armstrong. The ground at Hampton had been well prepared by a remarkable agent of the American Missionary Association, Lewis Lockwood, who had supported the school already established there by Mary Peake, daughter of a mulatto woman and a French trader. When Lockwood arrived in Hampton, Mary Peake had forty-nine pupils enrolled. Lockwood's sensitive and intelligent response to the black culture of the Hampton Roads area created an atmosphere congenial to self-help and educational aspiration.

At twenty-six, Samuel Armstrong was an ideal person to build on that foundation. The son of Hawaiian missionaries, he had graduated from Williams College in the era of Mark Hopkins, joined the army, and commanded a black regiment. It was, he declared, a "grand thing to be identified with this Negro movement. . . . What nobler work has been given to man since the reformation?" Armstrong, as head of Hampton's Freedmen's Bureau, became increasingly disillusioned about the limitations of that agency in equipping free blacks to take care of themselves in an American society. Like so many other white Northerners, he came to the conclusion that only education would materially assist in the process. His solution was an institute for young black men and women that would prepare them for making a living. What the freed black needed, above all, were "habits of labor," in Armstrong's view. "Improvidence and laziness must be overcome by some propelling force; hence the manual labor feature of this school."

The institute would not attempt to make its pupils "accomplished scholars but to build up character and manhood."

When the school opened in 1868, it had fifteen students, and Armstrong soon found himself embroiled in a debate with those missionaries who believed that his intensely practical curriculum with its emphasis on manual work and practical skills was discriminatory. When Armstrong's efforts to support the school by the labor of the students were unsuccessful, he required that they work during the day and attend a "night school." The students thus worked two full days a week and attended classes the remaining time. Printing, blacksmithing, and farming were among the skills taught. Armstrong's philosophy, which he dinned into his students, was a simple one: "Spend your life doing what you can do well. If you can teach, teach. If you can't teach, but can work well, do that. If a man can black boots better than anything else, what had he better do? Black boots." Armstrong did not say what the trained teacher who was allowed only to black boots should do.

At Hampton Institute students, male and female, followed the same course of study. The first year covered reading, "analysis of sounds and vocal gymnastics, writing, spelling, first lessons in grammar, physical geography, with map-drawing . . . vocal music . . . gymnastics. The second year emphasized letter-writing and composition; drafts of business letters . . . agriculture and agricultural chemistry and the third year book-keeping, natural science," and actual teaching in model schools. At Hampton the girls called their fellow student, Booker T. Washington, High Waters because his trousers were so short.

Fisk College became famous for its Jubilee Singers, a chorus of male and female students who gave concerts all over the world and through their efforts raised enough money to build a handsome hall and contribute to the college's endowment. In England they sang for Queen Victoria, and in Germany for the Kaiser. One of the members of the group was America Robinson. When she departed on her world tour, she left behind her fiancé, James Burris. She wrote him love letters from the capitals of Europe, telling of life infinitely remote from the severe discipline of Fisk. He sent his photograph, and she replied, "The photo is *very very* good. The glasses give you a stern & scholarly appearance. You look already like a professor. . . . I cannot possibly look at it without kissing it." While the romance faded as

America lingered in Europe to pursue further studies, Burris's determination to become a professor survived. He taught mathematics at Fisk and Alcorn and then entered business and prospered, leaving his estate of $120,000 to Fisk at his death.

Thirty black colleges were founded in the years immediately following the end of the Civil War, most of them by the American Missionary Association and various Protestant denominations. Howard University was started by the Freedmen's Bureau, while Alcorn and Alabama A&M were state institutions. Howard, founded in 1867 and supported by Federal funds, was the most prominent of the black colleges. The presidents of black colleges were invariably white, the most notable exception being John Mercer Langston, who, after serving as head of the Howard Law School, became acting president in 1874.

The black colleges and universities were, for the most part, totally unsuitable for the students whose needs they were designed to serve. The founders, dedicated and unselfish men and women, did the best they knew how, but they brought with them the ideal of the small denominational liberal arts institution which was already an anachronism in the North. Charles Francis Adams, Jr., had described Harvard in the 1850s as dominated by empty forms and thoroughly indifferent to the needs of students. It is hardly surprising that the black colleges, modeled to a large degree after it and its New England and Western counterparts, should have been, in many instances, unhappy caricatures of the originals. Like the schoolteachers and missionaries who flocked into the South to redeem the victims of slavery from dirt and ignorance, the white professors who made up the faculties of black colleges wished to turn their students into replicas of the students of Amherst or Williams or Yale or, in the West, Grinnell or Antioch. In many black colleges Latin was required, and Greek encouraged. The *Essays* of Charles Lamb and Lord Chesterfield's *Letters* were not uncommonly embedded in the curriculum. Simon Smith, for example, wrote proudly to the friend who had sponsored him: "I have recently taken up Horace, Xenophon's Memorabilia of Socrates, Grecian and Roman Antiquity. . . . I also have Latin and Greek prose compositions. Every Monday I have a lesson in the Greek Testament. . . ." The professors and administrators, who, often at considerable sacrifice, entered a world infinitely exotic and basically incomprehensible, were certainly not to blame. They did the best they knew how, and through personal concern and affection for their students they undoubtedly did a vast amount of simple human good. But the view of the world and of learning which they brought with them was one which had little relevance for their students. If anything, it often served to alienate those black men and women who were exposed to it from the generality of their people and not infrequently sowed doubts in them about black equality. We now understand education to be not simply a process of passing on information or imparting "culture," but a more subtle and complex system for transmitting the "buried" values of a society. The system of learning created by white Protestant Americans was a confirmation of their social, economic, and theological convictions (it still is, of course), but that was not so apparent in the post-Civil War era and certainly not to the faculties and students of black institutions of higher learning in the states recently forced back into reluctant union with their Northern sisters. The nature of those institutions, so noble in their aspirations and so disappointing in their accomplishments, was symbolized by the library of Tougaloo University in Jackson, Mississippi, in 1970. The library had no copies of Harriet Beecher Stowe's *Uncle Tom's Cabin* or the writings of any of the famous Northern abolitionists, not to mention the works of nineteenth-century black writers and historians, but there were hundreds of scholarly monographs in various fields that reflected the research interests of the still largely white faculty, trained, almost with exception, in Northern graduate schools.

In the North such discontinuity between the needs and concerns of the students and the scholarly preoccupations of the teachers was obscured by a heavy overlay of nonacademic activities and relationships. The students in such institutions as Dartmouth and Princeton, however tedious and irrelevant their studies might be, would, after all, graduate into a world that validated and rewarded the simple fact of their attendance, a world in which their power and their superiority were unquestioned. The graduate of Fisk or Hampton or Tuskegee, on the other hand, entered a world in which the doors to social and professional advancement were tightly closed. If he entered at all, it was usually as the consequence of white "kindness" or white beneficence. What should have come to him as a right was from time to time conferred as a gift, as a concession. By the same token, if an "outstanding" black student, one of unusual intelligence and ambition, almost invariably from a respectable middle-class black family, was admitted to some white academic sanctum, it was with an effably self-congratulatory air of enlightened liberal policy, and it was assumed that the student or students so admitted would be filled with gratitude.

Even graduates from Oberlin, the oldest and most prestigious college to graduate black students, had difficulty finding suitable jobs. "During the past few years," one black student wrote, "some score or more of colored students have graduated from this college, yet none could obtain a class to teach." The black students were often segregated, and a student complained that he was told by the manager of the college dining hall, "You colored people will have to understand that if you board in this hall you must sit where I tell you and nowhere else. You will not be mixed in with the white boarders. You ought to consider it a great privilege to be admitted into the hall even."

We would not be misunderstood in regard to black colleges. They were the products of a wholly exemplary desire to do good. And good they did. They required substantial sums of money and the investment of many intelligent and useful lives. Black (and white) Americans are much the better for their existence. But the cruel irony is that inherent in the assumptions on which they were founded were serious distortions of reality that, on one level at least, added to the psychic burdens of being black in America.

Black leaders and white educators were, of course, sharply divided on the question of what black students should learn. The more liberal or radical abolitionists insisted that there should be no discrimination in education between blacks and whites. If both races were "equal," they should receive the same education, the best available. Their opponents advanced two arguments. One argument held quite properly, as we have noted, that the standard liberal arts education, stressing the classics and designed to turn out "gentlemen," was ill-suited to black needs; the other took the line that black people could not be expected to make up in a day the gap between the higher level of white culture and "slave" culture, or, more generally, what was referred to increasingly as Afro-American culture. The gap could only be closed, so the argument ran, one step at a time. The capacities of blacks would, for a generation or two, be best utilized in industrial tasks and the skilled trades, especially the building trades. Their education should, therefore, be directed toward such practical subjects as mechanics, carpentering, and engineering. Considering the alternative, it was hard to refute the argument for the practical. What made it even harder was the fact that highly educated blacks could not find jobs appropriate to their abilities. The result was a self-fulfilling prophecy. If you laid down as a first principle that blacks were not, by virtue of genetic flaw or because, as it came increasingly to be argued, they were still in some earlier stage of evolutionary development, if you stated this as a fundamental proposition, it followed that you could, with a relatively clear conscience, restrict black men and women to the most menial tasks in the society, assuring yourself meanwhile that such tasks were simply a preliminary stage in black development. In a generation or two blacks, if they were ambitious and industrious, if they dutifully observed and absorbed white manners and modes of behavior, might aspire to the higher levels of business and professional activity. Meanwhile, black college graduates, many of them more intelligent and better trained than their employers, worked as maids, cooks, chauffeurs, and butlers. For it turned out that the abundance of cheap black labor coincided most conveniently with the desire of a burgeoning white middle class for domestic servants, a need which, in the North, was met in part by floods of immigrant Irishwomen.

It was now the familiar "double bind." If ambitious young black men or women went to a liberal arts college like Tougaloo and learned Latin and German, they were suspected of wishing to rise above their proper station—the old charge of being "uppity." More serious, they could seldom find a career appropriate to their education, and finally, they were sometimes fatally infected with white prejudices toward the generality of their own people. If they accepted what we might call the cultural-apprentice notion and took the more humble "practical" route of the industrial school, they foreclosed any possibility of a more challenging career (and not incidentally a higher-paid one) regardless of what their innate capacities might be. Most disheartening of all, they found that the more desirable industrial jobs and the skilled trades were increasingly closed to them by the action of white unions determined to protect themselves from black competition or by the prejudices of white employers. Whether young blacks opted for a hopelessly irrelevant "classical" education at Tougaloo or Fisk or for an eminently practical education at Hampton, they found themselves confined to the jobs of janitors, maids, waiters, and cooks, jobs that white Americans for the most part scorned to perform. It seemed there was no escape for black people from the cage that white people constructed for them. Certainly those whites most determined to help them become good middle-class Americans—quickly or in the appointed time—impeded them less than those whites, North and South, who hated them and did their best to degrade and humiliate them.

Blacks like Samuel McElwee overcame every obstacle to get an education. Born a slave, McElwee learned to read by looking over his sister's shoulder while daughters of the household taught her to read. After working all day in the fields, he would study until twelve or one o'clock in the morning. After a brief interlude of teaching in a Mississippi school he went to Oberlin, where he supported himself waiting on tables and washing windows. Unable to carry on both his work and his studies, McElwee peddled *Lyman's Historical Chart and Family Bible,* sold medicine, and began the study of Latin, German, and algebra with a private tutor, walking ten miles two nights a week. Finally, in the fall of 1878, he was able to enter the newly established Fisk University.

But such cases, pointed to with pride, were rare enough. Perhaps the best that could be said for the education of Southern blacks was that it was the single area in which white intention made at least a modest approach to black needs.

43

Impeachment

While Southern blacks took advantage of the Reconstruction Acts to assert themselves politically with remarkable tenacity and surprising skill, President Johnson contended relentlessly with a Congress dominated by Radical Republicans. Johnson continued to insist that Congress, by refusing to seat the Southern Senators and Congressmen elected under the proclamations issued by him in the summer of 1865, was acting unconstitutionally and that all its legislation was, correspondingly, unconstitutional. In this doctrine he had the unqualified support of Gideon Welles. In Welles's view, Johnson's only error lay in failing to "exercise his undoubted authority in vindication of what he knows to be right, but defers, delays, and suffers. . . . From the tame, passive course which has been pursued, the administration has lost confidence and strength. It has to-day no positive, established, successful policy; displays no executive power and energy; submits to insults. . . ." Welles's advice to the President would have been "not to have executed the unconstitutional Reconstruction law,—to have assigned no military commanders to govern States in time of peace." The President, Welles believed, should have offered himself as a sacrifice for the sacred principles of the Constitution. Welles wished that "I could have been in his place. . . . It would have been a glorious privilege to have seized the horns of the altar, planted one's self on the Constitution, rallied the patriotism of the nation, immolated himself, if necessary, in defending the Government of his country and the integrity of the Union." Johnson chose a less dangerous course but one almost equally exacerbating to Republican nerves. Repeating the refrain of unconstitutionality, he accompanied it by constant acrimonious attacks on his opponents. Georges Clemenceau detected in the President a disposition to create crises. He was, in Clemenceau's words, "as greedy for stirring emotions as his compatriot Andrew Jackson, of dauntless memory." At each session of Congress, Clemenceau noted, the Radical Republicans "add a shackle to [the President's] bonds, tighten the bit in a different place, file a claw or draw a tooth, and then when he is well bound up, fastened, and caught in an inextricable net of laws and decrees, more or less contradicting each other, they tie him to the stake of the Constitution and take a good look at him, feeling quite sure he cannot move this time. . . . This has been going on now for two years, and though in the course of things it is inevitable that Samson will be beaten, one must admit that he has put up a game fight."

Johnson's hand was strengthened by the decision of the Supreme Court in the case of *ex parte Milligan*, in which the Court ruled that Lincoln had acted unconstitutionally in giving jurisdiction to military courts in places where civil courts were functioning. Justice David Davis, a friend of Lincoln's, declared for the Court: "The Constitution of the United States is a law for rulers and people, equally in war and peace, and covers with the shield of its protection all classes of men, at all times, and in all circumstances." It could not be suspended "during any of the great exigencies of government. . . . Martial rule can never exist when the Courts are open, and in the proper and unobstructed exercise of their jurisdiction." In its reaffirmation of the rule of law *ex parte Milligan* was one of the court's most important decisions, but it had the practical effect of making it vastly more difficult for a black man to get justice in the South. This became immediately evident when Johnson dropped all trials of civilians by military courts, which resulted in the freeing of a number of whites in jail for murdering blacks.

Thaddeus Stevens, in response, demanded that Congress "do something to protect these people from the barbarians who are now daily murdering them; who are murdering the loyal whites daily and daily putting into secret graves not only hundreds but thousands of colored people of that country."

In Johnson's third annual message he once more chided Congress for "the continued disorganization of the Union." The principal task following the end of the war had been the restoration of the rebellious states to the Union. The "executive department" and the "insurrectionary states themselves" had demonstrated their disposition to "repair the injuries which the war had inflicted. . . . Candor compels me to declare that at this time there is no Union as our fathers understood the term, and as they meant it to be understood by us. The Union which they established can exist only where all the States are represented in both Houses of Congress; where one State is as free as another to regulate its internal concerns according to its own will. . . . The Union and the Constitution are inseparable . . . and if one is destroyed, both must perish together. . . . To me the process of restoration seems perfectly plain and simple. It consists merely in a faithful application of the Constitution." Much of the address was given over to a detailed lecture on constitutional theory. Congress must promptly repeal the Reconstruction Acts, Johnson declared. Not only were they unconstitutional, but "Business in the South is paralyzed by a sense of general insecurity, by the terror of confiscation, and the dread of negro supremacy."

Congress, needless to say, was unmoved by the President's exhortations. The group of Radical Republicans seemed to George Templeton Strong to be "prepared to ride over President and Supreme Court both, unless they get out of its way. This looks," Strong added, "like a courageous adherence to principle very rare among the politicians." The movement to impeach Johnson, which had surfaced a year earlier, gained strength. Elizabeth Meriwether, who had gotten an audience with President Johnson in order to plead for the return of her confiscated property, encountered Ben Butler and Thaddeus Stevens also waiting in the anteroom of Johnson's office. The two men were busy in heedless consultation, and the Memphis woman heard Butler say, "Impeachment is the thing, I tell you, there is no other remedy." To which Stevens replied, "Whatever plan is adopted there must be no let up until we down the traitor." Besides Thaddeus Stevens, the principal advocate of impeachment was an Ohio Congressman named James Ashley who, as Ben: Perley Poore put it, "had begun life . . . as a clerk on the Ohio . . . driving sharp bargains with the plantation darkies . . . in exchange of cheap jewelry and gay calicoes for cotton and eggs." From this he had advanced to becoming a printer, a lawyer, and finally the editor of a Toledo newspaper. Failing at that, he opened a drugstore and ran for Congress. "He was a short, fat man, with a clean shaven face, and a large shock of bushy light hair, which he kept hanging over his forehead like a frowsy bang, threatening to obstruct his vision . . . a man of the lightest mental caliber." It was Ashley who, perhaps fortunately for Johnson, undertook to initiate and manage the first impeachment of a president in the history of the Republic. The critical question was: On what grounds should the President be impeached?

Rumors had been circulating for months that Johnson, believing Stanton to be in cahoots with the Radical Republicans, intended to replace him by a more loyal adherent. Certainly, Stanton was the only Cabinet member left opposed to the President's policies. But in March, 1867, Congress had passed the tenure of office bill making it illegal for the president to fire an officer of his administration, without the consent of the Senate, if that officer's initial appointment had required senatorial approval.

It was a measure of dubious constitutionality (subsequently to be judged unconstitutional by the Supreme Court) and was looked on, at least by some members of Congress, as a direct challenge to the President. Johnson took it as such, but he let month after month pass without taking any action against Stanton. On August 10, two weeks after Congress had adjourned, Johnson finally requested Stanton's resignation. Welles, who had long hoped for such an action, expressed dismay in his diary. After months and months of delay the President had acted without consulting his Cabinet. "Impulse, rather than reason or common sense" had governed. "The President is vigorous and active, but too late, and has attempted too much at once," Welles wrote. ". . . This whole movement of changing his Secretary of War has been incautiously and loosely performed without preparation. . . . I have sometimes been almost tempted to listen to the accusation of his enemies that he desired and courted impeachment."

Stanton refused to resign (Sumner sent him a one-word message —"Stick"), and Johnson suspended his recalcitrant secretary and appointed Grant to the post *pro tempore*. Johnson then added fuel to the fire by replacing Sheridan as commander of the Fifth Military District with General Winfield Scott Hancock, known to be more sympathetic to the views of white Southerners, and Daniel Sickles by General E.R.S. Canby in the Second Military District. The generals displaced by Johnson were enthusiastically received by large crowds wherever they appeared. At St. Louis an estimated thirty thousand people turned out in a procession more than two miles long to honor General Sheridan and express their displeasure with Johnson.

When Congress convened in December, a resolution to initiate impeachment proceedings against the President was voted down in the House, but the Senate, after the Christmas recess, refused to approve of the suspension of Stanton. When the Senate refused to approve Stanton's dismissal, Grant abandoned the office of secretary of war, to Johnson's rage. Stevens's comment on hearing the news was: "He [Grant] is a bolder man than I thought. Now we will let him into the Church." After a three-week interval Johnson removed (or tried to remove) Stanton and replaced him by General Thomas. The Thomas chosen to replace the recalcitrant Stanton was "not the fighting Thomas of Nashville," George Templeton Strong noted, "but the doubting Thomas [Lorenzo], of whose loyalty people talked unpleasantly during the early period of the War." Stanton, with the warm support of Schuyler Colfax, Speaker of the House, who assured him that he was guarding the Thermopylae of Reconstruction, refused to budge. He disliked Thomas (he had once vowed to pick him up with "a pair of tongs and drop him from the nearest window"), and when the general, the President's order in his hand, tried to oust Stanton from his office, the secretary of war called out troops. That night Thomas was heard to declare that if Stanton did not leave his office, he would evict him by force. When this word reached Stanton, he sent a marshal to Thomas's home to arrest him. After he had been released on bail, Thomas went to the War Department and once more ordered Stanton to leave. Stanton in turn ordered Thomas out. Suddenly the absurdity of the scene struck both men, and Thomas said, "The next time you have me arrested please don't do it before I get something to eat." Whereupon Stanton put his arm around the general's neck and the two claimants had a drink of whiskey. Rumors now circulated through the city that the President intended to call out the marines to oust Stanton, and Senator Zachariah Chandler in response rounded up a hundred armed men and came to reinforce the troops around the War Department.

Now Stevens renewed the call for impeachment, and on February 22 the House voted 126 to 47 to impeach. Stevens, too weak to walk, was brought to the Senate in an armchair. He hobbled into the chamber with a delegation of Congressmen, and there, "pale, emaciated, deathlike in appearance, but in a stern, vigorous voice and bold, lofty manner," he announced, "We do impeach Andrew Johnson, President of the United States, of high crimes and misdemeanors in office. . . ." When Butler assisted Stevens to his chair, an unsympathetic observer was heard to say he was reminded of the devil assisting an old man in hell.

To a correspondent of *Blackwood's Magazine,* Stevens poured out his bitterness against Johnson and the Democrats. There was, he told his interviewer, "a moral necessity" for impeachment, "for which I care something; and there is a party necessity for it, for which I care more. In fact the party necessity is the moral necessity; for I consider that when the Republican party dies, this country will be given over to the so-called Democracy, which is worse than the devil."

The Senate, which would hear the trial, was described by Welles as "debauched, debased, demoralized, without independence, a sense of right, or moral courage. . . . The Constitution-breakers are trying the Constitution-defender," he wrote; "the law-breakers are passing condemnation on the law-supporter; the conspirators are sitting in judgment on the man who would not enter into his conspiracy, who was, and is, faithful to his oath, his country, the Union, and the Constitution. What a spectacle!"

Salmon Chase, presiding as chief justice of the Supreme Court, rose above partisan feelings and his remorseless political ambitions, to conduct the impeachment trial with fairness and dignity. The story was circulated that Chase favored Johnson because Johnson's conviction would put, as president pro tem of the Senate, Ben Wade in the President's chair and doubtless make him the Republican nominee in the forthcoming presidential race, thereby excluding Chase once again. It was also said that Kate Chase, the justice's daughter, had told her husband, Senator William Sprague of Rhode Island, that she would divorce him if he voted for Johnson's conviction.

As the trial went on, a shift in public opinion took place. Individuals like George Templeton Strong who felt a particular solicitude for constitutional government began to have serious misgivings. The *Nation* noted that Congress had turned Johnson into a "stupendous . . . villain. He started before them as simply a very indecent brawler . . . grew into a fornicator and adulterer, and then a seller of pardons, then a conspirator against the nation. . . . But all this was done by hint of hallooing and insinuating. No proofs were forthcoming."

Johnson's defense rested on two principal arguments. First, Stanton had been appointed by Lincoln, not by Johnson, and therefore the terms of the Tenure of Office Act did not apply to Johnson. Secondly, in firing Stanton, Johnson assumed that he would appeal to the Supreme Court and thus test the constitutionality of the Tenure of Office Act itself.

William Fessenden, James Wilson Grimes, and Lyman Trumbull led the opposition to conviction. Grimes had been the progressive Whig governor of Iowa who had established the free school system in that state and perhaps initiated more forward-looking legislation than any state executive of his era. When it was known that he intended to vote against conviction, he was subjected to enormous pressure, besieged with letters and telegrams, and warned that his political career would be at an end if he voted for acquittal. The massive attack may well have helped to bring on a mild stroke two days before the final vote. All the Senators and most of the Representatives were in the Senate chamber on May 16, 1867, when the vote on the eleventh article of impeachment, thought to be the strongest, was to be registered. Stevens was carried in in his armchair, Senator Jacob Howard of Michigan was brought in on a stretcher, and Grimes made his way to his seat with difficulty, assisted by friends. The first Republican to vote no was Fessenden. A few months earlier, Joseph Smith Fowler of Tennessee had declared that the Republican Party was itself guilty of treason in not impeaching Johnson. Now, denouncing the impeachment proceedings as "mere politics," he joined those opposed. The tally, for the most part, followed the expected course until it appeared that the crucial vote might be that of Senator Edmund Gibson Ross. Ross had been editor of the Lawrence (Kansas) *Tribune*. An outspoken supporter of Congressional Reconstruction and critic of Johnson, he had been elected to the Senate two years earlier. When a colleague had asked Senator Ross the day before the vote for whom he would be voting, Ross was reported to have replied, "Do not worry, I shall be voting on the right side tomorrow." During the voting he sat nervously tearing up sheets of paper. As the clerk called his name, he rose and said, "Not guilty." The vote was 35 Senators for conviction, 19 against, one vote shy of the necessary two-thirds for conviction. Seven Republican Senators had voted against conviction. Technically there were ten other articles of impeachment to vote upon, but the Senate adjourned for ten days.

While the opponents of impeachment were denounced for treachery and accused of having accepted bribes, the *Nation* praised them "not for voting for Johnson's acquittal, but for vindicating, we presume nobody but themselves knows at what cost, the dignity and purity of the court of which they formed a part, and the sacred rights of individual conscience." James Gordon Bennett wrote in the *New York Herald:* "Impeachment is broken down completely.

"So, with Lincoln murdered, with Chase pushed from his moral leadership of the party he made, with all the original heads of the great national movement out of the way, Butler, Sumner and Stevens had their vile hour and gloried in their political reign of terror. But the ninth Thermidor came soon, and their heads are in the sawdust."

Minor Meriwether was in Washington during the final stages of the impeachment trial and present in the Senate when the vote was taken. He noted that Stanton, "who had been watching the call with breathless interest, turned ghastly pale; as he rose to leave the chamber he staggered so that Gen. Logan took his arm and helped him away. . . . Poor old lame Thaddeus Stevens rose up and shambled out, neither asking [for] or receiving support; he limped out on his crutch, his face plainly showing the venomous but now futile hatred of Johnson and of the South which scarred his soul."

It was the opinion of John Roy Lynch, the black Congressman from Mississippi, that crucial votes were cast against the impeachment of Johnson by certain Republican Senators who could not stomach the notion of Benjamin Wade's being president of the United States. Wade, in Lynch's words, was "the sort of active and aggressive man . . . likely to make himself enemies of men in his own organization who were afraid of his great power and influence. . . ." Blaine had declared more than a year earlier, "There will be no impeachment by this Congress; we would rather have the President than the shallywags of Ben Wade."

It was an unhappy ending for Stevens's long and notable, if controversial, career. The *New York Herald,* always his enemy, described him as having "the boldness of a Danton, the bitterness and hatred of Marat, and the unscrupulousness of Robespierre" and warned that the Radical Republicans planned a coup d'état to replace Johnson with a triumvirate of Wade, Stevens, and Grant, with Grant assigned the role of Cromwell and Napoleon.

George Templeton Strong found some solace in the fact that Johnson's acquittal by the Senate denied him the martyrdom that he so avidly sought and was worth "many thousand votes to the Republican Party. . . . But it was an error," he added, indicating that he had once again changed his mind on the issue.

In July, 1868, Stevens gave his last speech in the House, where he had for so long held the attention of his colleagues by his passionate eloquence and his cutting tongue. Providence, he declared, had placed Americans in "a political Eden." He added: "All we have to do is avoid the forbidden fruit, for we have not yet reached the perfection of justice." He was fast approaching the grave. "But you sir," he said, turning to the Speaker of the House, Schuyler Colfax, "are promised length of days and a brilliant career." If Colfax and his colleagues could "fling away ambition and realize that every human being, however lowly-born or degraded, by fortune is your equal and that every inalienable right which belongs to you belongs also to him, truth and righteousness will spread over the land. . . ."

When Robert Dale Owen, converted to spiritualism, came to visit Stevens in his dying days and reported on his conversations with Daniel Webster, Henry Clay, and Stephen Douglas from the great beyond, Stevens replied, "Well, present my compliments to the defuncts and tell them for me that if they have nothing better to offer on the subject, I think that since they died they have not been in a very progressive state. Especially present my compliments to Douglas, and tell him I think he was the greatest political humbug on earth."

When Stevens was asked what sort of marker he wished for his grave, he replied, "I suppose, like the rest of the fools, we shall have to get something stuck up in the air; let it be plain." But he composed the inscription, and it read:

> I repose in this quiet and secluded spot,
> Not from any natural preference for solitude
> But, finding other cemeteries limited as to Race
>   by Charter Rules,
> I have chosen this that I might illustrate
>   in my death
> The Principles which I advocated
>   Through a long life:
> EQUALITY OF MAN BEFORE HIS CREATOR

"My life has been a failure," Stevens told Alexander McClure a few days before his death. "With all this struggle of years in Washington, and the fearful sacrifice of life and treasure, I see little hope for the Republic." To another reporter, he declared, "I have no history. My life-long regret is that I have lived so long and so uselessly."

When word came in the House on August 11 that the man who had dominated its deliberations for so long was dead, James Blaine was said to have whispered to a friend: "The death of Stevens is an emancipation for the Republican Party."

Ignatius Donnelly, the outspoken Congressman from Minnesota, perhaps pronounced his best obituary: "He never flattered the people. . . . On the contrary, on all occasions he attacked their sins, he assailed their prejudices, he outraged all their bigotries; and when they turned upon him he marched straight forward, like Gulliver wading through the fleets of the Lilliputians, dragging his enemies after him." Samuel Bowles, in the *Springfield* (Massachusetts) *Republican* of August 12, 1868, wrote: "When the hour came, the man was ready,—not with broad views, wise doctrines, good taste, faultless manners, or exemplary morals,—but resolute, shrewd, unsparing; willing to use friend or foe, careless of both, possessed with his cause and that alone, and equal to every occasion . . . he was a revolutionist in a period of reaction. . . . The new era of American nationality felt his powerful clutch and impetus, and the effect of his work will remain on our Constitution and polity, longer than that of Webster, or Clay, or of Calhoun."

Georges Clemenceau, who had watched enthralled while Stevens led the forces for impeachment, wrote: "For nearly eight months the country has been expecting the end of the desperate struggle which this extraordinary man has waged against age, grief, and a disease he knew was incurable. The nation has lost in him a great citizen. . . . Devoted heart and soul to the service of one ideal, the immediate abolition of slavery," he had pursued it with a single-mindedness nothing less than heroic. "It must be admitted," Clemenceau added, "that Mr. Stevens stands out as a man of only one idea, but that does not matter a whit, since he had the glory of defending that idea when it was trodden in the dust, and the joy of contributing largely to its triumph." To Clemenceau it seemed that a man could have no higher accomplishment than to have committed "his life and his soul" to the cause of racial justice.

The impeachment of Johnson marked a kind of watershed in post-Civil War politics. Men like Gideon Welles, for whom the preservation of the Constitution inviolate was the highest good and the most solemn obligation of every elected or appointed official, were immeasurably distressed by the reckless determination of the Radical Republicans to bring down the President. Congress had the votes to do virtually as it wished. Difference of opinion, however deep, animosities however corrosive, were not grounds for tampering with the document that contained the precious essence of America. Stubborn and intransigent as the President was, no fairminded man could charge him with treason. To which, of course, the Radicals replied, "Giving aid and comfort to the traitors of the South was treason enough." The Founding Fathers believed, as we know, that all power corrupts. The Radical Republicans, honest and dedicated as many of them were, had, it might be argued, more power than was good for them, and so, being human, they were tempted to misuse it. In that misuse they fatally weakened their own cause in the eyes of all Americans who believed that the war had been fought to preserve the Union, which to them was synonymous with the Constitution—Union-Constitution, they were, in essence, the same. Vengefulness, rather than the public good, appeared to be the motive behind impeachment. Had not the President been held in check or checkmate by the skilled chessplayers leading the congressional Republicans? What clear and essential political purpose was served by his humiliation?

Yet, when all is said and done, it is difficult to condemn the Radical Republican leaders. Mixed and unworthy as their motives, in some instances, may have been, they certainly had great provocation. The other vetoing President, Andrew Jackson, had vetoed eleven bills in eight years; Johnson had vetoed twenty in three years.

For many years now the efforts of the Radical Republican leaders to remove Johnson from office in the waning months of his administration have been used by unfriendly historians to indict them as vindictive and fanatical men. But when we consider how long and late they labored in behalf of the truest ideals of our national life when so many others were fainthearted or indifferent, we can, I think, be generous with their most conspicuous fault. The same fierce determination that sustained them in their fight for justice to the freedmen swept them into the impeachment fight.

Perhaps in the last analysis what the impeachment controversy most clearly demonstrated was a weakness in the American political system itself, which made it virtually impossible to remove a discredited president from office without convicting him of "high crimes and misdemeanors." In a parliamentary system Johnson would have fallen on a vote of no confidence by the end of his first year of office and been succeeded by a president who better expressed the wishes of his party.

It seems apparent that at some point Johnson decided that his only hope for succeeding himself lay with the Democrats. His belated firing of Stanton in the face of the secretary's reinstatement by Congress without consulting his Cabinet may well have been intended to rally the Democrats to his side by demonstrating that he could not be intimidated by the Radical Republicans. In addition, we have earlier noted strong indications of a martyr complex on the part of the President. The action in regard to Stanton was, in a sense, a challenge to Congress to crucify him if it dared. Where he misjudged the situation most seriously, it turned out, was in his hope that the Democrats would come to his support. Made overconfident by their success in October and November, the Democrats made a great show of being above the battle. They had their own political fish to fry. "There is little doubt," Georges Clemenceau wrote of the Stanton firing, "that Mr. Johnson reckoned wrong. The Democrats were leaving him on all sides. He made up his mind to stake everything on one play, and he lost, as far as one can judge."

When Charles Francis Adams, Jr. was asked, as a war hero, to give the Fourth of July, 1869, oration at Quincy, Massachusetts, the home of the Adams clan, he chose the theme of a "Double Anniversary" —that of '76, when America declared its independence of Great Britain, and that of '63, when the Emancipation Proclamation declared slavery at an end. He also acclaimed the defeat of Johnson's impeachment. To him it was a triumph of the law and the Constitution over the volatile passions of the moment. He made it clear that he had no sympathy with Johnson, "the object of an unprecedented popular odium, a chief magistrate who had shocked every sense of decency and humiliated every citizen—who was hated by the party in uncontrolled power and respected by no one. . . ." What was most striking was that, missing conviction by only one vote, he "was retained in office without a breath of resistance. . . . We may surely claim that this great episode will not discredit us in history."

44

The Election of 1868

Early in 1868, the presidential year, there was a widespread feeling that the Radical Republicans had pushed too far and too fast on the issue of black suffrage for the great majority of white Americans, but rather to George Templeton Strong's surprise, Congress seemed "unterrified by the alleged popular reaction against 'Radicalism.' I think there *is* such a reaction," Strong added, "and that it will prove formidable." Orestes Brownson, in his conservative phase, grumbled that the "eternal Sambo" preempted all other issues, and Walt Whitman had noted as early as February, 1868, in a letter to Moncure Conway: "The Republicans have exploited the negro too intensely, and there comes a reaction." The New York branch of the women's rights movement, angry over the fact that men like Wendell Phillips gave a higher priority to insuring the vote for black males than for white women, split with their New England cousins and pursued a more radical course, stressing the social and economic inequities in American life and muting their support for black suffrage.

John Van Buren, son of Martin, in the last public speech before his death declared that blacks were fit only to shine shoes and cut hair. The Democratic-controlled Pennsylvania legislature passed a resolution declaring: "The white race alone is entitled to the control of the

Government of the Republic, and we are unwilling to grant the negroes the right to vote." And in April, Michigan went, "unexpectedly, against negro suffrage by an overwhelming majority."

As Grant appeared to be a more and more likely rival of Johnson's for the Republican presidential nomination, Gideon Welles's diary took on an increasingly acerbic note in regard to the general. He suspected him of planning to establish a military dictatorship and noted: "It has been said he made a macadamized road from Washington to Richmond, which he paved with the skulls of Union soldiers. . . . I do not think he intends to disregard the Constitution," Welles added, "but he has no reverence for it,—he has no political principles, no intelligent ideas of constitutional government, and it is a day when the organic law seems to be treated as of less binding authority than a mere resolution of Congress."

As for Grant, he kept his own counsel. "We know next to nothing of his political notions, to be sure," George Templeton Strong wrote, "so choosing him is a little like buying a pig in a poke, but then his integrity has never been questioned, and a man who can conduct great campaigns successfully and without being even accused of flagrant blunders must possess a talent for affairs that fits him for any administrative office. Therefore, hurrah for Grant!"

The Republican National Convention met in May in Chicago under the chairmanship of General Joseph Hawley, in the interlude between the first and the final votes on the charges against Johnson. Hawley, known to be a confidant of Grant's, had been editor of the *Hartford Evening Press* before the war and an organizer of the Republican Party in Connecticut. He was a leader in the movement in Connecticut to erase the word "white" from the Constitution of that state. The Radical Republicans were uneasy about Grant's own views on Reconstruction but the Republican regulars overcame the doubts of the Radicals and nominated Grant, who was virtually unopposed, on the first ballot, with Schuyler Colfax named as his running mate.

Georges Clemenceau summarized the Republican platform as vindicating the actions of Congress and laying down that "every consideration of public safety, of gratitude, and of justice demands that the right of suffrage be guaranteed to the negroes in the rebel states, whereas the question of whether or not the negroes shall vote in the loyal states properly belongs to the people of those states to decide," a position that Charles Sumner described as "foolish and contemptible." Thomas Wentworth Higginson charged Northerners with being ready to let "the negro be a man in the South, to spite the white man, but not . . . that he should be a man at the North, when it offends their prejudices."

With the ratification of the Fourteenth Amendment there was a disposition in both parties to assume that the issue of black suffrage and the protection of black rights had been settled. The *New York World*, a Democratic organ, declared itself in support of Negro suffrage in the South on the grounds that it was already an accomplished fact and that a new and a Democratic Congress would not have the authority to undo it. Clemenceau found encouragement in this unexpected reversal of form. "If," he told his French readers, ". . . the two parties get together on this capital question, one important cause of the disagreement will have been removed, and the revolution which has been going on for eight months in American democracy will be theoretically accomplished."

With Grant nominated by the Republicans attention now shifted to the Democrats, who were to meet in New York in July to nominate their candidates. The front-runners were Winfield Scott Hancock of Connecticut, a war hero with a historic name known to be sympathetic to Southern whites, and George Hunt Pendleton. "His complete 'copperheadism,'" Georges Clemenceau wrote of Pendleton, "has long since made him odious to the Conservatives, while his inordinate affection for paper money alienates all capitalists of the Eastern states." Clemenceau described Pendleton as "a clever as well as a cultivated man, who exercises a kind of fascination over his circle."

In the wings hovered that perennial presidential hopeful Salmon Chase. Chase, for all his radical, problack notions, was "a *gold man* . . . whom the financial aristocracy of the country has always upheld," in Clemenceau's words.

When the Democrats met at Tammany Hall in New York City on July 9, George Templeton Strong noted that "the city is swarming with wild Southern and Western delegates . . . a rough lot—hirsute, porky creatures, in linen 'dusters,' with badges in their buttonholes." Party leaders, especially those from the West, were convinced that a War Democrat, untainted by Copperheadism, could carry the presidential election and, what was perhaps more important, assist in the election of a Democratic Congress. A complicating factor was the issue of gold versus greenbacks. The principal War Democrats had the handicap of being dangerously heretical on money matters. Originally described as a contest between "paper" and "specie," it was increasingly spoken of as a struggle between "greenbacks" and "gold." It was both a regional and a class issue in the main, but to the champions of specie it was a moral issue pure and simple. Specie was good; greenbacks were bad. Christian morality and indeed God Himself supported specie. Paper money, Gideon Welles wrote, "is a fiction, sustained by public confidence in part because there is a belief that it will ultimately bring gold. . . . Irredeemable paper is a lie; gold is truth."

Those politicians who flirted with the corrupt and corrupting greenback doctrines were simply yielding to popular clamor for a debased currency and degraded morals. When the Republican platform equivocated on the hard money, soft money issue, Carl Schurz felt a moral obligation to denounce that plank. "I think it is a barefaced, dishonest, rascally repudiation," he told a startled gathering of his Wisconsin Republicans, who had announced their support for paper money.

The principal Democratic problem was that the Copperheads, or Peace Democrats, had a strong hold on the affections of the party regulars, those political stalwarts whose hostility to the war had welded them into a company of kindred spirits. Persuaded with difficulty that their best chances lay with a moderate candidate not publicly identified with the Seymour-Vallandigham wing of the party, they suppressed their natural inclinations and reluctantly accepted Pendleton and Hancock as the most electable candidates. But when Pendleton and Hancock deadlocked through twenty-two ballots, the convention suddenly stampeded, like loco cattle, for Seymour, undoubtedly the least electable of all the leading Democratic candidates. In the words of Georges Clemenceau, "while Mr. Vallandigham's crew broke out into frenzied applause and shrieked with enthusiasm, Mr. Seymour rose and declared, in an even less resolute manner than before, that he could not accept the candidacy." But he was shouted down. "The trick was turned. Mr. Vallandigham, the man who was convicted of high treason to his country during the war . . . has succeeded in forcing on the Democratic party a candidate of his own choice," Clemenceau added.

Seymour's running mate was the able but impetuous Frank Blair, an anathema to Republicans and reputed to be a heavy drinker. "Western Democrats are much disgusted . . ." Strong wrote, "and think themselves out-maneuvered and swindled by the Manhattan Club and by New Yorkers generally."

"The Democrats and conservatives do not get reconciled to the New York nominations," Gideon Welles noted. "It was undoubtedly a mistake, but they must support it as preferable to Grant in his ignorance and Radicalism in its wickedness."

The nomination of Seymour served to give fresh emphasis to one of the most basic facts of the Civil War Era. The notion of a reasonably united "North" that defeated the South is a serious distortion of the facts. For whatever reason or combination of reasons, many "Northerners" living on the upper side of the Mason-Dixon Line (and north and west of the Ohio) were undeviatingly opposed to fighting to keep the South in the Union and, perhaps above all, to any interference with the South's "peculiar institution"—slavery. They felt so alienated from the major financial and social institutions of the Eastern upper-middle and upper classes that they were determined to contend against them to the bitter end and, in some instances, at the risk of their lives. The ostensible Civil War between North and South concealed or partially suppressed another war—that of the working men, the Irish, the Germans, the entrepreneurs, and small-businessmen of the Western states against the "moneyed interests of Wall Street," the bankers, the reformers, the champions of temperance, the graduates of Harvard and Yale, the "capitalists." As Clemenceau put it, in addition to representing the ideal of freedom and equality for Southern blacks, the Republicans were "the party of the industrial aristocracy, and for this reason . . . the rabid enemies of free trade. They are the authors of the incredible tariff, which would be unendurable except for the immense resources of this country and the abundance of paper money." Further, the Republican Party stood for "political centralization" and "Puritan intolerance," especially in regard to intoxicating liquors. For those groups that made up the Democratic Party the moral issue of slavery weighed but a feather as against the hatred of the nabobs and aristocrats. Suspended between Hancock and Pendleton, the mass of the Democratic delegates turned to Seymour and Valandigham. Political expediency, ingenious stratagems, even the counsels of common sense collapsed instantly before the opportunity to vent ancient animosities, come what might. It was the custom then, and later, to deplore the depth of party feeling, but attention has seldom been given to the deeper roots of that feeling. The massive racial prejudice of the Democrats, those of War and those of Peace, has often blinded historians to the "democratic" character of the Democrats. Slavery aside, it was clearly the party of the common man. But slavery, of course, could not be put aside. It was the incubus the Democratic Party could never get off its back, and *because* it could not, it was at a hopeless disadvantage in its competition for power with the Republicans. Every Republican error and misstep could be retrieved because the Democrats could not free themselves from the weight of their prejudices. The more bitterly Democrats attacked blacks, denounced them as gorillas and apes, savages and barbarians, the more doggedly the Republicans defended them, even, as time went on, those who gave away nothing in terms of racial prejudice to the Democrats. And the more the Republicans defended the blacks, in some instances going so far as to claim them superior in many respect to whites and superior in most respects to German and Irish immigrants and insolent mobs of rioting workers, the more deeply ingrained became the prejudices of the Democrats. It was not, of course, a new situation. For decades before the war the same contest had been fought—the immigrants and workingmen of the industrial North and West clasped in that extraordinary alliance with the semifeudal South. It is, indeed, impossible to calculate the degree to which that alliance, begun in the 1790s by Thomas Jefferson, has determined the course of our history. If the Democratic Party had been able to maintain itself without its Southern connection, it might have been a very powerful agent for social and economic reform and the history of late-nineteenth-century America might have then been very different. *But* without Southern votes, the Democratic Party could not have even challenged the hegemony of the almost equally odd alliance of Unionists, temperance advocates, Free-Soilers, capitalists, vegetarians, Puritans, protectionists, and hard-money men who made up, successively, the Federalists, National Republicans, Anti-Masons, Whigs, and, finally, Republicans. It was none other than Wendell Phillips who described the Republican Party as "shuffling, evasive, unprincipled, corrupt, cowardly and mean, almost beyond the power of words to describe, still," Phillips added, "a vote for Grant means the negro's suffrage recognized; a vote for Seymour means the negro disfranchised and another war." Georges Clemenceau put the matter precisely when he wrote: "The Republican party cannot abandon the negroes, under penalty of losing its excuse for existing."

One of the things that has clearly troubled liberal historians (and most historians have been liberal; a few radical) in trying to deal with the Era of Reconstruction is that the Republicans, the party of hard money, protective tariffs, and other "bad" things, are also the party of abolition and black equality, while the Democrats, the party of soft money, free trade, unions, the eight-hour day, and other "good" things, are also the party of remorseless hostility to black Americans. One suspects that historians, being only human (though it must be said they often write inhumanly bad books), would much prefer a scenario in which the good guys were plainly on one side and the bad guys on the other (provided, of course, that the good guys won out in the end). In such an arrangement, the good guys would be for abolition, black suffrage, equality, justice, free trade, the Union, women's rights, the eight-hour day, economic democracy, etc., while the bad guys would be against rights for free blacks, for economic exploitation, hostile to immigrants and the poor, etc. But history, fortunately, conforms neither to wishes of historians nor to logic.

It was soon evident that the Democrats had allowed their hearts to rule their heads. "They believed," Gideon Welles wrote, "the Radical measures were so atrocious that they could elect whoever was nominated, and therefore, having the organization, passed by all the War Democrats and nominated a Secession sympathizer."

Frank Blair, the brother of Montgomery Blair and the Democratic vice-presidential candidate, was quoted to the effect that "there is but one way to restore the Government and the Constitution, and that is for the President-elect to declare these acts [Reconstruction Acts] null and void, compel the army to undo its usurpations at the South, disperse the carpet-bag State Governments, allow the White people to re-organize their own governments." And the *La Crosse* (Wisconsin) *Democrat* declared that if the Democrats received a majority of "white" votes in the coming election they should "march to Washington . . . and take their seats, and reinaugurate the white man's government, in spite of man or devils. . . . If this brings bloodshed, then let blood flow!"

For the young Georges Clemenceau, the presidential campaign was a revelation of democratic politics. Reviewing the events of the preceding four years, he wrote: "The Americans, like all self-contained people, have an unbalanced streak in their nature. . . ." Normally reserved and even cold, they have imaginations which, "when once released, go all the further, and they indulge in the strangest of freaks." They seemed to Clemenceau "to save up their folly, instead of squandering it in small ways," and finally to pour it out "in the most extravagant quantities . . . every four years. . . . The pretext for the general universal dissoluteness of mind is the presidential election."

The press takes delight in its "untrammeled freedom of speech and of the press . . . freedom to jeer, to insult and deride and bear false witness, to arouse hatred and scorn of anything and anybody. . . . Everything contributes to enhance the interest of this mighty drama, in which everyone tries to play a role. . . . During this great carnival, when all human passions overflow, man's brutality requires much bloodshed before it is satisfied. . . . An account in detail of this amazing carnival would fill a volume," Clemenceau told his French readers. The rival politicians were "talking a great deal and saying very little . . . proving by God, the Bible, and history that Providence has always favored one party, and not the other, and invoking Greece and Rome to demonstrate the necessity of electing Mr. X." Clemenceau noted: "Any Democrat who did not manage to hint in his speech that the negro is a degenerate gorilla, would be considered lacking in enthusiasm. . . . That is the theme of all Democratic speeches." Marcus Mills Pomeroy, editor of the *La Crosse Democrat,* expressed the feelings of the irreconcilables when he wrote: "It is you, Republicans, who set up at the head of the nation a hideous clown, who became a shameless tyrant, a tyrant justly felled by an avenging hand, and who now rots in his tomb while his poisonous soul is consumed by the eternal flames of hell."

Blue was the color of patriotism and loyalty, the color of the Republicans. Clemenceau attended a blue parade in Philadelphia in October, 1868, in which it was estimated that more than fifty-five thousand people participated, "with every window full of flags, garlands, and inscriptions of one kind or another. . . . Numerous wagon loads of wounded soldiers, as well as one group of prisoners from Andersonville, displayed themselves proudly to the public gaze. . . ." The whole affair was said to have cost the Republican Party more than $200,000.

In New York the Democrats had their own mammoth parade, the chief features of which were allegorical floats, the most striking of which was a goddess of Liberty, "excellently draped and beautifully posed. She was a powerfully built Irish girl, wearing her red cap with an audacious air. . . ." During the last weeks of the campaign Frank Blair toured the Western states, "making endless speeches, which are doing immeasurable harm to the Democratic party by their exaggerations and ridiculous flights of oratory," Clemenceau wrote.

Gideon Welles noted: "Speakers are overrunning the country with their hateful harangues and excitable trash." The rumor spread that there was a substantial movement among the War Democrats to abandon Seymour and take on Chase as the party's candidate. When Welles contemplated what was clearly going to be a Democratic debacle, he laid much of the blame at the door of his old enemy Seward. "It was Seward who contributed to the retention of Stanton; it was Seward who counseled [Johnson] to submit and yield to Radical usurpation; it was Seward who broke down his Administration; it was Seward who drove him from the people," and finally, it was Johnson's dependence on Seward and Weed that had driven off the Democrats who might otherwise have supported him.

Despite the optimistic reflections of Clemenceau and others that the issue of black suffrage had been settled once and for all, news continued to filter north of actions of violence and intimidation directed against blacks, especially against blacks trying to exercise their political rights. In the Third Military District, which included Georgia, Alabama, and Florida, reports were received constantly of harassment and intimidation practiced against blacks attempting to vote. One such letter from a voter in Forsyth, Georgia, declared that "the white people won't let the colored people register their names nor vote. Last Saturday there was 250 colored people went up to the county seat to register their names and the Rebels run them off the place and would not let them register their names."

In the same state a white Republican, G. W. Ashburn, who had been active in helping freedmen organize, was murdered in his bed in a boardinghouse run by a black woman. Under pressure from General Meade, the military commander of the district, ten suspects were arrested. They made an odd bag—two policemen, two merchants, three clerks, a physician, a lawyer, and a black blacksmith. Before they could be tried, *ex parte Milligan* was invoked. They were freed, re-arrested by the civil authorities, and eventually freed without trial. In the words of one Georgian, it was all "a God-damned sight of fuss . . . made about killing that son of a bitch . . . and by God, there would be more of the same stripe missing."

Johnson had replaced Sheridan with General Winfield Scott Hancock as commander of the Fifth Military District. Under Hancock's administration, the murders of blacks increased sharply, and it was charged that in Louisiana alone more than a thousand blacks were killed in the weeks preceding the election of 1868. A week before the election, New Orleans was the scene of another racial riot. Welles, in his hostility toward the freedmen, dismissed all stories of Southern atrocities committed against blacks as "a mass of uncertain material, mostly relating to negro quarrels, wholly unreliable . . . rumors, scandal, and gossip. . . ."

In the election Grant and Colfax took twenty-six states with 214 electoral votes and a popular tally of 3,015,071, to the opposition's eight states, 81 electoral votes, and 2,709,613 popular votes. Republicans lost a number of seats in Congress, Benjamin Wade, a Radical stalwart, was not returned to the Senate from Ohio. Louisiana and Georgia were also lost by the Republicans.

Grant's margin was just 300,000 votes out of almost 6 million cast. To some observers it seemed evident that if the Republicans had nominated any candidate less popular than the savior of the Union or, conversely, if the Democrats had had the wit to nominate Hancock or Pendleton, the result might well have been a crushing setback for the Radical Republicans. As it was the Republicans and Democrats interpreted the outcome as they wished. Grant's victory was hailed by the *Congregationalist* as promising a "reign of order. The loyal Southerner, white or black, may sit hereafter under his own vine and fig-tree, none daring to molest him or make him afraid."

The Reverend Alexander Clark, a friend of Edwin Stanton's and a kind of minister without portfolio to the Radical Republicans in Congress, sounded a similar note in a Thanksgiving sermon to his Pittsburgh congregation. "There is a class of scant-idea-ed men who say that this is the white man's country," he declared. "So it is, but it is the black man's, the brown man's, and the red man's country, also. It is more the freedman's than the Irishman's, if birthright has any claim. Thank God, this glad Thanksgiving day, I can stand in a free pulpit and say to you in those free seats, that *this is everybody's country*. It is broad enough for all the kindreds, tribes and tongues; for rich and poor are here; while over all and first of all God is here; for at last it is God's country! And if he permits black men in it, he'll see they breathe its atmosphere, eat its bread, and enjoy it as creatures bearing his own image and destined to rise into his high heaven before their pale-faced fellows who hate them without a cause. Whoever hums this silly song, 'The white man's country,' deserves to be chased out of it by Indians; for if it comes down to a simple question of prior occupancy the copperskin's claim is best of all."

Georges Clemenceau was likewise convinced in the aftermath of the election "that the negroes will not be left to the mercy of their former masters, [that] America intends to make, and will make, out of its slaves, men, free men, citizens. . . . From the day when the Democratic party in a panic took refuge under the wing of Mr. Seymour, I foresaw, with everyone else, that it would slip back, step by step, into the blind, groping course it was following before the war. No one could keep it from sliding down hill. The Democrats simply will not understand that the revolution which has been carried out in spite of them is not of the kind that can be undone, and that there is no use reacting against it. The demand for the abolition of slavery was made not so much by the Republican party as by the conscience of the whole nation." It was easy enough to understand how Southerners, economically dependent on slaves and unable to envision a social system in which they might be free, should defend their "peculiar institution" to the bitter end. It was much more difficult to understand why millions of Northerners who had no slaves or any prospect of having any, should be almost equally fanatical in defending the institution. The Democrats, Clemenceau reported, "do not exactly wish for the return of slavery, and there are even a few who will admit if you press the point that a negro is a human being . . . they all deny most emphatically that he can possibly be made into a citizen. . . . Hence their idiotic desperation in the face of a destiny which they cannot escape. . . . When they took Mr. Seymour for their captain, they showed the world that they had forgotten much and learned nothing."

But in the opinion of John Roy Lynch, the black Congressman from Mississippi, the closeness of the popular vote encouraged the more irreconcilable element in the South to hold off from political activity (though not, it must be said, from constant acts of terrorism against black leaders and black voters) in the hope that another turn of the political wheel would put the Democrats on top and lead to the jettisoning of Congressional Reconstruction.

A month later an angry and embittered President delivered his final message to Congress, proposing an amendment to the Constitution to limit presidents to one six-year term and denouncing that body for undermining the Constitution. As Clemenceau put it: "For the last time, he indulged himself in the empty satisfaction of annoying the two Houses of Congress by saying disagreeable things to them in his official capacity." George Templeton Strong was among the critics of Johnson's final message to Congress. "That incorrigible malefactor, A. Johnson," he wrote, "has disgraced the country and disgusted all decent men by his very nefarious message, which both Houses rightly condemned as an insult." In the closing hours of the year 1868

Gideon Welles, secretary of the navy in a defeated and discredited administration, looked back over his years in office. To him there had been "much to impair confidence in the intelligence and integrity of the mass of the people to govern themselves. Under the influence of passion and led on by bad men, they hastily plunged into war." The Radical Republicans had "trampled the organic law under foot," and "in all this reckless wickedness" they had been "sustained by the people, and a majority of the next Congress is elected to support their wicked revolutionary proceedings."

Robert Ingersoll, active in Republican politics, remarked the night before Grant assumed office, "We can't run the machine merely by making faces at Andy Johnson." When the public had said, "Why in hell . . . don't we have peace in the South?" the answer was "Andy Johnson." "Why are not some of the traitors hung?" "Andy Johnson." "What the devil makes the roads so muddy—measles so mad —whooping cough so prevalent?" "Why G——d d——n it, Andy Johnson. We can sing this song only until tomorrow."

Johnson's bitterness was so great that he not only was unwilling to participate in Grant's inauguration—the inauguration of a man, as Welles put it, "we knew to be untruthful, faithless and false, a dissembler, a deliberate deceiver"—but prevented his Cabinet members from attending as well. Welles, at least, readily acquiesced. "The truth is," he wrote, "Grant is elected by illegal votes and fraudulent and unconstitutional practices." It was too much to witness the triumph of "this ignorant, vulgar man."

Johnson presents us with two related but distinguishable problems —the motivation for his policies and his behavior in attempting to give them effect. For the first, it must be remembered that Johnson was from Tennessee, a slaveholding state. He was also from a social class held in contempt by the planter aristocracy, and it was clear that he felt resentment and hostility toward the landed upper class. He was, in addition, a strong Union man, and it would not have been surprising if his Union feelings had their roots in his class resentment. Certainly there was never an indication in Johnson of sympathy with the condition of black people. That he was sincerely opposed to slavery we can readily accept, but beyond that, there is no evidence that he had any genuine concern for the plight of the freedman. Because the Union was paramount with Johnson, it is not surprising that he felt the preservation (or re-establishment) of the Constitution was his most solemn obligation as president. To Johnson that meant a scrupulous regard for the doctrine of states' rights, which in turn meant the restoration of the rebel states to the Union with all their rights as states intact. In any contest between what he conceived to be the rights of the white population of the South and the rights of the freedmen, Johnson's sympathies were all on the side of the whites. He had, to be sure, talked rather wildly in the closing months of the war about hanging Jeff Davis and other Southern leaders, but that was part of his spleen, his frontier political style. He had been a lifelong Democrat, and it is reasonable to assume that his suspicions of the old New England Whig elite from whom so many of the Republican leaders had been drawn was bone-deep; suppressed, not eradicated. When, under the influence of the austere, patriarchal Welles, Johnson had been convinced that the restoration of the Constitution was his patriotic duty, he became a dedicated man. Although Welles was only six years older than Johnson—sixty-three in 1865 as opposed to Johnson's fifty-nine—with his whitening beard and stern manner, the secretary of the navy was an imposing figure. The conviction of the assured, undeviatingly loyal Welles that the Radical Republicans were bent on destroying the Constitution in order to impose their own vindictive will on the nation had a strong, if not decisive, influence on Johnson.

In the matter of Johnson's behavior, the issue is clearly more complicated. Even Welles, generally uncritical of his superior, took note, time and again, of Johnson's secretiveness and indecision, of his readiness to listen patiently to his Cabinet members' often tedious discussions of questions of policy or strategy, and of his contrasting disposition to make the most critical decisions without consulting anyone. Welles observed shrewdly that Johnson sorely needed a confidant, but the President never assigned the role to him despite his obvious availability. There was, of course, the familiar question of the President's drinking habits. Certainly he drank and sometimes drank more than was good for him, but the drinking was symptomatic, not central.

There was clearly a touch of madness in Johnson, a reckless and demonic spirit that drove him to excess, to violent, hasty words and actions. Whether or not it could be attributed to his frontier origins, it was certainly characteristic of the frontier, especially the Southern frontier, where proverbially men's emotions were under slight constraint and where violence permeated every aspect of life. Along with a gambler's recklessness, there appeared to be in Johnson a desire to be punished, specifically to be martyred. Welles showed a remarkable insight into Johnson's martyr complex when he wrote in his diary on February 24, 1868: "I have sometimes been almost tempted to listen to the accusation of his enemies that he desired and courted impeachment." If his enemies laid traps for him, he seemed determined to spring them. He talked of hanging, hanging the rebels, hanging Sumner and Stevens and Phillips. He compared himself to Christ and Lincoln. He raged and raved until even the doggedly loyal Welles was disconcerted. Even if one feels that Johnson's devotion to states' rights and the Constitution was, in the context of the Reconstruction Era, wrong headed and obtuse, it was a legitimate position shared by millions of his fellow Americans. It was the way he proceeded to translate that devotion into political action that proved ultimately his undoing. To say that he would have been more successful, to say, indeed, that he might have triumphed had he been "tactful," is to misstate the case. Tact was quite beside the point. Deliberate abrasiveness and forthright provocation were the President's style. Since he believed his political adversaries were wicked men bent on destroying him, he missed no opportunity to strike out viciously at them. And each blow he delivered brought a dozen in return. He wished to be punished; Stevens wished to punish.

Every other issue was subsidiary to that. For those men like Stevens, Sumner, Henry Wilson, Trumbull, Hoar, and several dozen other radicalized Republicans who believed that at heart the Civil War had been brought on by the single, overriding issue of slavery and that freeing the slave and, beyond that, insuring justice for the freedmen, were ultimately the only justification for that terrible conflict and were, moreover, missions assigned them by the Almighty, there was no question of compromise, of faltering, or of turning back. The Constitution was, for them, an entirely secondary issue. If it was in the way of justice, it must be breached or kicked aside.

But what of the champions of the Constitution, of the sacred doctrine of states' rights? Well, of them it must be said, without equivocation or apology, that they cared more for the theoretical formulations of that document (as interpreted by them) than they did for the fate of 4,000,000 black people in the South. They were in love with abstractions and blind to injustice. They were wrong, as Stevens well understood, because in the long run the Constitution could not survive unless it could guarantee at least a rough approximation of justice to *all* Americans, regardless of the color of their skin. It still has not done that to the satisfaction of many fair-minded men and women, but it has at least proved capacious enough to incorporate that principle and to the degree that it has failed, the failure is certainly ours, not the document's.

It is the thesis of this volume that nothing could have changed or substantially modified the reaction of the white South to the freeing of its slaves. On the other hand, it seems reasonable to assume that a party or a powerful faction devoted to "states' rights" and, less emphatically, to reconciliation with the South would have manifested itself in the North, Johnson or no Johnson, and that such a party or faction led by a president of a mild and conciliatory temper, tactful and persuasive, might well have neutralized the radical advocates of justice for the freedmen and carried through a program of reconstruction that left to the South the "solution" of what was sometimes called, quite misleadingly, its negro problem or, equally misleadingly, the problem of negro domination. As we have had frequent occasion to note, the sympathy in the North with the needs and aspirations of the black people was extremely thin. To effect Black Reconstruction required the combined and reinforcing intractabilities of the white South and Andrew Johnson.

Andrew Johnson had a measure of revenge for his abandonment by the Republicans. In 1874 he ran for election to the Senate from the state of Tennessee. When the state legislature met in January, 1875, to elect a new United States Senator, the supporters of Johnson's two principal opponents became deadlocked. When Johnson was chosen by a majority of one on the fifty-fourth ballot, Democrats all over the country were ecstatic. The *St. Louis Republican* called his victory "the most magnificent personal triumph which the history of American politics can show," and when he took his seat in the Senate, he was greeted with general applause. Vice-President Henry Wilson, who, seven years earlier, had voted to impeach him, administered the oath of office. He had come back to the Senate, Johnson told a friend, with two purposes. One was to punish the Southern generals who had never, in his view, been sufficiently chastised, and the other was to make a speech in condemnation of Grant. The latter mission was fulfilled when Johnson attacked Grant for supporting the Reconstruction government of Louisiana. "The President finds a usurper in power, and he takes it upon himself to make the Government of the United States party to his usurpation. . . . Is not this monstrous in a free Government?" the new Senator asked. "Bid him disband his legions; return the commonwealth to liberty," he urged his colleagues, adding:

"How far off is empire? How far off is military despotism? ... Let peace and Union be restored to the land. May God bless this people, and God save the Constitution."

Two days later Congress adjourned, and Johnson returned to Tennessee, apparently satisfied that he had vindicated himself by his attack on Grant. Four months later he died of a stroke. In accordance with his wishes, he was wrapped in an American flag and his head placed upon his copy of the Constitution. He was sixty-seven years of age.

Hate is a dangerous emotion to indulge in, especially for politicians. In politics, of all places, inveteracy most readily invites disaster. Welles was, as his diary makes clear, the worst possible adviser to the already paranoid President. The secretary fed that paranoia as a keeper might feed a hungry lion.

When all is said and done, there was, after all, only one issue, simple, stark, inescapable. How far did justice and humanity require that the Republicans of the North go in attempting to protect the rights of the freedmen and women of the South?

45

The Soldier-President

Grant's inaugural address was brief. Reading it in a low voice and with a diffident manner, the President declared: "The office has come to me unsought; I commence its duties untrammeled. . . . I shall on all subjects have a policy to recommend, but none to enforce against the will of the people." There was much unfinished business left over from his predecessor's administration. "In meeting these it is desirable that they should be approached calmly, without prejudice, hate, or sectional pride, remembering that the greatest good to the greatest number is the object to be attained. This requires security of person, property, and free religious and political opinion in every part of our common country, without regard to local prejudice. All laws to secure these ends will receive my best efforts for their enforcement." In other words, where Johnson had left to the states the issue of "security of person, property . . . and political opinion," Grant made it clear that he thought these the responsibility of the Federal government and would not hesitate to intervene in those cases where "local prejudice" infringed those rights. Grant also took pains to express his concern for "the original occupants of this land. . . . I will favor any course toward them which tends to their civilization and ultimate citizenship."

The man who became the twenty-first president of the United States was (and remains) for Americans an enigma. Of his brilliance as a general there is little disagreement. As a president he has often been judged a disaster. But the matter is obviously more complex. To understand the task facing Grant, it is necessary to try to enter the mood or, as the Germans like to say, *Zeitgeist,* of the post-Civil War period.

There was, first, the matter of what might be called excessive expectations, of which we have already taken note—the belief that the end of the war would usher in a new age of justice and equality, of Christian brother- and sisterhood, of peace and prosperity. The sin of slavery had been expiated, the spirit cleansed; America had been reborn in the fiery crucible of war, purged and made whole. Completed. The schizophrenic break had been healed. Many Americans believed literally in the millennium; for many others to whom the millennium was a metaphor it was nonetheless eagerly anticipated.

But as months lengthened into years, contrary evidence accumulated at an alarming rate. Things had gone disconcertingly, even horrifyingly wrong. Capitalism, instead of being tamed and chastened, was more greedy and rapacious than ever. The tale of corruption appeared to be without end. The hoped-for reconciliation with a South freed of the taint of slavery and ready to cooperate with the victors to build a vigorous new society that would accord free blacks their rightful place as citizens and fellow Americans had proved illusory. Instead of reconciliation, there was unrelenting hatred, fanned and sustained by the determination of the Radical Republicans to see justice done to the ex-slaves.

The public temper, as we have seen, was volatile in the extreme. Even such solid characters as George Templeton Strong varied from month to month in their feelings about a variety of things, most particularly the status of free blacks in the South and how far the Federal government might legitimately go in extending protection to them without destroying the Constitution. It was a time of excruciating conflicts and almost unbearable tensions.

Remorseless, irrepressible, unyielding, the problem of blacks in the South refused to be solved, to go away, to allow any rest to the consciences of Northerners with consciences. Each day's news brought fresh tales of atrocities in the still-rebellious states, not all, of course, committed by whites against blacks—many blacks struck back in rage and fear—but all nonetheless distressing.

The country did not understand its own will, its own soul, its own fate. It seemed as if all the suffering, all the lives, all the money expended had simply produced a new nightmare, more knotty, more complex, more unsolvable than the old. It was difficult to suppress the terrible thought: Were not black people better off, after all, as slaves than as free persons stripped of the protections of the law, at the mercy of their former masters? If as slaves they were often beaten, they were seldom murdered if only because they were far more valuable alive than dead. Now whether or not they were alive or dead was a matter of indifference to the vast majority of Southern whites. Some expressed the wish to see them all exterminated.

That was the country to the leadership of which a somewhat reluctant Grant ascended, a country so deeply wounded and demoralized that it was beyond governing in any reasonable sense of that word. The new President had hardly moved into the White House before his own party started to unravel. The idealists went in a half dozen directions; only the pragmatists grouped themselves unflinchingly, like tribal warriors, around their chief.

The new President was totally untried as a politician. His highest values were loyalty to friends and the faithful performance of his duties. Politics are often described as the art of compromise. Grant was a man of implacable will, unable to distinguish compromise from retreat. He expected loyalty from Republican leaders in Congress much as he expected loyalty from the subordinate officers in the army.

Caught between those members of his party who took as their highest priority the preservation of black rights in the South, the most extreme of whom wished to see the freed blacks in power in every Southern state, and those Republicans who were increasingly uneasy about the role of the Federal government in state affairs, Grant was in a no-win position. In addition, his personal staff was composed of individuals of limited intelligence and dubious moral principles. If Grant was, on the whole, sympathetic with the aims of the Radical Republicans, he found them, with their self-righteous and moral rectitude, thoroughly uncongenial. Under such circumstances the Republican Party—never so much a party as a loose alliance of middle-class reformers and idealists whose only real bond was a common antipathy to slavery—began to come apart almost immediately. For one thing, the President showed a disconcerting disposition to ignore the leaders of his party. Like other generals turned politicians, he saw himself far more as a national than as a party leader. He wished devoutly to avoid the damaging split between the executive and legislative branches of the administration that had made a shambles of his predecessor's reign, but he lacked the political skills and deftness to do so. Perhaps no one could have held that fragile alliance together.

The first indication of the tone of his administration would, it was thought, be revealed by his Cabinet choices. Sumner, chairman of the Senate Foreign Relations Committee, seemed to many an obvious choice for secretary of state. There were half a dozen eminent Republican candidates. But Grant surprised everyone by choosing relative unknowns. George Boutwell was named secretary of the treasury, reassuring the hard-money men (Boutwell, for the excessive length of his speeches and his Massachusetts antecedents, had been nicknamed the Steady Wind Blowing Aft). Hamilton Fish was secretary of state (no one knew where he stood). And Grant's former aide, General Joseph Hawley, was secretary of war. Wendell Phillips, who had been strongly opposed to Grant's nomination, wrote: "Nothing can be told of the President's plans from his cabinet. On the contrary, its composition is a good sign that he has no plans. It is a cabinet that means nothing at all. . . . Everybody who had already been thought of is excluded. The President took the leftovers. But that does not signify, for it is our duty, the duty of the people, to tell them all what they must do." Clemenceau was of much the same mind. "Their mediocrity is probably the very quality for which the President values them," he wrote. "American democracy is a little afraid, and with some reason, of men of genius, of saviors guided by some mysterious inspiration, who are charged by Providence to think and act for other men."

One of the ablest new Congressmen in the Fortieth Congress was George Hoar of Massachusetts. Hoar was a descendant on his mother's side of Roger Sherman, the Connecticut shoemaker who became a leading figure in the American Revolution and one of the drafters of the Federal Constitution. His father, Samuel Hoar, was a prominent abolitionist in Massachusetts and a Congressman from that state. Born in 1826, George, the younger of two sons, graduated from Harvard in 1846 and Harvard Law School three years later. He had been one of the moving spirits in the founding of the Republican Party in Massachusetts.

The most popular man in the House was James G. Blaine, the Maine newspaper editor who, in Poore's words, "exercised a fascination over all." Blaine's "graceful as well as powerful figure, his strong features glowing with health, and his hearty, honest manner" were complemented by his "purity" of oratorical style and the "terseness . . . and strength" of his arguments.

Of Blaine, Hoar wrote: "He was born to be loved or hated. . . . In addition to the striking qualities which caught the public eye, he was a man of profound knowledge of our political history, of a sure literary taste, and a great capacity as an orator." When Benjamin Butler thought he had prevailed on Blaine as Speaker of the House to give him the coveted position of chairman of the Appropriations Committee and camped outside Blaine's door to insure his appointment, Blaine, hearing Butler was lying in wait for him, escaped through a window, hurried to the House, and rushed through the appointment of Henry Dawes.

Of his fellow Massachusetts politician Butler, who was a power in the House, Hoar had nothing good to say. Indeed, in his autobiography he devoted a substantial chapter to the major character defects in that swashbuckling politico, comparing him with Benedict Arnold, Aaron Burr, Robespierre, and Catiline. In Hoar's view, Butler was a classic instance of a man whose entire career was based on bullying and bluster. Butler was shrewd enough to base his power in Massachusetts politics on the powerless—"the poorer class of foreign immigrants." In an angry exchange in the Massachusetts legislature when the Speaker had on one occasion ruled him out of order, Butler had cried out: "I should like to knife that old cuss." Although a Democrat, he had done much to redeem himself in the eyes of the Republican leaders by his wholehearted support of the Union cause, helping thereby to prevent the Democrats from becoming simply the party of opposition. On the issue of the rights of the freed black, Butler never wavered.

When the impeachment proceedings against Johnson failed, Stanton resigned as secretary of war. Tired and ill, suffering from acute attacks of asthma, he nonetheless campaigned actively for Grant and was pleased when Roscoe Conkling wrote him that Grant had expressed a "strong feeling of friendship" for him. Back in Washington with Grant's election insured, Stanton was too weak to celebrate Christmas Eve with his second wife, Ellen, and their young children.

Stanton hoped for an appointment in Grant's administration, and when none was forthcoming, he gave way to gloomy suspicions about the genuineness of the President's Republican principles. His health and his finances both declined. Meanwhile, two vacancies appeared on the Supreme Court, and Grant, at the urging of Stanton's friends, and after some delay, offered one of the positions to Stanton. December 18 was Stanton's fifty-fourth birthday. Too ill to leave his bed, he was visited by the President and Vice-President Colfax, who informed him of his nomination to the Court. Barely able to hold a pen, Stanton wrote the next day to Grant: "It is the only public office I ever desired and I accept it with pleasure." He added that he was especially pleased to receive the appointment from Grant, "with whom for several years I have had personal and official relations, such as seldom exist among men." Four days later, on Christmas Eve, Stanton died. The day after Christmas his wife received a letter from Robert Lincoln. "I know that it is useless to say anything . . . and yet when I recall the kindness of your father to me, when my father was lying dead and I felt utterly desperate, hardly able to realize the truth, I am as little able to keep my eyes from filling with tears as he was then."

In George Templeton Strong's opinion, Lincoln, Stanton, and Grant "did more than any other three men to save the country. Good and evil were strangely blended in the character of this great War Minister. He was honest, patriotic, able, indefatigable, warm-hearted, unselfish, incorruptible, arbitrary, capricious, tyrannical, vindictive, hateful, and cruel."

The beginnings of a rupture between Grant and Sumner were to be found in the fact that Grant neither offered Sumner a position in his Cabinet nor did him the courtesy of consulting him about Cabinet appointments or about the appointments of ambassadors and consuls. Indeed, Grant began appointing obviously unqualified people, among them relatives, to various foreign posts. Welles greeted the news of the President's appointments with the comment that he was more interested in "horse-flesh" than in "brains or intellect. . . . Appointment of his friends to office is the extent of his ideas of administrative duties. . . ." Benjamin Butler commented that he could not make Grant comprehend the principal features of an amendment to the tenure of office bill. "But," said Butler, "he is stupidly dull and ignorant and no more comprehends his duty or his power under the Constitution than that dog," pointing to a small dog nearby.

The initial breach between the President and the party leaders was widened by Grant's strange infatuation with annexing Santo Domingo. Santo Domingo and Haiti occupied the island of Hispaniola. Political unrest had been endemic in the former Spanish colony, now a precarious republic racked by revolutionary upheaval. Buena ventura (Good Adventure) Báez had alternated as "chief of the republic" with his rival, Pedro Santana. In a game of political musical chairs, Báez had controlled the government 1849–53, 1856–58, 1865–66, 1868–73, with Santana dominating the intervals. It occurred to Báez that he might consolidate his shaky hold on power by, in effect, selling Santo Domingo to the United States through a treaty of annexation.

For reasons that remain obscure to this day, Grant became an enthusiastic accessory to the Báez plan. One of the difficulties with the Santo Domingo matter was that the slippery and unscrupulous Orville E. Babcock, the President's private secretary, was in the center of it. He imparted to the entire transaction a rancid air. Even Grant's Cabinet was opposed, and Secretary of State Fish offered his resignation on the issue. But the President could not be deflected. With the single-minded determination that had driven him through the bloody horror of the Wilderness campaign, he plunged stubbornly ahead, heedless of the obstacles in his path. The treaty annexing Santo Domingo was signed in December, 1869, just before Congress convened. As the Senators filed into Washington, Grant began twisting the arms of reluctant legislators. At a reception given by John Forney, publisher of the *Washington Chronicle,* Grant asked Carl Schurz for his support on the issue of the acquisition of Santo Domingo. The embarrassed Schurz replied unhappily that he could not, in good conscience, give it. Among his reasons was the fact that the "acquisition and possession of such tropical countries with indigestible, unassimilable populations would be highly obnoxious to the nature of our republican system of government" and would add to the difficulties already experienced with the Southern states.

In his first annual message to Congress the President enumerated the blessings of the citizens of the United States "with a territory unsurpassed in fertility, of an area equal to the abundant support of 500,000,000 people, and abounding in every variety of useful mineral in quantity sufficient to supply the world for generations; with exuberant crops, with a variety of climate adapted to the production of every species of the earth's riches and suited to the habits, tastes, and requirements of every living thing; with a population of 40,000,000 free people, all speaking one language with facilities for every mortal to acquire an education; with institutions closing to none the avenues to fame or any blessing of fortune that may be coveted. . . ."

Seven states had been restored to the Union under their new governments. Revenues were growing with each year, and the debt incurred by the war was being systematically reduced. Then entered that fatal apple of discord, Santo Domingo. "For more than a year . . . a near neighbor of ours, in whom all our people can not but feel a deep interest, has been struggling for independence and freedom," Grant said to his listeners. The United States had the "same warm feelings and sympathies" for Santo Domingo that it had displayed for the other American states that had shaken off the yoke of Spain. While Grant was careful not to call specifically for the annexation of Santo Domingo, he left no doubt of his own interest in the future of the former Spanish colony.

The President also urged Congress to play an active role in developing commerce with China and Japan, especially the latter since it had been a citizen of the United States who had played a crucial role in opening up that country to international trade. "In this connection," Grant declared, "I advise such legislation as will forever preclude the enslavement of the Chinese upon our soil under the name of coolies. . . ."

Shortly after the second session of the Forty-first Congress began, Fessenden, an important member of the Committee on Foreign Relations, died, and Sumner, chairman of the committee, replaced him with Schurz, knowing the Missouri Senator's opposition to the annexation of Santo Domingo. Sumner thus made himself the principal block to the ratification of the treaty. He and Schurz spent long hours planning the strategy to frustrate the President's wishes. To make matters worse, Sumner made a series of speeches ridiculing the President as only an arrogant and self-righteous man could, inflicting wounds that would never heal.

It was an unhappy and potentially disastrous development for the Republican Party. Johnson had claimed that Congress was too self-willed and vindictive to work with. Now it seemed that that body, by quarreling with Johnson's successor, was determined to prove him right. The United States needed Santo Domingo as much as it needed the proverbial hole in its head. The enemies of annexation were in the acutely embarrassing position of feeling obliged to oppose a president hardly settled in office, a man seen by many as the savior of the nation as well as of the Republican Party.

For six months the issue dragged on. Many Senators opposed to annexation recoiled from a showdown with Grant, and on these Sumner exercised all his considerable powers of persuasion. Finally, on June 29, 1870, by a vote of 28 to 28, far short of the necessary two-thirds, the treaty was rejected.

But Grant would not let the matter drop. The sources of his

infatuation with Santo Domingo are obscure, but it is clear that his own pride had become inextricably involved in the issue. He revived the project in his annual message to Congress in December, 1870, proposing that the island be annexed by joint resolution, a scheme that had unhappy memories attached to it from the bitter fight over the annexation of Texas in 1845. As the struggle went on, the members of Congress were forced, however reluctantly, to choose sides—for or against annexation; for or against the president of the United States and the leader of their party. So they divided. Those who cared nothing for Santo Domingo but everything for party unity moved over to the ranks of the President's supporters. Among them was the astute and skillful Oliver Morton. Searching for some face-saving formula, the peacemakers, led by Morton, proposed a commission to visit the island and report on the practicality of annexation. Morton assured Sumner that it was simply a way of letting the whole issue die, but Sumner was unbudgeable. He took the occasion for another attack on the President. One of Sumner's most effective charges was that Grant had given government jobs to legions of relatives and surrounded himself with inept and corrupt minions whose only claim to political preferment was that they were cronies of the President. "Thirteen relations of the President," Sumner pointed out, "are billeted on the country, not one of whom, but for his relationship would hold office. Beyond this list are other relations showing that this strange abuse did not stop with relatives but widened to include relatives of relatives."

Grant's friendship with Jay Gould and Jim Fisk, symbols of the corrupt manipulation of money and commodity markets, made him especially vulnerable. It was charged that the effort of Gould and Fisk to corner the gold market, which produced the "Black Friday" panic of September 24, 1869, had been connived at by Grant, who finally released $1,000,000 in gold to help restore equilibrium to the market.

The President made himself vulnerable by accepting handsome gifts, among them a carriage and pair of horses, from individuals seeking favors from his administration. His vulpine private secretary accepted such items as diamond shirt studs valued at $2,400 and a box of cigars with $1,000 inside. But the taint of corruption, or at least of laxness in matters of gift giving and taking, did not stop with the President and his official family. It pervaded every level of political activity down to the municipal, where the imaginative speculations of William Marcy Tweed and his "Forty Thieves" hung like a cloud over the country's greatest metropolis.

One more step remained to complete the rupture between Grant and the Radical Republicans. On the convening of the Forty-second Congress in March, 1871, the Senate caucus replaced Sumner as chairman of the Foreign Relations Committee with Simon Cameron, the cynical and venal Senator from Pennsylvania. It was a double affront to Sumner. A senior member of the Senate, the idol of the antislavery groups, one of the two or three dominating political figures in the country for a decade or more, Sumner was still a powerful presence, looming above his colleagues physically and intellectually, the great ravaged body slack, but the massive head still showing vestiges of his youthful beauty. Now he was deposed; not only deposed from his throne as chairman of the Foreign Relations Committee but replaced by a hack politician, notorious for shady deals and unsavory maneuvers.

In replacing Sumner, the Republican caucus was sending an unmistakable message about the importance of party loyalty. To be openly and publicly disloyal was to invite, if not insure, punishment. In making the point, the regulars widened the breach between the "radicals" and the "moderates," between the men of principle and the men of party, although the consequences would not at once be evident.

Whatever else might be charged against his administration, in the critically important realm of black rights Grant proved solid as a rock. The loss of Republican strength in Congress in the elections of 1868 was more than compensated for by the President's determination to enforce the Reconstruction Acts. He made clear from the beginning of his administration that he would employ whatever force was necessary to protect the rights of free blacks in the South. Ironically, as the hardcore of radical abolitionists died off, grew old and ill, or were defeated at the polls, more and more Republicans began to emphasize the issue of states' rights, and the President found himself increasingly isolated.

"Prejudice against the African race is dying out faster than anyone had dared to suppose it would," Georges Clemenceau wrote shortly before he returned to France in 1870. "Moreover, he [Grant] is pushing the theory of race equality even further, for he has unhesitatingly appointed negroes to various government positions. Out of five justices of the peace, whom he was called upon to nominate in the District of Columbia, two of his appointees are negroes. . . ." In addition, the President made himself available to black politicians from the South. "Although General Grant is openly trying to pacify the South," Clemenceau added, "it must be admitted in justice to him that, far from deserting the cause of the blacks, as Mr. Johnson did so promptly, he has surprised even the radicals by his insistence on not only preaching, but also practising the doctrine of the equality of the races. He is, in fact, the first President who has dared to give a black man a post in the administration." All this may seem modest enough in the perspective of relations between black and white Americans today, but the psychological effect, difficult though it was to measure precisely, was great. The most admired man in the United States had given dramatic emphasis to the issue of racial equality for black people. It is easy enough to say, as many of the Radical Republicans did, that he could have done more, that he fell far short of what they wished him to do, that what he did was done only to keep peace in the party; but that was not how blacks understood it. They came to believe that they had a friend and supporter in the White House. They felt that in part because, when the President received their leaders, he treated them without condescension, like men; explained to them the measures he felt obliged to take if they differed from their expectations; and assured them of his continuing concern for the needs and aspirations of their people.

Grant, in his inaugural address, had urged passage of the Fifteenth Amendment in order to secure the voting rights of Southern blacks. As early as March, 1866, Senator John Henderson had proposed an amendment, to supplement the Thirteenth and Fourteenth Amendments, which would declare that there should be no discrimination "against any person on account of color or race." He acknowledged that the Senate was not yet ready for such a step but predicted that within five years it must support it. "You cannot get along without it," he concluded. Now it was back on the Senate's docket several years ahead of time. The amendment encountered strong opposition among those members of Congress most devoted to the principle of states' rights, but the opposition was not limited to the champions of state sovereignty. A writer in the *Anti-Slavery Standard* pointed out that the amendment had no provisions to thwart "future State application of unequal tests of education and property." The freedmen were without adequate education or effective leadership, and the *Standard* predicted that "there will be no stone left unturned by which to encompass their political subjugation by the old ruling white class." Theodore Tilton predicted that the Southern states would "invent a dozen cunning schemes to defraud the negro of his franchise" under the terms of the proposed amendment.

The Radicals in the Republican caucuses in both chambers were not powerful enough to push through an amendment more to their liking, but they showed a strong disposition to block the Fifteenth Amendment as it stood. Sumner made his own views clear by proposing a section stating that "the right to vote, to be voted for, and to hold office, shall not be denied or abridged anywhere in the United States, under any pretense of race or color. . . ." All state or municipal laws "inconsistent herewith, are hereby declared null and void." Having taken his stand, Sumner rose to defend it. "Rarely have I entered upon any debate in this Chamber," he declared, "with a sense of sadness so heavy as oppresses me at this moment." It seemed to him that at the very moment when Congress should be most resolute, when victory was at last in sight, it was wavering. "Others may be cool and indifferent; but I have warred with Slavery too long, in all its different forms, not to be aroused when this old enemy shows its head under an *alias*. Once it was Slavery; now it is Caste; and the same excuse is assigned now as then. In the name of States Rights, Slavery, with all its brood of wrong, was upheld; and now, in the name of States Rights, Caste, fruitful also in wrong, is upheld." The South was apparently determined, with the complicity of the North, to "establish that vilest institution, a Caste and an Oligarchy of the Skin. . . . Vain are all our victories, if this terrible rule is not reversed, so that States Rights shall yield to Human Rights, and the Nation be exalted as the bulwark of all."

Surprisingly Wendell Phillips, as the undisputed leader of the old abolitionist coalition, played a crucial role in breaking the deadlock over the amendment by writing an editorial in the *Anti-Slavery Standard* calling for its passage as it stood. It covered "all the ground that the people are ready to occupy," he wrote in February, 1869. The effort of the Radical Republicans in the Senate to rule out all qualifications displayed "an utter lack of common sense . . . a total forgetfulness of the commonest political prudence [a quality in which, it must be said, Wendell Phillips had often been lacking]. . . . For the first time in our lives," Phillips added, "we beseech them to be a little more *politicians*— and a little less reformers." George Boutwell of Massachusetts, a member of the House, wrote Phillips: "That article saved the amendment. Its influence was immediate and potential. Men thought that if you, the extremest radical, could accept the House proposition they might safely do the same."

With the passage of the Fifteenth Amendment there was once more a general feeling among abolitionists that the problem of the black American was "solved." The antislavery groups, the seasoned veterans of a thousand abolitionist battles, could now be discharged, the "church" disbanded. The American Anti-Slavery Society, meeting in May, 1869, declared the amendment to be "the capstone and completion of our movement; the fulfillment of our pledge to the Negro race; since it secures to them equal political rights with the white race, or, if any single right still be doubtful, places them in such circumstances that they can easily achieve it." And when the ratification of the amendment was completed in March, 1870, Frederick Douglass gave full measure of credit to Phillips. "None," he wrote, "have been more vigilant, clear-sighted, earnest, true and eloquent. Without office, without party, only a handful at his back, he has done more to lead and mould public opinion in favor of equal suffrage than any man I know of." The act of dissolution of the American Anti-Slavery Society was left to its "father," William Lloyd Garrison, who had grown old and gray in the service of the cause, who, almost forty years earlier, had sounded in the first issue of the *Liberator* that stirring call "I am in earnest—I will not equivocate—I will not excuse—I will not retreat a single inch—AND I WILL BE HEARD." Heard he had been, perhaps more fatefully than any other American of the century. "Forty years ago this time," he reminded his audience, "I was lying in the cell of a Baltimore prison for advocating the glorious cause whose triumph we are here to celebrate. Yet I believe I was then quite happy in my mind and as confident in my spirit in that jail as today, because I saw the end which was the triumph we have met to celebrate." In his first address to the "colored citizens of Boston" he had promised them "that the time is not far distant when you and the trampled slaves shall all be free and enjoy the same rights in this country as other citizens. If you will hold on with a firm grasp, I assert that liberty, equality, every republican privilege is yours." The greatest struggle had been in the North, simply to win the right to preach the Gospel of Abolition. Now it was finished. "We have lived to see as great a miracle as ever we had read of. Who ever dreamed of seeing a nation, as it were, born in a day? Ten years ago the slave power seemed to be able to defy God." It seemed to Garrison that the black people of the South were taking the lead. "I believe it is the will of God," he declared, "that those States shall pass under the control of the colored people, and that they will lead off in a career of prosperity and honor and glory for our country."

Phillips, too, spoke in confident tones of the progress of the Southern black in self-government: "We have seen his right to State office vindicated at the point of the bayonet. We have seen him preside over State Senates, and take his place on the Supreme Bench of one of the original thirteen States. We have seen a negro fill the Senatorial chair at Washington left vacant by the chief of the Rebel Confederacy. . . . At length, panoplied in all the rights of citizenship, the negro stands under a Constitution which knows nothing of race, and for the first time in our history we can read without a blush our fathers' sublime declaration that all men are created equal. . . . We may yet live to see the day when a Presidential candidate will boast his share of negro blood. . . . Meanwhile, in his transition, he needs counsel, aid, education, land. Our long crusade for him is not therefore really and fully ended. We may break up our ranks, but we may not yet dismiss our care or lessen our interest. . . ."

Like the Anti-Slavery Society, the American Freedmen's Union prepared to go out of business. The *American Freedman,* the voice of the American Freedmen's Union Commission, ran an editorial in its December, 1868, issue, entitled "The Beginning of the End." The purpose of the union had been to "gather up the tangled skeins of the Freedmen's movement and weave them into a single strand; to incarnate in a national organization that spirit of humanity and enlarged patriotism which had before dwelt only in local Boards . . . and thus, in co-operation . . . to prepare the way more efficiently for the hour when the Southern States, freed from the last shackle of slavery, could establish, by legislative action, those educational institutions for which public charities, however generously provided and wisely administered, are but an imperfect substitute.

"This it has done. It has been a chosen channel of communication between private philanthropy and the Freedmen's Bureaus. Its schoolhouses have been planted in every Southern State. Its pupils are numbered by the thousands, and its constituents by the hundreds of thousands. Its mission is not yet accomplished, but it will be in a definitely short period of time." Peace between the North and South was "morally certain. . . . And that among the first-fruits of this assured 'peace' will be the provision of means for popular education at the South, can hardly be a matter of reasonable question." The salaried officers of the commission had been dismissed in anticipation of this happy day, and the remaining material and human resources of the commission were being expended "mainly on schools for the training of native or colored teachers."

Unquestionably the most dramatic development of 1870 was the emergence of a number of black politicians. Encouraged by the Reconstruction Acts, the passage of the Fifteenth Amendment, and the President's evident intention to support the rights of the freedmen and women, black voters flocked to the polls, and black politicians claimed their share of public offices.

Robert Elliott, chairman of the South Carolina Republican State Convention in 1870, set his sights on a congressional seat. Alonzo Ransier was chosen for the office of lieutenant governor. Three of the four members of the Republican Central Committee were blacks. The convention drew up a platform calling for "equality before the law, free speech, a free press, a free ballot, and free schools" and warmly endorsed President Grant.

When the Mississippi legislature met in January, 1870, the Reverend Hiram Revels was invited to open the Senate with prayer. "That prayer," John Roy Lynch wrote, "one of the most impressive and eloquent prayers that have ever been delivered in the Senate Chamber,— made Revels a United States Senator." The Mississippi House was made up of 107 members, of whom 30 were blacks; the Senate had 33 members, 4 of them black. Hiram Revels was the legislature's choice for the vacant Mississippi seat in the United States Senate, and early in February, 1870, he was sworn in, the first black Senator in the nation's history.

Of Revels's election to the Senate, George Templeton Strong wrote: "The world does move, and the arrogant folly of the Southern swashbucklers and fanatics in 1860 and 1861 gave it a shove such as it had not felt for centuries. . . . O Jeff Davis, ain't this a go? What do you think of the 'genman' who sits in your seat and represents your own—your be-yutiois, your chivalr-r-r-ric—state? To this have all your intriguings and blusterings and proclamations and conscriptions come at last!"

Joseph Rainey of South Carolina had the distinction of being the first black Congressman. He was followed by Robert Elliott, who easily won election in South Carolina's Third Congressional District. Elliott occupied the congressional seat held by Preston Brooks when he attacked Charles Sumner. Soon four more black Congressmen joined Rainey and Elliott: James Rapier from Alabama, John Lynch from

Mississippi, Alonzo Ransier and Richard Cain from South Carolina.

Cain was an imposing figure with sideburns curling along his cheeks and the confident and sonorous tones of a preacher. When, soon after his arrival, a North Carolina Congressman urged that free blacks be encouraged to emigrate, Cain replied, "The gentleman wishes that we go to Africa or to the West Indies or somewhere else. I want to enunciate this doctrine upon this floor. We are not going away. We are going to stay here and work out the problem. We believe that God Almighty has made of one blood all the nations upon the face of the earth. We believe we are made just like white men are. . . . I am clothed with humanity like you. I think, I reason, I talk, I express my views as you do. Is there any difference between us? Not so far as our manhood is concerned, unless it be in this: that our opinions differ and mine are a little higher up than yours." The freed blacks had been accused of laziness, Cain declared, but he had traveled throughout the South and seen who did the work. "Going along, I saw the white men doing the smoking, chewing tobacco, riding horses, playing cards, spending money; while the colored men are tilling the soil and bringing the cotton, rice and other products to market. Sir," Cain concluded, "we are part and parcel of this nation, which has done more than any other on earth to illustrate the great idea that all races of men may dwell together in harmony. We will take that time-honored flag which has been borne through the heat of a thousand battles. Under its folds Anglo-Saxon and Africo-American can together work out a common destiny, until universal liberty, as announced by this nation, shall be known throughout the world."

Robert Elliott recalled his emotions when he rose in Congress to give his maiden speech: "Everything was still. Those who believed in the natural inferiority of the colored race appeared to feel that the hour had arrived in which they should exult in triumph over the failure of the first man of 'the despised race' whose voice was about to be lifted in that chamber. The countenance of those who sympathized with our cause seemed to indicate their anxiety for my success, and their heartfelt desire that I might prove equal to the emergency." Elliott's subject was a bill to extend amnesty to those Southern whites excluded from political activity. Although a number of black leaders in his own state had supported removing such constraints, Elliott was strongly opposed. These same men, he argued, had condoned, if not actively encouraged, the Ku Klux Klan and its allied organizations devoted to intimidating and murdering blacks.

The *New York Tribune* upbraided him for implying that the "midnight riders and raiders in masks . . . are the ex-colonels, ex-legislators and ex-magistrates of the old slave holding regime. . . . If Mr. E. asserted that pears and watermelons are generally stolen by clergymen and deacons fifty to eighty years old, his mistake could not be more obvious." There is ample evidence that Elliott was right.

Each election of a black Congressman was hailed as a triumph by the Radical Republicans and was the occasion for bitter editorials in Democratic papers, North and South. The *Joliet* (Illinois) *Signal* declared: "Five Negroes in Congress! Five kinky-haired, long-heeled, thick-lipped semi-barbarians to sit in the halls of Congress and enact laws to govern thirty millions of intelligent Caucasians!"

The social life of the new black Congressmen was severely limited. A handful of Republican politicians invited their black counterparts to parties and receptions. More commonly, when a prosperous black man gave a party, white Republican Congressmen attended. When George Downing, the black caterer who ran the dining room in the House of Representatives, had a reception in honor of Hiram Revels, the Senator from Mississippi, the white members of the Mississippi delegation attended, along with a number of other Republican politicians. John Forney, publisher of the *Washington Chronicle*, gave a party for President Grant and his Cabinet and invited a number of blacks. The *New Era* speculated that "in the new and better life upon which we have now entered, the color of the skin will cease to be a bar to the recognition of gentlemanly qualities. . . ." The paper noted that Governor R. K. Scott of South Carolina took pains to receive black and white legislators with the same degree of courtesy and attention; "all alike, on such occasions, crowd around his luxurious refreshment tables where . . . no invidious distinctions are made." In Texas, when black members of the legislature were excluded from a "Grand State Ball" held in the legislative chambers, they protested vigorously but to no effect. Washington itself was a segregated city. Important as blacks were to the Republican Party, they were barred from the District's Republican Club. Although District laws forbade discrimination in restaurants, various subterfuges were devised to preserve them as white sanctuaries, such as "membership" or exorbitant food prices for black diners. A new law designated the District as a "territorial government," to be administered by a kind of minilegislature with a presidentially appointed governor and an upper and lower house.

Grant appointed three blacks to the upper house—Frederick Douglass, John Gray, a popular Washington caterer, and Adolphus Hall, a prosperous businessman. John Mercer Langston, head of the Howard University Law School, was appointed counsel to the District Board of Health.

The appearance of a black Senator and black Congressmen in Washington was, to a large degree, misleading. Far from marking an acceptance with white Southerners of black political activity, it served to stimulate ever-stronger resistance. While black legislators entered the front doors of state capitols and enjoyed for the first time the heady experience of political power, they and their black constituents were the objects of an increasingly violent campaign of terrorism.

Some black legislators like Emmanuel Fortune, who served for five years in the Florida legislature, enjoyed a certain immunity because of their reputations as dangerous fighters. Fortune was famous for his prowess with a rifle and pistol. Indeed, his house became, with the threat of the Ku Klux Klan, a fortress, and his wife and children were carefully drilled in how to help defend it. A rifle pit sunk in the floor was Fortune's post. Finally, after numerous narrow escapes Fortune took his family to Jacksonville, where he was elected city marshal five times and also chosen as an alternate delegate to the three Republican national conventions.

James Rapier, Congressman from Alabama, had served as United States commissioner to the Paris World's Fair. In Europe he had been treated with courtesy and respect, but in the United States he was constantly discriminated against. He could not go by train from Washington to Montgomery, he told his fellow Congressmen, without being denied access to a sleeping car and forced to ride "in a dirty, rough box with the drunkards, apple-sellers, railroad hands. . . . If we are compelled to lay over," he declared, ". . . I am turned away from the hotel, hungry and cold, to stand around the railroad station until the departure of the next train. . . . There is not an inn between Washington and Montgomery, a distance of more than a thousand miles, that will accommodate me to a bed or a meal."

Increasingly blacks, North and South, fought back against discrimination. When several New Orleans "men of color" were refused soda water at a confectionery, a large crowd of blacks gathered, whereupon, according to the *New Orleans Tribune*, "The fire alarm bells were rung and firemen with an engine and hose carriage and a large number of citizens soon arrived on the spot. They were armed and seemed well prepared to do work of death and blood. A general beating and knocking down with chairs and even children were not exempt." The black press carried a series of such stories.

Although the legislatures in most Southern states passed laws forbidding discrimination, the laws were widely defied. The South Carolina legislature, with a majority of black members, set a fine of $1,000 and up to three years' imprisonment for any act of racial discrimination. Francis Cardozo was so often refused accommodations in Pullman sleeping cars that he sued the Palace Car Company and won a letter from Mr. Pullman instructing any Pullman conductor to accommodate Cardozo. When he was refused a berth in a sleeping car in Augusta, Georgia (Georgia had no antidiscrimination laws), Cardozo produced Pullman's letter. The conductor told him that he could have a berth but that his traveling companions, who were black, would have to spend the night in the baggage car. Cardozo refused. The conductor asked for the letter, ostensibly in order to show it to his superior. Instead, he confiscated it, and when Cardozo, on a later trip, attempted to gain access to a sleeping car, the conductor barred his way and a gang of young whites closed in with the evident intention of dragging him from the train. Cardozo managed to elude them, but he was convinced that they intended to murder him.

In states with antidiscrimination laws, hotel and restaurant keepers hung out signs declaring that they were no longer public facilities but private homes which accommodated only "selected guests and personal friends."

Streetcars were also strictly segregated in Washington, D.C. Since the District was under the administration of Congress, Charles Sumner brought pressure on the standing Committee on District Affairs to write antidiscrimination clauses into the charter renewals of the streetcar companies. This piecemeal approach was supplemented by a law forbidding discrimination. Sojourner Truth, working in a community of freedmen in Arlington, Virginia, was one of the first to test the new law. Standing on a street corner, she signaled a trolley to stop, but the driver ignored her. Another passed without stopping. "She then gave three tremendous yelps, *I want to ride! I want to ride!! I WANT TO RIDE!!!!*" In the words of a friend accompanying Sojourner, "Consternation seized the passing crowd—people, carriages, go-carts of every description stood still. The car was effectually blocked up, and before it could move on, Sojourner had jumped aboard. Then there arose a great shout from the crowd, 'Hah! Hah! Hah!! She has beaten him,' etc. The angry conductor told her to go foward to where the horses were, or he would put her out. Quietly seating herself, Truth informed him she was a passenger. 'Go forward where the horses are, or I will throw you out,' said he in a menacing voice. She told him that she was neither a Marylander nor a Virginian to fear his threats; but was from the Empire State of New York, and knew the law as well as he did." Sojourner Truth rode the car to the end of the line and left it, saying, "Bless God! I have had a ride."

On another occasion Laura Haviland, a philanthropic white friend of Sojourner Truth's who was working in the same hospital, reported that when she and Sojourner entered a car, a man, "coming out as we were going in, asked the conductor if 'niggers were allowed to ride.'" When the conductor seized Sojourner by the shoulder and tried to expel her from the car, Laura Haviland took her other arm and said, "Don't put her out." The conductor asked if Sojourner "belonged" to Haviland. "No. She belongs to humanity," Haviland answered. "Then take her and go," the conductor replied, slamming Sojourner Truth against the door. Sojourner thereupon declared that she would not be treated like a dog and asked Mrs. Haviland to take the number of the car so that she could report the conductor to the police. The conductor backed down immediately, but when Sojourner reached the hospital and her arm was examined, it was found to have been wrenched from the socket. The Freedmen's Bureau furnished her with a lawyer. She sued the streetcar company, and the conductor was fired. The case "created a great sensation," Sojourner recalled, "and before the trial was ended, the inside of the cars looked like pepper and salt. . . . Now they who had so lately cursed me for wanting to ride, could stop for black as well as white, and could even condescend to say, 'Walk in, ladies.'"

By 1870 it was clear that Congressional Reconstruction would not work without the liberal application of Federal "force" to police the polls and at least to diminish the acts of violence and intimidation directed against blacks and Unionists. Moreover, the practical men— men like Blaine, Conkling, and Garfield—began to replace the older idealists of the Republican Party—the Sumners, Davises, and Stevenses. These men had little concern with the subtleties of constitutional theory. They were ready to use any means at hand to build up and sustain their party in the South. While they were not without concern for the rights of blacks, they were often disposed to use that concern as a cloak for strengthening their political hold on office. Above all, they were far more politically oriented and astute than their fellow Republicans. The Force Acts of 1870, 1871, and 1872 had as their purpose the Federal supervision of elections and election returns. Their passage was the consequence of the determination of Republican leaders that they should not be robbed of the political fruits of Reconstruction by elections controlled by fraud and violence. They marked another step in an escalating war between the Republican Congress and an unrepentent South. For every Northern move, the South had a riposte. Each force bill was met by a new Southern evasion or a new strategy designed to nullify the effects of the Reconstruction Acts. To each evasion the North replied with a new Force Act to plug a new loophole.

Each new application of "force" brought new defections from Radical Republican ranks. Far from experiencing the change of heart, the acceptance of the plain fact of Reconstruction that the Republicans constantly anticipated, the South seemed to grow more obdurate with each passing year. The question of how much strain the Constitution could bear was by no means a frivolous question. It was one thing to stretch it to its limits as an emergency measure, suppressing misgivings. It was another to do it year after year in the face of a series of emergencies that seemed to have no end in sight. With the Force Act of 1870 Carl Schurz signaled his defection from the ranks of Republican orthodoxy by a speech in the Senate in which he announced to his "party friends" that he felt the time had come "to bridle that tendency which we have so frequently had occasion to observe, to thrust the hand of the National Government into local affairs on every possible occasion and even to disregard and throw aside the most fundamental safeguards of popular rights for the correction of passing abuses." He declared himself "for State-rights as the embodiment of true and general self-government, and I am convinced," he added, "that this is the prevailing sentiment among the American people." The "exigencies of the civil war" had, "quite naturally, developed a tendency to accumulate and centralize power in the hands of the National Government," but the time had come when the tide must be reversed if the government were not to grow into an oppressive tyranny. He denied that the Constitution could be so construed as to permit Congress "to use the arm of the National authority for the purpose of realizing by force what conception each of us may entertain of the 'ideal republic.' " The party which attempted to carry such a revolution "much farther in the direction of an undue centralization of power," he warned, "would run against a popular instinct far stronger than party allegiance has ever proved to be."

Certainly Schurz, in his zeal to defend the Constitution, somewhat misstated the case. There is, after all, a considerable difference between protecting the rights of all citizens and undertaking by force to establish an "ideal republic." But he was doubtless right in his judgment of the temper of the country. And for a certainty, his speech marked the growing tensions within his party. To a modern reader who has lived through the era when a conservative Republican president of the United States has employed Federal authority to gain admission of black children to segregated white schools, the Force Acts will appear far less of a threat to republican government than would a demonstrable unwillingness to use the powers of government to insure justice for all citizens. But even if we concede, as this writer is certainly willing to do, the necessity of the Force Acts, the fact appears to be that nothing, in the long run, could have swayed white Southerners from their determination to put down blacks. The real question is not whether or not the Force Acts were justified in constitutional, legal, moral, or ethical terms, but whether or not there was, in the American people, and primarily in the people of the North, a determination to persist, come what might, in protecting the civil rights of Southern blacks. On that point the record appears unequivocal. Such a determination simply did not exist. Full justice could not be secured for black Americans in the Northern states.

Even the faithful began to entertain doubts. As the freedman gave increasing evidence of his determination to remain intractably black instead of becoming obediently "white," an increasing note of irritation and, indeed, disenchantment appeared in Northern Protestant journals. In 1869 the *Independent* printed a report from a clergyman who had toured the South: "If the colored people of the South are doomed to an inferior position, by their ignorance or their vices; they and their votes will be controlled by the more cultivated and competent whites; and no plans of reconstruction, no legislation at Washington, can permanently prevent this. In the long run, capacity is sure to secure position and power."

Whitelaw Reid, managing editor of the *New York Tribune* and one of the most influential men in the United States, wrote an editorial criticizing those Northerners who "have gone in too many instances into Virginia as into a conquered province, seeing no good in any but blacks, and burning to avenge the old wrongs of the negro by their actions and words. . . ." While this spirit should be honored, it was important to remember, Reid declared, "that there was something inherently good and worth saving in that much laughed at chivalry," that was "the grand old name of gentleman." When Thomas Wentworth Higginson read those words in his morning paper, he exploded. "That even the war should not have ended that miserable myth of Southern chivalry 'pure domestic morality' (faugh!), and all the distinction of 'high-toned gentleman!' " he wrote Reid. The latter, not a whit disconcerted by his friend's attack, replied, "I repudiate and abhor the doctrine that a minority composed of negroes and disreputable carpet baggers can permanently and safely govern a large majority in any American state," which had not been precisely Higginson's point.

When Thomas Wentworth Higginson's vivid account of his wartime experiences was published in 1870, it was as though it belonged to another era. William Dean Howells, who had already made himself something of an arbiter of the literary scene, praised it in the *Atlantic* because it was not "a celebration of the negro in any of his familiar aspects of martyr or hero, or present 'transitional state' of bore," but an "excellent and charming work of literature." That perhaps said it all—from passionate commitment to "charming literature." The problems, the needs, the despair of American blacks had passed from being the most critical moral issue facing the nation to the " 'transitional state' of bore."

46

William Marcy Tweed

While corruption was endemic in the post-Civil War period, it reached its most spectacular heights in New York City, already well acquainted with municipal skulduggery. It was hard to argue with George Templeton Strong's characterization of New York as "the most profligate city government in Christendom."

That thievery was not confined to New York is evident from Sidney George Fisher's comment on Philadelphia. "Our city government," Fisher wrote in 1867, "is utterly corrupt in all its departments and as a consequence the city is shamefully misgoverned, altho taxes are enormous and constantly increasing. The streets are dirty, ill-lighted and wretchedly paved, the police is so inefficient that there are two or three burglaries every night. . . . The prosecuting attorney is known to take fees from prisoners to screen them from justice, and the city councils are gangs of thieves."

Private defalcations rivaled public ones. The cashier of the Atlantic Bank in New York turned out to have embezzled securities worth $162,000. The president of the Brooklyn Trust, "prominent and public-spirited," a favorite law student of George Templeton Strong's father, had been similarly occupied and eventually committed suicide. His death led Strong to reflect on the misplaced emphasis in America on wealth and the competitive urge to get ahead. Every young man "hopes to win some prize in that great gambling house [of Wall Street]. . . . And so they grow up to be mere illiterate sharpers, with possible fine houses and fine horses and fine Newport cottages and without capacity to appreciate anything higher—men without culture and with damaged and dwarfed moral sense."

In the Bowery gamblers invaded the streets, working from portable tables with shell games and three-card monte. So-called concert saloons featured music and accommodating prostitutes, who put knockout drops in their patrons' drinks and robbed them. "Panel rooms" were brothels or seedy hotels where a whore's accomplice could come through a panel in the door to rob her john. The dram shop dispensed cheap liquor. A newspaper reporter wrote: "The money kings and the palaces of Broadway are worth visiting but to get an idea of the people who rule the metropolis, one must go down among the tenements and the drinking saloons of the whiskey wards. . . . The concert saloons were brilliantly lighted, and the girls were dressed in holiday attire, hoping thereby to entice many curious countrymen in their music dens. The 3,000 bar-rooms did a wonderful business, and a constant stream of ghastly forms shuffled through the doorway. . . . Every conceivable kind of merchandise was offered for sale on the sidewalks. . . . The gutters were occupied by dealers in old clothes. . . . In a corner sat an old woman grating horse-radish. . . . An endless procession of young ladies poured into the Bowery sweeping up and down the broad pavements." Pimps, dressed in flashy clothes and smoking expensive cigars, were called Bowery statues.

The police were in league with the criminals. The Fifth Precinct police connived with female pickpockets and split their takings. They shook down the numerous prostitutes, while corrupt judges took bribes to free thieves and robbers with political connections. In 1870 alone, seventeen thousand sailors were robbed, many of them from foreign ships tied up at New York docks. A judge before whom a captain brought a gaggle of prostitutes accused the officer of arresting the women for blackmail purposes and told him: "Break up the panel houses and gambling hells which abound in your precinct, and then look for these poor creatures. There are a number of panel houses of the worst kind in your precinct—this from my own knowledge. I dismiss these women."

Brothels ranged from the most luxurious to the most sordid. The ones on Broadway had such names as Dew Drop Inn, Assembly,

Canterbury, Oriental. Harry Hill's concert saloon was the most famous hangout on Broadway. Frequented by pickpockets, pimps, prostitutes, pugilists, and politicians, it featured a lewd Punch and Judy show, scantily clad waitress-prostitutes, and a "Virginia reel" in the course of which the women dancers removed most of their clothes.

Thousands of marginal poor were ragpickers who made their living picking through trash piles and dumps scattered about the city. The mark of their trade was a voluminous burlap bag into which they stuffed rags and paper with rag content to be reprocessed for more paper; as well as bones, scraps of metal, and any other items that could be sold to a junk dealer or utilized in some fashion. The ragpickers were seldom derelicts or chronic drunkards; more often they were men with families who lived in one of the half dozen or so shantytowns scattered about the city. They constituted a kind of fraternity of small-business men and women. Adjacent to the shanties were often garden plots with goats and chickens and, more rarely, pigs. In the upper Seventies in the 1870s the goats were such a hazard that the City Council passed a law banishing them, which read: "No goat shall be at large in any part of the streets, avenues, lanes, alleys, piers, wharves or public places in the City of New York under penalty of $3 for each such goat which shall be found at large. . . ." The abodes of the ragpickers were commonly known as Bone Alley or Ragpickers Row.

The census of 1870 reported the population of New York to be 942,292, of whom 419,094 were immigrants, 44 percent of the residents of the city. Fifty-five percent of the population lived in the city's slums. We have already taken note, on a number of occasions, of the splits between the different ethnic groups that made up the majority of the working class and the paupers—men and women most of whom today would be called unemployables: children, old people, the ill and crippled, chronic alcoholics, the insane, and hardened criminals.

The man who, more than anyone else, presided over this scene and whose imaginative defalcations insured him the attention of posterity was William Marcy Tweed. Tweed was born in 1823, the son of a furniture maker. He became an apprentice in the trade and helped organize the Americus, or Big Six, volunteer fire engine company, of which he was elected foreman. The post was an ideal springboard for Tweed into a series of public offices—alderman, Congressman, supervisor, school commissioner, deputy street commissioner, and state senator. Soon he had the city and then the state firmly in his grasp. His instrument was Tammany Hall and the Irish voters of the city, who dutifully performed the political chores assigned them by their chief. Abraham Oakey Hall, the mayor of the city, was Tweed's pliant tool, and his fellow conspirators included the city Board of Supervisors and most of the members of the state legislature.

The base was thus political. At elections, Tweed's strong-arm boys voted repeatedly under false names. John Morrissey, a professional gambler, an ex-prizefighter, a convicted burglar with a record of assault and battery and at least one murder charge against him, was one of Tweed's most trusted lieutenants. By 1870 Morrissey had a controlling interest in the Saratoga racetrack and ran several gambling houses decorated in the most lavish fashion imaginable, with every furnishing bearing Morrissey's monogram or a Tammany Hall tiger head. Morrissey was commonly in command on election day of the "repeaters," as well as of the "shoulder-hitters," thugs whose job it was to keep Republican voters away from the polls.

In one election Morrissey and his boys voted in the names of nine hundred blacks. When some of the blacks appeared and protested, they were arrested for trying to vote twice. A typical incident took place in the municipal elections of 1871. When a Republican poll watcher named Michael Costello objected to a repeater's voting and asked the police to arrest him, the Tammany election inspector gave the sign to four shoulder-hitters, who knocked Costello down and beat him badly. The police then arrested him for assaulting an officer.

In the New York elections of 1868 Samuel Tilden, at Tweed's behest, sent telegrams to the Democratic chiefs all over the state instructing them to wire Tweed as soon as they knew the tallies for governor in their districts; Tweed would thereby know how many votes to add to the New York City total in order to assure that his candidate, John Hoffman, would be elected governor. Horace Greeley charged Tilden: "Your name was used, without public protest on your part, in circulars sowed broadcast over the state, whereof the intent was to 'make assurance doubly sure' that the frauds here perpetrated should not be overborne by the honest vote of the rural districts. And you, not merely by silence, but by positive assumption, have covered these frauds with the mantle of your respectability. . . . you are as deeply implicated in them as though your name were Tweed, O'Brien, or Oakey Hall."

There was a kind of irresistible rascality about Tweed. At the height of his robberies, when he was state senator and president of the Board of Supervisors, he promised the voters that the board would "watch carefully over the financial interests of the county, and reduce the rate of taxation until this city became the most lightly taxed of any large city in the Union." Then he and Oakey Hall and city comptroller Richard B. Connolly approved bills of $6,312,500 for the new city hall, of which it was estimated later that $5,500,000 was padding in the form of kickbacks from contractors. A plasterer was paid $138,187 for two days' work, and a total of $2,870,464.06 for the balance of his laborers. One carpenter was ostensibly paid $360,747.61 for a month's labor.

The municipal judges, already notorious for their corruption, were an integral part of the Tweed machine. Any crook brought to court by some mischance could, in payment of an appropriate bribe, secure his freedom.

New Yorkers had always tolerated a fairly high level of municipal corruption. The respectable merchants and financiers of the city, as well as less savory figures like August Belmont, were accustomed to doing business with bosses. Indeed, George Templeton Strong wrote, the "Boss of New York" might in time "grow into permanence and figure in history like the doge of Venice." Tweed himself put the matter succinctly. "This population," he said, "is too hopelessly split up into races and factions to govern it under universal suffrage, except by the bribery of patronage, or corruption." Of such was the kingdom of Tweed.

By 1870 Tweed was reputed to be worth $12,000,000, all of it made at the public expense. Tweed's most daring plan was to push through a revised city charter, full of "jokers"—clauses designed to make it easier for him and his accomplices, primarily the mayor, Oakey Hall, and the comptroller, Slippery Dick Connolly, to line their pockets. One joker constituted the three men as a board of auditors to approve all city disbursements. Tweed secured the endorsement for the charter revision from the Citizen's Association, a group of leading businessmen, bankers, and philanthropists, including the now-venerable Peter Cooper, pioneer railroader and backer of the transatlantic cable. Then Tweed spent $600,000 to bribe the members of the state legislature. Five Republican state senators received $40,000 apiece; others accepted much more modest sums. According to Tweed, he bribed every legislator except two. One of the unbribed was Henry Genêt, the grandson of Citizen Genêt whose activities on behalf of the French Directorate had so infuriated Washington. Genêt, who was a plunderer in his own right, had been a henchman of Tweed's but was now in exile. Without Tweed's support (and doubtless at Tweed's behest) he found himself in jail for defrauding the city.

Under such circumstances, it was not surprising that Tweed thought he had covered all bases. He owned the mayor of New York City and all the principal appointed officials and most of those elected, the police force, the governor, and most of the newspapers. The majority of the city's journals received graft in the form of payment for official "notices," which were frequent and lengthy and often penned by Tweed on the subject of municipal reform. William Cullen Bryant's reforming *Evening Post* received $5,000 a month, and in a period of eighteen months $2,703,308.48 were paid out to newspapers in the form of advertising. The consequence was that most newspaper editors looked the other way.

When Charles Nordhoff, managing editor of the *Post*, took an anti-Tweed stand, Tweed insisted that he be fired. Even the supposedly incorruptible *Times* praised Tweed for his "reforms." "Senator Tweed is in a fair way to distinguish himself as a reformer," the paper declared, apparently without its tongue in its cheek. "Having gone so far as to champion . . . the charter, he seems to have no idea of turning back . . . he has put the people of Manhattan Island under great obligation." One of the directors of the *Times* was James B. Taylor, a partner of Tweed's in a printing company.

In addition to Tweed's Ring, there was a Brooklyn Ring which, when it was threatened with exposure by the *Brooklyn Eagle* (the paper of which Whitman had been for a time an editor), simply bought the *Eagle* and silenced it.

Tweed's most spectacular accomplice and sidekick was Jim Fisk. Fisk had started life as a peddler with his father, advancing to waiter in a tavern and then to a circus barker. Combining circus bravura with merchandising skill, he converted his father's drab van into a brightly decorated wagon equipped like a general store and soon had franchised several such vehicles. Arriving in New York in 1863, he literally took the town by storm. It was as though the city had been simply waiting for a smart and unscrupulous country boy to hit the big town. In his involvement with Tweed and Jay Gould, the banker and financier, Fisk's gift for high-level skulduggery proved irresistible. It was largely through his conniving that Gould was able to steal the Erie Railroad. Money rolled in, and Fisk showed a specular talent for spending it. He was reputed to have seven mistresses, the most notorious of whom was Josie Mansfield, who presided over what a historian of the period has called her "brothel-home," frequented by Tweed, Gould, and a host of politicos for whom she provided compliant young ladies.

Josie's handsome mansion was a block from Fisk's, and his in turn was adjacent to the Grand Opera House, which he bought for $820,000. German, Italian, and French opera and ballet troupes were imported to perform in it, and the young ladies of the companies often found that they were supposed to provide other services.

Perhaps the most incongruous ally of Fisk's was Daniel Drew, as notorious for his piety as Fisk was for his libertinism (one of his benefactions started the Drew Theological Seminary). When a minion of Drew's approached, by accident, an incorruptible state legislator with the offer of a modest $500 bribe, the outraged politician, who certainly deserves to be known to history—E. McKinney Glenn of Wayne County—tried to blow the whistle on the directors of the Erie Railroad. It turned out no one was listening. Glenn resigned and was re-elected. The episode was noteworthy for its rarity; as it turned out, it presaged the downfall of the ring.

Even George Templeton Strong had to confess to a kind of grudging admiration for Jim Fisk's splendid vulgarity. On New Year's Day, 1871, Fisk "made calls in a gorgeous chariot drawn by four high-stepping horses, with four smart footmen in flamboyant liveries. When he stopped before a favored house, his mamelukes descended, unrolled a carpet, laid it from the carriage steps to the door, and stood on either side in an attitude of military salute, while their august master passed by. It is a queer world," Strong added, "and this is a 'devilishly lively' community."

Edward S. Stokes was a wealthy New York playboy and sometime ally of Fisk's, who stole the affections of Josie Mansfield. Fisk in retaliation began to apply the heat to various enterprises of Stokes's. He had Stokes arrested on the charge of embezzling funds from an oil refinery in which both men had invested. These charges were dismissed, and Fisk was charged with and convicted of malicious prosecution. Josie Mansfield now entered the picture with a suit against Fisk for money which, she said, he owed her. Fisk replied with a perjured affidavit from a former butler charging Josie with improper sexual relations with him. Josie brought a charge of criminal libel, and Fisk appeared in court in a purple admiral's jacket with gold buttons. During an adjournment of the trial Stokes waited for Fisk at the Grand

Central Hotel, and as Fisk started up the stairs, Stokes shot twice, fatally wounding him. He died several days later, "amid the sobbings of Tweed, David Dudley Field, Jay Gould," and his doctor, Strong noted, adding that Fisk was "no loss to the community," an "opera impresario, 'commodore,' financier, roué, mountebank, corrupt to the core, with great facility of corrupting others, judges included. . . . Illiterate, vulgar, unprincipled, profligate . . . he was nevertheless freehanded with his stolen money, and possessed, moreover, a certain magnetism of geniality. . . . We are living in an age of ruffianism and of almost universal corruption," Strong added. "Life and property are as insecure here in New York as in Mexico. It is a thoroughly rotten community."

As Fisk's body in a colonel's uniform lay in his opera house, Stokes was arrested and charged with his murder. He was convicted and ordered to be hanged. On appeal the charge was changed to manslaughter in the third degree. Stokes was sentenced to four years in Sing Sing, but he was allowed to keep a coach and a pair of horses and go for rides through the countryside at night.

The most sensational social event of the spring of 1871 was the marriage of Tweed's daughter, Mary Amelia, to the heir of a distinguished Southern family. The press fastened on the wedding with an avidity willingly fed by Tweed, who gave them a list of his daughter's wedding presents. Judge George G. Barnard gave a gold, pearl, and diamond necklace valued at $1,000, and Tweed's state legislators and cronies competed with one another in the lavishness of their gifts. In all this ostentatious display, Jay Gould attracted attention by the tastefulness and modesty of his present, a set of silver, valued at only $250. The total value of the gifts was calculated by the thoughtful father of the bride at more than $700,000.

It may well be that in a nation somewhat inclined to conspicuous consumption and display, the wedding of Tweed's daughter set a standard never to be equaled. It challenged the wildest days of Nero's Rome or the extravagance of the Borgias and added an element of mind-boggling democratic vulgarity, unrivaled in any epoch of history.

Tweed now became the victim of a conjunction of odd circumstances. James Taylor, a director of the *Times* and a partner of Tweed's, died. The *Times* hired a relentless journalistic sleuth, an Englishman named Louis John Jennings, who made Tweed and his ring the special object of his attentions.

When the Democratic State Convention met in Rochester, it drew a swarm of thieves, pickpockets, prostitutes, and Tammany thugs. Tweed's man, John Hoffman, was nominated with Tilden presiding over the convention. Tilden had his watch stolen, and so many of the delegates were robbed—their losses totaled more than $15,000 —that they were advised to leave their hotel rooms and return to New York on the night train to avoid further exactions. The thieves took the train, too, robbed some of the passengers, and, when others left the train at waystations, left, too, and stripped their victims of watches, jewelry, wallets, and, in one instance, a woman's shawl. Word of the robberies was telegraphed ahead, and when the train reached Jersey City, it was met by police, who rounded up thirty-five suspects, most of them armed. One of the alleged robbers was Alexander Frear, a member of the State Assembly and commissioner of charities and corrections in New York City.

As election day approached, Senator Roscoe Conkling prevailed on Grant to order the 8th Infantry and two warships to New York, the infantry to help keep order and police the polling places to prevent intimidation and the warships presumably to underscore the President's strong personal interest in the outcome. Tweed, in response, called on his legions to keep order. "We know and feel," he declared piously, "that although an aggressive hand is upon us, yet we must, by a judicial exercise of law and order . . . show that New York is a law-abiding, and, as the world knows, a well-governed city." In a preelection rally August Belmont took his place on the platform beside Tweed and declared to an enthusiastic audience, "Never before have we been called up to vote for a ticket which commands so strongly our hearty and affectionate approval."

Tweed countered the growing charges of corruption by appointing a committee of leading financiers to make an investigation. John Jacob Astor was the chairman, and the committee included several of the richest men in the United States, among these Moses Taylor, who was president of City Bank, the owner of a fleet of merchant ships and a number of coal and iron mines. Edward Schell was one of the city's leading bankers. A few days before the election this blue-ribbon committee solemnly reported that, having examined the city's books, they were ready to "certify that the financial affairs of the city under the charge of the Comptroller are administered in a correct and faithful manner." The tycoons were either astonishingly naïve or in bed with Tweed. The result was to save the election for the Democrats.

"Gangs of repeaters paraded the streets," George Templeton Strong noted, "working openly and unchallenged. The echoes of Albany and Tammany roll from poll to poll and cheat for ever and ever."

Tweed's real nemesis was the brilliant young reformer-cartoonist Thomas Nast. The Boss was a cartoonist's dream. The oval face, sloping brows, deep-set eyes, bald head were, in their natural state, a cartoon representation of a shifty politician. Tweed's clothes hung so loosely on his corpulent body that he looked rather as though he had been inflated and then partially deflated. Oakey Hall, the slim, dandified mayor whose elegant pince-nez and dashingly tailored suits were a byword, was the perfect visual foil for Tweed.

Even at the time of his daughter's wedding Tweed's empire of corruption was beginning to become unraveled. Matthew O'Rourke, a would-be journalist, had wriggled his way into a job as county bookkeeper, and there he had made careful records of misspent funds, $2,500,000 in the space of a little more than two years. When O'Rourke tried to sell his material to several newspapers, he discovered he had a rival, Sheriff James O'Brien, Tweed's onetime beneficiary, who had procured records of his own from the comptroller's office and was also trying to find an outlet. The *Times* finally picked up the material and on July 8 began publishing an account of the ring's defalcations. Slippery Dick Connolly was apparently authorized by Tweed to offer Jones $5,000,000 to suppress the stories. His reaction smelled of panic. But even with the newspaper's revelations, it was not clear how Tweed and his allies were to be brought down. Frustrated New Yorkers began to talk of vigilance committees and lynching parties since the courts, thoroughly corrupt, seemed unwilling to act. Even the usually restrained *Nation* suggested that only the threat of "violent death" could persuade the pillagers to cease their pillaging. The ranks of the reformers were augmented by politicians and business leaders who had been afraid to speak out earlier for fear of punitive action by Tweed, whose bullies were notorious for beating and maiming critics of their leader. The anti-Tweed forces formed the so-called Committee of Seventy. William Havemeyer, a respected lawyer, and Charles O'Conor, an aged civic leader and also one of the most respected men in the state, joined the ranks. Congressman Robert Barnwell Roosevelt declared, "An aroused and outraged public is not patient," and suggested that force should be met with force, a doctrine that appealed to his young nephew Theodore. The reformers, by threats and intimidation, finally secured an injunction from

Judge Barnard preventing Tweed or any of his allies from raising or spending any public funds. In Tweed's words, "in the straitened condition of our credit, which was extended on every side, it broke us. You see our patronage had become so enormous and so costly that the injunction, which might not have troubled us at any other time, destroyed all our power to raise money from the banks or elsewhere, and left us strapped." Tweed later confessed that in the crisis he had thought of killing Jones or Jennings or committing suicide.

In the midst of this deteriorating situation, the state party conventions were held to nominate individuals for state offices and to lay the groundwork for the coming presidential election of 1872. The party which established control over the state would be in an excellent position to throw its weight behind its party's presidential candidate the next summer. The Republican convention was dominated by Conkling, who used Andrew White, the respected president of Cornell University, to block the reform-minded Greeley-Reid-Curtis forces and retain control of the party for the Grant regulars.

Tweed made one final effort to check the deluge at the Democratic State Convention, meeting once again in Rochester. This time Tilden, now a leader of the reformers, was the dominant figure. He delivered the opening address, attacking Grant for condoning corruption. "I do not wish to speak harshly of the illustrious soldier who fills the presidential chair," he declared. "He may not have been conscious of the fatal example he has set. But when the two ideas of personal gain and the bestowal of public office are allowed to become one . . . it is but a step to the sale of the greatest of trusts. Intellect, training, virtue, will soon succumb to wealth."

Meanwhile, a civil suit was filed against Tweed on an affidavit sworn to by Tilden. Tweed was arrested and freed on $1,000,000 bail posted by Jay Gould and others. Hall was arrested along with Tweed and then Connolly. Connolly jumped bail and made his way to Paris with an estimated $6,000,000. He bought a house in Paris and a château on Lake Geneva, and his daughter married a French count.

Tweed's first trial in 1873 resulted in a hung jury. His second trial resulted in conviction on fifty-one of fifty-five charges, and he was sentenced to twelve years in jail and a fine of $12,750. After a little more than a year on Blackwells Island the court of appeals reduced his sentence and set him free. A new suit for $6,000,000 was immediately filed against him, with bail set at $3,000,000, and he was put in the Ludlow Street jail. He escaped the loose surveillance of his jailers in

November, 1876, and fled to Spain. In Spain he was recognized, it was said, from Thomas Nast's cartoons, arrested, and, probably illegally, turned over to the captain of the USS *Franklin*. Back in New York, Tweed tried to plea-bargain, hoping to win freedom by telling all, implicating those involved with him. There were, as it turned out, far too many politicians fearful of being exposed who were determined to do everything possible to keep Tweed quiet. Proceedings were thus stalled until Tweed's death in prison in April, 1878, at the age of fifty-five.

Estimates of the loot siphoned off by Tweed and his accomplices have run as high as $200,000,000, with much more than $100,000,000 unaccounted for—a sum, allowing, as we say, for inflation, which would be well in excess of $1,000,000,000 in today's currency. As a jurist in one of Tweed's trials said, "The worst feature of it all . . . is that, notwithstanding all these crimes have been so clearly proven that no man can doubt their existence, nevertheless, the whole body of these conspirators against the city and its treasury go substantially unwhipped of justice."

Democracy, it turned out, not only could win a prolonged and bloody war and span a continent with a railroad and an ocean with a telegraph cable but could astound the world with corruption on an unprecedented scale. There was, indeed, a kind of breathtaking daring, one is tempted to say, a magnificence, about Tweed's undertakings. Not content to siphon off hundreds of thousands of dollars (millions by today's standards), Tweed and his accomplices went on to extract millions upon millions. Beginning by levying 15 or 20 percent on all municipal expenditures, they raised the ante to 30, 40, 50 percent. They became addicts, not so much of money, of which they soon had more than they had any hope of ever living to spend, as of thievery. It was the stealing, not the sordid rewards, they found irresistible. A country as great as the United States, a city as great as New York demanded thievery on a scale commensurate with its own grand dimensions—geographical, moral, political. To own a legislature, the legislature, in fact, of the nation's richest and most conspicuous state; to own judges and newspapers; to be able to buy up the country, even to put John Hoffman in the White House were clearly an intoxicating prospect!

William Marcy Tweed was the Rembrandt of municipal corruption, the Michelangelo of bribery. The richest, most powerful, most socially sanctified men in the nation bowed their necks to Tweed's large flat foot. Plainly Boss Tweed had qualities not revealed in any of the vast accumulation of "facts" about his remarkable operations; he had a gambler's daring, a range of imagination breathtaking in its boldness. For a time it seemed that he might corrupt the whole of the United States. It was, after all, only a step from the legislature of the state to that of nation. With enough money anything and anyone could be bought, or so it must have seemed to Tweed. Anyone, it turned out, but the dogged Jennings and persistent Nast.

Although the newspapers concentrated their fire on Hall, Connolly, Hoffman, and others who had been most flagrant in their thefts, it was apparent that many gentlemen and respectable Wall Street figures were, at least marginally, involved. The New York Yacht Club was an upper-class bastion where men like the Astors and William Blodgett exchanged drinks and courtesies and business dealings with Tweed and Hall, who, incidentally, was also a member of the exclusive Union Club. When Tweed and Hall began exchanging accusations, Strong noted: "skunk vs. rattlesnake." The hopes of men like Strong, who had suffered under a succession of corrupt Democratic regimes, were tempered by the consciousness that past municipal reforms had been short-lived. "We may succeed in breaking this Ring," Strong wrote, "but another will soon be riveted round our necks. A sordid and depraved community cannot govern itself without corruption. Cutting out a cancer . . . does not *cure* a patient whose blood is thoroughly poisoned. . . . When we the people learn (among other things) to consider wealth basely acquired and ignobly enjoyed a reproach and not a glory, we shall have a right to hope for honest rulers." Perhaps, as Strong suggested, corruption was the price cities like New York, Philadelphia, and Boston had to pay *for functioning at all*. Cities had grown so large and unwieldy, were made up of such concatenated elements, so severely split among class, economic, and national-racial lines as to be almost unmanageable. Clearly graft helped keep the wheels of the huge, cumbersome machines creaking along. Historians in recent years have emphasized the degree to which the corrupt political machines in large cities served the particular needs of immigrants and the poor. Seen in this light, graft was a kind of surtax imposed on the municipality to provide those services which the city government, had it been run with impeccable honesty, was not able, or intended, to provide.

47

The Klan

Though the plight of the freedmen and women of the South might have become "a bore" to William Dean Howells, it was a bitter reality to Southern blacks. In virtually every part of the South beyond the immediate reach of Federal troops, the lives of blacks who engaged in political activity, who tried to own property or start a business, or who in any way drew the unfavorable attention of whites were in continual danger.

The Reconstruction Acts had banned all military organizations except militia units, which in most Southern states were made up of blacks. To get around this prohibition, militant whites joined the volunteer fire companies, making them into quasi-military organizations that were increasingly used to intimidate black people. We have taken note of the terrorist tactics practiced by Southern whites on free blacks after the war. The Joint Committee on Reconstruction had compiled a horrendous list of such acts. Gradually they passed from random incidents of violence or repression to organized atrocities. Rifle clubs were added to volunteer fire companies. Intimidators were called bulldozers and cowboys. At Pulaski, Tennessee in December 1865, a group known as the Ku Klux Klan was founded. It was distinguished from its lesser-known rivals by an elaborate ritual and an extensive, political organization. The South Carolina counterpart was known as the Red Shirts. The latter group informed its members that "every Democrat must feel honor bound to control the vote of at least one Negro, by intimidation, purchase, keeping him away. . . . In speeches to Negroes you must remember that they can only be influenced by their fears, superstitions and cupidity. Treat them so as to show them you are the superior race and that their natural position is that of subordination to the white man. Never threaten a man individually. If he deserves to be threatened, the necessities of the times require that he should die. . . . Every club must be uniformed in a red shirt and they must be sure to wear it upon all public meetings and particularly on the day of election."

Elizabeth Meriwether, who had wholeheartedly joined with her husband in giving away much of the family fortune by freeing the slaves they had inherited and providing for them to be carried to Liberia, whose third child had been delivered by a black mammy and nursed by her black maid, exulted in the formation of the Ku Klux Klan. For a time, she wrote, white Southerners "felt powerless, in the face of over-whelming military forces, to prevent the carpet baggers from using the negroes as tools with which to exploit the South to the point of utter ruin and desolation . . . Under the evil counsel of the carpet baggers, the ignorant negroes became intolerably insolent and overbearing." In such circumstances, Elizabeth Meriwether wrote years later, "life in the South became one long nightmare; then a miracle happened—for surely the way the South escaped from that frightful nightmare was little short of miraculous." The miracle was the Ku Klux Klan, which ended the black "orgy of misrule and oppression" and "saved the South from such a devastation as no country has seen since the Duke of Alva laid waste the lowlands of Holland!" Elizabeth Meriwether's husband, Minor, who had freed his personal servant, Henry, after giving freedom to his plantation hands, and been so faithfully served by Henry during the war, was the principal aide to General Bedford Forrest in founding the Tennessee chapter of the Klan.

Attired in bed sheets, their horses' hooves padded, the silent Klan night riders played upon the superstitious fears of blacks by creating the illusion that they were the spirits of dead Confederate soldiers. It is doubtless true that the Klan began, in the minds of many of its more respectable members, as an effort to frighten bolder blacks into subordination and "obedience." But others undoubtedly had darker intentions from the first, and those blacks who saw readily through the mummery and refused to be "scared" were soon whipped or murdered. There followed a terrible and bitter struggle in which the Federal forces of occupation were initially powerless. The Klan boasted of being a secret order, an "Invisible Empire," and in large measure it was, although when Congress passed legislation outlawing the Klan, it proved possible to root it out in short order.

Elizabeth Meriwether disclosed, quite unselfconsciously, the real aims of the Klan. Protecting Southern womanhood proved a remarkably extensive undertaking. "The 'rebel' whites," she wrote, "were accused of 'intimidating' the loyal negroes from the polls, 'intimidating' them from sitting by white women in street cars, 'intimidating' them from elbowing white men off the sidewalks into the streets, etc." These were the unsufferable, unspeakable acts of black effrontery that whites were determined to extirpate. "The negroes who did any of these things, took seats by white women, went to the polls on election day to vote or shoved white men off the sidewalks . . . were not 'intimidated' at the time they committed the forbidden act"; they were protected by Union soldiers. "But negroes soon noted," Meriwether wrote, "that the Ku Klux ghosts paid visits only to such of their race as committed the forbidden acts; in extreme cases those ghostly visitors held ghostly trials at midnight in the depths of some dark forest and executed negroes by shooting or hanging before any of the million blue coated soldiers could interfere."

It seems not to have occurred to Elizabeth Meriwether that all legal and constitutional issues left aside, the "forbidden acts" she enumerated were hardly in the nature of capital offenses. Many of the "extreme cases" were blacks who refused to grovel and plead for their lives.

A black Mississippi state senator and former slave named Robert Gleeds described the Klan as having two objectives: "One was political, and the other was to hold the black man in subjection to the white man and to have white supremacy in the South. A paper published in Alabama said in plain words, 'We must kill or drive away leading Negroes and only let the humble and submissive remain.'" Assassinations of black leaders became more and more frequent. In 1868, not long after his participation in the state constitutional convention, Benjamin Randolph, chairman of the Executive Committee of the Republican Party of South Carolina, was shot in broad daylight. Armed whites visited the home of Thomas Jones of Greenville, South

Carolina, a teacher and an officer of the Union League, and threatened to kill him if he did not leave the county immediately. Each week the toll mounted. Joseph Rainey received a letter from the Klan written in red ink that read in part: "K.K.K. Beware! Beware! Beware! Your doom is sealed in blood. Special Order. Headquarters 17th Division, Cyclopian Cyclop Commandery. . . . Take heed, stay not. Here the climate is too hot for you. We warn you to flee. You are watched each hour. We warn you to go." Robert Elliott insured his life for $10,000 before he set out for Washington from Columbia, South Carolina.

Alan Colby, a member of the Georgia legislature in 1869, had been dragged from his bed in the middle of the night by white men, whipped and tortured for three hours, and then left for dead. His assailants, he told the congressional committee members, were among the most prominent men of the town—"one a lawyer, one a doctor, and some . . . farmers." They had tried first to bribe him to surrender his seat in the legislature, and when he refused, they set out to terrorize him. Colby never completely recovered from the beating, and when he tried to run again for the legislature, his house was "just peppered with shot and bullets."

Albert Richardson, another black Georgia legislator, was told by a friend, "They [the whites] intend to kill you. They say you are making too much money; that they cannot allow any nigger to rise up that way; that you can control all the colored votes and they intend to break you." That night a party of some twenty men came to Richardson's house. Some, he reported, "had on the regular old-fashioned doeface. Some had on black cambric with eye-holes. Some wore cambric caps." The raiders broke down the door and shot Richardson three times, while he in turn shot one of the invaders.

Hundreds of black farmers who had begun to prosper modestly were driven off their land and forced to take refuge in the larger towns and cities, where order was often preserved by Federal troops or where offices of the Freedmen's Bureau were located.

Elias Hill, a teacher and minister in York County, South Carolina, was a cripple (and the prototype for Albion Tourgée's hero in *Bricks Without Straw*). Klansmen broke into his house, dragged him out, accused him of having knowledge of the burning of white gins and homes, and struck him repeatedly when he protested that he was not involved. Hadn't he told black men "to ravish all white women"? "No." He was struck again. He must stop preaching, the Klan members told him, and he must put an advertisement in the *Charleston Daily News* renouncing Republicanism, or they would return and kill him.

Newspaper cartoons encouraged the notion that terrified blacks believed they were being "hainted" by ghosts. But the blacks knew well enough who their persecutors were, and many were able to identify them by familiar voices, by their walks and forms under the robes. Abe Lyon, a blacksmith, was killed for $600 in silver that he had saved to pay for his daughter's schooling. The autopsy counted thirty-three bullet holes in his body.

The Klan was described by its founders as "an institution of Chivalry, Humanity, Mercy and Patriotism." It has been estimated that in a three-year period its members killed some twenty thousand blacks, men, women, and children, besides administering innumerable beatings, whippings, and mutilations and burning or pillaging scores of black homes, schools, and churches. Blacks struck back whenever they dared. Many Klan barns were burned in a bitter and unrelenting warfare in which the odds were invariably on the side of the white raiders. Faith Lichen, one of the most outspoken blacks, urged Southern Unionists to "turn on your persecutors. Kill, burn and destroy. I know that you are without weapons, but there is one always by you—the torch. It is fearful, use it, hurl it with all your might into the mansions of the wealthy instigator, not into the huts of the poor tools."

Albion Tourgée, in *A Fool's Errand,* wrote: "So had the war and the lapse of half a decade changed this people, that in one State forty thousand men, in another thirty, in others more and in others less, banded together with solemn oaths and bloody ceremonies, just to go up and down the earth in the bright moonlight, and play upon the superstitious fears of the poor ignorant and undeveloped people around them. They became a race of jesters, moonlight masqueraders, personators of the dead. They instituted clubs and paraded by the hundreds, the trained cavalry of ghostly armies . . . having at their head the 'Grand Wizard of the Empire.' It was all in sport—a great jest, or at the worst designed only to induce the colored men to work somewhat more industriously from apprehension of ghostly displeasure. . . . Grave statesmen, reverend divines, legislators, judges, lawyers, generals, merchants, planters, all who could muster a good horse, as it would seem, joined the jolly cavalcade and rollicked through the moonlight nights. . . ."

The Klan was to Albion Tourgée, in the fictional person of

Colonel Comfort Servosse, "a new and terrible revelation. . . . He saw at once how this potent instrumentality might be used so as to effectually destroy the liberty of the newly enfranchised citizen, and establish a serfdom more barbarous and horrible than any on earth, because it would be the creature of lawless insolence.

"Of the slain," Tourgée wrote, "there were enough to furnish forth a battlefield, and all from those three classes, the negro, the scalawag, and the carpet-bagger,—all killed with deliberation, overwhelmed by numbers, roused from slumber at the murky midnight, in the hall of public assembly, upon the river-brink, on the lonely woods-road, in simulation of the public execution—shot, stabbed, hanged, drowned, mutilated beyond description, tortured beyond conception. And almost always by an unknown hand! Only the terrible, mysterious fact of *death* was certain. Accusation by secret denunciation; sentence without hearing! execution without warning, mercy, or appeal . . . more terrible still: in the treachery which made a neighbor a disguised assassin, most horrible of all the feuds and hates which history portrays." To Tourgée the "defense" offered by Southern whites "set up to rebut the charge, to mitigate the guilt . . . was sadder almost than the bloody facts themselves. . . . The bravest and strongest and best of the South gave it their recognition and support. . . . Thousands believed it a necessity to prevent anarchy and the destruction of all valuable civilization; others regarded it as a means of retaliating upon the government which they conceived to have oppressed them; while some others looked to it as a means of acquiring place and power."

Colonel Comfort Servosse, né Albion Tourgée, when he reflected upon the history of the Klan, "thought it an amazing piece of heroism that the colored man should so long have taken, not merely his own life, but the lives of his little ones in his hand and have gone to the ballot-box to deposit his ballot against such fearful odds of power. He thought that those who had died of one form of intolerance and another, since the time when a great nation falsely guaranteed to them safety, liberty, and the rights of citizenship; and the thousands who fell victims to the violence of Ku-Klux and Rifle Clubs, the natural barbarity which inaugurated and sustained the Repressive policy,— these thousands he deemed to have constituted an army of martyrs for those principles which he still believed, and of which he was once so proud. . . . It was not from hatred to the negro, but to destroy his political power and restore again their own insulted and debased supremacy that such things were done as have been related. . . . Pride the most overweening and a prejudice of caste the most intense and ineradicable, stimulated by a sense of injustice and oppression—both these lay at the bottom of the acts by which the rule of the majorities established by reconstruction legislation were overthrown. It was these things that so blinded the eyes of a whole people that they called this bloody masquerading, this midnight warfare upon the weak, the era of utterable horror, 'redeeming the South!' . . . For generations the South had regarded the uprising of the black, the assertion of his manhood and autonomy, as the *ultima thule* of possible evil. San Domingo and hell were twin horrors to their minds. . . . To prevent negro domination anything was justifiable. It was a choice of evils, where on one side was placed an evil which they had been taught to believe, and did believe, infinitely outweighed and overmatched all other evils in enormity. Anything, said these men in their hearts; anything, they said to each other; anything, they cried aloud to the world, was better, is better, must be better, than negro rule, than African domination. . . ."

The principal tactic of the blacks was defensive. When black leaders were threatened or rumors spread that local Ku Kluxers planned a raid, armed blacks gathered to defend the intended victim. In Avery, Alabama, the word that whites intended to burn the black schoolhouse got around. The building was promptly guarded around the clock by armed blacks. When the incendiaries came to the black village, they found their way blocked by Miles Prior with a dozen armed men. A fence surrounded the little settlement. "Don't any man fire," he told his little band, "until they put their foot over the fence." Faced down, the raiders withdrew, but for a year a kind of war raged around Avery, with white marauders prowling the area and firing into black houses, singling out Prior's home for special attention. Finally the whites turned to the law on the ground that the retributive burnings of white barns and houses had been done under the leadership of Prior. When he went to the neighboring town of Stevenson, the town authorities surrounded him and, after a desperate struggle, carried him off to prison. There Prior outwitted his captors and escaped.

One of the most sensational episodes took place at the town of Union Courthouse, Virginia. A white whiskey peddler was killed shortly before Christmas, 1870, by drunken black militiamen. Thirteen militiamen were arrested and jailed. The Klan appeared at the jail, seized the prisoners, carried them away, and executed them. This incident, perhaps more than any other, led to the formation of the Joint Select Committee to Inquire into the Condition of Affairs in the Late Insurrectionary States, which assembled nine volumes of testimony that made up a horrifying record of terrorism.

James Blaine wrote of the Klan that "in prosecuting their purposes these clans and organizations hesitated at no cruelty. . . . They whipped, maimed, or murdered the victims of their wrath. . . . Over two thousand persons were killed, wounded, and otherwise injured" in the state of Louisiana alone in the weeks preceding the election of 1868. In one parish the Ku Klux was said to have killed or wounded more than two hundred "Republicans," "hunting and chasing them for two days through fields and swamps. . . ." Twenty-five bodies were found in one spot. Reverdy Johnson, a famous Maryland lawyer and an ardent Southerner who had been engaged to defend Klan members apprehended by Federal troops, abandoned them to the mercy of the court. "I have listened with unmixed horror," he wrote, "to some of the testimony which has been brought before you. The outrages proved are shocking to humanity; they admit of neither excuse nor justification; they violate every obligation which law and nature impose upon man; they show that the parties engaged were brutes, insensible to the obligations of humanity and religion."

In the face of such wholesale intimidation of Southern blacks, the Civil Rights Act of 1871 authorized the President to use Federal forces in cases of insurrection or the breakdown of the agencies of the law. Grant, having waited for weeks for a bill to emerge from Congress, sent an urgent message to that body, pointing out that life and property were in danger in a number of states and requesting Congress to pass "such legislation as, in the judgment of Congress, shall effectually secure life, liberty and property in all parts of the United States." The resultant bill, which was at once known as the Ku Klux Klan bill, since it was an obvious effort to respond to the reign of terror instituted by the Klan, was bitterly attacked by the champions of states' rights. Joseph Rainey, the South Carolina Congressman who had himself been threatened by the Klan, defended the bill. "Could I exhume the murdered men and women of the South, Mr. Speaker," Rainey declared, "and array their ghastly forms before your eyes, I should not need remove the mantle from them because their very presence would appeal, in tones of plaintive eloquence, would be louder than a million tongues. They could indeed—

A tale unfold whose lightest word
Would harrow up thy soul. . . ."

Rainey challenged the opponents of the bill to justify their claim that the Constitution afforded no protection for the lives and property of the citizens of the nation. "If the Constitution which we uphold and support as the fundamental law of the United States is inadequate to afford security to life, liberty, and property,—if, I say, this inadequacy is proven, then its work is done, then it should no longer be recognized as the Magna Charta of a great and free people; the sooner it is set aside the better for the liberties of the nation." Robert Elliott was equally eloquent. Although the Democrats showed their contempt by ostentatiously laughing and talking during his speech and a number walked out of the chamber, one reporter wrote: "His manner was easy, his voice clear and penetrating, and his sentences, though delivered somewhat hurriedly owing to a desire to bring the argument within the hour's limit, had a finish and elegance not often heard in Congress oratory." Elliott cited such flagrant examples of attempted coercion as the resolution of the Democratic Club of Charleston that its members agree to "employ no mechanic who does not belong to the same Democratic organization, neither to patronize any mill, tannery or other place dependent on public patronage, owned or superintended by another than an out-and-out Democrat." He read from a Klan document: "*Resolved,* That in all cases of incendiarism ten of the leading colored people and two white sympathizers shall be executed in that vicinity."

It was not, of course, as the above passage indicates, simply blacks who were beaten or murdered. Joseph Rainey told of a well-known and highly respected doctor, a friend of Calhoun's, who had been attacked by a gang and shot seven times for no greater offense than being a Republican.

Acting under the provisions of the Civil Rights Act, Grant suspended the writ of habeas corpus in nine counties of South Carolina. Some 500 suspect Klansmen were arrested and brought to Columbia to appear before a Federal district judge. After a trial lasting two months, 55 of those indicted were found guilty and imprisoned. More than 5,000 Klansmen were arrested in various states under the provisions of the act, and for a time, the Klan and its imitators were suppressed.

Unless we are prepared to contend that the Southern portion of the United States produced a breed of individuals peculiarly prone to violence and brutality, we must give careful attention to the elements of pathology in the Southern temperament. It is appropriate here to remind the reader of some of our assumptions about Southern character. In the older Eastern seaboard region reaching from Virginia to South Carolina, the quasi-feudal character of plantation society with its strong emphasis on the code of personal honor, represented most dramatically by what we might call everyday violence, was expressed in the punishment of delinquent slaves. Certainly the constant physical punishment of black men and women cannot have been without profound effect on the psyches of masters and mistresses. The Deep South—Georgia, Alabama, Mississippi, and Louisiana—was, for the most part, without that tradition of gentility which moderated the behavior of the ruling class in such states as Virginia and South Carolina. There violence was more conspicuous and overt. The border slave states of Kentucky and Tennessee retained their frontier character long after the frontier itself had moved farther west, and violence, as we have had ample occasion to note, was endemic on every frontier. Indeed, if we keep in mind the almost perpetual violence in the forms of riots and mob action that was so evident in the larger Eastern cities—Baltimore, Philadelphia, and New York, specifically—we can perhaps begin to put Southern violence against blacks in a broader context of American violence in general. But there are obviously deeper and more complex roots to the violence practiced by whites against blacks in the post-Civil War period. Southerners, with their overweening pride, had been humiliated in front of their slaves, whether in specific acts of Yankee soldiers or in the more general sense of having been defeated and having had their slaves declared free. It seems reasonable to assume that those accumulated humiliations, like the accumulated wrongs of whites against blacks during two centuries of slavery, formed a kind of substratum of repressed hostility. In the view of the great majority of whites their actual physical safety, security of life and limb, rested on their maintaining an intimidating air of superiority over the black people who surrounded them. If that aura of invincibility, of white power, were dissipated, the tide of terror by which whites felt constantly threatened would, they believed, rise and engulf them.

In addition, there was the fact that the South had been materially as well as spiritually or psychologically devastated. Houses had been pillaged or burned, crops destroyed or left to rot in the fields, family fortunes wiped out, sons and husbands killed or wounded. The simple necessities of life were almost impossible to come by. Without putting too fine a point on it, many Southerners felt themselves materially ruined and morally degraded, left without resources to maintain themselves and without hope for the future. In this depressed state of mind, they saw the powers of the Federal government employed to place over them the very slaves who so recently had been their property. It is always alarming to see the powerless gain power. In the case of white Southerners that alarm was raised to the nth degree if for no other reason than their sense of the wrongs they had committed against their former slaves. The whole social and economic system of the South was based on the assumption of the perpetual and ineradicable inferiority of blacks. Now, it appeared, those same blacks were to rule their masters. In addition, there was an immense Southern rage against Yankees, the merciless instruments of their undoing, the destroyers of their plantations, their way of life, the lives of their sons and husbands. This rage could not, in the nature of things, be vented against its proper object—the despised Northerners. So it was vented against their instruments, the freedmen. Most bitterly resented of all were those free blacks from the North who came south to aid in the work of Reconstruction. In the minds of Southerners, they came, with their white allies, to gloat over the ruin they had caused and pick the choicest bits from the rubble.

So first there was a tradition of violence, an American tradition to be sure, but one specially nurtured in the South. Then there was an accumulation of white guilt and fear, a product of the slavery system, and, added to and working on that, humiliation and rage. But there was something still more fundamental in that strange equation. White Southerners, like black Southerners, were fighting for their lives, their culture, what we would call today their identity, a struggle as desperate in its own way as that of the freed blacks, perhaps, indeed, more desperate. The slaves had, after all, created their own culture, their own world; formed, in modern parlance, their own black consciousness, which existed independently of the white world, which was the center of their "real" life. They entered the white world in countless ways. *But the white world never penetrated the inner world of blacks, slave or free.* White Southern society, on the other hand, rested on slaves. It was wholly dependent on them. A white woman of the planter class could not iron a shirt or make a pot of soup. It defined itself in relation to "them," that race of whom, in fact, it knew so little. Emancipation was thus far more than simply setting free an enslaved people. It was an assault that penetrated to the deepest level of the white psyche, a level where the suppressed fear of blacks held sway. The ex-slave knew simply that he or she was free, although there was a vast degree of uncertainty and even a kind of terror in that knowledge. But Southern whites could not imagine what would become of them. The future was without definition or promise or hope. It seemed to hold only the threat of annihilation, not perhaps of the body—though hunger was not unknown—but of the soul, of their reality as human beings. We may not admire that reality, though there are many indications that we secretly envy it, but it was *their reality,* their self-definition. So it is not surprising that the white upper classes of the South reacted as they did. The poor whites were, in many ways, another story, but for the most part they allied themselves enthusiastically with aristocratic neighbors in the determination that all blacks should be "put in their place" at the bottom of the social and economic scale.

Historians sympathetic to the South have been disposed to argue that the racial hostility which has so disfigured the post-Civil War history of the South was the consequence of the determination of the Radical Republicans to foist black rule upon the South. By this reading, illiterate and untutored blacks, backed by Northern bayonets, were placed in charge of refined and cultivated whites, as punishment for the sin of secession. Elevated to positions they were totally unfitted to fill, they became the pliant tools of unscrupulous white adventurers, politicians, and financiers whose only interest was in further despoiling and humiliating the South. Ridiculous, where they were not danger-ous, the black politicians engaged in an orgy of corruption and misgovernment, while their constituents, the freedmen, raped South-ern women and burned the barns of white planters. In this scenario the freedmen demonstrated beyond dispute or cavil their incapacity not simply for "rule"—that was a foregone conclusion—but for participation in the political process at the lowest level. It thus followed that once the burden of Reconstruction had been shaken off, Southern whites were not only justified in excluding blacks but forced to do so in order to restore and preserve social order and its necessary concomi-tant, white dominance. In this reading of the Reconstruction Era, the rapacious Northern carpetbaggers who came to prey upon the South and their allies, the Radical Republicans, whose principal motive was revenge on the prostrate South, were the villains. Southern whites struggled heroically against enormous odds to defend the tattered remnants of the old order; the hapless freedmen were simply the dupes of Republican demagogues. They had to experience a second emancipation, emancipation from the influence of scheming and unscrupulous black leaders. Then, docile and humble once more, they would realize at last that their best friends were the Southern whites, who understood and loved them and were able to look after their interests far better than an officious Yankee. This is, of course, somewhat of a caricature of what, until relatively recently, was laid on as the true account of Reconstruction, but it is a reasonably close rendition in its essentials, and it is not entirely extinct at this moment.

The reader of this work will, I trust, be aware of how far wide of the extremely complex truth it, in fact, was. Or is. It is clear beyond question that Southern whites were convinced almost without exception that the freedmen were incapable of functioning as citizens of the Republic or, more specifically, of the respective Southern states and, having prejudged the case, were stonily determined not to cease from their labors, brutal and sanguinary as they might be, until they had re-established beyond question not the relative but the complete domination of whites over blacks. As we know today from the very different movements of dependent colonial peoples against white domination, there is no struggle more desperate and more unrelenting than the struggle of a people to preserve its own identity. This is what the white South thought it was doing, and this legitimized every horror and every terror. That these fantasies did not correspond with any perceivable reality is plain enough today and was indeed plain enough then if white Southerners had been able to take in what sight and hearing should have made obvious to them—that far from wanting to dominate, or even believing that, numbers aside, they had the capacity to do so, the black leaders and their constituents were remarkable for the temperateness of their language and the modesty of their aims. They wished, in the last analysis, no more than to have a voice in their own affairs and the same protections afforded to their persons and property as their white neighbors.

If we take seriously the figure of 20,000 to 40,000 Southern blacks murdered in the era of Reconstruction by individual Southerners or hunted down by rifle clubs, Red Shirts, Ku Kluxers, and the dozens of other vigilante bands that roved through rural counties, killing "uppity niggers," not infrequently, killing blacks who had done nothing to attract their animus other than to exist, and whipping and beating unnumbered thousands of others, we begin to get some indication of the courage and determination shown by black people in the pursuit of their rights, the right to vote being paramount among them. While there is ample evidence that some blacks were killed or beaten simply as a "warning" to their more politically aggressive brothers, it seems reasonable to assume that the majority of those singled out for punishment or assassination had given offense to some white man or men if only by presuming to own a gun, to look a white man in the face, or to try to vote.

April 16, 1872, was celebrated by the black citizens of Washington as the tenth anniversary of their emancipation. There was a splendid parade led by black District officials and featuring the Philadelphia Excelsior Cornet band, followed by a battalion of a hundred Howard College cadets in blue uniforms and white belts and several companies of Zouaves. The Lincoln Hook and Ladder volunteer fire company was favorably commented on by enthusiastic spectators. There were representatives of the various "workingmen's clubs" with the instruments of their trades in their hands and numerous pictures of Abraham Lincoln; a float with representations of the Twelve Apostles and the Goddess of Liberty. After being "saluted by the President and his Cabinet," the marchers gathered to hear an address by Robert Elliott. Elliott's message was a sobering one. "All history teaches that there is a constant reflux, or flowing back of the current of human events." (That in itself was a somewhat disconcerting doctrine in a nation committed to perpetual progress.) "There are in the moral as well as in the physical world, centripetal and centrifugal forces, the one tending to attract the good and the other to repel it." The "trite aphorism that 'revolutions never go backward'" was thus clearly in error. The ancient Israelites had succumbed to the Assyrians and Babylonians because "they proved false to the principle to which they owed their first deliverance [from the Egyptians]."

Elliott concluded his remarks on "this natal day of our freedom" by exhorting his listeners "to leave those who follow us a heritage enriched by our accumulation and adorned by our triumphs. . . . Let us lift ourselves to the height of our responsibilities . . . and fear no danger. . . . So living and acting we shall be worthy of the high privileges we possess, worthy to perform our part in preserving the temple of liberty, and in perpetuating our Republican institutions."

48

The Election of 1872

The activities of the Ku Klux Klan and similar organizations (it must be kept in mind that in sum total the more informal terrorist acts of rifle clubs, volunteer fire departments, and "bulldozers" undoubtedly resulted in more intimidation and violence against blacks than the far more conspicuous and better-publicized Klan) had succeeded in keeping Northern opinion inflamed and creating popular support for the Force Acts, but the acts themselves caused serious schisms in the Republican ranks, and these became more apparent as the election of 1872 approached. Horace Greeley, defeated in his bid for his party's nomination for governor at the New York State Republican Convention, organized what George Templeton Strong called a "schismatic convention," which nominated him. In addition, as we have noted, the ranks of the Radical Republicans suffered serious depletions from age and death. Stevens was gone, and Sumner was suffering from a serious heart condition and a disastrous marriage. After his mother's death in 1866, Sumner had married a much younger woman; he was fifty-five, and she was a widow of twenty-five with a seven-year-old daughter. Alice Mason Hooper had nursed Sumner at the home of a mutual friend when he was ill and had overcome his misgivings about marriage. They were married in the fall of 1866. On the day of their wedding, Sumner wrote a friend, "Today at 3 o'clock . . . and at the age of 55 [I] begin to live," and his old friend John Greenleaf Whittier noted, "Just think of it. Instead of taking his carpet-bag and starting off for the Washington cars, as aforetime, he went this winter, filling a coach with his family:—Mr. Sumner and Mrs. Sumner, and Mrs. Sumner's child, and Mrs. Sumner's child's nurse, and Mrs. Sumner's little dog!" Considered one of the most beautiful women in Washington, Alice Hooper Sumner was strong-willed, independent, and flirtatious. She involved her weary and often ailing husband in a giddy round of social events, dinners and parties and dances. It was soon said that the handsome Mrs. Sumner "leads the 'ton' in Washington." The wife of a Congressman wrote: "Sumner and his beautiful wife are themselves history and romance, they ought to be handsomely bound and opened a page at a time." But things did not go so well at home. Sumner was a bachelor—spoiled, demanding, and egotistical. Moreover, he could not keep up the pace set by his young bride. She grew increasingly contemptuous of him, and when he broke into tears, she derided him. She frequently went off to parties accompanied by Baron Friedrich von Holstein, a Prussian diplomat. Sometimes she refused even to tell Sumner where she was going. They separated, and rumors began to circulate in Washington, ranging from the story that Sumner was impotent to assertions that she was having an affair with Holstein. A friend of Sumner's secretary, Moorfield Storey, wrote, "Please ask Charley confidentially if his wife left him because he could not *perform the functions of a husband* . . ." while William Cullen Bryant wryly observed: "A woman is not content with a husband who is exclusively occupied with himself and his own greatness." Sumner grew increasingly bitter, describing his wife to a friend as "a bad woman—at home in the house a devil self willed and infernal; in every respect forgetful of her marriage vows. . . . No picture can adequately show the completeness of her vileness."

The Sumners were finally divorced in 1873, and Alice Hooper Sumner established herself in Europe, where she became a friend of another expatriate, Henry James, who praised "her great beauty (which on horseback is enormous)" as well as her "honesty, frankness and naturalness."

Accused of wishing to be president, Sumner wrote plaintively to Whitelaw Reid: "I beg you to believe that I do not consider myself a candidate for anything—unless it be the good-will of good men. . . . I have had enough of combat and am very weary."

Sumner's calamitous marriage was a kind of symbol of the disarray in Republican ranks. No party could have survived the disintegrative effects of Reconstruction in the South, corruption in the North, the division over hard and soft money, and the accumulations of scandals touching the administration itself. For better or worse, the President was tied to Roscoe Conkling's New York machine, and this alliance insured the enmity of Horace Greeley. Grant's determination to protect the rights of Southern blacks was seen increasingly as nothing more than a desire to insure his own re-election by keeping the Southern states in the Republican camp. The *Commercial* of Cincinnati noted: "The President's possibility of renomination rests with the carpetbaggers. . . . The intense solicitude of the President for the safety of the loyal men in the South means anxiety to secure the carpetbag vote." Oliver Morton stated the matter frankly: "Shall reconstruction be maintained, shall the colored people be protected in the enjoyment of equal rights, shall the Republicans of the southern states be protected in life, liberty, and property, are the great issues to be settled in 1872."

Corruption was another major issue. *Leslie's Weekly* declared in January, 1872: "The public ear is daily startled by stories of defaulting officials in Washington. . . . Since the formation of this government there has never been such a series of frauds, defalcations and peculations, either in number or in magnitude as have characterized the last three years. . . . And shall we have four more years of such misrule, such sordid self-seeking and greed—to crush out the very soul of this great and growing nation? God forbid. . . . Down with the Washington Ring!"

Increasingly Grant was depicted as a tyrant and an oppressor, determined to impose his will on the party and the country. The removal of Sumner from his chairmanship of the Foreign Relations Committee was pointed to in confirmation of the charge. Schurz, who had been Sumner's coadjutor in the Santo Domingo matter, wrote: "Another term of such arrogant assumption of power and wanton acquiescence may furnish the flunkies with a store of precedents until people cease to look for ordinary means of relief," a statement which seemed to imply a threat of force directed against the President. James Russell Lowell, after a visit to the White House, wrote: "I liked Grant and was struck with the pathos of his face; a puzzled pathos of a man with a problem before him which he does not understand." Neither, it might have been added, did anyone else. George William Curtis, the editor of *Harper's Weekly,* wrote a friend: "I think the warmest friends of Grant feel that he has failed terribly as President, not from want of honesty or desire, but from want of tact and great ignorance. It is a political position and he knows nothing of politics and rather despises them." The fact was that the Republicans could not "solve" the question of black rights, nor could they let it go. Democratic Congressman Durbin Ward of Ohio was confident that "from the very nature of things," the days of the "old Radical leaders" were numbered. "The Republican party is in the last stages of dissolution," he declared. "It drew its breath from the slavery question, and they must be buried in a common grave. The old issues being dead, the party has to face new ones, and it is too old and effete to grapple with them. . . . Its mission is finished, and it must go with its works to the dread ordeal of history."

The most serious defection from Republican ranks was that of Carl Schurz. Schurz, as we have seen, took the view that the Ku Klux Klan Act made a shambles of the Constitution. Now, as Senator from Missouri, a border slave state in which pro-Southern sentiment was still strong, he had his constituency to think of as well. Like others who opposed the act, he argued that the stories of Klan atrocities had been greatly exaggerated and laid much of the blame at the door of the corrupt Reconstruction governments. In doing so, Schurz staked out a new political territory, that of the Liberal, or independent, Republicans, men of conscience no longer willing to follow blindly the path laid out by the extremists of the party; men who also rejected the notion that the duty of Republicans was to support the administration at whatever cost to their convictions. "We desire peace and good will to all men," Schurz declared. "We desire the removal of political restrictions and the maintenance of local self-government to the utmost extent compatible with the Constitution as it is. We desire the questions connected with the Civil War to be disposed of forever, to make room as soon as possible for the new problems of the present and future."

Translated, the passage read: We want reconciliation with the white South even if the price for this is abandonment of the freed black; we believe in the doctrine of states' rights; we want to forget about the war; we want civil service reform, protective tariffs, hard money, and a climate favorable to business enterprise. Schurz's manifesto was another conspicuous straw that showed which way the political winds were blowing. His defection pointed up the replacement of the old, principled leadership of men like Sumner and Stevens, which, however self-willed, was sustained by an unshakable devotion to the ideal of social justice for all Americans, with the leadership of men of expediency, a company of politicians whose commitment was far more to retaining power than to a dream of justice and equality: Roscoe Conkling, dandified and ambitious; Schuyler Colfax; Oliver Morton; and Ben Butler. For such men the control of patronage was essential to their domination of the political machinery of their respective states. The reward for party loyalty was patronage.

Certainly the Ku Klux Klan Act was necessary if what was left of Republican power in the South was to be preserved against the constant erosion by terroristic tactics; it was justified on its own account as a last, almost despairing effort to protect the freed blacks. Although it had, initially, widespread popular support, a strong reaction soon set in, a reaction stimulated and encouraged by pronouncements like that of Schurz, who was soon joined by other Liberal Republicans. Horace Greeley's *Tribune* became the spokesman of the new faction. It was as though tension were building up along a geological fault line. Every act of Federal intervention to protect Southern blacks increased the pressure. As each new intervention proved inadequate, the feeling grew that such policies could not be pursued *ad infinitum* without bankrupting the country and perpetuating a kind of quasi war.

All this marked a subtle but critically important shift from primarily moral concerns to those of political expediency. It was as though the foundations of the large and impressive structure of Radical Republicanism had been eaten away and the building itself awaited only the slightest tremor to bring it crashing down in ruins. When the defections from the Radical Republicans (who would now much better be termed the Regular Republicans) were tallied, the results brought hope to Democratic hearts and gloom to the Republicans.

A minor issue dramatized the rupture. Charges had been made of improper sales of weapons to France in the Franco-Prussian conflict. Schurz made himself master of the episode and used it as a weapon to belabor the administration. Conkling stepped forward as the defender of the War Department, and Schurz took excessive pride in cutting him up. Now the break was official, in a manner of speaking. Schurz and his fellow Liberal Republicans began warning against the "calamity" of four more years of Grant. "I think,—in fact I firmly believe," Schurz wrote to Sumner in the fall of 1871, "—in case of Grant's nomination we shall have a third movement on foot strong enough to beat both him and the Democrats. I have commenced already to organize it, and when the time comes, I think it will be ready for action. . . ."

A new generation of young Southerners would be valuable recruits, Schurz felt. They hated Grant but cared little for the Democratic Party and were willing, Schurz believed, "to uphold the new order of things *in every direction,* if they are generously treated." The new party would be "composed of Republicans and former rebels." But that, it turned out, was simply Schurz's pipe dream. There was no such Republican constituency in the South.

Schurz convinced himself that in the West at least, the Democratic Party was disintegrating and its members were ready to be gathered up along with "Republicans who are not corrupted by patronage or frightened by official terrorism." As Frederick Bancroft and William Dunning, the editors of Schurz's *Reminiscences,* put it, "his ideal was a great moral uprising of the people, of such volume and scope as to sweep away the existing party machinery, with the corruption and abuses which it fostered, and to establish in its stead a new political order, in which intelligence, honesty and efficiency should have their due place in the conduct of government. . . ." The dream was both a reprise of the spirit of the young German revolutionaries of 1848 and a forecast of the "progressive" spirit of the last decades of the century, which sought to replace political jobbery with "intelligence, honesty and efficiency."

To Schurz and his allies the overriding issues became monetary policy and civil service reform. In their view the political corruption so evident at all levels of government was in large part fueled by the desperate and unending competition for offices, the buying and selling of which, or, more mildly, the passing out of which in return for political services, was one of the most conspicuous features of the American system. To such men civil service reform became a touchstone for the viability of republican government. It came simply to this: Could a democratic people purge themselves of massive corruption that threatened the credibility of the whole American experiment in self-government? Schurz's bill to reform the civil service, introduced on December 20, 1869, attracted strong support from such champions of reform as Lyman Trumbull and Charles Sumner, but it languished in the feverish atmosphere of congressional politics. Its opponents argued that it was not the time for innovations. The Republican Party was the party of patriotism and morality. Any measure, however justified in itself, which might work to the advantage of the Democrats, the party of treason and immorality, must be put on the shelf until better days. Schurz was determined to press the issue.

Not all Liberal Republicans shared Schurz's confidence in a new third party dedicated to political purity. Men like Lyman Trumbull wished simply to give "so imposing a demonstration of reform sentiment" within the party that Grant's supporters, realizing that they could not win without Liberal support, would jettison Grant for a reform candidate.

The heart (and brain) of the Liberal Republican movement was a group of liberal young newspaper editors who called themselves the Quadrilateral. It was made up of Murat Halstead of the *Cincinnati Commercial*, Henry Watterson of the *Louisville Courier-Journal*, Samuel Bowles of the *Springfield* (Massachusetts) *Republican*, and Schurz himself. Added to the original four were Horace White of the *Chicago Tribune* and Whitelaw Reid of the *New York Tribune*.

The Liberal Republicans, egged on by Schurz, held a mass meeting at Jefferson City in Schurz's home state on January 24, 1872, and passed resolutions urging that the Republicans endorse "amnesty, tariff reform and civil-service reform" and setting the date of May 1 for a meeting in Cincinnati to nominate a candidate for President on the Liberal Republican ticket.

Schurz was elected permanent chairman of the Cincinnati Convention in recognition of his leading role in the movement, and he exhorted the delegates to make no compromise with politics-as-usual. He warned the delegates of the consequences "if we attempt to control and use this movement by the old tricks of political trade, or fritter away our zeal in small bickerings and mere selfish aspirations. We must obey the purest and loftiest inspirations of the popular uprising which sent us here. . . . I earnestly deprecate the cry we have heard so frequently: 'Anybody to beat Grant!' There is something more wanted than to beat Grant." They must have a candidate of "superior intelligence coupled with superior virtue."

Only a handful of prospective candidates seemed to approach Schurz's severe criteria. The names of Charles Francis Adams, Sr., Lyman Trumbull, Horace Greeley, and David Davis, a justice of the Supreme Court and native of Illinois, were mentioned. Greeley, at sixty-one, was anything but a fresh face. Pompous, egotistical, and doctrinaire, with a record of erratic political behavior extending back over a number of years, he had slight appeal for Republicans, Regular or Radical, and less for the Democrats. Thomas Nast had made his rotund little figure and cherubic face with its fringe of white beard an object of ridicule in the pages of *Harper's Weekly*. Davis's services on the Court had been undistinguished, but at least they had served to keep him aloof from the bloody internecine battles of the Republican Party. To Schurz's mind Adams was the proper candidate for the new party. That fact in itself was a kind of conclusive commentary on the plight of the Liberal Republicans. Intelligent and able as Adams was, his prim New England air, dry and precise, his aloofness and lack of human warmth and affability, even his age—he was sixty-five—marked him as a representative of the old order, more a Whig than the standard-bearer of an aggressive new party. Trumbull, a youthful-looking fifty-nine, was simply a Western version of Adams. He bore, after all, two of the most honored New England names; his grandfather had been the famous Congregational minister and historian of Connecticut.

A serious schism appeared immediately in the ranks of the expanded Quadrilaterals when Reid made it plain that he was committed to his editor, Greeley. Schurz concentrated his efforts on trying to secure Adams's nomination. When B. Gratz Brown, governor of Missouri, learned that Schurz was trying to woo Missouri's ninety-five-man delegation to support Adams, he hurried to Cincinnati to block the move. There he joined forces with Reid to promote Greeley's candidacy.

Adams, for his part, took the line that he did not want the nomination and would take it only if it were offered to him with no strings attached. Then he made a characteristically Adams-like statement: "If the good people of Cincinnati really believe that they need such an anomalous being as I am (which I do not) they must express it in a manner to convince me of it, or all their labor will be thrown away." That, it turned out, was not enough.

In the first ballot Adams led by 203 votes with Brown second at 95. Brown rose and withdrew, urging his supporters to give their votes to Greeley. Greeley's vote then equaled Adams's, and after four more ballots and a good deal of the political jiggery-pokery that Schurz had counseled against, Greeley received the nomination, with Brown given second place on the ticket. The result was a shock to Schurz and indeed to all the idealists and reformers who had rallied to his call.

With Greeley nominated, Reid could afford to be magnanimous. He said to Watterson, who had been an Adams supporter: "I have won, and you people have lost. I shall expect that you stand by the agreement and meet me at dinner tonight." The dinner was not a cheerful one. "Frostier conviviality," Watterson wrote later, "I have never sat down to than Reid's dinner. Horace White looked more than ever like an ice-berg; Sam Bowles was diplomatic, but ineffusive; Schurz was a death's-head at the board; Halstead and I, through sheer bravado, tried to enliven the feast. But they would have none of us, nor it, and we separated early and sadly, reformers hoist by their own petard. . . . The Quadrilateral was knocked into a cocked hat. White-law Reid was the sole survivor. He was the only one of us who knew what it was all about."

The charges of the Liberal Republicans against Grant's administration, as listed in their platform, were five in number, beginning:

"The President of the United States has openly used the powers and opportunities of his high office for the promotion of personal ends.

"He has kept notoriously corrupt and untrustworthy men in places of power and responsibility, to the detriment of the public interest.

"He has used the public service of the government as a machinery of corruption and personal influence, and has interfered with tyrannical arrogance in the political affairs of states and municipalities. . . .

"He has shown himself deplorably unequal to the task imposed upon him by the necessities of the country, and culpably careless of the responsibilities of his high office."

There was more than one contradiction embedded in the document. The Grant Republicans were charged with having "kept alive the passions and resentments of the late Civil War, to use them for their own advantage; they have resorted to arbitrary measures in direct conflict with the organic law, instead of appealing to the better instincts and latent patriotism of the southern people by restoring to them those rights the enjoyment of which is indispensable to a successful administration of their local affairs." Then, some paragraphs farther on, the Liberal Republicans announced: "We recognize the equality of all men before the law, and hold that it is the duty of government, in its dealings with the people, to mete out equal and exact justice to all, of whatever nativity, race, color, or persuasion, religious or political." All very well, the Grant Republicans replied, but without the determination to intervene wherever "equal and exact justice" was threatened, the words were mere pious platitudes.

One of the final paragraphs dealt with civil service reform. The civil service had become, the platform declared, "a mere instrument of partizan tyranny and personal ambition, and an object of selfish greed . . . a scandal and reproach upon free institutions. . . . We therefore regard a thorough reform of the civil service as one of the most pressing necessities of the hour. . . ."

Schurz wrote to Samuel Bowles, the reformist newspaper editor who had backed Adams: "I cannot yet think of the results of the Cincinnati Convention without a pang. I have worked for reform in the largest sense of the word in good faith." But he had been betrayed by "just that tribe we thought we were fighting against, and the whole movement [was] stripped of its moral character and dragged down to the level of an ordinary political operation. . . ." Schurz's efforts to regain some degree of control over the Liberal Republican movement was an exercise in futility. He even tried to prevail on Greeley to refuse the Cincinnati nomination on the ground that another Liberal Republican ticket would soon be put forth more acceptable to the Democrats and reformers alike. Not surprisingly Greeley indignantly declined, and Schurz's rump session of some forty or fifty leading Liberal Republicans at the Fifth Avenue Hotel on June 20 served only to make clear that there could be no alternative to Greeley.

The process by which the Liberal Republicans found themselves saddled with Horace Greeley as candidate for president of the United States seemed to many of them quite inexplicable. It was somehow akin to the Democrats' ending up with Horatio Seymour four years earlier. George Templeton Strong wrote despairingly: "This is the most preposterous and ludicrous nomination to the Presidency ever made on this continent, except, perhaps Mr. George Train's, and that was made by himself alone. Horace Greeley's purposes are honest, but he is so conceited, fussy, and foolish that he damages every cause he wants to support."

Quixotic as the efforts of Schurz and the Liberal Republicans may appear in retrospect, there was about them an ineffable poignance. As we have seen, the Civil War had raised in the hearts of America's most brilliant and idealistic young men, most of whom had fought and many of whom had suffered wounds, hopes for a glorious new age. Charles Francis Adams, Jr., and his brother Henry had debated what roles they might best play in the renaissance of the reunited and purified states. James Beecher, younger brother of Harriet and colonel of a black regiment, had dreamed of a new age. Young Lester Ward, wounded in battle, organized his National Liberal Reform League to realize the frequently postponed promise of America. Oliver Wendell Holmes, Jr., wounded and lying on the "snowy heights of honor," had been sustained by the same vision. There were, in the aggregate, thousands of such young men and women who wished to be able at last to love America unreservedly. But all those hopes had been dashed.

Most disheartening of all to such idealists, of course, was the situation in the South. Every remedy seemed to contribute more to the crisis than to its solution. Millions upon millions of man- and woman-hours of dangerous and exhausting labors among the free blacks appeared hardly to have made a dent in the task of turning ex-slaves into middle-class blacks, restrained, clean, honest, thrifty, and ambitious. If all the energy expended in the cause of the freedmen had been available for more mundane political labors, the Augean political stables of the United States might have been swept clean. If the Northern bosses, the corrupted and their corrupters, could have consigned the young men and women of the country most zealous for reform to some kind of political limbo, they could have served the cause of corruption no better than it was doubtless served by their self-exile in the inhospitable South. On the other hand, there can be little question that the missionaries, teachers, agents of the Freedmen's Bureau, and all who devoted themselves unselfishly to the uplifting of the ex-slaves performed an essential service, not only for the blacks whom they went to serve but for their country. We dare not wish them elsewhere, and it may well be argued that they would all together have weighed little in the balance against the general corruption and demoralization. So perhaps, all other considerations aside, they were better off among the shanties, churches, schools, and cotton fields of the South. There, at least, the problems were clear enough and the emotional rewards were great for even the most modest successes—for an elderly black woman who learned to read her Bible or a black youth dispatched to Howard University or Hampton or, more rarely, to Harvard or Oberlin. There a Lucy Chase sustained by motherly old black Sukey could write: "They warm my heart, these warm-hearted people." There at least was love reciprocated and simple goodness simply expressed.

The debacle of the Cincinnati Convention was thus a much larger symbolic defeat, not primarily for the Liberal Republicans—they clearly deserved little better—but for the best of those hopes and dreams nourished by the hardship and suffering of the war and for the sense of a redeemed humanity engendered by it. I suspect it is not too much to say it broke many hearts and contributed substantially to the vague, ill-defined feeling of regret for lost opportunities and dissipated hopes that seemed to envelop so many of the most promising young men of the generation who came to their mature years after the war. It was almost as though the young idealists had bet their whole stake on the attainment of racial harmony and justice in the South and in losing lost an emotional investment of incalculable weight and value.

As a loyal party man George Hoar judged the defectors harshly. Years later he wrote that Sumner, Schurz, Greeley, and Trumbull had abandoned the party while the supporters of Grant had remained true. "They," he wrote, "purified the administration. They accomplished civil service reform. They helped to achieve the independence of American manufacturing. They kept the faith. They paid the debt. They resumed specie payment. They maintained a sound currency, amid great temptation and against great odds. To this result our friends who were independent of party contributed no jot or tittle."

Grant's enemies in the Republican Party, beating the bushes for an alternative candidate, mounted a campaign to draft Sherman as their party's candidate. When Schurz encountered Sherman on a ferryboat between New York and Jersey City in the early stages of the campaign of 1872 and mentioned the drive to make him a presidential candidate, Sherman broke out: "What do they think I am? A damned fool? They know that I don't know anything about politics, and am not fit for the Presidency. At least, I know it. No, I am not a damned fool. I am a happy man now. Look at Grant! Look at Grant! What wouldn't he give now if he had never meddled in politics! No, they must let me alone. They can't bedevil me!"

The Republican nominating convention which met at the Academy of Music in Philadelphia on June 5 was all harmony. Firmly controlled by the party's regulars, the delegates nominated Grant without dissent and applauded Oliver Morton's denunciation of the Liberal Republicans as the murderers of their own offspring. Henry Wilson replaced Schuyler Colfax, whose presidential ambitions had irritated Grant, as vice-president.

The Republican platform was a staunchly liberal one. It called for the vigorous enforcement of the Fourteenth and Fifteenth Amendments and supported civil service reform as well as pensions for veterans. It hinted at women's suffrage and endorsed a just and humane policy toward the Indians. Vague on fiscal policy and on protective tariffs, it included a special bid for the black vote, encouraging Frederick Douglass to declare: "The Republican party is the ship and all else is the sea."

Women, clearly, felt much the same way. The Republican platform gave some ambiguous hope for women's suffrage. The Liberal Republican platform was silent on the subject, largely out of deference to Henry Watterson, who was bitterly opposed and called the women advocates of suffrage "red-nosed angels" and "silly Sallies." So the women gave their support to Grant.

The activities of women during the war on behalf of the Union cause had added greatly to their visibility. As members of the women's auxiliary of the Sanitary Commission they had performed great services, not only in helping organize the fairs but in a variety of fund-raising activities and as nurses. They had made bandages, knitted socks and sweaters for healthy and wounded soldiers, collected petitions, taken the places of husbands and brothers who had gone off to fight. In the spring of 1863 Susan B. Anthony and Elizabeth Cady Stanton had founded the Women's Loyal National League for the primary purpose of collecting signatures on petitions calling for an act by Congress to support Lincoln's Emancipation Proclamation. When it was pointed out that such a statute might be repealed and that an amendment to the Constitution was a sounder course to follow, the league had turned its attention to circulating petitions calling for such an amendment. Two thousand women were soon busy, and within a month—by February 9, 1864—two blacks had brought into the Senate bundles containing more than 100,000 signatures. Six months later another 300,000 were added, the largest number ever collected in the name of a single cause.

Even women to whom the rights movement was an anathema discovered through their wartime activities new potentialities in themselves. George Templeton Strong's wife, Ellie, was among them, and Strong wrote proudly of her nursing: "The little woman has come out amazingly strong during these two months. Have never given her credit for a tithe of the enterprise, pluck, discretion, and force of character she has shown. God bless her. . . ."

After the war there was a great surge in the women's movement. William Lloyd Garrison and Wendell Phillips turned their attention to the issue of women's suffrage. Women sought admission to the professions, especially medicine and the law. In New Jersey David Macrae found "a lady, 'Doctoress' Fowler, acting as a public physician, with the reputation of being the most skilful, and having the largest and most lucrative practice in the district." In Chicago the *Legal News* was edited by a woman, and another was on the Board of Examiners for the Chicago High School.

"Application from three infatuated young women for admission to the Law School," George Templeton Strong had noted in his diary under the date of October 9, 1869. "No woman shall degrade herself by practicing law, in New York especially, if I can save her. . . . 'Women's-Rights Women' are uncommonly loud and offensive of late. I loathe the lot."

"The movement in favor of female suffrage seems to be gaining strength," Sidney George Fisher had written in 1867. "The idea is so absurd & repugnant to all feelings universally received of the true position of woman, that it would seem impossible for a scheme so extravagant to be seriously discussed. But we live in times when nothing is impossible except virtue, wisdom & moderation. Five years ago, Negro suffrage would have excited only scorn & ridicule from all parties as a monstrous and absurd notion, too wild to be entertained by any sane man, yet it is now the avowed policy of the ruling party of the country and will undoubtedly be forced upon the South, if that party can force it which destroyed slavery. The contest with the South," Fisher added in a significant sentence, "has caused an immense increase to the popular passion for liberty & equality, & under the influence of this excitement things will probably be done which it will be found difficult or impossible to undo when the madness is over & the evil results are evident."

When Susan B. Anthony and the delegates to the women's convention met in South Framingham, Massachusetts, on July 14, 1870, the meeting was reported typically in James Gordon Bennett's *Herald:* "The bold labor reformers, woman-suffrage advocates, spiritualists, and free and easy lovers, had their customary jamboree in Harmony Grove to-day."

The young Lester Wards set out to live the life of husband and wife free of the sex bias that characterized American marriage. "This woman suffrage question is destined to be the great issue of the next half century," Ward wrote in his diary. Soon he subscribed to *Revolution,* the radical feminist journal, which he and Lizzie read avidly.

The Reverend David Macrae was startled at the frequency and ease of divorce, especially in the Western states. In Chicago it seemed to him that marriages were more easily dissolved than business partnerships. He saw an advertisement by a Chicago law firm that declared it had obtained some 300 divorces, no charge unless the divorce was granted. Macrae was told that more than 250 marriages had been dissolved the previous year out of a population of scarcely 300,000. At the other extreme, only a handful of divorces had been granted in the state of South Carolina throughout its entire history. More disturbing to Macrae than the loosening of the marriage tie indicated by such statistics was the frequency of abortions. "It is impossible for any one to travel in the States," he wrote, "without becoming aware of the frightful prevalence of this practice. The papers swarm with advertisements of the requisite medicines. . . ." A doctor in a large Northern city told Macrae that he knew personally of thirty doctors who "devoted themselves to this species of murder," as the Scottish minister put it. A euphemism for one such place where abortions were performed was "Invalids' Retreat."

In reporting on a sensational scandal involving a love triangle and a murder in New York's higher social circle, George Templeton Strong remarked, "I fear there is a good deal of rather lewd practice among women of the upper middle strata," and William Wilkins Glenn was horrified at the general looseness in public morals. "Women tell me," he wrote, "that young girls now know of and discuss things about which young girls twenty years ago knew nothing." Talk of "free love," if not its practice, was rife. Victoria Woodhull and her sister, Tennie C. (or Tennessee) Claflin, provided the most radical critique of a capitalist economy and a sex-biased social system in their *Woodhull and Claflin's Weekly.*

All of these feminists' currents swirled around the election of 1872.

Militant women deplored Greeley's presidential ambitions and his refusal to support women's suffrage. Susan B. Anthony told the delegates at the women's convention in Baltimore that she hoped the convention would "cram suffrage down Horace Greeley's throat as he had forced Negro suffrage upon the South." It was a startling and significant passage and one which made clear both the movement's indignation at what seemed to its members their abandonment by the liberal political forces and their growing disenchantment with the Republican Party's preoccupation with the condition of Southern blacks. It was not even strictly accurate historically. Greeley had always had strong misgivings about "forcing" Negro suffrage on the South. Anthony's angry challenge also reminds us that the issue of women's suffrage vis-à-vis black suffrage had seriously split the movement.

The defection of the women to Grant was especially distressing to Greeley. "I . . . made myself ridiculous in the opinion of many whose good wishes I desired," he told George Julian, "by showing fair play and giving a fair field in the *Tribune* to woman's rights; and the women have all gone against me." He had been an abolitionist "for years when to be one was worth as much as one's life in New York; and the Negroes have all voted against me."

On the eve of the Democratic convention in Baltimore, a modest movement for Charles Francis Adams, Sr., was started, and as with the Liberal Republicans, Adams played hard to get. "I would accept a nomination by the Democratic convention at Baltimore," he cabled from London, "if the platform was good and the offer of the candidacy was spontaneous on the part of the convention."

William ("Extra Billy") Smith of Virginia and other Southern leaders lined up the halfhearted delegates for Greeley early, and when some objected on the ground that "Greeley did more than any one else to free the slaves," they were told: "That is the very reason why we want Greeley to try his hand at freeing southern white men." Smith, seventy-seven years old, colonel of the 49th Virginia Infantry during the war and briefly governor of the state, declared, "Give me Jew or Gentile, dog or devil, I care not which, so we can beat Grant."

The emphasis at the Democratic convention was for "peace and a true reunion." Greeley's sentence in accepting the Cincinnati nomination—"I accept your nomination in the confident trust that the masses of our countrymen are eager to clasp hands across the bloody chasm"—was widely and continuously quoted, and the delegates were constantly reminded that Greeley had signed Jefferson Davis's bond. Translated into Southernese, Greeley's statement might be read: Black Reconstruction was a mistake. If elected, I will leave the South to deal with the freedmen as it feels best. It is not the business of the Federal government to intervene. The key plank in the Democratic platform, which was adopted from the Cincinnati Convention, read: "We pledge ourselves to maintain the Union of these States, emancipation, and enfranchisement, and to oppose any reopening of the questions settled by the Thirteenth, Fourteenth, and Fifteenth Amendments of the Constitution." If the plank was a pious evasion in Cincinnati, it was an unabashed deception in Baltimore.

Of the 732 votes cast by a listless and dispirited convention on the first ballot, 686 were for Greeley. Although the *Tribune* reported that "shouts of applause went up at every mention of Greeley's name," another reporter admitted that the delegates' response was less than enthusiastic, attributing it to "the intense heat and the exhaustion of the delegates." Gratz Brown was chosen for vice-president.

When George Templeton Strong heard that the Democrats might endorse Greeley as their candidate for president, he wrote in his diary: "A party of cardinals running H. W. Beecher for Pope would be, in some respects, a less preposterous phenomenon. . . ." And when they did endorse him, he noted: "The Democrats at Baltimore have swallowed Horace Greeley whole, not without a few wry faces . . . and Horace Greeley (!!!) is Democratic(!!!) candidate for the presidency. 'Can such things be?' . . . Chivalry and Copperheadism hurrahing for Horace Greeley."

Sumner, although unwilling to come out in support of Greeley, made a bitter attack on Grant. "Our greatest senator has made the greatest speech of his life," the *Tribune* declared in unabashed self-congratulation. George Templeton Strong noted in his diary: "Sumner, the Ciceronian Thersites of the Senate . . . devotes an entire senatorial day to the laborious pelting of Grant with all the dirt he can lay his hands on. . . . This hot, heavy, malignant oration will do Grant little harm." Grant's response to Sumner's attack on him was reported to be that "if he were not President of the United States, he would hold Mr. Sumner personally responsible for the language and demand satisfaction from him," to which the little gamecock Babcock added "that if he were not officially attached to the Executive he would subject Mr. Sumner to personal violence."

With Sumner's defection, Thomas Nast pictured him in *Harper's Weekly* strewing flowers over the grave of Preston Brooks, and the editor of *Harper's Weekly*, George William Curtis, a Grant supporter, admonished Nast not to "introduce Mr. Sumner in any way into any picture" since "he was a dear friend, a man whose services to the country and to civilization have been immense."

When Blaine attacked Sumner for joining forces with "the ruffians who justified Preston Brooks in his brutal assault upon you . . ." Sumner replied, "You entirely misunderstand me when you introduce an incident of the past & build in it an argument why I should not support Horace Greeley. Never while a sufferer did any body hear me speak of him in an unkindness & now, after a lapse of more than half a generation I will not unite with you in dragging him from the grave . . . to aggravate the passions of a political conflict & arrest the longing for concord." Seven years had passed since the end of the war, a "natural period in human life. Can we not after seven years," he asked his colleagues, "commence a new life . . . ?"

Conkling rebuffed the criticisms of Grant. They were the evil product of "the greed and ambition of politicians and schemers . . . the sordid and the vile, who follow politics as the shark follows the ship. . . . Every thief and cormorant and drone who has been put out, every baffled mouser for place and plunder, every man with a grievance or a grudge, all who have something to make by a change, seek to wag an unbridled tongue or drive a foul pen." Conkling went on to quote Greeley from earlier days: "every one who chooses to live by pugilism, or gambling, or harlotry, with nearly every keeper of a tippling house, is politically a Democrat. . . ."

Those Democrats who could not swallow Greeley finally met at Louisville, Kentucky, on September 3; calling themselves the Straight-Out Democrats—they were called Duncan's Bourbons by their enemies—they tried to prevail on Charles O'Conor, the aged New York lawyer, to be their candidate, along with John Quincy Adams, brother of Charles Francis, Jr., as vice-president, but O'Conor declined.

Still another faction, made up of free-traders, Liberal Republicans, and a handful of Democrats, met at the Fifth Avenue Hotel in New York in a last, desperate effort to find an electable candidate. They denominated themselves the Liberal Republican Revenue Reformers Party and tried to prevail on William Cullen Bryant to be their candidate. Bryant, then seventy-eight, replied, "I would not commit the folly of accepting it." The Reformers then nominated William Groesbeck, an Ohio lawyer whose greatest claim to fame was his able defense of Johnson in the impeachment trial, and chose Frederick Law Olmsted as vice-president. They called for a more democratic method of nominating presidential candidates—"spontaneous nomination" they termed it—and the direct election of the president and vice-president.

The Prohibition Party fielded a candidate of its own since none of the other candidates was sufficiently strong on the temperance issue. (Greeley, of course, was a famous temperance man, but as a candidate of the Democrats he dared not mention the subject.)

George Francis Train, a New Englander who had made a great fortune in shipping and then become involved in the building of the Union Pacific, was one of that class of rich Americans who become, in later life, proponents of various eccentric or radical causes. He had been in France during the rise of the Paris commune and there became a convert to communism. The beauty of Victoria Woodhull attracted him to feminism and free love, and he endorsed the movement for Irish freedom into the bargain. He had himself "nominated" for president by some of his adherents and began campaigning around the country in his private railroad car, proclaiming communism and women's rights. Train's campaign did not prevent his friend Victoria Woodhull from running for president herself. Theodore Tilton had become one of Victoria's most eloquent apostles. As a spiritualist she had, he pointed out, conversed with the shade of Demosthenes, who had "prophesied to her that she would rise to great distinction; that she would emerge from poverty and live in a stately house; that she would win great wealth in a city crowded with ships; that she would publish and conduct a great journal; and finally, that to crown her career, she would become the ruler of her people."

The Greeley partisans wore long white coats and white top hats in imitation of their candidate. Greeley's major theme was that the time had come to bind up the wounds caused by the war. "Brothers," he said time and again, "we differed, we fought, the war is ended, let us be fellow countrymen and forget that we have been enemies." But, his adversaries replied, the South shows no disposition to forget. It gives every evidence of an unshakable determination to restore the old order—to hunt Unionists, blacks, and Yankees down, beat or kill or drive them out, and reinstitute a repressive and undemocratic regime in every state south of the Mason-Dixon Line. Is not reconciliation a two-way street? Is it asking too much to require that the South respect the rights and preserve the lives of whites and blacks whose only crime is loyalty to the United States?

One of the more reprehensible attacks on Greeley was directed against his signing of Jefferson Davis's bail bond. It touched a particularly sensitive nerve in Greeley, and he replied: "I tell you here that, out of a life earnestly devoted to the good of humankind, your children will recollect my going to Richmond and signing the bail-bond as the wisest act, and will feel that it did more for freedom and humanity than all you were competent to do, though you lived to the age of Methuselah." It was a characteristic Greeley utterance, self-important and self-righteous and in large part right, though blown considerably out of proportion. Certainly he reaped his reward, if reward it was. Without that powerfully symbolic act, he could never have won the Democratic nomination for president in 1872.

The Labor Reform convention met at Columbus, Ohio, at the end of February and nominated Judge David Davis of Illinois for president and Joel Parker of New Jersey for vice-president.

In May the Workingman's National Convention met in New York and nominated Grant and Wilson for president and vice-president, and in August the National Labor Reform Convention reconvened, this time in Philadelphia, to nominate Charles O'Conor for president and Eli Saulsbury for vice-president. (Both men declined to run.)

A month later the Colored Liberal Republican National Convention met at Louisville, Kentucky, with representatives from twenty-three states and "nominated" Greeley and Brown. There were, thus, in addition to the "regular" party nominating conventions, seven others. Counting the candidates of the National Prohibition Party and George Train and Victoria Woodhull, there were eight declared candidates.

All of which may, not unreasonably, be taken as an index to the disarray of American politics. Never in the history of the Republic had the country's political system seemed so close to disintegration.

American presidential campaigns had not been notable for truthfulness or restraint, but that of 1872 reached, if it were possible, new depths of mutual vilification and abusiveness. Thomas Nast's merciless caricatures of poor Greeley must rank as the most devastating in the history of political cartooning. *Frank Leslie's Illustrated Newspaper* commonly depicted Grant as a drunken tyrant.

Greeley, abandoned by the leaders of the women's movement and by black leaders, grew increasingly querulous, denouncing Union veterans for "rekindling the bitterness and hatred" of the war and describing black leaders as "ignorant, deceived and misguided." He even went so far as to suggest that he had second thoughts about slavery itself. In Ohio Rutherford Hayes noted in his diary: "Greeley's recent career of speaking . . . has been I think unwise on his part. It has helped us."

Gratz Brown, Greeley's running mate, gave several angry, rambling speeches to hostile audiences while obviously intoxicated. It was difficult to imagine how the combined Greeley forces could have performed more ineptly.

The split of the Liberal Republicans, or Reformers, from the Republican Party and the acquiescence of the Democrats to Greeley, plus the Tammany scandals, combined to give the Republicans their widest margin of victory yet. The Democrats carried only six states with 42 electoral votes to 286 for Grant. The popular vote was

3,597,132 to 2,834,125. "The Republican Party," George Templeton Strong wrote, "has secured such absolute control that it is not unlikely to run wild, abuse its power, disgrace itself, and fall to pieces. Someone has said that the safest of all majorities is a majority of one." Strong was remarkably prophetic. Greeley, of course, found no comfort in such speculations. He was conscious only that he had been overwhelmingly repudiated. He had also lost his wife, whose illness and death devastated him. Whitelaw Reid and his friends had taken over control of the *Tribune* during Greeley's campaigning. Under the strain of those multiple disappointments, Greeley's mind gave way, and his last days were spent in wild harangues against his enemies. His end was no less a tragedy for the fact that Greeley so often made himself absurd. He had, after all, been in the forefront of the forces of reform for more than twenty years, and he had made his newspaper the voice of virtually every philanthropic crusade in the nation from antislavery and temperance to peace and vegetarianism. He deserved a better fate than his determination to be president of the United States condemned him to.

The militancy of women was given dramatic emphasis by the determined efforts of a number of them to vote. In Rochester, New York, fifteen women, led by Susan B. Anthony, persuaded election officials to let them vote. (Anthony was subsequently fined $100 but refused to pay the fine, and the matter was quietly dropped.) In Norwalk, Connecticut, Sarah Huntington tried to vote but was turned away. In St. Louis, Virginia Moore sued election officials for $10,000 for refusing to register her as a voter. In Detroit, Michigan, Mrs. Mannette Gardner, who had voted in several previous elections, was denied the right to vote. In Oregon four women were allowed to vote, but their votes were not counted.

The desolation of the South did not stop Elizabeth Meriwether from espousing the cause of women's suffrage, which she did in a literary journal, called the *Tablet,* that she edited and published. When Susan B. Anthony was arrested in New York for attempting to vote, Elizabeth Meriwether decided to risk the outrage of her friends and family by voting in Memphis. "I had been taught in my history," she wrote, "that taxation without representation was tyranny—and in order to bring the question home to our people in the South, as Miss Anthony's arrest had done in the North, I determined to vote in Memphis." And so she did. To arrest a Southern lady of family and breeding was unthinkable. Southern chivalry would not countenance it. Elizabeth Meriwether was allowed to vote in the municipal elections and thereby deprived of martyrdom. But nothing changed in regard to the rights of women in Memphis or elsewhere in the South. Some impudent newspaper editors expressed now familiar horror at the thought of "our estimable female friends . . . being dragged into the corrupt cesspool of politics" and "unsexed" (as though she had not already been unsexed by being turned into a "pure, ethereal spirit"). Elizabeth Meriwether responded to such lamentations in a thoroughly down-to-earth spirit. "To say that love of politics can wipe [the maternal] feeling out of a woman's breast," she wrote in a letter to the *Memphis Appeal*, "is bosh. If a woman had to vote six times a day she would not love her baby one atom the less. Has Queen Victoria neglected her nine children because of politics?" she asked.

There was a final bizarre footnote to the nation's most bizarre election. Pinckney Benton Stewart Pinchback, the black politician, found himself, through astute maneuvering, in a position to hold the state of Louisiana for Grant. With the gubernatorial election deadlocked and both candidates claiming victory, Pinchback, as lieutenant governor, assumed the office of acting governor and applied to Grant for military support. He received the endorsement of the attorney general as "the lawful executive of Louisiana" and the promise of Federal troops to keep order. Appointed to the United States Senate by the State Assembly, which he dominated, Pinchback was denied a seat in that body on the grounds of his alleged career as a riverboat gambler and a conviction for assault and battery. Even so, he made his presence felt in the Senate chambers before his eviction, and a newspaper reporter who called him "a brown Mephistopheles" described him as "just perceptibly African, his eyes intensely black and brilliant" with "a sardonic smile" that gave him "an evil look, undeniably handsome as the man is. It seems," the writer added, "as though the scorn which must rage within him at the sight of the ignorant men from the South who look down upon him on account of his color, finds play imperceptibly about his lips." His manners were "a model of good breeding," and he was always impeccably dressed.

Another objection to seating Pinchback was that his black wife could not be received in Washington society. When months passed without the Senate accepting him, Henry Turner came to his defense in an article in the *New National Era*. "In natural genius and sweeping eloquence," Turner wrote, Pinchback was "the superior of half the Senators. . . ." He had saved Louisiana "from the voraciousness of

Democrats and Negro-haters" and was entitled to the support of Republican Senators. Whatever might be said of his past, "if Mr. Pinchback had been white he would have been seated with applause," Turner concluded. "The trouble is Mr. Pinchback is colored and he is smart." Finally, in 1876, the Senate rejected Pinchback, salving its conscience by awarding him $17,000 in back salary. Thwarted in the Senate, Pinchback nonetheless remained a power in Louisiana state politics for years to come.

The Republican victory in 1872 convinced many Southern whites of the old aristocracy that further resistance to Congressional Reconstruction was fruitless, and large numbers came into the Republican Party to try to guide it in a direction favorable to their interests. John Roy Lynch estimated that as many as 25 to 30 percent of Southern whites aligned themselves with the Republicans in the months immediately following the elections of 1872, among them "the best and most substantial men of that section," in Lynch's words. "After that election," he wrote, "the situation was accepted by everyone in perfect good faith. No one could be found in either party who was bold enough to express the opinion that the Congressional Plan of Reconstruction was a mistake, or that negro suffrage was a failure." It may be that Lynch rather overstates the case, but there is substantial evidence that his proposition was, in the main, true. The best evidence is to be found in the fact that a number of holdouts, Southern leaders and prewar political figures who had endorsed the notion of "masterly inactivity," came out of their self-imposed retirement and began to participate in Republican and Democratic politics.

49

Grant's Second Administration

With Grant's re-election the alienation of the liberal reformers in the party from the President was complete. Civil service reform, sound money, and an end to municipal corruption became their principal preoccupations. Increasingly Grant stood alone in his efforts to enforce the Fourteenth and Fifteenth Amendments and to protect black rights. The revelations of the various "rings," such as the Whiskey Ring in which Treasury Department officials were involved, helped discredit his administration further.

Even Grant's inaugural ball was a disaster. It had been planned for out-of-doors, and a large tent erected for the purpose, but the weather turned unseasonably cold. Ice formed in the beverages, the floral pieces were frozen, and the occasion was only partly redeemed by the fact that West Point cadets danced with the wives of the black Congressmen.

Corruption in all states and at all levels of government was, Reconstruction aside, the most conspicuous aspect of American society. In the period between 1869 and 1877, Massachusetts was as plagued by corruption as New York, New Jersey, or Pennsylvania. Three of Benjamin Butler's close political allies were convicted of crime and sent to the state prison. Still another fled to South America to escape prosecution for forgery. Another was indicted for frauds which resulted in the failure of a bank. To George Hoar, the principal hazard that faced the country was corruption, "which then, as always, followed a great war. Unprincipled and greedy men sought to get contracts from the Government by aid of influential politicians. This aid they paid for sometimes, though I think rarely, in money, and in contributions to political campaigns, and in the various kinds of assistance necessary to maintain in power the men to whom they were so indebted. This corruption not only affected all branches of the Civil Service, especially the War and the Navy and the Treasury, but poisoned legislation itself." Speaking in his hometown, Worcester, Massachusetts, in 1873, Hoar deplored "this poison, this rotting from the core, when the virtue of our public servants is corrupted. . . ." Such misdeeds were "far more dangerous to the Republic [than the late rebellion]. There is already danger that the operations of the Tweeds and Goulds in New York may be repeated on more gigantic scale at the national capital. The mighty railroads to whom our public domain has been so lavishly granted . . . afford infinite opportunity for plunder and corruption. All these are at the cost of the labor of the country. The increased tax falls in the end on the consumer."

In 1873 in Kansas a politician named Caldwell blatantly bought a U.S. Senate seat. A. R. Shepherd, a close friend of Grant's, was appointed head of the District of Columbia government by the President, and the whole administration of the city was soon a morass of maladministration and fraud. Secretary of War William Belknap sold the posts of Indian trader to the highest bidders. The most sensational peculation of all, of course, was the Crédit Mobilier. The Union Pacific and the Central Pacific Railroad companies had received large government grants to build the transcontinental railroad. Each road received, further, a thirty-year loan of government bonds to the value of $27,000,000. In addition, each company could mortgage its properties to the sum of $27,000,000. The government would extinguish all Indian claims and allocate to the railroads "ten alternate sections per mile within a twenty-mile limit of the line of the tracks." The government was presumably protected by the President's authority to appoint five government directors to the respective companies. The Crédit Mobilier was organized as a kind of holding company for the Union Pacific with common stockholders. The stock of the Crédit Mobilier was divided among the managers of the Union Pacific, who proceeded to mortgage the road for the full sum allowed by the government—$27,000,000—and, beyond that, to mortgage their land grants along the right-of-way for an additional $11,000,000. They then contracted with the Crédit Mobilier to build the Union Pacific's portion of the railroad for the total of the company's assets and divided the proceeds among themselves as dividends on the Crédit Mobilier stock. The Union Pacific was thus mortgaged to the hilt and without adequate funds to begin construction before the first mile of railroad was laid.

All this constituted a swindle as brazen as it was reckless, perpetrated by some of the most respectable gentlemen of the New York and Boston financial communities—the class of men in whose hands, Americans had been told since the founding of the Republic, should be placed the direction of public affairs on the ground that as disinterested and high-minded people of superior birth and education they would be far more trustworthy than those inferior to them in social rank and educational attainments. (It must be said parenthetically that few of the Founding Fathers took that view.)

What brought this extraordinary financial house of cards tumbling down (though it is hard to understand how it could have long stood) was that the thieves fell to quarreling among themselves about such questions as whether their criminal headquarters should be Boston or New York. The New Yorkers brought a suit in equity to enjoin Oakes Ames, the Massachusetts Congressman, and his brother Oliver from voting at a stockholder's meeting in New York. (Oakes and Oliver Ames had inherited their father's successful shovel-manufacturing business and had also made a killing in Western lands.) The corporate infighting which followed, marked by bribery and perjury, is too complex to detain us, but when the dust settled, the Ames brothers were in command. Thereupon a member of the defeated faction wrote a letter detailing the shenanigans to Elihu Washburne, who, because of his nose for sniffing out corruption, was known as the Watchdog of the Treasury, put the letter in the mails, and informed the opposition of his action. Knowing that the jig would be up if the letter reached its destination, the Ames faction capitulated and agreed to a board made up of criminals from New York as well as from Boston. The letter was retrieved from the mails, and Oakes Ames began to distribute the stock of the Crédit Mobilier around Congress, "where it would do the most good." The Congressmen were expected to pay for the stock at par value, but a dividend that would be greater than the original value of the stock was already pending. Buying a

$1,000 share was thus, in effect, getting it free. "A list of the men who were to be induced to take this stock was made out with wonderful and prophetic sagacity," in George Hoar's words. "It contained some of the ablest and most influential men in the two Houses of Congress. . . . It included men conspicuous for integrity as well as for ability." Blaine's name led the list, followed by Henry Wilson, Schuyler Colfax, Henry Dawes, George Boutwell, James Garfield, Roscoe Conkling, and John Logan of Illinois. The list thus contained the names of four men who were to become candidates for the nomination of their party to the presidency of the United States; one (Garfield) who was to become president; and two (Wilson and Colfax) who would become vice-presidents of the United States. (Colfax was, in fact, vice-president when the scandal broke.) The list included one Senator and three Congressmen from that citadel of moral rectitude, Massachusetts. Nine of the Congressmen involved subsequently became Senators. Of the eighteen men offered the stock, only four, including Conkling and Boutwell, refused to accept it. Henry Wilson's wife was given a share of the stock, but the Senate later insisted that, as soon as he learned about it, he had it returned.

When the whole unsavory business came out, it provided a field day for Thomas Nast and other political cartoonists, but a committee appointed by the Republican Congress to investigate the Republican culprits, not surprisingly, exonerated them. In the words of George Hoar, "All the persons who received any of the stock and told the story frankly at the investigation were acquitted of any wrong doing whatever, and never in the least suffered in esteem in consequence," a statement which, we might conjecture, probably said more about the general level of American politics than about the moral culpability of the individuals involved. Even Oakes Ames, manager of the deal, escaped with no more than a censure. Henry Wilson, it appeared to many, had been less than candid in his public declaration that he had never owned any of the stock in question, omitting to mention his wife's ownership. Schuyler Colfax was equally evasive and was found guilty of the minor offense of disingenuousness. The leadership of the Republican Party would have been decimated if any strict disciplinary action had been taken. Colfax's case was complicated by the fact that in the course of the investigation the committee unearthed the fact that the Vice-President had apparently accepted a bribe to help procure a government contract. Colfax had been the powerful and autocratic Speaker of the House for six years prior to his election as Grant's vice-president and was certainly one of the most influential political figures in the country. It is some comfort to note that the revelations of his wrongdoing finished him politically, though as far as any criminal proceedings against him were concerned, he got off scot-free. George Hoar noted a bit misleadingly in his autobiography that Colfax's term of office as vice-president "expired before any action could be taken, and he died soon after." Actually he died thirteen years later, a long "soon." Oakes Ames, an acute embarrassment to the Republican Party in Massachusetts, was more obliging; he did die "soon."

It was widely believed that Blaine, on receiving his stock, had said that "he should not be a dead-head." This was taken, not unreasonably, as assurance to Ames's agent that Blaine would help get the desired legislation through Congress. Blaine's defenders insisted it was a mere pleasantry, implying that he would take an active, though not illegal, interest in its affairs. It was also charged that Blaine had not been a merely passive figure in the transaction but had pointed out to those distributing the stock that he, as Speaker, had made a ruling that had "saved the road from hostile legislation." The most Hoar could bring himself to concede was that Blaine had made "an error of judgment, or of good taste." Although Blaine was, Hoar admitted, "a man of many faults and many infirmities," he was also "a brilliant and able man, lovable, patriotic, far-seeing, kind." He was also devoured by that dreadfully consuming presidential ambition that has warped the judgment and clouded the lives of so many otherwise decent and honest men.

Another unsavory scandal was lodged in the Treasury Department. Again it involved a Massachusetts political figure, an active supporter of Benjamin Butler's named John Sanborn, a special agent of the Treasury Department. Sanborn had been given a highly dubious contract to collect Federal taxes that had been evaded by the so-called Whiskey Ring. He had added to the delinquent distillers the names of several thousand other individual and corporate delinquents and had proceeded to collect from the defaulters $427,000, of which he received, by the terms of his contract with the Treasury Department, 50 percent, a substantial portion of which apparently went to political retainers of Benjamin Butler. When the fraudulent nature of the whole operation was exposed, the acting secretary of the treasury, William Adams Richardson, was allowed to resign. "It was unfortunate," George Hoar wrote in his account of the affair, "that nearly all the persons who were connected with this transaction were from New England, most of them from Massachusetts. . . ."

When Salmon Chase died, Grant offered the position of chief justice to Conkling, giving thereby another indication of his obtuseness in certain areas and perhaps revealing subconsciously his attitude toward the Court and the Constitution. Conkling turned down the offer. "I could not take the place," he wrote, "for I would be forever gnawing my chains." Politics, not law, was in his blood.

The Southern states, impoverished as they were by the war, had their own versions of the Crédit Mobilier, involving, in many instances, those very aristocrats who were most vocal in condemning the corrupt practices of carpetbaggers, scalawags, and "niggers." Indeed, in not a few instances bitter political rivals found themselves in bed with each other as members of one of the numerous rings that sprang up like mushrooms wherever it seemed possible to turn a dubious dollar. In South Carolina, for instance, the Blue Ridge Railroad, revived by infusions of public money, drew in ex-Governor James Orr and Matthew Calbraith Butler, a Confederate major general, connected to all the best families, a leader in Klan activities, and Senator-to-be. The Blue Ridge was merged with the Greenville & Columbia, and the members of the legislature bribed with some $90,000, spread around to insure passage of the inoffensive-sounding Revenue Bond Scrip Act. So much corruption was involved that it would take a modern-day Solomon to apportion the blame properly. Mixed in was a move to impeach Governor Robert Scott, who had carried the great seal of the state off to New York, where, allegedly under the influence of bad whiskey and loose women, he was prevailed upon to issue and sign a batch of new bonds.

A leader in the Blue Ridge Railroad faction, "Honest" John Patterson, a Pennsylvanian, was a classic carpetbagger, an unscrupulous robber of the state's treasury on a grand scale. Patterson worked hand in hand with Governor Scott. When Scott's defalcations resulted in the attempt to impeach him, Patterson reputedly spent $50,000 to buy up the votes to exonerate him. Blacks proved as susceptible as whites. One black man explained his acceptance of money for his vote thus: "I've been sold in my life eleven times. This is the first time I ever got the money."

The cost of getting a $2,000,000 appropriation voted for the Alabama & Chattanooga Railroad was $5,000 to the white chairman of the legislative committee and $50 to black legislators. The charges of corruption were not confined to the legislators, who issued worthless bonds and filled their pockets with the proceeds. Business interests, North and South, were eager corrupters of anyone willing to be corrupted. Northern financiers supplied the money that smoothed the way for the Alabama & Chattanooga Railroad, and banking interests in New Orleans crowded the halls of the state legislatures to lobby for bills that would enrich them. A Congressman visiting Columbia, South Carolina, reported: "Even the old aristocratic class, to whom we have been taught to attribute sentiments of chivalric honor, have not scrupled to bribe officials." In the view of one visitor, the willingness of aristocratic whites to offer bribes to black officials was a consequence of "the contempt which the old property-holding class feels for the freedmen and all who cooperate with them politically. This gives to the bribery of such persons, in the eyes of the old native class, the semblance of the purchase of a slave."

William Whipper, who had spoken so eloquently on behalf of enfranchising women in the state constitutional convention, soon became one of governor Scott's closest aides. Whipper's sisters-in-law, Catherine de Medici, Charlotte Corday, and Louise Muhlbach, were the leaders of black society in Columbia. Their house was furnished with "beautiful carpets, elegant furniture, tasteful pictures, and a one thousand dollar piano; photograph albums filled with the choicest Rembrandts lay in profusion on an Italian marble table."

A colored militia captain in the city gave a ball attended by the "youth and beauty of colored society . . . with a sprinkling of whites." Governor Scott, it was noted, "makes no distinction among members of the legislature (125 of them are colored); all taken equally by the hand with the graceful urbanity for which his honor is distinguished."

Franklin Moses, Scott's successor as governor, was soon called the Robber Governor. He bought the greatest mansion in Columbia, with stately columns and inlaid marble floors, and ran up, among other debts, $2,000 in unpaid butchers' bills. It was estimated that his total indebtedness was in excess of $225,000, and he set about to recover this sum and whatever he could amass in addition. A white resident of Columbia recalled seeing the governor often seated in "a handsome landau drawn by a spanking pair of high-stepping horses, and containing four Negro wenches arrayed in low-neck and short-sleeves. . . ." Moses would stop at a saloon on main street, go in and get champagne and glasses, "and right there in the public sidewalk enter into a perfect orgy with the dusky belles." Despite the racial bias evident in such accounts, Northern and Southern readers alike delighted in them. They were offered as evidence of the absurdity of black social pretensions and the unfitness of black politicians for leadership, though they might have been more reasonably interpreted as instances of ordinary human frailty.

Moses's peculations resulted in a warrant for his arrest. To defend him, he hired as his attorneys, Robert Elliott, his political ally, and Daniel Chamberlain, his rival, and called out four companies of colorfully garbed black Zouave militamen to protect him.

A group known as Union Reformers arose to try to defeat the corrupt Republicans. Richard Cain, deeply concerned about the continuing reports of corruption in his home state, wrote in the *Beaufort* (South Carolina) *Republican* of November 23, 1871: "We know that the colored men of this State will have to bear the odium of all the crimes or misdemeanors of the whites who manipulate the finances. This government of South Carolina is in the hands of white men, placed there by colored men's votes. If there is stealing being done, they do it. If there is robbery of the State of its millions, it is not the Negro who does these things. . . . Is it not the duty of the people to rise up in their might and select another class of men to guide the State? There must be a change. There must be a uniting of all honest men of every class and race in the State for honest government." The protests and exhortations of men like Cain were futile. As the finances of the state grew grimmer and its employees were paid in worthless scrip, it was the black people who, as usual, suffered the severest hardships. The land commissioner of South Carolina, C. P. Leslie, instructed to buy up land for distribution to black farm families, engaged instead in speculation, "leaving the poor laboring people homeless, barefooted and in rags," in the words of a black leader. Leslie was forced to resign, and it was left to Francis Cardozo, as state treasurer, to try to put the affairs of the Land Commission in some sort of order.

In Texas a black leader, James Washington, complained in the pages of the *New National Era* that black politicians had been corrupted by their white counterparts. "Our leading men in the legislature," he declared, "proved themselves corrupt and sold themselves for gold. They were all, with a few exceptions, crazy on railroads. . . . If you can get some of our Northern friends to come here and help us to educate the colored people that they will not sell themselves for gold, try to induce them to come. . . ."

A reform movement made up of dissident blacks and white Republicans opposed to Scott's administration held a convention in South Carolina, denounced the governor, and demanded reform of the government. The Union Reform Convention was led by Martin Delany, who came out strongly against the acceptance by blacks of white Republican leadership. "I take the ground," he declared, "that no people have become great people who have not had their own leaders, and black men must have black leaders. We have the strength and we want a fair share of the offices. We don't want more than one half; we don't want a colored governor, for our good sense tells us differently . . . but we want a lieutenant governor, and two colored men in the House of Representatives and one in the Senate and our quota of state and county offices."

Alonzo Ransier joined Delany in calling for the Republican Party to reform itself. "We find ourselves today, as a race," he told his black constituents in Charleston, "passing through a crisis. The colored people of the United States, with all the grand achievements of the past ten years, are today passing through the crisis of their political history in this country. We present to the world a noble spectacle, a record unparalleled in the annals of any people similarly situated. No race has been subject to such scathing criticism; no people have had such tremendous disadvantages to labor under. And I feel free to say, no race in a similar position could have acquitted themselves more creditably." It rested with the black voters, he declared, "to remove every just cause of complaint, remembering that by every unworthy man you elevate to office, by every scoundrel you keep in office, you justify the public opinion in the country adverse to the well-being of the Republican party in this State, and to the fitness of the colored man for the franchise."

Elliott switched his support to Daniel Chamberlain, and at the next election Chamberlain was elected governor by a substantial majority. Moses began a long decline, becoming a drug addict and an alcoholic before his death in Massachusetts in 1906.

Chamberlain, a graduate of Yale and a Union officer with a distinguished war record, was only thirty-five years old when he gained the governor's office. He spoke in support of Republican policies, reminded his listeners that in his administration no act which betrayed "a vindictive spirit, or which displays the old spirit of caste," had been passed. When the Republican Party came to power under the Reconstruction Acts of Congress, it faced an "appalling task." In addition to the "inveterate prejudices and habits" inherited from two centuries of slavery, "around them were the fresh wastes and ruin of desolating war. The passions, the hatreds, the sufferings of the long struggle, were still fresh in the hearts and memories of our people. . . . Surely, if ever a difficult task fell to human hands, it was the reconstruction of the civil and political fabric of our State, out of the materials which slavery and war had left us." Chamberlain would not claim "that no acts have been done, during the past two years, of doubtful expediency and propriety. I am not anxious to claim that there have been no instances of incompetency, of dishonesty, of corruption among those who have been trusted with public office." But he did insist that under the most difficult circumstances, the Republicans had compiled a record that they could be proud of. Chamberlain placed special emphasis on the increase in public spending for the support of "free schools." In 1866 the state had appropriated $13,600 for the University of South Carolina, $25,000 for the support of schools, and a total of $6,000 for the education of the deaf-mute and blind, and the care of the insane. In 1869, $200,000 had been spent on free schools, $37,500 for the university, and $8,000 for the care of the deaf-mute and blind—a total of $245,500, contrasted with $44,600 three years earlier. There were 625 schools in operation and 23,299 pupils in attendance. Cruel and archaic laws had been repealed, including "that disgraceful remnant of legal barbarism, imprisonment for debt." Laws had also been passed to protect the property of married women and the claims of mechanics to payment for services performed.

Before the war the average expense of a session of the South Carolina legislature was $20,000. In the six years following Congressional Reconstruction the average annual expense was $320,000. The session of 1871 spent $617,000. At the beginning of Reconstruction the state debt was less than $1,000,000. Five years later it was more than $17,500,000. "Public offices," Chamberlain wrote, "were objects of vulgar, commonplace bargain and sale. Justice in the lower and higher courts was bought and sold. . . . State militia on a vast scale was organized and equipped in 1870 and 1871 solely from the negroes, arms and legal organization being denied the white Democrats." The Klan, "brutal and murderous to the last degree," was "the gangrene of incapacity, dishonesty, and corruption in public office." A major part of the misappropriated funds was spent on fancying up the legislative chambers until they resembled a high-class bordello. Two hundred and six expensive cuspidors, "richly decorated and marked House of

Representatives," were ordered from a New York firm at a cost of $1,800. Six "fine black Belgian marble" clocks cost $885; and a "walnut and gilt mantel mirror for Speaker's room, carved, with palmetto, shield and eagle," came to $960. Legislators had been notoriously generous to themselves, but in a state many of whose citizens lived in poverty or on the edge of it, such extravagance seemed insupportable.

In every state charges of corruption were continually and loudly made by outraged Southern Conservatives or Democrats. The truth of the charges varied. That there was widespread corruption is as undeniable as is the fact that many black politicians were involved in it. It could hardly have been otherwise. We have already taken note of the general corruption in American politics. In every state in the Union the partisan political press was filled with lurid accounts of public misdoings, many true and many designed simply to advance the cause of a candidate or a party. It can be said with equal certainty of the Reconstruction governments that in most instances the charges of misuse of funds and of political corruption were vastly overblown for political purposes. Of the hundreds of charges leveled, few were ever proved in courts of law. It can also be said with confidence that the old planter aristocracy, which sang so loudly about malfeasance in office, was in many instances itself deeply involved, especially in the railroad schemes that tempted prospective investors with promises of quick and easy riches in the postwar South as well as in the North. We are faced with the by-now-familiar black-man-in-a-ditch syndrome: The white man drunk in a ditch is an example of human frailty; the black man drunk in a ditch is an example of the inherent depravity of blacks. It is clear that many of those busy indicting black politicians of the Reconstruction Era expected a far higher level of political morality from them than from white counterparts. A black politician on the take was thus not simply an individual lacking in some essential element of self-restraint; he was a *black* man giving evidence of the thievish inclinations of his race. Slaves stole chickens and pigs; black politicians stole tax revenues and railroad bonds.

In fairness to the white Southerners, it must be said that they lived in many instances in penury, in ruined economies that they were trying desperately to rebuild. Thus, they had far less tolerance for the thievish propensities of their politicians, whatever the color of their skin, than, say, prosperous New Yorkers had for the far more spectacular larceny of *their* political leaders. In a number of instances the Reconstruction governors from the North—carpetbaggers by

Southern definition—were men of far more intelligence and ability than the average politician. That certainly was the case with General Adelbert Ames, senator and then governor of Mississippi, and of Daniel Chamberlain of South Carolina.

Both Chamberlain and Ames made valiant efforts to clean up the corruption in their respective states, and in these efforts they were aided by some of the ablest of the black politicians. If black ministers and teachers like the Cardozos, Revels, Turner, Elliott, and Delany were touched by scandal, it was doubtless the price they had to pay for engaging in politics. Certainly all were men whose abilities were demonstrated beyond any reasonable doubt. The stereotype that has been most often presented is that of illiterate blacks pushed into positions of power and responsibility by scheming whites—venal carpetbaggers from the North and treacherous scalawags from the South, supported by Federal bayonets and all combining to corrupt and manipulate the ignorant freedman. Readers familiar with such men as Henry Turner, the Cardozo brothers, Jonathan Gibbs, Richard Cain, the Lynches, and several dozen other leading black politicians will be aware of how far from the truth the familiar stereotype is. At the same time the truth itself is infinitely complex. Conditions varied from state to state, depending on a number of factors, such as the character of those Southern white politicians who undertook to work with their black counterparts, the relative numbers of blacks and whites in the state legislatures, the degree of experience and sophistication of the black politicians, and, perhaps most important, the aims of the Northern white Republicans who came South to assist or exploit the free blacks (human nature being what it is, some who came to assist remained to exploit).

In addition to these manifold troubles, the country, early in 1873, was devastated by another of the periodic financial panics that were by now so familiar an aspect of American economy. It all began with the fall of "the great house of Jay Cooke & Company, with its affiliates and auxiliaries. . . ." as a consequence of reckless stock manipulation. A panic spread on Wall Street. Anxious speculators crowded the street despite rain, so that to George Templeton Strong, viewing the scene from Broadway, it appeared "a compact mosaic of shiny umbrellas, like a bed of mushrooms." There was a run on the Union Trust, and soon other banks were under siege from nervous depositors. The Stock Exchange closed its doors for ten days, and banks got permission to be

PANIC
OF
1873

open for only an hour or so at a time to slow down the withdrawal of funds. The secretary of the Union Trust Company skipped town with $250,000 of the company's dwindling assets. On September 24, 1873, Strong reported "the street . . . not excited but faint, sick, prostrate, and resigned to the approach of some indefinite calamity." Soon factories and mills were closed, and unemployed workers were parading with demands for jobs or some form of public assistance to keep their families from starving. The depression, it was soon evident, was worldwide; it was due, in large part, to reckless overexpansion and a host of get-rich-quick schemes. The Chicago and Boston fires were contributory causes. Two years earlier, on Sunday, October 8, 1871, a fire had started in a stable in Chicago, spread to a nearby lumberyard, and soon was out of control, consuming stores, theaters, hotels, and warehouses as well as numerous public buildings and private residences. It was twenty-four hours before the firemen could get control of the blaze. By that time 2,100 acres of the city had been burned—some 5 miles north and south—17,500 buildings were destroyed, and 100,000 people were homeless. The loss was greater than the terrible New York fires thirty years earlier. Chicago was the commercial center of the Middle West, and the devastation wrought there by the fire introduced a spirit of apprehension and anxiety among businessmen from New York to San Francisco. The *Nation* declared: "At the close of business on Monday, a gloomy atmosphere, an undefined sense of dread and terror, overhung the entire financial community and the ablest, calmest, most conservative did not hesitate to express their fear that the catastrophe of Chicago will prove the beginning of widespread financial and commercial difficulty. . . . The destruction of so large an amount of property at Chicago has a most disastrous effect, and tends to destroy credit in every direction and to precipitate a panic."

Thirteen months later, almost to the day, a terrible fire swept Boston, destroying most of the buildings in a sixty-five-acre area in the center of the city, including a majority of the city's warehouses. Where the pride of the "solid men of Boston" had stood, "there is nothing," the *Nation* reported of that fire, "but rubbish remaining. . . ." The Boston preacher Phillips Brooks wrote a friend: "Everybody has suffered, almost everybody severely. Very many have lost all. . . . Street after street went like paper. There were sights so splendid and awful as I never dreamed of and now the desolation is bewildering."

The fires did not, as it turned out, abate the rage for speculation, although they greatly increased its hazards. The Franco-Prussian War caused a decline in foreign purchases of American agricultural products, and a depression in England, with the consequent attempts of British investors in American industrial plants, ranches, and mines to liquidate their holdings, were also contributing factors.

Among those who suffered from the depression were freed blacks struggling to establish themselves as self-supporting farmers. "Purchases of large tracts of land are being made," the *South Carolina Missionary Record* reported, and freedmen were "building up homesteads and becoming taxpayers, producers and good citizens." The problem of financing black land purchases was solved in part by Congress's establishment of the Freedmen's Savings and Trust Company with forty-one branches in the Southern states. Within three years the bank had 44,395 depositors, whose total deposits rose to $55,000,000 by 1873. But the depression toppled the bank. It turned out that many of its loans, a number of which had been made to whites, were uncollectible. Frederick Douglass took over its direction in a desperate effort to retrieve something, even putting $10,000 of his own money into the venture. But it was too late. The bank failed. "It has been the black man's cow, but the white man's milk," Douglass wrote Gerrit Smith; "bad loans and bad management have been the death of it." It was a devastating setback to black aspirations. "The hope of everyone seemed to center in the Freedmen's Savings Bank," William Wells Brown wrote. " 'This is our bank,' said they and to this institution the intelligent and the ignorant, the soldier, farmer, day laborer and poor washerwoman all alike brought their earnings." After its failure many of the depositors, according to Brown, simply quit work, convinced that the cards were hopelessly stacked against blacks' achieving even the most modest degree of economic dependence. A number who had counted on their savings to complete payments on houses and farms were forced to abandon them.

One effect of the depression was to take a good deal of steam out of politics. The registration of voters in the city of New York alone fell by twenty-five thousand. The feeling of apathy infected most classes, but the well-to-do continued to spend money with abandon as though there were to be no tomorrow. In the great cities the fashionable stores were crowded as Christmas approached, and the contrast between the hectic buying of the affluent and the condition of the unemployed poor was generally remarked upon by the newspapers. The November elections of 1873 resulted in Democratic landslides in many states. "The Republican defeat is a Flodden or Bull Run," George Templeton

Strong noted. "But it may scare the party into better behavior and so prove a blessing in disguise."

With all this, a process was going on in the consciousness of the country (including indeed, the South) that anticipated relinquishing the "black question" to the South as quickly and unobtrusively as possible. The last of the great champions of black equality was Charles Sumner, already compromised in the eyes of many black leaders by his abandonment of Grant. (George Hoar recalled walking with the President across Lafayette Square. As they passed the handsome house Sumner had bought for his beautiful young wife, Grant shook his fist at it and said, "That man who lives up there has abused me in a way which I never suffered from any other man living.")

Sumner persisted in his efforts to get through Congress a civil rights bill that would provide a last measure of protection for blacks. He had first introduced the bill in 1870. He tried again in 1871 and once more in 1872, when he included a provision to give amnesty to former Confederate officers and officials. The act stipulated that no public facilities, including cemeteries or schools, could discriminate on the basis of race, color, or previous condition of servitude. Once more the bill was defeated. Stripped of his committee positions, viewed by many Republicans as a traitor to his party, devastated by the ruin of his marriage, he had to bear the final ignominy of having power wrested from him by the execrable Ben Butler in his home state of Massachusetts, where he had been ranked only slightly below the Deity for almost twenty-five years. He retained his Senate seat by the narrowest of margins. He had been suffering from acute attacks of angina, the pain of which could be relieved only by injections of morphine. He was sixty-three, and his large frame and massive head showed the ravages of years of combat. Like Stevens before him, Sumner suffered from an acute sense of personal failure. Yet he was determined to try once more to push a comprehensive civil rights bill through Congress. One of the bill's principal opponents in the House of Representatives—certainly its most dramatic opponent—was Alexander Hamilton Stephens, the former vice-president of the Confederacy, now a Congressman from Georgia.

Stephens represented the more liberal spirit of the South. He had opposed secession and after the war argued against the notorious Black Codes. He had been an outspoken enemy of the Klan and supported the franchise for blacks who owned property. In poor health, he was brought to the floor of the House on January 5, 1874, in a wheelchair and made a plea to his colleagues not to impair further the doctrine of states' rights or force upon the South yet another measure designed to transform its social order. Many of his colleagues listened to Stephens sympathetically. The states' rights argument was one to which they were especially susceptible. Robert Elliott was given the task of rebutting Stephens. The word had spread throughout the city that the black Congressman was to reply to the Southern leader, and the galleries of the House were packed. General Sherman was among the listeners as Elliott began to speak. "No man could have had a more exciting theme, or a more exciting occasion," Elliott wrote later. "I must speak under the eyes of crowded galleries, in the presence of a full house, and of many distinguished strangers, attracted by the novel interest of such an occasion.

"While I am sincerely grateful for this high mark of courtesy that has been accorded to me by this House," he began, "it is a matter of regret to me that it is necessary at this day that I should rise in the presence of an American Congress to advocate a bill which simply asserts equal rights and equal public privileges for all classes of American citizens." He advocated the bill not because he was black, he assured his colleagues, but "because it is right." Elliott went on to detail the contributions of black Americans to the history of the Republic—in the American Revolution, at the Battle of New Orleans, and in the Civil War itself. He marshaled an impressive array of citations —Francis Lieber, the most distinguished scholarly interpreter of the Constitution; Alexander Hamilton, his adversary's namesake. Much of Elliott's fire was directed against James Beck, a Congressman from Kentucky, who maintained that the Federal government had no right to intervene in the affairs of the states. Having made a shambles of Beck's argument, Elliott turned back to Stephens. As long as Stephens had confined his opinions, on "matters touching human rights, to his study or the columns of newspapers," he had, for his years and services, enjoyed a degree of immunity from attack. "But," Elliott declared, "when he comes again upon this national arena and throws himself with all his power and influence across the path which leads to the full enfranchisement of my race, I meet him only as an adversary; nor shall age or any other consideration restrain me from saying that he now offers his Government, which he has done his best to destroy, a very poor return for its magnanimous treatment, to come here and seek to continue, by the assertion of doctrines obnoxious to the true principles of our Government, the burdens and oppressions which rest upon five millions of his countrymen. . . ."

For John Harris, the member from Virginia who had earlier declared that his remarks were intended for only the white members of Congress, Elliott had a sharp riposte. "Let him feel that a Negro was not only too magnanimous to smite him in his weakness, but was even charitable enough to grant him the mercy of his silence. . . . Assuring the gentleman that the Negro in this country aims at a higher degree of intellect than that exhibited by him in this debate, I cheerfully commend him to the commiseration of all intelligent men the world over—black men as well as white men. . . . (Laughter and applause from the floor and the gallery.)

"The results of the war, as seen in reconstruction, have settled forever the political status of my race. The passage of this bill will determine the civil status, not only of the Negro, but of any other class of citizens who may feel themselves discriminated against. It will form the capstone of that temple of liberty, begun on this continent under discouraging circumstances . . . until at last it stands in all its beautiful symmetry and proportions, a building the grandest which the world has ever seen, realizing the most sanguine expectations and the highest hopes of those who, in the name of equal, impartial, and universal liberty, laid the foundation stones."

Elliott concluded his oration with the scriptural story of Ruth. Like her, black Americans were ready to say to their white countrymen: "Intreat me not to leave thee, or to return from following after thee: for whither thou goest, I will go; and where thou lodgest, I will lodge: thy people shall be my people, and thy God my God: where thou diest, will I die, and there will I be buried: the Lord do so to me, and more also, if ought but death part thee and me." (Great applause.)

Certainly, there have been few more dramatic exchanges on the floor of the House of Representatives. The champions of the bill, not surprisingly, declared that Elliott had demolished his opponents, and a modern reading will suggest a similar verdict. Certainly that was the judgment of the Republican members who surged forward in such numbers to congratulate him that they "formed in line in the aisle and moved up to his seat in a column."

Many journals and newspapers throughout the North printed the speech in whole or in part. The *New National Era*, the paper edited by Frederick Douglass's son, devoted the front page to the speech, and the *National Republican* declared: "No more dignified, skillful, exhaustive tearing down of the false theories raised by caste alone has ever been witnessed in legislative halls."

A few weeks later Richard Cain, Elliott's fellow editor, ten years his senior, and a graduate of Wilberforce University, spoke forcefully in behalf of the civil rights bill, telling of numerous incidents in which he and other black Congressmen had been refused service in restaurants and hotels and the humiliations they had experienced. Blacks did not wish "social mixing" or amalgamation, he insisted; they wished simply "all the rights and immunities" belonging to citizens. They wished their "manhood."

As weeks of desultory debate dragged on, James Rapier, the Alabama Congressman, added his voice, expressing his disappointment over the "protracted discussion." Apparently it was impossible to convince some white Congressmen that the exclusive preoccupation of black men and women was not "amalgamation" with whites. Did the whites believe that the Constitution would be invoked to force a white woman to marry a black man against her will or vice versa? "Just think," Rapier said, "that the law recognizes my right upon this floor as a law-maker, but that there is no law to secure to me any accommodations whatever while traveling here to discharge my duties as a Representative of a large and wealthy constituency. Here I am the peer of the proudest, but on a steamboat or car I am not equal to the most degraded. Is not this most anomalous and ridiculous?"

John Roy Lynch, in turn, discussed the question "from three stand-points—legal, social, and political." Like Rapier, Lynch directed his attention to the charge that the bill was designed "to bring about social equality between the races. I can . . . assure that portion of my democratic friends on the other side of the House, whom I regard as my social inferiors," Lynch declared, "that if at any time I should meet any one of you at a hotel and occupy a seat at the same table with you, or the same seat in a car with you, do not think that I have thereby accepted you as my social equal. Not at all. . . ." Lynch went on to tell of an incident involving a refined and intelligent black woman who had been turned out of a railroad car. "Mr. Speaker, if this unjust discrimination is to be longer tolerated by the American people, which I do not, cannot, and will not believe until I am forced to do so, then I can only say with sorrow and regret that our boasted civilization is a fraud; our republican institutions a failure; our social system a disgrace; and our religion a complete hypocrisy."

Lynch was perhaps more effective in his attack on the "exploded theory of white supremacy and negro inferiority. . . . The gentleman from North Carolina admits, ironically, that the colored people even when in bondage and ignorance, could equal, if not excel the whites in some things—dancing, singing, and eloquence, for instance." Assuming, for the sake of argument, that the Congressman was correct, Lynch asked, why should blacks excel in these areas and not in others? "The answer is an easy one: You could not prevent them from dancing unless you kept them constantly tied; you could not prevent them from singing unless you kept them continually gagged; could not prevent them from being eloquent unless you deprived them of the power of speech; but you could and did prevent them from being educated for fear they would equal you in every other respect."

Sumner, meanwhile, continued to suffer from angina. He struggled to complete his *Works*, an edition of his speeches, letters, and essays, although, as he wrote Longfellow, it had become "a load and mill-stone, under which time, income, strength, every thing seem to disappear." He was lonely and seized eagerly on visitors. Wendell Phillips called on him; when it came time for Sumner's hot footbath and Phillips tried to leave, Sumner begged him to stay, declaring that he would take his treatment only if Phillips remained. The Massachusetts legislature, aware of Sumner's failing health, rescinded a motion of censure against him passed originally under the influence of Butler and the Republican regulars. When Sumner received word of the legislature's action, a black friend, J. B. Smith, noted, Sumner wept "as I never saw a man weep before" and said, "I knew Massachusetts would do me justice."

As Sumner left the Senate chambers on March 10, 1874, he experienced the now-familiar pains. "I have a toothache in my heart," he told a fellow Senator. "I think I shall go home." There he had another serious attack. His physician gave him two successive injections of morphine to ease the pain. Friends, hearing that he was sinking, began to gather at his home. George Hoar, his ally in many legislative battles, came to his bed, and Sumner murmured something about his bill: "You must take care of the civil-rights bill, my bill, the civil-rights bill, don't let it fail." When Frederick Douglass came to see him, he repeated his injunction. Just before his death he turned to Hoar and said: "Judge, tell Emerson how much I love and revere him." Hoar replied: "He said of you once, that he never knew so *white* a soul." A world of irony was in the word.

Hearing of Sumner's death, George Templeton Strong wrote in his diary, "an able, accomplished, and unwise man. . . . He was too self-conscious and, perhaps, too cultivated and scholarly for the American people." Republicans, white and black, vied to honor the dead hero of abolitionism. The tragedy of his last years could not dim the luster of his achievements on behalf of black people. Since Stevens's death and the elevation of Henry Wilson to the seat of the presiding officer of the Senate in his role as vice-president, Sumner had been the last representative in Congress of the antislavery legion that had run Congress for more than a decade. To everyone's surprise and to the chagrin of many Southerners, Lucius Quintus Cincinnatus Lamar, the hard-line Mississippi Senator, came forward as one of his principal eulogizers. "There is a certain Orientalism in the mind of Mr. Lamar," James Blaine wrote, "strangely admixed with typical Americanism. He is full of reflection, full of imagination; seemingly careless, yet closely observant, apparently dreamy, yet altogether practical." Lamar defended himself in a letter to an indignant Alabaman by explaining that his purpose had been twofold—to express a genuine appreciation of Sumner's remarkable gifts as a political leader and also to disarm the Radical Republicans and thereby help defeat the civil rights bill. Lamar had set out to try to discover some common ground between the Northern and Southern Senators, but he had "found among the New Englanders & a few N. Westerners creatures egotistical, monstrously harsh & proud, with souls shut against every thing like commiseration, tenderness & charity, cynical, inexorable & contemptuous for the suffering people of the South." On the other hand, some Congressmen were much more favorably disposed, "but they are apprehensive & distrustful of reactionary measures if we get such control," Lamar added. ". . . They fear that the negroes will be put into a position of legal & civil subordination and an alliance formed with the Northern Democrats to reverse the results of the war."

Men like Lamar and Hampton had supported Horace Greeley against Grant in 1872 in the hope of putting to rest the Northern anxieties about an alliance between Southern and Northern Democrats to undo the results of the war. (The North was as obsessed with the specter of that alliance as the South was with the notion of "Negro domination.") The results were not at all what the South had hoped for. Now the death of Sumner seemed to Lamar to provide an opportunity to send a clear and unmistakable message to the North, saying: We wish to acknowledge that we have been defeated and that we accept the consequences of that defeat; we intend to live by its terms even to according the freedmen their rights and their political roles until it is as clear to the North as to the South that they are incapable of responsibly exercising those rights and performing those roles. Lamar was baffled by the fact that his fellow Senators from the North *simply could not hear what their Southern colleagues said*. It was evident in their faces, in their postures, and even, in the more extreme cases, in gestures or acts expressing indifference or contempt. But everything said about Sumner was sure to get immediate attention in the North, "especially," he wrote, "among those classes who have never given us a hearing." Moreover, Sumner, in Lamar's view, "had become an advocate of amnesty & peace & fraternity with our people. He had been deposed by the Conklings, Chandlers, Mortons, Grants & Butlers from the leadership of his party & was very strongly in sympathy with our people. . . . His death was a source of great regret to many of the best friends of the South."

Despite Lamar's efforts, the civil rights bill was passed by the Senate in April, a few weeks after Sumner's death and undoubtedly as a consequence of it. The House, however, balked, and it was not until a year later—March 1, 1875—that it was passed by both houses and signed into law. Soon it would be a dead letter.

One of the most widely reprinted eulogies of Sumner was that of Robert Elliott, delivered in Boston's historic Faneuil Hall, where Sumner had first drawn public attention to himself by a brilliant antislavery speech delivered at a meeting held to protest the annexation of Texas. Twenty-nine years later a black Congressman from South Carolina pronounced his "panegyric": "Mr. President, Ladies and Gentlemen: The boon of a noble human life cannot be appropriated by any single nation or race. It is part of the common wealth of the world; a treasure, a guide and an inspiration to all men in all lands and through all ages." The dead hero belonged to that company of "mighty spirits moving in new majesty and power on their great missions of Truth and Love. . . . Charles Sumner, in his mortal limitations, was an American; more narrowly, he was a Massachusetts man; more narrowly still, he was a white man; but today what nation can claim him, what State shall appropriate him, what race shall boast him? He was the fair consummate flower of humanity. He was the fruit of the ages. He was the child of the Past and the promise of the Future." He was uniquely the benefactor of the "colored race. To other men his services may seem only a vast accession of strength to a cause already moving with steady and assured advance; to us, to the colored race, he is and will ever be the great leader in political life, whose ponderous and incessant blows battered down the walls of our prison house, and whose strong hand led us forth into the sunlight of Freedom.

"Fellow-citizens," Elliott concluded, "the life of Charles Sumner needs no interpreter. It is an open, illuminated page. . . . He carried morals into politics. And this is the *greatness* of Charles Sumner,—that by the power of his moral enthusiasm he rescued the nation from its shameful subservience to the demands of material and commercial interests, and guided it up to the high plane of justice and right. . . . The blessings of the poor are his laurels. . . . Be it ours to walk by the light of this pure example."

Frederick Douglass wrote Elliott a few days later that he was "proud that one of my race, contumed and scorned for ages, has been able to make a speech at Faneuil Hall, Boston, in all respects so worthy of the place and the occasion. . . . The thought brings satisfaction to my heart and to my grey hair." And the *South Carolina News and Courier* addressed an open letter to Elliott, asking him "who wrote the speech on the Civil Rights Bill [and] . . . the eulogy of Sumner which you delivered as your own composition?"

50

The End of Reconstruction

George Templeton Strong's gloomy prophecy that the vast Republican margin of victory in 1872 might in fact signal the demise of the party proved amazingly prescient. The disarray of the Democrats and the Liberal Republicans obscured the extent to which the electorate in general had withdrawn its support, always fragile, from Reconstruction.

The death of Sumner was followed, a few months later, by the midterm elections of 1874, which gave unmistakable indications of the way the wind was blowing. General John Adams Dix, who had won the gubernatorial race in New York by a majority of 55,000 only two years earlier, was defeated by Samuel Tilden by a margin of 50,000, a shift of more than 100,000 votes. The new House was Democratic, while the Senate remained Republican. Even Massachusetts returned a Democratic governor, and Senator Carl Schurz was defeated in Missouri.

George Templeton Strong wrote in October, 1874: "Western elections have disheartened the Republicans and also the third-termites, whoever they are." The reaction was broad and deep. Everywhere Republicans were displaced by Democrats who only two years earlier had been abysmally beaten. November brought "a Waterloo or a Sedan to the Republicans. Total rout, North and

South. . . . There has been no such discomforture since Bull Run." In Strong's analysis of the debacle, the people were dismayed by the continuing bad state of business, "disgusted by abuses of power and bad management in Louisiana and other Southern states, by stories (half true, at least) of corruption and extravagance at Washington, and . . . nervous about a 'third term' and 'Caesarism.' . . ."

There were strong indications that Grant intended to try for a third term. With this prospect, Schurz and his Liberal Republican allies began to cook up a plan to put the senior Charles Francis Adams forward as a candidate of both parties. But the House passed, by a great majority, a resolution opposing a third term, and the Adams project was quietly dropped.

Schurz, however, continued to dream of a revival of the fortunes of the Liberal Republicans. After he had been ousted from the Senate, he wrote a friend: "I see some reason to hope that the year 1876 will present an opportunity for a movement such as that of 1872 ought to have been." E. L. Godkin of the *Nation,* Samuel Bowles, and the younger Adamses (Henry and Charles Francis) met in New York with Schurz in April to explore the possibilities of a third party dedicated to reform. For a time it appeared that Rutherford Hayes, candidate for governor of Ohio against the incumbent, William Allen, a soft-money man, might be their champion. Charles Francis Adams, Jr., wrote Carl Schurz that it was in Ohio that "our battle for '76 is to be lost or won. I do verily believe that if you could be turned into Ohio this year . . . a wholly new face would be put on the relations of parties to public questions in the conflict of next year." The "weapon with which to kill" Allen was the German vote, Adams said, adding that "it is the only effective weapon at hand, and you are its holder." With Schurz's strong support Hayes won the election by a narrow margin. "I got home morning," Adams wrote Schurz, "serene in the knowledge that 'Old Bill Allen's gray and gory scalp was safely dangling at your girdle." As governor of one of the largest states in the Union and a sound-money man Hayes immediately became a prime candidate for the Republican nomination since party stalwarts were searching desperately for a candidate to run against the popular governor of New York, Samuel Tilden.

Grant told John Roy Lynch, when he asked him after the election why he had refused to send Federal troops to Mississippi to protect black voters, that a delegation of prominent Republicans had called on him and told him that the Republicans would lose Ohio to the

Democrats if Federal troops were used. "I should not have yielded," Grant said. "But it was duty on one side and party obligation on the other. I hesitated but yielded to party obligation. If a mistake was made, it was one of the head and not of the heart. That my heart was right and my intentions good, no one who knows me will question."

Having expressed his misgivings about his action, Grant went on, in Lynch's account, to speak of his anxieties about the future of the country. When the war ended, Grant had assumed that four great issues were settled. First, slavery had been abolished; secondly, the indissolubility of the Union had been permanently established; thirdly, "the notion of absolute and independent sovereignty" of the states had been put to rest; and finally, a "national sovereignty had been . . . created and established, resulting in sufficient power being vested in the general government not only to guarantee to every State in the Union, a Republican form of government, but to protect, when necessary, the individual citizen of the United States in the exercise and enjoyment of the rights and privileges to which he is entitled under the Constitution and laws of his country. . . . In other words, so far as citizens of the United States are concerned, the States in the future would only act as agents of the general Government in protecting the citizens of the United States in the enjoyment of life, liberty, and property." This had been the ground on which Grant had undertaken to act, but he found increasing resistance among the leaders of his own party to such a conception of state versus Federal power.

It appeared to Grant that the augmentation of the powers of the legislative branch at the expense of the executive could only result ultimately, or even immediately and directly, in an accretion of power by the states, a development which would in effect nullify much of what the Northern victory had achieved. The ruthless intimidation of black voters in Mississippi, which in effect denied the Federal government and deprived blacks of their constitutional rights, was, in the President's view, "only the beginning of what is sure to follow. I do not wish to create unnecessary alarm, nor to be looked upon as a prophet of evil," Grant concluded, "but it is impossible for me to close my eyes in the face of things that are as plain to me as the noonday sun."

States' rights had too powerful a hold on the popular imagination in the North and West as well as in the South to be readily exorcised. The concept dogged the steps of Reconstruction, haunted the councils of the Republican leadership, seduced the justices of the Supreme

Court. Apparently killed by the war, at least in the minds of men like Grant, it rose again to work its mischief. Grant's idea of the powers of Federal government, at least as they applied to the protection of the constitutional rights of individual citizens regardless of the states they happened to reside in, was seventy-five years ahead of public feeling and, perhaps even more important, of a majority of the Supreme Court. The bedrock inescapable fact seems to be that the weight of public opinion, as well as of judicial opinion (the two can never be too far apart in any event), was decidedly on the side of a somewhat watered-down version of the traditional states' rights doctrine and very substantially against doing anything further to protect the rights of Southern blacks. The falling away of longtime champions of the black cause was, we have argued, in part the result of weariness over the apparently interminable struggle with an intractable South and in part the result of disillusionment at the failure of the freedmen to become "white" as rapidly as their advocates had hoped. Once we have moved past the abolitionists, we have to keep in mind that the vast majority of Northerners felt contempt or hatred for all blacks and, in most instances, found it much easier to identify with the white champions of the "Lost Cause."

In John Roy Lynch's analysis, the decisive event which led to a complete turnabout in white Southern attitudes was the Democratic victory in the midterm elections of 1874. He called it "a clap of thunder from a clear sky." After the elections of 1874 the conviction spread that "the Democratic party was the only channel through which it would be possible in the future for anyone to secure political distinction or receive official recognition. . . . Many of the parting scenes that took place between the colored men and the whites who decided to return to the fold of the Democracy were both affecting and pathetic in the extreme," Lynch wrote. In a nearby county the black president of the local Republican club, Sam Henry, who had recently formed a political alliance with Colonel James Lusk, "a conspicuous and influential representative of the Southern aristocracy," went to plead with the colonel not to abandon the Republican Party and, in effect, the blacks who had supported him. Henry argued that while he could not become a Democrat, Lusk could, without danger to himself or his family, remain a Republican. Lusk replied that "no white man can live in the South in the future and act with any other than the Democratic party unless he is willing and prepared to live a life of social isolation and remain in political oblivion. . . . I am compelled to choose between you, on one side, and my family and personal interests, on the other."

Events appeared to have vindicated the most intractable Democrats. Reconstruction was *not* to be a permanent fact. A determined effort could regain everything that had been lost. Leading Southern white Republicans defected by the hundreds. "Subsequent to 1872 and prior to 1875 proscription and social ostracism had been completely abandoned," John Roy Lynch wrote. "A Southern white man could become a Republican without being socially ostracized. . . . Cordial, friendly and amicable relations between all classes, all parties, and both races prevailed everywhere. Fraud, violence, and intimidation at elections were neither suspected nor charged by anyone, for everyone knew that no occasion existed for such things. But after the State and Congressional elections of 1874 there was a complete change of front."

Lynch overstates his case, but there may well have been a substantial element of truth in it. If things were not as amicable prior to 1874 as he suggests, it is certainly true that the situation deteriorated rapidly thereafter.

The Southern strategy heretofore directed primarily at the intimidation of blacks now shifted to an effort to influence Northern opinion. James Chesnut, husband of Mary, called for a convention of "citizens . . . in favor of honest and good government" in the fall of 1874. A Taxpayers' Convention met in South Carolina, and a delegation went to Washington to present its case to Grant. "Negro misrule," the delegates argued, was the cause of all the woes of their state. The Northern press took up the cause of the white Carolinians with enthusiasm. The picture painted was that of a courageous and abused people fighting for honest government and the most basic rights of citizenship against a phalanx of dishonest carpetbaggers bent on despoiling them. The power of the carpetbaggers was depicted as resting, in turn, upon the votes of ignorant and illiterate blacks, susceptible to Republican demagoguery. The campaign was remarkably successful. Thomas Nast, usually a sympathetic portrayer of Southern blacks, drew caricatures of comic black legislators, engaged in ridiculous harangues.

Francis Cardozo drafted a reply to the Taxpayers' charges in behalf of the black members of the State Central Committee, pointing out in detail that the increase in the South Carolina budget was far less than the committee had stated and that much of the difference lay in such items as the cost of free schools, a lunatic asylum, and a home for black orphans. The largest budget increase occurred in the item labeled "sundries," which had grown from a prewar $184,427 to $444,787. Perhaps the most telling point of Cardozo's paper was found in his breakdown of the cost of government per citizen: $2.05 in the prewar period, when the free population was only 301,214, the vast majority white, and $1.67 in the postwar period, under "the so called corrupt Radical rule" when there was a free population of 705,606. But the Northern press, now hot on the trail of "Negro misrule," ignored Cardozo's rebuttal. The Associated Press refused to send it over its wires.

The *New York Tribune* dispatched one of its ace journalists, James Shepherd Pike, known to be sympathetic to the cause of emancipation, to South Carolina to report on conditions at the state capital. A former Maine politician, Pike had been an antislavery man for years, an early Republican, and Lincoln's minister to the Netherlands. As Washington correspondent for Horace Greeley's *Tribune* Pike supported William Lloyd Garrison's call for the North to secede from the Union and thus free itself of the corruption of slavery. As was true of many abolitionists, Pike's feelings about blacks were profoundly ambivalent. In 1860, while insisting that "a great democratic republic cannot forever submit to the anomaly of negro slavery in its bosom," he added that when slavery was abolished, "the ignorant and servile race will not and cannot be emancipated and raised to the enjoyment of equal civil rights with the dominant and intelligent race; they will be driven out." All this is of more than ordinary importance since Pike's visit to South Carolina in 1873 resulted in a lurid series of newspaper articles portraying the corruption and demoralization of that state. The book that followed, entitled *The Prostrate State: South Carolina Under Negro Government*, was widely read and helped pave the way for the demise of Reconstruction. Perhaps equally important, it became a standard text and reference work on Reconstruction and was used by later historians sympathetic to the South to justify the suppression of blacks in all the Southern states. Thus, the degree of antiblack prejudice that Pike carried with him and that may be assumed to have influenced, if it did not seriously warp, his views of the political activities of the freedmen became of considerable importance.

Pike's prose is full of patronizing or contemptuous descriptions of South Carolina blacks. At the same time it is a thoroughly schizophrenic book that can, in fact, be read two ways. Pike often compares black politicians very favorably to their white counterparts.

Writing just about Virginia, Pike described the "throngs of blacks out after dark" in Richmond and the "jolly countenances of the Negro wenches in the street." In the Virginia House, Pike heard a "colored member 3/4ths black" give a very able analysis of a tax bill to the apparent surprise of "venerable Old Virginia gentlemen," who observed the "self-contained, half saucy, half intelligent expression" of the black legislator with "chagrin."

In Wilmington, North Carolina, Pike was favorably impressed with "the thrifty & capable darkey," whose presence inclined him to anticipate a "future for the race quite different from that bred from the old pro slavery idea of universal inferiority." It seemed clear to Pike that the freedman understood very well that without aggressive political participation his rights would be denied him. "The darkey," he wrote, ". . . is not so much of a fool as he is of a philosopher in his politics."

There seemed to be general agreement even among those Southerners most offended by black political activity that when the places of carpetbaggers had been "filled by colored men, the change has been advantageous to the State." Standing on the floor of the South Carolina House, beside a "snug-built, round-headed, young black man" with "full eyes, thick lips, and woolly hair," Pike asked him about a large "showy kind of white man" who was speaking. "Oh," the black legislator answered, "that is a chuckle-head from—. He has got about as much brains as you can hold in your hand." Pike wrote: "My pride of race was incontinently shocked. Here was a new view. It was no longer the white man deriding the capacity of the negro. . . . It was Sambo proclaiming the white man's inferiority."

Pike was quick to acknowledge that the black legislators understood those bills that affected their interests very well, such as a bill to combat the Ku Klux Klan and one to establish free schools. It seemed to him that, as in most legislative bodies of whatever color, the talk was interminable, and the action very modest. The black orator was "more vivacious," Pike noted, "than the white, and, being more volatile and good-natured, he is correspondingly more irrepressible. . . . He notoriously loves a joke or an anecdote, and will burst into a broad guffaw on the smallest provocation." Moreover, the black lawmakers were masters of parliamentary maneuver and "quick as lightning" in "detecting points of order." Order was maintained with difficulty, but Pike conceded that the black legislators had "a genuine interest and a genuine earnestness in the business of the assembly which we are bound to recognize and respect. . . ." What they were doing in essence, it seemed to him, was enacting a kind of drama, far richer and more colorful than the comparatively pedestrian routines of their white legislative counterparts. The drama, Pike wrote, "means escape and defense from old oppressors. It means liberty. It means the destruction of prison-walls only too real to them. It is the sunshine of their lives. It is their day of jubilee. It is their long-promised vision of the Lord God Almighty. Shall we, then, be too critical over the spectacle? Perhaps we might more wisely wonder that they can do so well in so short a time." Pike was also well aware of the most basic anomaly in the position of the blacks—that they had no economic power to undergird their political power. "The old slave-holders still own their lands," he noted. "The negroes were poor and unable to buy, even if the land-owners would sell. This was a powerful impediment to the development of the negro into a controlling force in the State."

Having described, in his early chapters, the surprising capacity of South Carolina black legislators, Pike went on to dwell on the corruption of that body and to argue that "the ignorant, thievish, immoral, stupid, degraded black man, is . . . no better than the white man of the same description." Pike emphasized that while there were clearly able black men in the legislature, as competent as their white counterparts, their constituency—the black voters who elected them—was usually illiterate and often profoundly ignorant of political and social issues. The disproportionate influence of the black population could not and should not be perpetuated indefinitely, he argued. "Although revolutions do not go backward," he wrote, "we feel that a state of things at once unequal and unnatural cannot endure. The whites must have in one way or another their relative weight in public affairs, not only in respect to the claim of numbers, but of the still weightier claims of property, intelligence and enterprise." Pike added: "The black is a child of vice and ignorance and superstition in South Carolina as well as in Africa. . . . Races of men exhibit the same general characteristics from age to age." If white South Carolinians failed to reclaim their state from the rule of corrupt black politicians and their white carpetbag abettors, they would give evidence of the lack of "manliness, the courage, and the energy of South Carolina white men" and testify against "the claims of Anglo-Saxon blood." In the place of the old aristocratic society stood "the rude form of the most ignorant democracy that mankind ever saw, invested with the functions of government. . . . It is barbarism overwhelming civilization by physical force. It is the slave rioting in the halls of his master, and putting his master under his feet. And, though it is done without malice and without vengeance, it is nevertheless none the less completely and absolutely done."

Pike was not alone in his indictment of black politics. Even some of the most ardent white missionaries recanted. William French, son of Mansfield and Arista French, two of the earliest and most ardent of Gideon's Band at Port Royal, was ready to concede by 1874 that the experiment in black rule had been a failure. "There can be no doubt," he wrote, "but what this reactionary feeling in favor of those who sought the dissolution of the Union, is a manifestation of the sympathy felt by the best classes at the North for a kindred people who, they are convinced, have for the last ten years been subject to state governments forced upon them of the most degraded nature."

Many of the more literate blacks had the intuition, if not the conviction, that their sudden and intoxicating powers would be short-lived. They were practical and hardheaded enough to realize that they were being maintained in power only by the bayonets of Federal troops and that the moment Northern resolution weakened they would be at the mercy of their former masters. This intuition led to two modes of action. One emphasized the importance of securing all the legislative reform possible, especially in the way of liberalized state constitutions, so that it would be difficult for white politicians, when they regained control of the state governments, to excise such reforms as proper care for the insane or free public education. The other mode inclined some black leaders to fall in with the schemes of white Republicans, carpetbaggers, and scalawags to feather their own nests by pillaging already greatly depleted state treasuries. In many instances both courses of action were pursued, sometimes by the same individuals —enlightened and progressive reforms and boldface robbery of public money. As we have seen, the whole postwar atmosphere encouraged corruption on an extravagant scale. This was especially true in the South, where the chaotic social, political, and economic conditions corrupted idealists and tempted men of principle to dabble in dubious ventures. Many foreign travelers to the United States in the period before the Civil War had commented on the fact that corruption was the oil that kept the wheels of the democratic political machinery turning. Sidney George Fisher lamented the fact that in Pennsylvania even the most innocuous legislation could be gotten through the state legislature only by bribery of its members. New York had been notoriously corrupt for decades. Fernando Wood had held New York City in thrall by highly imaginative forms of bribery and corruption. There was hardly a state legislature throughout the land untainted by the breath of corruption. Generally speaking, Americans demanded only that it not be so blatant as to attract widespread public notice. When that happened, reformers rose up in righteous anger and drove the scoundrels from the particular temples of democracy that they had been profaning, and everyone took the line that this sort of thing was quite the exception in American politics.

Thus, it was not surprising that there was considerable corruption in the governments established under the banner of Congressional Reconstruction. Finally, there was more than enough corruption to go around after the governments of Black Reconstruction were overthrown and the Bourbon aristocrats restored to power. Corruption recognizes no distinctions of color, class, or even, it might be said, sex. At the same time two things should be kept in mind in regard to the corrupt practices of Southern legislatures in the period of Congressional Reconstruction. In only two states—South Carolina and, for a brief period, Mississippi—did blacks constitute a majority of the legislature, and even in those states, in the matter of misuse of public funds, black politicians simply followed the lead of their white colleagues. Moreover, they did so under the admittedly shaky rationale that they were merely getting back some of their own. Southern whites had ripped off the black man for centuries; now blacks had a chance to participate in some ripping off on their own account. Finally, Southern whites in all instances made the most of every peculation, however minor. A battery of hostile newspapers stood ready to pounce on every defalcation and blow it up to maximum size in order to demonstrate the incapacity of the Republican governments.

The shrewdest black politicians, men like Francis Cardozo, knew that they were playing a risky game; that they were in a sense, however much idealism may have in fact been mixed in, not much more than pawns in a white political game. In such a climate that keen sense of survival bred into every Southern black dictated that you got what you could when it was available. In slavery you stole a ham if the opportunity presented itself and stored it away in the quarters. In freedom you stole a railroad, especially if encouraged to do so by whites. Francis Cardozo had said all that needed to be said on the subject. "The old aristocracy and ruling power" would sooner or later by one means or another "get into power," and when they did, there would be little enough for black people. So you got what you could—liberal laws and white money—when you could. That was what slavery had taught, and only a fool would believe that it would ever be otherwise.

Encouraged by the results of the elections of 1874, Southern Democrats redoubled their efforts in every state not only to gain political power but to drive blacks out of the political arena entirely. In Laurens County, South Carolina, the "colored citizens" petitioned Governor Chamberlain for protection. The Laurens County of 1876, they assured him, was not the county of four years earlier. "For then a black man and the poor white man could dare to say who he would cast his ticket for, without being starved, whipped or shot to death. But now he neither dares to speak or act without being in extreme danger. . . . No week passes without some of our people are either whipped, chased or shot at by night riders." When Robert Greener, professor at the University of South Carolina, tried to address black voters at Newberry, more than fifteen hundred Red Shirts filled the town square. They tried to bar Greener's way to the platform, and when he forced his way through, they formed a wall of mounted men between him and his audience. As Greener tried to speak, the Red Shirts shouted epithets at him, shook their fists, and denounced him as a "damned radical liar." After the Newberry meeting, Greener and the party of blacks who accompanied him to afford him some protection took the train to Abbeville. Red Shirts, with pistols prominently displayed, pushed into the car Greener was riding in and crowded menacingly around him. Members of rifle clubs filled the streets of Abbeville, and Greener and the blacks who had turned out to hear him speak retreated to a fairground a mile or so from town, where they were undisturbed. Greener carried his own pistol in his coat pocket, and his hand was constantly on it. In Laurens, Greener and his followers found the town full of Red Shirts, but in his words, "The colored people came in on mules and horses, charging and rearing in the same manner as the Democrats. That was the only place they were so determined." Outnumbered almost ten to one, the blacks literally took their lives in their hands to demonstrate their determination not to be intimidated.

In areas of the state where blacks outnumbered whites by large margins, they were far more assertive. Black women armed themselves with clubs and accompanied their men to the polls to be sure that they voted Republican. John Mustifer testified to a congressional committee that his sister accompanied her husband to the voting place and swore that if he voted Democratic, she would "kill him dead in his sleep." Mustifer's son was engaged to be married, but his fiancée refused to marry him when she learned that he had voted for the Democratic ticket. John Bird was threatened by a band of women who seized him with cries of "Kill him. He is a Democratic man."

At other polling places, whites armed with rifles and shotguns turned blacks away while they themselves voted repeatedly. In Edge-field County it was estimated that a thousand blacks were barred from the polls, while so many whites voted more than once that two thousand more votes were counted than the number of registered voters in the county. In spite of all the efforts at intimidation, Chamberlain was re-elected, as were Francis Cardozo and Henry Haynes as state treasurer and secretary of state respectively, while Robert Elliott was elected attorney general.

The Reconstruction governments of Texas, Arkansas, Mississippi, and Alabama all had fallen to the Democrats by the end of 1874. In Louisiana the White League created a paramilitary force and attacked the blacks of Grant Parish, killing two hundred of them in an orgy of brutality. A white man was reputed to have said after the "battle": "We shan't have no more trouble with niggers in Grant Parish. When as clean a job is made in every parish in the State we shall begin to have some quiet and niggers will know their place."

The situation of blacks in Choctaw County, Mississippi, had deteriorated to the point where anyone who dared to engage in political activity was threatened with summary execution. "The colored people," a resident of the county wrote, "are in such a state of fear that life itself is almost insupportable. We cannot have our churches, our schools, nor any social intercourse with each other, unless watched and insulted by white men. We are not permitted to own guns to protect our premises from intruders, nor our crops from destruction by beasts and birds."

A few months later the White League clashed with the black state militia in New Orleans. The militiamen were routed, and for five days the league controlled the city until Federal troops arrived to restore order. In the fall election the league was out in force, warning blacks, "If you don't vote our way you had better not go home for we are going to kill every damn nigger that votes the radical ticket today."

In Coahoma County, Mississippi, in the fall of 1875, hundreds of armed whites roamed the countryside, hanging and shooting blacks suspected of Republican sympathies. Monroe Lewis was dragged from his bed and a rope was placed around his neck; he was forced to say his prayers and was then shot. Charles Green, an old black man, was forced to cook for a party of a hundred whites, one of whom then shot him "to try his gun out." At Clinton a meeting of black Republicans was surrounded by heavily armed whites. Fighting broke out, and a number of unarmed blacks were shot. The next day, according to the testimony of a black farmer named Eugene Welborne, the whites "just hunted the whole country clean out. Every man they could see they were shooting at him just the same as birds. . . . A good many they killed and a good many got away." Many of the whites were from Alabama. Mississippi blacks appealed to Governor Ames, who asked Grant for Federal troops to keep order. Grant's attorney general refused, adding, "The whole public are tired out with these annual autumnal outbreaks in the South." Denied government assistance, Ames recruited seven state militia companies, five black and two white. A black state senator, Charles Caldwell, was captain of the first black company mustered up, and Welborne, who had witnessed the Clinton massacre, was his lieutenant. For a time it seemed as though open warfare might ensue, but Ames, under heavy pressure, accepted a "Peace Agreement" under the terms of which the militia was disbanded in return for a Democratic promise to conduct fair and open elections. With the militia disbanded the harassment and, worse, the murder of blacks resumed. Richard Gray, a candidate for the office of treasurer in Noxubee County, was attending a political rally when an elderly white man he had known for years walked up to him, declared that he had been insulted by him, and slapped Gray in the face. At that point "a young man named Pierce walked right up and fired on me," Gray later testified. "He shot me and I fell."

Charles Caldwell, making a final appeal to Ames, reported that the "Peace Agreement" was utterly without effect. The whites, he wrote, "said they were going to beat us at this election. They said that at the meetings, on the stumps and at the schoolhouses around the country. They said they would carry the county or kill every nigger. They would carry it if they had to wade in blood." The whites of Coahoma County made good their boast. Two years before, 1,300 Republican votes had been counted; now only 230 were recorded. In nearby Yazoo County, where there had been 2,500 Republican votes in the previous election, only 7 were recorded.

Caldwell himself was marked for assassination. On Christmas night he walked downtown after dinner for a constitutional. A white acquaintance asked him to have a drink. He refused, but the friend persisted. Caldwell was guided into a nearby bar. He and his acquaintance touched glasses, and at that instant Caldwell was shot. "Take me out of the cellar," he called out. "I want to die in the open air and not like a dog closed up." So he was carried into the street, and his body soon riddled by more than thirty bullets. Still alive, Caldwell asked to see his wife before he died. When the request was refused, he drew his coat about him and said, "Remember when you kill me you kill a gentleman and a brave man. Never say you killed a coward." A few hours later Caldwell's brother, Sam, was intercepted and killed "for fear he would go out of town and bring in people and raise a fuss." That night, while Margaret Caldwell sat by the bodies of her husband and brother-in-law, a band of whites who called themselves Modocs after the Modoc Indians came to her house, and, in her words, "they went into where the dead bodies laid, and they cursed them, those dead bodies, and they danced and threw open the windows and sung all their songs, and challenged the dead body to get up and meet them. They carried on like a parcel of wild Indians over those dead bodies. They carried on all that in my presence, danced, and sung and done everything they could."

The dance of the "Modoc Indians" around the bodies of Charles Caldwell and his brother was an act in which hatred was compounded by fear. It was a rite of exorcism designed to free the dancers of the rage and terror that possessed them. Perhaps more than any other recorded incident of white violence against blacks in the Era of Reconstruction, it gives us an insight into the psychopathology of white Americans (for the event could as well have happened in the North). Fear is the parent of violence. It is fear that drives men and women to the most dreadful of deeds. White Southerners could not declare that fear—to do so would have diminished them—but it was evident in every act of racial violence. When fear rests on the knowledge of grievous injustice, it is especially remorseless. Charles Caldwell would not crawl or beg for his life; he died like a brave man—a gentleman. To his murderers that was the most frightening fact of all.

Toward the end of a discussion of Black Reconstruction the *Augusta* (Georgia) *Chronicle* addressed black Georgians thus: "Let not your pride . . . flatter you into the belief that you ever can or ever will, for any length of time, govern the white men of the South. The world has never seen such a spectacle. . . . Your present power must surely and soon pass from you. Nothing that it builds will stand, and nothing will remain of it but the prejudices it may create." For almost a hundred years the words seemed prophetic. It appeared that nothing but an inheritance of black bitterness and white fear had remained. But what men have once acted on, be the actors black or white, what they have suffered for and given their lives for become a kind of moral capital for their descendants to draw upon, an inheritance which, neglected or forgotten, nonetheless lies waiting to be reclaimed by the rightful heirs.

George Templeton Strong died on July 21, 1875, at the age of fifty-four. He kept up the entries in his marvelous diary until a few weeks before his death. His last days were shadowed by failing health and an unhappy dispute with his older son, Temple, who left home in April after a row with his father. "Strange he should prefer a garret to the luxury and indulgence of home," Strong wrote. "But I suppose it is the same feeling that makes boys long to be Robinson Crusoes and get shipwrecked on desert islands. Were he not a Bohemian to the backbone, I should be sure he would sicken of this experiment within a month. Strange and sad that this unforeseen rupture should have occurred and should have become something very like permanent, incurable schism in less than thirty days. I fear I shall never hear poor Temple's oboe tootling up-stairs any more."

Temple's "Bohemian" defection was a kind of symbolic schism, a generational break, a young man's desperate flight from the world of the *haute bourgeoisie* to the fickle arms of Art, a flight that was part of a vast migration of young men of Temple Strong's generation to the wilder and wider realms of self-expression. It was exceedingly poignant that George Templeton Strong's particular experience of that general hegira should have cast a shadow over the last days of a man whose own deepest commitment had, after all, been to the muse Calliope.

The class of young men who flocked to Brook Farm in the 1840s, to Oberlin or Antioch to join the embattled legions of abolitionists or Bronson Alcott's vegetarians, or who ventured to foreign shores as missionaries, now withdrew to pursue one or more of the muses. The bolder and more enterprising followed Horace Greeley's advice and went west. Others became professors and doctors, bankers and lawyers; a few became ministers and a few tycoons. An inordinate number, as always, wished to become writers, novelists if possible, journalists if necessary. If politics was a wasteland, social life a bore and a fraud, there was Art, splendid and infinitely alluring, above and beyond the Philistines and the Pharisees. So it was to the standard of Art that thousands of upper- and middle-class youths of both sexes repaired—to make it, to contemplate it, to write about it, to revel in it, to produce, they hoped, a renaissance of American art that would astonish the world.

There were no national eulogies for Strong, although the New York newspapers, about which he had such ambivalent feelings, took notice of his distinguished career of service to his church, his college, his city, and his country. We shall miss him in the years ahead.

Sidney George Fisher had died four years earlier, almost to the day—July 25, 1871—at the age of sixty-three. Inflation and bad investments had brought a nightmare of debts in their train, and he suffered acutely from gout, a painful form of arthritis, for the relief of which the doctor prescribed marijuana, a drug that Fisher found delightful. Fisher's son, Sidney, had also become alienated from his father. His father's death left young Sidney and his mother destitute. Bet died a year later, in part, it seems, of malnutrition, at least according to her son's diagnosis. Sidney changed the spelling of his first name to Sydney, went, through the good offices of his relatives, to St. Paul's School, Trinity College, and Harvard Law School. He became an amateur historian and the author of a number of "true" books on American history—e.g., *The True History of the American Revolution*—achieving thereby the literary fame his appealing but impractical father had coveted.

51

A Disputed Election

As the presidential election year of 1876 opened, the Republicans were in search of a candidate. The field was not a promising one. James Blaine of Maine and Oliver Morton of Indiana appeared as the leading prospects. The Liberal Republicans—who preferred now to call themselves Independents—began at once to try to find an alternative to the Republican war-horses, tainted as they both were with the accumulated corruptions of the Grant regime.

Blaine, apparently trying to draw public attention to himself as the leading contender for the presidential nomination, made a bitter attack on the ex-Confederates for their intractability and stubborn unwillingness to concede an inch on the rights of Southern blacks. All true, of course, but Blaine made the mistake of dwelling on the horrors of Confederate prisons, implying that they were consciously used, like cannons and muskets, to kill off Union soldiers. It appeared almost at once that he had gone too far. The North wished to forget the iniquities of the South and the plight of the freedmen. Schurz wrote to Samuel Bowles a few days after Blaine's speech: "It seems almost as if Blaine had virtually killed himself as a candidate, as I always thought he would. He may seemingly revive, but I am sure he will die of too much smartness at last." The message conveyed by the reception of

Blaine's speech was not lost on other Republican presidential hopefuls or on those ambitious for lesser offices: Reconstruction was dead or dying.

Blaine had also made another serious blunder. The Federal elections bill was brought before Congress in the waning weeks of the spring session of the Forty-third Congress by the Radical Republicans, who were determined to leave it behind as a guarantee that the voting rights of Southern blacks would be protected. John Lynch was confident that the bill would have passed both houses if it had not been for Blaine's unexpected opposition. Blaine's opponents were convinced that he had scuttled it in order to prevent Grant, who was backing Roscoe Conkling for the Republican presidential nomination, from gaining additional power that might have enabled him to block Blaine's nomination. If that was his plan, the effect was quite different from what Blaine had anticipated. The Southern Republicans were so indignant at what they viewed as his defection that they determined to do all they could to block Blaine's nomination.

Blaine had a different and more logical explanation for his opposition to the bill when Lynch quizzed him on his motives months later. It was his conviction, he said, that if the bill had passed, the Republican Party would have suffered a crushing defeat in the presidential election of 1876. "We could not have saved the South even if the bill had passed," Blaine said, "but its passage would have lost us the North; indeed, I could not have carried even my own State of Maine, if that bill had passed." To add to Blaine's liabilities the so-called Mulligan letters were spread around by unfriendly newspapers on the eve of the Republican nominating convention. James Mulligan was a clerk for a Boston financier named Warren Fisher, and the letters which he made public seemed to indicate hanky-panky on the part of the Speaker of the House—money received for political favors performed. Although Blaine, hoping to defuse the issue, read the letters on the floor of Congress and attempted to explain them away, in the increasing clamor for reform they wounded him fatally.

The party regulars were further compromised by the revelations about Grant's protégé, Secretary of War Belknap, who, accused of accepting bribes, resigned in March but was, notwithstanding, impeached by the House.

With Blaine under a cloud and the party machine discredited, Schurz and his fellow reformers began to search for a strategy and a candidate with whom to block his nomination. Blaine, aware of what was in the wind, sought Schurz out, practiced all his famous charm upon him, and finally, unable to secure a pledge of support, threw his arm around Schurz's neck, and said, "Carl, you won't *oppose* me, will you?" That, indeed, was Schurz's intention, and in April he and his closest allies, among them Horace White and William Cullen Bryant, issued a call for a gathering of Independents at the Fifth Avenue Hotel. Invitations went out to three or four hundred Liberal Independents or Independent Liberals, and some two hundred appeared, "among them," Schurz's editors wrote, "college presidents and professors, clergymen, men of letters, philanthropists and others of light and influence." President Theodore Dwight Woolsey of Yale presided, and the conferees unanimously adopted a statement written by Schurz calling, in ringing tones, for reform and ruling out, as candidates they would support, any of the politics-as-usual crowd, implicitly Blaine, Morton, and Conkling. The stage was thus set for a dark horse, and Schurz felt he had an ideal equine in Rutherford Hayes, the hard-money reform governor of Ohio who owed a considerable debt to Schurz for insuring him the German vote in the gubernatorial election. The price for the support of the Independents was that Hayes should pledge himself to a hard-money policy, civil service reform, and the end of Northern intervention in the affairs of the South. To Schurz the last stipulation meant that the Constitution would be restored, states' rights once more honored, and a beginning made in binding up the wounds caused by a tragic war and its tragic aftermath. To black Americans like Robert Elliott, Richard Cain, Francis Cardozo, John Lynch; to black Congressmen and state legislators and the much larger company of black political leaders in small towns and rural villages throughout the South; to the considerable army of black and white teachers and missionaries, it meant abandonment to their fate at the hands of a white South which had never slackened or deviated in its determination to place "free" blacks in a condition of complete and unqualified subordination, where the vaunted protections of the Fourteenth and Fifteenth Amendments could not reach.

When the Republican nominating convention met in Cincinnati, Blaine was the early favorite. As the party's platform was drawn up, it became increasingly evident that its drafters were determined to soft-pedal the issue of Reconstruction. Frederick Douglass tried, in vain, to hold the delegates to their commitment to protect the rights of black people. "What does it all amount to if the black man, after having been made free by the letter of your law . . . is to be subject to the slaveholder's shot-gun? . . . I sometimes wonder that we still exist as a people in this country; that we have not all been swept out of existence, with nothing left to show we ever existed. . . . When you turned us loose, you turned us loose to the sky, to the storm, to the whirlwind, and, worst of all . . . to the wrath of our infuriated masters. The question now is, do you mean to make good to us the promises in your constitution?" The answer, of course, was no. And even Douglass's friends might have reminded him that after the Emancipation Proclamation he had declared that all the freedman wanted was to be left alone to work out his own destiny. Douglass would have replied, and doubtless did if anyone reminded him of his earlier views, that the essence of the problem was that the Southern whites would not leave the blacks alone to find their own way. They interfered so egregiously and so bloodily that humanity cried out for the North to intervene.

As the delegates proceeded to the business of nominating a candidate, it became evident that Blaine's strength was more apparent than real. The Southern Republicans were adamantly opposed because of Blaine's opposition to the Federal elections bill. They gave their support to Senator Morton. Robert Ingersoll of Illinois, who placed Blaine's name in nomination, gave such a stirring speech that for a moment it appeared as through the convention might be stamped for Blaine (he had 285 votes on the first ballot to 61 for Hayes), but the tide began to turn, and on the seventh ballot the delegates nominated Hayes.

The support of Hayes was by no means unanimous among the reformers, the Independents. Many of them preferred Governor Samuel Tilden of New York, the Democratic nominee. The senior and junior Charles Francis Adamses were among that company. To men like the Adamses it was not important whether a Republican or a Democrat became president as long as the winner was a hard-money man. Gustave Koerner of Illinois, a supporter of Tilden's, wrote to Schurz: "We want both parties to nominate hard-money men, so that, in either case, the election of a Republican or Democrat, one of the great objects of the Liberal Republicans, would be accomplished."

Schurz's efforts went into trying to persuade Hayes to place as much distance as he could between himself and such Republican regulars as Blaine, Morton, Simon Cameron, and Zachariah Chandler. "The cry for a 'change' is immensely powerful," he wrote to Hayes. "People say Governor Hayes is an honest man, but what good will it do to elect him if his administration is controlled by Morton, Conkling, Cameron, Chandler, Blaine, etc.—and off they go where they are sure of a 'change.'" Instead of fending off the regulars, Hayes, taking his cue from Blaine, devoted most of his efforts to raising the specter of Southern intransigence and rebellion.

In the midst of the presidential campaign an event which cast a pall over the nation took place. Hamburg, South Carolina, was an all-black town. When the whites in nearby communities began to organize rifle and saber clubs, the mayor or "intendant" of Hamburg, John Gardner, had written to Governor Chamberlain asking permission to raise and arm a company of black militia to protect the town from white raiders. With Chamberlain's approval, Gardner set about to form an infantry company—Company A of the 18th National Guard, with eighty-four members. On July 4, 1876, with Company A drawn up in the town square, Matthew Calbraith Butler, "general" of the Sweetwater Sabre Club in Edgefield, rode into Hamburg at the head of his "club" and made as though to drive through the formation of black militiamen. When Dock Adams, commanding Company A, protested, Butler replied that "this is the rut I always travel and I don't intend to get out of it for no damned niggers." Seeing that Butler was trying to provoke a fight, Gardner ordered the men to open ranks and allow the Sabre Club to pass. The matter did not end there. Butler brought charges against Adams for obstructing the highway. On the day of the trial Hamburg was filled with heavily armed white men. Butler demanded that the men of Company A give up their firearms in order to prevent a clash. Adams refused, saying that the arms belonged to the state. He then discovered that Butler had surrounded the town with several thousand armed men. The intention was clearly to destroy Company A, but Adams managed to extricate a portion of his little band. All night long Butler's men brought in blacks who had been hunted down around the town, often with the aid of bloodhounds, and confined them in a house they had commandeered. As dawn approached, Butler declared, "Well we had better go to work and kill all the niggers we have. We won't be able to find that son of a bitch," referring to Adams. The captives were carried one by one across the railroad tracks under the pale light of the moon and shot while their executioners sang "We're going to redeem South Carolina today." So occurred the Hamburg Massacre in the midst of nationwide celebrations of the country's centenary.

Governor Chamberlain denounced the massacre unsparingly. "If you can find words to characterize its atrocity and barbarism, the triviality of the causes, the murderous and inhuman spirit which marked it in all its stages, your power of language exceeds mine," he wrote to Senator T. J. Robertson. "What hopes can we have when such a cruel, bloodthirsty spirit waits in our midst for its hour of gratification? Is our race so wantonly cruel?"

Grant declared: "The scene at Hamburg, as cruel, bloodthirsty, unprovoked, and as uncalled for as it was, is only a repetition of the same that has been pursued in other Southern states within the last few years, notably in Mississippi and Louisiana. Mississippi is governed to-day by officials chosen through fraud and violence, such as would hardly be accredited to savages, much less to a civilized and Christian people."

Robert Elliott and other black leaders in the state called a Convention of Colored People to protest the massacre. Elliott was the author of "An Address to the People of the United States," supported by the convention. The address called on the American people "to place upon this wanton and inhuman butchery the indelible stigma of public abhorrence." Elliott also exhorted "the business men and property holders of the state to bend their energies toward the removal of this deadly nightshade of mob law and violence." A few weeks later Elliott, in his role as chairman of the Republican State Committee, urged black voters to "endure to the end as you have heretofore done in peaceable silence the threats of democracy, and look forward patiently to that restoration of human reason and truth which will speedily follow your certain success in the approaching election."

Chamberlain appealed to Grant for Federal troops. Meanwhile, the Democrats had the good sense to nominate for governor one of the most popular and able men in the state—Wade Hampton—to run against Chamberlain. Hampton, the grandson of the Revolutionary hero of the same name and a war hero in his own right, had displayed a genuine concern and interest in the fortunes of the freedmen, although his attitude toward them was, not surprisingly, that of a kindly patron rather than an open advocate of their rights. With their war-hero candidate as their standard-bearer, the South Carolina Democrats set out on a campaign of terrorism calculated to keep thousands of black voters from the polls and insure a Hampton victory. Gun clubs and "baseball clubs," the only purpose of which was to harass and, on occasion, murder blacks, were formed all over the state. Groups of armed whites appeared at Republican rallies, heckling and threatening the Republican candidates.

Hampton gave no support to the program of coercion. He devoted his efforts to a tour around the state, accompanied by a bodyguard of Red Shirts, and was greeted everywhere with rebel yells. He assured any blacks who appeared at his rallies that he would protect their rights and reminded them that as early as 1865 he had advocated a limited black suffrage. As governor, he promised, he would not take away "one single right enjoyed by the colored people today. . . . They shall be the equals under the law of any man in South Carolina."

In those Southern states still under Republican control the story was much the same. White politicians were not satisfied with simply regaining power. In many instances they hunted down the surviving black leaders vindictively, as though to assure that they would never challenge white supremacy again. Tunis Campbell, a freeborn native of Massachusetts, a Methodist minister, and coadjutor of Henry Turner, was a state senator in Georgia. Four years earlier Campbell had married a black man and a woman who, it was claimed, was white. Since mixed marriages were against Georgia law, the Democrats arranged for Campbell's arrest and prosecution. He was handcuffed and taken to jail. Two other black legislators were tried on the charge of rioting in their own church and convicted on the basis of testimony, in Henry Turner's words, that would not "have convicted the devil before a jury of angels." Campbell wrote to the chairman of the National Executive Committee of the Republican Party describing the tactics of the Democrats. "Just before every election they commence trying to intimidate by arresting all prominent colored men. As usual they have arrested me again."

To many voters Hayes and Tilden appeared like Tweedledum and Tweedledee, with little to choose between them. When the votes in the presidential election were counted, Tilden had a popular majority of 250,000 votes, but the outcome of the election rested on the disputed electoral votes in three states—South Carolina, Florida, and Louisiana. In each of the three states in question, both Republicans and Democrats sent in returns certifying their party the winner. In the Forty-fourth Congress the Democrats were in control of the House, and the Republicans of the Senate. After weeks of acrimonious and futile debate, both houses on January 25, 1877, approved the Electoral

Count Act, which created an electoral commission made up of five Senators, five Representatives, and five justices of the Supreme Court. Four justices—two Republican and two Democratic—were to be designated by the legislative members, and they, in turn, were to choose a fifth justice. The only member of the Court without a strong party affiliation was David Davis of Illinois. He was thus chosen as the fifteenth, and thus presumably deciding vote, but on the eve of the convening of the commission Davis resigned from the Court on the ground that he had been elected Senator from his home state. The remaining justices of the Court were all Republicans. Joseph Bradley, a Republican with strong Southern sympathies, became the fifteenth member.

John Roy Lynch opposed the appointment of the commission, suspecting that behind it lay a deal. "I had a suspicion," he wrote, "that it was the outgrowth of an understanding which would result in abandonment of Southern Republicans by the national administration."

Lucius Quintus Cincinnatus Lamar of Mississippi gave a clue to the direction in which the wind was blowing by publicly declaring that "it was more important that the South should have self-government than that the president should be a Democrat." Democrats around the country, convinced that their party was in the process of being robbed of its legitimate victory, threatened to march on Washington and unseat Hayes if the commission decided against Tilden. When the commission announced its findings in Florida, the first state the returns of which were scrutinized, the Republican electors were validated by a straight party vote, 8 Republicans for, 7 Democrats against. There was now every reason to assume that the results would be the same in the two remaining states, and the Democrats in the House began a series of parliamentary moves to try to forestall such an outcome. The Northern Democrats found their Southern colleagues disconcertingly reluctant to join forces with them. They were apparently engaged in negotiations with the Hayes's forces directed toward ending, for all practical purposes, Congressional Reconstruction. This could be achieved most simply and directly by an understanding with the Republican contender for the presidency that he would not use Federal troops to oversee or enforce the three amendments and the various acts of Congress intended to guarantee the civil rights of Southern blacks.

In South Carolina, where Wade Hampton had run against Daniel

Chamberlain, Democrats and Republicans, both charging fraud, began to organize the General Assembly. When the Democrats, convinced they were victorious, formed a procession to march to the statehouse, they found the way blocked by the Republican sergeant at arms and the Republicans ensconced therein. They thereupon found a hall, elected a speaker, and organized themselves into the state legislature. When the "Republican House" recessed, the Democrats occupied the vacated chambers. The Republicans returned, filed into the chamber, and what came to be known as the Dual House began its sessions, each faction scrupulously ignoring the other and purporting to conduct the official business of the state. Bedding and food were brought in, with additional guns and ammunition since most of those present were armed.

When the more absurd aspects of the standoff became evident, the gathering took on the character of a game. Whiskey and brandy flowed, and the black members began a songfest in which many of the white representatives of both parties joined. Under the rumored threat of Governor Chamberlain to deputize a band of black "counter-Red Shirts" the Democrats finally vacated the statehouse, declaring that they would abide by the judgment of the State Supreme Court. The Republicans immediately ruled that Chamberlain had defeated Hampton and inaugurated him as governor. The Democrats, meanwhile, did the same for Hampton, who told Robert Elliott that it was "the duty as well as the interest of leading colored men like myself [Elliott] to refuse our support and countenance" to Chamberlain because "I [Hampton] can protect the people of this State, black and white alike, while Chamberlain cannot protect either. . . . Governor Chamberlain cannot protect his own life. I have had to protect him from the just indignation of the people, and if I were to take my hands off the brakes for an hour, his life would not be safe." Given the mood of the angry Democrats, Hampton's analysis was doubtless correct.

Chamberlain and his supporters saw the proverbial handwriting on the wall. Six Republicans, Elliott and Cardozo among them, wrote him they were in agreement "in counselling you to discontinue the struggle" in the face of the abandonment of the Southern Republicans by the "National Administration." With understandable bitterness, Chamberlain composed an "Address to the Republicans of South Carolina": "Today—April 10, 1877—by order of the President whom your votes alone rescued from overwhelming defeat, the government of the United States abandons you, deliberately withdraws from you its support . . . and by the withdrawal of troops now protecting the State from domestic violence, abandons the lawful Government of the State to a struggle with insurrectionary forces too powerful to be resisted." He accused the Republican Party of "the abandonment of Southern Republicans, and especially the colored race, to the control and rule not only of the Democratic party, but of that class at the South which regarded slavery as a Divine Institution, which waged four years of destructive war for its perpetuation, which steadily opposed citizenship and suffrage for the Negro."

Those members of Chamberlain's administration, like Elliott and Cardozo, whose elections to various offices had not been challenged, refused to resign but were subsequently forced to vacate their offices by Hampton on the uncertain ground that he had a right to be served by officers of his own party. The Democrats then demanded the resignations of enough Republicans to establish their party's dominance in both houses of the Assembly. Hampton adopted a conciliatory policy toward South Carolina blacks, appointing a few black Democrats to offices where they would give little offense to whites. John Sherman, secretary of the treasury in Hayes's Cabinet, gave Elliott a position on the Federal payroll as a customs inspector at Charleston, and the black politician continued to be a minor power in Republican politics throughout the remaining years of the century, addressing the Republican National Convention in Chicago in 1880 and working to line up black delegates for Sherman's own presidential bid.

The fate of other black politicians varied greatly after the end of Reconstruction. Alonzo Ransier, who had served in Congress and had been lieutenant governor of the state and an outspoken champion of the reform of the corrupt practices of the legislature, ended his days as a street cleaner in Charleston.

Joseph Rainey, who served four terms in Congress, was appointed an internal revenue agent in Charleston, resigned in 1881, and went to Washington to become a stockbroker. He failed disastrously, suffered from a physical breakdown, and returned home to Charleston, where he died in 1887. He was fifty-five years old at the time of his death; Ransier was forty-six.

Richard ("Daddy") Cain, the oldest of the black Reconstruction politicians, had had a successful career as a minister and missionary of the African Methodist Church and became, after Reconstruction, a bishop of that church, as well one of the founders and the president of Paul Quinn College in Waco, Texas. He died in Washington, D.C., at the age of sixty-two.

William Whipper practiced law in Beaufort, South Carolina, which had a heavy black population, and fought with Robert Smalls for political leadership in the county. Whipper, who had been in business in Philadelphia before the war and active in the Underground Railroad and about whom the taint of corruption clung most persistently during Reconstruction, was finally made a probate judge. He and Robert Smalls were among five black delegates to the South Carolina constitutional convention of 1895. Almost thirty years earlier the two men had been present at the constitutional convention, held under the wing of Congressional Reconstruction, which had framed such a liberal and farsighted state constitution.

Robert Smalls proved to have the strongest hold on his predominantly black constituents of all South Carolina blacks and was returned to Congress until 1887. Thereafter he became a customs inspector in Beaufort.

Daniel Chamberlain moved to New York and became a successful corporation lawyer. Chamberlain offers us one of the most revealing readings on the remarkably volatile attitudes toward Reconstruction that have appeared in successive decades of our history. In 1890 his view of Reconstruction had changed so markedly that he could write: "My sympathy and my judgment are with the Democratic party. . . . The negro has been helped as no race has ever been helped before. He was set free by others, not by his own efforts. He was enfranchised by no efforts of his own. He had full opportunity to build up and protect his liberties. The whole power of the United States was at his call for eight years, and what was the result of it all? Am I wrong when I say the result was that the negro showed only weakness and unfitness for the task laid upon him?"

Yet a decade later, when the *Atlantic Monthly* devoted a whole issue to Reconstruction, Chamberlain's feelings seemed to have changed again. He did not hesitate to indict the South for its "harsh treatment of the emancipated negroes, in laws, in business, and in social relations. The effect of this folly," he noted, "was decisive at the North. Added to this was the fatuous course of President Johnson. . . ." Yet it seemed to Chamberlain in reviewing the debates in Congress over Reconstruction that under all the philosophical arguments lay "the will and determination [of the Republicans] to secure party ascendancy and control at the South and in the nation through the negro vote. . . .

"If there is any interest still attaching to the writer's view," Chamberlain wrote in 1901, "he is quite ready now to say that he feels there was no possibility of securing permanent good government in South Carolina through Republican influences." For all that went awry, Chamberlain blamed Thaddeus Stevens and Oliver Morton. That the Democratic triumph in 1876 left an unhappy legacy Chamberlain readily admitted. "The ballot debauched in 1876," he wrote, "remains debauched; the violence taught then remains now, if not in the same, in other forms; the defiance of law learned then in what was called a good cause survives in the horrid orgies and degradation of lynchings."

Yet Chamberlain, though he asked for understanding and compassion, could not muster any for those who devised the "congressional scheme of reconstruction," men characterized by their "unspeakable folly, blind party greed, their insensate attempt to reverse the laws which control human society." Chamberlain's own prejudices are clear enough from his statement that "literary, scientific, or what we call the higher education" was wasted on the Negro or, worse, was "a positive evil to him." He should, instead, be trained "in the three R's; and after that, skill in handicraft, in simple manual labor." Such a lot for blacks was "fixed not by us, but by powers above us." This from a man who had known intimately and been a political ally of blacks like Francis Cardozo, Martin Delany, and Robert Elliott.

When, near the end of *A Fool's Errand,* Colonel Comfort Servosse is forced to leave the South by the ending of Congressional Reconstruction, Albion Tourgée has his hero reflect: "When the power of the Nation is withdrawn, the struggle was at an end. Failure was written above the grave of the pet idea of the Wise Men. . . ."

But what of the abandoned blacks? the Reverend M. Martin asked his former student. To Servosse it seemed necessary that many Southern blacks should "flee from the scene of servitude," presumably to the West, and he confessed that he was surprised that they had not done so. It seemed to him that the ex-slaves must endure a time comparable to the Israelites' forty years of wandering in the wilderness, in the course of which "individual self-reliance, and collective hardihood and daring" could develop and grow. They must "leave more than one generation in the wilderness, before they regained the rights which were promised them, and which they for a little time enjoyed."

Martin, reflecting on Servosse's words, expressed his anxiety that Southern blacks might well, stimulated by their "suddenly-acquired freedom, . . . attempt an exodus [to the North] which will yet upset all our finely-spun theories, and test, at our very doors, the humanitarianism of which we boast." Servosse would not be surprised. "There is something marvelous and mysterious in the history of the African race in America. . . ."

Something further must be said about the man who left the office of president after eight stormy years. Grant has generally been given low marks by historians for his performance as president, but it is important to distinguish between Grant and his administration. Perhaps Grant's greatest mistake as president was his stubborn insistence on the annexation of Santo Domingo. It was a serious error, which alienated Sumner and Schurz and accelerated the fragmentation of the Republican Party. On the other hand, Grant remained unbudging in his determination to use the powers of the Federal government to enforce the law of the land, specifically the Fourteenth and Fifteenth Amendments—to protect the rights of black citizens in the South. On this issue his party deserted him as its most able and energetic spirits devoted themselves instead to the cause of hard money and civil service reform.

Two years after he left office, Grant wrote: "I did not want the Presidency, and have never quite forgiven myself for resigning the command of the army to accept it; but it could not be helped. I owed my honors and opportunities to the Republican party and if my name could aid it, I was bound to accept." And having accepted, he remained true to his trust to the end of his administration.

52

The Centennial Exhibition

The year 1876 was the centennial year. A hundred years had passed since the signing of the Declaration of Independence, and it was necessary to take notice of that momentous fact. (Of course, if we consider that the country actually "started" with the framing of the Federal Constitution and the election of George Washington as president in 1789, it was only eighty-seven years old.) In less than three generations the United States had been transformed beyond the most extravagant imaginings of a people naturally given to extravagant imaginings. There were old men alive in some numbers who had been born during Washington's administration. There were hundreds of thousands of Americans whose fathers had been actors in the drama of the American Revolution and the establishment of the Federal government. Charles Francis Adams, Sr., promoted as a Liberal Republican candidate for president in the elections of 1872 and 1876, was the grandson of the second president of the United States. Everything had happened yesterday, so to speak. The United States had consisted of the thirteen "original" states strung out along the Atlantic seacoast when Washington began his term of office. Now there were thirty-six states and six vast "territories" covering a substantial part of the continent. A land area of 864,746 square miles had grown to 2,969,640 square miles; a population of less than 4,000,000 to more than 40,000,000.

By 1870 the value of manufactured products was more than $4,000,000,000, or $1,300,000 in excess of the value of farm products. In the twenty years from 1850 to 1870 the value of manufactures had increased more than 300 percent. In commerce the story was much the same. The trade of the city of Chicago alone amounted to $450,000,000 annually. There were 80,000 miles of telegraph line, and Western Union employed more than 1,000 people in New York City alone. The enumeration could go on and on (and did)—agricultural output, industrial productivity, miles of railroad lines, tons of pork and beef and grain, minerals, coal, a steady flow of fuel oil. Such figures, constantly reiterated, produced a kind of statistical euphoria. All in all it was, Americans agreed, the most astonishing era in history.

However, 1876 was not a good year. The country had still not recovered from the severe Depression of 1873. Tens of thousands of workingmen were unemployed, and the various private relief agencies dedicated to relieving their distress were still taxed to their limits. Inflation had eaten away at the incomes of those fortunate enough to have jobs. Corruption was rampant. The large cities, crammed with immigrants, many of them out of work and desperately poor, were centers of crime and disease. In New York, Boston, and Philadelphia it was unsafe to be out on the streets after dark. On the Great Plains the Indians were resisting the intrusions of the railroads and being ruthlessly suppressed by generals and soldiers who had recently won victory for Northern arms—Sherman and Sheridan most conspicuously. At the beginning of the year the nation was faced with a murky and prospectively dangerous political situation as the resurgent Democrats, in a mood verging on the openly rebellious, prepared to challenge Republican hegemony. Plans for the centennial celebration had, of course, been under way for several years, and no one is recorded as having suggested calling it off merely because the country was in a mess. Quite the contrary. The determination was, rather, to make it into an orgy of self-congratulation, a great pageant celebrating the astonishing achievements of the United States.

A congressional bill, passed in 1871, authorizing the celebration declared that it was "fitting that the completion of the first century of our national existence shall be commemorated by an exhibition of the natural resources of the country and their development, and of its progress in those arts which benefit mankind, in comparison with those of older nations. . . ." The sentence was at best ambiguous. It seemed to say that the United States had developed "those arts which benefit mankind" to an extent far in advance of "older nations."

It was generally agreed that Philadelphia, where the Declaration had been signed, was the appropriate place for such a celebration despite some grumbling from Boston, and more than four hundred acres of Fairmount Park were set aside for exhibition buildings. It was soon decided by the exhibition commissioners, headed by ex-General Joseph Hawley, to "make the affair international instead of merely national—an exhibition of the products of all nations" in order to encourage "friendly intercourse" between nations and "new and still greater advantages to science and industry, and at the same time to serve to strengthen the bonds of peace and friendship which already happily subsist" among the nations of the world.

While it was true that international or "world" fairs had become something of a fad (Great Britain had had one in 1851, and Paris and Vienna had followed suit), the decision to "internationalize" the exhibition was a significant one. The American attitude toward the Old World had been, in the early years of the Republic, that it was hopelessly benighted, sunk in vice, and saddled with reactionary politics. There was, as we have often had occasion to note, the assumption that revolutionary upheavals, patterned on America's own Revolution, must soon usher in an age of enlightened democratic politics. The revolutionary ferment of the late 1840s and the triumph, in most instances, of reactionary regimes had, in conjunction with the Civil War, produced a less sanguine and more realistic temper in Americans vis-à-vis their relations with Europe.

Even more important was the fact that the industrial revolution had disclosed a commonality of interest among the industrialized nations stronger, at least for the moment, than any ideological differences. The electric light, the steam engine, the locomotive, the telephone, and the telegraph proved surprisingly "international," quite as accessible to the citizens of repressive monarchies as to their democratic cousins across the Atlantic. Americans might pride themselves on their accomplishments in the realm of technological innovation, but it was clear that they held no monopoly. Samuel F. B. Morse had worked closely with the French physicist André Marie Ampère, whose discoveries in electrodynamics were essential to Morse's development of the telegraph. European inventors, if usually less concerned with the practical applications of their work, were often well in advance of

Americans in the theoretical formulations that underlay the inventions themselves.

In inviting foreign nations to participate in its centennial birthday celebration, the exhibition's commissioners gave notice that the United States was abandoning its notorious provincialism and acknowledging its place in the international community. In so doing, Americans had, of course, no notion of giving up their denunciations of kings, dukes, and lords or their disposition to make invidious comparisons between the political institutions of the Republic and all other less favored forms of government.

Of all the foreign workmen and representatives in Philadelphia, the Chinese and Japanese were subjects of the greatest interest. Artists and cartoonists rendered them, and journalists described them (though communication was difficult, if not impossible). Chinese immigration was already a political issue, and *Harper's Weekly* took the occasion to point out that "in spite of the murmurs that have arisen concerning the presence of John Chinaman in our land, much can be said in his favor. In the first place, he is an eminently economical institution. His habits, his tastes, his pleasures, even his vices are cheap. His frugality is worn into his very bones . . . undoubtedly 'Chinese cheap labor,' rather than bad morals is at the foundation of the hue and cry that has arisen against the melancholy wearers of the pigtail. As merchants the Mongolians are not successful. They lack the restless spirit of venture through which the Caucasian produces such fabulous results. . . . But, as a laundryman is the 'heathen Chinee' peculiarly successful."

Harper's Weekly assured prospective visitors that Philadelphia could provide ample accommodations. In addition, there would be French, German, and Italian restaurants and "doubtless . . . others where the Chinaman and the Japanese can indulge their somewhat peculiar proclivities in the way of dishes. . . . There will be ample provision for every variety of taste."

Five principal buildings were erected at a cost of $4,444,000. Individual states and territories, as well as foreign countries, built their own more modest structures, 185 in all. There were seven "departments" in the American exhibitions: Mining and Metallurgy, Manufactures, Education and Science, Art, Machinery, Agriculture, and Horticulture. A point might be made about the departments and their order. Mining and Metallurgy represented the most sensational new technological breakthrough. The apparently limitless mineral resources of the Rocky Mountain region—gold, silver, and copper—in addition to the great coal mines of Pennsylvania and the Appalachian chain and the iron ores of the Great Lakes region, combined with new techniques of metallurgy, promised unlimited economic expansion and vast wealth. As late as 1820 only 356 tons of anthracite coal had been mined; by 1870 the output was 25,000,000 tons and another 25,000,000 tons of bituminous. Pennsylvania turned out 72 percent of the total. The value of copper produced in Western mines was over $5,000,000 a year in 1870. Some 220,000,000 gallons of petroleum were exported in 1875, primarily as kerosene, and as much consumed in the United States. From the discovery of gold in California to the centennial, well over $1,000,000,000 in gold had been panned or mined, and the annual yield of silver was calculated at more than $100,000,000 per year.

Education and Science were combined, suggesting that the most powerful component in education was "science," or, as Jefferson had argued in his espistolary debate with John Adams, that the two were virtually synonymous. Thirteen million pupils attended school, half of them in public institutions.

"Art" preceded "Machinery, Agriculture, and Horticulture." Art was thus verified as an essential element in society. It was both the status symbol of the new class of industrial tycoons and the refuge of those younger Americans who could not bear the crassness and materialism of American life. The latter class made Art and revered it as a revelation of man's higher spiritual life; the former bought it (primarily in Europe) to display its taste and wealth. The prominence of the Art Gallery at Philadelphia bore impressive witness to the determination of the promoters of the celebration (and perhaps more to the determination of their wives) to demonstrate to the world that the United States valued "culture" as much as money.

The Horticultural Hall performed somewhat the same function. (It was described as a "fairy palace" with its light and airy design and delicate ornamentation and its "grand conservatory alone constituting a world of beauty to all lovers of nature.") Flowers, shrubs, and trees were, after all, indications of refined sensibility, of leisure and of prosperity. In addition, the nineteenth century was mad about botanizing. John Burroughs, who had been successively a journalist, treasury clerk, and bank examiner, was a friend of Walt Whitman's and author of the first book on Whitman and his work, *Walt Whitman, Poet and Person*. Burroughs was already well known for his nature writing, and he had recently begun the work in hybridizing that was to make him almost as famous as his friend Edison. The Horticultural Hall was thus both a symbol, like the Art Gallery, of growing American sophistication and a reminder of the nation's love affair with nature, albeit in a tamed and domesticated, or "managed," version that combined the "natural" with the "scientific" and thus, like advances in metallurgy, demonstrated a fruitful partnership of man and nature.

The exhibition's logistics were as impressive as its buildings. Streetcar lines that could carry 12,000 passengers an hour were laid, and special railroad tracks and cars provided for another 24,000 per hour. A narrow-gauge railroad conveyed visitors around the grounds, while wheelchairs were provided for those too weary of foot to cover the almost four hundred acres of exhibits. A modern architectural historian has called the exhibition "a characteristically American organization of space . . . here was displayed the principle of regulated flow—of energy, of materials, of people."

Equally indicative of the spirit of the times was the demand of women that there should be a separate hall devoted to their achievements. Some women demurred on the ground that such an undertaking was unnecessarily pushy and aggressive; others objected on the ground that women's achievements should properly find their place with those of men—to create a separate category was demeaning to women because it suggested they could not compete with their male counterparts. Promoters of a women's hall replied that it was masculine prejudice, not feminine inferiority, that made it impossible for them to be adequately represented. Beyond that there was the simple fact that a women's hall would dramatically demonstrate the determination of women to have an equal share in the work and wealth of the nation. An appeal was made for funds, and in three months more than $100,000 were raised to build a "pavilion" of some thirty thousand square feet to display the accomplishments of women "in homes, asylums, missionary fields at home and abroad, sisterhoods, industrial schools, and in the cause of temperance and moral reform." In addition, there were numerous examples of women's crafts, especially needlework, and a first-rate etching by Queen Victoria.

As time approached for the opening of the "great Centennial Exhibit," the commission was racked by charges of extravagance and inefficiency. The funds required to complete the plans appeared to be $10,000,000 short of those on hand. Congress and prominent philanthropists were appealed to, and the opening was delayed from April

19, the date of the Battles of Lexington and Concord, to May 10. Philadelphians awoke that day to find lowering skies which threatened rain. Huge crowds nevertheless filled the streets, and flags flew from every staff, from every window and balcony. The Women's Work Committee led the procession of those entering the grounds of the exhibition, "each decorated with a silver star," followed by the representatives of foreign powers. The band played "Hail, Columbia," the sun came out, and the President and Mrs. Grant appeared on the platform with the emperor and empress of Brazil—the only monarchs that could be enticed to the exhibition—to the accompaniment of "The Grand Centennial March" composed especially for the occasion by the German composer Richard Wagner.

Bishop Matthew Simpson, a prominent Methodist, pronounced the invocation and gave special attention to the "women of our land. May the light of their intelligence, purity and enterprise shed its beams afar, until, in distant lands, their sisters may realize the beauty and glory of Christian freedom and elevation."

John Greenleaf Whittier had composed the "Centennial Hymn," which was sung by a thousand voices:

> Beneath our Western skies fulfil
> The Orient's mission of good-will
> And freighted with love's Golden Fleece,
> Send back the Argonauts of peace.
>
> For art and labor met in truce,
> For beauty made the bride of Use . . .
> Oh! make Thou us, through centuries long,
> In peace secure, in justice strong. . . .

There was a cantata by the Georgia poet Sidney Lanier; then the President made a brief and largely inaudible speech, the American flag was unfurled over the Main Hall, and Handel's "Hallelujah Chorus" was given a rousing rendition. The Centennial Exhibition had begun. Perhaps the most potent symbolic act was the switching on of the great Corliss engine that provided power for all the machinery of the exhibition by President Grant and the emperor. *"Now,* Mr. President," said George Corliss. "How?" asked the President. "By turning that little wheel six times." The President did as bidden, and like a story from ancient mythology, vast powers began to flow to the eight thousand machines—"countless wheels turning, bands beginning their rounds, cogs fitting their places, pistons driving backward and forward and up and down." A great exhalation of breath, a sigh of joy and astonishment, rose from the thousands of spectators.

The inventor of the machine, George Corliss, was a man of the new industrial age. Born in Easton, New York, in 1817, he had gone to work in a cotton factory at the age of fourteen, attended Castleton Academy in Vermont, started a country store, and invented a machine for stitching leather. After moving to Rhode Island at the age of twenty-seven, he began to make greatly improved reciprocating steam engines. Like Elias Howe, the sewing machine tycoon, Corliss was a brilliant promoter of his own inventions. He overcame the skepticism of prospective clients by offering to take as pay for his steam engines the savings in fuel for a given period of time, typically a year. His engine was judged the best in the world at the Paris and Vienna exhibitions. A member of the Centennial Commission representing Rhode Island, Corliss offered to build a steam engine of 1,400 horsepower, far beyond any engine in existence, to drive all the machinery in the exhibition. Spending more than $100,000 of his own money, Corliss designed an engine that did all he had promised. Its gear wheel alone was 30 feet in diameter, and the machine, when assembled, weighed 700 tons. Monsieur Frédéric Auguste Bartholdi, a French sculptor (who would one day design a mammoth statue entitled "Liberty Enlightening the World") reported to his government that the Corliss steam engine "belonged to the category of works of art, by the general beauty of its effect and its perfect balance to the eye." William Dean Howells, the editor of the *Atlantic Monthly,* an arbiter of American literary tastes, was even more lyrical. "It rises loftily," he wrote, "an athlete of steel and iron with not a superfluous ounce of metal on it; the mighty walking beams plunge their pistons downward; the enormous fly-wheel revolves with a hoarded power that makes all tremble; the hundred life-like details do their office with unerring intelligence. In the midst of this ineffably strong mechanism is a chair where an engineer sits reading his newspaper, as in a peaceful bower. Now and then he lays down his paper and clambers up one of the stairways that cover the framework, and touches some irritated spot on the giant's body with a drop of oil, and goes down again and takes up his newspaper; he is like some potent enchanter."

Like the Erie Canal, fifty years earlier, the Corliss steam engine, more than any other feature of the Centennial Exhibition, was taken to represent the triumph of American democracy. It was the perfect demonstration of the pragmatic temper of American inventors who, untrained in schools and colleges, displayed a native ingenuity that was taken as confirmation of the superiority of the American political and social system.

Indeed, inventions appeared in such profusion it was almost impossible to keep track of them. In the decade of the 1860s, four years of which were taken up by the war, 79,612 patents, or more than two thirds of the number granted in the whole history of the Republic, had been issued.

If the Corliss steam engine was by far the most spectacular piece of machinery, there were many others of impressive size and arresting beauty. In addition, there were on exhibit the "four new wonders of the world"—the "Electric Light, the Telephone, the Phonograph, and the Microphone." The electric light had "aptly been pronounced the brightest meteor that has flashed across the horizon of promise during the present century." Many people believed that the age of gaslighting, scarcely a generation old, was already drawing to a close and that night would be turned into day by this wonderful agent. "Although numerous experiments in electrical lighting have been conducted in Europe it remained for the 'wonder-working brain of Mr. Edison' to adapt these to practical use and produce a light which is alleged to be the most steady, clear, inexpensive, and reliable, of any electric light yet produced," a dazzled journalist wrote. Whether or not electricity could ever be made cheap and reliable enough to illuminate dwellings, it had already demonstrated its utility "in halls and other public buildings of considerable size."

In March, 1876, only a month or so before the Centennial Exhibition opened, Professor Alexander Graham Bell had taken out a patent for the telephone, thereby "affording fresh evidence of the versatility of American inventive genius." English inventors had preceded Bell, but the American had "democratized" the telephone by producing an improved instrument, "a marvelous apparatus" which made possible "cheap and instantaneous articulate communication." Bell, born in 1847 in Edinburgh, Scotland, and educated at the University of Edinburgh, had come to the United States at the age of twenty-five. Carrying on his father's work in the instruction of deaf-mutes, he had become professor of vocal physiology at Boston University. Before he was thirty, he had perfected his form of the telephone as an outgrowth of his efforts to invent some kind of voice box for mutes. Like Corliss and Edison, Bell showed a business shrewdness equal or superior to his inventiveness. The telephone and its offshoot, the phonograph, also invented by Edison, promised, according to a contemporary journalist, "the captivity of all manner of sound-waves heretofore designated as 'fugitive,' and their permanent retention; their reproduction with all their original characteristics at will, without the presence or consent of the original source, and after the lapse of any period of time; the transmission of such captive sounds through the ordinary channels of commercial intercourse and trade in material form, for purposes of communication or as merchantable goods, the indefinite multiplication and preservation of such sounds, without regard to the existence or non-existence of the original source; the captivation of sounds, with or without the consent of the source of their origin." The journalist concluded: "These five features may well be said to constitute a mechanical marvel hitherto undreamed of."

A Californian at the exhibition was astonished "at seeing a man before an apparatus apparently in the process of printing letters. He was demonstrating a typewriter, and I dictated to my wife half a dozen lines which he rapidly typed on paper," the awed visitor reported.

The Art Gallery, containing works of famous painters and sculptors from all over the world, was a central feature of the exhibition. Italy and France were well represented, but unfortunately some of the paintings and statues were of nude men and women, and a number of visitors to the gallery were shocked and offended. Indeed, some furious defenders of public morals physically attacked the offensive works. Portions of certain sculptural pieces were knocked off by walking sticks or umbrellas. Canvases were defaced. There was a scandal. *Harper's Weekly* depicted the vandals as donkeys. The gallery was closed to the public, and when it reopened, all canes and umbrellas had to be checked at the door.

The American infatuation with the novel, the bizarre, and the oversized was much in evidence. In addition to a Connecticut clock which weighed six tons and had eleven hundred wheels and cogs, the largest of which measured four feet in diameter, there was a statue of the "Sleeping Iolanthe" by Mrs. Brooks of Arkansas, carved in butter and weighing fourteen pounds; the largest cigar in the world; and the smallest steam engine. A popular exhibit was that of Charles Hires, who made root beer on the spot from genuine roots. The Smithsonian Institution showed "every kind of American bird" in a tasteful arrangement, as well as "every kind of fish, mollusk, reptile and quadruped." Pennsylvania contributed two blocks of coal, weighing, respectively, two and a half and five tons. Representatives of various Indian tribes were present, "their habitations, manners and customs" colorfully displayed. William Dean Howells was unimpressed, noting that the "false and pitiless savage faces" of the Indians excused the "mouldy flour and corrupt beef" that the government's Indian agents were allegedly feeding the Sioux.

Prominent among the exhibits were George Washington's camp bed, clothes, pistol, and sword; Lafayette's silver pitcher; John Adams's desk; and the original draft of the Declaration of Independence, "not to be touched."

Foreign nations had sent elaborate displays of those products for which they were most noted—Switzerland, watches; Canada, furs; Sweden, glasswork and wood carvings; Japan, "her multitudinous porcelains and bronzes." France contributed "its selectest elaborations in almost every department of knowledge and handicraft," including the famous Gobelin tapestries.

Instruction was leavened with entertainment. There were trials of new steam plows and reapers and exhibitions of farm animals—horses and mules, sheep, swine, goats. Most impressive of all was the poultry—dazzling feathered mutations and permutations: huge Cochin Chinas, Brahmas, Buff Orpingtons, the more svelte Leghorns, Hamburgs, and Majorcas, the top-knotted Polish and Houdans, the comfortable Barred Rocks, and the New Hampshire Reds. There was an international regatta on the Schuylkill, which flowed near the grounds. Temperance organizations held their conventions—the Sons of Temperance, the Washington Society, the newly formed Women's Christian Temperance Union, the Knights Templar. Musical associations met and competed and entertained. Americans, already mildly addicted to baseball, watched with amusement a series of international cricket matches. There were rowing regattas and rifle matches. The emphasis on sports was, in fact, notable. Sports were to be a conspicuous new element in the Age of Desire. Heretofore "sport" had meant hunting and fishing, practical exercises that produced food, if not as primary goal, at least as a most agreeable by-product. Now sport came to be something engaged in for its own sake, for pleasure or health. It was associated with "games" that people, mostly youths, "played." General Abner Doubleday had been given credit for inventing baseball at Cooperstown, certainly one of the most notable American inventions. New England youths had, from colonial days, played a game that was a kind of hybrid of rugby and soccer. Out of it developed a game called football which, like rugby, involved kicking and running with the ball, and, in 1869, Princeton and Rutgers had played the first formal game of the new sport at New Brunswick, New Jersey. Four years later, at a gathering which included Columbia, Yale, Princeton, and Rutgers, a uniform set of rules was adopted. Baseball was the common man's game; football was for the sons of the Eastern upper class.

On the periphery of the exhibition grounds a "Shantyville" sprang up, containing shooting galleries, freak shows, games of chance, and other licit and illicit pleasures.

The ultimate moment, the center and climax of the Centennial Exhibition, was, of course, "the Anniversary-Day," as it was called, the Fourth of July itself, "which numbered the first hundred years of the greatest republic upon which the sun ever shone," in the words of the centennial's official historian. "To say that the festal ingenuity of nearly forty States and forty millions of people, with their tens of thousands of cities, towns and villages, fairly spent itself, in efforts to commemorate the Wonderful Anniversary, is only faintly expressing the fact," the same chronicler wrote. "It was a festival of oratory, music, poetry, parade, bells, illuminations, regattas, cannon, banners, hallelujahs and huzzas." Congress had adjourned to participate in the celebration. Grant, worn out with greeting dignitaries, did not attend, and his absence was widely and unfavorably commented on. The Senator, Thomas Ferry, president pro tem of the Senate and acting Vice-President since the death, in 1875, of Henry Wilson, appeared in the President's behalf.

Dr. Oliver Wendell Holmes's "Welcome to the Nations" was sung by a great chorus. Bayard Taylor read his "The National Ode," and William Evarts delivered the oration. Richard Henry Lee, grandson of the Revolutionary patriot, read the Declaration of Independence from the original document, which was then held aloft, "cheer following cheer at this rare spectacle."

The ceremony was interrupted by five advocates of women's rights, who, having secured press passes, made their way to the podium and handed Ferry a Declaration of Women's Independence, which Susan B. Anthony, rising from the musicians' stand, read aloud as Bayard Taylor was attempting to deliver his long, turgid "The National Ode."

Many people who deplored the continuing hostility between

North and South were heartened by a message from the City Council of Montgomery, Alabama, "the birthplace of the Confederate government," which extended "a cordial and fraternal greeting to *all the people of the United States,* with an earnest prayer for the perpetuation of concord and brotherly feelings throughout the land."

All over the country lesser pageants celebrated the great day. In Chicago militant workers rallied to proclaim "greater revolutions" on behalf of the laborer and call for an end to capitalism. In Boston the Declaration of Independence was read by Brooks Adams, brother of Henry and Charles Francis, Jr., son of Charles Francis, and grandson of John Quincy. Faneuil Hall was festooned with flags and hung with a banner that proclaimed: "The city of Boston—the Cradle of Liberty; may Faneuil Hall ever stand a monument to teach the world that resistance to oppression is a duty. . . ."

The firing of the first centennial salute was an honor that fell to Eastport, Maine, the easternmost point in the United States and thus the first spot to observe the rising sun. Carl Schurz led a parade of the German citizens of St. Louis. San Francisco devoted three days to "varied and magnificent festivities which included a mock bombardment of the city's forts."

The day following the celebration, word reached Washington that General George Custer and five companies of United States cavalry, numbering some 270 troopers, had been killed at Little Bighorn by a band of Sioux led by Sitting Bull. Three days later newspapers carried accounts from South Carolina of the Hamburg Massacre. Each event, in its own way, anticipated the future. The destruction of Custer and his troopers gave fresh impetus to the inevitable—the final, conclusive military defeat of the Plains Indians. The Hamburg Massacre foreshadowed the systematic stripping of Southern blacks of whatever residue of political and civil rights remained to them at the end of Reconstruction.

Before the gates were closed in November, a few days after the disputed presidential election, almost 8,000,000 visitors had paid the price of admission (fifty cents for adults and twenty-five cents for children). There were, in addition, 2,000,000 free admissions, making a grand total of some 10,000,000 visitors, or roughly a fourth of the country's population, although it must be assumed that many attended more than once. In the month of October alone more than 2,660,000 people were admitted.

Among those not enchanted with the centennial activities was a

Princeton freshman named Woodrow Wilson, who wrote: "The American *Republic* will in my opinion never celebrate another Centennial. At least under its present Constitution and laws. Universal suffrage is at the foundation of every evil in this country."

One of the most important and elusive consequences of the international aspect of the Centennial Exhibition was the demonstration of genuine interest on the part of Americans in other and more exotic cultures. With all their braggadocio and provincialism Americans have commonly displayed a disarming capacity to respond sympathetically to other peoples. Part of this openness to the alien or unfamiliar was undoubtedly a residue of the "radical universalism" of the American Revolution, which advertised itself as the precursor of innumerable "coming revolutions" designed to produce a redeemed, Christianized democratic world. Part was due to the indefatigable labors of the legions of missionaries, whose reports of exotic lands (now often accompanied by "slides") to their home congregations had vastly expanded the awareness of remote lands. And part, of course, was attributable to the fact that the United States was itself a "congress of nations." In this spirit the immigration of large numbers of Chinese had stimulated an interest in Chinese culture.

The Japanese aesthetic sense was somewhat in the nature of a revelation to visitors of artistic sensibility. Initially an object of humor and ridicule, the Japanese Pavilion, with its simple and harmonious beauty, made a deep impression. Americans, indeed, were among the first "foreigners" to respond to the "democratic" Japanese print.

The Centennial Exhibition, dominated as it was by Corliss's marvelous engine, is as good a moment as any to mark the advent of the industrial era in America. Its roots went back several decades, indeed by some readings several centuries, and its apogee was to be a generation or more in the future, but its implications were beyond calculation. To put the matter as simply as possible, the industrial era changed the existential basis of society by creating whole new categories of *desire*. The Anglo-Indian philosopher Raimundo Panikkar has argued that one of the fundamental features of primitive, or tribal, societies is the absence of *desire*. The primitive man "does not desire something 'else' or something 'more' than what is; indeed, there is no room for anything else." It is difficult for the primitive man to *imagine* (the prerequisite, it might be argued, to desire) something that he does not have. The terrible and irresistible intrusion of the white man, the posttribal man, into tribal society was represented by the introduction of an *infinity of things to be desired.*

The industrial revolution was, of course, much more than a revolution in the means of production. It was a revolution in the human psyche. It inaugurated an era of virtually limitless *desire.* On the one hand, it rearranged and reorganized the productive agencies of society—people and raw materials—and rationalized the means of production by establishing a new relationship of man to his work, by grouping people and machines in a new kind of space called a factory. But essential to its existence and to its proliferation was the creation of what was soon called a market. A market is nothing more or less than the desire of large masses of people for things that they do not have and that, in the strictest sense, they do not need. Even things that they did need—food, clothes, and housing—were made more exotic, more costly, endowed with vastly greater dimensions of desirability. An earlier emphasis on saving, conserving, utilizing, improvising shifted to buying and consuming. Earlier Americans had, as we say today, authenticated themselves by thrift and prudence. In the Gospel according to Benjamin Franklin, "a penny saved was a penny earned," a verification of the individual's ability to rise above the common human temptation to spend the penny. The new ethic declared a penny spent to be an expression of the confidence of the spender that there will be another penny to replace it; it is an assertion of his potency, of the reality of his own existence. Living in a society organized around the act of spending, he is proving himself a worthy citizen. The more pennies he can spend, the deeper his own sense of gratification, of success in the terms in which the larger society has defined it.

In a consumer society spending is the ultimate act of gratification. In these terms we might say that the two most significant events of the nineteenth century were the opening of Alexander Stewart's department store in New York City in 1846 and Montgomery Ward's first catalogue, issued in 1872. Stewart, by collecting a hitherto unimagined array of desirable objects of every kind and price, was the first great stimulator (and satisfier) of American desire. But the stimulus was limited to native New Yorkers of the upper classes and a relative handful of other Americans (and European travelers) mobile enough to get to New York and prosperous enough to have anything left to spend once they got there. Montgomery Ward's catalogue, on the other hand, sought people out in the separateness of their homes. Desire arrived with the mailman. Montgomery Ward manufactured few of the alluring items that it advertised in its irresistible catalogues; it simply warehoused and distributed the items it collected from the manufacturers. In its own way it was as brilliant (and American) an invention as the telephone or the incandescent lamp. It made possible an enormous expansion of desire to the most remote Dakota farm, to a dusty Southern town, to a Western mining camp. What has come to be called capitalism depended on two essential elements—limitless desire and the constant circulation of money so that the desire could be, if not fulfilled (that would be the end of the system), at least to a modest degree appeased. The industrial era thus created a new human type—the buyer, or, as we have come to call him/her, the consumer, a poor creature whose desires always exceeded his/her means, except in the cases of the wealthiest 2 percent, who, able to satisfy all their material desires, often suffered from a terrible feeling of futility and purposelessness.

If the Centennial Exhibition celebrated, for the most part, the material achievements of American democracy and was pervaded by the Secular-Democratic spirit with its rather simpleminded worship of science and progress (to be achieved through education), it also ushered in the Age of Desire and sanctified the new man, the consumer.

53

Religion

The war had accentuated the religious revival set off by the Depression of 1857. As we have seen, many evangelical ministers viewed the struggle in a twofold light—as punishment for national sins, the gravest of which was slavery, and thus purifying and redemptive, and also as the apocalypse foretold in Revelation, the first act of the millennium. The redemptive Christian theme ran through most of the Radical Republican literature. The Reverend George Prentiss, minister of one of New York City's leading Presbyterian churches, declared that "the blessings of a new era of Christian light and liberty" could not come about merely through congressional legislation, "however wise and beneficent; all the agencies of Christian faith and philanthropy, untiring prayers, every form of pious labor and self-sacrifice, the pulpit, the press, the church, the school, innumerable men, women and children even who love Christ and His cause, must be added to complete and crown the glorious work."

The major Protestant denominations, with the possible exception of the Congregationalists, had flunked the test of social conscience posed by the slavery issue. With the advent of the war, most made a belated ecumenical effort to get on the antislavery band wagon. The Christian Commission, an uneasy affiliation of Protestant denominations, was formed to promote piety. It seemed to George Templeton Strong simply "one of the many forms in which the shallowness, fussiness, and humbug of our popular religionism are constantly embodying themselves." But Strong was equally indignant with his own Episcopal church, full of secession sympathizers, for its failure to take a bolder line on the war. "Now, at last," he wrote indignantly, "when they and their people are confronted by the most wicked of rebellions and the most wilful of schisms on the vilest of grounds, the constitutional right to breed black babies for sale, when rebellion and schism are arrayed against the church and against society in the unloveliest form they can possibly assume—the church is afraid to speak. . . . Alas for my dreams of twenty years ago!"

Many ministers believed that the war was a challenge, perhaps a last opportunity for the Protestant churches to align themselves with radical social reform. The Reverend Alexander Clark, Methodist minister in Pittsburgh, assured his congregation that it was not "a mere little select company of the saved and sanctified who are expecting to employ all their time and talent to keep themselves from backsliding into a lost condition. They are bound together for a more neighborly purpose—to do good to others—to represent Christ in the winning power of his life—to reconstruct society—to Christianize the world." The Church must have so much of the spirit of Christ as "to invigorate, to cheer, to comfort, to illuminate, to exalt and to bless communities of common people."

Evangelism was much in evidence. Chicago produced a rival to Henry Ward Beecher, the Reverend Dwight Moody, a whirlwind Christian, whose influence was felt primarily through the Young Men's Christian Association. When the association's "costly hall" caught fire, Moody started making the rounds of "Christian merchants" to rebuild it even before the fire was extinguished. "This is only a spectrum of the lightning Christianity of Chicago," David Macrae wrote. Moody was famous for his missionary work among the poor and unchurched of the city. Macrae accompanied him to one of the mission schools that Moody had founded. He had, he wrote, "rarely beheld such a scene of high-pressure evangelization. It made me think irresistibly," he added, "of those breathing steamboats on the Mississippi, that must either go fast or burst. Mr. Moody himself effervesced about the school the whole time, seeing that everybody was at work . . . and inspiring everyone with his own enthusiasm." Moody declared: "I look on this world as a wrecked vessel. God has given me a lifeboat and said to me, 'Moody, save all you can.'"

Spiritualism enjoyed a remarkable revival. Everyone, it seemed, was experimenting on Ouija boards. Victoria Woodhull had started her exotic career as a spiritualist. Even skeptical Carl Schurz was drawn in, at least for a moment. Summoned to Washington by President Johnson without explanation, Schurz had stopped off in Philadelphia to visit a friend from his revolutionary days in Germany, Dr. Heinrich Tiedemann. The Tiedemanns' fifteen-year-old daughter was believed to be clairvoyant. The Tiedemanns had lost two sons in the war, and the doctor, "although belonging to a school of philosophy which looked down upon such things with a certain distain, could not restrain a sentimental interest in the pretended communications from his lost boys," Schurz wrote, "and permitted spiritualistic experiments to be made in his family." Different deceased persons were called upon, but they replied with discouraging platitudes—"they lived in a higher sphere," were "happy," were "often with us," and so on. When Schurz was invited to summon a spirit in whom he was interested, he asked for Schiller. What did Schurz wish of him? the spirit asked through the medium. A verse from one of his works. The girl then wrote in German two lines from *Wallensteins Tod:*

> Gay music strikes my ear. The castle is
> Aglow with lights. Who are the revelers?

"We were all struck with astonishment," Schurz wrote. They looked up the line from the poem, which the girl assured them she had never read.

Next Schurz tried to communicate with Lincoln. Why, Schurz asked, had Johnson summoned him to Washington? The answer: "He wants you to take an important trip for him." Should he consent? Schurz asked. "Do not fail," Lincoln replied. Had Lincoln anything else to say to him? "Yes, you will be a Senator of the United States." From what state? Missouri. This seemed to Schurz stranger still, since he was a resident of Wisconsin.

As we have seen, the Protestant churches of the North raised millions of dollars to support the work of the freedmen's aid societies, to start schools and employ teachers in the South, and to establish the thirty or so black colleges in the South. This work was carried on through the Reconstruction years and, in the case especially of the black colleges, for decades thereafter. Foreign missionary activity sponsored by the churches also increased notably. The Near East, Hawaii, Africa, and India continued to be expanding missionary fields, and Young J. Allen, a Georgian, pioneered in the comparatively new missionary field of China. He laboriously taught himself Chinese and opened a small missionary chapel in Shanghai in 1863. By 1866 he could count only twenty converts, the rest to whom he had preached having been "excluded from the church on account of evil conduct, adultery, smoking opium and persistently breaking the Sabbath."

One of the most influential missionary leaders, the Reverend Rufus Anderson, wrote that Christianity was the bearer "of the blessings of education, industry, civil liberty, family government, social order, the means of a respectable livelihood, and a well-ordered community. . . . Our idea of the propagation of the gospel by means of missions is, to an equal extent, *the creation among heathen tribes and nations of a highly improved state of society, such as we ourselves enjoy.*"

Herman Melville, having witnessed the activities of missionaries on Tahiti, had a different view. "The fiend-like skill we display in the invention of all manner of death-dealing engines," he wrote, "the vindictiveness with which we carry on our wars, and the misery and desolation that follow in their train are enough in themselves to distinguish the white civilized man as the most ferocious animal on the face of the earth. . . . So far as the relative wickedness of the parties is concerned, four or five Marquesas Islanders sent to the United States as missionaries might be quite as useful as an equal number of Americans dispatched to these lands in a similar capacity."

Religious life does not take place exclusively in institutional settings. Outside the churches a profound change was taking place in the way in which many young middle- and upper-class intellectuals viewed the world.

Sidney George Fisher had never been an orthodox Quaker. He considered himself a transcendentalist, and, as he grew older, his reflections on the meaning of life were increasingly "philosophical" rather than theological. If "philosophy" was "an interesting and absorbing study," it was "not cheerful; it oppresses the mind with a profound feeling of the mystery of life, ourselves, our purpose & our fate," he added. "Life becomes more solemn, more earnest, more crowded with thought & emotion as we approach that period when it is to cease altogether on this scene." He found some consolation in trying "to reach the limits of science, to recognize our ignorance, to follow the track of masterly logic and to have one's mind opened to the grand & profound mystery of nature & of our own souls. . . . I have not much time before me," he wrote in his fifty-sixth year, "and ere long this familiar scene, with its work, its hopes and enjoyments, will pass away and perhaps be exchanged for a freer and larger existence. I enjoy it now, this sense of moral and intellectual being, this communion with the great mind of nature, and cannot conceive that I shall not, somehow or other, enjoy it always. This feeling of the present, this fore-sense of the future, fills my days with deep satisfaction & lifts me above the external things of life, I care not for wealth, I am not eager for reputation or position, it suffices that I live & think & feel and that I shall always do so."

Fisher reflected on "how much of what appears to be the not-me is really the me. . . . This point of time then is life. . . . There is no such thing as life except [consciousness] & no such thing as death except the inability to think. If the ability remains after death, death is continuous life, not more wonderful than our earthly continuous life thro successive changes from infancy to age." Why then did men fear death? "Because we shrink from the idea of annihilation if the mind really dies, and because we dread unknown changes if it does not. We love life, therefore we hate its opposite. . . . We have a profound sense of the dignity and worth of our souls, and cannot bear the thought that they are of so little worth as to perish utterly & be cast among the 'wastes of time.' Moreover, we love life not in the abstract only, but this earthly life, this beautiful world, this familiar scene, wife & child & property, our work, our plans and thought, and change, even for continued life in the unknown, is terrible to us."

Fisher's reflections have a decidedly modern ring about them. Even George Templeton Strong, though he remained a devout Episcopalian, felt obliged to read Darwin and reconcile the Englishman's theories with his own theology. In this spirit he delved into Darwin's *Descent of Man.* "To me," he wrote, "as a 'poor ignorant cretur,' the popularity of Darwinism among physicists seems no less amazing than the late epidemic of so-called spiritualism among the Polloi. The theory is unscientific because it is without a scintilla of evidence. From the harmonies and analogies that underly the whole realm of organic life, Darwin infers the descent of the higher species from the lower. He might as fairly infer the descent of gold from lead from the properties they have in common."

The findings of geology, which postulated a vastly longer history of the planet than that suggested by Genesis, Strong found thoroughly compatible with Christian doctrine. Viewing the fossils collected by John Strong Newberry, the new Columbia paleontologist, Strong was moved to reflect that "the period that separates the pyramids from the last Fifth Avenue brownstone front dwindles to a point when we think of the ages that have passed since any one of Newberry's trilobites gave his last flop or wiggle and settled down into the fast stratifying mudflat on which rested the waters of his native estuary. . . ." Strong saw no reason, in Christian doctrine, to resist the findings of the geologists. "Even if we think ourselves bound to search the Scriptures for physical science and that the Bible was meant to instruct us therein, its teachings are *not* contradicted by geology, while its revelation of the infinity of Creative Power is thereby most awfully enforced and illustrated. . . ."

When we come to the generation that fought the Civil War, the skeptical spirit is much more evident. On the Southern side, it is plain that the Reverend Colcock Jones, father of the colonel who was his namesake, was seriously disturbed by his son's lack of religious faith. "Daily does my soul go out to the precious Saviour in anxious cries for your salvation," he wrote. "When, my son, are you going to consider the interests of your immortal soul? Are you daily reading the word of God? Do you pray?"

The matter was much the same between Oliver Wendell Holmes, Sr., and Captain Holmes of the Massachusetts Regiment. When Captain Holmes was lying wounded on the battlefield near death, as he believed, he felt an impulse to recant his agnosticism and embrace that Christian faith which was such a solace to his parent. He had even discussed with his father, who was distressed by his infidelity, the possibility of "a deathbed recantation." But his "Philosophy" came to his rescue. Even though he was to "take a leap in the dark," he believed that "whatever shall happen is best—for it is in accordance with a general law—and *good & universal* (or *general laws*) are synonymous terms in the universe. . . ." He said to his friend Henry Sturgis, "Well Harry I'm dying but I'll be G. d'd if I know where I'm going." To which the more pious "Sturge" replied, "'Why—Homey—you believe in Christ, don't you' . . . with a brief exposition of doctrine argumentively set forth. . . ."

Theodore Winthrop, who was killed in the fighting at Big Bethel in one of the first engagements of the war, was a descendant of John

Winthrop, presiding elder of the Puritan Commonwealth and author of "A Modell of Christian Charity." Winthrop, thirty-three at the time of his death and a graduate of Yale, had already established a modest reputation as an author and connoisseur of art. Like so many upper-class youths of his generation, he was an avowed "infidel." As George Templeton Strong put it, "that brave, brilliant, and unfortunate young fellow used to avow his disbelief in the commonly received doctrines of Christianity with more frankness and freedom than good taste."

At almost the same time another young veteran, disabled in war, a farm boy from Illinois by way of Towanda, Pennsylvania, was throwing off his religious swaddling clothes. Lester Ward kept a diary which featured his intense physical relationship with his adored Lizzie. He read Paine and Voltaire for his own revelation and later Darwin. He and Lizzie subscribed to the feminist journal *Revolution*. When Lizzie got pregnant before they wished for a child, Ward noted dutifully that she had an abortion. Later he shared the housework and his wife's pleasure in their baby boy. He took the affirmative side in his debating society on the question of the "errors in theology" (Christians were not only those who believed in the divinity of Christ; Socrates and John Stuart Mill were both Christians in any proper meaning of the word, Ward maintained). Early in 1869 he cut off his beard and mustache. It was a more than casual act. It was as though, by doing so, he had cut himself off from an older age mired in religious obscurantism and outmoded notions and stepped forward into a new era, the age of Mill and Darwin, of reforms based on scientific principles rather than the muddled desire to "do good." (He and Lizzie continued, however, to "amuse" themselves with their Ouija board.) Like all proper, liberally educated young Americans, Lester Ward decided that he wished, above all other possible careers, to be a writer, and he began a book "devoted to the great cause of education."

In the spring of 1869 Ward wrote in his diary: "I have attained the most cherished object of my life, a college education." A few days later, debating the question of abolishing capital punishment, Ward confounded even the liberal thinkers of the lyceum "by demanding the abolishment of all punishment and declaring the integrity of man."

A few months later he and his friends founded the National Liberal Reform League for "the dissemination of liberal sentiment; the opposition to all forms of superstition; the exposition of all fallacious moral and religious doctrines, and the establishment of the principles of mental, moral, and religious liberty, as embodied in the Declaration of Independence and the Constitution of the United States." The main objects of their attack were to be "the leading doctrinal teachings of the so-called Catholic and Evangelical Protestant Churches," and their goal was to promote "the triumph of reason and science over faith and theology" in order to enable Americans "to unite in a powerful cooperative alliance for practical results." The association was to be secret, and the identity of its members carefully concealed. It sought recruits from the ranks of those who shared similar principles —"Liberals, Skeptics, Infidels, Secularists, Unitarians, Socialists, Positivists, Spiritualists, Deists, Theists, Pantheists, Atheists, Freethinkers, all who desire the mental emancipation of mankind from the trammels of superstition. . . ." The first issue of the league's magazine, under the editorship of Ward, appeared in March, 1870.

Charles Francis Adams, Jr., had read John Stuart Mill on Comte and had plunged into Darwin at almost the same time Lester Ward was reveling in Paine and Voltaire. "I emerged from the theological stage, in which I had been nurtured, and passed into the scientific," Adams wrote, adding that "from reading that compact little volume of Mill's . . . I date a changed intellectual and moral being." It is worth noting that while Mill and Darwin were Adams's emancipators, Paine and Voltaire performed the same service for Ward. We may, I think, take the experience of these two idealistic young Americans, so strikingly different in their training and education, as marking, in dramatic fashion, the rise of a new religion of science and progress. While it was true that it had a history that reached back at least to Thomas Jefferson, it had been, if not precisely submerged by evangelical Protestantism, at least intertwined with it and much moderated in its basically anti-Christian bias. Transcendentalism, which had so eroded orthodoxy, had at the same time constantly reaffirmed its faith in a universal moral order, talked constantly of God and spirit, and insisted that its mission was to reveal a truer and purer Christianity. Now the young intellectuals of the post-Civil War period struck out boldly against the whole structure of Protestant Christianity, liberal and orthodox alike. The order in the universe was not moral, after all, but scientific and progressive. To discover the truth, one read Paine and Darwin, not Ezekiel and Paul.

While Charles Francis Adams, Jr., "emerged from the theological stage . . . and passed into the scientific," his father remained firmly rooted in an older tradition. Writing to his namesake about the political genius of John Quincy Adams, the elder Adams gave it as his opinion that "the first and greatest qualification of a statesman . . . is the mastery of the whole theory of morals which makes the foundation of all human society. The great and everlasting question of the right and wrong of every act whether of individual men or of collective bodies. The next is the application of the knowledge thus gained to the events of his time in a continuous and systematic way."

In the new dispensation, science replaced morality. Or it became the new morality, to which, as George Templeton Strong pointed out, every question might be confidently referred.

We can take the manifesto of the National Liberal Reform League as a classic early expression of the aggressively secular spirit that would dominate American intellectual life for the next century. It did not seem to occur to Lester Ward and his allies and successors that they were, for all practical purposes, establishing a religion of their own, the religion of science and reason. Or re-establishing it, if we take Thomas Jefferson to be its principal American expositor. It is not too much to say that the failure of Ward and his friends to distinguish between, on the one hand, the inability of the ruling bodies of the principal Protestant denominations to come to grips with the issue of slavery and, on the other, the far deeper Protestant Passion for redeeming Americans (and ultimately the world) from all moral and spiritual deficiencies (a passion of which Ward, it might be said, was the residuary legatee) would mark virtually all subsequent scholarly treatment of the pre-Civil War era.

The obvious reason for this failure to discriminate between the churches and "the faith" was that the new secular religion of science and reason wished to lay claim to the spirit of "liberal reform." To do that, it had both to postulate a "rational" human nature (such a rational human nature lay, as we have seen, at the center of the Secular-Democratic Consciousness, which in turn had inherited or adapted it from the Enlightenment) and to attack "the Catholic and Evangelical Protestant Churches" as strongholds of superstition and obscurantism, not only ignoring the central role of Protestant Christianity in our history but assailing it as a symbol of intellectual nullity and political reaction.

Science was science; natural laws were natural laws. The sentimental intervention of well-intentioned people could only cause confusion and demoralization. The trouble with religion was that it was "unscientific." It dealt with unprovable matters such as faith and hope and the world hereafter. You could not use it as a guide to social problems any more than you could use the Sermon on the Mount to regulate economic activity. What was needed to reorder human society was a "social science," not the Christian social science of John Humphrey Noyes, but *the dispassionate study of the way things were*. But that, of course, was not necessarily the way they must continue to be. The old utopian vision could not be entirely suppressed. The argument that developed among the believers in the new religion of science, which they, of course, did not understand to be a religion at all but simply the bald, unvarnished scientific Truth, was comparatively subtle. Would the process, the millennia-long struggle of the fittest to survive, in and of itself produce the highest possible human order, or should human intelligence, as a product of that evolutionary process, undertake to shape and modify it? That, it may be said, was to be for the next hundred years or so the single overriding issue among those scholars and intellectuals who denominated themselves social scientists. Was it the responsibility of those students of man as a social being simply to urge that nothing be done to impede the evolutionary process by philanthropic tinkerings? Or must they, having learned something of how the process worked, aid and abet it? Oil and repair it; modify it when it appeared to be working badly? How much could one do to help the needy, the oppressed, the weak—as we would say today, the losers? The answer of many conscientious and intelligent Americans came to be "nothing." Simply clear the tracks. Remove the underbrush that has sprung up under the misguided ministrations of reformers and "do-gooders." Since it can't, in any event, be deflected, let nature take its course. In America, one of the principal corollaries of that doctrine was not "abandoning" so much as "leaving" the blacks of the South to their own devices, to the remorseless workings of the law of survival. So a number of things as diverse as "pure" ideas and the more diffuse workings of social and economic tendencies combined to prepare the way for "abandoning" Southern blacks and, once they were abandoned, to soothe the conscience of the North for having done so.

The notion of "progress," always an important component of the American consciousness, more and more replaced redemption. The irrepressible moral issue of slavery had forced many Americans to think and talk in terms of good and evil and interpret American history as a struggle against the forces of darkness. Now the evil had been eradicated. The evolutionary doctrines of Darwin, so far as they were understood, were applied to the social life of human beings and, depending in part, of course, on whose interpretation one favored, were taken to reinforce the Enlightenment conviction that man was a rational creature and that human society was perfectible and progressive. This being the case, one school of "social" Darwinians took the view that all aspects of man's common social and economic activity should be left "free" to respond to its own internal laws. There must be free competition, free trade, freedom for all social units from the individual to the giant corporation and nations themselves to respond to the challenge of their environments. In the remorseless functioning of this "progress," the fittest would survive and the race be thereby improved.

Finally, there was a more subtle but perhaps in the long run more important ideological element. This was the erosion of the faith of young liberal intellectuals in the notion of Christian equality and brotherhood. As we have noted, the religion of science, the prophet of which was Darwin, replaced the religion of traditional Christianity with startling rapidity in the years immediately preceding and following the Civil War. As long as the major doctrines of Protestant Christianity had dominated the "common mind" or consciousness of Americans, a redemptive notion of human nature prevailed, a notion which held that God had created all human beings in His image. No people, no race or nation could be, therefore, by its "nature" inferior to any other. And none inherently "superior." The only "operative" difference was Christianity. There were, to be sure, heathens who had never heard the Word of God and thus dwelt in spiritual and moral darkness, but they had always before them the hope of redemption. No devout Christian could rest until the light had been revealed to those in darkness. As we have had numerous occasions to note, not all Christians by any means held to such a doctrine, and many who did were troubled by what appeared to them evidences of racial inferiority among black people. But we have also taken note of the fact that among the great majority of abolitionists, who, after all, counted in their ranks a very substantial number of the best educated and most "enlightened" Americans, there was a firmly held conviction that it was the deprived and servile status of the blacks in the United States, free and slave, North and South, that accounted for what appeared to be black inferiority.

"Science," on the other hand, professed to be concerned with nothing but the "evidence." Empirical facts, not moral principles, ruled the universe. The "facts," it was soon said, all pointed to the inherent "racial" inferiority of black people and indeed all non-Anglo-Saxon people. The new science of anthropology measured brain capacity, facial hair, and other indices that were taken to indicate that certain races were higher in the evolutionary scale than others and thus "naturally" and unequivocally superior. It was this "scientific" argument for black inferiority that most offended George Templeton Strong. "The Negro can be taught reading and writing and the first four rules of arithmetic, to be sure," he wrote, "and he is capable of keeping a hotel. He can fight like a hero and live and die like a Christian." The modern apostle of science replies: "But look at his facial angle, sir, and at the peculiarities of his skeleton, and you will at once perceive that his place is with the chimpanzee and the gorilla, not with man. Physical science is absolutely infallible you know. No matter what the Church, or the Bible, or human instincts, or common sense may seem to say on any subject, physical science is always entitled to overrule them. It is very true that the science of 1863 has reversed or modified about 250,000 of the decisions it gave twenty years ago, but that makes no difference."

Samuel Gridley Howe was more susceptible to the claims of science. Howe had labored long and unselfishly in the abolition cause (as well as in virtually every other reform movement of the day), and he had held fast to the notion of the "black-as-redeemer of white America." But by 1863 he had begun to have misgivings. The scientist he knew best was the Swiss biologist Louis Agassiz, one of the most famous members of the Harvard faculty. Troubled over the prospective problems of emancipation and reconstruction, Howe wrote to Agassiz to solicit his opinion about the enfranchisement of freed blacks. Agassiz warned him against giving freedmen the vote. He believed that blacks were "indolent, playful, sensual, imitative, subservient, good-natured, versatile, unsteady in their purpose, devoted and affectionate" (rather as Moncure Conway had described them) but that they had never given any evidence of the capacity for self-government. "I cannot," Agassiz wrote, "think it just or safe to grant at once to the negro all the privileges which we ourselves have acquired by long struggles." Agassiz was not a Darwinian—he was a polygenist, believing in the simultaneous creation of different races in different geographical environments—but he and the other advocates of polygeny came out on racial matters pretty much where the Darwinians did. In fact, because the polygenists were disposed to believe that the different races of man had, in the main, remained biologically "fixed" since their creation, they saw no hope that the presently inferior Negroid peoples could ever "evolve" toward the superior Caucasians. But what Agassiz's apparently dispassionate and "scientific" appraisal of the Negro temperament did not reveal was his own strong personal dislike of black people. When he arrived in the United States in 1846, he wrote his mother of his shock on first encountering blacks—the servants in the hotel where he stayed. Looking at them, he found all his beliefs about the "confraternity of the human type" shaken. "In seeing their black faces with their thick lips and grimacing teeth, the wool on their head, their bent knees, their elongated hands, their large curved nails, and especially the livid color of the palms of their hands, I could not take my eyes off their faces in order to tell them to stay away. And when they advanced that hideous hand towards my plate in order to serve me, I wished I were able to depart in order to eat a piece of bread elsewhere, rather than to dine with such service."

In portions of his reply to Howe, deleted from his published papers by his wife, Agassiz expressed his fears about miscegenation. "The production of half-breeds," he wrote, "is as much a sin against nature, as incest in a civilized community is a sin against purity of character." The issue of miscegenation, as Agassiz's letter suggests, became part of the hidden agenda of the racial question. At the center of the issue lay white anxiety about black sexuality. It was general knowledge in the North that the masters of Southern plantations and their male offspring indulged themselves with the "lascivious" and sexually uninhibited female slaves. As the two races approached "equality," what would prevent the mixing or "amalgamation" of the races? An almost hysterical anxiety began to manifest itself about preserving the "purity" of not just Caucasian but specifically Anglo-Saxon blood, which was threatened not merely by miscegenation but, what was almost as bad, by mixture with the blood of "lesser" breeds—Latins, Slavs, and indeed any of a dozen or more of those immigrant groups pouring into the United States in such alarming numbers. The particular form that this anxiety took in the South was not so much fear that white males would continue to seek the beds of black females—that, after all, had been sanctioned for generations, and the evidence of the practice was everywhere—but that black males, believed to have a sexual potency equivalent to that of black women, would seduce white females. The nature and history of that anxiety are too vast to attempt to map here. Suffice it to say that into that dark, phantasmagorical subterranean world of American sexual fantasy there dropped the rape-seduction anxiety that had to do with the "pollution" of white females and white blood by black males.

The effect of Darwinian notions on liberal and even radical reformers can be measured by Georges Clemenceau's parting reflections on the future of blacks in America. Clemenceau had been, since his arrival in the United States, an unwavering champion of the rights of blacks. Several times he recorded his, as it turned out, premature conviction that their rights had been at last secured to them through this piece of congressional legislation or that. In 1869 he wrote: "the blacks must henceforth work to better themselves. They have the right to education, they must learn; they have the right to work, they must work; lastly, they have civil and political rights which are effective weapons, they use them in their own defense. They must gird up their loins, and struggle for existence, for their physical as well as their moral existence. In a word, they must become men. . . . In this ruthless struggle for existence carried on by human society, those who are weaker physically, intellectually or morally must in the end yield to the stronger. The law is hard, but there is no use in rebelling. European socialists who complain, not without reason, that some men are too well armed for this struggle, and others too ill, will not have modified this struggle, nor its causes, nor its conditions, nor its results, when, if ever, they succeed in putting nearly equal weapons into the hands of everyone. . . . As for the Republican party, which has done so much for the negroes in so short a time, considering the strength of the prejudices it had to combat, it will remain in power as long as its work is threatened, as long as the solution it has evolved for the question is not universally accepted by the conscience of the country. Once this result has been accomplished," Clemenceau concluded, "its role will be over and there will be another transformation in the two great parties which rule the American Republic."

The passage is worthy of our close attention. Clemenceau's call for blacks to prove themselves, to "become men," contained first, the dominant nineteenth-century ethic of self-improvement, which, if it had originated in the United States, had spread wherever democratic ideals had taken root. On the other hand, his adherence to the Darwinian "law" of survival, of "ruthless struggle for existence," a law without exception or exemption, gave the game away at once. It was no more than what the South had been saying. White Southerners were superior to black Southerners in education, training, culture, natural abilities, inherently and finally. Therefore, blacks must submit to the race which had proved and every day confirmed its superiority. That was the inescapable law of human development. But what of the fact that blacks, like the depressed and exploited working classes of Europe, were not "armed for the struggle" but were denied the weapons by which to prove themselves worthy? To that question, Clemenceau offered no answer.

The worm of doubt that gnawed not so much at Clemenceau's dedication to the rights of black people but at his confidence in their capacities gnawed at his American counterparts as well as at that very class of people who, in an earlier generation, had provided the cadres of the abolitionist army.

If many of the young men of the Civil War generation lost their faith in traditional (or untraditional) Christianity, it was, generally speaking, otherwise with the young women. Christian ideals and rhetoric continued to characterize the movement for women's rights, finding its most conspicuous expression in the Women's Christian Temperance Union, a vast agency of general reform.

We have noted earlier that under the influence primarily of Emerson the lecture came to replace the sermon as a channel for the transmission of truth. The debating and literary societies which sprang up in every small town in the decades following the war were also centers of secularism. Their prototype was Boston's Radical Club, which was made up primarily of clergymen and laymen. Emerson and Bronson Alcott were members, as were Whittier, the historian John Fiske, Oliver Wendell Holmes, Jr., and Thomas Wentworth Higginson. The group discussed such topics as "Indian Ethics," "Religion and Art," "The Immanence of God." Wendell Phillips spoke on the "limitations of human nature"; he took the line that "democracy is not a good government, but it is the best we can get while we have only this poor, rotten human nature to work with." It was an odd topic for the club, most of the members of which had been distinguished for their unfaltering optimism. It awakened the echoes of Puritan orthodoxy, of original sin and man's fatally flawed nature. The date was 1874. The war had been over for almost a decade, and the hopes that had been engendered by that vast struggle had already gone glimmering. The situation of blacks in the South had steadily deteriorated, and what perhaps was even more disheartening, business of the most ruthless and rapacious variety was firmly in the saddle. Thus, the Radical Club, which was far from radical, was an anachronism, the vestige of an era when despite slavery (or perhaps, paradoxically, *because* of it), the future seemed full of promise.

To say that by 1870 the Protestant Passion, which had informed all important reform movements of the first half of the century, was spent would be to overstate the case, but it was certainly true that it would never again exert anything like the same kind of influence. The great majority of Americans would continue to find a home in one or another of the constantly proliferating Protestant sects or old-line denominations, but the intellectual leadership that had distinguished the Protestant Passion in the decades prior to the Civil War would take a dramatically different turn. The Beechers, Channings, Parkers, Ripleys, et al. would leave no true successors. The effort to define America's mission in Christian-moral terms would give way to evolutionary scientism—the search for laws of human progress or social development. There would be, certainly, able and distinguished preachers, spokesmen for popular religion, revivalists and evangelicals, but the intellectual quotients in all such enterprises showed a marked decline from the earlier era.

Henry Ward Beecher's Plymouth Church had always been a refuge for liberal eccentrics. The summer of 1874 witnessed one of the strangest dramas in American history. For months Victoria Woodhull and her sister Tennessee Claflin had, in their *Woodhull and Claflin's Weekly,* been hinting at a sexual liaison between Henry Ward Beecher and Elizabeth Tilton, the wife of his sometime assistant and successor, editor of the *Independent,* the eccentric Theodore Tilton. Tilton had at least flirted with the free-love and communistic doctrines of the Claflin sisters and Stephen Pearl Andrews, the eccentric Texan whose antislavery sentiments and widely publicized efforts to convert Texas into a free state had forced him to leave his native state. Andrews had settled in Boston, where he invented a practical system of "phonography" or shorthand. Moving to New York, he founded the science of universology and developed a universal language which he called Alwato. A friend of Horace Greeley's, who was susceptible to any new nostrum, and an ally of the Claflins, Andrews had found a sympathetic ear in Henry Ward Beecher and Theordore Tilton.

Victoria Woodhull accused Beecher of "preaching every Sunday to twenty of his mistresses." Finally she narrowed the charge down to adultery with Theodore Tilton's wife, Elizabeth. George Templeton Strong was pleased to note that Woodhull had been arrested on the charge of libel and of sending obscene material through the mail and, unable to raise $8,000 bail, had been confined in the Ludlow Street jail.

Victoria Woodhull's animus against Beecher was due primarily to the fact that he had failed to respond to her letters asking him to intervene to prevent her from being ejected, on the grounds of her bad reputation, from the hotel in which she was living. Apparently Beecher's sister Isabella was the original source of the Claflins' information. Beecher felt obliged to respond to their charges, and he did so by that eminently safe recourse of appointing a committee made up of four devoted parishioners to investigate them. Before the committee could make its report, Tilton added fuel to the fire by publicly making the charge of adultery with his wife against Beecher and producing letters from Beecher to Mrs. Tilton, apologizing in abject terms for some injustice or indiscretion on his part. Elizabeth Tilton then weighed in with a series of distraught and somewhat contradictory stories which, again, confirmed the charge of adultery. Beecher denied the charges, his committee declared him innocent, and Tilton sued him for $100,000 for "criminal conversation" with his wife.

The case went to trial in January, 1875, and dragged on until June, titillating (or horrifying) the country with fresh revelations.

George Templeton Strong expressed a conviction common to many Americans not directly under the influence of the most famous preacher of the day when he wrote: "The Beecher pot still boils. People begin to say that whether Tilton is lying or not, Plymouth Church is a cage of unclean birds. Beecher's profound abasement for some wrong or other done to Tilton is the ugly feature of Beecher's case. . . . But Mrs. Theodore Tilton avers in her manifesto that her life was embittered by Theodore's 'free love' affiliations, teachings, and practices, and that he caused her home to be infested by vermin of the Victoria Woodhull species whom he patronized and cultivated."

To Strong it was difficult to distinguish between the wickedness of the Claflin-Andrews crowd and the more general looniness of the Plymouth Church-goers. He considered the church a "nest of 'psychological phenomena,' or, in plain language, 'lunatics.' Verily," he wrote, "they are a peculiar people. They all call each other by their first names and perpetually kiss one another."

When the jury finally retired to consider its verdict, the country had been treated to a symbolic drama of very considerable potency. The jury split nine to three for acquittal, but there was no acquittal for Beecher. The reputation of a man many considered the foremost spiritual leader of the age had been irredeemably tainted. It was not just Beecher himself who was on trial. The whole Beecher family, starting with the redoubtable Lyman, had occupied a position on the center stage of nineteenth-century America. There were Harriet and the formidable Catharine, the presiding spirits in the reform of the American home, their volumes of *Domestic Economy* best sellers decade after decade. There was the Claflin connection—the free-love doctrines, the communist affiliations, the role of the sisters in organizing the first international labor union under the uneasy aegis of Karl Marx and Friedrich Engels. Next only to Garrison and Wendell Phillips, Beecher had been the leading voice in the abolitionist crusade. The *Independent,* the most widely read journal of antislavery and general reform, was a kind of extension of Beecher's famous church, with a congregation of tens of thousands devoted to their inspiring leader.

The identification of any ecclesiastic with a sexual scandal is always particularly titillating to the laity, smacking as it does of hypocrisy unmasked and sin in sanctified places, but like the lamentable end of Greeley and Sumner's death in political eclipse, the Beecher fiasco had in it substantial elements of the tragic. Moreover, it served, though certainly few contemporary Americans marked the point, to accentuate the unhappy mess of American sexual attitudes and the general disarray of the reform movement. On top of the apparently endless chronicle of political corruption, of exploitation of the public by railroad tycoons, the manipulation of the commodity markets by vulpine speculators like Drew and Fisk, the rise of "infidelity," and the unsolvable muddle of race relations in the South, the sexual morals of the greatest Christian spokesman in the nation had been called into question. It seemed that there was no public figure, however revered, who, on closer inspection, did not turn out to have feet of clay. Tilton, Andrews, the Claflin sisters, women's rights, free love, communism. It all was profoundly unsettling. Reform, if it had not been exactly respectable, had, prior to the Civil War, at least conformed to certain tenets of middle-class respectability. Now the country suddenly was full of the wildest eccentrics—men like George Francis Train and nutty Stephen Pearl Andrews—who seemed to totter on the edge of sanity. It was being said with increasing stridency that America was done for, finished, washed up, about to go the way of the Late Roman Empire into that perdition which awaited all nations mired in luxury, materialism, greed, and selfishness. It was small wonder that the generation that had fought for the Union, fought for equality, for a truer humanity, for a nation it could finally "love," experienced the profoundest disillusionment. Those young men didn't give a rap for Henry Ward Beecher. Sixty-two years old, he appeared to most of them hardly more than an amusing relic of an earlier age. But his fall from grace was another kind of fall, a fall of the old spirit of Congregationalism, the end of the era of zealous middle-class Christian reform, the death knell of the Protestant Passion. Beecher had twelve more years to live. Most of his congregation stood by him, and his denomination formally exonerated him, but his vast power over the mind and conscience of Americans was gone. The process had, to be sure, started with his defection from the Radical Republicans, but the Tilton affair completed it.

There was another symbolic implication in the trial. The despised Claflins, representing for respectable Americans all that was wicked and scandalous in their alliance with Cornelius Vanderbilt and in their muckraking journal, had brought down the epitome of that very respectability which condemned and, on occasion, jailed them in an effort to stop their outrageous tongues. Seen in one perspective, the strange conjunction of the "psychological phenomena" of Beecher's followers with the Claflin-Andrews crowd appears rather like some new spirit struggling to be born. A world in which people "call each other by their first names and perpetually kiss one another" was, clearly, a world in the distant future, but in the midst of the moral and intellectual chaos of postwar America that oddly ill-assorted group gave an intimation of it. It was as though a cosmic prestidigitator had drawn back the curtain of his magic show to give his audience a brief glimpse of the future.

The greatest achievement of Protestant Christianity, or at least that portion of it which I have called the Church of Abolition, was the abolition of slavery. At the same time the inability of the old-line denominations—the Presbyterians, Baptists, Congregationalists, Episcopalians, and Methodists—to cope with the issue of slavery greatly diminished their influence. Although they remained strongholds of personal piety and individual redemption, their broader social importance was curtailed. As we have seen, they put their material and human resources primarily into churchly institutions, into denominational schools, colleges and seminaries, into orphanages and charitable hospitals, and, of course, most strikingly into missionary work—at home with freed blacks and Indians, abroad in the already well-established missionary fields in the Near East, India, and Africa, and, farther afield in the newer missionary areas of the Far East, most notably China and Japan. The established churches also put considerable effort and energy into the relatively noncontroversial area of temperance reform. Individuals in the women's rights movement and, indeed, in most other areas of "reform" continued to find their essential motivation in Christian doctrines and Christian ideals, but the type of young men and women who had constituted the indomitable legions of the abolitionists failed to establish another "church" or discover another mission as demanding and rewarding as the Church of Abolition. By the end of the century it was evident that a good measure of that spirit had moved west and south to provide the moral foundations for populism. "Godless" capitalism, with its ruthless and un-Christian exploitation of the farmer, reawakened some of the evangelical fervor that had characterized the great days of abolitionism, but in the runaway fragmentation of Protestant sects and denominations there was a marked disposition to turn inward to an increasingly sterile moralism and a rigid fundamentalism, evidences of an essentially beleaguered mentality rather than the redemptive vision that had given the Protestant Passion its remarkable power.

As far as the relations between Protestants and Catholics were concerned, they continued to be marked by an unrelenting hostility. Protestant and Catholic soldiers had fought side by side in the Union army, and some had looked forward to a reconciliation, at least in the United States, of the two great divisions of Christendom after the war, but it was not to be. The fact that corrupt big-city machines were commonly in the hands of Irish and German Catholic politicians while the "reformers" were almost invariably Protestants exacerbated feelings.

Harper's Weekly, the great liberal journal of reform which espoused the cause of Southern blacks, of Indians (with careful qualifications), of women (with similar reservations), was unrelenting in its attack on the Irish and, to a lesser extent, the German Catholics. A typical editorial in *Harper's,* entitled "The Plunderers of New York," used the publication of a book on the Tweed Ring to indict the "Roman Catholic rulers" of New York. The book revealed "how rapidly the debt rose; how rapacious were the Irish officials, judges, sheriffs, police; what enormous plunder was carried off in a few years," all the work "of a single nationality. . . . The prisons and almshouses are filled by the adherents of a single Church, that does little for its own poor while its wealth is enormous . . . and but for our Roman Catholic population, our

ANTI — Irish Harpon's Weekly

crime and pauperism would be diminished by two-thirds. . . . It appears therefore . . . that the Roman Catholic Church . . . is the chief cause of the whole series of public robberies. . . . Wholly incapable of self-government, our Irish Catholic citizens and a foreign Church have filled New York with crime and covered it with an unendurable load of taxation." The only avenue of relief was "to unite the whole Protestant . . . community in a single body" and "drive from power the foreign sect." The wonder is that a religious war did not erupt on the streets of New York City in the years following the end of the war. Of course, there was a war, a war of the despised and denounced Irish against the Protestant establishment, a war in which the "Irish Democracy" captured the city and exacted an enormous ransom from those they considered their oppressors.

In the matter of the capacity of blacks and immigrants in general to participate in the political life of the Republic, science was soon producing "evidence" that they were genetically inferior to white Anglo-Saxon Americans. To many Americans born in that state of grace it followed that all possible political and social inhibitions might thus be placed on the "less fit," lest they pollute the "more fit." Such notions as "brotherhood" were plainly irrelevant to scientific considerations. George Hoar, born in 1826, was only nine years older than Charles Francis Adams, Jr., but he belonged to the world of the senior Charles Francis, and he spoke for the classic Christian belief in brotherhood when he wrote in his autobiography: "How our race troubles would disappear if the dominant Saxon would but obey, in his treatment of the weaker races, the authority of the fundamental laws on which his own institutions rest! The problem of to-day is not how to convert the heathen from heathenism, it is how to convert the Christian from heathenism; not to teach the physician how to heal the patient, but how to heal himself. The Indian problem is not chiefly how to teach the Indian to be less savage in his treatment of the Saxons, but the Saxon to be less savage in his treatment of the Indian. The Chinese problem is not how to keep Chinese laborers out of California, but how to keep Chinese policies out of Congress. The negro question will be settled when the education of the white man is complete."

54

Reconstruction Reconsidered

Our first task is to say a word about why Radical Reconstruction took place at all. Our second to account for its demise. Our third to assess its significance.

Two of the most revealing works on Reconstruction are, not surprisingly, by black authors. John Roy Lynch, with whom we are already well acquainted, was a handsome, elegantly dressed mulatto with courtly manners, a friend and confidant of Grant's and other prominent Republicans'. While Lynch's argument in *The Facts of Reconstruction* that the elections of 1874 came like "a thunderclap," shattering the alliance that was taking shape between black and white politicians in the South, is certainly an oversimplification of the end of Reconstruction, his account of the cooperation between the old planter aristocrats and their black counterparts, men like Lynch and Cardozo, undoubtedly has much truth in it. He spoke of it as a bond "that the institution of slavery with all its horrors could not destroy, the Rebellion could not wipe out, Reconstruction could not efface, and subsequent events have not been able to change." Lynch reminds us that there was an "upper class" of black leaders, many of them very conscious of blood ties to the planter class, who, to a degree, shared the patronizing and paternalistic attitudes of that class toward the "poor whites." Black men, especially mulattoes and those who bore distinguished Southern names, felt, like Lynch, that given the support of the Federal government, they could in time come to terms with the wellborn, refined, intelligent element in the South—the gentlemen —and, accepting their leadership, cooperate with them and, while enjoying a lesser share of political power, deliver the votes of their black constituents, thereby preventing middle-class and "poor" whites from gaining political ascendancy. Lynch and his like-minded black allies realized that such an alliance depended on the Federal government's insuring the right of blacks to vote. Without that guarantee, without the black vote to deliver, the "upper-class" black politician —Cardozo or Lynch—was powerless and must in time be disregarded.

Lynch insisted that the freedmen much preferred members of the old ruling class to Northerners as well as to middle-class and lower-class whites, the much-abused scalawags. "When the partiality of the colored man for the former aristocrats became generally known," he wrote, "they—the former aristocrats—began to come into the Republican party in large numbers." In Georgia the way was led by a member of the prominent Longstreet family; in Virginia, by John Singleton Mosby, the famous guerrilla leader.

When Lynch wrote his book on Reconstruction in 1913, he argued that what he had predicted in 1874 had come to pass. The poor whites, far outnumbering the planter class, had taken political and economic control of the South. Lynch is also persuasive in his insistence that the notion of "black domination" was a white fantasy. In Lynch's words, "the white men knew that the colored men had no desire to rule or to dominate even the Republican party. All the colored men wanted and demanded was a voice in the government under which they lived, and to the support of which they contributed, and to have a small, but fair, and reasonable proportion of the positions that were at the disposal of the voters of the State in the administration." The high tide of black political involvement in Mississippi had come with the elections of 1872. John Lynch estimated that out of 72 counties in the state, each with an average of 28 public officials, not more than 5 out of every 100 were black men. In addition, "the state, district, county and municipal governments were not only in control of white men, but white men who were to the manor born, or who were known as old citizens of the State. . . . There was, therefore, never a time when that class of white men known as Carpet-baggers had absolute control of the State Government" or, indeed, any of the smaller units of public administration.

Lynch, as we have noted earlier, remained a power in the Republican Party as long as blacks voted in substantial numbers.

William Sinclair, the author of *The Aftermath of Slavery*, had been born a slave in 1858 and was thus a representative of the first generation of black leaders to have grown up in the post-Civil War period. He and his mother had been sold from his home in George-town, South Carolina, early in the war, when Sinclair was only four years old. After the war he went to a school run by Northern missionaries and then on to Claflin University in Orangeburg, South Carolina. When the University of South Carolina in Columbia, for generations the locus of higher learning for young Carolina gentle-men, was desegregated, he attended there. As soon as Reconstruction ended, black students were ejected, and Sinclair went on to Howard University, where he took a B.A. and a degree in theology, and then to do graduate work at Andover Theological Seminary. At Andover he won a prize for his dissertation and delivered the commencement address. He subsequently worked as a missionary teacher under the auspices of the American Missionary Association and studied medicine at the Meharry Medical College in Tennessee. For a time he was on the staff of Frederick Douglass Memorial Hospital in Philadelphia and then became financial secretary of Howard University.

Sinclair's book, published in 1906, was one of the earliest and most powerful attacks on the then-prevailing "white" and predominantly Southern interpretation of Reconstruction, and it was plainly prompted less by scholarly considerations than by a renewed Southern attack on black voting rights and the rising tide of racial prejudice through-out the North, especially in the academic world. It is agreeable to report that Thomas Wentworth Higginson, then eighty-two years old, wrote the introduction to Sinclair's book. Although Higginson entered a mild caveat at Sinclair's indictment of segregated Southern schools and Jim Crow in general, on the grounds that the North in his lifetime had been as segregated and that Southern segregation would, in time, also be swept away, he called the book "in almost all respects admira-ble," crediting it with showing much "more thoroughness in dealing with both sides [black and white] than any book recently produced by a Southern white man. . . ."

It was Sinclair's basic thesis, as, indeed, it was that of virtually all writers on Reconstruction whatever their conclusions, that slavery had left "a heritage of complicated and vexatious problems, the just and righteous solution of which will tax to the uttermost the patience and firmness of the nation." Above all, Sinclair wished to do justice to North and South alike, to white and black.

What is perhaps most valuable about Sinclair's book is the author's clear perception of the various stages at which even modest compliance by the South in Congressional Reconstruction would have satisfied Northern opinion and ended Federal intervention. In no other prominent work on Reconstruction is the role of Southern obduracy so explicitly stated, with the exception of W. E. B. Du Bois's *Black Reconstruction*, and it is clear that Du Bois owed a considerable debt to his older colleague.

Like Lynch, Sinclair attacked the Southern contention that the freedman sought to dominate the white. He makes clear that Southern blacks were realistic enough to know that they did not have the basis in wealth or population to dominate a single Southern state.

At the heart of Congressional Reconstruction was the fact that it was, in essence, not a policy at all but a series of pragmatic responses to the continuing racial crisis in the South.

Northern politicians seemed to have entertained no doubts that, given the facts that the South had been completely and decisively defeated, and the slaves set free, there would evolve a new social and economic order in which the freedman had an appropriate role. What this order would be no one was exactly sure, but the most common adumbration was of a "mixed" economy of small farms worked by black and white farmers, rather on the model of the classic New England farm, supplemented by a rapidly expanding industrial and commercial sector, staffed in large part by Northern technical know-how and receiving massive infusions of Northern capital. While some Northern capitalists might have viewed the South as simply fair financial game, the theorists assigned them the role of instructors and developers of a backward agricultural society whose mission it was to draw the South into the nineteenth century. Without a servile work force it was assumed that the South would have to develop a wholly

new economic base and, as a corollary, a new social order. Albion
Tourgée has his "self"-hero, Comfort Servosse, explain to his wife his
reasons for moving to the South: "Slavery has been broken up, and
things must turn into new grooves; but I think the country will settle
up rapidly, now that slavery is out of the way. Manufactures will spring
up, immigration will pour in, and it will be just the pleasantest part of
the country. I believe one-fifth of our soldiers—and that the best part
of them too—will find homes in the South in less than two years, just as
soon as they can clear out their old places. . . ." Only by "such
intermingling of the people of the two sections," Servosse declares,
"can we ever become one, and the danger of future evil be averted."

What few, if any, Northern politicians foresaw was the astonishing
tenacity of the Southern whites in attempting to reconstruct not a new
social and economic system but the old one under conditions as little
altered as possible. The Southerner was struggling to reassert his old
identity; indeed, he could imagine no other. Those who could imagine
another went north or west and, like Charles Colcock Jones, became
professionals or businessmen. Those who stayed dug in for a long
fight, confident in their hearts that they could outlast their invaders, in
time drive them out, and assume control of their own affairs.

Blissfully unaware of the depth and tenacity of Southern resistance, the Radical Republicans set out to "reconstruct" the South. In the
words of Georges Clemenceau, "most of the radicals of today [1870]
embarked on the abolitionist sea without any clear idea of where the
course would lead; that they arrived at their present position only after
being forced from one reform to another."

It was a process of what we might call negative reciprocity. Each
defiant act of resistance to black rights on the part of the South
provoked a congressional reaction that carried matters much farther
along on the road to the enfranchisement of blacks than the vast
majority of Northern whites had initially had any intention of going.
Congressional Reconstruction was, in essence, a pragmatic response, a
reflex action, in which specific legislative bills constantly outstripped
their theoretical or philosophical enunciation.

It has been widely argued that the North's most basic motive in
developing the policy of Congressional Reconstruction was revenge
—to punish the South. To the advocates of the punitive theory of
Reconstruction (which was certainly the Southern theory) Thaddeus
Stevens is an essential figure.

"I know," Stevens declared, "that there is a few of all classes, from the priest to the clown, which has more sympathy for the murderer on the gallows than for his victim. I hope I have a heart as capable of feeling for human woe as others. I have long since wished that capital punishment were abolished. But I never dreamed that all punishment could be dispensed with in human society. Anarchy, *treason,* and violence would reign triumphant."

It was unfortunate that Northern political rhetoric recurred so frequently to the theme of "punishment"—that the South should be *punished* for its transgressions. It gave credibility to the Southern charge that the North's much-vaunted solicitude for the freedman was, in fact, nothing more than the determination to use him to chastise the rebels. On the other hand, we can hardly be surprised or excessively critical of the Northern disposition to feel that, since the South had visited a catastrophe of almost inconceivable proportions on the country through its determination to preserve and extend the institution of slavery, it deserved to be punished. The spirit of revenge, if not attractive, is virtually universal in the race, and one could not deny that, given the provocation, the North showed commendable forbearance in dealing with the defeated South. The other point that must be kept in mind in regard to the theme of punishment is that those Radical Republicans whose concern for the rights of black Americans had been demonstrated beyond cavil by years of devoted labors in the cause were well aware of the shallow and tentative character of their colleagues' and their constituents' commitment to equality for blacks, North or South. Clearly it was much easier to generate public support for Congressional Reconstruction by emphasizing the theme of punishment than by stressing the importance of establishing and maintaining the rights of the freedmen.

Carl Schurz indignantly rebutted the argument that the granting by Congress of the franchise to Southern blacks was merely or even primarily punitive in purpose. "I may say," he wrote in his *Reminiscences,* "that in all my intercourse with various classes of people . . . I have never heard it mentioned or suggested, still less, advocated, as a punitive measure. It was never in itself popular with the masses —reason enough for the ordinary politicians to be afraid of openly favoring it." This passage, if generally true, is somewhat ingenuous. The punitive aspect of black enfranchisement may have been secondary with Thaddeus Stevens, for example, but the punitive temper was unmistakably there. Schurz went on to argue that two types of Republicans concurred in the enfranchisement of Southern blacks—

on one hand, the "doctrinaires" like Sumner and Stevens and, on the other, those who, presumably like Schurz himself, "after a faithful and somewhat perplexed wrestle with the complicated problem of reconstruction, finally landed,—or, it might almost be said, were stranded —at the conclusion that to enable the negro to protect his own rights as a free man by the exercise of the ballot was after all the simplest way out of the tangle, and at the same time the most in accordance with our democratic principles of government."

What was perhaps most important was the fact that Southerners never wavered in their conviction that the enfranchising of the freedmen was a punitive measure. In *Bricks Without Straw*, Albion Tourgée quotes a Southerner as declaring that the black was made a voter "simply to degrade and disgrace the white people of the South. The North cares nothing about the negro as a man, but only enfranchises him in order to humiliate and enfeeble us. Of course, it makes no difference to the people of the North whether he is a voter or not. There are so few colored men there, that there is no fear of one of them being elected to office, going to the Legislature, or sitting on the bench. The whole purpose of the measure is to insult and degrade. But only wait until the States are restored and the 'Blue Coats' are out of the way, and we will show them their mistake."

Too much emphasis can hardly be placed on Schurz's point that the enfranchising of the freedmen "was never in itself popular with the masses." In the period from 1865 to 1869 there were no less than eleven referendums in eight Northern states on the issue of black suffrage, of which only two—Iowa and Minnesota—were successful. Pennsylvania, New Jersey, and Illinois did not even put the issue to the vote. Black suffrage was defeated in Connecticut, New York, and Ohio. When a Republican legislature ratified the Fifteenth Amendment in New York in 1869, it was promptly replaced by a Democratic house, which voted to rescind the ratification. The percentage of blacks in the Northern states varied from a high of 3.2 in New Jersey (one of the Northern states which failed to ratify the Fifteenth Amendment) to 1.2 percent in New York. In Illinois, where prejudice against blacks was strong, the percentage of blacks in the population was 1.1.

Must we not come back to this as the most basic issue of all? The North had required the South to do something, the South had every reason to believe, that the North, under even roughly similar circumstances, would have refused to do itself—that it had indeed demonstrated its determination *not to do.* In this, the North was hypocritical and, in its heart, knew itself to be. The precondition of the North's acting in good conscience on behalf of Southern blacks was that it should itself accept, in evident and unmistakable ways, the full equality, the "brotherhood" of Northern blacks. And this the North had not the slightest intention of doing. What was the North to say to the South's challenge: Where are your black judges, sheriffs and state legislators, Congressmen and Senators? The argument that the North had not a large enough black population to justify representation was a weak reed to lean upon. The North had a substantial number of educated and able black men as well qualified for office as any white man. A Henry Turner from Philadelphia or a James Lynch from Boston proved himself an able politician, but he had to come south to do so.

It has become a modern commonplace to say that the Republicans abandoned and betrayed the Southern blacks by jettisoning Reconstruction for reasons of political expediency, but the fault lay far deeper. The great majority of Northerners had never accepted the claim of brotherhood that the antislavery forces avowed (and even they, of course, had been far from unanimous on the subject). Lydia Maria Child, at seventy-six the grand old lady of abolition, wrote to a friend a few years after the end of Reconstruction that the "antislavery struggle" seemed to be "completely . . . forgotten by the people, and even the terrible expenditure of blood and treasure, which followed it, is fast sinking into oblivion. . . . The lamentable misfortune is that emancipation was not the result of a popular *moral sentiment,* but of a miserable 'military necessity.' It was not the 'fruit of righteousness,' and therefore it is not 'peace.' "

There was also, of course, the fact that it became increasingly apparent that the Republicans needed the black vote in the South to retain power. The desire of Northern politicians to avail themselves of the vote made it possible for a small band of dedicated Radicals to push the Reconstruction Acts and the Fourteenth and Fifteenth Amendments through Congress. As often before, self-interest and idealism formed an uneasy political alliance, but it was a precarious union at best, and almost from the first it had been subject to severe strains. The reader must keep in mind that the Democratic Party was surprisingly strong in the North. The Democrats had, after all, threatened throughout the war to gain control of the government and bring the war to an end. For a time even ardent Republicans despaired of victory in the election of 1864, and it seems clear that only a string of Federal military triumphs secured the election for Lincoln.

It was George Templeton Strong's conviction that, had the South during the last year of the war "made anything like a show (however fraudulent and illusory) of willingness to talk about 'reconstruction' on any terms—conservation or restoration of slavery, for instance—at any time before Lincoln's reelection, they would have enabled Northern traitors to make a fearfully damaging diversion in their favor. There would have been ruinous division here. Lincoln would have been defeated. The national government would have passed into the hands of friends of the South." Without the electoral votes of the reconstructed states of the South, the Republicans would have been forced to yield the reins of government to the Democratic opposition. In the absence of the reckless and often violent opposition of the South to the barest rudiments of justice for the freedmen—an opposition which culminated in the atrocities of the Ku Klux Klan—Reconstruction might have been quietly buried several years before its actual demise.

It took the convergence of half a dozen elements—the desire of the Republicans to hold onto power; the fanatical and immovable determination of the South to reduce the freedmen to a condition of slavery in all but name; the intractable and finally infuriating policies of President Johnson; a widespread desire to punish the South that grew stronger and stronger in the face of Southern intractability; the political pressures created by the vast network of freedmen's associations; and, perhaps above all, the skill and tenaciousness of the leaders of the Radical Republicans in Congress—it literally took all these unpredictable elements to effect those modest improvements in the condition of the freed slaves that could be counted by the "end" of Reconstruction.

In his speech to the final meeting of the American Anti-Slavery Society in Boston in 1870, William Lloyd Garrison had called that apparent victory in the long fight for equality for black Americans a "miracle." It was certainly not too strong a word. It was indeed a miracle. That the miracle had to make peace with reality, that the political legerdemain which men like Sumner and Stevens, Davis, Wade, Fessenden, Trumbull, and dozens of others had displayed, balancing always on the most precarious of political high wires, must in time run out, was hardly surprising. What was surprising was that in the face of the indifference or outright opposition of the vast majority of Americans, it had happened at all. I suspect it is not too much to say that a few thousand or at the most a few hundred thousand Americans, out of some 40,000,000, saved the soul of the nation, so far as we may have been said to have had a soul. (Walther Rathenau, the German politician, said in 1925: "America has no soul and will not deserve to have one until it consents to plunge into the abyss of human sin and suffering.")

I have argued that the framing and ratification of the Federal Constitution took place by the narrowest of margins at the last moment when the Classical-Christian Consciousness had sufficient confidence and authority to create such a document. The emancipation of all Americans, black and white, from the incubus of slavery took place by perhaps an even narrower margin. It was never the will of a clear majority of the American people that the slaves of the South should be free, not to mention equal. So while it is true that blacks of the South were in a sense abandoned, to put the matter that way obscures the achievements of those responsible for freeing them and fighting for their rights with great skill and resourcefulness through the most troubled and chaotic decade of our history. It was probably the case that those rights could never be fully realized until a new consciousness had formed in white Americans in regard to the rights of "other" Americans and until black Americans gained sufficient confidence in their own powers to assert their rights as American citizens—and, it must be said parenthetically, until our sense of nationhood was stronger than our obsession with states' rights. In the last analysis, it was, as Sumner and Stevens and Grant pointed out, the specter of states' rights which stayed the hand of those Federal police powers needed to protect blacks' rights in the South.

No essential reform movement can be sustained indefinitely by the will of a relatively small group of people. If it does not find a legitimate place in the system, it must languish. Truman Marcellus Post, a Congregationalist minister from Missouri, wrote as early as 1866: "It is a sad truth that men, for the most part, are not heroes or martyrs. From the extraordinary tension requisite to act the part of such, they must in time relax from sheer exhaustion."

Finally, it must be said, most emphatically, that one of the main reasons Congressional Reconstruction lasted as long as it did was the enormous prestige of the man responsible for administering it. Of the approximately ten years that the Era of Reconstruction lasted,

GRANT CENTRAL

Ulysses S. Grant was president for eight. No other Republican president could have overcome the widespread misgivings of Northern voters over what appeared the problack bias of Congressional Reconstruction. Grant's tremendous popularity served to obscure the shallowness of the public support for the policies of the Radical Republicans and sustained Radical Reconstruction far longer than would have been the case had any other man held the office. One by one the Liberal Republicans abandoned the cause, most commonly in the name of states' rights, until Grant and Sumner, bitter enemies, were left like two great monoliths deflecting the current. Death carried Sumner away, and only the President was left. John Lynch's report of his conversation with Grant is thus given an added poignance. It was as though Grant had foreseen all that was to come in the undoing of the Union victory. States' rights had no appeal to him; he saw the issue as a purely reactionary trend, which, of course, it was. But the dilemma remained. The constituency was never there. The Republican Party could not stake its future indefinitely on acting as policeman of the South.

It might be well at this point to review the principal causes of the end of Reconstruction. The most basic reason for the end was in the beginning—Southern intractability. The *Meridian* (Mississippi) *Mercury* put the matter succinctly: "We would like to engrave a prophecy on stone, to be read of generations in the future. The Negro, in these States, will be a slave again or cease to be. His sole refuge from extinction will be in slavery to the white man."

William Sinclair wrote to the same effect: "To the colored people freedom came as a boon from heaven, a special gift of God, an answer to the agonizing prayers of centuries. It was a treasure above all price. But the white people of the South took a different view of it. They loved freedom for themselves and would die in defence of it; unfortunately, however, they regarded the freeing of the colored man as a wrong to the white man. . . . And so the chief efforts of Southern leadership have been to curtail the freedom of the colored people, to minimize their liberty and reduce them as nearly as possible to the condition of chattel slaves."

Almost as important as Southern obduracy or the shallowness of Northern support for black rights was the profound residual commitment in the North to the idea of states' rights, a principle which, it might be argued, was violated by *all* the Reconstruction Acts, as well as, in the opinion of many Americans, by the Fourteenth and Fifteenth

Amendments. In his speech of July 22, 1872, Carl Schurz spelled out the basic states' rights anxiety. "Seven years have elapsed since the close of the Civil War," he declared. "No thinking man can have watched the progress of things in the South without having gathered instructive experience. It must have become clear to all of us that the development of the new order of society there cannot be secured wholly by an extraneous pressure, which would involve a change in the nature of our institutions, but must ultimately be left to the workings of local self-government." The "enfranchisement of the emancipated class" was, Schurz insisted, "an irreversible fact. Every sane man recognizes that. . . ."

The freedmen of the South needed to be protected, but for the Federal government to intervene in the internal police of a particular state was clearly unconstitutional, "a stretch of power so great that no State in the Union ought to tolerate it—so great it ought to be resisted by every peaceful means," Thomas Wentworth Higginson wrote in 1876.

Leaving the South, Comfort Servosse, broken in health and old before his time, sadder and wiser, visited his old teacher and friend the Reverend Enos Martin. The two men discussed the future of the Republic. Martin incautiously expressed the opinion that the war and Reconstruction had at least put to rest the issue of states' rights. "On the contrary," Servosse replied, "the doctrine of 'State Rights' is altogether unimpaired and untouched by what has occurred, except in one particular: to wit, *the right of peaceable secession.* . . . 'And is this all that has been gained by all these years of toil and struggle and blood?' asked the old man with a sigh." The basic, everlasting issue was that of the black man's rights of citizenship, Servosse insisted. "You think the 'irrepressible conflict' is yet confronting us, then?" Martin asked. "Undoubtedly," Servosse replied. "The North and the South are simply convenient names for two distinct, hostile and irreconcilable ideas. . . . We tried to build up communities there [in the South] which should be identical in thought, sentiment, growth and development, with those of the North. It was A FOOL'S ERRAND."

We have mentioned earlier the attrition of the original "principled" and idealistic Radical Republican leaders—old-line abolitionists as varied as Zachariah Chandler of Michigan, Henry Winter Davis, and Benjamin Wade, not to mention Stevens and Sumner, and their replacement by men like Schuyler Colfax, Roscoe Conkling, and Benjamin Butler. We must make a further distinction between the

Radical Republicans in Congress and the old-time abolitionists whose agents, in a sense, the politicians were. Without the tireless efforts of the abolitionist lobbies, the Radical Republicans in Congress would never have ventured as far as they did.

The majority of the abolitionists had, as we have seen, a thoroughly romantic notion of blacks based on a relative handful of courageous, intelligent, and ambitious slaves who made their way to freedom, usually by thrilling escapes. To the abolitionists, the slave was not just a cruelly exploited individual; he was a surrogate for the Christ, Jesus, the suffering servant. The slave contained a saving element of humanity or spirituality (represented, for example, in slave spirituals) desperately needed in a crass and materialistic society. "God has given to man a higher dignity than the reason," Theodore Tilton declared. That was man's moral and religious faculty. "We have need of the negro for his . . . aesthetic faculties," he added. "We have need of the negro for his music. . . . But let us stop questioning whether the negro is a man. In many respects he is a superior man. In a few respects, he is the greatest of men. I think he is greater than those men who clamor against giving him a chance in the world, as if they feared something from the competition."

In both Harriet Beecher Stowe and Tilton there is more than the suggestion that the black is a "saving" figure. The abolitionists, like virtually all other American reformers, were convinced that their reform was not simply a matter of doing justice to an oppressed and degraded people, not merely the fulfillment of Christ's teaching of human brotherhood, but the essential means of redeeming a fallen world. They thus loaded black men and women down with a vast weight of hopelessly unrealistic expectations. Not only had the freed blacks to make their way in the profoundly prejudiced and generally hostile, highly competitive white world (which, however much the abolitionist may have exalted the "gentler" black "faculties," admired and rewarded very different qualities), but they were also expected, by the great majority of the abolitionists at least, to redeem America from greed, materialism, and infidelity.

The English journalist William Hepworth Dixon, a caustic and perceptive critic of the folkways of Americans, wrote in 1867: "In their flowery prose, the New England teachers had bestowed upon their negro client in the South an emotional nature far above anything that his poor white brother in the North could boast. On the hard and selfish side of his intellect, a white man might be cursed with keener power; the point was moot; but in all that concerned his moral nature,—the religious instincts, the family affections, the social graces —the negro was declared to be a softer, sweeter, and superior being. He was far more sensitive to signs and dreams, to the voices of birds, to the cries of children, to the heat of noon, to the calm of night. He had a finer ear for song, a quicker relish for the dance. He loved colour with a wiser love. He had a deeper yearning after places; a fresher delight in worship; a livelier sense of the Fatherhood of God." To Dixon, these "fancy pictures of the negro—drawn in a New England study"—were "a thousand miles" from the much more complex reality of "a rice-field and a cotton plantation."

The black man had to bear a burden of white hopes and expectations hardly less constricting than the burden of his contempt or anger. It was, in part at least, in the shadow of such illusions that thousands of idealistic whites *and* Northern blacks went south to assist in the transition from slavery to freedom, from serfdom to citizenship. As we have seen, the reality they encountered was both sobering and often demoralizing. The ex-slave was a vast way from the black abolitionists that the Northern reformers had known—a William Wells Brown, a Robert Purvis, a John Mercer Langston, a Martin Delany, or a Frederick Douglass. It was soon clear that turning black field hands into informed voters and cultivated scholars was a far more demanding task than the missionaries of liberal white culture had imagined. The "culture shock" of the Northern idealists, the "fools," as Albion Tourgée called them and himself, was considerable. It was not, of course, that blacks were inferior to whites but that they had their own dense and, to the white Northerner, virtually impenetrable culture.

Considering the white abolitionist illusions about Southern blacks, we might say that the "abandonment" of Southern blacks by the Northern liberal-radical abolitionist alliance and the termination of Reconstruction had its roots in the highly romantic image of blacks that no reality could validate. It certainly could be reasonably argued that much of what Northern idealists hypothesized about black temperament was true, but it was true in a manner and in a context that Northern teachers and missionaries found very difficult to deal with. There were, to be sure, the merest hints of all these matters in the letters and reports of teachers and missionaries to friends and relatives in the North, but gradually a substratum of disillusionment built up in the minds of Northern Radical Republicans.

Not only had the freed black failed to emerge from slavery as the redeemer of white society, more loving, more sensitive to beauty, more intuitive, more open, less materialistic, less competitive, a kind of racial antidote to capitalism; but he (and she) had also remained, for the most part, stubbornly black.

To most middle- and upper-class Americans the problems of Southern blacks grew dimmer and dimmer when contrasted with the more immediate problems of municipal corruption, a destructive "spoils" system in government, and, increasingly, Republican agitation over the issue of hard money. Money, as we have noted, came to evoke the same kind of moral passion that had once been invested in abolition.

The issue of protective tariffs was much the same. William Cullen Bryant's Democratic *New York Post* called protectionism "a policy of war, by its very nature. It seeks the advantage of one nation at the expense of others," and Clemenceau was equally caustic in his comments on the American passion for protective tariffs. "When an industry is interrupted for a couple of weeks," he told his French readers, "importation of foreign goods is given as the reason, and men set to work to frame a new tariff law. Owing to this custom, people have to pay ridiculous prices for articles of primary necessity . . . and a few big men in the East have grown exceedingly rich." For most Republicans protectionism was an article of faith only slightly less binding than hard money.

Not without influence was the barrage of Southern propaganda on the theme of the corruption of the Reconstruction governments and the misrule of the blacks, carpetbaggers, and scalawags. Vastly exaggerated as it was, funneled through Democratic papers and ultimately Republican papers as well, it had a substantial cumulative effect. James Pike's *The Prostrate South* is credited by many historians with driving one of the last nails in the coffin of Reconstruction. In the speech in which he abandoned the cause of Reconstruction, Carl Schurz cited as one of his reasons "the rule of unprincipled and rapacious leaders at the head of the colored population [which] has resulted in a government of corruption and plunder, and gives no promise of improvement."

We must also take account of the precariousness of the Republican alliance. "The Republican Party," E. L. Godkin wrote in the *Nation*, "is often called jokingly or contemptuously, 'the party of great moral ideas,' and it *is* essentially a party of ideas, while the Democratic party is essentially now, whatever it may once have been, a party of habits,

prejudices, and traditions." The fact is, of course, that "habits, prejudices, and traditions" are far more enduring than "great moral ideas."
The Democratic Party was, above all, the party of "the people," black
people aside, and that notion, vague as it was, compromised as it was,
had a remarkable capacity for survival. The Radical Republicans,
Sidney George Fisher wrote, "belong to the conservative classes, whilst
those who oppose the scheme are Democrats, each contradicting thus
the principles of its own party for the sake of partizan success, the
Republicans because they hope to gain the Negro vote in the South &
elsewhere in the next elections, and the Democrats, because if they
advocated Negro suffrage they would lose the Irish vote."

Finally, there was a more subtle but perhaps in the long run more
important ideological element. This was the erosion of the faith of
young liberal intellectuals in the notion of Christian equality and
brotherhood. As we have noted, the religion of science replaced the
religion of traditional Christianity with startling rapidity in the years
immediately preceding and following the Civil War. While it it
impossible to establish a direct link between the erosion of traditional
Protestantism and the end of Reconstruction there can be no doubt
that the shift toward a "scientific" view of the world was detrimental to
the black cause.

In the last analysis it was that unexpected Southern tenacity which
unnerved the Radical Republicans. They were well aware that their
constituents would not allow them unlimited time and money to
reconstruct the South. The system was expensive, and Americans had
other things on their minds than justice for Southern blacks. What told
most heavily against Reconstruction in the long run was simply that it
did not work. For ten years it had dragged on, racked by scandals,
never appearing any closer to some acceptable resolution of apparently unresolvable problems. So the wonder was not that it was abandoned
but that, through a favorable conjunction of crass political ambitions
and idealistic aspirations, it ever started and, having started, survived
for a decade after the war.

Certainly the end of Reconstruction came as no surprise to black
leaders like Francis Cardozo. Cardozo had predicted, in the South
Carolina constitutional convention of 1867, that the wealth and
intelligence of the white South would one day reassert its political
dominance.

As we have argued throughout this work, there was never in the
North, from the earliest days of antislavery agitation to the last, a

constituency for the abolitionist leaders. They always worked, as it were, in the air, suspended above the cockpit of American politics. It was only through shaky alliances with peripheral groups—temperance enthusiasts, Free-Soilers, vegetarians, nativists, and other assorted political odds and ends—that they made any headway politically (and many, of course, eschewed politics entirely as a compromise with the devil). By remarkable organization and indefatigable labors, they sustained the cause. But all their efforts would have come to nothing had not the South cooperated so splendidly by seceding and making the preservation of the Union the issue. Only under the stalking-horse of Unionism could the cause of abolition have made any substantial headway. It required the resolution of a Lincoln to bring the issue to the terrible test of battle and then, in the name of strengthening the Union cause, to free the slaves, partially at least.

In the discussion with the Reverend M. Martin that concludes *A Fool's Errand,* Comfort Servosse reaffirms his faith "in the cause for which he had struggled, and believed in the capacity of those with whom he had worked to achieve for themselves, at some time in the future, a substantial freedom; but in that struggle he could do but little. It would hang in doubt for generations; and that, in the mean time, that haughty, self-reliant, and instinctively dominant element which had already challenged the Nation to a struggle of strength, had been defeated, and *out of disaster had already wrested the substantial fruits of victory,* would achieve still greater triumphs, and would for an indefinite period dominate and control the national power."

Having attempted to account for the causes of Reconstruction and its demise, we are left with the perennial question of whether or not, considering it was doomed to failure, it would have been better had it never been attempted?

A number of historians, most of them, it must be said, Southerners, have taken that line. They have argued that the policy of Lincoln or of Johnson, who, it was said, was simply carrying out the policy Lincoln would have followed had he lived, would much better have prevailed. The South would than have come back into the Union in good spirits and reasonably good temper. The blacks would soon have abandoned any lofty and mistaken notions about the implications of being "free" and resumed their old relationship with their former masters, minus only the formal fact of slavery. Gradually, as the former slaves demonstrated beyond question their ability to function as citizens, their rights would have been extended by tolerant and sympathetic whites, and in time they would have shared all the privileges of citizenship in the Republic.

First, as we have already suggested, even before Reconstruction had taken shape, it was abundantly clear that white Southerners were determined to employ every stratagem, legal and illegal, to keep their ex-slaves in a subordinate and dependent condition and "reconstruct," as nearly as possible, the economic and social system that the war had disrupted. Reconstruction, we have argued, can perhaps best be seen as a response to the intractability of the South. It thus seems as safe as any generalization a historian can make to say that without Radical Reconstruction Southern blacks would not have had even a taste of political power and civil rights. Very well, but would they not at the same time have been spared an enormous amount of hardship and suffering? Would not the lives of many black leaders and many of their followers have been spared? Would Johnson's policy of reconciliation with the white South not have been infinitely more humane; far less costly in blood and money? The proponents of this view spoke vaguely of a day in the distant future when all blacks might participate more fully in the democratic process. But there was never in the South the disposition to give the freed blacks a chance, to concede to them the rights that even the poorest whites enjoyed, to give them the tutelage and guidance, the encouragement and support that Tourgée-Servosse insisted they needed in order to become responsible members of Southern society. And this one fact makes a mockery of the argument that the Radical Republicans did the freedmen a grave and indeed disastrous disservice by forcing black political activity on the South, thereby encouraging false hopes and expectations on the part of black people and bringing about a backlash of Southern resentment and hostility that was most prejudicial, in the long run, to the blacks themselves. Certainly there is an element of truth in this proposition. Unquestionably the hostility of white Southerners toward the freed-men was augmented very substantially by the experience of being, or considering themselves to be, "under black rule." On the other hand, no careful student of the era can avoid the conviction that even without Radical Reconstruction the white South would never have conceded to the freedmen a fair measure of political and economic power.

Despite the ugly stains of corruption, far more modest, certainly, than those that besmirched the escutcheon of New York City, idealistic whites and blacks together had remarkable accomplishments to their credit. Thousands of schools were opened, many of them short-lived and of indifferent quality, to be sure, but in the aggregate giving hundreds of thousands of black children a sense of their own potentialities and of new possibilities for their race, cruelly frustrated as those aspirations may have been. Hundreds of black politicians were elected or appointed to offices of importance and responsibility, and most of them discharged their duties far better than their detractors had predicted or would, in retrospect, admit. Constitutions were written, and laws enacted, in some instances years in advance of the rest of the nation in their humane and liberal spirit. More than thirty black colleges were established by Northern missionaries, and the handful of students who found their way to them became leaders of their people. The thousands of white "fools" who joined Albion Tourgée in fighting for the education and the rights of black people performed what was, on all counts, the most important collective act in our history. They symbolized the noblest spirit in the perpetually renewed dream of human equality and brotherhood, a spirit which we like to think is characteristically, though not uniquely, American. They were joined by uncounted numbers of black men and women, many of whom showed extraordinary courage in asserting the rights that every white American took for granted. Hundreds of thousands of Southern blacks voted when simply to cast a ballot was at the least to invite economic retribution and at the worst to risk one's life.

The simple act of voting was an act of enormous symbolic potency. There was a slave mentality, as we have had occasion to note often before—a sense of profound and hopeless inferiority that had so distressed Fanny Kemble when she encountered it among the slaves on her husband's Georgia plantation. Sarah Chase told of rebuking an old black woman in Florida for calling her fellow blacks "niggers." "We *are* niggers," she replied. "We always was niggers, and we always shall be; nigger here, and nigger there, nigger do this, and nigger do that. We've got no souls, we are animals. We are black and so is the evil one . . . we'se nothing but animals and niggers. Yes we'se niggers! niggers!"

In such a context, to vote was to assert one's manhood and one's humanity. Albion Tourgée has his hero, George Nimbus, say to his crippled preacher friend, Eliab Hill, after having registered to vote: "I reckon I'se free now. I feel ez ef I wuz 'bout half free anyhow. I wuz a sojer, an' fought fer freedom. I've got my house 'an bit o' lan', wife, chillen, crop, an' stock, an' it's all minę. An' now I'se done been registered, an' when de 'lection come off, kin vote jes' ez hard an' ez well an' ez often ez ole Marse Desmit [his former master] I hain't felt free afore—leastways I hain't felt right certain on 't. . . ."

William Sinclair listed the five most important consequences that, in his opinion, followed from the enfranchising of the freedmen. First "it established the sovereignty of the nation"—that is to say, by enabling the Republican administration to consolidate its power, it insured that that national government would be supreme over the states. As a corollary, "it utterly destroyed all that was vicious, mischievous, and menacing in the doctrine of state rights." If this judgment was excessive, it was certainly the case, nonetheless, that the more negative aspects of the states' rights creed were given a sharp, if temporary, check, although, as we have seen, the doctrine proved to be far from dead. Giving the vote to the freedmen was both the occasion and the consequence of the Fourteenth and Fifteenth Amendments by means of which the freed black "wrote his own citizenship ineffaceably into the Constitution. . . ." The enfranchised black also made possible "the adoption of free constitutions in the Southern states" under which the states were reunited with the Union, and, finally, but not least, "it gave the South its first system of Free Public Schools, a benefaction and blessing of incalculable value." Sinclair might well have gone on to name a number of other enlightened bits of social legislation, some incorporated in the state constitutions, others enacted in subsequent statutes.

Although it was not recognized at the time, the brief period of black enfranchisement demonstrated conclusively the most basic premise of democracy—that people, not just educated people, but people in general, people literate or illiterate, human beings of whatever color or degree, have the capacity for political activity which, in its simplest terms, is nothing more than indicating the conditions that they feel are most favorable to their needs, to, we might say, their humanity. They know the difference between justice and injustice, between rights and wrongs, and they are often capable of making shrewder judgments than their better educated and more sophisticated compatriots. If we accept the notion of original sin at least as a metaphor—that is to say, that all human beings have a disposition, as William Manning put it, to "self-aggrandisement," to the indulgence of selfish desires—we will avoid sentimentalizing or romanticizing the notion of "the people." But there is an accumulation of evidence in the form of careful observation and literary insight that, although living close to the social and economic margins of a society may degrade and demoralize people, it may also, under certain conditions (generally where human activity is supported and dignified by a well-defined religious and moral structure) make them more sensitive, compassionate, and courageous.

It is clear that in the period of Reconstruction black people, debased as they had been by slavery, validated that premise. We can perhaps more readily perceive that fact since in the march of democracy that Tocqueville had predicted and for which he had made the United States a case study, many nations with very low rates of literacy have embraced the democratic principle that the simplest human justice requires that all members of a society be represented in the political process. The irrefutable evidence for support of this proposition is to be found in the state constitutions drawn up under the governments mandated by Congressional Reconstruction, especially when they are contrasted with the repressive documents framed by the various Southern states in the period of Presidential Reconstruction. The constitutions framed in the period of Black Reconstruction were not, to be sure, exclusively or even primarily the work of the black members of the respective constitutional conventions, but men like James Lynch, Jonathan Biggs, and the Cardozo brothers were the intellectual equals and in many cases the superiors of their white colleagues, Republican or Democratic. Most important, Black Reconstruction confirmed the unity of the race. There was, as we have seen, a tendency for middle-class blacks, whose personalities and values had been derived directly from reform-minded whites of the abolitionist persuasion, to draw back from the exotic life of Southern blacks. It took a particular kind of heroism for men like Henry Turner and James Lynch to identify themselves with the mass of illiterate blacks south of the Mason-Dixon Line. The fact that such men played the roles they did is far more significant than the fact that some of them succumbed to the temptations of power and behaved little better than their white counterparts.

If all this be true, the question that has so preoccupied students of the period—was Reconstruction a mistake and, if not a mistake, a betrayal of black aspirations?—can perhaps be laid to rest. We care, then, not so much for the motives of those who devised Reconstruction (those motives appear, as in most political events, to have been a combination of the altruistic and the self-interested) or even for the reasons (or the guilt) associated with its abandonment. It obviously became an essential element in the complex equation of American history. It projected a possibility; anticipated a fulfillment, a fulfillment, one must say, which still has not been achieved. It is bitter to have to say that *American blacks have not yet regained the power and influence that they enjoyed in the Reconstruction Era,* although they have demonstrated their capacity to exercise it. The reasons are many and by no means simple, and they have in large part to do with the success of white Americans in erasing the story of black achievements from our collective memory, white or black, so that in a popular or public sense those achievements wait to be rediscovered, to chasten white arrogance and strengthen black pride. That they have been obscured, misunderstood, or forgotten is, of course, less important than *the fact that they happened.*

It might be said that simply being a black man or woman in white America was, and is, a form of heroism in itself. In Reconstruction blacks asserted the "manhood" that they insisted was their birthright. They proved themselves capable, beyond reasonable dispute, of filling a wide range of public offices with, to be sure, the shadings of competence and incompetence common to all officeholders. Where they succeeded, they were treated as notable exceptions; where they failed, it was attributed to the deficiencies of their race. Black Reconstruction or, specifically, the role of blacks in Reconstruction is, I suspect, the most enthralling, dramatic, and tragic story in our history. From the black perspective so much was achieved and so many hopes were engendered, and in the end everything was lost and forgotten. Or appeared to be. But buried history has a curious way of reasserting itself.

It is black Americans who have changed our perspective and renewed our interest in the era of Reconstruction. Thomas Wentworth Higginson wrote that no dependent and subordinate people in history had ever had freedom bestowed on them. They had always won it. Perhaps it must be the same, he reflected, with American blacks. The Civil War and the "Reconstruction" that followed it bestowed freedom on American blacks. It proved a mixed blessing. Although it could not be sustained, it had to be proffered or the long fight of the abolitionists to free the slaves would have remained an incomplete promise. Reconstruction certainly appeared to end in a devastating defeat, and for almost a hundred years it was easy enough to believe it had all been a ghastly mistake. But in 1955, when an obscure black woman named

Rosa Parks refused to go to the back of the bus in Montgomery, Alabama, it turned out that the spirit of Black Reconstruction was still alive. Time had brought its fulfillment, and Southern blacks, with or without white allies, were ready at last to claim their full heritage as Americans.

It was as essential that Congressional, or Black, Reconstruction be undertaken as it was inevitable that it must fail. So, to the question: "Was Black Reconstruction a mistake?" we can answer with considerable confidence, "Considering the alternative, emphatically *no.*" Tragic as its aftermath was for Southern blacks, their remarkable achievements and, above all, the determined courage so many of them displayed in claiming and trying to exercise their constitutional rights as American citizens became a residual part of the black memory and what we call today black consciousness. White Americans, never having really absorbed the nature or understood the significance of those black achievements, promptly forgot them. So far as they retained some dim impression of "the tragic era," it was dominated by stereotypes of rapacious "carpetbaggers," turncoat "scalawags," pretentious, corrupt, and semiliterate black politicians, and rampaging black mobs. Black politicians like John Roy Lynch and black scholars and journalists like Carter Woodson and William Sinclair did their best to correct the distortions, but white historians brushed their work aside as special pleading, unscientific and nonobjective. And when, in the decades immediately prior to the civil rights movement and the subsequent black power movement, white "revisionist" historians began to present a more accurate and more sympathetic assessment of Black Reconstruction, academic history had become too narrowly specialized to reach the general public. Thus is it absolutely true that one of the most dramatic episodes in world history and certainly the most dramatic era in American history since the Revolution itself has been, for generations, primarily a battleground for conflicting schools of academic historians rather than what it should more properly have been—an inexhaustible reservoir for black and white Americans alike of people and incidents demonstrating the indestructibility of the human spirit. In the nineteenth century the precious words "freedom," "equality," and "brotherhood" could be spoken with true existential power only by black Americans and their white allies. *They* were the true heirs of the Revolution. They still challenge us to make good its promise—"the consequent emancipation of a world," in the words of the Reverend Samuel Thacher.

Americans belong to a larger human category—that of the race or species—and no people should be more conscious of this larger "membership" because the nation was created by "all the nations of the earth" coming to it and, in so coming, the people of those nations vastly enlarged the world's collective notion of man's common humanity, the possibilities of what Wyndham Lewis called "Cosmic Man." The dream of black-white brotherhood which inspired the efforts of the abolitionists of both races still waits to be fulfilled. It will be realized when white Americans lay claim to the black heroes and heroines of our past —men and women like Salomon Northrup, Robert Purvis, Sojourner Truth, Harriet Tubman, Frederick Douglass, Henry Turner, William Wells Brown, Charles Caldwell, and hundreds of others, men and women who fought for the most treasured principles of America—not simply as "black" heroes and heroines but as American heroes and heroines. When white Southern schoolchildren (and of course, Northern and Western as well) can respond sympathetically to the stories of a Charles Caldwell and a Robert Elliott, understanding them to have been courageous fighters for the rights of all Americans regardless of color, we may finally begin to be worthy of the principles we have professed since our birth as a nation.

At the end of *Bricks Without Straw*, Albion Tourgée takes note of a colony of free blacks headed for Kansas to try to establish a cooperative community. "So," he writes, "day by day, the 'irrepressible conflict' is renewed. The Past bequeaths to the Present its wondrous legacy of good and ill. . . . The soil which slavery claimed [Kansas], baptized with blood, becomes the Promised Land of the freedman and poor white. . . . Ignorance marvels at the power of Knowledge. Love overleaps the barriers of prejudice, and Faith laughs at the Impossible."

John Jay Chapman, great-great-grandson of John Jay, first chief justice of the Supreme Court, grandson of John Jay, the abolitionist and pacifist opponent of the Mexican War, and of Maria Weston, one of the great women reformers of the century, was a mordant critic of American life. Chapman wrote in 1912 of the "Anti-slavery Legend" that it "will reflect the spiritual history of any mind that looks into it; it is a mirror of the soul. It is a sort of thesaurus of moral illustration."

The same can be said of antislavery's extension into the Era of Reconstruction. There, too, it is "a mirror of the soul."

55

Conclusion

The Civil War was an event too vast to comprehend, an event that on both sides at once rose to mythic proportions—for the South it became the "Lost Cause," the story of innocence besmirched, of chivalry betrayed; for the North the story of treason vanquished and overweening pride humbled. As it had been almost too much to bear, it became too much to encompass, too much ever fully to tell, although the histories, the memoirs, the autobiographies, and soon even the detailed military and naval records began pouring out almost before the last gun was fired, praising, explaining, accusing, exonerating, denouncing, as though by the mere volume of uncountable pages the depths of the reality of the war could be plumbed. Our understanding of its meaning was various and contradictory then, and it has never ceased to be so in all the interminable retellings. Every argument, every explanation offered at the terrible moment of trial by fire has been refurbished, usually more than once, and offered up again. It was a necessary war, an unnecessary war; a cleansing by fire; a war to preserve the Union; a war to free the slaves; both; neither; a corruption of the spirit; an act of aggression by the capitalist North against the agrarian South; and on and on.

Distinguishable from, if closely related to, the notion that the war was a form of punishment or penance for the sin of slavery that could not end until the price had been paid in full was the idea that the war would be a cleansing experience for Americans that, in Carl Schurz's words, it might be counted on to lift the people "above the mean selfishness of daily life," to stop the growth of "the 'vile, groveling materialism' which is so apt to develop into a dominant tendency in a long period of peace," and to turn "the ambitions of men into channels of generous enthusiasm and lofty aspiration." It failed, of course, to do so.

Historians have grown to maturity and lived to ripe old ages defending one explanation of the war or another. To the classic and by now elaborately defined "positions"—one is tempted to write "entrenchments"—of Northern and Southern historians have been added the fortresses and citadels of the economic historians, Marxist and non-Marxist, and now the psychological historians, the quantifying, computerized historians, and the cultural historians (the war was due, as Gideon Welles suggested, to too much reading of Scott's novels), and, of course, black historians and white historians distributed rather randomly among the different schools (none of the black historians, to be sure, prepared to argue against the slavery-as-principal-cause camp). One recalls again Herbert Butterfield's statement, "Sometimes when the human race has gone through one of its colossal chapters of experience, men in the aftermath have been so appalled by the catastrophe, so obsessed by the memory of it, that they have gone back to the story again and again, finding new angles of research, new aspects of the matter to reflect upon, as one generation succeeds another. . . ." Here, certainly, is a case where the seriousness of the trauma can be judged by the multitude of diagnoses it has produced. Most curiously it stands at the center of our history and will always stand there no matter how many subsequent generations or centuries our history may run.

I have said earlier that, in a real sense, the nation could not truly begin until the twin issues of slavery and secession had been laid to rest. Everything before was tentative, beclouded by the apparently unsolvable issue of black servitude. The profoundest questions—what it means to be human, the relations of the various races of man to each other, the meaning of equality and democracy—all were in abeyance, all waited to be resolved by the outcome of the most titanic internal struggle a nation had ever experienced. We have only to try to imagine a United States or, indeed, a world in which black slavery still exists to understand the enormity of the issue. Those historians who have deplored the Civil War as a "mistake" have offered us a multitude of assurance, all unsupported, of course, by anything but the flimsiest conjectures, that the South would in time have come to abandon slavery of its own free will. Every scrap of evidence speaks otherwise. The South had grown with each passing decade more defiant and determined in its defense of slavery, and the status of blacks, free and slave, North and South, had grown correspondingly worse. The only basis on which one could argue that this process must suddenly reverse itself was a blind faith in moral progress as an absolute, irresistible force in history. But we have had too many terrible regressions in our own century to believe the progressive triumph of reason and freedom in human affairs.

The Civil War and Reconstruction are the epic drama of American history, our *Iliad*, our War of the Roses, our Thirty Years' War rolled into one. Young idealists like Charles Francis Adams, Jr., and Lester Ward believed the end of the war would presage the dawn of a new age and the final fulfillment of the continually renewed, perpetually deferred promise of America. But the hopes were defeated; the promise failed. Instead of an era of Christian brotherhood, of equality, of justice and freedom for all without regard to class or race, the country entered into an age of widespread inequality, of social, economic, and racial injustice, of brutal repression of the freedmen and women of the South. The last Indians were driven from the plains and mountains of the West, herded into reservations, buried in an avalanche of white settlers moving relentlessly westward to possess a land that once had seemed too vast to fill up—Jefferson had predicted that more than a hundred generations must pass before white Americans would encompass it; it would take scarcely four. Corrupt political machines corrupted rapacious entrepreneurs—or vice versa; it was often hard to tell. It turned out that the fruits of the sacrifice of hundreds of thousands of lives, North and South, was not to be reconciliation, nationhood strengthened and affirmed, but unremitting hatred on one side and a series of military responses on the other.

Looking back from the perspective of the end of the century, Carl Schurz conceded that the nation emerged from the war with "a saved and strengthened Union, the abolition of slavery, and an invigorated consciousness of national power," but it was also the case that the war aroused and gave play to many baser impulses. Rather than give a new birth to unselfish idealism, it called forth "a greedy craving on the part of a great many to use the needs of government and the public distress as an opportunity for making money by sharp practices." It produced a " 'materialistic' tendency far worse than any we had known among us before," giving birth to "an era of absorbing greed of wealth, a marked decline of ideal aspirations, and a dangerous tendency to exploit the government for private gain."

But, that was clearly only half the story. In the face of a burgeoning industrialism that threatened to reduce them to subhuman elements in the process of production, workers fought for their share of the enormous pie. Desperate farmers took on the railroads. Angry and determined women battled for *their* rights. Above all, the nation (no longer the precarious "Union") grew at an accelerating pace, and prospered to such a degree that it seemed that all mistakes could be remedied, all failures redeemed.

Acknowledgments

The Era of Reconstruction is such a complicated and controversial period that I found myself particularly dependent on the advice and guidance of scholars in the field. The dean of Reconstruction historians, C. Vann Woodward, was kind enough to discuss with me current research trends and recommend specific works that might prove useful. James McPherson, of the Princeton history department, was also very helpful in his comments on the abolitionists and with suggestions for further reading. John Dizikes and Herman Blake read crucial chapters. Leon Litwack's *Been in the Storm So Long* was illuminating, as were Peggy Lamson's *Glorious Failure*, a biography of Robert Elliott (although I must say he seemed to me far more a success than a failure); *Nobody Knows the Trouble I Seen;* and Harold Hyman's *The Radical Republicans and Reconstruction, 1861–1870*. Most useful was Willie Lee Rose's marvelous monograph *Port Royal; Experiment in Reconstruction.*

Index

About the Author

Page Smith was educated at Dartmouth College and Harvard University. He has served as research associate at the University of California at Los Angeles and at Santa Cruz, where he was Provost of Cowell College. He is now Professor Emeritus of that university, as well as co-director of the William James Association. Dr. Smith is the author of *The Historian and History; Daughters of the Promised Land: Women in American History; As a City upon a Hill: The Town in American History;* the highly acclaimed two-volume biography *John Adams,* which was a selection of the Book-of-the-Month Club, a National Book Award Nominee, and a Bancroft winner; *A New Age Now Begins* and *The Shaping of America,* both Main Selections of the Book-of-the-Month Club. *Trial by Fire* continues Dr. Smith's extensive *People's History* of the United States, of which *A New Age Now Begins, The Shaping of America,* and *The Nation Comes of Age* are the first volumes. Page Smith lives in Santa Cruz, California.

MD8M

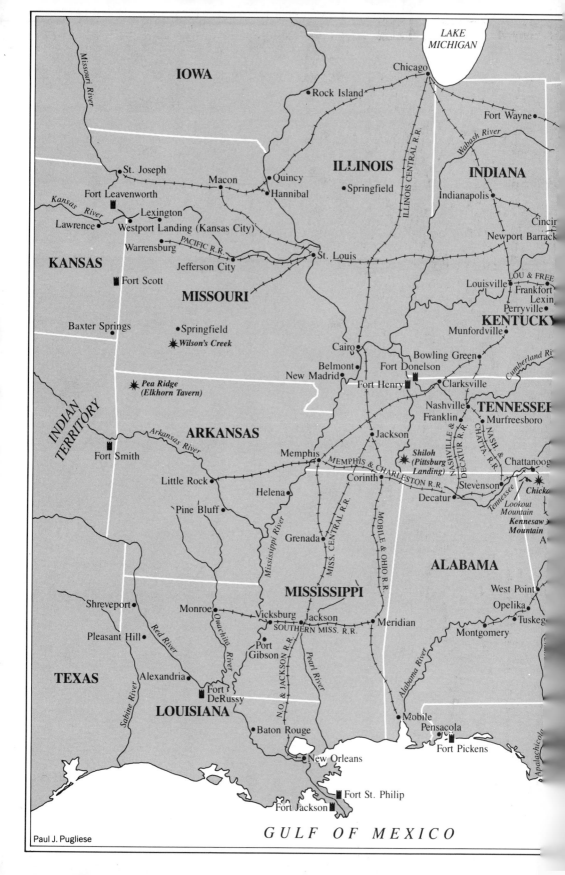

Paul J. Pugliese